FIELDING'S CARIBBEAN CRUISES

Fielding Titles

Fielding's Alaska Cruises/Inside Passage
Fielding's Amazon
Fielding's Australia
Fielding's Bahamas
Fielding's Belgium
Fielding's Bermuda
Fielding's Borneo
Fielding's Brazil
Fielding's Britain
Fielding's Budget Europe
Fielding's Caribbean
Fielding's Caribbean Cruises
Fielding's Caribbean East
Fielding's Caribbean West
Fielding's Europe
Fielding's European Cruises
Fielding's Far East
Fielding's France
Fielding's Freewheelin' USA
Fielding's Guide to the World's Most Dangerous Places
Fielding's Guide to Kenya's Best Hotels, Lodges & Homestays
Fielding's Hawaii
Fielding's Holland
Fielding's Italy
Fielding's Las Vegas Agenda
Fielding's London Agenda
Fielding's Los Angeles Agenda
Fielding's Malaysia and Singapore
Fielding's Mexico
Fielding's New York Agenda
Fielding's New Zealand
Fielding's Paris Agenda
Fielding's Portugal
Fielding's Rome Agenda
Fielding's San Diego Agenda
Fielding's Scandinavia
Fielding's Southeast Asia
Fielding's Southern Vietnam on Two Wheels
Fielding's Spain
Fielding's Thailand Including Cambodia, Laos, Myanmar
Fielding's Vacation Places Rated
Fielding's Vietnam
Fielding's Worldwide Cruises
The Indiana Jones Survival Guide

FIELDING'S CARIBBEAN CRUISES

Harry Basch,
Shirley Slater
and
Joyce Wiswell

Fielding Worldwide, Inc.
308 South Catalina Avenue
Redondo Beach, California 90277 U.S.A.

Fielding's Caribbean Cruises 1996

Published by Fielding Worldwide, Inc.

FIELDING WORLDWIDE INC.

PUBLISHER AND CEO **Robert Young Pelton**
GENERAL MANAGER **John Guillebeaux**
MARKETING DIRECTOR **Paul T. Snapp**
ELECTRONIC PUBLISHING DIRECTOR **Larry E. Hart**
PUBLIC RELATIONS DIRECTOR **Beverly Riess**
ACCOUNT SERVICES MANAGER **Christy Harp**
PROJECT MANAGER **Chris Snyder**
DATABASE PUBLISHING MANAGER **Jacki VanderVoort**

EDITORS

Kathy Knoles **Linda Charlton**

PRODUCTION

Martin Mancha **Gini Sardo-Martin**
Ramses Reynoso **Craig South**

COVER DESIGNED BY **Digital Artists, Inc.**
COVER PHOTOGRAPHERS—Front **Jim Raycroft/Tropical Stock**
Back **Princess Cruises**
INSIDE PHOTOS **Harry Basch, Shirley Slater, Carol Lee, Benford Associates, Grenada Tourist Office, Karen Weiner, Escalera Associates, Robinson, Yesavich & Pepperdine, Inc., Trombone Associates, Corel Professional Photos, Colin Bessonette**

Inquiries should be addressed to: Fielding Worldwide, Inc., 308 South Catalina Ave., Redondo Beach, California 90277 U.S.A., Telephone *(310) 372-4474*, Facsimile *(310) 376-8064*, 8:30 a.m.–5:30 p.m. Pacific Standard Time.

ISBN 1-56952-070-4

Printed in the United States of America

Letter from the Publisher

In 1946, Temple Fielding began the first of what would be a remarkable new series of well-written, highly personalized guidebooks for independent travelers. Temple's opinionated, witty and oft-imitated books have now guided travelers for almost a half-century. More important to some was Fielding's humorous and direct method of steering travelers away from the dull and the insipid. Today, the Fielding Travel Guides are still written by experienced travelers for experienced travelers. Our authors carry on Fielding's reputation for creating travel experiences that deliver insight with a sense of discovery and style.

Authors Harry Basch and Shirley Slater have personally been aboard all ships reviewed in Fielding's *Caribbean Cruises* and have taken more than 200 cruises during the past 15 years. Their vast cruise experience will provide you with inside information and hopefully guide you to more enjoyable cruise vacations.

Joyce Wiswell has tackled the daunting task of giving the reader a balanced overview of each Caribbean island. Along with highlighting the unique personality of each island, she brings a youthful enthusiasm and a true love of the Caribbean to the book.

Today the concept of independent travel has never been bigger. Our policy of *brutal honesty* and a highly personal point of view has never changed; it just seems the travel world has caught up with us.

Enjoy your Caribbean cruise adventures with Harry, Shirley and Joyce.

RYP

Robert Young Pelton
Publisher and CEO
Fielding Worldwide, Inc.

What They're Saying About *Fielding's Guide to Worldwide Cruises*

"...an appealing combination of humor, lesser known but interesting facts about various cruise ships, appropriate information about various ports and perceptive critiques of the ships themselves. It is a very fresh approach to the subject and is much more colorful, lively and interesting than many cruise guides of the past. In addition to being informative, it really makes for good reading ... (It) reveals information which will be helpful to agents, particularly those that have not been cruise oriented."

Lawrence J. Frommer, Frommer Enterprises
travel agency owner for 33 years,
travel agent consultant and cruise specialist

"Shirley and Harry's cruise knowledge is unsurpassed. They clearly and concisely cover all the bases with surprising candor and refreshing good humor. If you have space for only one cruise guidebook in your library, it should be this one."

Charles Doherty, Managing Editor,
Cruise Travel Magazine

"If a useful, accurate and entertaining cruise guide can be compiled—and I have never been convinced it could—Shirley Slater and Harry Basch have brought it off for Fielding. Five star plus is no more, replaced by a point of view, a fresh layout and, yes, some wit. Bravo!"

John Maxtone-Graham, Marine Historian,
author of *The Only Way to Cross* and *Liners to the Sun*

Shirley Slater and Harry Basch are the "travel agents'" travel agent, as far as cruise information is concerned ... they are frank and upfront as to what the public wants to hear."

Duke Butler, President,
Spur of the Moment Cruises

"This entertaining and useful guide will make even the most hardened land-lubber want to set sail. Slater and Basch have redefined cruise guide books."

Paul Lasley & Elizabeth Harryman,

ON TRAVEL RADIO

ABOUT THE AUTHORS

Shirley Slater and Harry Basch

Called by the *Chicago Sun-Times* "America's premier cruise specialists," Shirley Slater and Harry Basch are an award-winning husband-and-wife travel writing and photography team whose work has been published internationally since 1976. They are editors of Fielding's *Cruise Insider*, a quarterly news-and-reviews journal about the cruise industry, as well as authors of Fielding's *Worldwide Cruises* and *Freewheelin' USA*.

As contributing editors for the trade magazine *Cruise & Vacation Views*, their monthly ship reviews are read throughout the travel agent community. They have also written ship reviews for trade publications *Travel Weekly*, *TravelAge* and *ASTA Agency Management* magazine.

Their syndicated column "Cruise Views" has appeared regularly in the *Los Angeles Times* and other major newspapers for 15 years. They have also contributed to magazines such as *Bon Appétit, Vogue, Modern Maturity, Travel & Leisure, Islands, Travel Holiday*, as well as various auto club and inflight publications.

At the 60th World Travel Congress in Hamburg, Germany, in 1990 the couple was awarded the prestigious Melva C. Pederson Award from the American Society of Travel Agents for "extraordinary journalistic achievement in the field of travel," the third time the award was given and the first time it was awarded to freelance writers.

Joyce Wiswell

Joyce Wiswell has been writing about travel for more than 15 years. Various writing assignments have taken her to nearly every state in the union, as well as China, Hong Kong, the Philippines, Thailand, Europe, and, of course, throughout the Caribbean. Her work has appeared in numerous magazines and newspapers. Wiswell is also the author of Fielding's *Las Vegas Agenda*, Fielding's *Eastern Caribbean,* Fielding's *Western Caribbean* and Fielding's *Caribbean.*

A native of New Jersey, she is a magna cum laude graduate of Connecticut's Quinnipiac College. After paying her dues as a magazine writer and editor in New York City for eight years, she fled for life in California, where she lives happily in Santa Barbara. When not traveling, she putters in the garden and pampers her cats, and worries unduly about both when on the road.

Fielding Rating Icons

The Fielding Rating Icons are highly personal and awarded to help the besieged traveler choose from among the dizzying array of activities, attractions, hotels, restaurants and sights. The awarding of an icon denotes unusual or exceptional qualities in the relevant category.

Ratings	Fielding Award	Author Selection	Money Saver	Expensive	Quality	Warning	Danger	Inexpensive	Mild Disapproval
	Spacious	Cramped							
Cultural	Museum/ Art	Interesting Architecture	History	Book Reference	Artistically Important	Musically Interesting	Cultural Archeology	Crafts	Theatre
Sights	Picturesque	Great Scenery	Market	Beaches/ Resorts	Cultural	Fortress	Castles	Church	
Where to Stay	Simple	Luxurious	Cottage	Bed & Breakfast	Scenic	Business	Honeymoon	Chateau	
Travel Tips	Arrival/ Departure	By Air	By Water	By Train	By Car	Bus/Local Transit	Barge	River Boat	Calendar
	Itinerary	Compass	Kids						
Activities	Downhill Skiing	X–country Skiing	General Sports	Water Sports	Sailing	Scuba Diving	Snorkeling/ Diving	Deep-sea Fishing	Freshwater Fishing
	Swimming	Hiking	Walking	Relaxing	Golf	Tennis	Horseback Riding	Cycling	Workout
Special Interest	Mystery	Singles	Romantic	Nude Beaches	Lecture	Spectacular Cuisine	Wine Tast- ing	Shopping	Nightlife
	Cafe Stops	Gardening	Pro Sports						

TABLE OF CONTENTS

Once Ashore

LIST OF MAPS

Florida
Miami
Gulf of Mexico
Straits of Florida
Grand Bahama
Freeport
Bimini Islands
Nassau
Cay Sal Bank (The Bahamas)
Andros Island
Cancún
Mérida
Yucatan Peninsula
Isla de Cozumel
Yucatan Channel
HAVANA
Matanzas
Pinar del Rio
Santa Clara
Cienfuegos
Cuba
Isla de la Juventud
Mexico
Cayman Islands (U.K.)
Guantánamo Bay Naval Station
Chetumal
George Town
Montego Bay
Jamaica
Belize City
Guatemala
Belmopan
Swan Islands (Hon.)
Usumacinta
Puerto Barrios
Puerto Lempira
Honduras
Cayos Miskitos (Nic.)
Puerto Cabezas
Guatemala
Tegucigalpa
Isla de Providencia (Col.)
Nicaragua
Islas del Maíz (Nic.)
Isla de San Andrés (Col.)
San Salvador
El Salvador
Bluefields
SAN JOSE
Puerto Limón
Costa Rica
Bocas del Toro
Colón
Panama
PANAMA

Caribbean Region
National Capital
Territorial Capital
Secondary City
State/Nat. Boundary
0 100 200 300 400 km
0 100 200 300 mi
©FWI 1995
The Bahamas
Atlantic Ocean
San Salvador
Rum Cay
Crooked Island
Mayaguana
Acklins Island
Turks & Caicos Islands (U.K.)
Grand Turk
Great Inagua
Guantánamo
Windward Passage
Cap-Haïtien
Santiago
Dominican Republic
Haiti
Santo Domingo
Port-au-Prince
es Cayes
Mona Passage
Isla Mona (R.)
San Juan
Puerto Rico (U.S.)
British Virgin Islands
U.S. Virgin Islands
Anguilla
St. Martin (Fr.)
Sint Maarten
St. Barthélemy (Fr.)
Saba (N.A.)
Antigua and Barbuda
St. Johns
Basseterre
St. Kitts & Nevis
Montserrat (U.K.)
Guadeloupe (Fr.)
Isla Aves (Ven.)
Roseau
Dominica
Martinique (F.R.)
Fort-de-France
Castries
St. Lucia
St. Vincent and The Grenadines
Kingstown
Barbados
Bridgetown
Netherland Antilles
Aruba
Curacao
Bonaire
Willemstad
Islas Los Roques (en.)
La Blanquilla (en.)
Grenada
St. George's
Isla de Margarita (Ven.)
Isla La Tortuga (Ven.)
Tobago
Trinidad
Port of Spain
Santa Marta
Maracaibo
Cartagena
Caracas
Barcelona
Venezuela
Caribbean Sea

Sailing There

by Shirley Slater & Harry Basch

A NOTE ABOUT THE STARS

The first thing you will probably notice as you leaf through this **brand-new, all-new** *Fielding's Caribbean Cruises* is the rating system.

When the star rating system was originally initiated, ships were simpler and the top-ranked vessels somewhat less sophisticated in food, service and cabin amenities. As ships improved, the star ratings started pushing the envelope, everyone crowding the top and hardly anyone back at the average or beginning.

Now you'll find a new **One-to-Six** Star rating system reflecting a much wider range of cruise offerings in the marketplace than ever before in history. Herewith, we proudly introduce the **first-ever Six-Star cruise ships,** offering the best cruise ship experiences in the world.

THE BEST OF 1996

Six-Star Ships in the Caribbean

Ultra-deluxe vessels with sophisticated cuisine, excellent service, far-reaching and imaginative itineraries, and a highly satisfying overall cruise experience.

Crystal Symphony	**Crystal Cruises**
Queen Odyssey	**Royal Cruise Line**
Radisson Diamond	**Radisson Seven Seas Cruises**
Royal Viking Sun	**Cunard Line**
Seabourn Pride	**Seabourn Cruises**
Seabourn Spirit	**Seabourn Cruises**
Sea Goddess I	**Cunard Line**
Sea Goddess II	**Cunard Line**
Silver Cloud	**Silverseas Cruises**
Silver Wind	**Silverseas Cruises**

Five-Star Ships in the Caribbean

Stylish, comfortable ships, each vessel or class with its own distinct personality catering to a variety of different audiences with a high overall quality in its price range.

CostaClassica	**Costa Cruises**
CostaRomantica	**Costa Cruises**
Crown Princess	**Princess Cruises**
Dreamward	**Norwegian Cruise Line**
Ecstasy	**Carnival Cruise Lines**
Fantasy	**Carnival Cruise Lines**
Fascination	**Carnival Cruise Lines**
Horizon	**Celebrity Cruises**
Imagination	**Carnival Cruise Lines**

Maasdam	**Holland America Line**
Regal Princess	**Princess Cruises**
Royal Odyssey	**Royal Cruise Line**
Royal Princess	**Princess Cruises**
Rotterdam	**Holland America Line**
Ryndam	**Holland America Line**
Sagafjord	**Cunard Line**
Sensation	**Carnival Cruise Lines**
Star Odyssey	**Royal Cruise Line**
Statendam	**Holland America Line**
Vistafjord	**Cunard Line**
Wind Spirit	**Windstar Cruises**
Wind Star	**Windstar Cruises**
Windward	**Norwegian Cruise Line**
Vistafjord	**Cunard Line**
Zenith	**Celebrity Cruises**

Best Buys at Sea

- **The Carnival Fleet**, providing a big, splashy **Las Vegas/Theme Park experience for the whole family** at affordable prices.
- **The Celebrity Fleet**, offering the finest cruise ship food and service in handsome, tasteful surroundings at an excellent value, **the best large-ship buy afloat**.
- *Dreamward/Windward* from **Norwegian Cruise Line**, well-designed ships with a feeling of intimate spaces in sophisticated surroundings for young to middle-aged couples and singles.
- **The Holland America Line Fleet, the most beautiful traditional cruise ships at sea**, a solid value for the money with tasty, imaginatively served food and warm friendly service, classy and classic.
- *Nordic Empress* from **Royal Caribbean Cruise Ltd**., an **outstanding short-cruise experience** for first-time cruisers because of a tactful and caring staff that make you feel at ease.
- **The Silverseas Fleet**, looks expensive until you **see what you get for your money**, with airfare, all beverages and tips included.

Best Ships for Families with Kids

1., 2. Both **Big Red Boats** from **Premier Cruise Lines**, with Bugs Bunny aboard and a full gamut of fun and games for all ages.

5. *Sky Princess* from **Princess Cruises** for its big, comfortable playroom, kiddy pool and well-trained counselors.

Most Romantic Ships at Sea

Cunard's *Sea Goddess I* and *Sea Goddess II* give you a free, unfettered, laissez-faire cruise with a few like-minded romantics looking to **rekindle romance or launch a new love affair**. Take your lover along with you, however, since the ship rarely carries single passengers; recommended for couples only.

Silversea's *Silver Cloud* and *Silver Wind* are larger than Sea Goddess, so there's more anonymity if you really want to hide out, plus **those lovely private balconies** the Sea Goddess ships don't have. Couples are best, but there have been a few unattached males and females on both sailings we've made with them.

Windstar Cruises' *Wind Star* and *Wind Spirit* seem to attract a lot of handsome couples of all ages, but the **romance here comes from the sails**, from sitting alone together on the big gray-and-yellow cushions on the stern deck in the dark in the balmy tropical breezes.

Holland America Line's *Rotterdam* offers a different kind of romance, the romance of an ocean liner with polished woods and parquetry floors and two-level nightclubs; senior singles might find romance on a personal level, but also **young couples who could get caught up in the lushly romantic art deco atmosphere**.

The *Sea Cloud* from Special Expeditions is romantic in every sense of the word, particularly if you've booked one of the two owner's suites, where cereal heiress Marjorie Merriweather Post and her husband E.F. Hutton sequestered themselves (separately) in lavish 1930s splendor. If you're stuck in one of the newer, cheaper, smaller cabins, spend your free time **cuddled together on the big, blue-cushioned "blue lagoon" on the fantail**.

Costa Cruises' *CostaRomantica*—the name doesn't hurt but the spare and elegant suites with private verandas that are named after operas are among the most romantic digs at sea. Burled brierwood furniture and cabinetry, gauzy white bedroom, **an electronically-operated floor to ceiling window shade for total privacy, plus a large whirlpool tub, discreet butler service,** terrycloth robes and reclining deck chairs on the veranda. Yes!

Outer Space: The Sweetest Suites at Sea

1. **Cunard's** *Vistafjord* with its pair of dazzling, duplex penthouses complete with private sauna, outdoor hot tub on private veranda, two marble bathrooms with Jacuzzi tubs, wet bar and treadmill for a morning workout.
2. **Crystal's** two Crystal Penthouses on the *Crystal Symphony*, separate living rooms, dining area, large private veranda, big walk-in closets, extra guest half-bath, wet bar, Jacuzzi tub, lovely cabinetry.
3. The Royal Suite on *Legend of the Seas* from **Royal Caribbean Cruise Ltd.**, with a huge white piano dominating one corner of a spacious living room, green marble compartmented bathroom, wet bar, long private veranda, full entertainment center—drop-dead gorgeous.
4. *Maasdam/Ryndam/Statendam* from **Holland America**, a single huge owner's suite on each ship has a wide private veranda, separate living room, dining room and bedroom, huge walk-in closet, compartmented bath, butler pantry to have meals prepared in suite.
5. The Royal and the Princess Suites on *Royal Princess* from **Princess Cruises**, big elegant marble bathrooms, wide veranda, light, bright and airy, handsomely furnished.

Splashy Ships for Watersports

- *Black Prince* from **Fred. Olson Line** for its Marina Park that extends from the stern of the ship at anchor with teak decks, enclosed swimming pool and watersports galore.
- *Club Med 1* with a similar watersports platform sans pool.
- **Norwegian Cruise Line** for its super Dive-In Program.
- **Seabourn Cruises** with its watersports platform with pool.
- **Sea Goddess Cruises** with a watersports platform sans pool.
- **Windstar Cruises** for its watersports platform.

Best Ships for Singles

Under 30: Windjammer Barefoot Cruises

Try the special Singles Sailings that promise equality between the sexes.

Females Under 30: Carnival Cruise Lines

These ships attract a lot of single guys under 30.

30-50: Royal Caribbean Cruise Line

A good mainstream place to meet.

Women 50-up: Royal Cruise Line

Dancing hosts, dress-up evenings and live music almost around the clock.

Men 50-up: Royal Cruise Line, Cunard

Try being a dancing host.

Most Off-the-Wall Onboard Events

1. **Toga Night on Costa Cruises**, when virtually everyone on board dons a custom-made toga (with or without street clothes under them) and makes like Messalina and Claudius.
2. **BLT night on Tall Ship Adventures'** *Sir Francis Drake*, when everyone dons buccaneer, lingerie or toga, including the captain.
3. **Men's Knobby Knees Contests on Carnival** ships, and many other vessels as well.

The Best Cruise Lines For Buffets

1. **Holland America Line**, consistently the best day-in, day-out Lido food service.
2. **Celebrity Cruises**, the prettiest arrangements and most convenient layouts, plus wine by the glass on a rolling cart.
3. **Crystal Cruises**, outstanding special theme buffets and great deck grills.
4. **Majesty Cruise Line** for its Piazza San Marco deck bar.
5. **Cunard's** *Sea Goddess* for its imaginative deck food.

Three Worst Buffets at Sea

1. Embarkation buffet on **Princess Cruises'** *Regal Princess.*
2. Lunch buffet aboard **Regal Cruises'** *Regal Empress.*
3. Any buffet on **Commodore's** *Enchanted Isle.*

Three Best Theme Buffets at Sea

1. Italian deck buffet on **Crystal's** ships.
2. Norwegian seafood buffet on **Cunard's** *Royal Viking Sun*.
3. The Bavarian Brunch on **Cunard's** *Sagafjord* and *Vistafjord*.

Best Spas at Sea

- **Celebrity's** *Century* has created the most innovative health, beauty and fitness center afloat.
- **Nautica Spas aboard Carnival's megaships** offer 12,000 square feet of space, with a huge glass-walled gym and fulltime instructor, aerobics room, beauty services, spas with skylights overhead.
- **The Roman Spa and health and fitness centers aboard NCL's** *Norway* with lavish indoor pools like a Roman bath.
- **The Solarium aboard Norwegian Caribbean Cruise Ltd.'s** *Legend of the Seas*, with a glass canopy-covered pool, water jets, Roman marble everywhere.

Best Alternative Restaurants

An alternative restaurant is an option to dine occasionally somewhere other than the ship's regular dining rooms, where you usually have assigned seating.

1. **An Evening at Don Vito's** aboard the *Radisson Diamond* from **Radisson Seven Seas Cruises** serves up a delicious (and fun) all-Italian evening in a casual atmosphere.
2. **Prego Restaurant** aboard **Crystal Cruises'** *Crystal Symphony*, also Italian and very elegant.
3. **Tivoli Restaurant**, an intimate and romantic little Italian restaurant aboard **Cunard's** *Vistafjord* with candlelight.

Best Cruise Entertainment at Sea

- **Carnival's** *Fascination* **and its production of "Hollywood"** is one of the most spectacular shows we've ever seen at sea, dazzling with its company of 18 singers and dancers and flawlessly professional.
- **Princess Cruises' new "Mystique,"** a sensational production with 23 performers, including nine acrobats, set under the sea in Atlantic with scenery that "grows" in front of your eyes, is a knockout.
- **Crystal Cruises' elegantly costumed "Cole"** aboard the *Crystal Symphony* sets a new high for class acts.
- **Norwegian Cruise Line** offers well-performed Broadway shows like "Will Rogers Follies," "Dreamgirls," "Grease," "George M" and "Pirates of Penzance" on the stages of its ships; the classic *Norway* has a particularly fine theater with balcony and orchestra seating.

Maximizing Mini-Cruises

For Singles

- **Carnival's** *Ecstasy* from Miami to the Bahamas.

- **NCL's** *Leeward* from Miami to the Bahamas and to Mexico's Caribbean.
- **Regal Cruises'** *Regal Empress*, sailing from New York on party cruises in summer, from St. Petersburg on four-, five- and six-day sailings in winter.

For Couples

- **RCCL's** *Nordic Empress* from Miami to the Bahamas.
- **Radisson Seven Seas'** *Radisson Diamond* on a few special short sailings in March and April in the Caribbean aboard a super-luxury ship.

For Seniors

- **Dolphin's** *OceanBreeze* from Miami to the Bahamas (beginning in May, 1996).
- **Regal Cruises'** *Regal Empress*, sailing from New York on party cruises in summer, from St. Petersburg on four-, five- and six-day sailings in winter.

Six Best Floating Dining Rooms

Besides serving the finest food at sea, each of the following ship dining rooms has additional special qualities.

1. **The prettiest**: The Grand Dining room aboard **Radisson Seven Seas'** *Radisson Diamond.*
2. **Best service**: Galley Dining Room, **Radisson Seven Seas'** *Song of Flower.*
3. **Most convivial**: The Dining Salon aboard **Cunard's** *Sea Goddess I* and *Sea Goddess II.*
4. **Most eclectic menus**: **Royal Cruise Line's** *Queen Odyssey.*
5. **The most formal service**: *Seabourn Pride* and *Seabourn Spirit.*
6. **Most spacious dining room**: **Cunard's** *Royal Viking Sun.*

Good Ships for First-Timers and Why

Budget

Dolphin Cruise Line's *OceanBreeze* and *SeaBreeze* are clean, comfortable, affordable vintage vessels.

Moderate

Seawind Cruise Line's *Seawind Crown* offers a good Southern Caribbean itinerary on a classic and comfortable ship that also carries some free land stays to extend your vacation.

RCCL's *Nordic Empress* offers top-drawer surroundings, excellent entertainment and good food and service with tactful attention to first-timers.

Norwegian Cruise Line's dive-in and onboard sports programs, themed dinners and costume evenings on all ships add energy and direction to the overall experience.

Splurge

Traditionalists think **Radisson Seven Seas'** twin-hulled *Radisson Diamond* is a funny-looking ship, but it's great for first-time cruisers who want a top-drawer luxury sailing with space (sizable cabins, wide hallways) and stability (no seasickness on here!)

Special Experiences at Sea

Royal Cruise Line

—provides a full enrichment experience for its passengers, particularly older couples and singles, with heart-healthy menus available, gentlemen hosts and New Beginnings sessions.

Inaccessible Vessels for Wheelchair Passengers

ACCL	*Caribbean Prince, Mayan Prince, Niagara Prince*
Clipper Cruises	*Nantucket and Yorktown Clipper*
Club Med Cruises	*Club Med 1 & 2*
Regal Cruises	*Regal Empress*
Special Expeditions	*Polaris and Sea Cloud*
Star Clippers	*Star Clipper and Star Flyer*
Tall Ship Adventures	*Sir Francis Drake*
Windjammer Fleet	All sailing ships

INTRODUCTION: LOOK WHO'S AFLOAT

At twilight aboard the timeless Rotterdam, this romantic couple at the rail might be shipboard companions of Noel Coward.

> *"Why do the wrong people travel, travel, travel*
> *And the right people stay at home?"*
>
> **Noel Coward song lyrics**

Even the late Noel Coward, the most urbane and unflappable cruise passenger one can imagine, probably would have been rendered speechless at who and what's afloat these days.

On the decks he frequented, there were no earphone-wearing joggers or aerobics classes, just stately promenaders (the kind who nod only after being properly introduced) or dozing readers wrapped in steamer rugs. Certainly nobody ever requested a no-smoking table or a low-calorie lunch.

Coward definitely would have raised an eyebrow at cruise-ship dress codes allowing gentlemen to appear at dinner not only without black tie but without any tie or jacket at all. And he hardly could have imagined couples stealing away after dinner to screen a video in their cabin instead of dancing cheek to cheek to the ship's orchestra.

Suddenly four million Americans a year were going down to the sea in ships. And they weren't all wealthy retirees and they weren't all looking for love and attention. They were all ages, from all economic groups, singles, honeymoon couples, working couples on a budget, families with small children, grandparents with grandchildren.

We've been on cruises with—

- Amanda at 2 and Amy at 86
- High rollers and bingo buffs
- A fitness nut who found out she could cruise on a spa ship cheaper than going to a famous spa for a week
- Surfers, divers and joggers who run their daily mileage on deck
- A septuagenarian learning to operate a computer
- A purple-haired teen-aged punk rocker who spent more time on the deck than in the disco
- Bird watchers, whale watchers and girl watchers
- Women competing to see who could stuff the most ping pong balls into their bikinis
- A tycoon who has a long stretch limousine waiting to take him sightseeing in every port
- Best-selling novelists and supermarket checkers, retired teachers and circus owners, movie stars and mechanics—and none of them have ever been boring—or bored.

To Cruise Or Not To Cruise

A girl never really looks as well as she does on board a steamship, or even a yacht.

Anita Loos, Gentlemen Prefer Blondes, 1925

Life aboard cruise ships used to be thought of as a sedentary vacation for the very old and very rich, who reclined on wooden deck chairs reading books and sipping bouillon when they weren't wearing tuxedos and eating caviar.

Then along came the slick TV version, based on the premise that all a lovelorn individual had to do was get on board the "Love Boat" and the captain and his meddlesome staff would make everything smooth sailing. All problems would be settled, true love would triumph and, since the ship never seemed to move anyhow, no one's hairdo would even get mussed.

The real world of cruising today is volatile, ephemeral, constantly changing as lines are acquired, new ships come into service and old ships are retired or sold down the river into ignominious retirement as hotels or casinos.

Cruise lines are selling you a dream. And anyone old enough to remember the days of radio knows that the images the aural programs created in the mind were stronger, more dramatic and more compelling than the pallid stuff that came along later on TV. The power of your dream, your imagination, creates a challenge that the cruise industry is trying to meet. Sometimes they do, sometimes they don't.

Getting Real

TV commercials and brochures about cruises all promise the same unexcelled excursion into the glamour life.

TV commercials and glossy color brochures about cruises all promise the same thing—an unexcelled excursion into the glamour life, with romantic evenings, a perfect tan, six or eight gourmet meals a day, and intermittent forays into picturesque and exotic ports of call where the sun always shines, the shopping is splendid and the natives friendly and photogenic.

Oddly enough, more often than not, it works out that way.

But based on some of the complaints we've had from readers over the years, several of them signed up for a cruise that should have been advertised more like this:

"You'll have fun aboard the friendly, 30-year-old *SS Rustbottom*, which failed her last five sanitation inspections in spite of heavily spiking the drinking water with chlorine...Our bottom-of-the-line cabins are so small you have to take turns getting dressed inside, and our menus are created by a Miami-based computer programmed to give you the maximum number of calories for the lowest possible cost... Our inexperienced and incompetent staff could not care less about your comfort or pleasure, and the residents of our popular ports of call make their livelihoods by harassing you in the streets to purchase their overpriced souvenirs."

What are some of the things that make passengers angry?

First and foremost seem to be promises the passenger felt were implied in the brochure or claimed were actually made by the travel agent prior to the trip. Ambiguous terms like "first class," "deluxe," "elegance"—and, of course, the ever-popular "five-star-plus," the monster created by this very guide—typical hyperbole churned out by ad agency copywriters who may never have been aboard the ship—are echoed bitterly by disappointed letter-writers who expected something grander than they received.

Some expectations appear unrealistic to more experienced cruisers—24-hour room service does not necessarily mean hot four-course meals are served in the cabin at 3 a.m., for instance, and no cruise-savvy travel agent would promise clients they could spend the entire disembarkation and turn-around day aboard the ship in their cabin until time to catch their evening flight home.

One of our favorite reader complaint letters was from a female attorney celebrating her 40th birthday on her first cruise. The ship was one of the former Royal Viking Line vessels, always top of the line in food and service, but the attorney was suing to have the price of her cruise refunded because at breakfast every morning the waiters persisted in offering her a silver tray of pastries despite the fact that she had told them she was on a diet.

Hey lady, get a life!

Take a Vacation from Vacations

The real pleasure of a cruise is not having to do anything you don't want to do.

At some point in every traveler's life, there comes a moment, bittersweet as the end of a love affair, when the vacation is over, the workaday world is looming and there's nothing you need worse than a vacation to recover from your vacation.

Next time, maybe you should take a cruise.

Cruise lines spend a lot of time and money telling us about the unending procession of meals and the nonstop fun and games, when the real pleasure of a cruise is not having to do anything you don't want to do—except attend the obligatory lifeboat drill at the beginning of the cruise.

No packing and unpacking to move from one hotel to another, no cars to rent or trains to catch, no lunchtime arguments about which restaurant or picnic spot looks more appealing, no bungled hotel reservations on a weary midnight arrival in Budapest because a convention of Bulgarians came to town.

Coming back to your ship after a day ashore is like coming home. Your waiter knows how you like your breakfast eggs, your steward knows what time you go to dinner so he can turn your bed down and put a chocolate on your pillow.

A travel agency that specializes in cruises can help you select the ship and itinerary that's best for you, as long as you make your wishes and your budget considerations clear to them. Don't just ask for a Caribbean cruise and take whichever one is mentioned first. Ships and ports of call vary tremendously, and everybody loses if you don't enjoy yourself.

Take the right cruise, and you'll come home rested and happy. Of course, you will be expecting to be served breakfast in bed the first few days home, and you'll miss finding that good-night chocolate on your pillow.

FOOTNOTE

"I rather wished that I had gone first class," Evelyn Waugh wrote about sailing from Port Said aboard P&O's Ranchi *in 1929. "It's not that my fellow passengers were not every bit as nice as the Port Said residents had told me they would be, but that there were so many of them."*

Future Trends

Passengers on today's cruise ships are far from sedentary, with deck games, gyms, spas and aerobics classes always available.

If we can believe present trends, passengers of the future are going to be healthy, wealthy and wise.

Healthy, because virtually every ship menu afloat is offering low-calorie, low-fat and vegetarian options; because more and more cruise lines are banning smoking in their dining rooms and show lounges; and because well-equipped fitness centers and aerobics classes are as common as casinos. We're also seeing more stringent inspections of water and air conditioning systems and tougher restrictions on food handlers following the 1994 Legionnaire's disease scare on the *Horizon* and the shigella outbreak on *Viking Serenade.*

Wealthy, (well, at least less poor), because money-saving early booking discounts that let you cut costs from the published brochure rate are in effect closer and closer to sailing time; no matter how late you book, have your travel agent check to see if you qualify. Frequent cruisers can qualify for free cruises with accrued cruise days from Cunard, and Seabourn passengers in the line's WorldFare program may purchase blocks of 45 to 120 cruise days at a reduced price and use them on any cruises over a period of three years.

Wise in the ways of the world, because there is more of it to see by ship than at any time in recent history.

Fear of Cruising

A lot of people who think nothing of buying a package coach tour to a foreign country, driving the car across the continent or booking a week at a resort hotel on the recommendation of a casual friend over lunch, shy away from the idea of taking a cruise. Why?

Here's what they tell the pollsters:

Five Common Excuses

1. "I'm scared I'd get seasick."
2. "I can't plan my vacations that far in advance."
3. "I'd feel uncomfortable—I wouldn't know what to wear or how much to tip or which cabins were good."
4. "I'm afraid of gaining weight with all that food around."
5. "What if I don't like the ship? Then I've wasted my whole vacation."

Five Quick Answers

1. If your previous seagoing experience is limited to sailboats, fishing boats or a hitch in the Navy, modern cruise ships equipped with stabilizers that eliminate much of the rolling motion may surprise you. Fewer than five per cent of the passengers on any cruise complain of motion sickness; medications are readily available on board if you're bothered by *mal de mer.* (See Scoping Out Seasickness and Sidestepping Seasickness, page 60.)
2. If there's one thing there's plenty of, baby, it's cruise ship cabins in 1996. A good travel agent can book you on almost any ship for any destination on short notice—sometimes with a deep discount.
3. If you're bugged by the unfamiliar, a cruise is the least complicated vacation you'll ever have to deal with; it all comes in one neat prepaid package. You don't need a special wardrobe for cruises; chances are, everything you need is already in your closet. (See Eleven Tips to Lighten Your Luggage, page 51.) Tipping suggestions are spelled out on board toward the end of the sailing (also, see Tipping, page 63) and there's a checklist on what to look for in a cabin (see Choosing A Cabin on page 38.)
4. Every ship offers a variety of seafoods, salads, fruits and vegetables, along with low-calorie, low-fat dishes. Some offer full spa menus. Even on small ships you'll find exercise classes and a full array of gym facilities. You could come back home in better shape than when you left. As for temptation, repeat after us—"Just because I

paid for it doesn't mean I have to eat it all." (See How to Avoid Pigging Out at Sea, page 43.)

5. Selecting the right ship is the biggest single decision you'll have to make. Don't let anyone tell you all cruises are alike—they're not—or that Brand X Cruise Line is "the best" because there's not one single "best." The best cruise for you is the one you'll enjoy the most. See Choosing A Cruise, page 37 and How To Read A Brochure, page 33, below.

FOOTNOTE

Nearly 15 years ago when we first began writing our cruise column, a brusque California businessman planning his first cruise called us. He said he'd asked three travel agents which was the best cruise line–the first said Princess, the second said Carnival, the third said Sitmar (now defunct). So he called us to find out which of those three was the best. When we tried to counter by finding out something about him and what kind of cruise experience he was seeking, he screamed angrily into the phone, "I knew it! You don't know any more about it than those travel agents!" And he hung up.

The New Cruisers

More and more young singles and couples are discovering cruises as a fun and affordable mini-vacation.

A funny thing happened to ocean liners on the way to the 21st century—they got democratized.

The great and famous ships that carried royalty, heads of state, the Astors and the Glorias (Swanson and Vanderbilt) in first-class luxury, relegating to second and third class all other passengers from potato-famine Irish immigrants to '50s college students, have turned into one-class cruise ships where everyone on board is equal, more or less.

Meanwhile, the transatlantic jumbo jets that hastened the demise of ocean liners have become almost a parody of the old class system themselves, fawning over first-class passengers with sofa-sized seats and leg rests, personal video monitors and champagne and caviar, and cramming everyone else into steerage, where bodies are jackknifed into tortuous positions, babies cry all night and unidentifiable foods in plastic compartments are slapped down at intervals on wobbly trays.

Even a decade ago, the change was apparent, as cruise lines began to notice the huge numbers of first-timer cruisers aboard. Carnival's president, Bob Dickinson, then vice president of sales and marketing, pointed out in 1985 that 70 to 75 percent of all his line's passengers were first-time cruisers. "We don't think we're in the cruise business; we're in the vacation business." He went on to predict—correctly—that Carnival would have a 10-ship fleet by 1995.

The mini-cruise market, offering short, affordable getaways, was booming with Eastern Cruise Line's *Emerald Seas* (now the *Sapphire Seas*) sailing from Miami to the Bahamas and Western Cruise Line's *Azure Seas* (now Dolphin's *OceanBreeze*) cruising down to Ensenada from Los Angeles.

A lucrative and previously untapped new market was discovered— couples and singles from the world of young, upwardly-mobile professionals; baby boomers with income and leisure time for longer vacations; blue-collar and clerical workers who appreciated one up-front, all-inclusive ticket price for a vacation as luxurious as any they could find at a land-based resort and often less expensive.

In contrast to the retired and/or wealthy passengers who make up the rosters on around-the-world cruises, the new cruise passengers are looking for mini-vacations at sea, comparing a weekend cruise to a weekend spent in Nassau, Palm Springs, Las Vegas or Atlantic City.

You'll get the picture the minute you step aboard a cruise ship these days. Hardly a ship leaves dock without announcing a party for singles within a day or two of sailing, and guest hosts are on board many vessels expressly to dance, play bridge and socialize with unattached women.

If you're one of the new cruise passengers, you can count on more and more variety in the world of cruises. The day is not far off when you'll be able to cruise anywhere you wish for the length of time you prefer at a price you can afford, not once in a lifetime but once or twice a year.

Short Sails, Big Sales

The burgeoning mini-cruise market is the fastest-growing segment of cruising today as more and more first-timers decide to try the waters. They like the idea of sampling the experience for a few days before booking a longer sailing.

Short cruises seem to fit today's lifestyles, too, with people opting for several small vacations throughout the year rather than one big one. The newest wrinkle is family reunion cruises aboard mini-cruises where nobody has to host, cook or clean—and you can get a group discount as well. For every 15 or so people, there's usually a free or discounted escort or organizer's ticket.

The four major mini-cruise home ports are Miami, Port Canaveral, Ft. Lauderdale and Los Angeles.

FOOTNOTE

David Gevanthor, former president of now-defunct SeaQuest Cruises, once said about first-time cruisers starting out on modest ships or sailings, "That's like saying you start off buying a Ford and gradually work up to a Mercedes, and that ignores a guy that buys a Mercedes for his first car. Price is not a determiner; it's the lifestyle and desires of the client that determine what kind of cruise they take."

Anatomy of a Cruise Ship: A Curmudgeon's Guide

The funnel or stack is where the cruise line displays its logo and sends out its combustion gases; never sit downwind of the funnel without checking first for soot.

The Basics

- The **FUNNEL** or **STACK** is where the cruise line displays its logo, such as Princess Cruises' sea witch with flowing hair or Costa Cruises' blue-and-yellow C or Celebrity's big white X, Greek for Chi or C. The stack also carries away the ship's combustion gases and occasional bursts of black smoke. When wearing white pants, **never sit in a deck chair downwind of the funnel** without checking first for soot.

- The **GANGWAY** is the external stairway or ramp leading to the ship from the shore. It is also the place where the ship's photographers take pictures of passengers embarking or disembarking in every port, thereby creating a traffic jam in both directions.

- The **LIFEBOATS** are the orange and white vessels that hang outside your cabin window blocking your view if your travel agent doesn't know how to read a deck plan. Some lines like Crystal and Princess point out in their brochures where a cabin view is partly or entirely obstructed and reduce the price accordingly. Some lines, however, sketch the boats in on the deck plan but fail to point out or reduce the price on partially obstructed views. And still other lines fail to indicate the lifeboats at all, leading to *Titanic*-tinged visions.

Deck Areas

- The **SWIMMING POOL** on some ships may be mistaken for a footbath or an ornamental fountain. Fancy pool areas with swim-up bars, waterfalls and other pool novelties tend to get clogged up with passengers under 16.
- Many of the newer ships have a **JOGGING TRACK** on a sports deck high atop the ship. Some of these are so short that it takes 13 (on *Radisson Diamond*) or 14 (on *Queen Odyssey*) laps to make a mile. **Never, under any circumstances, book a cabin under the jogging track.**
- Some ships have a **CHILDREN'S WADING POOL** which can be identified by its singular lack of children, who prefer to spend their time belly-whopping into the adult pool.

Shuffleboard can reach fever pitch on a classic liner like the Rotterdam.

- **SHUFFLEBOARD** is a popular deck game that can reach fever pitch on a classic liner like the *Rotterdam*. On other ships, some passengers mistake it for hopscotch.
- The **Promenade** is the deck that goes all the way around the ship, giving passengers a chance for a brisk, breezy walk. Six or seven times around usually equals a mile. **Do not attempt to exchange pleasantries with a grim-faced walker counting laps.**

Lounges and Public Rooms

- The **SHOW LOUNGE** in the daytime is the setting for line dancing lessons, bingo games and port information lectures, but in the evening becomes Broadway and Las Vegas with musical extravaganzas or, all too often, the last refuge of magicians, jugglers, puppeteers and ventriloquists last seen on the Ed Sullivan Show.
- The **CINEMA** is where recent movies are screened; on Royal Cruise Line ships and Cunard's *Sagafjord* and *Vistafjord* it is also considered an ideal spot to nap after lunch. On the Big Red Boats, passengers under 12 vie with each other for the record number of times they can come and go opening the entry doors wide enough to wipe out the image on the screen.
- The **DISCO** is the place to meet junior officers in white uniforms late at night. On older ships like the *Dolphin IV*, *OceanBreeze* and *SeaBreeze* it's located deep in the bowels of the vessel and in the daytime looks like a place where Dracula would sleep. On Carnival ships it flashes with neon and rock videos and throbs with amplified sound. **Never book a cabin over, under or beside the disco.**

The disco is the place to meet junior officers in white uniforms late at night. Never book a cabin over, under or beside the disco.

- The **PHOTO GALLERY** is where the ship's photographers mount the pictures of passengers they've snapped at odd moments throughout the cruise. It's always crowded with people buying photos they want to keep and others buying photos they don't want anyone else to see.
- The **TEEN CENTER** is a euphemism for a video games arcade that is frequently filled with males far past their teens. A modern refinement introduced by Carnival's *Holiday* recently lets the kids use their own ship ID card to access the games in lieu of dogging dad for more quarters; the charge goes right into the billing computers along with dad's bar bills and mom's shipboard shopping.
- The **DUTY-FREE SHOPS** are the places to buy Lladro porcelain, Rolex watches, sequinned garments and other useless items. Essentials like toothpaste, aspirin and sunblock are harder to find since the profit margin is considerably smaller.
- The **SHIP'S CASINO** is a philosophical proving ground where optimists arrive and pessimists depart. A real gambler heads for the roulette table, taking a chance on whether the sea motion is in his favor or against it.
- The **LIBRARY** on most ships is the place to find books to read. It is also populated by competitive trivia quiz aficionados looking up answers in order to win still another bookmark or key chain. **You can tell how much your cruise line trusts you by noting whether the glass cases are locked or unlocked**.
- The **CARD ROOM** is the refuge of avid bridge players whose conversation beyond bids is limited to port of call observations such as, "It's only Hong Kong, shut up and deal." **Only a masochist should let himself be roped into being a fourth for bridge after lunch**.
- **ELEVATORS** on ships should be avoided at all costs, since the exercise of going up and down stairs is a major defense against weight gain. Elevators should only be used in an emergency except, of course, they do not operate during emergencies.

CRUISE SHIPS

1. **Jogging Track,** Sunrise Deck
2. **Bar,** Sports Deck
3. **Suites,** Sports Deck
4. **Restaurant,** Resort Deck
5. **Cafe,** Resort Deck
6. **Restaurant,** Entertainment Deck
7. **Gambling,** Entertainment Deck
8. **Lounge,** Promenade Deck
9. **Restaurant,** Plaza and Promenade Decks

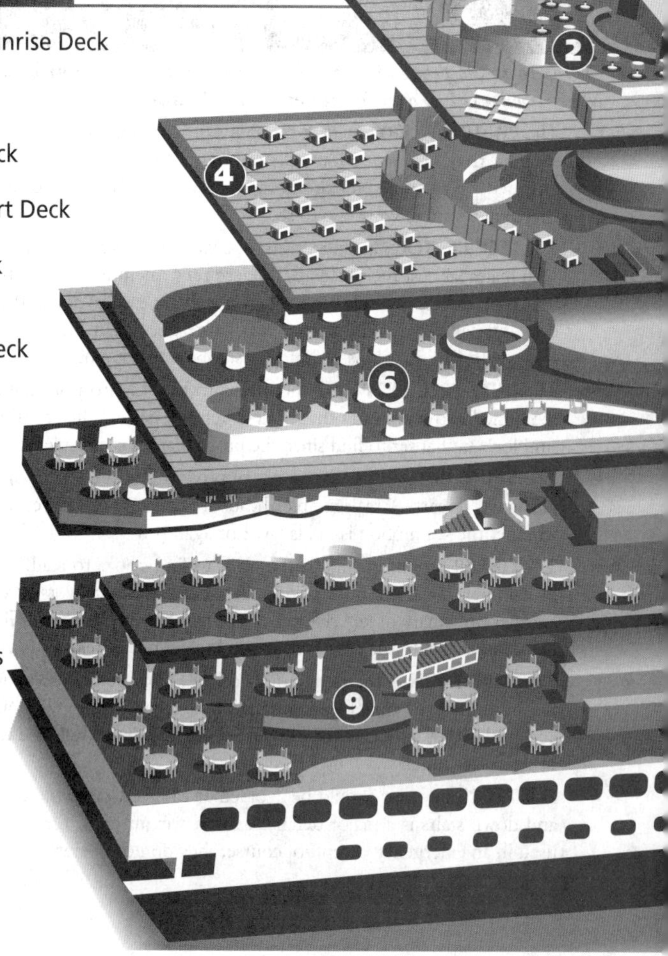

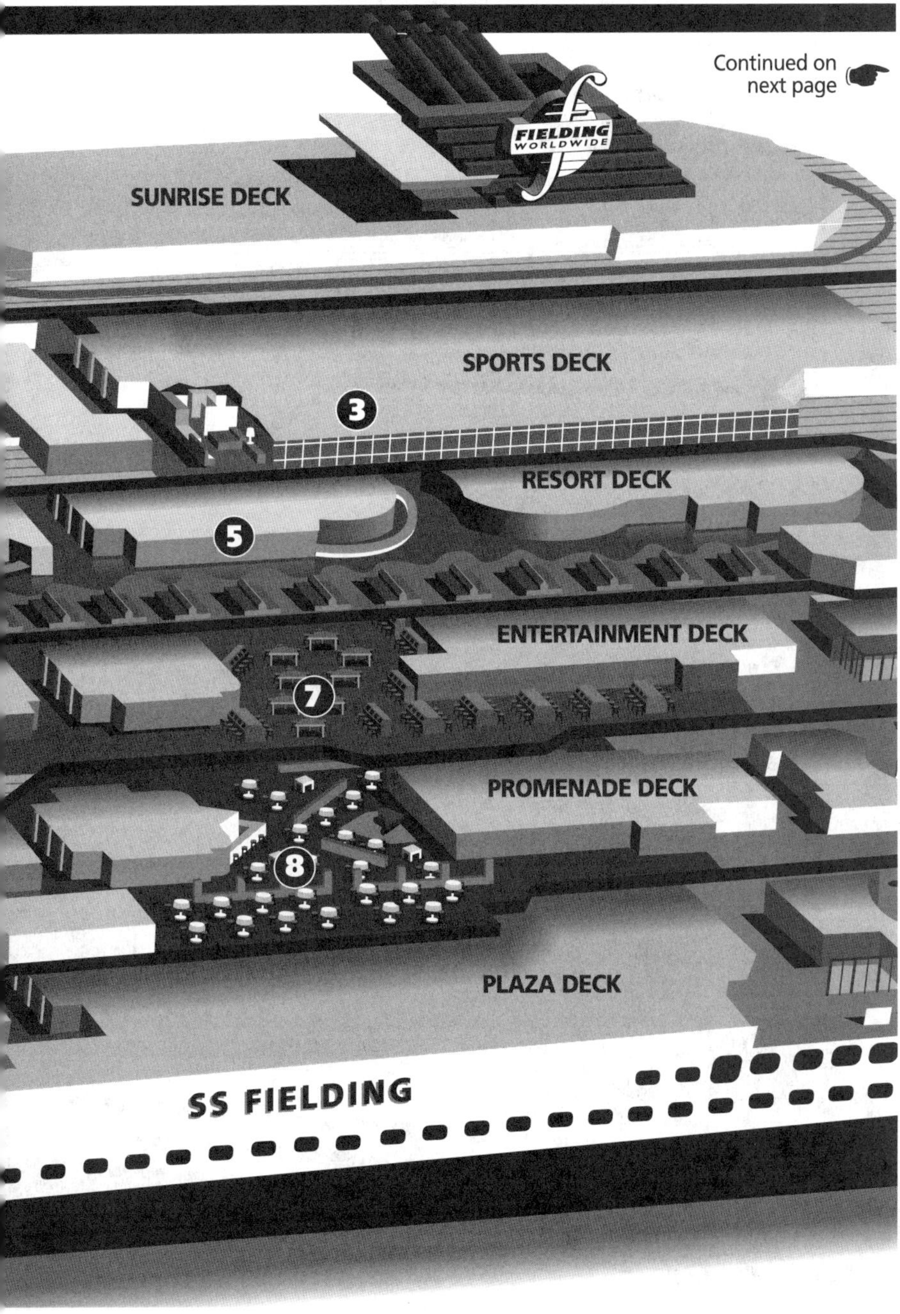
Continued on
next page
FIELDING
WORLDWIDE
SUNRISE DECK
SPORTS DECK
3
RESORT DECK
5
ENTERTAINMENT DECK
7
PROMENADE DECK
8
PLAZA DECK
SS FIELDING

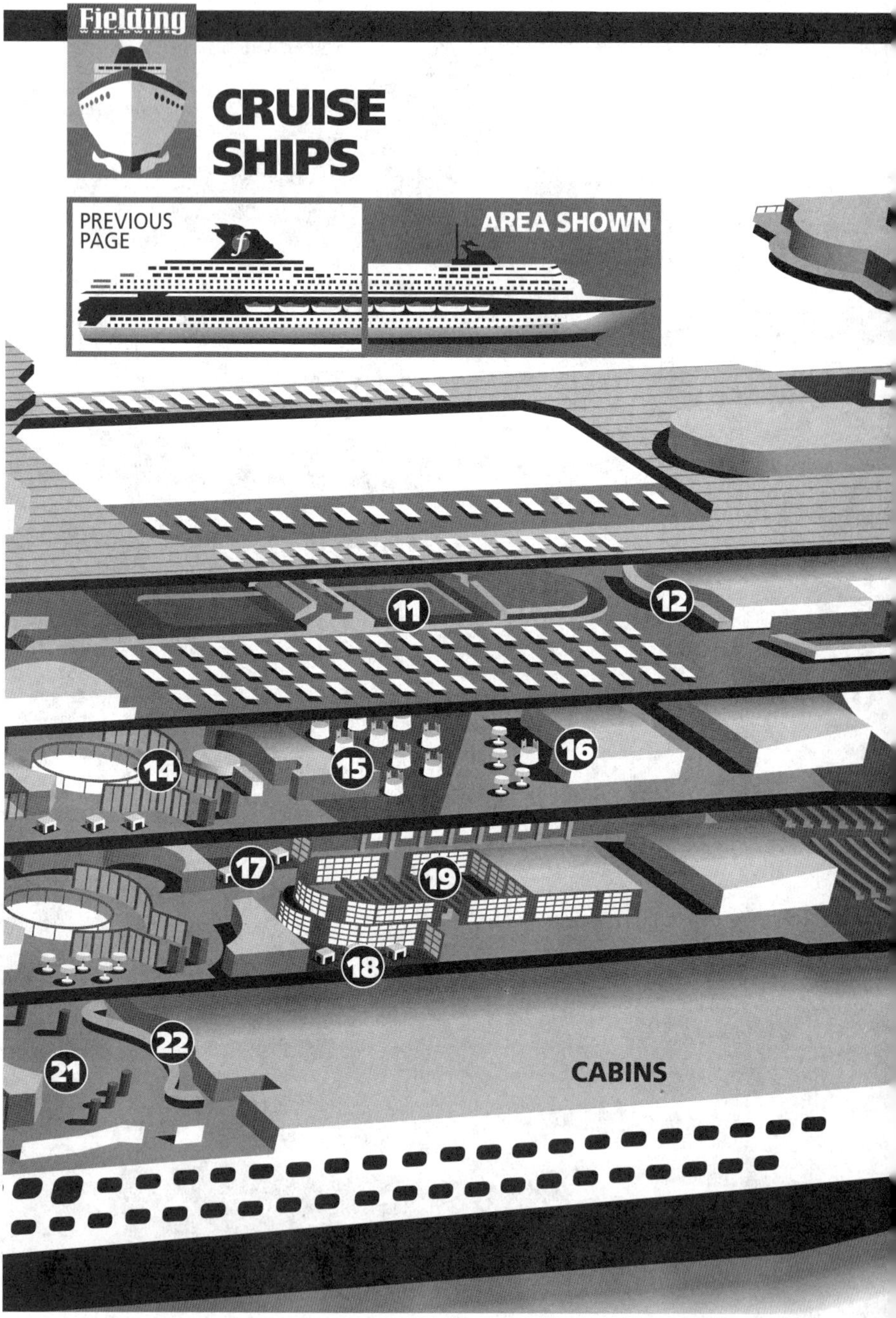
Fielding
WORLDWIDE
CRUISE
SHIPS
PREVIOUS
PAGE
AREA SHOWN
11
12
14
15
16
17
18
19
21
22
CABINS

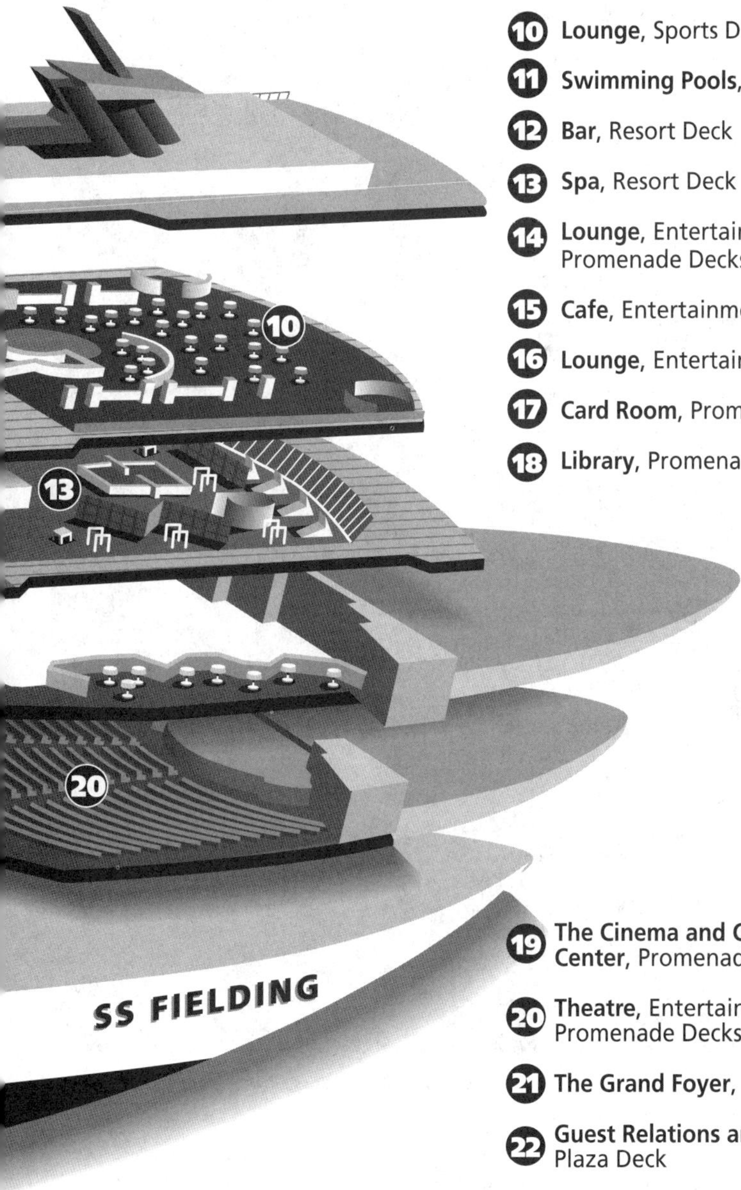

10 **Lounge**, Sports Deck

11 **Swimming Pools**, Resort Deck

12 **Bar**, Resort Deck

13 **Spa**, Resort Deck

14 **Lounge**, Entertainment and Promenade Decks

15 **Cafe**, Entertainment Deck

16 **Lounge**, Entertainment Deck

17 **Card Room**, Promenade Deck

18 **Library**, Promenade Deck

19 **The Cinema and Conference Center**, Promenade Deck

20 **Theatre**, Entertainment and Promenade Decks

21 **The Grand Foyer**, Plaza Deck

22 **Guest Relations and Lobby**, Plaza Deck

Elevators come in all shapes and sizes, including this neon-lit glass elevator on Carnival's Fantasy.

- The **BEAUTY SALON** is where all the women on board gather between 5 and 7 p.m. on formal nights. Naughty hairdressers direct them back to their cabins via the deck, where the wind destroys the comb-out and everything has to be done all over again.

All About Cabins

- **CABINS** come in all shapes and sizes, mostly small. As a rule, the higher the deck location, the higher the price, but **the smoothest ride is amidships (in the middle) on a lower deck**.

- If you go into your cabin and see a square or rectangular panel of glass with light coming through, you have an **OUTSIDE CABIN** with a window. If the glass is round, it is a **PORTHOLE**. If you fling the curtains open and find yourself facing a blank wall, you have an **INSIDE CABIN**.
- Windows and portholes in the cabin cannot be opened, except on very ancient vessels such as the Mayflower. Occupants of premium-priced **OUTSIDE CABINS ON PROMENADE DECK** are always admired by passers-by who look into the windows as they stroll by. On some ships the glass is covered with a special tinted film so outsiders see their own reflections during the daytime. But after dark, the situation is reversed, with the cabin occupants starring in their own X-rated TV shows for the passersby outside.
- Each cabin has a private bathroom with tub or shower, wash basin and **VACUUM MARINE TOILET**, which flushes with a loud "whoooosh." The best-designed have the flushing device situated where it cannot be activated until the top of the toilet is closed, an essential safety feature for absent-minded passengers.
- Before plugging a hair dryer or other **ELECTRICAL APPLIANCE** into a wall socket, **check whether the ship's electrical system is 110 volts and AC (alternating current) or 220 volts and DC (direct current)**. Plugging one of the former into one of the latter may blow more than the hairdo. Many ships carry voltage converters that will solve the problem; check with the purser's desk.
- Each cabin also has an individual **TEMPERATURE CONTROL KNOB**. When your choices are limited from cold to colder or hot to hotter, call Housekeeping to send up a repairman.
- **CABIN WALLS** on all but the newest ships can be very thin, and an entertaining alternative to a TV set or radio. The disembodied voice that gives greetings or commands from the cabin walls is usually the cruise director on the public address system, unless he's droning on about sea temperatures and windspeeds and nautical miles, in which case it's the captain. A panel of knobs located near the bed can tune in shipboard music programmed by overworked staffers at the reception desk who play "The Sound of Music" for three days in a row.
- Shipboard **CLOSETS** are designed to remind passengers that they should have left behind half the clothes they brought.
- Somewhere within the closet or under the beds are the **LIFE JACKETS**, which appear humorous at first glance but are extremely important should there be a problem at sea. **Always attend the life boat drill and never leave without learning to don the jacket properly, check for the whistle and light, and find which life boat is yours**.
- None of the many **PAPERS** which arrive under the cabin door is junk mail. Each has some message to impart, whether it is the full schedule of activities for the next day with the suggested dress code for the evening or a 20 per cent discount on perfume or gold chains in the gift shop. **Read all papers shoved under the door, no matter how boring they appear. One might be an invitation to dine at the captain's table**.

Service Areas

- The **PURSER'S DESK** is usually located in the lobby. It's the desk with the long line of people waiting to register a complaint, break a $100 bill into singles or buy postage stamps.
- The **SHORE EXCURSIONS DESK** is where you go to buy overpriced bus tours of minor Mexican cities which always stop at the cathedral, the cliff-divers and then an hour-long shopping opportunity at the gift shop of the guide's cousin.

- The **RADIO ROOM** is where you arrange to pay $15 a minute to send a fax to your office or make a call home to your answering machine and find out bad news that ruins your vacation.

The dining room — this one is aboard RCCL's Viking Serenade — is a favorite shipboard gathering spot.

The Dining Room

- **TABLES** rarely come with only two chairs but most often in fours, sixes, eights or even tens. **Couples who worry about being bored (or boring) are safer at tables of six or more**. After dining together throughout the cruise, passengers always wind up sending Christmas cards to each other.
- **MEAL SEATINGS** are the arbitrary times the cruise line has decided its passengers will eat. **MAIN** or **FIRST SEATING** offers lunch at noon and dinner at 6 or 6:30, but breakfast is at 7 a.m. **SECOND** or **LATE SEATING** passengers dine fashionably at 8 or 8:30, breakfast at a comfortable 8:30 or 9 in the morning, but can't have lunch until 1:30. This is why three-hour deck buffet breakfasts and lunches were invented.
- **SECOND SEATING** is preferred by really dedicated gourmands, who can fit in early riser's coffee and a few samples from the buffet breakfast before reporting for the regular dining room breakfast. Then morning bouillon at 11 settles any remaining hunger pangs until time for a hot dog or hamburger from the deck grill as an appetizer for the buffet lunch. Lingering over the 1:30 lunch fills the empty moments until teatime, with cocktail hour, dinner and midnight buffet left to round out the day—and the figure.
- Passengers who demand **SPECIAL DIET MENUS**—low in fats, calories or salt—at the beginning of a seven-day cruise usually throw abandon to the winds about Wednesday, then wonder why their shipboard diet plan didn't work.
- Ships that serve **MIDNIGHT BUFFET** at 10:30 p.m. rank high on the senior circuit. Swinging singles should seek vessels like Carnival's with midnight buffet at midnight, followed by the night owl buffet at 2 a.m.

The Only Ten Nautical Terms You Ever Need to Know

1. **Port**: the left side of the ship when you're facing the pointy end.
2. **Starboard**: the right side of the ship when you're facing the pointy end.

3. **Forward**: toward the front, or pointy end.
4. **Aft**: toward the back, or blunt end.
5. **Bow**: the pointy end.
6. **Stern**: the blunt end.
7. **Tender**: a boat carried aboard the ship that can ferry you ashore if the ship is not tied up at the dock; to use the boat to ferry passengers ashore.
8. **Gangway**: the detachable outside stairway from the ship's deck down to the dock or tender.
9. **Embark**: to get on a ship.
10. **Disembark**: to get off a ship.

Questions to Ask Yourself Before Calling a Travel Agent

Before you sail away into the sunset, you need to know what you want and be able to communicate that information to a travel agent, since virtually all cruise lines prefer or require bookings to be made through agents. Read these questions and know the answers to them before you call the travel agent. It will make her job much easier and ensure that you'll get the right cruise for you. For additional information on cruises and the Caribbean, get a copy of Fielding's *Worldwide Cruises* and Fielding's *Caribbean* available at your local bookstore or call *1-800-FW-2-GUIDE.*

1. What are you looking for—sunny island beaches, duty-free shopping, a stress-free, do-nothing getaway, a razzle-dazzle good time with plenty of entertainment?

You can get them all on a cruise, but not necessarily on the same ship. Try to be specific as to what you want. A working couple with young children might opt for a family cruise, giving them quality time with the kids and still the chance to be alone together while the youngsters join in special shipboard youth programs. On the other hand, a grade-school teacher seeking a break from workaday reality would probably want to set sail in exactly the opposite direction from ships that carry hundreds of romping children.

2. How long can you be away?

Cruises can be three-day weekend sailings, seven-day cruises, 14-day sailings, even 100-plus day world cruises. First-timers usually opt for three to seven days, frequent cruisers for a longer period of time.

3. Are you traveling as a single, one of a pair, or part of a group of family and friends?

Others may have different needs or desires, so confer with them before making any decisions. A ship good for singles may not work so well with family groups.

4. What do you want in the way of shipboard lifestyle?

Decide what you think are the most important elements of a good vacation, jot them down and have them handy when you make your initial call to a travel agent. While many stressed-out travelers picture a cruise ship as a place to lounge quietly by the pool with a good book, they may be ready after a couple of days for livelier activities. Virtually all cruise ships today offer gym equipment, aerobics, lectures, shoreside golf and tennis, dancing, bridge or crafts classes and even shopping.

5. Do you want a large, medium-sized or small ship?

Big ships have more entertainment, bigger casinos and spas and longer lines; medium-sized ships have scaled-down versions of the same. Small ships are more apt to be free of regimentation and rigid dress codes, but you may be on your own for entertainment. Small to mid-sized vessels usually provide a more relaxed ambiance, while glittering megaliners throb with music and bright lights most of the night. But there's not a vessel afloat that doesn't have a sunny, secluded corner for reading or a lively spot around the bar for socializing.

6. Do you want a classic (read older) or contemporary (read newer) ship?

Most new ships will remind you of a chain resort hotel like Hyatt or Marriott, complete with atrium, glass elevators and identical modular cabins, while ships built 20 or more years ago have ocean liner looks, odd-sized cabins and nostalgic promenade decks.

7. Do you want frequent opportunities to wear your nicest party clothes, or would you prefer to stay casual day and night?

Super-deluxe small ships are quite dressy, expedition and sailing ships casual, and big ships usually have two dress-up evenings a week. Sometimes people who work in an office that requires business attire every day welcome the indulgence of casual sailing or adventure cruising where the only dress code may request "no bathing suits or bare feet at dinner." But bear in mind that even very dressy small luxury vessels may have a watersports marina off the stern that unfolds when the ship is at anchor for swimming or windsurfing.

8. Do you want to go island-hopping on a ship that stops at a lot of ports or spend your time relaxing aboard ship?

If relaxing is more important, look for itineraries that designate one or two days at sea during a seven-day cruise. You'll still have ports to visit but can get some rest in between.

9. What do you want to learn about the places you'll visit?

If the history, culture, flora and fauna is important, look to expedition ships that emphasize natural history lectures and birdwatching boatrides. Adventure and expedition cruises always seem to attract a lot of doctors, lawyers, teachers and other professionals who diligently attend all the lectures, then happily splash ashore in rubber landing craft to go on nature hikes. If you prefer to know where to pick up brand names like Rolex, Lladro or Colombian emeralds, any big mainstream cruise ship will fill the bill with its "guaranteed shopping" programs subsidized by the very merchants being recommended.

INSIDER TIP

Don't let price be the major factor when you choose your first cruise, especially if you assume all ships and cruises are alike. They're not, and the difference of $20 a day could mean a huge improvement in the quality of your shipboard experience. Once you've taken a couple of cruises, then you can afford to experiment, but a first-time cruise experience that doesn't meet your expectations could turn you away from cruising for good. A smart travel agent will try to steer you toward the most positive cruise experience for you and your family; that means future repeat business for the agent.

How to Read a Brochure

Whenever a new flock of brightly plumaged cruise brochures arrive, we find ourselves leafing through them and visualizing, not the romantic days at sea they portray, but an overworked copywriter in a tiny cubicle high atop a metropolitan office building.

Our fantasy copywriter, thesaurus at the ready, stares through a dirt-streaked window at a rainy sky between bouts of turning out hyperbolic sentences about "hibiscus-scented nights" and "elegant lounges where the decor is luxurious and plush."

Sometimes we wish cruise lines would spend a little less on the four-color pages and take the poor copywriter out on a cruise someday. It would certainly help clear up the vague and overblown prose.

In the meantime, however, the safest path for a potential cruise passenger is to skim the prose lightly and **CONCENTRATE ON THE PICTURES AND CHARTS**—you'd be surprised how much information you can glean from them—and then turn immediately to **READ THE "FINE PRINT"** on the inside back pages for the real nitty-gritty.

First, take a careful look at all the color photos. Don't get lost in reverie, imagining yourself standing on the deck with that Technicolor tropical drink in your hand—that's the intention of most successful advertising photography.

Instead, first **STUDY THE MODELS**, those beaming, bronzed beauties in each shot, then notice the slightly out-of-focus "real people" in some, but not all, of the backgrounds. The models represent the line's idealized version of their perfect prototype passengers, while the people in the background are real passengers on board during the photo shoot. If the ship seems suspiciously empty, the real passengers were all chased away so they could photograph the models alone. If the background people and the foreground people look as if they would be invited to the same party, you have a cruise line that is marketing realistically.

Next, flip quickly through the entire brochure to **GET AN OVERVIEW**. Where is the emphasis? If you see lots of nightlife and casino shots, the company is trying to tell you they're proud of the ship's after-dark entertainment. Where you see smiling waiters and cabin attendants, the line is telling you you'll get special treatment from their staff. If you see smiling children and their happy parents, the line is tipping you off that they welcome families on board. And if you see lots of food pictures, they're telling you, Miss Scarlett, you'll never be hungry again!

The **ITINERARY TABLES** are also valuable sources of information. If the copywriter extols a particular Caribbean island where you'll get a breathtaking view from atop a volcanic mountain in the island's center, and the itinerary says you dock at 9 a.m. and sail at noon, there's no way you'll see that view. And if your Greek Islands cruise arrives in Hydra at 9 p.m. and departs at 10:30 that same evening, you won't have many slides to show the folks back home.

Watch out for the little **ASTERISKS THAT DENOTE "CRUISE BY"** for some ports or islands. While you may get a look at them through binoculars or telephoto lenses, you won't set foot ashore.

If the itinerary has two cities shown, one of them in parentheses you can expect a long bus ride from the port town to the destination city.

Be sure, too, to note the **DAY OF THE WEEK** you're scheduled to arrive in each port. If there's a special museum you want to visit, check to be sure it's open on the day you're there. If you're counting on some serious shopping in St. Thomas, remember that stores are closed on Sundays, except for a few that open for a quick couple of hours in the morning when a ship is in port.

DECK PLANS are helpful in spotting extra niceties on board that aren't always promoted—the library, card room, sauna and spa, beauty and barber shop, hospital, covered decks and enclosed galleries.

DINING ROOM DIAGRAMS can tip you off as to how close together the tables are and if there are many tables for two available. Note that on older ships the dining room is usually on a lower deck, where your only view is of closed draperies backlit with fluorescent tubing to give the illusion of daylight.

What **ABOUT THE FOOD** on board? A discerning gourmet can usually tell from the photographs. Don't waste too much time studying the overwrought, gelatin-encased gala buffet; it's as standard on mass market seven-day Caribbean ships as the deck chairs and about as tasty.

In today's more health-conscious world, salmon has supplanted beef as the food photo of choice in cruise brochures, and more space is given to appetizers and small plate dishes than main courses or gala buffets, suggesting to the nervous first-timer that he won't necessarily gain weight on this ship.

You can usually tell from the pictures whether the cruise line will go out of its way to offer an interesting excursion ashore or simply **sell you a three-hour bus tour**.

CABIN SIZE is better determined from deck plans than photographs. In the latter, the photographer is usually shooting with a wide-angle lens while braced in the doorway or crouching in the shower. These lenses can distort a standard-sized berth into a bed fit for Magic Johnson.

And watch out for the brochure that shows **ONLY PICTURES OF DESTINATIONS AND CLOSE-UPS OF ATTRACTIVE MODELS DRINKING CHAMPAGNE**. Unless the ship was still under construction or undergoing extensive refitting when the photos were made, you suspect, maybe rightly, that they're trying to hide something from you.

After practicing a while with the pictures and diagrams, you should be in fine shape to tackle the prose and read between the lines. For additional assistance, check out **The Brochure Says** and **Translation** segments for each ship in the ship review section.

CHOOSING A CRUISE

Sometimes equating a ship with a hotel can help a first-time cruiser visualize it better; this soaring atrium lobby from Royal Caribbean's Nordic Empress may remind you of your favorite Marriott.

Pick a Ship, Any Ship

OK, you say, a cruise sounds great. Where do I sign up?

That's like saying a hotel is a hotel, book me a room. If you're a Ritz-Carlton regular, you might not be happy at the Motel 6. We feel a lot of otherwise experienced travelers might be more comfortable with cruising if they could equate a cruise line with a hotel company, so we've taken a bit of poetic license to give you a chance to relate your favorite type of land accommodations to the possibilities at sea. Bear in mind, however, that although ships are looking more and more like land hotels, the cruise ship experience is often superior, especially in service and entertainment, to its shoreside equivalent.

Bed-and-breakfasts	**American Canadian Caribbean Line** **Clipper Cruises**
Club Med	**Club Med Cruises** **Star Clippers** **Windjammer Barefoot Cruises**
Four Seasons	**Silversea Cruises**
Holiday Inn	**Premier Cruises** **Sun Line**
Howard Johnson	**Dolphin** **Regal Cruises** **Commodore**
Hyatt Regency	**Princess Cruises** **Costa Cruises**
Inter-Continental	**Royal Cruise Line** **Celebrity Cruises**
Marriott	**Royal Caribbean Cruise Ltd.** **Norwegian Cruise Line**
MGM Grand	**Carnival Cruises**
Relais & Chateaux	**Windstar Cruises** **Sea Goddess** **Radisson Seven Seas**
Ritz-Carlton	**Seabourn** **Crystal Cruises** **Cunard Royal Viking Sun** **Sagafjord** **Vistafjord**
Small Luxury Hotels	**Renaissance Cruises**
Westin	**Holland America Line**

Choosing a Cabin

Prices for the cruise are determined by the **cabin category**, which in turn is based on **deck location**, **amenities**, whether the cabin is **outside** (with a porthole or windows) or **inside** (with no daylight), and sometimes, but not always, on cabin **size**.

Don't expect to snap up the bottom-priced loss leader (the one advertised in big print in the ads) because some cruise ships may have only four or six of these, long since allotted or sometimes assigned to cruise staff or entertainers.

Standard cabin amenities always include a **bed** or berth for each passenger, closet and **storage** space, some sort of table or **dresser, private bathroom facilities** (except on P&O's *Canberra* and some sailing ships) with toilet, sink, tub or shower. Most have **individual temperature controls, telephone and radio and/or TV**.

Grand suites like the Royal Suite aboard RCCL's Majesty of the Seas *have many pleasurable extras such as separate living and sleeping areas and entertainment centers.*

Pleasurable extras in upper price categories may include **private verandas**, suites with **separate living room** and bedroom, **mini-refrigerators**, sitting areas and **picture windows**.

Families with children or several people traveling together will save money by booking cabins with third and fourth upper berths, pull-down bunks that go for much less money (sometimes free) than the first two beds in a cabin.

Disabled travelers will find most vessels have one or more cabins that are specially configured to take care of wheelchairs with **wider doors, turning space, an absence of sills and grab rails in the bathroom**.

Dining Room Know-How

Your cruise ship dining room will operate in one of three ways:

1. **Totally open seatings**, usually on small or ultra-luxury vessels, in which the passenger arrives within a given time frame and sits where and with whom he pleases.

2. **Single meal seatings**, in which the passenger arrives within a given time frame and occupies an assigned table for the duration of the cruise.

3. **Two meal seatings**, in which passengers are assigned to dine at a particular table at a specified time, usually 6 p.m. or 8:30 p.m. for dinner, with breakfast and lunch comparably early or late as well.

The two-seating arrangement is the most common. You'll probably be asked at the time of booking which you prefer, but there's no guarantee you'll get it. If you don't get **a card with a specified dining time and table number** in advance or find it in your cabin when you arrive on board, go immediately to the maitre d'hotel in the dining room or another designated area and arrange your seating.

Some ships offer in addition to the regular dining room an alternative restaurant available at no extra charge but by reservation only.

Second seating times are the most in demand on Caribbean cruises. Don't be upset if you don't get your first choice on a cruise, particularly if the ship is full, but if it means a lot, **chat quietly with the maitre d'hotel, expressing your desire while tactfully holding a $20 bill** and you may be able to negotiate a change.

You can request first or second seating, a smoking (on those ships that still allow smoking in the dining room) or nonsmoking table and the table size you wish. Most first-time cruisers request tables for two, which are relatively rare, but find they enjoy being seated at a larger table for six or eight. The most potentially problematic table size is for four. If you can't stand your tablemates and want to move, be decisive—**make your move at the end of the very first dinner**. Don't wait a couple of days to see if they get more charming. They won't.

Some ships offer alternative restaurant dining by reservation; there is no charge except sometimes a request to tip at point of service. This enables passengers seated at a large table in the regular dining room to have a private dinner for two or an opportunity to dine with new acquaintances.

Cruise Line Cuisine

It seems to us that TV's "The Love Boat" was on the wrong track. Episode after episode, the passengers seemed to spend an inordinate amount of time falling in and out of love. You hardly ever saw anybody agonizing about what to order for dinner.

But if you took a poll of real-life cruise passengers, you'd find more of them looking forward to encountering a lobster thermidor than a shipboard romance, and to lighting into a dish of cherries jubilee instead of starting a flame in someone's heart.

Italian buffet night brings a major dessert display.

Cruise ship brochures entice us with full-color photographs of voluptuous midnight buffets, centerfolds of sensuous bananas flambe, lush melons and wicked croissants on a bedside tray. Is it any wonder we bound up the gangway anticipating a tryst with a tournedos of tenderloin Rossini?

In the fantasy world of cruise-ship advertising, every meal is a gourmet feast fit for a king, or even a restaurant critic. But in the real world on board, that's not always the case.

Think for a minute about your favorite little gourmet restaurant, the place you go once or twice a year to celebrate a special occasion. Does it serve two full dinner seatings an evening to between 500 and 1000 people, plus offering breakfast and lunch?

Does it operate a cafeteria on the side, along with a tearoom, half-a-dozen bars with snacks and hot hors d'oeuvres, a specialty pizzeria or ice cream parlor, and a catering service that produces beach picnics, deck barbecues and delivers meals to your door?

Is it atop a remote mountain peak or on an island in the middle of the ocean, hundreds of miles from a reliable source of food supplies?

No? Then don't try to compare most cruise ship cooking to a three-star *Michelin Guide* restaurant. Of course, there are a few exceptions (see Six Best Floating Dining Rooms, page 10).

Small ships, on the other hand, usually turn out tastier food because they don't have to deal with as much volume, but on the down side, their menus are usually more restrictive.

Five Food Fanatic Tips About Ships

1. Most large ships serve high-quality **hotel banquet food**, most often capably prepared and attractively served. You'll encounter a few truly memorable dishes, some mediocre ones and, at least once during your cruise will be served something unidentifiable that you're sure you didn't order until the waiter affirms that it is indeed the chef's version of gazpacho or pecan pie.

2. Before you sign on the dotted line with your friendly neighborhood travel agent, ask to **see some menus** from the ship you're considering—not prototype menus like some publish in their brochures, but actual menus that have the date printed on them from a recent cruise, preferably one the agent picked up during her cruise. (Because you fussy eaters are not going to accept an agent's recommendation unless she's been aboard that ship, at least for lunch, are you?)
3. Most mass market, mini-cruise and seven-day Caribbean lines have **rotation menu plans** that are not repeated during a single cruise but rather follow each other every seven or 14 or 21 days. Theme evenings are popular—French night with onion soup and *escargots* and *coq au vin*, Italian nights with antipasto, pasta and veal scaloppine, American nights with shrimp cocktail, corn on the cob and roast turkey with cranberry sauce. **In this book, such cuisine is referred to as Themed**.
4. Once on board, **shop around early in the cruise** for the location of the breakfasts, lunches and snacks that really sing out to you, and once you've found a winner, stick with it. Menus are usually posted ahead of time, so you can do your window-shopping in advance.
5. **Talk to your waiter**, and if he's good, learn to trust him. He's there to make you happy; his tip depends on it. Let him know what you like and dislike early in the cruise, and he'll always lead you through the menu. We treasure a memory of one of our first cruises, a Sitmar waiter named Tony who delivered the luncheon dish we'd ordered but materialized a few minutes later with another dish we hadn't ordered, murmuring, "I thought you might like to taste this one, too." Our choice was wrong; his was right.

FOOTNOTE

Cruise line food has improved tremendously in the 15 years we've been covering the scene. We remember a Dutch chef on the Rotterdam *world cruise in 1985 who was going to retire at the end of that 100-day journey, and went to bizarre extremes not to repeat a single dish during the entire cruise. By the time we got on for the last leg, he was down to truly terrible combinations.*

Five Tips on Reading a Shipboard Menu

1. See if it gives you **a variety of lunch options** from brunch-type dishes if you missed breakfast (omelets, for instance) to lighter fare (sandwiches and main-dish salads) to something hearty if you're hungry.
2. Check the **light or low-calorie recommendation**. We saw a ship once listing the day's diet special as Cobb Salad, that high-fat, high-calorie concoction of chopped bacon, blue cheese, avocado, and eggs with a gloppy-thick dressing. You'd never lose weight on that diet.
3. See how much **fresh food versus canned** or preprepared dishes they offer. Fresh catch of the day may be prefrozen, but that's to be expected unless you're cruising in Alaska. Watch out for that long list of seven appetizers, most of them tinned juices.
4. See if they're pulling out all their stops on the dessert menu. A lot of lines cut food costs by **stuffing passengers with sugary sweets** and stodgy starches—you'll note the macaroni salads and jello on the buffets—spending about $1.98 a day per passenger on raw materials.
5. Eye the dish descriptions carefully to make sure the line isn't **blanding out all the dishes** with cream-based sauces instead of fresh herbs, garlic or imaginative seasoning.

INSIDER TIP

Check the nationality of the ship's officers, chef or dining room staff. Princess ships have British and Italian officers but an Italian dining room and galley staff, so you can expect continental cuisine with a definite Italian accent. Greek ships are going to serve continental dishes plus Greek salads and appetizers and at least one Greek menu a cruise. The Norwegians like to put out lavish seafood smorgasbords somewhere along the way.

How to Avoid Pigging Out at Sea

1. Shop around, reading posted menus in advance and **checking out the entire buffet display** before plowing in.
2. **Don't stuff yourself**. Help save the whales by not being one; let the fishes finish your food.
3. Unless your metabolism is fantastic, **skip a meal every now and then**, substituting teatime for lunch or scheduling an hour in the disco before judiciously checking out the late buffet.
4. **Beware of Greeks** (or Italians or Jamaicans or Austrians) **bearing dishes**; a soulful-eyed waiter usually has his tip rather than your figure in mind when he coaxes you into ordering an appetizer, soup, salad, fish, meat and two desserts.
5. **Steer clear of piña coladas** and any other drink you can't see through or that has an umbrella in it. Opt instead for mineral water or diet soda, a glass of wine or light beer.
6. Take advantage of **the exercise classes and spa**; you've paid for them just as much as you have all that food you feel compelled to eat.
7. You'll find **vegetarian and low-fat** or low-calorie dishes on practically every menu these days, as well as a wider range of fish and poultry and less red meat.
8. If we want a vegetarian dinner, we sometimes order a plate of all the **side vegetable dishes** on the menu rather than the same old boring steamed cauliflower, broccoli and carrots.
9. Try ordering **dishes without the sauce**. Contrary to the famous Jack Nicholson "whole wheat toast" scene from *Five Easy Pieces*, most waiters will be happy to bring you sauce on the side or lemon wedges instead of salad dressing.
10. When you lunch on deck, plan to wear your bathing suit or shorts, and **check out the row of slender young sylphs and Adonises by the pool** (or for that matter, the not-so-slender ones) for positive reinforcement before you fill your plate.

Ship Sanitation Inspections

A great deal of attention is being paid these days to the "green sheet" ship sanitation inspection scores from U.S. Public Health's Center for Disease Control that are issued every two weeks.

It's laudable that the Center for Disease Control is carrying out the program because it keeps the cruise lines on their toes, making them train and carefully observe the galley employees, who may speak a dozen different languages.

The way food is handled from its very arrival aboard the ship to its storage, as here in the food storage lockers on Cunard's* Vistafjord, *and its final holding and preparation can affect the ship sanitation score.

But by **the time the score has been published, it's history**, and the infraction has been corrected long ago. As a rule, ships are inspected every six months, but may go a year or even longer without a reinspection unless the cruise line requests one. Many cruise lines employ a trained sanitation expert to establish and monitor their own sanitation practices.

The only real value of the scores for a potential passenger is as a longtime study of a specific ship over a couple of years. If the vessel is a consistent failure, then chances are its galley and sanitation practices are sloppy.

A single 30-point infraction causes the ship to fail automatically, since 86 out of a possible 100 is the passing grade. Improper methods of handling food are responsible for most major point losses, with temperature violations in food holding, preparation and serving areas the most critical.

Unannounced inspections are carried out at regular intervals on foreign-flag ships that call even occasionally in U.S. ports. When a ship fails, it can (and almost always does) request a reinspection as soon as possible to show the problem has been cleared up.

We went through all the "green sheets" for a one-year period between July 1, 1994, and June 30, 1995, and found an interesting pattern. Some of the cleanest and most highly-regarded ships were occasionally among the failures. The super-deluxe *Seabourn Pride*, which scored a 74 on February 19, 1995, but was retested March 21 and scored a 94; the spic-and-span *Rotterdam*, which scored a 78 on April 18, 1995, but bounced back with a 93 on May 24; and the stately *Sagafjord*, which failed with an 81 on April 23, 1995, but rescored a 96 on June 12. On the other hand, some vintage budget ships—notably the *Regal Empress* from Regal Cruises—held a score of a 95 during most of the time period, dropped to an 86, still passing, during a later period, and scored a 97 on the June 24, 1995, inspection. This despite the fact that before its first scheduled sailing from New York, officials went down to the dock and handed out flyers pointing out sanitation levels so low passengers might not wish to sail with her.

Ships most commonly fail on the last inspection before they're sold or transferred, probably because the crew is less motivated. Brand-new ships or new cruise lines (the latter the case with Regal Cruises) are usually given a couple of preliminary inspections with notes before getting a published score. "It's not unusual for a new ship to fail, because generally you have a lot of new people with new equipment," one of the inspectors told us.

At the time the *Horizon* went through a well-publicized incident of Legionnaire's disease in the summer of 1994, it carried a score of 94, and its reinspection after the incidents netted it another 94. The *Viking Serenade*, inspected on July 18, 1994, scored 92, and when reinspected January 6, 1995, four months after its widely publicized gastrointestinal outbreaks of early September, still received a passing grade of 88.

The CDC inspectors have improved the quality of ship sanitation tremendously over the years, as well as carrying on an education program for kitchen workers who may come from a culture with different sanitation standards. Very few land-based restaurants could score an 86 or better under the CDC standards, according to former program head Tom Hunt, who had previously been a restaurant inspector. Unless a ship consistently fails over a period of time, there's no real way of determining whether a passenger might suffer a gastrointestinal illness aboard.

In fact, we were inadvertently once the cause of a ship sanitation rating failure when photographing the dining room of Royal Cruise Line's previous *Royal Odyssey* for a food magazine. The chef had stuck a bouquet of fresh flowers in the walk-in refrigerator to keep them fresh until the shoot, and the CDC inspectors on the surprise inspection seized them as a major infraction—non-food items stored with food items.

Six Questions About Ship Sanitation Scores

1. Does anyone ever score a perfect score?
Yes, the first ship to make 100 on the numerical listings, which were initiated in 1989, was Carnival's *Fantasy* on April 30, 1990, followed by Windstar's *Wind Spirit* which scored 100 on August 27, 1990. More recently, *Crown Dynasty*, now *Cunard Dynasty*, scored 100 on February 8, 1994.

2. What's the lowest score ever recorded?
The lowest one we've found was a 23 for Epirotiki's *Oceanos* back in 1989; that ship sank off the coast of South Africa in 1991.

3. Can the CDC keep a ship from sailing because of poor sanitation?
Cooperation is voluntary on the part of the ship being inspected. The vessel sanitation program cannot forbid a ship with extreme sanitation problems to sail until its problems are corrected; it can only recommend that it not sail.

4. Who pays for these inspections?
The cruise lines themselves.

5. Are all cruise ships inspected?
The CDC's jurisdiction covers all ships carrying 13 or more passengers that sail in international waters. It does not include U.S.-flag vessels sailing in U.S. waters like those of American Hawaii, Delta Queen Steamboat, Alaska Sightseeing/Cruise

West, or American Queen. Those ships are the responsibility of the Food and Drug Administration and the state health departments within their cruising areas.

6. How can I get a copy of the latest scores?
Via Internet, FTP.CDC.GOV//PUB/SHIP_INSPECTIONS/SHIPSCORE.TXT, or by calling ☎ *(404) 332-4565* and requesting Document No. 510051.

Safety of Life at Sea

Commonly called SOLAS, Safety of Life at Sea regulations govern cruise ships that call at U.S. ports. Whenever a new ship comes into service, or enters a U.S. port for its first call, it must undergo a rigorous set of inspections by the U.S. Coast Guard covering fire safety drills, use of emergency equipment, crew drills and detailed examinations of the condition and safety of the vessel's hull and its machinery. After the initial series of inspections, the ships are reinspected quarterly. Unlike the CDC inspectors described above, the Coast Guard has the power to detain a ship from sailing if it is deemed unsafe for its passengers. One recent incident was when the newly-refurbished and not-quite-finished *QE2* was detained for 37 hours in New York in December of 1994, a case subsequently hotly disputed between Cunard and the U.S. Coast Guard.

The Coast Guard's Traveling Inspectors team boards ships with emergencies to investigate causes, such as those numerous incidents in the summer of 1995—ships running aground, engine room fires, main engines down and sweltering passengers aboard ships with no electricity, air conditioning or hot food. There were few injuries and no loss of life reported in any of the incidents, but in some of the vessels the backup equipment went out as well, which is unusual on modern ships. The Coast Guard set up a task force in July, 1995, to conduct a full review to determine what caused the rash of accidents and what could be done to avert them in the future.

Oddly, only one of the summer's reported incidents occurred on a ship built before 1987.

Still, stringent new SOLAS regulations being implemented beginning in 1997 seriously affect the cruise industry, because they require detailed (and costly) amendments and additions to older vessels, from sprinkler systems to freon-free air conditioning systems and low-level lighting systems. Vintage ships like Carnival's *Festivale*, for instance, would need more than $10 million to bring it up to the new standards, line executives said recently.

INSIDER TIP

Many of the older ships are being sold to operators abroad to sail exclusively from non-U.S. ports, and so do not come under U.S. Coast Guard inspections and SOLAS regulations. Be cautious about buying a bargain cruise on a ship that sails only from Mediterranean or Asian ports if you're concerned about ship safety.

Where in the Caribbean Do You Want to Go?

No poll, rating system or expert travel agent can tell all potential cruise passengers that any one experience is "best." A well-worn truism says neophyte cruisers care most about ports of call, veteran cruisers about which ship. In either case, you'll want to concern yourself about more than where you're going and how much it's going to cost.

Five Hints for a Hassle-Free Cruise

1. The shorter the cruise, the younger and more casual the group on board is likely to be. For most first-time cruisers, the **introduction to cruising is aboard a three- or four-day mini-cruise** from Florida or California.
2. If you want a smooth, trouble-free sailing, **avoid any shakedown, inaugural, maiden voyage or first sailing on the heels of major renovations**. Although some ships have sailed through these with flying colors, this is when the vessel is most vulnerable to plumbing, heating, air conditioning and water pressure problems.
3. If you are considering booking a ship that never sails from a U.S. port and your travel agent has no firsthand knowledge of it, take some time to **check it out before putting down a deposit no matter how tempting the price**. Some lesser-known vessels or very low-priced sailings may feature discounted cabins left over from a group or charter, or a cruise marketed primarily in another country, and you could find yourself odd man out. Also, these vessels are no longer inspected regularly by the U.S. Coast Guard and could represent a safety hazard.

With waiters and stewards to whom English is a second language, like this Greek bartender aboard Royal's Crown Odyssey, ***speak slowly and distinctly when ordering something.***

4. When dealing **with waiters and stewards** to whom English is a second or third language, speak slowly and distinctly and **be ready with an alternative word** when they don't understand your initial request. That way you'll be spared the problem one infuriated passenger had with her Scandinavian stewardess who did not know what a "cantaloupe" was; if the passenger had switched to the word "melon," she would have gotten a serving of breakfast fruit instead of the envelope that was delivered by the bewildered Norwegian.
5. **Read the fine print** at the end of the company brochure and on the back of your ticket/contract, and you'll find **the line is not responsible for missed ports of call**, changed itineraries or liabilities in connection with independent contractors such as airlines and ground tour operators.

Money Matters

With so many brand-new, enlarged and refurbished ships sailing the cruise routes in this year of economic uncertainty, **it's a buyer's market**.

Almost every day we see still another cruise line ad promising some new bonus or discount, everything from free airfare to and from the port to a shipboard credit for bars and shops, from early booking discounts to last-minute impulse cut-rates.

The hard truth is, they're not filling up all those new cabins, and you, the potential passenger, stand to benefit. We'll have **a glut of cruise cabins** in 1996, but the major lines are already gradually phasing out their old vessels with an eye to the stricter new safety regulations being implemented in 1997. The fall 1994 leveling-off of passenger numbers after a decade of steady rises combined with the disappointing 1995 season, suggests **1996 is the year to find a great cruise bargain**.

EAVESDROPPING

One of our readers, Walter J. DeFranco of Lakewood, California, suggested some years ago that tourist-class cruising, especially to Alaska, should be introduced "for retired people on limited income and working people in the $25,000-a-year class." DeFranco says, "Who needs five or six meals a day, top entertainment, fine wines, swimming pools etc.?" He suggested movies for entertainment, all-buffet meals, less steward service in cabins, and an across-the-board price of $100 a day with tipping optional. How about it, cruise lines, anyone think that's viable?

Seven Ways to Protect Yourself from Travel Scams

1. **Be skeptical**. If an offer seems too good to be true, it probably is. Unsolicited "prizes" you get through the mail or over the phone promising a free cruise usually involve your calling in and giving someone your credit card number or paying a "service fee" for a trip that never materializes.
2. **Follow up**. If you book through a discount agency's 800 number, don't send them checks or money orders. Use a credit card, but only after ascertaining that the cruise line rather than the agency will process the charge. Verify the reservation by demanding the vendor's confirmation number.
3. **Never give out your credit card number on the phone to someone who called you**.
4. **Don't buy a cruise from a toll-free 800 telephone number if you haven't checked them out**; it's better to visit the office in person and **talk face-to-face with a travel agent**. Several major cruise travel agencies with 800 numbers, some of them in business for years and regarded as reliable, went bankrupt suddenly in the last year or two, leaving clients high and dry and cruise-less.
5. Check any agency you're dealing with to see if they're **members of professional travel organizations** such as ASTA (American Society of Travel Agents), ARTA (Association of Retail Travel Agents), CLIA (Cruise Line International Association) or NACOA (North American Cruise-Only Agencies).
6. **Double-check with the cruise line** itself to confirm bookings and all payments.
7. When in doubt, **call the National Consumer's League Hotline**, ☎ *(800) 876-7060.*

GETTING READY TO GO

If you have a special occasion to celebrate, let the line know ahead of time and they'll bake you a cake, as Cunard did for this couple.

Timetable

Two Months or More Ahead of Time:

—Get a passport (see Appendix, page 67) or get your old one renewed if it's within six months of expiring.

—Apply for any visas you may need for ports of call. Some countries let you travel on a group visa so long as you stay with group excursions when ashore. If you want to strike out on your own, check to see if you need an individual visa. Then get it either through a visa service (usually quite costly and time-consuming) or, if you're in a city where there is a consulate or embassy from the country you're planning to visit, go down in person and apply. It takes only a few days, as a rule.

When Your Tickets Arrive:

—Sit down and examine carefully everything in the package, because there may be forms you need to fill out and mail or fax back to the line. At the very least, there are forms that you should fill out at home before leaving rather than at the check-in counter at embarkation, when you may be holding up a long line. And there will be valuable information dealing with life aboard the ship, wardrobe and how to communicate with you on the ship for those at home.

—Give a copy of the satellite communications telephone number for the ship to whomever should contact you in an emergency, and threaten violence if they call when there is no emergency. (There's nothing scarier than to be relaxing aboard a ship miles from land and have the radio officer ring your cabin with a call from home.)

—If you're traveling independently to the ship, take with you the name and telephone number of the port agent for the city of embarkation, because sometimes a ship isn't where it's supposed to be when you arrive.

The Day or Night Before:

—Pack your bags, being sure to affix to each one the baggage tags the cruise line has sent, with your name and cabin number clearly written on each.

The Day of Your Flight or Transfer to the Ship:

—Get to the airport (or the ship) comfortably early in case there's a traffic delay. Pay careful attention to boarding time and sailing time instructions. If you're too early, you'll sit around on a folding chair in a large terminal waiting until you can board.

Carry casual clothes to wear on deck in the daytime, like this couple aboard the **Star Clipper;** *bathing suit coverups are always useful.*

Eleven Tips To Lighten Your Luggage

1. Lightweight Bags: We carry soft-sided but durable bags in small to medium sizes, tucking in an empty folding bag to bring dirty laundry or souvenirs back home. Try never to carry more than you can handle yourself, since you may arrive in some primitive place where there are no porters or baggage carts, as in the Miami airport. While a ship doesn't care how much baggage you bring on board, the airline that gets you there can be sticky about overweight luggage. Also, cabin closet and drawer space may be limited on smaller ships or in lower category accommodations.

2. List: Work out a wardrobe list in advance to avoid those just-in-case clothes that get thrown in at the last minute and never worn. Remember that separates multiply, you can wear an outfit more than once, and sticking to basic color combinations means fewer shoes and accessories to coordinate.

3. Laundry: Virtually every cruise ship has a laundry, either self-service or send-out. Daytime clothes are casual and if they're washable as well, you don't need to take many. Dry-cleaning is available on most of the newer ships, and you'll often find irons and ironing boards in self-service laundries or from the housekeeping department for last-minute touch-ups.

4. Layering: Bulky garments add weight and take up space; instead, layer lightweight garments for air-conditioned areas and cool mornings on deck. You'll have more wardrobe variety as well. Wear your bulkiest clothing and shoes to the ship to save having to pack them.

5. Lightweight fabrics: Carry more light natural fibers such as cottons and linens to tropical climates; avoid synthetics, which tend to cling and don't breathe. Silks are nice for dressy evenings but wrinkle in the humidity on shore.

6. Location purchasing: Since you're going to be tempted by clothing in ports of call—T-shirts, caftans, pareus—you might as well plan for it. Take fewer casual items and shop with a clear conscience.

7. Little sizes: No, we don't mean clothing but toiletries; save those samples that come in the mail or buy the smallest possible tubes and containers before leaving. All but a few ships have complimentary toiletries in the cabins; we've tried to point out those that don't. (See Five Things You Won't Find Aboard under the cruise ship you're sailing aboard.)

8. Less is more: We've long ago limited gifts and souvenirs for friends back home to small, unbreakable, easily packed items such as scarves, flat placemats, leather goods including wallets or belts, rather than outsized, fragile items that have to be hand-carried.

9. Libraries: Don't carry a collection of hardbound best-sellers to read aboard; every ship has a library of some sort. Tuck a paperback or two into your luggage and then trade with someone else when you've finished.

10. Logic: Carry essentials including passport, tickets, traveler's checks, cash, extra glasses, cameras and prescription medications in hand baggage you always keep with you; never put them in a suitcase that may be checked.

11. Leave it out when in doubt: We've never yet come back from a cruise without at least one garment we carried and never wore. Other passengers usually don't notice if you're wearing the same thing several times; it's the pleasure of your company, not your wardrobe, that counts.

For many people, dressing up for formal night is a special part of the cruise.

Wardrobe Tips: Sequins Don't Wrinkle

Chances are, everything you need to pack for your cruise is already in your closet—(we know this doesn't make a good argument for someone using the cruise as an excuse to buy some smashing new clothes)—because people on ships wear the same clothes as people on land, regardless of what some department store fashion buyers seem to think.

In the daytime, casual shorts and T-shirts or jogging suits pass muster all over the ship, and in the evening, dress-up clothes of the sort you'd wear to a dinner party or nice restaurant will do just fine.

On the most classic and elegant ships, the dreaded words "formal night" do mean a tuxedo, dinner jacket or dark suit for a man, and a cocktail outfit or evening dress for women, but a blazer or sports jacket and tie for men, a dress or pantsuit for women, will be acceptable on most big Caribbean mass market lines such as Carnival, RCCL or NCL.

A few lines such as Star Clipper and Windstar ask only for "casual elegance" in the evenings and never require a jacket or tie. And Windjammer Barefoot Cruises in their clever little "Windjammer Survival Booklet" (☎ 800-327-2601 to get a copy) says "With us dressing for dinner means putting on a clean T-shirt."

Five Essentials to Pack in Your Hand Baggage

1. Prescription medications in their original containers.
2. Sunblock and a hat.
3. An extra pair of prescription eyeglasses or contact lenses.
4. A sweater to combat overzealous air conditioning on board.
5. Proof of citizenship—passport, copy of birth certificate or voter registration card; a driver's license is not acceptable.

Nice to Take Along

1. Camera and film (if you're a novice, practice at home with a roll or two before you leave).
2. Lightweight binoculars.
3. Small, packable guidebooks for the area.

INSIDER TIP

It's a good idea not to pack anything firm whether valuable or not in your checked baggage. In several major airports that handle a lot of cruise traffic (including New York's JFK) cameras and jewelry have a way of disappearing between the time the bag comes off the plane and when it gets into the baggage area.

Air/Sea Packages

If you've bought an air/sea package, the travel agent or cruise line has forwarded your air tickets to you a distressingly short time before departure. Neverthless, take a moment and double-check the departure times and other details to be sure they coincide with the date and departure time of the cruise. If you're traveling with a spouse, you may or may not be seated together on the plane, since the block of tickets is run through a computer that couldn't care less about your marital bliss. If this happens to you, see if another member of your group will change seats with one of you if you're all clumped together.

Your route between home and the port may also be circuitous because of the airline hub system. If there's a long way to get there, you can count on that being your route. Should you have plenty of frequent flyer miles, you could book the cruise at the cheaper cruise-only price and use your mileage to get to and from the port. The only downside there is if your cruise is cancelled at the last minute, the cruise line would probably not refund you the value of your lost mileage.

Arriving at the Airport of Your Port City

With an air/sea package, you will find somewhere in the arrival airport a uniformed meet-and-greet holding a sign with the name of your ship or cruise line on it. She may be at the gate or in the baggage area. She will tell you to claim your luggage and then mill about with the rest of your group until everyone has his or her bags, or until the couple whose bag was lost go to the baggage window and fill out the lost luggage forms.

Then you'll all be led as a group to your vehicles, and the meet-and-greets will supervise loading you and your baggage into the same or different vehicles. It's not a bad idea for a couple traveling together for one to get into the bus and get a seat for the two of you and the other watch the baggage until it is actually put into a vehicle.

Arriving at the Pier

The main difference between the port of Miami and the port of Los Angeles is that you'll be surrounded by porters to help you with your luggage at the former, and you'll be surrounded by passengers trying to find a porter at the latter. The porter will ferry your baggage from the taxi to the baggage-loading area for the ship, or, if you've arrived by transfer on an air/sea package, the meet-and-greets will see to its transfer. Again, it's a good idea to keep an eye on your bags as they're transferred.

You'll be ushered into a large hall where a lot of people are milling about or standing in line. There will be from one to 10 counters with letters of the alphabet above them. Queue up under the letter for your surname; if you are a couple with different surnames, as we are, select the shorter of the two lines. You will turn in your cruise tickets, passports, and (please, please, please) your already-filled-out forms, give them a credit card to imprint for on-board charges, and they in turn will give you a boarding card, perhaps a cabin key and part of your ticket. You will then be directed to the security point where you'll put everything through the machines again, just as you did at the airport. (If you're carrying 1000 ASA film for your cameras, this second X-ray dose could damage the film.)

INSIDER TIP

You'll be expected to turn in your passport to the purser's staff when checking in aboard a ship and should not expect to see it again until the morning you disembark, except in certain Baltic and Black Sea ports where you pick it up from the purser and immediately turn it in to the port security officers at the bottom of the gangway. They return it to you when you come back to the ship and you turn it back into the purser's office.

Security

Cruise passengers have gotten accustomed to the same security drills as airline passengers, running baggage through the X-ray devices and showing a boarding pass to reboard the vessel. The newest precautionary safety measure introduced on some lines recently is the requirement of a photo ID to back up the usual boarding card for passengers boarding and reboarding the ship.

Shipboard security officers like this Holland America stalwart stand at the gangway when ships are in port to enforce the "No Visitors" rule.

Visitors who have not made previous arrangements are not permitted to board most ships in port. If you want to invite a friend on board for lunch or a drink, be sure to ask well ahead of time at the purser's desk if it can be arranged.

Boarding

You will follow a long line of people carrying their hand baggage along an interminable gangway, perhaps up some stairs or an escalator, perhaps along a covered walkway, to the point where a strip of tape has been stuck across the floor and a man with a camera will order you to stop by a life ring and smile. Try to look as cheerful as you can, because this photograph will be put on display the next day for everyone on the ship to see.

When you cross over the threshold from the gangway into the ship, you will be simultaneously greeted with a smile, handed some sheets of paper that you don't have anywhere to put, told to watch your step and watch your head, and have a white-gloved steward try to wrestle your hand baggage off your shoulder while asking you your cabin number. He'll lead you to your cabin, where you may or may not be greeted by your cabin steward or stewardess, who introduces himself or herself politely and explains how to turn on the TV and flush the toilet.

Check to see that your dining table assignment card is waiting in your cabin; if not, go immediately to the maitre d'hotel and arrange it. The Rotterdam ***dining room here shows the variety of table sizes available.***

The First Five Things to Do After Boarding

1. Check the shipboard program to see when the lifeboat drill is held and what time the welcome-aboard buffet lunch service shuts down.
2. Be sure your dining table assignment is set. If not, hie yourself to the maitre d's table and get one.
3. Go to the spa or beauty salon in person to book all upcoming appointments for hair, nails, massage and facials.

4. Hurry to the library to check out that new best-seller or videotape you want to see; if the library is not staffed and things are locked up, make a mental note of what you want and check the shipboard program for the first opening time.
5. Unpack.

On Board

—Establish credit for your shipboard account.

On check-in or after boarding, you'll be asked to leave a credit card imprint to establish your shipboard charge account. Most ships make it impossible to spend cash until check-out time. (On a few small vessels without a completely computerized billing system, you may find that sales revert to cash at midnight the night before disembarkation to facilitate billing.) The purser's office slips a bill under your cabin door the last night of the cruise, usually long after bedtime, and you don't need to stop by the desk at all unless you have a question about it.

Every ship sailing today has some sort of gym and fitness center, as well as indoor and outdoor pools where water exercises are held; this is aboard the lap pool on Princess Cruises' **Royal Princess.**

Spas

Almost every ship today sails with some sort of gym or fitness center; a jogging or walking track, either a specially surfaced ring around an upper deck or the passenger promenade deck; a daily exercise program that includes aerobics and other energetic activities; and a menu that includes designated low-fat, low-salt, low-calorie dishes. In addition, most have a full range of beauty, hair, nail and spa services, including manicures, pedicures, massage, steam baths, hydrotherepy, facials, herbal wraps and even mud/steam baths. The bigger the ship, the more the facilities.

Like most casinos, shops and photographic services, spas and beauty shops at sea are operated by concessionaires. Steiner of London, which dates back to 1903 when the company got its first royal warrent for hairdressing, has the lion's share of ship contracts, some 104 vessels at last count.

Passengers are urged to book massage and beauty services as quickly as possible after boarding, since the best times go quickly. Busiest days are when the captain's formal welcome aboard and farewell parties are held.

Five Ways to Get Invited to the Captain's Table

1. Occupy the most expensive cabins aboard.
2. Be a many-time repeat passenger.
3. Be rich and/or famous, a travel agent or a member of the media.
4. Be an extremely attractive blonde, preferably Norwegian.
5. Have your travel agent make the request, describing you as a rich, famous, beautiful, Scandinavian, blonde travel writer.

The Lifeboat Drill

A mandatory lifeboat drill for all the ship's passengers and crew will be called within 24 hours after sailing from the port of embarkation. You will be told to go to your cabin and get your life jacket, then report to your lifeboat station as designated on a sign affixed to your cabin wall or door. Sometimes you report to a public lounge on the ship, sometimes directly to your boat station on deck. Crew members will be posted in each stairwell and hallway to direct you to your station. It is requested that you not use the elevators since in a real emergency, they might be disabled. The signal to gather for the lifeboat drill is seven short and one long blast on the ship's whistle. You stay at your station until released by the crew member in charge. Don't worry about struggling into your life jacket in the cabin; a crew member will help you at the boat station if you need assistance. Smoking and drinking during lifeboat drill is prohibited.

Steer clear of the ship's casino, like this one aboard RCCL's Majesty of the Seas, *as well as the bingo games, if you're on a tight budget.*

Five Money-Saving Tips On Board

1. Take along your own soft drinks, wine or liquor (or buy them along the way in port) for pre-dinner libations in your cabin (but don't take your own drinks into the

ship's public areas—that's a no-no). A few lines state that bringing your own liquor to your cabin is not allowable, but we've yet to see it enforced.

2. Ask the shore excursion staff about ways of doing your own sightseeing program ashore instead of buying a costly shore excursion; a group of four can sometimes negotiate a Caribbean island tour with a local cab driver for less than the cost of four excursions, and a couple can walk around a port town on their own and catch the highlights, using the shore excursion booklet as a guide.
3. If you have kids along, persuade them to participate in the youth programs and activities rather than hang out in the video arcades, where quarters have a way of melting away quickly.
4. Steer clear of the casino and bingo games on board if you're on a tight budget, or set aside the amount of money you can afford to lose and don't dip any deeper.
5. If your shopping resistance is low, concentrate on sightseeing instead; otherwise you'll end up with bulky shopping bags full of things that are not as irresistible as you thought when you get them home.

INSIDER TIP

To get better service than the other passengers doesn't cost a thing; just read a crew member's name tag, look him in the eye, call him by name, smile and say thank you and show an interest in him as an individual. And remember the name next time without having to look at the name tag.

KEELHAUL

Many cruise lines now offer "port lecturers" who hand out maps to what they call "recommended" shops where the merchandise is "guaranteed." All this means is that the shops listed on the maps have paid to be listed and give commissions to both the "lecturer" and the cruise line. Most promise a 30-day opportunity to return or exchange defective merchandise, but any legitimate shopkeeper should promise the same. Too many passengers read these maps without realizing they are commercial ventures, and become fearful of going into a "non-guaranteed" shop and getting ripped off.

Shore Excursions

A few cruise lines, primarily expedition vessels, include shore excursions in the base price, but aboard most ships, you'll be offered a variety of optional group port tours that may range from an inexpensive walking tour to a costly helicopter flight.

Early in the sailing, the shore excursions director will hold one or more sessions to describe the tours as well as shopping pointers and ways to tour on your own. You're usually given a printed form with the excursions and prices on them, which you fill out and turn in to the shore excursions office. The excursions are then charged against your shipboard account, and the tickets or vouchers delivered to your cabin. Take care of your tickets and remember to have them along with you, "ripped and ready" as one shore excursions manager used to say, when you go ashore to take the tour. No ticket, no tour.

If you're on a budget, you'll want to weigh carefully which excursions to take and which to skip. Consider taking your own walking tour in a small port rather than getting on a bus or in a van with the others. The shore excursions manager can usually give you some advice.

Remember too that certain excursions have limited participation, so if there's something you can't live without, get to the shore excursions office as soon as possible after that tour is open for booking. Some cruise lines will let your travel agent book a tour for you ahead of time so you're guaranteed a spot.

Scoping Out Seasickness

The recent removal of the Transderm Scop seasickness "patch" from the market was a better-late-than-never move for this often-dangerous drug perceived as innocuous by its users because it resembled the harmless and familiar Band-Aid. Over the years we've encountered numerous serious medical incidents because of the patch, whose main medical ingredient was scopolamine. The former prescription-only medication carried a lengthy cautionary sheet in fine print inside each package which we are confident few if any of its users ever read. Adverse reactions ran from dryness in the mouth (two-thirds of its users) to disorientation and loss of memory, particularly in older users.

There are much safer and equally effective treatments for seasickness, as well as some unusual remedies, included in the following roster:

1. Sea Band or Travel Garde bracelet-like knit bands worn around the wrist at acupressure points to relieve symptons of nausea.
2. Ginger root capsules, available in health food stores or Asian pharmacies, taken before meals.
3. Nonprescription antihistamine remedies such as Dramamine, Antivert or Bonine can be taken one or two hours before sailing but may cause drowsiness.
4. Some shipboard doctors recommend a Dramamine injection, which works more quickly than an ingested tablet for a sudden or severe onset of seasickness.

Sidestepping Seasickness

But we have a more revolutionary cure for seasickness—a malady we must confess we've never suffered, but we do have sympathy for its victims. Here are three things to do if you're worried about a little mal de mer.

1. Select the right ship.
2. Sail the smoothest waters.
3. Sleep in the steadiest beds.

Pick a ship with little rolling and no pitching motion, such as the unique twin hulled *Radisson Diamond*, which moves smoothly (if rather slowly) through the water with little discernible side to side motion and no back to front motion. Fixed inboard stabilizers counteract both roll and pitch, and pitch and heave are reduced because the water is funneled between the two pontoons of the catamaran-like ship.

The sail-cruise vessels such as the Windstar and Club Med ships have computer-trimmed and operated sails that keep the ships at an even keel when they proceed under sail, with heeling kept well under 6 percent.

Ships with a deeper draft (the measurement of the ship's waterline to the lowest point of its keel) usually perform better in rough seas than ships with shallow drafts. For instance, Norwegian Cruise Line's *Norway*, built as the transatlantic liner *France*, has a 35-foot draft that forces her to anchor rather than come alongside in her Caribbean ports but sure does make getting there smoother.

The smoothest ride on most ships is on a lower deck in an amidships cabin. The higher-priced sun and boat deck cabins give more bounce and roll. But book a cabin too close to the bow or stem, and you may feel every swell. Taking an outside cabin near the waterline bothers some cruisers, because the seas slosh across the little round window like a washing machine in the laundromat.

Ten Tips for First-Time Photographers

1. Take your camera manual with you on the cruise so if you have problems, a more experienced photographer on board can help you figure it out.
2. Always take a set of spare batteries and have them along with you when you go ashore.
3. When photographing people on deck or ashore against bright backgrounds, use your flash to fill in extra light on their faces.
4. Don't rest your elbows or camera against the ship's rail to steady it; the ship's vibrations will make your photo blur.
5. If you want to shoot pictures through the window of a tour bus, put your camera as close as possible to the glass without touching it; be aware tinted windows can cut down on your light and alter the colors of the subject. And using the flash will give you a beautiful picture of a white light in the bus window.
6. On deck, in small boats and Zodiacs, carry a plastic bag to slip over your camera to keep the salt spray from splashing it.
7. If you're traveling with a borrowed camera, get it far enough in advance so you can shoot a practice roll and develop it before leaving home.
8. When photographing lounge shows or lecturers indoors on a cruise ship, be aware how far the light from your flash will carry; it may be necessary to move forward into a better position to get your shot, but do it quietly and don't block anyone else's view. Some ships do not allow flash pictures during a show and almost all ban the use of video cameras.
9. If you hold your camera firmly in both hands, push your elbows against your rib cage, begin mentally counting backwards from 10 to 1 and midway squeeze the camera button strange as it may sound, you can get a steadier shot in a low light situation.
10. Think in terms of telling a story with your cruise photographs—photograph the life ring with the ship's name on it, your cabin, your waiters and stewards, even yourself in the mirror dressed for the captain's dinner.

Where to Complain

Cruises score higher on passenger satisfaction surveys than any other form of leisure travel. But if things go wrong, the worst thing you can do is seethe silently and complain to your travel agent after you get back home, or mutter about it to fellow passengers. That only aggravates the annoyance.

The purser's or hotel manager's desk, usually in the main lobby, as here aboard* Renaissance III, *is the place to take your complaints in most cases.

Instead, when you have a specific problem during your cruise, take it immediately to the person responsible for that area of service, speak calmly and explain the situation in a reasonable tone of voice.

—Cabin or cabin service complaints should go to the housekeeper; if it doesn't work out, go to the hotel manager.

—Dining room complaints should be taken up with the maitre d'hotel or the dining room captain responsible for your table area; if you don't get satisfaction, go to the hotel manager or chief purser.

—Ship charges or procedures should be discussed with the purser's desk or information desk.

—Always point out any problems or complaints on the questionnaire you're given at the end of the cruise. Everyone up to and including the chairman of the board and the ship owner read these whenever there is a serious complaint. And don't be coerced by an anxious waiter or steward to give an excellent rating when not warranted just because he says he may lose his job as a result.

KEELHAUL

We give a punishing Keelhaul Award to those litigious passengers who threaten to sue cruise lines because there happened to be a hurricane or storm at sea that spoiled their vacation. When was the last time they sued Holiday Inn or Marriott under similar circumstances?

THE END OF THE CRUISE

Despite the highly polished service, the cadre of dining room stewards aboard the **Seabourn Spirit** *does not accept gratuities.*

Tipping

It used to be that any article on shipboard tipping—"shipboard gratuities," as the cruise line brochures like to call it—dealt simply with whom, how much and when. At some point in his disembarkation lecture, the cruise director would say, "So many passengers have asked us about whom and how much to tip..." and launch into an easy-to-compute per-person-per-day figure for the waiters and the cabin stewards.

Then you would go back to your cabin and figure out how much to tip each, get some change and slip that amount into the little envelopes that had a way of appearing in your cabin just when needed. You might put a little extra cash in for someone who was extra solicitous, knock off a little from someone else who had done less than you expected.

That was the way it used to be.

In the late 1970s, Holland America Line, which trains its own employees at special hotel schools in Indonesia and the Philippines, implemented a "no tipping required" policy. "We don't say tipping is not permitted," a line spokesman explained, "simply that it is not required. A passenger is free to tip any of our serving personnel if he wishes, but those personnel are not permitted to solicit tips in any fashion."

Then in 1984, Sea Goddess Cruises came along with an even more explicit rule—"If you are concerned about tipping, the Sea Goddess concept is quite simple: gratuities are discouraged."

Seabourn went them one further in 1990; the company "strictly prohibits all staff for any solicitation or acceptance of gratuities."

Even more astonishingly is that we were getting excellent service on all three lines, erasing that notion that the word "tip" was an acronym "to insure promptness."

Well, if that isn't the case, what is a gratuity? Is it a voluntary reward for extra-special service, or is it, as in most European hotels and restaurants, a percentage charged for service and as routine a part of the bill as taxes? And if that's so, why couldn't it be added into the base cruise fare?

An automatic up-front payment would eliminate the problem crew members face called "stiffing"—a passenger leaving no tip whatsoever on a cruise where tipping is expected.

Aboard Royal Cruise Line's *Queen Odyssey*, a Seabourn-style vessel, tips are automatically calculated and added to the passenger's shipboard account. And on most ships, bar service charges of 15 percent are automatically added to the drink tab. Cunard established a policy a couple of years ago of letting passengers who were uncomfortable with the matter of tipping pay the usual amount up-front.

On Crystal's ships, you can even charge your tips on your shipboard account and receive in exchange small printed cards to sign and present to your waiters and cabin steward, who later turn them in for cash. This relieves you of adding and multiplying chores and the necessity of going down to the purser to get change.

Some of the confusion about tipping comes from ships with open-seating policies. Since you may have a different waiter each time, how do you know whom to tip?

The Greek stewards' union requests each passenger set aside a prescribed amount that is pooled and divided among the crew under a prescribed formula. The usual argument that a crew member will work harder if he's hoping for a tip doesn't apply here, since everyone's going to get the same. (Insiders say peer pressure shapes up any lazy stewards on a Greek ship.)

Some of the smaller American ships and expedition vessels also use the pool system for tips.

Anytime we mention tipping in our newspaper columns, the mail is fast and furious, very little if any of it defending the practice of tipping. The most audible complaints come not from first-timers but veteran cruisers.

Here are some of the questions raised—Should the person who eats breakfast and lunch from the self-service buffet and goes ashore for dinner when the ship is in port be expected to leave the same amount as the passenger who shows up in the dining room for all three meals every day? And should the couple in the small inside cabin on the lower decks give the same steward's tip as the couple in the big boat deck suite?

These are questions for which there are no easy answers. In the meantime, to find out the recommended tip amounts for each ship, check that ship's listing in the guide.

The Last Day: Don't You Love Me Any More?

Everyone at your table has hugged goodbyes the night before, after each has discreetly handed out the tips in their proper little envelopes and expressed a heartfelt thanks to the dining room stewards. The evening is always long and loud after a short cruise, with everyone getting in their last few hours of drinking and gambling and dancing, and quiet and downbeat after a long cruise, when the difficult transition to going home has to be made.

Bags go into the hall at midnight or sometime before 6 a.m. They'll be gathered up and ferried to a central area on the ship and transferred ashore after the ship has been secured the next morning.

No passengers are permitted to disembark until all the luggage has been unloaded and put ashore.

INSIDER TIP

Obvious as this may seem, you must be scrupulously careful setting aside the clothing you need to travel in the next day, all the items including shoes and underwear, before putting your bags outside your door for collection. You won't see them again until you're back on shore. Pajamas are not proper debarkation attire.

Breakfast service is more limited on disembarkation day, with the added aggravation in American ports that the tea is terrible because there's so much chlorine in the water in case the kitchen has a surprise public health inspection, and there are no poached eggs because for some mysterious reason, the kitchen cannot poach eggs if the public health inspectors are aboard.

If your waiters are friendly but a little withdrawn, it's because, on many ships, they're the same busy beavers that spent the night lugging luggage down the halls and so have had maybe two hours of sleep maximum. Your tablemates, your best friends for life during the past week or so, may seem inordinately concerned with airport and getting home details, but you all exchange addresses and phone numbers.

You say goodbye a dozen times to everyone while you're milling about waiting for the ship to be cleared by customs and immigration and for your group's turn to depart.

Getting Off

You have been given color-coded baggage tags depending on aircraft departure times or ongoing arrangements, and your baggage will be waiting in the customs hall in the color-coded group. Do not panic; it is probably there somewhere. Gather it up, getting a porter if you need one or lugging it out by yourself if you don't.

You will have been given a U.S. customs form to fill out, which you will turn in at the gate as you leave. Most cruise ships arriving in U.S. ports have customs and immigration officials on board who have precleared your passport and customs forms before you disembark the ship.

INSIDER TIP

It's a good idea to take a close look at your bag before setting it out in the hall. When you get on the dock, you'll see a dozen just like it. The idea is to pick up the one belonging to you. We have seen passengers wandering around with no idea of what their bags actually look like.

Going Home

If you're on the air/sea package, your return to the airport and home will be very similar to your arrival, with the meet-and-greets on hand with their signs and advice. If you're in the port of Miami or Ft. Lauderdale and flying with a major airline, after you claim your baggage and clear customs at the port, you can trundle it right over to the airline's baggage truck at the pier and check it in there, trusting it will arrive in your home airport when you do. It usually does.

THE NUTS AND BOLTS

How to get a passport:

Apply in person at one of the 3500 clerks of court or post offices which accept applications, or at one of the 13 passport agencies in the United States.

Present two passport photographs (go to a photographer who specializes in these), a photo ID with your signature such as an active driver's license, and proof of citizenship or nationality—a certified copy of a birth certificate, a Certificate of Naturalization or an expired U.S. passport.

Pay $65 if you're over 18, $40 if you're under 18, and turn in or mail in the completed printed form you were given to fill out. If you're renewing your passport, pay $55.

How to select a travel agent:

Take as much time and care with your choice as when choosing a mate, looking for intelligence, warmth, patience, friendliness and diligence. A knowledge of basic geography is helpful too.

Look for professional associations; the agent should be a member of ASTA (American Society of Travel Agents), ARTA (Association of Retail Travel Agents), CLIA (Cruise Lines International Association) and/or NACOA (National Association of Cruise Only Agents). The latter specialize in cruises, but it does not mean they are more qualified on the subject than "full service" agents, only that they are specialists.

Whenever you book a cruise ticket through an agent, the agent receives a commission from the cruise line, not from you. There may be surcharges on other agency services, however, with the recent airline caps restricting the commission an agent can make from booking an air ticket.

How to go through immigration:

Have your passport ready and in your hand.

Be sure you're in the correct line; signs often indicate certain lines are restricted to airline crews, nationals of that country or members of European Community nations only.

When you near the immigration officer, be sure to remain behind the taped or painted line on the floor until the person ahead of you has finished and left.

Answer any questions asked, but don't volunteer comments, and don't fidget while he's examining your passport.

How to go through customs:

Have ready any receipts for large purchases you may have made on the trip.

Fill out the requisite form honestly.

Be prepared to open any bags or suitcases if requested, but never hesitate or ask the officer if he wants it opened, even when the man in front of you has had to open his.

Trip cancellation insurance:

This covers you if you have to cancel your cruise at the last minute, after the full fare has been paid and the cancellation penalties kick in, because of illness, death in the family or business emergencies.

Travel agents usually recommend a client take this insurance; some of the more cautious even ask a client who refuses it to sign a form indicating they were offered the insurance. Cruise lines, while not wanting to appear heartless, point out that while an emergency of this sort may happen once in your lifetime, it happens to them every sailing.

Vaccinations and medications:

If you are going to exotic areas of the world, check with your doctor or public health authorities about any medications or vaccinations recommended for travelers to that region. Remember that if you eat and sleep only aboard the cruise ship you will not be taking the same risks as someone on a trek or a safari.

Port Taxes:

Those friendly tropical islands who love tourists also love slapping on huge port taxes, also sometimes called "head taxes," for visitors. The highest one we've encountered in North American waters is Bermuda's $60 a passenger.

Some sharp-eyed cruisers may note that the cruise line's port taxes fee may actually exceed the total of the individual ports' actual taxes. The usual explanation for this is administrative costs, whatever that means.

Pre- and post-cruise packages:

Most cruise line brochures have add-on pre- or post-cruise packages for the cities of embarkation and disembarkation. If you're interested in such a package, discuss it with your travel agent to be sure the hotel being used is one you would like and that the price is less than you could get on your own. The upside of these packages is that they usually include transfers, which could save a lot of money in some cities.

UP-FRONT AND PERSONAL

Your Guide to Our Guide

The main body of this book is a thorough compilation of cruise lines, ships and alternative cruises to the Caribbean, with major ships reviewed, plus details on dozens of other smaller and alternative vessels. The last section of the book rates Caribbean ports and provides an overview of each island.

The cruise companies—most are cruise lines but a few are marketing companies who represent various foreign cruise lines—are described first, in alphabetical order, and following each company's description the ships are then described individually or, in the case of identical sister vessels, in a group, but rated individually.

You may note in the book and even within certain segments of it information repeated several times, because we feel many readers will dip into the book at random rather than read it in sequence.

Eight Terms You May Meet for the First Time in This Guide

1. Repositioning—When a vessel moves seasonally from one cruising area of the world to another, it makes a "positioning" or "repositioning" cruise; because the ship has to make the journey whether passengers are aboard or not, the cruises may be discounted, offer an eclectic and unusual itinerary or a lot of leisurely days at sea.
2. Refit—The redecoration or remodeling of a vessel, which can be in drydock (the ship above the waterlevel so hulls can be repainted) or wetdock (the ship in the water). "Soft furnishings" are all the upholstery, draperies, sheets, towels, tablecloths and so on. "Cosmetic" refits are sort of like face lifts—they don't make the ship's life longer, just help her look a little fresher.
3. The Jones Act—The term commonly applied to the 1886 Passenger Service Act, an obscure turn-of-the-century passenger cabotage act designed to protect American shipping by not permitting any foreign-flag vessel to transport people between two points in the United States without calling at one or two foreign ports in between. Since there is very little American passenger shipping left, movement has been underway to strike out the antiquated law, but cargo shipping interests zealously

protect it because they feel if it were struck down it would threaten their cargo shipping as well.

4. U.S.-flag ship—For a ship to qualify as a U.S.-flag vessel, it must have been built and registered in the United States, be staffed by a primarily or totally American crew and never have been re-flagged to another country. The only exception to this rule was made in 1979 by Congress for American Hawaii's *Independence*, which lost its U.S. flag when it was sold to a Hong Kong shipping company.

5. Flags of convenience—A euphemism for ship registrations made in Panama, Liberia, the Bahamas, Cyprus and other nations with low ship taxes and non-hindering union requirements by ship owners who want to save money.

6. Cruise-only—The fare quoted is for the cruise itself and does not provide an air transfer from your home town to the port where you board the ship. You're responsible for getting yourself to the port on time, and getting yourself back home afterwards.

7. Air add-ons—Usually extra fees added on top of a cruise fare that may (or sometimes may not) already include some airfares. The usual routine is to book an air/sea package through the cruise line whenever it's available since the airfare will usually be lower than you could negotiate on your own. But some travelers want to use frequent flyer awards or fly a specific airline or upgrade to business or first class. While upscale lines may offer this option in their air add-ons, the normal cruise line is going to fly you in the cheapest seats on the most inconvenient schedule that can be blocked out. They don't like it; you don't like it. They're at the mercy of the air carriers, and that's why you don't get your air tickets until a few days before you leave on your cruise.

8. Meet-and-greets—These are land-based employees of the cruise line who do all the gathering up and shuttling of passengers between the airport and the ship. They are usually in a uniform of some sort and always carry a sign or clipboard with the name of your cruise line or ship on it. When you see them, check to make sure they have your name on their clipboard list or you may not get a seat on the bus that will take you to the ship.

Eight Things to Remember

1. Report Card—the ratings for ship cabins, food and entertainment based on the way your high school English teacher used to grade your book reports.

2. Average Price PPPD—the average per person per day price, based on double occupancy, for the cruise ship cabin under review.

3. The Bottom Line—Personal observations and ruminations about the vessel or cruise line under review.

4. GRT—Gross Registered Tonnage, not a ship's weight, but rather a measurement of a ship's enclosed cubic space which tallies all revenue-producing areas aboard for the purpose of harbor dues.

5. Passengers—Cabins Full—the maximum number of passengers aboard if all the beds, including upper berths, are filled.

6. Passengers—2/Cabin—The normal complement of passengers with two passengers to each cabin.

7. PSR—Passenger Space Ratio, a figure reached by dividing the number of passengers carried into the Cross Registered Tonnage, which gives a general idea of how much total enclosed space is available for each passenger; a sort of seagoing comfort index.

8. Seating—The number of meal seatings per evening; most ships have two seatings, a first, early or main seating, and a second or late seating. When there is a single seating, passengers often have some latitude in arrival time, unlike two seatings, which require on-time arrival.

The Ratings

When the *Fielding Worldwide Guide to Cruises* first began in 1981, the late Antoinette DeLand initiated the rating system of stars. As new authors for the cruise guides, we have decided to simplify the system somewhat by eliminating all the pluses but adding an extra star.

The present authors have been aboard all the ships rated with black stars and anchors in the following pages, and the **black star ratings** reflect our personal opinion of the ship and the cruise experience it offers.

The **white stars** represent ships that are in transition from one company to another, which we have been aboard in the vessel's earlier life, or new vessels that are sister ships to existing, already inspected vessels due to come on line in 1996.

The **anchor ratings** were created by the publishers to reflect a cruise experience that was enriching and rewarding aboard an adventure, expedition, river or coastal vessel where the pleasure of the journey far exceeds the physical quality of the cruise vessel. A few ocean-going ships that offer expedition and educational sailings will carry both star and anchor ratings.

Unrated ships are those the authors have not been aboard in the ship's present incarnation, most of them new ships not yet on line.

★★★★★★	The ultimate cruise experience
★★★★★	A very special cruise experience
★★★★	A high quality cruise experience
★★★	An average cruise experience
★★	If you're on a budget and not fussy
★	A sinking ship

AMERICAN CANADIAN CARIBBEAN LINE, INC.

461 Water Street, Warren, RI 02885
☎ *(401) 247-0955, (800) 556-7450*

History

Captain Luther Blount of Blount Marine in Warren, Rhode Island, founded ACCL, "the small ship cruise line," more than 30 years ago. He grew up in a fishing family and when he was 17, influenced by reading Gifford Pinchot's book *To the South Seas,* set out for the Galapagos as part of the crew aboard a 30-foot yacht. "We never got there—the boat got shipwrecked—I don't know how my folks ever let me go." The energetic New England octogenarian (when we first interviewed him by phone in 1989, he said, "I'm 74 but I only look 58") built his own three vessels, plus several that sail at present for Alaska Sightseeing/Cruise West. His offbeat itineraries demand "a good sea boat that can't draw over six feet, and it has to go through the Erie Canal so the top has to fold down flat." His ships also have a stern swimming platform with steps to get in and out of the water, a mini-sailboat for passenger use in the Caribbean, a motorized skiff to take passengers ashore when the bow landing feature is not used (see below) and a glass-bottom boat to let passengers view underwater life.

—Inventor of the bow-landing ramp; the vessel noses into shore and opens a forward ramp, allowing passengers to walk from the ship directly onto land. Inventor of the retractable pilot house, which folds down to allow the vessel to sail under low bridges such as those on the Erie Canal.

Concept

To create ships that can offer a maximum of 90 passengers a chance to go where larger vessels can't, to provide a casual onboard ambience so passengers and crew get to know each other well, and to take people on "real adventures close to home," like the Erie Canal, Belize and Guatemala, Costa Rica, Nicaragua, Honduras, Trinidad and Tobago, the Orinoco, and a cruise between New Orleans and Chicago. The line says it's destination-oriented rather than ship-oriented.

Signatures

The unique bow-landing ramp and retractable pilot house, plus extremely shallow drafts, allow the ships to go under low bridges, into shallow waters and disembark passengers almost anywhere.

A BYOB (Bring Your Own Bottle) policy, because Blount doesn't believe in making money off a bar. The cruise line provides soft drinks and snacks, but passengers who want a cocktail or glass of wine have to bring their own.

Gimmicks

After a passenger takes nine cruises with ACCL, his tenth cruise is free. This alone keeps 'em coming back year after year, comparing notes on how near they are to their freebie.

Who's the Competition

In the Caribbean, Blount's vessels compete (only slightly) with Clipper Cruises.

EAVESDROPPING

Captain Luther Blount: "I haven't gone whole hog in borrowing a lot of money and getting in the hole by trying to do too much, (and) I haven't tried to be the biggest guy on the lot." He makes it a point of pride to build a new ship only when he can do it without borrowing money.

Who's Aboard

Couples and singles, most of them in the golden years beyond retirement, with an aversion to dressing up, gambling, hanging around bars and watching floor shows. Instead, they enjoy getting closeup looks at exotic parts of our own hemisphere. They love swimming and snorkeling (although none of them would make the *Sports Illustrated* swimsuit issue), exploring archeological ruins and visiting remote primitive villages, and all of them look forward to their 10th cruise with the company.

Who Should Go

Basically, the people who are aboard, plus middle-aged couples who'd like to go snorkeling.

Who Should Not Go

Young couples and singles, families with small children (or teenagers, for that matter) or anybody who wants to live it up.

INSIDER TIP

The ships do not permit any passengers under 14 years of age.

The Lifestyle

Very casual, just as Captain Blount intends. No need to ever dress up, or even change clothes between the day's excursion and the evening's dinner unless you really want to. The closeness between passengers and crew that the boss advocates is nearly unavoidable, since these vessels are quite compact with a paucity of public space. Basically there's a dining room and a nearby lounge, and that's it except for open decks. Passengers sit where they wish at large informal tables in the dining room and food is served family-style, so everybody gets to know everybody pretty quickly, if only from passing the salt. Despite the absence of a bar, cocktail hour is diligently observed every night before dinner, with mixers and nibbles in abundance. The bottle-owners write their names on their bottles and stow them in the lounge between cocktail hours. Smoking is permitted only on the deck on the *Niagara Prince* and only on deck and in designated cabin areas aboard the *Caribbean Prince*. Entertainment, when it occurs, may be a folkloric company on shore or a musician brought on board at a port of call. Or a passenger may play the piano or do birdcalls. Some shore excursions are free, some sold at a modest charge from $15-$30.

Wardrobe

Very casual, anything you'd wear to the Kmart, but polyester with elastic waistbands is very popular. These passengers are people who aim at practicality, traveling light and skipping wrinkles—they are not interested in being fashion plates. However, the men may don a tie or bolo (string tie) and the women put on a dress or pantsuit on a special evening. There is one very sophisticated couple we know who love these cruises and do like to dress up, so there are exceptions.

Bill of Fare

It's American home cooking served family-style, and the quality relies heavily on what chef is in charge, but even if one of the less talented is in the galley, there's always plenty you will like. Once in a while a beach barbecue is scheduled, and coffee and snacks are available 24 hours a day. One special treat if you're in cabins near the galley is to smell the coffee brewing and breakfast cooking early in the morning. **Rating: C**

EAVESDROPPING

"The best thing about these ships," says a handsome La Jolla matron who sails them regularly, "is that you can go barefoot all the time."

Discounts

INSIDER TIP

The big sellouts, available on a first-come first-served basis, are positioning and exploratory cruises, which are offered at a flat rate of $125 a day per person to a limited number of passengers who dine with the crew. Sailings planned for 1996 include St. Thomas to Trinidad, and Trinidad to Bonaire. Call ☎ (800) 556-7450 for dates and details.

The Bottom Line

ACCL delivers just the sort of unpretentious, friendly and adventuresome cruise they promise, and the price is right. Loyal repeaters cite the casual lifestyle, the friendliness of the other passengers and the fact the vessels can go where nobody else can is the main reasons they continue to book. One regular calls the trips "senior citizen camping at sea."

Caribbean Prince ⚓⚓⚓
Mayan Prince ⚓⚓⚓⚓
Niagara Prince ⚓⚓⚓⚓

In Guatemala, bouncing along a dirt road in the back of a banana truck on one of ACCL's offbeat excursions, we stopped by the roadside and bought a fresh heart-of-palm, a huge chunk four feet long and big around as an elephant foot, for about 50 cents, but when we presented it to the ship's chef—whose forte seemed to be blueberry muffins and chocolate chip cookies—he studiously ignored our plea to let us make it into a salad for dinner. Later we heard a suspicious splash that we suspect was our heart-of- palm being tossed from the galley window.

While the three ships are not identical, they are quite similar to each other with comparable furnishings (functional) and decor (no-nonsense). Our first cruise with them was also our only cruise in tiny inside cabins; we had one each. Shirley is claustrophobic and had to leave the bathroom light on all night with the shower curtain pinned across the open doorway to pretend it was a window with a street light outside, and Harry went into hibernation in the soothing darkness, sleeping some mornings until nearly noon.

The cabins we're talking about are the ones we call "the terrible 20s," the tiny bottom-category forward cabins on the lowest deck with numbers in the 20s.

The ship layouts are simple—a Sun Deck on top with the pilot house, top category cabins and deck space, a Main Deck with more cabins, the galley, dining room and lounge, and the lower deck (except on the *Niagara Prince*), with crew quarters and "the terrible 20s."

The Brochure Says

"We at ACCL have been offering the traveling public 'adventure' cruises for 29 years, but we've done so with certain self-imposed restrictions. We believe in challenging trips, but never at the expense of your well-being, your wallet or your general comfort and peace of mind."

Translation

This is Captain Blount speaking bluntly—as is his wont—to his passengers. On the back page, there is also a paragraph that begins, "American Canadian Caribbean Line believes in honesty, reliability and good business ethics." You get a very strong sense of honor, decency and character with this line.

FOOTNOTE

When Princess Cruises objected to the proposed name of Mayan Princess *for Blount's new ship, he promptly announced, "The ship will undergo a sex change operation." It was christened* Mayan Prince.

Cabins and Costs

Fantasy Suites: **Report Card: NA**

Are you kidding?

Small Splurges: **Report Card: C-**

Average Price PPPD: $205 plus airfare.

We'd recommend springing for the biggest cabins you can afford on these ships. The Sun Deck amidships cabins are usually the costliest but not always the biggest so check the brochure diagrams carefully. Dimensions and furniture arrangements are given. Cabins on the *Niagara Prince* measuring 12 feet by eight feet are the largest in the fleet, along with the Sun Deck cabins aboard the *Caribbean Prince*, which come in at 11 feet by eight and a half. They have two lower beds (some of which can be made into a double berth if the request is made at the time of booking), picture windows, a closet, a couple of stools and a dresser, as well as a very compact bath with a European-style hand-held shower which (if you don't handle it right) will drench the entire bathroom.

Suitable Standards: **Report Card: C**

Average Price PPPD: $185 plus airfare.

Main Deck outside cabins are perfectly acceptable, but we wouldn't recommend the inside ones unless you're interested in hibernating. You'll find the usual two lower beds, perhaps a desk/dresser and stool, a closet and the compact bathroom with European hand-held shower.

Bottom Bunks: **Report Card: F**

Average Price PPPD: $122 plus airfare.

We told you about "the terrible 20s," but there's one cabin on the *Mayan Prince* and *Caribbean Prince* that's even cheaper, the A Cabin. It's beside the galley, which means an early morning wake-up from the minute the chef starts rattling those pots and pans. It's also somewhat smaller than even "the terrible 20s" and we can't in good conscience recommend it.

Where She Goes

The *Mayan Prince* starts 1996 with a series of 12-day Panama cruises between Balboa and Colon, followed by the positioning cruise (see previous "Insider Tip,"), then three 15-day spring Intracoastal Waterway itineraries. Summer sailings include some New York/Hyannis Islands programs and the Saguenay River, which segues into Fall Foliage sailings.

The *Niagara Prince* cruises the Caribbean and Orinoco River in the winter, then spends late spring sailing between New Orleans and Chicago on a Rivers of America itinerary. Summer Erie Canal cruises between Chicago and Warren, RI, meld into fall, and the year finishes with another Chicago-New Orleans sailing.

The *Caribbean Prince* winters in Belize with a dandy cruise for divers and snorkelers, then sails between Belize and Roatan, Honduras, for still more watersports fun before repositioning up the Intracoastal Waterway for a summer series of Saguenay sailings and the ever-popular fall foliage cruises.

FOOTNOTE

In fine print under the description of each cruise is the note: Every effort will be made to follow the published itinerary–wind, weather, tide and the good Lord providing. ACCL reserves the right to change, omit or add stops, change the route or consume extra days.

The Bottom Line

While we have a tremendous admiration for Captain Blount and his practical, no-ripoff approach to cruising, we have to caution readers that these ships are not for everybody. If you don't like mixing and mingling, you may not be happy aboard. You get to know everybody pretty well because there's nowhere to get away from them but in your cabin. You need to be footloose (or barefoot) and fancy free, able to take schedule changes or little annoyances in your stride. And look, at these prices, if you're a happy camper, you can earn your free cruise in no time.

Fielding's Picks

Gathering Points

1. The Lounge, where passengers stash their booze, names neatly written on the bottles, and there's usually somebody who suspects somebody else has been sampling his stash. Pretzels, cheese puffs and potato chips are in good supply.
2. The Dining Room, where passengers may dine on a single seating (where the timing is usually the same as early seating on other ships) and the crew dines at the second seating.
3. The Sun Deck, the place to stand to see the sea, where a stretch of tarpaulin may serve as shade because it's "low bridge, everybody down" on some sailings.
4. The Pilot House, where passengers are permitted to visit a couple at a time (it's too small for any more people than that) and see "who's driving the boat."
5. The bow-landing ramp, the entrance and exit in many ports.

Good Reasons to Book These Ships

1. The above-mentioned honor, decency and character.
2. To buy nine cruises and get the tenth one free.
3. To see The Americas first.
4. The price is right.
5. On the *Niagara Prince* in most cabins, the windows open.

Things You Won't Find On Board

1. A swimming pool.
2. A bar.
3. A casino.
4. A ventriloquist.
5. Sequins.

CANAVERAL CRUISE LINE, INC.

751 Third Avenue, New Smyrna Beach, FL, 32169
☎ *(904) 427-6892*

Stunning Bahaman sunsets are a treat for cruise passengers.

History

The *Dolphin IV* was purchased from Dolphin Cruise Line by Kosmas Shipping Corporation in July, 1995, to be repositioned to Port Canaveral for two-day cruises to the Bahamas as part of a week-long Florida land/sea package. Present plans are to retain the name of the ship, *Dolphin IV*. The ship leaves Dolphin service after its December 29 New Year's cruise and is expected to enter service for Kosmas in late February, 1996, after a drydocking and cosmetic refurbishment.

Dolphin IV ☆☆

The most delicious things on the ship are the breadsticks, which disappear all too quickly from the breadbaskets. At the captain's table (where we joined an astonishingly large group of 19) the captain is given his own personal basket of them, from which no one had the audacity to swipe one. After making the breadsticks disappear, the captain entertained his guests with after-dinner magic tricks with coins and cigarettes.

The ship, built in 1955 as the *Zion* for Zim Israel Line, was turned into the *Amelia de Mello* for Lisbon-Canary Islands service in 1966, laid up in 1971, sold to a Greek company in 1972 and renamed *Ithaca*, then sold again in 1979 to operate as the *Dolphin IV* under a joint agreement between Ulysses Cruise Line and Paquet. In 1984, Dolphin Cruise Line was formed to operate the vessel, which made three- and four-day cruises to the Bahamas out of Miami. For 1996, it is scheduled to make two-night sailings from Port Canaveral to Grand Bahamas Island.

Cabins and Costs

Fantasy Suites: **Report Card: NA**

N/A

Small Splurges: **Report Card: C-**

Average Price PPPD: $238 cruise-only.

There are some modest suites on the ship, five of them on the topmost passenger deck and four of them on the deck below the major public areas. Suites 500 and 501 are rather cramped, with double beds against the wall on one side and a sofa, coffee table and closet so close together you have to clamber over the coffee table to put clothes in the closet or sit on the sofa. Suites 513 and 515 are a little larger, but the view is partly obstructed from hanging lifeboats. In all the suites, the sofa makes into a bed, but we can't imagine how it opens up—there's no room.

Suitable Standards: **Report Card: D**

Average Price PPPD: $198 cruise-only.

Most of the cabins are just big enough for two lower beds, a dresser and bathroom with shower, but some also have upper berths.

Bottom Bunks: **Report Card: D-**

Average Price PPPD: $105 cruise-only.

The lowest-priced are inside cabins with upper and lower berths, five of them deep down into the ship and forward, where the ride is bumpier.

Where She Goes

In 1996, the vessel is scheduled to sail from Port Canaveral to Grand Bahamas Island on two-night cruises, sold as part of a land package that also includes three days in Orlando theme parks and two days at the beach.

The Bottom Line

It's a high density ship with long lines for buffets, for teatime, or any other time food is set out. Still, it has a pleasing personality, and the large numbers of first-time cruisers aboard always seem to be having a wonderful time. We do hope the new owners will refurbish the deck areas, which really need work. The teak is badly worn and oil-spotted. And the self-service buffet, which is tucked into a niche just inside from the pool area, is laid out very inefficiently, forcing the lines to circle the room and come back out the same narrow door. At breakfast, they add a second outdoor buffet on deck which cuts down some on the traffic.

Fielding's Picks

Favorite Places

1. The main lounge has a large metal dance floor and chrome-framed tub chairs that supplement long banquettes around the outside perimeters.
2. The library, with locked cases of books, a strip mirror wall and movable chairs, doubles as a film-screening room.
3. The casino, with one roulette wheel, three blackjack tables, a Caribbean stud table and 71 slots.

4. Two small plunge pools surrounded with tiny blue tiles ornament the aft end of the public rooms deck.
5. A disco buried deep in the bowels of the ship has a shiny, sunken dance floor and mirrored posts.

Things You Won't Find On Board

1. Elbow room at your dining table when the ship is full.
2. A peaceful game in the video games room; all 11 are about shooting, wrestling, fighting or car chases.
3. A performers' dressing room; they have to change in the card room off the main lounge. (At that, it's better than the old Royal Viking ships, when dancers used the public ladies' room to change costumes.)
4. Space to swim a lap in the swimming pools.
5. A cabin designated wheelchair-accessible.

Carnival®

3655 NW 87 Avenue, Miami, FL 33178
☎ (305) 599-2600, (800) 327-9501

Carnival designer Joe Farcus stands amid the flash and dazzle of his signature atrium lobby.

History

"The most popular cruise line in the world," as the slogan goes, was founded by Ted Arison, who had sold an air-freight business in New York in 1966 and headed back to his native Tel Aviv to retire. According to Arison's son Micky, now chairman and CEO of Carnival, his father never intended to go into cruising, but once he was back in Israel, he took over the management of a struggling charter cruise operation and turned it into a success.

When that vessel, a ship called *Nili*, was returned to the Mediterranean because of the owner's continuing financial difficulties, Arison had several cruises booked but no ship. As Micky tells it, "Ted heard the *Sunward* was laid up in Gibraltar, so he called (Norwegian shipping executive) Knut Kloster and said, "You've got a ship, I've got the passengers, we could put them together, and we'd have a cruise line.' So in effect, they started NCL (Norwegian Cruise Line) that way."

When that partnership dissolved in 1972 after some disagreement between the principals, Arison went out and bought the *Empress of Canada*, renamed it *Mardis Gras* and started Carnival Cruise Lines. The line's first sailing with 300 travel agents aboard ran aground. There was nowhere to go but up.

Today Carnival Cruise Lines operates a fleet of 10 ships with five more scheduled to arrive by 1998. Parent company Carnival Corporation also owns all or part of three other cruise lines, Holland America, Windstar and Seabourn. Founder Arison, an intensely private billionaire and philanthropist, has retired to Israel but still keeps an active eye on the company. *Mardi Gras* and *Carnivale* have also retired from the fleet; both were sold to Greek-owned Epirotiki Lines.

Carnival went public in 1987 and is traded on the New York Stock Exchange.

—The largest cruise line in the world, based on the number of passengers carried.

—Claims the largest staff of trained and qualified youth counselors in the industry (80 fulltime employees) to handle some 100,000 kid cruisers a year.

—First cruise line to build a dedicated performance stage in the show lounge (*Carnivale*, 1975).

—First cruise line to use TV commercials on a saturation schedule during the network news hour around the country (1984).

—Paid off a $1,065,428.22 "MegaCash" jackpot to two cruisers from Alaska (aboard the *Jubilee*, March 1994).

—Introduces the world's largest passenger ship, the 100,000-ton, $400 million *Carnival Destiny*, in fall, 1996.

Concept

The fledgling company took off when Arison and a young vice president of sales and marketing named Bob Dickinson created a new concept. They cut prices and added casinos and discos to attract more passengers. By loosening the traditional structure of the cruise market with its formality and class distinctions, they created the "Fun Ships" concept for a vast new cruise audience, a segment of the population that had never cruised before. The company calls itself a "contemporary product" aimed at a mass market, and the cruises are meant to tap the fantasy element to stimulate passengers rather than soothe them, turning the ship into a theme park for adults. Carnival's architect, Joe Farcus, the Michael Graves of the cruise industry, says, "The ships give people a chance to see something they don't in their ordinary lives...Instead of sitting in a theater watching, they're in the movie."

EAVESDROPPING

"Carnival is Wal-Mart, value-oriented for Middle America, for the masses, and it always meets their expectations," cruise industry analyst Jim Parker told the Miami Herald in a 1993 interview.

Signatures

Carnival's distinctive winged funnel painted in bright red, white and blue is instantly recognizable in warm water ports all over the Caribbean and Mexico and soon will be in Alaska as well. Chosen originally as a design statement, the funnel, which vents the smoke off to each side, surprised everyone when it actually worked.

Almost as recognizable is the bright blue corkscrew slide into the amidships pool on every "Fun Ship."

Splashy, fog-and-laser shows with contemporary pop music and spectacular dancing are a regular feature aboard Carnival ships; the bigger the ship, the bigger the show.

FOOTNOTE

Carnival's ship designer Joe Farcus, famous for his splashy "entertainment architecture," got his start with the line when a Miami architectural firm he worked for was contracted to go to Greece in 1975 to turn the Empress of Britain *into the* Carnivale. *When Farcus' boss got sick and no one else in the office was free to go, the young architect got the job, and the rest, as they say, is history.*

Gimmicks

Smiling waiters in tropical colors circulate around the decks on embarkation day with trays of Technicolor drinks in souvenir glasses, which first-time cruisers sometimes accept without realizing they have to pay for them. And kids in the $1 million virtual reality entertainment complex aboard the *Holiday* can activate the high tech games by using their passenger I.D. cards; they don't need to go get money from Mom or Dad, once the initial use has been approved.

Who's the Competition

In the Caribbean, Carnival competes with Royal Caribbean and Norwegian Cruise Line for under-40 couples and singles in the seven-day market and goes head-to-head with both in the mini-cruise market out of Miami and Los Angeles, as well as competing with Premier Cruises out of Port Canaveral. The line still perceives land-based resorts as its primary competition, and exerts a lot of effort to entice first-time cruisers. Dickinson himself says the former competitors are all "moving upscale" and leaving the field to Carnival and what he flippantly calls "the bottom feeders," low-budget cruise lines with old ships.

Who's Aboard

Despite the line's early reputation for swinging singles' party ships, Carnival attracts a broad spectrum of passengers from newlyweds to families with small children to middle-aged couples to retirees. About 60 percent are first-time cruisers, down from 80 percent in the 1980s, and some 23 per cent have taken a Carnival cruise previously, up from nine percent in the 1980s.

Families comprise a large part of the line's mini-cruise business.

Who Should Go

Families with children and teenagers will find plenty of diversions for the kids aboard, but there's also a well-thought-out Camp Carnival program with youth counselors that divides them into four age groups—toddlers two–four (on all ships except the *Tropicale* and *Festivale*), intermediates five–eight, juniors nine–12 and teens 13–17. They'll find playrooms stocked with games and toys, a full program of daily activities at sea including special aerobics classes and karaoke parties, a kiddies' pool tucked away on its own deck area and the trademark slide at the adult pool (see "Signatures"). Babysitting is usually available as well.

Plus: Anyone who likes to spend a weekend in Atlantic City, Nassau or Las Vegas, anyone who wants to show off some new clothes and stay up late dancing, or anyone who adores glittering high-rise resorts.

Who Should Not Go

People whose favorite cruise line was Royal Viking; early-to-bed types; or anyone allergic to twinkle lights and neon.

The Lifestyle

About what you'd expect if you've seen the Kathy Lee Gifford commercials—you know, "If they could see me now..." (Gifford says that when she auditioned for the job she almost didn't get it; she was sixth down on the list of performers they wanted to see.)

While the ships are glitzy, they are also very glamorous if you like bright lights and shiny surfaces, and the humor and whimsy Joe Farcus brings to the designs comes closer to *gee-whiz*! than *omigod*! The casinos and the spas are among the biggest at sea, the disco stays open very late, there's often an X-rated midnight cabaret comedy show, singles get-togethers, honeymooner parties, around-the-clock movies on the in-cabin TV set, plenty of fitness classes, trapshooting, shuffleboard, knobby knees contests, ice carving demonstrations, bridge and galley tours and all the other usual shipboard folderol.

INSIDER TIP

No passengers under 18 years of age are permitted to travel without a parent or adult guardian, and new I.D. cards issued to every passenger, including youths, flags a bar computer to report an underage wanna-be drinker.

Wardrobe

While Carnival ships are a bit less dressy than more traditional lines, many of the passengers look forward to dressing up on the one to two formal nights a week, when formal dress or a dark suit is suggested. You will see more sequins and tuxedos those nights than sport coats without a tie. The pattern is usually two formal nights, two informal nights (the line suggests sport coat and tie for men) and three casual nights that call for resort wear. For daytime, almost anything goes (or almost nothing, if you opt to sunbathe in the secluded upper deck topless sunbathing area). To go ashore in the Caribbean, casual, comfortable clothing and good walking shoes are best. Don't forget to take a sun hat and sunblock.

Bill of Fare

From a predictable mainstream seven-day menu rotation on its ships featuring Beef Wellington and Surf 'n Turf several years ago, the line has made some changes in its menus after finding a 300 percent increase in the number of vegetarian entrees ordered and a 20 percent rise in chicken and fish. Fewer than half the passengers order red meat these days, says Carnival's food and beverage director; a popular fresh fish "catch of the day" is now offered on every dinner menu.

That's not to say Beef Wellington and Surf 'n Turf have disappeared—they haven't—but rather that menus have moved a little closer to the cutting edge without scaring diners with huitlacoche mushrooms or fermented soybean paste; "Fun Ship" fans will still encounter those ubiquitous theme nights (French, Italian, Caribbean and Oriental) and flaming desserts parade, and children can order from their own special menus of familiar favorites.

Three-quarters of all the passengers opt for buffet breakfast and lunches rather than going to the dining room to their assigned seating, so a much wider range of casual, self-service options has been added, from a 24-hour pizzeria on the new *Imagination* to across-the-fleet salad bars, hot daily breakfast and lunch specials, made-to-order pasta stations and spa cuisine. Table service has been upgraded in the buffet areas as well.

All the shipboard dining rooms are smoke-free on Carnival. You can breakfast in bed and order simple menu items like sandwiches and fruit and cheese 24 hours a day from room service. Big midnight buffets are followed by a second mini-buffet at 1:30 a.m. on these late-night ships.

Cuisine Report Card: B+

NO NOs

The brochure warns that Carnival passengers are not permitted to bring alcoholic beverages of any kind aboard the ship or to consume any beverages purchased in a foreign port in the public rooms or on deck.

Showtime

Lavishly costumed, fully professional entertainment as good as (often better) than you'd see in Las Vegas is one of the line's hallmarks. The company produces its own musical shows in-house with high-tech lighting, sound and special effects. Different shows are featured on different ships (much as the Broadway shows on Norwegian Cruise Line ships vary from one vessel to another) so if you're a fan of big production shows, you'll want to cruise them all sooner or later.

Three different live bands and a piano bar are usually playing around the ship in the evening, along with a steel drum or calypso band on deck at midday in the Caribbean.

The only lecturers you'll run across on the Caribbean sailings are the people who tell you where to shop.
Entertainment Report Card: A+

Discounts

Super Savers let you deduct up to $1000 per cabin from the listed brochure rates if you book early. Savings amounts are reduced over time based on demand, so earliest bookings get the lowest rates. Some restrictions apply.

The Bottom Line

Carnival is not just for party-time singles any more. The new generation of sleek megaliners that began with the *Fantasy* in 1990 and continues through the *Ecstasy*, *Sensation*, *Fascination*, *Imagination*, *Inspiration* and two more in that class due in 1998 are real crowd-pleasers.

While the public areas pulse with their abstract sensory stimulation, fiber optics, neon, Tivoli lights, state-of-the-art stagecraft and virtual reality machines, there are a few quiet areas to get away from it all—in the massage rooms, the indoor whirlpool spas, the top deck jogging track or the outdoor deck wings aft behind the indoor Lido Deck bar. Cabins are adequate in size and comfortably free of glitz, with all-day movies and room service, although not so cushy you'll spend your whole cruise there rather than hitting the bars and casino.

On the other hand, if you want a quiet, relaxing cruise, better book another cruise line, because these are the "Fun Ships." While they're not to our own particular cruising taste—we find it hard to spend more than three or four days aboard before the color, lights and pinging slot machines get to us—most Carnival passengers think they've died and gone to heaven. For flat-out fun-and-games cruising, nobody does it better.

Celebration's *sister ship* Holiday

Celebration ★★★

Covered promenade decks take passengers from bar to casino to disco.

This ship has a wide starboard "boulevard" with the casino and lounges on port side; the earlier *Tropicale* has a more traditional center casino flanked by enclosed promenades on either side like the *Festivale*. The *Celebration* offers many of the design features of the later Fantasy class, with veranda cabins forward on a top deck, then a Lido deck with amidships pool, two interior decks with lounges, dining rooms and showroom, then below them, all the other passenger cabins.

These are also the vessels that discreetly offered an "Adults Only, No Jogging, Top-Optional Sunbathing" deck, and pioneered the line's recycling separation of garbage.

FOOTNOTE

The Celebration *made headlines in mid-1995 with an engine room fire that caused no injuries but inconvenienced passengers because the main engines were shut down, taking off the air conditioning and lights and driving sweltering passengers to sleep out on deck. The upside is, everyone got a two-day cruise back to Miami aboard the* Ecstasy *with an open bar, a full refund check before they disembarked and a voucher for a free seven-day cruise in the future.*

EAVESDROPPING

An excited family group boarding the Holiday was cautioned by one of their party, "Now remember, everybody needs to take a Valium." We hope she meant dramamine.

The Brochure Says

"People that cruise with Carnival are all very different people, with unique tastes. It's the job of our cruise staff to make sure that there are hundreds of different activities and ways to have fun aboard our 'Fun Ship.' So there's truly something for everyone."

Translation

Take your pick—an average day at sea offers you 14 eating opportunities (including two late-night buffets), eight screenings of the day's feature film on the cabin TV, six exercise sessions, bingo, Knobby Knees Contest, trivia quiz, disco, passenger talent show, sing-along piano bar, Newlywed and Not-So-Newlywed game, calypso, pool games, trapshooting, ice carving demonstration, poker games, skin care demonstration and shopping opportunities, plus all the bars and lounges, the evening production show and late-night cabaret or comedy show and the casino.

Cabins and Costs

Fantasy Suites: **Report Card: B**

Average Price PPPD: $347 including airfare.

Each ship has 10 Veranda Deck suites with sliding glass doors that lead to private balconies, separate sitting area with L-shaped sofas that can make into an additional bed, elegant wood cabinetry, large TV set, twin beds that convert to king-sized, a slightly larger than standard bathroom with tub and shower and a walk-in closet.

Small Splurges: **Report Card: C**

Average Price PPPD: $264 including airfare.

The Empress Deck category Nine outside doubles are just one deck down from the dining rooms, show lounge and shops, and two decks down from the casino, disco and other lounges. If you run back and forth a lot and are too impatient to wait for the elevator, the convenience might be worth the slightly higher tariff. Otherwise, the size and furnishings are identical to all the other standard cabins. See "Suitable Standards," below.

Suitable Standards: **Report Card: C**

Average Price PPPD: $245 including airfare.

You'll find twin beds that can convert into a king-sized bed, wall-mounted TV set, corner table, chair, two stools, desk/dresser, closet, bath with large shower.

Bottom Bunks: **Report Card: D**

Average Price PPPD: $199 including airfare.

The cheapest cabins are in category One on the two lowest cabin decks, 19 of them altogether, with upper and lower berths, wall-mounted TV, chair, stool, desk/dresser with drawers, closet and bath with shower.

INSIDER TIP

Prices listed under Cabins and Costs (above) are based on seven-day fares. Three-day cruises will run slightly higher per day, four-day cruises slightly lower.

Where She Goes

The *Celebration* sails every Saturday year-round from Miami to the Eastern Caribbean, calling in San Juan, St. Thomas and St. Maarten.

The Bottom Line

While not as shiny as when they were brand-new, these vessels are holding up pretty well; the age shows primarily in deck and cafeteria areas where the natural teak is spotted from food spills. Housekeeping aboard is generally good.

The buffet meal service has been expanded beyond the original closet-sized pantries to add a big salad bar that holds Continental breakfast makings in the mornings. Despite the gimmicks, they have a more nautical feeling than the newer ships, especially in the Lido Deck bar and grill rooms with resin-covered wood tables decorated with period luggage tags and other cruise memorabilia, coils of rope, the suggestion of a tugboat and a big red, white and blue funnel in the middle of the room.

Fielding's Picks

Good Reasons to Book This Ship

1. The fun and games.
2. The high-quality entertainment.
3. To play MegaCash, the biggest slot jackpots at sea.
4. To enroll the kids in Camp Carnival.

Things You Won't Find On Board

1. Smoking in the dining rooms.
2. Elbow room in the little stainless steel closets where the buffet hot foods are served.
3. Single cabins.
4. A cinema.
5. A passenger with nothing to do.

Ecstasy ★★★★★
Fantasy ★★★★★
Fascination ★★★★★
Imagination ★★★★★
Inspiration ☆☆☆☆☆
Sensation ★★★★★

"All I can say is, Wow!" sings spokeswoman Kathy Lee Gifford in the Carnival commercials, and passengers walking for the first time into these ships with their soaring seven-deck atriums, glass elevators and moving sculptures are saying the same thing—except for an occasional, "Oh my God!" from those who pretend to more refined tastes.

On the Fantasy, the huge clear-glass skylight in the dome ceiling seven decks above drenches the atrium with natural light during the daytime, but as dusk approaches, the room is suffused with color from miles of neon tubing that circle every level of the space. The effect is strangely impressive, but disorienting, something like walking into a giant jukebox. If you don't like the color, hang around for a while and it will change.

This is no place like home.

Toto, I don't think we're in Kansas any more.

Are you listening, Elvis? Las Vegas is alive and floating.

The *Fantasy*-class ships are all virtually identical in superstructure and deck plan, but each is dramatically different inside. We find ourselves doing a lot of standing by the rail looking down, both inside from the upper atrium levels down into the lobby, watching the glass elevators glide up and down, and outside from the upper decks down into the amidships pool deck with its acres of bronzing bodies in all shapes and sizes, at kids (and adults) trying out the bright blue water slide, at the impromptu dancers in bathing suits who always begin to gyrate on deck when the band comes out on the raised stage.

The 12,000-square-foot Nautica spas with their large whirlpool spas and well-equipped gyms are among the best at sea.

On the topmost deck is a rubberized jogging track, then down one deck on Veranda Deck is the huge Nautica spa with one of every exercise machine known to man, 26 suites with private verandas and on the aft deck, a sunbathing area and pool with two Jacuzzis.

One deck down on Lido is a large glass-walled self-service cafe with indoor and outdoor dining and the amidships pool area with its stage.

The Promenade Deck and Atlantic Deck contain most of the bars, lounges, showrooms and dining rooms, along with a galley on Atlantic Deck that makes the aft dining room a you-can't-get-there-from-here proposition. Directly behind that dining room is the teen club and children's playroom, and on the deck just above, the wading pool, all completely removed from the adult areas of the ship. Forward on the same deck is a second dining room, a small lounge and library, the atrium, shops and the main level of the showroom. One deck up on Promenade is the showroom balcony, the atrium, a vast casino on port side and an enclosed "avenue" on starboard side with sidewalk cafes and bars, another lounge and a disco, then still another lounge and a cabaret showroom aft.

The remainder of the cabins are on four decks below Atlantic; the base of the atrium with the ship lobby and information desk is one deck down on Empress. Three banks of elevators and three sets of stairs access the cabins.

These are "get up and get out and have fun" ships; the cabin TV runs the same daily feature over and over in any 24-hour period, and with only a minimal library of books, you mustn't expect to snuggle down and read.

CHAMPAGNE TOAST

On the Imagination, *the exquisite hand-set mosaics in Venetian glass sparkling with bits of gold-leaf-covered glass are framed in gilded wood to cover tabletops and inset in the granite floors. And don't overlook (as if you could) the gilded, bosomy Sphinxes staring down from the walls around the upper atrium levels.*

The Brochure Says

"The best vacation on land or sea! Children have plenty to do on a "Fun Ship" cruise. Relax on acres of sun splashed decks. Kick up your heels to one of our many live bands. Pamper yourself with our Nautica Spa program. Our attentive staff will wait on you 24 hours a day. Savor a fabulous array of food from around the world. We bet you'll have a great time in the largest casinos at sea. Enjoy lavish Las Vegas-style entertainment."

Translation

Every sentence is accompanied by a picture making the intent very clear—"Children" are eating pizza with a youth counselor serving them and no hovering parents in the background. "Relax" shows rows of sunbathing bodies holding flower-garnished drinks. "Kick up" depicts a pair of sedate middle-aged couples doing what kids today call close-dancing, meaning they're dancing while holding each other in their arms, like people over 50 do sometimes. "Pamper" shows shapely young bodies, mostly female, on gym machines with smiling male instructors. "Our attentive staff" is a waiter serving breakfast in bed to a happy couple. "Savor" shows a table of six-plus passengers (the table edge is cropped, but a six-top is the smallest table you can usually find on these vessels). "We'll bet" is a croupier at the roulette wheel with a lot of happy couples, all of whom seem to think they're winning. "Enjoy lavish Las Vegas-style entertainment" depicts a bevy of chorines in pink feathers and towering headdresses. Altogether, it's Cruising 101 Illustrated for first-timers.

INSIDER TIP

Sometimes passengers are so hypnotized by the dazzle that they just stand there staring indecisively at the elevator buttons, the buffet selections, the ice cream dispensing machine, the coffee dispensing machine, lost in space or reverie. You may have to nudge them to move them along.

FOOTNOTE

There are 226 slot machines, 23 blackjack tables, three craps tables, two roulette wheels and a giant wheel in the Crystal Palace Casino on the Ecstasy.

EAVESDROPPING

Designer Joe Farcus says passengers should feel romance, excitement and the anticipation of boarding a new ship, "and when they come on board, I don't want them to be disappointed; when they leave, I want them to feel they got more than they expected."

Cabins and Costs

Fantasy Suites: **Report Card: A**

Average Price PPPD: $347 including airfare.

The *Fantasy*-class ships have some of the best veranda suite buys at sea, with 28 Upper Deck veranda suites and 26 Veranda Deck demi-suites. But opt for the top—one of the Upper Deck suites with separate sitting area is big enough for entertaining and furnished with an L-shaped sofa, two chairs, coffee table, cocktail table, built-in wood cabinetry that includes a mini-refrigerator, glassware and TV with VCR, and a teak-floored private veranda with lounger, two chairs and a small table. The bedroom area has twin beds that can convert to queen-sized bed and marble counter desk/dresser with five drawers. The bath is fairly large with a marbleized counter, inset porcelain sink, Jacuzzi tub and tile walls and floor. There's an entry with walk-in closet, one full-length and two half-length hanging spaces, shelves and a large safe.

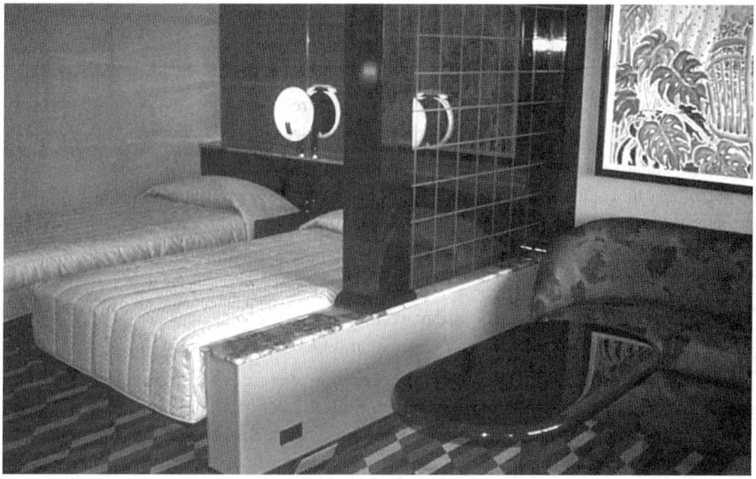

Fantasy-class suites like this veranda suite on the* Imagination *are good buys for the money.

Small Splurges: **Report Card: A**

Average Price PPPD: $318 including airfare.

The demi-suites on Veranda Deck have twin or queen-sized beds, big windows, private veranda with two chairs and a table, sitting area with sofa, table and chair and a bath with tile shower. Some have partially obstructed views due to hanging lifeboats.

Suitable Standards: **Report Card: B**

Average Price PPPD: $245 including airfare.

Carnival's standard cabins are consistent throughout this class, 190 square feet with twin beds that convert to queen-sized, dark gray carpeting thinly striped in bright colors, an armchair and matching stool, a built-in corner table, wall-mounted TV set and desk/dresser with four drawers. The closets have one enclosed and one open full-length hanging space plus shelves. The tile bath has a big shower, a counter around the sink and a glass-doored medicine cabinet.

Bottom Bunks: **Report Card: D**

Average Price PPPD: $199 including airfare.

The lowest category cabins are insides with upper and lower berths placed perpendicular to each other, considerably smaller than the standards (the brochure calls them "cozy"), similar closet space and a tile bath with shower. There are only nine of these on each ship, plus 28 more with upper and lower berths in higher price categories than are slightly roomier.

EAVESDROPPING

Carnival president Bob Dickinson: "We say we're 'Fun Ships'; we're not trying to be Royal this or Platinum that. People don't want to spend their vacations with the Queen Mum."

Where She Goes

The *Ecstasy* sails from Miami every Friday on three-day cruises to Nassau and every Monday on four-day cruises to Key West and Playa del Carmen/Cozumel.

The *Fantasy* sails every Thursday and Sunday from Port Canaveral on three- and four-day cruises calling in Nassau; the four-day sailing also visits Freeport.

The *Fascination* cruises the Southern Caribbean on year-round itineraries leaving San Juan every Saturday and calling in St. Thomas, Guadeloupe, Grenada, La Guaira/Caracas and Aruba.

The *Imagination* sails every Saturday from Miami to the Western Caribbean, calling in Playa del Carmen/Cozumel, Grand Cayman and Ocho Rios.

Beginning April 28, the *Inspiration* sails every Sunday from San Juan into the Eastern Caribbean, calling in St. Thomas, St. Maarten, St. Lucia, Barbados and Martinique. Prior to that, the ship's debut sailing March 22 is a 15-day Panama Canal cruise from Miami to Los Angeles, calling in Cartagena, Colombia; Caldera, Costa Rica; Acapulco, Puerto Vallarta and Mazatlán, Mexico, followed by a 15-day cruise from San Francisco to San Juan departing April 13 and calling in Puerto Vallarta, Acapulco, Caldera, Curaçao and St. Thomas.

The Bottom Line

These ships come to life at night when the dramatic colors and lighting are highlighted against the many glass surfaces. They are tactile (touch the surfaces of the chairs, tables, walls and floors on *Imagination*), aural (changing sounds of nature—the surf, rain, wind and chirping birds—wash by on *Sensation's* Sensation Boulevard) and intensely visual (fiber optics and neon panels "jump off" the walls as passengers walk by on the *Sensation*).

Elsewhere in this book, we call the *Fantasy* a lava lamp for the 1990s, but we mean it in a fond sense. This series of ships is constantly amazing and amusing, thanks to the ingenuousness and genius of Joe Farcus, whose own innocence and clarity of image keep them from being vulgar.

Are they gaudy? Sometimes. Do they tread dangerously close to maxing out? Perhaps. But they can match the much-praised pair of Crystal ships in marble, crystal and glove leather, dollar for dollar, ton for ton. Whether they strike you as glitzy or glamorous depends on your own individual taste, but they're never boring. Carnival delivers precisely what it promises, and if you've seen its advertising, you should already know whether it's the right cruise line for you.

Fielding's Picks

Fabulous Spaces

1. The Old Curiosity Library aboard the *Imagination* boasts replicas of Bernini's altar columns from St. Peter's in Rome along with genuine and reproduction antiques to give the atmosphere of an antique shop.
2. Also on the *Imagination*, the classy Horizon Bar & Grill with its 24-hour pizzeria (also serving calzone, Caesar salad with or without grilled chicken and garlic bread), jukebox, elegant cast aluminum chairs, granite and aggregate floors, Matisse-like hand-painted fabric tabletops under resin, fresh flowers, cloth napkins and silverware already on the tables and lots of drinkable wines by the glass.
3. Diamonds Are Forever on the *Fascination* is a James Bond take on a disco, with fiber optic diamonds on the walls and ceilings, tabletops that glitter with handset "diamonds", and carpets woven with diamond shapes; the black granite floor and banquette bases emit smoke/fog at night when the disco is going full blast. It's hot, hot, hot!
4. The Universe show lounge aboard the *Fantasy*, which in the words of one passenger "looks like it's ready to blast off" with its carpet covered with comets and swirling ringed planets, its black upholstery flocked with tiny, intensely bright metallic microchips in red, blue, silver and gold, and its ability to turn from a gigantic stage with a 33-foot turntable in the center to a ballroom closed off by a wall of beveled gold mirrors with a sunken orchestra pit that rises to eye level.
5. The 12,000-square-foot Nautica spas on every ship with Steiner of London beauty services from facials to aromatherapy and massage, an abundance of state-of-the-art exercise machines facing a glass wall overlooking the sea, sauna and steam rooms, fully mirrored aerobics room and big twin Jacuzzis lit by the sun through an overhead skylight.

Off-the-Wall Places

1. Cleopatra's Bar on the *Fantasy*, patterned after an ancient Egyptian tomb, with stone floor, hieroglyphics on the walls, gilded sarcophagi and full-sized seated and standing Egyptian gods and goddesses. In the center of the room is a glossy black piano bar, and as random laser lights spotlight details around the room, you half expect to hear a chorus of "My Mummy Done Ptolemy."
2. Cats Lounge on the *Fantasy*, inspired by the set for the musical of the same name, with oversized tin cans and rubber tires, bottle cap and jar lid tabletops, and walls lined with soap and cereal boxes; you enter through a giant Pet milk can and the band plays atop a giant rubber tire laid on its side.
3. Touch of Class piano bar on the *Sensation*, entered through a doorway framed by hands with long red fingernails; the same supporting hands cup the barstool seats (making for some funny images from the back when the stools are filled) and support cocktail tables, while the walls are covered with ceramic tile handprints.

4. The movie star mannequins spotted all around the *Fascination*, from Vivien Leigh and Clark Gable standing by the faux fireplace in the Tara Library to Bette Davis sitting in a corner booth of the Stars Bar with her ubiquitous cigarette, amid delightful Al Hirschfeld drawings under glass on the tops of the small white cafe tables. Passengers stand in line to photograph each other hugging a movie star; it's a big hit.
5. The 88 Piano Bar aboard the *Fascination* with its mirror-tile piano and myriad miniature piano-replica cocktail tables.

Good Reasons to Book These Ships

1. To have fun in an unintimidating, relaxed atmosphere without worrying about picking up the wrong fork or wearing the wrong clothes.
2. To try to win a million dollars.
3. To eat, drink, gamble, dance and watch movies all night long if you want to; it's your vacation.
4. To show the snapshots of the ships to your neighbors back home "so they can see you now..."
5. To get married on board (the line can arrange it) and spend your honeymoon at sea, all for less than a formal church wedding at home would probably cost; call Carnival's Bon Voyage Department at ☎ *800-WED-4-YOU* for details.

Things You Won't Find On Board

1. Lavish gift toiletries, even in the suites; all you get is a sliver of soap.
2. A table for two in the dining room.
3. A lot of books in the library.
4. A cruise director who spells Knobby Knees (as in the contest) with a "k"; every program we've seen calls it "Nobby Knees."
5. An atrium sculpture that doesn't move; some of them are inadvertently hilarious.

Festivale ★★

The future of the Festivale, *the only ship in the fleet that Carnival didn't build from scratch, is in question this year, but that's nothing new for this vessel. A decade ago, when the Holiday-class ships were still on the horizon, the* Festivale's *future was described as uncertain as well, but in those days two other vintage ships, the* Mardi Gras *and* Carnivale, *were still in the fleet. Now they're gone to Greece, settlement in the divorce suit between Carnival and Epirotiki after a brief partnership, and the* Festivale *is the only one left from the original trio.*

Built in 1961 as the Transvaal Castle *for Union Castle Lines, it carried mail and passengers between Southampton and Durban, South Africa, then was transferred to South African Marine Corporation and renamed* Vaal. *Carnival bought it in 1977.*

Company executives say it would cost more than $10 million to bring it up to the SOLAS (Safety of Life at Sea) requirements for 1997. That, coupled with the fact that the new Inspiration *is set to pick up the* Festivale's *popular Southern Caribbean itinerary, does not bode well for its future in North American waters. On the other hand, there's always Greece.*

The *Festivale* is long and sleek with ocean-liner lines and vestiges of its previous decor, including a remarkable art deco-style steel stairway, but don't expect a classic cruise experience. This is Carnival's basic "Fun Ship" sailing without the technological toys of the newer ships. It has a lot of sunbathing deck, two swimming pools aft and a small wading pool forward.

Most of the cabins are fairly spacious, although more than half of them are insides. The dining room, typical of vessels from this vintage, is amidships on a lower deck without windows. Lounges can get crowded with a party bunch aboard, but you can usually find stretch-out room on deck.

The Brochure Says

"With sleek lines and an intimate atmosphere, the *Festivale* is classic cruising at its best."

Translation

It carries fewer passengers than the other Carnival ships (except *Tropicale*) and still shows off some original art and woodwork.

Cabins and Costs

Fantasy Suites: **Report Card: C**

Average Price PPPD: $347 including airfare.

Ten suites with private verandas on Veranda Deck have twin beds that can be converted to king-sized, plus a sitting area with sofa that makes into a third bed. The bathroom has a tub.

Small Splurges: **Report Card: C**

Average Price PPPD: $255 including airfare.

Two forward-facing cabins on Veranda Deck are the biggest accommodations aboard, larger even than the more expensive veranda suites. Both have queen-sized beds.

Suitable Standards: **Report Card: D**

Average Price PPPD: $249 including airfare.

Category Seven standards carry the same price for inside or outside cabins, because the outsides are down on Main Deck near the dining room and the insides on upper decks near the public rooms and pool deck. You'll have to be specific here as to whether you want twin beds or a queen-sized bed; they're not convertible. In many of them, lavatories are in the main cabin rather than the bathroom.

Bottom Bunks: **Report Card: D**

Average Price PPPD: $199 including airfare.

There are only a handful of cabins in the bottom-most category, 11 to be exact, all with upper and lower berths and all on lower decks. Again, you can expect lavatories in the main cabin rather than in the bathroom.

Where She Goes

The *Festivale* stays on her seven-day Southern Caribbean itinerary from San Juan until it's taken over by the new *Inspiration* April 28. On April 29, the ship is scheduled to pick up a seven-day year-round itinerary from San Juan, sailing on Mondays to St. Thomas, Antigua, Barbados, St. Lucia, St. Kitts and St. Barts.

The Bottom Line

With the prices the same as on the glitzy new megaships, the *Festivale*, which shows its age in cabin plumbing, is overpriced. It's suitable for young, first-time cruisers who are not demanding, but how you gonna keep 'em on the *Festivale* after they've seen *Fantasy*?

Fielding's Picks

Favorite Gathering Places

1. The Veranda Deck pool, where everyone pulls their sun loungers into a circle like wagon trains around a campfire.
2. The Gaslight Club Casino and Cafe, where a darkish period feeling prevails, is flanked by two enclosed promenades.
3. The Fanta-Z Disco with its mirrored ceiling and lighted dance floor that blinks in rhythm with the music.
4. The Copacabana Lounge, a vivid parrot carpet and bamboo bentwood chairs lend a tropical look, enhanced by a sunshine-bright ceiling.
5. The Tradewinds Lounge, all rattan tub chairs and ceiling fans; you half-expect to see Peter Lorre in a fez peering from behind a potted palm.

Good Reasons to Book This Ship

1. To travel aboard a vintage ship built for ocean crossings.
2. To walk up and down that magnificent steel staircase.
3. To meet the (man, woman) of your dreams at the singles' party (it does happen sometimes).
4. To book one of the modestly priced, fairly sizable cabins with third and fourth berths for the kids, who can travel for $419 apiece.
5. To sail with her before she's banished from the "Fun Ship" kingdom.

Tropicale ★★★

When Ted Arison announced in 1978 that he was ordering his line's first brand-new ship, the 36,674-ton Tropicale, *20,000 tons was considered large for a cruise ship. The wisdom of the day was that he'd never fill it. (Today the* Tropicale *is the smallest ship in the fleet.)*

When it was delivered in 1982, he further confounded industry insiders by taking it out of the Caribbean and positioning in on the west coast for Mexican Riviera cruises out of Los Angeles. It wasn't very long until the vessel was operating at 100 percent-plus capacity.

Now—although the ship has been there before under charter—this year is the first time Carnival is in Alaska with a 100 per cent "Fun Ship" product.

The smallest ship in Carnival's fleet, the *Tropicale* might appeal particularly to people who like the "Fun Ship" cruise style but don't want to sail on megaships. With only 1022 passengers and a single dining room with two seatings, it's a little easier to get to know fellow passengers, at least by sight.

Some of the details on the *Tropicale* reflect design styles of older vessels, and again may have been influenced by the *Festivale*. The dining room, for instance, is on a lower deck with no windows, making it an awkward three-deck climb up to the show lounge, which is forward on Empress Deck.

At the same time, it modestly forecasts some of the bells and whistles that would distinguish the later new ships—the Exta-Z disco with its glass dance floor lit from below, the swimming pool with a slide leading down into it, the distinctive split T-shaped funnel that vents the smoke off to each side.

Cabins are modular, virtually the same size in all categories except for the slightly larger top deck veranda suites.

Cabins and Costs

Fantasy Suites: **Report Card: B**

Average Price PPPD: $381 without airfare.

The veranda suites with private balconies are best, especially if there's a glacier or Northern Lights sighting on your side of the ship. The suites contain twin beds that convert to king-sized in a separate sleeping area, with a comfortable sitting area as well. There is a pulldown upper berth and a sofa that makes into a bed, in case you want to take two additional family members along. The private veranda has a couple of chairs, the bath has a tub, and a low room divider separates sleeping and sitting areas. It could work as a family suite, especially since the kids (or adult occupants) would pay only $599 apiece for the cruise.

Small Splurges: **Report Card: NA**

There's nothing that really qualifies; all the rest of the cabins are standards, and prices change only according to the deck and whether the cabin is inside or outside (Carnival calls the latter Ocean View cabins).

Suitable Standards: **Report Card: C**

Average Price PPPD: $285 plus airfare.

Upper Deck outsides in category Eight offer windows and twin beds that convert to king-sized beds. A corner table, wall-mounted TV set, chair and desk/dresser with drawers, closet and bath with shower are what you get. Eleven cabins have been modified for the physically challenged and provide 32-1/2 inch-wide doors.

Bottom Bunks: **Report Card: C**

Average Price PPPD: $242 plus airfare.

A few bottom-price insides with upper and lower berths are on the *Tropicale* with furnishings similar to all the other ships in the fleet. The good news is they're larger than on most other vessels, the bad news is there are only nine of them.

Where She Goes

The *Tropicale* cruises the Western Caribbean on seven-day sailings every Friday from New Orleans, every Sunday from Tampa (passengers can board in either city and make a full week-long cruise), calling in Grand Cayman and Playa del Carmen/Cozumel. This itinerary ends with the sailing of April 28.

November 14, the ship makes a 14-day Panama Canal transit between Los Angeles and San Juan, with calls in Puerto Vallarta, Zihuatanejo/Ixtapa, Acapulco, Caldera, Curacao and St. Thomas.

The Bottom Line

The ship is in very good condition except for some worn natural teak decking that appears to be gradually being replaced.

The enclosed promenades on each side of the casino make a comfortable and attractive place to sit. It's certainly cheerful enough with its school bus yellow and black chairs and floor squares, inset with a Mondrian-pattern carpet in primary colors on the floor and walls, along with plastic-topped tables in red, yellow, blue and purple.

Celebrity Cruises, Inc.

5201 Blue Lagoon Drive, Miami, FL 33126
☎ *(305) 262-8322, (800) 437-3111*

***A passenger volunteer assists executive chef Walter Lauer in a cooking demonstration aboard the* Meridian.**

History

The Greek-based Chandris Group, founded in 1915, began passenger service in 1922 with the 300-ton *Chimara*, and by 1939 had grown to a 12-ship family-owned cargo and passenger line. In the post-World War II years, the company acquired a number of famous cruise liners, most of which have been retired. Under the Fantasy label (see "Fantasy Cruises"), the company operates the *Amerikanis* and sometimes the *Britanis*, the latter at press time under U.S. government charter in Cuba, as low-priced, mass market cruise vessels.

In April 1989, Chandris formed Celebrity Cruises with the intention of creating an upscale division with a premium cruise product. The *Meridian*, a massive makeover of the classic liner *Galileo Galeilei*, debuted in April 1990, followed the next month by the all-new *Horizon*. In April 1992, sister ship *Zenith* followed.

In October of that same year, Chandris formed a joint venture with Overseas Shipholding Group (OSG), a large publicly-held bulk-shipping company, and entered into the next expansion phase, ordering three 70,000-ton ships to be constructed by Joseph L. Meyer in Papenburg, Germany. The first of these, the innovative *Century*, was set to debut at the end of 1995, followed in the fall of 1996 by sister ship *Galaxy*.

—Chandris introduced the fly/cruise concept in the Mediterranean in the early 1960s.

—Pioneered fly/cruise packages in the Caribbean in 1966.

—Celebrity pioneered affiliations with land-based experts from London's three-star Michelin restaurateur Michel Roux to Sony Corporation of America to create innovative onboard products and programs.

Concept

Celebrity from its beginning has aimed at presenting the highest possible quality for the best price, and offers luxury service and exceptional food with a very solid value for the money spent. These stylish ships illustrate the decade's new values—luxury without ostentation, family vacations that don't just cater to the kids and close-to-home getaways that provide pure pleasure.

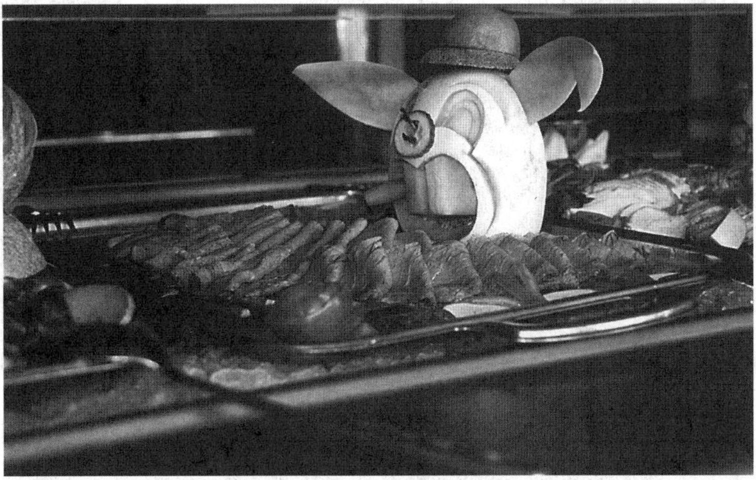

Celebrity's celebrity came in part from its exceptionally good food, created and supervised by Guide Michelin three-star chef Michel Roux; here, a whimsical touch adorns a buffet dish at lunchtime.

Signatures

Perhaps the single best-known feature of this fleet is its superlative cuisine, created and supervised by London master chef Michel Roux, a longtime *Guide Michelin* three-star chef, who takes a hands-on approach, popping in for surprise visits to the ships, training shipboard chefs in his own kitchens and sending key supervisory personnel for regular culinary check-ups.

Gimmicks

The Mr. and Mrs. icebreaker game. At the beginning of each cruise, a man and a woman on board are chosen to represent Mr. and Mrs. (*Horizon, Zenith, Meridian, Century*). During the cruise, passengers are encouraged to ask individuals if they're the Mr. and Mrs. selected, and the first to find them gets a prize. In the meantime, everyone gets acquainted. Anyone for musical chairs?

Who's the Competition

In its brief six years of service, Celebrity has managed to virtually create a class of its own by providing a product priced competitively with Princess and Holland America but with a level of food, and sometimes service, that approaches Crystal Cruises. Previously, the line limited its itineraries to Caribbean and Bermuda sailings, but this year is expanding to include Alaska and Panama Canal sailings, and very likely will enter the Mediterranean in 1997 with its mid-sized *Meridian*, oldest vessel in the fleet.

Who's Aboard

Young to middle-aged couples, families with children, and, aboard the *Meridian* on certain early-season sailings from southeastern ports, groups of senior citizens from Florida retirement communities who request early sitting dinners that start at 5:30 instead the normal 6 or 6:30 p.m. In winter season, Celebrity attracts some European and French Canadian passengers as well. Although the line is only six years old, it has many frequent cruisers with double-digit sailings.

Who Should Go

Anyone looking for a good value for the money; discriminating foodies who will find very little if anything to complain about; families with children; couples of all ages. When the line was first introduced in 1990, Al Wallack, Celebrity's senior vice president for marketing and passenger services, had several suggestions: "People who are joining country clubs but not necessarily the most expensive or exclusive country club on the block;" passengers of the former Home Lines and Sitmar ships who did not merge into Princess and who like "ships that look like ships, ships that have a European quality."

Who Should Not Go

Anyone who calls for catsup with everything or after perusing the menu asks the waiter, "But where's the surf and turf?"

The Lifestyle

Upscale without being pretentious, sleek and fashionable without being glitzy, the Celebrity ships offer a very comfortable seven-day cruise that is outstanding in the areas of food, service and surroundings. Evenings aboard are fairly dressy, with jacket and tie for men requested on both formal and informal nights; only casual nights suggest a sports shirt without jacket. Meals are served at assigned tables in two seatings.

Book a suite and you get all-day butler service; take the kids along during holiday and summer sailings and you'll find well-trained youth counselors on board. Ladies looking for a dancing partner will find social hosts on many sailings.

Evenings the ships present musical production shows and variety shows (except when they are docked in Bermuda, which does not permit professional entertainment other than live music on cruise ships in port), recent feature films, and duos or trios playing for dancing or listening in small lounges around the ships. Daytimes bring popular culinary demonstrations by the executive chef, arts and crafts lessons, trapshooting, napkin folding, golf putting, lectures on finance or current affairs, a trivia quiz, basketball, exercise classes and bingo.

Wardrobe

A seven-night cruise normally schedules two formal nights, in which the line suggests "both men and women may prefer more dressy attire, such as an evening gown for women and a tuxedo or dress suit for men." In our experience aboard the line's ships, a cocktail dress or dressy pants suit for women and a dark suit or blazer with tie will be acceptable. There is also a tuxedo rental service aboard the *Zenith*.

Two nights are designated informal, and men are asked to wear a jacket and tie, women a suit or dress, and three casual nights when a sport shirt and slacks are acceptable for men, dresses or pantsuits for women.

Daytime wear is casual, with good walking shoes a must. in spring and fall take a jacket or sweater, hat or scarf, there's often a cool breeze blowing.

A rolling cart of wines available by the glass serves the buffet restaurants.

Bill of Fare

Celebrity's executive chef, Vienna-born Walter Lauer, who goes from one ship to another constantly checking quality, describes it as "creating something new, where you can't cook everything in advance. Here there is the chance to do something new, more of the high standards in cuisine." One example: All the stock for soups is made from scratch on board rather than using prepared bases as many cruise kitchens do.

Lauer's mentor, Michel Roux, says, "The most important thing is to have a very good quality product and to rely on cooking skill more than the richness of the product." Fresh ingredients cooked to order figure prominently, and the menus are changed every six months.

Basically, the idea of serving simple but sophisticated dishes prepared from fresh ingredients as close as possible to serving time was revolutionary in the basic banquet/hotel catering kitchens of big cruise ships. But it succeeds splendidly. Usually if we find two or three dishes a meal that tempt us we're happy, but we could cheerfully order one of everything straight down the menu on these ships.

For lunch you might find a vegetable pizza or minestrone to start, then a main-dish salad of romaine with Mediterranean tabouli, hummus and pita bread garnished with garlic chicken; a piperade omelet with ham, tomatoes, peppers and onions; broiled ocean perch; roasted chicken with Provencale potatoes; spaghetti with fresh tomato sauce; grilled calf's liver with bacon and onions.

Dinner could begin with New England clam chowder or a pasta tossed with cilantro, oregano, ancho chile and fresh cream; a low-fat version of coquilles Saint-Jacques on vegetable tagliatelle; a pan-seared darne of salmon; roast lamb with garlic, thyme, fresh mint and olive oil with country roasted potatoes; broiled lobster tail or prime rib of beef. The dessert menu always includes one lean and light suggestion, along with fruit and cheese, pastries, ice creams and sorbets and a plate of showcase sweets presented to each table by the waiter, who describes them in mouth-watering detail. Full vegetarian menus are offered at every lunch and dinner.

A substantial 24-hour room service menu, gala midnight buffets, Caribbean barbecues on deck, continental breakfast in bed, late morning bouillon and afternoon tea are other meal options during a typical cruise.

Lunchtime buffets are reminiscent of Impressionist paintings, with displays of fresh fruits and vegetables, woven baked baskets holding bread and wonderfully crunchy homemade breadsticks, fresh and crisp salads, a huge display of fresh vegetables, a rolling cart of wines by the glass, cold and hot main dishes and plenty of desserts. **Cuisine Report Card: A+**

A variety of entertainment from production musicals to, as here, classical string quartets in the Horizon's *Centrum.*

Showtime

The production musical shows have a lot of verve and are well-performed and well-costumed; they follow the usual musical revue formats with salutes to Broadway and/or Hollywood, but with fresh looks at vintage shows like *Hair* and *Jesus Christ Superstar.* Variety performers, musical soloists and duos and a Caribbean band round out the evening entertainment. Daytimes are chock-a-block with games, movies, lectures and exercise classes. The new *Century* and *Galaxy* introduce still more technological marvels from rooms with "video wallpaper" to a nightly light-and-sound spectacular. **Entertainment Report Card: A**

Discounts

Special advance purchase fares are available for passengers who book well ahead of time; ask a travel agent for details.

The Bottom Line

In today's world with value for the vacation dollar so important, it's comforting to sail with a cruise line that delivers high quality food and service on a stylish ship at moderate prices. We sense welcome and commitment from every employee, even the cleaning crew who polish the brass and chrome and the deck crew who pick up dirty dishes and wet towels more promptly than on many ships. All the ships in the line, even the not-built-from-scratch *Meridian*, have our highest recommendation for quality for the money.

Century — Unrated
Galaxy — Unrated

Celebrity's chairman John Chandris calls his new pair of babies "the ships I've always wanted to build...ships for the next century" and tags them super-premium, saying they are for "discriminating consumers who demand the highest quality experience at the best possible value."

There are a lot of exciting new features on board. Take the state-of-the-art spa with its hydropool underwater "air beds" to give the body a weightless sensation and jets of water that provide neck massages as well as another spa area with jets of water at different heights that are similar to a standup Jacuzzi. Along with the usual hydrotherapy and thalassotherepy is a seagoing first—a mud, steam and herbal treatment called rasul. All the AquaSpa programs can be booked in advance with a travel agent.

A lounge called Images utilizes "video wallpaper," hundreds of changeable, custom-designed backgrounds that can be punched up on a wall-sized video display system to change the room's ambiance from tropical palms to low-light jazz club to sports bar or wine cellar, whatever background fits the activity of the moment. Around one end is a series of interactive gaming booths big enough to seat several people at a time.

For showtime, there's a Broadway-style theater with row seating, orchestra pit and four-deck fly loft for scenery. A glazed dome in the Grand Foyer changes in a slow transition from dawn to daylight to sunset to night, when astronomically correct "stars" appear in the dome "sky."

Sony Corporation of America has created exclusive interactive guest services, touch-screen information kiosks, in-cabin entertainment systems, telephonic video service and special teleconferencing equipment for meetings.

Cabins and Costs

Lavish penthouse suites measuring 11173-square feet offer a private veranda with its own outdoor hot tub, a living room, dining room, butler's pantry and 24-hour butler service, master bedroom with walk-in closet, living room with wet bar and entertainment center and a guest powder room supplementing the marble bath with spa tub.

All cabins contain safes, mini-bars, hair dryers, direct dial telephones and color TV sets, and the smallest is 171 square feet. Some 61 suites and cabins have private verandas.

Where She Goes

The *Century* sails alternating Eastern and Western Caribbean itineraries from Ft. Lauderdale every Saturday. The Eastern Caribbean sailing calls in San Juan, St. Thomas, St. Maarten and Nassau, while the Western Caribbean program visits Ocho Rios, Grand Cayman, Cozumel and Key West.

Horizon ★★★★★
Zenith ★★★★★

Revisiting a ship you've known from its birth is sort of like being a godparent to a child and watching it grow up. The first time we saw the Zenith, *at the Joseph L. Meyer shipyard in Papenburg, Germany, she was unprepossessing, a huge brooding structure of dark red steel with bare stairways, dangling wires and cords. Then, at her inaugural sailing in 1992, she was an elegant beauty decked out in expensive if understated finery, and when we saw her again not long ago she was prettier than ever, lovingly polished and primped within an inch of her life.*

The* Horizon's *Rendezvous Lounge is a popular before-dinner cocktail spot.

The *Horizon* and *Zenith* are very similar sister ships, with a few modifications on the interior of the *Zenith*—an expanded health club, a much larger forward observation lounge and ten more passenger cabins (including two additional suites), giving her a higher gross registry tonnage than the *Horizon*. The children's playroom was moved to a higher deck on the *Zenith*, and the topmost deck's Mast Bar eliminated, along with Fantasia, the teen center ice cream and juice bar, which is replaced by a meeting room on the *Zenith*. The *Zenith* also has warmer colors and more woodwork in its decor.

Because most of the cabins aboard are modular design, insides and outsides are virtually identical in size (around 176 square feet) and furnishings, with the cabin's deck position determining the price.

FOOTNOTE

The Horizon *made the headlines in the summer of 1994 with a mysterious outbreak of Legionnaire's disease that was believed to be caused by bacteria in the ship's Jacuzzis; one hospitalized passenger died and some two dozen were taken ill. The ship was taken out of service two weeks for extensive testing and was then approved to sail with a clean bill of health from the Centers for Disease Control. CDC officials said at the time that Legionella bacteria are "extremely prevalent" and are found in "an estimated one-third of offices and half the air-conditioning towers in the U.S." The bacteria can be eradicated with chlorine treatments or by heating water to 176 degrees Fahrenheit.*

FOOTNOTE

The Zenith *was at the time of its completion the largest ship to be built in Germany since World War II. The* Century *takes that title now.*

INSIDER TIP

In the back of the balcony, tall barstools around a tall table look inviting to latecomers to the shows, but those seats don't swivel and are clumsy to get into and out of; move on down to a regular seat, but avoid the front row of balcony seats where the wooden balcony rail is right at eye level.

The Brochure Says

"Attention to detail...you notice it the minute you come on board."

Translation

The care and attention to detail goes beyond the design and decor into every part of the service. At a second seating luncheon our waiter was removing the cover plate when he noticed a tiny spot on the tablecloth underneath it and, horrified, immediately began apologizing profusely as he removed all the tableware, tore off the offending linen and snapped on a new cloth, then reset the entire table. When we tried to make a joke about it, he said, "No, this is very serious, and this is my mistake; I'm terribly sorry."

Cabins and Costs

An outside deluxe cabin aboard the Zenith.

Fantasy Suites: **Report Card: A-**

Average Price PPPD: $549 including airfare in the Caribbean.

The two top suites, called Royal Suites on the *Zenith* and Presidential Suites on the *Horizon*, are 510 square feet with separate sitting room (the one we like has caramel leather sofas and chairs), glass dining table with four chairs, wood and marble counter, TV set and big windows; the bedroom has twin or king-sized beds, walk-in closet with generous storage space and built-in safe, and a second TV set. The marble bathroom is not large but does have a Jacuzzi bathtub. And there's butler service, hot cabin breakfasts if you wish, fresh fruit replenished daily and a welcome bottle of champagne.

Small Splurges: **Report Card: A-**

Average Price PPPD: $440 including airfare in the Caribbean.

Deluxe suites, 18 on the *Horizon* and 20 on the *Zenith*, have two lower beds or a king-sized bed, sitting area with two chairs or loveseat and chair, glass table, large window and small TV, as well as a long marble-topped desk/dresser with chair. The bathroom is very like the one in the bigger suites (see "Fantasy Suites" above). Perks: Butler service, terrycloth robes, hot breakfasts served in-cabin, fresh fruit, a welcome bottle of champagne.

Suitable Standards: **Report Card: B**

Average Price PPPD: $306 including airfare in the Caribbean.

Most standard cabins measure 176 square feet and have two lower beds or a double, two chairs, table, window, large built-in desk/dresser, TV set and bath with shower. Four outside wheelchair-accessible cabins on each ship have generous bedroom and bathroom space for turning, a big shower with fold-down seat, extra-wide doors and ramp access over the low bathroom sill.

Bottom Bunks: **Report Card: B**

Average Price PPPD: $260 including airfare in the Caribbean.

The cheapest insides are also 176 square feet with two lower beds or a double, two chairs, table, TV, wide dresser and bath with tile shower and white Corian self-sink and counter. A vertical strip of mirror on the wall where a window would be lightens and brightens the space. Some have third and fourth fold-down upper bunks.

Where She Goes

In winter the *Horizon* makes seven-night Caribbean sailings from San Juan calling at Barbados, Martinique, Antigua, St. Thomas and Catalina Island.

The *Zenith* operates seven-day Eastern Caribbean cruises round trip from Ft. Lauderdale calling at San Juan, St. Thomas and St. Maarten that alternate with Western Caribbean cruises calling at Ocho Rios, Grand Cayman, Cozumel and Key West. From January 6 through April 13 the *Zenith* will sail from San Juan on seven-day cruises calling at St. Thomas, Guadeloupe, Grenada, La Guaira and Aruba.

The Bottom Line

When the line was first introduced, executives were careful not to over-hype the new product and bombard the public with extravagant promises. Instead, they let the product speak for itself, and it did—in volumes. Early passengers commented that they had not expected so much for the price, and Celebrity's reputation grew quickly among knowledgeable cruise passengers looking for a good buy.

After sailing aboard all the line's ships, we find very little to criticize, other than the captain's formal parties with their tepid, watery, premixed cocktails; and we often wish, in dining rooms aboard other ships, we had one of Celebrity's menus facing us instead.

Fielding's Picks

Great Spaces

1. The shipshape navy-and-white nautical observation lounges high atop the ships and forward, America's Cup on the *Horizon* and Fleet Bar on the *Zenith*. Lots of wood and brass trim and snappy blue chairs with white piping around the edges.
2. The self-service cafe, with two indoor and one outdoor buffet line with an inviting array of dishes at breakfast and lunch, waiters on hand to carry passengers' trays to

the tables, and a rolling wine cart of vintages available by the glass at lunchtime. The floors are wood and tile, the seats a pretty floral pattern.

3. Harry's Tavern, named for company president Harry Haralambopoulos, is a small Greek taverna decorated with a mural depicting a Mexican fountain splashing under Greek trees occupied by South American parrots on a Tuscan hillside.
4. The elegant Rainbow Room on the *Zenith*, with its cabaret/nightclub ambience, wood-toned walls, gently curved bar, raised seating areas and blue leaf-patterned upholstery.
5. The show lounge offers optimum sightlines in most areas, with seven different seating levels on the two decks facing the large raised stage; multimedia projections and high-tech lighting design enhances the well-costumed shows.

Good Reasons to Book These Ships

1. Because the *Horizon* may very well be the best restaurant in the Caribbean this winter.
2. Because they represent perhaps the best value for the money in the whole world of cruising.
3. Because they take service seriously (see "Translation").
4. Because there's an excellent health center where you can work off the calories.
5. Because the whole family can experience a top quality cruise experience without mortgaging the farm.

Things You Won't Find On Board

1. Hot breakfasts served in standard cabins; you only get it in suites.
2. Private verandas.
3. Permission to bring your own alcoholic beverages aboard for cabin consumption; the brochure spells this out as a No No. You're expected to buy your drinks on board. (Other cruise lines permit passengers to use personal supplies while in the privacy of their cabins.)
4. A hungry passenger.
5. A cinema. Movies are shown daily on the cabin television.

Meridian ★★★★

"I believe ships have a soul," says the Meridian's *Captain A. S. Varsamis. "You go on ships all these years and you can feel it." His ship started life in 1963 as the* Galileo Galelei *for Lloyd Triestino and sailed between Genoa and Sydney. She was acquired by Chandris in 1984 and was sailing as the* Galileo *when we first saw her a year later. There's not a lot of the old ship left on the* Meridian*—she was dismantled and rebuilt from the hull up—except her soul, but we agree with Captain Varsamis. You can feel it when you stand at the rail on a wind-tossed night sailing from Bermuda.*

This smooth-sailing former ocean liner has a 29-foot draft and a top cruising speed of 24.5 knots, so it's one of the fastest ships at sea. The deck crew scrubs down the teak early every morning, when determined early-morning walkers do their mile or two if they don't mind working their way through the water and suds.

The *Meridian* has a longer, sleeker line than the newer *Horizon* and *Zenith*, with the dining room on a middle deck amidships and the show rooms and lounges one deck above. The topmost decks house the skylight suites, swimming pool and whirlpool spas and a self-service cafe that doubles as a late-night disco.

FOOTNOTE

Sister ship of the Galileo Galilei *was the* Guglielmo Marconi, *also built in 1963 and now sailing as the* Costa Riviera.

The Brochure Says

"The decor: inviting and perfectly understated. Put simply, you feel right at home. Except at home, you don't have a steward bringing you whatever you need, whenever you need it."

Translation

Rather than setting out to astonish, Celebrity works quietly, training its staff to serve meals or make cabins in precisely the same way time after time after time. A most recent sailing five years after the first one found all the details we had admired from the beginning still in place, still being done exactly the same way, down to the presentation of various breakfast teas in a wooden chest.

Cabins and Costs

Fantasy Suites: **Report Card: B+**

Average Price PPPD: $342 in Bermuda plus air add-ons.

Eight romantic Skylight Suites on the top deck let you look up at the night sky. The sitting area is beside floor-to-ceiling windows with sofa, two chairs, coffee table and a long built-in wood dresser/desk with 16 drawers. Two lower beds or one double, a wide nightstand with three drawers and a big cabinet/console, plus a closet with four doors opening to full- and half-length hanging sections, shelves and a safe, can stow plenty of wardrobe for a week—even for Ivana Trump. The bath, just barely big enough, is marble with a spa tub. Occupants of suites have the use of terrycloth bathrobes during the cruise, fresh fruit daily, a complimentary bottle of champagne as well as the services of the butler.

Small Splurges: **Report Card: B+**

Average Price PPPD: $313 in Bermuda plus air add-ons.

A pair of category Two deluxe junior suites on Atlantic Deck are as large as the top-ranked Skylight Suites, and represent a best buy (on our cruise, one of them was occupied by two cabin-savvy travel agents). You'll find a sitting area, two lower beds, two chairs, a big closet, lots of storage shelves, mini-refrigerator and bathroom with tub.

Suitable Standards: **Report Card: C**

Average Price PPPD: $242 plus airfare in Bermuda.

Category seven outside cabins are on Caribbean Deck, one deck below the dining room, with a choice of twin beds or a double bed (have your travel agent specify which you want when booking), desk/dresser with five drawers, and bath with shower. Some of the vintage bathroom fixtures and mirrors—including a round chrome porthole-shaped mirror and a big mirror on a stand—date from the *Galileo*. All cabins have hair dryers, complimentary toiletries, bottles of mineral water, TV sets and most have safes. Cabins on Europa, Caribbean and Bermuda Decks have portholes rather than windows.

Bottom Bunks: **Report Card: C+**

Average Price PPPD: $142 plus airfare in Bermuda.

The lowest-priced category 14 inside cabins offer double beds or upper and lower berths, with two dressers, plenty of storage. There are only six of them.

Where She Goes

The *Meridian* cruises in the Caribbean in winter on 10- and 11-night sailings from San Juan, alternating a 10-night itinerary calling at Aruba, La Guaira, Grenada, Barbados, St. Lucia, Martinique, St. Maarten and St. Thomas with an 11-night program visiting La Guaira, sailing into the Panama Canal, then calling at San Blas, Cartagena, Martinique, St. John and St. Thomas.

The Bottom Line

With slightly lower prices than Celebrity's newer ships and far-reaching Caribbean winter itineraries, the *Meridian* offers a good opportunity to passengers who want to see a lot of Caribbean islands on one cruise.

Cabins aboard are fairly spacious and the food, as we have said before, is excellent. When the ship is full, however, the dining room gets a little crowded, with less space between tables than on the line's new ships.

A nice additional touch: In the suites, daily lunch and dinner menus, along with wine lists, are delivered in mid-morning.

Fielding's Picks

Favorite Places

1. The Rendez-Vous Lounge always seems to be full of happy passengers comfortably ensconced in coral tub chairs at little marble tables to wait for dinner one deck below, to dance to a duo alternating rock 'n roll, Big Band favorites or 50s pop like "Blue Moon"—hey, a keyboard synthesizer helps—or watching a cooking demonstration or playing team trivia.
2. The Marina Cafe makes a pretty set-up out of buffet lunch, with an arrangement of wine bottles and grapes and a huge display of fresh vegetables at the entrance, then a chef in a crisp white toque carving a roast, plus salads, cold cuts and vegetables decorated with carved characters created from squash and onions, along with half a dozen hot dishes and a dessert table of sweets, including sugar-free pastries.
3. A two-level cinema that plays recent films on a reasonable schedule that lets someone who's missed everything since *Forrest Gump* play catch-up.
4. Two glass-enclosed promenade deck areas called Palm Court are divided into smoking areas on one side and nonsmoking on the opposite, with bamboo chairs and marble-topped tables, perfect for needlepoint, reading or having a quiet chat.
5. Interlude Bar, a great hideaway with pretty peach chairs and comfortable leather barstools, just the spot for a tête-à-tête.

Good Reasons to Book These Ships

1. The food, the food, the food, the food, the food!
2. The best martini at sea (from Franco in the Rendez-Vous Lounge).
3. A smooth and even ride in seas that can sometimes get rough.
4. A fresh and delightful production show called *Fifty Years of Broadway*.
5. A courteous and caring crew from the captain on down.

CLIPPER

In The Spirit Of Adventure

7711 Bonhomme Avenue, St. Louis, MO 63105
☎ (314) 727-2929, (800) 325-0010

History

Founded in 1982 in his native St. Louis by travel entrepreneur Barney A. Ebsworth, who also founded Intrav tour company, Clipper Cruises owns and operates two small ships, the 138-passenger *Yorktown Clipper* and the 100-passenger *Nantucket Clipper*, both U.S. flag vessels built in Jeffersonville, Indiana. The company is privately held by parent company Windsor, Inc., a real estate and investment company.

The first ship on line was the 104-passenger *Newport Clipper*, which introduced the line's signature Colonial South cruises in 1984. That vessel was subsequently sold and now sails as *SeaSpirit* for a cruise line of the same name.

The two ships cruise the waterways of North and Central America from Alaska to Costa Rica, the Caribbean to New England, with an emphasis on local culture, art, history, golf and swimming and snorkeling off the side of the ship, depending on the cruising region.

Nantucket Clipper ***passengers spot a whale.***

Concept

Clipper uses small, shallow-draft vessels to explore America's waterways, tying up in small, out-of-the-way ports as well as urban areas in walking distance of the sightseeing. The line prides itself on being "a thoughtful alternative to conventional cruising," stressing substance over slickness, naturalist and lecture programs over musical productions and bingo and sneakers over sequins.

Clipper president Paul U. Duynhouwer likes to point out the misconceptions about adventure cruising—"Elitist, expensive, far away and long are common misconceptions," he says. Clipper, on the other hand, makes soft adventure trips that are as short as seven days and more affordable than many of the exotic journeys other lines offer.

Signatures

Clipper was one of the early providers of golf theme cruises with its southeastern U.S. itineraries offering passengers a chance to play courses like Kiawah Island, Palmetto Dunes, Wild Dunes, Dataw Island, Osprey Cove and St. Simons Island Club, all during a one-week cruise.

Open-seating meals served by friendly young Americans, many of them just past college-age, are prepared by chefs trained at the famous Culinary Institute of America in Hyde Park.

Gimmicks

Clipper Chippers—warm chocolate chip cookies served at teatime and other times.

Who's the Competition

While Clipper offers a fairly unique product because of the scope of its itineraries, it does compete somewhat with Special Expeditions in Alaska, Costa Rica, Panama and Mexico's Sea of Cortez, as well as rivaling American Canadian Caribbean Line in the Virgin Islands in winter. And the all-American style of its food and service, as well as an emphasis on lesser-visited ports and cruising areas, competes with Alaska Sightseeing/Cruise West in Alaska.

Who's Aboard

Couples and singles past 40, many from the south and midwest, dominate the passenger list. What the passengers have in common is an interest in history, culture and nature, and a desire to learn more about the world around them. They are destination-oriented rather than pleasure-driven, and would show little interest in a casino or production show, even if Clipper were to offer them. Most represent household incomes of over $70,000 with substantial discretionary income. They're the sort of people who would wear a name badge if issued one.

Who Should Go

We think more younger couples would enjoy the ship as much as their elders, the same people who would take a bicycling tour through a wine region or stay in bed-and-breakfast establishments. Also, Clipper would appeal to people who have taken package tours or bus tours because they feel safer being escorted around but are tired of that much regimentation, packing and unpacking.

Who Should Not Go

Families with young or restless children, because there are no places on these ships for them to get away; everyone congregates in one large indoor lounge more suitable to quiet adult activities. Because the ships have no elevators, they are not appropriate for travelers who require wheelchairs or walkers to get around.

The Lifestyle

Single seating meals with no assigned tables allow passengers to get acquainted more easily than on large ships, and many of the Clipper crowd find they have a great deal in common. Most days the vessels are in port for all or part of the day, with a range of organized excursions and suggestions for on-your-own activities. Naturalists and lecturers are scheduled frequently to talk about special features of the ports of call, and if there is any entertainment, it is apt to be someone from shore performing folk songs or playing jazz.

Wardrobe

Day dress is casual but in the east coast preppy or country club style, with topsiders, golf pants, plaid Bermuda shorts and such. Zippered windbreakers, soft hats rather than billed caps and sensible shoes are worn ashore. While there is no specific dress code, passengers usually dress up a bit for dinner, and men will sometimes wear jacket and tie.

Bill of Fare

As mentioned above, chefs from the Culinary Institute of America are responsible for preparing the excellent contemporary American cuisine on board. We've found the food uniformly good and the menus consistent in their appeal and variety. Half-portions can be ordered for people with small appetites and "light" dishes are offered on every menu. Much of the food is prepared with fresh ingredients from scratch—including homemade crackers served with the day's soups.

A delectable—and very rich—Flourless Chocolate Cake is one of the specialties:

1 pound butter

1 cup brewed espresso or coffee

1 cup granulated sugar

1 pound semisweet chocolate chips, chopped

8 eggs

Bring butter, coffee and sugar to a boil. Remove from heat and stir in chocolate chips until melted. Mix in beaten eggs and pour into a buttered 10" springform pan. Bake at 350 degrees for 30 to 35 minutes. The cake should be wobbly but dry to the touch.

Cool and cover with Ganache:

4 cups heavy cream

2 pounds semisweet chocolate chips

Bring the cream to a boil and remove from the heat. Add chocolate chips and mix until melted. Pour over the cooled cake.

Rating: B+

FOOTNOTE

A free 21-minute video is available for loan from Clipper for any potential passenger who'd like a closer look at the vessels and the life aboard them. Rather than using models as most cruise lines do, the video features actual Clipper passengers. Call ☎ (800) 326-0010 to borrow a copy.

The Bottom Line

These are rewarding and enjoyable cruises, with many surprises and delights to be discovered on the way to Caribbean ports. The cruises are especially delightful when a passenger is following a subject of particular interest—whether golf, Civil War history, great art museums, Native American legends and lore, snorkeling or restored historic rail cars on a combination cruise/train journey into Mexico's Sea of Cortez and Copper Canyon.

Nantucket Clipper ⚓⚓⚓⚓⚓
Yorktown Clipper ⚓⚓⚓⚓⚓

A cruise along the coast of Maine aboard the Yorktown Clipper *brings back indelible memories of a lunchtime when a humpback whale mother swam by, her nursing calf clinging to her, lazily flapping her white fins in a backstroke wave just outside the dining room windows. On other days, we'd search out the lobster pound in every port, and feast on fresh steamed one-and-a-quarter pounders, promising each other it was in lieu of dinner—and then dinner was always so tempting we'd eat it anyhow.*

The *Nantucket* and the *Yorktown Clippers* have four passenger decks reached by stairs; there are no elevators. Topmost is the Sun Deck, with lounge chairs and good observation points; it doubles as an outdoor dining venue from time to time, and, on the *Yorktown Clipper*, also has four passenger cabins. The Promenade Deck, as its name implies, is wrapped all around by a covered promenade, and cabins on this deck open directly to the outdoors, a boon except when it's raining. Lounge Deck has a forward observation lounge and an outdoor bow area in front of that, along with passenger cabins, some opening into an inside hallway, others at the aft end opening to the outdoors. Main Deck is where the dining room is located, along with additional passenger cabins. All cabins are outsides with windows or portholes.

The Brochure Says

"Lifestyle on board is casual and unregimented. The crowds, commercial atmosphere and hectic activities so often associated with conventional cruise ships are nowhere to be found on Clipper. Your fellow travelers are likely to remind you of the members of your own country club."

Translation

None needed; it's a very precise description of the lifestyle and passengers.

Cabins and Costs

Fantasy Suites: **Report Card: NA**

Nothing on board really qualifies for this category.

Small Splurges: **Report Card: B**

Average Price PPPD: $440 plus air add-ons.

The category Five outside double staterooms, three on *Nantucket Clipper* and eight on *Yorktown Clipper*, are the most expensive digs aboard, primarily because of being slightly larger with more desirable deck locations. Like all the other Clipper cabins, they contain twin beds, bath with shower, desk/dresser with chair plus windows rather than portholes.

Suitable Standards: **Report Card: C**

Average Price PPPD: $340 to $400, plus air add-ons.

Same as the above (see "Small Splurges") except slightly smaller, the category Two, Three and Four cabins are very similar but vary slightly in price. The category Fours have twin beds in an L-configuration with a bit more floor space, while the others have the two beds parallel to each other with a small desk/dresser in between. All three categories have bath with shower only and windows instead of portholes.

Bottom Bunks: **Report Card: C**

Average Price PPPD: $315 plus air add-ons.

The lowest-priced cabins on board are forward on the lowest passenger deck and have portholes instead of windows. Otherwise, each contains twin beds arranged parallel to each other with a small desk/dresser and chair in between. Baths have shower only.

Where She Goes

In the winter the ships are in the Caribbean, then the *Nantucket Clipper* heads north along the golf course route March 30, followed by Colonial America and Civil War Battlefields sailing April 20, then more coastal U.S. and Canada itineraries. September 13, the art capitals cruise sets sail from Boston. Aboard the *Yorktown Clipper*, highlights of the season include spring and fall Copper Canyon and the Sea of Cortez sailings (April 12 and 19 and November 15). Summer is spent in Alaska, with a September 7 departure for The Folklore and Natural History of British Columbia and Southeast Alaska. Costa Rica and Panama are highlighted with spring and fall repositioning sailings.

The Bottom Line

While the prices could be regarded as slightly higher than average—and there's no early booking discount advertised—the value is there. The vessels are comfortable, attractively decorated and always spotlessly clean, although when the ship is full, the lounge sometimes feels crowded. In a few areas they visit—notably off the coast of Maine—the shallow draft causes more ship motion than some passengers might like. The other downer is getting from the Promenade Deck cabins, which open onto a covered deck, down to the dining room when it's raining. But the food, service, itineraries and overall experience are so delightful that little annoyances about space or rain in the face seem minuscule. We like these ships very much.

Fielding's Picks

Favorite Places

1. The tasteful Dining Room, just about everyone's favorite hangout three times a day, plus when it doubles as a cinema after dinner some evenings and the crew makes a batch of fresh popcorn.
2. The Observation Lounge, where passengers socialize, listen to lectures, play cards and games, write letters and do needlepoint, is prettily decorated in pastels and subdued pale tones. This is where the chocolate chip cookies are served at teatime.
3. The Promenade Deck, good for getting in a mile walk if you don't mind counting double-digit laps.
4. The bow observation area, a good place to watch for whales and dolphins where you might sip a cup of hot coffee or glass of iced tea.
5. The Sun Deck, where you sit in lounge chairs and observe the scenery, is also the place where a New England clambake may be dished up.

Good Reasons to Book These Ships

1. To get tee times at the south's top golf courses.
2. To get special tours of art museums conducted by your own shipboard art experts.
3. To enjoy some genuinely warm and friendly American service and delicious American food.
4. To meet other people around the same age who share the same interests.

Club Med® Cruises

40 West 57th Street, New York, NY 10019
☎ *(212) 977-2100, (800) 453-7447*

History

The vacation phenomenon that is Club Med started in the summer of 1950 in a small tent village on the island of Mallorca and has grown to more than 100 all-inclusive vacation villages around the world. In February 1990 the company introduced the first of two five-masted sailing ships, the *Club Med 1*, built by France's Société Nouvelle des Ateliers et Chantiers du Havre, the yard that also constructed the three Windstar sailing ships. Similar to the Windstar ships but larger, and also with computer-trimmed sails, the Club Med ships are sleek, handsome vessels carrying 376 passengers.

—At 14,745 tons, a length of 617 feet and a draft of 16.5 feet, they are the world's largest sailing ships.

The same emphasis on watersports as in the land clubs can be found aboard the Club Med ships with their marine platforms.

Concept

To offer a cruise vacation aboard a motor/sailing ship in "unparalleled comfort and elegance" with a relaxed atmosphere that "fosters freedom, intimacy and camaraderie."

Signatures

Some 64 to 77 GOs, *gentils organisateurs*, or "congenial organizers," as in the Club Med land resorts, operate as a sort of free-wheeling social staff aboard each ship.

Gimmicks

Usually once a cruise there's a shoreside lobster picnic lunch, along with a water-skiing exhibition by the GOs.

Who's the Competition

While the Club Med vessels are similar to those of Windstar, the lifestyle aboard differs because of the very strong presence of the GOs, who function as cheerleaders, entertainers and quasi-passengers. The end result is part-cruise, part-Club Med land village experience. Therefore, the real competition Club Med ships face is from Club Med land resorts.

Who's Aboard

Young to middle-aged singles and couples, families with children over 10 (kids under 10 are no nos), watersports enthusiasts, honeymooners, and destination-oriented young vacationers primarily from Europe and North America.

Who Should Go

Anyone young at heart who enjoys sun, sand, surf and sails, who has a sense of adventure, a dislike of formality but an appreciation for luxurious, if unpretentious, accommodations and surroundings.

Who Should Not Go

Children under 10.

Mrs. Pritchard, author James Thurber's quintessential cruiser: "If you travel much on cruise ships you are bound, sooner or later, to run into Mrs. Abigail Pritchard. She is not one woman, but many; I have encountered at least fifteen of her." Mrs. Pritchard, who appreciates Cunard, would be confused at the absence of a professional cruise staff, the lack of dress code and the babel of different languages with French predominating.

The Lifestyle

Dress is casual, but two Gala Night dinners call for dressier garb. There is no assigned seating for meals. A variety of indoor and outdoor, self-serve and full-service restaurants are on board, plus the Hall Nautique, a watersports marina that can be lowered astern when the ship is at anchor. Daily ports of call are visited by passengers who shuttle ashore by tender to go to an island beach or shops or restaurants.

Wardrobe

Daytime dress is casual aboard ship and on shore, and topless sunbathing is popular aboard with both passengers and female GOs. Bathing suits and coverups are the most common daytime garb. While recent Club Med brochures show a formally dressed couple on deck, we can't recall seeing anyone wearing black tie on our cruise. "Stylish resort attire" is what is requested for evening, and a jacket without tie on men, a long skirt or silk slacks on women is about as dressy as it gets normally.

Bill of Fare

An open-air snack bar, self-serve restaurant for breakfast and lunch plus a full-service restaurant for lunch and dinner offer meal choices for French-accented cuisine. A complimentary table wine is served at both lunch and dinner in generous quantity, with a wine list available offering premium wines for purchase. The cooking when we were aboard was more Continental rather than nouvelle. A room service menu offers additional choices at a surcharge—smoked fish, caviar and sandwiches.

Cuisine Report Card: B

Showtime

As in the land Club Meds, the GOs perform a lot of the entertainment, lip-syncing to records and donning funny hats with the same enthusiasm Judy Garland and Mickey Rooney used to put into their shows in grandpa's barn in the old MGM movies. Sometimes a steel band from shore comes aboard.

Entertainment Report Card: D

Discounts

Land/cruise combination packages can save money when purchased as a package, but the cruise line does not routinely offer discounts.

The Bottom Line

Club Med has begun to diversify its land product during the last several years, emphasizing certain resorts for "romance and friendship" for couples and singles, and others as "togetherness" for families. Another recent creation is a separate brochure marketing Club Med's Finest, listing nine of the club's most luxurious resorts, plus the two Club Med ships, promoting them as upscale destinations. And this seems to be the precise placement for Club Med Cruises, which in the early days did not seem to be able to decide whether it wanted to be a cruise line or a floating Club Med vacation village. It is, in fact, both, but an upscale, luxurious version, one of Club Med's Finest.

Club Med 1 ★★★

Her first captain, Alain Lambert, loves the Club Med 1. *"She's like a fish, just like a fish when she's running. She's lovely. She puts her nose in the water, she likes the water." Her maximum list is two percent but he can control it from one degree to five degrees. "If I have sportive passengers, I can put it five degrees." The combination of sails and engine saves seven tons of bunker fuel a day. Twenty tons are consumed in the average day. The ship makes 14 knots under motor and sail with favorable winds, and he can raise or lower the sails in one-and-a-half minutes. "She's very stable."*

Waterskiing demonstrations are performed by Club Med's GOs.

Instead of a professional cruise staff, pursers, hotel managers, entertainers and such, the cruise is run by a team of 64 to 77 energetic young men and women from various parts of the French-speaking world called GOs (for *gentils organisateurs*) who seem to be having more fun than anybody. Rather than hotel staffers in the traditional sense, they function as quasi-guests, taking part in the same activities with the guests. When they're not water-skiing or leading passengers in songs and dances, they're sunbathing by the pool or rehearsing lip-sync songs for shows. The chief purser/hotel manager is called the *chef de village*, or head of the village, and he may spend more time polishing his mono waterski technique than his hotel-keeping skills, while the ship's doctor may spend his days checking out scuba equipment to the passengers if no one is ill.

INSIDER TIP

Newlyweds on the Club Med ships get a bottle of sparkling wine, two bar coupons, two T-shirts and a VIP gift basket, plus a cocktail party with the chef de village. Honeymooners must be spending one week or longer aboard, must travel within three months of their wedding, must present their marriage certificate when checking in and should request the gift package when booking.

The Brochure Says

"The whisper of the wind along the sails above. On every side, a sea of ultramarine grandeur. Under your feet, eight elegant decks of Burmese teak...All the romance of the sea is yours when you fly on the wings of the wind in these sleek white ships."

ANNOYANCES

Passengers wanting to stretch out in lounge chairs by the pool may find them already occupied by the GOs.

Translation

The only problem is, you'll have to get up early in the morning to experience it since the ships tend to spend most of each day in port with the sails furled.

Cabins and Costs

Fantasy Suites: **Report Card: NA**

There is nothing on board that fits this category.

Small Splurges: **Report Card: A**

Average Price PPPD: $526 including airfare from New York in the Caribbean.

Suites (two measuring 321 square feet each on the *Club Med 1*, with the same basic furnishings as standards (see "Suitable Standards," below) are also available.

Suitable Standards: **Report Card: A**

Average Price PPPD: $325 including airfare from New York in the Caribbean.

All the *Club Med* cabins are outsides with portholes rather than windows and measuring 188 square feet, with white walls, mahogany trim, twin beds that can be made into a queen-sized bed and space module bathrooms that are trim and sleek with excellent pulsating shower heads. Some 23 cabins have a third upper berth. Furnishings include a long dresser/desk with six drawers, a mirror wall, wide counter, built-in TV set fitted into a wooden base (most of the programming is in French) and a hotel-type folding suitcase rack. Niceties include attractive art, reading lights over the beds, hair dryers, terrycloth robes, fresh fruit in each cabin and Club Med label toiletries. A stocked mini-refrigerator and mini-bar carry price lists for the contents. Except for continental breakfasts, room service carries a charge.

Bottom Bunks: **Report Card: NA**

There are no accommodations that fit this category.

INSIDER TIP

You have to join Club Med with a nonrefundable, one-time-only initiation fee when booking your cruise and pay an annual membership fee. Think of it as just another port tax.

EAVESDROPPING

"A real babble tower," is the way one of the Club Med executives described their 64 GOs that come from all over the world.

Where She Goes

Club Med 1 spends winters in the Caribbean, sailing from Fort-de-France, Martinique, and summers in the Mediterranean. Length of sailings varies from three to seven nights with land package combinations available. A few special Christmas holiday sailings may be seven to 15 nights.

The Bottom Line

While more emphasis has been placed on English-speaking personnel aboard the ships, these cruises still favor French-speaking passengers. Passengers have to hustle to get to the best deck chairs, watersports gear and barstools ahead of the GOs. While the ships are lovely in every way, the food perfectly acceptable and the wines drinkable, we find the bar prices extremely high and some of the GOs irritating. Club Med ships are primarily for the young at heart who want a casual, active holiday, or anyone who had the time of their lives at summer camp.

COMMODORE CRUISE LINE

Western Caribbean–Yucatan

4000 Hollywood Boulevard, South Tower, Suite 385, Hollywood, FL 33021
☎ *(305) 967-2100, (800) 237-5361*

History

In mid-1995, a financial group headed by Jeffrey I. Binder bought Commodore Cruise Line from its owners, Finnish-based EffJohn International, for $33.5 million, which included the line's two ships, *Enchanted Seas* and *Enchanted Isle.*

This transaction, plus Cunard's acquisition of the former *Crown Dynasty*, now the *Cunard Dynasty*, temporarily marked the end of EffJohn's longtime cruise operations in North America which at one time or another had included Bermuda Star Line (which was merged with Commodore in 1989) and Crown Cruise Line. (NCL's new *Leeward* is EffJohn owned.)

The vessels owned by Commodore are very likely the most-named passenger ships in the world. They started life as the *Brasil* and *Argentina* for New York-based Moore-McCormack Lines in 1958 in South American service. The *Brasil* became the *Volendam* and the *Argentina* the *Veendam* for Holland America in 1972, but after a year of service were laid up and subsequently the former *Argentina* was chartered out to Agence Maritime International, which, for some mysterious reason, renamed her *Brasil*, according to Arnold Kludas in *Great Passenger Ships of the World, Volume 5.* After that, things get even more confusing, but according to our reckoning, *Enchanted Seas* has had 11 names, *Enchanted Isle* 10. Two of them came out of waffling when Bermuda Star Line couldn't decide between *Bermuda Queen* and *Queen of Bermuda*, announcing first one and then the other, and later, on the same ship, Commodore was going to call her *Enchanted Odyssey* but decided it sounded too much like Royal Cruise Line's ships. (See "Footnote," below.)

After a brief stint as a Russian hotel (*Hotel Commodore*, moored on the Neva River in St. Petersburg), the *Enchanted Isle* was returned to service in the Caribbean in 1995. The *Enchanted Seas* was drydocked for much of 1995 but was scheduled to return to service December 17. The *Enchanted Seas* was leased to World Explorer Cruises to replace that line's *Universe* for 1996.

FOOTNOTE			
1958	*Brasil*	**1958**	*Argentina*
1972	*Volendam*	**1972**	*Veendam*
1975	*Monarch Sun*	**1974**	*Brasil*
1977	*Volendam*	**1975**	*Veendam*
1984	*Island Sun*	**1976**	*Monarch Star*

FOOTNOTE

1986	*Liberté*	**1978**	*Veendam*
1987	*Canada Star*	**1984**	*Bermuda Star*
1988	*Bermuda Queen*	**1990**	*Enchanted Isle*
1988	*Queen of Bermuda*	**1994**	*Hotel Commodore*
1990	*Enchanted Odyssey*	**1995**	*Enchanted Isle*
1990	*Enchanted Seas*		

Concept

The new Commodore aims "to provide top quality service to the markets we serve," according to the line's new chairman and CEO, Fred A. Mayer. The budget-priced cruises are slated to sail from New Orleans year-round.

Signatures

A distinctive line logo features the gold braid sleeve insignia of a commodore.

Gimmicks

In 1993-4, the line used a distinctive jazzy, neon-bright campaign called, "Tell Reality to Take a Hike," with some of the most innovative cruise brochure graphics in the industry. It was a shade more hip than the ships. In 1995 they went back to slimmer, more conservative brochures.

Who's the Competition

Since the ship is slated to sail from New Orleans year-round, the line will compete head-to-head with Carnival's Tampa/New Orleans sailings on the *Tropicale* except in summer, when that ship repositions to Alaska. The present published price for Commodore is priced below the *Tropicale's*, however, which will attract a price- rather than quality-driven market.

Who's Aboard

Lots of first-time cruisers drawn by the low prices and port-intensive itineraries. When we were aboard during the summer, there was an even mix of families with children, young and middle-aged couples and a good sprinkling of singles who seemed to have a grand time.

Who Should Go

People looking for a casual, moderately-priced getaway to the Western Caribbean.

Who Should Not Go

Veteran cruisers fussy about food and service.

The Lifestyle

When we were aboard, the ships were under the previous ownership and management, so styles may change for 1996. Generally, things follow a traditional medium-sized cruise ship pattern, with self-service breakfasts and lunches available as well as dining room meals. A cruise staff leads fun and games, and helps with the evening's entertainment. This line has been noted particularly for theme cruises, which have not yet been announced by the new owners.

Wardrobe

Plan to dress on the casual side of traditional. Two formal nights a week would find some men in tuxedos or dinner jackets but more in suits or sport jackets with tie. Women, as usual, can get by with just about anything except shorts.

Bill of Fare

Again, the food we had was under the previous regime, but should probably be similar under the new owners. The passengers generally don't complain about the food (but some self-styled gourmets might). Portions are generous and service is usually friendly if not always proficient. The self-service buffet meals—breakfast, lunch and tea—were less appealing than the dining room meals. Generally dinners offer a couple of appetizers plus fruit juices, several soups, a couple of salads and four main-dish choices, including a Lite Cuisine selection. Desserts are showy, on the rich and elaborate side. **Cuisine Report Card: C**

NO NOs

Shorts, tank tops and bare feet are not permitted in the dining room.

Showtime

Evening musical and variety shows are supplemented with lots of cruise staff-led fun and games, from horse racing and bingo to audience participation lip sync shows, line dancing lessons, trapshooting and wine and cheese parties.

Entertainment Report Card: C

Discounts

Early booking discounts require a $250 per person deposit or a full payment 90 days prior to the confirmed sailing date. Groups traveling together also qualify for discounts.

The Bottom Line

The ship has fairly spacious cabins, many with third and fourth berths good for families with children. The relatively deep draft means it rides well, an asset in the sometimes-rough Gulf of Mexico. Although the ship is generally clean and attractively furnished, it's on the basic side, without such finishing touches as art in the cabins and hallways.

Enchanted Isle ★★

Here and there on this ship, you can still glimpse a touch of the original vessels, or at least the Holland America version of them, with wood paneling, old wooden dressers with recessed vanity areas, etched glass folding panels to close off a bar area and bits of odd architectural details in the self-service cafes. We remember the Liberté *(now the* Enchanted Seas*) when it was newly restored for American Hawaii's short-lived Tahitian cruises in the mid-1980s and introduced the first 24-hour self-service buffet and deli. In what is now the Great Sound Lounge was a drop-dead chic disco filled with plaster 1930s bathing beauties perched around the room.*

The ship has been through many name and design changes through the years. The cinema deep down in the ship was turned into a disco. Cabin configurations, however, are virtually the same with high density passenger numbers vis-a-vis the open deck space and public room areas.

The Brochure Says

"You could pay as much for a room, and nothing more, at a Caribbean resort. Instead, enjoy a complete vacation. All your meals, orchestrated by Master Chefs, from tender steaks and elaborate desserts to lighter fare like grilled seafood. Snacks beside the swimming pool. Entertainment, a nightclub, fitness center and exercise classes. Wide decks for jogging or sunrise strolls. Counselors for kids during the summer and holidays. And at each port of call, new worlds to discover."

Translation

Commodore is very specifically aiming at budget-conscious first-time cruisers divided between taking a cruise or staying in a resort.

Cabins and Costs

NOTE:

The prices below are based on 1995 brochures, because no 1996 brochures had been prepared, or even decided on, by the new owners and management as we go to press. We expect them to be slightly (or even substantially) higher for 1996.

Fantasy Suites: **Report Card: NA**

There are no cabins aboard the ship that would qualify in this category.

Small Splurges: **Report Card: C**

Average Price PPPD: $207 plus air add-ons.

The same cabins are called superior deluxe on one ship and suites on the other, but we'll just call #356, a large forward-facing cabin with three windows a splurge, with a double bed, sitting area, desk/dresser with drawers, nightstands, good closet space and large tiled bathroom. The room is spacious and light. Some of the cabins in this category have old wooden dressers that look as if they date from Holland America days.

Suitable Standards: **Report Card: C**

Average Price PPPD: $137 plus air add-on.

Since the ship was built in the days before modular cabins, don't expect any two standards to be exactly alike. Many have portholes and most are fairly spacious, with two lower beds (some can be put together into a queen-sized bed, others should be specified as twins or double bed when booking), desk/dresser with drawers, fair closet space and in designated cabins, there is a tub in the bathrooms.

Bottom Bunks: **Report Card: D**

Average Price PPPD: $99 plus air add-ons.

Category 11 insides have upper and lower berths but are fairly spacious. They're not very luxurious, but then they're not very expensive either.

Where She Goes

The planned schedule for 1996 has the *Enchanted Isle* sailing every Saturday from New Orleans, calling in Playa del Carmen and Cozumel, with alternate calls in either Grand Cayman and Montego Bay, or Key West.

The Bottom Line

Until the end of 1995, prices were quite moderate, with some cabins coming at under $100 a day per person, double occupancy, but that's almost certain to change under the new ownership.

If you're a first-time cruiser, don't anticipate a ship that looks like, say, the ones in Carnival's TV ads or the ones you loved on "The Love Boat." This is an old ship and shows its age in some spots on deck and in the cheaper cabins on the lower decks. There's a lot of sound seepage between cabins as well. But it has a deep draft and rides fairly smoothly in rough seas, and the air conditioning was overhauled a couple of years ago and should still be working O.K.

Fielding's Picks

Social Spots

1. The observation lounges high atop the ship with a row of windows facing forward, a piano bar and late-night cabaret shows. Tub chairs, cocktail tables, a small bar with three stools and a large round center sofa furnish them.
2. The Monte Carlo casino is spacious but looks as if it's made up of several smaller rooms, with roulette, blackjack, Caribbean stud and slot machines.
3. The Grand Lounge on the *Enchanted Isle* has some vintage wood paneling and a marble dance floor along with some murky upholstery on the banquettes and chairs and lots of columns which spoil the sightlines during shows.
4. Barnacle's Bar in the Bistro (try to say that three times real fast!) on the *Enchanted Isle* is a popular gathering spot for daytime drinks (and checking out the singles action).
5. Neptune's Disco on the *Enchanted Isle* replaced the cinema so now they project movies on the back wall of the disco.

Good Reasons to Book This Ship

1. The prices are very modest, as low as any you'll find anywhere these days—based on 1995 published brochure prices, before any discounting and dealing!
2. To be able to sail from New Orleans on Saturday and have a full week in the Western Caribbean.
3. To find low-priced cabins big enough for a family of four to move around in (so long as you avoid the really small ones down on Dolphin Deck).
4. To sample some theme cruises from Mardi Gras to Country and Western, Jazz, even Polka (left over from the days of the *Boheme*!)
5. To see how well they used to build ships in Pascagoula, Mississippi.

COSTA *Italian Style* CRUISES

80 Southwest 8th Street, Miami, FL 33130
☎ *(305) 358-7325, (800) 462-6782*

Costa's distinctive bright yellow stack with a blue "C" is seen in many Caribbean ports.

History

The parent company of Miami-based Costa Cruises is Costa Crociere of Genoa, which started back in 1860 with a family business that imported olive oil from Sardinia, refined it and exported it all over Europe. When patriarch Giacomo Costa died in 1916, his sons inherited the family business and bought a freighter to transport their oil themselves. By 1935 they had eight freighters.

They started passenger service after World War II with the the 12,000-ton *Anna "C"* cruising between Genoa and South America. A fleet of three others was added in just four years—the *Andrea "C"*, *Giovanna "C"* and *Franca "C"*.

The first brand-new ship came in 1957-58 when Costa constructed the 24,000-ton *Federico "C"*, now sailing as Dolphin's *SeaBreeze*. In 1959 they moved the *Franca "C"* to Florida and entered seven-day Caribbean cruising. It wasn't long before their entire fleet began spending winters in the Caribbean.

Today, with one of the youngest fleets in the Caribbean, Costa markets tropical cruises in winter and Mediterranean cruises in summer. The line's present fleet (including the *Mermoz*) will number 10 with the arrival of the *CostaVictoria* in July.

—Introduced three- and four-day cruises to the Bahamas from Miami (*Anna "C"*, 1964).

—Based a cruise ship in San Juan and began the first air/sea program between the U.S. mainland and Puerto Rico (*Franca "C"*, 1968).

—Launched "Cruising Italian Style" with toga night parties (*CostaRiviera*, 1985).

FOOTNOTE

Costa's Bianca "C", *originally built as* La Marseillaise *for a French shipping company, burned and sank at the mouth of the harbor in St. George, Grenada, in 1961. You can still see the statue Costa erected in the harbor to commemorate the kindness and hospitality of the Grenadians, who took the 725 passengers and crew into their homes for two days until a rescue vessel could arrive. The statue depicts Christ of the Depths, and is a copy of the original statue in Portofino, Italy, dedicated to scuba divers. One crew member and two passengers died as a result of the fire, and another crew member was never accounted for.*

Concept

"Italian Style by Design," Costa explains as "a product that combines the sophisticated elegance of a European vacation with the fun and spirit of the line's Italian heritage."

Signatures

The distinctive bright yellow stack with a blue "C" and a blue band across the top makes a Costa ship easily recognizable in any port in the world, especially on the new ships, with their clusters of three narrow vertical yellow stacks.

The use of "C" (meaning Costa) following the ship's name in earlier days and the present use of the ship's name following the Costa name in one word, as in *CostaClassica*, emphasize the fact that this is still a family-owned, family-run company.

The piazza, or town square, comparable to the lobby in a major hotel, is the heart of every Costa ship.

Gimmicks

Roman Bacchanal, better known as "toga night," has progressed from a fairly primitive form—passengers tying on sheets taken from their beds—to a very sophisticated routine—ready-made togas handed out by cruise staffers who also pass around gilded laurel wreaths and such. From its very inception it's been wildly popular with North American passengers (they don't usually do it in Italy but offer a Venetian Carnival night instead). It used to be that on masquerade night, you often cringed in embarrassment if you had put on a costume and were one of the few—on toga night, you're embarrassed if you're wearing street clothes because you're very conspicuous. It's usually held the last night of the cruise, simplifying the what-to-wear question for people who pack before dinner. Also, at least one cruise director warns reluctant toga-wearers, "No sheet, no eat."

On Toga Night, almost every passenger dons one of the costumes, partly because it happens the last night aboard, when you've packed most of your clothes, but also because at least one cruise director threatens, "No sheet, no eat."

Who's the Competition

Costa used to face a lively competition from Sitmar and Home Lines, both Italian cruise lines that are now defunct, but doesn't really have to duke it out with Princess, despite Princess owning the former Sitmar ships; they appeal to different people.

Because of the stylish new hardware both lines have, we'd say Costa and Celebrity might compete in the Caribbean, since both are major names on the east coast.

Who's Aboard

Costa has always attracted a large segment of cruisers from the northeastern U.S., especially those with an Italian-American heritage. French and Italian passengers are numerous, especially since Costa added the *Mermoz* from Paquet French Cruises to its roster. Young to middle-aged couples, young families, retirees and often three generations from the same family may all be seen cruising Italian style.

Who Should Go

More young couples, especially anyone wearing an Armani label, would love the newest Costa ships, because they have the same spare elegance with their chic Italian furniture and uncluttered cabins. Opera fans will enjoy the bigger-than-life dining rooms with their strolling musicians and La Scala-painted murals that change by the evening from a medieval street to an Italian garden. Anyone who wants to travel with more Europeans than fellow Americans. Anyone who never said "Basta!" ("Enough!") to pasta.

Who Should Not Go

Cunard first-class transatlantic passengers who might find the energy and noise level a little high; anyone who dislikes pasta and pizza; anyone unwilling to don a toga when everyone else on board does; anyone who doesn't want a multi-cultural experience or can't stand to hear shipboard announcements broadcast in five languages.

The Lifestyle

Traditional cruise programs with an Italian accent characterize the Costa ships, with the usual dress code requests, two meal seatings, and a full onboard and shore excursion activities program. Lavish spas imitating Roman baths are on board the newer ships, and the pool decks encourage spending all day outside with cocoon cabana chairs, sidewalk-cafe tables and chairs, splashing fountains and lounge chairs with pale blue-and-white striped cushions. Overall, there's a lighthearted good humor on these ships, especially when a lot of unflappable Italians are aboard.

Because of the number of Europeans aboard in summer, Costa adds an American hostess program to perform as special liaison for the English speakers on board, usually a minority on European sailings.

Wardrobe

Costa says it would like its passengers to wear on gala evenings tuxedos or dark suits for gentlemen, evening gowns or cocktail dresses for ladies; there is at least one gala evening a cruise. On other evenings, men wear sports coats and slacks, ladies resort attire. In the daytime, casual resort wear is in order, including light cotton clothing and swimwear. Don't worry about toga nights if one is scheduled (they don't usually do it in Europe); the cruise staff delivers the costumes.

Bill of Fare

Meals are served at two seatings, with early or main seating at noon for lunch and 6:15 p.m. for dinner, and late or second seating at 1:30 p.m. for lunch, 8:30 p.m. for dinner. All dining room breakfasts and occasional lunches are designated open seating, which on these ships mean any passenger may arrive within a set time and be seated at whatever table has space. It's not unusual on the larger *Classica* and *Romantica* to find a queue forming 15 or 20 minutes ahead of time; some Costa passengers always seem to be worrying needlessly about when their next meal is arriving.

Food and service are usually good to excellent, with a captain or maitre d'hotel always willing to toss a salad or pasta especially for you at tableside. While the chef may be an Austrian and the waiters Croatian or Honduran instead of Italian, the spirit is there. "They're all Italians at heart," says Costa's president.

Whoever's in the kitchen, we've found the pastas generally outstanding, along with vegetarian eggplant dishes, flambe shrimp, breadsticks, salads, cheeses, fresh fruits, grilled veal chops and pasta-and-bean soups. Less successful on most ships are the pizzas (with the notable exception of the *CostaRiviera*, which has a fine pizzeria on board), some of the meats and the desserts. We particularly miss the Italian-style gelati that has been replaced with American commercial ice creams on several ships.

A fresh fish "catch of the day" is sometimes on display on a decorated cart at the entrance to the dining room on the *CostaClassica* and *CostaRomantica*.

Cuisine Report Card: B+

Showtime

Because passengers on board speak several different languages, Costa ships rely more on musical programs or variety performers like magicians, jugglers and acrobats rather than comedians or production shows that need an English-language narrative. The production shows we have seen aboard are produced by a British company and are handsomely costumed and well choreographed but seem dated beside some of the state-of-the-art shows coming out of Carnival, Princess and RCCL these days.

Films are shown on cabin TV sets throughout the day and evening on an alternating basis, and a late-night disco promises to keep going until the wee hours. Live music for listening or dancing is performed throughout the ships before and after dinner. In Europe, a small company of opera singers may be brought aboard to entertain for the evening.

Entertainment Report Card: B-

Discounts

Costa Cruise Savers offer special discounts on designated sailings, as well as special incentives for seniors, children, suite passengers and anyone booking two cruises back-to-back. Andiamo (Let's Go) Fares provide savings of $300 to $600 per person off the brochure rates for booking early. If one of two people booked in a cabin is 60 years old or older at the time of sailing, both passengers get an additional 10 percent off the Andiamo Fares for booking 90 days ahead of sailing. Children 12 and under sharing a stateroom with two full-fare adults pay only $99 each for the cruise.

The Bottom Line

Costa has been through several ups and downs in the last few years, as in 1992 when U.S. advertising and marketing executives for Costa attempted to abandon the very successful "Cruising Italian Style" concept for a new EuroLuxe label heralding the debut of the *CostaClassica*, proclaiming "a standard of elegance, entertainment and personal service so unprecedented, there wasn't even a name for it until now—EuroLuxe." While the new ship was dramatic and dazzling with its bare marble floors and sleek, stark ambience, its debut was marred by passengers who complained they had been promised plusher surroundings and more pampering from the service staff than they were getting.

But a change of U.S. executives and a return to the Italian-style theme led to a quick recovery, and by the time sister ship *CostaRomantica* was introduced a year later, most passengers took the marble floors in stride.

While the overall fleet goes back to the 33-year-old *CostaRiviera* and the 30-year-old *EugenioCosta*, the ships positioned in North America for Caribbean cruises are all recently built or rebuilt.

Costa offers a good, middle-of-the-road traditional cruise with an Italian accent—you should have a lot of fun aboard if you like Italian-American food and have an easygoing sense of humor.

CostaAllegra ★★★★

Venetian "canals" run along the pool deck of the* CostaAllegra *between the whirlpool and the swimming pool.

The *CostaMarina* was the first of the pair to debut, in the summer of 1990, an extensive rebuilding from the hull up designed by Italian architect Guido Canali. The same architect designed the *CostaAllegra*, which was built in 1992 on an existing hull. The result is a pair of high-tech, mid-sized ships that are cost-efficient and trim but without a lot of extra flourish and furbelows. This is not to say they're not attractive—on the contrary, they are extremely handsome, even whimsical—but they're not traditional. They have a trim, clean, almost austere design that lets the bones, the very skeleton of the ship, show through here and there.

The stern is cropped off in a vertical wall of glass which looks strange from outside but makes a lot of sense when you're sitting inside in the dining room or lounge looking out through all that glass. We recommend them to anyone who doesn't want to sail aboard one of today's megaships, but particularly to those younger passengers, Europeans and Americans, who have no preconceived notions of what a ship should look like.

The Brochure Says

"Sophisticated, stylish and architecturally stunning, the *m/v CostaAllegra* is a timeless masterpiece of color, light and water with an irrepressible Italian soul."

Translation

While the language is a bit effusive, we agree.

Cabins and Costs

Fantasy Suites: **Report Card: A**

Average Price PPPD: $427 in the Caribbean plus air add-ons.

On the *CostaAllegra* only, three forward-facing Rousseau Grand Suites offer a private veranda, separate living room with white sofa wrapped around two walls, wet bar, big portholes looking forward and mirrored walls. In the bedroom is a queen-sized bed and wood-toned walls, with a marble bathroom with toilet and bidet, Jacuzzi tub and separate stall shower, and a walk-in closet with dressing room area. The total space is 376 square feet. When you book a suite aboard at full tariff in the Caribbean, the second passenger pays the minimum cruise price.

Small Splurges: **NA**

No such category on the *CoastaAllegra*.

Suitable Standards: **Report Card: B+**

Average Price PPPD: $227 in the Caribbean plus air add-ons.

Most outside cabins aboard *CostaAllegra* in Category 7 on Gauguin deck have twin beds that can convert to queen-sized, two large portholes covered with solid shade and sheer curtains, walls covered in fabric wall hangings, a long desk/dresser with eight drawers plus a combination safe, color TV with remote control, three-drawer nightstands, bathroom with a futuristic round shower of clear curved plexiglass, gray marble counter with basin, big mirrors, good lighting and built-in hair dryer. The size is adequate but hardly generous at 156 square feet.

Bottom Bunks: **Report Card: C-**

Average Price PPPD: $185 in the Caribbean plus air add-ons.

Category Two inside cabins include some designated for disabled passengers (only on the *CostaAllegra*) with upper and lower berths; the others contain two lower beds that can be put together for a queen-sized bed, as well as furnishings similar to outside standards, including desk and chair. (See "Suitable Standards," above.) Inside cabins measure only 146 square feet.

INSIDER TIP

Playing the cabin radio is a good cover for your own in-cabin conversations, somewhat like a 50s spy movie.

Where She Goes

The *CostaAllegra* spends the winter in the Caribbean, sailing from San Juan every Saturday through April 20 with a new port of call every day, sometimes two ports—St. Thomas/St. John, St. Maarten, Guadeloupe, St. Lucia, Tortola/Virgin Gorda, and Serena Cay, Costa's private island off Casa de Campo.

The Bottom Line

Food and service in the dining room is quite good.

This ship is particularly well designed for younger passengers, with considerable space devoted to spa, gym and disco. There is a children's program and dedicated children's center on board.

Food and service in the dining rooms is quite good, with some tables for two available.

In the Caribbean, the great expanses of glass mean some parts of the ship—notably the disco and spa—get uncomfortably warm by late afternoon despite the air conditioning. Sightlines are not very good in the showrooms, but the entertainment is not always riveting anyhow.

The real pleasure of this ship is the fresh design, the open and inviting decks and public rooms and the ease with which even first-time cruisers can find their way around.

CostaClassica ★★★★★
CostaRomantica ★★★★★

The CostaClassica, *first of the two new ships, got off to a bad start because some former executives misled travel agents and potential passengers by tagging the new ship "EuroLuxe," creating the expectation of a plush Crystal-style ship rather than an austere but handsome contemporary Italian design. Expecting "luxury, elegance and sumptuousness," as the dictionary defines luxe, one disgruntled passenger looked at the bare marble floors and muttered, "The luxe stops here."*

The dining rooms change their looks when they change their background scenery, painted by a La Scala Opera House designer.

These sister ships are sleek and stylish with marble, tile, brass, polished wood, fountains and sculptures. So much hard surface lends a cool rather than warm ambience.

The ships have an angular bow, a boxy midsection and a rounded stern, with a vertical cluster of bright yellow funnels aft balanced by a forward glass-walled circular observation lounge set atop an all-glass deck housing the Caracalla Spa and amidships pool.

Two stairwells with bare stone floors and no risers provide the main vertical traffic flow through the ship, and on busy occasions like the lifeboat drill, sounds like changing classes at Woodrow Wilson Junior High.

Decks are handsome and well-designed. One pool is amidships, a second one aft, along with two Jacuzzis and several levels of teak decking for sunbathing.

The Brochure Says

"Created for those with a sense of adventure and an appreciation for style...(with) Italian hospitality, European charm and American comforts."

Translation

You can expect to find pasta and pizza; a cabin with TV, radio, hair dryer and safe; and a charming waiter who may just as likely come from Riga or Rijeka as Roma.

Cabins and Costs

Fantasy Suites: **Report Card: A+**

Average Price PPPD: $427 in the Caribbean plus airfare.

Among our very favorite suites at sea are the 10 veranda suites on each ship, particularly those on the *Romantica* named for operas. Each is 580 square feet with private veranda, living room with burled brierwood furniture, a kidney-shaped desk, a small round table, two tub chairs and a long sofa; a separate bedroom with queen-sized bed, elegant wood dresser with round brass-framed mirror; floor-to-ceiling white window shades operated electronically, gauzy white undercurtains and a tied-back sheer green curtain at the windows; large whirlpool bathtub, stall shower and double lavatories in a wide counter. Butler service, mini-bar, terrycloth robes and reclining deck chairs on the veranda. Romantic? Yes!

Small Splurges: **Report Card: A**

Average Price PPPD: $356 in the Caribbean plus airfare.

Mini-suites, on the *Romantica* only, measure 340 square feet and contain a couch, two chairs, desk and chair, floor-to-ceiling windows, queen-sized bed, single trundle bed, bath with Jacuzzi tub, stall shower and double lavatories. Butler service, mini-bar and terrycloth robes.

Suitable Standards: **Report Card: B+**

Average Price PPPD: $263 in the Caribbean plus airfare.

More spacious than on many ships, the standard outside cabins measure 200 square feet and contain two lower beds, most of which convert to queen-sized; a few designated cabins have fixed queen-sized beds only. White marble counters and built-in hair dryers are in all bathrooms, hanging and storage space is generous and the room has a dresser and a sitting area with two chairs and a table. Several inside cabins (cheaper than the price below) are designated wheelchair-accessible with extra-wide doors, bathrooms with pulldown shower seats and generous turning space.

The lowest-priced inside cabins on the CostaRomantica can sleep up to four in style and comfort.

Bottom Bunks: **Report Card: C**

Average Price PPPD: $156 in the Caribbean plus airfare.

The cheapest cabins aboard are insides with a lower bed and upper berth, with two chairs, small table, dresser, TV set and bath with space-age shower. There are only six on each ship and they are sometimes assigned to staff. The next category up has two lower beds and is only marginally higher in price.

Where She Goes

Both ships cruise the Caribbean in winter, with the *CostaClassica* sailing from Pointe-à-Pitre on seven-day cruises marketed exclusively to Europeans, calling at St. Lucia, St. Maarten, Tortola, Serena Cay, St. Barts and St. John.

The *CostaRomantica* makes alternate Eastern and Western Caribbean cruises out of Miami every Sunday through April 21, calling in Key West, Playa del Carmen/Cozumel, Montego Bay and Grand Cayman on the western itinerary, San Juan, St. Thomas, Serena Cay and Nassau on the eastern itinerary.

The Bottom Line

The "Italian by Design" theme emphasizes the architecture and decor of the ships and stresses Costa's Italian heritage, but most of the Italian waiters are gone, replaced over the years by other Europeans, many from the newly independent eastern countries and some of whom are still awkward with English.

Furnishings aboard are beautiful, with one-of-a kind high-style Italian chairs set about here and there like pieces of art.

In the dining room, despite the dangerous marble floors, meals are served on Limoges china and double-skirted Pratesi linen tablecloths while strolling musicians play. The food is most often very good.

Many standard cabins on the *Classica* have large wooden room dividers that steal floor space without adding any useful storage area; a better bet for couples are the cabins with fixed queen-sized beds and no room divider, the same size as the others but they seem much bigger.

Fielding's Picks

Easy Places

1. With a pool, an Italian sidewalk cafe, beach cabanas with striped blue-and-white curtains, a striking blue marble "Trevi" fountain and a thrust overhead runway from the jogging deck above overlooking all the action, it's La Dolce Vita time.
2. The heart of each ship is the piazza—on the *Classica* the Piazza Navona, on the *Romantica* the Piazza Italia—where everyone seems to gather, with an all-day- and-evening bar and lounge and music for dancing before and after dinner.
3. The dining rooms aboard change their looks on special evenings when the staff unfurls background scenery to turn it into an Italian garden or medieval city, ancient Pompeiian villas or Renaissance town; the backgrounds are painted by a scenic designer for the La Scala Opera House in Milan.
4. The big open-air cafe aft on each ship is covered with a sweeping white canvas awning and furnished with apple green wicker chairs and marble-topped tables, just like the Via Veneto.
5. The glass-walled discos high atop the ship and forward, like see-through flying saucers, double as observation lounges in the daytime.

CostaVictoria Unrated

The first of two more new ships for Costa, the *Victoria* is scheduled to debut in July. The 75,000-ton, 1928-passenger vessel comes out of the Vulkan Group's Shichau Seebeckwerft Shipyard in Bremerhaven, Germany.

The most striking area of the ship is expected to be the Observation Lounge, which spans four decks, with a waterfall and a floor-to-ceiling glass wall. The area will serve as the piazzetta, or town square, as well as a special events area and a theater for evening shows.

A second atrium in the Central Hall soars seven decks from the lobby up to a glass dome high atop the ship, with four glass elevators to sweep passengers to the upper decks.

A canvas-covered outdoor cafe similar to those on the *CostaClassica* and *CostaRomantica* is expanded to two decks on the aft end of the ship. Two swimming pools, a smaller splash pool and four Jacuzzis are on deck, as well as a tennis court and 1312-foot jogging track.

Fitness aficionados will find a super Caracalla Spa on board that includes an indoor swimming pool, Turkish bath, steam, sauna and fitness center.

Two dining rooms with two seatings each, a casino, centers for children and teens, a disco, library and show lounge are also planned.

Cabins and Costs

Six suites and 14 mini-suites are among the 964 cabins aboard; 60 percent are outside.

Where She Goes

CostaVictoria is scheduled to cruise the Greek Islands on seven-day itineraries out of Venice to Athens for her first summer season (July 14 through October 6) calling at Bari, Katakolon, Kusadasi and Volos then reposition to the Caribbean, beginning seven-day cruises out of Miami on November 10.

CRYSTAL CRUISES

2121 Avenue of the Stars, Los Angeles, CA 90067
☎ *(310) 785-9300, (800) 446-6620*

History

Los Angeles-based Crystal Cruises did the cruise line equivalent of coming from 0 to 60 in six seconds. Founded in 1988 by century-old NYK (Nippon Yusen Kaisha), one of the largest transportation companies in the world, the Japanese-financed company set up a long and elaborate program of introducing to the United States a new ship that was still two years away from completion.

The line's first ship, the 960-passenger *Crystal Harmony*, was built in the Mitsubishi shipyard in Nagasaki, Japan, and made its debut in Los Angeles in July, 1990, to great critical acclaim. A sister ship, the *Crystal Symphony*, built in Finland's Kvaerner-Masa Yard, made its debut in New York in May 1995.

—First line to offer two alternative dinner restaurants to all passengers at no surcharge (*Crystal Harmony*, 1990).

FOOTNOTE

Interestingly, this very upscale line deliberately chose as godmothers for its ships actresses that are better-known for popular television series than for feature films or theater, Mary Tyler Moore for the Crystal Harmony *and Angela Lansbury for the* Crystal Symphony.

Concept

From its inception, Crystal set out to define "luxury" by trying to provide the best of everything—food, entertainment, service and shipboard accommodation—and to offer "warm and personal service in an elegant setting." They say, "The line provides sophisticated travelers and experienced cruisers with an intimate and luxurious cruise experience."

Signatures

The turquoise seahorses on the Crystal stacks have become a recognized logo in most of the great ports of the world, and that particular shade is carried through on logo caps and T-shirts and other Crystal souvenir merchandise.

In the lobby of each ship is a "crystal" piano made of lucite, along with bronze-colored statuary, a waltzing couple on the *Harmony* and a pair of ballet dancers on the *Symphony*, and waterfalls with crystal cut-glass cylinders and Tivoli lights.

Gimmicks

Using costly Louis Roederer Cristal Champagne for special occasions like christenings.

Extension telephones in the bathrooms.

Who's the Competition

In its brief five years of cruising, Crystal has garnered an enviable reputation for service and overall quality, so that it virtually stands alone at the head of its class. It would have rivalled the former Royal Viking Line, and we do note some crossover from Cunard's *Royan Viking Sun*. It also attracts veterans of Princess and Holland America, as well as Seabourn and Sea Goddess.

Who's Aboard

Most of the passengers are successful couples between 40 and 70, with a sprinkling of older singles who enjoy the gentleman host program aboard. Very few of the passengers are Japanese, but those that do sail represent the upper strata of independent travelers rather than group tourism. Some 90 percent of the line's passengers are 45 and up with a median age of 60, and 80 percent are married. Of the line's total passengers, nearly half have traveled with Crystal before. A recent passenger list shows guests from the United States (primarily California), Canada, Saudi Arabia, Japan, Australia, Hong Kong, Mexico, Switzerland, Brazil, Germany and Belgium.

Who Should Go

Younger passengers and upscale first-time cruisers who will enjoy the excellent entertainment, the high quality of food and service and the only pair of Caesars Palace casinos at sea.

Who Should Not Go

Anyone who doesn't like to dress up and socialize.

The Lifestyle

These ships offer one of the finest versions of classic, traditional, luxury ship cruises available, with a fairly formal dress code and assigned dining at two seatings but with two alternative restaurants available most evenings as well by advance reservation. Lavish surroundings, pampering service, excellent housekeeping and superlative dining keep the same passengers coming back again and again. Daytime activities are frequent and fascinating, shore excursions very well handled and evening entertainment top-notch.

Wardrobe

Dressy, dressy, dressy. We're frequently carry-on people with only a little luggage, but we always check a large bag when we're flying to board a Crystal ship. Daytimes and shore excursions can be casual, but the passengers are almost always attired in smart casual, or casual elegance (what the Crystal handbook calls "country club attire.") Evenings, women wear cocktail dresses or dressy pantsuits for informal (what some lines now are calling "semi-formal") nights, while men don jacket and tie; on formal nights, women wear evening gowns (we saw as many long gowns as short ones on the inaugural of the *Symphony*) and men don tuxedos or dark business suits.

Bill of Fare

Creative contemporary cuisine, much of it prepared to order, comes out of the Crystal galleys, which are under the direction of executive chef Toni Neumeister, former executive chef for Royal Viking Line. A dinner menu will carry suggestions for a full menu recommended by the chef, a lighter fare menu giving the calorie, fat and sodium counts, a vegetarian menu and cellar master wine suggestions by the glass or by the bottle. Traditionally, you can choose from three or four appetizers (perhaps tempura fried softshell crab with red pepper aioli), two or three soups (maybe a chilled tomato soup with goat cheese quenelles), three salads, a nightly pasta special (like fusilli with zucchini, garlic, olive oil and onions) and four main dishes (say, seared fresh ahi tuna steak, crisp baby hen, grilled tournedos of beef tenderloin Rossini or roasted Scandinavian venison loin) plus a vegetarian option such as a baby eggplant stuffed with ratatouille. The dessert roster runs to five desserts (maybe a tarte Tatin with vanilla ice cream or a souffle Grand Marnier) plus a cheese trolley and various frozen desserts. A little silver tray of freshly made petits fours always arrives with the coffee service.

But that's only the dining room. There are also two alternative restaurants with special evening menus, one Italian and one Asian (Chinese on the *Symphony* and Japanese on the *Harmony*) and a wonderful assortment of casual buffet lunch choices from an elegant spread of cold seafoods and meats and hot dishes in the Lido Cafe to our favorite gardenburger, pizza, grilled hot dogs or hamburgers on deck. There's also an ice cream bar.

Cuisine Report Card: A

Showtime

The entertainment is dazzling, with highly professional productions that are constantly updated, along with prestigious lecturers, concerts, cabarets and game shows. Lecturers scheduled for 1996 sailings include journalist and author Pierre Salinger, ship historian Bill Miller, novelist Judith Krantz and former Los Angeles mayor Tom Bradley. Production shows are gorgeously costumed (some of the hand-beaded wardrobe pieces cost as much as $10,000 each) and beautifully choreographed and performed.

Entertainment Report Card: A

Discounts

Members of the Crystal Society (previous cruisers with the line) get a five percent discount good for any 1996 cruise, with no advance booking deadline. If you book a future cruise while you're aboard one of the ships, you get a discount of $250 to $500 per person, and your travel agent gets her full commission as well. Pay in full six months ahead of sailing time and you get an additional five percent discount.

The Bottom Line

There are only two possible criticisms demanding luxury cruisers could make—the two seating dining and the shortage of really generous closet space on very long sailings like the full world cruise. To the first, we'd point out that you could book the alternative restaurants for 7:30 or order dinner in your cabin for those nights when you didn't want to dine at your assigned table. To the second, we'd suggest if you're taking a really long cruise and you like to dress up, book as high a cabin category as you can, say one of the penthouses or penthouse suites.

The Crystal ships are for those who want—and are willing to pay for—the very best in a traditional big-ship sailing experience.

Crystal Symphony ★★★★★★

The highly successful Crystal ships have had only a few gaffes in their career—and our favorite is the Viennese Mozart Tea, which used to be presented as one of the highlights of the cruise. On the inaugural of the Crystal Harmony *in 1990, it was dazzling, with a string trio and all the waiters decked out in white wigs, gold lame frock coats and vests, long white stockings and slippers—visualize Tim Curry as Mozart in the film* Amadeus *and you get the picture. On our next outing aboard the* Harmony *in 1993, the procedure had gotten routine, and the Viennese Mozart tea on that sailing had only three of the waiters (the ones who looked as if they'd drawn the losing straws) garbed in white wigs and partial costumes, but wearing loafers and white tennis socks. The Manila Strings trio were only two, wearing their ordinary daytime garb of white pants and shirts. (The third musician was missing, Harry pointed out, because Mozart didn't write for guitar.) On the inaugural of the* Crystal Symphony, *there were no white wigs, gold lame vests and knee breeches in sight, just the table of elegant cakes and pastries. The wigs had caused near-revolution in the ranks of waiters, as had the costumes, so the whole fancy-dress thing was written off.*

This elegant ship with its sleek, graceful lines offers a lot of sensational cabins with private verandas, a plethora of posh public rooms and an easy-to-get-around layout. The public areas are concentrated on the top two decks and two lower decks with most of the cabins in between. An amidships pool deck is sheltered enough with its sliding glass roof and glass side windows that it provides a cozy sun-trap. By limiting the major "avenues" to one rather than both sides of a deck, the traffic flows neatly without sacrificing space that could be devoted to a shop or bar. Craftsmanship is meticulous. Comfortable cruising speed is 16 to 17 knots, but the *Crystal Symphony* on its inaugural was averaging 20.

An expansive amidships pool and raised whirlpool is surrounded by plenty of sunbathing area.

The Brochure Says

"From the moment you step aboard the gleaming white jewels known as *Crystal Harmony* and *Crystal Symphony*, you will feel you have arrived at a very special place and have been warmly embraced as part of the Crystal family."

Translation

They're serious about this, folks. There's something called The Crystal Attitude, a service philosophy that is a part of the intensive training each employee goes through, with motivational tapes and videos and classes for upper echelon employees in notable hotel schools like L'Ecole Hotelier in Switzerland and Cornell Hotel School. Crystal has the highest crew return factor of any cruise line, with more than 70 percent re-enlisting.

Cabins and Costs

Fantasy Suites: **Report Card: A+**

Average Price PPPD: $1324 with some airfare included.

The most lavish quarters aboard are the two Crystal penthouse suites, each measuring 982 square feet, with large sitting room, dining area, private veranda, wet bar, big Jacuzzi tub with ocean view, separate master bedroom with king-sized bed, big walk-in closets and a guest bath. There's butler service, of course.

Fantasy suites like the Crystal Penthouse with veranda aboard the* Crystal Symphony *are sought after by big spenders.

Small Splurges: **Report Card: A+**

Average Price PPPD: $722 to $906 with some airfare included.

Eighteen penthouse suites with verandas that measure a total of 491 square feet and 44 penthouses with verandas that measure 367 square feet are spacious and prettily furnished. Butler service is offered in all the penthouses, along with complimentary bar, cocktail hour canapes, and in-room dining with dishes that can be ordered from the dining room or either alternative restaurant.

Suitable Standards: **Report Card: A+**

Average Price PPPD: $495 with some airfare included.

The deluxe stateroom with private veranda is the most numerous of the cabin categories on board, with 214 cabins (on the *Symphony*) each measuring 246 square feet, with a private veranda, king-sized bed, loveseat sofa, chair, built-in desk/dresser with plenty of storage space, a safe, mini-refrigerator, TV/VCR, plus a large closet with built-in shoe rack and tie rack, and a marble bathroom with tub/shower combination, double sinks and two hair dryers. Seven staterooms for the disabled are available on the *Symphony*, four on the *Harmony*.

Bottom Bunks: **Report Card: A**

Average Price PPPD: $234.

Outside cabins without verandas on the *Crystal Symphony* are the lowest-priced digs aboard. The latter number 202, and some have restricted views due to hanging lifeboats.

INSIDER TIP

On all the above prices, an advanced booking fare can save up to 30 percent; these are capacity controlled fares and could be withdrawn at any time.

Where She Goes

The *Crystal Symphony* spends the first quarter of 1996 making the first-ever around-the-world cruise for the line, which positions the ship in Europe for a series of Mediterranean and Northern European summer cruises. A transatlantic crossing which visits the Canaries is set for late October, followed by transcanal and Caribbean sailings through the Christmas holidays.

The Bottom Line

While the ship's interior is handsome and dignified, the real sense of the luxury comes not from eye-grabbing architecture but rather fine attention to detail—items like the Wedgwood teacups in the Palm Court at teatime, Riedel hand-blown wine glasses in the Prego Restaurant, Villeroy & Boch china and Frette linens in the dining room, goose down pillows in each cabin, the designs on the Bistro plates and cups. Passengers are treated like adults rather than children at summer camp. Big-ship cruising doesn't get any better than this.

Fielding's Picks

Spectacular Spots

1. The Palm Court, a sunny, airy winter garden with wicker chairs and ceiling fans, potted palms and a harpist playing for tea.
2. The Avenue Saloon, the "in" bar on board (you can always tell the "in" bar because that's where the officers and the entertainers hang out) with its wood floors and Oriental rugs, green leather bar rails and movable stools.
3. Caesars Palace At Sea, a truly classy shipboard casino operation that actually (in the Vegas style) gives free drinks to players.
4. The spectacular Crystal Spa and Salon on the top deck with lots of glass windows, aerobics area, gym with lots of machines, sauna, steam and massage.
5. The elegant Prego Restaurant aboard the *Symphony*, the Italian alternative dining option, with its red-and-white striped pillars and high-backed blue armchairs tied with red tassels and cord, the very essence of a classy Venetian restaurant.

Good Reasons to Book This Ship

1. To tell all your friends about your cruise.

2. To show off your wardrobe and jewelry.
3. To be pampered by a happy staff who have the best crew accommodations at sea plus their own gym and Jacuzzi.
4. Cabin telephones with voice mail, and bathroom extension phones.
5. To have a private veranda, which will change your whole picture of luxury cruising.

Things You Won't Find On Board

1. Portholes; all the outside cabins have windows.
2. Anyone inappropriately dressed on formal night.
3. A bad attitude or discouraging word.
4. A lot of children, even though there's a youth and teen area provided.
5. A really unhappy passenger.

CUNARD

555 Fifth Avenue, New York, NY 10017-2453
☎ (212) 880-7500, (800) 221-4770

Cunard made headlines in 1994 when it acquired not only the posh* Royal Viking Sun *with its swim-up bar on pool deck but all rights to the prestigious Royal Viking brand name and its subsidiary labels.

History

"I want a plain but comfortable boat, not the least unnecessary expense for show," Samuel Cunard instructed the Scottish shipyard that built his 1154-ton wooden paddlewheel steamer *Britannia* in 1840. And when it set out on its maiden voyage from Liverpool to Halifax and Boston on July 4, with 63 passengers, 93 crew members and a cow to supply fresh milk on the voyage, the conservative businessman from Nova Scotia was more concerned about his cargo—he had a lucrative contract to carry Her Majesty's mails and dispatches across the Atlantic twice a month—than his passengers.

FOOTNOTE

One of the Britannia's *early passengers was novelist Charles Dickens, who sailed the North Atlantic through severe gales in January, 1842, describing his feelings tersely as, "Not ill, but going to be." His cabin contained "a very thin flat quilt, covering a very thin mattress, spread like a surgical plaster on a most inaccessible shelf," and the dining room was "not unlike a gigantic hearse with windows in the sides."*

That same year, Cunard quadrupled his fleet, eventually cutting down crossings from the usual six weeks of that era to two weeks.

FOOTNOTE

"Going to sea is a hardship," wrote one early Cunard executive in response to a query as to why the ships did not provide napkins in the dining room. "The Cunard Company does not undertake to make anything else out of it, and if people want to wipe their mouths at a ship's table, they could use their pocket handkerchiefs."

In its 156-year history, Cunard has operated more than 190 ships, including the famous *Queen Mary* and *Queen Elizabeth*, who saluted each other in the midatlantic as their paths crossed. They transported 4000 people a week between the U.S. and U.K.

In the late 19th and early 20th centuries, the Cunarders carried hundreds of thousands of immigrants from Europe to the U.S., and during World War II carried troops to and from Great Britain.

Cunard's* Mauretania *is remembered today with a striking 16-foot model displayed aboard the* QE2 *complete with lighted portholes.

But the 1920s and 1930s were the heyday of ocean liners. Cunard's legendary *Mauretania* with its four red-and-black stacks and lavish wood-paneled, plaster-ceilinged public rooms, ruled the waves through the twenties. The *Queen Mary* was star from the thirties to the waning days of transatlantic crossings in the sixties, with guests such as the Duke and Duchess of Windsor, in perpetual, glittering exile with their 75 suitcases and 70 trunks; Noel Coward; Rex Harrison; Rita Hayworth; Richard Burton and Elizabeth Taylor.

FOOTNOTE

After 31 years of service, the Queen Mary *was retired in 1967, exactly a decade since the number of transatlantic travelers crossing by air first outnumbered those crossing by sea. The* Queen Mary *is today a landmark moored at the city of Long Beach, California, serving as a hotel and tourist attraction.*

Samuel Cunard would probably not be surprised at the size and diversity of his company's present fleet—eight sea-going ships ranging from the 1814-passenger *QE2* to the deluxe little 116-passenger *Sea Goddess ships*, and five elegant river vessels—but he would probably be astonished to find that people book passage by sea not by necessity but for the sheer pleasure of traveling slowly, emulating those shadowy companions of another day who enjoyed an infinite supply of the one travel luxury we lack—time.

FOOTNOTE

Cunard has been a wholly-owned company of London-based Trafalgar House, PLC, since 1971.

—First company to take passengers on regularly scheduled transatlantic departures (*Britannia*, 1840).

—Introduced the first passenger ship to be lit by electricity (*Servia*, c. 1881).

—Introduced the first twin-screw ocean liner (*Campania*, 1893).

—Introduced the first steam turbine engines in a passenger liner (*Carmania*, 1905),

—Introduced the first gymnasium and health center aboard a ship (*Franconia*, 1911).

—Introduced the first indoor swimming pool on a ship (*Aquitania*, 1914).

—First cruise line to introduce an around-the-world cruise (*Laconia*, 1922).

—Held the record from 1940 to 1996 for the largest passenger ship ever built (*Queen Elizabeth*, 1940).

—The only cruise company to sail regularly-scheduled transatlantic service year-round (*Queen Elizabeth 2*).

—The first cruise line ever to offer three different around-the-world cruises at the same time (*QE2, Royal Viking Sun, Sagafjord*, winter/spring 1996).

FOOTNOTE

"Getting there is half the fun," was an ad slogan Cunard came up with in 1956 to promote its transatlantic crossings against the new competition from jet aircraft.

Concept

In the wide diversity of Cunard ships, the flagship *Queen Elizabeth 2* stands alone, providing an around-the-world cruise, regular transatlantic crossings and warm-water cruises.

The highly rated *Royal Viking Sun*, along with the prestigious *Vistafjord* and *Sagafjord*, offer very good quality food, service and accommodations at sea for the most demanding and sophisticated travelers.

Cunard's ultra-deluxe little *Sea Goddess* ships are among our very favorite vessels, because they give passengers the sense of sailing on their own private yachts.

In the mid-sized, moderately-priced range are two classic ships, the sparkling new *Cunard Dynasty*, making shorter cruises to popular destinations such as Alaska, the Caribbean and the Panama Canal, and the beloved, if somewhat vintage, *Cunard Countess*, which cheerfully cruises the Caribbean year-round with some interesting island ports of call.

Signatures

The distinctive red-and-black funnel that has characterized Cunard ships since the *Britannia* in 1840 has not been affixed to the *Royal Viking Sun* and the pair of *Sea Goddess* ships. The *Sun* retains the red RVL sea eagle, and the *Sea Goddess* ships carry a golden goddess.

The Cunard lion, rampant, wearing a crown and holding a globe in his paws, first appeared in 1880 when the company went public, and which, according to ship historian John Maxtone-Graham, rival sailors disparagingly called "the monkey wi' the nut."

Serving caviar and champagne in the surf is an eye-catching Sea Goddess tradition; here, passengers and crew wading at Jost van Dyke in the British Virgin Islands.

Gimmicks

Serving caviar from the blue two-kilo tins is a trademark/gimmick aboard the *Sea Goddess* ships, where it adorns the serve-yourself appetizer table at cocktail time and is fetched ashore by waiters in black tie and swim trunks on beaches in the Caribbean.

Who's the Competition

Cunard's purchase of the *Royal Viking Sun* eliminated much of the direct competition facing *Sagafjord* and *Vistafjord*; now the three of them compete with the Crystal ships. *Sea Goddess*, almost always mentioned in the same breath with *Seabourn*, is really more like Radisson Seven Seas' *Song of Flower* or the Silversea ships since the admittedly-steep fares include all the beverage service on board, still an optional extra with Seabourn.

Who's Aboard

Older couples and singles, most of them North Americans with an upper-range income, are typically aboard *Royal Viking Sun* while the *Sagafjord* and *Vistafjord* usually draw a more cosmopolitan and slightly younger crowd, a mix of North Americans, British and Germans.

Sea Goddess attracts almost exclusively couples who have money or want people to think they do and who may or may not be married.

Who Should Go

Anyone who loves luxury and can afford it should book one of the *Sea Goddess* ships, in the Caribbean, to be pampered with caviar and champagne around the clock as if it's your own private yacht. And aging baby boomers who've done well in business should reward themselves by sampling the *Royal Viking Sun*, *Sagafjord* or *Vistafjord* to see if that's how they want to vacation when they retire.

Who Should Not Go

It's interesting that with most cruise lines, the crossover from one ship to another is easily made, even with a size disparity, as with Princess Cruises' mid-sized *Pacific Princess* versus the very large *Regal Princess*. But with the Cunarders, even sister ships like *Sagafjord* and *Vistafjord* sometimes draw different patrons. And it's impossible to visualize a *Sea Goddess* passenger going over to the *Cunard Countess*, or even a *QE2* penthouse passenger who dines in the Queens Grill switching to the first seating in that ship's Mauretania restaurant. So when it comes to Cunard, "Who should not go on which ships?" is the real question, which will be addressed under the individual ships. (See "No Nos," under each ship.)

The Lifestyle

Because the lifestyle aboard Cunard vessels, unlike those of other cruise lines, varies depending not only on the ship but also the type of sailing—transatlantic, world cruise, warm-weather cruising—we'll describe it with each individual ship.

Wardrobe

Except for the *Cunard Countess* and *Cunard Dynasty*, which are termed "informal cruising," the Cunard ships call for a fairly dressy wardrobe. The exception, interestingly enough, is on a transatlantic crossing, when many businessmen, particularly Europeans, will wear a dark suit that doubles as business wear rather than a tuxedo. On the crossings, every night except first and last are formal.

Day wear aboard the ships is smart casual or "country club" garb. On informal nights, especially on the *Royal Viking Sun* and *Sagafjord*, some of the men wear madras jackets with bright linen pants in what we think of as a preppy or southeastern resort look.

Even on the least dressy vessels in the line, the *Cunard Countess* and *Cunard Dynasty*, it is noted in the fine print that "women prefer evening or cocktail dresses, or other formal attire, and gentlemen wear black tie or dark suit. On informal evenings, regular cocktail dresses for women, and jacket and tie for men are the norm." We wonder how one can tell the difference between a "cocktail dress" and a "regular cocktail dress."

Bill of Fare

The *Royal Viking Sun*, *Vistafjord* and *Sagafjord* all have good to excellent cuisine, especially the *Sun*, with some dishes cooked to order and a pleasurable range of choices, including the option to order special meals. Wine lists are outstanding on all three ships. *Sea Goddess* cuisine and service have always been superlative, even their deck buffet dishes. *Cunard Dynasty* and *Cunard Countess* serve a varied menu of popular Continental and international dishes in the dining rooms, along with buffet breakfasts and lunches in the deck cafe.

Cuisine Report Card:

A+ *Sea Goddess, Royal Viking Sun*

A *Vistafjord, Sagafjord*

B+ *Cunard Dynasty*

B *Cunard Countess*

Showtime

Cunard entertainment, while hewing to a general pattern, varies according to the size of the ship's show lounge facilities. The three classic stars—*Royal Viking Sun*, *Sagafjord* and *Vistafjord*—follow a traditional format of musical production shows and variety acts by magicians, ventriloquists, puppeteers and comedians, as well as audience participation game shows like Liars Club and Team Trivia. There's usually a dance team (yes, Velez and Yolanda live!) who perform on variety nights and teach dance classes during the daytime to groups or in optional private lessons. On the *Sea Goddess* ships, entertainment consists primarily of the passengers socializing with each other or dining alone in their suites, so except for a musical group that plays nightly for dancing, or a late-night cabaret artist, there is usually not much happening.

The entertainment aboard the mid-sized *Cunard Dynasty* and *Cunard Countess* also presents production shows and variety acts, but usually on a somewhat smaller scale. **Entertainment Report Card: B+**

Discounts

Cunard gives a 20 percent early booking discount to passengers who book and place a deposit on a cabin 120 days before sailing.

The Bottom Line

With the current policy of acquiring rather than building ships, Cunard has set itself apart from the other major cruise lines who are introducing new-builds almost annually. With eight ocean-going ships, Cunard is outnumbered only by Carnival, Costa and Royal Caribbean and stands equal with Holland America and Princess. The main difference is, all the other companies have new ships on order for the next several years.

Cunard Countess ★★

The Cunard Countess *used to offer a wonderful combination of Caribbean programs, a cruise and a resort stay, where you could book the* Countess, *get off in midweek at Barbados or St. Lucia and bop over to a Cunard-owned resort hotel, spend a week and then get back on the ship and finish your cruise. It was competitively priced with resort holidays and seemed a really good idea. But Cunard gradually got out of the hotel business, so the Sail 'n Stay Vacation went the way of the dodo.*

After her multiple makeovers, the *Countess* looks much as a vintage Hollywood star would; you can't look too closely under the cosmetics. Even though she's not as glamorous as the *Dynasty*, a lot of people love the ship, and she offers year-round low-key, relaxed cruising in the Caribbean at an affordable price. Basically easy to get around, she carries most of her cabins on the three lower passenger decks and the public rooms and deck areas on the three upper passenger decks. A recent renovation redid the vessel's air conditioning system and overhauled the stabilizers for a cooler, smoother ride, redecorated many cabins, put a new sound system in the show lounge and redecorated several public rooms.

The Brochure Says

"Let *Cunard Countess* transport you to a world of lush emerald isles afloat in a shimmering turquoise sea. Experience the quintessential Caribbean vacation, where palm-fringed beaches, splendid tropical weather and golden sunsets are a way of life."

Translation

Our passengers, many of them from the U.K. and Europe, come for the islands, beaches and sunshine, and don't care that our ship is aging.

Cabins and Costs

Fantasy Suites: **Report Card: NA**

Nothing on board qualifies for this category.

Small Splurges: **Report Card: B**

Average Price PPPD: $273 plus airfare.

A big spender could book the category A1 deluxe outside double rooms, one of the pair located amidships on Five Deck. What you get is a cabin nearly twice the size of the next category down, plus sitting area, mini-refrigerator, two lower beds, TV and bathroom with tub and shower.

Suitable Standards: **Report Card: C**

Average Price PPPD: $175 plus airfare.

Category C outside double cabins with windows have two lower beds and new bathrooms; some have a pull-down third berth as well. These are fairly basic although they were redecorated nicely on the last redo and had specially-commissioned watercolors added.

Bottom Bunks: **Report Card: D**

Average Price PPPD: $132 plus airfare.

The lowest-priced cabins aboard are the H category minimums, some with two lower beds, some with upper and lower berths, and baths with shower only.

Where She Goes

The *Cunard Countess* sails from San Juan every Friday year round, alternating between Caribbean capitals calling at Tortola, British Virgin Islands; St. John's, Antigua; Fort-de-France, Martinique; Bridgetown, Barbados; and St. Thomas, U.S. Virgin Islands, and 7-Day 7-Plus, visiting St. Maarten, Guadeloupe, Grenada, St. Lucia, St. Kitts and St. Thomas.

The Bottom Line

While not the prettiest ship to ever come along, the *Cunard Countess* is comfortable as an old shoe (but looks more like a new one, thanks to the recent renovations), non-fancy and non-intimidating. Her passengers come for the port destinations and the prices, which are very modest indeed in today's cruise world. Cabins are small, except for the very top pair, and walls are thin.

Fielding's Picks

Newly Refurbished Places

1. The Meridian Restaurant, looking better than ever after the most recent refurbishment, offers a few tables for two along with its more usual tables for four, six and eight.
2. The Showtime Main Lounge sparkles with its new sound system and reupholstered chairs and banquettes.
3. The Starlight Piano Lounge forward on Sun Deck has been completely redecorated.
4. The Outdoor Center has had its worn teak replaced and repaired and new tables and chairs installed, along with new lounge chair cushions.
5. The Satellite Cafe, which doubles as disco and casual buffet restaurant, has been perked up with new furniture.

Good Reasons to Book This Ship

1. To get a second week in the Caribbean with all-new island ports for half-price, except during the Christmas holidays, in cabin categories A1-F.
2. To take a popular country music cruise with the Cowgirl Hall of Fame and Pat Cannon's Foot & Fiddle Dance Company.
3. To sail from San Juan, where you can add on a two-night pre- or post-cruise package at the Condado Plaza Hotel and Casino for only $199 per person, double occupancy.
4. To earn Cruise Miles which can add up to discounts or free cruises.
5. You'll be able to find your way around it easily.

Things You Won't Find On Board

1. Private verandas.
2. Cabins designated wheelchair-accessible.
3. Single cabins (although some are small enough to qualify).
4. A self-service laundry.
5. A predominance of American passengers; the British usually outnumber them.

Cunard Dynasty ★★★★

We loved all three of the former Crown ships, and wish Cunard still had the Jewel *as well as the* Dynasty. *It's an ideal size, elegantly decorated, with very good food and entertainment and the only problem is a lot of people never heard of it.*

The pretty oval pool aboard the* Cunard Dynasty *is surrounded by a Palm Beach-style deck with comfy loungers and umbrella-shaded tables.

There used to be five mid-sized, moderately-priced ships in the fleet—the *Cunard Princess* (now sold to Mediterranean Shipping Company and under charter to Starlauro Cruises as the *Rhapsody*), the *Cunard Countess* and three leased ships built between 1990 and 1993 for Palm Beach-based Crown Cruise Line, owned by the Scandinavia-based Effjohn Group—*Crown Monarch*, *Crown Jewel* and *Crown Dynasty*. But the owners sold the *Crown Monarch* and the *Crown Jewel* to Asian-based operators, leaving only the three-year-old *Crown Dynasty*, renamed *Cunard Dynasty*, as the running mate to the 20-year-old *Cunard Countess*. The *Dynasty*, last of the former Crown vessels, is also the most dramatic, especially when you watch it sailing into a small or medium-sized port with its name painted in script in huge, eye-catching type against the white hull with a broad red band just above and, of course, the signature Cunard red-and-black stack.

The Brochure Says

"After dining amid magnificent sea views, take your seat for the Broadway-style revue. Dance in our lovely disco or choose your favorite game of chance in the casino. Watch a movie in the comfort of your cabin, or take a moonlight stroll on deck. Then, sample a delicacy or two from the Midnight Buffet."

Translation

It's all happening here, on a lovely ship that you share with fewer than 800 fellow passengers.

Cabins and Costs

Fantasy Suites: **Report Card: B+**

Average Price PPPD: $493 including airfare.

Top digs are 10 suites with about 350 square feet of area each, with teak-decked private balconies, separate sitting areas, mini-refrigerator and extra-large closets. (Two other suites have extra-large sitting areas with bay windows instead of private balconies if you prefer.) The two lower beds can be converted to one double, and the bath has a shower only.

Small Splurges: **Report Card: B+**

Average Price PPPD: $447 including airfare.

The seven extra-large category Two forward cabins on Deck Six give you a captain's-eye view of the sea through big angled glass windows, two beds that can be put together for a double, two chairs, cocktail table, dresser/desk and chair. These are about the same size as the Fantasy Suites above, but without the veranda.

Suitable Standards: **Report Card: B**

Average Price PPPD: $358 including airfare.

Category C standard outside doubles are available on three different decks, average 140 square feet with two lower beds that can convert to a double, remote-control color TV, safe, mirrored built-in dresser/desk, satellite telephone and bath with shower.

Bottom Bunks: **Report Card: C**

Average Price PPPD: $229 for the G, $183 for the H (as in, rare as hen's teeth), including airfare.

The two H category cabins would be so rare to be able to book—they're like the loss leader in a supermarket ad—that we might as well recommend the next category up, a 132-square-foot G inside double with two lower beds, TV, telephone and bath with shower.

Where She Goes

The *Cunard Dynasty* makes 11-day winter cruises from Ft. Lauderdale and Acapulco calling at Cozumel, Grand Cayman, Canal transit and Costa Rica. ten-day return cruises call at Costa Rica, transit the Canal, and visit Ocho Rios and Key West.

The Bottom Line

While big enough to give a sense of stability, the *Cunard Dynasty's* public rooms and lounges have an intimate ambience, so passengers can socialize easily. And its staterooms, while not overly spacious, are comfortable and handsomely furnished. There's something for everyone aboard this clean, pretty ship.

Fielding's Picks

Super Spaces

1. The drop-dead gorgeous five-deck atrium with its spiral staircase and trompe l'oeil mural of Italian colonnades with blue skies and clouds beyond, and down at the very, very bottom on a parquet floor, a white piano.
2. The Palm Beach-style deck with comfy loungers covered in blue-and-white striped mattresses, matching umbrellas to shade the tables and pretty oval pool.
3. The Rhapsody Lounge showroom with wood-backed banquettes in dark pink and purple tapestry fabric and matching carpet.
4. The surprisingly lavish Olympic Spa that offers seaweed body wraps, massages, body-composition analysis, makeup and hair styling and full beauty salon services.
5. The Marco Polo Cafe, the casual buffet-service restaurant with wicker chairs and a sunny tropical atmosphere.

Sea Goddess I ★★★★★★
Sea Goddess II ★★★★★★

When we asked the founder of Sea Goddess back in 1984 how he came up with the basic concept, an expensive and luxurious alternative to the usual sea vacation, Helge Naarstad, a handsome young Norwegian businessman, said, "I sat down and made a list of all the things I myself would like to do on a cruise." What Helge and his beautiful wife Nini like is, quite simply, the best of everything.

The little extras that you can take for granted aboard Sea Goddess include a special afternoon tea and grandly themed afternoon fruit-and-cheese buffets.

Well, setting out to create your own ideal vacation and give your passengers the best of everything does not necessarily guarantee a profit margin, certainly not when you're the first on the block to come up with such an unusual idea. So a financially-troubled Sea Goddess was acquired by Cunard Line in 1986, which had the wisdom not to change a thing, including the legendary largesse with champagne and caviar. All the alcoholic and non-alcoholic beverages consumed on board (except special-order wines) are included in the basic fare, as are the tips for the exceptionally fine staff. As the forerunner of the super-deluxe small ships, the *Sea Goddesses* are good but far from ideal, something their designers, Pettar Yran and Bjorn Storbraaten, would readily admit. The duo has created the interiors for virtually all the ships in this class—Seabourn, Silversea, *Song of Flower*, *Queen Odyssey*—and acknowledge that each subsequent ship got design refinements they learned from doing the previous one. Cabins are comfortable but not particularly large, closet space is sparse and bathrooms are strictly mainstream rather than upscale-sybaritic as on the Seabourn class vessels. But all in all, these are among only a handful of our very favorite ships at sea.

The Brochure Says

"A certain world travels on Sea Goddess: people whose lives are diverse, experience wide, tastes high. Worldly company fills the ship with the warmth, elegance and intimacy of a private club."

Translation

This is a Rorschach test. Read it and you'll know if you're right for Sea Goddess and Sea Goddess is right for you.

Cabins and Costs

Fantasy Suites: **Report Card: NA**

All the accommodations on board are suites.

Small Splurges: **Report Card: A**

Average Price PPPD: $971 plus airfare, all tips and beverages included, in the Caribbean. You can either opt for a suite-room or a suite. The latter is two suite-rooms, and would represent a splurge. In 410 square feet you get two entry halls, two full baths, a his and a hers, a large sitting room with two sofas and table and lots of built-in cabinetry, a bedroom with queen-sized bed, and a study or smaller sitting room with two chairs and large windows.

Suitable Standards: **Report Card: A**

Average Price PPPD: $642 plus airfare, all tips and beverages included, in the Caribbean. The suite-rooms are the standard outside doubles in these ships; there are 58 of them with about 205 square feet each. They contain an entry, bath with tub and shower, sitting area with sofa and chair, coffee/dining table, built-in cabinetry, mini-refrigerator, entertainment center, TV/VCR and stocked bar. The bedroom has a queen-sized bed, night tables, picture windows and vanity counter with stool and drawers. Closet space is adequate but not generous.

Bottom Bunks: **Report Card: NA**

See "Suitable Standards," above.

Where She Goes

Sea Goddess I cruises the Caribbean in winter, the Mediterranean in summer, with popular seven-day sailings roundtrip from Monte Carlo or between Monte Carlo and Venice or Rome. Autumn the vessel relocates to the Greek Isles and Turkey, then returns to the Caribbean.

Sea Goddess II cruises the Caribbean in winter with Indian Ocean, Southeast Asian and Alaska cruises the rest of the year.

The Bottom Line

The bathrooms and closets could be larger and the suites could have a private veranda, but there's little else we would change about these wonderful ships. They're not stuffy and not pretentious. Extra little surprises may include meals created by famous chefs (who just might be aboard to cook them for you), wine-tasting with famous vintners and unique shore excursions called Sea Goddess Exclusives. These ships fulfill the fantasies of sybaritic couples of all ages, but singles may find them frustrating.

DOLPHIN CRUISE LINE

901 South American Way, Miami, FL 33132
☎ (305) 358-5122, (800) 992-4299

History

Dolphin Cruise Line came about through a marketing agreement in 1979 between Peter Bulgarides, who formed Ulysses Cruise Line, and Paquet to operate the *Dolphin IV*. That agreement was terminated in 1984, and Dolphin Cruise Line was born to handle the ship.

A second ship, the former *Star/Ship Royale* from Premier Cruises, was acquired in 1989, and renamed the *SeaBreeze*, and when Admiral Cruises was disbanded by its parent company Royal Caribbean Cruise Line in 1992, Dolphin acquired the former *Azure Seas*, which it named *OceanBreeze*. The latter ship had been based in Los Angeles for more than a decade, making highly successful three- and four-day cruises to Baja California.

For three years, the company operated its trio of vessels, using the *Dolphin IV* for short cruises to the Bahamas and the other two for seven-day Caribbean sailings. In August 1995, Dolphin sold its *Dolphin IV* to Kosmas Shipping Group, Inc., a Florida-based company to Canaveral Cruise Line. The *Oceanbreeze* will be redeployed to Miami to take over the three- and four-day cruises to the Bahamas and Key West effective May 3, 1996.

Majesty Cruise Line, which operates the *Royal Majesty*, is also affiliated with Dolphin Cruise Line. Both lines are headed up by Captain Paris Katsoufis. Peter Bulgarides resigned as chairman of the board in 1994.

Concept

Dolphin feels it established itself as a leader in the three- and four-day cruise market early on by providing quality and value, as well as offering "quality service and gourmet dining" on all of its ships. The vintage Dolphin vessels still carry details from their ocean liner days such as teak decks, wood paneling, etched glass and polished brass.

Signatures

The distinctive blue dolphin on the ships' white stacks makes an easily recognized and identified logo.

Theme cruises such as Country Western sailings, '50s and '60s cruises, Motown, Oktoberfest, Big Band and Nostalgia are coming up in 1996.

On-board weddings were popularized by Dolphin and frequently take place on the ships.

Gimmicks

As the Official Cruise Line of Hanna-Barbera, Dolphin and Majesty ships are animated with cartoon characters such as Yogi Bear, Fred Flintstone and Scooby Doo.

Who's the Competition

Dolphin has long been a leader in the budget cruise arena and competes primarily in the price-driven market that also includes Commodore Cruise Line and Regal Cruises.

Who's Aboard

A great many first-time cruisers, family groups, singles, couples, many passengers in their 20s and 30s.

Who Should Go

Anybody who wants to sample a cruise to see what it's all about without having to make a big commitment in time and money should try one of the mini-cruises out of Miami.

Who Should Not Go

Fussy veteran cruisers will not like the very long lines that form anywhere food is being arranged, served or set out.

EAVESDROPPING

A man standing in line at tea time watching several family members heaping plates with cakes and sandwiches shakes his head in mock dismay and says, "I'm gonna hafta get some new springs for my car before I can drive the five of them back home."

The Lifestyle

The three- and four-day cruises are a little more hectic than the seven-day sailings, just because Dolphin tries to work in as many special activities as possible. The usual daily pattern always offers plenty of chances to eat, plus as many as eight shore excursions in port. Sports and exercise classes, movies, ping pong, dance classes, beauty salon demonstrations, napkin folding, fruit and vegetable carving, pool games, horseracing, tours of the navigation bridge, Name That Tune, captain's cocktail party, shore excursion sales, dance music, game shows led by the cruise director, a deck party under the stars, ice carvings, midnight buffet, disco and night owl movie—and that's just one day! Children's programs offer a variety of options from dolphin encounters to sand castle building and treasure hunts. The atmosphere on board is friendly, even ebullient, because people worried about whether they were going to have a good time realize they're having a great time.

Wardrobe

Dolphin is very kind to its first-time cruisers on the three- and four-day sailings, requesting that they dress up for formal night to meet the captain and go to dinner, then letting them change back to casual garb for the rest of the evening. Not many cruise lines do that.

Generally, they expect men to wear at least a jacket and tie for formal nights; a lot of men bring tuxedos or dinner jackets. They do not permit shorts in the dining rooms after 6 p.m. On evenings designated semi-formal, they also expect men to wear a jacket. On Tropical and Casual dress code nights, almost anything goes.

Bill of Fare

Dolphin has always impressed us with the quality and quantity of its embarkation day buffets when many more-expensive cruise lines are doling out sandwiches. Breakfast buffets on the pool deck usually include bacon, eggs, potatoes, French toast, fruit and pastries. Dinners are fairly predictable hotel banquet-type meals, but the homemade breadsticks are delicious and there are always a lot of rich, elaborate desserts that seem to please the multitudes. Menus rotate on a fixed basis and are changed "every couple of years." Midnight buffets are especially big on the three- and four-day sailings, with a themed version scheduled every night, Italian Buffet, Fruit Buffet and Farewell Buffet, plus the Magnificent Buffet on four-night sailings. There's usually a diet dish on every lunch and dinner menu.

Cuisine Report Card: B

Showtime

The three- and four-day sailings depend a lot on audience participation games including "The Newlywed and Not-So-Newlywed Game," along with disco and casino action, male nightgown competitions and cash bingo. On longer sailings there are mini-musical revues, variety shows and karaoke contests. The ship's orchestras play quite well for dancing.

Entertainment Report Card: C

Discounts

Dolphin's SaleAway Program promises, "The earlier you book, the more you'll save!"

The Bottom Line

These are good economy-priced ships for first-timers who want to take a mini-cruise or spend a week sampling popular Caribbean ports in a casual atmosphere. The staff is friendly and the food tasty, and the ships are kept very clean. The only vessel we felt badly needed some deck maintenance was the *Dolphin IV*, which the line has sold but will continue to operate for the new owners.

OceanBreeze ★★★

"We've never been on a cruise before," the young couple confided as they stood by the rail holding hands in the sunset. "Now we're going to save up for a longer one—14 days at least." He went on to say that he works as a mechanic for a municipal bus system; his wife bags groceries at a chain supermarket. Two chic and pretty African-American women who work for the post office were flirting with a Fijian bar steward, and a young punk rocker with purple hair spent most of his port time feeding the sea gulls perched on the ship's rail.

FOOTNOTE

One question we've been asked over the years is about timing—how we happened to get into the field of cruise writing 15 years ago before it was generally realized cruising would become a major industry. The answer is easy— Azure Seas *(and on the east coast,* Emerald Seas*) demonstrated back in 1981 that cruising is for everyone, not just the rich or retired.*

A very young Queen Elizabeth II christened this ship as the *Southern Cross* in 1954, when it made the Australia/New Zealand run from Great Britain. It featured several design innovations, including the placement of the funnel and engines at the aft end and the elimination of cargo holds; both features have become commonplace on nearly every passenger ship constructed since. The ship was laid up in Southampton in 1971, then sold to a Greek company in 1973 to be refitted as a cruise vessel named *Calypso*. She sailed the Mediterranean for five years, primarily with British vacation package tourists aboard, then was sold in 1980 to Eastern Steamship Lines and renamed *Calypso I*. In 1981, she was sold to the company's West Coast associates, Western Steamship Lines, named the *Azure Seas* and began sailing on three- and four-day cruises out of Los Angeles to Ensenada, Mexico. Eastern and Western Steamship Lines merged to become Admiral Cruises in 1986, which was subsequently acquired by Royal Caribbean Cruises and disbanded in 1992.

Still handsomely maintained, the *OceanBreeze* shows more than a bit of her art deco background as well as a touch of glitter and glamour from recent makeovers. Cabins are larger than on many ships in this price and age range.

The Brochure Says

"Sit back. Relax. Sip a colorful, tropical cocktail and get to know some new friends. Or get to know each other even better. There isn't a better time or place to do all the things you haven't done in years. This is the cruise to do it all. Or nothing at all."

Translation

Try it, you'll like it.

Cabins and Costs

NOTE:

These prices reflect the fares on the seven-day sailings through April 1996. When the ship begins its three- and four-day cruises in May, the per diems may change. Check before booking.

Fantasy Suites: **Report Card: B+**

Average Price PPPD: $335 plus airfare.

One of the 12 new penthouse suites they added on Boat Deck during a recent refit is called the owner's suite, and faces forward for a great view. With two big rooms—a living room with sofa and chairs, coffee table, minibar and TV, and a bedroom with queen-sized bed and plenty of storage, plus a bath with tub and shower—it's large enough to live in. The sofa makes into a double bed if you want to bring the kids along to share.

Small Splurges: **Report Card: B**

Average Price PPPD: $256 plus airfare.

The spacious Category 2 double outside cabins on Barbizon Deck are bigger, cheaper and more private than the pricier category 1 cabins on Atlantis Deck, a promenade deck where you have people going past your window all the time. Most have two lower beds or double, and many have a third pulldown berth. The bath has shower only.

Suitable Standards: **Report Card: B**

Average Price PPPD: $235 plus airfare.

The Category 3 outside double cabins on Caravelle and Dolphin Decks are adequate, although if you worry about motion sickness, we'd suggest avoiding the ones on Caravelle Deck, which are all forward from the dining room. A deck lower they're amidships for a smoother ride. Most of these have two lower beds but some of the choicest locations—# 239-244—have double beds instead and are near the elevators. Your bathroom will have a shower instead of a tub.

Bottom Bunks: **Report Card: C**

Average Price PPPD: $156 plus airfare.

The cheapest cabins aboard are the Category 10 inside doubles on Emerald Deck, and there are only two of them. They have two lower beds or a double and a shower in the bathroom.

Where She Goes

Until the sailing of April 14, the *OceanBreeze* cruises two alternating Southern Caribbean itineraries out of Aruba, calling one week in Dominica, Barbados, Martinique and

Curacao, and the next in Cartagena, with a cruise into the Panama Canal and stops in the San Blas Islands and Curacao.

Beginning May 3, the *OceanBreeze* will make three- and four-day cruises from Miami to the Bahamas and Key West, sailing on Fridays and Mondays. A repositioning cruise April 21 takes the ship from Aruba to Miami, visiting Curacao, Bonaire, Santo Domingo and Nassau.

The Bottom Line

A graceful and dignified ship, the *OceanBreeze* offers a good, medium-priced vacation at sea for first-time cruisers or anyone who wants to get away for a few days. Larger and smoother riding than the *Dolphin IV*, she should do very well on the three- and four-day mini-cruises out of Miami.

Fielding's Picks

Unforgettable Places

1. The elegantly refurbished two-deck casino with its art deco brass railings and light fixtures.
2. The Cafe Miramar, where buffet breakfasts and lunches are served and late-night cabaret shows sometimes happen.
3. The Mayfair Lounge with its wicker furniture, potted palms and ceiling fans evokes the past. Sunlit during the day, the bay windows offer pleasant sea views; softly lit at night with a pianist playing, it's an appealing spot for a quiet rendezvous.
4. On the other hand, the Rendezvous Show Lounge glitters and sparkles with the evening's main entertainment, which you watch from comfortable swivel tub chairs upholstered in a tight red-and-blue check that looks mauve from a distance. Don't sit behind a post or you'll miss some of the show.
5. The hard-to-find library has always been one of our favorites because it doesn't get much through traffic; books are locked in wood-and-glass bookcases and there are plenty of comfortable dark blue chairs and sofas.

SeaBreeze ★★★

The only mystery we kept bumping into was a sign in the main lobby, near the purser's desk, that said Pictures From An Exhibition. How classy, we said, perhaps an art show, an art auction is behind that locked door, or a lounge that presents classical music in the afternoons. The space was shown and neatly labeled in the deck plan bracketed by a pair of restrooms, with nothing more to illuminate it. Finally, the moment came when the doors were unlocked and open. It was the ship's photographer's display of the passengers arriving, shaking hands with the captain, coming down the gangway in port and posing in formal clothing on a dress-up night, perhaps the first time since the prom or the wedding pictures. Pictures From An Exhibition. Yes.

The *SeaBreeze* was built as Costa's *Federico C* in 1958 as a two-class ship, then became Premier's *Royale* in 1984. Dolphin acquired her in 1989. There are nine passenger decks, with cabins located on all but two, the topmost deck, where there is a buffet setup, and the bottom-most, where the disco is located. During its ownership of the vessel, Premier increased the density both by adding cabins in former deck areas and adding third and fourth berths, so that almost any cabin you book is likely to have additional overhead bunks. The idiosyncratic cabin layout means the configuration of the cabins varies; some have twin beds, some double beds, some bathrooms have tub and shower, some shower only.

CHAMPAGNE TOAST

To the hotel manager of the SeaBreeze, who not only keeps a superbly clean ship but who won't let passengers take their buffet breakfast and lunch trays from the cafe into the adjacent air-conditioned show lounge to eat. There's a sign on the door: No food permitted inside. That's the way it should be–If you want air conditioning, eat lunch in the dining room. If you want a buffet, eat it outdoors on the sunny or shaded deck. But don't spill your food and drink all over the lounges.

The Brochure Says

"As you'll find out, almost everything's included on Dolphin Cruise Line. So stop dreaming and wake up to Dolphin. One of the world's best cruise lines. And the best value in cruising."

Translation

The appeal is to first-time cruisers, reminding them that many more things are included in the basic fare on ships than they are accustomed to in resort hotels.

The dining room of the* SeaBreeze*, a very attractive, budget-priced ship.

Cabins and Costs

Fantasy Suites: **Report Card: B+**

Average Price PPPD: $236 plus airfare.

Seven suites on board are spacious, pretty rooms with king-sized bed, sitting area with sofa and chair, and a long built-in desk/dresser, along with two windows.

If you get B4, you'll have a view forward, a tile bath with tub and a frosted window in the bathroom, the last really rare on ships.

Small Splurges: **Report Card: B**

Average Price PPPD: $199 plus airfare.

Category 2 outside superior cabins are fairly spacious, some of them (# D8, for example) with built-in cabinetry from the 1960s, lovely old coatracks fitted onto the cabin walls with pull-out hangers, brass temperature gauges made in Milan with all the instructions in Italian, left over from the *Federico C* days. We like the cabin despite its obstructed view and its two additional overhead berths.

Suitable Standards: **Report Card: C**

Average Price PPPD: $189 plus airfare.

Category 4 cabins are outsides on the lower passenger decks with two lower beds or a double bed (specify which one you want when booking), bathrooms with shower and portholes instead of windows.

Bottom Bunks: **Report Card: D**

Average Price PPPD: $105 plus airfare.

The very cheapest cabins on board are two very tiny Category 11 inside cabins with upper and lower berths forward on Isolde Deck, the lowest deck with passenger cabins. (The only one lower is the Juliet Deck where the disco is located.)

Where She Goes

The *SeaBreeze* sails from Miami every Sunday on alternate seven-night itineraries to the Eastern Caribbean and the Western Caribbean. In the Eastern Caribbean, she visits Nassau, San Juan, St. John and St. Thomas, and in the Western Caribbean, she stops at Playa del Carmen/Cozumel, Montego Bay and Grand Cayman.

The Bottom Line

When we were aboard the *SeaBreeze* a few months ago, we were tremendously impressed at how clean and fresh she looks, especially given her age and her background as a veteran of the children's crusades over at Premier, when she was the *Royale*. Frankly, this ship is kept more spic-and-span than a lot of fancy new vessels built in the 1980s. It's a good economy-priced vessel for first-timers who want to sample a lot of Caribbean islands in a non-intimidating atmosphere.

Fielding's Picks

Special Places

1. The Water Music Whirlpool, a trio of Jacuzzi pools surrounded by rows of plastic loungers, is on the aft end of the Boheme Deck.

2. The Prelude Bar is an intimate little lounge with very comfortable swivel rattan barstools, a varnished teak floor and latticework walls, plus lots of healthy fresh green plants.
3. The Casino, with some rare five-cent slot machines among the 99 one-armed bandits, plus four blackjack tables, one Caribbean stud and one roulette.
4. Royal Fireworks Lounge, wide rather than deep, with curved sofas, wood tables, blue and mauve chairs and an oval dance floor in wood parquet.
5. The Carmen Lounge, a show lounge filled with swivel tub chairs in rose or sage, round wooden cocktail tables, bar with eight stools, and very poor sightlines.

Good Reasons to Book This Ship

1. The price is right.
2. The itineraries alternate from week to week—the Eastern Caribbean one week, the Western Caribbean the next—so you could add them together for a great 14-day full Caribbean tour, and take a substantial discount on the second week's price as well.
3. Let your kids meet Yogi Bear and Fred Flintstone.
4. To be one of the displays at Pictures From An Exhibition.
5. You could get married on board—and sail away on a wonderful honeymoon. Have your travel agent contact the Wedding Coordinator at Dolphin to find out about five different wedding packages from $275 to $750.

Things You Won't Find On Board

1. A chair apiece if you're not in a suite; in the cabins, you get one to share.
2. A look at the bottom halves of the chorus girls in the Carmen Lounge unless you're in the front row.
3. A table for two in the dining room; you'll be seated at a table for eight to 10. But look at the upside—you'll meet that many more people.
4. A movie projected on film; in the ship's cinema, videocassettes are what you get.
5. A horse in the Light Cavalry Arcade, which is occupied by 12 coin-operated video games.

EUROCRUISES
INCORPORATED

303 West 13th Street, New York, NY 10014
☎ *(212) 691-2099, (800) 688-EURO*

History

EuroCruises is the largest North American marketer of ships to Europe, representing 52 ships and ferries owned and operated by various European companies.

Among the most unusual ships it represents are the icebreakers *Nordbris* and *Polarstar*, which cruise to polar bear country in Spitsbergen on four- and seven-night cruises. The *Nordbris* carries 38 passengers, the *Polarstar* 25.

It's Black Prince from Fre. Olsen Cruise Lines sails the Caribbean in winter.

Black Prince ★★★

We still remember being stunned by the watersports platform on the stern of the Black Prince *that was added in the 1987 refit. That was ahead of Seabourn's collapsible wire mesh swimming pool but after Sea Goddess's more modest watersports platform.*

Fred. Olsen Cruise Lines' *Black Prince*, a favorite of the British cruise market, was built in Germany in 1966, and boasts not only one of the earliest watersports marina platforms but also the biggest—60 feet long when it's all in place. The Marina Park extends from the stern when the ship is at anchor to allow passengers to swim in a collapsible wire mesh pool with teak decking around it, or sail, waterski or windsurf off a watersports platform. It's used most frequently in the Canary Islands or in quiet Mediterranean and Caribbean bays away from shipping traffic.

The *Black Prince* has seven passenger decks, with cabins concentrated on four of them. The main public room deck is anchored with a lounge at either end and restaurants amidships.

The Brochure Says

"These days there are all sorts of holidays to choose from. Beach holidays and city holidays, cultural holidays and holidays crammed full of activities. But there's one break that combines them all and does it without you having to check in and out of countless hotels, jump on and off planes, trains and automobiles. It's a cruise."

Translation

None necessary.

Cabins and Costs

Fantasy Suites: **Report Card: NA**

N/A

Small Splurges: **Report Card: B**

Average Price PPPD: $267 plus airfare.

There are four larger-than-average deluxe double outside on the topmost Marquee Deck, attractively decorated, with two lower beds, a new in-house video system and bath with tub and shower.

Suitable Standards: **Report Card: B**

Average Price PPPD: $162 plus airfare.

Outside cabins with two lower beds may mean two real beds, one bed and one sofa, or one bed and one pullman bed that folds into the wall. These cabins have bath with shower only. There are also "family cabins" with a double bed, one lower and one upper berth; a wide range of inside and outside singles; and the possibility of creating a two-room suite out of certain adjoining cabins on Marina Deck.

Bottom Bunks: **Report Card: C**

Average Price PPPD: $103 plus airfare.

The little inside three-berth cabins are the low man on the *Black Prince* totem pole, with two lower beds and one upper berth. There is also fairly limited wardrobe space in the lower category cabins.

Where She Goes

The *Black Prince* sails in the Canary Islands and Morocco in winter, then repositions to the Caribbean for more winter sunshine, returns to the Canary Islands in springtime, heads north to Norway in midsummer, then to the Western and Eastern Mediterranean in late summer and fall. In the late autumn, the ship returns to the Canary Islands.

The Bottom Line

This is a sparkling clean, very sophisticated ship with a dedicated following in the United Kingdom. Cruises average 12 to 30 days in length, and discounts are offered for two back-to-back sailings as well as early bookings. The main problem we find is that most of the cabins don't offer a lot of wardrobe space, although the ship will store your "trunks and suitcases" down the hall in special closets for you.

Fielding's Picks

Favorite Principalities

1. The Aquitaine Lounge, a place to slip away and read in the daytime or sip before-dinner cocktails to piano music.
2. Neptune Lounge is where the evening entertainment happens with all those chorus girls, plus daytime fun and games when one of them just might be calling bingo.
3. The Video Lounge, where you can watch a movie on video (if you must).
4. The Marquee Restaurant is a top deck sidewalk cafe under canvas where you can breakfast or lunch alfresco.
5. The Sauna Deck, to steam out your aches, get a massage, exercise or have your hair done.

Good Reasons to Book This Ship

1. So you can become a member of the Fred. Olsen Cruise Lines Club and get perks on future sailings.
2. To take a games theme cruise, a whole sailing built around lots of Scrabble, Clue and Trivial Pursuit.
3. To visit the Canary Islands and Morocco for a little winter sunshine.
4. If you're over 62, you get a five percent senior discount; if you book certain soft sailings, you'll get 10 percent off.
5. To sail with the Norwegians to Norway.

Things You Won't Find On Board

1. Free 24-hour room service; there's a small fee for cabin service.
2. Ashtrays in the ship's indoor restaurant; smoking is not permitted there.
3. A visitor; Black Prince security systems do not permit them.
4. U.S. dollars; all accounts are run in pounds sterling.
5. Sloppy dressers; a jacket and tie are required for informal evenings, a dark suit or dinner jacket for formal evenings.

HOLLAND AMERICA LINE

300 Elliott Avenue West, Seattle, WA 98119
☎ *(206) 283-2687, (800) 426-0327*

***String trios play for teatime and after dinner, as here, aboard the* Statendam.**

History

One of the oldest and most distinguished of the cruise lines, Holland America was founded in 1873 as the Netherlands-America Steamship Company, a year after its young co-founders commissioned and introduced the first ship, the original *Rotterdam*, a 1700-ton iron vessel. The new ship left the city it was named for on Oct. 15, 1872, and spent 15 days sailing to New York on its maiden voyage. It carried eight passengers in first class and 380 in steerage. Only a few years later, because all its sailings were to the Americas, it became known as Holland America Line.

—A leading carrier of immigrants to the United States, Holland America transported nearly 700,000 between 1901 and 1914 alone; a steerage fare cost $20.

—After World War II, when middle-class Americans began touring Europe in large numbers, HAL concentrated on offering moderately priced tourist class service with two medium-sized ships that carried 836 tourist class passengers and only 39 first-class passengers.

—The line introduced educational and pleasure cruises to the Holy Land just after the turn of the century, and in 1971, suspended transatlantic sailings in favor of cruise vacations.

—The first line to introduce glass-enclosed promenade decks on its ocean liners.

—First line to introduce a full-service Lido restaurant on all its ships as a casual dining alternative.

—First cruise line to introduce karaoke, a sort of high-tech singalong (on the *Westerdam* in 1990).

—Through its subsidiary Westours, Holland America retains a strong tour profile in Alaska, and with another subsidiary company, Windstar, offers small-ship sailing vacations in Tahiti, the Caribbean and Mediterranean.

—In 1989, Carnival Cruise Lines acquired Holland America and its affiliated companies, but retains HAL's Seattle headquarters and separate management.

Concept

With its slogan "A Tradition of Excellence," Holland America has always had a reputation for high quality and giving full cruise value for the money, along with a strong program of security and sanitation. Since its acquisition by Carnival, the line has worked to upscale its product and sees itself now firmly entrenched in what is called the "premium" segment of the cruise industry, a notch up from mass-market lines such as Carnival but not in the highest-priced luxury segment.

HAL defines its premium status with such details as adding suites with private verandas to its four newest ships, *Statendam*, *Maasdam*, *Ryndam* and *Veendam*, along with more elaborate spas and advanced technology showrooms. The new vessels have also been designed to handle both short and long cruises equally well, with generous closet space and more-spacious staterooms.

There's also a strong undercurrent of "politically correct" behavior, consistent with its Pacific Northwest base, from specially packaged, environmentally safe cabin gift toiletries to taking a stand against the proposed Alaska aerial wolf-hunting program several years ago. The company also makes frequent, generous contributions to Alaskan universities and nonprofit organizations such as the Alaska Raptor Rehabilitation Center in Sitka.

Signatures

A "No Tipping Required" policy means that while tips are appreciated by crew members, they cannot be solicited. However, very few passengers disembark without crossing more than a few palms with silver.

The line's longstanding tradition of hiring Indonesian and Filipino crew members and training them in its own Jakarta hotel school results in consistently high-quality service.

The continuing use of museum-quality antiques and artifacts from the golden days of Dutch shipping adds dignity and richness to the ship interiors.

The classic ship names, taken from Dutch cities, are always repeated in new vessels, with the present *Statendam*, *Maasdam* and *Rotterdam* each the fifth to bear the name, the *Veendam* the fourth, the *Nieuw Amsterdam*, *Noordam* and *Ryndam* the third namesakes, and the *Westerdam* the second in the line with that name.

Gimmicks

The ubiquitous Holland America bag, a white canvas carry-all embellished with the company's logo and names of all the ships, can be glimpsed all over the world. Each passenger on each cruise is given one of these, so you can imagine how many frequent cruisers manage to amass. They're washable and last forever. "It's the single best investment we ever made," said one HAL insider.

Passport to Fitness, a folded card that has 48 separate areas to get stamped as the holder completes a qualifying activity, from the morning walkathon to aerobics class or a volleyball game. The prizes vary by the number of stamps, but are usually a Holland America logo item such as a T-shirt, cap or jacket. (We heard one eager-to-win passenger ask the librarian to stamp her passport for checking out a book about sports.)

Five Special Touches

1. Beautiful red plaid deck blankets.
2. Toiletries in each cabin wrapped in replicas of period Holland America posters and advertising art.
3. Museum-quality ship and seafaring artifacts in special display cases, along with antique bronze cannons and figureheads.
4. Fresh flowers flown in from Holland all over the ship.
5. Trays of mints, dried fruits and candied ginger outside the dining room after dinner.

Who's the Competition

Princess is the closest head-on competitor in the Alaska cruise market. In the Caribbean, Celebrity Cruises is a major competitor with Holland America. HAL is also in the league to compete in the premium market with Royal Cruise Line for senior couples and singles.

The line's classic ocean liner *Rotterdam* on its long cruises competes head-on with Cunard's *QE2*, *Royal Viking Sun*, *Sagafjord* and *Vistafjord*.

Who's Aboard

While they attract more and more younger cruisers and families, Holland America's basic passengers can still be defined as middle-aged and older couples who appreciate solid quality in food, surroundings and service.

Perhaps the most interesting are those who sail on the *Rotterdam's* long cruises, many wealthy, set-in-their-ways dowagers who cruise together year after year, throwing lavish cocktail parties and luncheons and competing to see who brings the most gorgeous gowns (and the most agreeable rent-a-male escorts).

Who Should Go

More younger couples and families should be aboard Holland America's sailings. Single women and families with children will find HAL is thinking of them—youth counselors coordinate activities for each age group, from an ice cream sundae party for the 5-to-8 set to teen disco parties and contests, and social hosts to dance with unattached women on all cruises 14 days or longer. Physically-challenged passengers will find suitable accommodations on board all the new ships, plus extra assistance from the attentive staff, who also lavish special care and attention on the elderly and small children.

Who Should Not Go

Young swinging singles looking to boogie all night or meet the mate of their dreams.

Nonconformists.

People who refuse to dress up.

The Lifestyle

A surprising amount of luxury and pampering go on aboard these ships, with string trios (two of them usually work each ship now) playing at teatime, white-gloved stewards to escort you to your cabin when you board, vases of fresh flowers everywhere, bowls of fresh fruit in the cabins, and most of all, what the Dutch call *gezellig*, a warm and cozy ambiance, defined with curtains in the cabins that can separate the sleeping area from the sitting area, friendly Dutch officers and caring Indonesian and Filipino crew members, who make it a point of pride to remember your name.

KEELHAUL

We're not sure who's doing what to whom in the suddenly hot art auction action at sea, but there must be gold in them thar prints, because there seems to be enough onboard revenue generated to allow Holland America to carry an art auctioneer as one of the cruise staff. Passengers who don't know much about art or auction bidding might be wise to stick to scarf-tying and napkin-folding demonstrations.

Wardrobe

Dress code follows a traditional pattern, with a week usually calling for two formal nights (and they do dress up on these ships, even in Alaska), two informal nights when men are expected to wear a jacket but a tie is usually optional, and three "elegantly casual" nights with no shorts, T-shirts, tank tops, halter tops or jeans permitted. During the daytime, comfortable, casual clothing—jogging outfits, shorts or slacks, T-shirts, bathing suits and cover-ups—are adequate deck wear.

***Holland America consistently produces some of the most attractive buffets at sea; here, breakfast aboard the* Maasdam.**

Bill of Fare

"Genteel tradition" is important to Holland America, from a chime master who announces dinner to the Indonesian bellman in the bellboy outfit (similar to the doormen in white at the Peninsula Hotel in Hong Kong) who holds open the doors between the Lido buffet and the deck for every passenger.

Holland America consistently produces some of the tastiest and most appealing buffets at sea, from the lavish Dutch-style breakfasts to wonderfully varied luncheons. In addition to a full hot-and-cold buffet in the Lido restaurants, chefs on deck will grill hot dogs and hamburgers to order, serve up make-your-own tacos, stir-fry-to-order and pasta of the day, plus a very popular make-your-own-ice-cream-sundae counter with a bowl of homemade cookies.

Because of the scope and popularity of the buffet service, dining room breakfast and dinner are served open seating, which means you can arrive within a specified time and sit with whom you wish.

Dinner menus have grown increasingly sophisticated. A typical dinner might include six appetizers (among them warm hazelnut-crusted Brie with apple and onion compote and French bread, bay shrimp coupe with cocktail sauce, smoked king salmon with horseradish cream and herb crostini), two soups (one may be five-onion cream with frizzled onions), three salads (including field greens with smoked duck, Asian pears and toasted pecans), six entrees, from a low-calorie, low-fat sauteed Alaskan snapper teriyaki or fresh halibut with asparagus and lemon pepper mashed potatoes to a parmesan-crusted chicken breast or a grilled New York steak with baked Idaho potato and onion rings. A cheese and fresh fruit course follows, then a choice of four desserts plus pastry tray, ice creams and frozen yogurts, and sugar-free desserts. Chocoholics will adore the Chocolate Extravaganza late show, served once during each cruise as a midnight buffet.

Children's menus offer four standard entrees—hamburger and fries, hot dog, pizza or chicken drumsticks—plus a nightly chef's special, perhaps beef tacos, fish and chips or barbecued ribs. The more urbane kid may prefer to order from the regular menu, but he can't sample the following winner for the line's executive chef in the seventh annual International Cruise Ship Recipe Competition:

Salmon Tart Scotch Mist

4 servings

1 pound thinly sliced salmon fillets

4 five-inch puff pastry discs, already baked (can use frozen ones)

1 ounce butter, melted

Sauce:

1 ounce butter

3 finely chopped shallots

1 ounce Scotch whisky

1/4 pint heavy cream

4 ounces unsalted butter cut into cubes

2 TB chopped fresh dill

Melt one ounce of butter in saucepan; add shallots and simmer until soft. Add whisky and reduce by half. Add heavy cream, bring to a boil. Whisk in the butter cubes a couple at a time. Add chopped fresh dill and salt and pepper to taste. Keep warm until serving time.

On each pastry disc, overlap slices of salmon, then brush with melted butter and place under a hot broiler for two to three minutes.

To serve, spoon a little of the sauce onto each plate, place the salmon tart near the center, and garnish with steamed baby vegetables, dill sprigs and rosemary sprigs.
Cuisine Report Card: A

CHAMPAGNE TOAST

*Holland America serves Seattle's famous Starbucks coffee on board all its ships; on the big new liners—*Statendam, Maasdam, Ryndam *and* Veendam*—after-dinner espresso is complimentary in the Explorer's Lounge.*

Holland America's distinctive logo is painted on the funnels of its ships.

Showtime

A more sophisticated level of production shows was introduced recently, with each ship featuring its own specially tailored programs. Aboard the *Maasdam*, for instance, the Los Angeles-produced musicals include costumes by award-winning whiz Bob Mackie and musical direction by Peter Matz (producer and arranger of many of Barbra Streisand's albums) and Earl Brown (musical director of "The Carol Burnett Show").

On the line's long cruises and world cruises, headliner entertainers such as Rita Moreno, Roy Clark, Victor Borge and Vic Damone, plus noted lecturers and even a Las Vegas-style ice skating spectacular, may show up on the program.

Entertainment Report Card: B+

Discounts

Early booking savings can take off 10 to 20 percent for passengers who book and make a deposit on a specified timetable, which may mean anything from one to six months ahead of time. An Early Booking Guarantee program promises 20 percent off on winter Panama Canal sailings booked before June 30, 1996. Passengers who book earliest get the lowest prices, and if a new money-saver is introduced after they book, their fare will be adjusted on request and verification. Past passengers also get added discounts and special mail offers on certain cruises.

The Bottom Line

This is an extremely high quality product with good fulfillment for the money, one that keeps getting better. As much as anybody in the business, Holland America delivers what it promises.

Officers are Dutch, with a no-nonsense attitude about safety and seamanship. The lifeboat drill is thorough and explicit, and cleanliness and sanitation are of an extremely high standard.

When we gave Shirley's parents their first cruise a few years ago for an anniversary gift, Holland America was the line we chose—and they're still saying it was the best vacation they ever had.

Maasdam ★★★★★
Ryndam ★★★★★
Statendam ★★★★★
Veendam ☆☆☆☆☆

The Dutch, or more precisely the Netherlanders, have lent their name to some decidedly unglamorous expressions—in Dutch, Dutch treat, Dutch uncle, Dutch courage. Over the years, they have given us cozy and cliche images of dowager queens in sensible shoes, herrings, Hans Brinker, Gouda and Edam cheese, windmills and respectable burghers staring out at us from museum walls and cigar boxes.

But these ships are not apple-cheeked little Dutch girls in wooden shoes and stiff white bonnets. They're sophisticated and very elegant women of the world who know who they are and what they're doing.

The newest HAL ships are ideal for long cruises, with spacious cabins, each with its own sitting area, and generous closet and drawer space. A variety of lounges, public rooms and outdoor spaces offer enough entertaining alternatives to ensure that passengers won't get bored.

A 26-foot Italianate fountain ornaments the three-deck lobby of the *Statendam*, and a slightly smaller version of the same also decorates the *Ryndam* lobby, while the *Maasdam*'s centerpiece is a monumental $350,000 green glass sculpture created by Luciano Vistosi of Murano, Italy, that looks as though it's made from Superman's kryptonite. The *Veendam*, scheduled to begin service May 25, will also have a towering glass sculpture in the lobby.

From the gangway level, a graceful curved stairway and an escalator (convenient but unusual aboard ships) take passengers up one deck to the front office and lobby, the bottom level of the three-deck atrium. Each ship shows off a $2 million art collection, along with dazzling two-deck theaters and showy glass-walled dining rooms, sizable spas and expansive deck areas.

CHAMPAGNE TOAST

For the charming artwork created for the Maasdam *by whimsical Danish artist Bjorn Windblad, especially in the beauty salon, where his mural of the Judgement of Paris (when the handsome youth Paris had to choose the most beautiful of the Greek goddesses) is accompanied by Windblad's handwritten note wishing that all the salon's clients will leave feeling like Aphrodite, the winner.*

The Brochure Says

"Floating resorts, our ships are our own private islands, destinations in themselves, offering everything you'd expect in a great resort on land. Fine dining. Dazzling entertainment. Activities galore. And it's all included in your cruise fare."

Translation

Holland America seems to be looking to appeal to a new group of passengers, younger, more resort-oriented people who may not have cruised before, by accenting entertainment, cuisine and variety. The previous emphasis on overall cruise value and nearly 125 years of service is still underscored as well.

Cabins and Costs

The lavish owner's suite aboard the Maasdam.

Fantasy Suites: **Report Card: A+**

Average Price PPPD: $1,098 including airfare in the Panama Canal; $1364 including airfare in Europe.

The penthouses on Navigation Deck, one on each ship, are huge—1123 square feet—ideal for entertaining with a living room with wraparound sofa, four chairs, big screen TV; a large private veranda, dining table that seats eight, butler pantry; separate bedroom with queen-sized bed, built-in dressing table and walk-in dressing room lined with closets. The marble bathroom has double sinks, a whirlpool tub, a steam bath/shower combination and separate water closet with bidet; there's even a custom-tiled guest bath.

Small Splurges: **Report Card: A**

Average Price PPPD: $463 including airfare in the Panama Canal, $370 with Early Booking Guarantee.

A deluxe outside double with private veranda in categories A or B measure 284 square feet and have a sitting area with sofa that can be converted into a third bed, a TV with VCR, minibar and a refrigerator, as well as a whirlpool bath. Both categories are identical, but the As are one deck higher than the Bs.

Suitable Standards: **Report Card: B**

Average Price PPPD: $365 in the Panama Canal with airfare; $292 with Early Booking Guarantee.

Each large outside double contains twin beds that can convert to queen-sized, a sitting area with sofa and chair, a desk/dresser with stool, coffee table, hair dryer, safe, large closet, and bath with tub/shower combination. Six wheelchair-accessible cabins, outside doubles with shower only, are also available.

Bottom Bunks: **Report Card: B**

Average Price PPPD: $315 including airfare in the Panama Canal, $252 with Early Booking Guarantee.

Even the cheapest cabins on the luxurious vessels are pretty good. Inside doubles are 187 square feet with sitting area sofa and chair, twin beds that can convert to queen-sized, a desk/dresser with stool, coffee table, hair dryer, safe, and a four-door closet. Bathrooms have showers only, and a floral privacy curtain between beds and sitting area.

Where She Goes

The *Statendam*'s 1996 itinerary begins with 10-day roundtrip Southern Caribbean sailings from Ft. Lauderdale through April 13, calling in St. John, St. Thomas, Dominica, Grenada, La Guaira (for Caracas), and Curacao. A 20-day autumn Panama Canal transit is scheduled for September 30, followed by another series of 10-day Southern Caribbean cruises and seven-day holiday sailings in late December.

A westbound transatlantic crossing by the *Maasdam* is scheduled for October 24, followed by 10-day Panama Canal and Caribbean Holiday cruises.

The *Ryndam* makes a series of 10-day Southern Caribbean cruises through mid-April from Ft. Lauderdale, John, St. Thomas and Nassau. On September 29, the ship is scheduled to return through the canal to the Southern Caribbean to resume its 10-day programs.

The *Veendam*, due to debut May with a series of seven-day Caribbean itineraries roundtrip from Ft. Lauderdale that alternate between the Eastern and Western Caribbean, spends its first summer in Caribbean waters. The Eastern Caribbean itinerary includes calls at Nassau, San Juan, St. John and St. Thomas, ending with two days at sea. The Western Caribbean program will calls at Key West, Playa del Carmen, Cozumel, Ocho Rios and Georgetown, Grand Cayman. The seven-day Caribbean program resumes at the end of October.

The Bottom Line

A musical production show aboard the* Statendam *illustrates HAL's younger, more energetic style that has emerged with the newest class of ships.

Traditionalists as well as luxury loving passengers should like these vessels, which gleam with softly burnished wood and brass, with the added zing of dramatic showrooms that are themed from Dutch masterpieces by Vermeer, Rembrandt, Rubens and Van Gogh.

While the decorous gentility will attract well-heeled older passengers, there's enough spark and energy to appeal to upscale younger couples and singles as well. Almost anyone should feel at home aboard, especially if home were a palatial mansion with a smiling staff.

The message these newest Holland America ships seem to be sending is that the company is aiming in the direction of other luxurious large-ship companies, such as Crystal Cruises. Both hardware (the new ships) and software (the food, service and ambiance) just keep on improving on this very fine line.

Fielding's Picks

Spectacular Places

1. The striking two-deck Rotterdam dining rooms on all the ships have a magnificent entry stairway ideal for making a grand entrance, window walls on three sides and a ceiling covered with a thousand frosted Venetian glass morning glories.
2. The sumptuous and subdued Rembrandt show lounge on the *Maasdam* is like walking into a tasteful 17th century drawing room full of fluted mahogany columns, Delft tiles and upholstery fabrics in red and blue shot through with gold threads.
3. The full promenade decks on all the ships, covered in teak and lined with classic wooden deck loungers, invite you to stretch out in the shade with a good book.
4. The handsome covered Lido Deck pool area with its retractable sliding glass dome, playful dolphin sculptures, spas and children's wading pools.

Good Reasons to Book These Ships

1. Sunbathers will like the blue terrycloth covers fitted to the loungers, much more comfortable for wet or oiled bodies than the usual plastic strips or removable cushions.
2. Buffets galore for nibbling and noshing, from an ice-cream-sundae bar to a make-your-own taco stand, free hot fresh popcorn at the movie matinees in the theater, the Chocolate Extravaganza late-night buffet, the hot hors d'oeuvres at cocktail time in the Crow's Nest, the Royal Dutch Tea, and a glass of fresh carrot juice from the juice bar in the Ocean Spa.
3. A good workout, from the Passport to Fitness program to a jog around the *Statendam* or a fast game of deck tennis on the *Ryndam* or *Maasdam*, with some aerobics, massage, sauna and steam treatments in the expansive Ocean Spa with its Stairmasters, treadmills, bicycles and free weights.
4. You'll have plenty of closet and drawer space to store your wardrobe, no matter how much you've over-packed.
5. The romantic little piano bars on board each ship, especially the *Maasdam's* elegant candy box of a room with rich gold and crimson curtains swagged from the ceiling like a pasha's tent.

Nieuw Amsterdam ★★★★
Noordam ★★★★

In May 1984, two new ships, the Noordam *and Sitmar's* Fairsky *(now Princess Cruises'* Sky Princess*) each made a debut cruise from Los Angeles to the Mexican Riviera a week apart along the same familiar route down to Puerto Vallarta and back. Cruise writers who were aboard both sailings had spirited arguments back and forth about which ship was prettier, the innovative* Fairsky*, the last big steamship to be built, or the solid, well-crafted and traditional* Noordam*. There was no decision, no winners or losers, although proponents of each went away certain their arguments had prevailed.*

A tile surround on the aft swimming pool aboard the* Noordam *keeps sunbathers cool.

The *Nieuw Amsterdam* debuted in 1983, the first new ship for Holland America in nearly quarter of a century, and, like her identical sister *Noordam* a year later, was built in

France's Chantiers d'Atlantique yard. Despite some noticeable vibration in certain areas, the ships are classy, traditional and comfortable, with museum-quality artifacts relating to sailing and the sea handsomely displayed.

All the cabins are relatively large with plentiful wardrobe space, from the minimum-priced insides to the deluxe staterooms with sitting areas. There are no large suites or private verandas. Outside cabins have windows on Main Deck and above; the portholes begin on A Deck and get more view-restrictive on B and C Decks. Inside cabins mark the imaginary "window" with fabric draperies that are always closed.

Once on board, passengers relax almost instantly in the spacious public rooms and tasteful, subdued decor. There's no glitz or jingle-jangle to bring in a jarring note, and the smiling, soft-spoken serving staff of Indonesians and Filipinos do nothing to break the mood. A few pockets of activity shelter night owls—the Horn Pipe Club on the *Nieuw Amsterdam*, the Pear Tree on the *Noordam*—but most passengers turn in fairly early.

The Brochure Says

"Attentive Filipino and Indonesian crew members offer gracious 'Five-Star' service, expecting no reward beyond your smile of thanks—because Holland America sails under a 'tipping not required' policy."

Translation

Note it does not say, Tipping not permitted. If you wanted to press the issue, you could claim tipping is not required on any cruise ship, but very obviously the passenger is expected to supplement the low base salaries on most major vessels with a tactfully "suggested" tip. Holland America does not permit its employees to "suggest" or even "hint" about a tip; instead, they simply provide excellent service the entire time you're aboard the ship, so that only a churl would even consider disembarking without dispensing some largesse.

INSIDER TIP

Happy Hour in the Crows Nest on the Noordam *is from 4:45 to 5:45 and from 7 to 8 p.m., with the first drink at the regular price and subsequent ones at half price. Drinks are accompanied by a generous assortment of hot and cold hors d'oeuvres.*

Cabins and Costs

Fantasy Suites: **Report Card: C**

Average Price PPPD: $575 plus airfare.

While there are no really big elegant suites aboard, the top category A cabins offer a great deal of comfort if not space. The wood furnishings are dark and polished, and all accommodations contain a king-sized bed, sitting area with sofa-bed, armchair, table, desk and double windows, as well as mini-refrigerator, closets with good storage space and bathroom with tub/shower combination. The down side is that every window in the A category cabins has a partially obstructed view from hanging lifeboats. The part you'll see through your window is only the top half, which still lets you see some of the sea.

Small Splurges: **Report Card: B**

Average Price PPPD: $470.

We'd recommend opting for a B or C rather than an A category on these ships, because you'll get the same or even more space, along with tub and shower and sitting area, and may not, depending on deck location, have to look out over hanging lifeboats. The best B cabins are 114 and 115 on Boat Deck, oversized quarters with double bed, and our favorite C cabins are those forward on Boat and Upper Promenade Decks with a captain's-eye view of the sea ahead. On the Boat Deck, cabins #100-103 are wheelchair-accessible quarters with bathroom grip rails, shower seat and low hanging closet rack.

An inside cabin on the* Noordam *is spacious and comfortable; notice the curtains that suggest a window may be behind them.

Suitable Standards: **Report Card: B**

Average Price PPPD: $383.

If you could nail down one of two E category Large Outsides (cabins E 711 or 716) you'd find a very big cabin with twin beds, large TV, long desk counter, leather headboards, and plenty of storage; these two cabins are almost double the size of the others in this category. The others are also OK, just not so big.

Bottom Bunks: **Report Card: C+**

Average Price PPPD: $232.

All the lowest-priced inside cabins have two lower beds and are the same size with the same furnishings as most of the other cabins aboard, including color TV, but on a lower deck (C Deck) and forward.

ANNOYANCES

This is really nit-picking, but the friendly, polite servers stand and chat with well-meaning passengers in the dining room, asking questions about their families and home towns, slowing down the service to a crawl sometimes.

INSIDER TIP

One of the best views of the stage is from the five rows of black leather theater seats in the center back of the main level of the show lounge, where latecomers are often put.

On the balcony level of the show lounges, late arrivals have to sit on the outer edges away from the railing in tables and chairs arranged in conversational groupings, and they do just that—make conversation while the show is going on at a volume that competes with the performers.

Where She Goes

The *Nieuw Amsterdam* makes seven-day Western Caribbean sailings from New Orleans in winter, calling at Montego Bay, Grand Cayman, Playa del Carmen and Cozumel.

The *Noordam* also makes seven-day Western Caribbean sailings in winter, sailing from Tampa and calling in Grand Cayman, Ocho Rios, Playa del Carmen and Cozumel.

The Bottom Line

While more than 10 years old, both ships are kept remarkably clean in the traditional Holland America shine-and-polish style. Where the age and wear shows is on the few outer deck areas covered with astroturf, with spots, splotches and patches all too apparent. Inside, however, housekeeping is of the sort our mothers used to describe as, "You could eat off the floor."

We like the glass bowls of fresh fruit in the cabins and batik bedspreads with matching privacy curtains, one of the cozy touches the Dutch call *gezellig*, as well as the comfortable places to sit all around the ship with antiques, ship models and old maps to study.

Fielding's Picks

Favorite Spots

1. The Crow's Nest, elegantly cozy forward observation lounges with hot hors d'oeuvres at cocktail time and piano music throughout the evening, as well as period ship models in plexiglass cases.

2. The Lido, where the art of the buffet comes to life; not only does everything look good enough to eat, but it really is. And you can make your own ice cream sundaes for dessert.
3. The Explorer Lounge on the *Nieuw Amsterdam*, with a wall lined with wooden ship figureheads holding lamps; this is where the Rosario Strings play after dinner while bar waiters offer espresso, cappuccino and liqueurs—on a tab, of course.
4. The Ocean Spa on both ships, with massage rooms, saunas, gym with bikes, rowing, treadmills and weights, and just outside, the pool and spas.
5. The broad natural teak deck all around both ships on Upper Promenade, with sheltered, covered reading spots and rows of traditional wooden deck loungers reminiscent of ocean-liner days.

Off-the-Wall

For the birds: The Partridge Bar on the *Nieuw Amsterdam* displays large paintings of peacocks on its back wall.

Good Reasons to Book These Ships

1. A tempting range of food opportunities, from light and healthful menus and sugar-free desserts to make-your-own-taco or ice-cream-sundae stations.
2. Hot, fresh popcorn served for movie matinees (but not evening screenings) in the theater.
3. The Dutch figures in traditional costume in the glass cases at the entrance to the Lido restaurant.
4. The broad expanse of Lido Deck in natural teak with fresh water swimming pool, wading pool and splash surround, only steps away from the hot dog/hamburger grill and the outdoor Lido Bar.
5. The classic Holland America tote bag, free to every passenger on every sailing.

Things You Won't Find On Board

1. A well-stocked library; if you want to read a current best-seller, bring it yourself.
2. A free self-service laundry; you pay $1 to wash your clothes, but soap and the dryer are free.
3. A bathroom mirror reflection in the designated handicap cabins if you're in a wheelchair; you can easily roll the chair under the sink rim, but can't see your reflection once you're there.
4. A good view of the stage from every seat in the two-deck show lounge, especially in the balcony; you'll have to search to find a good spot from which to see everything.

Rotterdam ★★★★★

It's still possible on the Rotterdam, *built in 1959, to see how it used to be divided into first and transatlantic classes (and could be again). A central stairway called "the secret staircase," inspired by stairs in the French chateau of Chambord, makes it possible for two people to go up or down on separate, adjacent stairs without seeing each other, except on the landings when sliding doors are open.*

The Dutch say* gezellig *for cozy, which describes these booths in the* Rotterdam's *Lido Cafe.

One of the true grande dames of the sea, the elegant *Rotterdam* has been renovated numerous times without losing her original character. The gleam of polished wood interiors, plush and leather lounge furniture will remind you of the splendid ocean-liner days, and the number of intimate bars and lounges around the ship, each with its own dance floor, suggests one of the favorite onboard activities.

But even sun-and-pool fans will enjoy it. An extension of the upper promenade deck adds a permanent cover to the Lido pool deck below, and a horseshoe shaped wooden bar with 16 barstools supplements the white plastic loungers and deck chairs and umbrella-covered tables around the blue-and-white tile pool. A covered grill on the starboard side turns out hot dogs, hamburgers and sandwiches grilled to order. Tea and coffee are served throughout the day in the Lido restaurant.

The flagship of the fleet, the *Rotterdam* is the fifth ship with this name.

EAVESDROPPING

A young Dutch officer just transferred to the Rotterdam*: "I told them, I'll do anything, work long months with a short vacation, just put me on the* Rotterdam *instead of one of those new hotels with a little hull wrapped around it so it'll float–the* Rotterdam *is a real ship!"*

The Brochure Says

"Holland America's Grand Voyage service begins the moment you step aboard. A string quartet plays. An officer smiles. A white-gloved steward escorts you to your stateroom, where everything has been laid out for your imminent arrival; personalized stationery, fresh flowers, even a plush terry robe to slip into."

Translation

Posh is an understatement on a long voyage aboard the *Rotterdam*, where every day seems to bring another special gift from the line. We'd suggest you carry an extra bag to bring them home in, except that HAL gives you a canvas carry-all as well.

Cabins and Costs

Fantasy Suites: **Report Card: A-**

Average Price PPPD: $311 plus airfare.

While not as plushly evocative as some of the public rooms, the A category staterooms aboard have king-sized beds, sitting area with sofa, two chairs and oval black granite table, a long dresser with 10 drawers, safe and shelves, mini-refrigerator, built-in dressing table and stool, separate dressing room and bath with tub and double sinks.

Small Splurges: **Report Card: B+**

Average Price PPPD: $299 plus airfare.

Deluxe outside double cabins in category B provide plenty of room and some of the custom cabinetry from the 1950s, including vanity tables with tall mirrors, built-in drawers and clips to secure bottles of perfume or other toiletries. A separate sitting area has a sofa and chairs with coffee table, and a dresser with nine drawers stores lots of clothing. Bathrooms usually have tubs and heated towel racks. We particularly like the forward-facing cabins on Boat Deck, B 33 and B 34, with three windows each.

Batik fabrics and built-in wood cabinetry decorate this standard outside cabin with portholes aboard the Rotterdam.

Suitable Standards: **Report Card: B**

Average Price PPPD: $247 plus airfare.

Because the original ship was built before modular cabins came into play, standard cabins vary somewhat in size and shape. All the standard doubles have two lower beds or double bed, private bath (some with tubs and heated towel racks), TV, batik bedspreads and curtains, a chair or two, built-in cabinetry with lower drawers and upper shelves, plus sometimes a pullout writing desk or vanity table.

Bottom Bunks: **Report Card: C**

Average Price PPPD: $183 plus airfare.

The cheapest economy inside doubles are category O, with upper and lower berths and bath with shower only. The ones we've looked at are very small, but still have a chair, dressing table with mirror, dresser with six drawers, some of them with locks, and a tile bath with shower only.

INSIDER TIP

Note that the Rotterdam *also has number of small single inside and outside cabins with one lower bed and bath with shower.*

Where She Goes

The *Rotterdam* is one of HAL's long-voyage vessels, setting out Jan. 18 on her 1996 Grand World Voyage, her 27th world cruise. She will visit 31 ports in 99 days, cruising the South Pacific, New Zealand, Australia, Asia and the Far East, Africa, the South Atlantic, South America and the Caribbean. Segments are available.

In the summer the ship will make seven-day sailings along Alaska's Glacier Route between Vancouver and Seward, calling in Ketchikan, Juneau, Sitka and Valdez, then head south Oct. 12 for a 50-day Grand South America Voyage that calls at Mexico, Guatemala, Costa Rica, Panama, Ecuador, Peru, Chile, Argentina, the Falklands, Uruguay, Brazil, French Guiana and Curacao. She finishes the year in the Caribbean with 10-day cruises roundtrip from Ft. Lauderdale to Aruba, Cartagena, the San Blas Islands, a cruise into Gatun Lake in the Panama Canal, and a call in Puerto Limon, Costa Rica, for San Jose.

The Bottom Line

This is one of our very favorite ships, and it makes us sad to note a few signs of age, such as the worn teak decking aft on Promenade Deck. Cozy, clean and comfortable cabins and gracious, understated public rooms; an around-the-ship promenade, part of it glassed in, lined with old-fashioned wooden steamer chairs; a plethora of fresh flower arrangements everywhere; a big, bright gym and sun room; the stylish, art deco nightclub and lounges—all add up to a classy and classic shipboard experience that cannot be duplicated. Please don't let them sell her down the river.

Fielding's Picks

Classic Places

1. The Ritz-Carlton Lounge, a two-deck nightclub that impeccably recalls the glorious days of ocean liners, with a shimmering 90-foot wall mural from 1959 with Aegean scenes and a grand curved staircase for a movie-star entrance. The furniture is upholstered in jewel-toned velvets in sapphire, emerald and topaz, and the dance floor is incised brass.
2. The two high-domed dining rooms, the La Fontaine decorated with ceramic scenes from the famous fables, and the Odyssey with ceramic scenes from Homer's epic poem.
3. The dual "secret staircase" left over from the days when the ship was divided into two classes, structured so people can go up or down at the same time without seeing each other.
4. The Ambassador Lounge, like a New York bar of the 1950s with its bull's-eye glass, long velvet banquettes, inlaid wood parquet dance floor and tiny red plush barstools for fashion-model derrières.
5. The easy-to-love Ocean Bar, one of the great small bars at sea, with its comma-shaped bar lined with stools and its handful of tête-à-tête cocktail tables.

Off-the-Wall Hideaways and Secret Spots

1. The Tropic Bar, a tiny pseudo-tropical late-night drinking-and-singalong spot tucked away behind the Ritz-Carlton night club. It's usually open only on long cruises.
2. An indoor swimming pool down on D Deck with marble benches, saunas and massage rooms nearby, tile fish on the pool bottom and sculptured fish on the walls.
3. The Sky Room, on Bridge Deck above the Sun Room, a little piano bar with overstuffed plush chairs (you can find the stairs leading up there near the Wireless Office).
4. A tiny terrace with tables and chairs outside the Sky Room, where nobody will ever think to look for you.
5. The shuffleboard courts outside the gym and sun room on Sun Deck, where spectators gather on wooden benches during the numerous hotly-contested tournaments.

Good Reasons to Book This Ship

1. To experience what the grand days of ocean-liner travel were all about.
2. To make a complete round-the-world cruise for 99 days starting Jan. 18 or a 50-day circumnavigation of South America that sets out from Los Angeles Oct. 12 and ends up in Ft. Lauderdale Dec. 1.
3. To admire the one-of-a-kind wood paneling and marquetry, the exquisite restored 90-foot wall mural of the Aegean that adorns the two-deck walls of the Ritz-Carlton nightclub, to seek out (behind the slot machines) the unique tapestry murals created for the 1959 ship in the former card room, now the casino, and the original wood chairs in a 1950s moderne design in the Queen's Lounge.
4. To read or write in the Reading Room with its dictionary stand, writing tables, wing chairs with batik upholstery and dark blue velvet hassocks piped with gold.
5. To get, perhaps, a last sad look at a ship of this type, should the corporate owners in their infinite wisdom decide not to make the sizable investment it would take to bring her up to the new SOLAS (Safety of Life At Sea) standards after her 1997 World Cruise.

Things You Won't Find On Board

1. A disco, although there are two piano bars.
2. A wheelchair-accessible cabin, although ramps are available to help get over the doorsills.
3. A children's playroom (don't bring the kids along on this ship).
4. An unobstructed sea view from the cabin windows on Sun Deck; they're partially blocked by hanging lifeboats.
5. A real fire in the fireplace in the casino.

Westerdam ★★★★

Built in Papenburg, Germany, by Meyer Werft as the Homeric *for now-defunct Home Lines, the* Westerdam *is Holland America's largest ship, thanks to a "stretching" from the same shipyard in 1989. How do you stretch a ship? Very, very carefully. Cut through the superstructure with acetylene torches, then check to make sure all the units have been completely severed by running a piano wire along the cut from top to bottom. Drop in a prefabricated midsection, then put it all back together again.*

The distinctive Sun Deck pool area with its sliding glass roof and enclosed glass-walled veranda offers optimum comfort both in Alaska's cool climate and the Caribbean when it gets hot and muggy. The same walls and roof that let in the sun and keep out the rain also hold in the air conditioning.

Nine passenger decks, two separate self-service buffet restaurants, two outside swimming pools, a two-deck showroom and a number of lounges keep the 1494 passengers well dispersed around the ship, while a wood-and-plexiglass dome with special lighting brightens the lower-deck dining room.

Perhaps a little less formal than the line's other ships, the *Westerdam* offers some competitive prices on seven-day cruises. The Big Apple teen disco and video center make this a good ship for families.

FOOTNOTE

The original Westerdam, *which made crossings between Rotterdam and New York from 1946 to 1965, had its keel laid in 1939, but when the Germans invaded Holland in 1940, work was suspended. The partly constructed vessel survived three sinkings at her berth during World War II before she made her maiden voyage. She was bombed by the Allies in 1940 and raised by the Germans, then bombed by the Dutch underground resistance forces in 1944 and again raised by the Germans, and sunk for the third time in 1945, again by the Dutch underground. After the war, the Dutch raised the vessel and completed construction. The first* Westerdam *was sent to be broken up in Alicante, Spain, in 1965.*

The Brochure Says

"It is a balmy Saturday afternoon as the *Westerdam* charts an easterly course through the Caribbean...First there will be two full days at sea. Great!"

Translation

Veteran cruisers treasure days at sea, lazy times when the ship is the destination and there's no getting up early to catch a shore excursion or rushing up and down the gangway in the tropical heat. Days at sea develop their own rhythms.

Cabins and Costs

Fantasy Suites: **Report Card: B+**

Average Price PPPD: $568; $483 with Early Booking Guarantee.

The five top suites on board are located on Lower Promenade Deck amidships, the traditional place for the most expensive cabins on classic vessels because the ride is smoother. Larger than two standard cabins, each of the suites has a separate bedroom with two lower beds that can convert to king-size, a living room with sofa bed that can sleep an additional two persons, as well as several comfortable upholstered chairs, a bathroom with tub and shower and some handsome cabinetry.

Small Splurges: **Report Card: B**

Average Price PPPD: $393; $334 with Early Booking Guarantee.

Deluxe double cabins in C category are long rooms with with separate sitting area which has sofa and matching chair, plus a sleeping area that can be set off with curtains that close. The entry hallway is lined on one side with two closets, on the other with tile bathroom with tub/shower combination. A desk/dresser with stool and a coffee table round out the furnishings.

Suitable Standards: **Report Card: C**

Average Price PPPD: $340; $290 with Early Booking Guarantee.

Standard outside cabins with two lower beds are somewhat smaller than the deluxe, without the sofa and sitting area, and bathrooms have shower only. There is a desk/dresser with good storage drawers and a mirror over and stool underneath.

Bottom Bunks: **Report Card: C**

Average Price PPPD: $302; $256 with Early Booking Guarantee.

The cheapest standard inside cabins, which are N category, have two lower beds that can convert to queen-sized bed, a nightstand, desk/dresser, TV set and bath with shower only, but are surprisingly spacious for bottom-of-the-line. However, there are only nine of these, so don't expect to nab one right off the bat. You may have to move up a grade or two on a popular cruise, but HAL has always been good about upgrading passengers when space permits.

Where She Goes

The *Westerdam* cruises the Eastern Caribbean in winter from Ft. Lauderdale on seven-day itineraries, calling in St. Maarten, St. John, St. Thomas and Nassau.

The Bottom Line

While the *Westerdam* is the only vessel in the fleet not built from the hull up by Holland America, she still has been rebuilt to fit almost seamlessly into the fleet. (A hint: If you're looking for her "stretch" marks, begin in the smaller dining room addition amidships on Restaurant Deck, the Bookchest library on Promenade Deck, the self-service laundries on Upper Promenade and Navigation Decks or the Veranda Deck and restaurant on Sun Deck.)

A very good value for the money, *Westerdam* provides bigger-than-average cabins and a sense of comfort throughout.

Fielding's Picks

Favorite Places

1. The beautiful Veranda restaurant with live music during luncheon and tea is one of the prettiest self-service cafes at sea; there's a second Lido Cafe two decks below.
2. The amidships Veranda pool area adjacent, with a sliding glass dome so you can sit comfortably in a lounge chair, loll in the Jacuzzi or swim in the heated pool even on a chilly day.
3. The 127-seat Admiral's Terrace balcony overlooking the main stage has some good sightlines for the evening's entertainment, but late arrivals have to stand to see the show. The 680-seat Admiral's Lounge below provides big, cushy theater-type seats and couches and is probably a better bet.
4. The volleyball and paddle tennis courts on Sports Deck, covered at the sides and top with nets, get a good workout on short cruises.
5. The 17th-century bronze cannon, cast in Rotterdam in 1634, once defended a Dutch admiral's warship, then lay at the bottom of the sea for 300 years until a Dutch fisherman dragged it up in his nets.

Good Reasons to Book This Ship

1. It sails to some of the most popular ports in the Eastern Caribbean—Philipsburg, St. Maarten; Nassau, Bahamas; and St. Thomas and St. John in the U.S. Virgin Islands.
2. To try and find the seams from the "stretch," which added 130 feet in length, 13,872 more gross registry tons and capability for 494 more passengers.
3. Because four laps on the all-around-the-ship Upper Promenade Deck make one mile.
4. Because for the price range the cabins are unusually spacious.
5. The little hideaway Saloon with a Victorian accent and singalong piano bar.

Things You Won't Find On Board

1. Private verandas.
2. An indoor swimming pool.
3. A single cabin.
4. Skimpy cabins for wheelchair users; designated mobility impaired cabins E002, D068, J021 and D087 are all on upper decks with plenty of extra turning space.
5. A long walk to an elevator; with four different locations along each deck, it's an easy stroll to a lift.

NORWEGIAN CRUISE LINE

95 Merrick Way, Coral Gables, FL 33134
☎ *(305) 445-0866, (800) 327-7030*

The sports bar on the* Windward *underscores NCL's emphasis on active and theme cruises.

History

Norwegian Caribbean Lines was founded in 1966 by Knut Kloster and Ted Arison (see Carnival Cruises, History, above) to create casual, one-class cruising in the Caribbean in contrast to the more formal, class-oriented tradition of world cruises and transatlantic crossings. That partnership soon broke up, however, leaving Kloster to begin a rapid expansion of the line while Arison went off to found Carnival Cruise Lines.

NCL's first ship was the *Sunward*, but the fleet soon grew to include the *Starward* (1968), *Skyward* (1969), *Southward* (1971) and, also in 1971, a replacement for the original *Sunward* called *Sunward II* (the former *Cunard Adventurer*).

But the real coup came in 1979 when the Kloster family bought French Line's *France*, which had been laid up in Le Havre for five years, made a major rebuilding to convert the former ocean liner into a cruise ship and renamed her *Norway*. From her debut in 1980, she was the flagship of the line, and the other four vessels came to be called "the white ships" for their white hulls that contrasted sharply with the dark blue hull of the *Norway*. (All the original "white ships" have been retired from the fleet, the last in September, 1995.)

In 1985, Kloster Cruise Limited, the parent company of Norwegian Cruise Line, bought Royal Viking Line, promising to make minimal changes to the highly respected company. Two years later, Kloster changed the Norwegian registry of the RVL ships to Bahamian, then a year after that closed down the long-time San Francisco headquarters and moved the entire operation to Florida.

In 1987, the former Norwegian Caribbean Lines changed its name to Norwegian Cruise Line with an eye to long-range marketing of Alaska, Bermuda and European cruises, and in 1989 acquired San Francisco-based Royal Cruise Line. This time, however, Kloster left the company in San Francisco with most of its executive roster intact.

The dismantling and sale of RVL happened in the summer of 1994, with the flagship *Royal Viking Sun* and the Royal Viking name, logo, past passenger list and general goodwill sold to Cunard, who promptly (but only briefly) named their new division Cunard Royal Viking Line (see Cunard, above). The *Royal Viking Queen* was soon transferred over to Royal Cruise Line and renamed the *Queen Odyssey.* Two earlier RVL ships, *Royal Viking Star* and *Royal Viking Sea*, had also gone to Royal to become *Star Odyssey* and *Royal Odyssey.*

In the late 1980s, Knut Kloster began taking a less active role in the company in order to pursue his dream of building the world's biggest passenger ship, the 250,000-ton, 5600-passenger *Phoenix World City*. Despite its detractors who say the project's dead, the giant ship may still be a viable possibility, pending funding.

—The first three- and four-day cruises to the Bahamas incorporating a private island beach day.

—First line to restage hit Broadway musicals aboard cruise ships; the *Norway*'s first production was "My Fair Lady."

—The official cruise line of the National Basketball Association, the Basketball Hall of Fame and the National Football League Players Association; NCL presents a number of sports theme cruises throughout the year (see Theme Cruises, page 433).

—First cruise line to broadcast live NFL and NBA games live aboard its ships.

Signatures

Theme cruises—especially the annual *Norway* jazz festival, now in its 14th year, and the sports theme cruises which are aboard all the ships.

The "Dive-In" program—the first and perhaps most successful of the watersports packages found on cruise ships combines onboard instruction and equipment rentals with shore excursions to snorkel and dive spots. A Sports Afloat T-shirt is given to participants in designated activities who accrue seven tickets by the end of the cruise.

INSIDER TIP

Note: At press time, Norwegian Cruise Line was in the process of changing its logo and ship livery.

Gimmicks

The line's award-winning advertising campaign built around a sexy young couple who look like they might star in lingerie or perfume ads and the slogan, "It's different out here." The campaign itself is great, but it could be argued they're barking up the wrong mast, because we've never seen that couple on an NCL ship.

Who's the Competition

The main competitors in all its cruising areas (now that Carnival has entered Alaska) are the ships owned by Kloster's old nemesis Arison and the rapidly-growing Royal Caribbean Cruise Line. The *Norway*, unique in the otherwise modern fleet because of her history as the famous ocean liner *France*, should be competing with other classic ships like the *Rotterdam* and the *Queen Elizabeth 2*, but with a year-round, seven-day Caribbean itinerary and the same food and entertainment as the rest of the NCL fleet, she doesn't.

Who's Aboard

A lot of sports-oriented young couples from the heartland; yuppies and baby boomers; jazz fans for two weeks every autumn on the *Norway*; people who want to see a Broadway show without actually having to set foot in Times Square.

Who Should Go

Young couples and singles looking for a first-time cruise; music fans who'll enjoy not only the two-week annual jazz festival but the annual blues festival and two country music festivals; TV quiz show fans to take the annual "Wheel of Fortune" cruise; comedy aficionados for the summer comedy cruise; rock 'n rollers for the 50's and 60's cruise; Big Band devotees for the November sentimental journey; and fitness buffs for the annual fitness and beauty cruise each fall aboard the *Norway*. (See Theme Cruises, page 433)

Young families who will appreciate NCL's "Kids Crew" program for kids 3 to 17, with special kids-only activities onboard and ashore. They're divided into four different age groups: Junior Sailors, 3–5; First Mates, 6–8; Navigators, 9–12; and teens, 13–17.

Who Should Not Go

Longtime cruise veterans looking to check out a new line, senior singles, and urban sophisticates who've "been there, done that."

The Lifestyle

"Elegant, yes; stuffy, never," was the way they described themselves a couple of years ago, and it's fairly apt. NCL's ships offer traditional cruising, with themed sailings (see Who Should Go, above), international themed dinners several times a sailing, live calypso music on deck, and something going on around the ship every minute. Not long after boarding, passengers are offered free spa demonstrations, free casino lessons, a rundown on the children's program for the week, a free sports and fitness orientation, dive-in snorkeling presentation and as many as three singles parties—one each at 8 p.m. for college-aged spring break celebrants and over-30 singles (a Big Band dancing session is usually scheduled at the same time for the over-50s set), plus a third at 11:30 for any singles that couldn't find a friend at the first two parties.

In other words, you'll stay busy aboard—and that's before the dozen or so shore excursions offered in each port of call!

Wardrobe

NCL calls for less stringent dress codes than its Caribbean competitors, good news for guys who hate to wear ties. A seven-day cruise usually calls for two formal outfits, two informal outfits and a "costume" for a theme country/western or Caribbean night if you wish. Short cruises schedule one formal night and two informal nights. Formal garb is described by NCL as "cocktail dresses or gowns for the ladies and the men wear a jacket and tie or tuxedo." On informal nights, "just about anything but shorts is fine." For daytimes, take along some exercise clothing, bathing suits, shorts, T-shirts and sandals, plus light cotton clothes and walking shoes for going ashore. NCL also reminds passengers not worry about clothes—if they forget something, they can buy anything they need in the shipboard shops.

Bill of Fare

The food is predictable big-ship cruise fare served in copious portions. We still remember a young couple from Pennsylvania we shared a table with on the *Norway*; he was a football coach and when he learned he could order more than one main dish, he regularly ate his way through most of the entrees every night, while his wife restricted herself to one entree but demolished one each of every dessert nightly.

The dinner menu usually provides five appetizers, three soups, two salads, a pasta and four main dishes, one of which is fish, along with a full vegetarian menu offered nightly. There are four desserts plus ice cream and fruit, and low fat, low calorie dishes are indicated on the menus with an asterisk. Dinners are served in two assigned seatings at assigned tables, with first seating 6:30 p.m. and second seating 8:30 p.m.

A welcome-aboard buffet is typical of lunchtime self-service offerings—a make-your-own taco table and a vegetarian buffet with hot and cold selections, plus carved roast beef, turkey goulash with rice and pre-cooked hamburgers, along with a dessert table and separate beverage service area.

An alternative restaurant called Le Bistro, on board the *Norway*, *Seaward*, *Dreamward* and *Windward*, requires an advance reservation and a tip to the waiter but makes no surcharge for the food. The menu, described as "South-Beach style" by the Miami-based line (meaning Miami Beach's trendy art deco district), offers for starters a Norwegian seafood medley, escargots, French onion soup or clam chowder, three salads including Caesar and a warm spinach, then a vegetable main course, two pastas and three main dishes—chicken Provençale, pepper steak Madagascar and veal medallions with a wine/herb sauce and polenta. Dessert choices include a warm apple tart, a chocolate dessert and a selection of fruit and cheese.
Cuisine Report Card: B

Showtime

NCL was the first cruise line to create a buzz about its onboard entertainment, presenting shipboard versions of popular Broadway shows from "My Fair Lady" to the relatively current "The Will Rogers Follies" and the popular revival "Grease." In addition to the Broadway shows, each ship presents a song-and-dance Sea Legs revue as well as variety performers on other evenings.

Also aboard: Q and A sessions with sports stars, several different lounges offering live music for dancing, art auctions, games, dance lessons, and pop psychology lectures about astrology or fashion colors.
Entertainment Report Card: A

Discounts

Early booking discounts knock off as much as 25 per cent of the cruise price; book 180 days ahead for a seven-day sailing, 120 days ahead for a three- or four-day cruise.

Children under two sail free; a maximum of two adults and two children per cabin is the limit for this offer.

The Bottom Line

These are good, moderately-priced traditional cruises that will particularly appeal to first-time cruisers, honeymooners, couples, families and singles up to the outer perimeters of Baby Boomdom. Filled with nonstop activities, music, very professional entertainment and sports-themed programs for watching or doing, NCL is never boring for middle-of-the-road mainstreamers, although very sophisticated travelers may (despite the "It's different out here" commercials) stifle a yawn now and again.

Dreamward ★★★★★
Windward ★★★★★

It was the water curtain on the Dreamward *that really grabbed attention. On the inaugural sailing, we sat in the front row scribbling notes about traffic "flow" and "splashy" production numbers while watching a dazzling revue staged behind a unique curtain of water. A Gene Kelly-lookalike splashed about in "Singin' in the Rain," marine creatures frolicked "Under the Sea" and not a drop of water fell on the front row. The water spurts from below like fountains or drizzles from above like rain, and the big finale incorporated fireworks, fog and film clips of Esther Williams swimming with cartoon characters Tom and Jerry.*

How do you make a big ship look like a little ship? The answer is clearly illustrated aboard NCL's new *Dreamward* and *Windward*, ships that carry 1246 passengers but offer so many intimate spaces they actually seem cozy. There are no soaring atriums or double-decker dining rooms; instead, three separate dining rooms that seat from 190 to 282 passengers appear to have more smaller tables seating two to four than big ones seating six to eight. Instead of a vast self-service buffet area, the ships have incorporated quick pick-up breakfasts and lunches into a small snack bar adjacent to the Sports Bar & Grill, with a continental breakfast and lunchtime hot dogs and hamburgers. Salads, desserts and beverages are laid out buffet-style. Many areas, including some of the dining rooms and deck sunbathing spots, have been terraced to give an illusion of smaller space but with more privacy.

INSIDER TIP

If you're not assigned to one of the dramatic terrace restaurants, you can still eat breakfast or lunch in one of them any time you wish, since those meals are served open seating at your choice of restaurant. And the view is even better in the daylight.

The Brochure Says

"No matter where you choose to go, you are certain to have a lot of fun getting there: full-court basketball, a jogging track and fitness center, golf driving nets, outdoor hot tubs, a two-story casino, a Sports Bar & Grill with ESPN, NFL and NBA games beamed in live, dozens of top-notch entertainers—they're all here, just waiting for you."

Translation

We're ready for the young and the restless, and double-dare anyone to get bored aboard.

Cabins and Costs

***Suite # 20 aboard the* Windward.**

Fantasy Suites: **Report Card: A**

Average Price PPPD: $599 including airfare in the Caribbean.

Top digs are six 350-square-foot grand deluxe suites with concierge service, all facing forward on three different decks for a captain's-eye view of the world. The living room is sumptuously furnished with a brocade sofa and three chairs, a long desk and dresser with eight drawers and glass coffee table. In the bedroom, you can choose either twin or queen-sized beds. The bathroom has tub and shower, and additional perks include a mini-refrigerator and a private safe.

Small Splurges: **Report Card: B**

Average Price PPPD: $452 including airfare in the Caribbean.

Penthouses with private balconies are 175 square feet inside plus a veranda that is large enough for two chairs and a table. A separate sitting area with love seat and chairs, floor-to-ceiling windows, twin or queen-sized bed, private safe, TV set, mini-refrigerator and concierge service are included.

Suitable Standards: **Report Card: B**

Average Price PPPD: $347 including airfare in the Caribbean.

Standard outside staterooms are virtually identical in size (160 square feet) and furnishings—sitting area and twin or queen-sized bed, TV set, built-in cabinetry—with the price varying according to deck location. "I'd advise clients to book one of the lower-category outsides," one travel agent told us, "because the differences in deck and amenities isn't that much." Accordingly, we'd recommend the D category outsides; get any lower on the totem pole and you're facing partial or full obstruction from hanging lifeboats. Six wheelchair-accessible cabins have shower seat and hand rails plus spacious turn-around room and no sills to impede the wheels.

Bottom Bunks: **Report Card: C**

Average Price PPPD: $297 including airfare in the Caribbean.

The lowest-priced cabins aboard are category J inside double cabins with two lower beds in 150 square feet of space. Needless to say, you shouldn't expect a sitting area with sofa.

INSIDER TIP

If you want to book a category A outside cabin and value your privacy, opt for those on Atlantic Deck instead of Promenade Deck. While Promenade Deck is considered posh by old-time cruisers, it also means the joggers and strollers are walking around the deck outside your windows day and night, while on Atlantic deck only the gulls and flying fish can look in while the ship's at sea.

Where She Goes

In winter, *Dreamward* offers a seven-day Western Caribbean program sailing Sundays from Ft. Lauderdale and calling in Grand Cayman, Playa del Carmen/Cozumel, Cancun and Great Stirrup Cay, NCL's own private island, for a beach day.

The *Windward* sails the Exotic Caribbean in winter on seven-day cruises from San Juan every Saturday, calling at Barbados, St. Lucia, St. Barts, Tortola, Virgin Gorda, St. John and St. Thomas.

The Bottom Line

This is a very special pair of ships, stylish enough for frequent travelers but accessible to first-time cruisers as well. They offer everything an active young passenger might wish without appearing intimidatingly huge. While the cheaper cabins are not as spacious as you might wish, they're a lot bigger than many NCL cabins used to be. And the fact that these vessels return to the human scale in contrast to the awesome new megaships is a great plus.

Fielding's Picks

The aft pool deck aboard the Dreamward *has terraced sunbathing.*

Fabulous Places

1. The sunbathing deck, not acres of astroturf lined with sunbathers sprawled everywhere, but lounge chairs arranged in a series of teak terraces separated by low wooden planters filled with clipped boxwoods, rather like an ampitheater.
2. Sports and Sky Decks include two golf driving areas, Ping-Pong tables in an enclosed alcove, a volleyball-basketball court and shuffleboard on rubberized mats, plus a full fitness center with sauna and massage.
3. The big forward Observation Lounge doubles as a late-night disco with marble dance floor and a pair of electronic route maps that show the ship's itineraries.
4. Le Bistro, originally a fourth dining room, has turned into a 76-seat specialty restaurant with no surcharge, only a request for advance reservations and a tip for the

waiter afterwards. It's a good place for a quiet dinner for two, perhaps celebrating a romantic occasion, or a place to get together with other new friends.

The Sun Terrace dining rooms aboard the **Dreamward** *and* **Windward** *offer sweeping views to the sea.*

5. The 150-seat Sun Terrace dining room, three levels set high atop the ship and aft, facing a wall of windows to the sea, and one deck below, The Terraces, 282 seats on several levels that also overlook the sea through an expanse of glass with a huge undersea mural on the back wall.

Good Reasons to Book These Ships

1. To meet jocks, both professional and amateur.
2. To sail aboard a ship christened by ex-first lady Barbara Bush (the *Windward*, 1993).
3. To luxuriate aboard a ship that was designed especially for new, younger cruise passengers who want everything a shoreside resort can offer, including an oceanfront room.
4. The Sports Bar & Grill, which brings in live sports telecasts from around the world daily on big-screen TV sets, with small snack bars not far away in a quiet corner if you want a hot dog with your beer or soda.
5. To venture aboard a young-minded ship into the Caribbean.

Things You Won't Find On Board

1. A single cabin.
2. A self-service laundry.
3. Anyone wearing shorts in the dining room after 6 p.m.
4. A giant atrium with revolving sculpture.
5. A lavish lunchtime deck buffet.

Leeward ★★★★

The much-postponed debut of the Leeward, *a major renovation of a Scandinavian ferry happened October 20. What passengers can expect is a 25,000-ton, mid-sized vessel carrying 950 passengers, more comparable to the now-gone "white ships" than NCL's present fleet.*

Two aft dining rooms with expansive window walls repeat the look of the popular Terrace dining rooms on *Windward* and *Dreamward*, while the main show lounge soars into a two-deck height. Piano bar, disco, casino, conference facilities and a fitness center are among the other features. The decor is charmingly art deco and the mid-size a definite plus.

Cabins and Costs

Two owners' suites and eight penthouses have private balconies and separate living and bedrooms, mini-refrigerators and concierge service. Six additional suites without private balconies are also aboard, as well as spacious inside and outside standard cabins averaging 175 square feet, including six designated as wheelchair-accessible. Cabin prices per person per day range from $192 to $553, based on double occupancy; airfare is included.

Where She Goes

The *Leeward* schedule calls for three- and four-day cruises year-round from Miami, sailing on Fridays on alternate itineraries to Nassau and Great Stirrup Cay, NCL's private island, and to Key West and Great Stirrup Cay.

On Mondays the ship sails to Key West, Cancun and Cozumel, through the sailing of April 29, then changes the summer itinerary to omit the call at Cancun through October 28, when it again reverts to the original four-day itinerary.

Norway ★★★★

Ship buffs and historians know the Norway *was built in 1962 as the* France, *the last of the great French Line fleet that also included the* Ile de France *and the* Normandie. *While the last major makeover added two additional decks that thickened her sleek line, she's still one of the most beautiful vessels at sea. She makes us think of the 1954 film* The French Line *with Jane Russell and a lot of U.S. Olympic athletes working out down by the indoor pool area, which has been remodeled lots of times since then but still looks glamorous. While most people visualize Jane Russell leaning against a shock of hay eyeing a baby-faced Billy the Kid in "The Outlaw", our favorite shipboard film is "Gentlemen Prefer Blondes," filmed aboard the* Ile de France *in 1953 with her co-star Marilyn Monroe.*

***The sybaritic Roman Spa aboard the* Norway.**

On our most recent *Norway* visit the ship looked very clean and spiffy from a recent makeover—she could rival any Hollywood star in number of facelifts, and she's only 34.

Over the years, new luxury cabins and penthouses have been added, each with big windows or private balconies overlooking the sea. But because of the ship's vintage, the original cabins come in all shapes and sizes rather than the neat, identical modules you find on new ships. It's worth spending some extra time studying the deck plan and cabin specifics to be sure you're getting the sort of cabin you want.

The heart of the ship is the International Deck with its enclosed promenade most of the way around on both sides, like fashionable boulevards lined with sidewalk cafes and elegant boutiques. Two separate dining rooms, remnants of the two-class ocean liner days, are divided by the galley in a you-can't-get-here-from-there arrangement, and cabins are dispersed throughout the 10 passenger decks in random configuration.

Even from a distance (she usually lies at anchor in her ports of call) you can recognize her twin stacks and dark blue hull.

The Brochure Says

"Ever since her launch as the *S.S. France*, she has been hailed for her plush splendor and architectural marvels. Now, after the finishing touches of a three-year, $60 million refurbishment...she has emerged with her classic features intact: the hand-laid tile mosaics, Art Deco murals, marble statuary, teak rails, two-story Broadway theater, and the magnificent Club Internationale ballroom."

Translation

The real joy of cruising on the *Norway* for a ship buff is to recreate some of the glory and nostalgia from an ocean liner, even a liner-come-lately like the *France*. In many of the cabins, touches remain from the original; some bathrooms still have the 1960s plumbing fixtures like old-fashioned bathtubs, heated towel racks and tile mosaics. And look for the five antique slot machines on exhibit in the new marble-floored casino, probably not from the original ship but antiques nevertheless.

INSIDER TIP

Enjoy the free ice cream from Sven's Ice Cream Parlor on the International Deck; passengers used to have to pay for it because, as one staffer said back then, "Otherwise it would be full all day with people eating ice cream." There was no crowd when we sampled some at 3 p.m. on a hot afternoon last spring—we were the only customers.

Cabins and Costs

Fantasy Suites: **Report Card: A**

Average Price PPPD: $778 including airfare.

While we admire the original two-bedroom, two-bath grand suites on Viking Deck (Jerry Lewis always occupied one of them when he was the headline entertainer on a cruise), today's luxury-loving passengers would probably prefer one of the two new owner's suites forward on the top deck. Each has its own wrap-around terrace; a living room with leather sofa and chairs, desk, tape/CD deck, large TV, fully stocked bar, marble table, built-in cabinetry, and plenty of room for entertaining; a bedroom with queen-sized bed, big walk-in closet, marble bath with Roman tub, marble floor, separate stall shower and powder room; and concierge service.

Small Splurges: **Report Card: A**

Average Price PPPD: $392 including airfare.

The junior suites on Pool Deck are marvelously light, bright rooms with three big picture windows, two lower, queen-sized or king-sized beds, sitting area with sofa and chair, dressing table with make-up lights and good mirror, mini-refrigerator, tub and shower, and concierge service.

This standard outside double cabin aboard the* Norway *is actually a bit more spacious than some in that category.

Suitable Standards: **Report Card: C-**

Average Price PPPD: From $271 to $307, including airfare.

Cabins vary widely, with the four standard outsides and one superior inside categories more or less falling into the standard cabin range. Each has a bed arrangement that sleeps two people in some fashion in lower beds, a bath with tub or shower, a chair, dresser, TV set and table. If you don't mind an inside, O 88 has a lot of room, twin beds, two dressers, two chairs and table.

Bottom Bunks: **Report Card: F**

Average Price PPPD: $214 in category N, $241 in category K, including airfare.

The category N inside doubles with upper and lower berths are the bottom-of-the-line on the *Norway*, and the one we looked at recently—V 248—we could not recommend, even to the most forgiving first-timer. A tiny space with a stool, TV set, single bed and overhead bunk, with fresh carpeting and upholstery but an original bathroom with shower only and the smell of bad drains. We'd suggest spending another $190 each for the week and take a category K inside like A 023 with a double bed and upper pulldown (making it workable even for roommates who want separate beds), chair, dresser, TV set and bath with shower only.

INSIDER TIP

Make sure your travel agent books a specific bed arrangement–twins, double, queen- or king-sized–because in many cabins on the Norway *beds cannot be put together.*

Where She Goes

The *Norway* follows the same seven-day itinerary year-round (except for the exceptions noted below), sailing from Miami on Saturdays and anchoring off St. Maarten, St. John, St. Thomas and Great Stirrup Cay, the line's private island in the Bahamas, for a beach day. In addition to the regular schedule are four seven-day cruises to the Western Caribbean scheduled for 1996—May 11, May 25, August 24 and November 2—when the ship visits Ocho Rios, Grand Cayman, Playa del Carmen, Cozumel and Great Stirrup Cay.

The Bottom Line

It's important for a potential passenger, especially an ocean liner aficionado, to make a clear mental distinction between the *Norway*, a seven-day mass- market cruise ship featuring dinner menus with fixed themes that rotate every seven days, and the *France*, an ocean liner that offered superb first-class food and service that rivaled the three-star Michelin restaurants of France on crossings in the 1960s. While the *Norway* offers extremely good seven-day Caribbean cruises for vacationers, honeymooners and first-time cruisers, you must not expect to sail in the legendary style of the French Line.

Fielding's Picks

Lovely Locales

1. The Club Internationale looks like the kind of nightclub Nick and Nora Charles would have frequented, except perhaps for the tuxedoed mannequin seated at the player piano and those gesso gods of the sea in the side niches. Elegant green and gold silk tapestry covers the banquettes and chairs, and original light fixtures from the 1960s still adorn the walls and ceilings.

2. The Champs Elysees on starboard side and Fifth Avenue on port side are almost as grand as the originals, enclosed promenades that let you saunter past shop windows glittering with jewelry, crystal, perfumes and sequinned gowns, even a fur shop, and a sidewalk cafe where you can sit down in white wrought iron chairs for a drink.
3. The sybaritic spa compound built around the ship's indoor pool, operated by Steiner of London, a 6000- square-foot Roman spa with hydrotherapy baths, steam rooms, saunas and aquacise pool with spa treatments sold individually or part of a package, plus a 4000-square-foot health and fitness center, basketball court and jogging track.
4. The charming children's playroom called Trolland on the Norway, still has its original fairytale wall mural from the *France*; three youth counselors are always aboard, but the number swells to seven during holiday sailings and summer.
5. The Saga Theatre is a proper theatre with its comfortable row seats and balcony, just the place to watch Will Rogers ropin' and chattin' in "The Will Rogers Follies," to catch the Gerry Mulligan Quartet during the jazz festival or the Shirelles singing "Dedicated to the One I Love" during a '50s and '60s theme cruise; the latter is scheduled this year for May 11 with equally great rock 'n roll era names.

Good Reasons to Book This Ship

1. To look for details from the original *S.S.France*. Where to start: The first-class dining room was the one now called the Windward, amidships on Atlantic Deck with its magnificent staircase for grand entrances; its original name was the Chambord Restaurant.
2. Because there's no extra charge for all that jazz—you can hear the world's greatest jazz musicians gathered together for concerts and impromptu jam sessions all over the ship at any hour of the day or night during the two-week annual autumn jazz festival.
3. To win a free T-shirt with seven vouchers proving you took part in seven Motion on the Ocean fitness and sports activities.
4. If you cruise before the fall of 1996, you can claim you've sailed on the world's biggest cruise ship; once the 100,000-ton *Carnival Destiny* arrives, *Norway's* record 76,049 gross registry tons falls into second place.
5. To enroll in a full spa program and get The Body Beautiful at the Roman Spa; each October there's a fitness and beauty cruise with top Olympic athletes and experts in fitness, health and beauty.

Things You Won't Find On Board

1. A gangway down to the dock in ports of call; passengers go ashore by tender, since the ship docks only in Miami.
2. A bad sport.
3. That nice couple you met on deck the other day; the ship is so big you'll want to get names and cabin numbers from anyone you'd like to see again.
4. A cabin designated single, although there are a lot of teeny-tiny ones that should be.
5. A self-service laundry (but can you imagine all the rich and famous who crossed the Atlantic on the *France* running down and washing their undies themselves?)

Seaward ★★★

Of all the ships in NCL's fleet, including the now-departed white ships, the Seaward *has been the hardest for us to warm up to, perhaps because of its cool, almost darkish interiors and upper decks, acres of painted metal and indoor/outdoor carpeting instead of teak. But a recent drydocking that added more pastels, mirrors and art work lightens it up, at least on the inside. Now, if they could do something about that painted metal Promenade Deck surface...*

This is a ship for the young and active, with a fitness center, golf driving range, a basketball court and a full, around-the-ship jogging track on promenade deck labeled with arrows so everyone runs or walks in the right direction (counter-clockwise). The Big Apple Cafe serves a lot of breakfasts and lunches for passengers too busy to go down to the dining room. Down on Atlantic Deck is a small children's playroom called Porthole. Traffic flow through the dining room areas moves smoothly along a port side walkway called Park Avenue that links the Four Seasons Dining Room with the Seven Seas Dining Room.

The Brochure Says

"She boasts a lounge featuring the Broadway hit musical 'Grease,' an extravagantly designed casino, and marvelous places to dance. As well as some of the finest four-star cuisine to be found anywhere..."

Translation

"Grease" was indeed playing on board during our most recent visit. The showroom is dark, cool and elegant, with generally good sightlines and row seats in back with pull-down drink tables fitted between the seats. The casino is also classy, but we're not sure what four-star cuisine is (the French food Bible Guide Michelin only goes up to three). However, there's a wide range of choices and what it lacks in subtlety it makes up for in copious portions.

INSIDER TIP

There's a tuxedo rental shop aboard if you've forgotten to bring one or don't own formal wear and want to dress up to match your wife's finery.

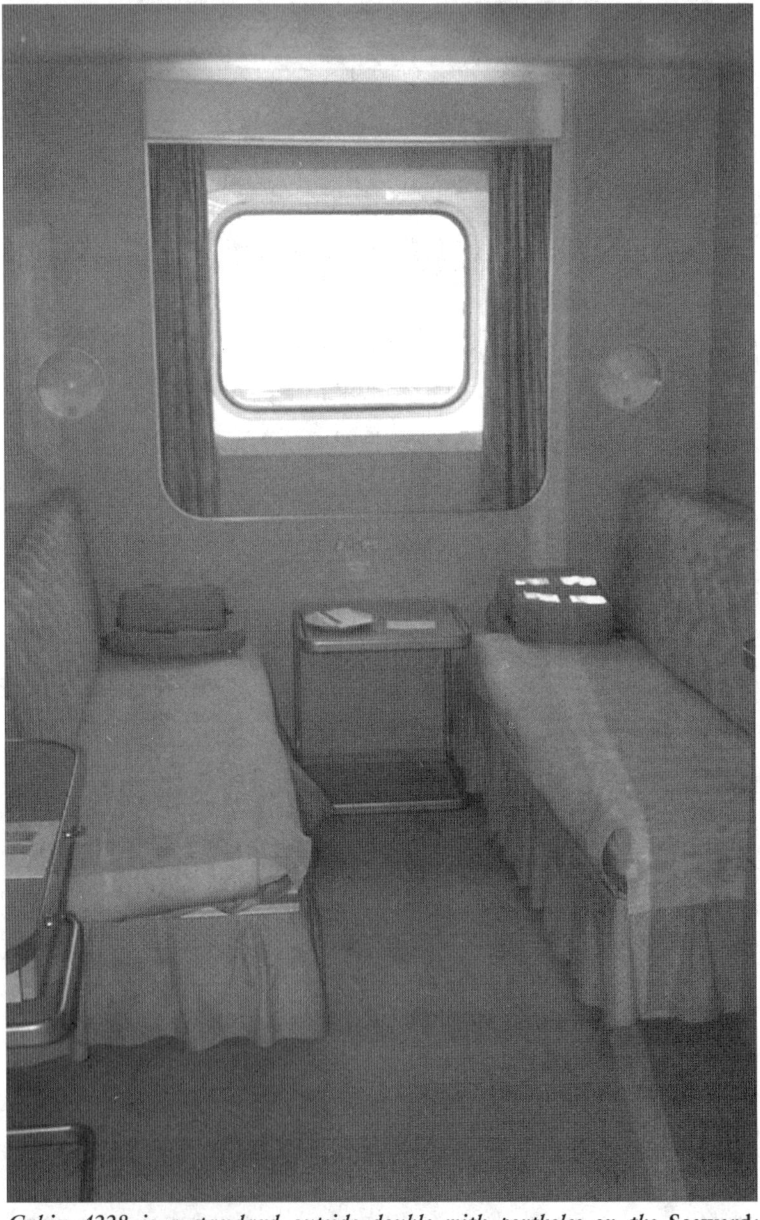

Cabin 4228 is a standard outside double with portholes on the **Seaward*****; lifejackets are laid out on the beds on embarkation day, when the boat drill takes place.***

Cabins and Costs

Fantasy Suites: **Report Card: A**

Average Price PPPD: $478 each for two occupants, including airfare.

Four newly added Owner's Suites sleep up to five passengers in 280 to 360 square feet, with sitting area with sofa double bed, dining area, separate bedroom, two TV sets, mini-refrigerator and bathroom with tub and shower.

Small Splurges: **Report Card: B**

Average Price PPPD: $399 including airfare.

Three forward deluxe suites on Norway deck share a captain's eye view of the scenery ahead, along with a sleeping area with two lower beds, sitting area with a sofa that can convert to a bed for an additional occupant, a mini-refrigerator, lounge chair and bath with tub and shower.

Suitable Standards: **Report Card: C**

Average Price PPPD: For category E outside doubles, $304 including airfare.

Twin sofa beds with a small table in between, a built-in cabinet tower with desk, four drawers, complimentary bottle of Evian, TV, ice bucket, slender full-length mirror and full hanging cabinet inside, as versatile a storage area as we've seen outside the Hold Everything catalogue. There are also two additional full-length hanging areas on the opposite wall, as well as a bathroom with tile floor, shower, and pastel bath fixtures. Cabin described is in category E.

Bottom Bunks: **Report Card: D**

Average Price PPPD: $245 including airfare.

Six category L cabins with a fairly large lower bed and a pulldown berth that folds up during the day because otherwise there's not enough room to walk between the beds. These cabins might work for two very slender, very close friends. There's also a built-in desk/dresser, a chair, TV set, a small table and a lime green cabinet tower (see Suitable Standards, above). And all cabins are issued a bowl of fresh fruit and a bottle of mineral water.

Where She Goes

The *Seaward* offers alternating seven-day Barbados Series and Aruba Series sailings roundtrip from San Juan every Sunday. The Barbados Series calls at Barbados, Martinique, St. Maarten, Antigua, St. John and St. Thomas, while the Aruba Series calls at Aruba, Curaçao, Tortola/Virgin Gorda, St. John and St. Thomas.

The Bottom Line

While this ship was one of the last to come out of the respected Wartsila shipyard in Finland before its subsequent conversion to Kvaerner-Masa Yard, the construction is not nearly so sturdy. In areas of the deck, you may step on a patch of thin, buckled steel plating under the indoor/outdoor carpet. The ship went through a major refurbishing in May, 1995, to freshen carpeting and upholstery, as well as adding additional suites. (Lavish suites are big sellers on this line that caters to so many honeymooners.) After being sentenced to the short-cruise market, which adds so much wear and tear to a ship, she needed a cosmetic make-over.

Fielding's Picks

Dramatic Spaces

1. The Crystal Court two-deck entry lobby with a fountain dripping water down glass pipes, slick white marble squares, wide dark green curved leather benches, plants, a rock garden—a dark, cool contrast to the bright, hot tropics outside.
2. Gatsby's is billed as a wine bar/nightclub, but when we were aboard recently in Miami, it was the setting for a small private wedding and luncheon, and showed it could be turned into the most romantic little restaurant at sea. It's pretty dreamy with its tall ladderback black chairs and round tables, granite floors and white piano.
3. Oscar's Piano Bar, with its very comfortable barstools, could entice a passenger to linger awhile around the curved piano bar, perhaps even join in on a chorus or two.
4. Hallways and landings, an often-ignored part of a ship's decor, here are filled with art, including pretty original water colors, wall hangings and majestic marble and granite, endowing the space with richness.
5. The Pool Deck with its shaded outdoor dining areas lashed with panels of fabric on the sides and ceiling, wood-trimmed tables and woven plastic armchairs.

Good Reasons to Book This Ship

1. The Chocoholic Buffet, served once a cruise at midnight, the chocoholic's witching hour, with every fantasy dessert you ever dreamed of.
2. To learn snorkeling with the well-organized, comprehensive Dive-In program.
3. Lickety-Splits ice cream stand, with free cones or dishes of ice cream in four flavors, plus sherbet, frozen yogurt and any toppings you'd like to add; open all afternoon.
4. Le Bistro for alternative dining at no extra charge except a tip for the waiter; an advance reservation is required, however. It's the place to be alone together for a special occasion or a quiet evening, or to get together with new-found friends.
5. To check out the seagoing mall called Everything Under the Sun, with lots of shops and gold chains by the inch.

P&O

P & O CRUISES

c/o Princess Cruises; 10100 Santa Monica Boulevard, Los Angeles, CA 90067-4189
☎ *(310) 553-1770, (800) LOVE-BOAT*

Princess Tours is a North American agent for P & O Cruises' new *Oriana*, the *Canberra* and the *Victoria* (the former *Sea Princess*).

History

Peninsular and Oriental Navigation Company is the oldest and largest of the British shipping companies, founded in 1837, shortly before Samuel Cunard founded his company. Cunard looked west to America, P&O looked east, first to Spain and Portugal, later to India. The founders of P & O, Arthur Anderson, a one-time Shetland Islands "beach boy" (itinerant worker) and Brodie McGhie Willcox, were serious young men only a few years away from poverty when they invested in their first ship, a small American schooner run aground near Dover which they salvaged. Soon they acquired additional vessels, including the steamer *William Fawcett*, usually credited as being their first passenger ship.

P & O's India-bound passengers in the 1840s had the option of traveling across the Suez overland three decades before the famous canal was built. First-class on P&O was the only socially acceptable way to travel to the raj.

In the 1880s, the *British Medical Journal* recommended sea voyages for health, and by 1898, a P & O poster was advertising a 60-day pleasure cruise to the West Indies.

Not only were generous quantities of food always included on the P & O sailings, but until 1874, unlimited quantities of wine, beer, spirits and mineral water were also included. On Sundays, sailing days and holidays, champagne was also thrown in. In the days before refrigeration, whole barnyards of live animals were taken along to be slaughtered and cooked as needed.

In 1914, P & O merged with British India Company. In 1932, the company had 41 cargo and passenger ships, only three pre-World War I, but in 1939 its ships, including 21 passenger vessels, were requisitioned by the government to serve as armed merchant cruisers and transports. In 1946, there were 13 left; eight had been sunk. Between 1946 and 1950, the government returned the requisitioned hardware to P & O, and in 1960, the first of two new ships debuted, the *Oriana*, followed a year later by the *Canberra*.

—The word "posh," according to popular lore, is said to have originated from the cabin reservation stamped P.O., S.H. for "Port Out, Starboard Home" for passengers traveling between England and India who demanded the coolest staterooms in each direction. Some authorities say that claim is without foundation; others say the word actually came into slang usage from the snobbishness of P&O passengers themselves.

—P & O claims it invented leisure cruising in 1844 when British author William Makepeace Thackery sailed around the Mediterranean on a free ticket to publicize the service and wrote a travel book about his cruise—*From Cornhill to Grand Cairo*—under the pseudonym Michael Angelo Titmarsh. He was not a happy camper—he hated Athens and was often seasick—and because his trip was during the religious holidays of Ramadan, he complained bitterly about missing all the grandly advertised wonders of the East, from the whirling dervishes to the harem at the seraglio in Istanbul.

—One of the three largest cruise lines in the world.

Concept

To take English-speaking passengers all over the English-speaking world and beyond, on world cruises, warm-weather getaway cruises and seasonal travels between a home on one continent and one on another.

Signatures

Cruising "British style," which appeals to many Anglophiles in North America in addition to the large number of travelers from the United Kingdom.

Gimmicks

The children's tea, an early supper served just to kids at 5:30, before the early seating dinner begins.

Who's the Competition

Naturally the Cunard ships compete head-on with the P & O ships, the difference being that P & O does not participate in active U.S. marketing except through companies like Princess Tours, while Cunard maintains very active U.S.-based offices.

Who's Aboard

Primarily British passengers, but some Americans, Australians, New Zealanders and others; families with children on holiday cruises; singles of all ages.

Who Should Go

The people that do, plus American and Canadian Anglophiles.

Who Should Not Go

Anyone who can't mix and mingle with people from another country; any passionately chauvinistic American who thinks everyone else is disadvantaged (much as the British used to feel about the rest of the world).

The Lifestyle

Since P & O virtually invented the pleasure cruise, many of the familiar traditions of the genre are practiced aboard these ships, from dress codes to shipboard games.

Wardrobe

We remember being aboard the *Victoria* when it was the *Sea Princess*, and a wealthy Texan showed up on a formal night in a resplendent custom-made outfit, a cowboy tuxedo in white with red patent leather lapels and matching red and white cowboy boots. The irate British at the next table summoned the maitre d'hotel and demanded that the Texan be sent back to his cabin "to change into proper attire." They may run around in frocks and undersized bathing suits and even terrycloth bathrobes all day long, but when black tie is required in the evening, they're sticklers for correctness.

Bill of Fare

The meal pattern is British rather than American, with kippers, kidneys and finnan haddie on breakfast menus, kedgeree and curries and such for lunch, along with a roast, called a joint. Afternoon tea is much more important than midnight buffet, and high tea (correctly used, the term means a light early supper rather than fancy little sandwiches and scones with cream and jam) a tradition for the children on board. The British like to see the entire array of silverware to be used for the meal arranged in front of them at the beginning, perhaps to scrutinize the setting to anticipate marrow on toast as a savory or the ever-so-fussy little mother-of-pearl server for caviar. And of course the sweet (dessert) comes before the savory (cheese, marrow or smoked oysters on toast or chicken livers grilled with bacon) that finishes the meal.

Cuisine Report Card: B

Showtime

Since P & O also invented the amusements that go with cruises—a letter written from before the turn of the century lists "quoits, bull, potato race, egg-and-spoon race, tugs-of-war, skipping contests, thread-needle races"—you can expect a daily quiz, team trivia games, a ship's mileage pool, duplicate bridge, even cricket games. Evenings offer music for dancing, some fairly routine production shows (except on the new *Oriana* with its professional theatrical stage) and the usual variety artists from Butlin's.

Entertainment Report Card: B+

Discounts

On some cruises early booking discounts on the *Oriana*, *Canberra* and *Victoria* should be available.

The Bottom Line

"Cruising British style" means less glitz and glamour in the decor but a more traditional shipboard experience. If you wonder what that's about, pick up almost any book by W. Somerset Maugham, (he's still famous, and quite obviously was a writer!) who traveled extensively by ship.

Victoria ★★★★

In the grand tradition of Hollywood films, where a classy, intelligent but plain Jane, usually played by Rosalind Russell, takes off her glasses, lets down her hair and suddenly becomes glamorous, Princess Cruises briefly turned P & O's stalwart Sea Princess *(now the* Victoria*), a sedate British dowager, into a Princess ship in 1987. This move infuriated the British, and after a relative brief whirl in her glamour garments, the* Sea Princess *returned to the fold. So great and long-standing was their wrath that eight years later the ship was renamed* Victoria *to erase any confusion in the U.K. that it might be one of those gaudy American Princess ships.*

This elegant and classic ship started life as the *Kungsholm* for Swedish American Lines, and was one of the last great ships built by John Brown on the River Clyde. Today the vessel combines a stateliness and solid seaworthiness with the big deck dazzle of a fun-in-the-sun ship. It has a lot of action for active outdoorsy types, two outdoor pools and one indoor one, plus a whirlpool spa, sauna and gym, and a special sports afterdeck with shuffleboard and quoits, table tennis and golf. There are enough bars and lounges on board to visit a different one every day of the week, and several big comfortable reading rooms overlooking the sea. Staterooms are unusually large and beautifully fitted, with enough closet and storage space for a three-month cruise.

The Brochure Says

"Her sleek lines reflect the elegance of her interior. As soon as you step on-board, you'll notice a little extra refinement, a touch more style. Wood paneling gleams in the subdued lighting. You'll see fine paintings and delightful floral arrangements everywhere you look. The *Victoria's* small size lets her slip into out-of-the-way ports, and gives you a chance to meet your fellow passengers."

Translation

None needed—well said!

Cabins and Costs

Fantasy Suites: **Report Card: A**

Average Price PPPD: $598

Six big suites added during the major refurbishment in 1986 are named for classic P & O ships and have sitting areas, double beds, mini-refrigerators and bathrooms with Jacuzzi tubs.

Small Splurges: **Report Card: A**

Average Price PPPD: $344

Spacious BA category cabins have sitting area, built-in desk/dresser with stool and mirror, twin or double beds, bathroom with tub.

Suitable Standards: **Report Card: B**

Average Price PPPD: $259

Many of the standard cabins have two lower berths, one of which folds away during the day to lend more space, while the other can be made up as a sofa. There are some tubs, some showers only in these middle categories. Some 16 inside and outside single cabins are a boon for the solo traveler, so often overlooked in today's new ships or hit with a hefty surcharge for occupying a double cabin alone.

Bottom Bunks: **Report Card: A**

Average Price PPPD: $212

Bottom category inside cabins on the lowest passenger decks are fairly spacious, fitted out with the lovely wood interiors like the other cabins are, and usually have a desk/dressing table and a chair as well as two lower beds, one of which folds away during the day.

Where She Goes

The *Victoria* does a series of Caribbean itineraries out of San Juan throughout the spring including one that offers a cruise into Gatun Lake in the Panama Canal.

The Bottom Line

A graceful and elegant classic ship since her days as the *Kungsholm*, the *Victoria* is an antidote to megaliners and glitz. If you're a traditional cruiser who loves polished wood interiors and glass-enclosed promenades, and you subscribe to British understatement, *Victoria* is your ship come in.

Fielding's Picks

Favorite Places

1. Warm wood paneling and finely detailed carpentry show the extraordinary custom work that went into the ship, especially in the International Lounge.
2. The Coral Dining Room is an attractive medium-sized room with two meal seatings and two entrances, one forward and one aft, for anyone who gets mixed up on the way to dinner.

3. The circular bar in the Carib Lounge is a popular gathering spot because the casino is nearby.
4. The International Bar is an intimate place for a drink or two with a very close friend.
5. The Starlight Lounge was our favorite venue for hotly contested Trivial Pursuit games; it helped that if only one table out of the six or eight teams got the right answer, the bar sent over free drinks.

Good Reasons to Book This Ship

1. It's a longtime classic and you can tell that by being aboard.
2. Two outdoor pools and one indoor one, plus whirlpool spa, sauna and gym, mean you can work out every day, and a special sports afterdeck provides an out-of-the-traffic area for shuffleboard and quoits, playing table tennis or driving golf balls.
3. Because if you book the right sailing far enough in advance through Golden Bear, you may be able to take the second person in the cabin along free.
4. Because there's a launderette and ironing room on virtually every deck.

Things You Won't Find On Board

1. TV sets in the lower-category cabins.
2. A children's program.
3. A hot breakfast served in your cabin; only continental breakfasts are offered by room service.
4. A private veranda.
5. A skimpy bathtub; all the cabins with tubs have those great deep British tubs.

PRINCESS CRUISES

10100 Santa Monica Boulevard, Los Angeles, CA 90067
☎ *(310) 553-1770, (800) LOV-BOAT*

A new tradition aboard the newest Princess ships is to stage the captain's cocktail party in the three-story atrium lobby.

History

While the popular TV series "The Love Boat" catapulted Princess Cruises to worldwide fame, the company had been a household name on the west coast, at least among cruise aficionados, from the 1960s.

In the winter of 1965-66, Seattle entrepreneur Stan McDonald chartered the 6000-ton *Princess Patricia* from Canadian Pacific Railway and offered cruises along the Mexican Riviera from Los Angeles. From the ship's name came the company name, Princess Cruises. The first season went so well aboard the "Princess Pat," as everyone began to call her, that McDonald soon chartered a newly-built Italian ship called the *Italia* and renamed her the *Princess Italia*. In 1968, the *Princess Carla* (the former French Line *Flandre*), then Costa's *Carla C*, was chartered, and in 1971 the *Island Princess* (the only one of these still in the fleet).

Then London-based Peninsular and Orient Steam Navigation Company, better known as P&O (see P & O under Cruise Lines, above), the largest and oldest shipping company in the world, eyed the action and decided to come into the cruise scene with its new *Spirit of London*, which it positioned on the west coast in the winter of 1972–73 to compete with Princess. There was little competition; McDonald continued to dominate Mexican Riviera cruising, despite one travel writer's comments that aboard the Princess Pat "the standard dessert was canned peaches" and the decor "was on a par with a good, clean $7-a-night room in a venerable but respected Toronto hotel."

So in 1974, P & O acquired Princess Cruises, including its key marketing staff, and set about upgrading the fleet hardware. The *Carla* and *Italia* went back to Costa Cruises in 1974, and the *Island Princess* was purchased outright. P & O's new *Spirit of London* was added to the fleet as the *Sun Princess*, and the *Sea Venture*, sister ship to the *Island Princess*, was acquired to become the *Pacific Princess*.

Things were already going well, but destined to improve even further when TV producer Doug Cramer showed up in 1975 with a new series he wanted to film aboard a cruise ship. *Et voila!* "The Love Boat" was born.

In 1988, continuing its "if you can't beat 'em, buy 'em" strategy, P & O/Princess acquired Los Angeles-based rival Sitmar Cruises, which added three existing ships and one nearly-completed new ship, *Star Princess*, to the fleet, to bring it up to nine vessels.

Today there are still nine Love Boats cruising the seven seas, five of them from the 1988 fleet, with a 10th, the 104,000-ton giant *Grand Princess*, due to arrive in the spring of 1997 to sail the Caribbean year-round. (A prudent move, since the ship is too big to go through the Panama Canal.)

—Parent company P & O claims it invented leisure cruising in 1844 when British author William Makepeace Thackery sailed around the Mediterranean on a free ticket to publicize the service and wrote a travel book about his cruise—*From Cornhill to Grand Cairo*—under the pseudonym Michael Angelo Titmarsh.

—One of the three largest cruise lines in the world.

—Offers the largest number of world-wide destinations of any major line.

—First to introduce all outside cabins with a high proportion of private balconies (*Royal Princess*, 1984).

—First major cruise line to introduce multimedia musical shows produced in-house.

—First to install a "black box" recorder on each of its ships for additional safety data in case of an incident at sea.

—Introduced easy-to-use phone cards to make local or long distance calls from anywhere in the world with a push-button phone; the card (good for $20 worth of phone time) was originally developed as a convenience for the Princess crew (sold across the fleet, July 1995).

—TV's "The Love Boat" is seen in 93 countries and heard in more than 29 different languages. The title comes from a book written by a former cruise director named Jeraldine Saunders about her life onboard.

FOOTNOTE

While the Pacific Princess *is the vessel most associated with "Love Boat" over the years, the pilot episode was actually filmed aboard the* Sun Princess, *the former* Spirit of London, *now retired from the fleet.*

Concept

"It's more than a cruise, it's the Love Boat," says a beaming Gavin MacLeod on the Princess commercials.

What does that make you think of? The TV series, of course, with its glamorous, friendly crew, never too busy to intercede in someone's love affair. Luxurious staterooms and elegantly garbed passengers. Nubile nymphs in bikinis. Exotic ports, perpetual sunshine and cloudless blue skies. In other words, the perfect vacation—a cruise.

With its varied fleet of vessels, ranging from the homey, mid-sized 610-passenger *Island Princess* and *Pacific Princess* to the new 1950-passenger *Sun Princess* and the upcoming 2600-passenger *Grand Princess*, the line feels it offers "something for everyone" from "endless activity" to "total relaxation."

FOOTNOTE

Princess says it has trademarked both the name Princess and the Love Boat slogan (see "Concept") and has in the past even brought legal action against two smaller cruise lines for infringement of copyright–American Canadian Caribbean Line for attempting to name one of its 90-passenger vessels Mayan Princess *(ACCL changed it to* Mayan Prince *rather than go to court) and now-defunct Ocean Cruise Line for advertising its* Ocean Princess *Antarctica sailings with the slogan "Cruise Antarctica with a Princess."*

Signatures

The line's distinctive stack logo, the "sea witch" with the flowing hair, provides instant identification when a Princess ship is in port. Just as distinctive, but less well known, is the Princess tradition of furnishing each of its new ships with an exquisite museum-quality million dollar-plus art collections from contemporary artists such as Andy Warhol, David Hockney, Robert Motherwell, Frank Stella, Laddie John Dill, Billy Al Bengston, Richard Diebenkorn and Helen Frankenthaler.

On-board pizzerias with special ovens serve up pizzas and calzone cooked to order aboard the line's *Crown Princess*, *Sky Princess*, *Regal Princess*, *Star Princess* and *Sun Princess*.

Gimmicks

Declaring St. Valentine's Day as Love Boat National Holiday aboard all the line's vessels, with renewal of vows ceremonies in which some 4000 couples participate. The holiday also features a poetry contest and reading, romantic feature films, a Hearts card game tournament and honeymooner and singles parties.

Who's the Competition

In Alaska, Princess has been competing head-on with Holland America for some years, and usually outnumbers HAL in ships positioned there for the summer. In the Caribbean, HAL is also a main competitor, but Love Boats face some Costa competition for fans of pizza, pasta and Italian waiters.

On more exotic itineraries, Princess is competing with Royal Cruise Line for upscale older couples and single women. Perhaps more significant is the small but discernible crossover from Princess to Crystal Cruises for some moneyed West Coast frequent cruisers.

Who's Aboard

Romantic couples of all ages who saw "The Love Boat" on TV; longtime loyals, both couples and singles, over 45; a group of younger couples who've met on board and continue to take vacation cruises together (see "Footnote" to follow); some families with children, who gravitate toward those ships that have dedicated playrooms and full-time youth counselors (*Sky Princess*, *Golden Princess* and *Star Princess*); people with glints of gold from head (hair coloring) to toe (gold lamé sandals or ankle bracelets), neck (gold chains) to fingertips (gold pinky rings, a gold lamé tote).

Who Should Go

Anyone who wants a very traditional cruise experience with a chance to dance and dress up; admirers of avant-garde Pompidou Center architect Renzo Piano, who designed parts of the *Crown* and *Regal Princess*; families whose teenagers like the pizzeria and the zany fountain drinks aboard the *Star*, *Crown* and *Regal*; young women who want to meet some Italians; anyone who loves pasta, pastries and cappuccino; fans of the Cirque du Soleil who'll adore the new avant-garde show *Mystique* on the *Crown*, *Regal* and *Star*. More younger passengers should be boarding, because Princess is becoming expert at giving them what they want, at least on the big new ships—a less-structured captain's cocktail party; music for listening and dancing all over the ship; lots of sundeck and water areas with swim-up bars, waterfalls, swimming pools and Jacuzzis.

Who Should Not Go

Anyone with children under 18 months of age (babies are not permitted on board); anybody who refuses to wear a tie on any occasion; anyone who would answer "Huh?" to the query, "Fourth for bridge?"

FOOTNOTE

Oops! A recent issue of Captain's Circle News, *a publication for Princess repeat passengers, ran a photo of two couples who met on a Princess ship and cruise together frequently; they're snapped by the ship's photographer on the gangway of a Princess ship in Nassau, but dominating the background is the unmistakable crimson hull of not a Love Boat but the Big Red Boat from Premier.*

The Lifestyle

Set in the framework of traditional cruises, a day aboard a Princess ship includes a plethora of activities and entertainment, from an exercise class in the gym or a facial in the beauty salon to language lessons, pool games, bridge classes, aquacise in the ship's pool, indoor and outdoor game tournaments, bingo, golf chipping, feature films in the ship's theater or in the cabin, port lectures, shopping lectures, cooking demonstrations, galley and bridge tours, fashion shows and karaoke singing. Even kids have their own karaoke contests, along with coketail parties, coloring contests and ice cream parties.

Many evenings are relatively formal aboard, with passengers wearing their finest clothes and jewelry and Italian or British officers hosting dinner tables, but other nights, such as the traditional London Pub Night, casual wear is prescribed and beer and pub dishes are on the agenda, along with rowdy music hall songs and dances.

Wardrobe

Princess passengers usually have two formal nights, two or three semi-formal and two or three casual nights during a week. For formal nights, men are requested to wear tuxedos, dinner jackets or dark suits and women cocktail dresses or evening outfits. Semi-formal evenings call for men to wear jacket and tie, women to wear dresses or dressy pantsuits.

On casual evenings, men may wear open-necked sport shirts, slacks and sports outfits; women, slacks, dresses or skirts. Daytime clothing can be quite casual, but coverups over bathing suits are expected for passengers walking through the ship.

Bill of Fare

Cuisine is Continental with an emphasis on Italian dishes. A pasta or risotto specialty is featured every day at lunch and at dinner, along with a low-fat, low-calorie selection and a vegetarian dish.

Late-night buffets aboard the Princess ships are themed, with fish and chips following London Pub Night, a pasta party, a pizza party, a champagne fountain and Crepes Suzette on French Night, and a gala buffet among the other offerings.

Meals are served in two assigned seatings, with dinners somewhere between 6-6:30 p.m. for first seating, 8–8:30 p.m. for second seating. Breakfast and lunch are also served at assigned seatings when the ships are at sea, but may be open seating when the ship is in port. Your travel agent should request your seating preference when booking. All Princess dining rooms are smoke-free.

Pizzerias that cook pizzas and calzones to order are aboard some of the line's ships (see "Signatures").

The captain's gala dinner may offer Sevruga Malossol caviar, shrimp cocktail, liver pâté Strasbourg and fresh fruit cup with Triple Sec, following by a choice of three soups, a salad, ravioli with porcini mushroom sauce, rock lobster tail, salmon en croute, pheasant breast flambé or tournedos, along with four desserts plus cheese and fruit. Wine prices aboard are generally reasonable.

The embarkation-day "snack" buffets we sampled recently varied wildly, from the *Sky Princess*, where the chef put out a lavish self-serve lunch of hot and cold dishes, to the *Regal Princess* with a disappointing assortment of dry sandwiches filled with gristly roast beef, salami, turkey roll or canned ham, along with pastries that looked like Laura Scudder jelly rolls. A regular deck buffet lunch on the *Crown Princess* in Cozumel offered a choice of cream Savoyarde soup, chili con carne, manicotti alla Sorentino, something we couldn't identify that was breaded and fried, hot dogs, pre-cooked hamburgers from the steam table, plus cold cuts and a salad bar.

Fortunately, meals in the dining room and pizzeria are usually somewhat better than the buffets. A dining room luncheon aboard the *Regal Princess* offered a choice of pasta shells with meat sauce, sautéed Alaskan rockfish, turkey scaloppine, a beef burger broiled to order or a tropical fruit plate. The *Golden Princess* provided seven generous if unexciting luncheon choices plus a pasta—ham omelette, fried catfish, vegetable cutlets, salami sandwich, chicken chow mien, London broil or chef's salad.

But with some notable exceptions—soups, non-creamy pasta dishes, pizzas made to order and special order dinner selections—much of the cooking consists of overly rich Continental clichés reminiscent of three-martini expense-account restaurants from the 1970s and not appealing to contemporary tastes. We feel the cuisine is the Achilles heel of this otherwise excellent cruise line.

Cuisine Report Card: C

CHAMPAGNE TOAST

Congratulations to Princess for maintaining family values by not serving alcoholic beverages to passengers under 21; the usual drinking age on most foreign flag vessels is 18.

Showtime

Princess pioneered elaborate multimedia shows with film clips projected onto screens beside the stage and pre-recorded "click track" sweetening to swell the musical accompaniment. As other lines began using many of the same techniques, the company started updating its entertainment to include Nolan Miller costumes (he did the wardrobe for TV's "Dynasty"), sometimes with as many as 60 costume changes a show (nearly as many as Joan Collins made each week).

The audience gets to participate in the popular "Love Boat Legends," playing on all the line's ships, with 24 passengers selected from volunteers who audition the first day, rehearse all week and join the cruise staff and entertainers in performing the last night of the sailing.

Perhaps the most sensational production is *Mystique*, an innovative and elaborately costumed production with a company of 23 performers, including nine European and Asian acrobats, set under the sea in Atlantis, with inflatable scenery that literally "grows" in front of your eyes; it's remarkable. *Mystique* appears only on board the *Crown Princess*, *Regal Princess* and *Star Princess*.

Big Band music, a splashy new Caribbean revue, a show-biz production called *Let's Go to the Movies*, a full lecture program, trivia quizzes, "Baby Boomer" theme nights, London Pub Night and A Night at the Races fill out the fun.

On the new *Sun Princess*, big-name entertainers are scheduled for some sailings.

Entertainmaint Report Card: A

Discounts

Love Boat Savers are discounts that take off from $299 to $999 per person from the cruise-only price, but the offer is restricted to residents of the U.S. and Canada. The lowest fares are for the earliest bookings; discounts may decrease as the sailing date approaches.

Frequent cruisers who belong to the Captain's Circle are mailed notices on special savings for designated sailings, including deals like two-for-one buys, 50 percent off for the second passenger in a cabin or free upgrades.

The Bottom Line

Princess prides itself on little extra details that make a cruise more luxurious, such as stocking each passenger cabin with robes to be used during the sailing, a bowl of fresh fruit replenished daily, CNN on cabin TV sets, designer toiletries, pillow chocolates and 24-hour room service.

Housekeeping aboard all the ships is excellent and service generally good, particularly in the dining room where Italian waiters and captains really seem to enjoy taking special orders and preparing tableside dishes such as Caesar salad and crêpes suzette.

All in all, these are good cruises for almost everyone except fussy foodies and families with infants.

Princess' familiar flowing-haired logo atop the funnel of the **Crown Princess.**

Crown Princess ★★★★★
Regal Princess ★★★★★

"Euclid alone / Has looked on beauty bare." Edna St. Vincent Millay

The most beautiful ship interior we ever saw was the Crown Princess *dome when it was under construction at the Fincantieri shipyard in Italy in early 1990. Architect Renzo Piano walked us through the pristine space that from the outside forms the "dolphin brow" of the ship. Inside it resembles what Piano called "the inside of a whale," with polished, rounded bone-colored ribs arching from ceiling to floor framing wide curved glass windows. As Piano talked about metaphor and magic, we stroked the silky, eggshell finish of the glossy plaster ribs.*

When we came back to Europe a few months later to sail on the maiden voyage, the dome was filled with slot machines and potted palms, red leather chairs and cocktail tables. It was never so beautiful again.

This elegant pair of ships, while similar in size to sister ship *Star Princess*, are far from identical to her. They were built in Italy's Fincantieri yard, while *Star Princess* came out of France's Chantiers d'Atlantique.

The *Crown Princess* and *Regal Princess* are unmistakable, even at a distance, because of their sloped, dolphin-like brow and strong vertical funnel. Controversial Italian architect Renzo Piano dislikes too much emphasis on the dolphin-like shape he designed—"A ship is a ship, it's not a dolphin."

The vertical funnel, a bold departure from the broad raked funnels on most of the Love Boats, he terms "a frank, clear, strong statement...and it works beautifully, by the way, to take the smoke away."

If an award were given for spacious cabins, these ships would win hands down. Cocktail lounges on board are lovely, as is a wine-and-caviar bar, a patisserie/sidewalk cafe in the lobby, a wonderful shopping arcade and a well-planned show lounge with fairly good sightlines except from the back of the main lounge.

CHAMPAGNE TOAST

On our most recent visit to these ships, the wood bars at eye level that had once sabotaged the observation facility of The Dome had been removed and lower wooden benches put in their places. Now the area really works as an observation lounge; finally, passengers are using it during the daytime as well as after dark.

The Brochure Says

"Her teak is from Burma, her marble from Carrera, and her fittings were forged by Italian craftsmen in shipyards over 200 years old...a masterpiece of the sea created by one of the world's most gifted architects."

Translation

Just what it says. These ships are the the last word in design and decor, luxurious, graceful, stylish and very comfortable, and they whisper about their $200 million-plus price rather than shout it the way Carnival's megaliners do.

EAVESDROPPING

One purportedly cruise-savvy matron to her friend just after boarding, "Don't they have to go three miles out before they can open the bars? I'm sure they do." (PS: They don't.)

Cabins and Costs

Fantasy Suites: **Report Card: A+**

Average Price PPPD: $450 with airfare on Caribbean sailings.

Top accommodations are the 14 suites, each with a double-size private veranda large enough for two lounging chairs with a small table between as well as a bigger table with two chairs, ideal for private breakfasts in the sun and sea breeze. A wide wooden doorway divides the living room with its sofa, chairs, tables and mini-refrigerator from the bedroom with its king-sized bed (which has a single mattress top rather than the two divided mattresses one usually gets when two beds are pushed together). Each room has its own TV set. A large dressing room lined with closets and enough storage space for an around-the-world cruise leads to the spacious marble bathroom with separate bathtub and stall shower. The toilet and second lavatory are adjoining, with another door that opens for the living room so it can double as a powder room when you're entertaining.

***A prettily furnished deluxe cabin on the* Regal Princess.**

Small Splurges: **Report Card: A**

Average Price PPPD: $400 with airfare in the Caribbean.

The category A mini-suites with private veranda are a bit smaller on both balcony and interior, but still very comfortable with bed (twins or queen-sized), sitting area with sofa and chairs, TV, mini-refrigerator, bath with tub and shower and spacious closet space.

Suitable Standards: **Report Card: A**

Average Price PPPD: $279 in the Caribbean with airfare.

Category GG outside double cabins forward on Plaza Deck provide queen-sized beds and a convenient location, but there are only four of them. All the standards contain amenities usually found only in suites—mini-refrigerators, remote-control TV sets, guest safes and walk-in closets. Baths have showers only. Other standards offer two lower beds that can be made into a queen-sized bed.

Bottom Bunks: **Report Card: A**

Average Price PPPD: $199 in the Caribbean with airfare for category M, $269 for category G.

Even the lowest category inside double cabin, the M category forward on Plaza Deck (only steps away from the lobby), measures 190 square feet and contains the same amenities and furnishings as the mid-range standards (see "Suitable Standards," above). The cheapest outside cabins are category G on Fiesta Deck with upper and lower berths and portholes instead of windows.

Where She Goes

Through the sailing of April 17, the *Crown Princess* cruises the Southern Caribbean roundtrip from Ft. Lauderdale on 10-day itineraries calling at Nassau, St. Thomas, Guadeloupe, Barbados, Dominica, St. Maarten and the private beach at Princess Cays.

The *Regal Princess* sails the Southern Caribbean roundtrip from San Juan on seven-day itineraries sailing every Saturday through April 6 and calling in Barbados, Mayreau for Princess' private beach, Martinique, St. Maarten and St. Thomas.

The Bottom Line

This is an exquisite pair of ships, with the only flaw, glimpsed on rare occasions, an undercurrent of staff "attitude" that makes us wonder if the mix of British and Italians always get along well together. Generally, though, everything runs smoothly. Newly embarking passengers are serenaded by a Filipino string trio and greeted by white-gloved stewards to escort them to their cabins. Everything you need to know is spelled out in the daily "Princess Patter" programs or advance cruise materials mailed ahead of time, making these very good vessels for first-time cruisers. With the improvements in The Dome (see "Champagne Toast"), Piano's vision seems clearer, although a lot of the magnificent view windows between the "whale ribs" are still blocked by slot machines. As for people who worry that there's nothing to do on a cruise, we'd like to take them on a stroll around these ships at almost any hour of the day or night, and they'd never fret again.

Fielding's Picks

Super Places

1. The chic 1930s-style cocktail lounges on promenade deck, the Adagio on the *Regal*, the Intermezzo on the *Crown*, where you half-expect to see Cary (but not Hugh!) Grant at the next table.
2. The Italian garden ambience in the Palm Court Dining Room on the Regal Princess, with its ivy-patterned carpet, pastoral garden murals and pastel rose and teal decor.
3. The Patisserie in the three-deck atriums, the true gathering spot on the ships (architect Piano had hoped The Dome would fill that function but it doesn't); you can get cappuccino and espresso all day long, accompanied by freshly baked pastries, and observe the comings and goings of fellow passengers.
4. The Bengal Bar aboard the *Regal Princess* takes you back to the raj with wicker chairs, ceiling fans and a life-sized Bengal tiger, plus some tiger balm—a menu of rare single malt whiskies or a classic Bombay Sapphire gin martini, all under $4.
5. The Presto Pizzeria on the *Crown Princess* with its Italian food-and-wine print red tablecloths, red-and-white glazed tile walls and natural teak floors, warm and inviting, serving five types of pizzas including vegetarian, plus calzones, garlic focaccio and Caesar salad, open 11 a.m. to 5 p.m., then again from 9 p.m. to 1 a.m.

Dancing in The Dome on the **Regal Princess.**

Off-the-Wall Things to Do

1. Order one of the zany drinks from the boldly illustrated menu in Characters Bar, perhaps the Strip & Go Naked or Ta Kill Ya Sunrise.
2. Converse with the talking elevators, which announce each deck and caution you when you exit to watch your step.
3. Check out the photo of ex-president George Bush on board wearing a *Regal Princess* cap and chatting with Captain Cesare Ditel; you'll find it with other trophies in the corridor between the library and the Stage Door lounge.

Good Reasons to Book These Ships

1. To see the spectacular shows, especially *Mystique*, go to the pizzeria afterwards, talk about the performance show with other audience members, then watch the stars come in for an after-show snack.
2. To get scuba certification in the New Waves program; the course costs $370 and passengers must sign up ahead of cruise departure or at the very beginning of the cruise.
3. To attend a captain's cocktail party where you don't have to stand in line for ages to shake hands and be photographed with the captain; on these ships everyone circulates throughout the three-deck atrium, drinks in hand, and anyone who wishes to be photographed can pose on the curved staircase for the ship's photographer.
4. To spend a day at a private beach in Mayreau or Princess Cays.
5. To get more spacious cabins for the money than almost anywhere else afloat.

Things You Won't Find On Board

1. A gym or spa with sea views.
2. Jogging permitted before 8 a.m.
3. Locked bookcases; Princess trusts these passengers not to steal books or games.
4. The best seats for the show in the front row; third row from the back, one level up from the main seating area, is better.
5. Captain Stubing (although his alter ego, Princess spokesman Gavin MacLeod, does show up sometimes).

Sky Princess ★★★★

The TSS Sky Princess, *constructed in 1984 in France's CNM shipyard near Toulon as Sitmar's* Fairsky, *was the last big steam turbine passenger ship to be built, probably the last that will ever be. TSS means turbine steamship, and while steamships are more expensive to operate than motor ships, they also offer a smoother, quieter ride. "She has an underwater body that is a masterpiece," said one of the officers who oversaw her construction. Smooth-riding but unfinished, she had to slip out of the shipyard in the dead of night, according to some crew members aboard at the time, because shipyard workers, fearful of losing their jobs when the project was done, were sabotaging their own work, building things during the daytime and breaking them again at night. The interior finishing was completed on the long crossing from France to Los Angeles.*

The welcome-aboard buffet on the* Sky Princess *was far more lavish than the other Love Boats.

Sky Princess was one of the early ships to be decorated by a team of designers, some of them noted for hotel rather than naval architecture. As a result, materials such as silk wall coverings, burled blond wood paneling, marble, Venetian glass and glove leather upholstery (instead of the Naugahyde prevalent then on many cruise ships) and subtle, harmonious shades of beige, gray, pale sage greens and soft rose were introduced into a sea of cheerful Scandinavian woolens in coral, marine blue and bright green. A recent refurbishment has kept the original design features virtually intact.

FOOTNOTE

When Sitmar operated the ships that became Sky Princess, Dawn Princess *and* Fair Princess *(only the* Sky Princess *remains in the fleet today) the late Boris Vlasov, who owned the line, insisted that white Swedish rubber rather than carpet lined all the stairwells, so passengers could see how clean everything was kept.*

The Brochure Says

"Passengers looking for comfort and understated elegance need look no further than the *Sky Princess*. Ultra-spacious, her casual, easy-going atmosphere pleases everyone from couples to teens."

Translation

Cabins aboard are larger than on the *Island*, *Golden* or *Pacific Princess*, the decor subtle, and the friendly Italian waiters like to joke with passengers. Children and teens find a lot to like aboard, including three pools, a fully supervised youth and teen center and the pizzeria, of course.

Cabins and Costs

Fantasy Suites: **Report Card: A**

Average Price PPPD: $829 including airfare.

Book one of the 10 AA category suites and you'll enjoy a private veranda as well as a separate living room with leather loveseat, four leather chairs, glass-and-chrome dining table, long marble-topped desk, stocked mini-bar and mini-refrigerator and TV. In the bedroom is a queen-sized bed (except Malaga and Amalfi suites, which have twin beds), robe and slippers, marble nightstand with four drawers, a dressing room with marble-topped table, three-way mirror, leather chair, big safe, built-in dressers with six drawers each, and two separate hanging closets with safes in each. The marble bathroom has a deep Jacuzzi tub.

Small Splurges: **Report Card: B+**

Average Price PPPD: $583.

Category B mini-suites on the Lido don't have private verandas but they do have picture windows, a bedroom with twin beds and wooden nightstand with two drawers, and a sitting room with long leather sofa, three leather armchairs, desk/dresser with marble inset, color TV, handsome marble lamp with linen shade, cabinet for bar glasses, mini-refrigerator, plenty of good mirrors, two full-length hanging closets with safe and bath with shower and long marble counter.

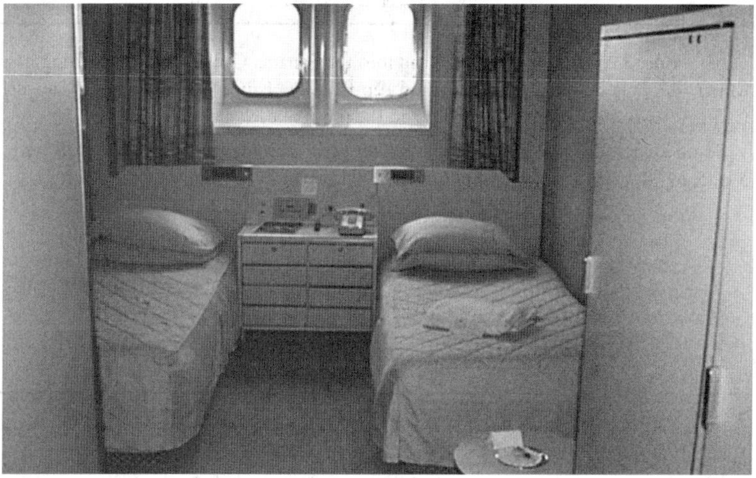

Cabin 148 is a Category C outside double.

Suitable Standards: **Report Card: C+**

Average Price PPPD: $303-$506, price varies depending on deck location and whether cabin is inside or outside.

All the standard inside and outside cabins are similar, with twin beds, nightstand, desk/dresser, two chairs, small table, generous closet space and bathroom with shower. Nearly half also have optional pull-down berths for third and fourth occupants. Six cabins are designated wheelchair accessible, including C 207 and C 208, outsides which are slightly larger than standards, with no lip on the doors, a shower with seat and pull bars, a roll-under sink, lower handles on the closets and a low-hanging rod accessible from a wheelchair; very wide inside with three windows.

Bottom Bunks: **Report Card: C+**

Average Price PPPD: $298.

The category M inside doubles are the least expensive accommodations on board, but are still fairly spacious and similar to the "Suitable Standards". Two lower beds, TV, very large closets, bath with shower, desk/dresser with chair and a second chair with small table.

INSIDER TIP

Library books must be checked in and out on the Sky Princess, *and anyone planning to abscond with an unfinished novel faces a $50 fine added to his cabin account.*

FOOTNOTE

Don't try this at home! The Love Boat cocktail is a blend of tequila, creme de cacao, Galliano, grenadine and cream.

Where She Goes

Sky Princess cruises the Caribbean and into the Panama Canal without transiting it in winter, offering 10-day itineraries round trip from Ft. Lauderdale, calling in Playa del Carmen/Cozumel, Limon, Cartagena and the private beach at Princess Cays.

Some longer 15-day Ft. Lauderdale-Los Angeles sailings are also available, calling in Montego Bay, Cartagena, Puerto Caldera, Acapulco and Cabo San Lucas.

The Bottom Line

This ship, one of the most elegant at the time of its inaugural sailing in 1984, has held up very well. The top deck indoor spa, including a whirlpool with raised stairs, was one of the first top deck, glass-walled spas; before that, indoor pools and a modest exercise area were usually found on a bottom deck amidships.

While the deck areas show their age in spots—worn astroturf, oil-stained teak—the interiors are as clean and pristine as when the ship was new.

Sky Princess is particularly good for families with children because the cabins with upper berths are spacious enough you won't feel cramped and because the child-care and teen programs on board are so well-arranged. The Youth Center is particularly pleasant, with linoleum floor, lie-down sofas and sturdy play tables. The Teen Center has lots of curved banquettes and game tables with industrial lamps overhead and a video game room with six games. The two dining rooms are light and bright with big windows. The buffets on this ship are much more elaborate than most of the others.

Fielding's Picks

Special Spots

1. Veranda Lounge, the venue for dancing before and after dinner, is a lovely room with its swirl marbleized carpet in gray and teal, with teal leather and fabric chairs, teal glass-topped tables with leather trim, sheer Austrian shades at the windows and pale wood walls.
2. The Pizzeria with its black bentwood chairs with red seats, big tile kitchen decorated with faux salamis, cheeses and hams, big round booths big enough for six or eight, and atop every table jars of crushed red pepper and oregano. For people who want a full lunch, a blackboard promotes a soup of the day and a pizza of the day.

3. The Horizon Lounge, an observation lounge with a forward-facing wall of windows, lots of cushy leather chairs in teal and caramel, and squashy cushions in the window ledges for additional seating with a view.
4. A beautiful library with two separate reading rooms, each with deep black leather chairs and wood-paneled walls, along with curved modern desks in wood and black leather for writing diaries or postcards.
5. The intimate little Melody Bar with its long granite bar lined with black leather swivel barstools, burled wood and mirrors on the walls, a perfect little hideaway for two.

Good Reasons to Book This Ship

1. The Pizzeria for its made-to-order pizza.
2. The big, lavish showroom with its thrust stage where you might see comedian Dick Gold, harmonica virtuoso Harry Bee, the juggling Zuniga Brothers and the Love Boat singers and dancers.
3. To buy some Lladro porcelain.
4. To compete in the passenger talent show.
5. To experience the smooth ride of the last passenger steamship ever built.

Things You Won't Find on Board

1. Alcoholic drinks available for 18-to-21 year-olds.
2. Silent elevators—the ones on the *Sky Princess* talk to you.
3. No full promenade deck all around the ship; the green astroturf-covered walking deck (no jogging) says 11 times around its perimeter is one mile and the textured dark red jogging track above the Sun Deck says 15 laps is a mile.
4. Marble bathroom counters on inside cabins.

Star Princess ★★★★

It was a unique experience to tour France's Chantiers de L'Atlantique shipyard in late 1988, to see a ship nearing completion that began life as Sitmar's FairMajesty *and by a stroke of a pen was turned into Princess'* Star Princess *overnight. That's why the* Star Princess *is not just like its sister ships* Crown *and* Regal. *When P&O bought Sitmar in July 1988, it acquired one ship under construction and two others on the drawing board, so because of the long planning and building time—two to three years—all three ships still carry many Sitmar characteristics, including Italian instead of British officers.*

Particularly memorable for us was sailing aboard the Star Princess *inaugural cruise with her godmother, the late Audrey Hepburn, as a fellow passenger.*

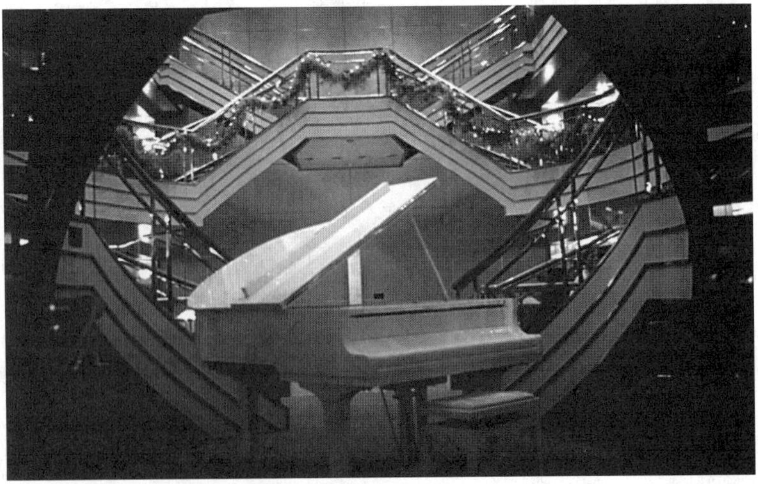

The atrium lobby and piano are framed by a dramatic staircase.

The *Star Princess* has one of the best pool-and-sun decks at sea. It runs most of the length of the vessel and stars two large swimming pools spanned by a raised sun deck. The area is filled out by an aft buffet cafe and a forward bar and pizzeria. Overall, she heralded a "new Princess," bigger, brighter, livelier than her predecessors, with a wider appeal and more accessibility to younger passengers than any of the previous ships from either Princess or Sitmar. A little more than a year after *Star Princess* first entered service, its median passenger age was seven years lower than the line's fleetwide average.

A three-deck atrium with a stainless steel kinetic sculpture dominates the amidships area. This is the vessel that first introduced the very popular La Patisserie cafe and pastry shop in the lobby area.

The spa, beauty salon, gym and massage areas, on the other hand, were relegated to below-decks without windows rather than given a prominent and sunny spot atop the ship as on the *Sky Princess*.

The Brochure Says

"...*Star Princess* also offers some of the largest standard staterooms in the industry. Connoisseurs of fine cruising will be dazzled by this modern-day floating resort."

Translation

An apt description. It's hard to think of anything you'd get at a big Caribbean resort hotel that you can't find on the *Star Princess*, except for sand between your toes.

Cabins and Costs

Fantasy Suites: **Report Card: A**

Average Price PPPD: $499 in the Caribbean including airfare.

The 14 AA category suites are top-of-the-line, measuring 530 square feet and named for popular Mediterranean ports. Inside the sliding glass doors is an open, L-shaped room divided into sitting and sleeping areas with sofa, two chairs, coffee table, queen-sized bed, nightstands and built-in desk. There's plenty of closet and storage space, two TV sets, a dressing room with mahogany built-in dressing table and large mirror, a spacious marble bathroom divided so the tub, separate shower stall and wash basin can be closed off to let the toilet and second wash basin double as powder room. A mini-bar is stocked with complimentary beverages, and a mini-refrigerator keeps everything cold.

Small Splurges: **Report Card: B**

Average Price PPPD: $442 in the Caribbean including airfare.

The 36 category A mini-suites are 370 square feet each, with private veranda, sitting area with built-in desk and counter as well as sofa and chairs, and a large bath with tub/shower combination.

Suitable Standards: **Report Card: A**

Average Price PPPD: $235-$316 in the Caribbean, including airfare.

All cabins aboard have twin beds that can be rearranged into one queen-sized bed, walk-in closet and separate dressing area, refrigerator and mini-bar, guest safe, terrycloth robes, hair dryers and color TV. Both outsides (with picture windows) and insides are the same size—180 square feet. Ten are designated wheelchair-accessible, and these measure 240 square feet with extra-wide doors and no thresholds.

Bottom Bunks: **Report Card: A**

Average Price PPPD: $214 in the Caribbean, including airfare.

The cheapest cabins are M category with two lower beds, only seven of them, located forward on Plaza Deck. Furnishings are the same as "Suitable Standards."

Where She Goes

Star Princess sails the Eastern Caribbean on a seven-day roundtrip itinerary out of Ft. Lauderdale, calling in Nassau, St. Thomas, St. Maarten and the private beach at Princess Cays in winter and spring.

The pool deck on the **Star Princess** *has a very popular waterfall.*

The Bottom Line

When a ship is this perfect for warm-weather cruising, we're puzzled as to why Princess sends it up to Alaska in the summer. But wherever it goes, it's a natural magnet for families and younger cruisers.

Sun Princess **Unrated**

The *Sun Princess* is the first of the new Grand Class ships for Princess, a 77,000-ton, 1950-passenger ship that will be followed in 1997 with sister ship *Dawn Princess*. Fairly deep-draft vessels at 26 feet, both ships come out of Italy's Fincantieri shipyard, which is also building the 100,000-ton-plus *Carnival Destiny*. The Italian-flag vessel is commanded by Italian officers, and carries an international crew of 900.

There's so much landscaping on board that the ship carries a full-time gardener as part of the crew.

A full-scale art-deco-style theater situated forward with tiered row seating and a 36-foot wide proscenium arch is supplemented by a second show lounge aft called Vista Lounge with a large dance floor/stage area.

A children's center "fun zone" devotes a lot of space to a splash pool, castle, doll's house, children's theater and ball jump, while a teen area called "Cyberspace" dings with video games and virtual reality machines.

Adults will find a huge casino with 150 slot machines plus poker, blackjack and roulette, with a wine-and-caviar bar located one deck below it. The classic pizzeria and the lobby patisserie Princess is noted for are also in place. Casual meals and dancing under the stars happen in the Horizon Court cafe, with indoor and outdoor eating areas, a dance floor and bar.

A swimming pool suspended between two decks has a pair of two whirlpool spas for relaxing under the stars, while a second pool amidships provides whirlpool spas, waterfall, island bar and nearby ice-cream stand. A paddle tennis court is built high atop the ship inside the funnel frame, and a wide teak promenade deck encircles the ship. Princess Links, an interactive golf simulator, features some of the world's most famous courses.

Cabins and Costs

Nearly 70 percent of the cabins on board have private verandas, and suites are furnished with wet bars, two TV sets, whirlpool spa tubs, separate shower and marble and stained glass trim. Cabin prices range from $206 to $521 PPPD, including airfare.

Where She Goes

The *Sun Princess* cruises the Western Caribbean in winter from Ft. Lauderdale, sailing Saturdays and calling at Princess Cays for a day at a private beach, Montego Bay, Grand Cayman and Playa del Carmen/Cozumel.

RADISSON SEVEN SEAS CRUISES

600 Corporate Drive, Suite 410, Fort Lauderdale, FL 33334
☎ (305) 776-6123, (800) 333-3333

History

This hybrid cruise line with three very different ships—what they have in common is superlative quality—came about through a series of marketing agreements. Radisson, of course, is a long-time hotel brand name which entered the cruise industry with the first major twin-hulled cruise vessel, the 354-passenger *Radisson Diamond*, owned by Finland's Diamond Cruise Inc., which debuted in 1992. Seven Seas is the San Francisco-based company marketing the elegant little 172-passenger *Song of Flower*, a Sea Goddess-like ship owned by Japan's "K" Line freight and container company under its "K" Line America subsidiary in New Jersey, and the 188-passenger *Hanseatic*, arguably the most luxurious expedition vessel in the world, owned by Germany's Hanseatic Cruises. Radisson Seven Seas Cruises was launched January 1, 1995, with 500 employees in the Ft. Lauderdale-based offices of the former Radisson Diamond Cruise.

—First cruise ship to be christened in the stern; it has no discernible bow. (*Radisson Diamond*, 1992, Greenwich, England).

Concept

Radisson Seven Seas says it aims to bring together three ultra-deluxe ships, exotic destinations worldwide and innovative shipboard programming to create three distinct styles of luxury cruising offering excellent service, intimate ambience and strong value for the dollar throughout the fleet.

Signatures

The *Radisson Diamond's* twin hull is an unmistakable sight in every port in the world, warranting at least a double-take if not a "What the hell is that?" Less known but almost equally unique is the ship's policy of using female rather than male servers in the dining room.

Song of Flower is among a handful of luxurious cruise vessels that distinguishes itself by not proffering tabs to be signed; virtually everything on board from bar beverages to tips is included. You pay extra only for laundry, beauty shop services, casino gambling and shop purchases. The distinctive blue lyre on the ship's twin funnels is now the logo for the entire line.

The *Hanseatic* is notable for its state-of-the-art environment-saving features, including an advanced non-polluting waste disposal system and a pollution-filtered incinerator which enable it to call in remote and environmentally sensitive areas.

Gimmicks

The *Radisson Diamond's* "An Evening at Don Vito's" is the liveliest and most delicious of all the cruise line alternative restaurants, with waiters in red aprons singing

"O Sole Mio" between serving up bites of everything that comes out of the special Italian kitchen that evening.

A "welcome back" libation greets *Song of Flower* passengers at the gangway when they return from grueling shore excursions—chilled champagne if it's a hot day in Southeast Asia, hot chocolate, hot buttered rum or mulled wine if it's a cold day in the Black Sea.

A "passenger bridge" on the *Hanseatic* is furnished with ocean charts and radar; in addition, passengers are free to visit the ship's real bridge whenever they wish.

Who's the Competition

The *Hanseatic* faces competition only from the *Bremen*, also a state-of-the-art expedition vessel which cruises with a similar mix of Europeans and North Americans. *Song of Flower* was competing mainly with the Sea Goddess ships until the debut of Silversea; now *Silver Cloud* and *Silver Wind*, although somewhat larger, are rivals. Seabourn and *Queen Odyssey* also provide a bit of competition but lack the all-inclusive policy that makes the other ships appealing to luxury-loving penny-pinchers. As for *Radisson Diamond*, that's a different situation entirely; it would seem to compete more with shoreside resorts and tours than other ships, except perhaps its own associate *Song of Flower*. Word of mouth has been the primary factor in attracting more and more passengers to these three vessels.

Who's Aboard

On all three ships, upscale middle-aged couples are the major passengers, along with older singles and younger, baby boomer pairs. *Radisson Diamond* has a number of group and incentive groups aboard on some sailings—the ship was originally created for that market but has found a huge acceptance from individual travelers as well. *Hanseatic's* luxurious version of soft adventures attracts a more cosmopolitan crowd than the earnest expedition types who like to rough it.

Who Should Go

People who don't like the idea of having to tip—tips are already included in the fares on all three vessels but passengers may offer additional money for special service at their own discretion.

People who worry about ship motion triggering seasickness should try the smooth-riding, twin-hulled *Radisson Diamond* with its four computer-operated, non-retractable stabilizers that correct pitch and roll after only one degree.

Who Should Not Go

There are some ship purists who would never set foot on the *Radisson Diamond* because of its boxy shape and twin hulls, and we can understand that reluctance, but it offers one of the finest food and hotel operations at sea, and when you're aboard, you're not really looking at its shape, are you?

The ships reserve the right to limit the number of children on board, but all except very mature teens and well-behaved 10-to-12-year-olds should not be aboard in any case.

The Lifestyle

What the three ships have in common is a small number of passengers in a relaxed but luxurious atmosphere with impeccable service and very good food. Entertainment, while it is provided, is a minor concern, as are casinos and gift shops, while enrichment lecturers, beauty services, fitness centers and alternative dining options are major on-board pluses.

Tips are included in the basic fares on all three ships, which makes the interrelationship between crew and passenger less forced, and all three provide a single open seating at mealtimes, letting passengers sit where and with whom they please.

Wardrobe

All three ships are relatively dressy, except that the *Hanseatic* says it wants the penguins to wear the tuxedos, and male passengers are perfectly O.K. in a dark suit. That's fine, but they also hint that they want him to be in a jacket, not necessarily with a tie, every night. The other vessels are a little more laid-back, with formal night meaning black tie or its equivalent, but casual nights dotted throughout the cruise where no jacket and tie at all are necessary.

Bill of Fare

The *Song of Flower* and *Radisson Diamond* outshine the *Hanseatic* a bit in the kitchen, but perhaps that's because they're dealing with a more homogenous passenger list and don't mind pushing the envelope when they've found something really interesting they want people to taste. On the *Radisson Diamond*, passengers are served beautiful meals in the most gorgeous dining room at sea, but when they wish, they can book the alternative dining experience, "An Evening at Don Vito's," a rollicking, finger-licking evening of home-cooked Italian food where you end up sampling a little bit of everything. The *Song of Flower* chefs and waiters are the ones we'd hire to run our own mansion if we were rich and famous.

Cuisine Report Card: Radisson Diamond A+, Song of Flower A+, Hanseatic B+

Showtime

Even on the *Hanseatic*, there's life after dinner, what with a quartet playing for dancing and an occasional folkloric troupe showing up to perform esoteric routines they learned from a Peace Corps volunteer. But showtime is not bigtime on these smallish ships, and it shouldn't be. We enjoy the Styleliner foursome that perform the music of Gershwin and Porter on the *Radisson Diamond's* scenery-less stage, as well as the amiable variety artists who double as shore excursion escorts on the *Song of Flower*, but these ships are not Broadway nor were meant to be. They're luxurious hideaways where you might just as soon spend an evening dining with friends or having dinner brought into your cabin and watching a video film.

Entertainment Report Card: B

Discounts

Early booking bonuses of $500 per person off the listed fares are in effect for the *Hanseatic* if you book by designated deadlines, and you get $500 off if you combine two back-to-back cruises. *Song of Flower* offers from $250 to $2050 per person for early bookings made 120 days before sailing, and includes free round-trip airfare and many shore excursions in its base rate. Combine two or more cruises back-to-back to total 15 nights and subtract another $1500. On *Radisson Diamond*, selected sailings deduct 50 percent of the fare of the second passenger in the cabin, plus adding airfare and free overnights on pre- and post-cruise stays.

The Bottom Line

We can think of no other cruise line that has three such dissimilar but very comparable ships. They're all small, intimate and upscale, with flawless European service and excellent food, fascinating itineraries and lavish accommodations. More remarkably, they give you a lot of value for the admittedly top-market prices. Strange bedfellows? Perhaps, but what they have in common is more important than how they are different from each other.

Radisson Diamond ★★★★★★

The first time we ever saw the Radisson Diamond *the brand new ship was moored in Tilbury, the Port of London, and right next to her was the long, sleek* Royal Princess. *The effect was like seeing the short wide robot R2D2 from* Star Wars *hanging around with Cary Grant.*

***The swimming pool on* Radisson Diamond.**

The *Radisson Diamond* has a unique SWATH design—Small Waterplane Area Twin Hull—with an extra-wide superstructure atop two pontoons. There are four special-design stabilizers, two forward and two aft, inside the well, permanent rather than retractable, and computer-controlled to negate rolling, pitching and heaving. The vessel roll is only one-fifth that of a conventional monohull ship with one-tenth of the noise and vibration levels, the captain says.

Inside, the extra-wide beam gives a great sense of spaciousness. A center atrium with stairs and two glass elevators makes it simple to get around the ship; all the passenger cabins and public rooms are clustered around it. A rubberized, nonskid jogging track, spa, beauty salon, fitness center, golf putting area and driving cage are on the upper deck areas, and a self-contained watersports marina allows passengers to go water-skiing, windsurfing, sailing or riding wave runners when sea and weather conditions permit.

The Brochure Says

"The *Diamond* is truly one-of-a-kind, the only twin-hull passenger vessel in the world. Her innovative design offers you a smooth and stable cruise. This unique configuration allows us to provide our guests with more spacious surroundings than any ship at sea."

Translation

They're so proud of their ship they've got to exaggerate a little. It is innovative and spacious, but not completely unique. There are several twin-hull passenger vessels that have been around longer than the *Radisson Diamond*, although none of the others are quite as large. The 49-passenger *Executive Explorer*, for instance, has been carrying passengers for more than a decade and was still in business when we saw her in Alaska a few months ago. And while the *Diamond's* passenger space ratio of 57.33 is impressive, it's still smaller than the *Europa's* 61.68.

Cabins and Costs

Fantasy Suites: **Report Card: A+**

Average Price PPPD: $932 including airfare from the east coast and two-night land package.

A hand-painted mural in the style of Henri Rousseau decorates each of a pair of master suites measuring 522 square feet, with a large sitting area with puffy pale blue leather sofa, two chairs, a full-sized desk, mini-refrigerator, fully stocked liquor cabinet and TV/VCR. A king-sized bed has a beige and blue coverlet with greyhounds stitched on it; a sliding etched glass panel can close off the bedroom from the entry hallway and closet area. On the private veranda outside are two chairs and a table. The bathroom has a double basin in a marble counter, separate water closet, stall shower and Jacuzzi tub.

Small Splurges: **Report Card: A**

Average Price PPPD: $643 including airfare from the east coast and two-night land package.

Most of the cabins on board have private balconies, and in 243 square feet you'll find queen-sized or twin beds, a sitting area with sofa, chairs and built-in desk, a marble bathroom with tub and shower—short, deep Finnish-style tubs—and TV/VCR, minibar and refrigerator and built-in dresser and storage area.

Suitable Standards: **Report Card: A**

Average Price PPPD: $521 including airfare from the east coast and a two-night land package.

The third cabin type aboard is the same size as the veranda cabin (243 square feet) but with a larger sitting area instead of the veranda. You'll have a white leather sofa and two chairs, built-in desk and dresser, wide window wall and marble bathroom with tub/shower combination. Two cabins are designated wheelchair-accessible.

Bottom Bunks: **Report Card: NA**

N/A

Where She Goes

The *Radisson Diamond* transits the Panama Canal between Puerto Rico and Costa Rica in winter, making nine-day cruises that visit St. Thomas, Curaçao, Cartagena and the San Blas Islands, along with a two-night overland excursion to San Jose and the Poas Volcano. These cruises are followed by a series of Caribbean sailings out of San Jose that range from four to 14 nights.

An art deco style bar with chrome barstools aboard the **Radisson Diamond.**

The Bottom Line

Despite the ship's unconventional looks, it offers a supremely appealing cruise experience. Our eleven days were gloriously relaxing without any ports of call. Why eleven days, you may ask? The ship's maximum comfortable cruising speed is only about 12 or 13 knots; she'd never win the Blue Riband.

Fielding's Picks

Splendid Spots

1. The Grill, a cluster of several teak-floored rooms with glass walls to the deck on both sides, where buffet breakfasts and lunches supplemented with cooked-to-order à la carte dishes are served at wooden tables; it turns into Don Vito's most evenings with red tablecloths, singing waiters and a constantly changing Italian menu.
2. In the coolly elegant Club, mushroom-colored leather chairs trimmed in ebony, mirrors and potted palms, lend a movie-set 1930s look; you expect to see William Powell and Myrna Loy make an entrance.
3. The most romantic dining room at sea is wide and airy and almost two decks high, with plenty of tables for two against an aft window wall, gilt frame armchairs with striped silk upholstery, art deco pillars and a 1930s frieze of figures, all in tones of copper, silver and bronze. On the evenings when candlelight dinners are served against a background of the fading sunset, it is indescribably lovely.
4. The Windows is a multi-level lounge with ice blue leather furniture, black granite bars and silver and gray barstools, a wide wood dance floor and raised stage with bandstand in front of a window wall; a lavish tea is set out here every afternoon.
5. The Constellation Center, a meeting room and lecture hall with rows of red leather chairs in blond wood frames; this is where art auctions, slide lectures and film screenings (with a big silver punch bowl of hot popcorn) take place.

Good Reasons to Book This Ship

1. If you're worried about ship motion that might cause seasickness, the twin hulls prevent pitching and rolling.
2. If you're a claustrophobe worried about ships being confining, check out the extra width and spaciousness.
3. To see a new series of Bettman Archive videos and catch up with some "Great Minds" from the prestigious Humphery Institute of Public Affairs when they lecture aboard.
4. If you love real Italian home cooking, "An Evening at Don Vito's" trattoria passes around trays of antipasto, followed by platters of lobster risotto, penne with porcini and tomato sauce and tortellini in butter and fresh sage—and those are just the starters. Then comes veal scaloppine with fresh vegetables and a rolling cart of Italian desserts like tirama su and cannoli, all of it served with generous complimentary portions of chilled Soave and Ruffino Chianti.

Things You Won't Find On Board

1. A bathtub you can stretch out in; the Finnish tubs are so short that tall bathers end up with their knees under their chins.
2. A place on deck where you can stand and watch the lines cast off; the configuration of the ship doesn't allow a view straight down to the water.
3. A traditional lifeboat drill; instead, passengers are shown where the jackets are stored on deck.

REGAL CRUISES

4199 34th Street, Suite B 103, St. Petersburg, FL 33711
☎ *(813) 867-1300, (800) 270-SAIL*

History

Regal Cruises was founded by executives from Liberty Travel and GoGo Tours in 1993 when the companies acquired the venerable *Caribe I*, "the happy ship" from Commodore Cruises, and turned it into the *Regal Empress* almost overnight. As it turned out, they may have started up too quickly, and with the crew consisting of half newly-hired tyros, the ship failed its first two sanitation inspections in May, 1993, when attempting to initiate its start-up "cruises to nowhere" from New York.

Throughout the summer, the crew tried to facilitate a demanding four-hour turnaround, and by the first season's repositioning for winter "cruises to nowhere" from Tampa, had gotten a general idea of how embarkations and disembarkations should work.

Concept

While a few longer cruises may be offered, Regal depends primarily on short-term "cruises to nowhere" for first-time cruisers and budget-minded vacationers.

Signatures

Two-day party cruises jamming onboard a capacity quota of the-more-the-merrier types.

Gimmicks

An adults-only spa to keep the kids out; candy bar bingo for the kids; 60s music and theme cruises with waitresses in poodle-cloth skirts.

Who's the Competition

There's nobody who can match the *Regal Empress's* low, low published brochure rates out of New York or St. Petersburg, Florida.

Who's Aboard

A lot of young first-time cruisers, singles and couples and families, party-hearty types who arrive ready for a good time.

Who Should Go

Just who's aboard, plus a New Yorker or West Coast Floridian who'd like a really low-priced getaway on a lovely old ocean liner with a friendly, if sometimes unpolished, staff.

Who Should Not Go

Traditional cruise veterans who have specific ideas about wardrobe and behavior; fussy eaters; people who demand top-notch service.

The Lifestyle

Cramming everything from cruises that's fun or interesting into the format. The line itself calls it "Regal Revelry on the High Seas" on the daily programs. There's a lot going on all day and a plethora of shore excursions, plus mealtimes happening every hour or so.

Wardrobe

The line specifies no tank tops or shorts in the dining room, but as often happens with first-time cruisers, they may forget to read the program and so enter in happy ignorance in inappropriate costume and are rarely corrected by the friendly crew, who don't want to hurt any potential tipper's feelings. What Regal Cruises would like to see are people who dress up a little bit for formal nights, even if it's only a jacket without a tie for men. The brochure models, always a tip-off to what the line imagines is right, are studiously casual but well-groomed, shown in polo shirts or sport coats without ties as a rule.

Bill of Fare

Feeding times are frequent on the *Regal Empress*, with early-bird coffee at 6 a.m., dining room breakfast 7 to 9 and poolside buffet breakfast 7 to 10. Lunch open seating buffets on shore days run from 11 to 1:30 in the dining room; on days at sea lunch is served later. Teatime with sandwiches and cookies is served at 4. First seating dinner is at 6, second seating at 8:15, and there is usually a midnight buffet.

The food is delivered in generous portions, but during our time aboard did not seem particularly well prepared, especially from the buffets, where meats were dry and tough from being too long on the steam table. We may have hit an off-period, however, because friends (actually, a friend—we don't know that many other people who have ever sailed aboard this ship) says it was acceptable to good during his cruise.

Cuisine Report Card: D

Showtime

The entertainment format follows the usual mass-market cruise pattern: lots of bingo and game shows with the cruise staff, dancing to the ship's orchestra, late-night disco with a DJ and a few variety artists of varying capabilities. The biggest hit aboard is the lip sync show in which passengers recruited ahead of time double in ship-provided costumes and wigs as, say, Sonny and Cher to mime "I Got You Babe" and suchlike amusements.

Entertainment Report Card: D

NO NOs

In the show lounge on the Regal Empress, *video and flash cameras are not permitted during the performance, the first two rows do not get drink service during the show and there is no smoking permitted in the entire lounge during the show.*

Discounts

They don't really need to offer discounts with their low brochure prices.

The Bottom Line

You get more than you pay for on this line, partly because of the lovely old ship itself, graceful and beautiful in many areas like the library and Mermaid Bar, plus the warm and friendly crew, from the captain and hotel manager down to the ebullient youth counselor Casey and the friendly Filipino crew. It's not a fancy cruise, and isn't meant to be. You're supposed to be ready for a good time or a party-time, and Emily Post ain't nowhere in sight. Let 'er rip!

Regal Empress ★★

Captain Uwe Bunsen, master of the Regal Empress, *has been at sea for 40 years and was for many years captain of the* Boheme *from Commodore Cruises, which now belongs to the Scientology group, and was 28 times in the Antarctic when he worked for Society Expeditions. But the former* Caribe I *is his favorite ship, and now he's back with her as the* Regal Empress. *"She's still one of the traditional ships, with beautiful design...only the plastic is missing."*

The *Regal Empress*, the former *Caribe I*, was built as the *Olympia* for the Greek Line in 1953 as a two-class ocean liner, making her maiden voyage from Glasgow and Liverpool to New York. In 1974 she was laid up in Piraeus, a victim of the overall cruise malaise brought on by the success of the transatlantic jet planes. In 1981, a German company purchased her and renamed her *Caribe*, but left her laid up in Piraeus, changing the flag from Greek to German. In 1983, with a major refit, she sailed from Piraeus to become the *Caribe I* for Commodore Cruise Lines. Very few changes have been made since she became the *Regal Empress*, so it's a wonderful experience for a ship buff to wander around and spot the beautiful spaces.

The Brochure Says

"We take pride in our decor, a study in quiet elegance with warm woods, tasteful fabrics and the occasional Art Deco touch. The *Regal Empress* boasts some of the largest staterooms afloat."

Translation

This is a lovely old ship and even the two-day party cruisers to nowhere fall silent when they peek into the elegant library. And for the money, you can get some very nice cabins. (See "Cabins and Costs".)

Cabins and Costs

A classic wood-paneled suite aboard **Regal Empress**; *you could almost imagine Fletcher Christian sleeping here.*

Fantasy Suites: **Report Card: B**

Average Price PPPD: $133 cruise only in the Caribbean.

While not huge nor unrelievedly lavish, there are two suites forward on Upper Deck that call back the grand old days of ocean cruising, even perhaps the captain's quarters on the *Mayflower*, but who's counting? The Admiral Suites forward on upper deck (accept no substitutes; there are other less admirable Admiral Suites on this ship), in particular the Commodore Suite # F, has a lovely wood interior, two rooms with the bedroom separate, windows facing forward, built-in dresser, glass coffee table, hair dryer, fresh flowers, mini-refrigerator, and the sofas in the sitting room convert to beds if you want to put friends or family inside at a reduced rate.

Small Splurges: **Report Card: C**

Average Price PPPD: $109 cruise only in the Caribbean.

The category Two deluxe mini-suites with mini-refrigerator, double bed plus two lower berths, sitting area with sofas, two windows and hair dryer are quite acceptable for the price.

Suitable Standards: **Report Card: C-**

Average Price PPPD: $101 cruise only in the Caribbean.

A category Four cabin on Upper Deck may have portholes instead of windows, twin beds and an optional upper berth, but you'll also find floral bedspreads, a chair, adequate closets and a bathroom with shower only.

Bottom Bunks: **Report Card: C-**

Average Price PPPD: $78 cruise only in the Caribbean.

In one of the lowest cabin categories, 10, in cabin B 24, you can find an inside with two lower beds, two dressers and two closets that will be perfectly adequate for a budget getaway for two.

Where She Goes

In the winter, *Regal Empress* sails from Port Manatee in St. Petersburg, Florida, on Mexico and Caribbean cruises to Key West, Cozumel and Playa del Carmen on four-, five- and six-day cruises, some including calls in Grand Caymen and Jamaica.

The Bottom Line

If the ship looks a little weary around the edges, think a little tenderness. She's had a long, hard life with party-time passengers who don't always appreciate her finer points. But for some impecunious people who would love to get even a tiny taste of what cruising is all about, this is a wonderful entry-level product—so long as you're not a cruise veteran who's just looking for a cheap thrill.

Fielding's Picks

Good Reasons to Book This Ship

1. The price, perhaps the lowest in all cruising today.
2. To poke around and discover some of the lovely little architectural and decorative surprises aboard.
3. If your budget is strapped and you need to get away for a couple of days of r&r.
4. If you'd like to take a cruise to Cozumel that doesn't cost too much.

RENAISSANCE CRUISES

1800 Eller Drive, Ft. Lauderdale, FL 33335
☎ *(305) 463-0982, (800) 525-5350*

History

Originally launched in 1989 by the Norwegian-based shipping company Fearnley and Eger, Renaissance began with an innovative idea—to build eight virtually identical 100-passenger luxury ships in a two-year period (actually, it took two-and-a-half years).

Before all the ships were completed, however, Fearnley and Eger foundered, filing for bankruptcy in May, 1991, and Renaissance was acquired by a partnership of Italy's Cameli Group and a holding company controlled by Edward B. Rudner, a travel entrepreneur who headed up Certified Tours and had a long association with Alamo Rent-A-Car.

Today, Renaissance operates six of its original eight ships, sailing them in the Caribbean, Mediterranean, Northern Europe, the Seychelles and African islands and Indonesia.

—First company to market a fleet of eight interchangeable ships.

—First cruise line to concentrate its marketing almost exclusively by direct mail to previous cruisers.

—First cruise line to charter a super-luxury airline to ferry passengers nonstop between Los Angeles and Antigua (aboard MGM Grand Air for *Renaissance III*, 1992).

FOOTNOTE

Between Fearnley and Eger's bankruptcy declaration in May, 1991, and the completion of the sale to the new owners in August, 1991, two of the line's ships were "arrested" (impounded), one in Antigua and the other in Europe. While the seizures were temporary, only until funds owed were paid out, the incidents created embarrassment for the new line.

Concept

Renaissance concentrates on destination-oriented seven- and 14-day cruises built around pre- and post-cruise land packages, on-board lecture programs to enrich the passenger's travel experience and in-depth shore excursions. The company describes the ships as having a "private club atmosphere," promoting open seating at mealtimes and the all-outside-suites configuration of the vessels. A shallow draft allows the Renaissance ships to go into ports larger ships must avoid.

Signatures

The repetition of the company name in the ship's names, each followed by its own Roman numeral, creates a strong identity factor for the line. With emphasis on the brand name rather than an individual ship, Renaissance is free to substitute one vessel for another or shuffle the fleet around when necessary. "Besides," the line's former president Mark Conroy (now president of Radisson Seven Seas) once quipped, "it's impossible to remember eight different names. I can't even remember the Seven Dwarfs."

Gimmicks

Renaissance often sells the destination more than the ship by distributing single-product flyers advertising only one cruise in detail rather than a full cruise brochure, and putting more pictorial emphasis on the scenery and activities at the destination rather than the ship and its lifestyle.

The direct mail brochures touting two-for-the-price-of-one sailings or freebies from roundtrip airfare to African safaris to low-cost upgrades to business class are designed primarily to attract the line's predominantly yuppie/baby boomer audience which can afford to buy whatever cruise it wants but which likes to feel it's getting something for nothing.

Who's the Competition

Nobody really fits into the niche where Renaissance has positioned itself, although there are certain similarities with Sea Goddess in ship size, open meal seatings and the all-suites concept, and with Windstar in a "casual elegance" dress code and day-long visits to beach-oriented islands. While a cursory glance at itineraries might bring some expedition lines to mind, Renaissance is strictly a mainstream "soft adventure" product with no bird-watching or desert hikes.

Who's Aboard

Well-traveled first-time cruisers who are booking for the itinerary rather than the ship; repeat Renaissance veterans who found out they loved the ships as much as the destinations; and bargain hunters who could never resist a two-fer. They're mostly couples, mostly between their late 20s and mid-50s, with an easy camaraderie with fellow passengers.

Who Should Go

Anyone who wants to travel to faraway places and be guaranteed a comfortable suite, good to excellent food and a non-regimented on-board life.

Who Should Not Go

Families with young children—there's nowhere for the kids to play or get out of the way of the adults; senior singles from Cunard or Royal Cruise Line ships who'll complain "there's nothing to do"; anyone expecting a big-time gambling and nightlife cruise—the casino is limited to one blackjack table and four slot machines and the entertainment is a musical trio playing for dancing.

The Lifestyle

People who like Sea Goddess, Radisson Seven Seas, Seabourn, Silversea and Windstar sailings will immediately be at home with the dine-when-you-wish and sit-where-you-like freedom; the tendency to treat passengers as adults rather than children who have to be constantly entertained and herded about (except during the overland portions, where some organization is essential); and the lack of a regimented dress code.

Wardrobe

The dress code calls for "comfortable elegance," meaning no jacket and tie is ever required although plenty of passengers do dress up in the evening. Resortwear is the operative word—things like silk shirts, linen pants, gauzy cotton skirts and the like.

Day wear is casual clothing from jogging suits to shorts and T-shirts, whatever is appropriate to the climate and destination.

NO NOs

The line specifically requests that jeans, shorts, T-shirts and tennis shoes not be worn in the dining room at dinner.

Bill of Fare

The cuisine is contemporary restaurant-style cooking, much of it prepared to order. While simple breakfast and lunch buffets are served on deck for people who don't want to change from their bathing suits, most passengers take all their meals in the dining room. At lunchtime, there is usually an expansive buffet of salads, shellfish, cold meats, sandwiches, breads, cheese and desserts, and guests are also offered a full à la carte menu for hot orders. All-day room service sandwiches are available in the cabins as well as Continental breakfast.

Low-calorie dishes are available every meal, and all dinners provide five main dish choices plus two always-available options, broiled steak with baked potato and broiled chicken.

During our three cruises with Renaissance, the food has always been good to excellent, but we have encountered some veterans in port during the past year that felt the quality of food they'd enjoyed on one ship had not been duplicated on a different ship. This may go back to the chef in the kitchen at the time, although a good head of operations should strive to keep things up to par throughout the fleet.

Cuisine Report Card: A-

Discounts

Past passengers get enticing two-for-one cruise buys or free airfare and overland package offers constantly in the mail, good if they book by a certain deadline. Groups qualify for discounts, and some frequent-flyer organizations also provide Renaissance discounts.

The Bottom Line

On our most recent sailing, we found the basic Renaissance cruise experience that we had enjoyed twice previously still very much intact, with the same care to food and service that we found on earlier sailings. But despite the ships' handsome, spick-and-span interiors, the exteriors and deck areas always look as if they need more spit-and-polish maintenance than they get.

Given the moderate prices for the quality of accommodations, more people should sample Renaissance if they enjoy small-ship, unstructured cruising. Unfortunately, the line is still not as well known as it should be among the travel agent community or the general public.

Renaissance III & IV ★★★★
Renaissance V–VIII ★★★★

It was aboard the inaugural cruise of the Renaissance I *that we learned Krakatau is not east of Java, as the old movie title had it, but west of Java and east of Sumatra in the Sunda Straits. We had gone ashore on the hot black volcanic sand to photograph a beach picnic for a* Bon Appétit *article about small luxury cruise ships, and when we uncorked the sweating, chilled bottle of California Chardonnay to pour it into the glasses, half a dozen ragged Sumatran fisherman surrounded us, holding out their own cups for a sample. We wonder how many cruise lines besides Renaissance have put their passengers ashore on the black sand beach at Krakatau.*

The ship layouts are very simple, basically five decks, each with some cabins amidships and forward, and public areas concentrated aft. The lowest passenger deck houses the restaurant, the next deck up the lobby and main lounge, the next up the piano bar and casino, the next up the swimming pool, whirlpool spa and outdoor pool bar, and the topmost the sun deck, which is forward of the four top category cabins.

Renaissance III and *IV* are identical sisters, while *Renaissance V-VIII*, all identical to each other, are slightly larger than the first pair.

All accommodations on board are suites, but some are more suite-like than others. (See "Cabins and Costs", for more detail.) Tucked away here and there are a small beauty salon, a gift shop, card room, library, sauna and a couple of exercise machines in a makeshift gym area.

The Brochure Says

"Relax in...our intimate Piano Bar in The Club, or try your luck in the Casino. Peruse The Library full of best-sellers and current videos."

Translation

And all without taking more than ten steps in any direction.

Cabins and Costs

A standard cabin provides twin beds or queen-sized bed.

Fantasy Suites: **Report Card: B+**

Average Price PPPD: $500 in the Caribbean plus air add-ons.

The top-priced suites on these vessels are literally on the top and called Renaissance Suites. They have private verandas, sitting area with sofa, two chairs, cocktail table, mini-refrigerator and desk/dresser with TV/VCR in 250 square feet of space. The bed can be arranged as twins or queen-sized, and there's generous closet space, bathroom and, in some, separate dressing area.

Small Splurges: **Report Card: A**

Average Price PPPD: $327 in the Caribbean plus air add-ons.

Unless you're set on having a private veranda and don't mind portholes instead of windows, we think the best buys aboard these vessels are the Superior Suites on the III and IV, two large rooms with big walk-in closet and large bath with marble counter. They're 287 square feet, the biggest suites on any of the vessels, and conveniently steps away from the restaurant. On the V-VIII, they measure 210 square feet, have big windows and walk-in closets.

Suitable Standards: **Report Card: B+**

Average Price PPPD: $285 in the Caribbean plus air add-ons.

The standard suite is an outside suite with an average of 210 square feet, with separate sitting area with sofa and chairs, bath and plenty of storage space.

Bottom Bunks: **Report Card: NA**

There are no accommodations in this category on the Renaissance ships; the cheapest cabins are the suites described under "Suitable Standards," above.

The small casino aboard has one blackjack table.

Where She Goes

In the first year, the line proudly named just about every sea and continent in the world short of Antarctica, but as realism settled in, based on balance sheets and bookings, the itineraries were narrowed to a few choice spots in the world—the Seychelles, the Caribbean and Indonesia in the winter, the Mediterranean and the Baltic in summer. Ask not which ship goes where—they're all more or less alike and it doesn't really matter. Just call and request to be put on their brochure mailing list.

INSIDER TIP

You can save money over the brochure price by taking advantage of one of the many discount possibilities. (See "Discounts".)

The Bottom Line

While not quite in the league of Sea Goddess, Seabourn, Silversea and Radisson Seven Seas, Renaissance offers excellent itineraries and a pleasurable on-board experience. Three caveats: The shallow draft of these vessels means sometimes bumpy rides in rough seas. Exercise equipment and self-service buffets sometimes get short shrift on these compact little ships. Last time we were aboard, the buffet filled the space originally designated for the gym and the exercise equipment (both pieces) had been relegated to a covered outdoor area on a lower deck.

But worst of all, the "suggested tipping guidelines" are outrageous (see "Keelhaul", earlier in this section).

Renaissance cabins are large enough for entertaining.

Fielding's Picks

Favorite Spots

1. The pretty Restaurant (terminology can be basic on ships this small) has plenty of tables for two, but passengers often want to gravitate to larger tables as they get to know each other, so there are also 4s and 6s, some sofa/banquettes and very comfortable chairs.
2. The sleek beige piano bar called The Club, where afternoon tea is usually served, card games are played and the casino operates to a piano background when the pianist is not needed to fill out the trio in the lounge downstairs.

3. The Lounge is where passengers gather for lectures, pre-dinner cocktails and dancing, and after-dinner dancing.
4. The Lobby, a cool, comfortable spot where the information desk is located, as well as (on the III and IV), a seating area convenient for waiting for friends or sinking into to cool off after a hot visit ashore.
5. The Library, where books and videotapes can be taken out whenever you wish; all cabins have TV sets with VCR capability.

Good Reasons to Book These Ships

1. To go to some of the world's most exotic ports in complete comfort and ease.
2. To be guaranteed an outside suite, no matter how much or how little you pay.
3. To travel in a full, luxurious, well-planned land-and-sea program that is not a bags-in-the-hall-at-six a.m., everybody-on-the-bus-at-seven package.
4. To have the luxury of dining when and with whom you please instead of being regimented into a set time and table.
5. To get on that repeat passenger mailing list that sends you two-for-one offers.

Things You Won't Find On Board

1. A children's program or playroom; don't bring small children aboard because you'll be punishing yourselves, them and your fellow passengers.
2. Space for two people at a time in the swimming pool; these birdbath-size waterholes are strictly plunge pools to dip into and get wet.
3. Inside cabins.
4. Wheelchair-accessible cabins, although the vessel does have an elevator.
5. Roulette; the casino consists of one blackjack table and a couple of slot machines.

ROYAL CARIBBEAN

1050 Caribbean Way, Miami, FL 33132
☎ *(305) 539-6000, (800) 327-6700*

The signature Viking Crown Lounge and RCCL logo.

History

In 1969, three Norwegian shipping companies, I.M. Skaugen, Gotaas Larsen and Anders Wilhelmsen, founded RCCL for the purpose of offering year-round seven and 14-day cruises out of Miami. Now owned by Wilhelmsen and the Hyatt Hotels' Pritzger family of Chicago, Royal Caribbean Cruises Ltd. is a publicly traded company on the New York Stock Exchange.

The spring 1996 delivery of the *Splendour of the Seas* brings the line's total to 10 vessels. Just past its 25th anniversary, RCCL is definitely one a handful of major players in the cruise industry.

—First cruise line to commission three new ships expressly for the Caribbean cruise market, *Song of Norway* (1970), *Nordic Prince* (1971) and *Sun Viking* (1972).

—First cruise line to "stretch" a ship, cutting it in half and dropping in a new mid-section, then putting it back together (*Song of Norway*, 1978).

—First cruise line to commission a specially designed ship for three- and four-day cruises (*Nordic Empress*, 1990).

—First seagoing, 18-hole miniature golf course (on *Legend of the Seas*, 1995).

—First cruise line to open shoreside hospitality centers in popular ports where passengers can leave packages, make phone calls, bone up on local shopping or sightseeing, get a cold drink and use toilet facilities (1995).

—Owners of the three largest ships ever built expressly for cruising, the 73,941-ton sisters *Monarch of the Seas* (1991) and *Majesty of the Seas* (1992) and their predecessor, the 73,192-ton *Sovereign of the Seas* (1988). It's typical of the company's conservatism that the contract to build the two later vessels was not signed until the *Sovereign* had already been in service nearly a year and proved itself a money-maker. The size record falls in the fall of 1996 with the debut of Carnival's 100,000-ton *Carnival Destiny*.

Concept

Consistency is the key word here. RCCL aims to provide a cruise experience to mainstream, middle-of-the-road passengers that is consistent in style, quality and pricing, with a majority of the ships following a consistent year-round schedule. Rod McLeod, head of sales and marketing, calls it "the doughnut factor" from a travel agent who once commented that what he liked best about RCCL was that all the doughnuts on all the line's ships taste exactly the same.

Signatures

RCCL ships are easily recognized at a distance because of the Viking Crown Lounge, a cantilevered round glass-walled bar and observation lounge high atop the ships projecting from or encircling the ship's funnel; company president Edward Stephan dreamed it up after seeing the Seattle Space Needle.

FOOTNOTE

When RCCL sold its Nordic Prince *to British-based Airtours last spring, the new owners didn't get to keep the Viking Crown Lounge; the cantilevered signature bar was removed before delivery.*

Lounges, bars and restaurants on board are named for Broadway musicals and operettas, sometimes with unintentionally funny results, as with the *Sun Viking's* Annie Get Your Gun Lounge. (That's also a musical that few of today's RCCL passengers would remember.)

FOOTNOTE

We fantasize over musical titles they haven't yet used on the RCCL ships, like a dining room named for Grease *or* Hair, *or a gym called* Black and Blue.

Gimmicks

ShipShape Dollars, given out each time a passenger participates in an exercise or sports activity; with six you get egg roll. Actually, you get egg-yolk yellow T-shirts proclaiming the wearer ShipShape. Passengers compete wildly for them and proudly wear them for years afterward aboard cruise ships of competing lines.

Who's the Competition

RCCL competes directly with Carnival and Norwegian Cruise Line for Caribbean passengers, but it also vies price-wise with more upscale lines like Celebrity and Princess. The line's new megaliners have brought in a more glitzy sheen, with flashy gaming rooms created by a Las Vegas casino designer instead of a ship designer. The company has also gone head-to-head with Carnival in the mini-cruise market in south Florida, pitting its ladylike *Nordic Empress* against the neon-throbbing *Fan-*

tasy and glow-in-the-dark *Ecstasy*, and in Los Angeles, where its glitzy *Viking Serenade* is getting some lively competition from Carnival's even glitzier *Holiday*.

Who's Aboard

All-American couples from the heartland between 40 and 60, with new clothes, new cameras and nice manners; families with fairly well-behaved children; two or three 30-something couples traveling together; born-to-shop types who find the line's newer ships with their mall-like galleries familiar and comforting; clean-cut young couples on their honeymoons; single 20-somethings on holiday sharing an inexpensive inside cabin, more often females than males.

Statistically, the median age is a relatively low 42, with a household income from $40,000 to $75,000. One-fourth are repeat passengers, half are first-time cruisers. More Europeans, Australians and Latin Americans are also gravitating to the line.

Who Should Go

These are ideal ships for first-time cruisers because the staff and the signage instruct and inform without appearing to lecture, putting everyone at ease right away. Also for honeymooners, fitness freaks (except on the *Sun Viking* and *Song of Norway*, which don't have gyms), sunbathers, big families on a reunion and stressed-out couples who want some time together in a resort atmosphere. Baby Boomers and their juniors 25 to 45 years old will always be warmly welcomed: RCCL wants YOU!

Who Should Not Go

Dowager veterans of the world cruise.

Small ship enthusiasts.

Anyone who dislikes regimentation.

The Lifestyle

RCCL's ships follow a traditional cruise pattern, with specified dress codes for evening, and two meal seatings in the dining room at assigned tables for a minimum of four and a maximum of eight or ten; very few if any tables for two are available. A day-long program of games, activities and entertainment on board is supplemented by shore excursions that emphasize sightseeing, golf and watersports.

Wardrobe

RCCL makes it easy for passengers by spelling out dress-code guidelines in the brochure. A normal seven-day Caribbean cruise has four casual nights where sport shirts and slacks are suggested for men, two formal nights where women wear cocktail dress or evening gowns and men wear suits and ties or tuxedos, and one or more theme nights where passengers may don '50s or country/western garb if they wish. During the daytime, comfortable casual clothing—jogging outfits, shorts or slacks, T-shirts, bathing suits and coverups—is appropriate on deck but sometimes not in the dining room.

NO NOs

No bathing suits, even with coverups, are allowed in the dining room at any time. Shorts, jeans and tank tops are not permitted after 6 p.m.

INSIDER TIP

Tuxedos are for rent on board most RCCL ships; ask your agent to check when booking if you think you may want to rent one.

Bill of Fare

Non-threatening, special-occasion food is produced by an affiliated catering company on a rotating set menu that is similar but not identical on the different ships. There's a wide variety and good range of choices, and the preparation is capable if not inspired. Dinner includes seven appetizers (four of them juices), three soups, two salads, five main dishes and six desserts (three of them ice creams). On a typical day main dishes may include crabmeat cannelloni, sole Madagascar, pork loin au jus, roast duckling and sirloin steak. In addition, a nightly vegetarian menu, a kids' menu and a ShipShape low-fat, low-calorie menu are offered.

Our very favorite from the latter seems tailored to The Ladies Who Lunch—it starts with a shrimp cocktail without sauce, then consomme, hearts of lettuce salad with carrot curls and fat-free dressing, followed by poached fish and vegetables, then rich, sugary Key Lime Pie with a whopping 12 grams of fat per slice.

Except on cruises of 10 days or longer, when cabin occupants can order from set lunch or dinner menus, 24-hour room service is limited to breakfast and cold snacks such as sandwiches, salads and fruit-and-cheese plates. Breakfast and lunch buffets are served in a self-service cafeteria with hot and cold dishes available, and early morning coffee, afternoon tea and midnight buffets fill out the legendary eight-meals-a-day format.

Captain Sealy's menu for kids includes fish sticks, peanut butter and jelly sandwiches, tuna fish, pizza, hamburgers and macaroni and cheese, plus chocolate "ship" cookies.
Cuisine Report Card: C+

CHAMPAGNE TOAST

Just like their competitors, RCCL bar waiters on embarkation day on Caribbean cruises are hustling around with trays of brightly colored fancy drinks in souvenir glasses, but unlike some of their competitors, they prominently display signs showing the drink price at $4.95 so an unwary first-timer doesn't assume that they're free.

Showtime

The major production shows produced by the line, complete with Broadway-style playbills and computerized light cues, are sensational on the bigger ships with their state-of-the-art technical facilities. Unfortunately, on the smaller vessels, the shows still come out of the under-inspired and overworked south Florida production companies and suffer from make-do stagecraft and poor sightlines. Passengers entertain each other at karaoke nights, masquerade parades and passenger talent shows, and pack appropriate garb for country/western night and '50s and '60s rock 'n roll night.
Entertainment Report Card: A/C

Discounts

Booking six months in advance earns discounts of 10 to 20 percent off the brochure rate.

The Bottom Line

Very nice but over-priced, especially when the line's consistency of pricing puts its older vessels in the same general range as its newer ones. Cabins are small throughout the fleet except in the newest Project Vision ships, but are very quiet in all the newer ships, thanks to modern soundproofing techniques that provide a 42-decibel reduction in the walls and 40 at the door from hallway noise. RCCL delivers a consistency across the fleet just as they intend to, even though the ships represent four different design groups and sizes.

Legend of the Seas ★★★★★
Splendour of the Seas ☆☆☆☆☆

They call it "The Ship of Light" and claim it has more glass than any other ship afloat, more than two acres of windows, from the atrium hotel lobby with its soaring glass elevators to a Roman spa with clear crystal canopy that can be opened to the air or covered against temperature extremes. The two-deck dining room walls are glass, the Viking Crown Lounge wrapped around the ship's funnel is almost all glass, and a glass-walled cafe that doubles as observation area is high atop the ship and forward. People who cruise on glass ships should take along their sunglasses.

The most talked-about feature on* Legend of the Seas *is its nine-hole miniature golf course, the first at sea (the only problem is, parts of it keep slipping into the sea in bad weather).

Legend of the Seas and its sister ship *Splendour of the Seas* are the first of a projected six vessels in RCCL's Project Vision series, ships that are slightly smaller but considerably faster than the line's giant *Sovereign*, *Monarch* and *Majesty*. They cruise at 24 knots as compared to the usual 20 or less, allowing passengers a longer time in port or shorter transits between ports.

Despite their size, these ships give the impression of intimacy, particularly in the soaring seven-deck Centrum with its glass skylight ceiling, where each deck level has its own small sitting areas, library or cardroom.

The Brochure Says

"Your accommodations aboard the *Legend of the Seas* are exceptionally roomy and comfortable, with large staterooms, more expansive public areas and more cabins with verandas."

Translation

Cabins are a bit bigger than the previous RCCL norm, although the one we occupied, called a Larger Outside, begged the question, Larger than what? The ship's extra width gives a greater sense of space throughout the ship. The passenger-space ratio of 38.32 is much higher than on the line's megaships.

KEELHAUL

The gaudy casino with Tiffany stained glass lamps over the tables, tacky carpeting and far too many pinging slot machines and neon lights resembles early downtown Reno.

Cabins and Costs

Fantasy Suites: **Report Card: A+**

Average Price PPPD: $650 including airfare on some sailings.

The 1148-square-foot Royal Suite with its gleaming white baby grand piano is drop-dead gorgeous, from its private veranda to its sumptuous marble bathroom with separate WC and bidet, three wash basins, stall shower and oval Jacuzzi tub. For entertaining, there's a wet bar, mini-refrigerator, full entertainment center with TV, VCR, CD and the rest of the alphabet. Two sofas, two chairs, a glass dining table for four, separate bedroom with king-sized bed, easy chair and super storage space.

Small Splurges: **Report Card: A**

Average Price PPPD: $534 each for two, $316 each for four, or $225 each for seven, including some airfare.

The two family suites, each with two bedrooms, two baths (one with tub and one with shower), private veranda, sitting area with sofa-bed and chair, and a pull-down berth, big enough to sleep seven and certainly comfortable enough for four.

A spacious Category D deluxe outside cabin on* Legend of the Seas *has sitting area and private veranda.

Suitable Standards: **Report Card: C+**

Average Price PPPD: $330, with airfare included some sailings.

Category F Larger Outsides provide twin beds that can convert to queen-sized, a sitting area with loveseat, small glass table with a brass wastebasket fitted underneath, nice built-in cabinetry, desk/dresser with three big drawers on one side, three little ones on the other, two nightstands with two drawers each and floral curtains with sheer drapery underneath. A small TV set, closet with one full-length and two half-length hanging areas, safe, full-length mirror and cabinet with shelves above make the basic unit more spacious and comfortable than on most RCCL ships. Bathrooms have showers only.

Wheelchair Accessible:

Seventeen cabins from Standard Insides to C category suites are designated accessible for the physically-challenged; all are near elevators. Doors are an extra-wide 32 inches across; there are no doorway sills; the bathrooms have shower stalls with stools and grab bars, and both bathrooms and passenger corridors are wide enough for a wheelchair to turn around.

Bottom Bunks: **Report Card: C**

Average Price PPPD: $250 apiece for two, $187 apiece for four, with airfare included on some itineraries.

Even the standard quad insides with two lower and two upper berths have a sitting area with TV and a little space to move around. Storage is adequate, if not overly generous, and you can always take turns sitting on that cute little sofa.

CHAMPAGNE TOAST

For outstanding attention to disabled passengers: the large number of wheelchair-accessible cabins (17); Braille elevator signs; special cabin kits for hearing-impaired passengers with strobe-light door knocker and telephone ringer, mattress-vibrator alarm clock, telephone amplifier and enhancing FM receivers for sound in the show lounge.

Where She Goes

The *Legend of the Seas* transits the Panama Canal on 10- and 11-night sailings between San Juan and Acapulco in winter, then sails to Hawaii in spring and fall, and spends summers in Alaska cruising the Inside Passage.

Splendour of the Seas is scheduled to debut in the Caribbean in March with a 10-night inaugural sailing, then reposition to Europe for the summer for a series of 12-night cruises. For the winter, the ship returns to the Caribbean with a San Juan home base, Saturday departures and a new Southern Caribbean itinerary that will probably include Aruba and Curaçao.

The Bottom Line

Despite a less than awesome debut in May, 1995, due to a rough springtime crossing that dumped a large section of the miniature golf course into the Atlantic, plus delays in completing the interior, *Legend of the Seas* and her upcoming sister look like moneymakers for the company. They feel like smaller ships than they are, because of the number of intimate areas tucked away here and there.

Cabins are somewhat more spacious than on previous RCCL ships—even another 24 square feet is a bonus. A total of 17 staterooms are designated for the disabled. Practical touches like removable coat hangers, some with skirt clips, along with good mirrors and makeup lighting will be appreciated, too.

Since several different designers created the public areas, there is a pleasurable variety of decorating styles. Deck areas are handsomer than on the line's megaships. There are canvas-shaded seating areas and pools with arcs of water spraying, although the golf course takes up a lot of sunbathing area.

We can already hear the cash registers ringing as this formerly conservative company starts crowding Carnival on the outer edges of Glitz World.

Fielding's Picks

Fabulous Places

1. A spectacular solarium with a "crystal canopy" sliding roof, pool with water jets and spas, Roman marble floors and walls, fountains, even a convivial marble bar; also there—a full spa, gym and beauty salon, steam baths and saunas.

2. The first 18-hole golf course at sea, in miniature of course, complete with water hazards, sand traps, halogen lights for night play, wind baffles and a clear dome roof in bad weather; reserved tee times, club rentals, $5 a game or $25 for unlimited play throughout the seven-day cruise.
3. The Centrum, the seven-deck, glass-ceilinged heart of the ship with two glass elevators, marble terraces and champagne bar.
4. The two-level Romeo and Juliet Dining Room, where diners are surrounded by glass walls and a dramatic curving stairway lets well-dressed couples make a dramatic entrance.
5. That's Entertainment theater, the best showroom at sea from an audience point of view because all the seats are good—and comfortable. High-tech professional shows, an orchestra pit and retractable 50-screen video for multimedia productions.

Off-the-Wall Fun Facts

1. Sitting in the Viking Crown Lounge on these ships puts you at eye level with the Statue of Liberty.
2. If these two ships sailed through your neighborhood at normal cruising speed, they'd be ticketed for exceeding 30 mph.
3. The steel used in *Legend of the Seas* could build two Eiffel towers.
4. The ships are twice as wide as Rodeo Drive in Beverly Hills, and twice as long and three times as high as the Hollywood sign.
5. Passengers on a seven-day cruise on *Legend of the Seas* devour 4200 chickens, 2150 bagels, 3065 pounds of watermelons, 600 cases of beer and 383 cases of soda.

Good Reasons to Book These Ships

1. If you've always wanted to play miniature golf at sea.
2. If you like translating basic Latin phrases like those adorning the marble walls of the Solarium—Bene Lava, Omnia Vincet Amor, Genius Loci and Carpe Diem.
3. To enjoy the excellent collection of original art on board, 1939 pieces altogether.
4. To hit the steam room and sauna, Jacuzzi and stand-up Solarium Bar.
5. To stargaze from a special deck with state-of-the-art starwheels that rotate on a "star-time" clock mechanism to show where constellations are in synchrony with real time and place. The cruise staff has been trained to explain it.

Things You Won't Find On Board

1. A self-service passenger laundry.
2. A golf cart on the 18-hole course.
3. A bad seat (or a smoking seat) anywhere in the show lounge.
4. A lot of space around your dinner table.
5. Public rest rooms in the Viking Crown Lounge.

Majesty of the Seas ★★★★
Monarch of the Seas ★★★★

One of the most fascinating phenomena of late twentieth-century life is the mall, that vast enclosed emporium of shops, bars, theaters and restaurants that has become a meeting place for teenagers and a weekend and evening destination for the young and upwardly mobile. In a sheltering, climate-controlled environment, surrounded by glittering options for spending money, people get dreamy-eyed and slow-moving. Majesty of the Seas *and her sister megaliner* Monarch of the Seas *remind us a lot of hangin' out at the mall.*

Starting with the first ship in this series, the slightly smaller *Sovereign of the Seas*, RCCL concentrated on positioning the cabins forward and the public rooms aft so that passengers can make their way vertically from, say the cocktail bars to the dining room to the show lounge to the casino, and horizontally from their cabins to the public areas.

But we would still recommend that a passenger traveling from a modest B deck inside forward cabin to the sports deck area atop the ship aft take along a compass and a brown bag lunch.

The plus side of big is that the soaring sense of space makes these huge ships especially appealing to first-time cruisers accustomed to hotels and resorts. And you shouldn't get lost too often—a three-dimensional plexiglass ship directory is set in each elevator/stairwell landing to help passengers find their way around.

They're good for kids because of the way the age groups are divided into five-to-eight-year-olds, "tweens" eight to 12, and teens from 13 to 17. Teens can hang out at their own soft drink bar with its adjacent video games center and even run the special effects and light show in the teen disco.

A whole new subculture of passengers has developed around these megaships. They call themselves Trekkies (after the "Star Trek" TV series) in honor of their own journeys into space.

FOOTNOTE

The stylish glass doors on the rest rooms are modestly frosted in the center with an inch of clear glass running around the edges; they offer an unobstructed view inside for inadvertent voyeurs.

INSIDER TIP

People in bathing suits should avoid settling into those handsome woven plastic mesh bar seats at the pool bar if they don't want waffle patterns on the back of their thighs when they stand up again.

EAVESDROPPING

"Isn't this something!," gushes a 40ish blonde woman in awe as she enters the Majesty *lobby at embarkation. "I'll certainly enjoy this week. You just can't believe it's a ship!"*

The Brochure Says

"Big-city dazzle with its elegant dining rooms...as tall as the Statue of Liberty...unlimited freedom to curl up with a good book, eat all the ice cream you want (and) tell the kids to ship out..."

Translation

It's a big ship but you're going to kick back and have a great time. Head up to the Viking Crown Lounge and fantasize being on eye level with Miss Liberty (only in your imagination, since these ships don't sail into New York). Dazzling, come-hither bright lights and a sense of action draw young and first-time cruisers who know how to have fun. As for good books, see "Insider Tip" below.

For unlimited ice cream, the line's *Nordic Empress* with its own free ice cream bar might be a better bet. But you can certainly tell the kids to ship out, with three child care programs that split age groups between 5 and 8, "tweens" 8 to 12, and teens. The last have their own club and disco called Flashes, created by a line that realizes teens are only a decade or so away from buying cruises for themselves. Attention must be paid.

OFF-THE-WALL

The On Your Toes nightclub/disco on the Majesty of the Seas *with its neon signage, optical illusion glass-and-neon entryway and state-of-the-art DJ station strains to send a "with it" message which is sabotaged by the saccharine central sculpture of a pair of ballet dancers.*

INSIDER TIP

The elegant library aboard has 2,000 books, an impressive number until you realize the ship carries 2354 passengers, presumably leaving 354 people with nothing to read during the cruise. Check out your book ASAP.

CHAMPAGNE TOAST

To the splendid new ShipShape Center, open daily from 8 a.m. to 8 p.m., with a padded floor and enough space so aerobics and exercise classes don't have to be scheduled on deck or in one of the lounges, as on many vessels.

Cabins and Costs

The Royal Suite on* Majesty of the Seas *is a true fantasy suite and great for entertaining.

Fantasy Suites: **Report Card: A**

Average Price PPPD: $571 including airfare.

The Royal Suite, #1010 on both ships, provides ideal digs for anyone who wants to entertain in nearly 1000 square feet indoors and out. A separate living room with private veranda, dining table with six chairs, L-shaped sofa and two chairs, wet bar stocked with liquor, soft drinks and snacks and an entertainment center with CDs and VCRs headlines the suite. In the bedroom is a king-sized bed, lovely wood dresser, a marble bathroom with double basins, Jacuzzi tub, stall shower and walk-in dressing area with large safe.

Small Splurges: **Report Card: B+**

Average Price PPPD: $457 per person for first two passengers, $107 per person for third and fourth sharing the suite. Includes airfare.

The Family Suite, #1549 on both ships, has two bedrooms and two baths, adequate sleeping, lounging and wardrobe space for a close family of five, with private veranda, sitting area, master bedroom and bath, and second bedroom with two lower beds, a pulldown berth and small bathroom with shower.

Suitable Standards: **Report Card: C**

Average Price PPPD: $321 including airfare.

F is the predominant category of standard outside double cabins, each with its twin beds in L-shaped configuration, the ends at the L overlapping by 18 inches. In the 127 square feet, you'll find one chair (flip a coin for it), a small TV set, a tripod glass-topped table with a brass wastebasket as its base (we tried to chill champagne in it but were sternly corrected by a Bahamian stewardess), a built-in cabinet with four drawers, a closet with one full length and two half-height hanging areas plus drawers and a safe and a small tidy tile bath with shower.

Wheelchair Accessible:

Two inside category N cabins and two outside category D cabins are designated as physically-challenged accessible. They're larger than others in their price category, with good turning room for the wheelchair, and twin beds with pastel covers, along with sofa and chair. The baths have no sills, and provide grab rails by the toilet and in the shower, along with a pull-down plastic seat. Some low hanging closet racks are accessible, but the safe, located on an upper shelf, would be out of reach for someone in a wheelchair.

Bottom Bunks: **Report Card: C-**

Average Price PPPD: $229 including airfare.

With the modular cabin design common to new ships, the cheapest digs often offer two lower beds and a bathroom identical to those in higher-priced categories. The bottom-dollar beds are in category Q, insides that measure only 114 square feet and are situated well forward on the lowest passenger cabin deck, but hey, they're livable unless you hit a heavy storm, which could toss you out of bed.

FOOTNOTE

At the French shipyard a week before delivery of the Monarch of the Seas, *a group of American media touring the vessel were bemused to note that in the Ain't Misbehavin' Lounge, the life-sized sculpture of the noted black pianist with his derby hat was labeled Fats Domino instead of Fats Waller.*

Where She Goes

Majesty of the Seas sails year-round, seven-day Western Caribbean round-trips from Miami (Sundays) calling at Playa del Carmen and Cozumel, Grand Cayman, Ocho Rios and, depending on the cruise, Labadee, Haiti, or CocoCay, Bahamas, for a beach day.

Monarch of the Seas sails year-round seven-day Southern Caribbean round-trips from San Juan (Sundays) calling at Martinique, Barbados, Antigua, St. Maarten and St. Thomas.

The Bottom Line

The acres of astroturf and anodized bronze loungers, glittering shops and glass elevators, leather sofas, potted palms and lobby pianist make the *Majesty* and *Monarch of the Seas* look more like Marriott of the Seas to a purist.

While the cabins and interiors are as spotless as ever, the deck housekeeping has been lax on the ships we've been aboard lately, particularly *Majesty of the Seas*, with old maraschino cherry stems stuck in the astroturf, corn flake crumbs in the chair cushions in the Windjammer Cafe at lunchtime and abandoned beer bottles by the rail. A well-decked-out lady deserves better than this.

Solid mainstream ships, the *Majesty* and the *Monarch* set out to impress from the moment a passenger boards, just as Carnival does, but they aim for a slightly more sophisticated audience. Only dedicated traditional ship buffs will find much to grouse about here.

Fielding's Picks

Great Space Stations

1. The Centrum, a four-deck lobby with two glass elevators, a two-level marble floor and a pianist, looking for all the world like a Hyatt Regency hotel lobby.
2. Boutiques of Centrum, 10 storefronts in the shopping gallery circled like pioneer wagons around a campfire, each with its own character and line of duty-free products. In the center of it all, a plaza with luggage-brown leather chairs where non-shoppers can sit and wait—just like at the mall.
3. The tri-level show lounge (A Chorus Line on *Majesty*, Sound of Music on *Monarch*) with its curved cantilevered box seats, eye-catching murals and neon entrance signage adds glitz to this fairly conservative line, although kilowatt-wise, it can't compete with the Casino Royale.
4. The spacious Schooner Bar, everybody's favorite piano bar, with a decor that includes plank floors, brass ship lamps, ship models in plexiglass cases and spars and rigging. While the house music is closer to "My Way" than "Blow the Man Down," it's still pretty nautical.
5. The two-deck Windjammer Cafe is open to the sea, with an enclosed cafe forward and a covered, outdoor cafe amidships, sheltered with window walls and a glass dome overhead; unique "waterfall" columns sandwich a cascade that ripples through plexiglass cases and towers of glass blocks.

Nordic Empress ★★★★

Our favorite memory of the Nordic Empress *was sitting on our cabin's private veranda late one Saturday night in the summer of 1990 when the then-new ship ship was docked in Nassau, and watching the equally new* Fantasy *from Carnival, docked across the way, change colors as its computer-programmed neon tubing strung throughout the vessel shifted from red to blue to fuchsia to lime to pink. The* Fantasy, *a sort of lava lamp for the 1990s, serves to delineate the differences between the two, the first brand-new ships that had ever been scheduled for profit-generating three- and four-day cruises.*

Until then, only the oldest vintage vessels from a line were shoved over into that high-density, high-attrition market once perceived as a one-time-only whoopee cruise for guzzling undergraduates and singles on the make.

Now, suddenly, right before our eyes, the whole scene had changed, and we were witnessing the cruise equivalent of a stare-down confrontation between genteel Melanie Wilkes and flamboyant Scarlett O'Hara.

The *Nordic Empress* actually started on the drawing board as a rather pretentiously named vessel called *Future Seas*, designed expressly for three-and four-day cruises for a now-defunct company called Admiral Cruises, an affiliate of RCCL.

Company executives define the differences on the mini-cruise vessels:

—"We try to cram a seven-day cruise into three days."

—More hectic.

—In port daily.

—More steak and lobster, fewer unfamiliar dishes on the menu.

—"Passengers want to eat and drink as much as they would in seven days." (Passengers also spend roughly the same amount of disposable income for on-board extras as they would in seven days.)

—Deck plan must be easy for the passenger to learn and find his way around in a limited time.

***Pool deck areas are shaded with canvas umbrellas on the* Nordic Empress.**

The Brochure Says

"A cascading waterfall. Lush tropical plants. The kind of sunlight you never get back home. Wait. This isn't an exotic port. This is your ship. The Centrum Lobby, actually."

Translation

The heart of the ship is a hotel-like lobby that connects to all the passenger decks and so helps passengers learn their way around. (It's no fun when you're on a three-day cruise and can't find your cabin for hours.) The Centrum, as it's called, is drop-dead dramatic, a great place for photographing each other. (It's also a good backdrop for a wedding, if you have romance in mind. See page 55, "Getting Married Aboard".)

CHAMPAGNE TOAST

For their subtle how-to's for first-timers: at the first night's dinner, the waiter, busboy and headwaiter introduce themselves to each table, each explaining what his particular duties are so the uninitiated cruiser doesn't have to worry about which server to summon for a glass of water or a cup of coffee. Cabin stewards greet each arriving guest and point out cabin features, and the welcome-aboard presentation on embarkation day introduces personnel from the ship's shops, sports and fitness program, beauty shop, casino and photography concessions to explain the services and prices, and that there's no charge for being photographed unless you want to buy the finished picture.

Showtime on the **Nordic Empress.**

Cabins and Costs

Fantasy Suites: **Report Card: A**

Average Price PPPD: $623 including airfare.

The one-bedroom Royal Suite is big enough for entertaining with a wet bar, large dining or conference table, curved sofa and chairs, teak-floored veranda, walk-in closet, Jacuzzi tub, and separate marble-and-glass shower. While the price is about

$100 a day more than the owner's suites, the Royal Suite incorporates space from an owner's suite and two standard cabins.

Small Splurges: **Report Card: B+**

Average Price PPPD: $406 including airfare.

One of the 56 category C deluxe outside cabins with private balcony, two lower beds which can be arranged as one, a sofa, chair and coffee table, built-in dresser/desk, good reading lamp, built-in vanity table and terrycloth robes.

Suitable Standards: **Report Card: B**

Average Price PPPD: $316 including airfare.

Cabins were designed with women in mind, according the ship designers, who say females comprise 60 percent of all cruise passengers. There's generous counter space in the bathroom, subdued pastel fabrics, floral watercolors and a beauty table with its own makeup lights. H and I category cabins have twin beds that convert to queen-sized, color TV, built-in dresser with stool, one chair, good storage space and small bathroom with shower only.

Bottom Bunks: **Report Card: C**

Average Price PPPD: $233 including airfare.

Q category cabins forward on B deck are the bottom-dollar digs; expect all the standard cabin amenities in a slightly smaller space.

Where She Goes

Year-round (Fridays) three-day roundtrips from Miami to Nassau and CocoCay.

Year-round (Mondays) four-day roundtrips from Miami to Freeport, Nassau and CocoCay.

The Bottom Line

The *Nordic Empress*, like Carnival's glittering new short-cruise megaships, is attracting a whole new set of first-time cruise passengers of all ages and ethnic backgrounds, a welcome sight in an industry that spent too many years competing for the same narrow stratum of cruise regulars.

This ship offers a gentler, quieter version of the party cruise without soft-pedaling the fun. On both three- and four-day itineraries, passengers have a full day at the beach on a private island for swimming, snorkeling, sailing and windsurfing with a calypso band and beach barbecue lunch, while competitor Carnival provides a day at sea to enjoy (read: spend money in) the ship's games, bars, shops and casinos.

The *Nordic Empress* is highly recommended for first-time cruisers of all ages, including families and three-generation groups. It's a good introduction to mainstream cruising.

Fielding's Picks

Sensational Spots

1. The Centrum, a nine-deck open atrium with a glass skylight on top, then a waterfall that cascades, sometimes framed in glass or caught up in pools, sometimes splashing free, faced with pink begonias and white marble and a crystal-drop sculpture of a ship's prow, all of it best viewed from the two glass elevators.
2. The two decks of the glass-walled Carmen Dining Room, the first of the nearly one dozen double-deckers now at sea, with a great view of the port as the ship sails away. It's bright and airy for breakfast and lunch, and spectacularly lit at dinnertime when musicians on a raised marble platform serenade diners.
3. The tri-level Casino Royale with 10 blackjack tables, two roulette tables, two craps tables, 40 sit-down poker machines and 220 slot machines is catnip for sporting cats.
4. Kids Connection Playroom has a slide that lets small children fall into a sea of brightly colored plastic balls; there's also a cave-like hidden TV room with carpeted seating levels, great for watching scary videos like *Jurassic Park.*
5. The Strike Up the Band Showroom in coral tones with white marble and gleaming brass cantilevered curved balcony boxes is lovely to look at, and a wooden thrust stage with splendid turntable and technical equipment offers state-of-the-art stagecraft. The only flaw is the over-exuberance of curved rails in the balcony that limit access and force late arrivals to vault over the railings into their seats.

Things You Won't Find on Board

1. The usual blank wall in inside cabins. Where the window would be on an outside cabin, the line has decorated with artwork and vertical fabric and plexiglass strips framing wall sconces.
2. A panoramic ocean view from outside cabins amidships on Mariner Deck (cabin 7100–7652, plus cabins 7032 and 7352) because lifeboats are hanging outside the windows. For the same price, ask your travel agent to book category F cabins well forward or aft to avoid the obstructions.
3. A library or card room.
4. A self-service laundry.
5. Consistently good sightlines in the show lounge; arrive early so you don't have to sit in the balcony.

Song of America ★★★

It was a windy but memorable December day in 1982 in Miami when opera star Beverly Sills christened Song of America. *It took the durable diva five swings before she broke the bottle of champagne across the bow. Moments before, she had cautioned the crowd of well-wishers not to spill anything on "my carpets—I like to run a tight ship." At the time, Wartsila-built* Song of America *was the biggest cruise ship ever constructed in Scandinavia, and perhaps the only modern Caribbean ship to boast an ex-president (Jimmy Carter) and his family as passengers on the maiden voyage. The Carters still return periodically, but also travel aboard the* Sovereign of the Seas, *where Mrs. Carter is godmother.*

A deluxe cabin on* Song of America *with its own sitting area and desk/dresser.

Unlike this ship's many fervent fans, we dismissed her as Nordic high-tech razzle-dazzle when she was new because of her popsicle interior colors, but in a more recent renovation, some of the original orange cabin furnishings have been muted to beige tones and the former grape-and-raspberry upholstery in the Can Can Lounge and Guys & Dolls Lounge has quieted down as well. It's been some time since the Schooner Bar was introduced and the outdated cinema removed (now that the cabins have color TV sets for video movies) in favor of a conference and meeting area and expanded casino. The soundproofing has been beefed up since the early days as well.

Traditionalists like the long sleek lines compared to today's shoebox shapes, and sunbathers find plenty of room to stretch out on the expansive Compass and Sun Decks. For nightlife, the ship has three spacious lounges for shows, music and dancing, plus the smaller Schooner piano bar.

The Brochure Says

"We'll do everything, so you have the option of doing nothing. We'll clean up your room (twice a day), cook for you (six times a day), entertain you and take you to far-away places with strange-sounding names."

Translation

A cruise is an easy vacation, because you buy everything in a neat package, even your round-trip airfare and transfers. You have a cabin steward who cleans your cabin twice a day, replacing towels and refilling the ice bucket, and you can eat every couple of hours if you concentrate. Best of all, your cruise ship takes you to exotic spots like the U.S. Virgin Islands where the inhabitants speak English and welcome U.S. dollars.

Cabins and Costs

Fantasy Suites: **Report Card: B**

Average Price PPPD: $464 including airfare.

The Owner's Suite, #7000, on Promenade Deck, is double the size of the deluxe outside suites, with sitting area with sofa, chairs and coffee table; mini-refrigerator, color TV, twin beds and an optional third berth, wide desk/dresser, three picture windows and bathroom with tub. On the down side, you're overlooking a public deck area from your picture windows.

Small Splurges: **Report Card: C+**

Average Price PPPD: $407 including airfare.

A deluxe suite in B category, not as lavish space-wise as the Owner's Suite, but comfortable enough, with sofa, chairs, desk/dresser, color TV, separate sleeping area with twin beds and big window, and bath with tub.

Suitable Standards: **Report Card: C-**

Average Price PPPD: $307 including airfare.

The modular cabin design means all standards are virtually identical, with the category and price difference reflected in the deck location. The H category A deck outside doubles have two lower beds (one sofa/daybed and one fold-up twin) except for cabins 3207–3210, 3147–3150 and 3013–3018, all of which have twin beds that can be put together into a queen-sized bed. Most of these also have a pulldown third berth. All have bathrooms with shower only.

Bottom Bunks: **Report Card: C**

Average Price PPPD: $235 including airfare.

The B Deck inside doubles in the forward part of the ship, Q category, are the lowest-priced accommodations. Each has two lower beds that can be put together to make a queen-sized bed, a bath with shower, wall-mounted color TV set and a desk/dresser with stool.

INSIDER TIP

Only about half the cabins on board have twin beds that can be converted to queen-sized beds, so specify your preference when booking.

Where She Goes

Song of America cruises the Southern Caribbean from San Juan in winter, sailing on Saturdays and calling in St. Croix, St. Kitts, Guadeloupe, St. Maarten, St. John and St. Thomas. In summer, she sails to Bermuda from New York every Sunday, and spends one day in St. George's, then two-and-a-half days in Hamilton.

The Bottom Line

This long, sleek beauty is one of only three classic non-mega-sized ships remaining in the rapidly-growing RCCL fleet, and it has retained its popularity over the years, with some loyals claiming as many as two dozen sailings aboard since its debut.

Because the cabins are on the small side (around 120 square feet for standard doubles), the passenger space ratio is a modest 26.8, but deck areas and lounges are spacious and comfortable, and warm-weather cruisers shouldn't have to spend too much time in their rooms.

Anyone sensitive to cigarette smoke may find, as we do, that although the Viking Crown Lounge with its expansive (and unopenable) glass windows offers dramatic sea and sunset views, it also retains the smell of smoke despite the line's zealous attempts to clean and freshen the air.

Song of Norway ★★

RCCL was certainly music-minded when it launched its first ship with rooms named after musicals—South Pacific Lounge, The King and I Dining Room, My Fair Lady Lounge—but the first time we went aboard this ship in the early 1980's, we were struck more by the Kool-Aid colors everywhere, raspberry, tangerine, lemon-lime and strawberry. All these, fortunately, have gone the way of RCCL's old cash-only policy. (The company was one of the last to institute a credit card policy for onboard purchases, a sure way to raise revenue but nervous-making for the conservative Norwegians.

(We asked them once why they charged a refundable $15 for checking a book out of the library. "Because someone might steal it," was the answer.)

Now with the SuperCharge card, passengers can take a cashless cruise, using the card for drinks, gift shop purchases, beauty shop services—yes, even that refundable book checkout deposit.

When the *Song of Norway* debuted back in 1970, she had a capacity for 740 passengers, probably considered quite enough in those days, but the demand was soon such that the line decided to lengthen the vessel in 1978 in the first-ever "stretching" operation (see "History") and now carries 1004 passengers. Second-smallest in the fleet (only *Sun Viking* is smaller), she manages to retain some intimacy but is big enough to give passengers a sense of choice when they're out and about, with three big lounges and a good expanse of deck space, plus a full round-the-ship promenade.

We wish we could say passengers get a sense of personal space as well, but most of the cabins are quite small—around 120 square feet—with the exception of three modest suites.

INSIDER TIP

You have to walk up an outdoor stairway to get into the Viking Crown Lounge, something that can really destroy your hairdo on a wet or windy evening.

The Brochure Says

"Like the beautiful and cultured countries she visits, our *Song of Norway* is known for her understated elegance...No wonder she visits such irresistible places—otherwise, you might never go ashore."

Translation

She's not very glitzy or glamorous, but you'll find her comfortable enough as a floating hotel to take you to some places you want to go without packing and unpacking all the time.

Cabins and Costs

Fantasy Suites: **Report Card: C**

Average Price PPPD: $499 including some airfare.

The Owner's Suite, while a little short on fantasy, is the biggest accommodation on board (266 square feet) with sitting area, mini-refrigerator and bar, larger-than-usual wardrobe area, bathroom with tub and shower and two lower beds that cannot be pulled together for a queen-sized bed.

Small Splurges: **Report Card: C**

Average Price PPPD: $374 including some airfare.

The category C deluxe staterooms are up around the Owner's Suite but a bit smaller. Still, they're adequate, with two lower beds and bathroom with tub. Strollers along the Promenade Deck outside the window add an additional diversion.

Suitable Standards: **Report Card: C-**

Average Price PPPD: $305 including some airfare.

Lots of "outside staterooms" and "larger inside staterooms" (read "smallish cabins") are in the mid-range categories on A and B decks. Expect a double or two lower beds, sometimes configured in an L-shape in the larger ones, or parallel in the smaller ones.

Bottom Bunks: **Report Card: D-**

Average Price PPPD: $254 including some airfare.

Q category bottom-of-the-line inside cabins have a single double bed suitable for petite romantics who don't want any sunlight coming in to wake them up. Bathrooms have showers only. There are only four of these.

INSIDER TIP

Young singles shouldn't plan on crowding four into a cheap inside cabin, no matter how appealing the prices are, without taking into consideration how little dressing, showering and storage space is available. If you travel really *light, however, you might be able to manage it.*

Where She Goes

Song of Norway makes seven-night Mexican Riviera cruises in winter roundtrip from Los Angeles, calling in Cabo San Lucas, Mazatlán and Puerto Vallarta. In early May, it joins the *Legend of the Seas* in Alaska, cruising the Inside Passage on 10- and 11-night itineraries with eight ports of call through mid-September, after which it resumes the winter Mexican Riviera schedule.

The Bottom Line

A sentimental favorite with both RCCL's executives and its repeat passengers, *Song of Norway* nevertheless shows her age in dated furniture and interior design and lack of specialized facilities now common on RCCL ships—for instance, there is a gym but it's tiny.

Standard accommodations still feature what we call the "interlocking knees" double cabin, from a long-ago RCCL brochure photograph that showed an attractive pair of models ensconced in that small, chairless cabin, gamely smiling, one sitting on each bed facing each other with, yes, their knees interlocked.

And this high-density vessel has a low passenger-space ratio, meaning when the ship is full, which it frequently is, conditions can get crowded.

Overall, this ship is best for competitive types, who can vie in the fitness/sports program to win free T-shirts and visors; couples, who can rekindle romance in the very cozy cabins; and kids, who fit into the upper Pullman-style berths easier than adults.

A future is still possible for ships of this size and vintage in European cruising, where many of the vessels are older and smaller, but RCCL has opted to replace her in Europe with the bigger, glossier *Splendour of the Seas*, so her days may be numbered.

Sovereign of the Seas ★★★★

In the awesome five-story open lobby, brass-trimmed glass elevators glide up and down, their gleaming reflections glancing off marble walls. Elegantly-clad guests lean against a brass railing to look far below at a white baby grand piano where a man in a red coat is playing light classics beside three fountain pools. Almost every major city has one of these grand hotels with majestic staircases and soaring, ethereal space. The only difference is, this one is scheduled to sail off into the Caribbean sunset at 5:30.

The pool deck on* Sovereign of the Seas *after embarkation.

Sovereign of the Seas was the largest ship ever built for cruising when it came into service in 1988. Like its newer sister ships *Monarch of the Seas* and *Majesty of the Seas*, it has a "bigger than life" theatricality and showy design that lends excitement. From the moment its mostly youngish, often first-timer passengers first board, they have the sense of arriving at a major resort. It's ideal for couples, singles and young families shopping for a Caribbean vacation that just happens to be aboard a cruise ship.

How far does the average passenger have to walk between the show lounge and the midnight buffet on a ship that is almost three football fields long? Theoretically, only a short stroll and a stairway or elevator separate the chorus girls from the cheesecake, because the ship's design concentrates the public rooms aft and the staterooms forward.

In fact, your evening could go something like this: You start at the bottom in your assigned dining room (Gigi is on A Deck and Kismet on Main Deck), then walk up one deck to the casino, to the lower level of the show lounge or the shops, then up another deck if you want to sit in the show lounge balcony or have a quiet drink in Finian's Rainbow Lounge or the champagne bar. Walk up one more deck to catch the late show in the Music Man Lounge, then up another deck to check out the disco. Finally, if you want a nightcap in the Viking Crown Lounge, catch the elevator outside the disco and ride three more decks to the top of the ship. Whew!

FOOTNOTE

When this ship was new, we speculated about how many hands a captain can shake at a captain's cocktail party. RCCL set two parties for each of the two dinner seatings, so that the captain had to press the flesh of only 1141 passengers in two shifts, while his second in command was in another lounge handling the other half.

The Brochure Says

"Big. You may wonder if that's what you want in a cruise ship. Won't you get lost just trying to find your stateroom? Not with Royal Caribbean—there's always a staff member who'll point you the right way—or take you there."

Translation

None necessary.

FOOTNOTE

When this ship was brand-new, we saw her docked in San Juan as we sailed in on another vessel. The passengers lining the rail wondered aloud what it was, until one man proclaimed, "I know, that's the new Severance of the Seas!"

Cabins and Costs

Fantasy Suites: **Report Card: A**

Average Price PPPD: $571 including airfare.

The Royal Suite, #1010, some 1000 square feet of luxury, with private veranda, whirlpool tub, living room with wet bar, refrigerator and entertainment center—plus plenty of room for entertaining, and a big walk-in closet with generous storage space and personal safe.

Small Splurges: **Report Card: B**

Average Price PPPD: $414 including airfare.
One of the eight Bridge Deck suites, with large windows, sitting area with sofa and chairs, two lower beds plus a sofa-bed for a third person, mini-refrigerator and bath with tub.

Suitable Standards: **Report Card: C**

Average Price PPPD: $314 including airfare.
In categories F and G, you'll find twin beds in an L-configuration, small tripod brass-and-glass table, one chair, desk/dresser, bath with shower and skimpy storage space in an area approximately 120 square feet.

Bottom Bunks: **Report Card: C**

Average Price PPPD: $228 including airfare.
The Q category inside cabins forward on B Deck are the cheapest on board, with two lower beds in parallel configuration, bath with shower, one chair and dresser.

Where She Goes

The Eastern Caribbean itinerary aboard *Sovereign of the Seas* is for sophisticated cruisers who like the luxury of leisurely days at sea, with only two ports of call, plus two beach days at RCCL's private islands, Labadee, Haiti, and CocoCay, Bahamas. The ship sails every Saturday from Miami, calling in San Juan and St. Thomas.

The Bottom Line

We're still not crazy about the vertical stacking that puts the cabins forward and the public areas aft. While it saves long strolls down hallways (unless your cabin is well forward) it still means a lot of stair climbing for impatient passengers who don't want to wait for the elevators.

Families with teenagers would be wiser to book one of the four newer ships—*Monarch, Majesty, Legend* or *Splendour*—because all of them have better youth facilities than *Sovereign.*

Other than that, however, you'll probably find *Sovereign of the Seas* is like your favorite resort hotel gone to sea, with everything aboard but the golf course; you'll have to book RCCL's new *Legend of the Seas* for that.

One Maritime Plaza, Suite 1400, San Francisco, CA 94111
(415) 956-7200, (800) 622-0538

History

Royal Cruise Line was established in 1971 in San Francisco by co-founding partners Barney A. Ebsworth, a travel entrepreneur who also founded INTRAV tour operations, and Greek shipping executive Pericles S. Panagopoulos, with the plan to construct super-deluxe cruise ships for U.S. West Coast passengers. The first ship, the 450-passenger *Golden Odyssey*, made its debut in 1974 under charter to INTRAV but did not make its first sailing for Royal until May 1975. In the meantime, travel industry veteran Richard Revnes joined the line September 1974 to head up the new marketing division. "Rev," as he was called by everyone, was instrumental in putting together Royal's successful air/sea packages and other innovations in sales, marketing and shipboard programs. He took over the presidency of RCL in 1978, and held that post until he died of cancer in 1990. The co-founding partnership split in 1977 and Panagopoulos bought out Ebsworth.

The dazzling new *Crown Odyssey* was introduced in June 1988 by a proud Panagopoulos, who said he had dreamed of her, his idea of a perfect cruise ship, since 1981. But a little more than a year later he sold the cruise line and its ships for a rumored $200 million to the Norwegian company now called Kloster Cruise Limited, owners of Norwegian Cruise Line and (at that time) Royal Viking Line.

—Although Cunard now owns the Royal Viking name, logo and last flagship (*Royal Viking Sun*), Royal Cruise Line has three of the five former RVL ships—the *Sea*, now *Royal Odyssey*, the *Star*, now *Star Odyssey*, and the *Queen*, now *Queen Odyssey*. Princess has the remaining one, the former *RVL Sky*, now *Golden Princess*.

—RCL pioneered air/sea cruising to Europe by building a 450-passenger ship specifically the size to accommodate the passengers of a 747 (*Golden Odyssey*, 1974).

—Pioneered the social host program for cruises (1982).

—Introduced the first major alternative dining program, created by former food and beverage director Chris Tsardoulias from American Heart Association guidelines and called "Dine To Your Heart's Content" (1986).

—Introduces the first full-ship spa-at-sea sailing completely dedicated to gourmet spa cuisine with no other food options aboard (*Queen Odyssey*, January 1, 1996).

Concept

Like Royal Viking Line, Royal Cruise Line started out by concentrating on upscale, older West Coast-based passengers, offering exotic cruises all over the world with well-run air/sea packages and a lot of hand-holding when transporting passengers to the ships. The line feels it has distinguished itself through 20 years of commitment to value, an incomparable Greek crew, worldwide itineraries and a spirit of innovation. Royal's very high number of repeat passengers have come to expect coddling from their Greek stewards, ports of call they haven't visited before, top-notch bridge lecturers, lots of amiable dancing hosts, and a sensible, low-fat, low-calorie menu for dinner, followed, of course, by a butter-nuts-and-syrup-drenched Greek sweet their favorite waiter persuades them to try.

Signatures

The Heart's Content menus; the New Beginnings program for promoting health, happiness and well-being and designed especially for travelers who want to revitalize themselves physically, emotionally and psychologically.

The distinctive gold crowns on the stack that symbolize Royal Cruise Line.

Gimmicks

A cadre of gentlemen hosts on board to dance with the ladies; Greek dancing by the crew (and passengers dragged onto the dance floor) on the line's Greek Night.

Who's the Competition

As Royal moves more and more upscale, it is edging into the territory of Cunard's *Royal Viking Sun* and *Sagafjord*, the two Seabourn ships (with its *Queen Odyssey*, an almost identical vessel to *Seabourn Pride* and *Seabourn Spirit*) and the Crystal ships, which also concentrate on an upscale West Coast market, although one slightly younger than Royal's traditional passengers.

Who's Aboard

Five or six years ago, the answer would have been easy—couples and singles, the latter mostly females, past 55, who like dancing, shopping, socializing and bridge-playing. But now, with most of the fleet made up of former Royal Viking ships providing some penthouse suites with private verandas and single-seating meals, Royal's poised to catch those RVL veterans who resist going over to Cunard.

And the *Queen Odyssey* is bringing in an entirely new audience for Royal, younger (40+), more sophisticated couples—often first-time cruisers but otherwise well-traveled—who take advantage of discounted prices to sample the deluxe product.

Who Should Go

Pretty much the same passengers who do. Upwardly mobile sophisticates, couples only, should check out the lavish and sybaritic *Queen Odyssey*, which goes at a deep discount through the end of 1996.

Who Should Not Go

RCL's not really for families with young children, or even teenagers, young singles looking for romance, or any woman who doesn't own something with sequins.

The Lifestyle

These are dress-up-and-have-fun ships, with lively cocktail hour action and lots of dancing before and after dinner, even at teatime some days. A full range of daily activities, escorted shore excursions that most people seem to sign up for, and escorted air programs to and from the ship mean passengers don't have to worry about details, or hardly think at all. Life enrichment lectures are big aboard, as are innovative features such as Jean-Michel Cousteau's under water program with Passages International, in which divers with mikes and video cameras go underwater as surrogates of the passenger audience, who watch the whole thing on a screen in the ship's lounge live, in color, with interactive dialogue.

Wardrobe

The apparel worn on these ships is definitely dressy. Men are requested to wear jackets every evening after 6 p.m., either a suit or sport coat and slacks, while women are expected to wear cocktail or evening dresses. Although there may be an occasional evening designated casual, you are expected to be well-turned-out at all times. Two designated formal evenings have most men in tuxedos or dinner jackets, most women in sequins or long gowns. A Pastel Night "for the ladies" has been around since the 1970s; women are expected to be pretty in pink. And Greek Night, a time-hallowed tradition, calls for something in blue and white.

Bill of Fare

While our favorite Royal Cruise Line meals have been special-order Greek lunches or dinners prepared and served with great panache, we were delighted with every meal we had aboard the new *Queen Odyssey* on a recent sailing and would give that ship the highest recommendation for cruisers to whom food is extremely important.

The special low-fat, low-calorie, low-salt Heart's Content menus are available on all the ships and are fairly tasty (although you can still sometimes see the Greek waiter's face fall when you order one—you'd think they were getting tipped by the number of calories you ingest rather than the number of days you're aboard.)

The menus in general are cosmopolitan, with a Greek salad always available by request in the dining room whether on the menu or not. There are several alternative areas for breakfast, including Yianni's Hearth for fresh-baked cinnamon buns, and four or five lunchtime venues from the top deck outdoor grill's gyros (spit-turned lamb) on pita bread with tangy yogurt dressing to soup-and-a-sandwich set up near the card room so as not to interrupt the bridge games. All the ships except the *Crown Odyssey* offer leisurely single-seating meals.

Cuisine Report Card: A+ for Queen Odyssey, B+ for the others

Showtime

Aboard the *Queen Odyssey*, a sextet of singers and dancers may present an evening of Cole Porter or George Gershwin, while on the larger *Crown Odyssey* with its full technical stage full-scale production shows are often featured.

The *Royal Odyssey* and *Star Odyssey* have had their sightlines improved with a new raked floor design. A pre-dinner big band show with vintage vocalist Beryl Davis had enthusiastic dancers from the audience filling the stage around the singer, which doubles as a dance floor. (While dinner is served at a single seating, shows are presented before and after dinner to cut down on the crowds in the lounge.)

Dancing, in fact, is a major part of a Royal cruise, and the guest gentleman hosts are always on the dance floor. (One newly recruited host, we heard, got so worn out he left the ship in Mexico before his cruise was finished.)

Aboard the *Crown, Star* and *Royal Odysseys*, lectures are provided on every cruise, covering world affairs, nature, photography, art history, music, food and wine.

Entertainment Report Card: B+

Discounts

Early booking discounts range from 15 to 50 percent, depending on the sailing, and passengers who pay in full nine months ahead of time can discount 7 percent of the already discounted fare. There's also a Stay and Save bonus for combining cruises.

The Bottom Line

With a very high repeat passenger factor of 30 to as much as 80 percent, depending on the cruise, Royal is obviously giving its passengers what they want. And with the debut of its world cruise this year, 102 days aboard the *Royal Odyssey*, the line shows its intention to be a serious contender in the upper segment of cruising.

RCL has always attributed much of its success to its Greek officers and crew—back in 1988, Revnes said, "Above anything else that we do, I think the warmth of the stewards and the feeling of family, of wanting to be hosts, is the most important. Anybody can build a beautiful ship but without the feeling of family, (it doesn't work.)"

Queen Odyssey ★★★★★★

The most delicious cruise we ever took was aboard this ship the last year it was the Royal Viking Queen, *a 14-day culinary extravaganza with French superstar chef Paul Bocuse, chefs from Le Cordon Bleu in Paris, the winemaker from Chateau Lafite Rothschild and the ship's own brilliant chefs. We think of it as a 10-pound cruise.*

The marina deck and mesh swimming pool can be set up for watersports when the ship is at anchor in calm seas.

The *Queen Odyssey* (the former *Royal Viking Queen*) bears a close resemblance to the two Seabourn ships; it was originally, in fact, supposed to be a third Seabourn until that company decided to stop with two. Kloster then ordered it for Royal Viking Line, where it debuted in 1992. The $86 million vessel was termed at the time "the highest investment per cabin or per berth in the cruise industry."

Designer Bjorn Storbraaten detailed for us the changes he made on the Queen—"We tried to make the colors warmer, and we have created more colors in the cabins. We took the glass band, the streamlined glass windows around the Seabourn ships, and replaced them with painted tubes against a dark blue background. On the funnel, we altered the mass and straightened out the bow."

In the lobby area are a series of four murals depicting scenes of shipboard life aboard traditional ocean liners in the 1920s, and there is a hand-painted glass globe outside the dining room. A board room with long table and 20 chairs fills the place where a card room and business center are located on the Seabourn ships, and Storbraaten feels the larger suites, especially the two owner's suites, were improved on the *Queen*.

The Brochure Says

"Maybe you've dreamed of discovering secluded yacht harbors and uncrowded ports aboard a small, private yacht."

Translation

This is the recurring fantasy that brings passengers aboard ships like this one, the Seabourn and Silversea ships, Sea Goddess and Radisson Seven Seas, and the dream itinerary is usually along the French and Italian Rivieras. But with more and more super-deluxe "small, private yachts" making that run every summer—we count nine in the list above, and that doesn't include the Windstar, Club Med and Star Clipper ships—how uncrowded can these ports remain?

INSIDER TIP

While there have been plenty of spa cruises over the years, this is the first time we can remember one, even one led by the redoubtable Sheila Cluff, that makes it nearly impossible to cheat on your diet. But the 212-passenger Queen Odyssey *sets sail Jan. 1 (how about that for an appropriate date?) with an all low-fat, low-calorie galley, delicious, gourmet dishes that will help you shed pounds without cravings. Call Royal for more details.*

Cabins and Costs

Fantasy Suites: **Report Card: A+**

Average Price PPPD: $1744.

The most lavish quarters aboard this sumptuous ship are the two 590-square-foot owner's suites with private verandas and big, gracious living rooms. A long built-in curved sofa and several upholstered tub chairs offer plenty of room for entertaining, and there's a dining table with four chairs for those evenings when you prefer to dine in, along with a TV/VCR, a separate bedroom with queen-sized bed, its own TV/VCR, walk-in closet, white marble bathroom with tub, shower, robes, hair dryer and safe, stocked bar and a guest bath.

Small Splurges: **Report Card: A**

Average Price PPPD: $1258.

The St. Paul-de-Vence and Venezia penthouse suites, 310 square feet each, have a spacious living room with long sofa and several chairs, dining table with two chairs, twin or queen-sized beds, small private veranda, separate dressing room with generous storage and a marble bath with tub and shower, stocked bar, TV/VCR and safe.

Suitable Standards: **Report Card: A**

Average Price PPPD: $893 plus small air add-on in the Med.

The standard suites aboard measure a generous 277 square feet, with marble bathrooms that contain and tub/shower combination and walk-in closets with plenty of storage space, plus queen-sized bed, hair dryers, a safe, mini-refrigerator, color TV/VCR, sitting area with sofa, chairs and hassocks enough for six, 24-hour room service and big picture window.

Bottom Bunks: **Report Card: NA**

There are no bottom bunk categories on this ship; standard suites (which they call Super Deluxe Suites S3) are the cheapest.

INSIDER TIP

You can host a bon voyage party in your cabin if you're sailing from a U.S. city where you have friends. You're allowed up to 10 visitors in your cabin, or you can host a private party in one of the public areas for up to 25 people. Have your travel agent write to the Operations Department at Royal Cruise Line at least three weeks ahead of time.

Where She Goes

Queen Odyssey starts the year in the Caribbean with a Jan. 1 spa-at-sea cruise that's guaranteed no-cheating because the ship will serve only low-fat, low-calorie spa cuisine. She spends the rest of January and February sailing the Caribbean from Barbados or San Juan, then makes a couple of Panama Canal transits that visit Costa Rica in March before setting out for her transatlantic crossing in early April.

The Bottom Line

This ship, while quite expensive, has been for each of the three times we've sailed aboard—twice with Royal Viking and once with Royal Cruise Line—absolute perfection in food, service and comfort in the standard suites. The best way to book is to take advantage of the early booking discounts—40 to 50 percent off—paying scrupulous attention to deadlines. With the prices per day, even in the costly Mediterranean, cut in half to $450 or so a person, that should mean the *Queen Odyssey* can successfully compete with many lesser cruise products.

SEABOURN
CRUISE LINE

55 Francisco Street , San Francisco, CA 94133
(415) 391-8518, (800) 929-4747

History

The buzz started in 1987 with a full-color ad in the travel trades depicting the dapper and distinguished Warren Titus, recently retired head of Royal Viking Line, clad in a tuxedo and standing on a pier at night to announce the impending arrival of a new super-luxury cruise line to be called Signet Cruises. But while the new company's first ship was still under construction, it was learned a small Texas-based company had registered the name Signet Cruises, presumably in case they might start a cruise line in the future. So the fledgling new line, owned by young Norwegian industrialist Atle Brynestad, changed its name to Seabourn and—the cliché is inevitable—the rest is history.

On a rainy mid-December morning in 1988 in San Francisco, ambassador and former child star Shirley Temple Black smashed the customary bottle of champagne against the bow of the 200-passenger *Seabourn Pride* with aplomb (to the rhythm of what some of us imagined was "On the Good Ship Lollipop") and later requested a tour of the engine room.

The *Pride* was followed in 1989 by almost-identical sister ship *Seabourn Spirit*; both achieved great acclaim, especially in the luxury travel press. In 1991, Carnival Cruise Lines, having long touted an upscale "Tiffany product" they intended to introduce, purchased 25 percent of Seabourn, and may acquire an additional 25 percent in 1996.

—First cruise line to implement a timeshare-at-sea program called WorldFare, in which passengers purchase 45, 60, 90 or 120 days of Seabourn cruising and use them over a period of 36 months on any cruises (1993).

FOOTNOTE

A seagoing timeshare concept was first discussed in 1979 when Seattle-based United States Cruises Inc. owned the SS United States, *but that obviously never came to fruition.*

Concept

To offer discriminating passengers all the amenities they expect aboard a full-sized cruise vessel of 10,000 tons carrying 200 in an onboard ambiance that is "casual, but elegant." Service is "warm and friendly, but impeccable. And there is absolutely no tipping."

Signatures

The blue-and-white shield logo that adorns the double funnels of both ships.

The Signature Series of shore excursions, custom-designed especially for Seabourn passengers. The Celebrity Chefs series that brings well-known chefs from restaurants around the world to prepare signature dishes or special menus to complement the ship's already superb cuisine.

EAVESDROPPING

Then-mayor of San Francisco Art Agnos, touring the newly christened ship with its godmother Shirley Temple Black and other local officials, quipped, "If the Pilgrims had come over on the Seabourn Pride *rather than the Mayflower, they never would have gotten off the ship."*

Gimmicks

Seabourn WorldFare advance purchase plan in which a passenger can buy a certain number of days aboard and use them within three years on any cruises offered by the line.

Who's the Competition

The usual suspects, of course. The most direct competition is Royal's *Queen Odyssey*, which is a virtual clone of the two Seabourn ships, and which could certainly compete in the areas of food, service and entertainment when we were aboard in early 1995. Silversea Cruises will give Seabourn a good run for the money passengers if it maintains its present high quality product (which, unlike Seabourn, includes all beverages in a less-pricey base fare) and keeps prices down. And of course, the one and only Sea Goddess, which had a four-year head start on Seabourn.

EAVESDROPPING

Carnival CEO Micky Arison to Seabourn founder Atle Brynstad, "No one has ever tried to copy Carnival (the most profitable of Carnival Corporation's three cruise lines) but everyone tries to copy Seabourn (at that time, the least profitable)."

Who's Aboard

Veteran cruisers from Royal Viking and Sea Goddess, first-time cruisers who only want the best and can afford it, a few families traveling in three-generational groups with interconnecting suites, ranging in age from thirtysomething two-income professional couples to retired CEOs. About half the passengers on any cruise are under 50. On our several cruises with Seabourn, we've met English country squires, San Francisco restaurateurs, Hong Kong journalists, a young California-based New Zealand executive, a romance novelist, a noted jazz musician, and numerous doctors, dentists, lawyers, financiers and psychoanalysts. They're more often old money rather than nouveau riche. Passengers are always falling into small-world conversations, finding they have close mutual friends or children attending the same schools. It's a small world in that tax bracket.

Who Should Go

Anyone who books a suite at the Pierre, lunches at The Club in Pebble Beach, has a house in Vail or a condo in Deer Valley. Clubby and very posh, these ships are for couples who are rich and successful. If you want to see a cross-section of typical passengers, ask the line to send you a copy of their pretty publication for repeat passengers called Seabourn Club Herald. There, on several back pages, are color photographs of recent passengers—Stirling Moss, the legendary British motorcar racer; actress Rhonda Fleming; Teddy Roosevelt's granddaughter Sarah Gannett—along with a number of the rich and unfamous.

Who Should Not Go

Children or even restless teenagers would not find places to go and things to do on these ships. Anyone unwilling to dress for dinner would be out of place. And anyone who doesn't know what "out of place" means should certainly not go.

The Lifestyle

The ships are large enough to give passengers a sense of privacy when they wish but with a variety of indoor and outdoor spaces to be social or be secluded. Obviously the luxuriously comfortable cabins with seating areas, TV/VCR and full meal service entice passengers to spend more time inside. Days are casual, with many passengers lounging on deck in bathing suits reading a book, but evenings get much more formal. There are not many organized activities on board since passengers prefer to plan their own time, but they will attend outstanding lecturers.

Wardrobe

While daytimes may be spent in casual, but never sloppy, garb, people dress up in the evenings, not because a dress code tells them they must, but because they like to, and because they are at ease in tuxedos and dressy gowns, silk or linen suits and top-label sportswear.

The Veranda Cafe on the* Seabourn Spirit *is a delightful place to have breakfast on a sunny morning.

Bill of Fare

Sophisticated contemporary cuisine prepared a la minute (when it's ordered) and served in small portions to encourage passengers to try the suggested menu rather than simply one or two dishes. We remember one chef's suggestion menu from Stefan Hamrin that we followed all the way through—an avocado fan with jumbo shrimp and scallion sauce, followed by creamy onion garlic soup with croutons, then a field salad of arugula and radishes, roast rack of spring lamb Dijonnaise, and hot macademia nut soufflé with Tia Maria sauce. The food was light enough and the portions small enough that we were satiated but not stuffed at the end of the meal.

Mornings you can breakfast on deck under the shade of a canvas canopy or inside the jade green-and-white marble Veranda where the fresh fruits are arranged on the buffet like gemstones and the thinly sliced smoked salmon and gravlax are draped like silk with caper beading.

The recipe for a delectable raspberry dessert was given to us by Seabourn chef Stefan Hamrin when we were writing a *Bon Appétit* article about luxury cruise ships in the Mediterranean several years ago.

Raspberry Parfait

10 servings

5 egg whites

1/4 cup sugar

1 1/8 cups sugar

4 ounces (1/2 cup) water

3 pints fresh raspberries

1/2 cup sugar

1 tsp lemon juice

4 cups whipping cream, whipped stiffly

Beat egg whites and 1/4 cup sugar together until stiff peaks form. Cook 1 1/8 cups of sugar with 4 ounces water to soft ball stage (when a bit of the mixture dropped into a cup of cold water forms a soft ball).

Carefully add this sugar syrup in a thin stream to the beaten egg whites, beating all the time to incorporate it, until the mixture is evenly cool.

Purée the raspberries and strain through a fine sieve to remove the seeds. Combine raspberry purée with 1/2 cup sugar and lemon juice and fold into the egg white mixture.

Finally, gently fold in the whipped cream and place in a mold or freezer form; place in freezer for several hours until firm. Serve with additional raspberry purée and whipped cream if desired.

Cuisine Report Card: A+

Showtime

When the ships began operation, the evening's entertainment was done by the Styleliners, a quartet of singers who perform music by Sondheim, Porter, Berlin, Gershwin and other notables in a choreographed concert style. The ships still offer musical caberet shows on the modest stage using the variety of principal artists performing during the cruise, as well as bringing in regional entertainers from the ports of call. Lecturers from celebrity chefs to contract bridge teachers, jazz artists, pianist-humorist Victor Borge and other celebrities. TV personality Dick Cavett, actress Brenda Vaccaro, Paris-based food writer Patricia Wells and astronaut Wally Schirra were among the recent guests.

Entertainment Report Card: A

Discounts

Seabourn never allows the "D" word to creep into a discussion, but a rose by any other name can still save some money on a cruise. Repeat passengers in The Seabourn Club get "savings on the cruise tariff" of 10 percent from having made a previous cruise, plus 5 percent off the fare for friends they bring along who occupy a separate suite. Cumulative days of cruising with the company also brings "substantial fare reductions," and anyone who completes 140 days aboard the ships gets the next cruise of up to 14 days free. An "early payment program" means if you book and pay for your cruise 12 months ahead of time you save 10 percent, six months ahead of time and you save 5 percent. A "single traveler savings option" on certain cruises reduces the normal 200 percent surcharge to only 110, 125 or 150 percent.

The standard suite-like cabins aboard **Seabourn Pride** *and* **Seabourn Spirit** *are large enough to have friends in for cocktails.*

The Bottom Line

When the *Seabourn Pride* had been running for a year and the *Seabourn Spirit* just introduced, we asked Warren Titus about the difference between operating Seabourn and operating Royal Viking. "It's much easier for us to cater to a single strata of people...They basically come from the same background and tastes...and it's so much easier to satisfy people on this ship than on a Royal Viking ship with a variety of cabins and prices."

Seabourn ships are the ultimate in patrician elegance without ever being stuffy. Your dinner table partner might turn out to have a title preceding his name, but he's unlikely to ever mention it. Everything works on these ships from the food to the service to the ambiance. You get, quite simply, a superbly satisifying cruise experience.

Seabourn Pride ★★★★★★
Seabourn Spirit ★★★★★★

Day after day, time after time, we find ourselves agreeing that there is nowhere else on earth we would rather be than right here, right now, aboard the Seabourn Pride *listening to Page Cavanaugh at the piano playing "Rainy Day" at cocktail time in the understated elegance of The Club.*

Notes from the inaugural sailing
December 1988

Nothing makes the folks at Seabourn madder than to hear their 10,000-ton cruise ships called "small," "little," or "yacht-sized." They have, as Warren Titus pointed out on the first sailing of the *Seabourn Pride*, "all the amenities and facilities of a full-sized cruise ship but only for a few people." Everything here is scaled to the human passenger rather than cruise industry statistics, and they spent a lot of time determining what the experienced cruise passenger who books the upper end of the market would like. Suite-rooms are a spacious 277 square feet with very lavish bathrooms and sitting areas large enough to host six people comfortably at cocktail time. There are all sorts of beautiful public rooms and deck spaces, along with, at one time, a mysterious flying saucer-like device called the Star Observatory, where passengers could climb in and lie back on cushy leather seats to star-gaze through a telescope; that's not easy on a moving ship, which is why we've never saw anyone try it.

The Brochure Says

"To some, Seabourn may be expensive; but Seabourn is not overpriced. Some cruise lines say they provide a 'Seabourn-like' experience at half price. We know it can't be done and so do you. New and so-called luxury cruise lines are cropping up and claiming five stars even before their ships are launched. At the same time, old and established cruise lines, as we knew them, are either disappearing or being modified and downgraded in price wars that offer the 'deal.' The authentic Seabourn Experience is a good value for the money, because we believe we provide an experience that exceeds your expectations."

Translation

This is an example of what we meant when we said above that Seabourn is "the ultimate in patrician elegance without ever being stuffy." They're not above taking off their white gloves to duke it out with the competition.

Cabins and Costs

Fantasy Suites: **Report Card: A+**

Average Price PPPD: $1780.

Owner's Suite Type E (there are two per ship) are 575 square feet with veranda, large living room with curved sofas, chairs and coffee table plus a dining table with four chairs, a marble bath with tub and twin sinks plus a second half-bath for guests, and a separate bedroom with all the amenities listed below (see Suitable Standards).

Small Splurges: **Report Card: A+**

Average Price PPPD: $1330.

Each of the 16 Regal B suites is 400 square feet with a small private veranda, queen-sized bed in a separate bedroom, curved sofas and chairs in the living room and lots of built-ins, plus all the amenities listed below (see Suitable Standards).

Suitable Standards: **Report Card: A+**

Average Price PPPD: $1025.

The standard suite-rooms are 277 square feet each with a five-foot picture window placed low enough on the wall that you can lie in bed (either twins or queen-sized) and watch the sea. A tapestry-print sofa, three chairs and two round stools provide plenty of guest seating, along with a mini-refrigerator, full array of crystal and a fully stocked liquor cabinet. The coffee table can be raised to dining table height if you want to dine in, and there's a walk-in closet with lots of storage, a built-in dresser/desk with drawers and mirror, and a marble bathroom with tub, twin sinks set in a marble counter and a mirrored storage area for toiletries.

Bottom Bunks: **Report Card: NA**

There's no such thing on Seabourn ships.

EAVESDROPPING

Famous Last Words Department: A quartet of San Francisco travel agents, invited for the christening-day tour of the Seabourn Pride, *walked from the gangway into the reception hall and turned up their noses at the last-minute touch-ups of artificial greenery to replace plants damaged in the stormy crossing, accepted a glass of champagne from a white-gloved waiter and flounced into the Magellan Lounge, where they sat at the back table just long enough to empty their glasses. "Hmph," one sniffed, "I don't like this room; it's too dark." "Well, this ship'll never touch the Sea Goddesses," her friend commented. "I've seen enough—ready to go?" And away they went, back down the gangway without looking at anything else.*

FOOTNOTE

We have had innumerable conversations with heads of certain ultra-deluxe cruise lines about why they don't include as largesse the relatively inexpensive duty-free bar drinks (even if it's house brands only) and dinner wines like Song of Flower, *Silversea and Sea Goddess ships do, and the answer we invariable get is, "The passengers who don't drink don't want to subsidize those that do."*

Where She Goes

The *Seabourn Pride* offers a coastal California cruise, on Aug. 13, then a transcanal to San Juan, a repositioning from San Juan to New York and a quartet of New England Canada cruises before heading for the Caribbean and Amazon for November and December.

The *Seabourn Spirit* starts 1996 with a 60-day Grand Cruise Around South America, available in three segments, then offers a couple of Caribbean cruises before setting on its transatlantic sailing March 28 to Lisbon.

The Bottom Line

Yes, it's expensive, but not even the worst nit-picker could find anything to complain about with the food, service and accommodations. And there are really exotic and interesting itineraries for 1996, calling at some rarely visited ports, along with appealing mix-and-match cruises that can be combined for a sizable savings. Go for the standard suite-rooms unless you want to splurge to get a veranda. When you head for the deck, there's a steward in white shirt and tie to turn your deck chair toward the sun hourly or spritz you with mineral water. In the evening, you can slip away for cocktails in the club while the pianist plays your favorite sentimental song, or don something dazzling for dinner dancing between courses in the restaurant. Or enjoy breakfast in bed while gazing at the sea through a five-foot picture window with its own automatic window washing system.

Fielding's Picks

Unforgettable Places

1. A watersports marina that can be thrust out from the ship when it's at anchor, letting passengers swim in a giant submersible steel mesh tank with its own teak deck around it, or go windsurfing, sailing or waterskiing.
2. Forward on the top deck is the Horizon Lounge with wrap-around glass windows, cushy blue leather chairs and couches, a polished granite bar, a radar screen for passengers to play with and a computer-animated wall map of famous historic voyages as well as itinerary information.
3. The Sky Bar, a wooden bar with a circle of barstools around it plus wooden tables and lower stools fixed on the teak decking, is one of the most popular gathering spots on the ships.
4. The Club, cool white and beige with wood, marble and woven textures, is equally handsome in the daytime with sunlight streaming in its glass dome or in the evening with the shades lowered and a pianist playing Duke Ellington compositions.
5. The Restaurant, with quiet, comfortable tables placed well apart, tapestry-patterned chairs and silky curtains; a pianist plays during dinner and there's a small dance floor for those evenings when dinner dancing is scheduled and passengers take a turn around the floor between courses.

Good Reasons to Book These Ships

1. Because service is so good you don't have to lift a finger; you can let things come to you, rather than having to go fetch them.
2. Because you can buy an air/land program that includes economy-class airfare or optional upgrades, premium hotel accommodations, hospitality desks at the hotels and transfers to and from the ship.
3. Because tipping is not only not requested, but not permitted.
4. The little extras that mean a lot—bathrobes, hair dryers, combination safes, walk-in closets with four different kinds of hangers, personalized stationery, a sewing kit with the needles already threaded, a 24-hour room service menu that includes everything from sandwiches to grilled steaks, complete sets of bathroom towels in two colors, peach and pewter gray, and exquisite almond-scented toiletries.
5. Instead of aspic-encased show buffets and parades of baked Alaska, you can find sevruga caviar whenever you want to order it, fresh broiled sea bass, sautéed pheasant breast with Calvados sauce, chocolate truffle cake.

Things You Won't Find On Board

1. A lap swimming pool; the smallish pool is adequate but wedged between the Veranda Cafe and a stairwell. The Jacuzzi is more popular than the pool.
2. A view of undersea life in the underwater viewing room on the bottom deck when the ship is moving; all you see are bubbles.
3. A delay on getting your laundry and dry cleaning back; same-day service is available.
4. A surprise when you get to the dining room; copies of the menus are delivered daily to the cabins so you can plan ahead.
5. Bar drinks and dinner wine included in the fares; you'll pay extra for those.

SEAWIND CRUISE LINE

4770 Biscayne Boulevard, Miami, FL 3137
☎ *(800) 223-1877*

History

Seawind Cruise Line was founded in 1991 by a mix of Portuguese, Swedish and Greek interests to market the classic Portuguese ocean liner *Vasco de Gama* in the Caribbean on sailings out of Aruba. Until mid-1995, the ship retained the name *Vasco de Gama* while it sailed as and was marketed under the trade name *Seawind Crown*. Now it is officially *Seawind Crown*, and the double names painted on the bow are gone.

The ship was christened in Aruba on Aug. 11, 1991, by Maria Kyriakidis, wife of charterer Takis Kyriakidis, whose charter agreement was abruptly terminated Sep. 20, 1991. The then-owners, doing business as Trans World Cruises, picked up the charter themselves, and the ship resumed sailing Oct. 6, 1991, under the direction of Bo Paulson, George Potamianos and Jan Hygrell. Paulson and Hygrell represented the Swedish shipping giant Nordisk, which sold the vessel in July 1995, to a group of New York investors named Capital Holiday.

Concept

Sailing from Aruba with two alternating southern Caribbean itineraries at modest prices in a very gracious and spacious classic liner.

Signatures

The dual names on the ship's bow certainly made it stand out in a crowd, but, alas, that whimsical touch is gone now. There's an elegant wood-paneled chapel that can be used for weddings or renewal of vows. And there's always the Great American Cookout/Picnic on deck with down-home American music from barbershop quartets and such.

Gimmicks

Honeymoon and anniversary celebrations for people married within seven days of their cruise or couples celebrating an anniversary during the cruise.

Who's the Competition

With Dolphin Cruise Line withdrawing the *OceanBreeze* from Aruba in May to take over the *Dolphin IV's* three- and four-day sailings from Miami, there'll be little real competition year-round for Seawind except in the general Caribbean marketplace itself.

Who's Aboard

A mix of 70 percent veteran and 30 percent first-time cruisers drawn by the price and itinerary, many of them young to middle-aged couples. The median age aboard is 45-50.

The ship also attracts a sizable contingent of Europeans, Latin Americans and Asians.

Who Should Go

Veteran cruisers will love the classic ship and the excellent itineraries, while first-timers will find all the traditional cruise touches they expect presented in an un-glitzy fashion. An extra bonus for island collectors: If you take the two cruises back-to-back, you'll visit eight islands.

Who Should Not Go

Passengers who need a wheelchair-accessible cabin; there are none aboard. Families with small children, since there's no children's program or counselor. Anyone who thinks it's not a Caribbean cruise if it doesn't call in St. Thomas.

Teak and tile ornament the pool deck of this classic Portuguese liner.

The Lifestyle

Basically, a traditional cruise pattern is followed, with exercise classes, musical and variety show entertainment, skeet-shooting, scuba and snorkel lessons. There are two formal nights during the week.

EAVESDROPPING

Travel agent on board: "My cabin I can get to in three minutes. On a three-day cruise on those big ships, you spend the whole three days trying to find your way around. Everything is right here—you don't have to walk five blocks just to get to the lounge."

Wardrobe

Casual island resort wear is proper daytime and shoreside apparel.

There are two formal nights aboard during each week, the captain's welcome-aboard and farewell parties, which call for men to wear a tuxedo, dinner jacket or suit, or at least a jacket and tie.

Bill of Fare

The food is generally good, but the caterers lean toward large show buffets, flaming desserts and displays to impress first-time cruisers. There are some innovative Caribbean and Latin American dishes, as well as a couple of Greek specialties, that show up from time to time to supplement the run of oxtail consomme, duckling à l'orange and cherries jubilee. There are two meal seatings at assigned tables. First dinner seating is usually 6:30, the second at 8:30.

Cuisine Report Card: B

Showtime

There's a lot of entertainment with different musical productions nightly from Vanoff Productions of Miami, featuring feather-clad chorus girls who, when they exit, leave the stage looking like it's molting season. Caribbean bands play poolside in the daytime, and a combo plays dance music in the Panorama Lounge. Movies run daily in the cinema and on the cabin TV sets.

Entertainment Report Card: C+

Discounts

Seawind does some aggressive marketing, with advance purchase rates for anyone booking with a deposit 60 days ahead of sailing and a discounted second week for anyone booked 14 days back-to-back. A special Aruba land package called Free-Aruba adds on a free seven-night resort stay in Aruba at La Cabana All-Suite Beach Resort and Casino for passengers who have booked in cabin categories A through D. If you buy a cheaper cabin, in categories E through G, you'll still get three nights free at La Cabana. The airfare is included in that package too. You can also, if you prefer, opt for a free Caribbean wilderness adventure in Dominica or St. Lucia. If you cruise five nights on board in a cabin category A through G, you get four nights in Dominica's The Castaways (a beach and dive resort) or Fort Young Hotel (an urban hotel built in an old fort). If you cruise five nights on board in cabin categories A through D, you get seven nights free in The Harmony (a 30-room hotel at Rodney Bay) or Orange Grove Hotel (a hilltop hotel with its own private beach below) in St. Lucia.

The Bottom Line

This is a very good buy for anyone interested in cruising on a mid-sized classic ship to Caribbean islands a little off the beaten track.

Seawind Crown ★★★★

It was an object lesson in how not to initiate a new cruise line—compared with, say, Crystal, which spent more than two years paving the way. The erstwhile charterer picked up the ship in a dock in Aruba at the end of a chartered Brazilian cruise (and some of the Brazilians refused to get off, so they sailed on the inaugural with us). He also flew out from Miami carrying two tons of excess baggage that consisted mostly of printed materials for the vessel. The costumes for the entertainers were impounded by Aruban officials (probably because of all the feathers), and the final blow came when the line's new president, while describing to the press all the 11th-hour travail, picked up a packet of sugar to sweeten his coffee and saw that it was marked Premier Cruise Line, a rival line that shares the same catering company.

The *Seawind Crown*, previously the *Vasco de Gama*, was built as the *Infante dom Enrique* in 1961 for the Portugal-to-Mozambique service and was laid up in Lisbon in 1976 after the African colony won its independence from Portugal and there was no further need to transport bureaucrats and their families back and forth.

In 1988, a major refurbishment supervised by George Potamianos was done in Greece to turn the ship into the *Vasco de Gama*, the name of the street in Lisbon where George lives. It would be interesting to ship buffs to make a walk-through figuring out which areas were what when it was a two-class ship. We got some clues from George. The smaller Madeira Restaurant adjoining the big dining room was the first-class dining room, the casino the first-class bar. There were even separate children's playrooms, presumably so the kids of the first-class passengers didn't have to associate with the kids of the second-class passengers. Turns out they didn't pray together either, since there was a second-class chapel where the mural behind the pool is located now. The existing chapel is, of course, the old first-class chapel. There was even, George said, a Tourist Class B, the next thing to steerage, and a lot of the cabins didn't have private baths in the old days. He also built what we believe is one of the few seagoing squash courts, but it was supplanted not long ago, alas, by an ordinary mirrored gym and fitness center.

The Brochure Says

"A half-century ago, when cruising was still the exclusive domain of the very rich, there was a certain style of life aboard cruise ships, a simple, classic style of service that is rarely found in the world today. Here, in the balmy waters of Seawind's Caribbean, time has stood still, and thoughtful, gracious service still awaits you."

Translation

Although the international crew may represent as many as 34 different nationalities, there is a warmth and friendliness from them that most cruisers will enjoy.

Cabins and Costs

Fantasy Suites: **Report Card: B**

Average Price PPPD: $420 including airfare and free Aruba land stay.

The two owner's suites are spacious apartments with a large living room and separate bedroom, lots of windows facing forward, a couch that can convert to additional sleeping, coffee table, two chairs, color TV set, mini-refrigerator, built-in desk and entry hall. In the bedroom are two single beds, a long built-in table with console and nightstands, two large closets, and a huge bathroom with two wash basins, tub and shower and storage shelves.

Small Splurges: **Report Card: B**

Average Price PPPD: $335 including airfare and free Aruba land stay.

Also on the topmost deck are eight suites not quite as large as the owner's but very handsomely furnished, part of the 12 suites that were created out of 24 original cabins in the 1988 refurbishment.

Suitable Standards: **Report Card: C**

Average Price PPPD: $263 including airfare and free Aruba land stay.

In category H, fairly good-sized cabins with chest, dresser, three closets, optional overhead bunks, and bath with shower.

Bottom Bunks: **Report Card: B**

Average Price PPPD: $192 including airfare and free Aruba land stay.

The very lowest-priced category are the 32 inside cabins with upper and lower berths, a small three-drawer chest, dresser, TV, mini-refrigerator, terrycloth robes, hair dryers, bathroom with shower, a large mirror, altogether quite adequate unto the need.

FOOTNOTE

On the inaugural sailing of the Seawind Crown, *everyone was so frantic and flustered that the theme from "Gone With The Wind" played over and over on the cabin radios, every day of the cruise until Friday, when someone, perhaps a bored Brazilian, put on samba tapes, which then played nonstop for the remaining two days.*

Where She Goes

The *Seawind Crown* sails two alternate itineraries in the Caribbean out of Aruba, one week calling in Curaçao, Grenada, Barbados and St. Lucia, and the next week visiting Antigua, Guadeloupe, Barbados and Dominica, giving a real collector eight islands in 14 days, including Aruba.

The Bottom Line

We like the ship and the line for the money they charge, and the Free-Aruba package makes it a very good buy, throwing in on one package price roundtrip airfare, a seven-night cruise and overnight stays in Aruba, the number of nights and type of hotel depending on the accommodations you booked aboard the ship. There are also new packages for Dominica and for St. Lucia, which let you cruise five nights on the ship, then stay in an island resort for four to seven nights and fly home from that island. That's a creative solution to the problem of airlift into Aruba to get the passengers all in and out. The impending departure of the *OceanBreeze* will help alleviate that problem, perhaps.

Fielding's Picks

Super Places

1. The chapel, a quiet, elegant little room on an upper deck, with an original inlaid wood mural outside, where passengers can participate in a renewal-of-wedding-vows ceremony.
2. The Panorama Lounge, used for cabaret acts and dancing in the evenings.
3. The spiffy lower-deck gym, replacing a unique squash court but probably more popular among the North American passengers.

4. The Taverna doubles as a casual breakfast and lunch buffet area but is a bit small to handle the passenger numbers. However it makes a warm and cozy hideaway between meals.
5. The pool deck has a raised platform for the musicians, a horseshoe-shaped bar, white plastic loungers, chairs and tables, plus a large, lap-sized swimming pool; there's a second, smaller one on the deck above.

Good Reasons to Book This Ship

1. To go back to the days of elegant transatlantic liners.
2. The price is right.
3. The itineraries let you discover a lot of the Southern Caribbean on a seven-day cruise.
4. You can get a free Aruba, St. Lucia or Dominica vacation before or after your cruise; see Discounts, above, for details.
5. Cabins are spacious and the ship never feels crowded.

Things You Won't Find On Board

1. That wonderful squash court that used to be there.
2. Two names painted on the bow—with the new ownership, it's now officially the *Seawind Crown*.
3. A self-service laundry.
4. Theme cruises.
5. Ushers in the cinema.

SILVERSEA CRUISES

110 East Broward Boulevard, Ft. Lauderdale, FL 33301
☎ *(305) 522-4477, (800) 722-9055*

History

Founded in 1992 by the Francesco Lefebvre family of Rome and the Vlasov Group of Monte Carlo, the former owners of now-defunct Sitmar Cruises, Silversea built its line around two 296-passenger super-luxury vessels instead of returning to big-ship cruising in the Sitmar style.

The *Silver Cloud*, which debuted April 2, 1994, and the *Silver Wind*, which debuted Jan. 29, 1995, were designed by Norwegian architects Pettar Yran and Bjorn Storbraaten, who also designed the interiors of the Seabourn and Sea Goddess ships as well as the renovated *Song of Flower* for Radisson Seven Seas Cruises.

—The Silversea name ties in with the Vlasov Group's 80-year-old British-based shipping company called the Silver Line.

—V.SHIPS, Inc., of Monte Carlo, also part of the Vlasov Group, provides many cruise lines around the world with officers and crews and other operational services.

Concept

The intent to provide full all-inclusive packaging in one price, including onboard beverage service, all gratuities on board, port taxes, baggage handling and selected shore excursions. Air/sea packages also factor in air travel, transfers, porterage and a choice of overnight or day deluxe five-star hotel room prior to embarkation. All-inclusive fares are available on cruise-only or air/sea packages. Free shuttles between the port and town are also offered in many ports of call.

Signatures

The Silversea Experience—a special shore excursion that is included for all passengers that explores some special aspect of local culture or hospitality, perhaps dinner in a Victorian castle, a private wine tasting in Bordeaux or a Turkish wedding party with camels and belly dancers and a lavish picnic in a pine forest.

Gimmicks

Special affiliations with prestigious companies lets Silversea produce themed sailings such as a series of Le Cordon Bleu voyages featuring chefs from the famous Paris cooking school preparing meals and demonstrating culinary techniques, along with wine tastings conducted by the head of Domaines Lafite Rothschild.

Who's the Competition

It's pretty obvious that Silversea's competition is other players in the small-ship ultra-luxury market. But with larger ships, a higher proportion of private verandas, increasingly finer food and service, and all-inclusive fares at very competitive prices, this newcomer can give Seabourn, Sea Goddess, Royal's *Queen Odyssey* and Radisson Seven Seas a run for the money.

Who's Aboard

Everybody from Charlton Heston (guest-starring in a recent film festival aboard the *Silver Cloud*) to your friendly neighborhood travel agent (if your zip code is 90210). On one recent sailing aboard the *Silver Wind*, the guest list ranged from two college-age passengers from New Jersey traveling with their parents to an Italian principessa and a number of doctors and professors; passenger home addresses included the United States, Britain, Hong Kong, Italy, Germany, The Netherlands, Mexico, Bermuda, Switzerland and Austria. Passengers are predominantly middle-aged couples, many of whom have sailed aboard some of the other super-luxury lines.

Who Should Go

Anyone who likes a lot of options, with, say, a choice of lunch in the dining room, on the canvas-shaded terrace of the Terrace Cafe, on the private veranda of your cabin or ashore in a waterfront cafe; people who stay in Relais & Chateaux hotels; people who want individual service and attention.

Who Should Not Go

Anyone whose idea of a really great meal is a Big Mac with fries; anyone whose all-time favorite vacation was a week at Disney World or a weekend in Las Vegas; anyone with small children, because there's no program or playroom for kids on these ships.

The Lifestyle

Life on board the Silversea ships will feel familiar to any veteran of the other super-deluxe vessels—luxurious, sociable, stress-free without schedules and regimentation. Two well-traveled British couples on a recent sailing around Italy never got off the ship.

Shipboard activities are low-key, ranging from nine fitness classes a day to a printed quiz, duplicate bridge, trivia, a galley tour or water volleyball. A sports marina that can be opened off the stern of the ship when it is at anchor allows passengers a chance for windsurfing, snorkeling and sailing from the ship. A larger-than-average swimming pool on board is long enough for modest laps.

Arriving guests find chilled champagne, fresh flowers and a bowl of fruit in their suites, as well as a fully stocked bar and mini-refrigerator. With a high ratio of staff to passengers (one crew member for every 1.5 passengers) and an extremely high passenger-space-ratio of 56.75, you can anticipate a leisurely, pampering cruise experience. But many veteran travelers say the detail they appreciate most about an all-inclusive cruise is the freedom from signing bar chits or figuring out tips.

Wardrobe

The Silversea ships are fairly dressy with passengers fashionably attired daytimes as well as evenings when we've been aboard (except for a couple of elderly Brits who wandered around most of the day in the terrycloth robes from their cabins). Formal wear is requested for two evenings a week, with most men wearing either a tuxedo or dinner jacket and women in their most glamorous outfits. It's telling that the daily programs do not find it necessary to tell passengers exactly what formal dress requires. Informal dress, usually requested two or three nights out of seven, calls for men to wear a jacket and tie, while casual garb on the remaining evenings is still fairly dressy on these ships. Anyone who doesn't feel like dressing for dinner can always order dinner from the dining room menu to be served course-by-course in the cabin.

Bill of Fare

The cuisine is contemporary, restaurant-style cooking with a nice mix of simple and sophisticated dishes and an emphasis on fresh foods. Very early or late risers will find coffee, tea, pitchers of freshly-squeezed orange and grapefruit juice, and fresh-baked croissants and other pastries in the Panorama Lounge on an upper deck between 6 and 11 a.m., followed by bouillon and crackers at 11. Full breakfast and lunch buffets and a la carte menu of hot dishes is set out daily in the Terrace Cafe, and The Restaurant serves all meals on an open seating arrangement that lets guests arrive when they wish and sit where they please. In addition, a special themed dinner may be served in the Terrace Cafe or on deck once or twice a cruise.

Cuisine Report Card: A

Showtime

The entertainment aboard usually includes a couple of variety acts, a team of magicians and a puppeteer, for instance, plus some singers and dancers, usually a quartet of Americans called the Styleliners who present music from the Gershwin/Cole Porter era as well as more contemporary show tunes and pop music, or the Matrix Dancers, a British group that perform scaled-down versions of traditional cruise production shows.

A pianist or harpist is on hand to play during teatime and dinner, a quartet plays for dancing, the casino is open when the ship is at sea and films are screened on cabin TV sets or available anytime day or night in the library for your cabin VCR.

Entertainment Report Card: A

Discounts

Besides a full air/sea, all-inclusive package price, Silversea also offers an early booking incentive of 10 percent off for passengers who book and pay a deposit four months ahead of sailing date; a combination cruise program that saves up to $3,000 off the published air/sea fare for passengers booking two or more consecutive sailings; and an advanced payment bonus for 15 per cent when payment is received in full six months prior to sailing.

The Bottom Line

These all-inclusive, very luxurious ships should appeal to almost everyone who's extra-demanding about food, accommodations and service. With a sizable contingent of former Royal Viking Line personnel in the hotel operations on Silversea, you can expect the same quality that RVL always provided. The vessels themselves are well-designed, with spacious decks and public rooms, very comfortable suites, many of them with verandas, and alert and personable cabin stewardesses. A concierge is always on duty to help with any shipboard or shoreside requests. For what it costs, Silversea sailings represent a very good upscale cruise buy. (One passenger recently figured that he saved $1813 on items included in the 11-day air/sea package that he would have had to pay for on similar lines without inclusive packages.)

Silver Cloud ★★★★★★
Silver Wind ★★★★★★

While we thought the Silversea concept was excellent, we didn't consider it really earthshaking, at least not until the day we drove back to Monte Carlo, having spent the day touring the Silver Cloud, *under construction at the shipyard in Genoa, to learn that at the same time we were aboard the ship, the Northridge earthquake, the most costly natural disaster in the history of the U.S., was taking out parts of the Los Angeles area. While we found nothing damaged when we got home, we still think of that 6.8 temblor every time we board a Silversea ship.*

The pretty pink dining room of the* Silver Cloud *serves very good cuisine cooked a la minute.

On check-in, passengers find a bottle of champagne in the suite, chilling in a silver ice bucket, a bud vase of fresh flowers, maybe orchids, a mini-refrigerator stocked with Evian and soft drinks, a liquor cabinet with several large bottles of different spirits, an epergne of fresh fruit, foil-wrapped chocolates on turndown, a mini-refrigerator (to keep the champagne cold if you don't want to drink it then), and a full set of glassware in a cocktail cabinet. Everything is replenished frequently. The only extra expenses you'll have are laundry and dry cleaning, the casino, shopping and extra-premium wines and champagnes if you want to pay a surcharge. Otherwise, the wines they pour with meals are quite acceptable; there are usually two or three choices.

The layout of the sister ships makes it easy to find your way around—Vista Suites, The Restaurant, photo shop and self-service laundry on the lowest passenger deck, then The Bar, casino, boutique and entry lobby on the next deck up, along with Veranda Suites. Take one more deck up the stairs or one of the elevators to the main lobby, show lounge, card room, concierge and information desks. The Terrace Cafe, fitness center and beauty salon are one more deck up, then the pool deck and Panorama Lounge. High atop the ship is a walking/jogging track and the glass-walled observation lounge.

The Brochure Says

"Silversea cruises are truly all inclusive as everything you could possibly desire on board is included in your fare: All suite accommodations, complimentary alcoholic and non-alcoholic beverages, select wines with lunch and dinner, all gratuities, all port taxes, 24 hour room service, in suite a la carte dining, all entertainment, on board lectures and a special shoreside event."

Translation

Who could ask for anything more?

CHAMPAGNE TOAST

A glass of the bubbly to Silverseas for including port taxes in their all-inclusive fare. This annoying and oft-times overpriced head tax is almost always an extra on other ships.

INSIDER TIP

There are two suites for the physically challenged on the Silver Wind *(640 and 643) but none on the* Silver Cloud.

Cabins and Costs

Fantasy Suites: **Report Card: A+**

Average Price PPPD: $1054 for full air/sea package; $944 for air/sea package on Grand Suite with one bedroom.

The term could aptly apply to virtually all the accommodations on board these ships, certainly any of those with a private veranda, but if you really wanted to book the top digs, one of the 1314-square-foot Grand Suites should do fine. A two-bedroom suite with three small private verandas, a huge living room and a second smaller sitting room, dining area with ocean view, entertainment center with CD, TV, and VCR, mini-refrigerator, two walk-in closets and two marble bathrooms with full-sized tubs.

Small Splurges: **Report Card: A+**

Average Price PPPD: $899.

The Silver Suite (three to each ship) is usually the first to be booked on board these ships. At 541 square feet, it's almost twice the size of the standard suites, and has a large veranda, big living room and dining ell, a separate bedroom, walk-in closet and marble bath with tub. Also inside: Twin beds that convert to queen-sized, an entertainment center, two TV sets, VCR, refrigerator, cocktail cabinet, writing desk, wall safe, dressing table and lots of storage space.

Suitable Standards: **Report Card: A**

Average Price PPPD: $624.

We regard the Silversea Veranda Suite as standard, and the Vista Suite (without veranda, see below) as slumming because we love being able to sit out in the fresh sea breezes anytime day or night. The Veranda Suite has 295 square feet, including a small private veranda, with the sitting area adjacent to the veranda and furnished with sofa, three chairs, table, built-in desk/dresser, entertainment center, mini-refrigerator, cocktail cabinet, wall safe, walk-in closet, dressing table with hair dryer, twin or queen-sized bed and marble bathroom with tub.

Bottom Bunks: **Report Card: A**

Average Price PPPD: $400.

Despite our flip comment above, booking a Vista Suite is not exactly slumming, even if it is the lowest-price cabin category on the ships. With 240 square feet of space and all the furnishings detailed above except the private verandas (see Suitable Standards, above) it would be quite acceptable.

Where She Goes

The *Silver Cloud* spends most of the year in Southeast Asia, Europe and the East Coast of Canada and the U.S. before finishing out the winter in the Caribbean.

The *Silver Wind* starts the year in the Caribbean and South America with seven-, 10-, 11- and 14-day cruises, including a Buenos Aires-to-Valparaiso sailing Jan. 31, then makes a transatlantic crossing from Barbados to Civitavecchia (for Rome) April 26 to start the summer European season.

***Looking down at the pool deck from the jogging track on the* Silver Cloud.**

The Bottom Line

After a tentative start, Silversea has really come a long way. The infusion of new staff from the Royal Viking ships and *Song of Flower* has sharpened the hotel staff, and the kitchen is turning out a more-polished version of contemporary cuisine than at the beginning.

At the same time, it's a comfortable, non-intimidating cruise experience where everything is done just right without someone hovering at your elbow all the time.

While not as showy as Seabourn (you won't find silver cloches lifted in unison in the dining room here) or as sybaritic as Sea Goddess (we haven't run across serve-yourself tins of caviar among the canapes), Silversea ranks right up there on our happy vacation roster.

Fielding's Picks

Fabulous Places

1. The natural teak pool deck with its 30 x 12 foot swimming pool, long enough for modest laps, two Jacuzzis, sunny and shaded lounging areas, long wooden bar with wood barstools in one corner, loungers covered with blue/white striped cushions and tables with umbrellas.
2. The hideaway Observation Lounge high atop the topmost deck sits out on its own like a glass bubble furnished with wicker chairs, glass tables, cactus gardens and monitors showing wind speed and other operational ship's data.

3. The elegant double stairway with brass rails that is the heart of the ship; if you look up from each landing you can see the shape of a ship's keel overhead.
4. The Bar and the adjoining Parisian Lounge, Art Nouveau-style with art glass insets and Erte painted figures on each side of the stage, elaborate period lamps with wrought iron and copper trim, and glass doors etched with champagne glasses and bubbles.
5. The Terrace Cafe, more like your favorite restaurant than a ship's casual buffet cafe, with wood walls and green and yellow tapestry print chairs, lots of green plants and fresh cut flowers.

Good Reasons to Book These Ships

1. Because everything is included in one neat package (see "The Brochure Says", above).
2. Because a special Silversea Experience is included with every cruise; our favorite was on the *Silver Cloud* when we were taken to a pine forest near Antalya for spectacular Turkish wedding feast—Turkish wines, two dozen cold appetizers, six or eight different kind of kebabs grilled over charcoal, a table of desserts and fresh fruits, and a costumed wedding couple who rode through the trees on decorated camels greeting guests while folk dancers and belly dancers performed on a small open-air stage.
3. For an extremely smooth ride despite the vessels' shallow drafts; in the Aegean we didn't notice any motion until we looked out and saw a 40 mph wind blowing the lounge chairs all over the deck.
4. For a toning and trimming spa routine with Steiner of London, including the only thalassotherepy tub on a ship this small; massage and beauty treatment rooms, saunas and steam rooms, ionotherapy, and nine exercise classes a day plus personal training consultations.
5. For a very well-rounded introduction to super-deluxe cruising in a non-pretentious atmosphere.

Things You Won't Find On Board

1. A snob; despite the elegance, all the passengers are very friendly and socialize easily.
2. A baby; the line doesn't permit infants under one and severely limits small children under three.
3. Enough days at sea; no matter how well-planned the itineraries, passengers never feel they have enough free time to luxuriate aboard these lovely ships.
4. A crowded shore excursion bus; the line's routine is to book enough tour buses to allow everyone to spread out and be comfortable with a maximum of 60 percent of the seats occupied and a carry-on kit of mineral water, soft drinks and disposable washcloths.
5. A closet hanger with skirt clips; nitpicking, we admit, but on board both *Silver Cloud* and *Silver Wind* (a year apart) we've requested these from housekeeping and have been told "they're on order."

SPECIAL EXPEDITIONS

123 South Avenue East, Third Floor, Westfield, NJ 07090
☎ *(908) 654-0048, (800) 348-2358*

History

Launched in 1979 as a travel company offshoot of Lindblad Travel by Sven-Olof Lindblad, son of the late expedition pioneer Lars-Eric Lindblad, Special Expeditions has also carved out its own very special niche in expedition cruising. Sven bought the division in 1984 and acquired the line's first ship, the 80-passenger *Polaris*, the former *Lindblad Polaris*, in 1987, followed by the *Sea Lion* in 1989 and the *Sea Bird* in 1990. With Captain Hasse Nilsson, longtime captain for the Lindblad vessels, Sven co-owns the *Swedish Islander*, a 128-foot ship that carries 45 passengers around the Stockholm Archipelago for a program called "Impressions of a Swedish Summer," putting them up overnight in small country inns. Special Expeditions is also the best-known North American charterer of the famous sailing yacht *Sea Cloud*, built for cereal heiress Marjorie Merriweather Post.

Concept

The logo for Special Expeditions, a giant eye in dark blue, "stands for a different way of looking at the world, with more of an in-depth perspective," says Lindblad. Many of the places his expeditions visit are fresh and fascinating, not always as gee-whiz name-dropper stops but visited rather for their own unique environments, and the company's excellent expedition leaders and naturalists devote considerable time and attention to interpreting them for passengers.

Signatures

The blue eye logo on the stack of the line's flagship *Polaris* and the sides of the smaller *Sea Lion* and *Sea Bird*.

Zodiacs, inflatable rubber landing craft used to explore ashore or venture in close to icebergs and cliffs of nesting seabirds.

Allowing a serendipitous flexibility in the schedule when something special occurs.

Including all shore excursions and sightseeing, as well as some transfers and shore meals, in the basic fares.

A generosity of spirit in refusing to exploit on-board revenue—visits to the ship's doctor are free and the staff frequently offers free drinks or beer and wine with meals.

Gimmicks

Publishing individual brochures for each sailing or series of similar sailings rather than an entire catalogue of cruises by the year.

Who's the Competition

The *Polaris's* classic competitors in the expedition field are the *Explorer* from Abercrombie & Kent, once its Lindblad Travel stablemate, and Society Expeditions' *World Discoverer*. In Alaska and the Pacific Northwest, the *Sea Lion* and *Sea Bird* come head-to-head with Alaska Sightseeing/Cruise West's very similar small vessels, which offer fewer expeditioning extras than Lindblad. The *Sea Cloud*, in our opinion, has no competition; it stands alone.

Who's Aboard

Mostly seniors and retirees who have the time and money for expeditioning and the thirst to learn more about the world around them.

Who Should Go

Birdwatchers of the world—these are some of the most fantastic voyages for birding we've ever been aboard; whale watchers and wildlife spotters; photographers; more young people who enjoy hiking and ecotourism.

Who Should Not Go

Families with very young children—there's no program for children and no place for them to play.

People with wheelchairs or walkers—these ships have no elevators but do have numerous steep stairs and gangways to negotiate.

The Lifestyle

The overall ambiance is one of fun and discovery, due in part to the energetic young naturalists and expedition leaders. Dress is casual, and single-seating meals are served at unassigned tables. Aboard the *Polaris*, you'll be able to have your hair done, see a doctor or take a sauna, but don't expect a swimming pool, cabin TV set, casino, slot machines or after-dinner entertainment. You may, however, go ashore on an uninhabited island for a barbecue dinner or set out in a glass-bottomed boat on a balmy moonlit night to sip champagne while drifting over luminous seas sparkling with rainbow-colored fish, or go swimming or snorkeling from empty beaches in clear turquoise waters. You'll also go back to school if you wish—and everyone does—attending lectures, reading supplementary materials and watching films and slides when not actually ashore or in a Zodiac exploring.

Wardrobe

Very casual, sturdy expeditioning clothes—jeans, twills, shorts and T-shirts, swimsuits, sweaters, depending on the climate, plus sturdy shoes for deck wear and hiking ashore and rain gear in some climates. Most passengers take along one sort of dress-up outfit, not black tie and sequins but more on the order of bolo tie and knit dress.

Bill of Fare

Food is not an obsession with Sven-Olof's passengers—most require only that it be healthful, substantial and digestible with no strange seasonings or ingredients a lifelong New Englander can't recognize. The chefs do a nice job in spite of the guests. Meals are served at a single open seating, allowing passengers to sit where and with whom they please. They do, however, as we have observed over the years, tend to stake out the same table and tablemates for most of the cruise.

Cuisine Report Card: B

Showtime

Unless you count the nightly 7 p.m. "recap"—the recapitulation of what happened today and the forecast of what may or may not happen tomorrow—as entertainment, these ships have none.

Entertainment Report Card: N/A

The Bottom Line

Special Expeditions has moved ahead carefully and cautiously, concentrating on its strong suits rather than trying to spread itself too thin and offer too many different options to its dedicated repeaters, many of whom sailed with Sven's father before him. It is a solid, predictable cruise product of very high quality and dignity, worth every penny of the sometimes substantial price.

Polaris ★★★, ⚓⚓⚓⚓⚓

Expeditioners would rather actively participate than passively observe, would be more intent at a slide lecture on seabird migration than a big-money game of jackpot bingo and are unruffled when schedules and itineraries are juggled without notice because of weather conditions or other unexpected problems. There's little ostentation—dressing for dinner may mean changing into clean clothes, and the only one-upmanship practiced at cocktail time is about rare birds spotted or offbeat destinations visited previously.

Homey, low-key and comfortable, the 82-passenger *Polaris* provides single-seating meals at unassigned tables for four or six, allowing everyone a chance to get acquainted, and wide windows in the dining room mean no one has to miss a whale sighting during lunch. On one *Polaris* cruise, our well-traveled fellow passengers, many near or past retirement age, included an archeologist from New Mexico, a New York architect, a Hollywood screenwriter-director, a rice farmer from California's central valley, attorneys, university professors and stockbrokers.

The Bahamian-registry ship is sturdy rather than glamorous, but the cabins are well-furnished and comfortable and the Filipino service staff and Swedish officers friendly and efficient. The captain usually allows visitors on the bridge on an informal basis.

FOOTNOTE

The Polaris *was the only cruise ship that passed through the Panama Canal during the U.S. military action against Panama's president Manuel Noriega in 1989. The ship was already in the canal when the firing started, and was stalled at the locks nearest Panama City for an hour or so, with some gunfire and a lot of helicopters flying overhead. The passengers were brought inside and below decks since there was shooting going on. "It was terrible for our bird list," one of the naturalists observed later.*

The Brochure Says

"Where can you snorkel on the largest barrier reef in the New World, search for toucans and howler monkeys in the rain forest, discover vibrant native cultures, and walk among the temples of ancient Mayan cities? You can do all this between Panama and Belize—a region of coral reefs, wildlife reserves, archeological treasures and welcoming people."

Translation

This is the strong suit aboard the *Polaris*, the chance to explore and discover all the wonders listed above. If you take all the shore excursions—they're included in the fare—you'll discover at least three-quarters of what they promise, if not a hundred percent. Unlike many cruise line brochures, those of Special Expeditions never promise what they don't have a good chance of delivering.

Cabins and Costs

Fantasy Suites: **Report Card: B**

Average Price PPPD: $775 plus airfare.

The owner's suite has two full-sized beds and a lot of space (but it's no bigger than the slightly cheaper #321 down the hall). Sitting areas are handsomely furnished in navy blue with sofa and matching chair piped in red, and there is a desk/dresser with its own chair and a coffee table. Two windows.

Small Splurges: **Report Card: B**

Average Price PPPD: $683 plus airfare.

The aforementioned #321 (see above) has much the same decor and furniture as the owner's suite and is also convenient to the public area and decks. Two windows.

Suitable Standards: **Report Card: B**

Average Price PPPD: $470 plus airfare.

The largest category of standard cabins is Category 2 with 22 examples, all but one with windows instead of portholes. (Cabin #101 one deck lower has a porthole). All cabins are outsides. Twin beds, windows, a desk/dresser with chair, lamp and telephone, and bathroom with shower are typical of this category.

Bottom Bunks: **Report Card: C**

Average Price PPPD: $415 plus airfare.

Four outside doubles with portholes instead of windows are the lowest-priced cabins aboard, and contain the same general decor and furniture arrangement as the suitable standards, above. Your portholes will sometimes look like washing machines when seas are churning.

Where She Goes

The *Polaris* starts the year in Central America where she transits the Panama Canal between Panama and Costa Rica with "A Journey on the Wild Side" itineraries, then crosses the Atlantic in April to Lisbon to begin her cultural and historical explorations of Europe, including the islands of Britain and Ireland and the Norwegian Fjords. Then she sets out for the Scandinavian and Canadian Arctic before turning south toward the Caribbean.

The Bottom Line

Basically it's a no-frills cruise with some largish, some smallish cabins, lectures and slide shows on every subject from seabird migration to the life cycle of lichens; inflatable rubber landing craft to take passengers ashore on deserted islands or navigate through narrow river channels; and no-nonsense dinners, briskly served and sometimes eaten without a change of clothes from the last expedition of the afternoon. But the ship is a favorite of well-traveled people for its warmth and friendliness. It's expensive, but we've never been disappointed with a cruise aboard the *Polaris.*

Fielding's Picks

Good Reasons to Book This Ship

1. To get an incomparable introduction to an exotic corner of the world that is unique.
2. To travel with like-minded fellow passengers who care intensely about nature and the environment.
3. To listen to some of the brightest and best naturalist/lecturers on the expedition circuit.
4. To be able to scoot around the seas of the world in Zodiacs or the ship's own glass-bottomed boat.
5. To be able to go on the "open bridge" and look at the radar and navigation charts and chat with the officers.

Sea Cloud ★★★★, ⚓⚓⚓⚓⚓

While any vessel with white sails puffed by the wind is romantic, the sailing yacht Sea Cloud *is the most romantic of all the tall ships, not only because of her grace and beauty, but also because of her history. The yacht was built for a glamorous heiress by a fabled financier who loved her, became a nursery garden of delights for a child who would grow up to become a famous actress, and was briefly a home during the holidays for many of the world's rich and famous, as well as the rich and infamous. The legendary ship went on to become the toy of a Latin American dictator, a playpen for movie starlets, then an impounded derelict rotting away in Panama before being rescued by a group of German yachtsmen who restored her to her original glory.*

The *Sea Cloud* was built for $1 million in 1931 in the Krupp yard in Kiel, Germany, and was the largest privately-owned yacht in the world when she was delivered to cereal heiress Marjorie Merriweather Post and her then-husband financier E. F. Hutton. The four-masted barque was first named *Hussar V*, since she was fifth in the series of yachts Hutton had built under that name. (See Windjammer Barefoot Cruises, the *Mandalay*, page 387 for the *Hussar IV*.) Their daughter, actress Dina Merrill, remembers in her childhood spending six months of every year sailing around the world with guests such as the Duke and Duchess of Windsor.

FOOTNOTE

Marjorie rented a large warehouse in New Jersey where she chalked out the deck plan on the floor and endlessly arranged and rearranged the antique furniture until it suited her, then transferred it to the ship. All the bric-a-brac and ornaments were glued to the mantels and tabletops where she meant for them to stay.

The Brochure Says

"The *Sea Cloud's* graceful style still inspires awe and admiration today, whether in port or under sail. And the exhilaration of being on board, under full sail in warm tropical waters, is without comparison."

Translation

You're an instant celebrity in any port when you disembark this unique and glamorous vessel, and you'll find yourself fending off street vendors in the Caribbean who think you must be very, very rich.

FOOTNOTE

Rafael Trujillo had come into possession of the Sea Cloud *by trading a 44-passenger Viscount propjet to Marjorie for it. He then put a cannon on the side of the yacht, named it* Angelina, *termed it a man-of-war and rented it back from the Dominican Republic's Navy for $1 a year. His favorite illegitimate son Ramfis took it to college with him when he was enrolled in law school in Southern California. When Trujillo was assassinated in 1961, family members and loyal aides fled the country aboard the yacht with some $5 million in cash and the dictator's body in an elaborate mahogany coffin in the smoking room. After they were intercepted by a Dominican Republic gunboat, the dictator's body was permitted to go on for burial in Paris' Pere Lachaise cemetery while the yacht–and presumably the $5 million–was returned to the country to become the* Patriot.

The elegant owner's suite aboard the sailing yacht* Sea Cloud *has marble fireplaces (non-working) and gold faucets.

Cabins and Costs

Fantasy Suites: **Report Card: A+**

Average Price PPPD: $1184 plus airfare.

Owner's Suite #1, decorated in Louis XVI style with a marble fireplace (non-working), marble bathroom with gold faucets, French canopy bed with damask covers, chairs and ottomans in satin brocade, flower-etched mirrors and gilded moldings, is sumptuous and spacious.

Small Splurges: **Report Card: A+**

Average Price PPPD: $1070 plus airfare.

Suite #7 is warm and sophisticated with its softly burnished pale pine paneled walls and lower wainscoting accented with darker wood strips. The bath, a bit smaller than those in the two owner's suites, is marble with gold faucets on the tub. Best of all, there's a deep, walk-in closet with handcrafted storage cubicles.

Suitable Standards: **Report Card: C**

Average Price PPPD: $656 plus airfare.

Now, here's the rub. There are only eight original staterooms on the ship; the remaining 24 were built in a refit when the ship was turned into a cruise vessel. They are divided into Categories A and B. The As are "large outside staterooms" which means they're slightly bigger than the tiny B cabins, and contain two lower beds with storage drawers built in underneath, a window, a built-in dresser with four drawers, and a small bathroom with shower. There is no desk, table or chair, nor anywhere to sit except on the beds, but you do get a hair dryer, terrycloth robes, a bowl of fruit, fresh flowers and a bottle of German champagne. In these cabins, you take turns getting up, showering and dressing, then one of you goes outside so the other can get up, shower and dress.

Bottom Bunks: **Report Card: C-**

Average Price PPPD: $570 plus airfare.

B Category staterooms are furnished similarly to A, above, but are somewhat smaller.

Where She Goes

Special Expeditions' cruises with the *Sea Cloud* for 1996 include four Caribbean cruises beginning Feb. 3, 10 and 17 and March 16. Sailing from Antigua the *Sea Cloud* will cruise among the Windward Islands, call at Carriacou, Tobago, St. Lucia, Dominica and Iles des Saintes.

The Bottom Line

The food, prepared by German and Austrian chefs, is delicious although menus are limited in scope. Set dinner menus are posted in the mornings; if passengers spot something they don't like, they report promptly to the bartenders, who double as major-domos, and a substitute dish or entire menu will be arranged. Breakfasts are self-serve affairs set up in the dining room; lunches are elaborate buffets of hot and cold dishes with complimentary wines and beer usually eaten on the Lido deck, and dinners are formally served on linen-covered tables by candlelight, again with complimentary wines. Despite the cozy little shipshape cabins, we would go again tomorrow; it's that special.

Fielding's Picks

Glorious Places

1. The Main Deck, natural teak with brass trim, glossy wood-paneled walls and polished benches, above which you can watch young sailors, male and female, climb the rigging to set the sails in the time-honored fashion.
2. The Lounge with its elegant wood bookcases, piano and oil paintings of classic tall ships doubles as part of the dining room during candlelight dinners.
3. The dining room with its original carved wood ceilings and panels and elegant wood-and-upholstery chairs is where the captain invites each passenger to dine at his table one evening during the cruise.
4. The Lido, a big deck shaded with a tarp, is where you sit out in the breeze and enjoy the casual buffet lunches. Complimentary wines are served at lunch and dinner.
5. The Blue Lagoon, a big cushioned area aft on the middle deck where lolling sunbathers recline on a raised platform upholstered with puffy blue mattresses.

Off-the-Wall Places

1. Owners Suite # 1 is Marjorie's own suite, grandly done up in marble and gold.
2. Owner's Suite # 2 was E. F. Hutton's equally grand but more masculine quarters, pine-paneled with a Carrera marble fireplace.
3. Suite # 4, all its furnishings original, was where the Duke of Windsor slept when he and the Duchess cruised with Mrs. Post to Cuba. (We don't know where the Duchess slept.)
4. Suite # 7 was Dina's bedroom and nursery, with a lavish marble bathroom and walk-in closet.
5. We're not sure which cabin was occupied by Zsa Zsa Gabor in the 1950s when her friend Ramfis Trujillo had the yacht anchored off the coast of Santa Monica, but people ashore still remember waking up one morning to see a banner hanging

across the Sea Cloud's side painted in foot-high bright red letters, "Zsa Zsa Slept Here."

Good Reasons to Book This Ship

1. Because it's there.
2. To pretend to be one of the rich and famous, if only by getting up and going out on deck early in the morning to make believe it's 1935 and this is your own private yacht.
3. To explore the Caribbean or Mediterranean on a sailing expedition with all shore excursions included.
4. To have an unimaginably wonderful experience that you'll never forget.
5. To sleep in the bed where the Duke of Windsor once slept.

Things You Won't Find On Board

1. A wheelchair-accessible cabin; with no elevators and extremely steep stairs, this vessel should not be booked by anyone with limited mobility.
2. A children's program; children should not be aboard this ship because there's nowhere for them to play or be looked after.
3. A casino.
4. A beauty shop.
5. A swimming pool, although sometimes when the ship is at anchor, the gangway is lowered for passengers to swim in the Caribbean.

STAR CLIPPERS, LTD.

4101 Salzedo Avenue, Coral Gables, FL 33146
☎ *(305) 442-0550, (800) 442-0551*

History

Swedish-born yachtsman and shipping executive Mikael Krafft introduced the first of his two classic square-rigged, four-masted clipper ships in June 1991, in the reverse order from what he had planned. Since the name of his company is Star Clipper, he naturally intended to debut the *Star Clipper* first, but found himself embroiled in litigation with St. Louis-based Clipper Cruise Line over the proprietary use of the name "Clipper." The Missouri-based Clipper, which operates motor vessels, not sailing ships, claimed the use of the word entailed copyright infringement. So the *Star Flyer* debuted first (same ship, different name) while the case was pursued, then settled by the time the *Star Clipper* arrived in the Caribbean at the end of 1991.

—The tallest ships in the world (226 feet in mast height).

Concept

To experience the essence of sailing in its purest form, says the line, on a ship where computerized systems have not replaced human hands in the ancient ritual of raising sails.

Signatures

The 30 sails with 36,000 feet of canvas snapping taut in the wind is as distinctive an image as a cruise line could wish.

Daily sail-training classes conducted on both ships teach sailing a square rigger to every interested passenger and award diplomas of Nautical Achievement on the final night of the cruise.

Gimmicks

The taciturn parrot named Captain Loreto was brought on board *Star Flyer* and trained to talk by owner Mikael Krafft, but the trauma of actually sailing resulted in long spells of silence in the early days. Later, either he perked up or another parrot replaced him, because he became loquacious and a popular feature of the ship.

Who's the Competition

Traditional sailing vessels such as the *Star Clipper* ships differ from the windcruiser vessels such as the Windstar and Club Med ships but would attract some of the same thirtysomething couples because of the romance of it all. Classic tall ships such as the Windjammers lack the luxurious cabins and public rooms the Star Clippers provide. "Wow," one Windjammer veteran said about the *Star Clipper*, "this is so luxurious compared to Windjammer," which she described as "sort of like camping out with cold showers and stuff."

Who's Aboard

Sophisticated travelers who are successful and live well but may not have taken a cruise before; sailing enthusiasts from both Europe and America; mostly couples. It may be a person who made a safari in Africa last year who wants to cross the Atlantic on a square-rigged sailing ship this year.

The average passenger is 47, a professional, married. Half are first-time cruisers.

"A lot of our passengers," one executive says, "are people who have done a bare boat charter in the Caribbean and the wives have found out it wasn't as much fun as they thought; the husband was out fishing while the wife was in scrubbing the head."

Who Should Go

A New Jersey travel agent we sailed with aboard the *Star Clipper* said she would gear the ship toward people to whom relaxation is paramount, to couples in their mid-30s and older, to outgoing singles and to honeymooners when the ships call at romantic ports. Or to someone who doesn't cruise but takes a condo in Maui or goes skiing in Aspen for a week.

Who Should Not Go

The ships are not appropriate for people in wheelchairs or who have difficulty walking, since there are no elevators and plenty of stairs and extra-high sills. Bookings for children under 8 years old are also discouraged.

The Lifestyle

There's a wonderful sense of casual camaraderie aboard, appealing to anyone looking to unwind from a stressful job. The ports are colorful and interesting with few "must see" destinations so the obligation of shore excursions is removed. Most passengers set out on their own to stroll through the ports, perhaps lunching or dining ashore. Passengers are allowed to lend a hand with the sails if they wish, and, when seas permit, the ship anchors for swimming, sailing and windsurfing from the gangway platform. Informal classes in navigation and sail-handling are also offered. A team of sports directors supervises aerobics classes, snorkeling lessons and diving trips for passengers with certification.

Wardrobe

Dress is casual aboard, although some passengers don fashionable resortwear for dinner. Jackets are never required, but shorts and T-shirts are not considered acceptable at dinner. The term "casual elegance" crops up in the brochure a couple of times. The right footwear is particularly important, with rubber-soled deck shoes of some sort essential for getting around the ropes and gear on deck.

Bill of Fare

Out of necessity, food is less elaborate aboard sailing vessels because the galleys are smaller and don't allow banquet-type catering preparation. Breakfasts and lunches are often served buffet-style with a choice of several hot and several cold dishes, and dinner is served course by course but with a limited selection—two appetizers, one soup, one salad, a pasta, a choice of two main dishes and two desserts plus ice cream. A table of hot and cold hors d'oeuvres is set out on deck daily at 5:30.

Cuisine Report Card: B

Showtime

To supplement a resident singer/pianist, local entertainment is brought on in some ports. In the Mediterranean, a pair of opera singers from Elba entertained during dinner one evening. Another night, a Corsican quartet headed up by a Dean Martin lookalike in a pin-striped suit played European pop music and American '50s rock for dancing on the deck under the stars. TV sets in the cabins play movies during the day and evening on two channels when the hotel manager remembers to load the videos. A 24-hour news crawl is updated regularly.

Entertainment Report Card: C

Discounts

From time to time, special pricing promotions on designated sailings may also include one category upgrades for early booking and special air/sea package fares. Have your travel agent inquire.

The Bottom Line

One important detail to remember is that sailing ships do not stick to itineraries as steadfastly as bigger cruise liners, since winds and sea conditions may necessitate last-minute port changes. But flexibility is part of the fun.

***A passenger lends a hand with the sails aboard the* Star Clipper.**

Star Clipper ★★★★
Star Flyer ★★★★

Sailing represents romance to a woman, adventure to a man, we were told while standing at the rail of the Star Flyer *off the Isle of Wight in 1991. The new ship had just sailed from Belgium and along with a BBC-TV crew and some British press, we sailed out from Southampton to meet her. At the last minute, we were given permission to come aboard, and climbed up the Jacob's Ladder against the steep, sheer side of the ship for what seemed a mile before being pulled over the rail onto her deck.*

While passengers are not usually permitted to climb the Jacob's Ladder up the side, they can venture out on the bowsprit, which has a safety net underneath, to lie back and see the ship's sails from that vantage point, to stand on the outdoor bridge and watch the helmsman at work, or go out in an inflatable Zodiac landing craft to photograph the ship under full sail. The Star Clippers are very hands-on vessels for passengers, who lend a hand with the sails if they wish. The forward deck is where the serious work goes on; amidships and aft deck are swimming pools and lounging chairs for serious sunning.

The Brochure Says

"Perhaps nothing stirs the spirit so much as the romantic era of the great clipper ships. Today, a new name proudly carries on the tradition of the tall ships with two new sailing vessels—the first passenger sailing vessels to be classified by Lloyds since the early 1900s."

Translation

It's rare and wonderful to be able to sail aboard a square-rigger and recall the brief days of the clipper ships, the two decades between the California Gold Rush of 1849 and the opening of the Suez Canal in 1869. These classic vessels, built by Scheepswerven Langerbrugge in Ghent, Belgium, were rated A-100 by Lloyds, and passed U.S. Coast Guard inspection on the first try, a rarity in the port of Miami.

Cabins and Costs

Fantasy Suites: **Report Card: NA**

Average Price PPPD: N/A

There is a "secret" owner's suite on board—at the extreme aft end of Clipper Deck—that is never put on the market but only used as a special charity auction item or for the CEO on incentives and charters. With a queen-sized bed, sofas, mini-refrigerator, TV in a built-in cabinet, four bedroom portholes, a large closet, a marble bathroom with a gold faucet Jacuzzi tub and porthole, it's pretty lavish. There's even an escape hatch to the pool deck above.

Small Splurges: **Report Card: B+**

Average Price PPPD: $370 plus airfare.

Category 1 cabins aft on Sun Deck near the pool have twin beds that can be put together into a queen-sized, a mini-refrigerator stocked with complimentary beverages, and a large bathroom with Jacuzzi tub. Four portholes are built up high so no one looks in while walking past. Cellular satellite direct-dial phones are in every cabin, along with TV/VCR and hair dryers.

Suitable Standards: **Report Card: B**

Average Price PPPD: $320 plus airfare.

We booked a category 2 double with a king-sized bed (two lower beds pushed together with a thin fill mattress across the top) and built-in storage underneath. A built-in corner chair has a drawer underneath, and there's fairly good hanging space, one full-length about two feet wide and one half-length, a safe and three open shelves below, plus a third cupboard that is all open shelves top to bottom. The bathroom has a medicine chest, some counter space around the sink (with a faucet water control that you push on but goes off by itself just when you're ready to rinse your toothbrush), and a shower that also saves water by turning off just when you've soaped up.

Bottom Bunks: **Report Card: C**

Average Price PPPD: $213 plus airfare.

Standard inside cabins with upper and lower berths have plenty of shelving, wall lamps and privacy curtains across doorway; these are the only cabin category aboard that doesn't have TV sets.

Where She Goes

Star Clipper is based in Barbados year-round, setting out every Saturday for seven-day sailings on two alternate itineraries, one to Tobago, Grenada, Cariacou, St. Vincent and

St. Lucia, the other to Union Island/Tobago Cays, Bequia, Dominica, Martinique and St. Lucia. *Star Flyer* is based in St. Martin in winter.

The Bottom Line

The Star Clippers spend more time under sail than the modern windcruisers, particularly in the Caribbean out of Barbados where the winds are favorable; the *Star Clipper* is under sail at sunset every day but one, and spends a full 36 hours nonstop under sail on alternate weeks in the Tobago Cays, a real treat for a sailor. While the service in the dining room may not be as polished as on the Sea Goddess, these ships are beautiful and unique, and will provide a lifetime of wonderful memories of being under sail.

Fielding's Picks

Fine Places

1. The Tropical Bar, outdoors with a white tarp covering the area, two fixed high wood tables with six built-in wood and chrome barstools at each, plus a big outdoor bar with 16 wooden stools around it.
2. The Library, cozy and comfortable, with a non-burning fireplace, a belle époque fixture from a 19th century home in Ghent, print armchairs, fixed wooden tables, cream leather sofas, oil paintings of sailing ships, CD player, and lots of hardback books and games.
3. The Piano Bar has a royal blue carpet and 12 blue leather and brass stools at the indoor marble-topped bar (which connects with the outdoor bar so one bartender can work them both). Tables, paisley-covered chairs and built-in leather banquettes make this a comfortable place to chat, and you can look through portholes into the underwater pool.
4. The dining room has royal blue carpet with a rope pattern, rose flame print chairs with wood and wicker backs but no arms, tables for six and eight and side booths set up for four but big enough for six. It's open seating, so you can sit where and with whom you wish.
5. The bowsprit, the perfect place to slip away to see the ship's sails in full glory; there's a net underneath for safety.

Good Reasons to Book These Ships

1. The romance of it all.
2. To learn how to sail a square-rigger.
3. To kick back and relax in a luxurious but unstuffy setting.
4. To have a once-in-a-lifetime experience at the cost of an ordinary cruise.
5. To take a 35-day repositioning cruise from Rhodes to the Thai island of Phuket, sailing through the Suez Canal, the Gulf of Aden, the Arabian Sea, the Indian

Ocean, the Bay of Bengal and the Andaman Sea aboard the Star Flyer (see Where She Goes, above).

Things You Won't Find On Board

1. A casino.
2. A beauty shop.
3. Laundry service (they can send it out for one-day service in certain ports).
4. Smoking permitted in the cabins.
5. An elevator.

SUN LINE CRUISES

One Rockefeller Plaza, Suite 315, New York, NY 10020-2090

(212) 397-6400, (800) 872-6400

NOTE: Sun Line Cruises and Epirotiki Cruises announced a merger in August 1995, to form a new cruise company called Royal Olympic Cruises, to begin sailing in March 1996. Under the agreement, both companies would continue to own their own vessels.

History

Sun Line was founded by the late Ch. (Charalambos) A. Keusseoglou in 1957, after he had been a co-founder and former executive vice president of now-defunct Home Lines. Keusseoglou had been in the shipping industry since he left the Greek Army in 1947, going first to Sweden to work with Swedish American Line, then becoming one of the founders of Home Lines later that same year, along with Swedish American Line and Greek interests. He worked with Home Lines until after the acquisition of his first vessel for Sun, a Canadian frigate he turned into the yacht-like *Stella Maris I* in 1959. This ship was followed by the *Stella Solaris I*, then in 1963 the present *Stella Maris* replaced the original and four years later the *Stella Oceanis* was added to the fleet to replace the *Stella Solaris I*. In 1973, the flagship *Stella Solaris* was put into service, bringing the fleet to its present three ships.

The Marriott Corp. acquired an interest in Sun Line in 1971, but the family purchased back those shares in 1987.

Isabella Keusseoglou from the beginning has taken the responsibility for decorating the line's ships and hiring the cruise staff and entertainers, and with her sons and daughter in key executive positions, has overseen the operation of the cruise line since her husband's death in 1984.

In August 1995, Mrs. Keusseoglou, with George Potamianos of Epirotiki Cruises, made a joint announcement of the merger of the two companies into a new cruise line to be called Royal Olympic Cruises. Two of the three present Sun Line ships will compose two-thirds of the upscale Blue Ships division of the new company, while the third, the little *Stella Maris*, will be made available for charter under the auspices of the new line. The New York marketing offices will remain in the Sun Line quarters in Rockefeller Plaza, while operations will be headquartered in Epirotiki's Piraeus offices.

Concept

To create itineraries to take passengers to "the unusual and the unexpected," with destinations in Greece and Turkey, the Caribbean and South America, and the services of a warm, loyal Greek crew, many of whom have been with the line for years.

Signatures

"Luxury Cruises in the Exotic Zone," with winter sailings up the Amazon and into the Yucatan, timed to coincide with special events from Carnival in Trinidad to the Maya Equinox at Chichen Itza.

Gimmicks

The hot homemade potato chips served in the Bar Grill room on the *Stella Solaris* keep passengers like us coming back.

Who's the Competition

Under the new merger with Epirotiki, this pair of Greek lines could perform very solidly in the Aegean, at least until the Greek version of the Jones Act is eroded, as industry watchers expect it to be, because of demands from European Community members who would like to see their ships be able to make roundtrip cruises out of Piraeus. Orient Lines' *Marco Polo*, the surprise entry this summer in the Mediterranean, at about the same size and a slightly lower price range than the *Stella Solaris*, could be competition. But if Celebrity's *Meridian* is repositioned to the Mediterranean in 1997, it would be the toughest competition for the upscale Blue Ships because of the extremely high quality of its hardware, food and service.

Who's Aboard

The *Stella Solaris* appeals mainly to older, more experienced cruise passengers, many of them frequent travelers with the line. Sometimes 45 percent of the passengers aboard are repeaters. Young couples and singles, particularly in the Greek Islands, like all three ships.

Who Should Go

The new line's division between Blue and White Ships should broaden the market base for both Sun and Epirotiki and reach more of the land tour travelers to the Aegean, including more young singles, couples and families.

Who Should Not Go

Any curmudgeon who won't join in the Greek dancing on Greek Night.

The Lifestyle

The Greek Islands and Turkey itinerary on Sun Line ships is the perfect answer for people who worry that "there's nothing to do" on a cruise. With its port-intensive itinerary, onboard lecturers and land guides, it's the most information-packed trip imaginable, so long as your stamina and curiosity hold up.

"I'd never book honeymooners on this cruise," one American travel agent sighed after a morning tour in Delos and an afternoon in Mykonos.

Passengers are a cosmopolitan lot, particularly in Greece, but language groups are sorted out and multilingual guides travel with each group. Social hosts accompany many of the cruises aboard the *Stella Solaris* in winter, when there are more days at sea and an older clientele aboard.

Wardrobe

Both the Aegean and the South American cruises are casual by day, somewhat dressy by evening. The line suggests that on formal nights men wear dark suits or tuxedos and women gowns, cocktail dresses or dressy pantsuits. On informal nights, men are expected to wear suits or jacket and tie, while women are requested to don dresses, skirts or pantsuits. Casual evenings call for slacks and sportshirts for men, similar attire for women. There are usually two formal nights, one informal night and four casual nights during a seven-night cruise. Laundry and pressing services are available on board but there is no dry cleaning.

Bill of Fare

While the food is variable, depending on the chef aboard, the Greek dishes are always uniformly delicious, and we've found the deck buffets tasty as well.

The chief steward, if alerted the day before, can arrange a light cuisine or special order meal. Dinners usually provide three main dish choices, fish, fowl and meat, plus light or vegetarian fare, and a passenger can always order broiled chicken or grilled steak on the spot if nothing on the menu seems appealing. All breads and desserts are made on board, and hot homemade potato chips and thick, creamy homemade yogurt are two of our favorite treats.

An appealing deck buffet offers Greek salad, cold meats, hamburgers, moussaka, batter-dipped fried zucchini, fruit and cheese, in case you want to get an early start on an afternoon ashore.

Cuisine Report Card: B

Showtime

Mrs. Keusseoglou usually selects both the cruise staff and the entertainers who work on board and tends to keep certain passenger favorites over the long haul, including the charming and talented Caesar, a cocktail pianist. During our several cruises aboard, we've seen every sort of entertainment from the infamous Mr. Blackwell doing wildly popular fashion makeovers for volunteers from the audience to a dance team so exquisitely untalented they could bring back Velez and Yolanda. Magicians, ventriloquists and other variety artists are usually aboard, along with some really gifted performers such as jazz artists Steve and Bonnie Cole.

Entertainment Report Card: B

Discounts

Early booking discounts from 10 to 50 percent, depending on itinerary and departure date, are offered by Sun Line. Royal Olympic Cruises had not established a discount policy as we went to press.

The Bottom Line

The Sun Line ships are well-suited to the new Royal Olympic venture, and the marketing clout of the combination should be good for both companies. But there's a wide disparity in shipboard style between the two lines, and we wonder how that will be reconciled. We would like to think the Blue Ships will reflect the careful, warm and fastidious service so typical of Sun for all these years.

Stella Solaris ★★★

It's hard to imagine anything more romantic than a balmy evening at midnight standing at the rail of the Stella Solaris *with moonlight rippling on the Aegean Sea. Even the captain had fallen in love with one of his American passengers during one of these Greek Islands cruises and later got married aboard his own ship. Yes, these week-long sailings are exhausting, exciting, exotic, fulfilling and hectic—and they're also very, very romantic.*

The largest of the three Sun Line ships is *Stella Solaris*, built in 1959 as the *Stella V*, then the *Camboge*, with eight passenger decks and a great expanse of teak decks aft. The topmost Lido deck is where you'll find the swimming pools, sunbathing loungers and Lido Bar. Down one deck from here are the suites, with a full around-the-ship promenade deck outside and a small reading and card room aft that doubles as a meetings venue. The main public lounges are on Solaris Deck, with the dining room and galley forward, a couple of bars, the lobby and purser's desk amidships, and the main lounge and a piano bar aft. Below are cabins, plus a cinema, gym, beauty shop, disco and hospital.

The Brochure Says

"Our Greek officers and crew are experts when it comes to welcoming you on board in the true tradition of Greek hospitality."

Translation

The new merger of Sun and Epirotiki becomes the largest Greek cruise company, Royal Olympic Cruises, who have taken the blue and white of the Greek flag as their colors and it will set you sailing with that wonderful crew.

INSIDER TIP

Better take those free Greek dancing lessons when they're offered, because on Greek night, you can count on being whirled out on the floor by an enthusiastic crew member.

FOOTNOTE

Celebrity passengers aboard Stella Solaris *have included Cary Grant, Rock Hudson, Jimmy and Rosalyn Carter, Eva Marie Saint and Ernest Borgnine, in whose honor the staff screened "The Poseidon Adventure."*

Cabins and Costs

Fantasy Suites: **Report Card: B+**

Average Price PPPD: $397 plus airfare.

The 34 deluxe suites on Boat Deck have various configurations, but all usually contain a large sitting area with sofa and chairs and coffee table, plus built-in wood cabinetry, and a bedroom with twin or queen-sized bed, huge walk-in closet and spacious bath with tub and shower.

Small Splurges: **Report Card: B**

Average Price PPPD: $360 plus airfare.

Smaller deluxe suites amidships on Ruby Deck have the advantage of the smoothest ride aboard as well. Two lower beds, four small closets, sitting area and bath with tub and shower, and, on this deck, portholes instead of windows.

Suitable Standards: **Report Card: B**

Average Price PPPD: $295 plus airfare.

Superior outside doubles on Emerald Deck also have portholes, plus two lower beds, built-in desk and dresser, stool, bathroom with tub and shower, and, in some, the possibility of booking adjoining cabins.

Bottom Bunks: **Report Card: D**

Average Price PPPD: $192 plus airfare.

The least expensive digs are the Category 11 inside cabins on Sapphire Deck, which do not have elevator access; you have to walk down from the elevator on the deck above. These cabins are small with upper and lower berths and bath with shower only.

EAVESDROPPING

Captain Michael Benas, for many years master of the Stella Solaris, *when asked about passengers fraternizing with crew, chuckled, "When we miss a passenger, we call the crew cabins."*

Where She Goes

Stella Solaris spends the winter in the Caribbean and South America, sailing from Ft. Lauderdale through the Caribbean and into the Amazon Jan. 2 on a 14-day cruise with a special theater festival at sea on board, then between Manaus and Galveston through February. A pair of 12-day Panama Canal sailings from Galveston Feb. 28 and March 25 is interspersed with a seven-day Western Caribbean itinerary on March 11 and the special Maya Equinox Cruise March 18.

The Bottom Line

With a deep 28-foot draft and steam turbine engines, the *Stella Solaris* offers a very smooth ride. Safety procedures get high marks as well, with a thorough boat drill that includes lowering the launches in front of the passengers at each boat station. One of the main assets of this ship is also one of its problems—the Greek dining room stewards who have been here forever sometimes get more involved in the logistics of "Head 'em up, move 'em out" on open seatings than is appropriate with a ship of this class. Bear in mind, too, that the *Stella Solaris* is one of those ships that changes personality by season. The longer winter voyages attract older, more affluent passengers than the seven-day summer sailings. Some of the winter passengers come back every year, stay on board 40 or 45 days and may not get off the ship in ports they've seen before. "They don't care where the ship goes," said one longtime staffer, "they want to travel with their favorite steward."

Fielding's Picks

Familiar Places

1. The Grill Room Bar with its classic dark leather sofas and chairs, its horseshoe-shaped bar and clubby New York ambience, is one of our favorite spots at sea.
2. The Solaris Lounge is divided from the Piano Bar by an open sculpture wall and furnished with gold plush chairs and patterned plush banquettes, plus raised seating levels around the sides of the room facing the dance floor and stage.
3. Teatime takes place in the Piano Bar with a pianist playing pop and show tunes as waiters serve tea and cookies. A long, low bar with wide view windows behind it offers a great view of the sea.
4. The pool deck has two overlapping oval pools surrounded by a sunning platform, umbrella-covered tables and sun loungers.
5. The dining room with its wide windows lets you watch the scenery while you're cruising, or you can puzzle over the murals of legends and heroes decorating the walls.

Good Reasons to Book This Ship

1. Because the same Greek waiters, stewards and bartenders seem to have been here forever.
2. Because the ship never feels crowded, even when it's full.
3. For unique special event cruises such as the Maya Equinox Cruise, when passengers visit the El Castillo Pyramid in Chichen Itza on March 21 for the vernal equinox, when the setting sun makes a pattern of seven triangles, one appearing at a time, along the north face of the temple, depicting the mystic descent of the "feathered serpent" that illustrates the arrival of the Maya god Kukulkan on earth.

4. To take a seven-day crash course in Greek history and culture.
5. To socialize with some of Sun's celebrity passengers.

Things You Won't Find On Board

1. TV sets in most of the cabins except suites.
2. A bumpy ride in rough seas; the deep draft of the ship adds a lot of stability.
3. A chance to sit where you want to at open seating breakfasts and lunches, when the waiters rush you into whatever empty space is up.
4. Plenty of soundproofing between cabins; many allow eavesdropping through the walls.
5. A wheelchair-accessible cabin.

TALL SHIP ADVENTURES

1389 South Havana Street, Aurora, CO 80012
☎ *(303) 755-7983, (800) 662-0090*

History

The three-masted schooner *Sir Francis Drake* was constructed in Germany in 1917 as the *Landkirchen* and carried copper from Chile around Cape Horn to Europe. Then, with an engine added in the 1920s, it spent 40 years carrying cargo in the Baltic and North Seas. In 1988 Eckart Straub and Captain Bryan Petley purchased the vessel and renamed it after the dashing English buccaneer. Captain Petley, a New Zealander, has been sailing since he was 13, and brings a cheerful, offbeat attitude of fun that rubs off on all the passengers.

—One of fewer than 100 tall ships remaining that was built to transport cargo solely under sail.

Concept

"We advertise ourselves as a middle-of-the-road soft adventure," says Captain Petley, "not as luxurious as the Star Clippers or *Sea Cloud* but a bit less basic than the Maine Windjammers or the Windjammer Barefoot Cruises." What he means is that the cabins are carpeted, air-conditioned and have private bathrooms, but you can still show up to dinner barefoot and in shorts.

Signatures

The B.L.T. party, every Tuesday night, when passengers are required to wear (1) Buccaneer dress, (2) Lingerie or (3) Toga.

Gimmicks

Pirate's Punch is free.

Who's the Competition

Probably the Windjammer ships come the closest in style and authenticity, but the cabins don't all have private facilities on those vessels.

Who's Aboard

Young to middle-aged couples and singles, with a median age in the mid-40s, but they can be as young as 20 or as old as 80, plus an occasional family with children over 8. Captain Petley discourages children any younger than 8.

Who Should Go

People who want to relax. One veteran of many Tall Ship Adventures says, "The first day you're a little uptight, the second day you begin to unwind and by the seventh day, you don't have a clue what's happening in the world and you don't care."

Who Should Not Go

Fussbudgets and nitpickers; clothes horses; shoppers (there are very few shopping stops on the itinerary); people who hate sun, sand and sea.

The Lifestyle

The usual drill in the U.S. and British Virgin Islands is to sail in the mornings, anchor at midday and have lunch on the beach, spending the afternoon snorkeling, swimming, windsurfing, sailing or waterskiing. Dinner is served on board, and afterwards the captain and whoever wishes to join him usually go ashore "to where the bands are" and party. For a 10-minute video preview of the ship, send a refundable $15 deposit to Tall Ship Adventures (address above).

Wardrobe

Anything goes. Bare feet and shorts are acceptable dinner attire except perhaps on the Sunday night captain's dinner. "That's when I dress in my uniform," Captain Petley says.

Bill of Fare

In the tiny galley below decks, the chef prepares a mix of popular standards including hamburger and barbecued ribs with elegant lobster sandwiches on homemade bread or Caribbean-accented specialties such as chicken-and-shrimp stir-fry and West Indian baked chicken. Lunch is often served on the beach, and deck barbecues are popular. This is chef Patrick Browne's recipe:

Chicken and Shrimp Stir-Fry

4 to 6 servings

1 cup diced raw chicken breasts, skin and bones removed

1 cup chopped raw shrimp, shells and veins removed

Salad oil

1 cup each thinly sliced and chopped fresh cabbage, carrots, broccoli, cauliflower and onions, or other vegetables if preferred

Seasoned salt

Soy sauce

Hot steamed rice

Heat 1-2 TB oil in wok or large deep skillet until smoking, then drop in chicken and shrimp and cook, stirring constantly, two minutes. Remove from oil with slotted spoon and keep warm. Put vegetables in oil and stir quickly to mix, then cover and steam just until vegetables are crunchy-tender, about 15 minutes. Ten minutes into the cooking, return the chicken and shrimp to the pan, add seasoned salt and soy sauce to taste and cook an additional five minutes or so. Serve over hot rice.

Cuisine Report Card: C

Showtime

Going ashore after dinner to small island nightclubs with the unflappable Captain Petley.

Entertainment Report Card: N/A

Discounts

Early booking bonuses up to 20 percent are available on certain cruises; call the company for details. A group of 10 to 19 passengers gets a 5 percent group discount, while a group of 20 or more gets a 10 percent discount. Spring 1996 seven-day British Virgin Island cruises from Tortola are discounted 10 percent on sailings between April 6 and June 1; call for details.

The Bottom Line

This is Captain Petley's ship, run in his own inimitable fashion. He formerly sailed as a captain with Windjammer and describes one primary difference between his ship and theirs: "They sail at night every night and stop during the day. We sail during part of the day and anchor at night."

Sir Francis Drake ⚓⚓⚓⚓

The first time we saw the Sir Francis Drake *was in the Boston Harbor during the Tall Ships celebration in 1992, and even there amid so many vessels its three masts stood out above the crowd.*

You won't get lost aboard the ship if you can just remember which companionways go where. There are only 14 cabins, a dining room, a lounge and the open deck, but a recent refitting has spruced it up, and if you had 33 like-minded friends could probably arrange your own charter. The last going price we heard was $4000 a day, which would work out to about $118 apiece a day if you had the full 34 people.

The Brochure Says

"• It's swimming and watersports and relaxing on the beach.

• It's sunfish sailing and windsurfing and fabulous sunsets.

• It's picnics on the beach and snorkeling and diving.

• It's delightful parties and dancing the nights away.

• It's exploring tropical islands and exciting ports of call.

• It's making new friends that will last a lifetime."

Translation

There's the answer to the question, What's there to do?

EAVESDROPPING

"The people we get don't ever want to go back on a floating hotel or a wimp cruise again," says Captain Bryan Petley.

Cabins and Costs

Fantasy Suites: **Report Card: C-**

Average Price PPPD: $199 plus airfare.

There is one luxury suite on board, contoured into the aft corners of the vessel, not huge but it certainly seems spacious beside the others. Anyhow, the bed is big enough for two, it's carpeted, air-conditioned and has a wall-mounted chest for a modicum of storage.

Small Splurges: **Report Card: C-**

Average Price PPPD: $170 plus airfare.

Small is the operative word here. You can book the next category down, a double bed with upper twin (there are six of these), carpeting, air conditioning and private toilet and shower.

Suitable Standards: **Report Card: C-**

Average Price PPPD: $170 plus airfare.

Side-by-side twin beds mean only one of you gets up and gets dressed at a time; there are four of these, with very compact bathrooms.

Bottom Bunks: **Report Card: D**

Average Price PPPD: $142 plus airfare.

And you thought the small splurges were small! Three of these with upper and lower bunks are pretty basic; one is aft, opposite the suite, and the other two forward, but you can't get from the aft one to the forward ones without going up, across the next deck and back down.

Where She Goes

While the captain changes itineraries frequently, he stays in the Caribbean, usually around the British Virgin Islands. The most recently announced routes for 1996 have the ship sailing from Tortola on the first, third and fifth Saturday of each month to most of the little islands in the BVI, and on the second and fourth Saturdays to the rest of them. In summer, the ship sails between Simpson Bay, St. Maarten, and English Harbour, Antigua, visiting St. Barts, Tintamarre, Statia, St. Kitts and Nevis southbound, and Antigua's snorkeling beaches, Barbuda's coral reefs and the remote volcanic island of Saba on the northbound route. Combine both itineraries and you can knock off 10 percent from your 14-day cruise.

The Bottom Line

The *Sir Francis Drake* is a handsome old ship, especially after its recent refurbishment, but housekeeping is not always pristine and the casual lifestyle may verge on the raffish occasionally. Still, the prices are very low, the beach activities super and the food isn't bad either. If you're not fussy and want a relaxed and relaxing barefoot cruise, you should try it.

Fielding's Picks

Shipshape Spaces

1. The lounge, which doubles as bar, video room, gift shop, TV room, library, gathering spot and lecture hall. (Only kidding—they don't do lectures aboard.)
2. The deck, clean, natural teak bleached to a weathered gray, is ringed with chairs, lounges and small tables.
3. The dining room, elegantly wood-paneled and prettily redecorated in beige with wood armchairs.
4. The bowsprit has a safety net underneath that can support a foolhardy passenger or two.
5. The deck bar, sometimes the setting for an onboard wedding.

Good Reasons to Book This Ship

1. To join Captain Petley at the Tuesday night B.L.T. (buccaneer, lingerie or toga) party; he himself may appear in filmy lingerie with his captain's bars pinned to one spaghetti strap.
2. It's a good blend of land and sea vacations for a watersports-and-party crowd.
3. Because all you need to pack are shorts, T-shirts and tennis shoes.
4. Because you can cruise through the unspoiled British Virgin Islands.
5. Because you can take a seven-day cruise for as little as $796 if you get in on an early booking discount.

Things You Won't Find On Board

1. Room service.
2. A concierge.
3. Anybody with a stuffy attitude.
4. Anyone wearing pantyhose and high heels—except maybe on B.L.T. Night.
5. An elevator.

WINDJAMMER BAREFOOT CRUISES, LTD.

1759 Bay Road, Miami Beach, FL 33139
☎ *(305) 672-6453, (800) 327-2602*

History

In 1947, Captain Mike Burke, just out of the U.S. Navy after serving four years in submarines, says he headed first for Miami, then after a few drinks, on to the Bahamas with $600 back pay in his pocket. He woke up the next morning on the deck of a 19-foot sloop with no money and a splitting headache. He had bought a boat. He named it the *Hangover.*

Soon Burke found himself taking paying friends and guests on cruises to the Bahamas, and after a year or so of that, combined his entrepreneurial skills with his love of tall ships and founded Windjammer Barefoot Cruises. His first boat was a 150-foot schooner named *Janeen* that had been run aground. Burke fixed her up and renamed her *Polynesia I.* By 1958, his fleet numbered four, *Polynesia I*, *Polynesia II*, *Brigantine Yankee* and his prize, the *Yankee Clipper*, originally built for German industrialist Alfred Krupp and confiscated as a prize of war by the U.S. in 1945.

Burke says his secret is to buy the ships in bad shape and then fix them up. In that way he acquired his present fleet of six tall ships (the newest, the former *France II*, new name pending, is scheduled to debut in mid-1996) and one motor vessel, *Amazing Grace*, his supply ship. His six children have joined him in his company.

—The largest single fleet of tall ships in the world (six). Burke says the Norwegian government comes in second with three tall ships.

FOOTNOTE

The Polynesia I *was confiscated by Fidel Castro in 1971 when a storm blew her off course into Cuban waters and government officials seized her. Burke had to bail his crew out of jail in Cuba; fortunately, there were no passengers aboard. But Castro kept the vessel as his own private yacht.*

Concept

To provide "memorable, affordable vacations for would-be "ol' salts of all ages" where informality rules. Passengers set their own pace, doing as much or as little as they like, from helping hoist a sail to lolling in the sun doing nothing.

Signatures

The logo tall ship and the word "barefoot" in the company name describe the product clearly to would-be passengers. Four or five designated singles cruises are among each year's big sellers, in which an entire sailing is devoted only to singles, sometimes within a certain age bracket, and always promising an equal mix of men and women. The line claims five marriages so far from couples that have met on singles sailings. Their longtime sailaway anthem is "Amazing Grace."

Gimmicks

"Drinker's Doubloons" are tokens you buy from the bartender on board to pay for drinks without having to carry cash around.

"Story hour" is the daily morning briefing (8:45 a.m.) from the captain, telling you what is likely to happen during that day.

Who's the Competition

The only really comparable product is Tall Ship Adventures' *Sir Francis Drake* (see above) but with only one ship, it doesn't really put a dent in Windjammer's business. None of the more upscale sailing ship cruise lines—Star Clipper, Windstar or Club Med Cruises—come close to the bargain prices and informality on board the Windjammers.

Who's Aboard

The company says, "Singles, nearlyweds, newlyweds, retirees and families alike," which pretty much covers the waterfront.

Who Should Go

People who love sailing and the sea and want to meet like-minded folks.

Who Should Not Go

Tradition-mined cruisers; Sea Goddess veterans; anyone susceptible to mal-de-mer; infants and toddlers.

NO NOs

Open bottles of personal liquor in the cabins are not permitted; smoking is forbidden anywhere except on the open decks; and flip-flops are not advised for deck and island wear.

The Lifestyle

"Barefoot" is the operative word here; you'll never need dress-up clothes or even shoes, if you don't feel like wearing them. Free Bloody Marys before breakfast, Rum Swizzles at sunset, free wine with dinner (which is served in two seatings), and always time for a party. Passengers may help the crew with the sails or take a turn at the helm, and swimming, diving and snorkeling are favorite pastimes. Cabins range from dorm-like rooms to doubles to suites, most but not all with private bathroom facilities.

Wardrobe

As little as possible, because the cruises are very casual with no dressing up even considered, let alone required, and because there's very little storage space in the cabins. Take plenty of bathing suits, shorts and T-shirts, perhaps a long-sleeved shirt and long pants or skirt to cover up from the sun.

Bill of Fare

The food is hearty, simple and family-style. Breakfasts feature freshly baked breads and pastries, preceded, if you wish, by a complimentary Bloody Mary. Lunch may be a picnic on the beach or a buffet on deck. At cocktail time, hors d'oeuvres are served with rum or soft drinks, and dinner includes wine, beer or soft drinks of your choice. A late-night snack provides "midnight munchies." Many of the dishes have a Caribbean accent, including these ribs:

Guava Glazed BBQ Spare Ribs

6 servings

3 racks baby back ribs

6 cloves of garlic, minced

1 TB dried thyme

4 bay leaves, crumbled

2 TB dried parsley

1 TB ground allspice

2 TB liquid smoke

2 ounces soy sauce

4 ounces white wine

Parboil ribs for 10 minutes to rend fat. Combine the remaining ingredients into a marinade. Pat ribs dry with paper towels, then place in baking pan and brush liberally on both sides with the marinade. Cover and bake at 325-350 degrees for one hour and 30 minutes, basting with marinade from pan every half-hour. Remove from oven, cool pan drippings and prepare Guava Glaze. Finish on a grill (or return to the oven at 450 degrees); brush frequently with Guava Glaze.

Guava Glaze

1 cup pan drippings with fat removed

4 TB guava jelly

1 Scotch bonnet or jalapeno pepper minced
or, 1/2 TB West Indian hot sauce

Defat the drippings by pouring them from the baking pan into a saucepan and putting ice cubes in until the fat congeals on the ice. Then remove ice and fat, return pan to heat and reduce the drippings by half. Add jelly and minced pepper or hot sauce and continue reducing until sauce reaches a thick consistency.

Cuisine Report Card: C+

Showtime

Drinking Rum Swizzles and nibbling hot hors d'oeuvres on deck is the evening's pre-dinner entertainment. What you do later is up to you.

Entertainment Report Card: N/A

Discounts

Windjammer Club members ($25 initiation fee) get to take along a friend on a fall cruise for half-price on the "bosom buddy" program, good through early December.

The Bottom Line

Windjammer delivers exactly what it promises its passengers, which explains its high repeat factor, with one loyal who's passed his 160th sailing. Like Carnival, you know pretty much what you're getting so you can figure ahead of time whether it's what you want. The prices are right and the supply of food and grog plentiful; what's not to like?

Amazing Grace Unrated

The supply ship *Amazing Grace*, built in 1955 in Scotland as the *Pharos* and acquired by Windjammer in 1988, is a former British Navy motor vessel that sails on 13-day voyages between Freeport, Bahamas and Trinidad. She rendezvous with Windjammer's tall ships and delivers their monthly supplies, just as she once delivered supplies to lighthouse keepers along the rugged North Sea coast in Scotland on weekdays and entertained royalty at tea on weekends.

A period dignity has earned her the nickname "Orient Express of the Caribbean," and both a smoking room and a piano room with fireplace have been preserved in their original style. A spacious deck gives passengers room to move around or relax with a book.

Cabins and Costs

Cabins are somewhat larger than on the tall ships, a few with twin or double beds. Some have private toilet facilities and some offer a wash basin in the room and toilet down the hall. The **Fantasy Suite** equivalent is Burke's Berth, which has a sitting room, sleeper sofa, TV/VCR and CD stereo with tape player and honor bar, a separate bedroom with double bed and a marble and teak bath with its own Jacuzzi.

Suitable Standards with private toilet and shower facilities include cabins 1BB, 1BI and the Officer's Deck cabins. All have upper and lower berths.

Bottom Bunks would include 1TP, 2TP and 2BP; the first two have twin beds and wash basin, porthole and desk or vanity, the latter upper and lower berths with porthole and wash basin.

Prices for the 13-day cruise range from $950 to $2800 per person, double occupancy, the latter, of course, for Burke's Berth. Add $100 a person for sailings between the first of November and the end of May. Calls are made at any of nearly three dozen islands between Freeport, to the north not far off Florida, and Trinidad.

Fantome ⚓⚓⚓⚓
Flying Cloud ⚓⚓⚓⚓
Mandalay ⚓⚓⚓⚓
Polynesia ⚓⚓⚓⚓
Yankee Clipper ⚓⚓⚓⚓

"Romantic" is the word most commonly used to describe sailing ships, perhaps because these age-old craft take us back to what we imagine as a more stress-free time. Shirley says white canvas sails puffed by the breeze are the perfect accessory to romance, far better than a ruffled parasol or a bearskin rug, because they seem to make most men act like Mel Gibson.

This fleet of tall ships—the four-masted stay-sail schooner *Fantome*, built in 1927 for the Duke of Westminster; the *Flying Cloud*, a former French naval cadet training ship decorated by General Charles de Gaulle for sinking two Japanese submarines when she was carrying nitrates from Tahiti; the *Mandalay*, the former luxury yacht of financier E. F. Hutton, originally the *Hussar IV* and predecessor to the famous *Sea Cloud*; the *Polynesia*, a former Grand Banks fishing schooner acquired by Windjammer in 1975, previously the *Argus*, subject of a National Geographic feature and an Allen Villers book; the two-masted sailing ship *Yankee Clipper*, probably the only armor-plated yacht in the world, built in 1927 for German industrialist Alfred Krupp as the *Cressida*; and the former *France II*, a meteorological research and exploration vessel owned by the French government, being converted into a four-masted ship.

FOOTNOTE

The Fantome *was purchased by Aristotle Onassis from the Guinness Brewing family to present as a wedding gift to Princess Grace and Prince Rainier. When he wasn't invited to the wedding, he didn't send the gift. Captain Mike picked her up in 1969 as the flagship of his fleet.*

FOOTNOTE

The Yankee Clipper, *originally a yacht named* Cressida *built for German munitions king Alfred Krupp, hosted Adolf Hitler during World War II, was acquired by the Vanderbilt family after the war and raced regularly off Newport Beach, California, as the* Pioneer, *once clocked at 22 knots under sail. She's still considered one of the fastest tall ships sailing.*

The Brochure Says

"Informality rules! T-shirts and shorts are all you'll need to pack, so trash the tuxes and ballgowns. Stow your gear in your air-conditioned cabin. From dorms to Honeymoon Suites, all feature modern amenities. Who said anything about roughing it?"

Translation

This is the ultimate in casual cruising, and Windjammers multiple repeaters like it like that. Some of the cabins are pretty basic, however, and while everything is more or less air- conditioned, the modern amenities aboard may or may not include a private toilet facility.

Cabins and Costs

Fantasy Suites: **Report Card: B**

Average Price PPPD: $187 plus airfare.

The best digs (apart from Burke's Berth on the *MV Amazing Grace*, above) would be the Honeymoon Suite aboard *Flying Cloud*, which is below Main Deck with its own private entrance, windows, a queen-sized bed, mini-refrigerator, private toilet and shower, TV/VCR, CD and wet bar.

Small Splurges: **Report Card: C**

Average Price PPPD: $170 plus airfare.

The Admiral's Suite on the *Fantome* with a queen-sized bed, private bathroom with toilet and shower and a mini-refrigerator, relatively lavish comfort for Windjammer.

Suitable Standards: **Report Card: C-**

Average Price PPPD: $154 plus airfare.

Par for the course double cabins on the Windjammers are compact but livable, as in the *Yankee Clipper's* Main Deck cabins with upper and lower berths, mini-refrigerator, picture window, private toilet and shower.

Bottom Bunks: **Report Card: D**

Average Price PPPD: $107 plus airfare.

There's a wide range to choose from on the fairly basic Windjammers. Typical would be the Bachelor/ette dorm rooms on the *Polynesia* or *Flying Cloud*, which sleep six in bunks with a private shower and toilet for the dorm. It's sold to all-male, all-female or a family of five or six.

Where She Goes

There's never a hard and fast schedule on the Windjammers; that's part of their charm. The captain chooses where to go based on a certain group of islands, and every time there's a fifth Monday in the month, it's a Captain's Choice cruise hitting all his top favorites.

The *Fantome*, based in Antigua, checks out the British, French and Dutch West Indies, visiting from among them St. Barts, St. Kitts, Nevis, Montserrat, Guadeloupe, Iles des Saintes and Dominica.

The *Flying Cloud* covers the British Virgin Islands from its home in Tortola, choosing among Jost van Dyke, Beef Island, Virgin Gorda, Peter Island and Norman Island.

The *Mandalay*, home-ported in Grenada and Antigua, visits the Windwards and the Grenadines, selecting from Nevis, Montserrat, Iles des Saintes, Dominica, Martinique, St. Lucia, St. Vincent, Bequia, Canouan, Mayreau, Palm and Carriacou.

From Sint Maarten, the *Polynesia* sails out to see Anguilla, St. Barts, Saba, Statia, St. Kitts, Nevis and Montserrat.

The *Yankee Clipper* is based in Grenada and sails to several of the following islands: St. Vincent, Bequia, Canouan, Mayreau, Union, Palm and Carriacou.

The Bottom Line

Prices are very modest on the Windjammers, so much so that if it's a special occasion like a honeymoon, you should spring for the best you can afford. If you're footloose and fancy free, book anything and spend your spare time on the deck. Don't worry about sailing experience; you don't need it. Just go with the flow. If you're concerned about getting seasick, take a dramamine or other approved medication in the prescribed amount of time before boarding rather than waiting until you feel queasy. But bear in mind that seasickness is much rarer than people think—neither of us has ever experienced it in more than 200 cruises in some of the roughest seas in the world. (See Seasickness, page 60 for more about the malady and the treatment.)

Fielding's Picks

Fun Places

1. The *Mandalay* interior, extensively renovated in the style of its period (the 1920s) has always been considered one of the most luxurious private yachts in the world. Reminiscent of the *Sea Cloud* in her original rosewood-paneled cabins and marble bathrooms, and of the modern-day ultra-luxury vessels with a pair of suites with private verandas.
2. The *Fantome's* dining room is a trim and shipshape wood-paneled area with comfortable booths and resin-coated tables.
3. The deck on any Windjammer, where you sun, hang out, chat or read, meet your fellow passengers or learn about sails and charts from the captain during a sailing lesson.
4. The beach, a frequent part of any Windjammer cruise, where you may have a barbecue or buffet lunch, a swim or rum and nibbles at sunset.
5. The deck bar, where you check in with your $10 paper doubloon and have the bartender nick it with a hole punch every time you buy a drink.

Good Reasons to Book These Ships

1. To take advantage of the modest prices that include a lot of things other lines charge extra for such as sunset cocktails and wine with dinner.
2. To take a singles cruise and meet the mate of your dreams.
3. To learn how to handle the sails on a tall ship.
4. To see (and be seen in) the Caribbean aboard a classic ship, which automatically makes you a celebrity.
5. To kick back and relax and take off your shoes.

Things You Won't Find On Board

1. Elevators.
2. Jacuzzis.
3. Fitness centers.
4. Swimming pools; they claim theirs is the Caribbean sea.
5. Casinos.

WINDSTAR® CRUISES

A HOLLAND AMERICA LINE COMPANY

300 Elliott Avenue West, Seattle, WA 98119
☎ *(206) 281-3229, (800) 258-7245*

History

In Helsinki, Finland, in the early 1980s, ship designer Kai Levandar and his Finnish workshop group came up with a number of revolutionary cruise vessel concepts, including several that looked like major high-rise urban hotel towers floating on a ship-like hull, somewhat similar to the long-in-progress Phoenix World City project. But following a suggestion from an imaginative entrepreneur named Karl G. Andren, owner of Circle Line sightseeing boats, they created a design in 1983 called Windcruiser, a motor-sailing vessel with computer-trimmed sails.

In 1984, Andren contacted a French-born, Miami-based cruise line veteran named Jean-Claude Potier to make a feasibility study and find a yard to build it. Potier, who subsequently became the line's president, announced the project, Windstar Sail Cruises, in December 1984, and hired a French shipyard (Societe Nouvelle des Ateliers et Chantiers du Havre) to build it and French architect-designer Marc Held to create an interior design. The French government assisted in the financing.

Jean-Claude Potier saw romance in the design. "A sailing ship, unregimented, not organized, fun, an experience in feeling, not glittery, beautiful." He coined the term "casual elegance" to describe the onboard dress code for the vessels.

The 148-passenger *Wind Star* was the first of the trio, debuting in 1986 to immediate acclaim. The *Wind Song*, to be based year-round in Tahiti, followed in 1987, and the *Wind Spirit* in 1988. Andren sold the company to Holland America Line in August 1988, and Carnival Cruise Lines subsequently acquired Holland America in January 1989, and with it Windstar. Potier departed not long afterward, and the company subsequently changed its name to Windstar Cruises, eliminating the word "Sail." The ships do a substantial number of charter and incentive sailings.

In 1990, a new division of Club Mediterranee called Club Med Cruises introduced the first of two similar but larger motor/sail vessels, *Club Med 1*. (See Club Med Cruises, page 127)

—First cruise passenger vessels with computer-operated sails.

FOOTNOTE

How does it work? Sails on these sophisticated 440-foot, four-masted ships are set and trimmed by computers that monitor wind velocity and direction and control heeling to less than six degrees. This, in combination with the usual cruise-ship stabilizers and bow thrusters, gives the comfort of a cruise vessel with the romance and grace of a sailing ship. If you want to see it work, the captain welcomes passengers to the navigation bridge anytime.

Concept

A relaxed, non-regimented, non-dressy version of a cruise with an emphasis on watersports, tropical and Mediterranean ports and an upscale onboard lifestyle.

Signatures

The four-masted sailing vessels maintain an open bridge with passengers permitted to come inside and watch the computers trim the sails.

Gimmicks

In some seasons on certain itineraries, two of the ships may meet to sail side-by-side, so each vessel's passengers can photograph or videotape the other.

Who's the Competition

Windstar has found itself a fairly solid niche with a lot of repeat passengers in the younger, non-traditional cruise area. Club Med Cruises competes in all three of Windstar's cruising areas, Tahiti, the Med and the Caribbean, but attracts a slightly different crowd and more Europeans. Star Clippers, although more traditional sailing vessels, also compete somewhat with Windstar, but Windjammer Barefoot Cruises is not a strong competitor.

Who's Aboard

Mostly urban thirtysomething-and-up couples in high-pressure jobs out to relax. A few sailing enthusiasts (but purists turn their noses up at computer-trimmed sails), a lot of destination-oriented passengers (particularly on the Tahiti itinerary). One executive described the average Windstar passenger as 45, affluent, well-traveled, pays a lot of attention to travel plans and is interested in the sports activities available. He may or may not have taken a cruise before.

Who Should Go

Anyone who wants to have an upscale but casual resort sort of holiday. The ships are beautiful and the cabins and bathrooms efficient and well-designed. All are identical, so there's no problem deciding what cabin category you'll book.

Who Should Not Go

Sometimes there are families with children on board, but this doesn't work as well with kids under 12 because there's nowhere for them to call their own and they end up belly-flopping in the swimming pool and being general nuisances. The line discourages toddlers and young children specifically. Also, because there's no elevator, anyone with mobility impairment should not book because getting from cabin to breakfast cafe can mean climbing as much as four flights of stairs.

The Lifestyle

There is no regimentation. No mileage pool or deck games, no ship's photographer treading on the punch line of your best joke to ask everyone to sit closer together, no table assignments or specified meal seatings, no waiter choruses of "Happy Birthday" in the dining room, no tipping required, and no dress code beyond the genially vague "casual elegance."

These are ships for those who eschew a standard cruise, for couples who want to be alone together on a remote island beach instead of a bus tour of St. Thomas, for erstwhile or would-be skippers who like to stand on the bridge with the captain instead of lying in the sun, and for anyone who would rather snorkel and go windsurfing than play bingo or line up to photograph the midnight buffet.

Wardrobe

"Casual elegance," the ambiguous dress code term suggested by Jean-Claude Potier, has been variously interpreted over the years, but generally means elegant resort wear with jacket and tie optional. You see a lot of open-necked silk shirts and linen pants on both men and women. Daytime wear is very casual, usually a lot of shorts and swimsuits, and going ashore garb, except in the fashionable Mediterranean resorts, is equally basic.

Bill of Fare

With Los Angeles' super-chef Joachim Splichal, owner of Patina, creating his signature cuisine on board all three ships, you can count on delicious fare. Splichal is not the type to wander away after stamping his name on a menu; the name of the cuisine concept is "180 Degrees from Ordinary." Consider marinated salmon with horseradish, potatoes and creme frâiche; chilled gazpacho with cilantro creme; roast young chicken with creamy polenta, artichoke, truffle oil and crispy Parmesan chips; chocolate croissant pudding with Wild Turkey bourbon sauce.

The seating at meals is open, meaning you arrive when you wish and sit where and with whom you please. Besides the dining room, there is a casual buffet cafe atop the ship where breakfast and lunch is served; it doubles as a cabaret or disco late at night.

Cuisine Report Card: A

Showtime

Entertainment is too organized a concept for the Windstar ships, but there is usually a trio playing for dancing and a small casino, as well as a large library of videotapes, some of them X-rated.

Entertainment Report Card: NA

Discounts

The Advanced Sailings Advantage Program allows discounts up to $1153 per person on 1996 sailings for early bookings on a first-come first-save basis; a limited number of cabins is available. From time to time, two-for-one sailings are also announced. For 1996, the Oct. 20 Yachtsman's Adventure, a 13-day transatlantic crossing from Funchal, Madeira, to Bridgetown, Barbados, goes for $1348 per person, double occupancy, for a limited number of the earliest bookings, for example. The best idea is to get on the Windstar mailing list, either by requesting it from the 800 number above or by being a repeat passenger. Then you'll get all the information as soon as the deals come up.

The Bottom Line

Since the emphasis is on low-key camaraderie and offbeat, noncommercial ports of call, people looking for nightlife, disco and casino action and born-to-shop types should opt only for other itineraries. While the sails initially attract the passengers, it is the pleasurable experience—friendly, relaxed and low-key—along with the very nice staff and crew, that keeps everybody on board happy. Windstar is a real winner.

Wind Spirit ★★★★★
Wind Star ★★★★★

They are most uncommon cruise ships, their long, trim hulls cutting through the indigo sea like a knife through silk, their sails catching the breeze and rising like romantic whispers from four tall white masts. The ports of these dream ships are fantasies themselves, fragments of the world's surreal estate—the wave-worn black sand beaches of Tahiti where Paul Gauguin spilled out his life painting women as lush as overripe mangoes...the fortress fastness of Elba, where Napoleon would sit for hours on a cold marble bench in a prim little garden staring across the sea toward France...the elemental water-smoothed stones of The Baths rising from the sapphire-and-turquoise Caribbean Sea at Virgin Gorda.

Sleek and sexy, these high-tech 148-passenger ships are fitted out like yachts, with dark wood and brass, rich colors and glove leather. The futuristic gray modular bathrooms, a marvel of design by France's Marc Held, make you want to say, "Beam me up, Scotty!" when you step into the shower. Casual elegance is the keynote for the lifestyle on board. A coverup over your bathing suit will allow you to lunch in the handsome glass-walled Veranda Cafe, and after a busy day ashore or a bare-feet-and-bikini day in the sun, you can slip into sandals and something loose, soft and silky for evening.

FOOTNOTE

On the 1986 maiden voyage of the Wind Star, *in Mustique, William F. Buckley came over from his yacht and requested permission to board, and David Bowie wangled an invitation to lunch. In St. Lucia, Princess Margaret admired the ship, and Colin Tennant, Lord Glenconnor, was so enchanted he invited the ship and its passengers to spend the afternoon at his private beach (later to become the posh resort Jalousie) with his pet elephant Bupa, along with steel drummers, fire eaters, limbo dancers and acrobats.*

Twilight on the Wind Star.

The Brochure Says

"It's not like any other travel experience you've ever known. The sails are your first clue that it's different."

Translation

If you've booked this vessel for a vacation and didn't know about the sails—let's face it, they no longer mention them in the company name—you may not notice they're there until a shadow suddenly falls across your body when you're sunbathing, and you look up with faint annoyance.

Cabins and Costs

Fantasy Suites: **Report Card: NA**

All the cabins aboard are fantastic but not in the sense Fantasy suites implies.

Small Splurges: **Report Card: A**

Average Price PPPD: $581 plus airfare.

There is an owner's suite, cabin # 107, that is somewhat larger than the standard cabins and sold at a 30 percent higher price than the standard cabins.

Suitable Standards: **Report Card: A**

Average Price PPPD: $449 plus airfare.

All the cabins on board, with the single exception of the owner's suite (see above) are identical, clean-lined and efficient rooms that have twins or queen-sized bed, color TV with VCR, mini-refrigerator and bar, makeup table, safe, desk, bookshelves and drawers. Bathrooms have space-age showers, hair dryers, plenty of counter space and thick terrycloth robes. Some have a pull-down third berth and some an adjoining private door to make a two-room suite.

Bottom Bunks: **Report Card: NA**

This category does not apply; all cabins have two lower beds.

Where She Goes

The *Wind Star* alternates north and southbound Caribbean cruises out of Barbados in winter, visiting Nevis, St. Martin, St. Barts, Montserrat and Martinique on the northbound itinerary, and Bequia, Carriacou, Grenada, Tobago, Tobago Cays and St. Lucia on the southbound. In summer, *Wind Star* cruises the Mediterranean out of various ports on 10-, 11-, 12- 13-, and 14-day sailings.

The *Wind Spirit* cruises the Virgin Islands in winter from St. Thomas, visiting St. Croix, Saba, Montserrat, St. Barts, Virgin Gorda and St. John, and in summer sails the Greek Islands and Turkey.

The Bottom Line

These unique vessels, which capture the imagination of all who see them, the admiration of all who sail on them, have changed the face of small-ship cruising, offering an alluring alternative to sophisticated travelers looking for a fresh and more personal vacation experience. They have our highest recommendation.

Fielding's Picks

Fun Places

1. The lounge is filled with natural light flooding in from a large skylight in daytime, and furnished with a lot of comfortable chairs and sofas in convivial conversational groupings.
2. The glass-walled veranda is a casual breakfast and lunch cafe that sometimes doubles as a disco when somebody can figure out where to turn on the fog machine and turn out the lights.
3. The restaurant is a charming room with wood paneling and windows that let in the view. While there are plenty of tables for two, the ambiance onboard is such that during the week or so of the cruise, passengers tend to clump together in larger and larger groups at dinner.
4. The outdoor piano bar is conveniently close enough to the outdoor bar that joining in on a familiar song is irresistible.
5. The instruction wheel is on the top deck, a fixed ship's wheel that offers some sailing lessons to passengers, and makes a dandy place to be photographed.

Good Reasons to Book These Ships

1. Romance, romance, romance.
2. To eat the delectable cuisine of Joachim Splichal without having to pay the Patina price.
3. To use the watersports deck in the balmy Caribbean.
4. To enjoy an unusually smooth ride, even in notoriously temperamental waters.

Things You Won't Find On Board

1. A cruise director leading the fun and games.
2. A children's program.
3. An inside cabin; all accommodations have a view.
4. Anyone nudging you for a tip; tipping is at the passenger's discretion.
5. An elevator.

THE CARIBBEAN CRUISE

Everybody has the image of what they'd like to do on a Caribbean cruise.

The Caribbean is **the most popular cruise area in the world**, drawing more than half of all cruise passengers. The appeal of its always warm and sunny weather is obvious, especially when most North Americans are shivering on a cold winter day. But the Caribbean, once considered seasonal sailing, is **big-time all year round in cruising** as more and more families take summer vacations afloat.

For some, a Caribbean cruise is the most comfortable route to a multi-island **shopping spree to stock up on duty-free items** from liquor to perfume, jewelry to cameras. For others, it's **a handy sampler of beaches and resort hotels** to check out for future vacations, or coral reefs and clear turquoise or cerulean water for diving or snorkeling,or a multicultural dip into a dazzling variety of languages, currencies, architecture and tropical foods.

Most cruise ships offer several basic shore excursions for sale for each port of call—a **general island tour that will include scenery, history and a shopping stop**; a boat excursion that may be anything from a rum punch party raft to a yacht cruise that stops at an uninhabited island to a submarine ride; and a beach, snorkeling or resort visit. On some islands, golf, tennis or helicopter sightseeing is also available.

Since per-person prices for excursions range from $15 to $85 or more, a large family or group of three or four friends may choose to negotiate **an independent island tour with a local cab driver** or hire a cab to go to and from the beach. Be sure to agree on the price before getting into the vehicle; on many islands the fares are fixed and posted.

On the other hand, passengers making their first trip outside the mainland U.S. or who are uneasy or uncomfortable about striking out on their own, will probably prefer the shore excursions sold on board the ship in order to travel with a group from the ship and have the services of an English-speaking guide.

Select your excursion choices carefully, because on many ships the tickets are not refundable if you change your mind about going.

Five Tips for Caribbean Touring

1 **Don't overtax yourself** in the hot, humid weather. An excursion that sounds super while you're sitting in the air-conditioned lounge may not be as nice when you're standing in the broiling sun, say, at St. Lucia's Soufrière looking at bubbling volcanic mud pots and sniffing sulphur.

2 **Never take a full-day tour if a half-day tour will do**. You see almost exactly the same things on both; the full day just throws in a longer shopping stop and a hotel buffet lunch that's not nearly as good as what you get on the ship.

3 Unless you're a tireless trouper with unlimited funds, don't sign up for everything, or they'll all start running together in your memory. **Every island offers an island tour, whether there's anything interesting to see or not**.

4 If **you hire a cab** to take you to a remote beach for a swim, make a deal to have him wait (otherwise you might not get a cab back before the ship sails) and **don't pay him until you get back** to the pier.

5 Don't succumb to the urge to have your hair done in **cornrow braids** on the first day of your Bahamas cruise if you plan to spend the second day in the sun and water; you could get some painful, serious sunburn on your scalp.

Big, Mid-sized or Little Ship?

Big splashy megaliners carrying as many as 2600 passengers ply the waters of the Caribbean all year, with sophisticated spa facilities, glittering casinos, nightclubs with Las Vegas-style entertainment, shopping mini-malls and experts to teach you everything from bridge to line-dancing to aerobics or *tai chi*. There's never a dull moment, you'll get to know at least two or three other couples in your age range pretty well by sharing mealtimes at the same table, and you can have a drink in a different bar almost every day of the cruise.

Mid-sized ships carrying 500 to 1000 passengers have a lot of the same features but scaled down in size and glitz a bit. Many of these are older ships that still have real cinemas instead of films running on your cabin TV set, and full, all-the-way-around-the-ship promenade decks for brisk morning walks. These vessels are more likely to offer midmorning bouillon and a white glove afternoon tea than the big babes above. You may spend more time reading or sunning on deck, and you may get to know more people than just those at your dinner table since you see them frequently on deck and at lectures and activities.

The **small ships** that cruise the Caribbean can be divided into several types:

- **Ultra-deluxe**, with posh cabins, dressy evenings and a minimum of organized entertainment and activities.
- **Expedition ships**, with basic cabins, not much dressing up but lots of lectures on the environment, flora and fauna and inflatable landing craft to take you to island beaches.
- **Casual ships**, from sailing craft to bow-landing exploration boats, where everybody gets to know everybody else, almost anything goes in the way of clothes, and you get to go swimming and snorkeling.

How Long?

Bahamas cruises generally last three or four days and may be combined with a land tour such as an Orlando Theme Parks stay.

The most typical Caribbean cruise is a seven-day round trip sailing from a Florida or Puerto Rican port and offering an Eastern Caribbean, Western Caribbean or Southern Caribbean itinerary. Those that sail from San Juan or other island ports like St. Thomas, Aruba, Antigua, can sail more of the "deep Caribbean" than ships that have to spend a first and last day just getting there from south Florida. Many ships have two alternate itineraries so a passenger can sign up for 14 days, two back-to-back seven-day cruises, without repeating ports of call.

Ten Best of the Best in the Caribbean

1 **Most elegant beach barbecue**: Aboard Cunard's *Sea Goddess I* where waiters in white mess jackets and swim trunks serve champagne and caviar to passengers wading in the surf at Jost van Dyke in the British Virgin Islands, followed by a lunch of grilled fresh Caribbean lobster, steaks, even plebeian hot dogs and hamburgers.

2 **Adventuring with the rich and famous**: Sailing on the unique four-masted sailing yacht *Sea Cloud* with Special Expeditions' splendid shore excursions in search of rare flora and fauna, or swimming off the lowered gangway at a quiet anchorage. Once owned by cereal heiress Marjorie Merriweather Post, the yacht maintains its 1930s ambience, complete with marble fireplaces (nonworking) and gold faucets on the tubs in the grandest suites.

3 **Best fantasy beach**: The Baths at Virgin Gorda, where small-ship passengers may arrive by Zodiac or bow-landing tender—or overland by van—then swim among the boulders and into the hidden grottos or snorkel offshore.

4 **Most casual cruise**: Forget about tuxedos. If you don't even want to wear shoes on your vacation, check out Windjammer Barefoot Cruises and their classic sailing ships. You can sleep out on deck, if you wish, and there's a free Bloody Mary for breakfast every morning.

5 **Best port performers**: The stylish and handsome Ballet Folklorique of Martinique, who come aboard to perform on many ships that call in Fort-de-France.

Most elegant beach barbecue is the caviar-and-champagne beach picnic aboard Cunard's Sea Goddess I *at Jost van Dyke.*

6 **Busiest port**: If you like crowds, you'll love Charlotte Amalie, St. Thomas, where four to seven cruise ships a day may call and you can hardly move inside the popular shops.

7 **Rarest ports of call**: If you want to name-drop, see if you can find a ship that calls at any of the following islands—Anguilla, Saba, Barbuda, Montserrat, Nevis, Marie-Galante and Canouan. A few do.

8 **Best private island beach day**: Royal Caribbean's Coco Cay in the Berry Islands of the Bahamas, with a day of exploration and watersports—snorkeling with underwater cameras, diving, rides on watercycles, rocket rafts and pedal boats, underwater caves and nature trails to explore, native straw markets for shopping, steel drum bands and a lavish barbecue buffet for lunch.

9 **Best whole family experience**: A day at Port Lucaya with The Big Red Boat, swimming with dolphins, joining a junkanoo, hanging out with Bugs Bunny, scuba diving, straw markets and parasailing.

10 **Best island spotting**: Two swivel telescopes are bolted to the handsome teak decks aboard the *Club Med 1* for spotting distant islands or identifying ships that pass in the night (or day).

Rating the Ports of the Bahamas

Freeport/Lucaya, Bahamas ★★

Language:	**English**	*English Spoken?:*	**Yes**
Currency:	**B$=US$**	*US$ ok?:*	**Yes**
To town:	**Walk, taxi, tender, depending on dock or anchorage**		

Only 60 miles from Florida, Freeport is the **closest foreign port to the United States**, and as such, has long been a major **shopping port-of-call for day cruises** off the Florida coast. It's full of **tacky shopping bazaars**, which is a pity, since Grand Bahama Island also has 660 miles of beaches with watersports, snorkeling, golf and tennis plus birdwatching at Rand Memorial Nature Centre and Garden of the Groves. Shore excursion options here range from swimming with dolphins ($$$) to dancing to a junkanoo band ($). Lucaya has a highly developed stretch of beach for cruise ship daytrippers with watersports, dolphins and rum party cruises.

Nassau, Bahamas ★★★

Language:	**English**	*English Spoken?:*	**Yes**
Currency:	**B$=US$**	*US$ ok?:*	**Yes**
To town:	**Walk**		

The Duke and Duchess of Windsor were posted to what they regarded as a colonial backwater during the turbulent days of World War II. These days, Nassau is a bigtime cruise port, especially for three- and four-day cruises sailing from the U.S. For many Americans, it is their very first foreign city, and despite the daytrippers, they still manage to scrape up some charm with **horsedrawn carriage city tours** and **the freewheeling straw market**. Your ship is steps away from downtown, so **duty-free shopping is a snap**. If you want to explore the **nightlife**, sign up for a tour to Paradise Island, or do it on your own by taxi. **Good buys** include British woolens and china, Colombian emeralds, hand-embroidered Irish linens, Gucci bags and Rolex watches. **Shore excursions** usually include the Seaworld Explorer semi-submarine ($$), a snorkeling expedition ($$), diving ($$, certification required), catamaran cruise ($), city and island tour ($), Coral World tour ($), beach tour ($) and a look at the marching flamingos at Adastra Gardens ($).

Rating the Ports of the Caribbean

St. John's, Antigua ★★★

Language:	**English**	*English Spoken?:*	**Yes**
Currency:	**EC$**	*US$ ok?:*	**Yes**
To town:	**Walk, taxi**		

Your ship will call in either St. John's or out at English Harbour near Nelson's Dockyard National Park, an excursion bus tour or taxi ride away from the capital of St. John's. Feisty, cricket-loving Antigua claims **365 beaches**, one for every day of the year, but yachting is an even bigger draw for the world's yachtsmen, who come from everywhere for **Sailing Week in April**. Traffic moves on the left, and roads are rough, potholed and poorly marked. Since taxis are fairly expensive, **shore excursions** may be cheaper than a cab tour here. Choose from the Nelson's Dockyard and island tour ($$), a half-day bus ride with time allowed for shopping and exploring at English Harbour ($$), and a swimming and beach tour ($$). Windsurfing, waterskiing, sailing, snorkeling and diving to see the wreck of the *Andes* are sometimes also available. **Good buys** include attractive silk-screened cotton garments at Coco's and the West Indian Sea Island Cotton Shop in St. John's. Ask whether prices quoted are in U.S. or EC dollars, since they use the same symbol and it takes nearly three of the latter to make one of the former.

Oranjestad, Aruba ★★★

Language:	**Dutch, Papiamento**	*English Spoken?:*	**Yes**
Currency:	**Guilder**	*US$ ok?:*	**Yes**
To town:	**Walk, taxi**		

Dutch-style buildings painted in pastel and tropical colors lend Aruba a distinct charm, but outside town it's flat and desertlike with dry, hot winds, dotted with cactus and weird, windblown divi divi trees. **White sugar-sand beaches** lined with palm trees stretch for seven miles along the west coast, a short taxi ride from the port. Good buys include Delft pottery, Swiss watches, pens, jewelry and hand embroidered linens. The **Hyatt Regency Aruba** with its lush gardens and waterfalls makes a good place to lunch. **Shore excursion** options include a not terribly interesting island tour ($$), the excellent Atlantis submarine ride ($$$), the Seaworld Explorer semi-submarine ($$), and a routine glass bottom boat ride ($). Divers should head directly for the submerged wreck of a WWII German freighter ($$$). Windsurfing ($$) and the new sport of sandsurfing ($) are other possibilities. Bustling Aruba is now independent from its erstwhile Dutch Leeward cousins Curaçao and Bonaire; the three were once called the ABCs.

Bridgetown, Barbados ★★★★★

Language:	**English**	*English Spoken?:*	**Yes**
Currency:	**B$**	*US$ ok?:*	**Yes**
To town:	**Taxi, long walk**		

The colorful new Bridgetown port area makes shopping fun and easy, and has turned Barbados into one of the best day calls in the Caribbean.

The **new port area** in Bridgetown makes this one of the most appealing home ports or day calls in the entire Caribbean. **Great shops**—Caribbean Sounds, Duty-Free Liquor, Colombian Emeralds, Local Colour, plus **free samples** of a lot of local liqueurs (it's ok, you're walking back to the ship), a restaurant and a tourist information office. If you want to **lunch ashore**, you have two very different options—a posh hotel like the elegantly renovated **Sandy Lane Hotel**($$$) and the funky **Brown Sugar Restaurant** ($), near the **Barbados Hilton** on the outskirts of Bridgetown, with a moderately-priced sampling of the best of Barbados food from **fried flying fish** to homemade soursop or coconut ice cream. Stroll afterward on the sugar-fine beach by the Hilton amid the sheltering shade of palm trees. **Shore excursions** here include a city and island tour ($$), an underground walk through Harrison's

Cave ($$), a Jolly Roger rum party cruise along the coast ($$) or an Atlantis submarine ride ($$$).

Kralendijk, Bonaire ★★★★

Language:	**Dutch, Papiamento**	*English Spoken?:*	**Yes**
Currency:	**Guilder**	*US$ ok?:*	**Yes**
To town:	**Walk**		

The sandy desert island of Bonaire, noted primarily for its snorkeling, also has miles of empty beaches and an easygoing ambiance.

Bonaire sits atop a coral reef, making it one of the **best snorkeling and diving destinations** in the Caribbean. Not many cruise ships call here, which is a mixed blessing. Its very isolation and serenity makes it one of the most appealing places in the Caribbean. **Eco-tourism** outweighs commercial development by policy. and Bonaire's visitors are primarily **divers, snorkelers, hikers and birdwatchers**. There's little in the way of duty-free shopping, evening entertainment or organized shore excursions. Roads are narrow and often rough, but there's not much traffic; an adventurous visitor could **rent a four-wheel drive vehicle** and drive all around the island in a day, looking at bright **pink flamingos** feeding in salt ponds, prowling the 13,500-acre Washington-Slagbaai National Park in search of **Amazon parrots** and bright green and yellow native parakeets, or go underwater to look at Redlip Blennies, Parrotfish and Trumpet Fish. Divers head for the submerged 1000-ton freighter *Hilma Hooker* in Angel City, to the double reef at Alice in Wonderland and to Thousand Steps. A number of dive operators are based in Bonaire including the famous pioneering company that operates **Captain Don's Habitat**, where you can book a Bonaire Night dinner and folk dance on Tuesdays.

Willemstad, Curaçao ★★★

Language:	**Dutch**	*English Spoken?:*	**Yes**
Currency:	**Guilder**	*US$ ok?:*	**Yes**
To town:	**Taxi or long walk**		

Sailing into Curaçao brings everyone out on deck to snap photographs of the pastel old Dutch buildings.

One of the pleasantest arrivals in Caribbean cruising is sailing into Willemstad past rows of **pastel old Dutch gabled houses**, most of them turned into duty-free shops. It's so **charming and easy to get around** that there's little point in taking the pedestrian city and island tour ($$) around the outlying desert terrain unless you're avidly curious about Curaçao or want to taste **the island's eponymous orange-flavored liqueur** at the distillery where it's produced. **On your own walking tour**, the don't-miss details are the Queen Emma Pontoon Bridge and the floating market nearby, lined with brightly painted schooners that sail over from Venezuela or Colombia to sell fresh fruits, vegetables and fish. Across the street is a local **open-air crafts market**, and steps away the pedestrian shopping mall chockablock with **duty-free shops**. Penha & Sons, in a building dating from 1708, sells perfumes, clothing and cosmetics. Divers will love Curaçao's 12-1/2 miles of coral reefs, and snorkelers will find **the largest protected underwater park in the Caribbean**, with 16 marked and 10 unmarked trails.

La Romanna, Dominican Republic ★★★

Language:	**Spanish**	*English Spoken?:*	**Some**
Currency:	**Peso**	*US$ ok?:*	**Yes**
To town	**Tender, shuttle bus**		

The famous resort of Casa de Campo is a regular port of call for Costa's Caribbean cruises, which use one of the resort's beaches as a private out island.

Little La Romanna on the island's eastern edge, adjacent to the **world-famous resort Casa de Campo**, is a popular port of call for Costa Cruises. Golf on a Pete Dye course, tennis in the "**Wimbledon of the Caribbean**," horseback riding and polo at The Equestrian Center, fishing, clay pigeon shooting, swimming and a shopping and sightseeing excursion to the Old World fantasy village of Altos de Chavon are all shore excursion options here, but if **a passenger does not buy a shore excursion, he doesn't get to go to the resort** itself, only to the cruise line's private beach resort. **Elegant shopping**, hardly budget but very artistic one-of-a-kind items, especially some stately amber and silver necklaces, can be found in the Altos de Chavon village. Amber is one of the Dominican Republic's best buys.

Puerto Plata, Dominican Republic ★

Language:	**Spanish**	*English Spoken?:*	**Some**
Currency:	**Peso**	*US$ ok?:*	**Yes**
To town	**Walk or taxi**		

The Dominican Republic occupies half of the island of Hispaniola; the other half is Haiti. Despite its lush landscapes, rivers, white sand beaches, coral cliffs and old Spanish towns, the country still remains largely undiscovered by Americans outside a few resort hotels.

In Puerto Plata, there's not much to do except **shop for amber** or **head for the beach**, unless you're one of the passengers on Costa's new *CostaPlaya* **headed to Cuba** on the first regularly scheduled cruise calls to that island in a long time. **Shore excursions** here are usually limited to guided mini-bus tours that are not terribly interesting, and even the price of amber has escalated in recent years. If you want **to eat ashore**, you can find grilled chicken and plantain chips in the cheap restaurants, good local seafood in the expensive restaurants.

Santo Domingo, Dominican Republic ★★

Language:	**Spanish**	*English Spoken?:*	**Some**
Currency:	**Peso**	*US$ ok?:*	**Yes**
To town:	**Taxi**		

Santo Domingo, the capital, has a lot of history, including the claim that Columbus, whose son was governor here, is or was at one time buried in the 1514 cathedral, oldest in the New World. As the **oldest city in the New World**, Santo Domingo can also claim the oldest house, street, hospital and university. The major **shore excursion** here, of course, is a tour of the Old Town and the appropriately old monuments ($). **Beaches are about half an hour away**; lively, anything-goes Boca Chica is the most popular. The food is quite good in the Dominican Republic, with shrimp, chicken and beef readily available. Local *empañadas* (pastry turnovers) filled with ground beef are sold from street carts and served in restaurants.

Portsmouth, Dominica ★★★

Language:	**English**	*English Spoken?:*	**Yes**
Currency:	**EC$**	*US$ ok?:*	**Yes**
To town:	**Shuttle bus, taxi**		

Dominica is going the way of eco-tourism rather than high-rise development, so more and more cruise ships are discovering this lush and unspoiled island.

Eco-tourism is the name of the game in lush and unspoiled Dominica, beginning to see a number of cruise ship calls thanks in part to a **new port facility** constructed at the north end of the island near **Cabrits National Park** and the town of Portsmouth. Previously, the few cruise ships that called usually arrived in the capital city of Roseau, and some still do call there. Rain forests, national parks, **rare birdlife and equally rare surviving Carib Indians** are among the highlights of "the nature island," headed up since 1980 by the Honorable Dame Eugenia Charles, the only female prime minister in the Caribbean. **Shore excursions** usually include a walking tour of the renovated Cabrits fortress ($ or free) or a drive to the rain forests and the Carib Reservation, where the last remaining Carib Indians still live ($$). An adventurous visitor can **rent a beat-up Jeep** in town ($$) and cover a surprising amount of territory in a day. The drive along the coast between Portsmouth and Roseau is scenic, as is the Layou River Valley, inland from Roseau, but the roads are sometimes rough and potholed. **Get a local driving license** at the police department before setting out.

George Town, Grand Cayman ★★★

Language:	**English**	*English Spoken?:*	**Yes**
Currency:	**CI$**	*US$ ok?:*	**Yes**
To town:	**Tender from ship**		

The **Switzerland of the Caribbean** has even more banks than duty-free shops, and the Cayman Islands dollar is often worth more than the U.S. dollar, so check prices carefully if you're tempted to shop here in the **posh, duty-free shops**. Locals live well, there are a lot of U.S. expatriates who moved down to stay with their money. Traffic moves on the left in this British Crown Colony. **Shore excursions** include the wildly popular **Stingray City Tour**, a snorkel-with-stingray opportunity that also includes snorkel equipment and instruction ($$), Scuba two-tank dive ($$–$$$, **bring certification**), Seaworld Explorer Semi-Submarine Tour ($$), Atlantis Submarine ($$$), a cruise aboard the Calypso Mermaid ($$), snorkeling ($$) and an island tour ($$) that includes Seven Mile Beach, the turtle farm, a black coral factory and a brief stop in **Hell**. (Locals find it amusing.) On your own, cab it to the Hyatt Regency Grand Cayman, a splendid resort hotel **on the sand at Seven Mile Beach**, or walk around in town hitting the shops. Then, perhaps, sit on the terrace at **Jamin**, a few steps away from the dock, sip a cold soda or beer and **crunch on conch fritters** while admiring your ship at anchor.

The harbor at St. George's, Grenada, is one of the loveliest in the Caribbean; the area where the bright boats are tied up is called the Carenage.

St. George's, Grenada ★★★

Language:	**English**	*English Spoken?:*	**Yes**
Currency:	**EC$**	*US$ ok?:*	**Yes**
To town:	**Walk**		

There's no way, José, no matter how tough you may think you are, to get out of Grenada without forking over a dollar or two for the must-buy souvenir from this spice island, a tiny **handwoven basket filled with local nutmegs**, cloves, mace and other spices. Because they're dried and not fresh, you can bring them back into the United States, and they make cheap, compact and **unusual gifts for friends at home**. Have your camera ready for the sail into this **picture-book harbor**, one of the prettiest in the Caribbean, and stroll around the Carenage in the harbor to shoot the vividly painted fishing boats, each with its own special name painted on the bow, while fending off spice sellers along the way. (It doesn't do any good to hold up the baskets you already bought; the Grenadans think you can never have enough souvenir spice baskets.) **Shore excursions** include the island tour ($$), often with a driver who gives his memories of the 1983 U.S. invasion of Grenada, a stop at Grand Etang National Park, and a half-day beach tour to two-mile-long Grand Anse Beach, easy enough to do on your own with a taxi, either a regular cab from town or a water taxi from the Carenage, across to the beach. For divers, the **biggest shipwreck in the Caribbean** is here, an Italian cruise ship called the *Bianca C* from Costa that caught fire and sank in 1961; a 350-pound grouper was living in the smokestack, the last we heard. Take a break at The Nutmeg to sample **the island's famous rum punches** with fresh grated local nutmeg on top. Two will make you careen along the Carenage back to your ship.

The Grenadines ★★★★

Language:	**English**	*English Spoken?:*	**Yes**
Currency:	**EC$**	*US$ ok?:*	**Yes**
To town:	**Tender from ship**		

A treasure chest of **100 or so craggy green islands** set like emeralds in the sapphire blue sea, a yachtsman's treasure with some of the best sailing in the world. Sail cruisers, small expeditioners and champagne-and-caviar ships all stop here, especially at the **jet-set island of Mustique** and the whaling outpost of Bequia, where the few surviving whalers like to share their memories with interested visitors. Best buys, if you can afford them, are the **elegantly hand-**

crafted boat models to order. (Queen Elizabeth has one.) The **silk screen fabrics** from The Crab Hole are also attractive. Carriacou, an offbeat call for smaller vessels, also has traditional boat builders at work. **Mayreau**, which provides a beach island day for many of Princess Cruises' Caribbean passengers, is privately owned and very tiny. **Palm Island**, even smaller and also privately owned, is filled by a resort called the Palm Island Beach Club. Small vessels occasionally call there. None of these islands offers organized shore excursions. Your best bet is to stroll around or hire a local taxi (often an open-bed pickup) for a bumpy but fascinating look around.

Pointe-à-Pitre, Guadeloupe ★★★

Language:	**French**	*English Spoken?:*	**Some**
Currency:	**Franc**	*US$ ok?:*	**Yes**
To town:	**Walk**		

The dock in Guadeloupe is adjacent to the heart of Pointe-à-Pitre, and one of the Caribbean's top restaurants, La Canne à Sucre, is only steps away.

One of the best restaurants in the Caribbean is only a few steps away from the dock in Pointe-à-Pitre, if you can afford it and are there in the evenings when it's open—the sophisticated **La Canne à Sucre** ($$$). But real Caribbean food freaks swear by the ebullient female Creole chefs who run simple restaurants with local cooking, often in their own homes. You have to call ahead in order to get directions and be sure the place is open; ask locals what's currently good. The cooks proudly parade through the streets during **the annual Cooks' Festival every August**, wearing their traditional Madras headdresses and beating on pots and pans with kitchen utensils. Butterfly-shaped Guadeloupe is really two islands, Grande-Terre, more heavily populated, with a gentle landscape, and sparsely settled Basse-Terre with rugged, mountainous terrain. **Shore excursions** include an island tour ($$), with a visit to a rustic rum factory, a short hike to a waterfall in the national park and a brief shopping stop in town.

Iles Des Saintes ★★★

Language:	**French**	*English Spoken?:*	**Little**
Currency:	**Franc**	*US$ ok?:*	**No**
To town:	**Tender**		

The seldom-visited Iles des Saintes are clean, colorful and totally French.

For cruise ship day trippers from small sail cruise ships like Star Clippers, Windstar and Club Med, going off on your own and strolling around is the real pleasure—walking down a narrow road with more chickens than cars, photographing brightly painted fishing boats and whimsical cottages with flower gardens in the front yard, swimming or snorkeling in clear waters, **lunching on conch or sea urchins** or a French-style court bouillon of fresh fish. These eight tiny, idyllic islands off Guadeloupe inhabited by fishermen descended from Breton sailors who arrived more than a century ago are **like going back to yesterday's French West Indies**. Some French is handy if you want to have dialogue or commerce with the islanders.

Montego Bay, Jamaica ★★

Language:	**English**	*English Spoken?:*	**Yes**
Currency:	**J$**	*US$ ok?:*	**Yes**
To town:	**Taxi, shuttle**		

Skip the town itself unless you're really into local crafts and local food (the **jerk chicken at the Pork Pit** near Doctor's Cave Beach is to die for!) because you'll have some heavy hustling by vendors (including ganja—locally-grown marijuana—if you're under 50) and what many perceive as a lot of attitude. Some of the island's most elegant resorts are in the vicinity, including **Round Hill, Half Moon Bay** and **Tryall**. **Shore excursions** include rafting ($$) which we can't recommend since some tourists were robbed and shot while on a group excursion on the Rio Grande a couple of years ago; a visit to **Rose Hall Great House** ($$), said to be haunted by a "white witch" who murdered three husbands; a half-day at a private beach club ($$); golf at Half Moon Bay ($$$), snorkeling ($$), scuba ($$$, **certification required**) or trimaran sailing to Doctor's Cave Beach ($$), within walking distance of the Pork Pit.

Climbing Dunn's River Falls near Ocho Rios is the must-do shore excursion in Jamaica; give your guide your camera to carry and he'll snap a picture of you.

Ocho Rios, Jamaica ★★★

Language:	**English**	*English Spoken?:*	**Yes**
Currency:	**J$**	*US$ ok?:*	**Yes**
To town:	**Walk**		

Ocho Rios gets **more cruise ship calls** than Mo Bay these days. The **top shore excursion** is a splashy 600-foot climb up Dunn's River Falls ($$). **Wear a bathing suit under your street clothes** and take a camera; your guide will carry it up the climb for you and snap your picture as a bonus. Slightly longer tours may include a combination of Carinosa Gardens, Fern Gully and Dunn's River Falls ($$), Prospect Plantation ($$) to see bananas, coffee, pineapple, sugar cane and other tropical plants growing; or coastal yacht cruises ($$-$$$). As we said in the copy above about Mo Bay, **we cannot recommend river rafting** ($$) since two Pennsylvania men were robbed and shot on one of those in a group tour a couple of years ago. Craft vendors are sometimes aggressive in the streets around the port, some pushing you to buy ganja. **Ask about prices**, since **the Jamaican dollar sign is written like the U.S. dollar sign**, and vendors hope you'll pay in the more valuable U.S. dollars without double-checking. The smoothly-functioning port facility is within walking distance to malls and craft markets, and if your mouth is set for some **spicy jerk chicken and ice-cold Red Stripe beer**, the Jerk Center is a short stroll from the ship; just ask the cruise staff how to find it.

Fort-de-France, Martinique ★★

Language:	**French**	*English Spoken?:*	**Some**
Currency:	**Franc**	*US$ ok?:*	**Yes**
To town:	**Long walk, taxi**		

Despite the sultry heat and the rather longish (about a mile) and dull (except for the stunning Schoelcher Library) walk into town, we usually grit our teeth and hoof it because the local cabbies, heavy on attitude, are now charging **$8 to drive you into town**, nearly double what it was a couple of years ago. On our most recent visit in the spring of 1995, the cab drivers would not let the prearranged tourist buses come into the port to take the passengers on the island tours unless the cabs could get half of the pre-sold shore excursion business. The fact that the tour guides are fluent in English and history of the island and many cab drivers hardly speak English at all didn't seem to bother them. If you're comfortable driving a small rental car on a French-speaking Caribbean island and can arrange the rental ahead of time, we'd recommend going out on your own if you can't take the usual half-day island tour. The single most dramatic event in the history of the island, **the eruption of Mt. Pelée** in 1902 that killed 30,000 people from gas fumes, with the only survivor a prisoner in an underground cell, is dramatically illustrated in the local museum in St. Pierre. You can **buy French perfumes**, cosmetics and Lalique crystal at air-conditioned duty-free havens like Roger Albert's gigantic shop.

Cozumel, Mexico ★★★

Language:	**Spanish**	*English Spoken?:*	**Yes**
Currency:	**Peso**	*US$ ok?:*	**Yes**
To town:	**Walk, taxi or tender**		

At Cozumel's new port facility two miles from the old town, vendors promote tropical drinks made from luscious fresh fruits.

On a busy winter or spring day, the port of Cozumel may be **chockablock with cruise ships**, some of them tendering from anchorage into the town dock in the heart of little San Miguel, others alongside at the new dock facility a couple of miles away with its own port shopping complex. On a Western Caribbean itinerary, Cozumel is the star, and the drill is that your ship usually calls first briefly at the port of Playa del Carmen on the mainland just long enough for **the shore excursions to Maya ruins** to disembark, then sails on to the island of Cozumel. The local shops have really gotten tarted up the last few prosperous years, but traces of the funky old Mexican village that used to be here are still in evidence. The handsome **Inter-Continental Hotel** is a short cab ride from the new pier and makes a nice place to lunch at the outdoor bar by the pool. If you're in the middle of town, try the casual, inexpensive **Palmeros** on the main square by the crosswalk to the town pier. Snorkeling and shopping head the list of things to do in Cozumel. **Good buys** include fine black coral jewelry made locally, hand-embroidered garments, carved alabaster knick-knacks, straw hats and bags, woven hammocks, brightly painted pottery and the ubiquitous T-shirt in all its guises. **Shore excursions** may offer a ho-hum island tour ($$), interesting but hardly riveting; snorkeling on famous Palancar Reef ($$), which includes instruction and equipment; a one-tank dive at the Santa Rosa Wall ($$$, **certificate required**); or a beginner dive at Paraiso Reef ($$), including instruction and equipment.

Playa del Carmen, Mexico ★★★

Language:	**Spanish**	*English Spoken?:*	**Yes**
Currency:	**Peso**	*US$ ok?:*	**Yes**
To town:	**Walk**		

Tulum, shown here, is the easier, half-day tour; it usually takes all day on the bus or an expensive roundtrip flight to visit Chichen Itza.

Playa del Carmen is used primarily as a disembarkation port for passengers taking in **the wonders of the Maya ruins** at Tulum or Chichen Itza, but it's also possible to visit the resort beach strip at Cancun ($$) on an excursion from Playa del Carmen, although few ships offer the option. More common is **an all-day excursion to Tulum's Maya ruins** by the sea and **the "sacred lagoon" of Xel-Ha**, with a box lunch provided by the ship ($$). Even more spectacular (and pricey) is the flight tour to Chichen Itza's ruins ($$$) to see the pyramid of Kukulcan, the ball court, Temple of the Warriors and Well of Sacrifices. The bus tour to Chichen Itza from Playa del Carmen is **more than three**

hours each way, and using a video camera at any of the ruins carries a surcharge of around $10. **Take a bottle of mineral water** from the ship to sip as you're walking around the ruins. If you have a whole day in Playa del Carmen, as ships occasionally offer, you'll find a good beach right by the pier backed by a pretty pink resort hotel, and not far away, south of Tulum, **Sian Ka'an Biosphere Reserve**, one of the UNESCO World Heritage Sites, with tropical forests and marine habitats protecting endangered mammal, bird and reptile species. Guides are on the premises to take you around ($$$).

San Juan, Puerto Rico ★★★★

Language:	**Spanish**	*English Spoken?:*	**Yes**
Currency:	**US$**	*US$ ok?:*	**Yes**
To town:	**Walk to old town, taxi elsewhere**		

Most cruise ships dock at the edge of San Juan's colorful Old Town at one of the city's spiffy new piers (or the old one) but if there's an overflow, your ship may sometimes be a mile or two away in an industrial port area. The Old Town is the main point of interest, and something you can easily do on your own unless you want a guide to fill you in on all the history. Pick up the latest copy of *Que Pasa* magazine (free but you'll have to ask for it) from the tourist information office near the dock. **Ship buffs should make a detour** (by taxi) over to the **Radisson Normandie Hotel**, a great eccentric art deco hotel designed to look like one of the French Line ships. The famous **Caribe Hilton** is a half-block away if you want to walk over there for a look. **Shore excursions** include a half-day Bacardi Rum Factory tour in combination with a visit to El Morro Castle and Old San Juan ($$), a city tour of new and old San Juan ($), a drive through the El Yunque rain forest ($$), golf at Cerromar Beach ($$$), deep-sea fishing ($$$), horseback riding with beach visit and barbecue lunch included ($$$), snorkeling ($$) or diving ($$$ for a one-tank with certification required, $$ for a first-timer's dive with equipment and instruction). Nightclub or casino evening tours ($$) are also offered when a ship stays in port until midnight or later, but the last one of these we took (spring of 1995) was **dreadful, a lot of milling about and waiting for the cultural show in a stuffy, sleazy, smoke-filled casino** and nowhere smoke-free you could even sit down and get a quiet drink. We ditched the tour and took a cab back to the ship, where it was much nicer.

Gustavia, St. Barts ★★★★★

Language:	**French**	*English Spoken?:*	**Yes**
Currency:	**Franc**	*US$ ok?:*	**Yes**
To town:	**Tender from ship**		

Quiet beaches and sheltered inlets like this make St. Barts a favorite hideaway of the rich and famous.

This lovely little island is the kind of French tropical island we used to dream about—gorgeous sandy beaches, **discreet topless sunbathing**, secluded resorts and restaurants, **chic shopping for Paris labels** and a glamorous, if laid-back, clientele. Now we just hop aboard one of the small, elegant cruise ships that visits there, rent a mini- Moke or Jeep ($$) and take off for the day for a beach or two and whatever hotel is trendy favorite of the year. In 1995, it was **Le Toiny**, where we sat on the terrace watching the cobalt blue swimming pool shimmer and seem to slip seamlessly over the edge into the twinkling sea beyond. We ate grilled fresh fish, nibbled a plain green salad and drank an icy bottle of Muscadet, and tried to be suave enough not to raise an eyebrow at the $100 check. (No, no soup, no dessert, no coffee, just the fish and wine.) Off-the-wall fun in St. Barts (the real name is St. Barthélemy but nobody calls it that) includes parking on the hill above the airport and watching the planes barely clear the top of your head, then nose steeply downward to **land downhill on an STOL runway**! You could, of course, also spend your time wandering through the cool and costly shops of Gustavia checking out Cartier, Cardin, Animale St. Tropez, Hermés, Libertine, Hervé Leger and so on. Absolutely fabulous, darling!

St. Croix, U.S. Virgin Islands ★★★

Language:	**English**	*English Spoken?:*	**Yes**
Currency:	**US$**	*US$ ok?:*	**Yes**
To town:	**Walk to Frederiksted; shuttle to Christansted**		

St. Croix is the largest of the U.S. Virgin Islands, with an underwater national park for snorkeling and a lot of duty-free shops with less crowds than St. Thomas.

Only a few very small ships such as those from Renaissance and Sea Goddess can dock in the capital city of Christiansted. Large cruise ships usually come alongside or anchor off the second city of Frederiksted, across the island, whose port **was rebuilt recently** after severe damage from hurricane Hugo. **St. Croix is different** from sister islands St. Thomas and St. John, lower key, more affordable, with a wide range of beaches and watersports. It's Teddy Kennedy's Caribbean hideaway; you may run into him at **Duggan's on the Reef** chowing down on chowder or a flying fish sandwich. Only a few miles offshore is **Buck Island Reef National Monument**, the only underwater national park in the United States, with its marked underwater snorkeling trails. Shopping is best in Christiansted; shuttle service across the island is usually available for a nominal fee. **Shore excursions** here usually include an island tour and visit to Whim Great House ($$), a rum-tasting tour to the Cruzan Rum Distillery ($$), golf at a Robert Trent Jones course ($$$), horseback riding in the rain forest and at the beach ($$$), sailboat ride ($$), snorkeling at Buck Island ($$) or scuba at Long Reef ($$$, certificate required).

St. John, U.S. Virgin Islands ★★★★★

Language:	**English**	*English Spoken?:*	**Yes**
Currency:	**US$**	*US$ ok?:*	**Yes**
To town:	**Tender from ship**		

You'll disembark your big cruise ship in the early morning and board the tender for a balmy shuttle into the village of Cruz Bay, then be herded by groups into the local "taxis," the backs of pickup trucks with canvas-shaded benches built across them. Never fear, it's cool and nice once you head out into the woods, far nicer than an air-conditioned bus with windows that don't open. The **drivers are congenial**, stopping whenever anybody wants a photo, chatting about life on the island and just generally being cool and laidback. **Shore excursions** to Trunk Bay ($$) board these St. John taxis for a ride through pristine forest to an immaculate white sand beach fringed with coconut palms. If Trunk Bay looks crowded, ask the driver if he can drop you off at Hawksnest Bay (one cove closer to Cruz Bay) instead, and tell him to pick you up when he fetches the rest of the group from Trunk Bay. Slip him a tip, of course. If you lose your tour group, you can take one of the frequent ferries from Cruz Bay back to Red Hook on St. Thomas, then grab a cab back to the dock. Just remember your ship's sailing time and allow at least three hours to get back to St. Thomas. **Campers should check out Cinnamon Bay Campground** for future visits, two bays beyond Trunk Bay, if the driver will take you farther; some of these national park sites have cottages or rental tents and can be reserved in advance. The famous ecologically-oriented **Maho Bay Campground** is a bit farther away and a lot of drivers won't go in there because the road is so bad. It sure keeps out the riffraff.

Basseterre, St. Kitts ★★★★

Language:	**English**	*English Spoken?:*	**Yes**
Currency:	**EC$**	*US$ ok?:*	**Yes**
To town:	**Taxi shuttle from dock**		

There's no way you can take a shore excursion in St. Kitts and miss the island's pride and joy, the fortress at Brimstone Hill.

We think one of the **most charming shore excursions** in the whole Caribbean for first-time visitors is the half-day island tour ($$), which usually includes a visit to the restored 17th century British fortress at Brimstone Hill, called the Gibraltar of the Caribbean because it was never conquered. You'll glimpse at least a couple of the 125,000 **wild vervet monkeys** that run amok all over the island (they're in a roadside cage on the way into town), and have a chance to buy a few garments at **Caribelle Batik**, where silkscreen fashions are produced in the manor house of a 17th century plantation. There's even a quick tour around the raffish capital with its Caribbean versions of Big Ben, Piccadilly Circus and Pall Mall. While going around on your own isn't difficult, there's little need to do so when the **island tour is so well done**. The favorite local beaches, none of them up to the sandy classics on some of the other islands, include Banana Bay, Cockleshell, Conaree Beach, Frigate Bay and Friar's Bay, the last open to both the Atlantic and the Caribbean with some wild surf. While Nevis is very near here, it's almost impossible to get over there and back on a day tour from your ship because of local transportation times.

Castries, St. Lucia ★★★★

Language:	**English**	*English Spoken?:*	**Yes**
Currency:	**EC$**	*US$ ok?:*	**Yes**
To town:	**Taxi**		

The Pitons, twin peaks on the island of St. Lucia, and the still-active volcano of Soufriere are at the less-visited end of the island.

Lovely, lush St. Lucia has two ports, and most ships, because of size, must call at the less-interesting capital of Castries rather than anchor off the town of Soufrière at the foot of the needle-like Pitons and the still-seething volcano on the other end of the island. A few small vessels are able to anchor off Soufrière and take passengers in by tender for shore excursions to the bubbling mud pots and steaming sulphur pools of the volcano, but major ships call only at Castries' handsome new port facility of Pointe Seraphine, with an assortment of **duty-free shops just steps away from the gangway**. Old Caribbean hands will like funky downtown Castries, where **the lively vegetable market** still has posters stapled around its perimeters forbidding urinating in public. **Shore excursions** offered here include a sailboat trip to Marigot Bay ($$) where *Dr. Doolittle* was filmed; a daylong boatride with lunch along the coast to see Soufrière and the Pitons from the sea ($$); a city and environs tour which includes a shopping stop at Bagshaw's silk screen studios ($$); and, on occasion, a daylong bus tour to Soufrière ($$), which we'd hesitate to recommend unless you're *really* into fumaroles.

Philipsburg, St. Maarten ★★★

Language:	**Dutch, Papiamento**	*English Spoken?:*	**Yes**
Currency:	**Guilder**	*US$ ok?:*	**Yes**
To town:	**Tender from ship**		

When you disembark your tender at the town pier in Dutch St. Maarten, the historic courthouse will probably be the first building you'll notice.

You'll land at the pier in the heart of town when you disembark the ship's tender, and getting around couldn't be simpler—there are **two main streets**, Front Street, the one nearer the water, and Back Street, the one farther away from the water. See how easy it is? But it's more complicated than it seems. The **schizophrenic 37-square-mile island is divided not quite equally between the Netherlands and France**; the French have more land but the Dutch have the international airport. But it's painless passing between the two sectors, just hail a taxi van, spend three bucks or so to ride up to Marigot and hail another one back to Philipsburg. The Dutch town has most of **the shopping and the casinos**, and the duty-free shopping here is pretty good; we'd stack it up against St. Thomas any day, except Americans get an extra break on the goods they buy in St. Thomas. The streets are usually thronged with shoppers and the occasional pickpocket. **Shore excursions** offered in Philipsburg include an island tour ($-$$), a sightseeing boat cruise up to Marigot, the French capital ($$), golf at Mullet Bay ($$$), **a cruise on an America's Cup yacht**—everyone loves this one—($$$), a sail and snorkel half-day aboard a catamaran ($$), snorkeling ($$) and a one-tank scuba dive to a reef at a depth of 50 to 60 feet ($$$, bring certification).

Marigot, St. Martin ★★★★

Language:	**French**	*English Spoken?:*	**Yes**
Currency:	**Franc**	*US$ ok?:*	**Yes**
To town:	**Tender from ship or shuttle from Philipsburg**		

Smaller ships sometimes call in Marigot on the French side of St. Martin, where a crafts and vegetable market often takes place in the town square.

This is the Gallic half of the island above, and a few valiant ships, notably the sail cruisers from Windstar and Club Med, still anchor in the bay here. The **waterfront area has been gentrified** in the last several years, and has turned what used to be a photogenic island vegetable market into a crafts and flea market with more junk than art. Still, the port area is lined with appealing (and expensive) sidewalk cafes that might make you think of the Côte d'Azur if you've never actually been there. **Culinary capital** of the island is the town of **Grand Case**, a short and inexpensive ride away on a local bus. **Stroll around town reading menus** to pick out a spot to lunch; we liked **Deep-Blue**, a casually elegant French Swiss spot with an open terrace by the sea, when we were last there, but there are a dozen others as well. Some **outdoor food sellers line the road** by Grand Case Beach if you prefer a snack. The island's **best-known clothing-optional beach** is Orient Beach, several miles east of Grand Case. You could also **take the ferry over to Anguilla**, where almost no cruise ships call, to have a look around, but you'd have to rush to squeeze it in.

St. Thomas, U.S. Virgin Islands ★★★

Language:	**English**	*English Spoken?:*	**Yes**
Currency:	**US$**	*US$ ok?:*	**Yes**
To town:	**Shuttle, tender**		

The streets of Charlotte-Amalie, St. Thomas, are lined with shops and touts hustling you to come into each one of them.

The **most popular cruise port in the Caribbean** has four different areas where your ship may be positioned—the main port at West India dock (a.k.a. Havensight), two miles east of downtown Charlotte Amalie; the Crown Point (a.k.a. Sub Base) about two miles west of downtown Charlotte Amalie, the downtown pier (only small ships like ACCL's *Mayan Prince* tie up here), and anchoring offshore, as the elegant *Norway* has to do every week on its call. From West India Dock the **shuttles will charge you around $3 a person** for the ride into town. If a little light shopping is the only thing on your agenda and you don't like crowds, we'd recommend you stroll from the pier into the very nice and usually **uncrowded shops of Havensight Mall**, where we promise you'll find a branch of virtually every major downtown shop with the same prices but without the touts crowding the sidewalks. **Liquor is a bargain** if you don't mind lugging it home, but **never check it with your baggage**. **Shore excursions** include a beach day at Magen's Bay or island tours in open-air jitneys ($-$$); Kon Tiki rum punch party boats, Coral World's underwater observatory or a beach expedition to St. John ($$); the Atlantis Submarine, helicopter tours or golf at Mahogany Run ($$$). The harbor with its turquoise water, rows of red-roofed white buildings climbing green hills, and fluorescent foliage—bougainvillea, hibiscus, yellow trumpets—is gorgeous. **Don't be tempted to rent a car** to ride around; you drive on the left and roads are narrow, winding and often unmarked. While Hurricane Marilyn wreaked havoc last September, the island should be back on cruise itineraries in 1996.

Kingstown, St. Vincent ★★

Language:	**English**	*English Spoken?:*	**Yes**
Currency:	**EC$**	*US$ ok?:*	**Yes**
To town:	**Walk**		

Lush, rural St. Vincent is primarily a banana port and administrative center for the Grenadines; you'll have a chance at an island tour to see the breadfruit.

A beautiful and unspoiled island with winding country roads and farming communities, St. Vincent really doesn't open itself up to the daytripper with limited time. In the port, you'll see **bananas being loaded onto Europe-bound freighters**, an activity that seems to go on night and day. A posh resort that is part of and at the same time not part of St. Vincent—it's on its own island with a severely restricted transportation policy—is **Young Island**; they only allow a few visitors on the private island at a time and you have to literally telephone from the boat landing to see if they'll let you come over or not. Frankly, when we finally were permitted to come over—hours after we first applied—we found it a bit **overrated if you're into creature comfort**. **Shore excursions** usually offered include an island tour ($$) that visits the botanical gardens dating from 1765, oldest in the Caribbean; you'll see a living **breadfruit tree brought back from Tahiti by Captain Bligh**. Diving and snorkeling tours ($$-$$$) to the Falls of Baleine, a 60-foot cascading waterfall spilling into a 15-foot-deep fresh water pool, are also sometimes available. **Stamp collectors** treasure St. Vincent's beautiful postage stamps; you can find them at St. Vincent Philatelic Services Ltd. in Kingstown.

Scarborough, Tobago ★★★

Language:	**English**	*English Spoken?:*	**Yes**
Currency:	**TT$**	*US$ ok?:*	**Yes**
To town:	**Walk or shuttle, depending on dock or anchorage**		

A golf course in Tobago—but you'll see more cricket than golf played here.

The new port facility in Scarborough accesses one of the prettiest beaches in the Caribbean, Pigeon Point. It used to be that small ships anchored off the point and took passengers ashore by Zodiac or tender, but that doesn't seem to happen much any more. On our most recent arrival, we were greeted by **a fine steel drum band** that seemed to consist mostly of local students, both male and female. **Shore excursions** accent the island's emphasis on **ecotourism**, with glass-bottom boat rides and snorkeling at Buccoo Reef ($-$$), an island tour ($$) visiting the capital of Scarborough, the 18th century English fortress of Fort George, the town of Portsmouth with its mysterious riddle on an 18th century tombstone inscription, and a modest history museum. **Offshore reefs attract divers and snorkelers**; local operators offer dive excursions to Buccoo Reef ($$$, **bring your certification**). Golfers will find an 18-hole course adjacent to Mount Irvine Bay Hotel.

Road Town, Tortola ★★★★

Language:	**English**	*English Spoken?:*	**Yes**
Currency:	**US$**	*US$ ok?:*	**Yes**
To town:	**Taxi, shuttle vans**		

We adore the British Virgin Islands, secluded and laid-back compared to the U.S. Virgin Islands, but with a distinctive character all their own. **Don't expect fancy or fussy**, glitzy or glamorous. What you get are pretty tropical islands with friendly people who are not in a bit of a hurry—heaven forfend—so you'd better not be either. Yachtsmen enjoy sailing around the 40 or so islands and cays, of which Tortola is the largest, as well as being the administrative center of the group. The **U.S. dollar is the official currency** here in these British islands. **Shore excursion options** are modest, with sailing, snorkeling and scuba ($$-$$$) heading the list, along with a tour to the Baths at Virgin Gorda ($$) or a glass-bottom boat ride over the **1867 wreck of the Royal Mail Ship *Rhone* near Salt Island** ($$). If you want to just walk around Road Town, Pusser's Company Store is the place to sample **killer rum drinks**, rated by number for strength, and buy tropical safari wear. If you can drive on the left and negotiate narrow, winding, potholed roads, a self-drive rental car tour of the island ($$) could take you to the beach at Cane Garden Bay, Sage Mountain National park, Soper's Hole, and **Apple Bay's Sugar Mill** and its beachfront restaurant **Islands** for lunch.

The streets of Port-of-Spain, Trinidad, are lined with handsome Victorians.

Port-of-Spain, Trinidad ★★

Language:	**English**	*English Spoken?:*	**Yes**
Currency:	**TT$**	*US$ ok?:*	**Yes**
To town:	**Walk**		

First there was **a single scarlet ibis**, feeding on a mud flat alongside some egrets and blue herons, then another and then after the guide anchored our boat 500 feet away so as not to scare them, they began coming home in flocks, like groups of flashily dressed commuters off the 6:19. Trinidad has some of the **best birdwatching** in the hemisphere, with 400 varieties, many of them rare or unique, plus 600 species of butterflies. Until not long ago, Trinidad was prosperous enough from oil and international business, but with a soft economy has begun to look at tourism, **primarily eco-tourism**. The few cruise ships that call here arrive at a handsome new cruise port in downtown Trinidad; walking is the best way to get around here since traffic still clogs the streets throughout the day. **Shore excursions** offered include an island tour with a visit to Maracas Beach ($$); an early morning or late afternoon visit to Caroni Bird Sanctuary to see huge flocks of those scarlet ibis described above ($$); or an occasional expedition to Asa Wright Nature Centre ($$), a rain forest bird sanctuary with more than 160 species, some very rare. If you hire a taxi to take you out to Asa Wright and back, make sure he knows where it is before you set out (our driver didn't) and agree on the price in advance. On your own in town, have **lunch at Veni Mange** (Come and Eat), a moderately priced spot in a tiny cottage on a side street where **two sisters cook up great local food**. If you can get here for the **pre-Lenten Carnival**, Trinidad's biggest tourist event of the year, you'll see a costume parade to rival Rio's.

Spanish Town, Virgin Gorda ★★★★

Language:	**English**	*English Spoken?:*	**Yes**
Currency:	**US$**	*US$ ok?:*	**Yes**
To town:	**Shuttle vans**		

Virgin Gorda is home of The Baths, as well as some off-the-beaten-path resorts.

The world-famous **Baths of Virgin Gorda** with their gigantic water-smoothed boulders and turquoise pools and grottos are the primary excursion here ($$). A boat brings you to Gun Creek, where you board an open-air safari bus or tourist van for an island drive which takes you through Spanish Town and ends at the Baths. You'll be let out at the top of the hill with a short walk down a narrow, uneven path into the area. Here you can explore, swim or snorkel amid the boulders for an hour or so before going back up the hill to get into your bus. A **sailing excursion** ($$$) aboard a 75-foot catamaran that sails around Peter, Pelican and Cooper Islands is also sometimes offered. After the cruise, the boat anchors off a sheltered beach for swimming, sunning or snorkeling. Laurance Rockefeller's famous **Little Dix Bay** has been a top luxury resort here since it opened back in 1964, but other famous resorts such as **Bitter End Yacht Club** and **Biras Creek** can only be reached by sea. Divers can explore Anegada Reef, the wreck of the *RMS Rhone* (where the film *The Deep* was shot) and the wreck of the *Chikuzen*. British entrepreneur Richard Branson owns **Necker Island**, a posh and private island with a 10-room hotel available for **$10,000 a night** for a maximum of 16 guests.

1996 THEME CRUISE CALENDAR

SHIP	CRUISE LINE	LOCATION	DATES
	CULINARY		
Sea Goddess I, II	Cunard	Caribbean	Dec 16, Jan 6
Wind Star	Windstar	Caribbean	Sep 26
	HEALTH & FITNESS		
Queen Odyssey	Royal Cruise	Caribbean	Jan 1
Norway	NCL	Caribbean	Oct 12
	MUSIC & ENTERTAINMENT		
	Big Band		
OceanBreeze	Dolphin	Caribbean	Feb 4, Apr 14
Norway	NCL	Caribbean	Nov 23
SeaBreeze	Dolphin	Caribbean	Dec 15
	Blues		
Norway	NCL	Caribbean	Dec 14
Atlantic	Premier	Caribbean	Jan 7
SeaBreeze	Dolphin	Caribbean Motown	Sep 8, 22
	Country Western		
Norway	NCL	Caribbean	Jan 13, Nov 9
Royal Majesty	Majesty	Caribbean	Apr 1, 5
SeaBreeze	Dolphin	Caribbean	Apr 28, May 5
	Fifties & Sixties		
Royal Majesty	Majesty	Caribbean Elvis 50s-60s	Jan 5, 8, May 12, Sep 8, Oct 6, Dec 6, 9
SeaBreeze	Dolphin	Caribbean	Jan 21, 28
Norway	NCL	Caribbean	May 11

SHIP	CRUISE LINE	LOCATION	DATES
	Jazz		
Norway	NCL	Caribbean	Oct 26 Nov 2
	Comedy		
Norway	NCL	Caribbean	Jun 8
	When Radio Was		
CostaRomantica	Costa	Caribbean	Jan 14
	MYSTERY		
Sagafjord	Cunard	World	Jan 28
	PROFESSIONAL SPORTS		
Royal Majesty	Majesty	Caribbean	SuperBowl—Jan 26 Hall of Fame Base-ball—Feb 2, 5 LPGA Golf—Oct 20 Sports Bonanza—Oct 27
Norway	NCL	Caribbean	Football—Feb 24 Hockey—June 22 Basketball—July 13 Baseball—Nov 16
Dreamward	NCL	Caribbean	Ski—Sep 28 Motorsports—Dec 1 Pro beach volley-ball—Dec 8
	WINE		
Wind Star	Windstar	Caribbean	All of Mar
	SPECIAL EVENTS		
	Valentine's Day		
Princess (Fleetwide)	Princess		All of Feb
	Greek Festival		
Royal Majesty	Majesty	Caribbean	Sep 22
	Irish Festival		
Royal Majesty	Majesty	Caribbean	Mar 15
OceanBreeze	Dolphin	Caribbean	Mar 17
	Octoberfest		
SeaBreeze	Dolphin	Caribbean	Oct 6
Royal Majesty	Majesty	Caribbean	Oct 20

GODMOTHER QUIZ

Reprinted from Fielding's *Cruise Insider*, Volume 1, Number 4

Match the names of the superstars and world figures on the left with the ships each has christened (thus becoming its "godmother") on the right.

1. Lauren Bacall	a. *Seabourn Pride*
2. Audrey Hepburn	b. *Star/Ship Oceanic*
3. Princess Diana	c. *Royal Viking Sun*
4. Angela Lansbury	d. *Crystal Harmony*
5. Liza Minnelli	e. *Crystal Symphony*
6. Margaret Thatcher	f. *Royal Majesty*
7. June Allyson	g. *Crown Princess*
8. James and Gloria Stewart	h. *Regal Princess*
9. Gloria Estafan	i. *Royal Princess*
10. Whoopi Goldberg	j. *Star Princess*
11. Mary Tyler Moore	k. *Nordic Empress*
12. Shirley Temple	l. *Radisson Diamond*
13. Sophia Loren	m. *Song of America*
14. Kiri Te Kanawa	n. *Maasdam*
15. Beverly Sills	o. *Windward*
16. Barbara Bush	p. *Dreamward*
17. Diana Ross	q. *Monarch of the Seas*
18. Minnie Mouse	r. *Viking Serenade*

ANSWERS: 1, q; 2, j; 3, i; 4, e; 5, f; 6, h; 7, n; 8, c; 9, k; 10, r; 11, d; 12, a; 13, g; 14, l; 15, m; 16, o; 17, p.; 18, b.

CARIBBEAN CRUISE LINE CONTACTS

American Canadian Caribbean Line	(800) 556-7450
Carnival Cruise Lines	(800) 327-9501
Celebrity Cruises	(800) 437-3111
Clipper Cruise Line	(800) 325-0010
Club Med Cruises	(800) 453-7447
Costa Cruise Lines	(800) 462-6782
Crystal Cruises	(800) 446-6620
Cunard Crown	(800) 221-4770
Cunard Royal Viking Line	(800) 221-4770
Dolphin Cruise Line	(800) 222-1003
EuroCruises	(800) 661-1119
Fantasy Cruises	(800) 437-6111
Holland America Line	(800) 426-0327
Norwegian Cruise Line (NCL)	(800) 327-7030
P & O Cruises (Princess Cruises)	(800) LOVE-BOAT
Princess Cruises	(800) LOVE-BOAT
Radisson Seven Seas Cruises	(800) 333-3333
Regal Cruises	(800) 270-SAIL
Renaissance Cruises	(800) 525-5350
Royal Caribbean Cruises Ltd. (RCCL)	(800) 327-6700
Royal Cruise Line	(800) 622-0538
Seabourn Cruise Line	(800) 929-4747
Seawind Cruise Line	(800) 258-8006
Silversea Cruises	(800) 722-6655
Special Expeditions	(800) 762-0003
Star Clippers	(800) 442-0551
Sun Line Cruises	(800) 872-6400
Tall Ship Adventures	(800) 662-0090
Windjammer Barefoot Cruises	(800) 327-2600
Windstar Cruises	(800) 258-7245

Once Ashore

by Joyce Wiswell

THE CARIBBEAN

What is it about the idea of a tropical island that sets our pulses racing and hearts swooning? It's the lure of palm tree-dotted beaches, no doubt, and a sea so incredibly clear you can inspect your pedicure in five feet of water. It's balmy evenings when trade winds caress your hair, soothe your spirit and make everyone look and feel sensuous. It's the sheer romance of escaping the bills and the boss, not worrying about windchill factors, and having only to decide if it's time to turn over and tan your back or if you're up to a night dive.

While a rose may still be a rose no matter what it's called, lumping the Caribbean islands together under one category is, categorically, unfair. Each island has its own history, its own culture, its own unique personality. Seen one, seen them all is not the reality of the Caribbean.

While the many islands of the Eastern Caribbean are strewn closely together as if a giant tossed a handful of land into the sea, those of the West are generally much more spread out, with miles of deep blue sea between landfalls. These destinations are famed for their superior diving and untamed natural beauty. Some, such the Dominican Republic, are very poor, which means cheap prices for tourists but also accompanying pangs of conscience.

With the notable exception of hot, humid weather and that alluring crystalline sea, Aruba has no more in common with the Mexican Yucatan than Arkansas has to California. See the individual island chapters to determine which jewel of the Caribbean is right for you.

Caribbean Planner

The Affordable Caribbean, *(8403 Colesville Road, Silver Spring, MD 20910;* ☎ *(301) 588-2300)* is a monthly newsletter that reports on last-minute deals and other Caribbean bargains. If you travel to the Caribbean frequently and have a flexible schedule, it's well worth the $49 annual subscription cost.

Land Excursions

Some islands are so tiny you'll easily get around on foot. Others use the golf cart as the preferred mode of transportation. Several have excellent bus systems and good taxi fleets—it varies widely by island. For details, see the "Getting Around" section in the directory in the back of each island chapter.

Taxi service

Some islands have metered cabs, but many more use standardized fares. In those cases, always ask what the trip will cost before you get in. If you're hiring a cabby for a day's sightseeing, you'll usually be able to negotiate a fare. On some islands, such as St. Martin, fares increase dramatically at night. In others, they disappear by midnight. If you're relying on taxis, be sure you'll be able to catch a cab in time to make it back to the ship. Always treat your cab driver with courtesy and respect. You should anyway, but it can especially pay off when you hit it off and the cabby—virtually always a native—turns you on to interesting facts and places you'd never otherwise find.

Packing

As humidity is quite high throughout the Caribbean, bring natural fabrics; lightweight cotton is the best. Casual clothes are fine just about anywhere both day and night (when it's not, it's noted in the hotel or restaurant description). An exception are historic churches, which generally have a no-shorts rule. Respect this custom; it's especially easy for women, who can wear a light sundress.

The nights are generally warm and sultry, but some clubs and restaurants will invariably overdo the air conditioning, so tuck in a jacket or sweater. If you're going to be trekking through the jungle or rainforest, obviously you want sturdy shoes and raingear. Don't forget to bring a beach bag to hold your suntan lotion, hat or visor and a few dollars for lunch (your carry-on bag can serve this purpose).

Bring sandals or flip-flops for the beach (the sand gets hot!) and good sneakers for touring around. Lots of villages have cobblestone streets, and the old forts usually have dubious pathways, so you'll appreciate sturdy shoes. Unless you're into tottering around on high heels, you can leave them at home; flat dressy sandals will do even at the finer resorts.

Consider buying a sarong once you arrive. These large, colorful pieces of rectangular cloth can be tied in a variety of ways, from halter dress to shirt, fold up into practically nothing, are easy to handwash and make great souvenirs to boot. You'll find them in all the shops and marketplaces.

You'll also find lots of hats, mainly straw, and it's a good idea to pick one up. The sun is very strong throughout the region, and just because you are dutifully sightseeing rather than lazing on the street doesn't mean you won't get burnt.

The sunbathers on many islands go topless; whether or not you do too is a personal choice. However, it's considered rude to go to a nude beach and keep your clothes on. In any event, wearing swimsuits anywhere but the pool or beach is generally a no-no, and men, please spare us the sight of your hairy (or otherwise) chest in public places.

Other essentials include mosquito repellent, a portable water bottle, strong sunscreen and film. You'll generally save a lot of money by buying these items stateside rather than on the island. Smokers, on the other hand, can usually score cigarettes much cheaper on the islands, often even compared to the duty-free shops. (Remember you can legally bring only one carton back into the U.S.)

When to Go

Common holidays such as Christmas and Easter are celebrated throughout the Caribbean. In addition, virtually every island has a large carnival, usually in February before Lent. These giant parties consist of parades, imaginative costumes, food festivals, sports competitions and general fun. Trinidad and Martinique's are among the most elaborate. The following guide summarizes the holidays and festivals unique to each island.

Antigua

Carnival is late July to early August, a time when locals celebrate their nation's heritage with dancing, parades and calypso bands. The last week of April is Sailing Week, one of the premiere sailing events of the world. Other holidays are Easter Monday, Labor Day (May 1), Whit Monday (June), Caricom Day (July 3), Independence Day (November 1) and Boxing Day (December 26).

Aruba

Carnival is mid-to-late February, an island-wide celebration with street dancing, parades, live bands and the crowning of Carnival Queen. Aruba also celebrates Good Friday, Easter Monday, National Anthem and Flag Day (March 18), Queen's Birthday (April 30), Labor Day (May 1) and Boxing Day (December 26).

Barbados

Crop Over, which celebrates the completion of the sugarcane harvest, takes place for three weeks in July, with special events such as a large parade, craft exhibitions, the Bajan Cultural Village, folk concerts, calypso competitions and the Grand Kadooment, the grand finale with street dancing and fireworks. There's also the Jazz Festival (January), Gospelfest (May), Holetown Festival (February) and the Oistins Fish Festival (Easter weekend). Also observed are Good Friday, Easter Monday, Whit Monday, Errol Barrow Day (January 21), May Day (May 1), United Nations Day (first Monday in October), Independence Day (November 30) and Boxing Day (December 26).

Belize

St. George's Caye Day, Independence Day and Pan American Day are all celebrated nationwide with special events. The Cashew Festival (May) in Crooked Tree Village pays homage to the tasty nut. The Sea & Air Festival in San Pedro, held each August, is a musical extravaganza with competing bands from across Central America.

Public holidays include Baron Bliss Day (March 9), Good Friday, Holy Saturday, Easter Monday, Labor Day (May 1), Commonwealth Day (May 24), St. George's Caye Day (September 10), Independence Day (September 21), Columbus Day (October 12), Garifuna Settlement Day (November 19) and Boxing Day (December 26).

British Virgin Islands

The Spring Regatta takes place in mid-April. The three-day race is the second leg of the Caribbean Ocean racing Triangles. The first week of August is given over to the Summer Festival, with parades, street dancing, bands and more. BVI also celebrates Commonwealth Day (March), Easter Monday, Whit Monday, Sovereign's Birthday (June), Territory Day (July 1), St. Ursula's Day (October 21) and Boxing Day (December 26).

Cayman Islands

Pirate's Week, held late October, is a grand affair of swashbucklers ho-ho-hoing throughout George Town. Other holidays include Ash Wednesday, Good Friday, Easter Monday (third Monday in May), Constitution Day (first Monday in July) and the Monday after Remembrance Sunday (November).

Curaçao

Carnival starts in late January with parades, dancing, music and other events. In March, the Regatta attracts boat racers from the world over. Other holidays are Chinese New Year (January), Harvest Festival (March), Good Friday, Easter Monday, Queen's Birthday (June 30), Labor Day (May 1), Curacao Flag Day (July 2) and Boxing Day (December 26).

Dominica

Carnival occurs the Monday and Tuesday before Ash Wednesday, with the usual costumes, parades and merriment. Other holidays are Good Friday, Easter Monday, May Day (May 1), Whit Monday, August Monday (first Monday in August), Independence day (November 3), Community Service Day (November 4) and Boxing Day (December 26).

Dominican Republic

There's a big Merengue Festival each late July-August where locals perform and dance to the spirited music in Santo Domingo (a smaller one is held each October in Puerto Plata.) Holidays include Our Lady of La Altagracia (January 21), Durate's Birthday (January 26), Independence Day (February 7), Restoration Day (August 16) and Our Lady of Las Mercedes (September 24).

Grenada

Carnival takes place each August and includes five days of steelband competitions, the crowning of the king and queen, street dancing and jump ups, costumed bands and a parade. The Carriacou Regatta, also held each August, is three days of boat races between Grenada and Carriacou and Big Drum Dance performances. The Rainbow City Festival, also in August, takes place in Grenville with cultural events and street dancing. Other holidays: Independence Day (February 7), National Day (March 13), Labor Day (first Monday in May), Emancipation Day (first Monday in August), Thanksgiving (October 25) and Boxing Day (December 26).

Guadeloupe

Carnival starts in early January and runs through Lent, with a giant party on Ash Wednesday. The Mardi Gras-style celebration is among the Caribbean's wildest. The Cook's Festival (Fete des Cuisinieres) takes place each August and includes a five-hour banquet (tourists welcome), singing, dancing and women parading in Creole costumes with baskets filled with island specialties and trimmed with miniature kitchen utensils. Other holidays include Easter Monday, Labor Day (May 1), VE Day (May 8), Slavery Abolition Day (May 22), Ascension Thursday (late May), Pentecost Monday (June), Bastille Day (July 14), Assumption Day (August), All Saints Day (November 1) and Armistice Day (November 11).

Jamaica

Carnival happens islandwide in April with costume parades, reggae and calypso concerts and dancing in the streets. Negril has its own carnival each

May with a float parade, concerts, a mento band competition and Jonkanoo and gereh dancing. Each August, the Reggae Sunsplash International Music Festival in Montego Bay draws flocks of people. Jazz fans have a similar party in June in Ocho Rios. Public holidays include Ash Wednesday, Good Friday, Easter Monday, Labor Day (May 23), Independence Day (first Monday in August), National Heroes Day (third Monday in October) and Boxing Day (December 26).

Martinique

Carnival is among the best in the West Indies. It starts each January and includes six weeks of pageants, parades, special events and all-night parties called zouks. The festival is especially lively as Ash Wednesday nears, and, unlike most other islands, continues on this day. On Shrive Tuesday (also known as Mardi Gras), revelers costumed as "red devils" parade around La Savane in Fort-de-France. Other holidays include Easter Monday, Labor Day (May 1), Slavery Abolition Day (May 22), Ascension Thursday (late May), Pentecost Monday (June), Bastille Day (July 14), Assumption Day (August), All Saints Day (November 1) and Armistice Day (November 11).

Puerto Rico

In January, the annual San Sebastian Street Festival turns Old San Juan into a giant fiesta. Carnival happens each February with parades, costumes, coronations of queens and the traditional coastal burial of the sardine. Festival Pablo Casals celebrates the Spaniard (who lived here many years) with cultural concerts each June. Inquire upon arrival about the numerous patron saint and folklore festivals that take place throughout the year in various villages. Public holidays include those observed in the U.S., as well as Three King's Day (January 6), Eugeio de Hostos' Day (January 9), Martin Luther King's Birthday (January 16), Emancipation Day (March 22), Constitution Day (July 25) and Discovery Day (November 19).

St. Barthélémy

Carnival occurs in late February with a week of celebrations, including a pageant for Prince and Princess and a Mardi Gras costumed parade. The Festival of St. Barthélémy takes place each August to honor the island's patron saint. Boats are blessed and there's a regatta, public ball and fireworks. Fete-du-Vent takes place in the late summer with fishing contests, lotteries, dances and fireworks in the village of Lorient. Other public holidays: Easter Monday, Labor Day (May 1), Armistice Day (May 8), Ascension Thursday, Pentecost Monday, Slavery Abolition Day (June 27), Bastille Day (July 14), Assumption Day (August), All Saints Day (November 1), All Souls Day (November 2) and Armistice Day (November 11).

St. Croix

Christmas is celebrated over 12 days, from December 25 through January 6. Besides the big day itself and New Year's Eve, there's the Feast of the Three Kings, a colorful parade through Christiansted on January 6. There's also two carnival days on the last Friday (for children) and Saturday (for adults) in April. Besides the holidays celebrated in the U.S. the island observes Three King's Day (January 6), Transfer Day (March 31), Organic Act Day (June 20), Emancipation Day (July 3), Hurricane Supplication Day (July 25), Hurricane Thanksgiving Day (October 17), Liberty Day (November 1) and Christmas Second Day (December 26).

St. John

Carnival is celebrated on the last Friday (for children) and Saturday (for adults) in April. The Atlantic Blue Marlin Tourament, held each August, draws anglers from around the globe. Besides the holidays celebrated in the U.S., the island observes Three King's Day (January 6), Transfer Day (March 31), Organic Act Day (June 20), Emancipation Day (July 3), Hurricane Supplication Day (July 25), Hurricane Thanksgiving Day (October 17), Liberty Day (November 1) and Christmas Second Day (December 26).

St. Kitts

Carnival, which happens in late December-early January, is a week-long festival with queen shows, calypso competitions, float and costume parades and street dancing. Public holidays are Carnival Last Lap (January 3), Good Friday, Easter Monday, Labor Day (first Monday in May), Whit Monday, Queen's Birthday (second Saturday in June), August Monday (first Monday in August), Culturama Last Lap Day (August 8), Independence Day (September 19) and Boxing Day (December 26).

St. Lucia

Carnival is a two-day affair in February with parades, music, costumes and partying. National Day in December is celebrated with cultural and special events. Public holidays are New Year's (January 1 and 2), Independence Day (February 22), Good Friday, Easter Monday, Emancipation Day (August 7), Thanksgiving (October 2) and National Day (December 13).

St. Martin/Sint Maarten

On the French side, Halloween is a wild affair in Grande Case, where everyone dresses up and goes wild. Carnival occurs in February right up through Ash Wednesday with parades, election of the Queen, and Shrove Thursday, a Mardi Gras-style festival with street dancing in Marigot and Grande Case. On the Dutch side, carnival is celebrated in late April and early May with beauty contests, food competitions, calypso concerts, parades, bright costumes and jump ups. Other holidays include Queen's Birthday (April 30), Labor Day (May 1), Ascension Thursday, Pentecost Monday, Bastille Day (July 14, French side), Assumption Day (August) and Concordia Day, when both sides celebrate their peaceful coexistence (November 11).

St. Thomas

Carnival, held just after Easter, is an island-wide event with steel bands, jump ups, parades and Mocko Jumbies—people dressed as spirits and perched precariously on very high stilts. Charlotte Amalie sees most of the fun. Besides the holidays celebrated in the U.S., the island observes Three King's Day (January 6), Transfer Day (March 31), Organic Act Day (June 20), Emancipation Day (July 3), Hurricane Supplication Day (July 25), Hurricane Thanksgiving Day (October 17), Liberty Day (November 1) and Christmas Second Day (December 26).

St. Vincent

The large Carnival takes place each July with steel and calypso bands in fevered competition, the crowning of the king and queen, jump ups and lots of fun. Other holidays include St. Vincent and Grenadines Day (January 22), Good Friday, Easter Monday, Labor Day (May 2), Whit Monday, August Monday, Independence Day (October 27) and Boxing Day (December 26).

Trinidad & Tobago

Carnival, which is centered on Trinidad but also spills over to Tobago, is among the Caribbean's greatest celebrations. Held each year on the Monday and Tuesday right before Ash Wednesday (February or early March), it's a huge party with amazing handmade costumes, parades, calypso competitions and a Kiddie Carnival (held the previous Saturday). Other holidays are Good Friday, Easter Monday, Whit Monday (June 7), Corpus Christi (June 18), Labor Day (June 19), Emancipation Day (August 1), Independence Day (August 31), Republic Day (September 24) and Boxing Day (December 26).

Yucatan Peninsula

Carnival is celebrated for three days before Ash Wednesday in both Cancun and Cozumel with all the usual merriment. On Holy Cross Day (May 3), construction workers mount decorated crosses on unfinished buildings, with fireworks and picnics at building sites. Christmas celebrations generally start on December 16. Public holidays include Constitution Day (February 5), the birthday of Benito Juarez (March 21), Labor Day (May 1), Battle of Puebla (May 5), Independence Day (September 16), Day of the Race (October 12) and Revolution Day (November 20).

Secret Tips for Caribbean Survival

Duty-Free Does Not Necessarily Mean Cheaper

The term "duty-free" (a shopper's best friend) means that retailers are not required to pay import taxes on certain items, so they can pass these savings directly along to the consumer. Often that translates to prices 30 to 40 percent cheaper than in the U.S. Even islands not officially duty-free still often have duty-free shops at the airport or around the island, such as St. Lucia's Pointe Seraphine. Furthermore, on your way to an island, you can shop duty-free in major U.S. airports by showing your boarding pass.

While most duty-free items are truly a bargain, it isn't always necessarily so. Cigarettes, for example, often cost close to $17 per carton at airport duty-free shops, and you can often do better on the island itself (and even in some U.S. supermarkets). If you're planning to buy expensive French perfume or a good piece of jewelry, do some comparison shopping before leaving the U.S. to see how prices stack up. Remember, if the product is defective, you'll have a much easier time getting satisfaction from your local store than a little shop in the Caribbean.

Good duty-free bargains can generally be found on French perfumes, Dutch porcelain, Swiss crystal, fine bone china and woolens from England, linens and gemstones, especially emeralds. Prices are especially good on European-owned territories such as St. Martin. St. Barts, Martinique and Guadeloupe for French items and Anguilla, Antigua, Montserrat, Nevis, St. Kitts, Grenada, St. Lucia, St. Vincent and the British Virgin Islands for goods from England.

Health Precautions

There are very few health risks throughout the Eastern Caribbean. In most cases, the water is safe to drink (even if it doesn't taste so great); always inquire on the ship if you're not sure. They'll give you an honest answer—the last thing these people want is a bunch of sick guests on their hands.

The biggest health threat in the Caribbean—as, alas, the world over these days—is from AIDS and other sexually transmitted diseases. Use condoms! It's best to bring them from home because they are not always as readily available on smaller islands as we've grown accustomed to seeing them in the U.S. Latex condoms offer much more protection than those made of lambskin.

It's always a good idea to carry along a small bottle of stomach medicine such as Mylanta, diarrhea aids such as Pepto Bismol or Imodium and pain relievers like aspirin or Tylenol. Don't assume you'll be able to find such items on the island. (No problem in St. Thomas, but lots of luck on Saba.) If you require injections, bring your own sterile syringes and consider buying disposable ones from a U.S. pharmacy before you leave.

Fortunately, malaria is generally no longer a threat (except possibly in the Dominican Republic and Haiti), which is good news, since you can count on providing lots of free meals for mosquitoes and no-see-ums.

Watch out for the sun, it's going to be a lot stronger than you think, especially on overcast days when you may forget to apply sunscreen. Though getting a killer tan is high on many tourists' list of things to do, start slowly with a strong sunscreen, then once you work up a good base tan, gradually switch to a lower number. (Of course dermatologists recommend no tan at all, but let's deal with reality.)

The high humidity will probably make you perspire more than usual. Drink lots of fluids to avoid dehydration (water is best) to replace the sweat you're oozing through your pores.

Guests on cruise ships invariably go wild the first night with all those exotic drinks, then pay dearly for it the next day. Keep that in mind as you order your fourth pina colada.

Buying prepared food from street vendors is generally safe, but do check out the operation. Is the meat kept refrigerated? Are the utensils clean? When buying bottled water, especially on the street, check that the tamper-proof band is intact. Some unscrupulous vendors will refill bottles with tap water.

Weather—or Not

Californians cope with earthquakes and mudslides, East Coasters deal with blizzards and ice storms and Midwesterners have bitter cold and flash floods. In the Caribbean the enemy is the hurricane.

Hurricane season is an annual event that generally runs from June to September. Most turn out to be little more than pesky rainstorms or dramatic electrical displays, but some are deadly and should be taken dead serious. Thirty years ago, Hurricane Hattie was strong enough to literally rip a Belizean island in two, and Hugo devastated St. Croix, St. Eustatius, and other islands in 1989. In September, 1995, Luis and Marilyn wreaked havoc on several islands. Heed warnings of locals in regard to threatening weather.

Mother Nature's other biggest drawback is the high humidity that lingers on the islands all year long and is especially uncomfortable in the summer. It won't kill you (though it sometimes feels like it will) but take care to avoid overexertion and drink lots of water to keep hydrated.

Island Etiquette

While some of your best vacation photos will be candid shots of locals, keep in mind that many folks—older ones especially—often don't appreciate being part of your tourist experience. Always ask before snapping someone's photo and take a refusal with grace. (Although I do find it annoying that the old woman who makes johnny cakes at St. Croix's Whim Plantation refuses photos—rudely at that—since she is part of the attraction and you pay a hefty admission price to get in.) Kids, on the other hand, usually love to get the attention and will often ask YOU to take their picture. Indulge them, even if you're down to your last shot (better to fake taking the picture than hurt their feelings), and besides, you'll probably get some really cute shots.

Carry small bills when dealing with street vendors and in marketplaces where you'll be negotiating prices.

In museums and restaurants, keep your negative feelings to yourself (or at least whisper them to your companion) about the lousy artwork or crappy food. You may find you just hate conch, but remember that it's a staple in many island diets, so try not to be judgmental. On the other hand, if the food is truly inedible, you have every right to send it back.

No one should have to endure lousy service, but extra patience will be required in the Caribbean. Everything is on a slower pace, and that, alas, includes waitresses and cooks.

Respect local rules and customs regarding the formality of dress. In most cases shorts and T-shirts are just fine, but most churches ban them, even if you're just ducking in for a quick peek. Bathing suits are nearly always improper anywhere but on the beach or at the pool. If you want to go topless, make sure it's considered acceptable on the island.

Make a genuine effort to speak the language on islands such as Guadeloupe, where English speakers are rare. No matter how terrible your syntax or pronunciation, such efforts are greatly appreciated, and people will be much more apt to help you out than if you just walk up expecting them to speak your language.

Above all, do your fellow countrymen a big favor, and don't act like the Ugly American. It's no wonder everyone thinks we're all rich the way some U.S. travelers flash around large bills and expensive jewelry. (And actually, if we can afford a Caribbean cruise—even on the cheap—we are pretty rich compared to most locals.) Be sensitive to the fact that on most of these islands, life is much simpler and less materialistic. Remember, too, that you are a guest in this foreign land. Sure, you're paying for it, but that doesn't mean you've bought the right to impose your values on people of different cultures.

Here's a huge generalization, but it does apply: Islanders are usually quite reserved and will often avoid eye contact, especially on the street. However, it's amazing how far a smile and a "good day" will go. Try it, and you'll be pleasantly surprised—and left all atingle in good feelings.

ANTIGUA

Farming on Antigua has shifted from sugarcane to fruits and vegetables.

Antigua starts with an A—a letter that could be easily used to spell either attitude or adventure. Formerly a British Colony, Antigua comes wrapped with a British frostiness that finds its way into the cool, distant smiles of waiters, hotel clerks and even shopkeepers. But, with nary a day of rain, and miles and miles of glorious beaches, the island still boasts enough attributes of paradise to keep American, Canadian, British and German millionaires heading for the super-deluxe resorts on its southern and western shores. Today, the island also attracts a broader base of tourists, and can accommodate all budgets, from the backpacker to the honeymooner, the latter always looking to save money at no sacrifice of romance. Color and music explode in August when Carnival comes to the streets of Antigua, filling the air with calypso competitions, steel bands and fanciful costumes. Since flying is the easiest way to reach the Caribbean—some airlines fly direct—Antigua is the best place to start a Caribbean vacation; from here, you can always charter a sailboat and fan out to neighboring islands. In fact, during the last weeks of April (or beginning of May), when international yachting fans congregate for Antigua's annual Sailing Week—the premier nautical event in the Caribbean—some hearty travelers actually chuck their flight ticket home and hitch a ride on one of the many colorful sailboats bobbing in the harbor.

Bird's Eye View

Sprawling over about 108 square miles, Antigua is the largest, most developed and most visited of the Leeward Islands. Together with Barbuda and Redonda, an uninhabited rocky inlet, it forms the independent nation of Antigua and Barbuda, within the Commonwealth of Nations. To the south lies the French island of Guadeloupe; to the southwest lies the British dependency of Montserrat and to the west, the island of Nevis. The capital is St. John's, with a population of about 36,000. The island of Antigua itself is divided into six parishes. Travelling through the island, you will be able to discern clearly the variety of regions as you pass from the hilly ranges in the southwest to the almost desertlike cacti in the northeast to the enormous bush and woodland in the interior. **Boggy Peak**, its highest elevation, rises to 1330 feet. There are 365 talcum-soft white beaches fringed with palm trees, among the most beautiful in the West Indies.

History

The Siboney Stone people were the first to graze the terrain of Antigua with settlements dating back to 2400 BC. Arawaks lived on the islands between A.D. 35 and 1100. Columbus discovered the island on his second voyage in 1493, naming it Santa Maria de la Antigua. The absence of freshwater springs persuaded French and Spanish colonists to sail on, and by 1632, the English had successfully established colonization. Apart from a brief French invasion in 1666, the three islands of Antigua, Barbuda and Redonda have all remained British. The first large sugar estates were established in Antigua by Sir Christopher Codrington in 1674, who convinced the natives on Barbuda to raise provisions for the plantations (a village in Barbuda bears his name). As production increased forests were cleared for cultivation and African slaves were imported by the boatloads. (Today many Antiguans trace the lack of rainfall to this early forest devastation.) A vicious cycle of drought led eventually to barren lands, testimony of which can be seen in the ruined towers of sugarcane throughout the island. Abolition arrived in 1834, but the former slaves found they could barely subsist due to a lack of surplus farming and an economy that was based on agriculture and not manufacturing. Poor labor conditions and growing violence led to the organization of unions in 1939. A strong political Labor Party emerged seven years later,

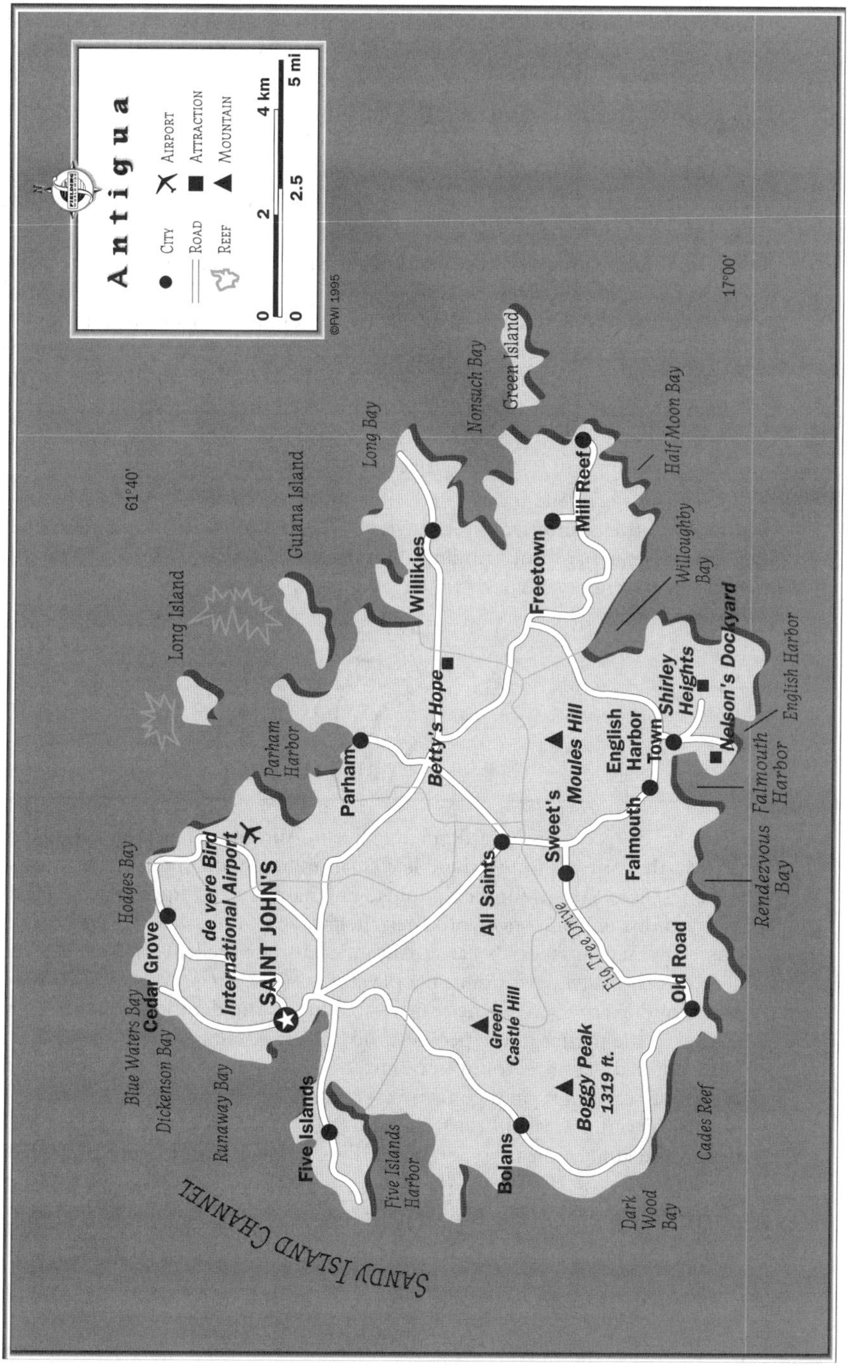
Antigua
City
Road
Reef
Airport
Attraction
Mountain
0 2 4 km
0 2.5 5 mi
©FWI 1995
61°40'
17°00'
SAINT JOHN'S
de vere Bird International Airport
Cedar Grove
Hodges Bay
Blue Waters Bay
Dickenson Bay
Runaway Bay
Five Islands
Five Islands Harbor
Bolans
Boggy Peak 1319 ft.
Green Castle Hill
All Saints
Parham
Parham Harbor
Long Island
Guiana Island
Long Bay
Willikies
Betty's Hope
Nonsuch Bay
Green Island
Half Moon Bay
Mill Reef
Freetown
Willoughby Bay
Shirley Heights
Nelson's Dockyard
English Harbor
English Harbor Town
Falmouth Harbor
Falmouth
Moules Hill
Sweet's
Rendezvous Bay
Fig Tree Drive
Old Road
Cades Reef
Dark Wood Bay
SANDY ISLAND CHANNEL

catapulting Antiguans into the 20th century. During World War II, Antigua was selected as a military base and American servicemen arrived in droves. Until 1959, Antigua was administered as part of the Leeward Islands, until attaining associated status with full self-internal government in 1967.

Since 1990 scandal and accusations of corruption have rocked the Antiguan government, including misuse of public funds and a series of arson attacks and murders investigated by Scotland Yard. In 1990 the governments of Antigua and Barbuda became embroiled in a scandal where they were accused of being involved in the sale of weapons to the Medellin cartel of drug traffickers in Colombia.

Today Antigua maintains strong links with the U.S., having actively assisted in the U.S. military intervention in Grenada in 1983. Since 1982, both Antigua and Barbuda have intensified their programs of foreign relations and have agreed that the People's Republic of China could open an embassy. In 1990 Antigua opened relations with Russia and in April 1983 with the Ukraine. Today both islands are constitutional monarchies, with executive power invested in the British sovereign and exercised by the Governor-General, who is appointed on the advice of the Antiguan prime minister.

Since the sugarcane industry fell off completely in 1972, tourism has monopolized the economy. In recent years, touristic activities have undergone a tremendous expansion, bringing the number of tourists who visit yearly to nearly half a million (half of which are cruise passengers).

People

As of a 1993 census, 65,000 people live in Antigua, 85 percent of them of African descent, although there is a small minority of English, Portuguese, Lebanese and Syrian. On first glimpse, the natives of Antigua may seem formal and distant, but once you crack the facade of formality, a warm, generous character surfaces. Because Antigua has an excellent harbor and easy access to the outside world, its people are quite used to traveling and are well aware of current events. The relative stability of the democracy has been reflected in the nature of the people, who are considered among the leaders in the Caribbean family. About one-third of all Antiguans live in or around the capital of St. John's, on the northwest coast. The remainder are spread evenly throughout the island, in more than 40 small towns and villages. Most own some kind of property, even if it is just a small shack in the countryside.

To delve more deeply into the Antiguan character, read Jamaica Kinkaid's devastating profile of the island and its people called *A Small Place* (1988).

Beaches

You could spend several lifetimes exploring the 365 beaches in Antigua. Beyond West Bay's Seven Mile Beach, the nearest beach to St. John's is Fort James, not conducive to swimming because of its milky film and rough waters. Nevertheless, on weekends, it gets very crowded. Farther out is Dickenson Bay, with numerous hotels along the strand section off the beach. On the peninsula west of St. John's, past the Ramada Royal Antiguan Hotel, are several picturesque beaches. **Galley Bay**, past Five Islands, is secluded and pristine, especially popular with joggers at sunset. A spectacular beach is **Galleon**, near English Harbour, though you'll need a car or taxi to get there. One of the most beautiful in the Caribbean is **Shoal Beach**, famous for its uninterrupted stretch of silvery powder. The four **Hawksbill** beaches at the end of the peninsula are attractive crescent shapes (one is a nudist beach). **Dark Wood Beach**, on the road from St. John's to Old Round around the southwest coast, is quite pleasant, with a bar and overpriced restaurant.

What Else to See

Although St. John's, the capital of Antigua, looks a bit tatty these days, there are areas being developed for tourism and worthy of a stroll, particularly **Redcliffe Quay**, a picturesque district full of historical buildings and now duty-free stores, souvenir shops and new restaurants. Cruise ship passengers tend to crowd into **Heritage Quay**, off the harbor, where there is also a casino and a big-screen TV satellite.

If you're looking for a cool interior to escape from the sun, dip into the city's **Anglican Cathedral**, rebuilt several times due to earthquakes. No matter where you stand in St. John's, you can see the twin towers. The present building was rebuilt in 1843.

Fascinating weekly lectures are given at the **Museum of Marine and Living Art**, where you can view exhibits of sea shells, shipwrecks and even pre-Columbian history. A tour of the English Harbour is a must if you have any sort of maritime fetish. The area has been designated as a national park. The best view of the harbor is from **Limey's Bar**. Take the footpath that leads round the bay to **Fort Berkeley** for a great view that you'll share with grazing goats. Nearby, the future King William IV spent his nights at **Clarence House** when he served in the Navy during the 1780s. Overlooking the English Harbour, at Shirley Heights, are the ruins of 18th-century fortifications. It's best to go

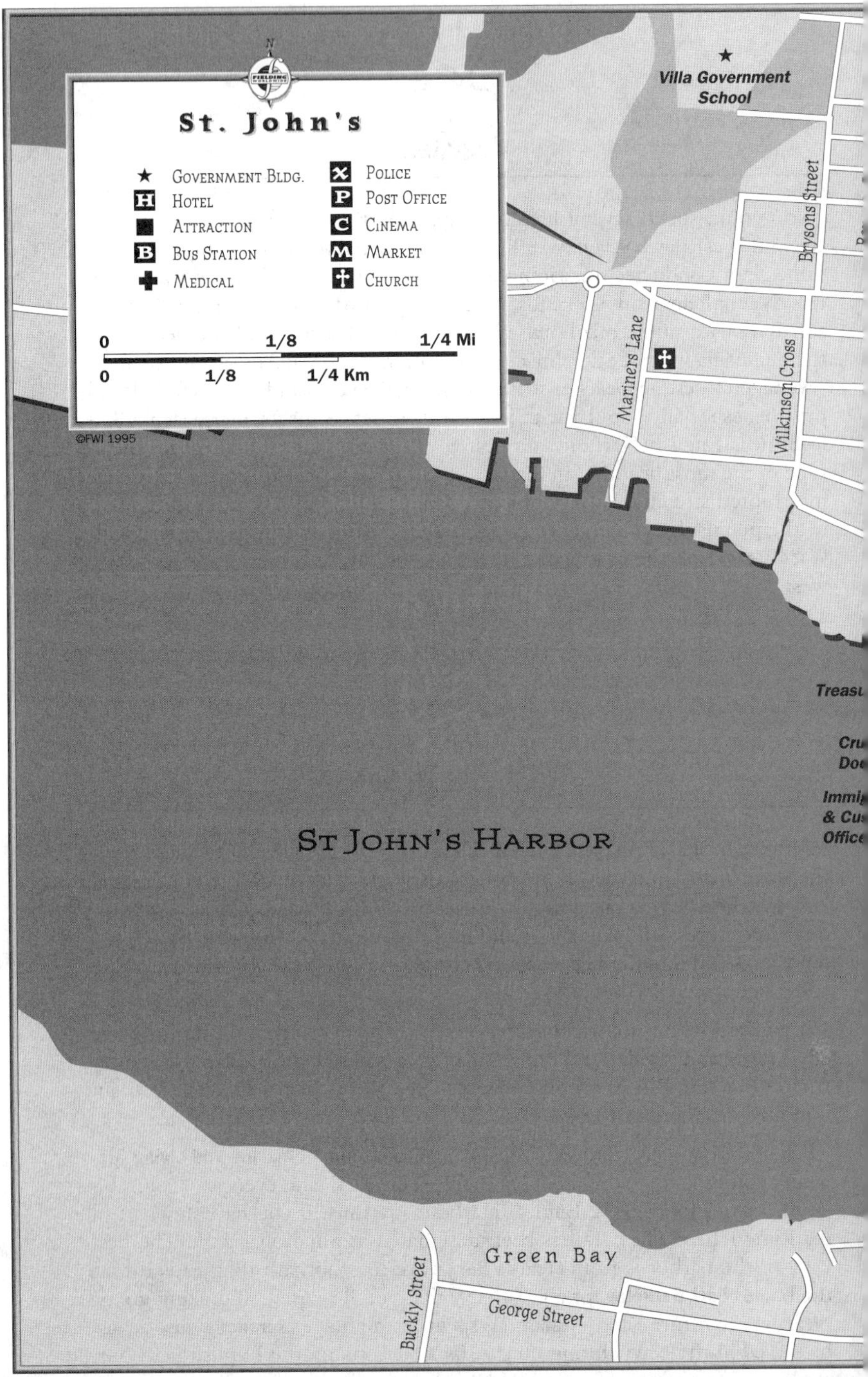
St. John's
Government Bldg.
Hotel
Attraction
Bus Station
Medical
Police
Post Office
Cinema
Market
Church
0
1/8
1/4 Mi
0
1/8
1/4 Km
©FWI 1995
Villa Government School
Brysons Street
Mariners Lane
Wilkinson Cross
St John's Harbor
Green Bay
Buckly Street
George Street

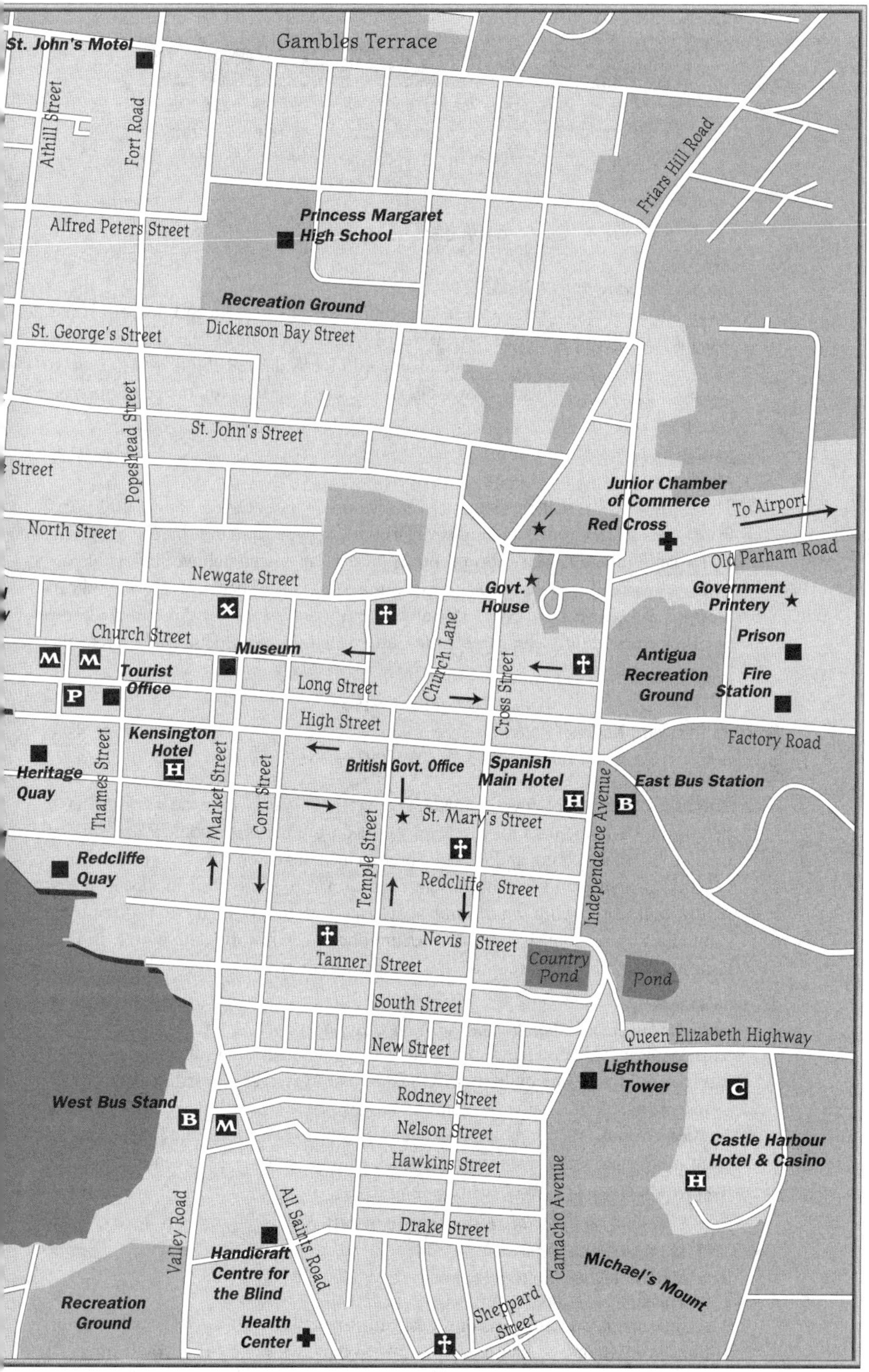
St. John's Motel
Gambles Terrace
Athill Street
Fort Road
Friars Hill Road
Princess Margaret High School
Alfred Peters Street
Recreation Ground
St. George's Street
Dickenson Bay Street
Popeshead Street
St. John's Street
Street
Junior Chamber of Commerce
Red Cross
To Airport
North Street
Old Parham Road
Newgate Street
Govt. House
Government Printery
Church Street
Museum
Church Lane
Prison
Tourist Office
Long Street
Cross Street
Antigua Recreation Ground
Fire Station
High Street
Factory Road
Kensington Hotel
Thames Street
Market Street
Corn Street
British Govt. Office
Spanish Main Hotel
Heritage Quay
East Bus Station
Independence Avenue
St. Mary's Street
Temple Street
Redcliffe Quay
Redcliffe Street
Nevis Street
Tanner Street
Country Pond
Pond
South Street
New Street
Queen Elizabeth Highway
Lighthouse Tower
Rodney Street
West Bus Stand
Nelson Street
Castle Harbour Hotel & Casino
Hawkins Street
All Saints Road
Valley Road
Camacho Avenue
Drake Street
Handicraft Centre for the Blind
Michael's Mount
Recreation Ground
Sheppard Street
Health Center

on Sundays when the steel bands play at the bar on the lookout point called the Battery. Prepare yourself for very loud music.

Best View:

Even Antiguans still flock to the top of the Shirley Heights installations to view the fabulous sunsets. You can see the English and Falmouth harbors in the foreground and the hills and coast of Antigua in the distance. On a clear day you can see as far as Redonda, Montserrat and Guadeloupe.

City Celebrations

Carnival

Various locations, ☎ (809) 462- 194.

What began some 20 years ago as a celebration to welcome Queen Elizabeth II has become a full-fledged annual festival with 11 days of art shows, parades and partying. The main event is "Juve," when some 400 locals dance behind steel and brass bands. Held in late July and early August, you can pick up a full program once on the island.

Sailing Week ★★★★

English Harbour.

The Caribbean's premiere yachting event is now in its 27th year. Some 200 boats from 25 countries pour into English Harbour for five races, and there's lots going on for landlubbers as well—food vendors, beach dancing and above all, lots of partying (and lots of cops to keep things from getting out of hand). For $30 you can dress up and attend Lord Nelson's Ball at the Admiral's Inn, but those in the know say it's a bit too stuffy compared to the unabashed goings-on elsewhere. Held the last week of April.

Historical Sites

Nelson's Dockyard National Park ★★★★★

Nelson's Dockyard, English Harbour, ☎ (809) 460-1005.
Hours open: 8 a.m.–6 p.m.

This pretty spot is the only Georgian-style naval dockyard left in the world. It has a rich history as home base for the British fleet during the Napoleonic Wars and was used by Admirals Nelson and Hood. The area includes colonial naval buildings, nice beaches, ancient archeological sites and lots of nature trails. Short dockyard tours, nature walks of varying length and boat cruises are offered daily. Check out the Admiral's House, a lovely inn and museum of colonial history, then have a drink at their popular bar. Children under 16 admitted to the park for free.

St. John's Cathedral ★★

Newgate Street and Church Lane, St. John's, ☎ (809) 461- 82.

This Anglican cathedral has a sorrowful history. Originally built of wood in 1683, it was replaced by a stone building in 1745, then destroyed by an earthquake in 1843. Replaced in 1847, it was once again heavily damaged by earthquake in 1973. Restoration continues as funds are available. The figures of St. John the Baptist and St. John the Divine were taken from a French ship in the early 19th century, and the iron railing entrance dates back to 1789.

Museums and Exhibits

Dow's Hill Interpretation Center ★★

Near Shirley Heights, English Harbour.
Hours open: 9 a.m.–5 p.m.

The multimedia presentations of the island's six periods of history, from Amerindians to slavery to independence, are unique to the Caribbean. Bring your camera, as the views from the observation platforms are spectacular. $2 for kids under 16.

Museum of Antigua and Barbuda ★★

Church and Market Street, St. John's, ☎ (809) 462-1469.
Hours open: 8 a.m.–4 p.m.

Mainly intended for the island's children but worth a look if you're in the neighborhood, this small museum spotlights Antigua's geological and political past. Some interesting exhibits include a lifesize Arawak house, a wattle and daub house, models of sugar plantations and Arawak and pre-Columbian artifacts. There's also a decent giftshop selling local arts and crafts, books and historic artwork. Donation requested.

Tours

Jolly Roger

Redcliff Quay, English Harbour, ☎ (809) 462-2064.

This is the largest sailing ship in local waters—108 feet long—and a great way to spend the day. A "pirate" crew will have you walking the plank, dancing the limbo, eating, drinking, and in general making merry as you sail the seas.

Sports

The **Antigua Sailing Week** is a major Caribbean event, held at the end of April through the beginning of May.

All you have to do is head for the English Harbour to meet some of the hundreds of yachties who cruise in from all over the world. Most hotels now arrange day-sailing excursions. Numerous dive facilities are located along **Dickenson Bay**, and certification courses are available. The watersports concession located there can also reserve a deep-sea fishing expedition. Windsurfing is generally best accomplished on the eastern shores; regattas are regularly planned, so ask about. Most of the big hotels have tennis courts, and many visitors return for the Antigua Tennis Week in late April or May. Rates for balls and rackets are exorbitant. Golfers will find an 18-hole course at the **Great Valley Course**, near St. John's. Horseback riding can be arranged through your hotel, as there are several stables and resorts with their own horses and equipment. The southeast countryside is rife with trails and a great half-day trek can be made to **Monks Hill**. Also attractive is the ride around **Half Moon Bay** that circles around Mannings and overlooks Soldier Point on the Atlantic.

Golf

Two locations, English Harbour.
Hours open: 8 a.m.–6 p.m.

The island has only two golf courses, so it won't be hard to make your choice. At **Half Moon Bay Hotel** ☎ *(460-4300)* there are nine holes (2410 yards, par 34), with more challenging conditions at **Cedar Valley Golf Club** ☎ *(462-0161)*. Their 18-hole, par-70 course has some lovely views of the north coast. Green fees are $30 and cart rental is an additional $30.

Watersports

Long Bay Hotel, Long Bay, ☎ (809) 463-2005.

If it involves getting wet, they have it at the **Long Bay Hotel**, where nonguests can rent equipment for scuba (experienced only), snorkeling, sailing, etc. They also offer snorkel trips (four minimum) to a few small islands, though conditions are great just off the beach, thanks to Long Bay's double reef. Also check out **Shorty's** ☎ *(462-6066)* where they have all kinds of watersports and glass-bottom excursions; and **Halycon Cove Watersports** ☎ *(462-0256)*, where you can water ski. Both are at Dickenson Bay.

Windsurf Shop

Lord Nelson Beach Hotel, Dutchman's Bay, ☎ *(809) 462-3094.*

Here's your chance to try this ever-popular sport; they guarantee you'll be whisking around on your own after $50 and a two-hour lesson. (And in case you mess up, they have radio-assisted rescues.)

Where to Eat

Fielding's Highest Rated Restaurants in Antigua		
★★★★★	La Perrouche	$18–$35
★★★	Chez Pascal	$22–$29
★★★	Coconut Grove	$15–$30
★★★	Colombo's	$22–$32
★★★	Le Bistro	$22–$26
★★★	Le Cap Horn	$10–$20
★★★	Redcliffe Tavern	$7–$20
★★★	Warri Pier	$7–$40

Fielding's Special Restaurants in Antigua		
★★★★★	La Perrouche	$18–$35
★★★	Colombo's	$22–$32
★★	Brother B's	$6–$15
★★	The Wardroom and Pub	$8–$30

Fielding's Budget Restaurants in Antigua		
★★	Brother B's	$6–$15
★★	Hemingway's	$7–$15
★★	G & T Pizza	$7–$19
★★★	Redcliffe Tavern	$7–$20
★★★	Le Cap Horn	$10–$20

Antigua has rarely suffered for the lack of good restaurants, but new additions are always cropping up. Prices for a top-class dinner aren't cheap; expect to fork over at least $95 for two in the most expensive places. Spices, influenced by East Indian and creole cooking, are liberally added and tend to run on the hot side. Look for specialties such as banana and cinnamon pancakes with Antiguan rum syrup, sea urchin flan, and lump crabmeat with avocado and lemongrass.

For steel bands and a barbecue on Sundays, reserve first and then head to **Shirley Heights Lookout**, housed in a restored 18th century fort with a memorable view of Nelson's Dockyard and English Harbour.

Admiral's Inn **$$$** ★★

Nelson's Dockyard, English Harbour, ☎ (809) 460-1027.
American cuisine. Specialties: Pumpkin soup, red snapper.
Lunch: Noon–2:30 p.m., entrees $10–$25.
Dinner: 7–9:30 p.m., entrees $10–$25.

Like the Copper and Lumber Store Hotel alongside it, the Admiral's Inn is so long on atmosphere and history, the food doesn't have to be good to be worth a visit. But thankfully, that is not the case here, especially for a silky pumpkin soup. Some never get as far as the restaurant, preferring to stay in the dark bar or sit under the old trees outdoors, looking out at the convoys of ships in the harbor. Those so inclined can eat here three times a day, and breakfast, served daily from 7:30 to 10:00 a.m., is a terrific deal. Closed September through mid-October.

Big Banana Holding Co. **$$$** ★★

Redcliffe Quay, St. John's, ☎ (809) 462-2621.
Italian cuisine. Specialties: Pizza, conch salad.
Lunch: Noon–4 p.m., entrees $6–$30.
Dinner: 4 p.m.–midnight, entrees $6–$30.

A lot of locals and tourists homesick for pizza flock here at all hours. The pies in question are rather pricey and not very exciting, but the location, in the interesting and trendy Redcliffe Quay shopping center, helps. All in all it's considered very proper to sit under the whirring fans and just sip a cool tropical drink (these are bright, frothy and potent). Salads, seafood dishes and fruit plates are also available.

Brother B's **$$** ★★

Long Street, St. John's,
Indian cuisine. Specialties: Pepperpot soup and fungi, pelleau, bull's foot soup.
Lunch: entrees $6–$15.
Dinner: entrees $6–$15.

A not-to-be missed touch of local color, Brother B's in Soul Alley (near the Museum) is the place to be to experience a taste of real Antiguan culture, hear the live buzz of other diners amiably feasting on local West Indian eats and freshly squeezed juices, and to tap to the beat of a hired band at noon.

Calypso **$$$** ★★

Redcliffe Street, St. John's, ☎ (809) 462-1965.
International cuisine. Specialties: Pumpkin soup, baked chicken with cornmeal.
Lunch: 10 a.m.–4 p.m., entrees $8–$25.

This open-air, lunch-only spot jumps weekdays, and is an accessible, friendly location to try West Indian specialties. These often include fresh seafood, sauteed or prepared in batter. Homey stews and soups with pumpkin or okra satisfy; the less adventurous can chow down on burgers and sandwiches.

Chez Pascal **$$$** ★★★

4 Tanner Street, St. John's, ☎ (809) 462-3232.
French cuisine. Specialties: Bisque de langouste, croustade de fruits de mer.
Dinner: 6:30–10 p.m., entrees $22–$29.

Lyon-born Pascal Milliat, previously the chef de cuisine at La Sammana, the swank five-star resort on St. Martin, owns and toils in the kitchen of this, his own chez with the ever-pleasant assistance of his spouse, Florence, who seats patrons. Dishes are classic French with a twist of "Antiguaise" sprinkled hither and yon. Vichyssoise is a popular starter.

Coconut Grove **$$$** ★★★

Dickenson Bay, St. John's, ☎ (809) 462-1538.
International cuisine. Specialties: Grilled local lobster, chilled gazpacho.
Lunch: 11:30 a.m.–3 p.m., entrees $15–$30.
Dinner: 6:30–10 p.m., entrees $15–$30.

A simple beachfront spot surrounded by tall coconut palms swaying in the breeze, this eatery is a choice spot for privacy, moonlight and a nicely grilled lobster caught fresh that day. Chicken, hearty chops, tangy soups and salads are also on offer.

Colombo's **$$$** ★★★

Galleon Beach, English Harbour, ☎ (809) 463-1452.
Italian cuisine. Specialties: Veal Scaloppine, carpaccio.
Lunch: 12:30–2:30 p.m., entrees $22–$32.
Dinner: 7–10 p.m., entrees $22–$32.

Only in the Caribbean can one eat spaghetti Bolognese or carpaccio in a fancy, thatched-roof hut and dance to a reggae band on the beach. But everything here is scrupulously good and the service is amiable. There are daily specials and a variety of wines.

G & T Pizza **$$** ★★

East Falmouth Harbor, Falmouth Harbour,
Italian cuisine. Specialties: Pizza, salads.
Lunch: Noon–4:30 p.m., entrees $7–$19.
Dinner: 4:30–10:30 p.m., entrees $7–$19.

Blend in with the seafaring crowd at this popular restaurant on the waterfront at the Antigua Yacht Club in Falmouth Harbour that serves tasty pizzas and salads for under $20. Seating is on informal picnic tables framed by palm trees, and day or night, entertainment is provided by sailboats and motorcraft on the oceanfront. G&T stays open until midnight for drinks, and there's a happy hour from 5-6 p.m.

Hemingway's **$$** ★★

St. Mary's Street, St. John's, ☎ (809) 462-2763.
International cuisine. Specialties: Lobster soup, tropical chicken with fruit salsa.
Lunch: 11:30 a.m.–4:30 p.m., entrees $7–$15.
Dinner: 4:30–10 p.m., entrees $7–$15.

Not very far from the sea in the traditional West Indian town of St. John's is this tropical Victorian house with a restaurant on the second floor. There's a lot of activity and people-watching opportunities on the porch, where frothy tropical drinks can be sipped. Nibble on lobster, salads, burgers and spicy chicken. Vegetarian specialties are also available.

La Perrouche **$$$** ★★★★★

Falmouth Harbour, ☎ (809) 460-3040.
International cuisine. Specialties: Whitefish with polenta, lobster with Bordelaise sauce.
Dinner: 6–10 p.m., entrees $18–$35.

This charmer is an ideal splurge restaurant, one of a handful on the island that boasts native French or French-trained chefs. The artist in question at this bloom-bedecked outdoor establishment is David Wallach, who served a stint at L'Esperance. Together with partner Mona Frisell, he creates a culinary palette of tropical colors and tastes each evening. Wallach imports a special whitefish chosen for its delicacy, and local lobster is used as a sauce ingredient. Desserts involve a small orchard of exotic fruits, including sweet "black" pineapple. Well-chosen wine list.

Le Bistro **$$$** ★★★

Hodges Bay, St. John's, ☎ (809) 462-3881.
French cuisine. Specialties: Red snapper baked in foil, seafood in puff pastry.
Dinner: 6:30 p.m.–10:30 p.m., entrees $22–$26.

Le Bistro, on the island's north shore, caters to residents with expensive villas in the area, but anyone with a fancy for fine cuisine can repair here for classic French dishes prepared with care. Lobster and red snapper are usually available, and made with cream, white wine and fresh herb sauces. The dining room is attractive and plant-filled.

Le Cap Horn **$$$** ★★★

Falmouth Harbour, ☎ *(809) 460-3336.*
French cuisine. Specialties: Seafood, pizzas, steak.
Lunch: Noon–6:30 p.m., entrees $10–$13.
Dinner: 6:30–11 p.m., entrees $13–$20.

A highly recommended Italian and French restaurant in a verdant outdoor setting en route to Nelson's Dockyard. Snacks, wood-fired pizza or more substantial meat dishes are available for decent prices. Dine early or late on the porch on daily specials for under $20.

Lemon Tree **$$$** ★★

Long and Church Streets, St. John's, ☎ *(809) 462-1969.*
International cuisine. Specialties: Cajun garlic shrimp, burritos.
Lunch: 10 a.m.–4 p.m., entrees $15–$25.
Dinner: 4–11 p.m., entrees $15–$25.

The atmosphere here is very South Seas, with a lot of wicker and wooden blinds, good for a cool-off drink or meal after a visit to the Museum of Antigua and Barbuda nearby. Graze Caribbean-style from a long menu of finger foods, Tex-Mex items and the usual lobster and chicken dishes, which vary in quality. Unfortunately, with a cruise crowd in attendance, service can be rushed. Good for music in the evening.

Lobster Pot **$$$** ★★

Runaway Bay, St. John's, ☎ *(809) 462-2856.*
Seafood cuisine. Specialties: Chicken in coconut milk and curry, fresh fish.
Lunch: entrees $7–$12.
Dinner: entrees $15–$25.

Even picky diners will find something to their liking at this airy eatery in Runaway Bay that does creative things with chicken and lobster at prices that won't leave you breathless. The substantial menu runs the gamut from hearty breakfasts to leafy salads, sandwiches and fresh local fish and shellfish. Commune with nature at tables on the seaside veranda; come early for these or reserve a seat.

Redcliffe Tavern **$$** ★★★

Redcliffe Quay Street, St. John's, ☎ *(809) 461-4557.*
Italian cuisine. Specialties: Barbecued chicken, pasta, fresh local seafood.
Lunch: 8 a.m.–3 p.m., entrees $7–$20.
Dinner: 3–7:30 p.m., entrees $10–$20.

Begin or end a shopping tour at the charming Redcliffe Quay complex in St. John's harbor with lunch or dinner or a snack at the Redcliffe Tavern. It's one of a handful of vintage structures that have been restored for commercial usage. Once an old warehouse, the Tavern sports antique hardware for decor, and the waitstaff serves good burgers or barbecue or pastas and freshly caught lobster. Architecture buffs and Anglophiles should find the surroundings especially appealing.

Shirley Heights Lookout **$$$** ★★

Shirley Heights, English Harbour, ☎ *(809) 463-1785.*
Seafood cuisine. Specialties: Pumpkin soup, lobster with lime sauce.
Lunch: 9 a.m.–4 p.m., entrees $15–$26.
Dinner: 4–10 p.m., entrees $15–$26.

Something festive is always happening in this two-story pub-restaurant amidst the ruins of Fort Shirley—especially on Sunday, when there's dancing and live bands that play for free from mid-afternoon on. Barbecued meats at decent prices accompany the tunes, and the views behind the Lookout are superb. The rest of the week, eat in peace upstairs or downstairs for breakfast, lunch or dinner. The second-floor dining room is a very intimate trysting spot.

The Wardroom and Pub **$$$** ★★

Nelson's Dockyard, English Harbour, ☎ (809) 460-1058.
International cuisine. Specialties: West African groundnut soup, shepherd's pie.
Lunch: 11:30 a.m.–4:30 p.m., entrees $8–$25.
Dinner: 6–11 p.m., entrees $18–$30.

Old Antigua hands will be pleased with the new face given the 18th-century Copper and Lumber Store Hotel in Nelson's Dockyard. Others should come at least once to savor the atmosphere and eat remarkably fine food at remarkably high prices, especially at dinner in the Wardroom on the ground floor. But American-style or English lunches and cool drinks are within most everyone's reach at the hotel's pub.

Warri Pier **$$$** ★★★

Dickenson Bay, St. John's, ☎ (809) 462-0256.
International cuisine. Specialties: Seafood linguine, marlin.
Lunch: Noon–6 p.m., entrees $7–$35.
Dinner: 6–10 p.m., entrees $7–$40.

Dine on marlin—"warri" is the local name—on a private pier belonging to the Halcyon Cove Beach Resort. This is a lovely setting poised high above the sand like a great wooden bird on the northern edge of Dickinson Bay, about a mile and a half from the airport. Undoubtedly, it's an excellent perch from which to observe the setting sun. Light meals of chunky fruit salads or burgers and seafood soups are substantial at lunch. Dinner gets somewhat fancier with grilled lobster and the like and luscious desserts.

Where to Shop

Redcliffe Quay and **Heritage Quay** now compete for tourist shoppers.The best shops are clustered on **St. Mary's Street** or **High Street** in St. John's. Duty-free items are omnipresent, and there are also some special Antiguan crafts such as rum, silk-screened fabrics, native straw work, and curios made from shells. Hot new clothing stores have also sprung up or expanded in the last year. Check easy-to-wear cotton and cotton/lycra styles for men, women and children at BAE stores in Redcliffe Quay. Also in Redcliffe Quay is the chic Debra Moises boutique, which carries husband-and-wife-designed sensations in flowing gauze and one-of-a-kind hair accessories (carried by Bergdorf's and Saks in Manhattan). For some strange reason, some shops in Antigua close on Thursday at noon.

Check out the Saturday fruit and vegetable market at the West Bus Station. You can also find a good selection of local handicrafts.

Antigua Directory

BUSINESS HOURS

Shops open Monday–Friday 8:30 a.m.–4 p.m. and Saturday 8 a.m.–noon or 3 p.m. Banks generally open Monday–Thursday 8 a.m.–2 and Friday 8 a.m.–4 p.m.

CLIMATE

The Antiguan climate is probably the best in the Caribbean, with so little rainfall that water shortage sometimes becomes a problem. Any rainfall is usually restricted to brief heavy showers. Constant sea breezes and trade winds keep the air fresh and the temperatures hovering around 81 degrees F, except in the hot season (May-November), when temperatures can rise to 93 degrees F. The mean annual rainfall of 40 inches is slight for the region.

DOCUMENTS

U.S. and Canadian citizens must show proof of citizenship (passport, birth certificate, or voter's registration) plus a photo ID, and an ongoing or return ticket.

ELECTRICITY

The majority of hotels use 110 volts, 60 cycles, same as the U.S. Some shaver outlets are 110-volt. Hotels generally have adapters.

GETTING AROUND

The best guides in Antigua are generally taxi drivers. Or stop by the taxi rank on St. Mary's Street. Buses don't go to the airport, or to very many beaches. Look for one outside Dew's or Bryson's supermarket. Barter for a price beforehand since there are no meters. And make sure you are both talking about the same dollars (Antiguan or American).

Buses tend to leave only when there are enough riders.

Hitchhiking during the day seems fashionable and safe.

Car rental agencies are numerous. Some hotels have their own rental car services. Others found at the airport include **Titi Car Rental** ☎ *(809) 460-1452*; and **Jonas Rent-A-Car** ☎ *(809) 462-3760*. If you plan to drive, be careful since Antiguan roads are notorious for potholes, crumbling shoulders and bad signs. Antiguan drivers are about as courteous as French ones, so drive defensively.

If you want to rent a car, you must purchase a license (about US $12), valid for three months by showing your own valid license to the agency.

Motorcycles and mountain bikes are probably the easiest way to see the island. Try **Ivor's** at English Harbour or **Sun Cycles** in Hodges (for bikes only).

LANGUAGE

English is the official language, though the special Antiguan lilt may make some words indistinguishable.

MEDICAL EMERGENCIES

Holberton Hospital, on the outskirts of St. John's, is a 220-bed hospital. Serious medical emergencies are usually flown off the island to Miami. Ask if your hotel has a doctor on call.

MONEY

The official currency is the Eastern Caribbean dollar (known as Bee Wee or EC). You get the best exchange rates at banks. Most establishments will accept American and Canadian dollars. Credit cards and traveler's checks are accepted at top hotels and many shops and eateries.

TELEPHONE

From the U.S., dial 809.

TIME

Atlantic Standard Time.

TIPPING AND TAXES

Most restaurants add a 10 percent service charge. When not included, tip 10–15 percent for waiters. Tip taxi drivers 10 percent.

TOURIST INFORMATION

The official tourist office is located on Long Street in St. John's. You can also find information centers at the airport, at the ship terminal in St. John's and at Heritage Quay. For more information call ☎ *(809) 462-0480; FAX (809) 462-2483.* In the United States call ☎ *(212) 541-4117.*

WHEN TO GO

Men's Tennis Week, a professional and amateur tournament is held in January. Women's Tennis Week, a professional and amateur tournament, is held in early April. Race Week, a week of boat races between sailors from all over the Caribbean, is held in late April. The Queen's Birthday is celebrated in June. Carnival is held during the week before the first Monday of August. Independence Day is Nov. 1. Independence Week Half Marathon is held in early November. Christmas and Boxing Day is Dec. 2 and 26.

ANTIGUA RESTAURANTS	PHONE	ENTREE	CR. CARDS
St. John's			
American			
★★ Admiral's Inn	(809) 460-1027	$10–$25	A, MC, V
French			
★★★ Chez Pascal	(809) 462-3232	$22–$29••	A, DC, MC, V
★★★ Le Bistro	(809) 462-3881	$22–$26••	A, MC, V
★★★ Le Cap Horn	(809) 460-3336	$10–$20	A, MC, V
Indian			
★★ Brother B's		$6–$15	None
International			
★★★★★ La Perrouche	(809) 460-3040	$18–$35••	A, MC, V
★★★ Coconut Grove	(809) 462-1538	$15–$30	A, DC, MC, V
★★★ Warri Pier	(809) 462-0256	$7–$40	A, MC, V
★★ Calypso	(809) 462-1965	$8–$25•	A, DC, MC, V
★★ Hemingway's	(809) 462-2763	$7–$15	None
★★ Lemon Tree	(809) 462-1969	$15–$25	A, DC, MC, V
★★ The Wardroom and Pub	(809) 460-1058	$8–$30	A, MC, V
Italian			
★★★ Colombo's	(809) 463-1452	$22–$32	A, DC, MC, V
★★★ Redcliffe Tavern	(809) 461-4557	$7–$20	A, MC, V
★★ Big Banana Holding Co.	(809) 462-2621	$6–$30	A, DC, MC, V
★★ G & T Pizza		$7–$19	A, MC, V
Seafood			
★★ Lobster Pot	(809) 462-2856	$7–$25	DC, MC, V

ANTIGUA RESTAURANTS	PHONE	ENTREE	CR. CARDS
★★ **Shirley Heights Lookout**	(809) 463-1785	$15–$26	AE, MC, V

Note: • Lunch Only

•• Dinner Only

ARUBA

Windsurfing is Aruba's most popular sport.

With the highest percent of repeat visitors in the Caribbean, there is something definitely addictive about Aruba. Something habit-forming *had* to inspire *Bon Appetit* readers to elect the smallest, but most developed of the ABC Islands, their all-time favorite destination in the Caribbean. Sure, there are nice beaches, dry sunny weather, and cool breezes, but how do you explain honeymooners who return *18 years in a row* to the same hotel? Only 50 years ago, Lago Oil workers, Dutch seamen and Norwegian whalers prowled the streets and busted up barrooms; today those besotted sailors have been replaced by half a million sunburned tourists a year, who seem to thrive on the big resorts, the 10 casinos, the 100 restaurants, and what seems to be the zillion duty-free shops. Simply, Aruba has raised the island packaged vacation to a strange, but wonderful art. If you stay at a big all-inclusive resort in Aruba, you can sleep, surf, sun, soak, wine, dine and shop without ever leaving the property.

Aruba is not exactly a pretty island, unless you've got a yen for tough scrubby land with lots of cacti. What it does have are temperate blue waters that give way to nearly every watersport imaginable—from parasailing and game fishing to jet skis, snorkeling and scuba. Because of the constant trade winds, windsurfing has become the number one sport, particularly during the end of May and the beginning of June, when the never-say-die converge for the annual Aruba Hi-Winds Pro-Am Windsurfing Competition. Even during the year, the die-hard surfers are a sight to behold, as they make their daily pilgrimage to the beach, en masse across Lloyd G. Smith Boulevard, their sails held high over tight gleaming muscles.

Bird's Eye View

The smallest of the ABC islands, Aruba lies 16 miles off the northeast coast of Venezuela, about a four-hour plane ride from New York. Sprawling over 74.5 square miles, the 20-mile-long island looks like a slab of ham pointing northwest to southeast toward South America. Like Bonaire and Curaçao, its sister islands, Aruba has scant vegetation, yet its outback, called *cunucu*, is a soul-stirring landscape. As the paved road gives way to gravel and finally to coral dust, a stark and arid terrain appears, punctuated by upended boulders, mauve dunes, crashing waves and an array of scrubby Aruban vegetation, from cacti *(kadushi)* tomnesquite *(kwihi)* to the wind-bent divi-divi trees *(dwatapana)*.Tiny bright red flowers called *fioritas* provide one of the few splashes of color. On the northwesternmost tip, at Kudarebe, the sand dunes make for excellent warm-weather sledding.

Dutch-gabled and pastel-pretty, Oranjestad, the capital, called Playa, is a dazzling yellow brick town. Shops line the main shopping street of Nassaustraat and Wilhelminastraat. About 7500 hotel rooms stretch along the five-mile strand of pure white sand on Palm Beach and in the smaller Eagle Beach and Druif Bay (both south of Palm, near Oranjestad). During the year, more than 540,000 tourists add to the native population of a mere 71,000.

History

When Spanish explorers arrived in the 15th century, the Caiquetios, a tribe of Arawaks, may have already been living on Aruba for more than 4500 years, having migrated there from their ancestral homes in Venezuela. The Spanish exiled most of them in 1513, though more immigration occurred around 1640, when the Dutch permitted the Indian population to live a free—if difficult—life in Aruba. Though the last full-blooded natives died out in 1862, remains of their villages, workshops and cemeteries can be glimpsed throughout the Aruban countryside. Many place names still retain their Indian origins, such as Arashi, Daimari, Jamanota and perhaps the

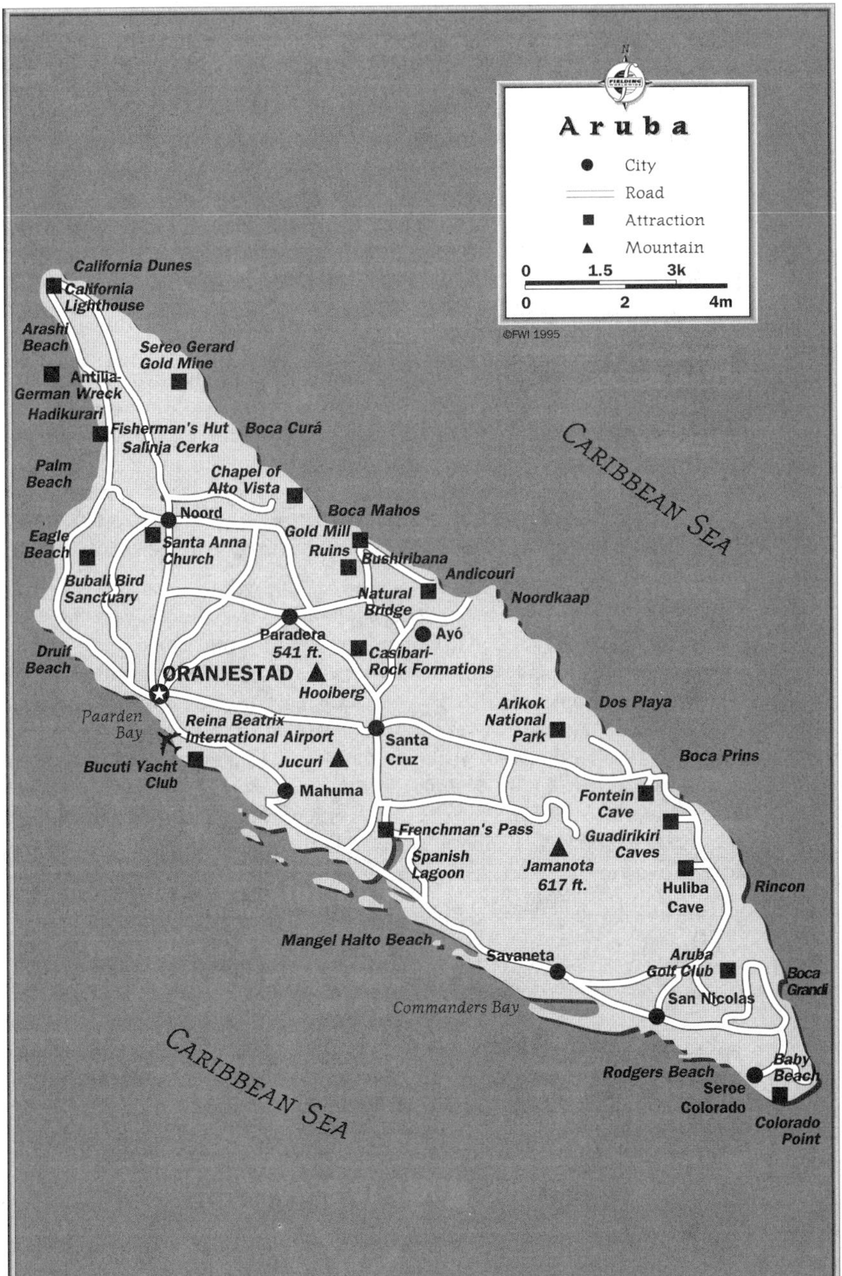
Aruba
City
Road
Attraction
Mountain
0 1.5 3k
0 2 4m
©FWI 1995
CARIBBEAN SEA
California Dunes
California Lighthouse
Arashi Beach
Sereo Gerard Gold Mine
Antilia-German Wreck
Hadikurari
Fisherman's Hut
Boca Curá
Salinja Cerka
Palm Beach
Chapel of Alto Vista
Noord
Boca Mahos
Eagle Beach
Santa Anna Church
Gold Mill Ruins
Bushiribana
Andicouri
Bubali Bird Sanctuary
Natural Bridge
Noordkaap
Paradera 541 ft.
Ayó
Druif Beach
Casibari-Rock Formations
ORANJESTAD
Hooiberg
Arikok National Park
Dos Playa
Paarden Bay
Reina Beatrix International Airport
Santa Cruz
Boca Prins
Bucuti Yacht Club
Jucuri
Mahuma
Fontein Cave
Frenchman's Pass
Guadirikiri Caves
Spanish Lagoon
Jamanota 617 ft.
Huliba Cave
Rincon
Mangel Halto Beach
Savaneta
Aruba Golf Club
Boca Grandi
Commanders Bay
San Nicolas
Rodgers Beach
Baby Beach
Seroe Colorado
Colorado Point
CARIBBEAN SEA

name Aruba itself, which some think is Arawak for "guide." Even the faces of modern Arubans—with their high cheekbones and tawny complexions—strongly reflect their native ancestry.

After being discovered by the Spanish explorer Alonso de Ojeda in 1499, Aruba was deemed useless along with its sister island Bonaire and Curaçao, and ignored for years. After the Spanish shipped off the resident male Indians to work the salt mines of Hispaniola, they began a limited colonization, turning the dusty mote into a large ranch and introducing horses, donkeys, sheep, dogs, goats, pigs, cats and chickens. In 1636, the Dutch took over and continued ranching. The English and the Spanish duked it out from 1792-1816, though the Dutch remained in control. Aloe cultivation and gold mining became important industries

In 1824 a lowly goat herder discovered the first gleaming nuggets of gold and started a tropical gold rush. Smelters were built and miners flooded the island. When the going got rough, major smelters shut down in 1914, but today there are those who still find nuggets. The real gold of Aruba became aloe vera, brought over from North America via Jamaica in the mid-19th century, a hardy succulent that adapted well to the climate. By 1900 Aruba had become the largest exporter of aloe vera, earning itself the nickname of Island of Aloe, for producing more than 90 percent of the world's supply. Today every Aruban home boasts its own small crop, using it as a natural laxative and wound-healer.

In 1924, oil refining arrived, ushering in an unprecedented era of prosperity. By 1985 the oil boom had gone bust, and the country's biggest employer Exxon went home, leaving the country its worst crisis, with 60 percent of the foreign exchange lost, 70 percent of the harbor space empty, and 40 percent of the population unemployed. In 1986, Aruba separated from its sister islands of the Netherlands Antilles (Curaçao, Bonaire, Sint Maarten, Saba and Statia), but still remained part of the Dutch Kingdom. This was a move favored by Arubans, but the time couldn't have been less favorable. It forced the island to totally depend on tourism. Government guarantees were given to the Hyatt, Sheraton and Holiday Inns—a plucky move that worked. Today tourism is Aruba's biggest industry, employing about half the population.

People

Arubans have legendary smiles and sunny dispositions—character traits tailor-made for tourism. In fact, Arubans are sometimes so helpful that they fight among themselves over who gets to help you. Acts of kindness are considered a way of life. Sociopsychologists have attributed this collective congeniality to several historical factors, including the relative absence of slavery and the benign Dutch intervention. Even the government has shown itself to be enlightened, and there seem to be no overt inequalities in service. As such, Arubans have a high standard of living, often earning as much as visiting tourists, so there is little resentment over spending habits (the downside of this is that nothing is cheap). About three-quarters of the people living full-time on the island are native-born. Racial intermingling has also had a long history here, starting with the Indian base, and adding 16th-century Spaniards, 17th-century Dutch, 18th-century Portuguese and French Huguenots and 19th-century African and Italian gold diggers, not to mention Americana oil technicians in the 20th century. The majority of Arubans are Roman Catholic.

Expect to find some Dutch customs and windmills on Aruba.

Beaches

Of the three ABC Islands, Aruba has the most beautiful beaches. All are open to the public free of charge. Avoid swimming on the east side because the surf can get dangerously rough. **Palm Beach**, considered by some to be one of the 10 best beaches in the world, is the hub of Aruban beachlife—interpret that as *crowded*—but it is also excellent for swimming and other watersports. **Fishermen's Hut**, north of the hotel strip, is the favorite hangout of the windsurfing crowd. Here you'll see a lovely view of neon sailboats bobbing madly in the wind. **Rodger Beach** is notable for its lovely palm trees, and **Baby Lagoon** on the west is unusually calm. A truly wondrous wide stretch of strand, **Manchebo Beach** seems to magically inspire women to fling their tops off. Other good beaches are **Bachelor's Beach** and **Boca Grandi** in the east, which is good for windsurfing.

Several yachts and catamarans offer cruises along Aruba's coast.

What Else to See

On the jagged, windy northern coast, the **Natural Bridge**, the largest in the Caribbean and Aruba's most noteworthy natural formation after the beaches, is one of the island's biggest attractions. Every bus and jeep stops here, so expect crowds. Honeymooners like to pose for photos as the waves surround the gaping coral bridge. The culturally starved can head for a trio of small but fascinating museums. The **Archaeology Museum** features artifacts from the island's Indian past. The **Numismatic Museum** showcases more than 30,000 coins from all over the world, including the rare jotin from 1798. (Brazil should have taken notice how the governor of the Netherlands Antilles Johan R. Lauffer solved a coin shortage at the time by cutting one coin into four pies; the word *jotin* is taken from the French *guillotine.*) The **Historical Museum** is housed in the island's oldest building, **Fort Zoutman**, built in 1796 by the Dutch. It's also the site of the weekly **Bonbini Festival**, held every Tuesday evening, featuring local music, dance, crafts and food.

BEST VIEW:

Schooner Harbor is a great photo op for its colorfully docked sailboats and open market where fishermen and boatpeople hawk their wares in open-stall markets.

City Celebrations

Carnival

Various locales around Aruba, Oranjestad.

The yearly party starts two weeks before Lent (usually in February). Don't miss the Grand Parade, held on the Sunday before Lent. Other festivities include street dancing and the crowning of the Carnival Queen.

Jazz and Latin Music Festival ★★★★

Various venues, Oranjestad.

This yearly festival, begun in 1988 and run under the auspices of the Aruba Tourism Authority, is a local favorite. Held every June, it attracts some big names.

Historical Sites

Fort Zoutman ★★★

Off Lloyd G. Smith Blvd., Oranjestad.

The fort, built in 1796, is the island's oldest building. The Willem III tower was added in 1868 and served as a lighthouse for decades. On the grounds is Museo Arubano, a historical museum in an 18th-century home that displays relics and artifacts found around Aruba.

Museums and Exhibits

Aruba Archeology Museum ★★★

Zoutmanstraat 1, Oranjestad.

Artifacts from the precolonial period—including some skeletons 2000 years old—are on exhibit at this small museum. Its founder, Martin Bloom, conducts interesting island tours (see "Special Tours/Excursions").

De Man Shell Collection ★★★

18 Morgensten St., Oranjestad.

The De Mans are proud owners of one of the world's largest private shell collections. Call ahead and if they're free, they'll let you check it out.

Numismatic Museum ★★

Irausquin Plein 2A, Oranjestad.

More than 3000 pieces of coins and currency from 400 countries from the private collection of J.M. Odor are on display.

Tours

Atlantis Submarines ★★★★★

Seaport Village Marina, Oranjestad.

Hours Open: 10 a.m.–3 p.m.

Not for the claustrophobic, but a great excursion for everyone else in a modern submarine that goes as deep as 150 feet below the sea to observe coral and fish along the Barcadera Reef. Trips depart every hour on the hour, and reservations are essential. The fee is $48 for adults, $34 under 16; children under four not permitted.

De Palm Tours ★★★

L.G. Smith Blvd. 142, Oranjestad.

If it involves showing tourists around Aruba, they're happy to oblige at De Palm. On- and off-road excursions start at $49.95 and include lunch and snorkeling; three-hour treks for hikers cost $25; deep-sea fishing starts at $220; horseback rides are $30 for two hours. They also do boat tours and snorkel excursions, with prices starting at $22.50.

Martin Booster Tracking ★★★

Diamontbergweg 40, San Nicolas.

Martin Booster, an archeologist who founded the Archeology Museum, personally conducts these interesting tours that explore the island's pre-Columbian roots. Via jeep, he'll take you far into the interior and regale you with tales of Aruba past and present. The tour generally departs at 8:30 a.m. and goes until 3:30 p.m.; the $40 price includes lunch.

Sports

Aruba's temperate blue waters give way to nearly every watersport—from parasailing to game fishing to jet skis, snorkeling and scuba, but the No.1 sport here is **windsurfing**. Consistent year-round winds and shallow flat waters make it one of the top sailboard destinations in the world, particularly good for beginners and intermediates. For 300 days of the year, guaranteed winds blow up to 20 knots. The prime location is **Fisherman's Huts**, north of the Holiday Inn on Palm Beach. For those not up to high winds yet, quieter waters are available farther south on Palm Beach, where there is also equipment and instructors. The most advanced head for **Bachelor's Beach**. During the end of May and the beginning of June, the hail-and-hearty converge here from around the world for the annual **Aruba Hi-Winds Pro-Am Windsurfing Competition**. Aruba is a haven for all watersports, but golf and tennis find lots of takers. Companies dedicated to well-organized sports activities can be found in major hotel lobbies. **Scuba diving** is probably Aruba's best-kept secret, and nowadays, many operators offer one-tank dives so you will have time for all your other pleasures. (For more information, see "Dive Sites" above.) **Sport-fishing** is big on the island, and half- and full-day charters can be arranged through one's hotel or directly from local operators. Less than a mile from shore, the sea is rich with kingfish, tuna, bonito, wahoo and blue and white marlin. **Boat excursions** for picnics and sightseeing are available on catamarans and glass-bottom vessels for viewing the corals—check with your hotel. Though yachting is not a big pastime here yet, there is a nautical club at the mouth of the Spanish Lagoon. **Horseback riding** is available daily on trails throughout the countryside, on paso fino horses imported from South America; the mounts of these finely trained horses are known for an unbelievably comfortable ride.

Aruba Sail Cart

Bushire 23, Oranjestad.

Hours Open: 10 a.m.–7 p.m.

Can't quite get the hang of windsurfing? This goofy sport is easy to learn instead. You'll be whisking about in no time on special carts equipped with a windsurf-type sail—fun! Costs about $15 for a half-hour.

Rancho El Paso

44 Washington, Oranjestad.

Here's the spot to come for trail rides on beautiful paso fino horses.

Red Sail Sports

Seaport Marketplace, Oranjestad.

The island's largest selection of watersport rentals, including scuba instructions and packages. One-tank dives start at $30.

Where to Eat

Fielding's Highest Rated Restaurants in Aruba

★★★★	Chez Mathilde	$16–$33
★★★★	Papiamento	$20–$33
★★★★	Valentino's	$16–$26
★★★	Brisas del Mar	$10–$30
★★★	Die Olde Molen	$15–$30
★★★	La Dolce Vita	$11–$32
★★★	Mi Cushina	$12–$24
★★★	Old Cunucu House	$14–$27
★★★	Que Pasa?	$12–$26
★★★	Talk of the Town	$18–$20

Fielding's Special Restaurants in Aruba

★★★★	Chez Mathilde	$16–$33
★★★★	Papiamento	$20–$33
★★★	Bali	$10–$20
★★★	Charlie's Bar	$7–$22
★★★	Old Cunucu House	$14–$27

Fielding's Budget Restaurants in Aruba

★★★	Steamboat	$7–$15
★★★	Bali	$10–$20
★★	Buccaneer Restaurant	$7–$23
★★★	Charlie's Bar	$7–$22
★★★	Mi Cushina	$12–$24

With more than 100 international restaurants, Aruba is becoming a Disneyland of cuisines. French, German, American, Swiss, Spanish—all are at your fingertips in Aruba. Plentiful supplies of Dutch cheese have inspired *keshi yena*—a stewed chicken-or-meat stuffed Gouda cheese pocket. From Indonesia, a former Dutch colony, came the lavish *rijsttafel* (rice table), an array of savory meat and vegetable dishes served with rice. From Spain, via nearby Venezuela, comes the delicious caramel dessert *flan quesillo.* You can, however, also eat strictly Aruban specialties, such as *sopi di yuana*—iguana soup—which tastes strangely like mom's chicken soup. *Funchi* (cornmeal bread) and *pan bati* (Aruban griddle bread made with cornmeal) are Amerindian specialties that accompany every Aruban meal. At the atmospheric Papiamento mi Cushina in Cura Cabai owned by native Wijke Maduro, a 10-minute drive from Oranjestad, you can go true Aruban—with specialties such as *keri keri* (finely minced fried shark) or *bestia chiquita stoba* (stewed lamb served with delicious freshly baked pan bati.) Other local delights worth trying include *pastechi* (cheese or meet-filled turnovers), wild hare stew and *cabrito* stew, a traditional seasoned feast of goat meat.When you get tired of exotica, head for the hotel coffee shops for American-style grub.

Arubans enjoy the people-to-people contact tourism has brought them.

Bali **$$** ★★★

Lloyd G. Smith Boulevard, #11, Oranjestad, ☎ (297) 8-20680.
Asian cuisine. Specialties: Indonesian Rijstaffel.
Lunch: Noon–3:30 p.m., prix fixe $10–$20.
Dinner: 6–11 p.m., prix fixe $10–$20.

Feast on almost 20 different Indonesian specialties while bobbing gently on the sea in this intricately decorated houseboat in Schooner Harbour. In what could be Aruba's most exotic dining experience, servers present dishes of varying intensity (but nothing is overly spicy), including *nasi goreng* or *bami goreng*, rice and noodles with egg, peas, chicken or beef. Lighter meals are also served, including Western-style sandwiches. No lunch is served on Saturday.

Boonoonoonoos **$$$** ★★

Wilhelminastraat 18A, Oranjestad, ☎ (297) 8-31888.
Latin American cuisine. Specialties: Ajaka (chicken in banana leaves), Jamaican jerk ribs.
Lunch: Noon–5 p.m., entrees $5–$13.
Dinner: 5:30–10:30 p.m., entrees $13–$33.

No, the eyes do not deceive, there really are four pairs of oo's in the name of this downtown restaurant, which means "extraordinary" in Jamaican patois. Located in a restored colonial home that's been brightly splashed with paint, cuisine covers the Caribbean in a large nutshell as conceived by Austrian chefs Kurt and Jacky Biermann. Signature dishes include Jamaican jerk ribs and a silky pumpkin cream soup; hungry diners will be more than satisfied with the Carib Combo platter, groaning with eight or nine dishes representing several Caribbean islands. The service is as good as the food. No lunch is served on Sunday.

Brisas del Mar **$$$** ★★★

Savaneta 22A, East Oranjestad, ☎ (297) 8-47718.
Seafood cuisine. Specialties: Broiled lobster, catch of the day.
Lunch: Noon–2:30 p.m., prix fixe $10–$30.
Dinner: 6:30–9:30 p.m., prix fixe $10–$30.

Bustling and jammed with locals, especially on music-filled weekends, Brisas del Mar is about 20 minutes away from downtown Oranjestad, but well worth the trek for spanking fresh seafood and some of the finest local dishes on the island. Reservations at this folksy beach shack are required because there are only 10 or so tables. A recurring special is a flavorful fish stew, loaded with whatever's fresh, in a tasty broth. Groups can order the Aruban special, a potpourri of lightly fried fish cakes, spiced minced shark, hot relishes, plenty of rice and corn pancakes.

Buccaneer Restaurant **$$** ★★

Gasparito 11-C, East Oranjestad, ☎ (297) 8-66172.
Seafood cuisine.
Dinner: 5:30–10 p.m., entrees $7–$23.

Moderately priced seafood generally satisfies the crowds of diners who come back again and again to this aquarium-laden, cozy restaurant located just a short jog from the large hotel strip in Noord. I've heard some complaints, though, about overcooked fish, so buyer beware. If you don't want to eat, there's a popular bar, and plenty of swimming marine life at which to gaze. European-style meat dishes are also available for seafood-hating companions. No lunch is served on Mondays.

Chalet Suisse **$$$** ★★

J.E. Irausquin Boulevard, Palm Beach,
International cuisine. Specialties: Dutch pea soup, veal in cream sauce.
Dinner: 6–10:30 p.m., entrees $15–$30.

For a change of pace, enjoy Old European specialties in a wood-panelled dining room that's a cool, comfortable spot protecting diners from the glare of the sun outside. Homey and rib-sticking dishes like Dutch split pea soup, veal and steak offer few surprises, but are exceptionally well prepared.

Charlie's Bar **$$** ★★★

Main Street 56, San Nicolas, ☎ (297) 8-45086.
American cuisine. Specialties: Grilled shrimp, churrasco.
Lunch: Noon–4 p.m., entrees $7–$18.
Dinner: 4–9:30 p.m., entrees $7–$22.

You too can become a part of history by hanging a hankie or old tennis shoe to join the hundreds of other artifacts on the ceiling of this 50-plus-year-old bar. It's located in the once-thriving ghost town of San Nicolas, former headquarters of The Standard Oil Company. Charlie's served as a watering hole for workers (no women were allowed then) and it now overflows with tourists seeking a cold brew (or something stiffer) and a simple lunch or dinner of fresh seafood or steak. Overseeing all this activity is Guus Dancker, who has manned the circular bar for more than 40 years.

Chez Mathilde **$$$** ★★★★

Havenstraat 23, Oranjestad, ☎ (297) 8-34968.
French cuisine.
Lunch: 11:30 a.m.–2:30 p.m., entrees $16–$25.
Dinner: 6–11 p.m., entrees $19–$33.

Every Caribbean island must have a bastion of haute cuisine, and this elegant and intimate beauty in a 19th-century town house is IT in Aruba. Dishes are prepared in the classic French style by a Dutch chef, including thick and juicy lamb or veal chops, pate, bouillabaisse, tournedos with peppercorns and lobster thermidor. The romantic setting comes complete with candlelight, fine tableware and classical music. No lunch is served on Sunday.

Die Olde Molen $$$ ★★★

J.E. Irausquin Boulevard, Palm Beach,
International cuisine.
Dinner: 6–10:30 p.m., entrees $15–$30.

Until the brisk winds that blow on the islands constantly threatened to ruin them, this authentic Dutch windmill among the high-rise hotels in Palm Beach sported real sails. Reassembled from an 1800s-era mill that was shipped over from the old country, this tourist attraction is now a restaurant serving international food with Aruban touches. Shrimp is often featured, prepared in a savory cheese sauce, as is pepper steak and liqueured ice cream desserts. Worth a visit for the aesthetic value.

La Dolce Vita $$$ ★★★

Palm Beach 29, Oranjestad, ☎ (297) 8-65241.
Italian cuisine. Specialties: Veal, snapper.
Dinner: 6–11 p.m., entrees $11–$32.

Life is truly sweet here, especially for weary shoppers hoofing it down the fashionable Caya Betico Croes, where this well-known Italian restaurant is located. After several hours perusing the almost duty-free jewelry and clothing shops, snag a table (after reserving ahead) in this refurbished private home for veal and red snapper prepared in different ways, or pastas and authentic Italian desserts and coffee drinks.

La Paloma $$$ ★★

Noord 39, Noord, ☎ (297) 8-62770.
Italian cuisine. Specialties: Conch stew with pan bati, caesar salad, red snapper.
Dinner: 6–11 p.m., entrees $13–$28.

A nice place to take the family for American-style Italian food, La Paloma is always full of patrons who like the huge menu chock full of pasta with red sauces and huge steaks, the brisk service and old-fashioned decor (chianti bottles!). The restaurant is housed in a low-rise building in the Noord area. If you want peace and quiet, this place isn't it. The bar is a popular watering hole.

Mi Cushina $$$ ★★★

Noord Cura Cabai 24, San Nicolas, ☎ (297) 8-48335.
Latin American cuisine. Specialties: Bestia chiquito stoba, pan bati.
Lunch: Noon–2 p.m., entrees $12–$24.
Dinner: 6–10 p.m., entrees $12–$24.

There are a handful of charming small restaurants serving home-style Aruban cuisine, which is not readily available outside of the islands; one of the best is Mi Cushina, or owner Wijke Maduro's "kitchen" and family museum. Occasionally, Maduro serves iguana soup or goat stew, but usually there is fresh fish like grouper or shark served lightly fried in cake form or minced with tangy sauce. A specialty is *bestia chiquito stoba*, or lamb stew in a Creole sauce. Entrees are reasonably priced because of the hearty portions, which include some of the best pan bati on the island.

Old Cunucu House $$$ ★★★

Palm Beach 150, Palm Beach, ☎ (297) 8-61666.
International cuisine. Specialties: Pan fried conch, cornmeal, pan bati.
Dinner: 6–10 p.m., entrees $14–$27.

Experience the Aruba of bygone days in this 1920s-style dwelling with a restaurant whose name means "old country" house. Tasty seafood is featured, as well as New York steaks and a few Aruban specialties. The atmosphere here is very relaxed and informal, amidst modern high-rise hotels that dwarf it. Even if you don't come to eat, there's a rustic bar with live and local entertainment on weekends.

Papiamento **$$$** ★★★★

Washington 61, Noord, ☎ (297) 8-64544.

Latin American cuisine. Specialties: Meat or fish cooked on hot marble, clay pot seafood.

Dinner: 6–11 p.m., entrees $20–$33.

This is possibly one of Aruba's "don't miss" experiences if only for the exquisite surroundings. Dining here is like being invited to a gracious private home—which this is. Lenie and Eduardo Ellis design their own handwritten menus, garnish their Continental dishes with fresh garden herbs, and have decorated the various dining areas with distinctive plantings and antiques. You can dine by the pool or request a single honeymoon table. Perennial favorites are available on the ever-changing menu.

Que Pasa? **$$$** ★★★

Schelpstraat Street 20, ☎ (297) 8-33872.

International cuisine.

Dinner: 6 p.m.–2 a.m., entrees $12–$26.

Hang with the locals at this funky cafe/art gallery in an eclectic Dutch house. The imaginative menu features dishes from all over the world—especially good are the pasta specialties, fresh fish, homemade soups and interesting appetizers such as bitterballen and sate ajam.The portions are huge and the service friendly. The walls are adorned with colorful Haitian art; if one strikes your fancy, you can buy it on the spot. This fun spot is a real winner.

Steamboat **$$** ★★★

Lloyd G. Smith, Oranjestad, ☎ (297) 8-66700.

International cuisine. Specialties: Buffet Brunch.

Lunch: Noon–5 p.m., entrees $7–$10.

Dinner: 5:30–11 p.m., prix fixe $15.

One of Aruba's best bargains is this buffet foodery in a shopping center near all the hotel action. Steamboat serves a large breakfast or brunch for under $8, and large sandwiches are available for lunch. Dinner is another all-you-can eat buffet that draws crowds (understandably) for $15 per person.

Talk of the Town **$$$** ★★★

L.G. Smith Boulevard 2, Oranjestad, ☎ (297) 8-23380.

American cuisine. Specialties: Prime rib, steaks.

Dinner: 5:30–11 p.m., entrees $18–$20.

This is an excellent stop for people with big appetites, with superb beefsteaks and prime rib feasts on Saturday nights for under $20. Located near the airport in a Best Western resort of the same name that resembles a Spanish hacienda, it's a surprisingly nice spot for quiet, intimate, candlelit dinners, and possibly the only restaurant in the Caribbean that's been awarded membership in the prestigious Chaine de Rotisseurs culinary society.

Valentino's **$$$** ★★★★

Palm Beach Road, Noord, ☎ (297) 8-64777.

Italian cuisine. Specialties: Mozzarella in carozza, penne del pastor.

Dinner: 6–11 p.m., entrees $16–$26.

Arubans like to come here to celebrate special occasions along with residents and guests at the chic Caribbean Palm Village Resort in Noord. The reason is delicious pastas—especially fettucini with salmon—intimate tables and gracious, friendly service. Before dining, patrons can unwind with drinks, then ascend to the second-story courtyard restaurant overlooking the pool and cooled by evening breezes.

Where to Shop

Oranjestad, the capital, is a shopper's haven. Shops line the main shopping streets of Nassaustraat and Wilhelminastraat, selling mostly duty-free products (minus the 8 percent duty), such as liquor, jewelry, electronics, crystal, china, perfumes and designer fashions. Shopping malls—**Holland Aruba Mall**, **Seaport Village Mall** and the **Strada Complex**—make for one-stop shopping while **Harbour Town** and **Port of Call Marketplace** cater to the cruise crowd. The best free-port shopping can be found at **Caya G. F. Betico Croes**.

Aruba Directory

BUSINESS HOURS

Shops open Monday–Saturday 8 a.m.–6 p.m. Alhambra Bazaar is open 5 p.m.–midnight. Banks open Monday–Friday 8 a.m.–noon and 1:30–4 p.m.

CLIMATE

Dry and sunny, Aruba boasts average temperatures of 83 degrees F, though trade winds make the heat seem gentler. Mosquitoes get frisky in July and August, when it is less windy.

DOCUMENTS

U.S. and Canadian citizens need to show some proof of citizenship—birth certificate, passport or voter's registration plus a photo ID; driver's license is not accepted. You must also show an ongoing or return ticket.

ELECTRICITY

Current runs at 110 volts, 60 cycles, as in the U.S.

GETTING AROUND

Taxis are plentiful, but the lack of meters requires firm negotiations with the driver before you take off. Drivers often know the city as well as private guides. Ask your hotel to recommend one. A dispatch office is also located at **Alhambra Bazaar and Casino** ☎ *(297) 8-21604*. You can also flag down taxis from the street. Rates are fixed (no meters) but you should confirm the price before you set off. All Aruban taxi drivers are specially trained guides; an hour's tour will run about $30.

Cars are easily rented on the island; you will need a valid U.S. or Canadian driver's license to rent a car; different agencies have various age requirements. You will save money if you rent from a local agency rather than from one of the well-known agencies. Among the best are **Hedwina Car Rental** ☎ *8-26442* and **Optima** ☎ *8-36263*. Avis, Budget and Hertz are all available at the airport.

Scooters are the best vehicle to toot around the island and are the most economical. You'll save money renting for two days or longer. **Ron's** ☎ *8-62090* and **George's** ☎ *8-25975* will deliver to the airport.

Inexpensive buses run hourly between the beach hotels and Oranjestad. The main terminal is located in South Zoutmanstraat, next to Fort Zoutman. A free Shopping Tour Bus departs hourly from 9:15 a.m.–3:15 p.m., starting at the Holiday Inn and making stops at all the major hotels on the way toward Oranjestad.

LANGUAGE

Arubans are pleasantly multilingual. The official language is Dutch; also spoken are English, Spanish, Portuguese and the local dialect called Papiamento.

MEDICAL EMERGENCIES

Horacio Oduber Hospital ☎ *8-24300* is a modern facility near Eagle Beach, with an efficient staff. Ask your hotel about doctors and dentists on call.

MONEY

The official currency is the Aruban florin (also called the guilder), written as Af or Afl. American dollars are accepted at most establishments, but it might be cheaper to pay in florins.

TELEPHONE

To call Aruba from the U.S., dial ☎ *011+297+8* followed by the five-digit number. Forget calling home from your hotel—surcharges can hike the price of an overseas call to exorbitant levels. Instead, head for SETAR, the local company, with several locations in Oranjestad and near the high-rise hotels in Palm Beach. From here, you can make phone calls using a card you purchase, and also send and receive faxes.

TIME

Aruba is on Atlantic Standard Time, year round.

TIPPING AND TAXES

Aruban custom is to charge a 10–15 percent service charge and 5 percent government tax. The total of these two charges is usually written into the "tax" slot on credit cards. If you want to give more for service, feel free, but it is not expected.

TOURIST INFORMATION

Aruba Tourism Authority, *A. Shuttestraat 2, Oranjestad, Aruba, N.A.* ☎ *011+297+82-3777*, FAX *83-4702*. From the U.S. call ☎ *(800) 862-7822*.

WHEN TO GO

New Year's is celebrated with an explosion of fireworks set off by the hotels and serenaded by strolling musicians and singers. Carnival is a blowout event, which starts two weeks before Lent, and culminates with a Grand Parade on the Sunday preceding Lent. National Anthem and Flag Day on March 18 is celebrated by displays of national dancing and folklore. A weekly Bonbini show in the courtyard of the Fort Zoutman museum on Tuesdays 6:30–10:30 p.m. also presents island folklore, song, and dance. The International Theatre Festival is an annual event; contact the tourist board for exact dates.

ARUBA RESTAURANTS	PHONE	ENTREE	CR. CARDS
Oranjestad			
American			
★★★ Charlie's Bar	(297) 8-45086	$7–$22	None

ARUBA RESTAURANTS	PHONE	ENTREE	CR. CARDS
★★★ Talk of the Town	(297) 8-23380	$18–$20••	A, DC, MC, V
Asian			
★★★ Bali	(297) 8-20680	$10–$20	A, MC, V
French			
★★★★ Chez Mathilde	(297) 8-34968	$16–$33	A, D, DC, MC, V
International			
★★★ Die Olde Molen		$15–$30••	A, DC, MC, V
★★★ Old Cunucu House	(297) 8-61666	$14–$27••	A, DC, MC, V
★★★ Que Pasa?	(297) 8-33872	$12–$26••	MC, V
★★★ Steamboat	(297) 8-66700	$7–$15	A, MC, V
★★ Chalet Suisse		$15–$30••	A, DC, MC, V
Italian			
★★★★ Valentino's	(297) 8-64777	$16–$26••	A, DC, MC, V
★★★ La Dolce Vita	(297) 8-65241	$11–$32••	A, D, MC, V
★★ La Paloma	(297) 8-62770	$13–$28••	A, MC, V
Latin American			
★★★★ Papiamento	(297) 8-64544	$20–$33••	A, MC, V
★★★ Mi Cushina	(297) 8-48335	$12–$24	A, DC, MC, V
★★ Boonoonoonoos	(297) 8-31888	$5–$33	A, DC, MC, V
Seafood			
★★★ Brisas del Mar	(297) 8-47718	$10–$30	A, MC, V
★★ Buccaneer Restaurant	(297) 8-66172	$7–$23••	A, D, DC, MC, V
Note: • Lunch Only			
•• Dinner Only			

BARBADOS

Large numbers of sailboats are available for charter in Barbados.

Three centuries ago, Barbados was called the "Brightest Jewel in the English Crowne," and today, this tiny coral island still gleams, not just as a "veddy British" trinket, but as a Caribbean treasure in its own right. After a long struggle to balance itself politically after declaring independence from Britain 30 years ago, Barbados is returning to a celebration of its own Bajan culture, interlacing the passion for cricket and afternoon teas with the more boisterous native traditions of rum, calypso and Rastafarianism. In 1993, the Human Development Report of the United Nations placed Barbados first among all developing nations in the world—the third year in a row—and tourists can't help but feel blessed by the efficiency of service, the top-class cuisine and the general enthusiasm of spirit. Long one of the most cosmopolitan and sophisticated islands in the Caribbean, Barbados is looking even spiffier these days as a building boom creates new hotels and restaurants by the dozens. Spearheaded by the Pemberton Resorts' new **Royal Westmoreland Golf and Country Club**, the construction of golf facilities, including an international school and six multimillion-dollar courses, will rank Barbados among the top destinations for golf in the world. Carnival and the annual Crop Over festival are the times when Barbados truly hangs loose, but those interested in getting away from it all can still find a wild and rugged Barbados tucked in the backcountry. A new Concorde charter service will allow travelers to reach Barbados in less the flight time normally required and will reap hundreds of saved dollars in an 8 day/7 night package at one of 15 luxury hotels on the island.

Bird's Eye View

A pear-shaped coral island that stretches 21 miles north and 14 miles east to west, Barbados is the most easterly of the complex of West Indies islands—a series of stepping stones that arch from South Florida to South America. Spanning a total of 166 square miles, Barbados boasts a remarkably varied topography—in an hour you can pass through the lush rain forest of St. Thomas, the rugged rocky coast of St. Joseph, and the gentle sloping capped hills of St. Andrew. The northernmost parish of St. Lucy is where the Caribbean and the Atlantic coast meet. Because Barbados is the first land hit by the westerly trade winds traversing the Atlantic, the air is fresh and invigorating, so much so that in the 19th century the island became known as the "sanitarium of the West Indies" because boatloads of Brits came to air out their vaporous lungs. Perhaps the good air explains the longevity of Barbadians, who on the average live well into their 70s.

History

When the Portuguese explorer Pedro a Campos discovered Barbados in the 17th century, he found the island totally uninhabited. As the sailor took in the lush tropical surroundings, he spotted fig trees with clumps of bushy roots hanging from branches that resembled beards. From that came the name Barbados, which in Portuguese means "the bearded ones." Long before the first European contact, Arawak Indians were said to be living on the island, but they were long gone by the time of the first British expedition in 1625. Two years later, 80 British settlers under the leadership of Captain John Powell settled at Jamestown (later renamed Holetown). Soon, conditions proved highly favorable for tobacco, cotton and sugarcane production, and thousands of African and European slaves were shipped over to till the fields. A strong fortress system (26 forts along 21 miles of coast) kept the island from invasion, and Barbados became the only island in the Caribbean to be under uninterrupted British rule for more than three centuries. In 1937, economic problems caused by the fluctuating price of sugar led to demonstrations in Bridgetown, which resulted in the establishment of a British

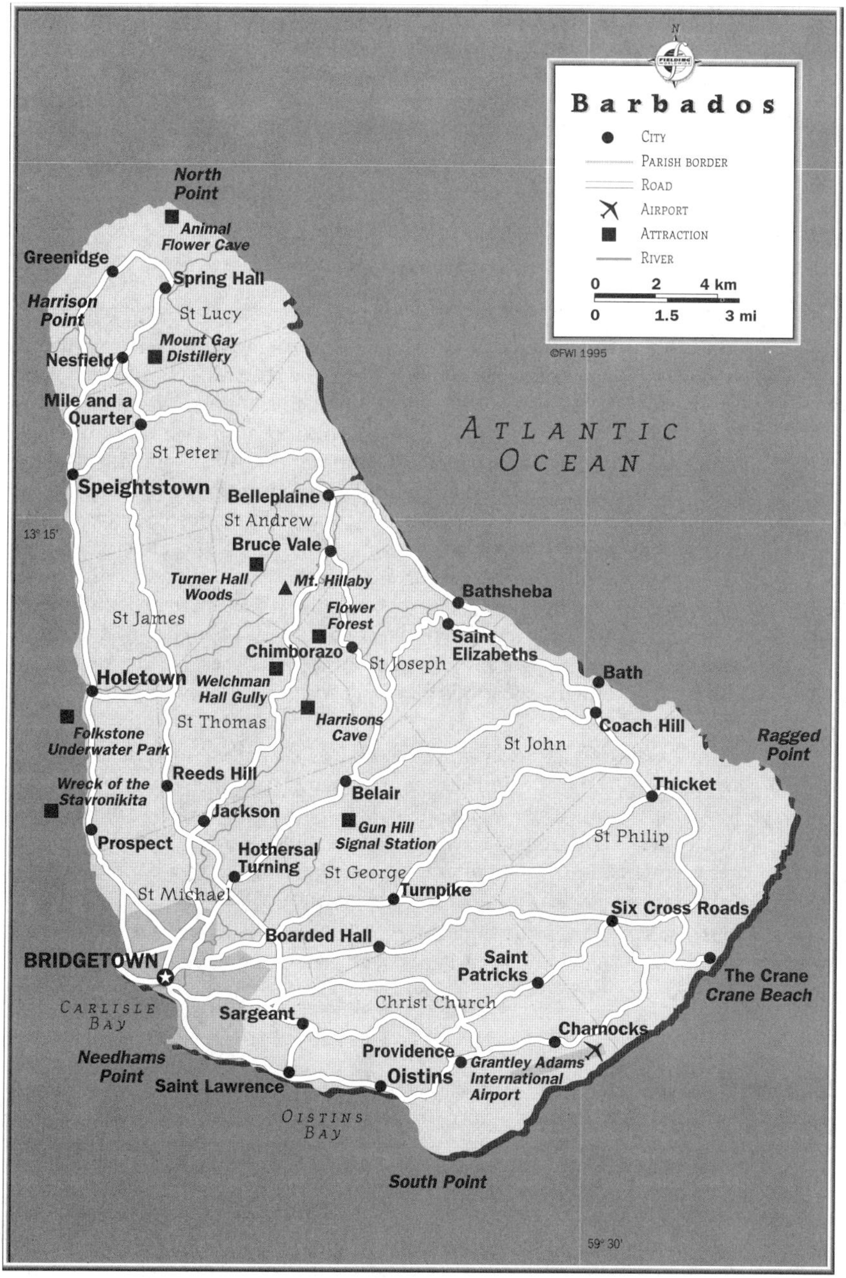
Barbados
City
Parish border
Road
Airport
Attraction
River
0 2 4 km
0 1.5 3 mi
©FWI 1995
Atlantic Ocean
North Point
Animal Flower Cave
Greenidge
Spring Hall
Harrison Point
St Lucy
Mount Gay Distillery
Nesfield
Mile and a Quarter
St Peter
Speightstown
Belleplaine
St Andrew
13° 15'
Bruce Vale
Turner Hall Woods
Mt. Hillaby
Bathsheba
St James
Flower Forest
Saint Elizabeths
Chimborazo
St Joseph
Bath
Holetown
Welchman Hall Gully
St Thomas
Harrisons Cave
Coach Hill
Folkstone Underwater Park
St John
Ragged Point
Reeds Hill
Belair
Thicket
Wreck of the Stavronikita
Jackson
Gun Hill Signal Station
Prospect
Hothersal Turning
St Philip
St George
St Michael
Turnpike
Six Cross Roads
Boarded Hall
BRIDGETOWN
Saint Patricks
The Crane
Crane Beach
Carlisle Bay
Christ Church
Sargeant
Charnocks
Needhams Point
Providence
Grantley Adams International Airport
Saint Lawrence
Oistins
Oistins Bay
South Point
59° 30'

Royal Commonwealth to the West Indies—a gesture that proved instrumental in bringing about social and political reform, including universal adult suffrage in 1951. Fifteen years later, Barbados received its full sovereignty.

Today Barbados is a British Commonwealth nation with a parliamentary system of government headed by an appointed governor-general and an elected prime minister. British influence extends to the courts, laws, language and place names.

People

Barbados is still a place where stately women carry umbrellas with pride, children peer from shutters, and men slam down dominoes on rickety tables. About 80 percent of the native population hail from African origin, another 15 percent are of mixed blood. Although Europeans represent only about 5 percent of the total population, a strong sense of British tradition still pervades, including a profound commitment to education (the island boasts a whopping literacy rate of 99 percent). Schoolchildren descended from slaves were taught to think of Barbados as Little England, and even in the most inland roads, you'll see children dressed in the mandatory school uniforms (pressed shirt and ties for both sexes), all color-coded in true British fashion. So strong is the Brit lifestyle here the afternoon tea is still habitually enjoyed, and passions for cricket and polo run deep. Along esplanades and streets, however, you might see locals playing *warri*, a traditional bead game from West Africa.

Driving around aimlessly is a way of life in Barbados—there's even a word for it: "buttin' 'bout." In fact, the best thing to do in Barbados is to throw away your map because asking and receiving directions can often be the prelude to new friendships or a spontaneous game of road tennis. If you really want to delve into the soul of Barbados, pick up a copy of the highly acclaimed novel *In the Castle of My Skin* by George Lamming.

One sad note: due to high unemployment, U.S. advisories have warned about purse-snatching, sexual crime and armed robbery. Avoid flashing jewelry and keep an eye on wallets and packs carried on the back.

Beaches

All beaches in Barbados are open to the public, even those abutting the high-priced hotels; local law requires that access to the beaches be open, either through the road or through the hotel's entrance. A beautiful drive through sugarcane fields will take you to the rugged, surf-pounding beaches

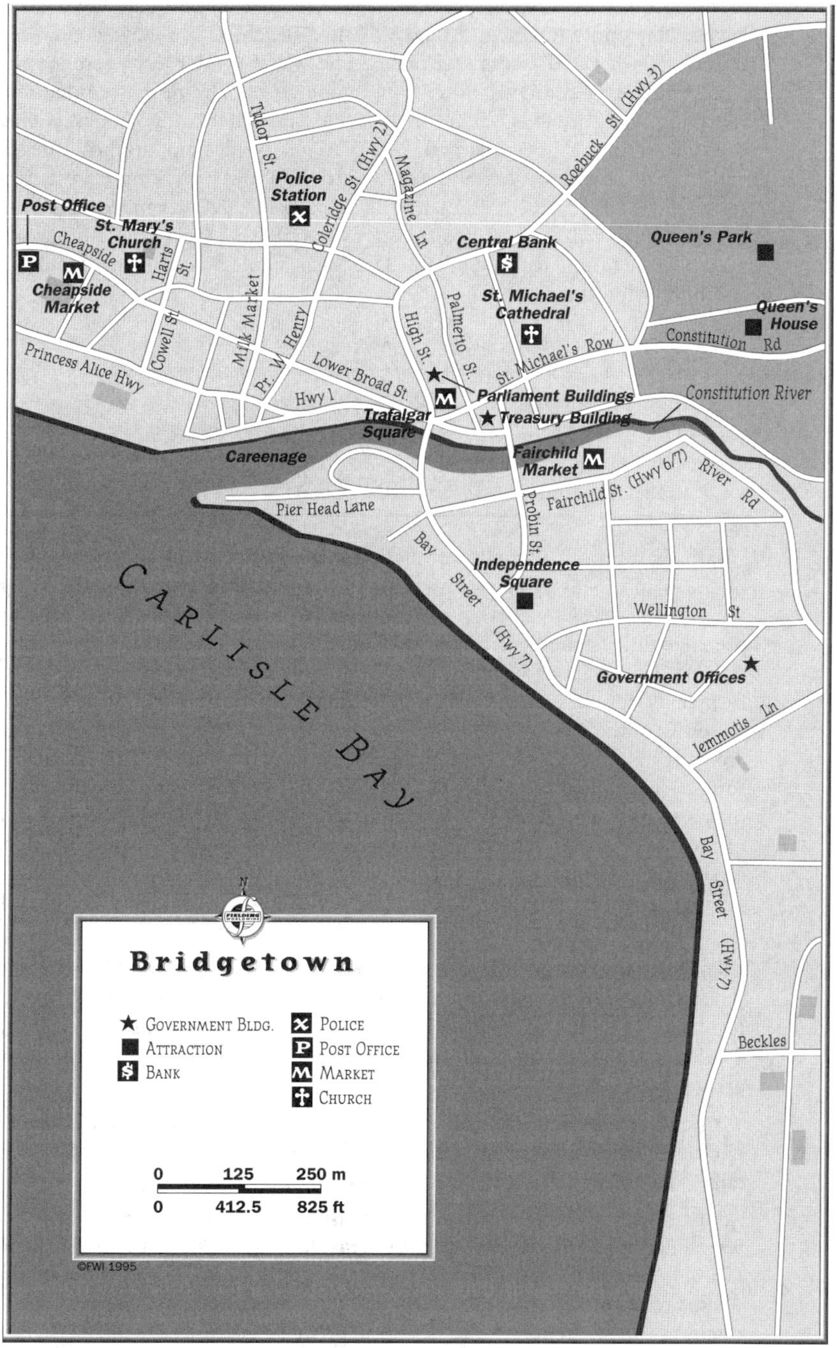
Bridgetown
Government Bldg.
Attraction
Bank
Police
Post Office
Market
Church
0 125 250 m
0 412.5 825 ft
©FWI 1995
Post Office
St. Mary's Church
Cheapside Market
Police Station
Central Bank
St. Michael's Cathedral
Queen's Park
Queen's House
Parliament Buildings
Treasury Building
Trafalgar Square
Careenage
Fairchild Market
Independence Square
Government Offices
Carlisle Bay
Constitution River
Tudor St.
Coleridge St (Hwy 2)
Magazine Ln
Roebuck St (Hwy 3)
Cheapside
Harts St.
Cowell St.
Milk Market
Pr. W. Henry
Lower Broad St.
Hwy 1
Princess Alice Hwy
High St.
Palmetto St.
St. Michael's Row
Constitution Rd
Pier Head Lane
Fairchild St. (Hwy 6/7)
River Rd
Probin St.
Bay Street (Hwy 7)
Wellington St
Jemmotis Ln
Beckles

of the east coast (North Point, Cove Bay and Archer's Bay), but most people prefer the calmer western beaches called the **Gold Coast** (Paradise Beach, Paynes Bay and Sandy Lane Bay, Treasure Beach, Gibbs Bay, Heywoods Beach, Rockley and Bentson Beach). The water most everywhere stays a comfortable few degrees below body temperature. The most secluded and charming hotel beach is behind the **Coconut Creek Club**, in St. James. **Mulins Bay**, just south of Speightstown, is a particularly pleasant nonhotel beach with a good restaurant-bar and a free outdoor shower. Parking is in the lot across the road. The most dramatic beach is most likely **Batsheba**, on the rugged northeast side, where foamy waves pound the shores with huge salt sprays. Here you'll see lots of old Barbadian families taking their weekend and holiday escapes.

What Else to See

Barbadian history and culture still lives vibrantly in the art and architecture of the island. Most visitors only visit the capital, **Bridgetown**, for shopping forays, but there are a few sights for which you might consider sacrificing precious time at the beach. **The Careenage**, a haven for the old clipper ships, still exudes an air of intrigue, although these days it has lost some of its former glory. Cars usually whiz by **Trafalgar Square**, but the stained glass windows of the **Public Building** represent the crowned heads of England, and are worth a quick look. The monument, dedicated to Admiral Horatio Nelson, celebrates his contributions to the island. It's rare to find Jewish houses of worship in the Caribbean, but the synagogue on Synagogue Lane is one of the oldest in the Western Hemisphere, erected on the site of an even older synagogue established by Brazilian Jews. From here, you could take a taxi to visit the garrison Savannah, especially if a cricket game or horse race is in full force.

Speightstown, on the west coast, has retained much of its colonial look and flavor. Two-story shops with Georgian-style galleries propped up by two-by-four pillars line the narrow street. Just to roam the sidewalks clogged with food vendors is an education in the vast variety of exotic tropical fruits that are available on the island.

An interesting excursion is to take a tram through **Harrison's Cave**, home of geologic formations of crystallized limestone. Streams, pools and waterfalls—one of them 40 feet—cause slow but steady erosion of the rock.

Anyone interested in antiques should visit a few plantation houses, some of which date back to the 17th century. **Drax Hall** is considered the oldest plantation house on the island, and many of the bedrooms and parlor of **Sunbury Plantation** look as if someone is still living there. **St. Nicholas Abbey** boasts an owner, Lt. Col. Stephen Cave, who will prove a true living legend if you corner him into conversation. To round out the history lesson, visit the **Barbados Museum**, which houses a fine collection of Barbadian furnishings, fine art and artifacts from the early days. The Barbados Heritage Passport, a package program, was recently expanded to 15 of the most outstanding cultural sites on the island (plantations, gardens, museums, mills, etc.). Run by the Barbados National Trust, the package offers entrance to all sites for $35, a 50 percent discount from regular admission prices.

BEST VIEW:

Grenade Hall, a restored 19th century signal station, surrounded by a user-friendly tropical forest, offers the most spectacular panorama of the island.

Historical Sites

Bridgetown

Francia Plantation ★★★

Highway X, St. George, ☎ (809) 429- 474.
Hours open: 10 a.m.–4 p.m.
This family house, still home to descendants of the original owner, provides an authentic look at old Barbados. Also worth checking out is the Sunbury Plantation Home in St. Philip *(☎ 423-6270)*, a 300-year-old home filled with fine antiques.

Gun Hill Signal Station ★★

Highway 4, St. George, ☎ (809) 429-1358.
Hours open: 9 a.m.–5 p.m.
This 1818 signal station was used by the British Army. Even if you're not into such things, the views from atop the highland are worth the trip.

Old Synagogue ★★★

Synagogue Lane, Bridgetown, ☎ (809) 426-5792.
Hours open: 9 a.m.–4 p.m.
Built by Jews from Brazil in 1654, the synagogue is the second-oldest in North America. It was partially destroyed by hurricane and rebuilt to its present state in 1833. The grounds include a cemetery, still used today, with graves of early Jewish settlers from as far back as the 1630s.

St. Peter

Morgan Lewis Sugar Windmill ★

Highway 2, St. Andrew, ☎ (809) 426-2421.
Hours open: 9 a.m.–5 p.m.
This historic spot provides a fine example of the windmills used to process sugarcane in the 17th-19th centuries. Nice views of the "Scotland District."

St. Nicholas Abbey ★★★

Cherry Tree Hill, St. Peter, ☎ (809) 422-8725.
Hours open: 10 a.m.–3:30 p.m.
This is Barbados' oldest structure, dating back to 1650, though it was actually an abbey only in the mind of a former owner, who dubbed it so in the 1800s. Two hundred acres of sugarcane surround the Jacobean-style great house of wood and stone.

Museums and Exhibits

Bridgetown

Barbados Museum ★★★★

St. Ann's Garrison, St. Michael, ☎ (809) 427- 201.
Hours open: 9 a.m.–5 p.m.
This unusually fine museum, housed in a former military prison, traces the island's history from prehistoric times to the present. Good exhibits on natural history, West Indian maps and arts and the slave trade. The grounds also include a decent gift shop and an excellent cafe.

Parks and Gardens

Bridgetown

Welchman Hall Gully ★★★

Highway 2, St. Thomas, ☎ *(809) 438-6671.*
Hours open: 9 a.m.–5 p.m.
A peaceful oasis owned by the Barbados National Trust, with acres of labeled trees and flowers, and possibly even a green monkey. The breadfruit trees are said to be descended from seeds brought by Captain Bligh.

St. Peter

Andromeda Gardens ★★★

Bathsheba, St. Joseph, ☎ *(809) 433-9261.*
Hours open: 9 a.m.–5 p.m.
This unique spot encompasses eight acres of gardens set into oceanfront cliffs. The emphasis is on unusual plants from around the world, and they have those aplenty, plus hundreds of orchids, hibiscus and palm varieties—plus a babbling brook winding throughout.

Farley Hill ★★★★

Farley Hill, St. Peter.
Hours open: 8:30 a.m.–6 p.m.
Very rugged grounds and the ruins of a once-grand plantation house mark this picturesque national park.

Flower Forest

Highway 2, St. Joseph, ☎ *(809) 433-8152.*
Hours open: 9 a.m.–5 p.m.
Set on an old sugar plantation in the scenic Scotland District, this park encompasses eight acres of flowering trees and shrubs. Great views of Mt. Hillaby, too.

Tours

Bridgetown

Atlantis Submarines Barbados ★★★★★

McGregor Street, Bridgetown, ☎ *(809) 436-8929.*
Hours open: 9 a.m.–6 p.m.
The perfect way to see the world below, without getting wet, is aboard an Atlantis submarine, which takes its passengers in air-conditioned comfort some 150 feet beneath the water's surface. The two-hour tour includes the sighting of a shipwreck. Recommended for everyone but the claustrophobic.

Harrison's Cave ★★★★★

Highway 2, St. Thomas, ☎ *(809) 438-6640.*
Hours open: 9 a.m.–4 p.m.
This is the island's biggest tourist attraction, and rightfully so, as these limestone caverns are unique to the Caribbean. Better yet, it's all tastefully done with discreet lighting that preserves the feel of the place. Don a hard hat (more for drama than necessity) and ride an electric tram through the immense caverns, which come complete with waterfalls and streams. Reservations are recommended.

Highland Outdoor Tours ★★★★

Bridgetown, ☎ *(809) 438-8069.*
Experience the real Barbados—far from the glittery resorts and tony restaurants—with this new tour operator that specializes in adventure travel. Options include a 2.5-hour Horseback Trek to the island's east coast for a bareback ride in the surf and a Caribbean lunch on the beach ($100); the Scenic Safari Hike, a five-mile walk through the pristine Scotland district and lunch on the beach ($70); and the Plantation Tour, a two-hour jaunt on a tractor-driven open jitney through some of the

Barbados' great plantations ($25). You can also tour the plantations via horseback ($50).

Jolly Roger Cruises ★★★★

Shallow Draft, Bridgetown, ☎ (809) 436-2149.

Lots of options for multihour cruises, including the Bajan Queen, a Mississippi riverboat replica that is the largest cruise ship of its kind and the only one offering sit-down dining. There are also two very fun pirate frigate replicas that offer snorkel trips and general merrymaking. Prices start at $52.50.

St. Peter

Animal Flower Cave ★★★

Highway 1B, North Point, ☎ (809) 439-8797.

Hours open: 9 a.m.–4 p.m.

The cavern takes its name from the small sea anemones that prettily open their tentacles, but don't expect to see too many nowadays.

Barbados Wildlife Preserve ★★★★

Highway 1, St. Peter, ☎ (809) 422-8826.

Hours open: 10 a.m.–5 p.m.

This walk-through preserve, essentially a monkey sanctuary run by the Barbados Primate Research Center, features free-roaming land turtles, peacocks, parrots—even a kangaroo. They also have good exhibits on the island's natural history and an interesting walk-in aviary.

Where the Rum Comes From ★★★★

Pick up from your hotel, St. Peter.

The wonderful world of rum is the focus of this tour, held each Wednesday from 12–2:15 p.m. You'll tour Cockspur, manufacturers of Barbadian rum for more than 200 years, then sip the potable and groove to a steel band while supping on a buffet meal.

Sports

Barbados is a perfect island for surf and turf sports. Hiking, as sponsored by the Barbados National Trust and the Duke of Edinburgh's Award Scheme, has nearly become a national pastime on Sunday mornings from January-May when group treks are arranged, according to skill and endurance. (For more information, see "Treks" above.) Horseback riders can enjoy a variety of trails through tropical forests; one spectacular ride is the 3-4 hour tour of the Villa Nova Plantation, which includes a hearty lunch. Tennis courts can be found at most of the major hotels, and there are usually facilities for night-playing.

Conditions for all watersports in Barbados rank among the finest in the Caribbean, especially windsurfing, which takes advantage of the sturdy trade winds between November and May and the shallow offshore reef off Silver Sands. Deep-sea fishermen have raved about the variety of barracuda, sailfish, marlin and wahoo. Resort certification in scuba can be arranged through **Sandy Beach Watersports**; check out its most recent scuba-holiday packages. Snorkeling is also favorable, especially in **Folkstone Underwater Park**, where visibility can range up to 100 feet most of the year.

Pemberton Resort's new **Royal Westmoreland Golf and Country Club**, is presently building a $30 million-dollar, 27-hole course over 500 acres in the hills overlooking the two adjacent Pemberton hotels—Royal Pavilion and Glitter Bay. Sandy Lane also updated its course and opened an international golfing school in 1993. The Barbados government has approved five more courses on the island's south coast.

Bridgetown

Dive Shop, The

Aquatic Gap, St. Michael, ☎ *(809) 426-9947.*
Hours open: 8:30 a.m.–4:30 p.m.
They offer great scuba excursions to colorful reefs and wrecks, with prices starting at $40 per one-tank dive. Beginners can take a resort course for $50, and deep-sea fishers can arrange a charter for $300 per boat per half-day.

Christ Church

Barbados Windsurfing Club

Silver Sands Hotel, Christ Church, ☎ *(809) 428-6001.*
Rent a windboard for $20 an hour, $40 per half day, or partake in a lesson to learn this challenging sport.

Fun Seekers, Inc.

78 Old Chancery Lane, Christ Church, ☎ *(809) 435-9171.*
You can rent motorbikes or bicycles here, or better yet, partake of a cruise aboard the 44-foot *Limbo Lady*. Lunch cruises cost $50 and include snorkeling; sunset sails are $40. They'll pick you up at your hotel if need be.

St. Peter

Caribbean International Riding

Auburn, St. Joseph, ☎ *(809) 433-1453.*
Hours open: 7:30 a.m.–6 p.m.
Trail rides on handsome horses range from a 75-minute jaunt ($28) to a three-hour tour of the historic Villa Nova Plantation, complete with lunch, for $88.

Sandy Lane Golf Course

Sandy Lane Hotel, St. James, ☎ *(809) 432-1311.*
This is the island's best, an 18-hole championship course with a famed 7th hole that has an elevated tee and wonderful views. Greens fees are $120 for $18 holes, $90 for nine.

Where to Eat

Fielding's Highest Rated Restaurants in Barbados		
★★★★	**Bagatelle Great House**	$30–$35
★★★★	**Carambola**	$20–$40
★★★★	**David's Place**	$9–$30
★★★★	**Ile de France**	$18–$38
★★★★	**La Cage aux Folles**	$25–$38
★★★★	**Pisces**	$15–$30
★★★★	**Raffles Old Towne**	$25–$35
★★★★	**The Fathoms**	$6–$29
★★★	**La Maison**	$23–$40
★★★	**Reid's**	$21–$40

Fielding's Special Restaurants in Barbados		
★★★★	**Bagatelle Great House**	$30–$35
★★★★	**David's Place**	$9–$30
★★★★	**La Cage aux Folles**	$25–$38
★★★★	**Raffles Old Towne**	$25–$35
★★★	**Reid's**	$21–$40

Fielding's Budget Restaurants in Barbados		
★★	**Chicken Barn, The**	$3–$11
★★	**Carib Beach Bar**	$6–$16
★★	**T.G.I. Boomers**	$4–$17
★★	**Atlantis Hotel**	$12–$17
★★★	**Koko's**	$12–$22

Barbados' restaurants are world-class, and can hold their own against any international cuisine.

Bajan cooking blends the ethnic influences of the British colonists, the Arawak Indians in residence on the island at the time of their arrival, and the African slaves imported between 1640 and 1807.

Flying fish—boiled, baked, stewed, fried, steamed or stuffed—is the island specialty, available on many menus. One of the hot spots is **La Maison**, tucked inside an old coral-stone Bajan house where the red snapper marinated in herbs and honey is reportedly sublime.

Wine bars and tapas are now the rage in Barbados. Tapas fanatics should head for the **Waterfront Café** in a restored coral-limestone warehouse on Bridgetown's inner harbor, where the young and gorgeous chow down on "fish-melts" (batter-fried flying fish roe) and lime squash while listening to great jazz. Lunch is also good since the view of the bay is spectacular.

Among the most romantic spots are **Carambola**, on the west coast (catch the sunset), and **The Mews** on the Gold Coast, where you can dine on the patio under a starry sky or inside the white stucco house brimming with tropical plants. Even more romantic is **Reid's**, a St. Peter restaurant with open sides that overlook manicured gardens filled with fountains and singing tree frogs called *coquis.*

Do stop by the supermarket and check out the huge variety of island spices. You'll also discover nine different brands of *mauby*, the local sugar-and-tree bark drink. Hot-sauce addicts can choose from at least 12 brands of local brew made from scotch-bonnet peppers, mustard, garlic, scallions and spices; visitors have been known to chug home a gallon or two.

Bridgetown

Bagatelle Great House **$$$** ★★★★

Highway 2A, St. Thomas Parish, ☎ (809) 421-6767.
French cuisine.
Dinner: 7-9:30 p.m., entrees $30–$35.

Diners too timid to experience the vibrant street scene on the Baxter Road, an open-air market in the heart of Bridgetown where vendors cook fish on hot fires, come to Bagatelle Great House, which duplicates this method with whatever's fresh that day. The restaurant is located within the former residence of the first governor of Barbados, and this is probably one of the island's more elegant dining experiences, with stellar service—though the food is less distinguished than the surroundings. Guests can eat downstairs or on a small terrace one flight above.

Brown Sugar **$$$** ★★★

Aquatic Gap, St. Michael Parish, ☎ (809) 426-7684.
Latin American cuisine. Specialties: Flying fish, Creole orange chicken.
Lunch: Noon-2:30 p.m., prix fixe $14–$25.
Dinner: 6–9:45 p.m., entrees $10–$25.

One of the better values on the islands, and a lovely one to boot, is this lush, terraced, tropical-style restaurant located a few miles south of Bridgetown. Smart businesspeople and others in the know dine here at lunch on weekdays when a West Indian buffet is available for $14.00. There are various soups, salads and stews to choose from, including pepper pot. Other offerings include flying fish, jerk chicken and pork and luscious desserts. Dinner is more of a Continental affair, with international touches added to local ingredients, like the popular Creole orange chicken.

Carib Beach Bar **$$** ★★

Sandy Beach, Worthing,
International cuisine. Specialties: Fish fry, barbecue.
Lunch: 11:30 a.m.–3 p.m., entrees $6–$16.
Dinner: 3–10 p.m., entrees $6–$16.

One of a string of economical beach bars that pop up on several locations around the islands, Carib is right on the sand at Sandy Beach, offering fish sandwiches and fresh seafood in a comfortable upstairs restaurant, and potent rum punches in the lower-level bar. Better yet are the Wednesday night fish fries and Friday barbecue buffet, which both start at 7:30 p.m. and cost around $10 for a substantial amount of food. A happening place that stays open fairly late. The restaurant closes at 7:30 on Sundays.

Chicken Barn, The **$** ★★

Highway 7, Worthing,
American cuisine. Specialties: Fried chicken.
Lunch: 10 a.m.–3:30 p.m., entrees $3–$11.
Dinner: 3:30–10:30 p.m., entrees $3–$11.

The Chicken Barn is a convenient quick lunch stop that serves fried chicken and decent burgers for a little over $1. In fact, the Barn is one of a group of inexpensive faster food establishments on Highway 7 not far from Sandy Beach in the town of Worthing, a great place for budget-minded travelers. You can also get salads and fish and chips for under $4.

Josef's **$$$** ★★★

Waverly House, St. Lawrence Gap, ☎ *(809) 435-6541.*
International cuisine. Specialties: Toast skagen, dolphin meuniere.
Lunch: Noon–2:30 p.m., entrees $10–$13.
Dinner: 6:30–9:30 p.m., entrees $25–$40.

Although Austrian chef and restaurateur extraordinaire Josef Schwaiger sold his well-loved namesake restaurant to open two other fashionable spots, the flame has passed splendidly to Swedish chef Nils Ryman. Ryman has kept Josef's more stellar creations on the mostly seafood menu, including the sublime dolphin meuniere, but has added some fine dishes of his own, namely a smorrebrod of shrimp with dill mayonnaise. It might be difficult to snag a dinner reservation, but a weekday lunch is a viable option for a smoked fish or chef's salad. No lunch served on weekends.

Waterfront Cafe **$$$** ★★

The Careenage, Bridgetown, ☎ *(809) 431-0303.*
International cuisine.
Lunch: 10 a.m.–2 p.m., entrees $8–$25.
Dinner: 2–10 p.m., entrees $8–$30.

The Waterfront Cafe is an inexpensive cool-off eatery on the Careenage, a small inlet for light craft. It serves Bajan-inspired quick meals like pepper pot soup, a copious appetizer platter and flying fish interspersed with familiar burgers and English pub food. There's music every evening, usually jazz, and a relaxed bar scene. Seating is either outdoors facing the water or in the dining room.

Christ Church

Da Luciano's **$$$** ★★

Staten, Christ Church, ☎ *(809) 437-7544.*
Italian cuisine.
Dinner: 6:30-10:30 p.m., entrees $19–$33.

A lot of care goes into the presentation and preparation of the Italian food served here in a handsome old home, Staten, a historical landmark near a white sand beach popular with locals. Starters include a mixed seafood platter and antipasto, and main courses and pastas are hearty and often infused with plenty of garlic.

David's Place **$$$** ★★★★

St. Lawrence Main Road, Christ Church, ☎ *(809) 435-6550.*
Latin American cuisine. Specialties: Baxter Street fried chicken.
Lunch: 11 a.m.–3 p.m., entrees $9–$13.
Dinner: 6-10 p.m., entrees $14–$30.

Wear loose clothing to eat this delicious Bajan food in a pretty cottage beside St. Lawrence Bay, where every table has an ocean view. A spicy fried chicken named in honor of the Baxter Street food vendors is a specialty, as is pepperpot and pumpkin soup. Huge helpings of rice and peas, cheese bread, potatoes and vegetables come with all the entrees, but you can't stop there. Make room for fantastic desserts like coconut cream pie if you can—you won't regret it.

Ile de France **$$$** ★★★★

Hastings, Christ Church, ☎ *(809) 435-6869.*
French cuisine. Specialties: Foie gras.
Dinner: 6:30-10 p.m., entrees $18–$38.

An innovative French restaurant located on the lush grounds of one of Barbados' traditional hotels, the Windsor Arms, Ile de France brings Gallic intensity to its slower-paced, old-fashioned surroundings. Many classic dishes are represented, including a definitive foie gras and ballotine de canard (one of the owners is from Toulouse), escargots de Bourgogne, and crepes flambeed at tableside. The atmosphere is sublime and unobtrusive, with candlelight, subtle lighting and music.

Pisces **$$$** ★★★★

St. Lawrence Gap, Christ Church, ☎ *(809) 435-6564.*
Seafood cuisine. Specialties: Red snapper caribe.
Dinner: 6-10 p.m., entrees $15–$30.

Flowers, greenery, an oceanfront table and an impeccable reputation for fresh seafood draws visitors to Pisces again and again. Red snapper caribe with tomatoes and shrimp is an ongoing special, although it may be difficult to choose an entree from the long and varied menu that invariably includes the catch of the day served any style, with a butter sauce or with Jamaican jerk seasonings. There's a refreshing gazpacho and a few meat, chicken and vegetarian dishes.

T.G.I. Boomers **$$** ★★

St. Lawrence Gap, Christ Church, ☎ *(809) 428-8439.*
International cuisine. Specialties: Flying fish.
Lunch: 11:30 a.m.–6 p.m., entrees $4–$11.
Dinner: 6-10 p.m., entrees $11–$17.

This very welcome (for variety and bargain prices) bar-restaurant near Rockley Beach serves three meals a day, including an all-American breakfast of bacon and eggs, french toast or an omelette (with coffee and juice) for $6.50. At lunch, burgers, deli and fish sandwiches and vegetarian dishes are offered for under $10. Dinner plates of steak or seafood are garnished with vegetables, rice or potatoes and soup or salad. It also serves the needs of party types and barhoppers with daiquiris and other blender drinks at the bar, which stays open until midnight.

Witch Doctor **$$$** ★★

St. Lawrence Gap, Christ Church, ☎ *(809) 435-6581.*
Latin American cuisine. Specialties: Pumpkin soup.
Dinner: 6:15-9:45 p.m., entrees $13–$30.

You'll think you're on another island when dining at this wild jungle-themed dining room serving spicy, innovative and traditional island cuisine. If the decor doesn't get to you, the good food will satisfy, including creamy pumpkin soup, seafood cocktail marinated in lime and flying fish.

St. Peter

Atlantis Hotel **$$$** ★★

Bathsheba, St. James Parish, ☎ *(809) 433-9445.*
Latin American cuisine. Specialties: Pepper pot stew, flying fish.
Lunch: Noon–3 p.m., prix fixe $12–$17.
Dinner: 7–9 p.m., prix fixe $15–$17.

You might go without a full meal for a week after the enormous Sunday brunch at the Atlantis Hotel, a traditional hostelry with a breathtaking sea vista. Although this dining room operated by owner Enid Maxwell serves set lunches and dinners at very reasonable prices, Sunday is when everyone (including tour groups) blows in. The tables groan with authentic "Bajan" specialties, including pepper pot stew (assorted meats in a rich broth, simmered for days), breadfruit, flying fish and rice and peas. If lines are overwhelming, try the Edgewater Hotel dining room nearby ☎ *(433-9902).*

Carambola $$$ ★★★★

Derricks, St. James Parish, ☎ *(809) 432-0832.*
French cuisine.
Dinner: 6:30–9:30 p.m., entrees $20–$40.

This old favorite is still wowing a select group who ooh and aah over the spicy Thai-French cuisine (a unique combination) served in a cliffside dining room, with the sea lapping 10 feet below. Carambola is located in a converted old home north of Bridgetown in St. James Parish, where chef Paul Owens and owner Robin Walcott have prepared and planned such delights as green or red curry chicken or filet of dolphin with dijon mustard sauce. It's too bad that only dinner is served, because the view is spectacular.

Koko's $$$ ★★★

Prospect House, St. James Parish, ☎ *(809) 424-4557.*
Latin American cuisine. Specialties: Pepper pot soup, seafood.
Dinner: 6:30–10 p.m., entrees $12–$22.

The chef here is a talented saucier, creating a symphony of flavors that accentuate the freshly caught shellfish and game garnishing the colorful plates. The beach setting is pretty, with tables set on the patio of a traditional Bajan house on the west coast of the island. The food is largely island-style, with pepper pot soup often on hand, as well as lightly fried shellfish cakes in a tangy citrus and mayonnaise sauce.

La Cage aux Folles $$$ ★★★★

Summerland Great House, St. James Parish, ☎ *(809) 424-2424.*
International cuisine. Specialties: Sesame prawn pate, orange peel chicken.
Dinner: 7–10:30 p.m., entrees $25–$38.

There aren't any showgirls with feathered plumes anywhere in sight at this eclectic Asian-Caribbean restaurant. The setting, in the Summerland Great House, a restored plantation, is entertainment enough. The food, luckily, plays a stellar role, with Chinese crispy duck, sesame prawn pate and orange peel chicken as predominant examples. There's a balcony for cocktails and a view of lush gardens, and an intimate antique-filled room for private parties within. Owners are experienced restaurateurs with establishments in London.

La Maison $$$ ★★★

Balmore House, St. James Parish, ☎ *(809) 432-1156.*
Seafood cuisine.
Dinner: 6:30–10 p.m., entrees $23–$40.

Comfortably positioned in yet another Great House on the St. James coast (will they ever run out of them?), La Maison has been wowing visitors and residents alike since it opened in the early 1990s with sophisticated, French-inspired seafood. Dining here is likened to a posh beach camp-out, with tables set out on the sand under a tent or indoors in a courtyard exposed to ocean breezes and views. The ever-changing menu may feature salmon with cream sauce, marinated flying fish and rich ice cream or chocolate desserts.

Raffles Old Towne $$$ ★★★★

1st Street, St. James Parish, ☎ *(809) 432-6557.*
International cuisine. Specialties: Curries.
Dinner: 7–10 p.m., entrees $25–$35.

Named after the Raffles Hotel in Singapore and inspired by British colonial exploits abroad, this highly regarded restaurant employs a big-game hunter theme in an intimate room close to the ocean in Holetown. Naturally, there are curries and chutneys, blackened fish and chicken, and a full-course dinner for $40. Raffles rates three "knives and forks" (the highest culinary honor) from the Barbados Tourism Authority.

Reid's **$$$** ★★★

Derricks, St. James Parish,
International cuisine. Specialties: Lobster.
Dinner: 7–10 p.m., entrees $21–$40.
Fresh fish, lobster and escargots in white wine and garlic are served to diners at this plantation building south of Holetown. Reservations should be made a few days in advance to enjoy manicured garden views, gurgling fountains and a well-chosen wine list.

The Fathoms **$$$** ★★★★

Paynes Bay, St. James Parish, ☎ *(809) 432-2568.*
International cuisine. Specialties: Lobster, octopus.
Lunch: 11 a.m.–3 p.m., entrees $6–$8.
Dinner: 6:30–10 p.m., entrees $15–$29.
Daring seafood dishes are the hallmark of this ocean-view, red-roofed spot on Paynes Bay, near Holetown. You can stick with a grilled lobster, stuffed crab or catch of the day, but octopus and sea eggs (white sea urchins' roe, prepared deviled or breaded) are sometimes on the menu. At night it's romantic with candlelight and crashing waves for sound effects; other times it's Bajan casual. Besides seafood, there are burgers, salads and pork crepes. With less than 25 tables in the dining area, make reservations well in advance.

The Mews **$$$** ★★★

Second Street, St. James Parish, ☎ *(809) 432-1122.*
Seafood cuisine. Specialties: Fresh fish.
Dinner: 7–10 p.m., entrees $20–$30.
This is one of two new restaurants opened by award-winning chef Josef Schwaiger, who sold his popular Josef's in St. Lawrence Gap. It's already very successful among his many admirers and assorted fish fanciers (Josef's specialty) who like to dine in a trellised garden on paupiettes of snapper and a sublime lime mousse. Before or apres dinner, walk across the street to **Nico's Champagne and Wine Bar**, ☎ *(809) 432-0832* for some bubbly or chablis by the glass.

Where to Shop

Even the shopping scene in Barbados has been recently spruced up, with the addition of more stores to an already bulging array of specialty boutiques, departments stores and resort-wear shops spread throughout the island. Even the beach peddlers have new kiosks. At the newly renovated cruise terminal (probably the best in the Caribbean), you can stroll through an attractive indoor shopping and entertainment arcade lined with 20 duty-free shops, crafts boutiques and restaurants—all designed to resemble a West Indian town with gingerbread cottages in pastel colors. Cruise passengers (and other foreign tourists) can choose among jewelry, liquor, china, electronics, perfume and leather goods, all duty-free for U.S. citizens (with savings of up to 40 percent off U.S. prices). There are also shops of Barbadian woodcarvings and fine art galleries as well as clothing and souvenir boutiques. Here you can also find a tourist information center, car and bike rentals, automated teller machines, florists, dive shops and a communications center with fax and phones.

Most resort hotels have a bevy of boutiques at their entrance or on premises, but prices are usually marked way up; you pay for the convenience (the Hilton and Sandy Lane do have interesting stock, however). If you're looking for department stores (and impressive ones for an island), head for downtown (especially **Da Costas Mall** with more than 50 stores), but branches can usually be found in resort communities as well as at **Holetown** and **Speightstown**, where you also find specialty boutiques of top quality and resort-wear shops. On the west coast, there is the **Sunset Crest** shopping mall.

Perhaps the most outstanding Bajan art you can take home is **pottery**. Native potters use clay from the area, eschewing cheap souvenir figurines and instead fashioning the traditional shapes used in Bajan kitchens, such as the monkey pot that actually makes water taste better since it can be stored at the proper temperature. The ramshackle town of **Chalky Mount**, high on a cliff overlooking Barbados' northeastern St. Andrew parish, is considered to be the epicenter of Bajan folk art. Here, every home has a potter's wheel and fathers pass down the craft techniques to their sons, a tradition that dates back 300 years. Best pottery can be found at **Chalky Mount Potter** ☎ *(809) 422-9619* and also at **Springer's Pottery** ☎ *(809) 422-9682.*

Other local crafts include black-coral jewelry, attractive wall hangings made from dried grasses and flowers, and straw mats, baskets and bags. Leatherwork is just beginning to find its place among Bajan craft art.

Barbados Directory

BUSINESS HOURS

Stores open weekdays 8 a.m.–4 p.m., Saturday 8 a.m.–1 p.m. Banks open Monday–Thursday 8 a.m.–3 p.m. and Friday 9 a.m.–5 p.m.

CLIMATE

Constant northeast trade winds keep temperatures between 75-85 degrees F year-round. The wet season, from June to November, is more humid than at any other time; September and October are the rainiest months. Weather can change quickly—in a cross trip on the island from west to east, you can start out with sunny skies and end up in a raging storm. Rainfall varies from 50 inches on the coast to 75 inches in the higher interior.

CRUISES

Cruise ships dock at the Deep Water Harbour's pier. Most folks on a limited time schedule head for Pelican Village to do some shopping. You can easily catch a taxi waiting at the dock. (The walk can get long and hot!)

DOCUMENTS

U.S.and Canadian citizens need to show proof of citizenship (passport, birth certificate, or voter's registration card, along with a government-issued photo ID, like a driver's license). Also required is an ongoing or return ticket.There is a departure tax of U.S. $12.50.

ELECTRICITY

The current is 100 volts, 50 cycles, as in the U.S., though the speed is somewhat slower. Hotels with 220 volts usually provide adapters.

GETTING AROUND

If you rent a car, you'll need your own license, plus a driver's permit issued at the airport by the police or your rental agency for a $5 fee. Take the insurance ($5 a day) if you're not sure you are already covered. Note that driving is on the left.

The most highly recommended car-rental agency is **National Car Rental**, Bush Hall, Main Road, St. Michael; ☎ *(809) 426-0603*. Cars will be delivered to a location anywhere on the island.

Also try **P&S Car Rentals** ☎ *(809) 424-2052 or 424-2907*, Pleasant View, Cave Hill, St. Michael; **Sunny Isle Motors**, ☎ *(809) 435-7979*.

In general, roads are well paved and locations well marked.

Taxi drivers are no longer naive on Barbados and know their way around know-nothing tourists. Ask your concierge or hotel management how much a particular trip should cost before you get in the taxi; otherwise you could get bilked.

Public buses are reliable and safe, but unbearably crowded at rush hours (8:30–9:30 a.m. and 3:30–6 p.m.). The route that runs down the south and west coast is an inexpensive way to see the island.

GUIDES

Although the more independent traveler prefers to rent his own car and toddle around on his own, hotels can arrange a personal guide for you if you want to see more of the island. Excellent service is offered by **Sally Shearn's VIP Tour Service** ☎ *(809) 429-4617*.

LANGUAGE

English is the official language, spoken with a pronounced island lilt.

MEDICAL EMERGENCIES

Top-class hotels usually have a doctor on call. Queen Elizabeth Hospital, located on Martinsdale Road in Bridgetown, is the preeminent training hospital in the Caribbean.

MONEY

The official currency is the Barbados dollar, worth about 50 cents in American currency. Most stores will accept American dollars and traveler's checks. However, to get your best rate, it's better to exchange your American dollars for Bajan ones at a bank.

TELEPHONE

Area code is 809.

TIPPING AND TAXES

Most restaurants add a 10 percent service charge. Feel free to tip extra if the service is especially fine.

TOURIST INFORMATION

The tourist office is located in the Harbour Industrial Park near the Deep Water Harbour in Bridgetown. You'll also find information posts at the airport and at the cruise ship pier at the Deep Water Harbour. They are only open weekdays. From the U.S. call ☎ *(213) 380-2198*.

WATER

Water is safe to drink in Barbados, pumped from an underground source in the island's coral reefs.

WHEN TO GO

Crop Over Festival in July and August is an islandwide celebration of Barbadian arts, food, music and dance, which harks back to the 19th century when the last of the year's sugarcane crop was feted. Three weeks of competitions, festivities, feasts and fairs celebrate the culture and history of the island. Kaddoment Day, a national holiday held on Aug. 1, is the culmination of the Crop Over Festival, with costumes, music, street dancing and fireworks. The Holetown Festival in February, commemorating the first settlement in 1627, is celebrated by a big street party, as is the Oistins Fish Festival at Easter. In November the National Independence Festival of Creative Arts (NIFCA) usually sponsors an annual month-long celebration of Barbadian talent competitions in art, music, song and dance. In July, the Sir Garfield Sobers International School's Cricket Tournament, named after a famous Barbadian cricketer, has become an international event, attracting worldwide participation.

Every Sunday year-round, traditional Sunday hikes are cosponsored by various charities, encouraging participants to walk at their own pace. Walks start at 6 a.m. and 3:30 p.m. Call the **Barbados National Trust** ☎ *(809) 428-5889*. On Sundays in January, **Barbados Horticultural Society's Open Garden Program** presents local gardeners displaying their gardens from 2–6 p.m. For more information, call ☎ *(809) 428-5889*. On Wednesday afternoons, January-April, **Barbados National Trust Open House Program** invites visitors to browse through the private homes of architectural and historical importance to the island.

The period between Christmas and Easter is the most popular time for tourists, though the British summer is busier than it used to be.

BARBADOS RESTAURANTS	PHONE	ENTREE	CR. CARDS
Bridgetown			
American			
★★ Chicken Barn, The		$3–$11	None
French			
★★★★ Bagatelle Great House	(809) 421-6767	$30–$35••	A, MC, V
International			
★★★ Josef's	(809) 435-6541	$10–$40	A, MC, V
★★ Carib Beach Bar		$6–$16	MC, V
★★ Waterfront Cafe	(809) 431-0303	$8–$30	A, MC, V
Latin American			
★★★ Brown Sugar	(809) 426-7684	$14–$25	A, DC, MC, V
Christ Church			
French			
★★★★ Ile de France	(809) 435-6869	$18–$38••	MC, V
International			
★★ T.G.I. Boomers	(809) 428-8439	$4–$17	A, MC, V

BARBADOS RESTAURANTS	PHONE	ENTREE	CR. CARDS
Italian			
★★ Da Luciano's	(809) 437-7544	$19–$33••	MC, V
Latin American			
★★★★ David's Place	(809) 435-6550	$9–$30	A, MC, V
★★ Witch Doctor	(809) 435-6581	$13–$30••	A, MC, V
Seafood			
★★★★ Pisces	(809) 435-6564	$15–$30••	A, MC, V
St. Peter			
French			
★★★★ Carambola	(809) 432-0832	$20–$40••	A, MC, V
International			
★★★★ La Cage aux Folles	(809) 424-2424	$25–$38••	MC, V
★★★★ Raffles Old Towne	(809) 432-6557	$25–$35••	A, DC, MC, V
★★★★ The Fathoms	(809) 432-2568	$6–$29	A, MC, V
★★★ Reid's		$21–$40••	A, MC, V
Latin American			
★★★ Koko's	(809) 424-4557	$12–$22••	MC, V
★★ Atlantis Hotel	(809) 433-9445	$12–$17	A
Seafood			
★★★ La Maison	(809) 432-1156	$23–$40••	MC, V
★★★ The Mews	(809) 432-1122	$20–$30••	A, MC, V

Note: • Lunch Only

•• Dinner Only

BELIZE

Mayan ruins throughout Belize continue to fascinate all who explore them.

Belize is not usually thought of as a Caribbean destination, located as it is in Central America between Mexico and Guatemala. But its huge barrier reef, second-largest in the world, makes it a haven for divers and fishermen. Add to that the mysterious appeal of well-preserved Mayan ruins, thick jungle teeming with exotic wildlife (including monkeys and jaguars), waters swum by the giant and gentle manatees and a system of caves beckoning to be explored, and it's no surprise that Belize has become *the* hot eco-tourism destination.

It's a designation Belizeans take seriously. As tourism continues its inevitable march through the country, both the government and concerned citizens are intent on ensuring that Belize remains wild and untamed. No one wants to see this nature-rich country succumb to the miles of concrete and luxury hotels that have overrun such spots as St. Martin and St. Thomas.

First-time visitors should keep in mind that Belize is about as Third World as they come. Even the "luxury" hotels of Belize City leave much to be desired when compared to the tony resorts that have become a Caribbean mainstay. It's best not to drink the water in most places, eschew ice in drinks

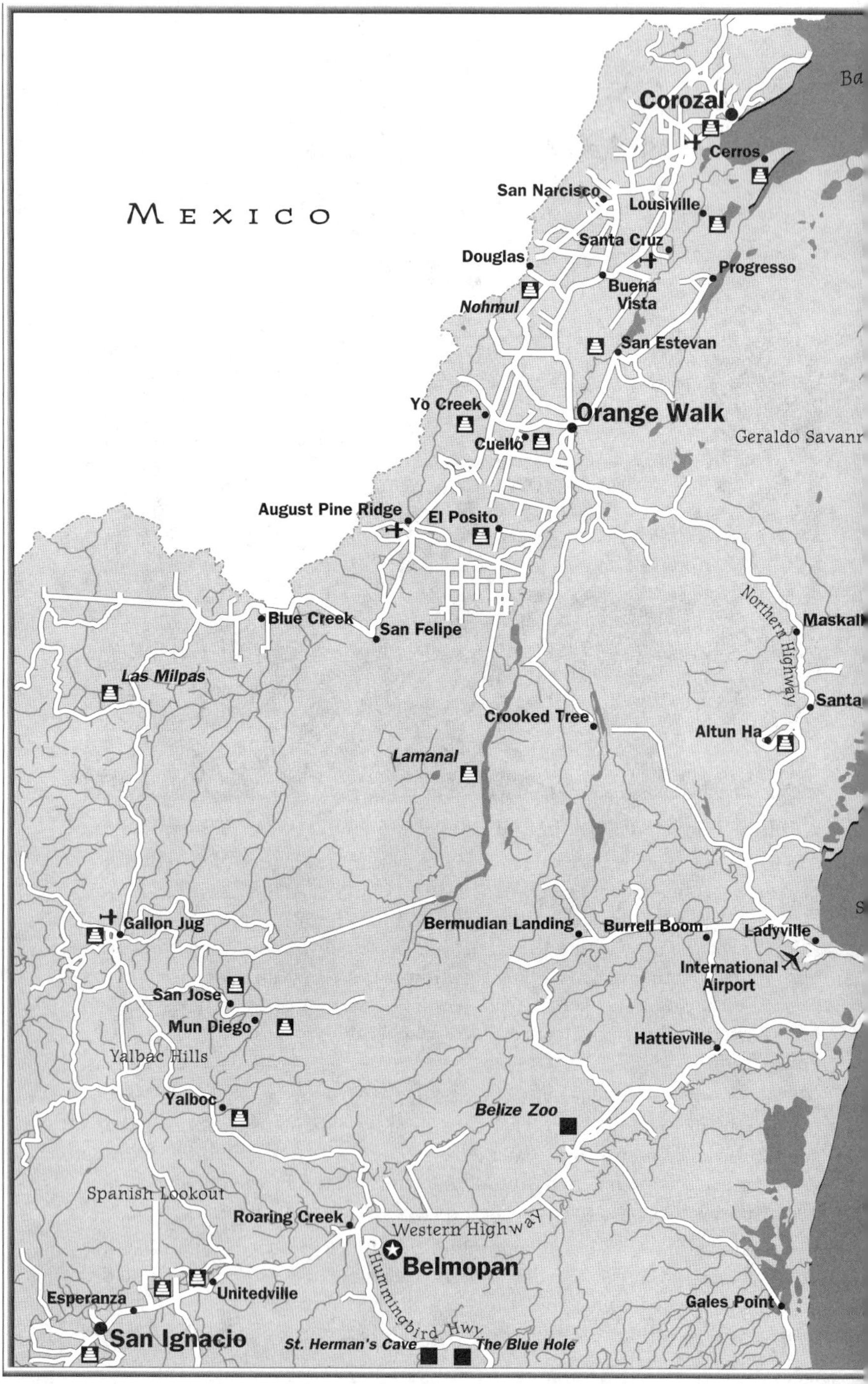
MEXICO
Corozal
Cerros
San Narcisco
Lousiville
Santa Cruz
Douglas
Progresso
Buena Vista
Nohmul
San Estevan
Yo Creek
Orange Walk
Cuello
Geraldo Savanr
August Pine Ridge
El Posito
Blue Creek
San Felipe
Northern Highway
Maskal
Las Milpas
Santa
Crooked Tree
Altun Ha
Lamanal
Gallon Jug
Bermudian Landing
Burrell Boom
Ladyville
International Airport
San Jose
Mun Diego
Hattieville
Yalbac Hills
Yalboc
Belize Zoo
Spanish Lookout
Roaring Creek
Western Highway
Belmopan
Hummingbird Hwy
Esperanza
Unitedville
Gales Point
San Ignacio
St. Herman's Cave
The Blue Hole

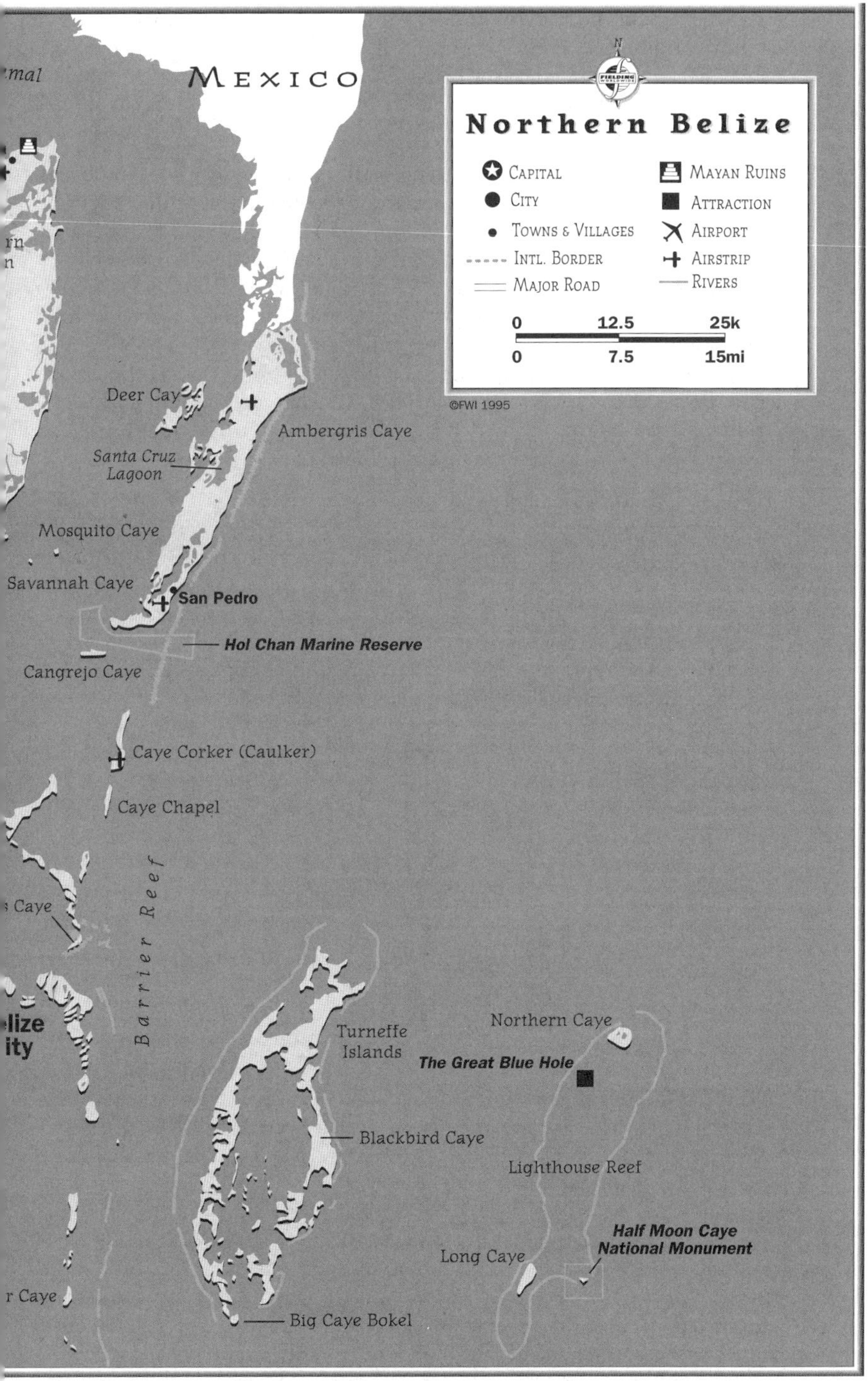

Northern Belize
Capital
City
Towns & Villages
Intl. Border
Major Road
Mayan Ruins
Attraction
Airport
Airstrip
Rivers
0 12.5 25k
0 7.5 15mi
©FWI 1995
Mexico
Deer Cay
Ambergris Caye
Santa Cruz Lagoon
Mosquito Caye
Savannah Caye
San Pedro
Hol Chan Marine Reserve
Cangrejo Caye
Caye Corker (Caulker)
Caye Chapel
Barrier Reef
Turneffe Islands
Northern Caye
The Great Blue Hole
Blackbird Caye
Lighthouse Reef
Half Moon Caye National Monument
Long Caye
Big Caye Bokel

and you should don enough insect repellant to kill a small army. Many roads are made of hard-packed sand filled with giant ruts, even the paved streets are horrendous, air conditioning is a rarity and the domestic airlines will give heart attacks to those who fear flying. Leave your memories of pampering trips to the Caymans and Martinique far behind, and prepare for an adventure of an entirely different ilk.

The democratic nation has two main parties, the United Democratic and the People's United, which local wags say exist only to throw the other out of power, mostly by exposing corruption. Sounds more than a bit similar to the United States, but in Belize, elections are really mainly by personalities and skeletons in closets—not issues. While some claim that enough money can open up any sensitive ecosystem to development, most hoteliers say they were pleasantly surprised that they never had to grease a palm to build their properties. The general consensus is that both parties are sincerely dedicated to preserving the country's natural assets. But Belize is a young and decidedly Third World nation, and it's fervently hoped that good intentions will not be forgotten in the heady lure of tourist dollars.

You, as a visitor, can help. Always stay on the trails, don't remove or disturb plants, don't touch or kick sand on coral, respect wildlife, use local guides when available and, very importantly, don't buy any sea turtle products; reptile skins and leather; birds, their feathers or skins; and furs of spotted cats (you'll never get them past customs anyway). As Belizeans struggle to cope with an influx of tourists, it's imperative visitors show them that they like the country just as it is. Belize will never have the sophistication of a San Juan or a Charlotte Amalie—and viva la difference!

Bird's Eye View

Sandwiched between the Mexican Yucatan and Guatemala, Belize is a small country, totaling just 8866 square miles (about the size of Massachusetts). It borders Guatemala to the west and the Caribbean Sea to the east. The country is well known for two features, one the work of nature and the other left by ancient man.

Lying just offshore is a large barrier reef, the longest in the Western Hemisphere and second in the world only to Australia's Great Barrier Reef. The reef stretches 200 miles from the Yucatan Peninsula to the Guatemalan border and is visable (as breaking waves) from most points on the mainland. There are also three coral atolls—**Turneffe Islands, Lighthouse Reef** and **Glover's Reef**—that give divers a total of 350 miles of reef to explore. Add more than 200 cayes (pronounced "key"), mostly uninhabited, and you have a true diver's paradise. The reef is also good for snorkelers, especially **Hol Chan Marine Reserve**, a five-square-mile underwater park with depths from 3 to 30 feet, located off the coast of San Pedro in **Ambergris Caye**.

The "other" Belize is on the mainland, an area rich in ruins from the remarkable Mayan civilization that lived in the area from 2000 B.C. to A.D. 1000. No one is quite sure what happened to these flourishing, advanced peoples, but a visit to at least one ruin is *de rigueur.*

In the north, the land is mostly flat, while the southern regions encompass the craggy **Maya Mountains**. Many rivers meander through the land, their banks lined with monkeys, parrots and toucans in the trees, their waters filled with manatees, crocodiles and trophy-size fish.

Much of the country is given over to jungle and rainforest, and numerous sanctuaries provide safe havens for howler monkeys (locally called baboons), jaguars, tapirs, pumas, ocelots, hundreds of bird species and other exotic creatures.There are caves to be spelunked, rivers to cruise, mangrove swamps to be explored and giant waterfalls to splash about in.

The Cayes

Belize's 100 or so cayes (pronounced "key") are mostly uninhabited, but several, notably **Ambergris Caye** (see separate section) and **Caye Caulker** cater to tourists, especially divers eager to explore the surrounding crystal-clear waters.

Located just 19 miles northeast of Belize City, Caye Caulker is a peaceful little island (five miles long and a half-mile wide) with streets of sand. The island is sliced in two by a narrow passageway called the **Split**, which was created by Hurricane Hattie in 1961. While tearing the island in two, Hattie created a small beach and excellent snorkeling.

The north section is given over to mangrove swamps and nesting birds; there's a total of 139 species, with more than 20 percent indigenous to Belize. It's in the south end where all the action takes place—though "action" is a relative word in such a quaint, laid-back place.

A handful of streets are lined with boutiques, clapboard houses, inns and wooden, slat-style lobster pots. There are only a few cars—most folks get around on golf cart (even the taxis), bicycle or foot.

The barrier reef is visible from most points in town and is the reason divers and fishermen flock here. **Hol Chan Marine Reserve** (also excellent for snorkeling), the famed **Blue Hole at Lighthouse Reef**, and a recently discovered underground cave system keep divers fascinated. Other nearby prime diving sites include **Pyramid Flats, Long Caye, Coral Caverns** and **Sergeant's Caye**. A popular day trip is to **Goff's Caye**, a tiny tropical island with exactly 13 palm trees.

History

It's interesting to think that when Jesus walked the Earth as man, some 750,000 Mayas lived in what is now Belize. They planted corn everywhere and built impressive cities and ceremonial centers of limestone. But, a thousand years later, as Europe entered the Dark Ages, the Maya civilization collapsed, for reasons still unclear.

Five centuries later, the Spanish captured Mexico and Central America, and the few Maya left were kept in virtual slavery. Today's jungles and rainforests developed and mahogany flourished. British pirates (called logcutters, then later, Baymen) arrived in the 1600s and went to work harvesting the highly valued mahogany. The Spaniards sent troops to kick the British out, but five tries later, the logcutters remained.

Finally, Spain signed a treaty with England granting the Baymen the right to cut wood between the Honro and Belize rivers. But when the Spanish governor of Yucatan tried to remove the Baymen from the Hondo River, England intervened with a fleet of ships and soldiers under the command of Admiral Sir William Burnaby.

No violence was necessary; the dispute had already been settled before the admiral arrived in 1765. Before leaving, though, he crafted Burnaby's Code, a constitution-like document that established the public meeting as the supreme lawmaking body. This code was honored until 1862, when Queen Victoria granted the settlement English colonial status, and the area became known as British Honduras. In 1870, British Honduras was named a Crown Colony.

Meanwhile, Maya refugees from Mexico began flooding into Belize and, among other things, introduced sugarcane. But sugar prices crashed in the 1880s, and World War I effectively killed the demand for mahogany. The colony became entrenched in poverty. It wasn't until after World War II, when Belizean soldiers came home with new ideas for the colony's future, that things started looking up.

On December 31, 1949, the British Government devalued the British Honduras dollar. That sparked the Movement of Liberation—formed the very next day—which finally succeeded in 1964, when the colony became a self-governing nation. The name was officially changed to Belize in 1973—it had been called that for years, though no what knows exactly where the word comes from or what it means. On September 21, 1981, Belize became an independent nation.

Today, the country is a democracy that belongs to the United Nations, the Commonwealth and the Non-Aligned Movement. The government is dedicated to opening the country to tourism while at the same time preserving its rich natural assets.

Mayan Ruins

Hundreds of years later, the scientific community continues to be baffled by the ancient Mayan civilization that lived in Mexico and Central America. Who were they? How did they erect such impressive buildings? And where did they all go?

Mayans inhabited the area from 2000 B.C. to 1000 A.D. They were a remarkably advanced people, well-honed in science, trade and art, and built sophisticated cities and temples. Between 250 and 900 A.D., the peak of the Classic period, literally millions of Mayans lived in Belize, which was considered the heart of the Mayan Empire. Mayan ruins are found throughout the country, some remarkably preserved—and many more, undoubtedly, sleeping far beneath the jungle floor. You'll easily find the major ruins on tourist maps or by asking at your hotel. The ruins feature incredibly steep steps—the reward for climbing to the top is awesome views, but take great care, as the stones are often quite slippery.

Located 31 miles north of Belize City, **Altun Ha** (Water of the Rock) is one of the easier explored ruins. It's also one of the country's most important, as the jade head found here is the national symbol of Belize. The head, the largest carved jade object in the entire Maya area, represents the sun god, Kinich Ahau, and is on the corner of every Belize dollar. Altun Ha was a major ceremonial center in the Classic Period and a vital trading center with Maya centers in the interior.

One of the most significant ruins is **Caracol** (The Snail), located south of San Ignacio. It wasn't until the 1980s that archeologists realized its importance as the "supreme" Maya city, after unearthing an elaborately carved altar stone that describes a victory by Caracol over Tikal, once considered the most important Maya metropolis. The impressive ruins include a *canaa* (sky palace) that rises 140 feet—the tallest man-made structure in Belize.

Located on the New River Lagoon, **Lamanai** (Submerged Crocodile) is one of the nation's largest ceremonial centers and had a long occupation, from 1500 B.C. to the 19th century, when the Spaniards came. Among the ruins are a sugar mill and two Christian churches.

La Milpa, in the Rio Bravo Conservation Area in northwestern Belize, is Belize's third-largest site, featuring more than 85 structures and 24 courtyards, including the enormous **Great Plaza**.

Cahal Pech (Place of the Ticks), located in the Cayo District on the west bank of the Macal River, is a medium-sized Maya center. The best reason to come here are the fantastic views of San Ignacio and the Belize River Valley.

Other important sites include **Lubaantun** (Place of Fallen Stones), a late Classic ceremonial center northwest of Punta Gorda (a 20-minute walk from the road); **Cerros**, a short boat ride from Corozal Town in the Bay of Chetumal, an important coastal trading center during the late Pre-Classic period (100 B.C.–A.D. 250); and **Xunantunich** (Maiden of the Rock), a major ceremonial center on a natural limestone ridge, located near the western border across the river from San Jose Succotz.

People

Belize's 200,000 residents are a blend of Creole (the majority at 60 percent), Maya, Mestizo (a mix of Spanish and Indian), Mennonites (conservative farmers and furniture makers), immigrants from India, and Garifua (black Carib Indians who perform ritualistic dances). There are expatriates from Europe, Asia and the United States.

Education is a top national priority, and 90 percent of the population is literate, though school is mandatory only until age 14. After that, students must pay to attend high school, a price out of reach of most Belizean families.

The people are generally friendly and open. A smile is invariably returned, and children who bump into you on the street will offer a sincere and polite apology. Though crime is a serious problem in Belize City, the rest of the nation is relatively safe—though, of course, care should always be taken when engaging strangers in conversation and carrying valuables.

Beaches

Belize has ancient ruins, renowned sportsfishing and wonderful diving—but not, alas, great beaches. Much of the coast is given over to mangrove swamps. Even on Ambergris Caye, which has a sandy coast dotted with swaying coconut trees, you generally can't swim off the beach unless you don't mind mucking about in sea grass and the guts of fish stripped clean by those who caught them. (Good swimming can generally be found at the end of the boat docks that jut from nearly every hotel.) To the south, Placencia has picturesque beaches, but again, sea grass keeps most swimmers out.

What Else to See

Belize may be small in size, but it's full of things to do and see. One of the more popular activities for visitors is swimming with manatees. Belize is said to have the largest population of the playful, shy sea cows in the world. **Excalibur's** *(59 Barrier Reef Drive (Front Street), San Pedro,* ☎ *(501) 26-3235)* offers a trip to **Goff's Caye**; en route, the boat stops to let snorkelers frolic among the manatees, which the company says are "100 percent guaranteed."

Caving is also popular; the rutted **Hummingbird Highway**, which links Belmopan and Dangriga, has several along its route. At **Caves Branch**, you can float on an inner tube through miles of underground river caves, many with Maya artifacts and wall carvings. Professional guides are mandatory; call ☎ *(501) 2-33903.* Also worth exploring is **St. Herman's Cave**, where spears, torches and pottery have been recovered. To get there, take the trail from Blue Hole, but beware, it's a killer. There are also caves to explore around San Ignacio in the Cayo District, including the Chumpiate Maya, a limestone cave with enormous Maya pottery that's been untouched for eons.

River trips through mangrove swamps are available from most destinations throughout the country. One of the best is along the **Monkey River**, south of Placencia. Chances are good you'll spot manatees, iguanas, howler monkeys and lots of exotic birds during the five-mile float. Part of the Bladen River Reserve, the Monkey is Belize's largest protected river.

If you're into butterflies, they've got them by the bushel at San Ignacio's **Butterfly Breeding Centre** *(☎ (501) 92-2037).* The chief attraction here is the blue morpho, known as the "Belizean Blue."

Wildlife of a wilder kind can sometimes be spotted at the **Cockscomb Basin Sanctuary** near Dangriga. This is the world's first and only jaguar preserve. The cats are nocturnal, so you probably won't see them by day, but overnight excursions can be arranged by calling ☎ *(501) 2-77369.*

Parks and Gardens

Belize Zoo ★★★★

Mile 30, Western highway, Belize City.

Hours open: 10 a.m.–5 p.m.

The Belize Zoo and Tropical Education Center was opened in 1983 by Sharon Malota, who was seeking a home for a small group of animals no longer needed by a natural film producer. Today the zoo totals 28 acres and has more than 100 species of native animals, including many endangered species such as the jaguar, tapir and howler monkey. The zoo is small by U.S. standards, but internationally respected for the good care its animals receive and the emphasis on education and conservation. Animals are enclosed in thatch-roof cages with lots of natural bush, so you'll go to some effort to spot them. Frustrating perhaps, but not nearly as depressing as a visit to a zoo where the poor creatures sit bored in concrete cages. The biggest attraction is April, a 500-pound tapir (Belize's national animal) who resides in her own pond and is a big hit with the many schoolkids who pass through.

Tours

Community Baboon Sanctuary ★★★★★

Bermudian Landing, near Belize City.

Hours open: 8 a.m.–5 p.m.

Don't come expecting large black monkeys thumping their chests—the animals here are the small howler monkeys (locally known as baboons). Called an "experiment in grass-roots conservation," the sanctuary comprises 20 square miles of eight villages, where some 130 landowners have voluntarily left trees intact at riverbeds and boundary lines to give the thriving population of howler monkeys a viable habitat. After touring the small but crammed museum on the Belize ecosystem, a guide takes you into the jungle, where chances are excellent you'll spot a family of the little rascals. The father of the group lets out a strange howl that sounds like water going down a rusty drain—hence the name. You'll also spot leaf-cutting ants industrially going about their business, and, alas, more mosquitoes than imaginable. Wear lots of repellant and bring your camera.

Crooked Tree Wildlife Sanctuary ★★★

two miles off the Northern Highway, near Belize City.

Located 33 miles northwest of Belize City, this bird sanctuary is home to the jabiru stork, the largest bird in the Western Hemisphere with a wingspan of eight feet. You'll also spot snail kites, snowy egrets, and five species of kingfisher, among other feathered friends. The 3000-acre park, founded by the Belize Audubon Society, has swamps, lagoons and waterways. Hire a local guide at the village of Crooked Tree for the best views of this fascinating slice of nature.

Tour Companies

Belize City.

Melmish Mayan Tours *(☎ (501) 2-45551)* in Belize City offers a variety of tours of Maya ruins, the Baboon Sanctuary, into the jungle and caves and along rivers. They're highly reputable and a pleasure to deal with. Other major tour operators in the city include **Mayaland Tours and Travel** *(☎ (501) 2-30515)*, **Belize Travel Adventures** *(☎ (501) 2-33064)*, **Belize Land Air Sea Tours** *(☎ (501) 2-2-73897)* and **Discovery Expeditions Belize** *(☎ (501) 2-30748)*. **Tubroos Tree Adventures** *(☎ (501) 2-33398)* offers specialty tours on natural history and archaeology, while **Native Guide Systems** *(☎ (501) 2-75819)* can tailor special tours for birding, kayaking and sightseeing. In San Pedro on Ambergris Caye, tour companies include **Island Adventures** *(☎ (501) 26-2697)*, **Rocks Inn** *(☎ (501) 26-2362)* and **Belize Visitor & Tours** *(☎ (501) 26-2728)*. In Placencia, Ellis Burgess is a laid-back guide who will take you just about any place you want to go in his plush red van. He's easy to find just by asking around. Other tour guides include **P.I. Tours** *(☎ (501) 62-3291)* and **Seahorse Guides** *(☎ (501) 62-3175)*. On Caye Caulker, try **Cari Search LTD** *(☎ (501) 2-22178)* for tours with marine biologists. The **Caye Caulker Tour Guide Association** *(☎ (501) 2-22285)* and **Harrison Tours** *(☎ (501) 2-22263)* offer general excursions, while **International Cultural Tours** *(☎ (501) 2-22285)* conducts tours with an emphasis on culture, ecology and local customs.

Sports

Besides trekking through the jungle, most athletic pursuits in Belize take place off its shores in the Caribbean Sea. Diving, of course, is the biggest attraction, But sports fishing is also immensely popular, and fishermen from the world over love to tell tales of the ones that got away—and the ones that didn't—in Belize.

Bonefishing takes place year-round along the coast and at offshore cayes. The most popular fishing spots are **Ambergris Caye** (where the fish averages three pounds), **Turneffe Islands** (where you can expect sizes of five pounds), **Tobacco Caye** and **Glover's Reef**. Trophy size is considered eight pounds. Fly fishing is the preferred method; a nine-weight fly rod, nine-weight floating rod and small fly are recommended. With spinning gear, use a six- to eight-pound line and small jig or hook and hermit crab as bait.

Placencia is the best spot to fish for permit, also found year-round closer to the reef and drop-offs on the flats. They average about 10 pounds, with trophy sizes about 30 pounds. Fly fishers should use a 10-weight rod, weight-forward floating line and 14- to 15-pound leader.

Other game to try for include tarpon (found April through November along the flats and cayes and June and July on the reef at Ambergris Caye), snook (found on flats close to the mainland from November through March), and, along the barrier reef, mutton and yellowtail snapper, grouper, jack crevalle and barracuda

Belize's many rivers—particularly the Sibun and Belize—also offer up great rewards. The quarry here is snook, tarpon, cubera snapper and jewfish, which can grow to 200 pounds. All can be found year-round, through the best time for tarpon is April and May when the fish spawn.

Fishing the flats costs about $100 to $250 for a half or full day. Full-day deep-sea fishing trips start at $350. River excursions go for $125 to $250 for a half or full day. A tip of $20 per full day of fishing is considered the norm.

Bring your own equipment, as tackleshops are few and far between. You'll have no problem finding a guide—the country teems with them. For more information, contact the **Belize Game Fishing Association** at ☎ *(501) 2-77044.* Also pick up *Destination Belize*, the nation's official visitor magazine, which supplied information for this section and contains a wealth of detailed tips for reeling in the big one.

Diving

Belize City.

There are more mosquitoes on Belize than diving companies, but not many more. The list of operators is far too long to include in these pages, but here are some of the larger companies. Ambergris Caye (San Pedro): **Old Island Divers** *(☎ (501) 26-2151 and (800) 258-3465)*, **Amigos del Mar** *(☎ (501) 26-2706)*, **Excalibur Dives** *(☎ (501) 26-3235)* **Blue Hole Center** *(☎ (501) 26-2982)*, **Tortuga** *(☎ (501) 26-2804)* and **Belize Dive Center** *(☎ (501) 26-2797)*. **Reef Seeker** *(☎ (501) 26-2804)* offers glass-bottom boat trips for snorkelers (rent your equipment before departing), and is unique in that even if just one person signs up, they'll still make the trip. Placencia: **Placencia Dive Shop** *(☎ (501) 62-3227)*, **Deep End Dive Shop** *(☎ (501) 62-3295)*, **Rum Point Divers** *(☎ (501) 62-3239)* and **Seahorse Guides** *(☎ (501) 62-3166)*. Belize City: **Blackline Marine Service** *(☎ (501) 2-33187)*, **Western Caribbean Live Aboard** *(☎ (501) 2-32810)* and **Blue Planet Divers** *(☎ (501) 26-76770)*. Caye Caulker: **Belize Diving Service** *(☎ (501) 2-22143)*, **Caye Caulker School of Scuba** *(☎ (501) 2-22292)* and **Frenchie's Diving Service** *(☎ (501) 2-22234)*.

Fishing

Belize City.

Fishing is big business in Belize, and you'll have no problem finding a guide to take you to the hot spots, be it along the barrier reef, off an atoll or along a river. Here are some of the major operators. Ambergris Caye (San Pedro): **Deep Sea Charter Fishing** *(☎ (501) 26-2911)*, **Amigos del Mar** *(☎ (501) 26-2648)*, **Captain Morgan's Retreat** *(800-447-2931)*, **El Pescador Hotel** *(☎ (501) 26-2398)* and **Excalibur Tours** *(☎ (501) 26-3235)*. Placencia: **Blue River Guiding** *(☎ (501) 62-3130)*, **Kingfisher Sports** *(☎ (501) 62-3175)*, **P&P Sport Fishing** *(☎ (501) 62-3132)*,

Seahorse Guides *(☎ (501) 62-3166)*, **Southern Guide** *(☎ (501) 62-3277)* and **Westby Sportsfishing** *(☎ (501) 62-3234)*. Belize City: **Belize Travel Adventures** *(☎ (501) 2-33064)*, **Belize River Lodge** *(☎ (501) 2-52002)*, **Discovery Expeditions** *(☎ (501) 2-30748)*, **Ramada Royal Reef Marina** *(☎ (501) 2-32670)* and **Zippy Zappy Boating Service** *(☎ (501) 2-75033)*. Caye Caulker: **Roque's Fishing and River Tours** *(☎ (501) 2-22014)* and **Allan Nunez Reef Trips** *(☎ (501) 2-22285)*.

Belize City

Blessed are those who expect nothing, for they shall never be disappointed. Keep that in mind when you visit Belize City, the nation's only urban area that's home to some 80,000 residents. Though it has some decent accommodations and a few sites worth seeing, the city is rundown, grungy and not especially worth visiting. Many folks leave immediately after clearing customs at Philip S.W. Goldson International Airport—and they're not missing much.

Still, the city does have some charms. It's cut in two by the narrow (and quite polluted) Haulover Creek, with three bridges spanning its width. The charming one is the **Swing Bridge**, which dates from the early 1900s. Nine men labor to open the bridge by hand crank each day at 5:30 a.m. and 5:30 p.m. Hours before, an array of boats, including some dubious-looking makeshift skiffs, line up and "park." It's a colorful sight.

Downtown's two main streets are called Albert and Regent. They're lined with cafes, shops, offices (it's strange to hear the clatter of typewriters) and outdoor vendors displaying a curious collection of goods—a typical stall has cheap tableware, pots and pans, racy comic books and large quantities of sexy lingerie. These entrepreneurs are mellow, letting passersby peruse their wares without the obnoxious pushiness that plagues Jamaica and the Bahamas.

What does plague the city is crime. Muggings and purse snatchings are all too common, and virtually every structure—even the expensive homes in the Caribbean Shores district—has bars on the windows. It's hoped the addition of tourism police and a new quick trial system with harsh punishments will put a dent in youthful crime. Recently, two boys aged 17 and 19 were sentenced to 14 years apiece for hitting a woman while stealing her gold chain.

Though it fronts the Caribbean Sea, the city has no beaches. You can stroll the seafront promenade and gaze with awe at the giant pelicans that hang out in the **Fort George** area. Also here is the **Baron Bliss Lighthouse**; Bliss, Belize's greatest benefactor, is entombed in front.

Sites to see in the city include the **Commercial Centre**, located at the southeastern corner of the Swing Bridge. This large, open building has vendors selling fruits, vegetables and some tacky souvenirs. A sign above its large planters begs, "please don't sit on the plants. Give them a change to grow." Apparently people do indeed park themselves atop the greenery because the poor things are struggling.

Government House, a green-roofed colonial structure, is one of the city's prettiest buildings. Located on the sea at the end of Regent Street, it houses visiting dignitaries. Nearby is **St. John's Cathedral**, the oldest cathedral in

Central America. Built in 1812–20 from bricks used as ballast on English ships, four Mosquito Coast kings were crowned here.

If you're dying to get pampered, make tracks for the **Acupuncture & Massage Center** at *3 Cork Street* in the Fort George area. The charming Chinese couple that owns the place gives a marvelous, hour-plus massage for just $20. They're also skillful acupuncturists; call ☎ *(501) 2-31017* for an appointment.

The city is currently undergoing an ambitious, $50-million beautification project. The money is being spent to redo roads, add sidewalks, revamp the fetid canal system and fund loans so property owners can fix up—or at least paint—their facades. As a banner on City Hall declares, "Belize City Council and Citizens Working Together for a Cleaner and Healthier Belize by the Year 2001." They have their work cut out for them, but also a fine spirit that's not to be discounted.

Ambergris Caye

Belize's biggest tourist region is on the island known as Ambergris Caye (pronounced "key"), located far to the north, just a few miles from the Mexican Yucatan. San Pedro, its biggest town, is a fun and funky place where the streets are made of sand, many shops and restaurants have sand floors and the preferred mode of transportation is the golf cart. Since the carts are incredibly expensive to rent ($15 an hour, $70 a day, $275 a week), most folks get around on foot—usually bare ones at that.

Tiny San Pedro has two main streets that only in the past few years were officially given names. Front Street is now Barrier Reef Drive but no one seems to recall the new name they gave Middle Street—which gives you an idea just how casual life here is. The town is small, but it's crammed with hotels, restaurants, an incredible amount of liquor stores and a slew of watersports centers for the chief attraction—diving. Nearly 50 wooden piers jut out from the shoreline to accommodate the many fishing and diving boats active in town.

San Pedro has no real attractions, just a gloriously laid-back aura characterized by people strolling about in the most casual of outfits with beers firmly clenched in hand. The beaches are pretty but not especially swimmable due to an overwhelming abundance of sea grass. If you're dying for a dip, just walk to the end of a pier and jump in where the sea is clear.

The town has a great nightlife, and, interestingly enough, Belize's only casino: an unassuming little joint called **Palace Video** *(☎ (501) 26-3570)* where they have a handful of video poker and slot machines. It's open daily from 1 p.m. to 2 a.m. They don't serve liquor and a sign outside warns against bringing in firearms.

One very cool spot is **Tarzan's** *(☎ (501) 26-2947)*, a disco whose sand floor gives way to a lighted dance floor. Two balconies upstairs overlook the action and a silly automated waterfall adds to the surrealness of the spot. It opens each night at about 8 or 9 and closes Monday-Wednesday at midnight and Thursday-Sunday at 3 a.m. If it's crowded enough, the owner will flick on the air conditioner. Music varies from reggae to disco to hard rock, while occasional entertainment features the likes of male strippers and wet tee-shirt contests. (They have to import the "talent" from Belize City as the locals watch, but don't participate.)

At the **Pier Lounge** at the Spendrift Hotel, they have crab races on Mondays (hermit crabs trying to maneuver an obstacle course) and the chicken drop on Wednesdays. This dubious event consists of blowing on a chicken's behind, then dropping it onto a numbered grid in hopes it will defecate on your number.

More sedate types make tracks for the **Sunset Bar** above the Lagoon restaurant. Open only from 5–7 p.m., it's simply a bunch of tables and chairs on the roof where you can lazily sip a beer and watch the sun drop. Also worth a visit is **Fido's**, where they serve the coldest beer in town. The restaurant is not great, but the bar, overlooking the beach and sea, is nice and casual. Resist the urge to play the two video poker machines here—they're a royal rip-off.

San Pedro is one of the few spots in Belize where you'll see conspicuous signs of prostitution. These working girls come over from Belize City looking for tourists willing to pay for a good time. Use caution: AIDS has infiltrated Belize, just like everywhere else.

Placencia

Placencia is one of the most laid-back places on Earth—and also one of the hardest to leave. It's here you'll find Belize's best beaches (though they're still not great compared to other Caribbean islands), a Garifuna village with its own distinctive culture dating back centuries and the happiest bunch of expatriates ever to plant their roots in a new land. The locals, mostly Creoles, peacefully coexist with these American and European entrepreneurs—mostly older hippies, younger deadheads, and others seeking the good life—but view them with a bit of bemusement. Most of the hotels here are owned and run for foreigners, but as long as they respect and employ the local community and treat nature with respect, no one seems to mind.

Placencia Village, which has about 500 residents, has earned its spot in the *Guinness Book of World Records* by having the world's narrowest street. The publishers must have been in a good mood when they made the entry—undoubtedly swept away by the area's charms—since this "street" is nothing more than a concrete sidewalk that winds past restaurants and though people's yards. It lasts just a mile or so, then ends abruptly and nowhere in particular. And that about sums up Placencia.

Visitors to the region would be remiss if they failed to make a visit to the neighboring town, **Seine Bight**, located four miles to the north. This Garifuna community follows ancient cultural traditions from Africa, speaks its own language (**Garinagu**) and generally keeps to itself. Visitors are welcome to wander through its maze of simple huts on stilts, however, and even participate in a healing dance if one's occurring. This ritual, performed only on "prescription" by the traveling Garifuna medicine man, involves the family of the ill dancing for three days and three nights straight. Afterwards, selected family members spend seven days and six nights in the temple—a wooden shack to the uninformed—and may not leave until that time has passed. As stated, tourists are welcome to watch and even dance, but must cover their head in a bandana and show respect for a ritual taken very seriously by those who practice it. Some 765 people, mostly related to one another, live in Seine Bight.

Like the Creoles, the Garifuna don't seem to mind the creeping stretch of tourism right in their backyard. Most of the area's nicest lodging is found just outside the village but so far the two distinct worlds live peaceably, with a good deal of mutual respect.

Visitors to Placencia are big on diving—there are 40 cayes offshore with colorful coral and teeming schools of fish. Catch and release fly-fishing for bone fish, snook and trophy-size permit is big. Also popular are excursions up the Monkey River, manatee watching in Placencia Lagoon (which separates the peninsula from the mainland) and night trips to the **Cockscomb Basin Wildlife Sanctuary** in hopes of spotting the elusive jaguar.

Placencians know how to party! Fun night spots include **De Tatch**, where they'll let you scribble your thoughts on the wall; the **Flamboyant**, where folks gather around picnic tables under a giant yellow flamboyant tree; **Tentacles**, a bar and restaurant on stilts right over the sea; and the **Dockside Bar**, where the breeze and the music is always good. People are friendly, the kids are adorable (they love getting their picture taken) and it takes just a few hours in this southern town to feel the stresses of the real world slip away in favor of the what-the-hell, live-and-let-live Placencian state of mind.

Where to Eat

Fielding's Highest Rated Restaurants in Belize

★★★★★	De Tatch	$3–$8
★★★★★	Lagoon	$8–$17
★★★★	Brenda's	
★★★★	Fort Street Restaurant	$7–$14
★★★★	Maxime's	$5–$22
★★★★	Micky's Place	$4–$19
★★★	Elvi's Kitchen	$3–$17
★★★	Franco's Restaurant	$5–$7
★★★	Little Italy	$4–$17
★★★	Tentacles	$6–$16

Fielding's Special Restaurants in Belize

★★★★★	De Tatch	$3–$8
★★★★★	Lagoon	$8–$17
★★★★	Brenda's	
★★★	Elvi's Kitchen	$3–$17

Fielding's Budget Restaurants in Belize

★★★★★	De Tatch	$3–$8
★★★	Franco's Restaurant	$5–$7
★★	Flamboyant	$3–$10
★★★	Elvi's Kitchen	$3–$17

Belize City

While the quality of water may be dubious, the food is not, and Belize City's restaurants run the gamut from gourmet rooms in hotels to tiny shanties on the side of the road. Most vegetables, meat and seafood are produced locally. Belizean food is generally spicy with a generous dose of peppers and cilantro. Some of the county's most famous dishes are *escabeche* and *relleno*, hardy soups of vegetables and chicken served with corn tortillas. You'll also see *granacho* on lots of menus—a corn fried tortilla piled with refried beans, cabbage, cheese and hot sauce. You may also spot *gibnut*, a small, furry animal that Queen Elizabeth bravely tried when she visited the country a few years ago.

A note to vegans: You'll have a terrible time trying to eat well in Belize. Bring your own food or prepare to live on salads of iceberg lettuce. Vegetarians who eat seafood fare much better.

Calypso Bar & Grill $ ★★★

Newtown Barracks, ☎ (501) 2-32670.
American cuisine.
Great views from this hotel restaurant built right over the sea. The menu offers American and Belizean dishes in a casual atmosphere. There are live bands on the weekends, when the joint stays open until 2 a.m.

Fort Street Restaurant $$ ★★★★

4 Fort Street, ☎ (501) 2-60116.
International cuisine.
Lunch: 11 a.m.–2 p.m., entrees $7–$8.
Dinner: 6–10 p.m., entrees $12–$14.
This intimate dining room pays homage to the film classic *Casablanca*, with a large poster of Humphrey Bogart standing guard. The eclectic menu features Continental and Belizean specialties such as lobster and steaks, as well as fresh seafood and vegetarian dishes. Save room for their famous "Death by Chocolate" cake. Also open for breakfast from 7–10 a.m.—don't miss the luscious french toast.

GG's Cafe and Patio $ ★★★

2-B King Street, ☎ (501) 2-74878.
International cuisine.
This charming restaurant in downtown Belize City has a pleasant courtyard where you dine under Belikin beer umbrellas. Owner George Godfrey makes great hamburgers, steaks and local dishes like skewered pork and rice and beans. Reasonable prices make this spot a winner.

Maxime's $$ ★★★★

2 Marine Parade, ☎ (501) 2-77400.
American cuisine.
Dinner: 6–10 p.m., entrees $5–$22.
Located on the fifth floor of the Radisson Fort George, this gourmet room has large picture windows overlooking the city and sea. Next door is a comfortable bar with a nice open-air balcony. The large dining room doesn't have much atmosphere—yellow walls, simple artwork, ceiling fans—but the service is decent and the food quite good. The menu offers a large selection of soups, salads and seafood. There's also pork and beef from the Cayo Hills and chicken from Mennonite farms. Most dishes cost $12 to $14.

Ambergris Caye

Long before tourism became the economic mainstay, San Pedro was a sleepy fishing village. Today's fishermen realize they can make more taking tourists out on deep-sea excursions than on fishing themselves, so ironically enough, local restaurants have a hell of a time getting fish. Nonetheless, you'll probably find a fair amount of tasty sealife on the menus, as well as luscious lobster dishes and the ever-popular rice and beans. **Elvi's Kitchen** may have turned into a tourist trap, but it still serves decent fare. For gourmet dining, try the upscale (but any standards) **Lagoon**. Great baked goods await at **Ruby's Cafe** on Front Street.

Elvi's Kitchen $$ ★★★

San Pedro, ☎ (501) 26-2176.
International cuisine.
Lunch: 11 a.m.–2 p.m., entrees $3–$17.
Dinner: 5:30–10 p.m., entrees $3–$17.

Elvi's has been open for 18 years, making it a San Pedro institution. Locals resent that it's become so popular and touristy, but the food is still quite decent and reasonably priced. The restaurant is quite atmospheric with a sand floor, picnic-style wooden tables, ceiling fans and a high thatched roof. The huge menu lists tons of seafood, chicken, meat and burgers. Don't miss the rice and beans. There's live music on Thursdays (Caribbean) and Saturdays (Mexican). They close each October for two weeks, so if you're in town then, call ahead.

Lagoon **$$** ★★★★★

San Pedro, ☎ (501) 26-2327.
International cuisine.
Dinner: 6–10 p.m., entrees $8–$17.
Wonderful food and professional service are the hallmarks at Lagoon, San Pedro's only true gourmet restaurant. The eclectic menu features international specialties, but this place is best known for its tasty seafood and lobster dishes. Lobster Lagoon comes with sweet butter liqueur creme sauce restuffed in the shell and served with mashed potatoes to die for, while lobster curry has a sweet coconut cream sauce with artichokes, mushrooms and onions, served on a bed of rice with almonds, raisins and bits of pasta. Also luscious is the green salad with pico de gallo and creamy Parmesan dressing. The restaurant has cute ice cream parlor-style wrought-iron chairs, cloth tablecloths and napkins, waiters in black tie (in San Pedro!) and the funkiest bar in Belize. Don't miss it. If you come early enough, go up to the third floor to the Sunset Bar, open only from 5:00-8:00 p.m., where the views are great and the drinks potent.

Little Italy **$$** ★★★

San Pedro, ☎ (501) 26-2866.
Italian cuisine.
Lunch: 11:30 a.m.–2 p.m., entrees $4–$17.
Dinner: 5:30–9 p.m., entrees $4–$17.
Keep in mind that this is not Italy, and you'll be satisfied with the Italian fare at this waterfront restaurant. You can sit outside overlooking the beach or in a large dining room with plastic red-checkered tablecloths, ceiling fans, candles and Italian operas on the stereo. You can order spaghetti for just $5, then add sausage, fresh fish or shrimp for another $4 to $12. The a-la-carte menu also features sandwiches, burgers, pizzas and lots of salads. There's a decent wine list, and good desserts like Caribbean Coupe—vanilla ice cream with fresh fruit and papaya rum. Service is excellent.

Micky's Place **$$** ★★★★

at the Hotel Playador in San Pedro, ☎ (501) 62-2223.
International cuisine.
Lunch: Noon–2 p.m., entrees $4–$10.
Dinner: 6–10 p.m., entrees $9–$19.
Located a few miles outside downtown San Pedro, near the Belize Yacht Club, this casual beachfront restaurant is a great choice for tasty lunches (the lobster salad is excellent) or romantic dinners. The menu features salads, seafood, steak, chicken and pork. Locals flock here on Thursdays, when they serve a huge Mexican platter of tacos and enchiladas.

Placencia

Placencia is primarily a fishing village, so you can expect lots of good seafood. You'll also have no trouble finding American-style burgers and sandwiches. **Brenda's** offers up ethnic fare as well as the antics of its owner, while breakfasts (and the house specialty drink) are killers at **De Tatch**. Italian prix-fixe dinners can be found at **Franco's**.

Brenda's **$** ★★★★

☎ *(501) 62-3137.*

Belizean cuisine.

The hours tend to vary at Brenda's, named for its owner, a wild and crazy young woman who deserves her own comedy special on HBO. The food's just great and the servings huge at this rustic wooden eatery. The menu varies but usually features local seafood, chicken and beef dishes. Brenda takes special requests and will keep you thoroughly entertained while you wait. Count on spending about $7 or $8 for an unforgettable meal.

De Tatch **$** ★★★★★

in the village,

American cuisine.

Lunch: from 6 a.m., entrees $3–$8.

Dinner: to 2 a.m., entrees $3–$8.

They don't come much cooler than De Tatch, a great bar/restaurant where locals congregate to listen to the great collection of 150 cassettes—everything from reggae to blues and jazz to folk, and especially Belizean punta music. The floor is sand and the walls are decorated with graffiti from travelers passing through, funny tee-shirts and the "Lost Souls of the Caribbean" collection of orphan shoes found on the beach outside. Besides the usual burgers and sandwiches, they have great coffee and yummy dishes like stuffed fry jacks (deep-fried flour dough stuffed with scrambled eggs, bacon, beans and cheese). If you're feeling daring, try a "Bye Yama"—a drink named after a big storm that has two shots of rum and cranberry juice. As they say, it comes out of nowhere, kicks you in the back and leaves. Be careful, because it takes exactly like Kool-Aid and goes down easy.

Flamboyant **$** ★★

in the village, ☎ *(501) 62-3322.*

International cuisine.

Dinner: to about midnight, entrees $3–$10.

Eat inside the cute little restaurant, or, better yet, outside under the giant flamboyant tree strung with Christmas lights from which this restaurant takes its name. The menu offers up Creole and American dishes such as burgers, chicken, lobster and shrimp. Like most Belize restaurants, the cole slaw is a treat!

Franco's Restaurant **$** ★★★

at Kitty's Place, near the airstrip, ☎ *(501) 62-3237.*

International cuisine.

Lunch: 11:30 a.m.–5 p.m., entrees $5–$7.

Dinner: 7–9 p.m., prix fixe $15.

Located upstairs with great views of the beach and sea, Franco's is a casual spot for simple sandwiches by day and pasta, seafood or meat four-course fixed-price dinners at night. The restaurant is spartanly decorated with such eclectic items as golf clubs, U.S. license plates and a portrait of Bob Marley. You can catch up on the news on the satellite TV at the bar, or just soak up the local gossip by eavesdropping on the chatty staff.

Tentacles **$$** ★★★

☎ *(501) 62-3156.*

Seafood cuisine.

Dinner: 6–10 p.m., entrees $6–$16.

Locals favor this thatched-roof cafe set on stilts on the water's edge. Dine on seafood, local dishes and even Italian fare at this very pleasant spot.

Where to Shop

Belize is not much of a shopper's paradise, though it's great fun to divide prices by two (one U.S. dollar equals $2 Belize), giving the feel that everything is on a giant 50 percent off sale.

The international airport in Belize City has a duty-free shop in both the departure and arrival lounges with great prices on designer perfumes, premium liquors and cigarettes. In the city itself, several hotels, notably the **Biltmore**, Radisson and Fort Street, have decent gift shops. Local artwork can be found at **Emory King's Art Gallery** and at **Rachel's**. The **National Handicraft Centre** *(☎ (501) 2-33636)* has a wide array of zericote wood carvings, black slate carvings, jippi joppa baskets and other crafts made by Belizean artisans. **Go Tees** *(☎ (501) 2-74082)* is a quaint, art deco-style shop with good Belizean art, clothing and gifts. On Fridays, Mennonite farmers bring their handmade furniture into the city; ask at your hotel to find them.

Shopping is decent at **San Pedro** on Ambergris Caye. Among the better hotel gift shops are those at the **Holiday Hotel** (where among the tee-shirts saying "you better Belize it!" are salves made from jungle plants that reduce the itch of mosquito bites or ease a stomach ache) and the **Belize Yacht Club**, where they sell very fine shirts with the resort's logo. Jewelry crafted from protected black coral, which grows just a quarter- to a half-inch in diameter every 100 years, can be found at the **Little Old Giftshop on Front Street** *(☎ (501) 26-2924)*, while ceramic iguana figurines, pottery, masks and original paintings, all done by artist John D. Westerhold, are at **Iguana Jack's** *(☎ (501) 26-2767)*, which also has the best logoed T-shirts in the country. Also well worth a visit is **Belizean Arts** *(☎ (501) 26-3019)*, located off Front Street next to Fido's Bar, where they have an excellent selection of jewelry, wood-carved animals and local artwork.

In the San Ignacio area, **Caesar's Place** *(☎ (501) 92-2341)* has a wide selection of arts and crafts, many made on the property; you can take a free guided tour of the workshop. Products from the rainforest and other Central American countries can be found at **San Iggy Gifts** *(☎ (501) 92-2034)* at the San Ignacio Hotel.

Belize Directory

All prices are in U.S. dollars.

CLIMATE

It's a subtropical climate, with constant trade winds from the Caribbean Sea. Summer temperatures average 75–85 degrees F, while winter is about 60–80 degrees F. Saltwater temperatures range from 75 and 84 degrees F. The rainy season is between June and August. The best time to come is October through May, though March can be overwhelmingly windy. Average humidity is 85 percent.

BUSINESS HOURS

Stores open weekdays 8 a.m.–noon and 1–5 p.m. Some also open Saturday. Banks open Monday–Thursday 8 a.m.–1 p.m. and Friday 8 a.m.–1 p.m. and 3–6 p.m.

DOCUMENTS

A passport and proof of return is required for entry. Visas are not necessary for citizens of the United States, Canada and nations of the European Economic Community. (Rules for other countries vary, so consult your local Belizean embassy or consulate.) Visitors are allowed to stay a month without extension.

ELECTRICITY

Current runs at 110 volts, the same as the United States and Canada.

GETTING AROUND

The best way to explore the mainland is by rental car—preferably a four-wheel drive (the roads are generally awful). If you're heading south, a four-wheel drive is mandatory. Prices start at about $65 per day. Virtually all rented vehicles have manual transmission and no air conditioning.

Taxis are cheap and plentiful. There are no meters but rates are standardized, so be sure to ask before you get in. Cost from the airport to Belize City is $15, and it's just $2.50 for most short trips.

Belize has a good and inexpensive bus system that connects all major towns, with buses leaving Belize City hourly to major towns in the north and west. It costs just $10—but it takes many hours to travel from Belize City to Punta Gorda. Most buses are now relatively modern and air conditioned, but if you tend toward car sickness, don't get near one! Most roads are filled with potholes and deep ruts, and also quite curvy.

LANGUAGE

English is the official language and spoken by virtually everyone. You may also hear Spanish, Maya, Creole and Garifuna. All media is in English.

MEDICAL EMERGENCIES

Belize City has a large hospital *(☎ (501) 02-32723)*. There are also hospitals in Orange Walk, Corozal, Dangriga, Punta Gorda and San Ignacio. To reach the police, dial 911. To get the fire department or an ambulance, dial 90.

MONEY

The local currency is the Belize dollar (BZ), though U.S. dollars are accepted everywhere. One U.S dollar equals BZ $2, a rate that is fixed. Unless specified otherwise, always assume posted and quoted prices are BZ. (If you say "U.S.?" the answer may just be yes, and you'll end up paying double.)

TELEPHONE

Belize's excellent telephone system belies its Third World status. Direct-dial service is available to virtually anywhere. For directory service, dial 113. For local and regional operators, call 114. For international operator assistance, dial 115.

TIME

Central Standard Time. Belize does not observe daylight savings time.

TIPPING AND TAXES

Service charges are generally not included on restaurant checks; 10 percent is the norm, with 15 percent for outstanding service. That's also true for taxis and tour guides. There is a seven percent government hotel tax, and a Value Added Tax (VAT) is expected to be implemented in 1996. Departure tax is $11.25.

TOURIST INFORMATION

The Belize Tourist Board *(☎ (212) 563-6011 and (800) 624-0686)* at *421 Seventh Avenue, Suite 701, New York, NY 10001* can supply information. Be sure to request *Destination Belize*, the official government tourist magazine, which is filled with good information. In Belize City, the Tourist Board is located at *83 North Front Street; ☎ (501) 2-77213.*

WHEN TO GO

In February (one week before the start of Lent), the Fiesta de Carnaval is celebrated nationwide, with an emphasis on cultural traditions. Groups compete in special dances called *comparsas*. February also sees the International Billfish Tournament and the San Pedro Carnaval, a Mestizo carnival made up of competing comparsas and lots of craziness. On March 9, Baron Bliss Day is a national holiday with horse and cycle races and a regatta. In May, the Cashew Festival in Crooked Tree Village pays homage to the cashew harvest season with live punta music, cashew wine, and Caribbean-style meals and games. May 24 is Commonwealth Day, which is celebrated nationwide as the Queen's birthday with lots of special events. Each June sees the Dia de San Pedro, a three-day festival honoring St. Peter, the patron saint of San Pedro. Activities include a boat parade, fiesta, jump ups, and the blessing of the fleet. San Pedro also hosts the International Sea & Air Festival each August, when bands from Mexico and Central America compete nightly. September is the most happening month, with Independence Day celebrated with cultural, religious and sporting activities, including the crowning of Miss San Pedro. St. George's Caye Day commemorates a 1798 battle in which the Spanish were defeated by slaves, Baymen and British soldiers. There are lots of parades, carnivals and concerts held throughout the nation. October sees the Belikin Spectacular, a billfish tournament, and Pan American Day in Orange Walk and Corozal with fiestas that celebrate Mestizo culture. In the southern regions, Garifuna Settlement Day occurs each November 19 with cultural dancing and festivals. Both Christmas and Boxing Day (December 26) are celebrated in Belize.

BELIZE RESTAURANTS	PHONE	ENTREE	CR. CARDS
Ambergris Caye			
Continental			
★★★★★ **Lagoon**	(501) 26-2327	$8–$17	
Italian			
★★★ **Little Italy**	(501) 26-2866	$4–$17	A, MC, V
Caribbean			
★★★★ **Micky's Place**	(501) 62-2223	$4–$19	A, MC, V

BELIZE RESTAURANTS	PHONE	ENTREE	CR. CARDS
★★★ Elvi's Kitchen	(501) 26-2176	$3–$17	A, MC, V
Belize City			
American			
★★★ Calypso Bar & Grill	(501) 2-32670		MC, V
Continental			
★★★★ Fort Street Restaurant	(501) 2-60116	$7–$14	MC, V
★★★★ Maxime's	(501) 2-77400	$5–$22	MC, V
★★★ GG's Cafe and Patio	(501) 2-74878		None
Placencia			
★★★★★ De Tatch		$3–$8	
★★★★ Brenda's	(501) 62-3137		
★★★ Franco's Restaurant	(501) 62-3237	$5–$7	MC, V
Creole			
★★ Flamboyant	(501) 62-3322	$3–$10	None
Seafood			
★★★ Tentacles	(501) 62-3156	$6–$16	

Note: • Lunch Only

•• Dinner Only

BRITISH VIRGIN ISLANDS

Up close views of marine life await novice and experienced divers on the British Virgin Islands.

BVI refer to themselves as Nature's Little Secrets. The country has never sought nor desired mass tourism, preferring to let the discerning traveler discover it. The quiet, unassuming attitude is felt the moment you step off the plane, reflected in the gentle nature of the people and the laid-back way of life. The *dolce far ninete* (nothing-to-do) philosophy reigns in the BVI, and those who require high-rise resort amenities, late-night bars and other externally generated entertainment should not even buy a ticket. Even at The Baths, BVI's most famous beach on its second-largest island, Virgin Gorda, there are no bustling beach cafes, souvenir shops or crowds. What BVI does have are miles and miles of nearly deserted, uninterrupted beaches, tiny coral coves perfect for diving, and even a few islands where the only place to stay is a luxurious private home that can rent for up to $8000 a day. For more reasonable budgets, a full week on the water in the BVI, sailing from island to island, under the direction of a well-trained captain, can run under $450 per person summer and fall. Essentially, the compactness of the BVI, the purity of the waters and the accessibility of facilities offer an unparalleled opportunity to experience as many different dive, snorkeling and trekking sites as possible in the shortest amount of time.

Bird's Eye View

Boats and kayaks are available for rent on BVI.

More than 40 islands, rocks and cays make up the complex called the British Virgin Islands, the most important being Tortola, Virgin Gorda, Beef Island, Anegada and Jost van Dyke. Lying 60 miles east of Puerto Rico and directly northeast of St. John, the islands harbor a population of only about 12,000 people stretched over 16 inhabited islands. From nearly any advantage point, the view is that of seemingly endless tropical islands stretching off into the horizon. The appearances of these islands range from sloping mountains cloaked with verdant green growth to scrub and cactus-covered hills layered with massive rounded boulders. Long stretches of palm-shaded beaches border much of the island's perimeters. Offshore rough-hewn rock formations poke their heads out of the water, providing perches for seabirds.

Tortola, the capital and largest island, is a good base for exploring the archipelago. The coastline snakes in and out, providing a wealth of anchorages and long, fine beaches. Hills angle up to a rocky spine, running the length of the island. On the moist north side of the island (exposed to the Atlantic), vegetation takes the form of a jungle, with aromatic flowering bushes.The highest point is the 1740-foot Mount Sage, a rain forest that is part of the BVI National Trust. The north side retains the air of old Tortola, with its quaint inns, rustic bars and isolated beaches. The island's West Indian roots can be seen in Road Town, where pastel-colored wood shops line Main Street and local chefs add Caribbean flavor to dishes such as conch fritters

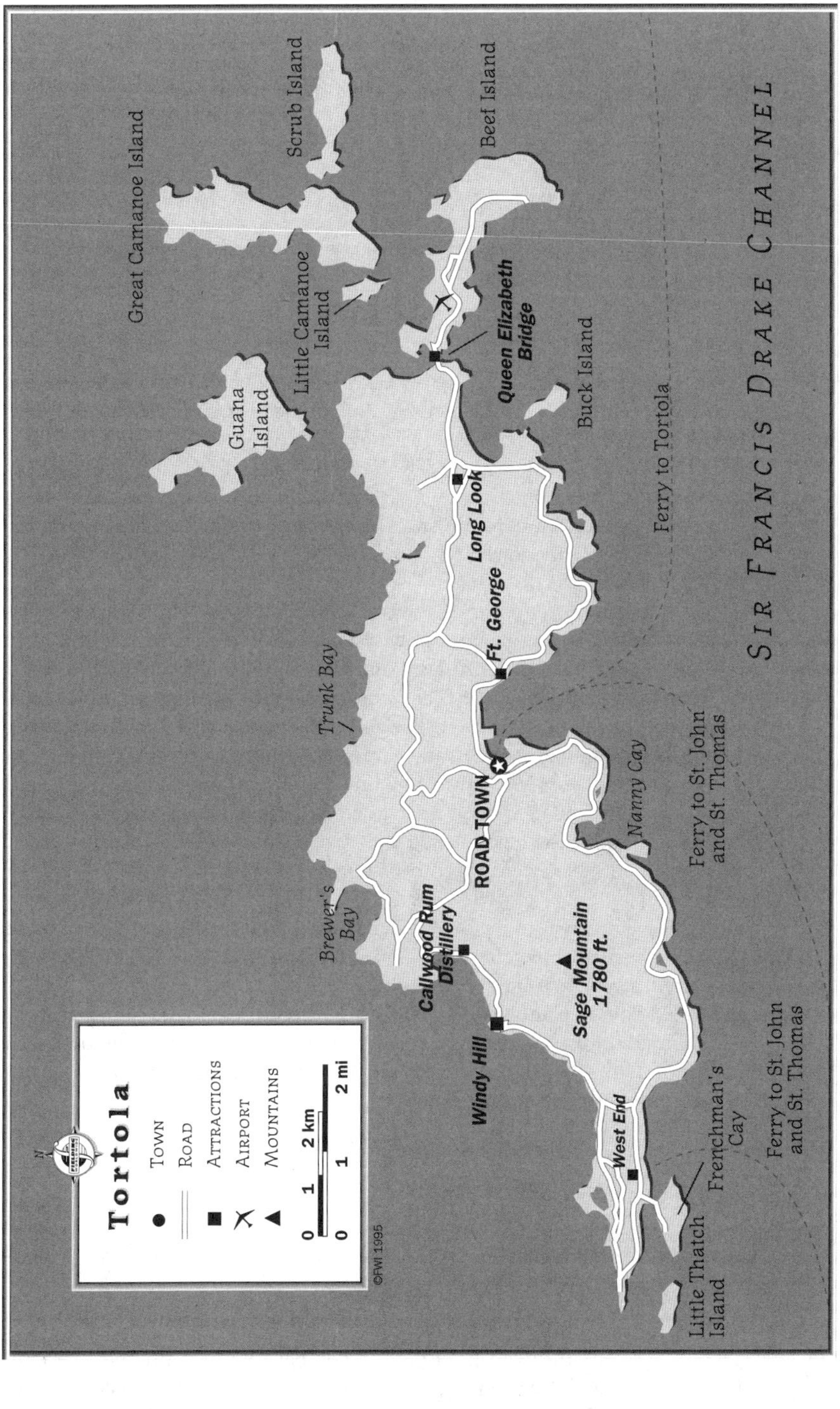
Tortola
Town
Road
Attractions
Airport
Mountains
0 1 2 km
0 1 2 mi
©FWI 1995
Great Camanoe Island
Scrub Island
Beef Island
Little Camanoe Island
Guana Island
Queen Elizabeth Bridge
Buck Island
Long Look
Ft. George
Trunk Bay
ROAD TOWN
Nanny Cay
Brewer's Bay
Callwood Rum Distillery
Sage Mountain 1780 ft.
Windy Hill
West End
Frenchman's Cay
Little Thatch Island
Ferry to Tortola
Ferry to St. John and St. Thomas
Ferry to St. John and St. Thomas
Sir Francis Drake Channel

and shrimp creole. Here, on the arid southern coast, facing the Sir Francis Drake Channel, one finds the stark beauty of foothills decorated with cactus and scrub bush. Protected yearlong from the brunt of the trade winds, this is perfect sailing territory, considered among the best in the world. Although the ocean is calm for much of the year, certain bays are famous worldwide among surfers for the fine waves during January and February.

History

The Virgin Islands were discovered by Christopher Columbus on his second voyage in 1493. Fascinated by the exquisite natural beauty of the islands, he named them *Las Once Mil Virgines* (the 11,000 Virgins) in honor of St. Ursula and her followers. The truth is, Columbus was the not the first human to set forth on the island. Prior to the European invasion, these islands had been populated by successive waves of Indian tribes migrating north from the Orinoco region of South America. Unfortunately, the arrival of the Europeans spelled the end of the native population; within a generation, there was not a trace of them. The occupation of the island by the Spanish and other Europeans followed a pattern similar to that of other Caribbean islands. For two centuries, control of the island was passed from one country to another while the islands remained mostly uninhabited. Many of those who balked at directly challenging the Spanish chose instead the path of piracy and pirateering, the most famous of whom were Sir John Hawkins, Henry Morgan, Jost Van Dyke and Edward Teach, better known as Blackbeard. These islands provided a secluded and safe anchorage for these brigands. Even today the legacy of piracy survives in the names of many islands and in the ever-persistent legends of buried treasure. Control of the Virgin Islands finally equalized with the Danish taking control of the western islands, now known as the U.S. Virgin Islands, while the British controlled the eastern set—so-named the British Virgin Islands. In fact, Tortola (BVI) is separated from St. John (USV) by less than two miles. From the 1700s to the mid-1800s, a plantation economy supported these islands. The remnants of the sugar industry can still be seen in the ruins of sugar mills hidden in the bush. In 1967, the BVI became a self-governing member of the British Commonwealth.

People

The people of the British Virgin Islands have an extraordinarily friendly reputation and will naturally extend you greetings as you stroll down the street. In fact, an islander can become quite hurt if you don't return the greeting. At the same time, Gordians and Tortolans are said to be somewhat retiring and not exactly prone to inviting travelers into their homes. Those who live in the interior mountains definitely tend to by shyer, but their lifestyle is also comparatively less pressured by touristic demands; these are older people in the mountain communities who still ride donkeys, make their own charcoal and harbor age-old superstitions about *duppies* or spirits. As tourism blossomed due to the efforts of established black families as well as spunky individuals, some of the island's women have become renowned for their cooking skills, in particular Mrs. V. Thomas who was decorated by the Queen of England for her guava jelly and mango chutney. As construction demands rise, traditional island occupations, such as stonemasonry and gardening, have begun returning, and sailors in the old school of sloops are finding another kind of work in more progressive boating. Because of the generous economic assistance received from Great Britain, islanders enjoy a considerable enthusiasm for, and strong identification with, their mother country.

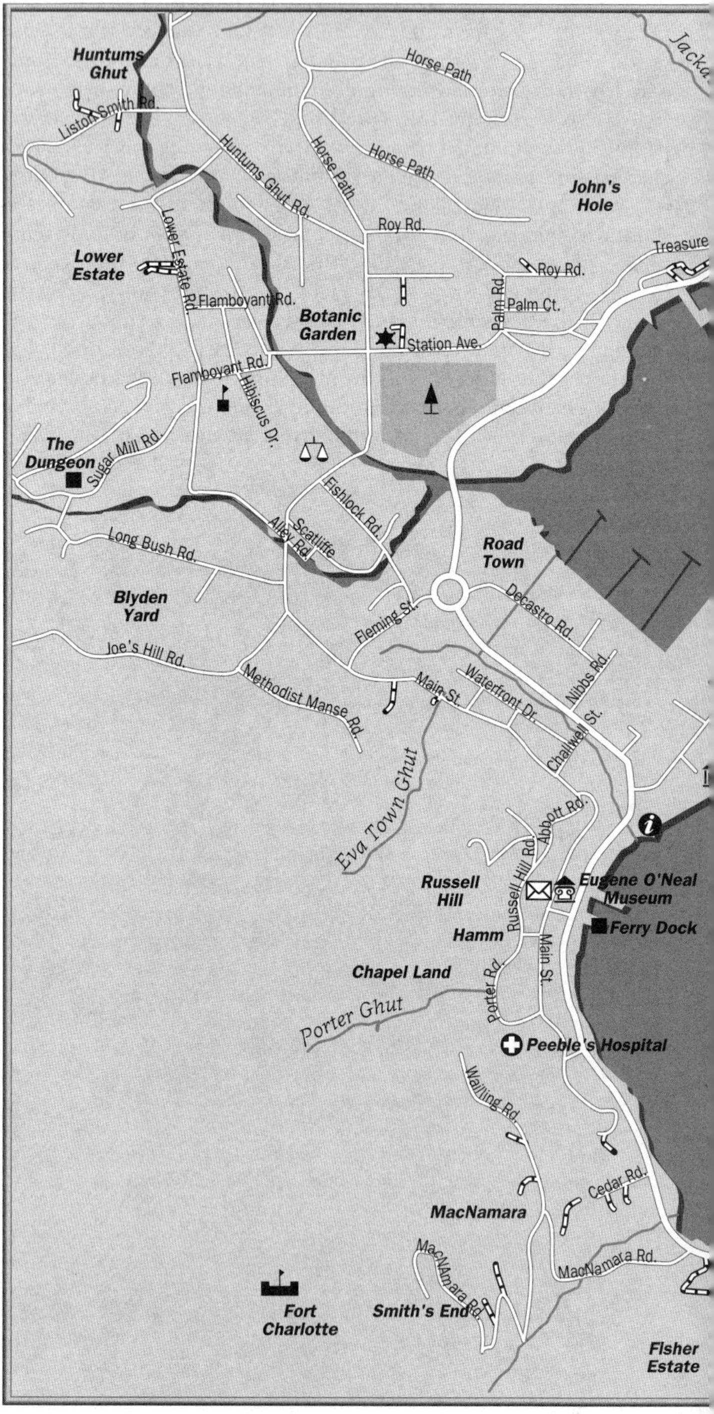
Huntums Ghut
Liston Smith Rd.
Horse Path
Huntums Ghut Rd.
John's Hole
Roy Rd.
Treasure
Lower Estate
Lower Estate Rd.
Flamboyant Rd.
Palm Rd.
Palm Ct.
Botanic Garden
Station Ave.
Hibiscus Dr.
The Dungeon
Sugar Mill Rd.
Fishlock Rd.
Scatliffe
Alley Rd.
Long Bush Rd.
Road Town
Blyden Yard
Decastro Rd.
Fleming St.
Joe's Hill Rd.
Methodist Manse Rd.
Main St.
Waterfront Dr.
Nibbs Rd.
Challwell St.
Eva Town Ghut
Abbott Rd.
Russell Hill
Russell Hill Rd.
Eugene O'Neal Museum
Ferry Dock
Hamm
Chapel Land
Porter Rd.
Main St.
Porter Ghut
Peeble's Hospital
Wailling Rd.
Cedar Rd.
MacNamara
MacNamara Rd.
Fort Charlotte
Smith's End
Fisher Estate

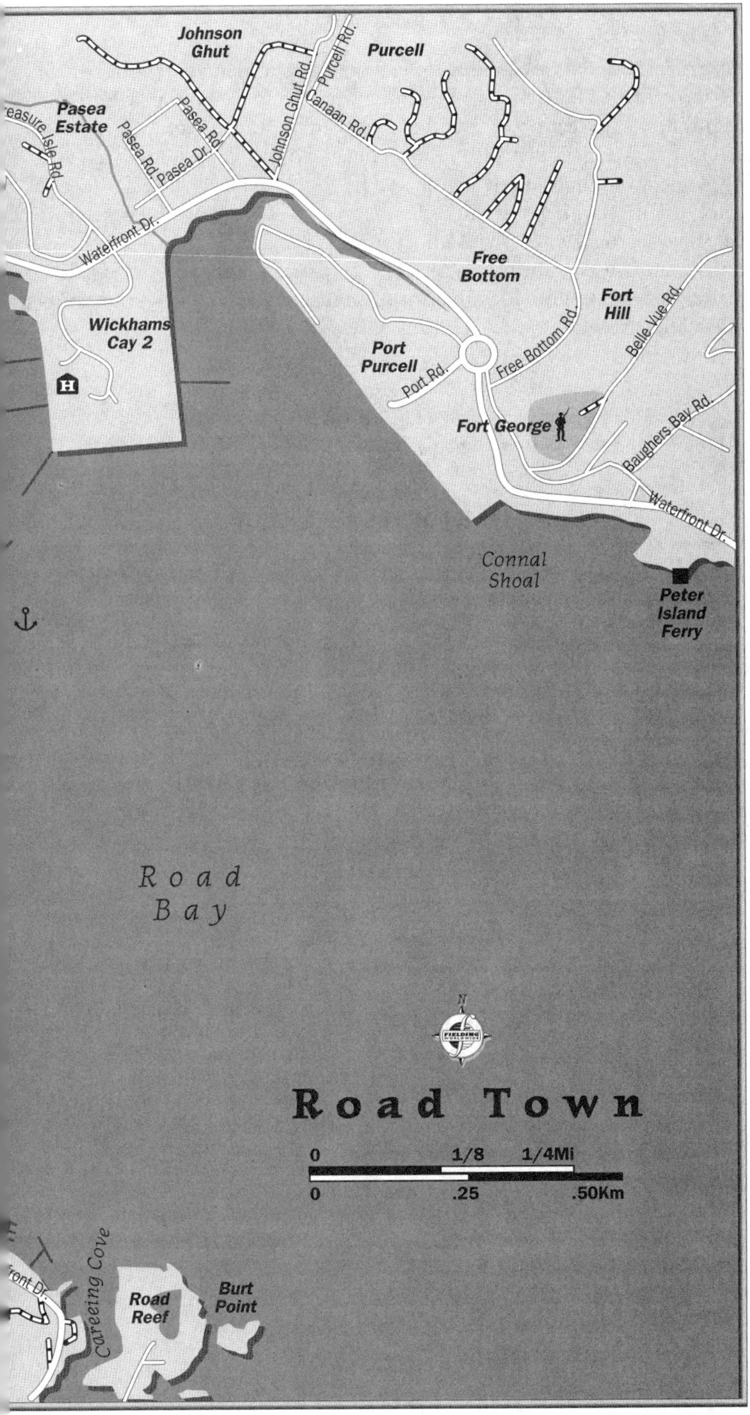
Johnson Ghut
Purcell
Pasea Estate
Treasure Isle Rd.
Pasea Rd.
Pasea Dr.
Johnson Ghut Rd.
Purcell Rd.
Canaan Rd.
Waterfront Dr.
Free Bottom
Fort Hill
Wickhams Cay 2
Port Purcell
Port Rd.
Free Bottom Rd.
Belle Vue Rd.
Fort George
Baughers Bay Rd.
Connal Shoal
Peter Island Ferry
Road Bay
Road Town
0 1/8 1/4Mi
0 .25 .50Km
Careeing Cove
Road Reef
Burt Point

Tortola

Twelve miles long by three miles wide, Tortola is home to three-fourths of the residents of the BVI. It's a refreshingly unaffected combination of the young and new, a reflection of a refined and contemporary approach to West Indian culture. Years of British rule have given Tortola a well-educated and worldly population, one largely unaffected by tourism. Nevertheless, most of the hotels are located here, about a dozen around Road Town. There are a couple of places to stay near Wickam's Cay I and II, on the southeast shore, and on the northwest shore at Apple Bay. In general, the crime rate is low and many residents seldom lock their doors, but it's not suggested that tourists follow their habit.

Beaches

The finest beaches and bays are located on the north side of Tortola. At the **West End**, where the majority of hotels are situated, are the Pirate's Pub and the Pusser's Pub; **Smuggler's Cove** to the north is an exquisite crescent-shaped strand. **Long Bay** and **Apple Bay** are notable; the latter is where surfers find their biggest waves (check out Bomba's Surfside shack made out of driftwood). **Cane Garden Bay** has a gently curving beach and is a popular anchorage. Good beaches are also located around **Beef Island**, the site of Tortola's airport, including the extremely dramatic **Josiah's Bay** and **Elizabeth Beach**. Outstanding, powdery beaches can be found on all the islands of the BVI. Snorkelers and divers can take full advantage of the crystal clear waters.

What Else to See

The best sights in the British Virgin Islands have to do with sun, surf and beach; anything else should be left for a rainy or hazy day. The Tourist Office can arrange a visit to **Road Town's Folk Museum** or the **rum factory**. Consider taking a frog-jumper's flight or quick cruise to one of the surrounding islands—you can make it back the same day. Most people come back from **Cooper Island** raving about the beauty, and if you get tired of the beach you can always trek through some fascinating trails. **Anegada**, reached best by small plane from Tortola's Beef Island, can also turn into a memorable day excursion, mostly for divers.

Museums and Exhibits

British Virgin Islands Folk Museum ★★★

Main Street, Road Town.

Hours open: 10 a.m.–4 p.m.

Housed in a traditional West Indian building, this museum showcases artifacts from Arawak Indians and the island's plantation and slave eras. There are also some interesting relics salvaged from the wreck of the RMS Rhone, a British mail ship that sank off Salt Island in 1867.

Parks and Gardens

J.R. O'Neal Botanical Gardens ★★★

Station Avenue, Road Town, ☎ (809) 494-4557.

Hours open: 8 a.m.–4 p.m.

Indigenous and exotic plants are beautifully showcased at this four-acre garden, which includes an herb garden and hothouses for orchids and ferns.

Mount Sage National Park ★★★★

Ridge Road, West End.

Located on the peak of a volcanic mountain, this 92-acre national park protects the remains of a primeval rain forest—most, alas, was cut down over the years. A graveled path will take you to the top, some 1780 feet up, the highest elevation in the British and U.S. Virgin Islands. A nice day trip.

Tours

Travel Plan Tours ★★★

Waterfront Plaza, Road Town, ☎ (809) 494-2872.

Island tours take about 2.5 hours and include all the hot spots. $50 per person.

Sports

Why bother with other sports when the sea treasures are as spectacular as they are on these islands? There are tennis courts at some hotels and horseback riding can be arranged through many hotels. Bare-boating (self-crew yacht chartering) is one of the biggest pastimes here, or you can charter a boat that comes equipped with a crew. Navigation is not difficult and the weather is usually so clear you can't get lost. (Note that bareboaters aren't allowed to travel to Anegada because of the dangerous route through the reef.) If you're not an educated sailor, think about taking a few classes at the **Nick Trotter Sailing School** at the **Bitter End Yacht Club, North Sound** ☎ *494-2745*. The best centers for fishing are **Salt Island, Anegada, Jost Van Dyke, West End, Tortola** and **Peter Island**. Bird-watchers should have a blast on **Virgin Gorda** and **Guana Island**, off Tortola.

Boardsailing B.V.I.

Long Look, West End, ☎ (809) 495-2447.

Learn the popular sport of windsurfing for $20 for a one-hour lesson. Boards can be rented for $155 a week. On Virgin Gorda, the Nick Trotter Sailing School at the *Bitter End Resort* ☎ *(809-872-2392)* offers courses and rentals.

Boating

Road Town, ☎ (809) 494-2331.

At the Moorings Resort, you can rent all manner of sailing yachts, from bareboat (no crew) to the works, with a skipper, cook and crew. Try Virgin Island Sailing, also in Road Town, for charters. Call from the States: ☎ *800-233-7936.*

Deep-Sea Fishing

Various locations, Road Town.

Sport fishers can arrange a charter or join a scheduled excursion. Captain Dale ☎ *(809-495-5225)* arranges trips out of Virgin Gorda.

Scuba Diving

Various locations, Road Town.

Several outfits will teach you the ropes and take you to the best underwater sports. On Tortola: **Baskin in the Sun** ☎ *(809-494-5854)* and **Underwater Safaris** ☎ *(809-494-3235)*. On Virgin Gorda, try **Kilbrides Underwater Tours** at the Bitter End Resort ☎ *(809-495-9638)*; two-tank dives cost $80–$90.

Shadow's Ranch

Todman's Estate, Road Town, ☎ *(809) 494-2262.*

Hop aboard a horse and venture along the beach or up to Mount Sage National Park. Prices start at $25 per hour.

Where to Eat

Fielding's Highest Rated Restaurants in British Virgin Islands

★★★★	**Biras Creek**	$40–$40
★★★★	**Brandywine Bay**	$20–$28
★★★★	**Capriccio di Mare**	$8–$15
★★★★	**Skyworld**	$7–$40
★★★★	**The Tradewinds Restaurant**	$18–$36
★★★★	**The Upstairs**	$10–$27
★★★	**Olde Yarde Inn**	$18–$30
★★★	**Sugar Mill**	$6–$28
★★★	**The Apple**	$15–$35
★★★	**The Bath and Turtle Pub**	$7–$30

Fielding's Special Restaurants in British Virgin Islands

★★★★	**Biras Creek**	$40–$40
★★★★	**Brandywine Bay**	$20–$28
★★★★	**Skyworld**	$7–$40
★★★★	**The Tradewinds Restaurant**	$18–$36
★★★★	**The Upstairs**	$10–$27

Fielding's Budget Restaurants in British Virgin Islands

★★	**Kilumba**	$8–$15
★★★	**Green Parrot**	$5–$20
★★★	**Toys Grand Cafe**	$5–$23
★★★	**China Garden**	$5–$24
★★★★	**Classic Eatery**	$5–$25

Excellent West Indian cuisine is available throughout Tortola; however, prices here are extravagant and can even give New York prices a run for the money, though the casual settings often belie the reality of the final bill. To save time, you'll probably want to stay around **Road Town**, where the majority of restaurants are located, but an excursion out to Sugar Mill on the northwest coast can end up a spectacular experience; even though the owners are American ex-pats, they've been highly acclaimed for their curried banana soup and cold rum soufflés. One of the best views, overlooking the town, can be had at **Skyworld** on the Ridge Road.

Resort food is not to be sniffed at on BVI, and some of the best dining can be found at both Virgin Gorda's **Bitter End Yacht Club** and **Biras Creek**, where diners will have breathtaking views. The menu at the **Peter Island Resort** changes every day, a combination of West Indian delicacies and continental favorites. For home-cooked meals and a big, generous heart, head for **Mrs. Scatlife's**, east of Sugar Mill at Carrot Bay, whose owner might serenade you with gospel music after dinner. English pub food can be had at **Pussers**, with locations in both Tortola and Virgin Gorda; while you're there, don't miss downing a Painkiller, made from Pusser's Rum, a local product, orange and pineapple juice, and coconut creme. Reservations at most popular restaurants are essential, especially at the smaller ones, which can book up fast.

Bing's Drop Inn **$$** ★★

Fat Hog's Bay, East End, ☎ (809) 495-2627.
Indian cuisine. Specialties: Conch fritters, fish stew.
Dinner: 6:30 p.m.–midnight, entrees $10–$20.

Do drop in to Bing's—and you'll probably make a local friend or two. Tasty home-style conch fritters and fish stew are specialties and more elaborate lobster, chicken and steak dishes are served as well. Come to dance and kibitz here after a meal elsewhere; it's a very unpressurized environment that stays open for snacks and drinks until midnight.

Brandywine Bay **$$$** ★★★★

Sir Francis Drake Highway, West End, ☎ (809) 495-2301.
Italian cuisine. Specialties: Homemade mozzarella, beef and lobster carpaccio, tiramisu.
Dinner: 6:30–9 p.m., entrees $20–$28.

For a special occasion, drive out a little east of Road Town to this hillside spot owned by Cele and David Pugliese for Tuscan food that's very widely praised. Whether it's local fish simply grilled with homegrown fresh herbs or an elaborately sauced roast duckling, everything is superb. Dining is on the terrace outside the once-private home that overlooks the Sir Francis Drake Channel. Hostess Cele will personally describe each entree on the menu while David prepares and arranges everything picture-perfectly (he's a former fashion photographer). Closed August-October.

Capriccio di Mare **$$** ★★★★

Waterfront Drive, West End, ☎ (809) 494-5369.
Italian cuisine. Specialties: Pastries, pasta and pizza, frozen granite.
Lunch: 11:30 a.m.–4 p.m., entrees $8–$15.
Dinner: 4–9 p.m., entrees $8–$15.

This new arrival is a welcome taste treat for seafood-dominated Tortola. A little sister operation to the popular Brandywine Bay, a bastion of *cucina fiorentina*, Capriccio di Mare is an informal Italian cafe—a place to sit and sip espresso or cappuccino and nibble pastries or sandwiches on foccacia bread. Pizzas with a choice of vegetable or meat toppings are also available, as well as pastas.

Chopsticks **$$** ★★

Wickham's Cay, ☎ (809) 494-3616.
Asian cuisine.
Lunch: entrees $10–$20.
Dinner: entrees $10–$20.

When you have a yen for Japanese (no pun intended), Chinese and other Asian (crossbred with West Indian) foods, and it's after 10 p.m., where you gonna go? Chopsticks, a cool spot with a veranda situated across from the Cable and Wireless office in Wickham Cay (you can also call mamma), has a good reputation for local fish and conch. All dishes are available for take-out. Open from 7:30 a.m. until late; hours vary.

Mrs. Scatliffe's **$** ★★★

Carrot Bay, West End, ☎ (809) 495-4556.
Indian cuisine. Specialties: Pot roast, chicken or pork, spicy papaya soup.
The former chef of the well-regarded Sugar Mill, a native Tortolian, operates this West-Indian restaurant on the deck of her home, a pastel-colored building with a tin-roof in Carrot Bay. Diners come for the set meal of four courses, which are prepared with fruits and vegetables from her own garden. Popular starters are fresh fruit daiquiris, followed by soup, home-baked bread, chicken in a coconut shell or curried goat, and more of that fresh fruit in her imaginative ice cream desserts. Entertainment follows, usually, a family sing-out.

Pusser's Landing **$$$** ★★

Sopers Hole, ☎ (809) 495-4554.
International cuisine. Specialties: Beef Wellington, guava chicken, nightly dessert specials.
Lunch: 11 a.m.–3 p.m., entrees $5–$9.
Dinner: 6–10 p.m., entrees $13–$25.
Diners can look out to the lights of St. Thomas from this waterfront restaurant in Tortola's West End, a fancier link in the Pusser's chain, serving black bean soup, West Indian ribs, roasted half-chicken in guava sauce and the signature Pusser's dishes, Beef Wellington with Bearnaise sauce and mud pie for dessert. Special events include dancing under the stars to a live band on Saturdays and all-you-can-eat shrimp dinners on Tuesday nights for $17.95. The potent Pusser's Painkiller may cure what ails you, but don't quaff too many or you'll be back in pain in the morning.

Pusser's Outpost and Pub **$$$** ★★

Main Street, ☎ (809) 494-4199.
International cuisine. Specialties: Beef Wellington, lobster club sandwich, mud pie.
Lunch: 11 a.m.–3 p.m., entrees $7–$9.
Dinner: 5–10 p.m., entrees $15–$25.
Enjoy varied international cuisine with the yachting set in this second link in the Pusser's (local rum) chain of eateries. The two-story establishment has a downstairs pub where the namesake libation can be quaffed, accompanied by sandwiches and snacks amid a boisterous atmosphere. Escape upstairs later to the Outpost for Beef Wellington prepared with choice cuts of beef tenderloin, mushroom duxelle and homemade pastry, served with Bearnaise sauce. Later, if you have room, down Pusser's famous mud pie, dessert-style or in a rum-Irish cream concoction.

Skyworld **$$$** ★★★★

Ridge Road, West End, ☎ (809) 494-3567.
International cuisine.
Lunch: 10 a.m.–5:30 p.m., entrees $7–$13.
Dinner: 6:30–10 p.m., entrees $23–$40.
A perfect remembrance of a Tortola visit is dining or having a drink before sunset and watching a technicolor movie in the sky at this dining room perched some 1000 feet above sea level. You can partake from chef George Petcoff's international menu of veal with capers, beautifully grilled local fish, passion fruit sorbets or less elaborate conch fritters or french fries and onion rings. At lunch enjoy the view from a different perspective with a sandwich on homebaked bread while casting an eagle eye on neighboring islands in the distance. Closed in September.

Spaghetti Junction **$$$** ★★

Waterfront Drive, West End, ☎ (809) 494-4880.
Italian cuisine. Specialties: Chilled roasted eggplant and plum tomatoes, veal scaloppine.

Dinner: 6–10 p.m., entrees $10–$25.

You can get spaghetti and other pastas in this cute joint located upstairs in a small blue building, built back a little ways from the sea in Road Town. Formerly a bar that overlooked the water, it is now separated from the ocean by new roads and office buildings—all in the name of progress. Yachties and others like it for its infectious grooves. The caesar salad, served with sun-dried tomatoes, isn't bad, either. Daily chalkboard specials and desserts.

Sugar Mill **$$$** ★★★

Apple Bay, West End, ☎ (809) 495-4355.
International cuisine.
Lunch: Noon–2 p.m., entrees $6–$12.
Dinner: 7–8:30 p.m., prix fixe $18–$28.

Bon Appetit columnists Jefferson and Jinx Morgan spent a lot of years cooking and writing about food and wine before they decided to buy a 300-year-old sugar mill in Apple Bay, converting it to a world-class inn and restaurant. The Morgans have wisely kept their menu small, allowing them to concentrate on the details of each dish, which usually includes a cold fruit soup and fresh fish in banana leaves with herbs from the Mill's own garden. Leave room for a scrumptious banana bread pudding with rum sauce when it's available.

The Apple **$$$** ★★★

Zion Hill Road, ☎ (809) 495-4437.
Indian cuisine. Specialties: Whelks in garlic butter.
Dinner: 6:30–9 p.m., entrees $15–$35.

An enterprising and talented Tortolian, Liston Molyneux, has opened a restaurant in his home in Little Apple Bay, on Zion Hill, preparing local dishes like uncommonly served whelks (a type of snail), and the more familiar conch. Lunches are varied and include curried chicken rotis (West Indian burritos), or crepes. An interesting Sunday barbecue of West Indian treats is also offered from 7-9 p.m. Closed in September.

The Fish Trap **$$$** ★★★

Columbus Centre, ☎ (809) 494-3626.
Seafood cuisine. Specialties: Prawns provencale, prime rib, teriyaki chicken.
Lunch: 11:30 a.m.–3 p.m., entrees $8–$14.
Dinner: 6:30–8 p.m., entrees $14–$25.

An informal, open-air terrace restaurant in Wickham's Cay that always has some good-value meals happening, the Fishtrap features barbecues on Saturdays and Sundays, prime rib on Sundays and local fish, shellfish, teriyaki chicken and other hearty, honest food the rest of the week.

The Upstairs **$$$** ★★★★

West End, ☎ (809) 494-2228.
International cuisine. Specialties: Filet mignon, roast duck.
Lunch: Noon–2 p.m., entrees $10–$16.
Dinner: 6–8:30 p.m., entrees $16–$27.

An intimate dining room with lovely views of the harbor, The Upstairs has received kudos from the likes of *Gourmet* magazine. The star of the Prospect Reef Resort, which is built on a coral reef, the restaurant offers simple but exceptionally well-prepared (and pricey) meals like local lobster served grilled as an entree or gratine as an appetizer. Service is attentive and gracious. Ask for a window table for stargazing.

Virgin Queen **$$** ★★★

Fleming Street, ☎ (809) 494-2310.
English cuisine. Specialties: Queen's pizza, shepherd's pie, bangers and mash.
Lunch: Noon–2 p.m., entrees $7–$12.
Dinner: 6–9 p.m., entrees $8–$16.

The Queen's pizza has been nominated for best in the islands, but it's also great finger food for sailors and other active types who like to quaff a few, throw darts at a board and shoot the breeze. There's a TV for background noise to go with the other fare offered—mostly English pub and West Indian food like bangers and mash, saltfish and shepherd's pie.

Where to Shop

In Road Town, the shopping hub is located on Main Street, starting at the **Sir Olva Georges Plaza**. Unfortunately there is no duty-free shopping, and you must sift through imported goods from Great Britain to find any bargains. **Pusser's Rum** (the "official drink of the British Royal Navy"), is one of the big island buys, available at the company store on Main Street. An aromatic excursion to the **Sunny Caribee and Spice Company** won't be time wasted, especially if you want to pick from the best selection of Caribbean spices and handicrafts on the island. Stop next door at the **Sunny Caribee Gallery**, which features fine artwork by islanders as well as handpainted furniture and wood carvings. If you need to supplant your vacation wardrobe, there are several boutiques including **Sea Urchin** in the Abbot Building, and **Kids in De Sun**, also in the Abbot Building, which specializes in tropical attire for children.

Resort Islands Near Tortola

Virgin Gorda

Huge boulders form a natural swimming pool and underwater caves known as The Baths of Virgin Gorda.

The most chic resorts of the BVI are located on Virgin Gorda, an eight-square-mile slab of scrub and cactus whose shape some say resembles a "fat virgin"—hence its name. Notwithstanding a brief gold rush in the 17th century, the idyllic island lay undiscovered until Laurence Rockefeller cruised the bay and decided to build his Little Dix Bay Hotel. Boats from Tortola regularly dock at the southern settlement of Spanish Town, where most of the 1500 islanders live. The best beaches lay south of Spanish Town, and in the extreme southeast you can find ruins of an old 19th-century copper mine. The road to the north of the island passes through Savannah Bay and Pond Bay before reaching Virgin Gorda's second town, Gun Creek. Below is North Sound, where two fine resorts are located.

The big attraction on Virgin Gorda is a spectacular series of massive granite boulders, the Baths, whose jumbled piles are backed by coconut palms. The stones, made of a granite that is not common to the Caribbean, are thought to have been carried there by glacial movement during the Ice Age. "Having nothing to do" is one of the major pastimes here, but if you say you're bored while staying at Little Dix Bay, they will scurry you off along the coast to a secluded beach, deposit you with drinking water, a picnic and an umbrella, and pick you up later.

Treks and Beaches

Virgin Gorda looks like two different islands north to south. The northern tip is mountainous, while the south is flat, with boulders blocking every curve. Everything above a thousand feet on Virgin Gorda is considered a national park. You'll find a self-guided trail at the 265-acre park at the forested peak near the island's center; it leads to an observation point. The lookout is the end of a paved road leading to Little Dix Bay resort. The first place most people head to are **The Baths**, where snorkeling in the limpid pools created by the pattern of the huge boulders is considered to be superb. (These days you may have to fight for space among the many cruise passengers who alight here; ask your hotel what their arrival schedule is.) Some hearty souls actually climb the island's tallest mount, the 1370-foot **Gorda Peak**; the trail boasts some unusual flora, including tropical orchids. Great treks can be made through **Devil's Bay National Park**; a 15-minute trail through a natural garden of native vegetation and massive boulders will take you to a fine secluded beach. Other beaches noted for their beauty include **Trunk Bay**, wide and sandy and reachable by boat or along a rough path from Spring Bay, a sandy beach north of Yacht Harbour. There is also **Mahoe Bay**, at Mango Bay Resort, with its gently curving beach and vivid blue water.

The greatest adventure in Virgin Gorda is to just get on a boat and explore the numerous other islands, such as **Necker**, **Mosquito**, **Jost Van Dyke** and **Anegada**. You'll usually find at least one resort on these islands, where you can have a fabulous lunch.

City Celebrations

Virgin Gorda Tours Association ★★★

Fischers Cove Beach Hotel, South Sound, ☎ *(809) 495-5252.*

Want to see the island but lack your own wheels? They'll shuttle you about, taking in all the high points, for $50. Two tours are offered daily; call for a schedule.

Parks and Gardens

Virgin Gorda Peak

South Sound.

The "peak" in the name rises some 1500 feet, making it the island's highest point. This 265-acre preserve is home to indigenous and exotic plants and has been reforested with mahogany trees. Hike to the top, then catch your breath at the observation tower, though foliage obscures the view.

Tours

The Baths ★

Lee Road, South Sound.

Gigantic house-size boulders strewn about have formed saltwater grottoes and small pools great for snorkeling. A new step and ladder system and a protected swimming area are welcome additions to this must-see natural wonder. This is by far the island's most-visited spot, so come early in the morning or late in the afternoon to avoid the crowds.

Sports

Beyond a tennis court at the Little Dix Bay resort, all other sports take advantage of the glorious seas. Most hotels will arrange diving, sailing expeditions, and deep-sea fishing; you can also find agencies at the Yacht Harbour or negotiate directly with crew members lolling about. At **Kilbrides Underwater Tours**, you can speed out to underwater caves, wrecks and coral forests in two 42-foot dive boats under the able direction of Bert Kilbride, considered a true pro in the area. Certification courses run about $60 and you can even get a video made of your dive. If you are interested in chartering a yacht, there are a couple of agencies beside the Little Dix Bay Resort. Both one-day trips and longer excursions can be arranged.

Where to Eat

For such a tiny island, the cuisine on Virgin Gorda can run to the superb, especially at the **Little Dix Bay Hotel** (the stupendous views from the dining terrace don't hurt either). At the **Biras Creek** hotel, dining is highly romantic, perched high on the hilltop, and the wine list is considered to be one of the best in the Caribbean. The best place to have Sunday brunch is **Pusser's Pub**, at Leverick Bay, on North Sound (good place for American-style hamburgers as well).

Biras Creek $$$ ★★★★

☎ *(809) 494-3555.*

International cuisine. Specialties: Half lobster any style, stilton with port.

Dinner: 7:30–9 p.m., prix fixe $40.

Dine in a stone "castle keep" with all-encompassing views of the Caribbean and Atlantic from the airy and luxurious main dining room of the tony Biras Creek Resort. The four-course, prix-fixe dinner menu changes each evening, but fresh half-lobster served grilled or poached with lemon or garlic butter is always available if requested by 4 p.m., for an extra $5. The well-chosen menus combine local specialties like conch with spicy mango chutney or pumpkin soup with rum. For a "veddy" English touch, stilton and port arrive shortly after dessert.

Chez Michelle $$$ ★★

The Valley, ☎ *(809) 495-5510.*

International cuisine. Specialties: Lobster remy, pastas.

Dinner: 6:30–9:30 p.m., entrees $16–$28.

An intimate Gallic spot amidst the surf and turf, Chez Michelle provides cozy, candlelit surroundings in a West Indian house near the Yacht Harbour. The specialty is local lobster, flambeed in cognac and served with a delicately rich mushroom sauce. Fresh pastas made in-house are justifiably popular, as is the rack of lamb.

Olde Yarde Inn $$$ ★★★

The Valley, ☎ *(809) 495-5544.*

International cuisine. Specialties: Seafood delight, fresh fish, grilled lamb chops.

Dinner: 6:30–8:30 p.m., entrees $18–$30.

The ambience is lovely at this garden restaurant in the Olde Yarde Inn, and the French-Continental food enhances the experience. Inn guests and others can dine here all day, starting with a breakfast menu that commences at 8 a.m. But the real draw is dinner, where classics like escargot with garlic butter or caesar salad for two can be paired with local fish of the day, or Caribbean lobster with lemon butter sauce. Desserts are all homemade and change frequently.

Pirate's Pub & Grill $ ★★★

Saba Rock,

American cuisine. Specialties: Barbecue, sandwiches, dessert drinks.

Lunch: Noon–4 p.m., entrees $5–$7.

Dinner: 4–8 p.m., entrees $5–$7.

It can get wild and woolly here some nights when the booze flows, but this informal pub is (relatively) kind to the pocketbook, serving a small menu of hefty sandwiches, ribs and chicken with all the trimmings for under $10, although a side order of potato salad at $2.50 is a tad much. Patrons are expected to drink their desserts here, downing such delights as raspberry pound cake and strawberry short cake blended at the bar. Entertainment is in the form of darts, or impromptu jam sessions with whomever washes up on the beach.

Pusser's Leverick Bay $$$ ★★★

Leverick Bay, ☎ *(809) 495-7369.*

American cuisine. Specialties: Filet of beef Wellington, mud pie.

Lunch: 11:30 a.m.–4:30 p.m., entrees $6–$10.
Dinner: 6–10 p.m., entrees $13–$24.
The Virgin Gorda branch of the popular Pusser's chain is located in a boisterously colored Victorian house, where familiar and tasty stateside favorites like nachos with guacamole and jalapeño pepper and cheddar fries are served with drinks. The chain's filet of beef Wellington is a specialty, served with fresh mushrooms and encased in pastry. There's also lobster, and pasta with vegetables. Desserts are huge and sweet, like mud pie with mocha ice cream and cookie crust, or the Mud Head, a chocolate and Pusser's rum concoction with gooey cream on top.

Teacher Ilma's **$$$** ★★★
The Valley, ☎ (809) 495-5355.
Latin American cuisine. Specialties: Calalloo, grouper.
Lunch: 11 a.m.–1:30 p.m., entrees $3–$10.
Dinner: 7–9:30 p.m., prix fixe $18–$25.
Teacher Ilma is Mrs. Ilma O'Neal, a veteran schoolmistress and now kitchen doyenne serving full-course dinners each night and lighter repasts at lunch. Located in her own home at Princess Quarters, Teacher presents genuine island favorites like conch, callaloo soup and roast pork to an appreciative culinary audience. Desserts might include pies and cakes made with exotic local fruits and nuts.

The Bath and Turtle Pub **$$$** ★★★
The Yacht Harbour, ☎ (809) 495-5239.
International cuisine. Specialties: Fried shrimp in coconut batter, specialty pizzas.
Lunch: 11:30 a.m.–5 p.m., entrees $7–$15.
Dinner: 6:30–9:30 p.m., entrees $11–$30.
A convivial bar-tavern, The Bath and Turtle has two happy hours a day, one midmorning, and another one before sundown. Drinks are usually fruity and tropical, accompanied by good pizzas (Mexican crabmeat, veggie and special of the day), a West Indian chicken sandwich with spicy local seasonings, filet mignon, lobster and burgers. The location is fine too, next to a shopping center and the local lending library. The Pub is open for breakfast from 8 a.m. and usually stays open until 9 p.m.

The Crab Hole **$$** ★★★
South Valley, ☎ (809) 495-5307.
Latin American cuisine. Specialties: Calalloo soup, stewed goat, rotis.
Lunch: 11 a.m.–3 p.m., entrees $6–$12.
Dinner: 6:30–9 p.m., entrees $10–$15.
One of a growing handful of West Indian restaurants in Virgin Gorda, The Crab Hole draws locals who come to chow down on home-cooking, island style, be it callaloo (local spinach) soup, spicy chicken curried rotis or plantains and rice and peas. There's lively entertainment as well on Friday and Saturday nights.

Where to Shop

The British Virgin Islands don't give American citizens the same duty-free break as do the U.S. Virgin Islands. There's not much to rave about here in terms of quality. Boutiques at Little Dix Bay and the Bitter End resorts carry the proverbial casual wear and souvenir merchandise. Along the Yacht Harbour you'll find another bevy of shops, including a few handicraft stores. Most of the work is imported from other islands, though you can find interesting buys on homemade preserves and spices.

British Virgin Islands Directory

BUSINESS HOURS

Stores open Monday–Saturday 9 a.m.–5 p.m. Banks open Monday–Thursday 9 a.m.–2:30 p.m. and Friday 9 a.m.–2:30 p.m. and 4:30–6 p.m.

CLIMATE

Little rain falls on this nearly-perfect temperate island, with temperatures hovering between 75 degrees F and 85 degrees F year-round. The constant tradewinds keep the humidity low. Even during the rainy season, rain usually arrives in 10-minute bursts that stop as fast they start.

CRUISES

BVI has become a ready port of call for many cruise liners. Many stop at Tortola and bring passengers aboard on small ships.

DOCUMENTS

Customs officials prefer visitors bring passports, but will accept proof of citizenship (birth certificate, voter's registration card, plus a photo ID). Travelers must also show an ongoing or return ticket. Departure tax by air is $5; by sea $4.

ELECTRICITY

Current runs 110 volts, 60 cycles, as in the U.S.

GETTING AROUND

Private ferry service between Caneel Bay and Little Dix Bay is provided by the island resorts three times a week. Public ferries are also available. They run Thursday and Sunday, between Cruz Bay and Spanish Town on Virgin Gorda. Call **Transportation Services** on St. Thomas, for information ☎ *776-62821*, $22 one way. A passport is required for travel between the American and British Virgin Islands.

Public ferries also make the 45-minute voyage from St. Thomas (Charlotte Amalie) to Road Town and West End on Tortola. Companies providing this service include **Smith's Ferry Service** ☎ *(809) 494-4495* and **Native Son** ☎ *(809) 495-4617*.

Transportation on Virgin Gorda is mainly by boat, often in the form of one of Little Dix's handy Boston Whalers.

Car rental prices can be exorbitant during high season because the demand is so high. As such, it's best to reserve a car before you arrive. Rates seems to change daily, so verify any last-minute adjustments at least two days before your expected pickup. Narrow dirt roads that are often not well lighted require sturdy wheels such as gurghels or jeeps. To rent a car, you must obtain a BVI license by presenting your valid hometown driver's license and shelling out $10. Though there are numerous local agencies, the best security is to stay with U.S.-based agencies that can verify mistakes in billing, etc. Among the best are **Avis** ☎ *(809) 494-3322*, **National** ☎ *(809) 494-3197*, **Hertz** ☎ *(809) 495-4405* or toll-free *800-654-3001* in the United States.

LANGUAGE

British English is spoken with a West Indian accent.

MEDICAL EMERGENCIES

The Peebles Hospital, Porter Road, Road Town; ☎ *(809) 494-3497* is a fully functioning facility with lab and X-ray machines. Hotels usually have a list of doctors on-call in Tortola.

MONEY

The American dollar is used exclusively.

TELEPHONE

To reach BVI from the U.S., dial *809* (area code) + *49* (country code) + local number. Area code is *809*.

TIME

Atlantic Standard Time throughout the year.

TIPPING

Waiters and taxi drivers both expect to be tipped 10–15 percent.

TOURIST INFORMATION

The **British Virgin Islands Tourist Board** on Tortola is located in the *Joseph Josiah Smith Social Security Building, Waterfront Drive, Road Town;* ☎ *(809) 49-43134*, FAX *(809) 49-43866*. Few hotels have phones in the room, so do ask in advance if you need one. Calls can be made with phone cards purchased from the Cable & Wireless company. In the United States call ☎ *(800) 538-8530*.

WHEN TO GO

The BVI Summer Festival in August is one of the island's biggest events, which includes two weeks of festivities, song, dance and parades. Also in August, fish enthusiasts can also attend the International Marlin Tournament at the Birch Creek resort. In November hop a ferry to Virgin Gorda's Bitter End Yacht Club when the Pro-Am Regatta sets sail. The annual Spring Regatta is a Caribbean-wide yacht race, featuring outdoor music and street fairs. For a schedule, call ☎ *(800) 835-8530* in the U.S. Easter is celebrated by a three-day festival in Virgin Gorda.

BRITISH VIRGIN ISLANDS RESTAURANTS	PHONE	ENTREE	CR. CARDS
Tortola			
Road Town			
Asian			
★★ **Chopsticks**	(809) 494-3616	$10–$20	A, MC, V
English			
★★★ **Virgin Queen**	(809) 494-2310	$7–$16	None
Indian			
★★★ **Mrs. Scatliffe's**	(809) 495-4556	$0–$0•	None
★★★ **The Apple**	(809) 495-4437	$15–$35••	A, MC, V
★★ **Bing's Drop Inn**	(809) 495-2627	$10–$20••	A, MC, V
International			
★★★★ **Skyworld**	(809) 494-3567	$7–$40	A, MC, V
★★★★ **The Upstairs**	(809) 494-2228	$10–$27	A, MC, V

BRITISH VIRGIN ISLANDS RESTAURANTS	PHONE	ENTREE	CR. CARDS
★★★ Sugar Mill	(809) 495-4355	$6–$28	A, MC, V
★★ Pusser's Landing	(809) 495-4554	$5–$25	A, D, MC, V
★★ Pusser's Outpost and Pub	(809) 494-4199	$7–$25	A, MC, V
Italian			
★★★★ Brandywine Bay	(809) 495-2301	$20–$28••	A, MC, V
★★★★ Capriccio di Mare	(809) 494-5369	$8–$15	A, D, MC, V
★★ Spaghetti Junction	(809) 494-4880	$10–$25••	None
Seafood			
★★★ The Fish Trap	(809) 494-3626	$8–$25	A, MC, V
Virgin Gorda			
North Sound			
American			
★★★ Pirate's Pub & Grill		$5–$7	A, MC, V
★★★ Pusser's Leverick Bay	(809) 495-7369	$6–$24	A, MC, V
International			
★★★★ Biras Creek	(809) 494-3555	$40–$40••	A, MC, V
★★★ Olde Yarde Inn	(809) 495-5544	$18–$30••	A, MC, V
★★★ The Bath and Turtle Pub	(809) 495-5239	$7–$30	A, MC, V
★★ Chez Michelle	(809) 495-5510	$16–$28••	MC, V
Latin American			
★★★ Teacher Ilma's	(809) 495-5355	$3–$25	None
★★★ The Crab Hole	(809) 495-5307	$6–$15	None

Note: • Lunch Only
•• Dinner Only

CAYMAN ISLANDS

Cayman Brac's 180-acre Brac Parrot Reserve is home to 500 rare parrots.

Cayman Islands is a scuba Eden. Due south of Florida and Cuba, the three small Cayman Islands were eclipsed for centuries by Jamaica (180 miles to the southeast), but have today zoomed into world-class status as divers, snorkelers, saltwater anglers, and beach-loving layabouts learn to love the high standard of living (20 percent higher than in the U.S.), the low crime rate, and the ingratiating good manners. The islands also draw travelers who need little nightlife and revel in the ease, peace and thriftiness of renting a condo by the beach. Reports of the Caymans having the best dive sites in the world have attracted more than 75,000 scubaniks a year (out of the 400,000 tourists who visit annually); the Cayman walls, particularly in the north, are said to rank next to Australia's Great Barrier Reef and the Red Sea in the excellence and accessibility of their sites. Money does seem to find its way here. *The Firm*, Hollywood's recent Tom Cruise movie about money-laundering on the Caymans, brought the Caymans a newfound publicity, at the same time erroneously suggesting an island lacking in moral conscience. What *is* conspicuously absent here are the traditional Caribbean straw-hat markets and open-air produce stands; instead, expensive Italian sandals have replaced the traditional bare feet, and native vendors have been usurped by sophisticated ex-pats who run the trendy boutiques. Still, the simple life can still bleed through on the Caymans, when the town's rooster is heard daily crowing from the veranda of the Old Courts Building at dawn.

Bird's Eye View

Grand Cayman, 22 miles long and eight miles wide, is the principal island of a complex that includes Cayman Brac and Little Cayman. About an hour's flight from Miami, Grand Cayman covers 76 square miles of land mass, though half of that is swamp. About 89 miles to the northeast of Grand Cayman lies Cayman Brac (the name means "bluff" in Gaellic), a limestone bluff rising from sea level to a height of 140 feet. Five miles west of Cayman Brac, the mile-wide Little Cayman lives up to its name, with a land mass of a mere 10 square miles.The capital of the islands is George Town, on the west side of Grand Cayman. No rivers cross the islands, but the vegetation is lush and tropical, dotted with coconut trees, thatch palm, Australian pine and seagrape.

West Bay Beach is the hub of tourism in Grand Cayman, an exquisite strand that gently curves around the western shore. Here, you'll find most of the resorts and hotels. An enormous coral reef surrounds North Sound, a massive bay in the west. Sting Ray City is the shallow habitat of two dozen western Atlantic stingrays whom Caymanian divers have fed and tamed to eat out of their hands.

History

Columbus discovered the Caymans in 1503 and dubbed them *Las Tortugas* for the enormous numbers of tortoises that would provide sustenance to English, Dutch and French sailors for centuries. (Las Tortugas somehow evolved into Los Caimanes, the Spanish name for a kind of tropical American crocodile). For a good 150 years after being sited, the Caymans were almost entirely avoided. They were remote, perilous to approach by sea, and their interiors were inhospitable—swampy and mosquito-infested in Grand Cayman, and hard and scrubby on Little Cayman and Cayman Brac. Among the few creatures that thrived here were crocodiles, called *caymanas* in the language of the Carib Indians. For a time the critters shared the island with such buccaneers as Sir Henry Morgan and Edward Teach (the original Blackbeard) who hid out in the islands while preying on Spanish and French ships. (Cayman history abounds with stories of sunken treasure and derring-do.)

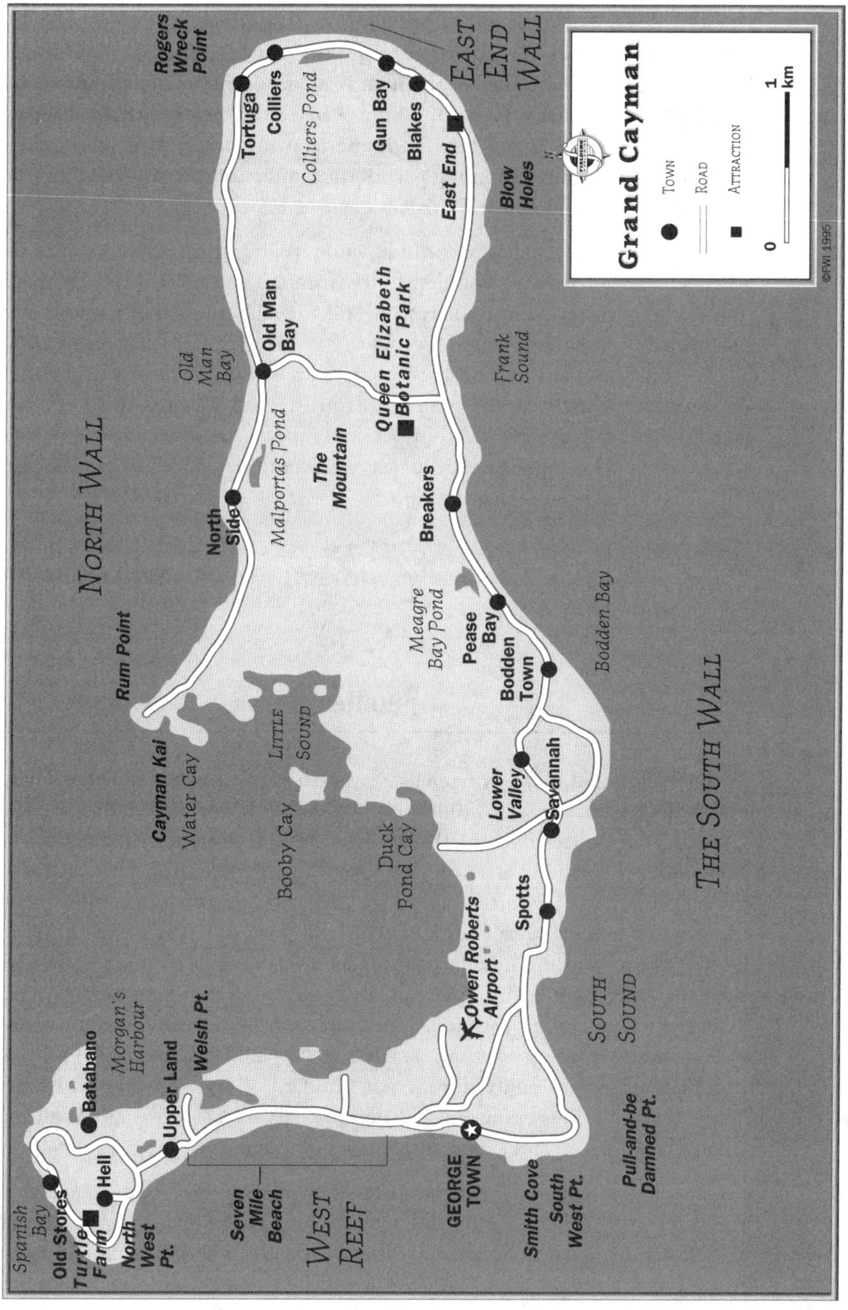
Grand Cayman
Town
Road
Attraction
0
1 km
©FWI 1995
North Wall
The South Wall
East End Wall
West Reef
South Sound
Little Sound
Rogers Wreck Point
Tortuga
Colliers
Colliers Pond
Gun Bay
Blakes
East End
Blow Holes
Old Man Bay
Queen Elizabeth Botanic Park
Frank Sound
The Mountain
Malportas Pond
North Side
Breakers
Meagre Bay Pond
Pease Bay
Bodden Town
Bodden Bay
Rum Point
Cayman Kai
Water Cay
Booby Cay
Duck Pond Cay
Lower Valley
Savannah
Spotts
Owen Roberts Airport
Batabano
Morgan's Harbour
Upper Land
Welsh Pt.
Spanish Bay
Old Stores
Turtle Farm
Hell
North West Pt.
Seven Mile Beach
GEORGE TOWN
Smith Cove
South West Pt.
Pull-and-be Damned Pt.

The abundance of meaty sea turtles made the islands a convenient provisioning stop, but by most accounts, the first real settlers didn't arrive until 1655, when deserters from Oliver Cromwell's army abandoned their platoon in Jamaica as the English were taking it from the Spanish. In 1670, Spain ceded both Jamaica and the Caymans to Great Britain. A century later, Grand Cayman had 933 residents, most of whom were slaves. After emancipation by Britain in 1835, the island became home to many other freed slaves; their descendants gradually becoming part of the families of the island, paving the way for the harmony that still exists today.

Just 33 years ago Jamaica chose independence, but the Caymans stayed on a British Crown Colony. The first tourists started to arrive in the Caymans during the 1950s while the roads were still bad, the insects voluminous and the electrical supply iffy. Legislation creating tax-investment havens in 1966 favored offshore banking and trust companies whose executives began seeing vacation promise in the islands. A tourist board, established in 1966, began strictly supervising hotel inspections, which has succeeded in raising and maintaining a high standard of service. About half a million people visit the Cayman Islands each year.

People

Nearly all the 30,000 Caymanians live on Grand Cayman, a fourth of them in George Town. About 1650 live on Cayman Brac and a mere 50 on Little Cayman. Their ancestry is an ethnic mix from 50 countries, including Jamaica, the U.S., and the U.K.The lilting brogue is a leftover from British seafarers centuries ago. The utter lack of racial tension on the island stems from the fact that neither sugar plantations or long-term slavery was part of the island's history, and the mixing of races seems to have been more fluid here than on other islands. In 1841, an observer noted that Caymanians were "strictly honest and industrious," and that even the wealthy were prone to walk around without shoes on. Today the simple life still seems to prevail, though Caymanians enjoy the highest standard of living in the Caribbean. There is little serious crime. And if the Caymans are short on native culture, locals make up for it for being congenial and tolerant.

Today lots of offshore investors park their money here because taxes and fees are few and client's identities are usually shielded by law. So profitable are the ventures that there are more than 50 banks and $435 million in assets here. Though the recent movie *The Firm* and its plot about money-laundering in the Caymans almost smudged the reputation of the island, locals insist such a scam can't happen here. They claim that anyone trying to deposit lots of U.S. cash would raise eyebrows among local officials.

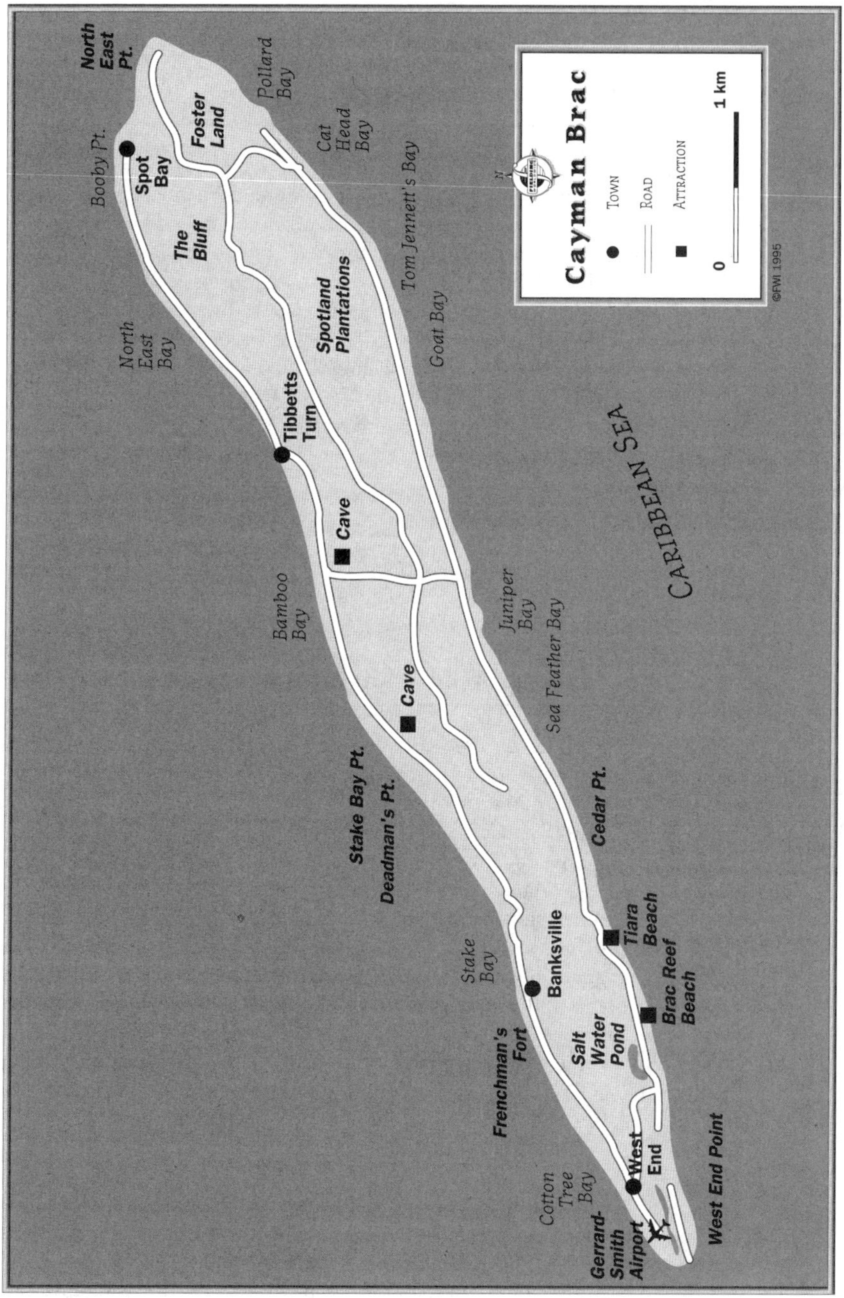
Cayman Brac
Town
Road
Attraction
0
1 km
©FWI 1995
North East Pt.
Pollard Bay
Foster Land
Cat Head Bay
Booby Pt.
Spot Bay
Tom Jennett's Bay
The Bluff
Spotland Plantations
Goat Bay
North East Bay
Tibbetts Turn
Caribbean Sea
Cave
Bamboo Bay
Juniper Bay
Sea Feather Bay
Cave
Stake Bay Pt.
Deadman's Pt.
Cedar Pt.
Banksville
Tiara Beach
Stake Bay
Brac Reef Beach
Frenchman's Fort
Salt Water Pond
West End
West End Point
Cotton Tree Bay
Gerrard-Smith Airport

Beaches

The beaches of the Caymans can be described in a few short words—powder-fine white strands with a handful of birds. **Seven Mile Beach** is considered one of the most fantastic beaches in the Caribbean, marked by a beautiful crescent shape and clear turquoise blue waters. Public buses operate hourly down the strand. North of the Holiday Inn, where most of the watersports facilities are based, is a public beach with small cabanas and tables and chairs. Most memorable sunsets can be seen from the beach at **Rum Point**, at the northeastern tip of North Sound, a sleepy little community of private homes and condos. **Little Cayman** is known for its long white beaches with nary a footprint to mar their beauty. For some reason, locals don't use the beaches much for sunbathing or swimming, so most of the strands are exquisitely private and not crowded.

What Else to See

There is little to dazzle the eye in regards to historical settings in Grand Cayman, but a jaunt around George Town should include a trip to the **Cayman Islands National Museum**, on the waterfront at Hog St. Bay, where you can view some 2000 artifacts about the island's history. If you get bored, the little library on Edward Street stocks English novels and magazines. To see more of Grand Cayman, you might consider renting a bike, motorbike or even a car. You can start out driving along Seven Mile Beach, past the residence of the island's governor and onto the West Bay. A stop at **Hell**, a formation of jagged burnt charcoal-colored rocks called iron-shore, has spawned a cottage industry of products imbued with "hell" themes. There is even a post office nearby where you postmark letters "from Hell." At the **Cayman Turtle Farm**, you can watch reptiles being hatched and raised (28,000 yearlings released into the sea last year) and scour the gift shop for turtle paraphernalia. Along the **South Sound Road**, you'll drive past some of the most attractive old wooden houses on the island. Bat fanatics can stop at their own **Bat Cave** (take the dirt road off the main road, to Bodden Town, heading east). A cliff overhanging the sea houses numerous caves; just beware where you walk. At the **Cayman Islands National Botanic Park**, you can hike over a 1.5-mile marked trail. The *Submarine Atlantis* at George Town Harbour—considered the stretch limo of the Caribbean—makes a sightseeing dive on a sophisticated vessel by a Creole pilot whose assistant entertains as you browse 100 feet down, among puffers, parrot fish and the reef life.

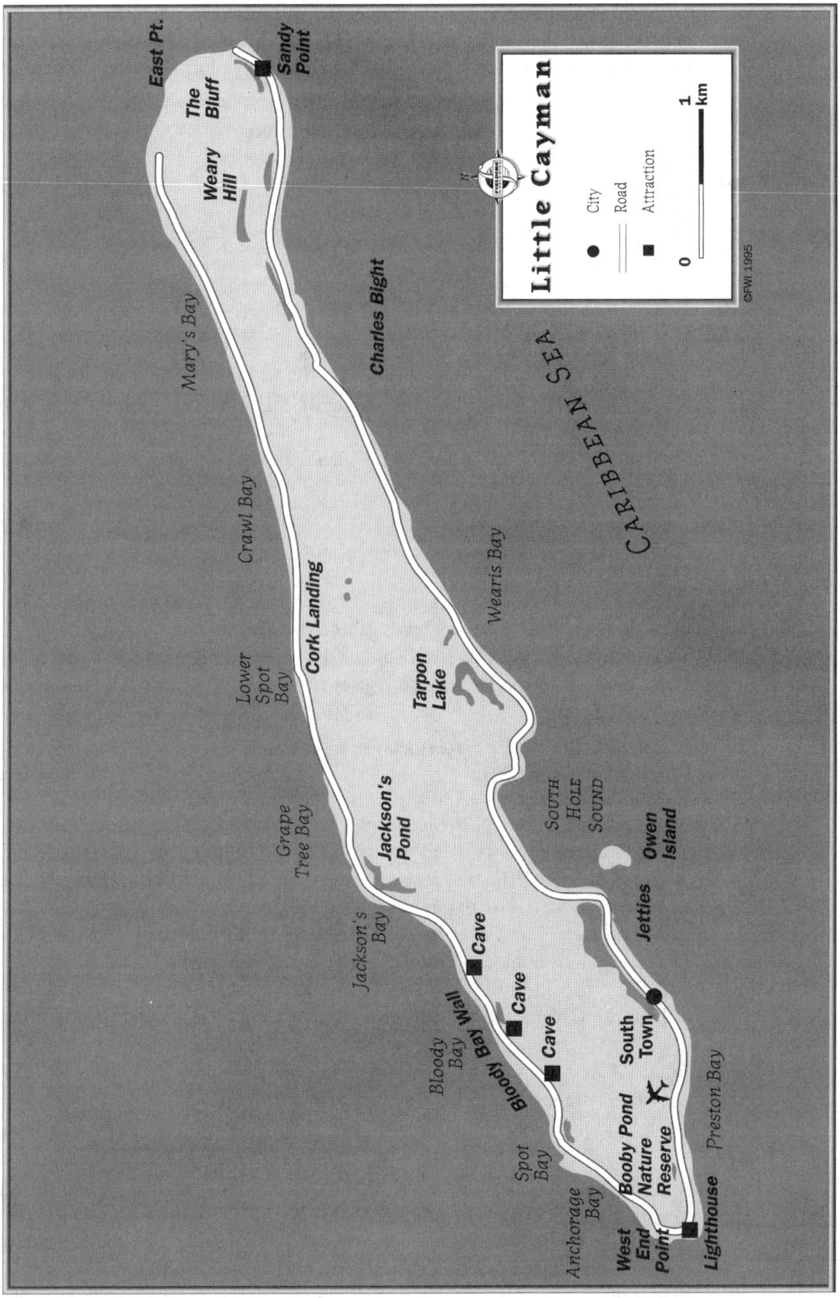
Little Cayman
City
Road
Attraction
0
1
km
©FWI 1995
CARIBBEAN SEA
East Pt.
Sandy Point
The Bluff
Weary Hill
Mary's Bay
Charles Bight
Crawl Bay
Cork Landing
Wearis Bay
Lower Spot Bay
Tarpon Lake
Jackson's Pond
Grape Tree Bay
SOUTH HOLE SOUND
Owen Island
Jetties
Jackson's Bay
Cave
Cave
Cave
Bloody Bay Wall
Bloody Bay
South Town
Preston Bay
Booby Pond Nature Reserve
Spot Bay
Anchorage Bay
West End Point
Lighthouse

City Celebrations

Pirates' Week ★★★★★

Various locations, Georgetown, ☎ (809) 949-5078.

To celebrate its history as a pirate haunt, this islandwide festival, held in late October, brings out the buccaneer in locals. There are costume parades, fishing tournaments, treasure hunts and the ever-popular kidnapping of the governor. Lots of ho-ho-hoing, and more than a few bottles of rum.

Museums and Exhibits

Cayman Brac

Brac Museum ★★

Stake Bay.

Hours open: 9 a.m.–4 p.m.

This small museum exhibits local antiques and relics from shipwrecks.

Grand Cayman

Cayman Islands National Museum ★★

Harbour Drive, Georgetown, ☎ (809) 949-8368.

Hours open: 9 a.m.–5 p.m.

Housed in an 1833 West Indian building on the waterfront—which in previous incarnations was a jail, courthouse and dance hall—this museum exhibits more than 2000 items detailing the history of the islands and its peoples. Students & Seniors $2.50.

Treasure Museum ★★★

West Bay Road, Georgetown, ☎ (809) 947-5033.

Hours open: 9 a.m.–5 p.m.

This small museum specializes in recovered artifacts from shipwrecks, with lots of pieces from the Maravillas, a Spanish galleon that sank in 1656. Among the exhibits are a seven-pound gold bar, dioramas of the islands' seafaring history and an animated Blackbeard the Pirate, who regales visitors with long-ago tales that may or may not be true.

Parks and Gardens

Queen Elizabeth II Botanic Park ★★★★

Center of the island, Georgetown.

Hours open: 7:30 a.m.–5:30 p.m.

This new interpretive woodland trail is less than a mile long, but packs a lot in a relatively small space. The trail passes through more than a dozen Caymanian landscapes, from wetlands to cactus thicket, logwood swamp to woodland and mahogany trees. There's also an iguana habitat partially funded by the World Wildlife Fund that is home to the endangered native blue iguanas, a crocodile swamp with 300-year-old fossil bones and a pond housing small freshwater turtles found only in the Caymans. Bird-watchers may spot Grand Cayman parrots, Northern Flicker woodpeckers, Vitelline warblers, Zenaida doves and Bananaquits. The Botanic Park is the first of several ambitious projects to protect the Caymans' environment. Future plans call for a network of preserves on Grand Cayman and a bluff-top tract atop Cayman Brac.

Tours

Atlantic Submarines Cayman ★★★★★

Goring Avenue, Georgetown, ☎ (809) 949-7700.

Not for the claustrophobic but memorable for everyone else, this modern submarine seats 46 people in air-conditioned comfort. It travels along the Cayman Wall at depths of up to 90 feet, giving nondivers a taste of the fascinating underwater sights. Night dives are especially recommended. Prices range from $79–$90; half that for kids under 12 (children under four are not permitted). Atlantis also operates two

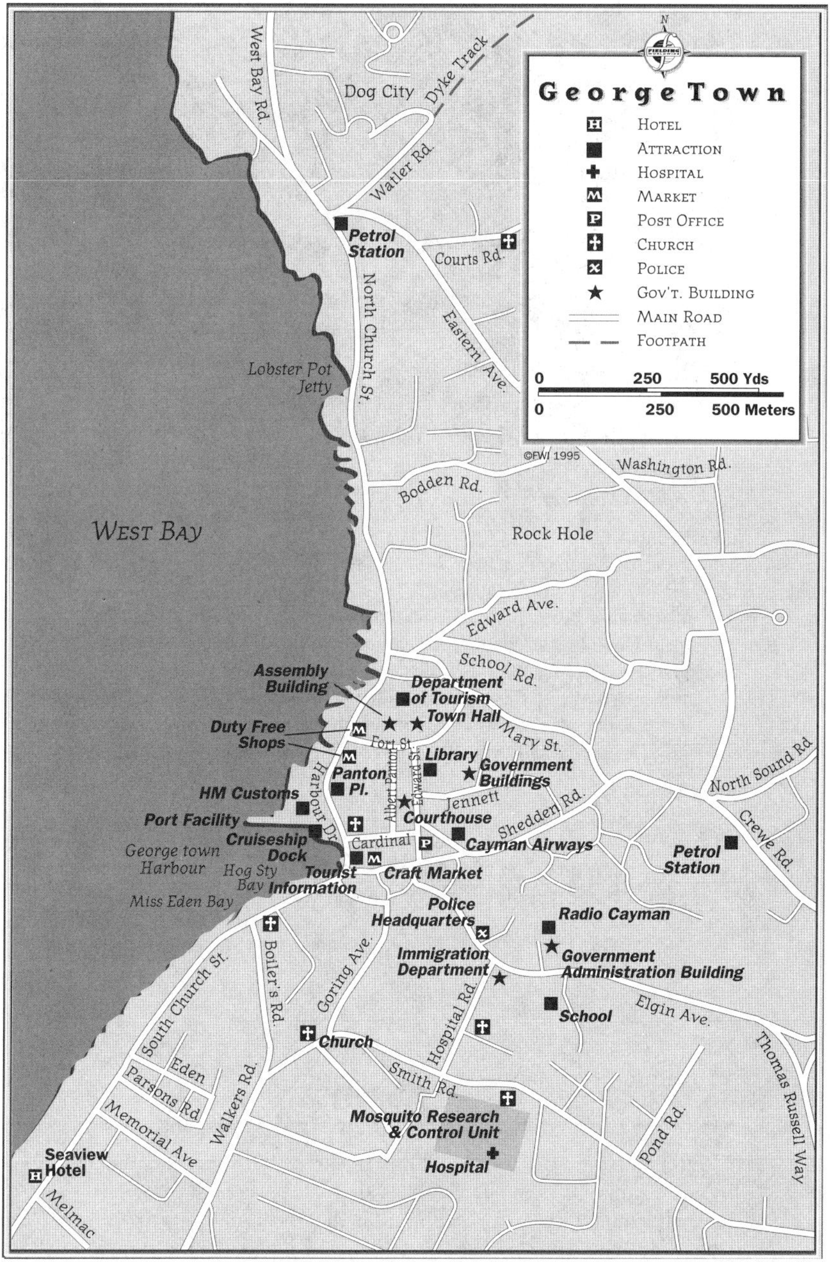
George Town
Hotel
Attraction
Hospital
Market
Post Office
Church
Police
Gov't. Building
Main Road
Footpath
0 250 500 Yds
0 250 500 Meters
©FWI 1995
West Bay
West Bay Rd.
Dog City
Dyke Track
Watler Rd.
Petrol Station
Courts Rd.
North Church St.
Eastern Ave.
Lobster Pot Jetty
Washington Rd.
Bodden Rd.
Rock Hole
Edward Ave.
School Rd.
Assembly Building
Department of Tourism
Town Hall
Mary St.
Duty Free Shops
Fort St.
Library
Government Buildings
Harbour Dr.
Panton Pl.
Albert Panton
Edward St.
HM Customs
Jennett
Courthouse
Port Facility
Shedden Rd.
North Sound Rd
Cruiseship Dock
Cardinal
Cayman Airways
Petrol Station
Crewe Rd.
George town Harbour
Hog Sty Bay
Tourist Information
Craft Market
Miss Eden Bay
Police Headquarters
Radio Cayman
Government Administration Building
Immigration Department
Boiler's Rd.
South Church St.
Goring Ave.
Hospital Rd.
School
Elgin Ave.
Thomas Russell Way
Church
Smith Rd.
Eden
Parsons Rd
Memorial Ave
Walkers Rd.
Mosquito Research & Control Unit
Hospital
Pond Rd.
Seaview Hotel
Melmac

research subs that go as deep as 800 feet and carry just two passengers at a time. This trip costs $275 per person; a highlight is the wreck of the cargo ship Kirk Pride.

The 12,000 green turtles at Cayman Turtle Farm on Grand Cayman range in size from two ounces to 400 pounds.

Cayman Turtle Farm ★★★

West Bay, Georgetown, ☎ *(809) 949-3893.*

Hours open: 8:30 a.m.–5 p.m.

The island's most-visited tourist attraction houses more than 12,000 green turtles, from hatchlings to giant specimens weighing 600 pounds. It's the world's only green sea turtle farm, and while it supplies turtle meat to local restaurants, it also strives to replenish their numbers in the wild. You can taste turtle dishes at the cafe, but skip the gift shop, as U.S. citizens can't import anything made of these endangered critters. Children 6–10 are half price and under 6 are free.

Sting Ray City ★★★★★

North Sound.

Some two miles off the northwest tip and 12 feet down live several dozen stingrays that await handouts from divers and snorkelers. They are relatively tame, but beware of their stinger tails! One of the Caribbean's most popular dive sites.

Sports

Watersports are the bread and butter—or is that the fish and crabcake?—of the Caymanian experience. Scuba is king, and there are three dive shops that have the capability of serving 75,000 divers annually. (For more information, see "Dive Sites"). The less-athletically inclined should definitely take a cruise on the island's famous submarine, the 28-passenger *Atlantis* ☎ *(809) 949-7700*, which dives up to 150 feet both day and night. Also consider a glass-bottom-boat trip—contact the Holiday Inn for information. Deep-sea fishing has caught on with a great passion in recent years. Blue marlin, bluefin and yellowfin tuna, wahoo, dolphin, tarpon, groupers, snappers, barracuda and the occasional shark are all potential catches. The prime fishing season runs from November-March, but fishing year-round remains good. In June, there is a Million Dollar Month sport-fishing competition, with a one-million-dollar prize (where *do* they get that money?) awarded to the angler who breaks the current world record for Atlantic blue marlin (the odds are probably longer than the New York Lottery). On Grand Cayman, Sunfish and Hobie Cats can be rented as well as 60-foot catamarans chartered with crew. Seven-Mile Beach receives the most cruises. North Sound, Spots Bay and Hub Bay have all proved safe for anchors, but boats must first register at the Port Authority in George Town if they want to come ashore. A yacht race is held annually in the spring for locals and visitors. Some hotels and condo complexes have tennis and there is an unusual 18-hole golf course called the Links. You can also do as the British bankers do—take in cricket, or polo, with all the gusto of an ex-pat.

Deep-Sea Fishing

Various locations, Georgetown.

Several outfits offer charters and excursions for deep-sea, reef, bone and fly fishers: **Crosby Ebanks** *(☎ (809) 947-4049)*, **Capt. Eugene's Watersports** *(☎ (809) 949-3099)*; **Charter Boat Headquarters** *(☎ (809) 947-4340)*, and **Island Girl** *(☎ (809) 947-3029)*. Serious fishermen and women should plan to visit Grand Cayman in June, when the Million Dollar Month fishing tournament is held, featuring international competitors and cash prizes. For details, contact Box 878, West Wind Building, Grand Cayman.

Golf

Two locations, Georgetown.

The island's newest course is the **Links at Safehaven** *(☎ (809) 947-4155)*, a par-71, 6519-yard championship course designed by Roy Case. Duffers can also tee off at **Britannia**, designed by Jack Nicklaus, which includes a nine-hole regulation course, an 18-hole executive course, and a Cayman course, in which special short-distance balls are used. Green fees are $25–$50; *☎ (809) 949-8020.*

Mastic Trail ★★★★★

Off Frank Sound Road, Georgetown, ☎ (809) 949-1996.

This newly restored 200-year-old footpath winds through a two-million-old woodland in the heart of the island. Just reopened in 1995, the trail is located west of Frank Sound Road, a 45-minute drive east from George Town. The two-mile trail showcases the Mastic Reserve's scenic wonders, including a mangrove swamp, woodland area, and traditional farms. Birders should be on the lookout for the Grand Cayman parrot, Caribbean dove, West Indian woodpecker, Cuban bullfinch, smooth-billed Ani and Bananaquit. The new nonprofit reserve now numbers 200 acres, with the plan of adding 800 more acres as funds become available. Guided tours, which are not recommended to children under six, the elderly and the infirm, last 2.5 hours and are limited to eight people, so reservations are essential. They are available Monday through Friday at 8:30 a.m. and 3 p.m. and on Saturday at 8:30 a.m.

Scuba Diving

Various locations, Georgetown.

Check out one of the following: Grand Cayman: **Dive Cayman BVI** *(☎ (809) 947-5133)*, **Parrot's Landing** *(☎ (800) 448-0428 or ☎ (809) 949-7884)*, **Quabbin Dives** *(☎ (800) 238-6712 or ☎ (809) 949-5597)*, **Sunset Divers** *(☎ (809) 949-*

7111), **Bob Soto's** *(☎ (809) 947-4631)*, **Don Foster's** *(☎ (809) 949-5679)* and **Red Sail Sports** *(☎ (809) 949-8745)*. Cayman Brac: **Divi Tiara** *(☎ (809) 948-1316)* and **Brac Aquatics** *(☎ (809) 858-7429)*. Little Cayman: **Southern Cross Club** *(☎ (809) 948-1099)*. Prices are generally about $40 for a single-tank dive; $55 for two tanks.

Windsurfing

Various locations, Georgetown.

Try **Cayman Windsurf** *(☎ (809) 947-7492)* or **Sailboards Caribbean** *(☎ (809) 949-1068)*.

Where to Eat

Fielding's Highest Rated Restaurants in Cayman Islands		
★★★★★	**Hemingway's**	$17–$23
★★★★★	**Lantana's**	$20–$34
★★★★★	**Ottmar's Restaurant**	$12–$25
★★★	**Crow's Nest**	$5–$19

Fielding's Special Restaurants in Cayman Islands		
★★★★★	**Lantana's**	$20–$34
★★★	**Crow's Nest**	$5–$19
★★	**Grand Old House**	$13–$34
★★	**Ristorante Pappagallo**	$14–$25

Fielding's Budget Restaurants in Cayman Islands		
★★★	**Crow's Nest**	$5–$19
★★	**Hog Sty Bay Cafe**	$5–$19
★★	**Corita's Copper Kettle II**	$10–$15
★★	**Cracked Conch**	$6–$25
★★	**Edd's Place**	$6–$25

Although most of the food is imported on this dry, scrubby island, the Caymans took top honors in the first annual Caribbean Culinary Competition in 1993. However, prices, in general, tend to be highly inflated in regards to quality (one plus is that portions tend to be enormous). Of course, fresh fish is the basis of most menus; the biggest Caymanian specialty is turtle in all its varied forms (turtles on the Cayman Islands are specifically bred for food). The best time to eat lobster is from August through January. Chef Tell, the TV cooking celeb, has his own restaurant on Church Street called **Chef Tell's Grand House**, which specializes in both German delicacies as well as tropical delights such as spicy fried coconut shrimp and deep-fried grouper in a minted yogurt-and-curry sauce. (Reservations are required and be prepared to spend between $15–$31 for a main course). **Hemingway's** in the Hyatt Regency on West Bay Road is considered to serve the best seafood around. For ambiance, try the **Ristorante Pappagallo**, set on a 14-acre bird sanctuary and housed in an elegant thatch and reed Polynesian tribal lodge—the Italian chefs work wonder with tropical products. Risk-takers should try the blackened alligator tail at **Benjamin's Roof** at Coconut Place, off West Bay Road. The best bargain bet is to splurge at lunch at the better restaurants. Supermarkets are more expensive than in the U.S. but now feature salad bars and prepared salads for about $4 per pound—perfect for picnics. Try **Kirks**, **Foster's Food Fair** and **Hurley's**, all located along Seven Mile Beach.

Cayman Brac

Edd's Place **$$$** ★★

West End, ☎ (809) 948-1208.
Asian cuisine.
Lunch: 7 a.m.– 4 p.m., entrees $6–$15.
Dinner: 4-11 p.m., entrees $10–$25.
A nice change from resort cookery on Cayman Brac is this restaurant and bar that's open early for breakfast and later on serves Chinese food and local favorites. If you phone the management, they'll arrange to pick you up, as there is no bus service, and taxis are expensive.

Little Cayman

Pirate's Point Resort **$$$** ★★★

☎ (809) 948-4210.
International cuisine.
Lunch: entrees $25–$35.
Dinner: entrees $25–$35.
Owner Gladys Howard, trained at Paris' Cordon Bleu, whips up wonderful seafood dishes supplemented by lots of local fruits and vegetables. You can try to recreate some of her dishes back home by buying one of her cookbooks.

Grand Cayman

Almond Tree, The **$$$** ★★★

North Church Street, ☎ (809) 949-2893.
Seafood cuisine. Specialties: Callaloo, conch, turtle steak.
Dinner: 5:30-10 p.m., entrees $14–$22.
An informal and reliable restaurant located just north of George Town, the Almond Tree is a good place to try turtle steak, which is unavailable stateside. More sensitive diners will find all types of seafood, including conch, lobster, filets and a popular all-you-can-eat main course extravaganza for under $15 on Wednesdays and Fridays. It's lit up dramatically at night with tiki torches.

Benjamin's Roof **$$$** ★★

Coconut Place, ☎ (809) 947-4080.
International cuisine. Specialties: Lobster bisque, cajun shrimp.
Dinner: 3-10 p.m., entrees $12–$30.
Greenery abounds in this cool spot in the Coconut Place retail center with a bar dispensing strong libations, a pianist in the corner and spicy blackened-cajun style fish and seafood, with barbecued ribs, lamb and pastas to round out the menu. Desserts are also notable for their richness.

Corita's Copper Kettle II **$$** ★★

Eastern Avenue, ☎ (809) 949-5475.
Latin American cuisine. Specialties: Conch, callaloo.
Lunch: entrees $10–$15.
Busy office workers grab a Jamaican-style breakfast and come back for lunch at this spic-and-span diner located in George Town. Simple, island-style fare includes conch and lobster burgers and local spinach soup. Hot peppers are sprinkled liberally here and there, so beware.

Cracked Conch **$$$** ★★★

Selkirk's Street Plaza, ☎ (809) 947-5217.

Seafood cuisine. Specialties: Cracked conch, conch fritters, key lime pie.
Lunch: 11:30 a.m.–3 p.m., entrees $6–$15.
Dinner: 6-10 p.m., entrees $10–$25.

Not a place for intimate conversation, the noisy Cracked Conch serves lots of seafood in dim, rather stark surroundings. But the food, especially conch, served lightly fried, is smashing. Burgers, soups and other fast meals are also available, and all meals are prepared for takeout.

Crow's Nest **$$$** ★★★

South Sound, ☎ (809) 949-9366.
Latin American cuisine. Specialties: Lobster, conch.
Lunch: 11:30 a.m.–2 p.m., entrees $5–$8.
Dinner: 5:30-10 p.m., entrees $12–$19.

Romance is in the air at this exquisite little eatery on the south point of the island, where diners eat with the ocean waves lapping behind them. Wonderful for a star-filled evening meal or view lunch, the Crow's Nest offers tasty, usually spicy dishes like chicken with hot pepper sauce, coconut fried shrimp and key lime pie. It's hard to believe that George Town is only four miles away.

Garden Loggia Cafe **$$$** ★★

West Bay Road, ☎ (809) 949-1234.
International cuisine. Specialties: Roast suckling pig, lobster.
Lunch: entrees $9–$16.
Dinner: entrees $16–$34.

This top-rated indoor-outdoor cafe facing an elegant expanse of greenery is noted for Sunday buffets replete with champagne and roast suckling pig, and a Friday night all-you-can-eat seafood spread. Otherwise, the bill of fare usually includes jerk chicken and seafood.

Grand Old House **$$$** ★★

Petra Plantation, ☎ (809) 949-9333.
International cuisine. Specialties: Grouper.
Lunch: 11:45 a.m.–2:30 p.m., entrees $13–$32.
Dinner: 6-10:30 p.m., entrees $20–$34.

This lovely gingerbread house in George Town is owned by jolly, red-cheeked TV celebrity Chef Tell Erhardt, who also labors in the kitchen. Cuisine is savory and often deep-fried, but good for a splurge. Erhardt uses herbs, curries and sauces liberally, but with a sure hand, as befits the island's No. 1 caterer. German specialties are also offered from time to time, reflecting the chef's heritage. Expect spaetzle and sauerkraut interspersed with local delicacies. Closed May through October.

Hemingway's **$$$** ★★★★★

West Bay Road, ☎ (809) 949-1234.
International cuisine. Specialties: Jerk chicken, lobster.
Lunch: 11:30 a.m.–2:30 p.m., entrees $17–$23.
Dinner: 6-10 p.m., entrees $17–$23.

Spectacular Seven Mile Beach looms blue in front of diners supping at this, the Hyatt Regency Grand Cayman's luxury dining room. The chefs here create nouvelle Caribbean dishes utilizing local fish, turtle steak and chicken, accompanied by lightly zingy herb and citrus sauces. Cocktails are creative and service is attentive.

Hog Sty Bay Cafe **$$$** ★★

North Church Street, ☎ (809) 949-6163.
English cuisine.
Lunch: 11:30 a.m.–5:30 p.m., entrees $5–$12.
Dinner: 6-10 p.m., entrees $12–$19.

A good, casual American-English style pub, the Hog Sty Bay Cafe in George Town Harbor is a relaxing perch for burgers and sandwiches or fish and chips. It's hard to miss the brightly painted bungalow that hums inside with a crowd of regulars who also like to come for the romantic sunset views and happy hour drinks. Breakfast is also served, with all the usual offerings plus Mexican-style eggs for added zing.

Lantana's **$$$** ★★★★★

West Bay Road, ☎ *(809) 947-5595.*
Mexican cuisine. Specialties: Conch fritters with ancho chile mayonnaise.
Dinner: 5:30-10 p.m., entrees $20–$34.

Lantana's is one of the island's most prestigious dining establishments due to its creative New Mexican-style food. Most dishes are prepared with flair by an Austrian chef, Alfred Schrock, who understands how well West Indian culinary treats blend with dessert hot sauces and condiments. Witness his lightly fried conch fritters with ancho chile mayonnaise and Santa Fe cilantro pesto pasta with seafood. A Viennese tarte tatin is scrumptious. Surroundings recall Santa Fe's Coyote Cafe.

Lobster Pot **$$$** ★★

North Church Street, ☎ *(809) 949-2736.*
Seafood cuisine. Specialties: Lobster, turtle soup.
Lunch: 11:30 a.m.–2:30 p.m., entrees $10–$25.
Dinner: 5-10 p.m., entrees $15–$28.

When the Hog Sty Bay Cafe is busy, this upper-level pub facing West Bay fits the bill. The Lobster Pot manages an intimate atmosphere despite its popularity and the tendency of servers to rush diners through their meals. Nevertheless, the food is good, encompassing lobster, salads and frozen tropical drinks. There's a dart board, natch, for diversion.

Ottmar's Restaurant **$$$** ★★★★★

West Bay Road,
International cuisine. Specialties: Fresh fish, rijstaffel.
Dinner: 6-10 p.m., entrees $12–$25.

Another excellent dining room run by an Austrian expatriate, Ottmar's in the Clarion Grand Hotel proffers classical-French cuisine like bouillabaisse and then turns around and offers a Dutch-Javanese rijstaffel (a spicy feast of 16 courses surrounded by steamed rice). The room is elegant and spacious, and conversations are carried on unheard by diners at neighboring tables.

Ristorante Pappagallo **$$$** ★★

Palmetto Drive, ☎ *(809) 949-1119.*
Italian cuisine.
Dinner: 6-10:30 p.m., entrees $14–$25.

Northern Italian cuisine is served in a series of thatched-roof huts facing a lagoon, surrounded by palm trees and wooden bridges. Despite the overwhelming atmosphere and chattering macaws in cages for background music, the food is reasonably good, with veal and seafood predominating. Even if you don't come to eat, it's a good spot for a cocktail.

The Wharf **$$$** ★★

West Bay Road, ☎ *(809) 949-2231.*
Latin American cuisine. Specialties: Seafood.
Lunch: Noon-2:30 p.m., entrees $21–$30.
Dinner: 6-10 p.m., entrees $21–$30.

The ultimate West Indian dining experience is a seafood supper on a huge deck overlooking the waterfront at the Wharf, which is justly famous for its sublime conch chowder and great service. Chef Tony Egger likes to pair fresh local seafare with Caribbean touches, including a seafood medley baked with a papaya sauce. Harp players rove from table to table, taking requests, and calypso bands play in the attached popular bar. Come at 9 p.m. to see them feed giant tarpon off the rear dock.

Verandah Restaurant, The **$$$** ★

West Bay Road, ☎ *(809) 947-4444.*
American cuisine. Specialties: Breakfast buffet.
Lunch: 6 a.m.–4 p.m., entrees $6–$15.
Dinner: 6-9 p.m., entrees $18–$32.
The only reason this restaurant in the Holiday Inn is mentioned is because it serves up a bountiful all-you-can-eat breakfast for $10, a great buy in bargain-starved Grand Cayman. This morning feast could easily get you through the rest of the day.

Where to Shop

You wouldn't go to Grand Cayman just to shop, but George Town does boast charming shops that offer the high-end designer luxury items; the bait is the duty-free status that makes imported crystal, china, French perfumes and British woolen goods seem a sometime-bargain. Casual resort wear in stylish designs can be found at **Mango Mames**, in Coconut Place on West Bay Road. For an unusual buy, take home some genuine gold pieces-of-eight and other ancient coins and artifacts recovered from pirate ships and turned into jewelry. The **Jewelry Centre** on Fort Street stocks the most complete collection of loose and set diamonds, as well as black coral (imported) and caymanite.

Cayman Islands Directory

BUSINESS HOURS

Shops open Monday–Saturday 9 a.m.–5 p.m. Banks open Monday–Thursday 9 a.m.–2:30 p.m. and on Friday 9 a.m.–1 p.m. and 2:30–4:30 p.m.

CLIMATE

With an average temperature of 79 degrees, the Caymans are pleasant year-round. High season runs from mid-December to mid-April, but July and August, when waters are clearest, are the prime times for diving.

DOCUMENTS

U.S. and Canadian citizens may show either a valid passport or proof of citizenship (voter registration or birth certificate with photo ID) and an ongoing or return ticket.

ELECTRICITY

The current runs 110 volt, 60-cycles, as in the United States.

GETTING AROUND

Taxis are omnipresent and rates are officially fixed. Since the islands are small and flat, bicycling and walking are pleasant alternatives to walking. Autos, are nevertheless, easy to rent. Major U.S. firms are here as well as local ones, such as **Just Jeeps** ☎ *(809) 949-7263.* Motorcycles and motorscooters are for hire at **Soto's** ☎ *(809) 947-4652.*
Driving is on the left side of the street.

LANGUAGE

English is the main tongue, though the accent is a highly musical melange of Irish, Welsh, Scottish and West Indian lilts.

MEDICAL EMERGENCIES

George Town Hospital ☎ *949-8600* is the only facility on Grand Cayman, located on Hospital Road. Cayman Brac has an 18-bed facility called **Faith Hospital** ☎ *948-2243*.

MONEY

The official currency is the Cayman Islands dollar, unique to the islands. Most tourist establishments accept U.S. dollars and credit cards. Local banks will cash traveler's checks. Keep track which dollars (American or Cayman) are being quoted on menus, etc. If quoted in Cayman dollars, the price will look a lot cheaper than it actually is.

TELEPHONE

Area code is 809. International calls can be made 24 hours a day. Local calls now use 7 digits (as opposed to 5 digits in the past).

TIME

Eastern Standard Time all year long, with no change during the northern shift to Daylight Savings.

TIPPING AND TAXES

Taxi drivers generally don't expect tips unless you've exhausted them with heavy bags.

TOURIST INFORMATION

The **Cayman Islands Department of Tourism** is located in the Harbour Centre in George Town ☎ *(809) 49-0623.*Tourist information booths can also be found at the pier and at the airport. In the U.S. call ☎ *(213) 738-1968* or *(212) 682-5582*.

TOURS

Half-day guided sightseeing tours (Turtle Farm, Hell, Governor's Residence, George Town) average $30 per person a half-day; a tour to the caves and blowhole sites on the eastern end is $45 per person; full-day tours including lunch and stops at all island sites average $65 per person. None include swimstops. An all-day snorkel trip with lunch averages $50 per person; a one-tank offshore dive is $30–$35, with all equipment, $35–40. **Evco Tours** ☎ *(809) 949-2118* offers six-hour tours around the island, as does **Greyline** ☎ *(809) 949-2791* and **Reids** ☎ *(809) 949-6311*.

WHEN TO GO

Pirates Week Festival in October is celebrated with parades, songs, contests and games; even businessmen arrive at the office dressed in costume. Million Dollar Month brings anglers from all over the world to compete in one of the world's biggest big-fish contests. Batabano, the weekend before Easter, is the island's cultural carnival weekend. Queen Elizabeth's birthday in mid-June is celebrated with a full-dress uniform parade, marching band and 21-gun salute.

CAYMAN ISLANDS RESTAURANTS	PHONE	ENTREE	CR. CARDS
Cayman Brac			
West End Point			
Asian			
★★ Edd's Place	(809) 948-1208	\$6–\$25	MC, V
Grand Cayman			
George Town			
American			
★ Verandah Restaurant, The	(809) 947-4444	\$6–\$32	A, MC, V
English			
★★ Hog Sty Bay Cafe	(809) 949-6163	\$5–\$19	A, MC, V
International			
★★★★★ Hemingway's	(809) 949-1234	\$17–\$23	A, MC, V
★★★★★ Ottmar's Restaurant		\$12–\$25••	A, MC, V
★★ Garden Loggia Cafe	(809) 949-1234	\$9–\$34	A, MC, V
★★ Grand Old House	(809) 949-9333	\$13–\$34	A, MC, V
★ Benjamin's Roof	(809) 947-4080	\$12–\$30••	A, MC, V
Italian			
★★ Ristorante Pappagallo	(809) 949-1119	\$14–\$25••	A, MC, V
Latin American			
★★★ Crow's Nest	(809) 949-9366	\$5–\$19	A, MC, V
★★ Corita's Copper Kettle II	(809) 949-5475	\$10–\$15•	A, MC, V
★★ The Wharf	(809) 949-2231	\$21–\$30	D, MC, V
Mexican			
★★★★★ Lantana's	(809) 947-5595	\$20–\$34••	A, D, MC, V
Seafood			
★★ Almond Tree, The	(809) 949-2893	\$14–\$22••	A, MC, V
★★ Cracked Conch	(809) 947-5217	\$6–\$25	A, MC, V
★★ Lobster Pot	(809) 949-2736	\$10–\$28	A, D, MC, V
Little Cayman			
Crawl Bay			
International			
★★ Pirate's Point Resort	(809) 948-4210	\$25–\$35	None

Note: • Lunch Only

•• Dinner Only

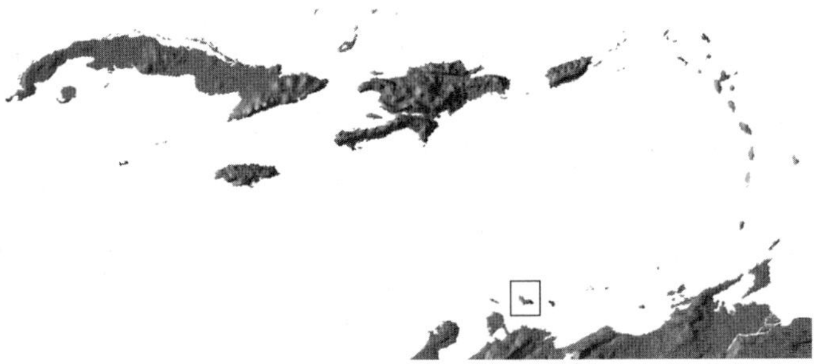

CURAÇAO

Curaçao offers great beaches, diving, excellent restaurants, shops and casinos.

The "C" in the ABC Islands (part of the five-island Netherlands Antilles federation), Curaçao is an excellent choice when one-half of the traveling couple dives and the other one doesn't. Beaches here are small and intimate; and the bustling harbor, expensive stores, excellent restaurants and lively casinos of the Dutch-inspired capital of Willemstad could tempt even a devoted diver to take off his wet suit.

The fact that Curaçao is such an excellent dive spot is one of the Caribbean's deepest guarded secrets. Because most hard-core divers naturally gravitate toward the diving mecca of Bonaire, Curaçao has become a poor relation when it comes to enticing divers from the U.S., but in truth, Curaçao attracts many Dutch recreational divers who might spend up to three weeks underwater. In fact, these Dutch scubaniks are rough-and-ready divers who love to wear "Sea Hunt" suits and go where no diver has gone before. With visibility from 60–150 feet and water temps 70-85 degrees F, the island offers a wide range of sites at every skill; and eco-sensitive divers, especially, will appreciate the permanent moorings of the 12-mile long **National Underwater Park**, where spearfishing is prohibited and the fish are just beginning to get used to the divers. No one should leave Curaçao, however, without a vigorous trek through **Christoffel Park**, where cacti grow over 10 feet tall and iguanas scurry underfoot before they are made into a delicious soup the whole island adores.

Bird's Eye View

At 171 square miles, Curaçao rates as the largest of the five islands in the Netherlands Antilles. Shaped like the arched wings of a great heron, it is located 35 miles north of the coast of Venezuela (which explains why it was long a tourist haven for Venezuelans before the rest of the world discovered it). The entrance of the harbor splits the main downtown area of Willemstad into two. Downtown, which is well developed and recently renovated, is the hub of Curaçao shopping and its vibrant colors and pastel-house facades are true picture ops. The contrast between the bustling Dutch-cobbled pastel fronts of Willemstad and the countryside is stark; once you leave the capital, the landscape takes on the color of brown and russet, studded with three-pronged cactuses, spiny-leafed aloes, and divi-divi trees. You can still see Dutch windmills pumping water to irrigate the arid fields. Since the island receives very little rainfall, much of its landscape looks like the Sonoran Deserts of the American Southwest. Continuing past East Point of Curaçao you will get to the tiny island of Klein Curaçao ("Klein" is little in Dutch.) There are two sides to the island: windward and leeward.

History

Long before Alonso de Ojeda set foot on the island in 1499, Arawak tribes—from the clan of the Caquetios called Curaçaos—were inhabiting the island. After Ojeda marked his claim, a Spanish settlement followed in 1527. A hundred years later, the Spanish unceremoniously left the island, leaving it in the hands of Holland, which deemed it a possession of the Dutch West Indies Company. The island's natural harbors and strategic location in the Caribbean inspired predatory interest among the French and British, who continually tried to send the Dutch packing, with little success. In 1642, a young Dutchman named Peter Stuyvesant became governor of the island, a mere three years before he took over governorship of the Dutch colony of New Amsterdam, today known as New York. During Dutch rule, the island was divided up into plantations. Not all were devoted to agriculture; some of the estates were utilized for salt mining. In 1863 emancipation freed the slaves. The island made waves on the international scene until oil was discov-

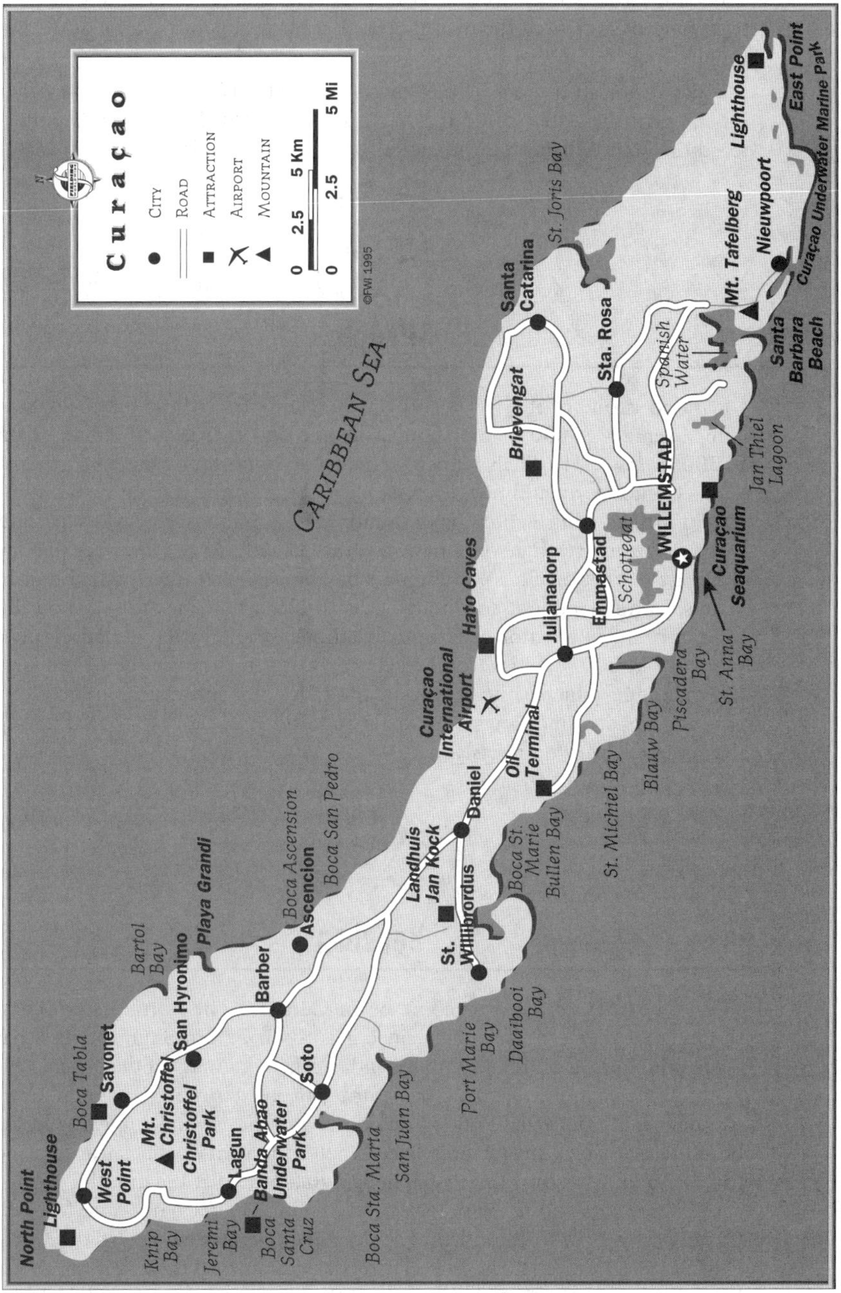
Curaçao
City
Road
Attraction
Airport
Mountain
0 2.5 5 Km
0 2.5 5 Mi
©FWI 1995
N
Caribbean Sea
North Point Lighthouse
West Point
Knip Bay
Jeremi Bay
Boca Santa Cruz
Boca Tabla
Savonet
Mt. Christoffel
Christoffel Park
Lagun
Banda Abao Underwater Park
Boca Sta. Marta
San Juan Bay
Soto
San Hyronimo
Bartol Bay
Playa Grandi
Barber
Port Marie Bay
Daaibooi Bay
St. Willibrordus
Ascencion
Boca Ascension
Boca San Pedro
Landhuis Jan Kock
Boca St. Marie
Bullen Bay
Daniel
St. Michiel Bay
Oil Terminal
Blauw Bay
Curaçao International Airport
Hato Caves
Piscadera Bay
St. Anna Bay
Julianadorp
Emmastad
Schottegat
WILLEMSTAD
Curaçao Seaquarium
Jan Thiel Lagoon
Brievengat
Sta. Rosa
Spanish Water
Santa Barbara Beach
Santa Catarina
Mt. Tafelberg
Nieuwpoort
St. Joris Bay
Lighthouse
East Point
Curaçao Underwater Marine Park

ered in Venezuela, and the Royal Dutch Shell Company, impressed with Curaçao's fine harbor potential, erected the world's largest oil refinery there. The industry lasted well into this century, attracting laborers from many nations who have created the melting pot that makes up Curaçao's population today.

Today Curaçao is part of the kingdom of the Netherlands. The other Dutch territories—Bonaire, Saba, St. Eustatius and St. Martin—are administered through Willemstad, the capital of the Netherlands Antilles.

People

Curaçao is one of the few islands in the Caribbean where the annual income averages $5000 or more (most people on other islands scrape by on $1500 or less). The Shell refinery remains an important element in the island's economy. In addition, Curaçao has obtained the reputation as an international banking center, with hundreds of millions of dollars passing through businesses that only have a phone and P.O. box number. Today there are 79 nationalities represented on the island, from Dutch, English, Spanish and Portuguese, to Chinese, East Indian and Venezuelan. About 80 percent of the population are Roman Catholics; the Jewish population totals today about 600. Rabbi Aaron L. Peller remains the head of the Mikve Israel-Synagogue, which is thought to be the oldest in continuance in the Western Hemisphere, since Jews from Spain and Portugal, via Brazil, were among the earliest settlers on the island.

Beaches

Good beaches are hard to come by in Curaçao. The northwestern coast should be avoided by swimmers since it is too rough, though the west has some calm bays good for swimming and snorkeling. Many of the beaches are private and charge a fee, but in return you get changing facilities, clean stretches and snack bars. Public beaches are notoriously unkempt. Avoid the beach near Willemstad (at the Avila Beach Hotel); it's artificial, gritty and too dense for good snorkeling. **Santa Barbara**, located at the mouth of Spanish Water Bay, is popular with locals and has full services. The Curaçao Yacht Club is close by. On the northwest side, **Boca St. Martha**, where the Coral Cliff Resort is located, exudes a certain peacefulness and the bay is gorgeous. **Knip**, farther up the coast, rates as one of the best on the island, with its large, sandy stretch; on weekends it can get crowded and noisy with music. **Playa Forti**, on the western tip, has dark sand and is good for swimming.

Klein Curaçao, a small, uninhabited island off East Point, makes a nifty day excursion; many charter boats and dive operators offer packages with lunch included.

What Else to See

Willemstad, capital of Curaçao, features Dutch-inspired architecture.

Willemstad is a port ready-made for cruise passengers. Shopping is the best in the Caribbean and most of the sightseeing can be seen within a six-block radius. The city is cut in half by Santa Anna Bay. On one side is the Punda, and the other side the Otrabanda (literally, "the other side"). The Punda is the touristic side, with its numerous boutiques, restaurants and marketplaces. The Otrabanda is more residential, the heart of the local Curaçao life.

To cross from one side to the other, you can either 1) ride the free ferry; 2) drive or take a taxi over the Juliana Bridge; or 3) walk across the Queen Emma Pontoon bridge.

One of the most fantastic views of Willemstad can be had standing on the Otrabanda side, looking back at the pastel-colored face of the other side, where spiffy rows of townhouses and gabled roofs attest to the Dutch heritage. The **Queen Emma Bridge**, beloved by the natives and affectionately called the Lady, is a 700-ft. floating bridge, the creation on the American consul Leonard Burlington Smoth, who made a small fortune off the tolls. Today there's no fee. Farther north is the 1625-foot-long **Queen Juliana Bridge**; the view from here is terrific, especially at sunset when the various colors of the dying sun turn the sea into a colorful palette.

The **floating market on the Punda side** is a must first stop. Early mornings Venezuela schooners park and unload their dazzling loads of fresh fruits, vegetables and freshly caught fish. The best time to see the arrivals is 6:30 a.m., but traffic bears up all day.

The **Mikveh Israel Emmanuel Synagogue** is the oldest temple still in use in the Western Hemisphere, founded in 1651. Twenty thousand visitors a year come to see the special floor of brilliant white sand, which signifies Moses' deliverance of his people to the Promised Land. Visit the museum, which displays Jewish artifacts from the centuries.

At the foot of the Pontoon Bridge is **Fort Amsterdam**, an 18th-century citadel that was once the center of the city. On the far side of the plaza stands the **Waterfort**, a 17th-century bastion that now houses, under the Waterfort Arches, one of the most delightful shopping malls on the Caribbean.

It will take a car to reach, but a visit to the **Curaçao Museum** will be worth it. On display are numerous Indian artifacts, as well as colonial and historical antiques. On the same road trip you can visit the **Landhuis Jan Rock**, a supposedly haunted house from the 17th century. Sunday mornings are the best time to come when the proprietor serves pancakes in the restaurant nearby.

A quick pass through the village of Soto in the northwest tip of the island is warranted. Past Soto a dry Arizona-type landscape is in evidence, with cacti and flamboyant dry bushes. The road continues out to Westpunt Highway, curving back south to Boca Tabla, where the sea has carved a fine grotto. It's a lovely place just to lie back and listen to the waves crashing against the rocks.

On the eastern side of the island, the **Curaçao Seaquarium** is as fun as it is informative. Forty-six freshwater fish hold more than 400 species of fish; nearby a man-made beach of white sand is good for young swimmers.

The **Senio Liqueur Factory** is the center of local production and distribution for the island's original Curaçao liqueur. The small open-air showroom is situated in a handsome landhouse. You can take a self-guided tour and read the story of the distillation process. Samples are offered and there is ample opportunity to stock up on your favorite flavors. A free tour of the Amstel Brewery is offered in nearby Salina—it's the only beer made from distilled seawater.

Craft demonstrations and folklore shows are held at **Landhuis Brivengat** on the last Sunday of each month. An Indonesian smorgasbord is served at the adjacent restaurant on Wednesdays. Dance bands play every Friday night for a party held on the veranda.

Historical Sites

Landhuis Brievengat ★★★

Brievengat, Willemstad.

This restored 18th-century plantation house has 18-inch-thick walls, watchtowers (where long-ago lovers met), and antiques of the era. The last Sunday of each month sees crafts demonstrations and folkloric shows, and there's live music on Wednesdays and Fridays. Located about 10 minutes out of Willemstad.

Museums and Exhibits

Curacao Museum ★★★

Van Leeuwenhoekstraat, Willemstad.

Housed in a former military quarantine hospital for those with yellow fever, this 1853 building displays art and Indian artifacts of historical significance. There's also a garden with specimens of all the plants and trees of Curacao, and the small Children's Museum of Science, where kids are asked to please touch.

Curacao Seaquarium ★★★★★

Bapur Kibra, Willemstad.

More than 400 species of fish and marine life—in fact, EVERY species native to the area—is on display at this excellent aquarium. You can touch some of the creatures and take a glass-bottom boat ride—the truly daring can enjoy the "Animal Encounters" in which divers and snorkelers feed sharks by hand through a thick (let's hope so) mesh fence. You can also swim with sting rays, angelfish and grouper—or just watch the fun from a 46-foot-deep underwater observatory.

Jewish Cultural Historical Museum ★★★

Kuiperstraat, Willemstad.

Located in two buildings constructed in 1728, this fine museum exhibits ceremonial and cultural objects from the 17th and 18th centuries used by one of the oldest Jewish communities in this hemisphere.

Octagon House ★★

Penstraat, Willemstad.

This small museum houses antiques and personal items of Venezuelan liberator Simon Bolivar.

Parks and Gardens

Christoffel National Park ★★★★★

Savonet, West Point.

Hours open: 8 a.m.–4 p.m.

This 4500-acre nature preserve is located on the island's highest point, crowned by 1230-foot-high St. Christoffelberg, the highest point in all the Dutch Leewards. Well worth a visit, but come early to avoid the overwhelming late-afternoon heat. The park includes 20 miles of one-way roads, hiking trails, a small museum, rare orchids, cacti, divi-divi trees, palms, lots of birds and wild goats, Curacao deer and donkeys.

Curacao Underwater Marine Park ★★★★★

Princess Hotel, East Point.

A wonderful spot for divers and snorkelers, this 12.5-mile unspoiled reef is a protected national park. Sights include two well-preserved shipwrecks and an 875-foot underwater nature trail. On a clear day, you can see almost forever—or up to 150 feet, anyway.

Tours

Curacao Liqueur Distillery ★★

Salinja, Willemstad.

The orange-flavored liquor chobolobo is produced here in a 17th-century landhuis (land house). Witness the process and sample the results. While in the area, head over to the Amstel Brewery, where beer is made from distilled seawater. Tours are conducted only on Tuesdays and Thursdays at 10:00 a.m., after which you can drink all you want for free (designate a driver!). ☎ *612944* for information.

Hato Caves ★★★★★

F.D. Rooseveltweg, Willemstad.

Hours open: 10 a.m.–5 p.m.

Just recently opened to the public, these limestone caves are imbedded with fossil coral formations. An hour-long guided tour takes you into several caverns and past Indian petroglyphs, active stalagmites and stalactites, and underwater pools. Neat!

Old City Tours ★★★

De Ruyterkade 53, Willemstad.

Interesting walking tours of Willemstad and its wonderful architecture are sometimes led by owner Anko van der Woude, a local expert on the island's history. The two- to three-tour trek costs $15. Old City also conducts harbor tours on a small fishing bark. Prices range from $10–$17.00.

Sports

Windsurfing is one of the most popular sports here, given a tremendous boost by the constant trade winds that cool the island and blow the divi-divi trees into shape. The Curaçao Open international Pro-Am Windsurfing Championship, attracting masters from around the world, is held annually here. The best windsurfing spot is on the southeast coast between Jan Thiel and Princess beaches, the site of the annual competitions. Novices should begin at the more protected lagoon Spanish Water. Sports fishing has become extremely fashionable in Curaçao, with anglers hoping to catch tuna, dolphin, marlin, wahoo, sailfish and others. Boats may be chartered, with half- or full-day trips, and can be arranged through most hotels, or at the marinas in Spanish Water. Only hook-and-line fishing is permitted in the Curaçao Underwater Park. Yachting is popular, and regattas are held frequently, but little sailing is commercially developed for visitors. Small crafts such as Sunfish are available through hotels.

Sports/Recreation

Cruises

Various locations, Willemstad.

Tabor Tours *(☎ 376637)* offers sunset cruises with wine and munchies, snorkel trips to Point Marine, and excursions aboard the Seaworld Explorer, a "semi-submarine" that cruises five feet below the water's surface. The 120-foot **Insulinde** *(☎ 601340)*, a rigged sail logger, offers sunset and afternoon sails. Finally, **Sail Curacao** *(☎ 676003)* has day and evening sails and snorkel trips. Bon voyage!

Curacao Golf & Squash Club

Wilhelminalaan, Willemstad.

Tourists and other nonmembers can golf on this nine-hole course only from 8 a.m.–noon Fri.–Wed., and Thur. from 10 a.m. to dusk. Greens fees are $15.

Watersports

Various locations, Willemstad.

Try one of the following: **Coral Cliff Diving** *(☎ 642822)* for dive and snorkel excursions and one-week courses on scuba, sailing and windsurfing; **Underwater Curacao** *(☎ 618131)*, a PADI-accredited dive shop; **Seascape Dive and Watersports** *(☎ 625000)* for snorkel and scuba trips and lessons, deep-sea fishing, water-skiing and glass-bottom boat rides; **Peter Hughes Diving** *(☎ 367888)* for diving, snorkeling and deep-sea fishing; and **Curacao High Wind Center** *(☎ 614944)* at the Princess Beach Hotel for windsurfing lessons and rentals.

Where to Eat

Fielding's Highest Rated Restaurants in Curaçao		
★★★★★	De Taveerne	$18–$32
★★★★★	L'Alouette	$18–$40
★★★★	Bistro Le Clochard	$20–$30
★★★★	Fort Nassau	$20–$28
★★★★	Rijstaffel Restaurant	$9–$20
★★★★	Seaview	$15–$30
★★★	Belle Terrace	$10–$24
★★★	La Pergola	$25–$35
★★★	Pirates	$15–$35
★★★	Wine Cellar	$20–$35

Fielding's Special Restaurants in Curaçao		
★★★★	Fort Nassau	$20–$28
★★★★	Rijstaffel Restaurant	$9–$20
★★★	Belle Terrace	$10–$24
★★★	Golden Star	$8–$26
★★★	Wine Cellar	$20–$35

Fielding's Budget Restaurants in Curaçao		
★★	Cactus Club	$4–$15
★★	Playa Forti	$5–$16
★★★★	Rijstaffel Restaurant	$9–$20
★★★	Belle Terrace	$10–$24
★★★	Golden Star	$8–$26

Dining in Curaçao is an international smorgasbord of delights, from French, Swiss and Italian, to Danish, Dutch, Indonesian, Creole, South American and junk-food American-style. Excellent food isn't cheap here, but when combined with some of the most romantic atmospheres in the islands, you'll feel the bill was worth it. Ensconced in a wine cellar in one of the old landhouse estates, **De Taveerne** is a must for anyone on a honeymoon who wants the soap-opera-dinner-by-candlelight-on-a-tropical-isle experience.

Bistro Le Clochard also rates high for romance, with its cozy, candlelit rooms tucked into an old fort overlooking the sea. For local dishes at bargain prices, prepare to trek a bit to **Golden Star**, on the coast road leading southeast from St. Anna Bay. Surroundings are humble, but such Curaçao delicacies as *kiwa* (criollo shrimp), *bestia chiki* (goat-meat stew) and *bakijauw* (salted cod) are superb. One of the best views of the island is at **Playa Forti**, in the extreme northwest of the island. Snorkel before lunch or dinner, then order a brimming plate of *ayaca*, a chicken-beef combo, stuffed with nuts, raisins, spices and olives, rolled up in a corn dough tortilla. *Funchi*, the local cornmeal staple, comes with everything.

'T Kokkeltje **$$$** ★★

F.D. Rooseveltweg 524.
International cuisine. Specialties: Split-pea soup, herring, Caribbean chicken.
Lunch: entrees $12–$27.
Dinner: entrees $12–$27.

Sample Dutch fare by the pool at the Hotel Holland located on the highway to the airport. The hard-to-pronounce name means cockles and this cozy restaurant serves marinated mussels when available. Other specialties to savor are split-pea soup, pickled herring and salads. There is also a dimly lit dining room for those who prefer it. Food is served from 7 a.m. to 10:30 p.m.

Belle Terrace **$$$** ★★★

Penstraat 130, ☎ (599) 961-4377.
Scandinavian cuisine. Specialties: Danish smorgasbord, keshi yena, barracuda.
Lunch: Noon–3 p.m., entrees $10–$15.
Dinner: 7–10 p.m., entrees $14–$24.

Eating out in Willemstad is very often a historic experience—one day it's breakfast high above the sea (never far away here) on a hilltop in a converted 18th-century fort, or, in the case of the Belle Terrace, right on the beach (albeit a rocky one) in a 200-year-old mansion, the former home of the island's governor. Sometimes the cuisine, which includes a smorgasbord at lunch, featuring salmon and other fish smoked on the premises, can be less than stellar, but with a setting like this, who cares? Breads and ice creams are homemade.

Bistro Le Clochard **$$$** ★★★★

Rif Fort, ☎ (599) 962-5666.
French cuisine. Specialties: Bouillabaisse, raclette, fondue.
Lunch: Noon–2 p.m., entrees $20–$30.
Dinner: 6:30–11 p.m., entrees $20–$30.

Dine in this traditional French/Swiss bistro, one of a number of restaurants built in the vaults of what is left of the old (early 19th century) Rif Fort near the harbor. As with many Willemstad restaurants, you may dine indoors or on the open-air Harborside Terrace. Various fondues reflect the tastes of the owner's wife (who is Swiss), and they include raclette with potatoes, pickles and onions, and bourguignone. There's also fresh fish, veal and lobster. The outdoor terrace is only open for dinner, and there's no lunch served on weekends.

Cactus Club **$$** ★★

6 van Staverenweg, ☎ (599) 937-1600.
American cuisine. Specialties: Fajitas, buffalo wings, cajun snapper.
Lunch: 11:30 a.m.–3 p.m., entrees $4–$15.
Dinner: 5–11:30 p.m., entrees $7–$15.

A transplanted, stateside-style after-work restaurant and bar, the Cactus Club doles out tasty burgers, shakes, nachos, pastas and fajitas to homesick Americans and locals who love the place, which is always full. Decor is Southwest-desert, but it's nice and cool inside.

De Taveerne **$$$** ★★★★★

Landhuis Groot Davelaar, Salina, ☎ (599) 937-0669.
French cuisine. Specialties: Salmon carpaccio, chateaubriand stroganoff for two.
Lunch: Noon–2 p.m., entrees $18–$32.
Dinner: 7–11 p.m., entrees $18–$32.

The owners of this innovative and highly regarded French restaurant in the Salina residential area have renovated a traditional old octagonal country mansion—the Landhuis Groot Davelaar, built in the early 18th century by a South American revolutionary—into an antique-filled mini-museum. Once the main house of a cattle-producing estate, it is one of many scattered throughout the arid countryside. Prime beef shows up on its tables in the form of platter-size steaks and chateaubriand for two. Closed for lunch on Saturdays.

Fort Nassau **$$$** ★★★★

Fort Nassau, ☎ (599) 961-3086.
International cuisine. Specialties: Smoked salmon, shrimp with red linguine in a spicy sauce.
Lunch: Noon–3 p.m., entrees $20–$28.
Dinner: 7–10 p.m., entrees $20–$28.

If you never dine anywhere else in Curacao, don't miss Fort Nassau, which sings with history even though some dishes may be overambitious and miss the mark at times. Perched like an eagle's nest above Willemstad and overlooking Santa Anna Bay, diners can see forever from here. Used as a fort by the Dutch in the late 18th century and by Americans in World War II, it became a restaurant in the 1950s. Cuisine runs the gamut from Asian to Italian, utilizing fresh fish, pasta and game in combination with local tropical fruits. No lunch served on weekends.

Fort Waakzaamheid Bistro **$$$** ★★

Seru di Domi, ☎ (599) 962-3633.
Seafood cuisine. Specialties: Veal curry, barbecued steaks.
Dinner: 5–11 p.m., entrees $17–$26.

An alternative to the often-crowded Fort Nassau, which gets inundated with cruise-ship passengers, this hilltop aerie in the Otrabanda was held captive many moons ago by the notorious Captain Bligh, probably in part because he was spellbound by the view. There is no need to dress up for this American-style tavern and bar, which is open for dinner only. There is a fresh fish and salad special daily, as well as barbecued steaks, scampi and veal curry.

Golden Star **$$$** ★★★

Socratesstraat 2, ☎ (599) 965-4795.
Latin American cuisine. Specialties: Carni stoba, stoba de Carco, grilled conch.
Lunch: 11 a.m.–1 p.m., entrees $8–$26.
Dinner: 11 p.m.–1 a.m., entrees $8–$26.

Go local in this deliberately tacky restaurant dive, which has the best authentic Antillean food in town. There may be no better place for carni stoba (meat stew), conch served lightly grilled or with vegetables, goat and criollo shrimp, accompanied with plenty of starchy and filling (and good) rice, fried bananas and funchi (cornmeal pancakes). Beer, especially locally brewed Amstel, is the preferred beverage with this food. Golden Star is open until 1:00 a.m.

L'Alouette **$$$** ★★★★★

Orionweig 12, Salina, ☎ (599) 961-8222.
International cuisine. Specialties: Cheese flan, seafood sausage.
Lunch: Noon–2:30 p.m., entrees $18–$30.
Dinner: 6–9 p.m., entrees $30–$40.

Amid beautiful, sleek surroundings, you can eat creative French cuisine and still keep your weight down at this sophisticated eatery specializing in the best ingredients available, embellished with light and springlike herbs and spices. Chef Maria

Eugenia Saban pays close attention to detail in this restored house in a residential area on the east side of the harbor. Specials that never change are her cheese flan duet with mushroom and basil sauces. Cuisine may be light, but portions are substantial and worth the high tariff.

La Pergola **$$$** ★★★

Waterfort Arches, ☎ (599) 961-3482.
Italian cuisine. Specialties: Smoked salmon with olive oil and cloves, grouper siciliana.
Lunch: Noon–2 p.m., entrees $25–$35.
Dinner: 6:30–10:30 p.m., entrees $30–$35.

A seaside Italian eatery in the trendy Waterfort Arches shopping center, La Pergola serves pizzas, fresh fish and desserts with a light hand—no heavy tomato or gloppy cream sauces here. Take your seat on the lovely terrace facing wraparound windows and watch the wavy action below, and feast on the likes of grouper Sicilian-style with a puttanesca sauce and conclude with an airy, angelic Zuppa Inglese. Closed for Sunday lunch.

Pirates **$$$** ★★★

Piscadera Bay, ☎ (599) 962-5000.
Latin American cuisine. Specialties: Paella, red snapper almendrado, ceviche.
Lunch: entrees $15–$35.
Dinner: entrees $15–$35.

In addition to an Indonesian restaurant, La Garuda, and bountiful buffets served on the Pisca Terrace bar facing a spectacular swimming pool, this newcomer to the Curacao Caribbean Hotel and Casino's dining scene might assure that its guests needn't leave this minicity-within-a-city resort on Piscadera Bay. Famous for theme-night parties, the hotel's latest successful scheme is Pirates, specializing in tasty Latin-style seafood, including paella and ceviche, served by a charming waitstaff in nautical garb.

Playa Forti **$$** ★★

Westpunt, ☎ (599) 964-0273.
Latin American cuisine. Specialties: Cabrito, fish soup, keshi yena.
Lunch: entrees $5–$16.
Dinner: entrees $6–$16.

If you find yourself in the northwest point of the island, dine at this clifftop retreat overlooking Playa Forti beach. It's a hangout for tasty criollo food, and a good place to try keshi yena, an island specialty of meats cooked with Creole sauce and covered with Edam or Gouda cheese. Other specialties to try are cabrito or goat stew, and funchi, or local cornbread. Sunsets are gorgeous here as well. Meals are served from 10 a.m. to 6 p.m.

Rijstaffel Restaurant **$$$** ★★★★

Mercuriusstraat 13, Salina, ☎ (599) 961-2999.
Asian cuisine. Specialties: Rijstaffel, bami goreng, jumbo shrimp in garlic sauce.
Lunch: Noon–2 p.m., prix fixe $9–$17.
Dinner: 6–9:30 p.m., prix fixe $13–$20.

A carryover of Dutch colonial days, rijstaffel is a banquet of up to 25 spicy and savory Indonesian-Javanese dishes surrounded by a mound of steaming rice. A delightful change from the usual steaks and surf and turf awaits at this restaurant in the Salina area, known for its nightlife. To eat here, get a group together and book a table several days ahead for a 16-to-25 dish feast that includes bami goreng (fried noodles, shrimp, meat and vegetables) and krupuk (gigantic shrimp chips). Vegetarian and a la carte dishes are also available.

Seaview **$$$** ★★★★

Waterfort Arches, ☎ (599) 961-6688.
Seafood cuisine. Specialties: Salpicon de mariscos, pepper filet.

Lunch: Noon–2 p.m., entrees $15–$30.
Dinner: 6–10 p.m., entrees $15–$30.
An amiable surfside spot located right in the heart of the Waterfort Arches, one of Willemstad's many converted old army posts and now a busy retail, nightlife and culinary bazaar, Seaview offers up spectacular ocean and sunset vistas from a breezy terrace or air-conditioned dining room. Its forte, naturally, is fresh-from-the-briny fish and shellfish, as well as prime meats, fresh vegetables and international dishes.

Wine Cellar **$$$** ★★★

Concordiastraat, ☎ (599) 961-2178.
International cuisine. Specialties: Roast goose, lobster salad, red snapper.
Lunch: Noon–2 p.m., entrees $20–$35.
Dinner: 5–11 p.m., entrees $20–$35.
Connoisseurs of fine wines repair here to master sommelier and rotisseur Nico Cornelisse's lair, a traditional, small (about eight tables) and comfortable Dutch home near the cathedral in downtown Willemstad. The voluminous wine list consists of vintages from the Alsace region of France, as well as Germany and Italy. To complement these refined labels are some hearty dishes to warm the blood, including filet of beef with goat cheese sauce, venison and roast goose. More delicate appetites will appreciate light seafood salads and red snapper. Service is attentive and personable.

Where to Shop

Curaçao is famed for its shopping, some of the best in the Caribbean, with more than 200 shops. Three of the main shopping streets are pedestrian malls with no traffic or exhaust, making strolling a joy. Cruise ships dock at the downside terminal, which is a short walk to the shopping center; when ships dock, stores stay open on Sunday and holidays. Right in the heart of Willemstad is the Punda shopping district in a five-block square. Since everyone speaks three or four languages, you won't have any trouble understanding shop clerks. Best of all, Curaçao has a very low duty (3 percent) on imported tourist items and no sales tax. No import duty is charged on locally made jewelry, handcrafts, art and antiques. Good bargains can be found on German and Japanese cameras, Swiss watches, Dutch Delft blue souvenirs, and Curaçao liqueur. **Little Switzerland** is the premier watch store in the Caribbean. Designer clothes can be found at **Penha 7 Sons**. The **Yellow House** handles the best stock of perfume on the island.

The most charming shopping center is the **Waterfront Arches**, an historic waterfront remodeled into a cove of quaint boutiques with exotic imports from Paris, Indonesia and South America.

Curaçao Directory

BUSINESS HOURS

Shops open Monday–Saturday 8 a.m.–noon and 2–6 p.m. Banks open Monday–Friday 8:30 a.m.–noon and 1:30–4:30 p.m.

CLIMATE

Like Bonaire and Aruba, its neighbors, Curaçao is to the south of the Hurricane Belt, making storms an extremely unusual occurrence. The island is constantly refreshed by trade winds blowing from 10–20 miles per hour and the temperature stays constant all year round, seldom fluctuating out of the mid-80s. Summer can be a few degrees hotter and winter a little cooler. Light, casual clothing is the rule. Hotels and casinos are air-conditioned so you may wish to bring fancier clothes, or a sweater.

DOCUMENTS

U.S. and Canadian citizens need to show proof of citizenship (passport, birth certificate, or voter's registration) plus a photo ID, and an ongoing or return ticket beyond the Netherlands Antilles.

ELECTRICITY

Current is 110–130 volts AC, 50 cycles. Outlets are American-style. Converters are not necessarily needed for American appliances, but hotels have supplies.

GETTING AROUND

Buses stop when you hail them and taxi rates are regulated by the government. Don't tip a driver unless he carries your shopping bags. Charges after 11 p.m. go up by 25 percent. You'll find lots of taxis waiting for passengers on the Otrabanda side of the floating bridge. If you want to make a tour by taxi, expect to pay about $20 per hour (up to four passengers allowed).

Rental cars are represented by **Avis** toll-free ☎ *(800) 31-2112*, **Budget** toll free ☎ *(800) 527-0700* and **Hertz** toll-free ☎ *(800) 654-3001*. Check your credit card to see if you can obtain insurance just by charging. To save money, reserve the car from the States before you arrive. Do note that all driving is on the right.

LANGUAGE

The native language is Papiamento, the official language Dutch, but most everybody speaks some form of English, as well as Spanish.

MEDICAL EMERGENCIES

The 550-bed St. Elizabeth Hospital is the main facility of the island.

MONEY

Official currency is guilder (Netherlands Antilles florin), noted as NAf. U.S. dollars and credit cards are accepted unilaterally.

TELEPHONE

Country code is *5999*. From the States, dial *011* (international access code), *5999* (country code) + local number. If you are calling from another Caribbean island, check to see if the same code applies. Within Curaçao itself, use only the six-digit number.

TIME

Atlantic Standard Time all year long.

TIPPING AND TAXES

Ten percent service charge is added to restaurant bills, but waiters appreciate an extra five percent.

TOURIST INFORMATION

The **Curaçao Tourist Board** has offices in *Willemstad at the Waterfront Arches* ☎ *613397, closed weekends, and 19 Pietermaai* ☎ *661600*. At all offices you can obtain brochures, maps and have questions answered by English-speaking staff. An office is also at the airport ☎ *668678* (open daily till last flight arrives). In the U.S. call ☎ *(800) 270-3350.*

WATER

Tap water, distilled seawater, is safe to drink.

WHEN TO GO

Carnival takes place in January, an unrestrained revel complete with costumes, parades and street parties. Best time is the weekend right before Ash Wednesday. The International Sailing Regatta is held in March.

CURAÇAO RESTAURANTS	PHONE	ENTREE	CR. CARDS
Willemstad			
American			
★★ Cactus Club	(599) 937-1600	$4–$15	DC, MC, V
Asian			
★★★★ Rijstaffel Restaurant	(599) 961-2999	$9–$20	A, DC, MC, V
French			
★★★★★ De Taveerne	(599) 937-0669	$18–$32	A, DC, MC, V
★★★★ Bistro Le Clochard	(599) 962-5666	$20–$30	A, DC, MC, V
International			
★★★★★ L'Alouette	(599) 961-8222	$18–$40	A, DC, MC, V
★★★★ Fort Nassau	(599) 961-3086	$20–$28	A, DC, MC, V
★★★ Wine Cellar	(599) 961-2178	$20–$35	A, MC, V
★★ 'T Kokkeltje		$12–$27	A, MC, V
Italian			
★★★ La Pergola	(599) 961-3482	$25–$35	A, D, DC, MC, V
Latin American			
★★★ Golden Star	(599) 965-4795	$8–$26	A, DC, MC, V
★★★ Pirates	(599) 962-5000	$15–$35	A, DC, MC, V
★★ Playa Forti	(599) 964-0273	$5–$16	A, MC, V
Scandinavian			
★★★ Belle Terrace	(599) 961-4377	$10–$24	A, DC, MC, V
Seafood			
★★★★ Seaview	(599) 961-6688	$15–$30	A
★★ Fort Waakzaamheid Bistro	(599) 962-3633	$17–$26••	A, MC, V
Note: • Lunch Only			
•• Dinner Only			

DOMINICA

Bananas, coconuts, grapefruit, limes and passionfruit are important to Dominica's economy.

Home to one of the finest primal rain forests in the world, Dominica has changed little since Columbus set foot on its shore some 500 years ago. Just as it was in 1493, there are still no sugar-white beaches, no resorts, no McDonald's, no duty-free stores and little nightlife. What Dominica does have is one of the world's last ocean rain forests, a flooded fumarole said to be the largest in the world, a lake covered with purple hyacinths, and so many species of trees that one of them is even named "no-name." Here is an earth of boiling lakes and mountain cascades, of desolate lava-ravaged landscapes, of forests dense with bromeliads and lianas, chataigniers and gommiers, of landscapes so dazzlingly accented with helicnia and anthurium blossoms that you could easily believe you're in the Garden of Eden. (The island receives so much rain—400 inches a year—that it may be the only nation in the world that exports water, but there is so much mist from the morning and evening showers that rainbows are as predictable as the sun.) Days on Dominica simply take on a different dimension than on other Caribbean islands. The Dominica experience is about fighting your way up treacherous mountain paths, shading yourself beneath chatannyé and mang blanc trees, boiling your body in hot sulfur springs, and tracking the two-note song of the sifflé montang. Quite frankly, Dominica is not for the faint-hearted or the out-of-shape tourist. Divers best know how to exploit a real surf-and-turf vacation—most take a two-hour tank dive in the morning, followed by some equally daunting land excursion in the afternoon. Simply, come to Dominica and expect yourself to be taxed to the max—you may need another Caribbean isle on which to recover.

Note: *Wide Sargasso Sea*, a darkly romantic novel by Jean Rhyss, took place on a plantation in Dominica. Made into a fiercely erotic movie, it is now available on video.

Bird's Eye View

Dominica's small Emerald Pool waterfall attracts hordes of tourists.

Not to be confused with the Dominican Republic, Dominica sprawls over a 29-mile by 16-mile rocky terrain, lying between Guadeloupe to the north and Martinique to the south.The island is part of the Caribbean Rim of Fire, those jagged terrains born of the violence of volcanic eruptions (Dominica was in fact formed by 15 such eruptions). Verdant-green mountains, some scaling up to 4700 feet, reach to the edge of the sea, as valleys actually dip under the sea, making for spectacular diving conditions as well as hot springs that provide natural spas. There is virgin rain forest with trees as straight as chimneys and tall as cathedrals growing in a tangle of ferns and epiphytes. Offshore, underwater pinnacles reflect the mountainous terrain above. A coral reef stretches along the south coast, attracting many species of tropical fish. In the interior, often cloaked by clouds of vapor, is **Boiling Lake**, near the Valley of Desolation in the 16,000-acre **Morne Trois Pitons National Park**. The lake is the second largest in the world, with temperatures that hover between

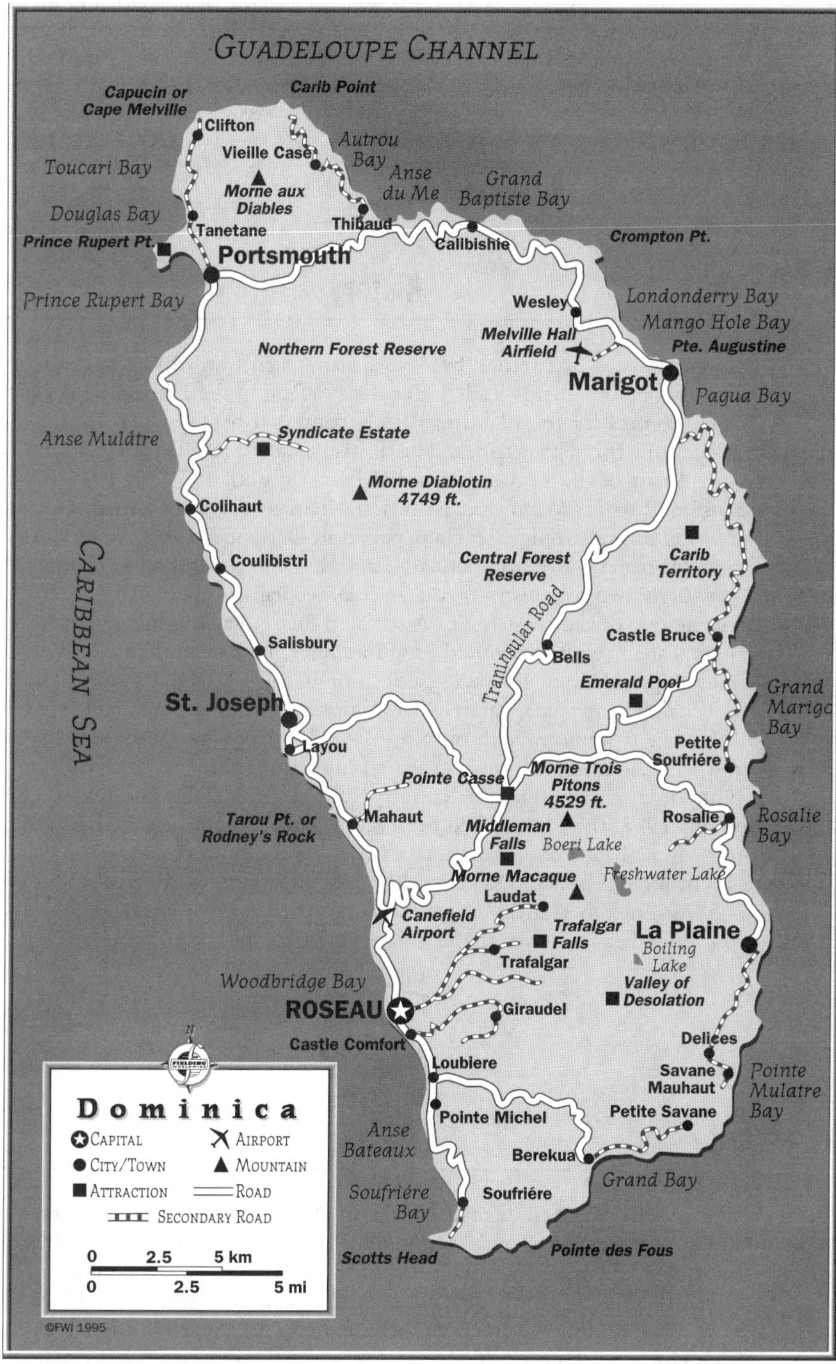
GUADELOUPE CHANNEL
Capucin or Cape Melville
Carib Point
Clifton
Vieille Case
Autrou Bay
Toucari Bay
Morne aux Diables
Anse du Me
Grand Baptiste Bay
Douglas Bay
Tanetane
Thibaud
Prince Rupert Pt.
Portsmouth
Calibishie
Crompton Pt.
Prince Rupert Bay
Wesley
Londonderry Bay
Mango Hole Bay
Melville Hall Airfield
Pte. Augustine
Northern Forest Reserve
Marigot
Pagua Bay
Anse Mulâtre
Syndicate Estate
Morne Diablotin 4749 ft.
Colihaut
Carib Territory
Coulibistri
Central Forest Reserve
CARIBBEAN SEA
Traninsular Road
Salisbury
Castle Bruce
Bells
Emerald Pool
Grand Marigot Bay
St. Joseph
Layou
Petite Soufriére
Pointe Casse
Morne Trois Pitons 4529 ft.
Tarou Pt. or Rodney's Rock
Mahaut
Middleman Falls
Rosalie
Rosalie Bay
Boeri Lake
Morne Macaque
Freshwater Lake
Laudat
Canefield Airport
Trafalgar Falls
La Plaine
Boiling Lake
Trafalgar
Woodbridge Bay
Valley of Desolation
ROSEAU
Giraudel
Castle Comfort
Delices
Loubiere
Savane Mauhaut
Pointe Mulatre Bay
Pointe Michel
Petite Savane
Anse Bateaux
Berekua
Grand Bay
Soufriére Bay
Soufriére
Scotts Head
Pointe des Fous
Dominica
CAPITAL
AIRPORT
CITY/TOWN
MOUNTAIN
ATTRACTION
ROAD
SECONDARY ROAD
0 2.5 5 km
0 2.5 5 mi
©FWI 1995

180-197 degrees F. In the lake basin, rainfall and water from two small streams seep through the lake's porous bottom to the lava, where it is heated to a boiling point. The small, beautiful Emerald Point and waterfall, in a forest grotto about 45 minutes from Roseau, is a 10- or 15-minute walk from the main Castle Bruce road.

History

Dominica was first settled by Arawaks and then Carib Indians, the latter who dubbed the island "Tall Is Her Body." During the 17th and 18th centuries, control for the island was hotly contested between the British, the French and the native tribes. The British finally prevailed and Dominica formed part of the Leeward Islands federation until 1939. In 1940 it was transferred to the Windward Islands and remained attached to that group until the federal arrangement was ended in December 1959. Under a new constitution, effective from January 1960, Dominica achieved a separate status with its own administrator and an enlarged legislative council. In 1967, it became one of the West Indies Associated States, gaining full autonomy in internal affairs with the United Kingdom retaining responsibility for defense and foreign relations. Following a decision in 1975 by the Associated States to seek independence separately, Dominica became an independent republic within the Commonwealth on Nov. 3, 1978. A program instigated in August 1991, granting Dominican citizenship to foreigners in return for a minimum of U.S. $35,000 in the country, caused considerable controversy, but by July 1992, the amount had been reduced and a quota set. By mid-1993, 466 people had taken advantage of the program, however, mostly Taiwanese. In foreign policy, Dominica has close links both with France and the U.S. As a member of the Organization of the Eastern Caribbean States, it contributed assistance to the U.S. intervention in Grenada.

People

Almost all of the people on the island of Dominica profess Christianity, and about 80 percent are Roman Catholics. There is a small community of Carib Indians on the east coast. The tourist industry is small and farming is the principal industry, heavily dependent on the banana, which is very vulnerable to weather conditions. In 1989 the island and its residents suffered greatly from Hurricane Hugo, but have now recovered. Much effort in the past several five years has made Dominica into one of the most active promoters of tourism in the Caribbean. As such, what hotels and restaurants may lack in efficiency is made up by a friendly, generous nature.

Beaches

Dominica has only a few beaches of any worth; the best bathing is done in rivers. The west coast does have some admirable strands, directly south of Prince Rupert Bay in the **Picard** area. On the Caribbean coast, the sand is black, as at Mero, where the Castaways Hotel is located. The closest beach to the city of Roseau is Scott's Head, a 20-minute bus ride away. White beaches best suited to swimming are located on the northeast coast, such as **Woodford Hill** (near Melville Hall airport) and **Hampstead**. The sand is a beautiful golden color at **Pointe Baptiste**. Most of the beaches, however, consist of black volcanic sand.

What Else to See

In Roseau, all the sights are within walking distance; don't miss the **Botanic Gardens** and especially the **Dawbiney Market Plaza**, which is chock full of art exhibits and local fruits and vegetable stands. You'll also find tourist information centers here. By the time you arrive, there may even be handicraft vendors.

Roseau, Dominica's capital, has made Old Market Plaza a pedestrian area.

Many people visit the Carib reservation in the northeast of the island where some interesting woven handicrafts, including authentic native baskets, are for sale. Also interesting is **The Point Cabrits National Park**, a double-peaked peninsula defining the northern edge of Prince Rupert Bay and the southern edge of Douglas Bay. It's home to **Fort Shirley** (originally named Prince Rupert's Garrison), a British fort dating back to the mid-1700s. Most fascinating is the series of crisscrossing paths from the sentry post to the armory to the garrison.

Parks and Gardens

Cabrits National Park ★★★★★

Portsmouth, ☎ (809) 448-2401.

Located on the northwestern coast, this gorgeous spot encompasses 1313 acres of tropical forests, swampland, beaches, coral reefs and various ruins. The best preserved is Fort Shirley, a 1770 military complex, which includes a small museum. Good for birding.

Morne Trios Pitons National Park ★★★★★

South-central region, Roseau, ☎ (809) 448-2733.

The 25-square-mile slice of nature is a primordial rainforest complete with famous Trafalgar Falls, reached by an easy 15-minute hike. There are some other great sights to see here, including a lake nestled in the crater of an extinct volcano, and Boiling Lake, a bubbling mass of mud that's seen only by the hardy—it takes four strenuous hours to trek there. The Emerald Pool Nature Trail is for more moderate hikers.

Tours

Guided Tours ★★★

Various locations, Roseau.

A number of outfits will take you around Dominica, from the city sights of Roseau to the rainforest, Traflagar Falls to Portmouth: **Wilderness Adventure Tours** *(☎ 448-2198)*, **Rainbow Rover Tours** *(☎ 448-8650)*, **Dominica Tours** *(☎ 448-2638)*, **Emerald Safaris** *(☎ 448-4545)*, **Ken's Hinterland Adventures** *(☎ 448-4850)*, and **Sun Link Tours** *(☎ 448-2552)*, which also offers sea excursions. Prices are generally in the $20 to $30 range.

BEST VIEW:

Stop for a pick-me-up drink at the Picard Beach Cottages and enjoy a spectacular view of Prince Rupert's Bay.

Sports

Although hiking predominates, Dominica also offers tennis, waterskiing, windsurfing and snorkeling. Scuba diving along walls plunging hundreds of feet and even in hot springs is especially popular. Two dive shops are **Waitikubuli** ☎ *(809) 44-82638* and **Dive Dominica** ☎ *(809) 44-82188.*

Sailing, windsurfing and deep-sea fishing are popular pastimes in Dominica.

Scuba Diving

Various locations, Roseau.

To arrange a diving excursion, try one of these: **Castaways Hotel Dive Center** *(☎ 449-6244)*, **Dominica Dive Resorts** *(☎ 448-2638)*, and **Nature Island Dive** *(☎ 449-8181)*. All offer classes and dive trips. Prices are generally about $65 for a two-tank dive, $90 for a resort course. They also rent equipment to snorkelers.

Where to Eat

Fielding's Highest Rated Restaurants in Dominica		
★★★★★	**La Robe Creole**	$7–$27
★★★★	**Evergreen**	$17–$20
★★★★	**Guiyave**	$8–$19
★★★★	**World of Food**	$2–$15
★★★	**Almond Beach Restaurant**	$8–$15
★★★	**Balisier**	$9–$22
★★★	**Callaloo Restaurant**	$6–$14
★★★	**Coconut Beach**	$10–$25
★★★	**De Bouille**	$5–$30
★★★	**Floral Gardens**	$14–$25

Fielding's Special Restaurants in Dominica		
★★★★★	**La Robe Creole**	$7–$27
★★★★	**World of Food**	$2–$15
★★★	**De Bouille**	$5–$30
★★★	**Floral Gardens**	$14–$25
★★★	**Papillotte**	$8–$19

Fielding's Budget Restaurants in Dominica		
★★	**The Mouse Hole**	$6–$10
★★	**Le Flambeau**	$4–$13
★★★★	**World of Food**	$2–$15
★★★	**Callaloo Restaurant**	$6–$14
★★★	**Orchard Restaurant**	$4–$17

Although Dominica is sandwiched between Guadeloupe and Martinique, a French style of cooking has not invaded the island. Flavors tend to lean toward the English (meaning basic and sometimes boring). Most people are too tired after hiking to care about anything but quantity. The best place to find a good meal is at a hotel; the tastiest are the ones at **Papilotte** and **Springfield Plantation**. Freshly caught fish is the smartest way to go, as well as local fruits and vegetables; the local pawpaw (or papaya) and christophine (Caribbean squash) are delicious. Beware when you see mountain chicken on the menu—here in Dominica, it isn't chicken at all, but the legs of huge frogs that burrow into the woods.

Almond Beach Restaurant **$$** ★★★

Calibishi, Roseau, ☎ (809) 445-7783.
Latin American cuisine. Specialties: Callaloo, chicken palau.
Lunch: Noon–2 p.m., entrees $8–$15.
Dinner: 6–8 p.m., entrees $8–$15.
A convenient village restaurant on the east coast, Almond Beach is a cool spot to stop for refreshing and exotic fruit and spice beverages made with anise or ginger. The view of the sea is just ahead, and meals include a savory chicken and rice dish, lobster or callaloo (dasheen) soup.

Balisier **$$$** ★★★

Place Heritage, Roseau,
International cuisine. Specialties: Chicken garraway.
Lunch: 12:30–3 p.m., prix fixe $9–$17.
Dinner: 7–10:30 p.m., entrees $13–$22.
Located in a modern, newish hotel on the oceanfront in Roseau, the Balisier is a view restaurant on the first floor, serving competently prepared local fish, curries and a specialty, Chicken Garraway, a moist breast rolled around a local banana and exotic spices. Pies are home-baked and tasty.

Callaloo Restaurant **$$** ★★★

63 King George Street, Roseau, ☎ (809) 448-3386.
Latin American cuisine. Specialties: Curried conch, callaloo.
Lunch: 11:30 a.m.–2:30 p.m., entrees $6–$14.
Dinner: 6:30–10:30 p.m., entrees $6–$14.
Chefs at Callaloo present home-style cooking on a terrace overlooking downtown Roseau. Like its namesake, the hearty soup made from the omnipresent dasheen (a spinach-like green) is made from scratch daily. There are daily specials, which often include conch prepared in a number of different ways.

Castaways Beach Hotel **$$** ★★

Mero Beach, Mero, ☎ (809) 449-6244.
Latin American cuisine.
Lunch: Noon–2 p.m., entrees $12–$18.
Dinner: 7–9 p.m., entrees $12–$18.
Dine informally by the ocean at this hotel restaurant popular for good breakfasts, tropical rum punches and the ubiquitous national dish of crapaud, or frog legs. Sometimes there is crab and conch, and although most of the food is freshly prepared, it varies in quality.

Coconut Beach **$$$** ★★★

Picard Beach, Portsmouth, ☎ (809) 445-5393.
Seafood cuisine.
Lunch: Noon–2:30 p.m., entrees $10–$15.
Dinner: 6:30–10:30 p.m., entrees $10–$25.
A casual sandwich and seafood eatery right on the beach located south of Portsmouth, the Coconut Beach serves as a yacht and boat stop as well as a watering hole for daytrippers passing through the island's second-largest town. It's also a good place to try rotis, or flatbread rolled around curried meat or vegetables.

De Bouille **$$$** ★★★

Victoria Street, Roseau, ☎ (809) 448-5000.
International cuisine. Specialties: Pumpkin soup, lobster.
Lunch: Noon–2:30 p.m., entrees $5–$14.
Dinner: 7–10 p.m., entrees $14–$30.

A baronial and stately restaurant serving a varied cuisine, De Bouille is ensconced in an old fort, now one of Roseau's finest hotels. Diners can feel history in the stone walls, which add plenty of atmosphere to go along with the pumpkin soup, seafood and steaks served here. A good place to spot local movers and shakers.

Evergreen $$$ ★★★★

Castle Comfort, Roseau, ☎ (809) 448-3288.
International cuisine. Specialties: Frogs' legs, crab.
Lunch: 1 p.m.–2 p.m., prix fixe $17.
Dinner: 6–10 p.m., prix fixe $20.

One of the island's most convivial spots, the Evergreen Hotel's dining room is open to non-guests for a prix-fixe five-course meal with a choice of soup and salad; entrees of chicken, frogs' legs and lamb; side dishes, relishes and homemade desserts. The owners, the Winston family, run a very tight ship, with excellent service all around.

Floral Gardens $$$ ★★★

Concord Valley, Concord, ☎ (809) 445-7636.
Latin American cuisine.
Lunch: 11 a.m.–3 p.m., entrees $14–$25.
Dinner: 7 p.m.–midnight, entrees $14–$25.

The name of this restaurant near the Carib Territory couldn't be more apt—the grounds are surrounded by amazingly fertile plants and flowers. Owned by a former prime minister and his wife, Floral Gardens serves creole and international specialties in a room overlooking the Pagwa River. Tour groups often stop here for refreshments, so service can be slow.

Guiyave $$ ★★★★

15 Cork Street, Roseau, ☎ (809) 448-2930.
Latin American cuisine. Specialties: Goat water, rotis.
Lunch: 8 a.m.–2 p.m., entrees $8–$19.
Dinner: 2–5 p.m., entrees $8–$19.

This informal eatery is a popular breakfast and lunch spot serving ham and eggs, French toast, and sandwiches during the week. Saturday's home-cooked creole food is a tradition, and that may involve goat water (a spicy meat stew), blood pudding, calalloo, pumpkin soup, and rotis. Guiyave is also THE local juice bar, squeezing out whatever's fresh that day, including tamarind, mango, or soursop, a tangy citrus fruit.

La Robe Creole $$$ ★★★★★

3 Victoria Street, Roseau, ☎ (809) 448-2896.
Latin American cuisine. Specialties: Mountain chicken, calalloo.
Lunch: 10 a.m.–3:30 p.m., entrees $7–$27.
Dinner: 3:30–9:30 p.m., entrees $7–$27.

Regarded as Dominica's fanciest restaurant, La Robe Creole, named after the native madras costume, serves a sublime callaloo soup with coconut and crab and an unforgettable rum punch. There's also pizza and chicken and tropical fruit and coconut pies. Patrons are prominent citizens who come to see and be seen in air-conditioned luxury, but as sometimes happens on this relaxed isle, service can be very slow.

Le Flambeau $$ ★★

Prince Rupert Bay, Portsmouth, ☎ (809) 449-5131.
International cuisine. Specialties: Creole pork chops, homemade ice cream.
Lunch: 7 a.m.–4 p.m., entrees $4–$6.
Dinner: 4–11 p.m., entrees $9–$13.

A pleasing change from exotic Creole specialties, Le Flambeau, located on the sand at the Picard Beach Cottage Resort, flips omelettes, pancakes and French toast to an appreciative crowd at breakfast. The rest of the day and well into the evening, pork chops and vegetarian specialties are available, and the fresh fruit ice creams are delightful.

Orchard Restaurant **$$** ★★★

31 King George Street, Roseau, ☎ (809) 448-3051.
Latin American cuisine. Specialties: Callaloo, conch.
Lunch: 11:30 a.m.–4 p.m., prix fixe $4–$17.
Dinner: 7–9 p.m., prix fixe $4–$17.

Hearty, complete meals for under $20 draw patrons to this informal downtown eatery, which also has a popular bar. Entrees like conch (called *lambi* here) are served with trimmings, which in this case involve rice, relishes, salads and whatever the chef has on hand. Those wishing to eat lighter can order a la carte sandwiches and soups, or get food to go. No dinner is served on Saturdays.

Papillotte **$$** ★★★

Trafalgar Falls Road, Trafalgar, ☎ (809) 448-2287.
Latin American cuisine. Specialties: Flying fish, callaloo soup.
Lunch: Noon–3 p.m., entrees $8–$19.

Paradise awaits in this garden of Eden near Trafalgar Falls, a haven for nature lovers; amateur botanists will be in seventh heaven. The Retreat's restaurant is only open to nonguests for lunch, but some selections from the small menu, like river shrimp and flying fish, are rarely available elsewhere. There's a hot springs pool on the premises where daytrippers can dip before or after meals.

Reigate Hall **$$** ★★

Mountain Road, Reigate, ☎ (809) 448-4031.
French cuisine. Specialties: Mountain Chicken.
Lunch: 12:30–2:30 p.m., entrees $7–$12.
Dinner: 7–10 p.m., entrees $7–$15.

High up on King's Hill near Trafalgar Falls is the Reigate Hall Hotel, a refurbished plantation home with an attached restaurant serving French and Creole specialties. Not unlike eating in a castle, guests enjoy coq au vin, scampi or mountain chicken in a formal atmosphere, but the waitstaff can be less than alert on occasion.

The Mouse Hole **$** ★★

3 Victoria Street, Roseau, ☎ (809) 448-2896.
Latin American cuisine. Specialties: Rotis, pastries.
Lunch: 10 a.m.–2:30 p.m., entrees $6–$10.
Dinner: 2:30–9:30 p.m., entrees $6–$10.

The cutely monikered Mouse Hole serves as the takeout-short order adjunct to its big sister, La Robe Creole, which holds court upstairs. There is a counter for sit-down service, but most patrons order rotis of curried chicken, sandwiches, pastries and small meals to go.

World of Food **$** ★★★★

48 Cork Street, Roseau, ☎ (809) 448-3286.
Latin American cuisine. Specialties: Fresh fish, lambi (conch).
Lunch: Noon–3 p.m., entrees $2–$15.
Dinner: 6–10:30 p.m., entrees $2–$15.

Literary lions will delight in the fact that this restaurant is located at the site of author Jean Rhys' birthplace. Owner Vena McDougal has turned it into a patio restaurant that brims with office workers at cocktail hour. Diners can sit under a spreading fruit tree and partake of local fish cakes, souse (black pudding) or reasonably priced sandwiches and soups.

Where to Shop

Martinique—Dominica isn't. There are no fancy imports or duty-free stores. Instead, you will have to scope out handicraft shops which, ironically enough, will render you some of the most fantastic souvenirs of your days in the Caribbean.

Dominica Directory

BUSINESS HOURS

Stores open weekdays 8 a.m.–1 p.m. and 2–4 p.m. and Saturday 8 a.m.–1 p.m. Banks open Monday–Thursday 8 a.m.–3 p.m. and Friday 8 a.m.–5 p.m.

CLIMATE

Climate is tropical, though tempered by the sea winds that sometimes reach hurricane force, especially from July-September. Average temperature is 80 degrees F., with little seasonal variation. Rainfall is heavy especially in the mountainous areas, where the annual average is 250 inches compared with 70 inches along the coast.

DOCUMENTS

Visitors will need a passport or proof of citizenship in conjunction with a photo ID as well as a return or ongoing ticket.

ELECTRICITY

The current is 220 volts/50 cycles, which means you must have a transformer with the proper plug adapters. Rechargeable strobes and lights should be charged on the stabilized lines most dive operators have available for his purpose.

GETTING AROUND

Taxis and buses are inexpensive and plentiful. Car rentals are available, but driving is on the left and the roads are narrow and twisting, often with a steep drop on one side and a steep rain gutter on the other.

LANGUAGE

English is the official language, but a local French patoi, or Creole is widely spoken. In part of the Northeast, an English dialect known as Cocoy, is spoken by the descendants of the Antiguan settlers.

MEDICAL EMERGENCIES

There are two main hospitals at Roseau and Portsmouth, with 242 and 50 beds, respectively.

MONEY

The official currency is the Eastern Caribbean dollar, but the U.S. dollar is accepted virtually everywhere.

TELEPHONE

The area code is *809*. To call Dominica from the U.S., dial *011* (international code)+*809* (country Code)+*44* (local access) +five-digit number. If you want to save money, head for the Cable & Wireless (West Indies) Ltd. company where you can make international calls, send faxes, telexes, teletypes and telegrams. You can also purchase phone cards here which can be used in pay phones. You can make both local and international calls from pay phones. (Avoid making long-distance calls from your room —if your room indeed even has a phone—as hotel surcharges and operator assistance can raise the bill even higher than the room rate.)

TIME

Atlantic Standard Time, one hour later than New York.

TIPPING AND TAXES

A 10 percent service charge is added to your bill by most restaurants. In addition, there is another three percent sales tax. If you feel inclined to leave more for service, do so.

TOURIST INFORMATION

For more information write to the **Dominica Division of Tourism** *(Box 293, Roseau, Dominica, WI; ☎ (809) 448-2186, FAX (809) 448-5840).* Mail from the States takes about two weeks to arrive.

WHEN TO GO

Carnival takes place the Monday and Tuesday preceding Ash Wednesday.

Labor Day is May 1. Independence Day is Nov. 1.

DOMINICA RESTAURANTS	PHONE	ENTREE	CR. CARDS
Bagatelle			
French			
★★ **Reigate Hall**	(809) 448-4031	$7–$15	A, MC, V
International			
★★★★ **Evergreen**	(809) 448-3288	$17–$20	A, MC, V
★★★ **Balisier**		$9–$22	MC, V
★★★ **De Bouille**	(809) 448-5000	$5–$30	A, MC, V
★★ **Le Flambeau**	(809) 449-5131	$4–$13	A, DC, MC, V
Latin American			
★★★★★ **La Robe Creole**	(809) 448-2896	$7–$27	D, MC, V
★★★★ **Guiyave**	(809) 448-2930	$8–$19	A, MC, V
★★★★ **World of Food**	(809) 448-3286	$2–$15	None
★★★ **Almond Beach Restaurant**	(809) 445-7783	$8–$15	D, MC, V
★★★ **Callaloo Restaurant**	(809) 448-3386	$6–$14	None
★★★ **Floral Gardens**	(809) 445-7636	$14–$25	A, D, DC, MC, V
★★★ **Orchard Restaurant**	(809) 448-3051	$4–$17	A, MC, V
★★★ **Papilotte**	(809) 448-2287	$8–$19•	A, MC, V
★★ **Castaways Beach Hotel**	(809) 449-6244	$12–$18	MC, V
★★ **The Mouse Hole**	(809) 448-2896	$6–$10	A, MC, V

DOMINICA RESTAURANTS	PHONE	ENTREE	CR. CARDS
Seafood			
★★★ **Coconut Beach**	(809) 445-5393	$10–$25	A, DC, MC, V

Note: • Lunch Only
•• Dinner Only

DOMINICAN REPUBLIC

The best place to tee off in Santo Domingo is the course at Casa de Campo.

The Dominican Republic is the granddaddy of the Caribbean. It can claim age rank over any other island in the region in nearly every category. It has the oldest city, Santo Domingo, in the New World; the oldest street, the oldest cathedral, the oldest university, and even the remains of the oldest hospital. Despite its intense historical interest, the country has lagged behind in tourism for decades due to the negative influence of Generalissimo Rafael Leónidas Trujillo, the former ruthless dictator who controlled the government for more than 30 years till 1961. His regime and the purposes of tourism were at cross-purposes, despite the building of several casinos; the presence of paramilitary troops on the streets didn't attract tourists in any case. Not until the mid-'70s did interest in the island return, as the government poured millions into renovating and building a viable touristic infrastructure. The American firm, Gulf & Western, also contributed to the building of a famous resort in the south as well as other hotels, expanding the number of available rooms and offering new luxury accommodations. These days annual tourists have swelled to more than 2 million, seeking many of the comforts of other islands—and at a fraction of the cost. The island is being heavily promoted today by tourist officials under the fantasy name "Dominicana," suggesting a calmer, less frantic paradise—not exactly the picture of bustling Santo Domingo where the crime rate has risen and tourists must travel with a big eye to caution. Electricity failures are common, which might be why many people head straight for outdoor treks—considered to be spectacular here. What the Dominican Republic excels in are beaches, a thousand miles' worth, anywhere from mountainous backdrops to powdery coves.

Bird's Eye View

The Dominican Republic, which shares the island of Hispaniola with Haiti, is situated between Cuba and Puerto Rico in the Caribbean Sea. An ecological wonder, the island harbors 14 national parks and seven reserves. Beyond the beaches are tropical forests and mountains sprinkled with more than 300 varieties of orchids, and 5600 other plant species, 36 percent of which are endemic. The highest peak is **Pico Duarte** at 10,400 feet, which ranks as the highest mountain in the Caribbean. **Lago Enriquillo**, an unusual saltwater lake 144 feet below sea-level, is home to a large reserve of American crocodiles. *Isla Cabrito*, **Goat Island**, which lies in the lake, has a research center where scientists collaborate with the National Zoo to increase the crocodile population. The capital and chief seaport is **Santo Domingo**, whose 12-block historical center, brings great charm to the island. The road from Santo Domingo leads through lush banana plantations and rice and tobacco fields to the groves of royal poinciana trees in the Cibao Valley, where the island's oldest settlement, **La Vega**, is located. A hundred miles north of the capital is the industrial city of **Santiago los Caballeros**, a center for tobacco leaf production. Once a dynamic town now turned sleepy, **Puerto Plata** in the northern coast is home to many of the island's most luxurious resorts.

History

One could say that the Dominican Republic is really a family affair. The great Christopher Columbus dropped anchor in the Dominican Republic on his first voyage in 1492; four years later, his brother Bartolomeo founded the colony of Santo Domingo; 13 years after that, Christopher's son became the colony's governor, serving as viceroy when the Dominican Republic, then the colony of Santo Domingo, was the provisioning port and jump-off place for some of Spain's greatest expeditions to the New World. The list of ex-

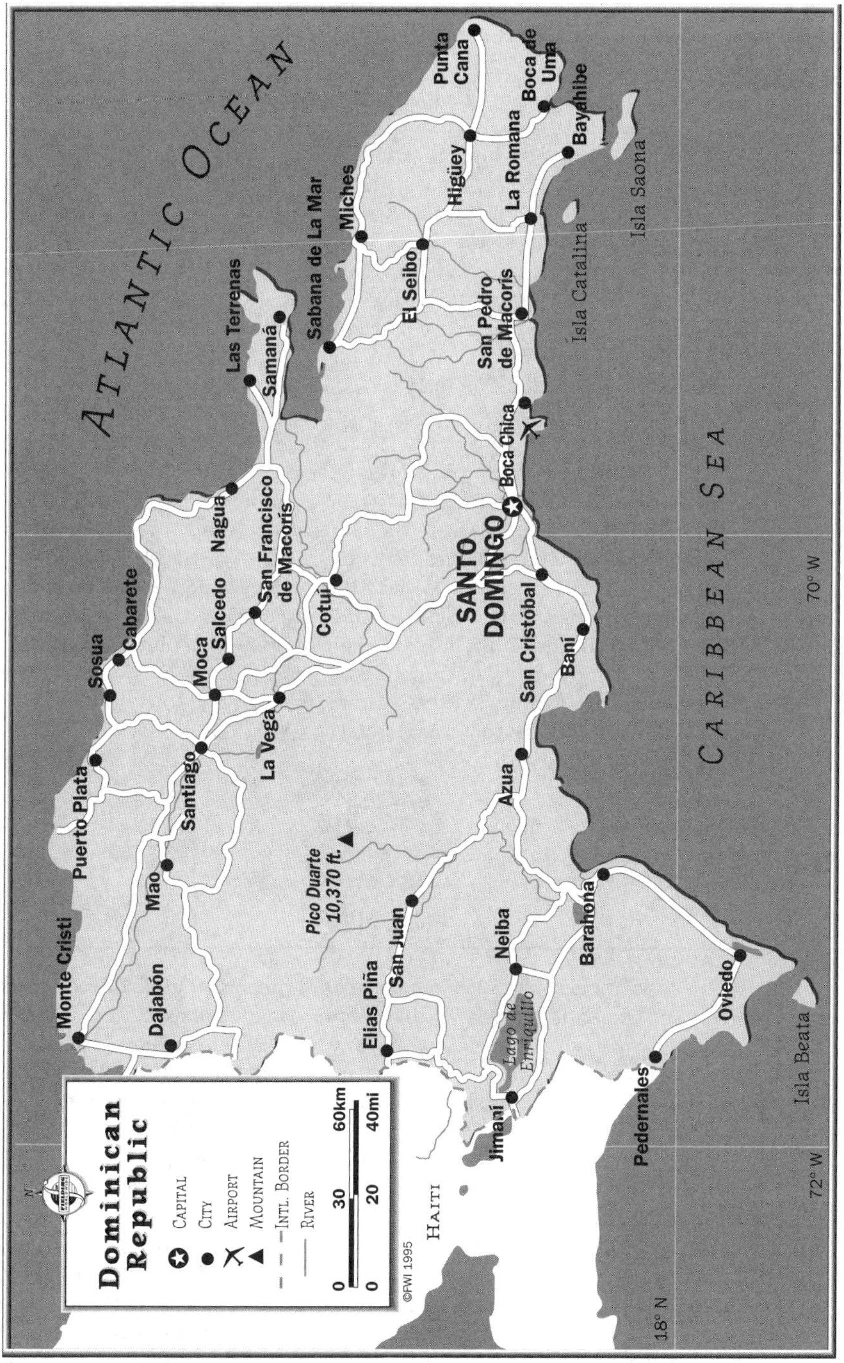
Dominican Republic
Capital
City
Airport
Mountain
Intl. Border
River
0 30 60km
0 20 40mi
©FWI 1995
Haiti
Atlantic Ocean
Caribbean Sea
Monte Cristi
Dajabón
Puerto Plata
Mao
Sosua
Cabarete
Santiago
Moca
Salcedo
La Vega
Nagua
San Francisco de Macorís
Cotuí
Las Terrenas
Samaná
Sabana de La Mar
Miches
El Seibo
Higüey
Punta Cana
Boca de Uma
Bayahibe
La Romana
San Pedro de Macorís
Boca Chica
SANTO DOMINGO
San Cristóbal
Baní
Azua
Pico Duarte 10,370 ft.
San Juan
Elias Piña
Neiba
Lago de Enriquillo
Jimaní
Barahona
Oviedo
Pedernales
Isla Beata
Isla Catalina
Isla Saona
18° N
72° W
70° W

plorers who sailed from this port is as impressive as a Hollywood A-list: Juan Ponce de Léon to Puerto Rico, Velasquez to Cuba, Cortés to Mexico. Even Sir Francis Drake put his mark on the port, attacking it, ransacking it, and then setting fire to it in 1586.

Over the next 300 years, the island changed hands between France, Spain and Cuba, and for a time it was even self-ruled in a phase called "Ephemeral Independence." Since winning its independence from Spain in 1821 and from Haiti in 1844, the Dominican Republic has been plagued by recurrent domestic conflicts and foreign intervention; between 1916 and 1924 it was occupied by American forces. In 1930 the country entered into a 30-year dictatorship led by General Rafael Leónidas Trujillo Molina, who ruled personally until 1947 and indirectly thereafter until his assassination in 1961. His death gave rise to renewed political turmoil, and an election in December 1962 led to the inauguration of Juan Bosch Gaviño, a left-of-center democrat, as president in February 1963. In the same year, Bosch was overthrown by a military coup; subsequently the military installed a civilian triumvirate which ruled until April 1965, when civil war erupted. Military forces intervened on April 28, 1965, and imposed a truce while arrangements were made to establish a provisional government and prepare for new elections. For the next 12 years the country was run by a moderate, Dr. Joaquin Balaguer, who then returned after one term for another two consecutive ones. Presently there are at least 10 different political parties representing diverse ideological viewpoints, including the Social Christian Reformed Party of 80-year-old Dr. Balaguer to the Dominican Revolutionary Party, a left-democratic grouping, to the right-wing Quisqueyan Democratic Party, the Dominican Communist Party (a traditionally pro-Moscow party), and the Dominican Popular Movement, which is pro-Peking.

People

The population of the island (more than 3 million) is a mixture of black, white and mestizo, but each of those terms come with a special island definition. *Blanco* (or white) refers to anybody who is white, white/Indian mestizo, or substantially white with either or both Indian and African mixture. *Indio claro* is anybody who is white/black mixed mulatto or a mestizo; *indio oscuro* is anyone who is not 100 percent black; *negro* is 100 percent African. The African and Afro-Cuban influence is deeply present in the song and dance of the island, with merengue the dominant beat, typically played by a three-man group. There are festivals throughout the year, and international merengue celebrations that attract music lovers from all over. Due to political unrest and an unstable economy (not to mention high unemployment) there is, sad to say, a level of violence that underscores society here; in the past few years, unruly demonstrations and strikes have marred the island's equilibrium. Because of the hard economic conditions, great care should be taken with one's valuables (from luggage to camera to purse) at all times.

Crime is quite prevalent, and tourists are often conned into various compromising situations (big and small). About a quarter of the population is employed in agriculture, and the farther you go from the main city, the more simple and less harried will be the people you meet. Almost all profess Christianity and 80 percent are Roman Catholics. There are small Protestant and Jewish communities.

Beaches

The Dominican Republic is known for its beautiful beaches.

A whopping 1000 miles of beaches await visitors, who often have a hard time just deciding which beach to pick for the day. Unfortunately, the beach closest to the city—**Boca Chica** (about 21 miles from the capital)—is also the most crowded, a veritable zoo on the weekends as locals and tourists alike invade the vanilla-white strands. In the past five years the fine white sands have gone from nearly deserted to a clutter of pizza huts, plastic beach tables and lounge chairs, and rental cottages full of screaming babies. The one thing that has remained protected here are the coral reefs, which serve to keep dangerous marine life from getting too close. As such, feel free to walk out in to the sea. Twenty minutes east of Boca Chica is **Juan Dolio**, with its powdery white beach. Here you'll find the Villas del Mar Hotel and the Punta Garza Beach Club. Other excellent beaches are the thumbprint-sized **Minitas** beach and lagoon, and the palm-fringed **Bayahibe**, only accessible by boat. This area, called **La Romana**, also houses the Casa de Campo Resort, which means it is usually crowded. The island's pride and joy is **Punta Cana**, a 20-mile sprawl (though it seems longer for its beauty), lined with shady trees and coconut palms. Here is located **Club Med**, the **Melia Punta Cara**, and the **Bavaro Beach Resort**. Primitive is the only description for **Las Terrenas**, tucked into the north coast of the Samaná peninsula. You'll be hard-pressed to find anything here other than tall palms, sea, mountains and sand. **Sosuá** could be pleasant since the waves are gentle and the sand white and soft, but the scene is marred by camping tents and hawkers selling cheap trinkets. The beach of the future is **Puerto Plata**, on the north Amber Coast, where there are excellent reefs for snorkeling and the horizon hasn't yet been marred by too much civilization. Windsurfers and waterskiers particularly love the conditions, and many fishing expeditions take off from here. Windsurfing conditions on **Cabarete Beach** are excellent; between June and October wind speeds at 20–25 knots and 3- to 15-foot waves attract some of the best windsurfers in the Caribbean.

What Else to See

The 12-block area known as the **Colonial Zone** is a must-see on any itinerary. The area today bristles with feverish activity, as people and cars jostle their way through the narrow cobbled streets, home to some of the finest restaurants, shops and galleries on the island. Strange how all the noise and confusion of the modern cityscape takes one immediately back centuries, when the city was yet a colony and a home port for pirates, colonists and great explorers. Most recently, the island has invested millions of dollars to renovate this area, and numerous sights are well worth the time to visit. Top on the list should be the **Alcázar de Cólon**, an imposing Renaissance castle, once the home of Don Diego Colon (aka Columbus). The antiques and tapestries did not all belong to Columbus, who lived here with his bride (some are even of the wrong century), but the total effect gives the feeling of life with the great explorers. Built in 1514, it was reconstructed and restored in 1957.

Across the street is the **La Ataranza**, the Royal Mooring Docks, once the colonial commercial district, and now home to several crafts stores, restaurants, and galleries. The **Museu de las Casas Reales** (Museum of the Royal House) presents exhibits that include replicas of Columbus' famous three ships, ancient maps, coats of arms, coaches and a royal courtroom, as well as Indian artifacts. The **Casa de Bastidas** (south on Calle Las Damas and cross Calle El Conde) boasts a beautiful courtyard full of tropical plants and temporary art exhibits that show unusually excellent pieces.

Make time to step inside the most wondrous **Catedral Santa Maria la Meno, Primada de America**, the first cathedral in America. In the nave are four baroque columns, carved to resemble royal palms, which for more than four centuries guarded the magnificent bronze and marble sarcophagus containing (somc Dominican historians claim) the final remains of Christopher Columbus. Started in 1514, the church was finally finished in 1540, its facade a heady mixture of late Gothic to Plateresque styles. The sarcophagus has been moved of late to the **Columbus Memorial Lighthouse**. (Actually, it was Columbus' last wish that he be buried in Santo Domingo.) After the French occupation, the Spaniards stole his remains from the cathedral and sent them to Cuba. Later, both Spain and Cuba claimed to have confiscated the bones of someone named Columbus, but nobody really knows whether it was Christopher (or even *the* Christopher) or one of his grandsons.

If you have time, stop by the Columbus Lighthouse, a newly constructed memorial that includes six museums, a laser-beam lighthouse, and a chapel (one more place that claims to hold the dear old bones of Columbus) and the **Parque Zoological Nacional**, a lake for water-bound birds and an open plains park where animals roam freely. Children particularly love the children's section and the caves that are perfect for prowling and hooting up a storm. One of the most romantic things to do on the island is to take the horse carriage ride through the **Jardin Botanico Nacional Dr. Rafael M. Moscoso**. Other excellent museums are the Museum of Fine Arts, the Museum of Natural History, and the Public Library. The Museu del Hombre Dominicano is an excellent way to absorb the main points of Caribbean history, but a working knowledge of Spanish would seriously help. On the fourth floor is a fantastic exhibit of masks and costumes that feature the various carnivals around the country.

Historical Sites

Alcazar de Colon ★★★

Calle Las Damas, Santo Domingo, ☎ (809) 687-5361.
Hours open: 9 a.m.–5 p.m.
Situated on the bluffs of the Ozama River, this is the castle of Don Diego Colon, Christopher Columbus' son, who was the colony's governor in 1509. Built in 1514 and reconstructed, after decades of neglect, in 1957, the 22-room house has 40-inch-thick limestone walls and 22 rooms filled with antiques from the 16th century.

Capilla de los Remedios ★★

Calle Las Damas, Santo Domingo.
Hours open: 9 a.m.–6 p.m.
The Chapel of Our Lady of Remedies was built in the 17th century in the Castilian-Romanesque style. Sunday masses begin at 6 a.m.

Cathedral Santa Maria la Menor ★★★

Calle Arzobispo Merino, Santo Domingo.
Hours open: 9 a.m.–4 p.m.
This is the first cathedral built in the Americas, begun in 1514 and completed three decades later. The Spanish Renaissance-style building has a gold coral limestone facade and houses an impressive art collection and a high altar of beaten silver. Sunday masses begin at 6 a.m.

El Faro a Colon ★★★★★

Av Espana, Santo Domingo.
Hours open: 9 a.m.–4 p.m.
The Columbus Memorial Lighthouse was completed in 1992 to celebrate the 500th anniversary of his "discovery" of the Dominican Republic.The impressive pyramid cross-shaped monument houses six museums on the explorer and the early days of the New World. It also reportedly contains the remains of Columbus. Several institutions around the world make similar claims. At night, the monument projects a huge cross on the clouds above that can be seen as far away as Puerto Rico.

Fort San Felipe ★★★

Puerto Plata.

This, the oldest fort in the New World, dates back to 1564. You can explore its small rooms and eight-inch-thick walls and be glad you weren't a prisoner here during Trujillo's rule. Lots of sidewalk vendors lend a tawdry air.

National Pantheon ★★★

Calle Las Damas, Santo Domingo.

Hours open: 10 a.m.–5 p.m.

This Spanish-American colonial-style building dates back to 1714 and was once a Jesuit monastery. A mural of Trujillo's assassination is on the ceiling above the altar, and the ashes of martyrs who tried to oust him in 1959 are preserved here.

Santa Barbara Church ★★

Av Mella, Santo Domingo.

Hours open: 8 a.m.–12 p.m.

This combination church and fortress, unique to the city, was built in 1562 and is worth a gander if you're in the neighborhood. Sunday masses begin at 6 a.m.

Torre del Homenaje ★★★

Paseo Presidente Belini, Santo Domingo.

Hours open: 8 a.m.–7 p.m.

The Tower of Homage in Fort Ozama was built in 1503, and was the place where condemned prisoners awaited execution.

Museums and Exhibits

Museo de la Familia Dominicana ★★

Calle Padre Bellini, Santo Domingo, ☎ (809) 689-5057.

See how the other (richer) half lived during the 19th century at this Museum of the Dominican Family.

Museo de las Casas Reales ★★★

Calle Las Damas, Santo Domingo, ☎ (809) 682-4202.

Hours open: 9 a.m.–5 p.m.

Two 16th-century palaces house the Museum of the Royal Houses, which spotlights Dominican history from 1492-1821. Exhibits include antiques and artwork, Indian artifacts, relics from two galleons sunk in 1724, pre-Columbian artwork, and replicas of Columbus' ships.

Museum of Dominican Amber ★★★

Calle Duante 61, Puerto Plata, ☎ (809) 586-2848.

Hours open: 9 a.m.–5 p.m.

A beautiful mansion houses exhibits on amber, the country's national stone, which is found only in the Dominican Republic, Germany and the former Soviet Union. You can buy amber pieces and jewelry at the gift shop. Guided tours are conducted in English daily.

Plaza de la Cultura ★★★★

Av Maximo Gomez, Santo Domingo.

This large, modern complex includes a theater, the national library and museums of Dominican man, natural history and modern art—each well worth a look. Guided tours of the complex are offered in English on Tuesday and Saturday afternoons at 2:30 p.m.

Parks and Gardens

Jardin Botanico Nacional ★★★

Arroyo Hondo, Santo Domingo.

Hours open: 10 a.m.–6 p.m.

This is the largest botanical garden in the entire Caribbean, with 445 acres of orchids, Japanese plants and trees, colorful flowers and 200 varieties of palms. You can tour it via foot, boat, train or horse-drawn carriage.

Los Haitises National Park ★★★★★

Samana, Santo Domingo.

A natural rainforest, pristine and primitive, with mangrove swamps, lakes and caves with Indian petroglyphs.

Tours

Acuario Nacional ★★★

Av de las Americas, Santo Domingo.

Hours open: 10 a.m.–6 p.m.

This is the Caribbean's largest aquarium, with lots of tropical fishes and dolphins swimming about.

Parque Zoologico Nacional ★★★

Av Maximo Gomez, Santo Domingo, ☎ *(809) 562-2080.*

Hours open: 10 a.m.–6 p.m.

Lions and tigers and bears roam in relative freedom at this 320-acre national zoo. There's also an aquatic bird lake, a pond teeming with crocodiles, a snake pit and a large aviary.

Sports

Although there is a plethora of sports activities on the island, most of the island's resorts have monopolized the organized programs. Cruise passengers may sometimes make use of their services, although some hotels offer their all-inclusive activities only to their own guests. Tennis is omnipresent (nets almost seem to be a national symbol). Windsurfing between June and October is delightful, particularly on Cabarete Beach. Bicycling is a passion on the island, and you can choose your destination according to your own skill and endurance—from pancake-flat beaches to steep hill and mountain roads. Small-boat sailing is limited, though most resorts can hunt up at least one ragtag vessel for rent. The golf courses on the island are among the best on the Caribbean, especially the 18-hole Peter Dye wonders at **Casa De Campo**. Two new 18-holers are being planned for the Punta Cana Beach Resort and the Bávaro Beach. The Playa Dorada hotels also boast their own 18-hole courses designed by Robert Trent Jones.

Canodromo el Coco

Av Monumental, Santo Domingo, ☎ *(809) 560-6968.*

Greyhounds race at this track about 15 minutes from Santo Domingo. Post times are Monday, Wednesday and Friday at 7:30 p.m. and Sunday at 4:00 p.m.

Golf

Various locations, Santo Domingo.

The best place to tee off is at one of the courses at Casa de Campo in La Romana; ☎ *(809) 523-3333* for details. Over at Puerto Plata, the Robert Trent Jones, Jr.-designed links are also good; ☎ *(809) 320-4340.*

Hipodromo Perla Antillana

Av San Cristobel, Santo Domingo, ☎ *(809) 565-2353.*

You can wager on a horse year-round at this racetrack. Post times are Tuesday, Thursday and Saturday at 3:00 p.m.

Watersports

Various locations, Santo Domingo.

Try one of these: Deep-sea fishing: **Andres Boca Chica Club** *(Boca Chica,* ☎ *(809) 685-4950)*, and **Casa de Campo** *(La Romana,* ☎ *(809) 682-2111).* Scuba diving: **Mundo Submarino** *(Santo Domingo,* ☎ *(809) 566-0344).* Boat rentals: **Heavens** *(Playa Dorada,* ☎ *(809) 568-5250)*, and **Casa de Campo** *(La Romana,* ☎ *(809) 682-2111).* Windsurfing: **CaribBIC Windsurfing Center** *(Caberete Beach,* ☎ *(809) 635-1155).*

Where to Eat

Fielding's Highest Rated Restaurants in Dominican Republic		
★★★★★	Casa del Rio	$14–$26
★★★★★	De Armando	$10–$22
★★★★★	Lina Restaurant	$15–$30
★★★★	Chopin	
★★★★	La Bahia	$10–$20
★★★★	Restaurant Montparnasse	$5–$20
★★★	El Alcazar	$9–$25
★★★	El Conuco	$8–$15
★★★	Pez Dorado	$18–$30

Fielding's Special Restaurants in Dominican Republic		
★★★★★	Casa del Rio	$14–$26
★★★★★	De Armando	$10–$22
★★★★	La Bahia	$10–$20
★★★★	Restaurant Montparnasse	$5–$20
★★★	El Conuco	$8–$15

Fielding's Budget Restaurants in Dominican Republic		
★★★★	Evergreen	$17–$20
★★★	Coconut Beach	$10–$25
★★★	De Bouille	$5–$30
★★★★★	La Robe Creole	$7–$27
★★★	Balisier	$9–$22

Dining out is a special event in the Dominican Republic—best done in elegant clothes (at the very least, don't go out dressed like a beach bum, unless you're on the beach); the rule is smart casual at lunch and dressier at dinner). The normal local time for dinner (Spanish style) is about 9 or 10 o'clock, but most American-style visitors cave in much earlier; luckily, restaurants usually open around 6 p.m. (as such, it will be easier to get a table in a popular restaurant if you eat early). Local dishes are spiked with Latin zest, especially the omnipresent paella, which is uniformly excellent. *Sancocho* is one of the most filling dishes, a thick stew made from five to seven different meats; if you eat it for lunch, you may be inclined to take a very long siesta. *Arroz con pollo* (chicken with rice) is a staple on every menu. *Plátanos*, or plantains, are cooked in a million different ways. A light delicious lunch might be a *tortilla de jamón* (spicy ham omelet). One of the most favored desserts is a hearty cornmeal custard called *majarete*. For to-die-for snacks that will ruin your diet and your cholesterol for many weeks, try *chicharrones* (fried pork rinds) or the less dangerous *galletas* (flat, biscuit crackers). The local beers are Bohemia, Quisqueya and Presidente, and the local rums are Brugal and Bermúdez. It's always a Dominican delight to salute the end of a good meal with a dark brown aged rum over ice, called *añejo*.

Among the resort hotels, the best chefs are at Dominican Fiesta (La Casa), the Sheraton (Antoine) and Embajador (Manhattan Grill). After 10 p.m. is when the night owls, dressed to kill, turn out for the post-supper stroll down the Malecón. Another delicious tidbit is the *bollito de yucca*, a postage-stamp-sized hors d'oeuvre made of ground yucca root and cheese—much tastier than it sounds. If you get homesick for American-style fixings, head for the hotel coffee shops, where a steak sandwich, hamburger, or simple fruit salad will soothe the aching palate. Remember to peel and/or wash any fruit you may pick up in the local markets.

Puerto Plata

Chopin $ ★★★★

Playas de Bavaro, ☎ (809) 221-2311.
cuisine.
This wonderfully romantic open-air restaurant at the equally romantic Melia Bavaro resort is reached via a short stroll through the rainforest. The restaurant offers a different buffet each night; Tuesday, for example, features Italian fare. Other nights you may find smoked salmon, paella or Spanish ham. After dinner, you're serenaded by a quartet from the Symphony Orchestra of Belgrade playing classical tunes. Lovely! Hotel guests on the meal plan pay $5.00, while the fee for non-guests is $25.00.

De Armando $$$ ★★★★★

Avenida Antera Mota 23, Puerto Plata, ☎ (809) 586-3418.
International cuisine. Specialties: Fresh fish, lamb in wine sauce.
Lunch: 11 a.m.–3 p.m., entrees $10–$22.
Dinner: 3–11 p.m., entrees $10–$22.
The pride of North Coast dining is this top-rated restaurant in a Victorian building, where guests are served international cuisine serenaded by a guitar and string trio. Specialties have included fresh sea bass prepared with shellfish or mushroom sauces, lamb marinated in red wine, steaks and lobster. The menu also features Dominican specialties like lentils and rice and green plantains.

Roma II $$ ★★

Calle Beller, Puerto Plata, ☎ (809) 586-3904.
International cuisine. Specialties: Pizza, octopus.
Lunch: 11 a.m.–2 p.m., entrees $6–$15.
Dinner: 2 p.m.–midnight, entrees $6–$15.
This plain but comfortably air-conditioned bistro with charming service serves an excellent array of pizzas, plain or fancy—cheese or perhaps shrimp, made on dough baked fresh daily. More challenging appetites might go for the octopus, a specialty here, served with a vinaigrette sauce, or with fresh tomatoes, or on pasta. Steaks and filets are also on the menu.

Santo Domingo

Cafe del Sol **$** ★★

Altos de Chavon Village, Altos de Chavon, ☎ (809) 523-3333.
Italian cuisine.
Lunch: 11 a.m.–4 p.m., entrees $8–$10.
Dinner: 6–11 p.m., entrees $8–$10.
This pretty rooftop cafe in the artists' colony of Altos de Chavon is a perfect stop for a light repast of pizza or salad.

Caribae **$$$** ★★

Camino Libre 70, Sosua.
International cuisine.
Dinner: entrees $20–$30.
Pick your own lobster or shrimp from myriad tanks in this unpretentious little restaurant in the gorgeous beach resort town of Sosua. The crustaceans you choose are all raised at the restaurant's private shrimp farm nearby. For accompaniment, a plate of organic vegetables from the same farm round out a healthy meal.

Casa del Rio **$$$** ★★★★★

Altos de Chavon Village, Altos de Chavon, ☎ (809) 523-3333.
French cuisine.
Lunch: 11 a.m.–4 p.m., entrees $14.
Dinner: 6:30–11 p.m., entrees $18–$26.
Possibly the most expensive restaurant in the Dominican Republic (and the chicest), Casa del Rio is just the place for resort dwellers at the nearby Casa de Campo to go for a night on the town, but many fans have no compunction about driving the 100 miles from Santo Domingo to eat here. Any why not—it's hard to resist dining in a tower room glowing with candlelight, overlooking the Chavon River. French chef Philippe Mongereau likes a challenge, and constantly experiments with Asian and Caribbean spices to dress up shellfish, meats and poultry.

Che Bandoneon **$$$** ★★

El Conde, ☎ (809) 687-0023.
Latin American cuisine. Specialties: Argentinian churrasco.
Dinner: 6 p.m.–midnight, entrees $15–$30.
Tango to this Argentinian charmer that nests in a restored home in the Old City area of Santo Domingo. Specialties include huge, choice cuts of ranch-style beef fillets or steaks. Seating is indoors or out on a pretty terrace, serenaded by troubadours playing the *bandoneon* (Argentinian accordion) for you. Desserts are rich and very French.

El Alcazar **$$$** ★★★

Avenida Independencia, ☎ (809) 221-1511.
International cuisine.
Lunch: Noon-3 p.m., prix fixe $9.
Dinner: 6–11 p.m., entrees $10–$25.
The noonday lunch buffet at the El Alcazar is an exotic and very reasonable dining adventure, with a bevy of international dishes and succulent seafood items available daily. World-renowned couturier (and local hero) Oscar de la Renta designed the interiors of the chic hotel-restaurant on a grand North African theme, with gorgeous fabrics, shells and mirrors for accents.

El Conuco **$$** ★★★

Calle Casimiro de Moya, ☎ (809) 686-0129.
Latin American cuisine. Specialties: Sancocho, chicharrones de pollo.
Lunch: 11 a.m.–4 p.m., entrees $8–$15.
Dinner: 6–11 p.m., entrees $8–$15.
This comically hokey but fun restaurant is situated in an ersatz thatched-roof house, where hanging artifacts from former diners provide a running commentary along

with the hearty country cooking (*conuco*). Fill up on rice and kidney beans, stews, cod and crunchy fried chicken bits while hammy waiters turn into musicians and/or dancers at the drop of a sombrero.

Fonda La Aterazana **$$** ★★

Calle Aterazana 5, ☎ (809) 689-2900.
Latin American cuisine. Specialties: Chicharrones de pollo.
Lunch: 10 a.m.–4 p.m., entrees $5–$20.
Dinner: 4 p.m.–1 a.m., entrees $5–$20.
Feel like a Spanish grandee in this whitewashed-stone building in the Aterazana section of the Colonial Zone, sharing seafood or crunchy fried Dominican chicken strips (more delicious than it sounds) with someone special. This bright and festive spot is often jumping with musical groups and dancers performing to a merengue beat.

Jade Garden **$$$** ★★

Avenida Sarasota 65, ☎ (809) 221-2131.
Chinese cuisine. Specialties: Peking chicken and duck.
Lunch: Noon–3 p.m., entrees $12–$22.
Dinner: 7:30–11:30 p.m., entrees $12–$30.
Considered one of the best Chinese restaurants in town, Jade Garden boasts Hong-Kong trained chefs who prepare Peking duck or chicken in a beautifully decorated room in the imposing Hotel Embajador.

La Bahia **$$$** ★★★★

Avenida George Washington, ☎ (809) 682-4022.
Seafood cuisine. Specialties: Kingfish in coconut sauce, conch.
Lunch: 9 a.m.–2:30 p.m., entrees $10–$18.
Dinner: 2:30–11:30 p.m., entrees $12–$20.
Completely unpretentious and a very popular local hangout, La Bahia sits quietly on Santo Domingo's wide seafront and park, surrounded by towering luxury hotels and convivial cafes. It's very difficult to choose from a huge variety of luscious sea creatures served here, but you can't go wrong with a fish and shellfish soup loaded with shrimp and lobster, or kingfish with a tropical coconut sauce. The prices are so reasonable for what you're served, it's almost beyond belief.

Lago Grill **$$** ★★

Casa de Campo, La Romana, ☎ (809) 523-3333.
American cuisine.
Lunch: Noon–4 p.m., entrees $5–$15.
Terrific breakfasts and lunches are served at this view spot on the golf course of the Casa de Campo resort. Happily for the many top stateside executives who stay here, they (and you) can have cooked-to-order eggs and omelets any style or an array of freshly squeezed juices from an exotic fruit bar. Dominican and Caribbean entrees, delicious burgers and sandwiches, and a copious salad bar are top choices for lunch.

Lina Restaurant **$$$** ★★★★★

Avenida Maximo Gomez, ☎ (809) 685-5000.
Spanish cuisine. Specialties: Zarzuela de mariscos, paella.
Lunch: 11 a.m.–4:30 p.m., entrees $15–$24.
Dinner: 6 p.m.–midnight, entrees $15–$30.
Before the Dominican Republic became a popular tourist destination, Chef Lina Aguado was already a legend; after serving as personal chef to long-reigning president Rafael Trujillo, she opened a small eatery which grew like Topsy into a hotel/restaurant that bears her name. Today, others with equal skill and passion have inherited the great cucinera's recipes for paella valenciana or cazuela de mariscos with Pernod, and interpret them with aplomb.

Meson de la Cava **$$$** ★★

Avenida Mirador del Sur, ☎ *(809) 533-2818.*
International cuisine.
Lunch: 11 a.m.–3:30 p.m., entrees $25–$30.
Dinner: 6 p.m.–midnight, entrees $25–$40.
In order to eat here, diners must descend to a cavern way below ground (some 50 feet), reached via a scary staircase. What's down under is some rollicking entertainment from a live band (contemporary and merengue) and simply prepared, unsurprising, but delicious food. Some people might find this sort of thing silly, but kudos must be given to whomever thought up this clever idea, which seems to be working. Reserve way in advance, and dress fashionably.

Neptuno's Club **$$$** ★★

Boca Chica Beach, Boca Chica, ☎ *(809) 523-4703.*
Seafood cuisine.
Lunch: 9 a.m.–2 p.m., entrees $10–$20.
Dinner: 2–10 p.m., entrees $10–$25.
Calm and warm waters and a short (about 45 minute) drive from the capital make Boca Chica Beach, where this little hut is located, popular with daytrippers. Neptuno's has a good reputation for fish stews and sauteed kingfish, although international meals are served as well.

Pez Dorado **$$$** ★★★

43 Calle el Sol, Santiago Caballeros, ☎ *(809) 582-2518.*
Chinese cuisine. Specialties: Chinese seafood.
Lunch: 11 a.m.–3 p.m., entrees $18–$30.
Dinner: 6–11:30 p.m., entrees $18–$30.
If you find yourself visiting the historical city of Santiago de los Caballeros, about two hours away from Santo Domingo, this restaurant serving seafood Chinese-style in a posh, comfortable room is one of the best dining choices in town. Perhaps afterwards, you can wend your way to a local dance club—after all, this is the birthplace of the merengue.

Reina de Espana **$$** ★★

Avenida Cervantes 103, ☎ *(809) 685-2588.*
Spanish cuisine.
Lunch: Noon–4 p.m., entrees $8–$20.
Dinner: 4–11 p.m., entrees $8–$20.
In a city where Spanish food is treated with respect, Reina de Espana, located in a restored home not far from the sea, manages to present more than just the average paella or seafood stew for discriminating diners. The menu traverses each region of Spain, with roast quail or suckling pig prepared as specials from time to time. But the old favorites like gazpacho are all represented and rarely disappoint.

Restaurant Montparnasse **$$$** ★★★★

Avenida Lope de Vega 24, ☎ *(809) 562-4141.*
Latin American cuisine.
Lunch: Noon–2 p.m., entrees $5–$18.
Dinner: 2 p.m.–midnight, entrees $11–$20.
Prominent local folk like to eat here, especially for lunch, making this creative Franco-Caribbean bistro a good place to observe them. But those not inclined to eavesdropping or voyeurism will still enjoy the unusual combinations of native vegetables like pumpkin and plantain pureed into creamy bisques or a vichyssoise. Decadent desserts like chocolate souffle are served all day and night—in true Dominican fashion, the place stays open late.

Vesuvio I **$$** ★★

Avenida G. Washington, ☎ *(809) 221-3333.*

Italian cuisine.
Lunch: 11 a.m.–2 p.m., entrees $8–$18.
Dinner: 2 p.m.–midnight, entrees $8–$20.
The Bonarelli family from Naples has been running this boisterous family restaurant on the Malecon since the 1950s. As they are not content to rest on past laurels, every visit brings a new specialty or improvements on old favorites. The voluminous menu features seafood and plenty of it, including crayfish with garlic, although veal scallopine with fresh herbs is worth noting. Decor is contemporary, with plenty of colorful marine life painted on the walls.

Where to Shop

Bargaining is as second nature as breathing in the Dominican Republic. If you don't bargain, you aren't respected; shopkeepers enjoy the cat-and-mouse game and even look forward to it. Don't disappoint them. At the same time, don't give in to a vendor's first, second, or third price—they can be hard-nosed because they know your time is precious and your wallet is on vacation. Before you go, bone up on a few choice phrases in Spanish, including the well-understood "Non!"

Everyone comes to the Dominican Republic hot on the trail of jewelry made from amber. The island boasts one of the world's largest deposits, and the prices for this translucent, semiprecious stone will make your jaw drop. (Don't succumb to the tourist disease called "souvenir overkill" when you see too many displays of them; they are lovely and will look special by the time you get your piece home.) A type of petrified resin taken from coniferous forests that disappeared from the Earth more than 50 million years ago, amber comes in many colors ranging from pale lemon to dark brown. Best buys are those which have a tiny insect or small leaves embedded inside. (Remember that childhood novel *Bug in Amber*?)

Santo Domingo's main covered market is called **El Mercado Modelo**. Located in the Colonial Zone bordering Calle Mella, it has lots of shops, eateries, bars and boutiques located in the restored buildings of La Ataranza, across from the Alcázar. It's lovely to walk down the Calle El Conde, Santo Domingo's main shopping street in the Colonial Zone, now sectioned off for pedestrians only. Some of the best shops here are far north of the Colonial Zone between Calle Mella and Av. Las Américas. Fine art galleries are located in the **Altos de Chavón**, with stores grouped around the main square. The **Tourist Bazaar** *(Calle Duarte 61)* in Puerto Plata boasts seven showrooms in a finely renovated old mansion. For good souvenirs and local jewelry, try **Calle Beller** (in the Plaza Shopping Center *at Calle Duarte and Av. 30 de Marzo.*) Avoid buying a tortoise shell since a U.S. customs official will confiscate it if he finds it in your bag.

Fine art galleries are located in the Altos de Chavón, with stores grouped around the main square. Among the best names are **Arawak Gallery** and **Novo Atarazana**. Other great home-crafted buys are hand-carved wood rocking chairs; they are sold unassembled and boxed for transport, so make sure you are handy with a screwdriver. For other woodcrafts, check out the stalls at the El Mercado Modelo. Macrame, baskets and pottery figurines are all reminiscent of the island's crafts.

Dominican Republic Directory

BUSINESS HOURS

Stores open weekdays 8 a.m.–12:30 p.m. and 2:30–5 p.m. and Saturday 8 a.m.–noon. Banks open weekdays 8:30 a.m.–4:30 p.m.

CLIMATE

The climate is subtropical; with an average annual temperature of 80 degrees in Santo Domingo, temperatures are generally between 66 and 88 degrees F. The west and southwest of the country are arid. Hispaniola lis in the path of tropical cyclones.

DOCUMENTS

In order to purchase a $10 tourist card, good for 90 days, visitors must present a valid passport or other proof of citizenship (birth certificate, voter's registration card, with an official photo ID such as driver's license). Cards may be purchased upon arrival, or through the consulate.

ELECTRICITY

Current is 100 volts, 60 cycles, as in the United States.

GETTING AROUND

Taxis are available and fellow travelers are usually open to sharing a taxi. Buses in Santo Domingo are called *públicos*, small blue-and-white or blue-and-red cars that run regular routes, stopping to let passengers on and off. The fare is two pesos. There are also *conchos* or *coléctivos* (privately owned buses) whose drivers tool around the major thoroughfares, leaning out the window and trying to seduce passengers onboard. (For this inconvenience you get to pay a peso less.) Privately owned air-conditioned buses make regular runs to Santiago, Puerto Plata and other destinations. Reservations can be made by calling **Metro Buses** *(Av. Winston Churchill; ☎ (809) 586-6063* in Puerto Plata).

Cars can be rented in the airports and at many hotels. The top names are **Budget** ☎ *(809) 562-6812*; and **Hertz** ☎ *(809) 688-2277*. Driving is on the right side of the street, but drivers here are maniacs, often driving down the middle of the road and passing dangerously whenever they feel like it. They are nice enough, however, to flash their light-on when they know the highway patrol is lurking about—the 50 mph. (80 kph) limit is strictly enforced. (Police have been known to stop drivers on the pretext of some violation and insinuate the need for a bribe. If you must drive around the unilluminated mountain roads at night, drive with utmost caution since many cars do not have headlights or taillights, cows stand in the middle of the road, and bicycles are rarely well lit. Gas stations are few and far between.

Motorbikes, called *motoconchos*, are a popular and inexpensive way to tool around the island, especially in such places as Puerto Plata, Sasúa and Jarabacoa. Bikes can be flagged down in road and town.

LANGUAGE

The official language is Spanish, so do as much as you can to bone up on Spanish before you go. Officially, nearly everyone involved in tourism speaks English, but it is sometimes a quizzical version and many people have trouble understanding English. Waitresses in coffee shops may simply drop their jaws when you speak to them in English. In the outlying areas, it is absolutely necessary to speak Spanish. Bring along a phrase book and keep it handy in your purse.

MONEY

Official currency is the Dominican peso. Most hotels and shops welcome American dollars as well as major credit cards and traveler's checks. Try to spend your pesos rather than having to exchange them back into dollars before you leave.

TELEPHONE

The country code is *809.* To call the Dominican Republic from the United States, dial *011* (international access), the country code *(809)* and the local number. Connections from the U.S. are generally made with ease and are clear. Calling from the Dominican Republic can become a headache—fast. There is a direct-dial system, but you should feel extraordinarily blessed to have it work right. Try dialing 1, then the area code, followed by the number.

TIME

Atlantic Standard Time year-round.

TIPPING

Restaurants add a whopping 21 percent government tax (which includes a 10 percent service charge) to all bills. In restaurants and nightclubs, an extra 5–10 percent above the service charge included on the bill will be greatly appreciated by the waiters and waitresses. Taxi drivers expect a 10 percent tip; tip more if you arrive alive.

TOURIST INFORMATION

The **Dominican Tourist Information Center** is located at the corner of *Avs. México an d30 de Marzo;* ☎ *221-4660* or *00-752-1151*. There are also information booths in Santiago (City Hall Av. Duarte; ☎ *582-5885* and in Puerto Plata Av. Hermanas Mirabel ☎ *586-3676*. You can also find a booth at the airport open daily. In the U.S. call ☎ *(212) 768-2481*.

WHEN TO GO

Merengue Week explodes in late July, the island's biggest rum-filled festival dedicated to the national dance. Carnival is held on February 27.

DOMINICAN REPUBLIC RESTAURANTS	PHONE	ENTREE	CR. CARDS
Puerto Plata			
Continental			
★★★★ **Chopin**	(809) 221-2311		A, DC, MC, V
International			
★★★★★ **De Armando**	(809) 586-3418	$10–$22	A, DC, MC, V
★★ **Roma II**	(809) 586-3904	$6–$15	A, MC, V

DOMINICAN REPUBLIC RESTAURANTS		PHONE	ENTREE	CR. CARDS
Santo Domingo				
	American			
★★	Lago Grill	(809) 523-3333	$5–$15•	A, DC, MC, V
	Chinese			
★★★	Pez Dorado	(809) 582-2518	$18–$30	MC, V
★★	Jade Garden	(809) 221-2131	$12–$30	A, DC, MC, V
	French			
★★★★★	Casa del Rio	(809) 523-3333	$14–$26	A, MC, V
	International			
★★★	El Alcazar	(809) 221-1511	$9–$25	A, DC, MC, V
★★	Caribae		$20–$30••	MC, V
★★	Meson de la Cava	(809) 533-2818	$25–$40	A, DC, MC, V
	Italian			
★★	Cafe del Sol	(809) 523-3333	$8–$10	A, MC, V
★★	Vesuvio I	(809) 221-3333	$8–$20	A, DC, MC, V
	Latin American			
★★★★	Restaurant Montparnasse	(809) 562-4141	$5–$20	A, DC, MC, V
★★★	El Conuco	(809) 686-0129	$8–$15	MC, V
★★	Che Bandoneon	(809) 687-0023	$15–$30••	MC, V
★★	Fonda La Aterazana	(809) 689-2900	$5–$20	A, DC, MC, V
	Seafood			
★★★★	La Bahia	(809) 682-4022	$10–$20	A, MC, V
★★	Neptuno's Club	(809) 523-4703	$10–$25	MC, V
	Spanish			
★★★★★	Lina Restaurant	(809) 685-5000	$15–$30	A, DC, MC, V
★★	Reina de Espana	(809) 685-2588	$8–$20	A, MC, V
Note:	• Lunch Only			
	•• Dinner Only			

GRENADA

Horseback riding is fun for adults and children on Grenada's beaches.

Grenada isn't called The Spice Island for nothing. Walk along The Carenage, the island's bustling waterfront, and you'll see dozens of turbaned black ladies selling their fragrant cloves, allspice, cinnamon and nutmeg with a merry song and a spiel. Aroma, it seems, takes on a seductive, almost musical quality on this tiny island, whose stunning natural wonders—lush mountain forests, cascading waterfalls and secret beaches—complete a delightful package that tourists are now discovering 12 years after U.S. troops quelled the Marxist-based coup. From rum shop to fishing village to market square, Grenada preserves the Caribbean the way it *was*, long before the American cultural intervention of Big Macs and Coke; best of all, tourist development, though viable, has been kept to a reasonable scale. It's here on Grenada that you can still glimpse women scrubbing laundry in the streets, goats and chickens vying with traffic and old native ladies wearing baskets of bananas on their heads. Beyond Grenada's 45-plus beaches, travelers can hike rain forest trails riddled with cascading rivers, seek out more than 450 flowering plant species and 150 varieties of birds, or just discover a new dive site. For refreshment, there's elegant dining in old plantation houses, where the delicious callaloo soup can be sampled in a hundred different ways, and for adventure, a few hours lost in the ramparts and tunnels of forts that the French and British built during their 100-year-old custody battle.

Bird's Eye View

In Grand Anse, no development may be taller than a coconut palm.

Sixty miles southwest of St. Vincent and 90 miles north of Trinidad, Grenada lies in the southernmost part of the Windward Islands, the smallest independent nation in the Western hemisphere. Egg-shaped, the island is 12 by 21 miles, volcanic in origin, with vegetation so thickly clad that it looks as if it is upholstered in deep green velvet. Its fertile volcanic soil springs forth a bounty of tropical fruits and vegetables and grows more species per square mile than anywhere else on the planet. In fact, the landscape is so lush that Grenada's residents regularly carry machetes as if the path they cleared today will be overgrown with green tangles tomorrow. The capital of St. George is one of the prettiest harbors in the Caribbean, with a pedestrian walk, The Carenage, which hugs the horseshoe-shaped harbor, inviting you for a stroll beside the sea. Several lofty lookouts—Fort George with cannons aimed seaward, Fort Frederick and Cemetery Hill—present splendid views of the town clambering up the slopes from the waterfront. The island, once a British Crown Colony, but now independent, also includes two other islands—Carriacou, with a very slight infrastructure, and Petite Martinique, famous as a pirate's haunt.

Grenada
City/Town
Road
Airport
Attraction
Mountain
River
0 3 6 km
0 2 4 mi
©FWI 1995
Ronde Island
Caille Island
London Bridge
12° 15'
Green Island
Sauteurs
Sandy Island
Caribbean Sea
Victoria
Tivoli
Gouyave
Mt. St. Catherine
2757 ft.
Grand Roy
Grenville
Concord Falls
Mt. Qua Qua
2373 ft.
Grand Etang Lake
The Seven Sisters
Mt. Sinai
2306 ft.
St. George's
Saint David's
Grand Anse Bay
La Sagasse Nature Center
Grenada
Wreck of the Bianca
L'Anse aux Epines
12° 00'
Glover Island
Calvigny Island
Hog Island
Atlantic Ocean
61° 45'

History

Grenada was discovered by Columbus on his third voyage in 1498. The French built Grenada's first settlement, first appeasing and then battling the native Carib Indians, the last of whom leaped to their death from Morne de Sauteurs, a rock promontory in the island's north coast, in 1651. Over the next century, Grenada was a battlefield between the French and British until the island was declared British under the Treaty of Versailles in 1783. Soon after, the island experienced the first rebellion led by a French plantocrat, Julien Fedon, resulting in the murder of 51 British colonists. (Fedon, who was never captured, remains a legend today in Grenada.) In 1838, the Emancipation Act freed Grenada's African slaves, forcing plantation owners to import indentured laborers from India, Malta and Madera. The descendants of this cultural stew live on today in the multiethnic cuisine, the French-African lilt to the language, and the British and French village names. Until 1958, the island remained a British colony, when it joined the abortive Federation of the West Indies. In 1967 it became a member of the West Indies Associated States, with Britain retaining responsibility. Many Grenadians were opposed to self-rule under Eric Gairy, the first Prime Minister, who was often compared to Haiti's Papa Doc Duvalier. Nevertheless, Gairy became a champion of the poor overnight, though he gained an irreverent reputation for some strange actions—for example, marching a steel band through an opponent's meeting and lecturing the U.N. about UFOs. In the early '70s, Maurice Bishop, a charismatic lawyer, just back from his studies in England, earned popular support as a human-rights activist when his New Jewel Movement convicted Gairy of 27 crimes in a mock trial that called for his resignation. Bishop, along with other members of his party, was mercilessly beaten by Gairy's police and thrown into jail for the night.

Such was the climate when Grenada (and its two dependencies, Carriacou and Petite Martinique) gained its independence from the British Commonwealth on Feb. 7, 1974. That very day management of the Holiday Inn pulled out, leaving an entire independence banquet in the hands of one pastry chef. By the late'70s, Gairy's economy was a shambles and his support diminished, even among the poor. On March 13,1979, Bishop staged the first modern coup in the English-speaking Caribbean while Gairy was off-island. The economy improved early in his tenure and countries around the world accepted Bishop and the new Jewel Movement as a governing force. Still, free elections were never held. Bishop fostered ties with Cuba and the Eastern Bloc countries, and as his friend Fidel Castro granted Grenada aid and labor to build a larger airport at Port Salines in the south, U.S. ties began to unravel. In 1983 Bishop was ousted by a more Marxist/Leninist member of his own party, Bernard Coard, who placed Bishop under house arrest and imprisoned some of his followers. At a rally to support the release of Bishop, members of the People's Revolutionary Army fired into the throng; today no

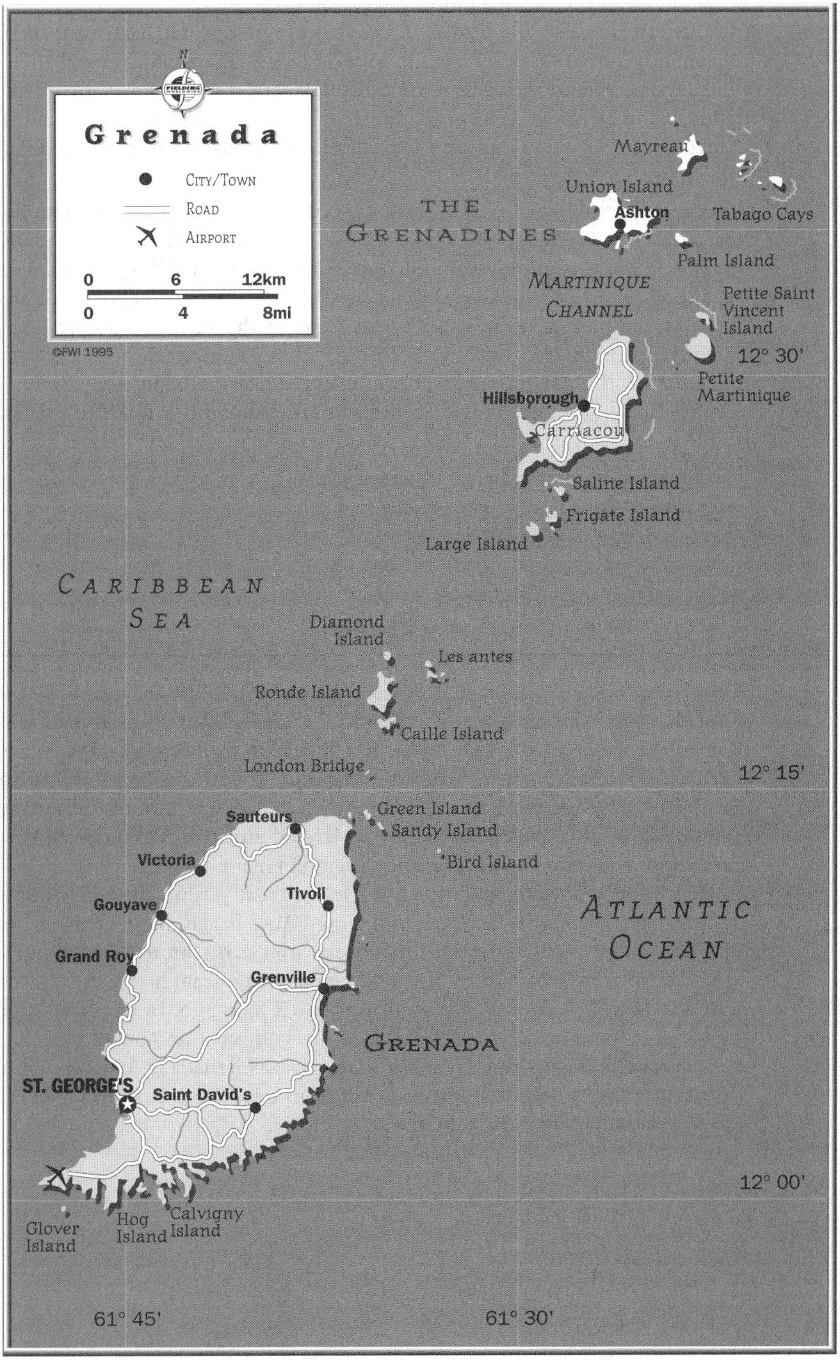

Grenada
City/Town
Road
Airport
0 6 12km
0 4 8mi
©FWI 1995
THE GRENADINES
Mayreau
Union Island
Ashton
Tabago Cays
Palm Island
MARTINIQUE CHANNEL
Petite Saint Vincent Island
12° 30'
Petite Martinique
Hillsborough
Carriacou
Saline Island
Frigate Island
Large Island
CARIBBEAN SEA
Diamond Island
Les antes
Ronde Island
Caille Island
London Bridge
12° 15'
Green Island
Sandy Island
Bird Island
Sauteurs
Victoria
Tivoli
Gouyave
ATLANTIC OCEAN
Grand Roy
Grenville
GRENADA
ST. GEORGE'S
Saint David's
12° 00'
Glover Island
Hog Island
Calvigny Island
61° 45'
61° 30'

one is sure how many men, women and children were killed. The U.S. government, using the subsequent brutal execution of Bishop as pretext, landed 7000 troops on Oct. 26, 1983, on the shores of Grenada, accompanied by the military forces of other neighboring islands—ostensibly to protect democracy and defend the lives of some 1000 Americans residing there, mostly medical students at St. George's University. The American troops were welcomed with open arms by most Grenadians who called the mission not an invasion, but an "intervention."

The aftermath of what has been considered a bad dream by Grenadians has been a stars-and stripes p.r. blitz—new bridges, a retrained police force, and a renewed sense of democracy. The Americans put the finishing touches on the airport, and in 1990 American Airlines began its daily run. Today Grenada holds democratic elections every five years, with five major political parties vying for votes. Among these are the Maurice Bishop Patriotic movement and Gairy's GULP. The once-exiled Gairy, well into his 70s, and virtually blind, promises that if he's elected, the Almighty will restore his vision.

People

Like other recently created Caribbean countries freed from colonial ties, Grenada must constantly test the political waters—a fact that explains why Grenadians seem so politically aware and fascinated by foreigners. Warm and witty, Grenadians are insatiably curious, often quizzing tourists on Clintonomics or the latest word on Michael Jackson. About 75 percent of residents are black, the balance being largely mulatto. Although most of the 91,000 residents live off the land, unemployment is a huge problem (estimated to be about 30 percent in 1990). As a result, crime, especially in the lagoon area between St. George's and Grand Anse beach, has increased; hoteliers warn guests not to walk on that beach after dark, but to take the lighted service road instead. Grenadians are very pro-American, however, and still grateful to the U.S. for the military invention 13 years ago. In fact, graffiti on the island still sings praises and thank-you's to "our saviour Ronald Reagan." Although there are no longer American troops on Grenada, you will run into lots of American students studying under palm trees at St. George's Medical School on the Grand Anse campus.

Beaches

Grenada claims 45 beaches, all free of charge to the public. All have fine white sand. The most famous is long and stunning **Grand Anse**, home to many of the island's resorts and hotels. Also in the south are **Calabash** and **Horseshoe**. If you are looking to pack a picnic lunch, head for **Levera Beach** on the northeastern shore, where you will find swaying palms and deserted stretches. Other good beaches are near Lance aux Epines. This is where the Atlantic and the Caribbean meet. The best beaches in Carriacou are **Paradise** and **Sandy Island**.

What Else to See

Grenada is full of natural wonders, but a stroll through the narrow streets and cobbled alleys of **St. George's**, the capital, should be a priority on your itinerary. There are centuries-old churches to explore and the **National Museum**, once a French garrison, where an antique rum still, wildlife specimens and even the personal effects of Josephine Bonaparte—including the marble tub she used as a child—are kept. The ramparts of Fort George tower over the Carenage and look out to sea—today it is the police headquarters. On Richmond Hill, marvel at the 18th-century military construction of Fort Frederick and drink in the view of the capital with a rum punch at the nearby Hotel Balisier. The best day to visit St. George's Market Square is on Saturday, when the plaza bustles with the brightest aromas and colors of the Caribbean. For a few dollars you can come home laden with baskets of cocoa balls (to make coca tea), sorrel, tannia, yams, limes, mangoes and luscious papayas. A tour of the **Doug Laldston Estate** near Gouyave will give you a glimpse into the secrets of nutmeg cultivation. Afterward, a dollar will get you into the Nutmeg Processing Station, where nuts and mace are separated and graded by hand, then stored in huge burlap bags.

Historical Sites

Fort George ★★★

Church Street, St. George's.

Built by the French in 1705 on a promontory to guard the entrance to the harbor, this old fort has lots of small rooms and four-inch-thick walls.

Museums and Exhibits

Grenada National Museum ★★★

Monckton Street, St. George's, ☎ (809) 440-3725.

Hours open: 9 a.m.–4:30 p.m.

Set in the foundations of an old French army barracks and prison dating back to 1704, this small museum has some interesting exhibits on the island's natural and historical past. Don't miss Josephine Bonaparte's marble bathtub!

Parks and Gardens

Annandale Falls ★★★★★

Main Interior Road, St. George's, ☎ (809) 440-2452.
Hours open: 8 a.m.–4 p.m.
Bring a picnic and your swimsuit (changing rooms are available) to this pretty spot, where water cascades down some 50 feet into a pool perfect for dips. There's a good gift shop on site with handicrafts and species native to the island.

Grand Etang National Park ★★★★★

Main Interior Road, St. George's, ☎ (809) 442-7425.
Hours open: 8:30 a.m.–4 p.m.
This rainforest and bird sanctuary, located in the island's interior between St. George's and Grenville, has lots of gorgeous, unspoiled scenery. Several trails wind throughout for easy to difficult treks. Don't miss Grand Etang Lake, whose 13 acres of cobalt blue waters are nestled in the crater of an extinct volcano.

Tours

Nutmeg Processing Plant ★★

Gouyave.
You'll never again take this little spice for granted after a half-hour tour of the processing plant. Nutmeg is Grenada's largest export and smells sweet, too.

FIELDING'S CHOICE:

The Tower was a fabulous plantation house built in 1917 by a Grenadian lawyer to please his bride. Today, the owners, Paul Slinger and his wife, Victoria, open their historic home to visitors for a $10 tour every Thursday. The Tower is full of antiques, including Hogarth prints collected by Paul's grandfather (who commanded the West Indian regiment in World War I). Situated on nine acres of land, the property is a veritable plantation of tropical fruits, samples of which are served during your tour along with a fruit punch.

Sports

Sailing is the premier sport on Grenada, particularly through the islands of the Grenadines, where the conditions are said to be some of the best in the world. Seagoing travelers always come back with great tales of derring-do, hidden coves and an occasional disaster. St. George has excellent equipment for rent, including Hobie Cats, Sailfish and Sunfish for short excursions. Numerous charter operations can arrange programs for any length or vessel (rates are about 20 percent lower in off-season). Sometimes the easiest thing is to hop a fishing boat to the nearby Hog Island or Calivigny. The Carriacou's Regatta, held in the first weekend of August, attracts classic seamen from all over the world who thrive on the ferocious competition.

Sportfishing is excellent November -May; several operators offer four-hour or longer charters. Several hotels have tennis courts, including Calabash, Coral Cove, Secret Harbor, Spice Island Inn and the Grenada Renaissance.

Grenada Golf Club

Frand Anse, St. George's, ☎ (809) 444-4128.

Not the greatest golf in the world, but since it's the only one on the island, it'll do. The nine-hole course has some nice views. Greens fees are a reasonable $20.

Watersports

Various locations, St. George's.

Scuba diving and snorkeling: **Grenada Aquatics** *(☎ 444-4129)*, and **Dive Grenada** *(☎ 444-4371)*. Boating: **Seabreeze Yacht Charters** *(☎ 444-4924)*, and **The Moorings** *(☎ 444-4548)*. Cruises: **Best of Grenada** *(☎ 440-2198)*. Deep-sea fishing: **Dive Grenada** *(☎ 444-4371)*, and the **Best of Grenada** *(☎ 440-2198)*. A major fishing tournament is held each January. On Carriacou, contact **Dive Paradise** at the Silver Beach Resort *(☎ 443-7337)* for watersports.

FIELDING"S CHOICE:

Every other Saturday a bunch of Grenadians known as the Hash House Harriers get together, split into teams, and set off on chases through glorious countryside on trails that always end up at Rudolf's, a bar next to the Carenage in St. George's. It's a great way to meet and mingle with those Grenadians not in good enough shape for the triathlon.

Where to Eat

Fielding's Highest Rated Restaurants in Grenada

Rating	Restaurant	Price
★★★★★	La Belle Creole	$22–$30
★★★★★	Morne Fendue	$17–$17
★★★★	Canbouley	$10–$30
★★★★	Coconut's Beach	$6–$26
★★★★	Nutmeg, The	$5–$20
★★★	La Source	$45

Fielding's Special Restaurants in Grenada

Rating	Restaurant	Price
★★★★★	La Belle Creole	$22–$30
★★★★★	Morne Fendue	$17–$17
★★★★	Canbouley	$10–$30
★★★★	Coconut's Beach	$6–$26
★★	Mamma's	$19–$19

Fielding's Budget Restaurants in Grenada

Rating	Restaurant	Price
★	La Sagesse	$6–$12
★	Rudolf's	$8–$15
★★★★	Nutmeg, The	$5–$20
★	Portofino	$6–$22
★★★★	Coconut's Beach	$6–$26

Few West Indians have mastered the art of adapting local fruits, vegetables, seafood and spices to Continental-style recipes as well as Grenadians have. The restaurant scene in Grenada, which traditionally centered around the major hotels, now includes newcomers that have added not only spice but variety to the island cuisine. The national dish, "oil down," concocted with breadfruit and salt pork wrapped in dasheen leaves and steamed in coconut milk, is delicious, but also don't miss tasting callaloo soup (made with the spinachlike leaves of the dasheen), christophine au gratni, pepperpot stew, and nutmeg ice cream (nutmeg is the main spice import of Grenada). All dining options are available, however, whether you choose to dine on possum and armadillo at the tin-roofed **Mama's** or eat international cuisine in the elegant **Canboulay**, overlooking the Grand Anse beach. American medical students from St. George's Medical School hang at **Red Crab**, a legendary fish-and-chips, beer-belly pub just outside the gates of the Calabash Hotel. Don't miss sampling a proper Grenadian rum punch, or a local candy called nutmeg cheese.

Bird's Nest **$$$** ★

Grand Anse Beach, Grand Anse, ☎ (809) 444-4264.
Chinese cuisine.
Lunch: 10:30 a.m.–2 p.m., entrees $11–$24.
Dinner: 2–11 p.m., entrees $11–$24.

A no-surprises, pleasant Chinese restaurant that also serves good sandwiches for lunch, Bird's Nest roosts near the airport and several hotels in Grand Anse. Specialties include sweet and sour chicken or fish, served with tasty fried rice. The restaurant is open on Sunday for dinner only, from 6 p.m. to 11 p.m.

Canbouley **$$$** ★★★★

Morne Rouge, ☎ (809) 444-4401.
International cuisine.
Lunch: 11:30 a.m.–2:30 p.m., entrees $10–$20.
Dinner: 6:30–10 p.m, entrees $20–$30.

For a grand night out in exotic surroundings, most visitors choose this festive restaurant with a view of the lights of the capital across the bay. The decor and the tropical-Asian cuisine reflect the heritage of Trinidad-born owners Erik and Ginalee Johnson, where spices, heady scents and Carnival are a way of life. The Johnsons really shine with shrimp prepared in interesting ways, including an Indonesian peanut and fruit satay. Desserts are memorable, especially a chocolate-orange mousse and a custard-filled coconut cake called "Oh Goood!"

Coconut's Beach **$$$** ★★★★

Grand Anse Beach, ☎ (809) 444-4644.
French cuisine. Specialties: Lobster, conch.
Lunch: 10 a.m.–6 p.m., entrees $6–$13.
Dinner: 7–10 p.m., entrees $13–$26.

As the name implies, guests can eat right on the beach in high style under palm-frond shelters, or in the dining room of a spiffy, native house with an open kitchen where the chefs deftly saute the catch of the day in gleaming cookware. Lobster with various butter sauces or lambi (conch) curry are mouth-watering choices, as are ribs, chicken or steak. A good lunch menu of crepes, salads or sandwiches offers most dishes for under $10.

Cot Bam **$$$** ★

Grand Anse Beach, Grand Anse, ☎ (809) 444-2050.
American cuisine.
Lunch: 9 a.m.–2 p.m., entrees $6–$30.
Dinner: 2–11 p.m., entrees $6–$30.

Savory, quick meals and a cold brew draw guests to this convivial bar and grill after a hard day at the beach. Since it's within strolling distance of all hotels on Grand Anse, why settle for room service? Snacks and plate meals include West Indian rotis, salads, shrimp and chips, etc.

Delicious Landing **$$$** ★

The Carenage,
Seafood cuisine.
Lunch: 10:30 a.m.–2 p.m., entrees $17–$24.
Dinner: 6:30–11:30 p.m., entrees $17–$24.

Although many eating establishments on this island boast enviable views, Delicious Landing may have the best one of all, situated right on the water's edge near St.

George's Harbor. Decently prepared seafood and fish is featured, but the sea vistas, breezes and excellent tropical drinks are the main reason to linger here.

La Belle Creole **$$$** ★★★★★

Grand Anse Beach, Grand Anse, ☎ (809) 444-4316.
Seafood cuisine. Specialties: Callaloo quiche.
Lunch: 12:30–2:30 p.m., entrees $22–$28.
Dinner: 7–9 p.m., entrees $25–$30.

Some of the most creative West Indian food is served in this airy terrace restaurant on the grounds of the Blue Horizons Cottages. For many years "Mamma" Audrey Hopkin earned a deserved reputation as the best Creole home chef in town, and now her sons have carried the torch with admirable results. Real men (and women) eat quiche here, which is an unusual combo of callaloo (dasheen leaf) and lobster or shrimp; there's also a veal roulade with crab and a tasty fish mousse. Desserts are equally imaginative—try the unique farine pudding, a custard made from cassava. An ever-changing fixed-price dinner of up to five courses, including dessert, is available nightly for $40. The service is as good as the food, and the atmosphere is perfect for lovers.

La Sagesse **$$** ★

Eastern Main Road, St. David, ☎ (809) 444-6458.
American cuisine.
Lunch: 11 a.m.–3:30 p.m., entrees $6–$11.
Dinner: 6:30–9 p.m., entrees $8–$12.

This small restaurant by the sea is part of the La Sagesse Nature Center, formerly the home of a cousin of Queen Elizabeth, now an inn and banana plantation. Fittingly, patrons can get a nice organic vegetarian platter or blended tropical fruit drinks. Other dishes include seafood, sandwiches and burgers. The calm waters here are only eight minutes away from the capital.

La Source **$$$** ★★★

Pink Gin Beach, ☎ (809) 444-2556.
Spa cuisine.
Dinner: 7:30–9:30 p.m., prix fixe $45.

Chef Richard Lovett gives new meaning to spa food at this tasty restaurant at the all-inclusive La Source. Thanks to wonderful entrees like vegetable cutlets coated with parmesan cheese and crab-stuffed chicken, you can pig out without an ounce of guilt. There's even a selection of low-fat desserts. Items like braised shank of lamb are also featured for those not watching their waistline. The prix-fixe dinner includes drinks and wine, appetizer, entree and dessert.

Le Karacoli **$$$** ★★

Grande-Anse Beach, Grand-Anse, ☎ (590) 28-41-17.
French cuisine.
Dinner: entrees $8–$25.

This bustling beachfront restaurant with an unlikely name (the snail) offers reasonably priced creole dishes (mostly seafood) to locals and the numerous tourists who have discovered the place. Try the crab backs stuffed with shrimp or enjoy a full-course meal with yams and vegetable accompaniments for $14. Service is gracious even during peak times.

Mamma's **$$$** ★★

Lagoon Road, ☎ (809) 440-1459.
Latin American cuisine. Specialties: Oil down, exotic small game.
Lunch: 8 a.m.–1:30 p.m., prix fixe $19.
Dinner: 7:30–11 p.m., prix fixe $19.

Yes, eating here is like Sunday dinner at Mamma's—if she was West Indian. But no one has to wait until the end of the week to dine here; Mamma's daughter Cleo and other family members set out a groaning buffet of some 20 local dishes in a friendly, boardinghouse atmosphere every day of the week. The menu features the overwhelming bounty of this verdant isle, including the pear-shaped christophene vegetable stuffed with crab, oil down (breadfruit, meats, callaloo in coconut milk) and curries. The daring can call ahead for a taste of stewed armadillo or iguana.

Morne Fendue **$$$** ★★★★★

St. Patrick's, St. Patrick's Parish, ☎ *(809) 442-9330.*
Latin American cuisine. Specialties: Pepper pot.
Lunch: 12:30–3 p.m., prix fixe $17.
Lunch at this history-laden plantation house may soon be a thing of the past, as owner Betty Mascoll, who has been holding court here for many years, is well into her 80s. So while you can, reserve a place at this traditional West Indian buffet and make friends with the repeat visitors and a faithful staff that prepares a mean pepper pot stew, peas and rice, stewed chicken and island vegetables every afternoon except Sunday. The house itself, built of native stone and decorated with family keepsakes, is a national treasure.

Nutmeg, The **$$** ★★★★

The Carenage, ☎ *(809) 440-2539.*
Seafood cuisine. Specialties: Nutmeg ice cream, conch.
Lunch: 9 a.m.–4 p.m., entrees $5–$15.
Dinner: 4–11 p.m., entrees $9–$20.
This well-known and widely visited restaurant with a view of seagoing vessels in St. George's Harbor features its heady namesake spice in a few specialties, including a nutmeg ice cream and rum punch. Otherwise, for a few dollars, sample local dishes like callaloo soup, lambi curry or fish sandwiches and fries, washed down with the locally brewed Carib beer.

Portofino **$$** ★

The Carenage, ☎ *(809) 440-3986.*
Italian cuisine. Specialties: Pizza, Pastas.
Lunch: 11 a.m.–2 p.m., entrees $6–$22.
Dinner: 2–11 p.m., entrees $6–$22.
A comforting plate of pasta plus a harbor view make this upper-level Italian charmer an unbeatable draw. Jazz often plays in the background, putting everyone in a relaxed mood. It's also a good place for the kids, who can choose from a wide variety of their favorite food: pizza. Lobster and veal dishes are also available.

Red Crab, The **$$$** ★

L'Anse aux Epines, Grand Anse, ☎ *(809) 444-4424.*
International cuisine. Specialties: Steak.
Lunch: 11 a.m.–2 p.m., entrees $10–$31.
Dinner: 6–11 p.m., entrees $10–$31.
This place should have been named the Plush Cow, because although it serves seafood, old-timers roll in here for the beefsteaks, which are the best on the island. It's located in the posh southern point of the island, in one of Grenada's original tourist developments. Travelers staying in the Grand Anse area can get here by car in five minutes.

Rudolf's **$$** ★

The Carenage, ☎ *(809) 440-2241.*
International cuisine. Specialties: Conch.
Lunch: 10 a.m.–2 p.m., entrees $8–$15.
Dinner: 2 p.m.–midnight, entrees $8–$15.
Although it's got a humming bar scene, Rudolf's features a large selection of seafood and steak dishes for those who want to eat here. It also helps that this pub eatery with a harbor view has some of the best prices in town—many dishes are under

$10. There are daily specials, usually lobster or conch (highly recommended), as well as sandwiches, salads and fish and chips.

Where to Shop

Shopping isn't duty free on Grenada, but sometimes bargains can get you very close. Special buys to bring home are spice baskets full of native-grown nutmeg, cinnamon, cloves, ground coriander, and others—perfect for Christmas gifts or for spiking the eggnog. At the **Grand Anse Shopping Center** (closest to the hotels) there are even spice vendors who stroll up and down the streets barking their prices (don't be shy about bargaining). Imported china can be found at prices 60 percent cheaper than in the States. You can find other shopping centers on the **Esplanade side of Fort George** and on **Melville Street**, facing the harbor. A good bakery and coffee shop is located in the **Le Marquis Complex**, in the Grand Anse district. Grenada shops open and close with their own schedules, but usually cater hours to cruise ships. Best time to visit the Granby Street food market on Market Square is Saturday.

Carriacou

Carriacou (Carry-a-COO) is a 14 -square mile island lying 40 miles northeast of St. George's, reachable by daily 10-minute flights in very small planes. Although administered by its own staff, the island is under the government of Grenada. The capital is Hillsborough and home to 4600. A postage-stamp paradise untouched by large-scale development, it boasts only 11 inns and guest houses with no more than 20 rooms in the largest. **Gramma's Place** on Main Street, an unofficial meeting place, serves breakfast and snacks. For dinner the **Callaloo Restaurant** is a find. The tiny museum was once a cotton ginnery, and the hillside cemetery is notable as a place where young girls tend their goats. The Scottish influence can be seen in the wooden schooners of local white cedar, while strong African roots vibrate in the drum song and dance unique to the island.

To get there, take a small plane from Port Salines International Airport in Grenada on inter-island flights from St. Vincent or from Barbados. You can also catch a ride on the mailboat or fishing boat or charter a private yacht. Everyone on Carriacou will be clamoring for American dollars, so don't worry about exchanging any.

Petite Martinique

A tiny burp in the sea is this third island in Grenada's troika. Fishermen know exactly where it is. To get here, best to hop a ride on a mail boat.

Grenada Directory

BUSINESS HOURS

Stores open weekdays 8:30 a.m.–noon and 2:30–6 p.m. Banks open weekdays 8 a.m.–noon and 2–4 p.m., but during the summer, hours are generally 8 a.m.–3 p.m.

CLIMATE

A dry and rainy season dominate Grenada's climate. April–December is the dry season; May–January the rainy, though showers are brief. Temperatures hover around 80 degrees F. There is blissfully little humidity because of the constant trade winds.

DOCUMENTS

U.S. citizens must present a valid passport or proof of citizenship (birth certificate or voter's registration card), plus a photo ID) and an ongoing or return ticket. All visitors pay a departure tax of $14.

ELECTRICITY

The official current is 230 volts, 50 cycles AC, so you must bring an adapter.

GETTING AROUND

Driving on the left, but risky for the twisting and sometimes poor roads over rough terrain. Instead, do as residents do, and get around on so-called buses, really vans that accommodate up to 14 in very cozy quarters. To make a sightseeing tour, hire a taxi and driver for a day, and head out to the forest reserve, waterfalls, small fishing village and great views.

LANGUAGE

Since Grenada was formerly under the British throne, natives speak English with a beautiful lilt. A local dialect mixes French with African slang.

MEDICAL EMERGENCIES

The General Hospital in St. George has limited facilities; you might find better advice at the Grenada University School of medicine ☎ *(809) 444-4271*, a privately owned, U.S.-managed school on Grand Anse Beach.

MONEY

The official currency is the Eastern Caribbean dollar (EC). Make sure you know which dollar is being quoted to you by a shopkeeper or taxi driver. Traveler's checks and major credits are also widely accepted. If you exchange at the local bank, you may end up in endless lines. If you pay big bills in dollars, the exchange rate will probably not be calculated in your favor.

TELEPHONE

Area code is *809*. To save money, head for the Grenada Telecommunications, Ltd., in St. George or use a special phone card on other telephones. Cellular phone service can be purchased through Boatphone ☎ *(800) 567-8336*.

TIME

Atlantic Standard Time, which is one hour later than New York time.

TIPPING

Expect a 10 percent service charge; no need to tip help further. At eateries leave a 10–15 percent tip. Only tip a taxi driver if he carries your bags.

TOURIST INFORMATION

Grenada Board of Tourism is located at The Carenage, St. George's ☎ *(809) 440-2001* and will answer questions, offer brochures and maps. Stop here if you are traveling on to other Grenadine islands. **Grenada Hotel Association Ross Point Inn, Lagoon Road, St. George's** ☎ *(809) 444-1353*. In the United States call ☎ *(800) 927-9554*.

WHEN TO GO

Don't miss Grenada's Carnival in early August, a four-day-to-night blowout of calypso songs and steel bands, and the traditional "jump-up" parades. Carriacou comes alive in early August for its annual Regatta. Also check out the ninth annual International Triathlon, usually held in January. Competitors come from as far away as Australia and Norway and it takes place along and near Grand Anse Beach.

GRENADA RESTAURANTS	PHONE	ENTREE	CR. CARDS
Grenada			
St. George's			
American			
★ Cot Bam	(809) 444-2050	\$6–\$30	A, D, MC, V
★ La Sagesse	(809) 444-6458	\$6–\$12	A, MC, V
Chinese			
★ Bird's Nest	(809) 444-4264	\$11–\$24	A, D, MC, V
French			
★★★★ Coconut's Beach	(809) 444-4644	\$6–\$26	MC, V
★★ Le Karacoli	(809) 444-4117	\$8–\$25••	MC, V
International			
★★★★ Canbouley	(809) 444-4401	\$10–\$36	A, MC, V
★ Red Crab, The	(809) 444-4424	\$10–\$31	A, D, MC, V
★ Rudolf's	(809) 440-2241	\$8–\$15	MC, V
Italian			
★ Portofino	(809) 440-3986	\$6–\$22	A, MC, V
Latin American			
★★★★★ Morne Fendue	(809) 442-9330	\$17–\$17•	None
★★ Mamma's	(809) 440-1459	\$19–\$19	None
Seafood			
★★★★★ La Belle Creole	(809) 444-4316	\$22–\$30	A, D, DC, MC, V
★★★★ Nutmeg, The	(809) 440-2539	\$5–\$20	A, D, MC, V
★ Delicious Landing		\$17–\$24	None

Note: • Lunch Only

•• Dinner Only

GUADELOUPE

Guadeloupe's Ste.-Anne offers white sand beaches and crystal clear water.

Guadeloupe is an island with split personalities. Beaches wash up against volcanoes, sugarcane sprouts next to mangrove swamps, the most luxurious hotels vie for competition with mere wooden huts. Even its population is divided among French apologists and African militants, plus a growing new sector clamoring for a united Carib identity. Guadeloupe's terrain is shaped like a two-winged butterfly, one side verdant mountains, the other rocky and ringed with white beaches. These days Guadeloupe is a paradise for those eco-adventurers who want to challenge themselves to the max. Diving is a matter of fierce honor among the French-operated industry, and certification courses are considered to be some of the toughest. An entire vacation could be spent trekking over 6000 acres within the national park. But the latest craze in Guadeloupe—a sport for which you need stamina, grit—and a big dose of humor—is cycling. The island terrain is perfect for the two-wheeler activity, which not only lets you see the countryside close up but permits the opportunity to compete with crazy French drivers—an experience that will leave you thankful to be alive.

Bird's Eye View

Guadeloupe is the most northerly of the Windward Islands group in the West Indies. Dominica lies to the south and Antigua and Montserrat to the northwest. A 659-square-mile archipelago, Guadeloupe is formed by two large islands, Grande-Terre and Basse-Terre, separated by the Riviere Salé, a narrow four-mile sea channel (but linked by a bridge) with a smaller island, Marie Galante, to the southeast, and another La Désirade, to the east. At 312 square miles, Basse-Terre (which means lowland) lies on the leeward side of the island, where the winds are calmer. The smaller, less mountainous Grande-Terre received the more dramatic waves and air currents typical to the windward side. There are also a number of small dependencies, mainly Saint Bart and the northern half of St. Martin.

History

Christopher Columbus stumbled upon Guadeloupe during his 1493 excursions, dubbing it Santa Maria de Guadeloupe de Estremadura in honor of a Spanish monastery with which he had close ties. Some 143 years later, the French landed, peopling the island with settlers who had to work in indentured conditions for three years to pay off their sea passage from France. Unfortunately, many proved to be unskilled and unacquainted with tropical farming, and the island soon fell into disrepair while nearby Martinique continued to prosper. The French Revolution inspired the settlers to revolt; they eventually declared themselves independent and even solicited the help of the British enemy. In response, the French government sent more than a thousand soldiers to whip the settlers into shape, expelling the British and executing more than 4000 Guadeloupian rebels on guillotines set up in the main squares. Under the Napoleonic reign, slavery was reinstated. In 1810 the British successfully reinvaded the island, handing it over to Louis XVIII during the Restoration, and returning when Napoleon came to power; the Brits finally surrendered the island for the last time when the French emperor was exiled to St. Helena in 1815. Since then, Guadeloupe has retained its distinct French flavor combined with a spicy West Indian allure. In September 1989, Hurricane Hugo struck the islands, causing widespread devastation and leaving about 12,000 people homeless. But by the mid-1990s the banana industry and the tourist industry had recovered and the majority are looking forward to prosperous years.

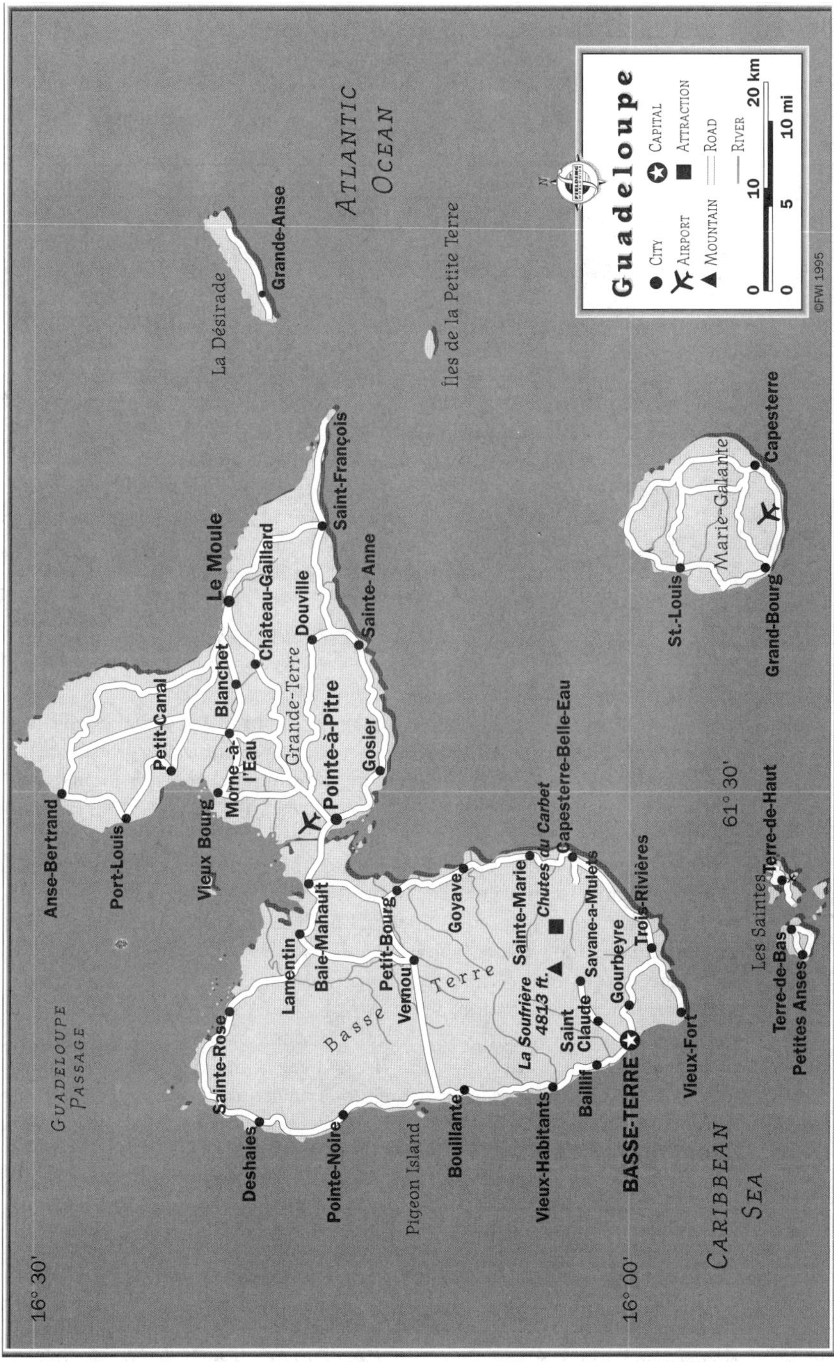
Guadeloupe
City
Capital
Airport
Attraction
Mountain
Road
River
0 5 10 mi
0 10 20 km
©FWI 1995
Atlantic Ocean
Caribbean Sea
Guadeloupe Passage
16° 30'
16° 00'
61° 30'
Grande-Anse
La Désirade
Îles de la Petite Terre
Saint-François
Le Moule
Château-Gaillard
Douville
Sainte- Anne
Blanchet
Grande-Terre
Petit-Canal
Anse-Bertrand
Port-Louis
Morne-à-l'Eau
Vieux Bourg
Pointe-à-Pitre
Gosier
Capesterre
Marie-Galante
St.-Louis
Grand-Bourg
Capesterre-Belle-Eau
Chutes du Carbet
Sainte-Marie
Goyave
Petit-Bourg
Baie-Mahault
Lamentin
Vernou
Basse Terre
Sainte-Rose
Deshaies
Pointe-Noire
Pigeon Island
Bouillante
Vieux-Habitants
La Soufrière 4813 ft.
Savane-a-Mulets
Trois-Rivières
Gourbeyre
Saint Claude
Baillif
BASSE-TERRE
Vieux-Fort
Les Saintes
Terre-de-Haut
Terre-de-Bas
Petites Anses

People

Bananas are the largest export for Guadeloupe.

The proximity of rugged natural resources has bred a spiritual people highly attuned to nature. The medicinal uses of plants and their spiritual properties is common knowledge, particularly among the older residents, but it takes some convincing to induce them to part with the secrets. What most characterizes the people of Guadeloupe, however, is a love of music. In recent years, beats born in Guadeloupe have taken flight onto the international scene, bringing forth a new generation of musicians who are being recognized on the world market. Influenced by black American radicalism in the 1960s, Guadeloupe artists began to redefine their relationship to *gqoka*, or slave music, thus transcending any negative connotations. Infusing the beat with a new political message, a new African-based identity was affirmed. For years a struggle between two musical factions divided musical techniques; one favoring heavy Afro-oriented drum beat while the other favored beguines played on European instruments. The group Kassav suddenly bolted into prominence in the '80s, uniting the two factions by using all matters of instruments and rocking the dance clubs of New York, Paris and Amsterdam. In their wake, many younger groups have been inspired. (For more information about the music of Guadeloupe, see the chapter "Caribbean Culture.")

Most of the locals of Guadeloupe profess Christianity and many are Roman Catholics. There is a segment of the population which is East Indian, but like their fellow islanders from Africa, they have lost the use of their language and speak only Creole. Most women don't even know how to tie a sari anymore. But Hindu worship still continues in the privacy of their homes. Offsetting the multiracial mixture is a small but significant group of whites called Blancs-Matignons, who steadfastly cling to racist attitudes.

Beaches

Most of Guadeloupe's beaches are lovely white strand open to the public at no extra charge. Hotels sometimes charge minimal fees for nonguests to utilize the resources of their changing facilities, including beach chairs and towels. Some of the best beaches, with long white stretches, are to be found in Grande-Terre. Gray volcanic sand characterizes the beaches in the southern tip of Basse-Terre; the color is gloriously golden as you move toward the northwest coast. Beaches on the windward (Atlantic side) are simply too rough for swimming; divers who use the water should be exceptionally skilled in maneuvering strong currents. Beaches are generally accessible by roads, paved and otherwise. The exception is Islet du Gosier, which is a blip off the shore of Gosier that welcomes nude bathers. It's a great place to plop yourself for a daylong picnic, and arrangements for watersports can be made through the Creole Beach hotel in Gosier.

Caravelle Beach probably wins the award for the most stunning in Guadeloupe—tropical beauty with an immense strand. The sand is exceedingly powdery. Reefs surrounding the beach make excellent conditions for snorkeling. **Club Med** makes use of one end of the beach, but the **Hotel La Toubana** in the hills above has snorkeling equipment for rent. Le Meridien Hotel also sports a fine beach at Raisin-Clairs, where equipment for water sports can be hired. Most popular with the weekend crowd—best to go during the week if you want seclusion—is **Anse de la Gourde**; you will find a restaurant and snack bar there. Lots of nude bathers head for **Tarare**, a private strand just before the tip of Pointe des Châteaux Another popular nude beach is **Place Crawen**, Les'Saintes' placid half-mile strand on Terre-de-Haut. Changing facilities are available a five-minute walk away at **Bois Joli Hotel**. A lovely "feet in the water" restaurant can be found on **La Grande Anse**, just outside of Dashaies, on the northwest coast of Basse-Terre. the Creole cuisine is excellent here at the **Karacoli Restaurant**. Along the western shore, you'll find lots of beaches in miniature, including the gray sands of **Pigeon Beach** and the blackish ones farther south. **Petit-Anse**, on Marie-Galante, is a beautiful large beach with gleaming gold sand that fills up fast on the weekends.

What Else to See

Point-a-Pitre is the Caribbean in double time. The city of some 100,000 people moves at a faster peace than probably any other Caribbean city, a maze of narrow streets, traffic pileups and honking horns. The city has paid its dues over the years, a victim of various hurricanes, earthquakes and other natural disasters, the last being Hurricane Hugo in 1989. Some French colonial structures still remain, but downtown has been recently renovated, and the new cruise terminal called Centre St. John Perse has brought a lively commercial feel with its numerous boutiques and restaurants.

First stop in the city should be at the **Tourist Office in Place de la Victire,** to pick up maps and brochures. Even outside the door you'll find lots of lively locals hawking anything from pots and pans to underwear. Fruits and vegetables can be bought from a bevy of women dressed in brightly colored costumes near the port. The local Marketplace, between the streets of St.John Perse, Freebault, Schoelchen and Peynier, is a beehive of activity for the purchase of the latest crops from the fields. Take time to meet the ladies of the market, whose beautiful smiles could light up anybody's day. Due to the presence of crowds, give attention to your handbag as you stroll through.

Two museums are worth a look. The **Musee St. John Perse** in a restored colonial house is a tribute to the 1960 Nobel Prize winner in literature, where you can read works of his poetry. Also check out the **Musée Schoelcher**, a memorial to Victor Schoelcher, a 19th-century Alsataon freedomfighter who was responsible for emancipation in the French West Indies.

The capital of the island, **Basse-Terre,** is significant for its port and its market, both situated along boulevard General de Gaulle. A fine colonial square houses several old structures at Champ d'Arbaud. A few beautiful hours can be spent strolling the gardens at **Jardin Pichon**. A short stop can be made to the 17th-century fort St. Charles and the Cathedral of our Lady of Guadeloupe. A look at the volcano in this area can be made from any number of picnic tables in the suburb of **St. Clade**. (For information on how to scale the mountain, see under "Treks" above.) Near the ferry landing for Les Saintes, the **Parc Archéologique des Roches Gravees** contains a collection of pre-Columbian rock engravings. Exhibits explain the engravings of folk and fauna symbols on the petroglyphs. The park, inside a handsome botanical garden, is a quiet haven for tourists who need to escape the bustle of Pointe-a-Pitre.

Take time to visit the islands lying directly offshore the mainland. Ferries run regularly to Marie-Galante, Desirade and Terre-Haut (see below for more information, after "Where to Shop"). Ferry schedules, however, can never be counted on, but check with the tourist office to find out the latest pseudo-itinerary. If you plan to spend time on some of these outposts, a good handle on French is necessary because you will be hard put to find anyone who speaks English. Most of your simple needs can be met with a finger pointed to your mouth or the word "toilette" (pronounced twa-lette). There's no need to carry much with you; in fact you can wear your bathing suit under your outer clothes, but you should bring a towel. The island of Dominica is just a short hop away on an airplane. The trip can be done in a day and excursions can be arranged ahead of time to save you wasting time on the island itself.

Historical Sites

Parc Archeologique des Roches ★★★

Trois-Rivieres.

Hours open: 9 a.m.–5 p.m.

At this peaceful spot near the wharf, displays interpret the rock engravings by Carib Indians that date back to A.D. 300.

Museums and Exhibits

Edgar Clerc Archaeological Museum ★★★

La Rosete, Moule.

This small museum displays artifacts from the Carib and Arawak Indians found on the islands of the Eastern Caribbean. Closed Wednesday afternoons and Tuesdays.

Musee Schoelcher ★★

24 Rue Peynier, Pointe-a-Pitre.

Displays highlight the personal papers and belongings of Victor Schoelcher, who, in the 19th century, worked to abolish slavery in the French West Indies.

Musee du Rhum ★★★

Bellevue, Sainte-Rose, Basse-Terre.

Hours open: 9 a.m.–5 p.m.

The Rum Museum showcases three centuries in the making of the quaff, which is produced with sugarcane. After a guided tour, you get to taste the potable, and, of course, buy some to take home. But perhaps the best reason to come here is to check out "la Galerie des Plus Beaux Insectes du Monde," where you can marvel at more than 5000 (safely dead) critters—from beautiful butterflies to spine-tingling spiders, roaches, and other huge creepy-crawlies. Those interested in the rum-making process should also check out the **Domaine de Severin in Sainte-Rose** (northern Basse-Terre, ☎ *590-28-91-86*). This distillery still functions with a paddle wheel; a guided tour takes you through each step of production. It's open daily from 8 a.m.–1 p.m. and from 2-6 p.m., and from 9 a.m.–noon on Sundays.

Musee St. John Perse ★★

Achille Rene-Boisneuf Rue, Pointe-a-Pitre.

Hours Open: 9 a.m.–5 p.m.

This museum in a restored colonial house contains the works of St. John Perse, a local boy made good who won the Nobel Prize in Literature in 1960.

Parks and Gardens

Floral Park ★★

Cabout, Petit-Bourg, Basse-Terre.

Hours open: 9 a.m.–5 p.m.

Le Domaine de Valombreuse is the official name of this Eden-like spot on the east coast of Basse-Terre. Numerous shady valleys house 300 species and 200 subspecies of flowers and a slew of exotic birds. The Park Restaurant is open daily for lunch, and there's a playground on site for little tykes. Admission is $5.00 for kids under 12.

Parc Naturel de la Guadeloupe ★★★★★

Route de la Traversee, Trois-Rivieres.

Covering 74,000 acres with 200 miles of trails, this national park has something for everyone: waterfalls, thick vegetation, nature walks and the centerpiece, La Soufriere, a smoldering volcano that last erupted in 1975. Stop by the Maison de la Foret for a look at the park's history (only, alas, in French) and a booklet on hiking trails. Wear rain gear, as this area gets some 250 inches per year. If you're interested in a guided hike tailored to your level, contact the **Organisation des Guides de Montagne de Caraibe** at ☎ *80-05-79.*

Zoological and Botanical Park ★★★

Route de la Traversee, Bouillante, Basse-Terre.

Hours open: 9 a.m.–4:30 p.m.

Located high in the hills of Basse-Terre, this reserve is home to myriad trees, bushes and creepers that lots of little critters like mongoose, iguana, land turtle, and raccoon (called ti-raccoon here) call home. Great views abound at Le Ti-Raccoon restaurant (open daily for lunch except Mondays), which serves up authentic creole cuisine. Admission for children is $3.00.

Tours

Aquarium de la Guadeloupe ★★★★★

Place Creole, Marina Bas-du-Fort.

Hours open: 9 a.m.–7 p.m.

This is the Caribbean's largest aquarium and considered to be France's third most important. Good exhibits feature everything from tiny fishes to giant sharks. While in the area, check out the 18th-century Fort Fleur d'Epee, complete with dungeons and spectacular views.

Sports

Strong currents and good winds make yachting a popular sport in Guadeloupe. Safe anchorages can be found at the offshore isles of Marie-Galante and Les Saintes—many people go here on day excursions. In the harbor are yachts of all shapes and sizes, which can be hired, chartered, crewed or bareboat, for any length of time. You can, through the services of **Le Boat**, a unique service, take one boat to an island and leave it there (ask the Tourist Office for more information). Windsurfing is also popular and lessons and equipment can be arranged through all the seaside hotels. Hotels also assist in arrangements for deep-sea fishing from boats based at the **Port de Plaisance Marina in Bas du Fort** ☎ *(590) 82-74-94.* Marlin and tuna are profuse in the waters off the west coast of Basse-Terre at Pigeon Island. The season for barracuda and kingfish is January to May. Horseback riding can also be arranged through **Le Criolo**, a riding school at St. Félix near Gosier. (For diving, trekking and cycling, see under the appropriate sections above.)

Golf Municipal Saint-Francois

St.-Francois.

The island's only golf course features 18 holes designed by Robert Trent Jones and an English-speaking pro. Greens fees for the par-71 course are $45.

Holywind

Pointe de la Verdure, Gosier.

Feeling daring? Fly along the coastline in an Ultra Leger Motorise, a lightweight seaplane.

Watersports

Various locations, Pointe-a-Pitre.

Check out one of the following. Scuba diving: **Chez Guy et Christian** *(☎ 98-82-43)*, **Aqua-Fari** *(☎ 84-26-26)*, and **Nauticase** *(☎ 84-22-22)*. On Isle des Saintes, **Centre Nautique des Saintes** *(☎ 99-54-25)*. Windsurfing: **Callinago** *(☎ 84-25-25)* and **UCPA Hotel Club** *(☎ 88-64-80)*. Deep-sea fishing: **Caraibe Peche** *(☎ 90-97-51)*, **La Rocher de Malendere** *(☎ 98-70-84)*, **Evasion Exotic** *(☎ 90-94-17)*, and **Fishing Club Antilles** *(☎ 86-73-77)*. Boat rentals: **Soleil et Voile** *(☎ 90-81-81)*, **Vacances Yachting Antilles** *(☎ 90-82-95)*, and **Locaraibes** *(☎ 90-82-80)*.

Where to Eat

Fielding's Highest Rated Restaurants in Guadeloupe

★★★★★	**Auberge de la Vielle Tour**	$23–$39
★★★★★	**La Canne A Sucre**	$18–$32
★★★★★	**La Plantation**	$14–$54
★★★★★	**Le Chateau de Feuilles**	$18–$29
★★★★	**La Rocher de Malendure**	$8–$18
★★★★	**Nilce's Bar**	
★★★	**La Louisiane**	$22–$30
★★★	**Le Poisson d'Or**	$14–$27
★★★	**Le Restaurant**	$25–$40
★★★	**Sucrerie du Comte**	$13–$35

Fielding's Special Restaurants in Guadeloupe

★★★★★	**Auberge de la Vielle Tour**	$23–$39
★★★★★	**Le Chateau de Feuilles**	$18–$29
★★★★	**Nilce's Bar**	
★★★	**Sucrerie du Comte**	$13–$35
★	**La Braise Marine**	$8–$30

Fielding's Budget Restaurants in Guadeloupe

★★	**Le Jardin Creole**	$4–$14
★★★★	**La Rocher de Malendure**	$8–$18
★★	**La Saladerie**	$7–$19
★★	**Le Amandiers**	$12–$16
★★★	**Chez Paul de Matouba**	$12–$18

Guadeloupe boasts some of the best creole cuisine in the Caribbean, and chefs care for their food with pride and love. Trust places that specialize in local foods—typically they'll say *cuisine créole*—and they reflect the obvious pride in creole style, the way a place would look in the French countryside if France were the Caribbean—which is precisely the case in Guadeloupe. Court bouillon is a lively fish soup, which makes a good starter. Rice and beans are often prepared in coconut water. Of the more than two dozen creole restaurants that thrive on the islands, there are a few that are considered out of this world. Among the best are **La Canne a Sucre**, in an elegant new location in the modern Centre St.-John Perse at the edge of the water (the brasserie down below is cheaper than the restaurant, which features red snapper with passion fruit mousse). **La Créole Chez Violetta** is also highly recommended. A voluptuous beachside lunch can be had at **Le Karacolo** restaurant in Deshaies (For more information, see the chapter "Caribbean Culture" under the heading Culinary Arts.

Basse-Terre

Chez Clara **$$$** ★★★

Ste. Rose, Ste. Rose, ☎ (590) 28-72-99.
Latin American cuisine.
Lunch: Noon–2:30 p.m., entrees $9–$27.
Dinner: 7–10 p.m., entrees $9–$27.

Like the jazz she once danced to, native chef Clara Lesueur's culinary improvisations are realized by years of perfecting basic techniques. Guests that patronize Clara's chez on Ste. Rose's seafront are fans of long-standing, guaranteeing a bit of a wait, but the refreshing rum drinks at the bar help ease the pain. Go easy on the cocktails so you can enjoy the Creole specials of lambi with lime and peppers, crayfish and crab backs. No dinner is served Sundays.

Chez Paul de Matouba **$$** ★★★

Riviere Rouge, ☎ (590) 80-29-20.
International cuisine.
Dinner: entrees $12–$18.

Enjoy a refreshing country lunch in this Creole restaurant in Matouba, formerly a Hindu settlement, in the mountains above Basse-Terre. The ambience here is similar to a fishing lodge, where diners enjoy a veritable marketplace of local greens and fresh seafood while a river runs outside. Specialties include *accras* (codfish fritters) with an incendiary sauce, or grilled *ouassous* (crayfish). Fixed-price meals under $20 are available.

La Rocher de Malendure **$$** ★★★★

Malendure Beach, Bouillante, ☎ (590) 98-70-84.
French cuisine.
Dinner: entrees $8–$18.

The vista from this upscale eatery perched on a bluff above Malendure Beach is Pigeon Island, a top diving locale and underwater reserve. If you can keep your eyes from the scenery, you'll be drawn to the the delectable creole treats on the fixed-price lunch that runs under $20—accras, barbecued chicken, crayfish in sauce and a beverage. Dinners are served Fridays and Saturdays only.

Grande-Terre

Auberge de la Vielle Tour **$$$** ★★★★★

Montauban, Gosier, ☎ (590) 84-23-23.
French cuisine.
Dinner: 7–10 p.m., entrees $23–$39.

Possibly the finest cuisine in Gosier can be found in the main dining room of the Pullman Auberge de la Vielle Tour. The view alone, of the Ilet du Gosier and its lighthouse in the distance, is worth the high tariff. Tables facing the wrap-around windows are, naturally, the most sought after, so request one way in advance. A la carte offerings include red snapper or catch of the day served with exotic fruit butters, or lamb loin roasted with herbs. A prix-fixe menu ($45) is also available.

Chez Violetta **$$$** ★★★

Perinette Gosier, Gosier Village, ☎ (590) 84-10-34.

French cuisine.
Lunch: Noon–3:30 p.m., entrees $11–$25.
Dinner: 7:30–11 p.m., entrees $11–$25.
One of the best-known tourist establishments in the islands is this restaurant serving traditional Creole specials in a room resplendent with baroque trappings. This mecca for delicacies like *accra* (cod fritters) and *lambi* (conch) is still going strong, even after the death of its creator Violetta Chaville. Service is by women in traditional dress. This is an excellent visual and culinary experience for first-time visitors.

Folie Plage $$$ ★★

Anse Laborde, Anse Laborde, ☎ (590) 22-11-17.
French cuisine.
Lunch: Noon–3 p.m., entrees $14–$18.
Dinner: 7–10 p.m., entrees $14–$18.
Local families flock to this restaurant/guesthouse in Anse Laborde on the north coast of Grand-Terre, especially on weekends, for a combination of beach-combing and grilled fish, court bouillon and chicken curry. If you're so inclined, rent a simple room from Madame Marcelin for under $50.

La Canne A Sucre $$$ ★★★★★

Quai No. 1, Point-a-Pitre, ☎ (590) 82-10-19.
French cuisine.
Lunch: Noon–2:30 p.m., entrees $18–$32.
Dinner: 7:30–10 p.m., entrees $18–$32.
This fine restaurant in Pointe-a-Pitre's port of Centre Saint-John Perse has a seagull's eye view of arriving ships, with a location on the quay. Patrons have a choice of dining in a ground floor brasserie on grilled lamb and mixed seafood platters, or upstairs in a tony, rose-hued chamber. Chef Gerard Virginius is fond of enhancing the finest seafood and poultry available locally with soursop and starfruit-infused vinegars and wine sauces.

La Louisiane $$$ ★★★

Quartier Ste. Marthe, St. Francois, ☎ (590) 88-44-34.
French cuisine.
Lunch: Noon–2 p.m., entrees $22–$30.
Dinner: 7–10 p.m., entrees $22–$30.
Located a few miles from the chic resort of St. Francois in Sainte Marthe, this bloom-filled hillside house has an established reputation for creative French-Antillean cuisine. Dinner for two can get pricey, but the experience is worth the splurge—specialties include shark prepared in a saffron sauce and pate of sea urchin roe.

La Plantation $$$ ★★★★★

Galerie Commerciale, Bas du Fort, ☎ (590) 90-84-83.
French cuisine.
Lunch: Noon–2:30 p.m., entrees $14–$54.
Dinner: 7–10:30 p.m., entrees $14–$54.
Guadeloupe's largest marina also boasts this well-known four-star establishment housed in two rosy, intimate dining rooms. La Plantation presents French classic cuisine with an emphasis on natural ingredients. Crayfish is a specialty, prepared in myriad ways—sometimes in a salad with foie gras, an unusual combination that works.

Le Chateau de Feuilles $$$ ★★★★★

Campeche, Anse Bertrand, ☎ (590) 22-30-30.
French cuisine.
Lunch: 11a.m.–3 p.m., entrees $18–$29.
Dinner: entrees $18–$29.

If you pass the remains of a crumbling old sugar mill in off-the-beaten-path Anse Bertrand, you're close to your goal—a four-star culinary landmark in an unlikely location—of a farm owned by chef-hosts Jean-Pierre and Martine Dubost. The atmosphere is like a house party, with a pool to swim in after lunch and a breathtaking choice of 20 flavors of rum, like a sophisticated Baskin-Robbins for adults. If you had a hard time finding the restaurant, don't indulge too much or you may never make it home. Dinner is served on Fridays and Saturdays, for a minimum of 10 people.

Le Poisson d'Or **$$$** ★★★

Rue Sadi-Carnot 2, Port Louis, ☎ *(590) 22-88-63.*
Latin American cuisine.
Lunch: 9:30 a.m.–4:30 p.m., entrees $14–$27.
Dinner: 6–9 p.m., entrees $14–$27.

The pride of the quiet fishing town of St. Louis is this cozy spot serving Creole specialties and seafood in a homey atmosphere. Specials change frequently, but usually feature crab farcis with spicy stuffing and homemade ice cream.

Le Restaurant **$$$** ★★★

Chateaubrun, Ste. Anne, ☎ *(590) 88-23-96.*
French cuisine.
Lunch: 12:30–2:30 p.m., entrees $25–$40.
Dinner: 7:30–9:30 p.m., entrees $25–$40.

Le Restaurant at the tropical village-style Le Relais du Moulin serves the usual Antillean-French dishes with some flair in an elegant dining room facing the resort's pool. Fixed price meals for $40 and a la carte offerings include grilled langoustes with herbs, blaff (fresh seafood in a spicy infusion) and lobster. After dinner, stroll the grounds; an old mill (moulin) dating back to the inn's plantation days makes a picturesque photo opportunity.

Les Oiseaux **$$$** ★★★

Anse des Rochers, St. Francois, ☎ *(501) 88-56-92.*
French cuisine.
Lunch: Noon–3 p.m., entrees $14–$29.
Dinner: 5–10:30 p.m., entrees $14–$29.

It's easy to imagine that you're in the South of France while dining on the terrace of this stone structure facing the sea, located a few miles south of St. Francois. The talented chef is a whiz with seafood, attesting to the popularity of his cassoulet de fruits de mer, and a cheeseless fondue of various fish and shellfish cooked with aromatic oils.

Sucrerie du Comte **$$$** ★★★

Comte de Loheac, Sainte-Rose, ☎ *(590) 28-60-17.*
cuisine.
Lunch: Noon–3 p.m., entrees $13–$35.
Dinner: 7–9:30 p.m., entrees $13–$35.

This pretty open-air restaurant, built of Brazilian woods and volcanic rock, is on the site of a former sugarcane factory and a small hotel that bears the same name. It's open all day for salads and sandwiches and offers such evening specialties as Tahitian fish with coconut milk, fish stew, mahimahi in parchment paper, and fresh fruit crepes. A good wine list accompanies the tasty dishes, many accented with local spices. On Sundays, the menu features traditional Creole dishes.

Victoria **$$$** ★★★

Cottage and Troical Club hotels, Le Moule, ☎ *(590) 23-78-38.*
French cuisine.
Lunch: 11:30 a.m.–2:30 p.m., entrees $7–$30.
Dinner: 7–10 p.m., entrees $10–$37.

Ceiling fans, coral-colored walls, and rattan furniture with blue seat cushions is the pleasing decor at this pretty open-air cafe across from the beach at la Moule. Choose from imaginative meat, chicken, and fish dishes with traditional heavy creams; the goat cheese salad is to die for. Besides the tasty food and fine wine list, a big plus is the fact they speak fluent English here—a rare find on Guadeloupe. Also open for breakfast from 7:00-9:30 a.m. daily; lunch hours can vary, so call first.

Where to Shop

The market at Pointe-a-Pitre is a bonanza of straw hats.

Guadeloupe is not a shopper's paradise—better to go to Martinique. What Guadeloupe lacks in merchandise, it more than makes up for in fun, however. Head for the street stalls around the harbor quay, in front of the tourist office and at the open-air market. The **Juan Perse Cruise Terminal** caters to the more sophisticated, and expensive tastes of cruise passengers; here you'll find a spanking new mall with about 24 shops. Avoid days when cruise ships are in port and start shopping early in the morning, before the noonday sun gets too hot.

Paying with traveler's checks and/or credit cards can sometimes reap you a 20 percent discount. French products, from crystal to cosmetics, perfume and fashions, are often less expensive than stateside, but if you are interested in brand names, check the prices at home before coming. Native craftwork can run from the junky to the intriguing; the best buys are salako hats made of split bamboo, straw baskets and hats, and wood carvings. Table linens made from madras are particularly fine. Even if you don't drink, bring back at least one bottle of Guadeloupe rum; there's sure to be someone back home who will love it. Best shops for rum are **Delice Shop** in Pointe-a-Pitre and **Ets Azincourt**.

In Pointe-a-Pitre, the main shopping streets are **rue Frébault**, **rue de Nozieres** and **rue Schoelcher**. Bas-du-Fort's two shopping districts are the **Mammoth Shopping Center** and the **Marina**, where you will find a good supply of both boutiques and restaurants. This is the place to come if you are in need of resort-wear fast. Duty-free shops can be found at the **Raizet Airport**.

Iles des Saintes

The sailing school at Petite Anse, Terre-de-Haut, offers half or full day windsurfing courses.

Terre-de-Haut is the largest island in an archipelago of eight islands called Les Saintes, off the south coast of Guadeloupe. The 35-minute ferry ride to reach there from Trois-Rivieres or 60-minute ride from Pointe-a-Pitre can be torturous due to choppy waves; take motion sickness pills if you are susceptible. Terre-de-Haut has but 1500 residents on its five-square-mile terrain; its largest city is Bourg with seerla boutiques, restaurants and gingerbread houses hugging the hillsides. Daring explorers can scope out secluded coves; there's even a nude beach at Anse Crawen, which has been compared to Rio de Janeiro for its beauty. A third of the island's economy is dedicated to tourism, so expect locals to be generous and friendly. Among the most important sites (there really aren't that many) is **Fort Napoléon**, leftover from the days when the English warred with the native population, and a nearby museum that houses a modern collection of paintings.

The real reason to come to Terre-de-Haut is to revel in its tranquil, laid-back charms. The quaint European-style village is a treat with its pastel wooden buildings (resist peeking in—many are private residences), friendly locals (who speak little English but are patient as tourists butcher their native French), decent restaurants, and limited shopping (note that virtually all stores close from noon to 2 or 3—or even 4 p.m.—for siesta). Don't miss the old Catholic Church at town center with its marble floor and high wooden ceiling; for five francs (about $1), you can light a candle in memory of a loved one. Then stroll up the street to **Chicken George's**, a local character who makes unforgettable (unless you drink too many) local punches. Also be on the lookout for **Kaz an Nou** ☎ *(590) 99-52-29* , where artisans make traditional wooden creole facades, the perfect souvenir to take home. While most of the island's beaches are not the greatest, the water is wonderfully clear and inviting. Be sure to check out Grande-Anse Beach on the Atlantic side, a lovely, lonely stretch you'll probably have all to yourself. The tide is much too strong for safe swimming (and signs forbid it), but it's the perfect spot for a picnic lunch.

The entire island has only about 30 cars; tourists get around on foot (easily done, though the trek up to Fort Napoléon is quite steep) or rent a motor scooter. You can arrange this just as you get off the ferry; expect to pay about $30 per day, including gas and insurance. You may plan to come just for the day, but just in case, pack an overnight bag. **Les Saintes** is magical, especially in the evening as the children play in the ferry square, locals emerge sleepily from their afternoon siestas, and atmospheric cafes prepare creole dinners; you'll be hard-pressed to bid au revoir to this enchanted isle.

What to See

Historical Sites

Fort Napoleon ★★★★

Bourg, Les Saintes.

Hours open: 9 a.m.–12:30 p.m.

This old French fort, wherein you can survey barracks and prison cells, is quite well preserved and a nice place to while away a few hours. All signage is in French, but you can buy an English brochure for $5.00—a bit of a rip-off after the $4.00 admission fee. Still, it's a nice spot, with many interesting exhibits inside—huge model ships, massive oil paintings depicting sea battles, and, oddly enough, a modern art museum—and breathtaking views and lovely botanical gardens outside. Look closely among the many varieties of cacti and you're sure to spot an iguana or two. Wear sturdy shoes as the ground is uneven, and bring lots of water if you plan to hike up the very steep road to the fort.

Sports/Recreation

Watersports in Les Saintes

Les Saintes.

Les Saintes may not have the most beautiful beaches in the Caribbean, but its crystal-clear waters beckon to be explored. For sailing excursions, try **Paradoxe Croisieres** *(☎ 590-88-41-73)* and **Atlantis** *(☎ 590-99-50-56)*. For general

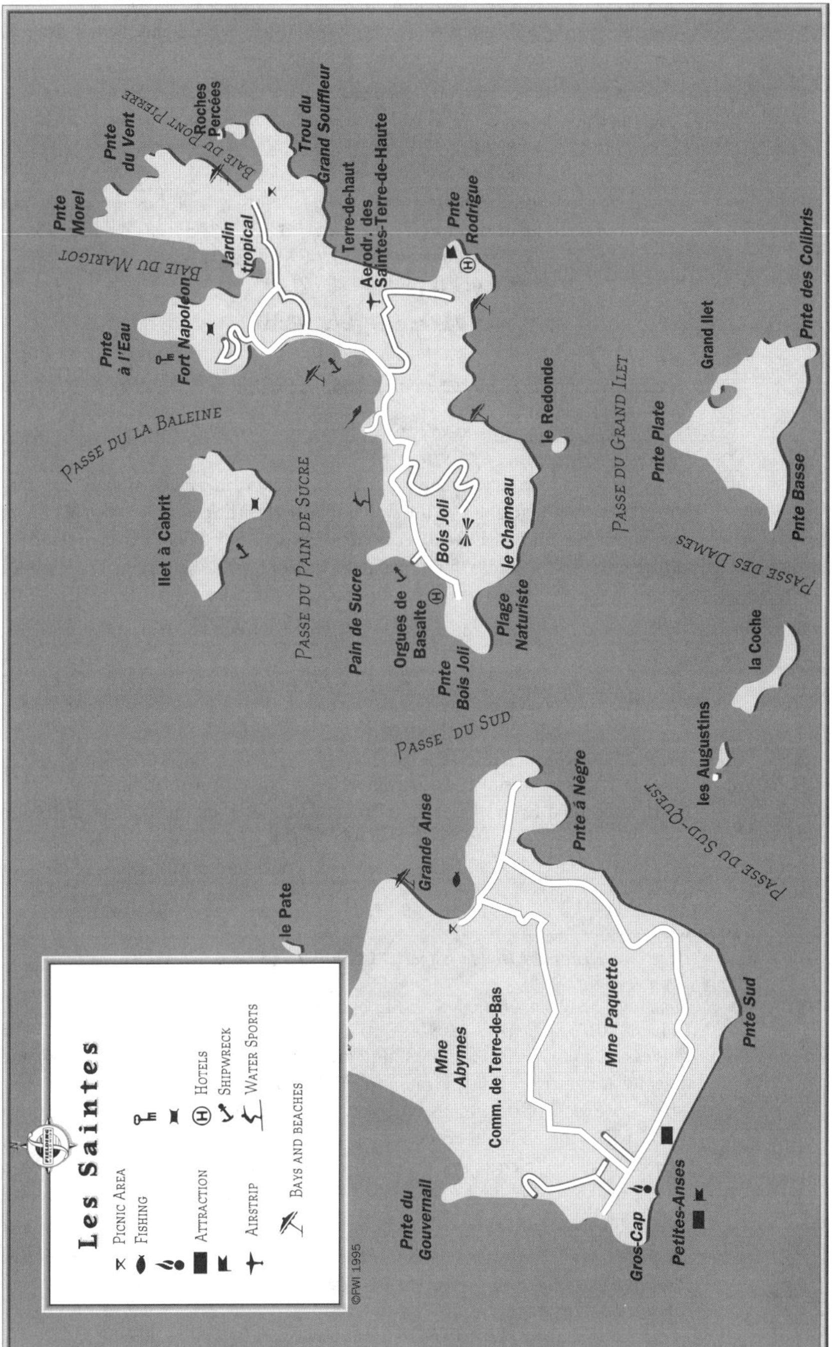
Les Saintes
Picnic Area
Fishing
Attraction
Airstrip
Hotels
Shipwreck
Water Sports
Bays and beaches
©PWI 1995
Pnte Morel
Pnte du Vent
Baie du Pont Pierre
Roches Percées
Trou du Grand Souffleur
Baie du Marigot
Jardin tropical
Terre-de-haut
Aerodr. des Saintes-Terre-de-Haute
Pnte Rodrigue
Pnte à l'Eau
Fort Napoleon
Passe du la Baleine
Ilet à Cabrit
Passe du Pain de Sucre
Pain de Sucre
Orgues de Basalte
Bois Joli
le Chameau
Plage Naturiste
Pnte Bois Joli
le Redonde
Passe du Grand Ilet
Grand Ilet
Pnte Plate
Pnte Basse
Pnte des Colibris
Passe des Dames
la Coche
les Augustins
Passe du Sud
Passe du Sud-Ouest
le Pate
Grande Anse
Pnte à Nègre
Mne Abymes
Comm. de Terre-de-Bas
Mne Paquette
Pnte Sud
Pnte du Gouvernail
Gros-Cap
Petites-Anses

watersports and diving, try **UPCA** *(☎ 590-99-54-94)*, Diving **Nautique des Saintes** *(☎ 590-99-54-25)*, **Land Maidonneuvre Guy** *(☎ 590-99-53-13)*. For pedal boat and canoe rentals, call **Lognos Paul** *(☎ 590-99-54-08)* and **Deher Daniel** *(☎ 590-99-52-42)*.

Tours

Guided Tours in Les Saintes

Les Saintes.

Terre de Haut is easily explored by foot or motorscooter—you can't rent a car. If you'd rather leave the navigating to someone else, try one of these operators, who provide island tours in small buses: **Procida** *(☎ 590-99-55-13)*, **Emilien Pineau** *(☎ 590-99-51-42)*, **Rose Rosette** *(☎ 590-99-50-61)*, **Sigiscar** *(☎ 590-99-53-08)*, and **Ch. Henri Vincent** *(☎ 590-99-51-79)*.

Where to Eat

La Saladerie **$$** ★★

Anse Marie, Terre de Haute, ☎ (590) 99-50-92.
International cuisine.
Lunch: Noon–2 p.m., entrees $7–$19.
Dinner: 7–9 p.m., entrees $7–$19.

As the name implies, guests can get a good green salad as well as seafood lightly grilled with fresh vegetables on the side at this lovely little oasis filled with plants and good music from owner Edward's eclectic CD collection. Prices are very reasonable for the great sea views, the high quality of the food, and the very gracious service. Save room for the luscious desserts, especially the fresh fruit sorbets. Highly recommended!

Le Amandiers **$$** ★★

Place de la Mairie, Terre de Haute, ☎ (590) 99-50-06.
Latin American cuisine.
Lunch: 11a.m.–2:30 p.m., entrees $12–$16.
Dinner: 7–11 p.m., entrees $12–$16.

This casual bistro is a superb base from which to while away the hours in the quaint Norman-flavored town of Bourg de Saintes, with its location right on the central square. A set-price lunch of local vegetables, salads, cod fritters and dessert is a bargain at $10. At dinner, sea-fresh selections like conch and crayfish keep visitors coming back for more.

Le Jardin Creole **$** ★★

Place du Debarcadere (the ferry pier), ☎ (590) 99-55-08.
Seafood cuisine.
Lunch: 9 a.m.–2 p.m., entrees $4–$14.
Dinner: 7–10 p.m., entrees $4–$14.

This casual spot is perfect for grabbing a quick bite before or after the ferry—or anytime, for that matter. Inside is rather plain, but outside, on the patio, patrons have a bird's-eye view of the goings-on below in the square; it's especially charming at night, when the children come out to play (and happily ignore the restaurant owner's pleas of "silence, si vous plait!") The menu offers up a large selection of crepes, steaks, mussels and smoked fish; I particularly liked the hardy fish pie with its golden, flaky crust. An added bonus: the owner speaks excellent English.

Nilce's Bar **$** ★★★★

Place du Debarcadere (ferry pier), ☎ (590) 99-56-80.
International cuisine.

This place debuted in June 1995 to instant success—I was there just three days after the grand opening, and it was mobbed! With good reason, too. Nilce, a beautiful Brazilian-born singer married to the owner of Village Creole (see Hotels), wows the crowd as she and an incredibly talented keyboardist belt out tunes from 6:00 p.m. nightly. The atmosphere is unmistakingly French—even the furniture came from an old French bistro—and depending on the crowd, there'll be local musicians jamming, abandoned dancing, and a hell of a good time for all. Set in an old house, the cafe serves American and French breakfasts and a tapas menu for lunch and dinner. Look for the old white building with fresh green trim and prepare for an evening of new friends and general merriment.

La Désirade

La Désirade, five miles east of Guadeloupe, was coveted by Columbus when he spotted the island on Nov. 3, 1493. The name he chose, which means "desired land" showed his true feelings about the exotic nature of the terrain. Ironically, the island became a leper colony for several years. Today it is a perfect place to escape with a picnic to one of the more beautiful beaches of **Souffleur** and **Baie Mahault**. Presently, the island is nearly pristine. In the main village of Grand Anse, there is a charming old church to visit and a hotel called **La Guitone**, where you can get a fine fish meal.

Marie-Galante

At 60 square miles, Marie-Galante is the largest of Guadeloupe's islands. The Caribs retreated here when they were driven from the mainland by the French; centuries later it's become a favorite haven for tourists, both local and foreign, who find the beach at Petit-Anse particularly charming. The island is the epitome of laid-back, though back in the 1800s it had a thriving sugar plantation industry. Ruins of sugar mills can be found all over the island. To get here, take the ferry from Pointe-a-Pitre, which drops you off at Grand Bourg, its largest city with a population of 8000, or one of the numerous short flights offered from Pointe-a-Pitre.

What to See

Museums and Exhibits

Chateau Murat ★★

Near Grand-Bourg, Marie-Galante.

After being destroyed by an earthquake in 1843, this 18th-century sugar plantation has been faithfully restored to its former glory. The mill is constructed of handhewn stone and houses the Ecomusee, an arts and traditions museum on island life. The adjoining botantic garden produces many of the medicinal herbs used on Marie-Galante.

Rhum Magaalda ★★★

Domaine de Bellevue, Capesterre, Marie-Galante.

This rum factory, located on the Bellevue property, dates back to 1821 and was completely rebuilt after being felled by a hurricane in 1928. The hospitable elderly owners welcome the public for impromptu tours—"just drop by and knock"—but come with a French phrase book, as they don't speak much English. Also bring lots of insect repellant—this place is charming, but crawling with mosquitos.

Sports/Recreation

Guided Tours of Marie-Galante

Marie-Galante.

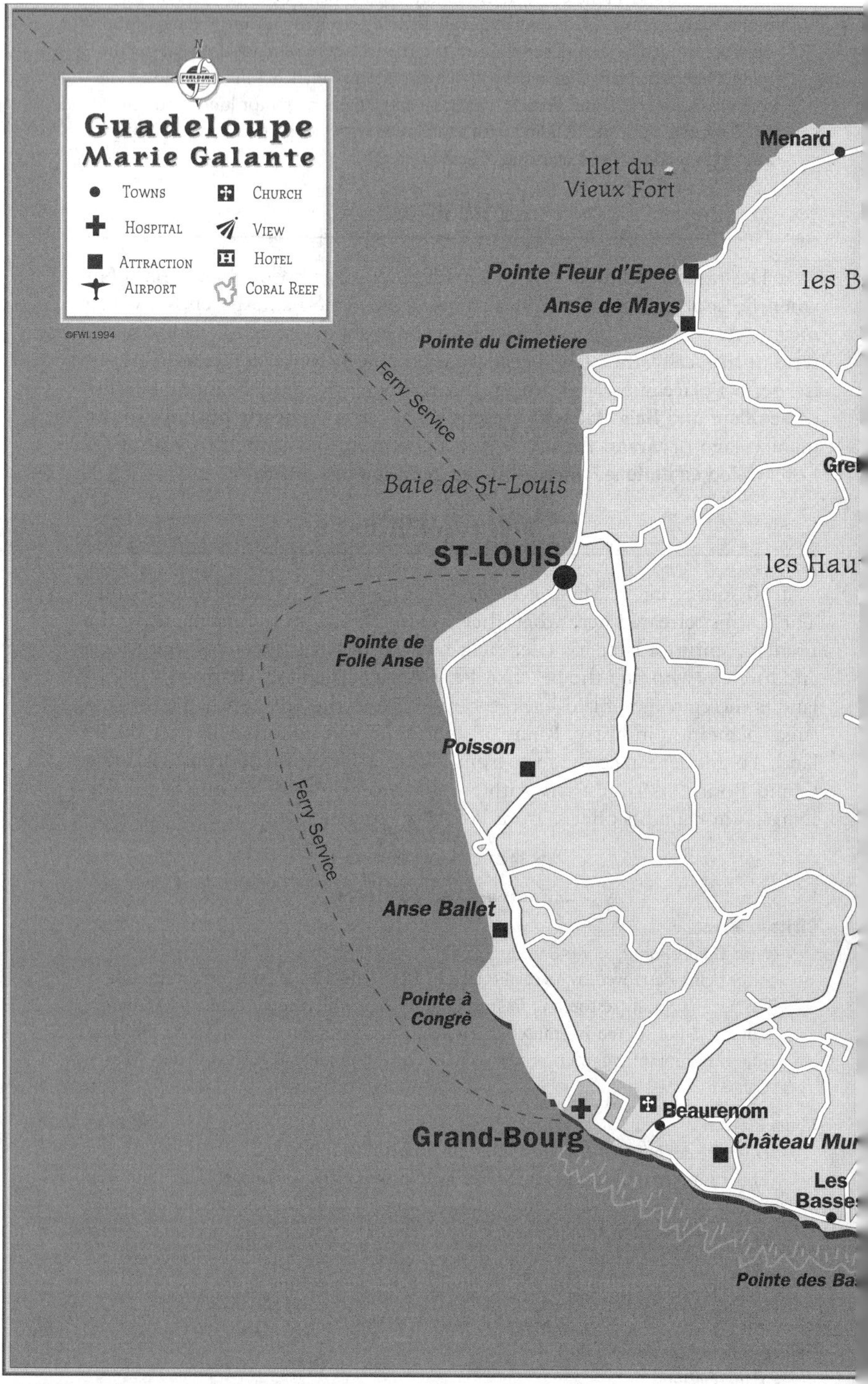
Guadeloupe
Marie Galante
Towns
Church
Hospital
View
Attraction
Hotel
Airport
Coral Reef
©FWI 1994
Menard
Ilet du Vieux Fort
Pointe Fleur d'Epee
Anse de Mays
Pointe du Cimetiere
Ferry Service
Baie de St-Louis
ST-LOUIS
Pointe de Folle Anse
Poisson
Ferry Service
Anse Ballet
Pointe à Congrè
Beaurenom
Grand-Bourg

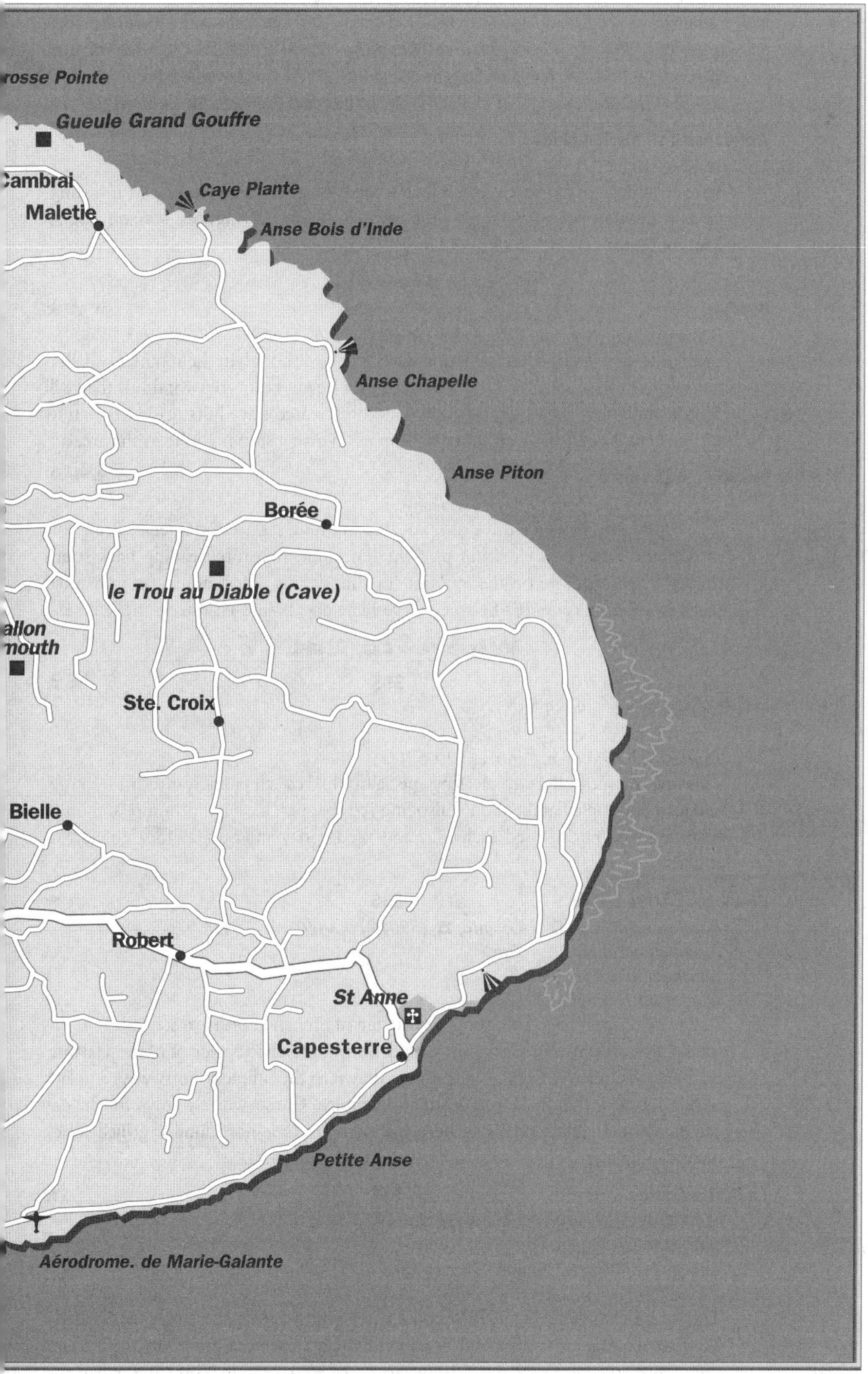
rosse Pointe
Gueule Grand Gouffre
Cambrai
Maletie
Caye Plante
Anse Bois d'Inde
Anse Chapelle
Anse Piton
Borée
le Trou au Diable (Cave)
allon
mouth
Ste. Croix
Bielle
Robert
St Anne
Capesterre
Petite Anse
Aérodrome. de Marie-Galante

The island is best explored by rental car, which costs about $50.00 per day. If you'd rather leave the driving to someone else, call one of the following: **Bavarday Philippe** ☎ *(590) 97-81-97*, **Jernival Roseline** ☎ *(590) 97-73-14*, **Glovert Gino** ☎ *(590) 97-34-18*, **Moysan Eugene** ☎ *(590) 97-31-05*, **Leveille Etiene** ☎ *(590) 97-72-97*, **El Rancho** ☎ *(590) 97-81-60*, and **Goram Frederic** ☎ *(590) 97-09-89*.

Watersports on Marie-Galante

Marie-Galante.

Take advantage of Marie-Galante's lovely beaches and inviting sea. For windsurfing, try **Fun Evasion** *(Capesterre, ☎ (590) 97-35-21)*; for diving, call **Maison Poullet Section Murat** *(Grand-Bourg, ☎ (590) 97-75-24)*.

Tours

Bezard ★★★

Between Etang-Noir and Grand Case, Marie-Galante.

This spot was still under construction when I passed though in the summer of 1995, but it should be open for 1996. It features a newly renovated windmill that will demonstrate how sugarcane is crushed, and re-created slave huts made from straw and goelette wood that will house boutiques. Worth a stop if you're in the area.

Sea Arch at Gueule ★★★★

The islands's northern tip, Marie-Galante.

It's well worth the scenic drive to reach this stunning sea arch at Gueule. Bring lots of film and beware of climbing past the fenceline. If you're heading back south toward Capesterre, be on the lookout for the island's oldest house, an unmarked shack made from cane. It's between Caye Plate and Pointe Pisiou, on the left.

Where to Eat

Auberge de la Roche d'Or **$$$** ★★

Capesterre, ☎ (590) 97-37-42.

International cuisine.

Dinner: 7:30–9:30 p.m., entrees $20–$30.

This inviting spot offers up pleasing specialties like conch pannes, breadfruit gratin, and iced pineapple flambe. You'll also find red snapper, local river shrimp, and other treats from la mer. Closed each May and Wednesday and Sunday for dinner year-round.

L'Auberge L'Arbre a Pain **$$$** ★★

Rue Jeanne d'Arc, Marie-Galante, ☎ (590) 97-73-69.

International cuisine.

Lunch: entrees $10–$30.

Dinner: entrees $10–$30.

It may help if you have a working knowledge of French in order to stay or eat at this small (seven room) inn located in Grand-Bourg, the civic center of Marie-Galante. But most visitors to this rural outpost are drawn to the simple country ways and lack of development that make this destination choice. Guests who fly down for the day can enjoy unique seafood dishes here, like octopus, or a more familiar grilled conch or seafood platter. There's also a five-course meal for $30.

La Braise Marine **$$$** ★

Face Plage de la Ferriere, Capesterre, ☎ (590) 97-42-57.

International cuisine.

Lunch: 11:30 a.m.–3:30 p.m., entrees $8–$30.

Dinner: 7–11 p.m., entrees $8–$30.

The menu changes daily at this casual eatery right across the street from one of Marie-Galante's most beautiful beaches. Expect to see sea urchin fritters, grilled fish, and creole blood sausages. If ouassou is offered, grab it. This large prawn-like delicacy, unique to the rivers of Guadeloupe and its islands, tastes like lobster and is just fabulous!

Guadeloupe Directory

BUSINESS HOURS

Stores open weekdays 9 a.m.–1 p.m. and 3–6 p.m. Banks open weekdays 8 a.m.–noon and 2–4 p.m. Some shops and banks are also open Saturday mornings.

CLIMATE

The climate is tropical with an average temperature of 79 degrees F. The more humid and wet season runs between June and November.

DOCUMENTS

If you're only staying up to three weeks, you need show only a current or expired passport (five years old or less) or proof of citizenship (voter's registration, birth certificate and official photo ID), as well as an ongoing or return ticket. Longer stays require a valid passport.

ELECTRICITY

Current is 220 volts, AC, 50 cycles. Adapters for U.S. appliances are needed.

GETTING AROUND

Taxis are plentiful and fares are set by the government. Between 9 p.m. and 7 a.m., fares increase 40 percent. You will have to be able to speak French to hire radio cabs.

Buses throughout the island run from 5:30 a.m.–7:30 p.m., and connect the island's major towns to Pointe-a-Pitre. Conditions are modern. Bus stops are included along the road and in shelters marked arrêtbus, but buses will often stop if you flag them down. Fares are inexpensive but the schedules are not reliable and they are often too crowded for comfort. Avoid riding them before and after school.

Since biking is a major sport here, you won't feel alone if you rent one. Bike rentals average about $10 a day, somewhat more for mountain bikes. Vespas are also good vehicles to rent, costing about $40 a day, plus a $200 deposit or a major credit card.

Cars are easy to rent on Guadeloupe. You may use your own driver's license up to 20 days; after that you need to obtain an international driver's permit. Roads are excellent here (more than 1225 miles), though the hairpins on Basse-Terre will take some careful negotiating. Natives drive well but fast, so be aware of passers. Stick with the top names like Hertz, Budget and Avis, in case there is trouble with your bill once you return home. In general, rentals here, about $60 a day, are a bit higher than on other islands. Check with your travel agent to see if prearranged rentals will save you money.

For some reason known only to Guadeloupeons (and even they're not too sure why), the three ferries that service Marie-Galante, Les Saintes, and La Desirade all offer virtually the same schedule. It's quite an amusing sight as they all pull into Point-a-Pitre at the exact same time and vie for passengers. Each leaves Pointe-a-Pitre at about 8 a.m. and departs for the return at about 4 p.m. Depending on the weather, the ferry ride can be quite rough, so take motion-sickness pills if you don't have great sea legs. Other times, it can be a smooth and exhilarating ride, especially if you sit on top in the open air. Call for information. **ATE** ☎ *(590) 95-13-43*, **Brudey Freres** ☎ *(590) 90-04-48*, and **Princess Caroline** ☎ *(590) 99-53-79*.

LANGUAGE

The official language is French. The African-influenced Creole is spoken by nearly everyone. Only some people speak English, so bring a French phrase book.

MEDICAL EMERGENCIES

There are five hospitals and 23 clinics in Guadeloupe. Your hotel or the tourist office can assist you in finding an English-speaking physician.

MONEY

The official currency is the French franc. The best exchange rate is to be found at banks or bureau de change; to convert francs back to dollars, you must go to a bank. For some reason, paying for purchases with dollar-denomination traveler's checks or credit cards may get you the best exchange rate.

TELEPHONE

The area code is *590*. To phone from Guadeloupe, buy a "telecarte," a plastic credit card sold at post offices and other outlets marked "Teleporte en Vente Ici." Use these cards on phones marked "Telecom." Operator-assisted calls and those made from your hotel room are much more expensive.

TIME

Guadeloupe is one hour later than Eastern Standard Time.

TIPPING

Restaurants and bars are required by law to add a 15 percent service charge. Most taxi drivers don't expect tips, especially if they own their own cars. Room maids should be tipped $1–$2, bellboys 50 cents–$1 a bag.

TOURIST INFORMATION

Brochures, maps and advice can be found at the Office Départemental du Tourisme de la Guadeloupe located near the waterfront in *Pointe-á-Pitre at 5 Pl. de la Banque*; ☎ *(590) 82-09-30*. The office is open Monday–Saturday. In the U.S. call ☎ *(213) 658-7462*.

WHEN TO GO

Between December and May. June–November is the humid and wet season.

GUADELOUPE RESTAURANTS	PHONE	ENTREE	CR. CARDS
Basse-Terre			
Basse-Terre			
French			
★★★★ **La Rocher de Malendure**	(590) 98-70-84	$8–$18••	DC, MC, V
International			
★★★ **Chez Paul de Matouba**	(590) 80-29-20	$12–$18••	MC, V
Latin American			
★★★ **Chez Clara**	(590) 28-72-99	$9–$27	MC, V

GUADELOUPE RESTAURANTS	PHONE	ENTREE	CR. CARDS
Grande-Terre			
Pointe-a-Pitre			
French			
★★★★★ **Auberge de la Vielle Tour**	(590) 84-23-23	$23–$39••	A, DC, MC, V
★★★★★ **La Canne A Sucre**	(590) 82-10-19	$18–$32	A, MC, V
★★★★★ **La Plantation**	(590) 90-84-83	$14–$54	A, DC, MC, V
★★★★★ **Le Chateau de Feuilles**	(590) 22-30-30	$18–$29	MC, V
★★★ **Chez Violetta**	(590) 84-10-34	$11–$25	A, DC, MC, V
★★★ **La Louisiane**	(590) 88-44-34	$22–$30	MC, V
★★★ **Le Restaurant**	(590) 88-23-96	$25–$40	A, DC, MC, V
★★★ **Les Oiseaux**	(501) 88-56-92	$14–$29	V
★★ **Folie Plage**	(590) 22-11-17	$14–$18	A, DC, V
Latin American			
★★★ **Le Poisson d'Or**	(590) 22-88-63	$14–$27	MC, V
Terre-de-Haute			
Terre de Haute			
International			
★★ **La Saladerie**	(590) 99-50-92	$8–$18	MC, V
Latin American			
★★ **Le Amandiers**	(590) 99-50-06	$12–$16	A, MC, V
Marie-Galante			
Marie-Galante			
International			
★★ **L'Auberge L'Arbre a Pain**	(590) 97-73-69	$10–$30	V

Note: • Lunch Only;
•• Dinner Only

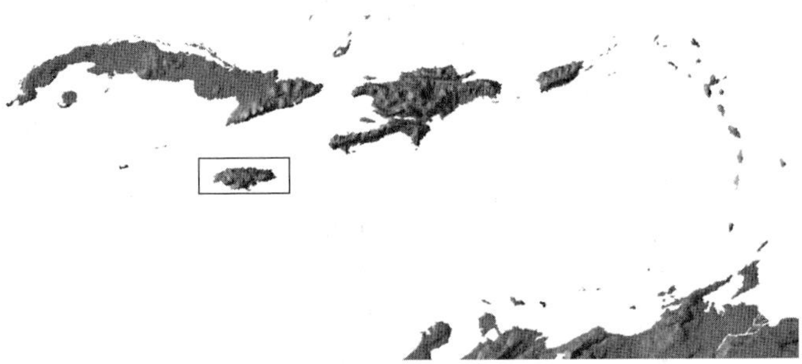

JAMAICA

Jamaica is famous for its magnificent waterfalls.

Rastas and reggae, jerk pork and ginger beer, cool mountains, hot beaches, damp jungles and the cold refreshing water of streams and rivers—Jamaica is a continuous dance of the senses. The island can be so stimulating, in fact, that when Ian Fleming created his immortal character James Bond here in 1952, he insisted on facing a white wall in order to avoid the distracting beauty of both women and landscape. Midwife to the great all-inclusive resorts that have given immediate pleasure a new definition, Jamaica today is fostering the growth of a new, less-traditional style of resort—small, private places away from the beaches that allow intimate glimpses of island life and culture. In a back-to-the-future gesture, many of the great houses of century-old sugar plantations are being renovated today with artistic aplomb, and a pioneer in this work is Chris Blackwell, the rock entrepreneur who made Bob Marley an international superstar; his luxurious 10-room Good Hope Great House, a 45-minute drive from Montego Bay high in Jamaica's lush green hills, gives you the opportunity to relax in the gentile atmosphere of a British country home, six miles from the beach. Ecologically, Jamaica is still a treasurehouse—rain forests, rivers, waterfalls, wetlands, coral reefs and caves are found in every corner of the island, and hundreds of miles of well-marked trails can run from the easy to the daredevilish. From Montego Bay to Ocho Rios, around the perimeter of the island, excellent conditions for all watersports make for exciting adventures, though one of the best is still the rafting sojourn down the Rio Grande River on a banana boat (a favorite pastime of Errol Flynn).These days, with a rising crime rate, you do need to take precautions in Jamaica, but once you sit down to a cold local brew and a big plate of Jamaican-style barbecue, shaded by a palm and served with the most gracious smile you can imagine, every care you've ever had will disappear in a wink.

Bird's Eye View

Located 700 miles southeast of Miami, 110 miles west of Haiti, and 90 miles south of Cuba, Jamaica sprawls over 4400 square miles, making it the third-largest island in the Caribbean. Like other West Indian islands, it was formed from the outcropping of a submerged mountain range. A mountain range, reaching 7402 feet at the Blue Mountain Peak, crosses the island in the east and descends westward; a series of gullies and spurs cross north to south. The north and west coasts harbor the majority of beaches, though a few good ones can be found in the south. The cultural and social pulse of the island, Kingston, the capital, is located in the southeast coast—one of the largest and best natural harbors in the world. Montego Bay, another landmark name in Jamaican tourism, lies in the northwest part of the island.

History

Columbus first glimpsed the north coast of the island in May 1494, landing in Montego Bay before he went back to Cuba. When he returned nine years later, stormy weather crippled two of his ships and he was forced to anchor at St. Ann's Bay, where he and his men were shipwrecked until the governor of Hispaniola retrieved them. In 1510, a permanent Spanish settlement was finally established under the orders of Don Diego, the son of Columbus, who was then governor of the West Indies, based in Santo Domingo. A new capital was erected in 1935 at Villa de la Vega (the Town on the Plain), now known as Spanish Town. In 1655, Britain, under Oliver Cromwell, challenged Spain's claim on the island, ultimately triumphing and establishing a head base at Port Royal, across the harbor from what is now Kingston. (The Spaniards fled to Windsor Cave, the home even today of many of their descendants.) The new headquarters at Port Royal became the hub of some of the most nefarious activities on the high seas, under the di-

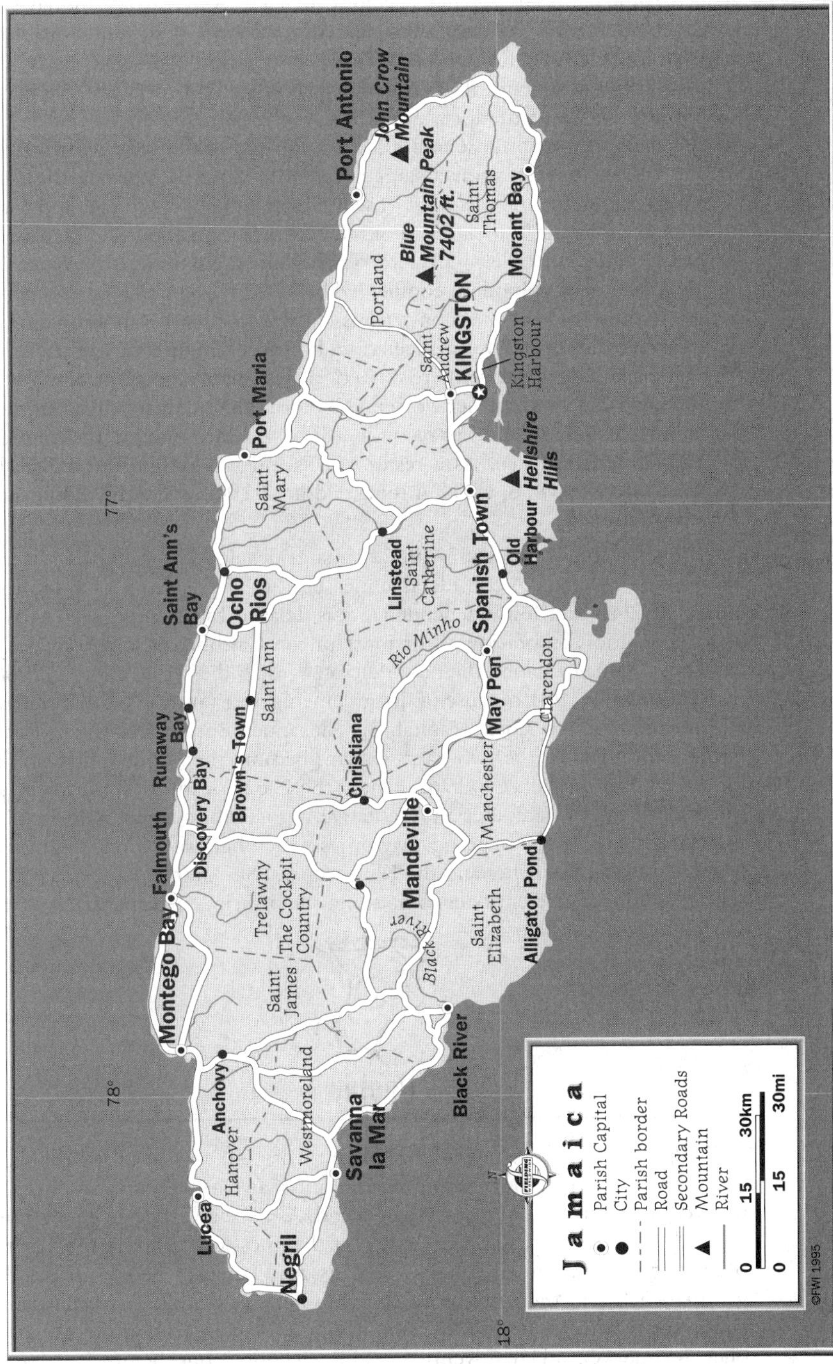
Jamaica
Parish Capital
City
Parish border
Road
Secondary Roads
Mountain
River
0 15 30km
0 15 30mi
©FWI 1995
78°
77°
18°
N
Negril
Lucea
Hanover
Anchovy
Westmoreland
Savanna la Mar
Black River
Montego Bay
Saint James
Falmouth
Trelawny
The Cockpit Country
Black River
Saint Elizabeth
Alligator Pond
Mandeville
Manchester
Discovery Bay
Runaway Bay
Brown's Town
Christiana
Saint Ann
Saint Ann's Bay
Ocho Rios
Rio Minho
May Pen
Clarendon
Linstead
Saint Catherine
Spanish Town
Old Harbour
Hellshire Hills
Saint Mary
Port Maria
Saint Andrew
KINGSTON
Kingston Harbour
Portland
Blue Mountain Peak 7402 ft.
Saint Thomas
Morant Bay
Port Antonio
John Crow Mountain

rection of the buccaneer Henry Morgan, whose sacking of the Spanish colony in Panama clinched England's claim to Jamaica. A massive earthquake in 1692 actually shook half the town—like Sodom and Gomorrah—-into the sea. The multi-ethnic, though black-based, population of Jamaica began to be born in the next centuries as sugarcane farming took root, and the need for imported labor in the form of black slaves became imperative. After Jamaica's slave population rose to 300,000 at the end of the 18th century, the ratio of blacks to whites was a staggering 15 to one. Included in the mix were free coloureds, the offspring of white men and slave women, and Maroons, descendants of free slaves. (For more information about the Maroons, see below under "People.") Slave revolts became a common occurrence in Jamaica, the largest, bloodiest conflict led by "Daddy" Sam Sharpe, a Baptist preacher whose oratory and convictions led the way to the abolishment of slavery in Jamaica in 1838. Emancipation, however, led directly to the fall of the sugarcane industry since there was a decided lack of labor. The condition of the freed blacks was further worsened by drought and unsteady economic conditions, leading to another revolt in 1865, which resulted in the murder of a government official. As a result, the island was designated a British Crown Colony in 1866, which it remained until 1944, when full adult suffrage was granted.

A British colony from 1655–1962, Jamaica developed a two-part system before World War II. A considerable measure of self-government was introduced in 1944, but full independence was delayed by attempts to set up a wider federation embracing all or most of the Caribbean Commonwealth territories. Jamaica joined the now-defunct West Indies Federation in 1958 but withdrew in 1961 because of disagreements over taxation, voting rights, and location of the federal capital. Sir Alexander Bustaments, one of the original founders of the two-party system, became the nation's first prime minister at independence in 1962. Under the 1962 constitution the queen is the titular head of state. Her representative, a governor general, is advised in areas bearing on the royal perogative, by a six-member privy council. Jamaica is divided into 13 parishes and the Kingston and St. Andrew Corporation, a special administrative entity encompassing the principal urban areas.

People

Like Brazil, Jamaica is a wonderful place to visit—if you don't get robbed. Jamaicans are a cheerful, generous bunch, full of an earthy humor and deeply inspired by the natural beauty of their island. As a society, they are inherently musical, with great artistic gifts—some of the finest craftwork in the Caribbean is done by untrained Jamaican artisans. And Jamaican people are deeply spiritual—it's said there are more churches per square mile than anywhere else in the world. Most are Protestant, though there are some Roman Catholics, Jews, Seventh Day Adventists, and Pentecostals, but the most apparent are the dreadlocked **Rastafarians**, a local minority cult best recognized by their long braided hair that resembles a rat's nest (Rastas take a religious vow not to wash their hair). Though they can often look a bit intimidating (their hairdos can look voluminous when they pull off their caps), they are nonviolent and do not eat pork; they believe the late Emperor Haile Selassie was a divine being, whose call for the end of racial superiority was connected to the belief that God would lead the blacks out of oppression and back to the Promised Land. Marcus Garvey, the ideologist born in St. Anne's Bay in 1887, is considered a prophet by the Rastas and is today a national hero.

The soul of Rastafarianism lives in the musical genre called reggae, Jamaica's most popular export known throughout the world. Over the years, such musical greats as Bob Marley, Peter Tosh, Jimmy Cliff and others have used reggae as political and spiritual inspiration through strong lyrics often disguised in meaning. Recently in Jamaica reggae has been supplanted by a newer genre called Dance Hall, which sports a heavier beat, and like American rap, tends to focus on urban violence and sex. Both musical forms can be heard throughout the island; beaches cannot be considered Jamaican if there isn't at least one jam session going on close by.

In the heart of the mysterious and rugged Cockpit country live the Maroons, descendants of escaped slaves who through incredible courage and cunning managed to evade capture for a century. The attitude toward this community is diverse—they have been called anything from the world's most successful revolutionaries to desperate villains and rogues. The peace treaty they eventually signed with the British still exists, like their culture, 250 years later. Hidden deeply inside the hills along a barely passable road, their isolated, self-governing enclaves are only slightly more accessible today. In the past there have been stories reported by travelers of being stopped along the road to Moore Town by Maroons armed with machetes demanding a payment of a road tax. (Being self-ruled, the Maroons can do anything—only in the event of murder are they subject to Jamaican jurisdiction). Their resistance has been buoyed by strong African religious beliefs and rites, and modern Maroon leaders are thought to be imbued with supernatural powers aligned not only to religion but to military prowess. Obeah, the ashanti-inspired system of belief, plays a major part in the Maroon tradition in Jamaica. The January Accompong Festival celebrates the victory of the Maroons over the English. To get to their enclaves is difficult and can often end in a futile search. (For more information, see below under the section "Porto Antonio—Treks")

There are many excellent Jamaican novelists whose fiction gives an excellent glimpse into the heart and soul of the people. *Abeng*, a novel by Michelle Cliff, explores the sensitive issues of race and class as seen through the eyes of a young girl. *Jamaica Farewell*, by Morris Cargill, is an honest portrait of the country and its people by a native newspaper columnist. Other fine writers include Olive Senior, H. Orlando Patterson and the poets Mervynn Morris and Dennis Scott.

INSIDER TIP

Note:. Illegal under Jamaican law, the "herb" locally called ganja (marihuana) is known to be a major source of income in the highlands. Officials, however, claim that ganja does not grow anywhere in the residential areas, adding that if it grows "anywhere," it is in the wilderness.

Beaches

The best way to acquaint yourself with the beaches of Jamaica—before even buying a ticket—is to rent a video of the first James Bond film, *Dr. No*—it's practically a travel promotional for the island's most beautiful strands. Then look for more specific information under the individual areas—Kingston, Montego Bay, Port Antonio—below.

Sports (Island-Wide)

Every imaginable water sport is available in Jamaica; the all-inclusive resorts are masters at accommodating guests to arrange any and all levels of expertise. With such luxurious countryside, however, the latest trends are to pursue challenging treks (see the "Treks" section, above)—from floating lazily down the White River (near Ocho Rios) or tooling down the Martha Brae River on an inflatable raft.

Kingston

For many tourists, Kingston on first sight is everything they don't want in a Caribbean isle—grimy, traffic-clogged, polluted, noisy, crime-ridden and irrespressibly raucous, but it is, nevertheless, the soul and spirit of most native islanders whose eyes wax over when they remember their childhood memories. This is where the ethnic melting pot first produced the crossbreeding that makes up the present heady spice called Jamaican society. What Kingston truly is today is Bob Marley turf, the undisputed (albeit deceased) king of reggae whose 1974 song "Lively Up Yourself" became the cry of the masses. Today you can't go anywhere in Kingston without making homage to his name; indeed, some travelers come to Kingston *only* for that. His dreadlocked statue stands in the middle of the square across from the National Arena and his records can be found in every store on the island. The **Bob Marley Museum**, ensconced into a 19th-century home on Hope Road, is a visual testimony to his life, struggles and musical influence.

To see the full variety of sights in Kingston, you will probably need to rent a car, or hire a taxi for the day. At the top of the itinerary should be the **Devon House**, a restored 19th-century mansion that first belonged to one of the Caribbean's first black millionaires, George Steibel. The **National Gallery of Jamaica** is a fine place to appreciate the island's art, from 17th-century portraits to impressionist paintings and sculptures. **Hope Botanical Gardens** is a lovely pace to stroll and enjoy the exotic flora of the island; Sundays are crowded but give you a chance to see Jamaican families in action. Across the harbor is **Port Royal**, or what is left of Port Royal, once the island's premier city in the 17th century when buccaneers ruled the waves. Henry Morgan, the British pirate, called the city his home, before it toppled, in 1692, into the harbor by an earthquake and subsequent tidal wave. There's still quite a lot left to see, including the cockeyed **Giddy House**, which has been tilting off-center since a 1907 earthquake, as well as **St. Peter's Church**, **Fort Charles** and the old **Naval Hospital**. At **Morgan's Harbor** marina you'll find a few restaurants, bar and small hotel.

West of Kingston is **Spanish Town,** Jamaica's old capital, with a few historical sites still standing. On the south coast, **Madeville** represents a quieter, calmer Jamaica. Bird-watchers will enjoy **Marshal's Pen**, an 18th-century greathouse set on a 300-acre wildlife sanctuary. Two of the best places to see the sunset are **Yardley Chase** and **South St. Elizabeth**. For touring the area as an ecologist, contact **South Coast Safaris** (on the Black Rover); ☎ *(809) 965-2513* for a 1.5 hour excursion covering 10 miles round-trip where you can photograph a variety of birds, crocodile and other wildlife. Special fishing tours can also be arranged.

Beaches in Kingston

Gunboat Beach is one of the most popular beaches around Kingston. A rare black sand beach is found at **Fort Clarence**, tucked into the Hellshire Hills southwest of the city. There you'll find changing facilities and live entertainment. Locals think nothing of driving the 30-odd miles for the special surroundings at **Lyssons Beach** at Morant Bay, whose golden sands gleam in the sun.

A delightful excursion is to hire a boat at the Morgan's Harbor Marina at Port Royal to cruise to **Lime Cay**, an island just beyond Kingston Harbor. Here is an ideal place to picnic, swim and sunbathe.

What Else to See

City Celebrations

Reggae Sunsplash ★★★★★

Jam World, Kingston.

The annual week-long party of all parties takes place each summer, usually in July. Lots of top-name reggae bands and groovin' folks. Book your hotel way in advance or you'll never get in.

Historical Sites

Devon House ★★★★

26 Hope Road, Kingston, ☎ (809) 929-7029.

Hours open: 10 a.m.–5 p.m.

This 1881 mansion is filled with period furnishings but the best reason to come is for the excellent crafts shops on the grounds. There are two restaurants and a great ice cream shop.

Museums and Exhibits

Bob Marley Museum ★★★

56 Hope Road, Kingston, ☎ (809) 927-9152.

Hours open: 9:30 a.m.–4:30 p.m.

The national hero's clapboard house was his home and recording studio for many years. Reggae fans will appreciate the collection of Marley memorabilia and consider this a five-star attraction. Those not into Marley's brand of music can pass.

Institute of Jamaica ★★★

12 East Street, Kingston, ☎ (809) 922-0620.

Hours open: 8:30 a.m.–5 p.m.

This museum has excellent exhibits on the island's history, with some impressive old charts and almanacs. It also houses the National Library.

National Gallery ★★★★

12 Ocean Blvd., Kingston, ☎ (809) 922-1561.

This waterfront gallery displays paintings, sculpture and other works of art by Jamaica's most famous artist, Kapo. Other artists' works include Edna Manley, Alvin Marriott, Isaac Belisari and Augustin Brunias.

Parks and Gardens

Royal Botanical Gardens ★★★

Hope Road, Kingston, ☎ (809) 927-1257.

A peaceful refuge from city life, these gardens encompass 50 acres. Most plants and trees are marked for identification.

Theatre

Little Theatre ★★★

4 Tom Redcam Road, Kingston, ☎ (809) 926-6129.

This theater presents a variety of dramas, musical and special performances. Each December 26-April they produce the LTM Pantomime, a variety show with song, dance and stories.

Theme/Amusement Parks

Anancy Family Fun ★★★

Negril, Kingston, ☎ (809) 957-4100.

This newer attraction consists of three acres of miniature golf, a fishing pond, go-carts and a nature trail. Geared toward kids.

Tours

Cruises

Various locations, Kingston.

Lots of choices for cruising the ocean blue. Montego Bay: **Paco Rabanne** *(☎ (809) 951-5020)*, the **Mary-Ann** *(☎ (809) 953-2231)*, the **Calico** *(☎ (809) 952-5860)*, and the **Rhapsody** *(☎ (809) 979-0104)*. Port Antonio: **Lady Jamaica** *(☎ (809) 993-3318)*. Ocho Rios: **Heave-Ho Charters** *(☎ (809) 974-5367)* and **Red Stripe** *(☎ (809) 974-2446)*. Negril: **Aqua Nova Water Sports** *(☎ (809) 957-4323)* and the **Lollypop** *(☎ (809) 952-4121)*. Excursions range from snorkel trips to catamaran sails to booze cruises with live bands.

Port Royal ★★

Near Kingston, Kingston, ☎ (809) 924-8706.

Hours open: 9 a.m.–5 p.m.

Now it's more touristy than anything, but this port used to be known as the "wickedest city in the world" because of its buccaneering past and frequent visits by Blackbeard. That all changed in 1692, when it was destroyed by an earthquake. There's lots to see in the complex, including St. Peter's Church, which dates back to 1725; the Archaeological and Historical Museum; a small maritime museum housed in the former British navel headquarters; Fort Charles, which dates back to 1656 and is the port's only remaining fort; and the Giddy House, permanently tilted after an earthquake.

Sports in Kingston

Yachting is one of the major activities in Kingston since there are so many attractive offshore islets in the area. A well-attended regatta is sponsored in August by the Morgans Harbor Hotel. If you belong to a yacht club at home, inquire whether you have privileges to participate. Ask at the Morgans Harbour Hotel regarding cruises around the harbor.

Many resorts have tennis courts. Public courts are available at the Ligunea Club across the road from the hotels in New Kingston. Squash can also be played at the Ligunea Club. Eighteen-hole golf courses can be found at the Caymanas Golf Club and the Constant Spring Golf Club.

Jamaica has a passion for **polo**. In the Kingston area, the Kingston Polo Club on the Caymanas Estates holds regular matches. For more information about activities at Chukka Cove, see "North Coast" below.

Golf

Various locations, Kingston.

Jamaica has lots of golf courses. The best by far are the links at Tryall, a PGA tour-approved, par-71 course that is considered one of the world's best. Call ☎ *(809) 952-5110*. Also in the Montego Bay area are the **Half Moon Golf Club** *(☎ (809) 953-2280)*, a spacious, par-72 course designed by Robert Trent Jones; **Ironshore Golf and Country Club** *(☎ (809) 953-2800)*, par 72 and known for its many blind holes; and **Wyndham Rose Hall Country Club** *(☎ (809) 953-2650)*, a par-72 course on the historic Rose Hall estate with an imaginative layout. In Kingston, try **Caymanas Golf Club**, *(☎ (809) 926-8144)*, a par 72 known for its very challenging 12th hole; and **Constant Springs** *(☎ (809) 924-1610)*, a par-70 course.

Horseback Riding

Various locations, Kingston.

Several operations offer horseback riding. Ocho Rios: **Chukka Cove Farm** *(☎ (809) 972-2506)*, $20 per hour; and **Prospect Plantation** *(☎ (809) 974-2373)*, $18 per hour. Montego Bay: **Rocky Point Stables** *(☎ (809) 953-2212)*, where 1.5-hour rides start at $38. Negril: **Horseman Riding Sables** *(☎ (809) 957-4474)*, $25 for two hours.

Watersports

Various locations, Kingston.

Check out one of the following operations. For scuba and snorkel, try **Fisherman's Inn** *(Falmouth, ☎ (809) 247-0475)*. Runaway Bay: **Jamaqua Watersports** *(☎ (809) 973-4845)* and **Sun Divers Jamaica** *(☎ (809) 973-2346)*. Negril: **Negril Scuba Centre** *(☎ (809) 957-4425)* and **Sun Divers Jamaica** *(☎ (809) 957-4069)*. Ocho Rios: **Sea and Dive Jamaica** *(☎ (809) 947-5762)*. Montego Bay: **Seaworld** *(☎ (809) 953-2180)* and **Sandals Beach Watersports** *(☎ (809) 949-0104)*. Port Antonio: **Lady Godiva** *(☎ (809) 993-3281)* and **Aqua Action** *(☎ (809) 993-3318)*. In addition to the above, **Resort Divers** *(☎ (809) 974-0577)* has six locations around the island. For deep-sea fishing, check out **Seaworld Resorts** *(☎ (809) 993-3086)* and **Sans Souci** *(☎ (809) 974-2353)*.

Where to Eat

Fielding's Highest Rated Restaurants in Jamaica		
★★★★★	Evita's	$7–$19
★★★★★	Reading Reef Club	$10–$24
★★★★★	Temple Hall	$25–$25
★★★★★	Trident Hotel Restaurant	$25–$50
★★★★	Almond Tree	$12–$26
★★★★	Blue Mountain Inn	$12–$24
★★★★	Norma's at the Wharfhouse	$26–$34
★★★★	Sugar Mill	$14–$31
★★★	De Montevin Lodge	$11–$18
★★★	Pork Pit	$2–$9

Fielding's Special Restaurants in Jamaica		
★★★★★	Temple Hall	$25–$25
★★★★	Almond Tree	$12–$26
★★★★	Blue Mountain Inn	$12–$24
★★★★	Norma's at the Wharfhouse	$26–$34
★★★★	Sugar Mill	$14–$31

Fielding's Budget Restaurants in Jamaica		
★	Chelsea Jerk Centre	$3–$5
★★	Chicken Lavish	$3–$5
★★	Hot Pot, The	$3–$4
★★★	Pork Pit	$2–$9
★★	Front Line, The	$5–$8

Blue Mountain Inn **$$$** ★★★★

Gordon Town Road, ☎ (809) 927-1700.

International cuisine.

Dinner: 7–9 p.m., entrees $12–$24.

This is probably one of Jamaica's most elegant dining experiences, set in an old coffee plantation house overlooking the Mamee River, located about half an hour from Kingston. It's a good excuse for women to air out a little black dress and men a jacket (ties are not required) while sampling continental cuisine that's impeccably prepared and served by a gracious staff. Steak and lobster thermidor and flambeed desserts are some of the old fashioned but delicious choices frequently on the menu.

Chelsea Jerk Centre **$** ★

9 Chelsea Avenue, ☎ (809) 926-6322.
Latin American cuisine. Specialties: Jerk Chicken and Pork.
Lunch: Noon–3:30 p.m., entrees $3–$5.
Dinner: 3:30–10 p.m., entrees $3–$5.

No, this isn't a self-improvement workshop for nerds on Chelsea Avenue - the Jerk Centre proffers blazingly hot barbecued chicken or pork that's been marinating for hours in a medley of incendiary spices that are a closely-guarded secret. Most dishes here are under $5 and come with sides of rice and peas (white rice with red beans). A half-chicken or pork slab can be packaged to go.

Devon House Restaurants **$$** ★★

Devon House, ☎ (809) 929-6602.
Latin American cuisine.
Lunch: 10 a.m.–4 p.m., entrees $6–$16.
Dinner: 4 p.m.–midnight, entrees $6–$16.

This former colonial mansion turned restaurant/coffee house/craft emporium is one of Kingston's most visited tourist sites. An incredible Jamaican breakfast is served on the breezy Coffee Terrace every day except Sunday. Diners saunter to a long table topped with red-checked country cloths for a buffet of beautifully carved fresh fruit, ackee and saltfish, cod fish balls and breads. Blue Mountain coffee and exotic juices are included. If you have room, pop into the adjoining I-Scream for a frozen concoction of soursop or mango.

El Dorado Room **$$** ★

17 Waterloo Road, ☎ (809) 926-9334.
International cuisine.
Lunch: Noon–2:30 p.m., entrees $7–$20.
Dinner: 7:30–11 p.m., entrees $7–$20.

The main dining room of the Terra Nova Hotel, a boutique style hostelry, provides a gracious ambience for local residents taking a breather from the vibrant Kingston restaurant scene. Picture windows look out onto the spacious grounds of the former private estate built in the early 20s. Seafood shines here, whether it's freshly-caught grilled lobster or red snapper in ginger sauce.

Gap Cafe, The **$$$** ★★

Hardwar Gap, Blue Mountain, ☎ (809) 923-7055.
International cuisine.
Lunch: entrees $12–$15.
Dinner: entrees $17–$22.

A visit to the Gap Cafe is a journey to another Jamaica—one where a fireplace may be glowing all year round, understandable at a height of 4200 feet. Gloria Palomino welcomes guests to sip Blue Mountain coffee and savor some of the best pastries on the island, served all day and at high tea on Sundays. Native guavas are used in the cheesecake, as well as soursop and passion fruit for the cakes and mousses. The Cafe, once an old fixer-upper, is now a cozy, flower-filled charmer decked out in tones of maroon and blue. There's a gift shop on the premises.

Hot Pot, The **$** ★★

2 Altamont Terrace, ☎ (809) 929-3906.
Latin American cuisine. Specialties: Fricassee Chicken, Saltfish and Ackee.
Lunch: 8 a.m.–4 p.m., entrees $3–$4.
Dinner: 4–10 p.m., entrees $3–$4.

A dandy place to try Jamaican specialties is this informal joint behind the Wyndham Hotel. The decor isn't much, but the authentic dishes are cheap and filling. The

Hot Pot serves three meals a day, including the legendary saltfish and ackee (a vegetable brought over by Captain Bligh of Bounty fame) for breakfast.

Indies Pub and Grill **$** ★

8 Holborn Road, ☎ (809) 926-5050.
Latin American cuisine.
Lunch: entrees $4–$12.
Dinner: entrees $4–$12.

This is the Jamaican version of a local pub, roosting companionably in a New Kingston neighborhood. The fare is nothing fancy: just burgers, fish and chips or pizza, but sometimes there's nothing better than rubbing elbows with office workers on a comfortable alfresco terrace. The Indies is a popular late night spot as well, it serves food and drink until 1:30 a.m. on weekends and until midnight the rest of the week.

Ivor Guest House **$$$** ★

Jack's Hill, ☎ (809) 977-0033.
International cuisine.
Lunch: entrees $18–$22.
Dinner: entrees $22–$30.

This cozy guest house/dining room on a hill high above Kingston boasts a million dollar view (at 2000 feet) and the chef prepares reasonably-priced lunches and dinners with a Jamaican flair. The terrace of this small colonial inn is a popular spot for high tea and cocktails on the open terrace. On a clear night, the lights of the city in the distance make strong men (and women) swoon.

Le Pavilion **$$$** ★★

81 Knutsford Boulevard, ☎ (809) 926-3690.
International cuisine.
Lunch: 12:30–3 p.m., prix fixe $16.
Dinner: 7–11 p.m., entrees $16–$26.

As hotel dining rooms go, Le Pavilion just might be the most popular downtown meeting spot. Sophisticated city dwellers flock here for high tea on weekdays while others like the seafood buffets on Fridays and the reasonably-priced three-course lunches with a variety of Caribbean and Continental meat and fish concoctions. No lunch is served on Saturday.

Minnie's Ethiopian **$$** ★

176 Old Hope Road, ☎ (809) 927-9207.
Latin American cuisine. Specialties: Gungo-Pea Stew, Festival Bread, Juices.
Lunch: entrees $10–$20.
Dinner: entrees $10–$20.

After a pilgrimage to reggae icon Bob Marley's Museum and Tuff Gong Recording Studio nearby, fans can repair to his former chef's eating establishment for some Rasta Ital food (mostly vegetarian, utilizing local bounty) prepared by Chef Minnie. The full name of this round wooden restaurant is Minnie's Ethiopian Herbal Health Food, and after a few freshly-squeezed juices and her signature gungo (pigeon pea stew, you'll feel truly cleansed.

Norma's at the Wharfhouse **$$$** ★★★★

Reading Road, Reading, ☎ (809) 979-2745.
Latin American cuisine.
Lunch: Noon–2:30 p.m., entrees $26–$34.
Dinner: 7:30–10:30 p.m., entrees $26–$34.

The finest restaurant on the island may be this historical dockside beauty created by Norma Shirley, Jamaica's most famous chef. Dine with influential Jamaicans and visiting celebrities while watching the action at a table set on the wharf of this 300-year-old warehouse, or in an antique-filled salon. Shirley, who owned a restaurant in New York, utilizes the rich bounty of the region to spectacular effect; the menu, which changes daily, often includes succulent smoked marlin with papaya or grilled deviled crab backs. The elegantly-dressed plates are a treat.

Temple Hall **$$$** ★★★★★

Temple Hall Estate, ☎ (809) 942-2340.
Latin American cuisine. Specialties: Fettucine Boston Jerk.
Dinner: 6:30–11:30 p.m., entrees $25.

Of the handful of gracious plantation homes on the outskirts of Kingston, The Restaurant at Temple Hall Estate is probably on most gourmet lists of "don't miss" experiences. For the most part the vast property is self-sustaining, growing most of the herbs and vegetables and raising the livestock for the scrumptious meals. Guests are provided with complimentary transportation by the owners, who like to put on a light show at night by illuminating the long driveway with torches. Reservations required.

Montego Bay

Known to locals as Mo' Bay, Montego Bay is the primary port of entry by air for Jamaica. It's here, along the shoreline, where Jamaican tourism was born. Once a sleepy town, it's burgeoned into the apotheosis of what some tourists feel is the Caribbean nightmare, but for others it's a town that epitomizes the bustling, sweaty, crowded charm of a Third-World port. Downtown is a joggerhead of traffic, people, vendors and markets.

Beaches in Montego Bay

Cornwall Beach is a man-made phenomenon to provide tourists with an alternative to the postage-stamp patch called Doctor's Cave Beach—once the hub of Montego Bay's social scene during its heyday in the'60s. The scene is still happening at Cornwall, but with so many locals and tourists, that if you're the kind of person who needs to see the color of the sand beneath your feet, stay away. These days Doctor's Cave itself is just too reminiscent of Florida to get our vote for exotica, but the five-mile stretch of vanilla-colored sand still has its charm, though its overexposure in the press has brought every loud obnoxious tourist out of the woodwork. On the plus side, the changing facilities can be useful and there is a large variety of junk food to choose from. **Walter Fletch Beach**, on the bay near the center of town, is very good for swimming, since it is well protected from the strong winds.

What Else to See

Historical Sites

Greenwood Great House ★★★★

Highway A1, Montego Bay.
Hours open: 9 a.m.–6 p.m.
One of Jamaica's greatest great houses, this one belonged to the Barrett family, of which Elizabeth Barrett Browning is a descendant. The early 19th-century mansion is nice to tour, filled with antiques, unusual musical instruments, rare books, custom-made china and portraits of the family.

Rose Hall Great House ★★★★

Rose Hall Highway, Montego Bay, ☎ *(809) 953-2323.*
Hours open: 9 a.m.–6 p.m.
Not as architecturally impressive as Greenwood, but this great house from the 1700s is filled with tales of murder and intrigue. It seems that mistress Annie Palmer seduced slaves and then killed them, as well as murdering three husbands. Her story

has been fictionalized in several books, which you'll find in the gift shop. There's also a neat pub in the basement.

Parks and Gardens

Columbus Park Museum ★★★

Queens Highway, Discovery Bay, ☎ (809) 973-2135.
Hours open: 9 a.m.–5 p.m.
This outdoor park, studded with pimento trees, has some interesting and eclectic exhibits. There are 18th-century cannons, a stone cross, a large mural of Columbus' landing in 1494, and displays on the history of sugarcane. Stop by if you're in the area, but don't bother making a special trip.

Rocklands Wildlife Station ★★★

Anchovy, St. James, ☎ (809) 952-2009.
Hours open: 2 p.m.–5 p.m.
This privately owned reserve is a must for birders (the rest can probably live without it). Doves, finches and other feathered creatures eat right off your hands.

Tours

Appelton Estate Express ★★★★

Appelton Estate Station, Montego Bay, ☎ (809) 952-3692.
All aboard the Appelton Express, an air-conditioned diesel railcar that chugs some 40 miles into the mountains. Along the way you'll pass Jamaican villages, coffee and fruit plantations, and wonderful scenery. You'll also tour a rum factory and get to taste the goods. The fee includes transportation from your hotel, continental breakfast, buffet lunch, and an open bar. The train departs at 8:50 a.m. on Monday, Thursday and Friday, and returns about 5:00 p.m.

JUTA Tour Company ★★★★

Claude Clarke Avenue, Montego Bay, ☎ (809) 952-0813.
This well-established tour company has offices all over Jamaica. They'll take you river rafting, on sea cruises, through great houses, and into Kingston.

Where to Eat

Georgian House **$$$** ★

2 Orange Street, ☎ (809) 952-3353.
International cuisine. Specialties: Pan-Barbecued Shrimp, Coconut Pie.
Lunch: Noon–2:30 p.m., entrees $22–$32.
Dinner: 6–10:30 p.m., entrees $22–$32.
This restaurant's private van will pick you up from your hotel to dine in an 18th century townhouse and art gallery. Once there, you can eat outdoors on the patio if you prefer a more casual atmosphere—in any case feel free to dress resort-casual. Specialties are from the sea; usually shrimp or spiny lobster, barbecued, or sauteed with vegetables, or in a wine sauce. Steaks and filets are also marvelous, the coconut pie is deadly, and the wine list is well-chosen.

Julia's **$$$** ★

Bogue Hill, ☎ (809) 952-632.
International cuisine.
Dinner: 6–10:30 p.m., prix fixe $35.
It's highly advisable to take this mountaintop restaurant's offer of a private van to pick you up at your door. Negotiating the steep road that leads to this estate above MoBay (800 feet or thereabouts) can be hazardous. Once ensconced in your seat, relax and enjoy a four-course dinner served by an attentive staff, while the lights of the bay and the city glow below. The mostly-Italian entrees of veal (usually Parmesan), chicken, or fish will include a salad, pasta, dessert and choice of beverage.

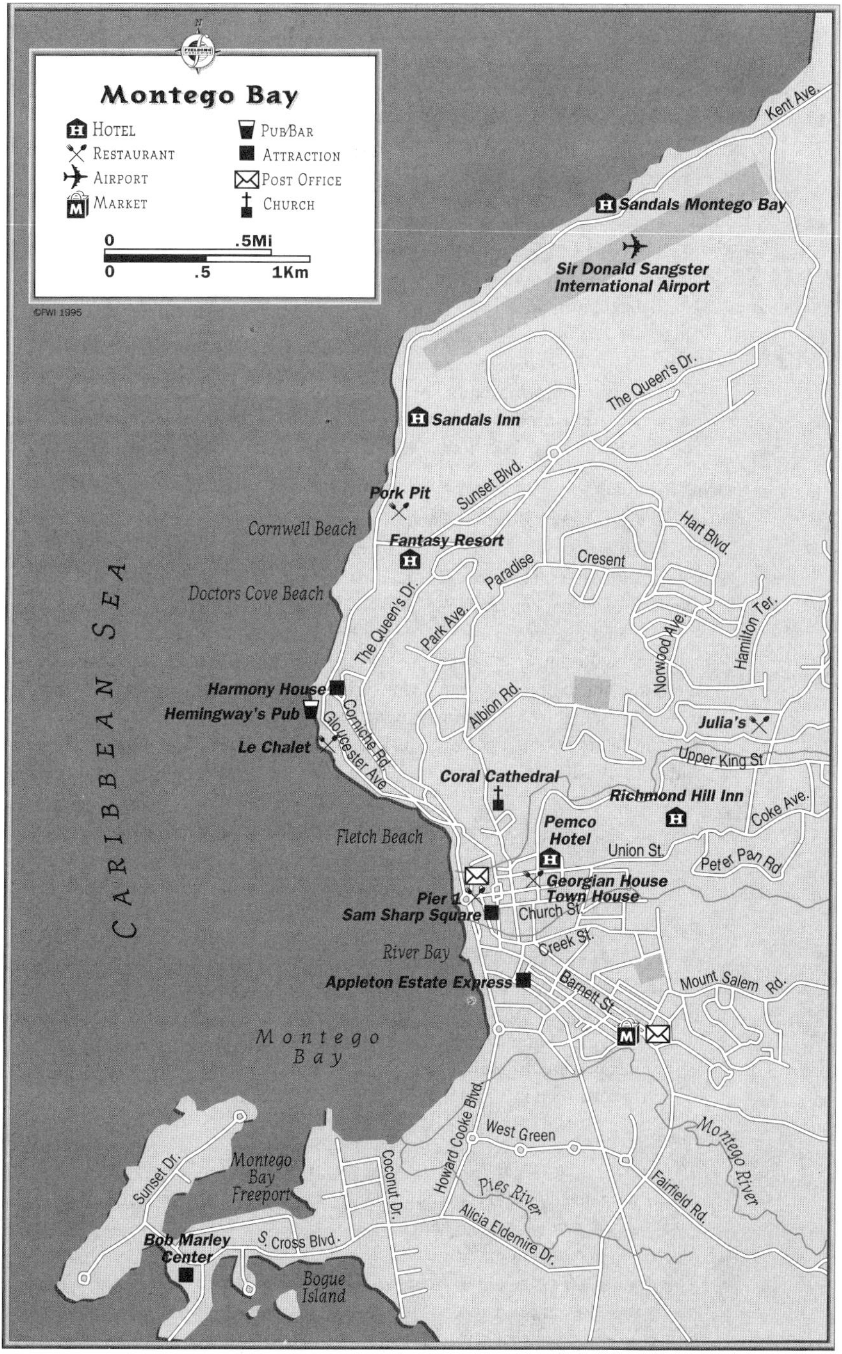
Montego Bay
Hotel
Restaurant
Airport
Market
Pub/Bar
Attraction
Post Office
Church
0 .5Mi
0 .5 1Km
©FWI 1995
Kent Ave.
Sandals Montego Bay
Sir Donald Sangster International Airport
The Queen's Dr.
Sandals Inn
Sunset Blvd.
Pork Pit
Cornwell Beach
Fantasy Resort
Hart Blvd.
Paradise
Cresent
Doctors Cove Beach
The Queen's Dr.
Park Ave.
Hamilton Ter.
Norwood Ave
CARIBBEAN SEA
Harmony House
Hemingway's Pub
Albion Rd.
Julia's
Corniche Rd.
Gloucester Ave
Le Chalet
Upper King St
Coral Cathedral
Richmond Hill Inn
Coke Ave.
Pemco Hotel
Fletch Beach
Union St.
Peter Pan Rd
Georgian House Town House
Pier 1
Sam Sharp Square
Church St.
Creek St.
River Bay
Appleton Estate Express
Barnett St
Mount Salem Rd.
Montego Bay
Howard Cooke Blvd.
West Green
Montego River
Sunset Dr.
Montego Bay Freeport
Coconut Dr.
Pies River
Fairfield Rd.
Alicia Eldemire Dr.
Bob Marley Center
S. Cross Blvd.
Bogue Island

Pier I **$$$** ★

Howard Cooke Boulevard, ☎ (809) 952-2452.
Seafood cuisine.
Lunch: 11 a.m.–4 p.m., entrees $16–$25.
Dinner: 4 p.m.–midnight, entrees $16–$25.

The cocktails and punches are fruity and potent, and the burgers are juicy; but even if kibble was served, the view from the waterfront bar would still be stellar. There's a tony dining room within where you can dine on well-prepared seafood and some hearty soups, chicken and steaks.

Pork Pit **$** ★★★

Gloucester Avenue, corner, ☎ (809) 952-1046.
Latin American cuisine.
Lunch: 11 a.m.–4:30 p.m., entrees $2–$9.
Dinner: 4:30–11:30 p.m., entrees $2–$9.

Eat fiery jerk pork, chicken or spare ribs picnic-style on benches or tables open to the sea breeze. Common accompaniments include local cornbread (called festival) and Red Stripe beer. Location is close to Cornwall Beach and the airport.

Reading Reef Club **$$$** ★★★★★

Bogue Lagoon, ☎ (809) 952-5909.
Italian cuisine.
Lunch: Noon–3 p.m., entrees $10–$24.
Dinner: 7–10 p.m., entrees $10–$24.

Located in a discreet, small (21-room) hotel situated halfway between Montego Bay and the Round Hill Resort, this Caribbean-influenced Italian restaurant reflects the tastes of the hotel's owner, JoAnne Rowe, a New York-born expatriate. These include a strange combination of pasta served with ginger that works quite well, judging by its popularity. Crayfish, seafood and steaks are other standards paired with local produce.

Sugar Mill **$$$** ★★★★

Rose Hall, ☎ (809) 953-2228.
International cuisine. Specialties: Bouillabaise, Smoked Marlin.
Lunch: Noon–2:30 p.m., entrees $14–$31.
Dinner: 7–10 p.m., entrees $14–$31.

Swiss chef Hans Schenck creates Jamaican-Continental specialties at this restaurant in a historical house with a terrace that overlooks the ocean and the golf course of the Half Moon Club. Marlin, a specialty catch of the area, is often smoked and served with pasta; bouillabaisse is spiced with local pepper and citrus sauces. Even if you're just passing through, come for a look at the remains of the old sugar plantation that have been incorporated into the grounds of this sleek resort.

Town House **$$$** ★★

16 Church Street, ☎ (809) 952-2660.
Latin American cuisine. Specialties: Red Snapper Baked in Parchment.
Lunch: 11:30 a.m.–2:30 p.m., entrees $13–$30.
Dinner: 6–10 p.m., entrees $13–$30.

This grand, 300-year-old Georgian building is a fun place to eat, especially in an art-filled, brick-walled cellar room, which is a novel change from the favored practice of dining alfresco. But that can also be achieved here on an outdoor terrace. Specialties include a signature fresh red snapper baked in parchment with a cheese and seafood sauce.

Negril

Negril became known to the world at large in the early'70s when it was a mecca for hippies, escapists, artists and visionaries who spent most of the day bonged out on the local weed. Located on the extreme northwestern point of the island, it has grown from a sleepy bohemian town to one of Jamaica's finest resort areas. The seven-mile stretch of pure-white, powder-fine beach dotted with sea grape and coconut palms has inspired many a fantasy, and numerous fashion shoots have been conducted here. For some unexplained reason, the sunsets here are extraordinarily spectacular, bursts of neon color across the horizon. Although there's little sight-seeing available, most visitors are just happy to relax and soak in the atmosphere. For the active, there are numerous watersports, superb scuba diving (see below), and fine snorkeling.

If you get to Negril, you must make an extra excursion to **Booby Cay**, a small island across from Rutland Point that attracts an inordinate number of nude bathers. Also spectacular is the sunset cruise on the *Sunsplash*, a 155-foot catamaran that can be booked through Sandals Negril. After you pass through town and head west to Negril Point, the resorts tend to get smaller and more quaint. Here the beach gives way to high limestone cliffs. At **Xtabi**, the sea caves cut into the cliffs to create a romantic setting that is ideal for sunset viewing. Everyone heads for **Rick's Cafe** —a terrific place to watch divers jump off from the cliff below and a perfect place to celebrate the glorious sunset, but if you don't like crowds, you won't love Rick's. If you're a night prowler, you'll find some of the biggest reggae stars in Jamaica performing throughout Negril until the wee hours. Recently, Negril, through the efforts of the Coral Reef Preservation Society, has instituted a very active mooring and education program. At present, 35 separate moorings virtually eliminate the need for anchoring.

Beaches in Negril

Negril Beach is seven long miles of heaven—everyone's idea of Eden. Unfortunately, much of it is fenced off today, especially the nude area. Fortunately, some resorts have had the foresight to build their properties overlooking the nude areas. The famous (infamous) singles-only club **Hedonism II** is located on this beach.

Divers enjoy the beautiful cliffs and caves at the west end of Negril.

Where to Eat

Cafe au Lait **$$$** ★★

Lighthouse Road, ☎ (809) 957-4471.
French cuisine.
Lunch: Noon–3 p.m., entrees $9–$29.
Dinner: 5–10 p.m., entrees $9–$29.
Located in a cottage resort on the West End, this authentic bistro (for Jamaica) features island-influenced, light French meals, including pizza and crepes (some made with callaloo), French bread, local seafood and French wines.

Chicken Lavish **$** ★★

West End Road, ☎ (809) 957-4410.
Latin American cuisine.
Lunch: 9 a.m.–4 p.m., entrees $3–$5.
Dinner: 4–10 p.m., entrees $3–$5.
Super informal, super cheap, and super delicious—with a juicy name like that what else can you expect? Once a local hangout jealously guarded by those in the know, the word is out about this unpretentious little spot on the beach renowned for toothsome fried chicken and curried goat.

Cosmo's **$** ★★

Norman Manley Boulevard, ☎ (809) 957-4330.
Seafood cuisine. Specialties: Curried Conch.
Lunch: 11 a.m.–4 p.m., entrees $5–$12.
Dinner: 4–10 p.m., entrees $5–$12.
Seafood is pretty much IT here, but what seafood! Owner-character Cosmo Brown specializes in conch, either stewed, curried or in a generous vat of soup. Since this chewy gastropod appears more often in other Caribbean islands, this is a good spot to try it. Otherwise, a grilled or baked escovitch (well-marinated in spices) whole fish is a popular choice. Cosmo's is situated in an informal, thatched-roof hut on a sparsely-populated East End beach.

Hungry Lion **$$$** ★★

West End Road.
Latin American cuisine.
Lunch: entrees $18–$30.
Dinner: entrees $18–$30.
The setting at this small and popular restaurant is as verdant and colorful as the Rastafarian Ital cuisine served here. Ital, which is based on local vegetarian ingredients, often features foods that display the Rasta colors of green, red and gold. At the Hungry Lion, if you dine outside by a fountain, you'll be surrounded by a greenhouse of flowering plants. Inside, the dining room is a living canvas of sophisticated tie-dye hues. A plate consisting of a marinated whole fish will be dressed with a hibiscus flower. It's that kind of place.

Paradise Yard **$$** ★★

Gas Station Road, ☎ (809) 957-4006.
Latin American cuisine. Specialties: Rasta Pasta.
Lunch: 8 a.m.–4 p.m., entrees $6–$15.
Dinner: 4–10 p.m., entrees $6–$15.
Life is fine at this relaxing open-air restaurant with a tin roof situated on the road to the port city of Savannah-del-Mar. You can get here early for a full-on Jamaican breakfast of saltfish and ackee, juicy local fruits and bammies (cassava bread). At lunch and dinner, ackee appears again in the Rasta Pasta—the golden vegetable (which tastes like scrambled eggs) is teamed with a thick tomato sauce and green peppers over fettuccine. There's also curried goat, pumpkin soup and enchiladas. This is a very authentic experience.

Rick's Cafe **$$$** ★

West End Road, ☎ (809) 957-4335.
Seafood cuisine. Specialties: Grilled Lobster, Fresh-Fruit Daiquiris.
Lunch: Noon–4 p.m., entrees $11–$28.
Dinner: 4–10 p.m., entrees $11–$28.
This famous (circa 1974) bar-restaurant-hangout is a scene and a place to be seen. One of the many draws here is a concept imitated from the La Quebrada divers in Acapulco—locals and visitors plunge some 25 feet into the sea from the cliffs at Rick's before emerging (it's hoped) for a papaya daiquiri. A tamer ritual takes place just before sunset when crowds of tanned and buffed young people pack the rock-

encrusted, palm-fronded terrace for fun and frolic and a last glimpse of old sol. You can also come here for lunch or brunch, but for that you can go anywhere.

Tan-ya's **$$$** ★

Norman Manley Boulevard, ☎ (809) 957-4041.
Latin American cuisine.
Lunch: 11 a.m.–3 p.m., entrees $5–$8.
Dinner: 6:30–10 p.m., entrees $8–$25.
This restaurant at the quietly elegant Seasplash Resort is where guests and others go to dress up (just a little) for French-inspired seafood and a creative way with lobster.

North Coast

About 30 miles east from Montego Bay, **Falmouth** gives you the feeling of being in a fairly quiet area while still maintaining proximity to the cities of Mo' Bay or Ocho Rios. This small 18th-century port town takes about a half-hour to explore on foot. There are a number of historical buildings that are interesting to see, such as the courthouse, a reconstruction of the 19th-century building, the customs office, the William Knubb Memorial Church, at George and King Street, and the 1796 parish church. Nearby is the **Good Hope** great house (leaving town, turn south), the 18th-century estate of John Thorpe, one of the richest Jamaican planters. The restoration of the main house and several outbuildings is exquisite, and it now stands as a fine hotel. Save time for a magnificent horseback ride through the countryside, over the estate's 6000 acres. Two miles east of Falmouth is the **Caribatik factory**, which is the artwork of a fine Jamaican artist, Muriel Chandler. At **Glistening Waters Marina**, east of Caribatik, you'll discover Oyster Bay, which glows with bioluminescence caused by microorganisms in the water.

Ocho Rios

Over the past 15 years, Ocho Rios has become one of the busiest, if most elite, tourism sites in Jamaica. Cruise ships dock nearly daily and a number of fine resorts are located here. Five outstanding beaches, excellent restaurants, abundant nightlife and lots of sports make the area ideal for those who want to escape the Third-World chaos of Kingston and Montego Bay. The town has fiercely hung onto its charm despite the massive development. The most exciting natural phenomenon near here is **Dunn's River Falls**, the internationally renowned stair-stepped falls that rush under the road and reappear to join the sea on the white beach to the left. Even if you don't throw yourself to the wetness in a fun tour of the falls, you must come to see its dramatic descent over the mountainside. Other natural attractions are plenty, from the Shaw Park Botanical Garden, where you can wile away a few hours studying the exotic tropical plants of the island.

If you're still feeling athletic, a terrific horseback riding jaunt can be arranged at the **Prospect Plantation**, which will take you through trails of citrus groves and coffee trees, and down by the banks of the White River. Jitney tours of the estate are free of charge. Rafting tours on the nearby White River are also available (see the section under "Treks.") Out on Annotto Bay, you'll find the 250-acre **Crystal Springs**, a natural garden replete with hundreds of birds, a myriad of tropical orchids, fierce waterfalls, rivers and a restaurant.

Beaches in Ocho Rios

Ocho Rios beach is giving Mo Bay a run for its money these days in terms of traffic. Mallard's attracts the most crowds, somewhat due to the presence of the Jamaica Grande hotel, which caters to the convention crowd. (Don't write us if you find yourself on the beach sitting next to someone with elks ears.) Turtle Beach is the adjacent strand, which has a very good reputation for swimming.

What Else to See

Historical Sites

Firefly ★★★

Grants Pen, St. Mary.
Hours open: 9 a.m.–5 p.m.

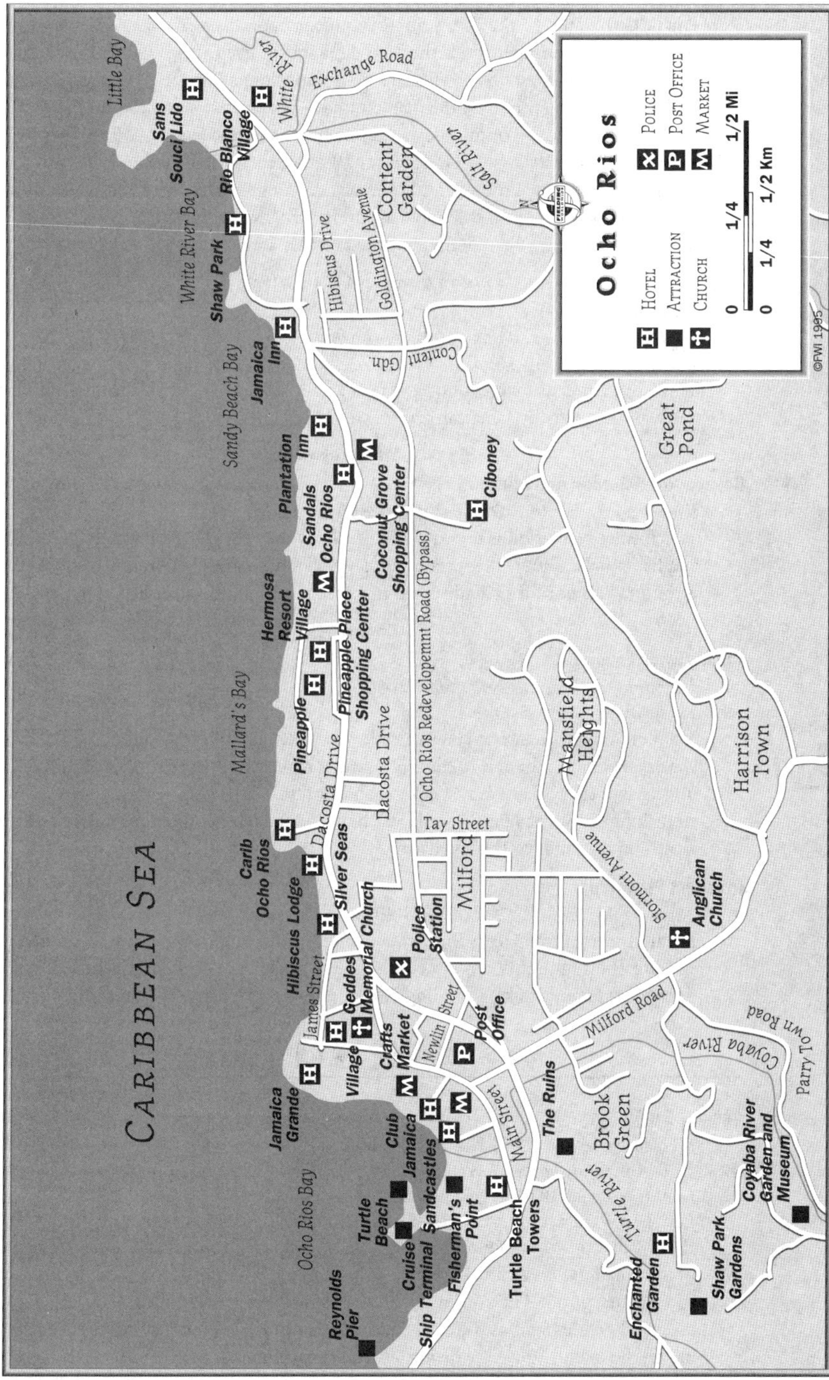
Ocho Rios
Hotel
Attraction
Church
Police
Post Office
Market
0 1/4 1/2 Mi
0 1/4 1/2 Km
©FWI 1995
Caribbean Sea
Little Bay
White River Bay
Sandy Beach Bay
Mallard's Bay
Ocho Rios Bay
Sans Souci Lido
Rio Blanco Village
Shaw Park
Jamaica Inn
Plantation Inn
Sandals Ocho Rios
Coconut Grove Shopping Center
Hermosa Resort Village
Pineapple
Pineapple Place Shopping Center
Carib Ocho Rios
Silver Seas
Hibiscus Lodge
Geddes Memorial Church
Police Station
Post Office
Crafts Market
Village
Jamaica Grande
Club Jamaica
Turtle Beach
Cruise Ship Terminal
Sandcastles
Fisherman's Point
Turtle Beach Towers
Reynolds Pier
The Ruins
Brook Green
Enchanted Garden
Shaw Park Gardens
Coyaba River Garden and Museum
Anglican Church
Ciboney
Harrison Town
Mansfield Heights
Great Pond
Milford
Content Garden
Exchange Road
White River
Salt River
Hibiscus Drive
Goldington Avenue
Content Gdn.
Ocho Rios Redevelopemnt Road (Bypass)
Dacosta Drive
Tay Street
Stormont Avenue
Milford Road
James Street
Newlin Street
Main Street
Turtle River
Coyaba River
Parry Town Road

This is the home of Sir Noel Coward, who spent the last 25 years of his life in Jamaica. Donated to the Jamaican government upon his death in 1973, the mansion remains unchanged since the actor and author lived there. Guided tours take you through the house to gawk at his bedroom, closets filled with clothes, antique furnishings and paintings by the man himself. His grave is also on the site, as well as a cafe and gift shop. Continue your literary tour at **Goldeneye** ☎ *(809-974-5833)*, located on the outskirts of Oracabessa, 20 miles east of Ocho Rios. This 15-acre beachfront estate was the winter home of Ian Fleming, creator of the James Bond books. He penned 14 of the popular novels here, five set in Jamaica. The house is much more modest than Firefly, but the grounds are gorgeous.

Museums and Exhibits

Harmony Hall ★★★

Highway A3, Tower Isle, ☎ *(809) 460-4120.*
Hours open: 10 a.m.–6 p.m.
This late 19th-century great house is now a gallery displaying high-quality paintings and arts and crafts by Jamaican artists.

Parks and Gardens

Coyaba River Garden and Museum ★★★

Shaw Park, Ocho Rios, ☎ *(809) 974-6235.*
This former plantation is now a private estate with lovely gardens, waterfalls, a river and fish ponds. The small museum displays relics from pre-Columbian days. *Coyaba* is the Arawak word for paradise and this spot is certainly a small slice of it.

Tours

Dunn's River Falls ★★★★

Highway A3, Ocho Rios, ☎ *(809) 974-2857.*
Hours open: 9 a.m.–5 p.m.
These much-photographed falls cascade down some 600 feet into the sea. The best way to experience them is to hire a guide and make a human chain that climbs right up the slippery rocks. Wear sneakers, and don't forget to tip your guide. You can stop along the way to dip in pools and be massaged by the tumbling water. There's a path on dry land for the less daring.

Prospect Plantation ★★★

Highway A3, St. Ann, ☎ *(809) 974-2058.*
Located just east of Ocho Rios, this working plantation can be toured via jitney. Among the highlights are sweeping views, gorgeous scenery, and lots of trees planted by famous folks, including Noel Coward and Charlie Chaplin.

Where to Eat

Almond Tree $$$ ★★★★

87 Main Street, ☎ *(809) 974-2813.*
Latin American cuisine. Specialties: Roast Suckling Pig, Pumpkin Soup.
Lunch: Noon–2:30 p.m., entrees $12–$26.
Dinner: 6-9:30 p.m., entrees $12–$26.
If you can stop swinging in the unique chairs suspended from the ceiling in the bar of this small inn on a cliff overlooking the sea, you'll find the food in the restaurant to be quite good. The Almond Tree has a real tree growing through its roof, a diverse clientele (famous rock stars have been known to swing in) and roast suckling pig on the menu. Soups are divine, especially the pumpkin. Drop in at the piano bar on the hotel grounds for some good tunes to accompany after-dinner drinks in a more subdued atmosphere.

Evita's **$$** ★★★★★

Eden Bower Road, ☎ (809) 974-2333.
Italian cuisine. Specialties: Homemade Pasta.
Lunch: 11 a.m.–4 p.m., entrees $7–$19.
Dinner: 4-11 p.m., entrees $7–$19.

Don't cry for Evita—in this instance, restaurateur Eva Myers - who has no trouble drawing in pasta lovers and others to this 1860s-era gingerbread house perched over Ocho Rios Bay. Many guests prefer eating on the terrace as the sun sets over the deep blue Caribbean waters. Some of the seemingly endless parade of pastas include a lasagne rastafari with bell peppers, tomatoes and ackee - the Rastafarian (and Italian) colors. Fresh and delicious fish, especially red snapper, steaks and ribs are also available.

Parkway Restaurant **$$$** ★★

60 Da Costa Drive, ☎ (809) 974-2667.
Latin American cuisine.
Lunch: 7:30 a.m.–4 p.m., entrees $6–$25.
Dinner: 4-11 p.m., entrees $6–$25.

This tropical diner-roadhouse in downtown Ocho Rios serves up some very reasonably priced and tasty Jamaican specialties to simple folk as well as prime movers and shakers. You can join them too, while watching local programming from the ever-present TV. Spicy Jamaican chicken or curries and banana cake or pie are popular choices.

Ruins Restaurant **$$$** ★

Da Costa Drive, ☎ (809) 974-2442.
Chinese cuisine.
Lunch: Noon–2:30 p.m., entrees $12–$33.
Dinner: 6-9:30 p.m., entrees $12–$33.

The cuisine is mostly American-Chinese (chop suey, chow mein, etc.), but the scene is the thing at this refreshing alfresco restaurant named after the ruins of an old sugar mill that once occupied the site. Expect a lot of fellow revelers marveling at the surrounding waterfalls and pools that are softly lit at night. Dress is casual, and there is a cocktail lounge in an adjoining building. Specialties include shellfish and lobster; but you can also order a steak. No lunch is served on Sunday.

Port Antonio

Port Antonio is a miniature island port built around two **picturesque harbors** that could have served well as a Hollywood set. Indeed, Port Antonio *was* nearly a Hollywood set, at least the winter stomping ground, for such luminaries as Ginger Rogers, Bette Davis, Clara Bow and such financial magnates as J.P. Morgan and William Randolph Hearst, who in the'20s,'30s, and'40s were drawn to the tropical exoticism and serene beauty of the bay. Port Antonio's biggest fan was actor Errol Flynn, who often could be seen prowling the bars at night. Strange architectural fantasies took shape in this town: the dream castle of architect Earl Levy, complete with turrets, over the shoreline east of the Trident Hotel, and the sprawling concrete mansion built by a Connecticut tycoon, now in crumbling remains. Ecologists won't want to miss the 282-foot deep lagoon called **Blue Hole** off Route 44, or **Somerset Falls**, in the gorge of the Daniel River, above Hope Bay (you can't find a more romantic trip than the gondola ride under the falls). Hiking up to the **Blue Mountains** is spectacular and offers a terrific vista (for more information, see under "Treks"). Only the hardiest climbers will make it to the top of **Reach Falls** at Machioneal (no wonder the name!), but the effort will be worth it since the falls are considered to be the most beautiful in Jamaica. Nonsuch Cave is a few miles to the southeast where there are fossils and other hieroglypic signs of the Arawak tribes. There is no public transportation available so you will have to take a taxi and ask the driver to wait (about $10 round trip). The entrance fee is $5.

Beaches in Port Antonio

The best beaches in Port Antonio are **Boston Bay** and **San San Beach**. A delicacy of the area is the eye-watering peppery jerk pork, which will drive you to down a beer as quickly as possible. Just follow your nose and eyes to the smoke-spewing shacks, where local chefs cook them right on the beach. Cave Beach is a notable place to plop east of the town. **Navy Island** is located in the harbor and boasts two nude beaches—take the jetty on West Street near Musgrave Market. The island, once owned by Errol Flynn, has a memorial gallery to his life and career, where you can view movie stills and screenings of his old films. Snorkeling is available for a small fee, but the currents are strong and the fish are few. A complete wedding ceremony can be conducted in the chapel (for more information contact ☎ *(809) 993-2667*).

What Else to See

Parks and Gardens

Athenry Gardens and Cave of Nu ★★★

Portland, Port Antonio, ☎ (809) 993-3740.
Hours open: 9 a.m.–5:30 p.m.
The Nonsuch Cave dates back some 1.5 million years give or take a century or two, and can be toured to see its stalagmites and stalactites. On ground level there are great views at the pretty flowering gardens. About 20 minutes from Port Antonio.

Crystal Springs ★★★

Highway A2, Port Antonio, ☎ (809) 993-2609.
This former sugar plantation is a privately owned estate that covers 158 acres. A peaceful spot to while away the hours, it has more than 15,000 orchids and lots of hummingbirds and other feathered friends. Bring binoculars.

Where to Eat

De Montevin Lodge **$$** ★★★

21 Fort George Street, ☎ (809) 993-2604.
Latin American cuisine.
Lunch: 12:30–2 p.m., prix fixe $11–$18.
Dinner: 7–9 p.m., prix fixe $11–$18.
Errol Flynn's chef used to rule the kitchen at this veddy British Victorian-style inn on Titchfield Hill (I don't think he paid much attention to what he was eating) but the food served here now is unadulterated Jamaican, prepared home-style; the number of courses that arrive depends on what you paid—the cheaper menus are just a tad over $10. Dishes include pumpkin soup, fricassee chicken, dessert and coffee.

Front Line, The **$** ★★

Boston Bay.
Latin American cuisine.
Lunch: entrees $5–$8.
Dinner: entrees $5–$8.
After leaving the chic resorts of Port Antonio (a town bereft of inexpensive eateries) travelers eagerly stop at Boston Bay beach for a soak and the best jerk barbecue on the islands. Of course, nothing is fancy, just a series of roadside stands vying for your attention—but the best one may be The Front Line, with the grills presided over by colorful pit men. Marinated chicken, pork or sausage swathed with a top secret sauce (lots of hot pepper and cayenne) is perfect with Red Stripe beer or rum.

Trident Hotel Restaurant **$$$** ★★★★★

Route A4, ☎ (809) 993-2602.
International cuisine.
Lunch: Noon–2:30 p.m., entrees $25–$35.
Dinner: 8–10 p.m., prix fixe $50.
It's a memorable experience to dine in the high-ceilinged restaurant of this 14-acre hotel. Here five course dinners are served on the terrace or in the main dining room by white-gloved waiters; the only sounds you hear are gentle murmurings from fellow guests and the softly-whirring ceiling fans above.

South Coast

The south coast is Jamaica's ecological haven—the place where Jamaicans long to visit when they go on holiday. Here you'll find some truly "undiscovered" beaches, though you'll have to do a bit of driving to get there. The South Coast is also known as the best place for **deep-sea fishing**, and boat trips sail out from Belmont to the offshore banks and reefs. The bay is so calm here that **snorkeling** is often an exciting experience. Southeast of Bluefield are simply some of the most pristine, unspoiled strands in all Jamaica, but unfortunately, a new Sandals resort is moving in soon. Transport from Montego Bay is easily arranged. If you take the A2 road past Scotts Cove, proceed to the town of **Black River**, one of the oldest on the island, once a thriving port during the 18th century for logwood dyes. Along the coast are some handsome colonial mansions presently being restored. The longest river in Jamaica, the Black River is perfect for canoe and **rafting** trips. If you stay on A2 instead of turning off at Black River, proceed past Middle Quarters to the left turn that takes you to the **Y.S. Falls**, a glorious unspoiled area in the middle of a plantation—be prepared for a 15-minute hike from where you park your car. (For more information on Black River and Y.S. Falls excursions, see above under "Treks").

Mandeville is a lovely, peaceful upland town with what locals feel is the best climate on the island. For some reason, there are no slums among the population of 50,000—its present prosperity is due to the production of bauxite/alumina. The village green is reminiscent of New England, with its Georgian courthouse and parish church; visit on Mondays, Wednesdays and Friday, if you want to see the market in full swing. Horseback riding, tennis, and golf on an 18-hole course are available.The Seventh Day Adventists run the Westici Health Foods store and also a vegetarian restaurant behind the church in the center of town. A craft center is located on Manchester Road.

Beaches

Bluefield Beach, near Savanna-la-Mer south of Negril, is the easiest to get to. Farther out, another gem is Crane Beach at Black River. Most secluded is **Treasure Beach** (a strand that truly lives up to its name), 20 miles along the coast beyond Crane. To the east of Treasure Beach is **Lovers Leap**, a gorgeous view, where legend has it that a plantation owner's daughter and her love, a slave, leaped to their death.

What Else to See

Museums and Exhibits

Arawak Museum ★★★

White Marl, Spanish Town, ☎ *(809) 922-0620.*
Hours open: 10 a.m.–5 p.m.
Located on the site of a large Arawak settlement, this small museum houses relics and artifacts from that era.

Jamaica People's Museum ★★★

Constitution Square, Spanish Town, ☎ *(809) 922- 620.*
Hours open: 9 a.m.–5 p.m.
This museum of native craft and technology houses farm implements, a sugar mill, an old fire engine and a hearse, as well as vintage prints, models and maps.

Tours

Milk River Mineral Baths ★★★

Milk River, Clarendon, ☎ *(809) 924-9544.*
Arthritis acting up? Rheumatism got you down? Liver ailing? Come for a half-hour soak in what is reportedly the world's most radioactive mineral waters, said to help all those conditions—and more. The baths are private and tepid at 90 degrees.

Somerset Falls ★★★

Highway A4, Hope Bay, ☎ *(809) 926-2950.*
Hours open: 9 a.m.–5 p.m.
Ride in a gondola to these scenic falls, located in a deep grove and surrounded by tropical rainforest. Wear your swimsuit so you can take a dip in the refreshing pools.

Where to Eat

The motto "Out of many, one people" goes as much for politics as it does for cuisine in Jamaica—for the influences that have gone into the dutchie, or cast-iron cooking pot, to create Jamaican menus, are many—the barbecuing techniques of the Arawaks, the African meat-preserving techniques in the country's best known dish, jerk pork; Spanish marinades meet New World vegetables in twice-cooked escovitched fish. British **cornish pastries**, which are meat-and-potato-filled pastries, have become Jamaican spicy beef patties. And the spices of Asia and the Levant come together in dishes such as curried goat. Today nouvelle cuisine is also dressing up traditional ingredients in trendy resort restaurants along the North Coast. Rastafarianism—Jamaica's contribution to 20th-century religion—has created a cuisine all its own, one that places the accent on nature's bounty. Rastas don't drink alcohol or eat meat, but their vegetarian cooking is delicious, including hearty vegetable stews with ingredients such as *calllallo* (a spinach-like vegetable), *chocho* (a pear-shaped squash), pumpkin and yams. Johnnycakes—flat, dense, unleavened breads—were a slave adaptation of British breads, while *bammie* was the Amerindian cassava bread that Columbus wrote about in his journals. Another newer addition is the popular Rasta Pasta, which features the

Rastafarian colors in the red of tomatoes, the green of bell peppers, and the gold of ackee, all served over pasta. One of the bases of Jamaican cooking is "poor folk's food," like codfish, stew peas and roast breadfruit. It takes some experience to learn to like boiled green bananas as a breakfast dish.

Other Jamaican delicacies include: *bun* (a dark fruitcake served with cheese usually at Easter time); *cowfoot soup* (spicy soup of cow trotters and vegetables, claimed by Jamaican men to be an aphrodisiac); *dunkanoo* (a dessert of grated corn, flavored with sugar, cinnamon, ginger, and coconut milk, and steamed in a banana leaf); *pepper rum* (a mixture of fiery Scotch bonnet chiles and dark rum, used as a seasoning); *matrimony* (a dessert that blends orange segments with star apple pulp in cream); *mannish water* (a heavy goatmeat and vegetable soup, flavored with white rum and hot peppers, and reputed to be an aphrodisiac); *rundown* (mackerel or codfish boiled in coconut milk and eaten with ashed onions and peppers); *Solomon gundy* (pungent spiced pickled herring); and *stamp-and-go* (batter-fried saltfish fritters, usually eaten as a finger snack).

In Kingston, Sunday brunch is special at Devon House, a restored historic home dear to many Jamaicans for its food and ice cream. Seated on the wide veranda of mansions such as The Coffee Terrace, with whirling fans overhead, you can indulge in fluffy yellow ackee, a Jamaican-grown tree vegetable, whose custardy flesh tastes and looks somewhat like scrambled eggs. This mixture of the savory ackee and salt fish harks back to the days of slavery when feeding the slaves was a major concern for plantation owners. **Jerked cooking** is a method of barbecue using well-seasoned meat, said to have originated with the Maroons, the fierce escaped slaves who retreated to the mountains of Cockpit Country and kept the British at bay for more than a century. They would roast pork over hot coals in earthen pits that were covered with branches of green pimento, or allspice, wood. The smoking wood is what provides the unique seasoning. At Boston Beach today, pit men such as Vasco "Kojak" Allen at Front Line #1, are famous for their grillwork, which includes jerked chicken, (pork, the classic dish), jerked sausage, and jerked fish.

In Ocho Rios, the **Ciboney Beach Resort** has some of the best options for dining: head for Orchid's, for pork chops filled with bread and chutney, or the alfresco **Casa Nina**, for ackee and callalloo. The **Ciboney Grill and Market Place** is designed like a Jamaican outdoor market with colorful food stalls.

In Montego Bay, the restaurant at the four-bedroom hostelry called **Norma's** at the Warehouse is a treasurehouse of delicacies, from smoked marlin with papaya salsa to roast loin pork with prunes. Desserts run the course between plantain turnover with brandied whipped cream or a vine-ripened papaya, with a drizzle of island grown ortanique (cross between an orange and a tangerine). Less fancy digs on the North Coast include the **Rite Stuff Café** and Caterers in Montego Bay's Westgate Plaza, where you can dig into curried goat, stew bee, or a steaming bowl of pumpkin soup. Meat patties, flaky turnovers stuffed with a savory chopped meat and herb mixture, are a favorite snack on this island of nibblers.

You won't know the cuisine of Jamaica until you make a stop at the island's hub of hedonism, Negril. Head for the **Hungry Lion**, one of the best spots on the North Coast to try Italian food, and at **Paradise Yard**, where you can indulge in a special Jamaican breakfast feast.

Where to Shop

Jamaica has some wonderful opportunities for committed shoppers; you may find yourself wishing you had brought an extra piece of luggage to handle the overflow. Duty-free shopping is available in the cosmopolitan areas, with good buys on perfumes, crystals and china. Stop at the crafts markets or roadside stands for more authentic goods. Excellent wood carvings sell generally for a modest sum.

Kingston is the New York City of Jamaica—nearly anything you can buy in Jamaica can be found here. You can choose from a luxury list of duty-free items or concentrate on local crafts made by well-skilled artisans. Despite a 10 percent General Consumption tax that has been added to all goods and services, **duty-free bargains** will generally reap you significant savings from back home in the States. (Of course, if you are vulnerable to such bargains, you should figure in the cost of buying things you probably wouldn't buy at home.) This duty-free wish-list in Kingston includes: Swiss watches, gold jewelry, camera, electronic equipment, liquor, cigarettes, fine European crystal, china, French perfume and British woolens. You must carry proof of identity with you to receive the duty-free discount. Best liquors to pick up include the Jamaican rums, Rumona (a rum liqueur), and the coffee-flavored Tia Maria. Royal Jamaican **cigars** are a connoisseur's delight, available at the airport as well as the pier. **Blue Mountain coffee** is the native brew, and will make one of the finest cups you have ever drunk. If you plan to do serious duty-free shopping, bring a list of comparative prices in the States, so that you don't go home and want to shoot yourself.

Local artists do excellent work in various media, but especially wood carvings, usually using *lignum vitae*, a rosy native hardwood. All kinds of objects are carved—from bookends to statues of saints (and Bob Marley) to furniture. You can pick up the best pieces in the crafts markets as well as at roadside stands on the north shore between Montego Bay and Falmouth. Straw work is also native to Jamaica, and good finds can also be found in basketry and batiks. Some of the best crafts at the best prices can be found at **Things Jamaica** at the Devon House (as well as at the airport); special buys are carved wood bowls and trays to reproduction of silver and brass historical pieces. Jamaican designers have quite a flair with resort wear, particularly using colorful fabrics silk-screened on the island. Silk batiks, sold by the yard, and so beautiful they can be used as wall art, can be found at **Caribatik**, the studio of the late Muriel Chandler, two miles east of Falmouth. Search through the shopping malls for fashionable clothes, such as at the New Kingston Shopping Mall, not far from the Pegasus hotel. If you need a new pair of sandals, try Lee's New Kingston in this mall.

You can't—don't even think about—leave Jamaica without buying a few reggae tapes. Records by some of reggae's greats including Bob Marley, his son Ziggy Marley, Peter Tosh and Burning Spear can be found at **Randy's Record Mart** at *17 N. Parade*—a legendary store where you can be directed to records by some of the new crop of up-and-coming stars.

Another shopping center for more mundane necessities is Lane's Shopping Mall (just one of half a dozen along Constant Spring Road). Hotel boutiques may have some cosmetics and toiletries, but they will be highly overpriced. Discover the pleasure of aloe-based Jamaican skin creams. They also make excellent gifts.

Jamaica Directory

BUSINESS HOURS

Stores open weekdays 9 a.m.–5 p.m. and Saturday 9 a.m.–6 p.m. Banks open weekdays 9 a.m.–5 p.m.

CLIMATE

Jamaica has a tropical climate with considerable variation. High temperatures on the coast are usually mitigated by sea breezes, while upland areas enjoy cooler and less-humid conditions. Jamaica lies in the hurricane zone, so always check weather reports before you come (even before you book). Rainfall falls plentifully throughout Jamaica; the heaviest season is in May and from August-November. In Kingston temperatures range from 6 degrees F in January to 81 degrees F in July.

DOCUMENTS

U.S. citizens need either a passport or other proof of citizenship (birth certificate, voter's registration) and a photo ID. All others need a passport. Departure tax is U.S.$5.

ELECTRICITY

Current is not consistent throughout the island. Some hotels feature 110, some 220. Adapters and converters are supplied by hotels who need them for foreign visitors.

GETTING AROUND

Taxis are best taken for short trips in Jamaica. You can always find a JUTA taxi and coach at most resorts. If you are planning an out-of-the-way excursion, arrange for the driver to pick you up afterwards and negotiate a good round-trip fare. Most taxis are unmetered. When in doubt, ask to see the rate sheet, which all cabs are supposed to carry.

Buses prove to be a cheap way to toot around the Kingston and Montego Bay areas; they run often but they are often unbearably overcrowded, hot and dirty. (Moreover, a tourist on a crowded local bus is often a sitting duck for crime; if you are wearing your camera and an "I Love Jamaica" T-shirt, you might as well just hand over your valuables before being asked for them.) Kingston bus fares range from $3 JDS to $7.50 JDS (about 15 cents to 35 cents in American currency) at press time. The fee depends on the distance traveled. You can tour the island on a bus, but here you will have to share aisle space with the local riffraff—meaning chickens on their way to getting their heads chopped off at market. Minibus jitneys also travel around the island, but they are unscheduled and you may have to flag them down in the street—not a reliable way to get somewhere on time. As a result, most people cave in and rent cars or hire a cab.

Car rentals are a good idea on Jamaica since the roads are well-paved and your own car will allow you to conduct your sightseeing at your own pace. You must be able, however, to handle that "British thing" of driving on the left; it takes getting used to, so be careful the first few days (the moment you "space out," a common occurrence on long trips or in new lands, you may find yourself veering to the right, which will be disastrous in the face of oncoming traffic. If you're driving with a companion, let them be a front-seat driver for a while and spot for you.) About a dozen agencies on the island offer rentals; among the best are **Avis** ☎ *(809) 926-1560*; **Budget** ☎ *952-1943*; and **National** ☎ *(809) 924-8344*. In Ocho Rios you'll find **Sunshine Car Rental** ☎ *(809) 974-2980*. In Port Antonio try **Eastern Car Rental** ☎ *(809) 993-3624*. Major international chains accept bookings through stateside toll-free *(800)* numbers. Always ask for a written confirmation (a fax will do) and be sure you bring it along. There have been numerous cases of lost reservations, and supply often runs low, despite the presence of 2800 rental cars on the island. Also remember to add the cost of gas to your expenses (no free gas) and a 10 percent government tax. Valid U.S. and Canadian licenses are acceptable, but many agencies have a 25-and-over age limit (ask before you book). Beware of Jamaican drivers who suddenly and unexpectedly turn macho and wipe the road with the tar of their tires. In such cases, it is always best to yield.

LANGUAGE

The official language is English. The unique Jamaican dialect, used by natives, is English with African and native words and a British inflection and tropical rhythm.

MEDICAL EMERGENCIES

The most efficient and advanced medical facilities are in Kingston, where you will find the country's largest hospital.

MONEY

The official currency is the Jamaican dollar, which has proven to be quite unstable in relation to the American dollar. American dollars are accepted in most establishments, but exchange rates will vary (also make sure when you are quoted a price, that you know which "dollar" is being used). All airports have exchange houses; best rates are found at banks. Major credit cards are accepted by most hotels and many restaurants, as are traveler's checks. When changing money, be sure you keep the receipt so you can change the money back before you leave.

SECURITY

Crime in Jamaica is lower per capita than in most large U.S. cities, but the city of Kingston is rife with incidents. Downtown Kingston is particularly bad, and you should never walk in the street after dark. Don't even think about going to West Kingston, even in a car with the doors locked. Don't ever leave money, wallets, purses or valuables such as cameras unattended at the beach. Police foot patrols are present in all the major tourist areas, so head directly for one if you sense trouble approaching. Also avoid standing in the middle of a street to hail a taxi; it's best to head for a shopping center or ask your hotel to arrange one ahead of time.

TELEPHONE

The area code is *809*. Direct telephone, telegraph, telefax and telex services are all available.

TIME

Eastern Standard Time throughout the year.

TIPPING

Most Jamaican restaurants add a service charge of 10 percent; always check first to see if it's included. If not, tip waiters 10–15 percent (depending on the service). It's not necessary to tip taxi drivers, although 10 percent of the fare is usually appreciated.

TOURIST INFORMATION

The main office of the Jamaica Tourist Board is in Kingston *(Tourism Centre Building, New Kingston, Box 360, Kingston 5; ☎ (809) 929-9200)*. There are also JTB desks at both Montego Bay and Kingston airports and in all resort areas. In the U.S. ☎ *(213) 384-1123.*

WHEN TO GO

Carnival is a recent addition to Jamaica, held oddly at Easter time. The annual reggae festival called Sun Splash is usually held in the middle of August, in Montego Bay, at the Bob Marley Centre. The Independence celebrations, also held for a week in August, are colorful blowout bashes (usually on Independence Day, Aug. 1). In October the annual International Marlin Tournament at Port Antonio attracts fishermen from all over the world and includes festivals other than fishing. Contact the Tourist Board for a twice-yearly calendar of events covering a wide spectrum of sports and arts festivals.

JAMAICA RESTAURANTS		PHONE	ENTREE	CR. CARDS
Kingston				
	International			
★★★★	**Blue Mountain Inn**	(809) 927-1700	\$12–\$24••	A, DC, MC, V
★★	**Gap Cafe, The**	(809) 923-7055	\$12–\$22	A, MC, V
★★	**Port Royal**	(809) 926-3690	\$16–\$26	A, DC, MC, V
★	**El Dorado Room**	(809) 926-9334	\$7–\$20	A, DC, MC, V
★	**Ivor Guest House**	(809) 977-33	\$18–\$30	A, MC, V
	Latin American			
★★★★★	**Temple Hall**	(809) 942-2340	\$25–\$25••	A, DC, MC
★★★★	**Norma's at the Wharfhouse**	(809) 979-2745	\$26–\$34	MC, V
★★	**Devon House Restaurants**	(809) 929-6602	\$6–\$16	A, MC, V
★★	**Hot Pot, The**	(809) 929-3906	\$3–\$4	V
★	**Chelsea Jerk Centre**	(809) 926-6322	\$3–\$5	A, MC, V
★	**Indies Pub and Grill**	(809) 926-5050	\$4–\$12	A, MC, V
★	**Minnie's Ethiopian**	(809) 927-9207	\$10–\$20	None
Montego Bay				
	International			
★★★★	**Sugar Mill**	(809) 953-2228	\$14–\$31	A, MC, V

JAMAICA RESTAURANTS	PHONE	ENTREE	CR. CARDS
★ Georgian House	(809) 952-3353	$22–$32	A, DC, MC, V
★ Julia's	(809) 952-632	$35–$35••	A, DC, MC, V
Italian			
★★★★★ Reading Reef Club	(809) 952-5909	$10–$24	A, DC, MC, V
Latin American			
★★★ Pork Pit	(809) 952-1046	$2–$9	None
★★ Town House	(809) 952-2660	$13–$30	A, DC, MC, V
Seafood			
★ Pier I	(809) 952-2452	$16–$25	A, MC, V
Negril			
French			
★★ Cafe au Lait	(809) 957-4471	$9–$29	MC, V
Latin American			
★★ Chicken Lavish	(809) 957-4410	$3–$5	MC, V
★★ Hungry Lion		$18–$30	MC, V
★★ Paradise Yard	(809) 957-4006	$6–$15	None
★ Tan-ya's	(809) 957-4041	$5–$25	A, MC, V
Seafood			
★★ Cosmo's	(809) 957-4330	$5–$12	MC, V
★ Rick's Cafe	(809) 957-4335	$11–$28	None
Ocho Rios			
Chinese			
★ Ruins Restaurant	(809) 974-2442	$12–$33	A, DC, MC, V
Italian			
★★★★★ Evita's	(809) 974-2333	$7–$19	A, MC, V
Latin American			
★★★★ Almond Tree	(809) 974-2813	$12–$26	A, DC, MC, V
★★ Parkway Restaurant	(809) 974-2667	$6–$25	A, MC, V
Port Antonio			
International			
★★★★★ Trident Hotel Restaurant	(809) 993-2602	$25–$50	A, MC, V
Latin American			
★★★ De Montevin Lodge	(809) 993-2604	$11–$18	None
★★ Front Line, The		$5–$8	None

Note: • Lunch Only

•• Dinner Only

MARTINIQUE

Martinique is the best place for bargains on French imports from perfume to clothes and crystal.

Martinique is a little bit of foie gras in the middle of the Caribbean. From the cuisine to the chic style of the women, to the lilt of the language, Martinique exudes the charm of its mother country—France. But add to that a decidedly West Indian cachet and shopping values that would make a Parisian's jaw drop open, and you have a tiny island nation waiting to be loved. Rising from beaches to rain forest to the heights of a volcanic mountain that wiped out an entire city in 1902, Martinique is rife with opportunities to dive, trek, sail, surf, parasail and about any other sport imaginable—from mountain biking to deep-sea fishing in some of the clearest waters in the Caribbean. The island has stayed ecologically pure enough to still boast good sightings of many birds in the mangroves, including the yellow-breasted sandbird, a symbol of the island. Best of all, tourism is just beginning to snap at the heels of this nearly forgotten island and locals are still green enough—business-wise—to have escaped becoming jaded. Of course, on an island such as this one, there will always be a few cases of French snoots, but try to ignore them and concentrate on the natural beauties.

Bird's Eye View

Fifty miles long and 22 miles long, Martinique covers 425 square miles. Of its neighboring islands, Dominica lies to the north and St. Lucia to the south; Miami is 1470 miles away. Martinique comes from volcanic origins, and today the 4575-ft. Mount Pelé in the Parc Naturel Regional de la Martinique is the only active volcano, situated in the northwest island. Most of the island is mountainous. In the center of the island lie the Pitons de Carbet and the Montagne du Vauclin is in the south. These mountains are linked by hills, and the airport is situated in the central plains area. The north of the island is covered by an enormous rain forest; banana and pineapples are cultivated there, while sugarcane dominates the rest of the island. Black sandy coves are found throughout the south and along the rugged coast open to the Atlantic, white and gray sands characterize the beaches facing the Caribbean and in the south. On the east coast, the peninsula of Caravelle, the oldest volcanic formation of the island, stretches into the rough Atlantic, boasting a mangrove swamp lined with a coral reef. The capital, Fort-de-France, is situated on the Baie des Flamandes on the western coast, while the burgeoning town of Lamentin is slightly more inland.

History

Columbus was stunned when he chanced upon Martinique—historians can't decide whether it was 1493 or 1502—but phrases like "the most fertile, the softest...the most charming place in the world" leave no doubt regarding his true feelings. Carib Indians were the resident locals on Martinique when Columbus happened by. Martinica was the name Columbus bestowed on the volcanic island, in honor of St. Martin. The Caribs called it Madinina, meaning "island of flowers." The Caribs proved too hostile for the Spaniards who moved on to other shores, but they continued to fight the French who settled on the island in 1635. Twenty-five years later the French signed a treaty with the Caribs who agreed to stay on the Atlantic side of the island; nevertheless, they were soon exterminated. The next 200 years was a struggle between the Brits and the French. In 1762 the Brits took control, only to pass it over in exchange for Canada, Senegal, the Grenadines, St. Vincent and Tobago. France remained with Guadeloupe and Martinique because they were knee-deep in the sugarcane. The English took over again between 1794-1802, at the request of plantation owners who needed assistance in the face of growing dissent among slaves. Slavery was

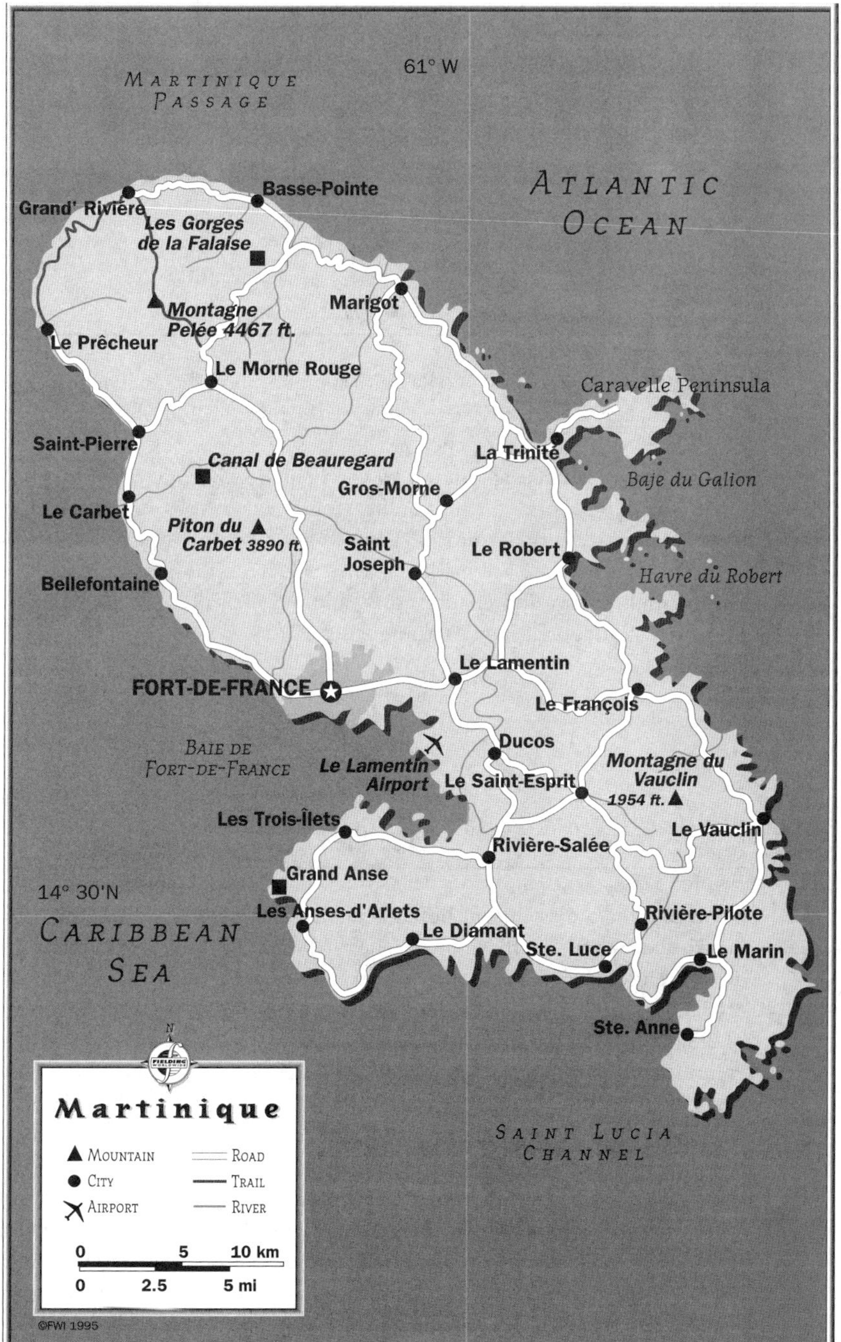
61° W
MARTINIQUE PASSAGE
ATLANTIC OCEAN
Basse-Pointe
Grand' Rivière
Les Gorges de la Falaise
Montagne Pelée 4467 ft.
Marigot
Le Prêcheur
Le Morne Rouge
Caravelle Peninsula
Saint-Pierre
Canal de Beauregard
La Trinité
Baje du Galion
Gros-Morne
Le Carbet
Piton du Carbet 3890 ft.
Saint Joseph
Le Robert
Bellefontaine
Havre du Robert
Le Lamentin
FORT-DE-FRANCE
Le François
Ducos
BAIE DE FORT-DE-FRANCE
Le Lamentin Airport
Le Saint-Esprit
Montagne du Vauclin 1954 ft.
Les Trois-Îlets
Le Vauclin
Rivière-Salée
Grand Anse
14° 30'N
Les Anses-d'Arlets
Rivière-Pilote
CARIBBEAN SEA
Le Diamant
Ste. Luce
Le Marin
Ste. Anne
N
Martinique
Mountain
Road
City
Trail
Airport
River
0
5
10 km
0
2.5
5 mi
SAINT LUCIA CHANNEL
©FWI 1995

abolished in 1848 by the French but not before a major slave rebellion occurred in 1879, encouraged by the French Revolution. Eventually, a new wave of immigrant workers from India began to change the dominant color of skin in the island's population. Martinique finally became a French Department in 1946 and a region in 1974.

People

There are about 369,000 people in Martinique, about half of which are living in the capital of Fort-de-France. A racially mixed batch of Africans, East Indians, whites and others, they are all considered citizens of France, and governed by a Prefect, appointed by the French Government. Unemployment is quite high, about a third of the people have no jobs. About a quarter of those employed are in tourism. To get a good glimpse of social life, hang out in the Savane, a 12-acre park of lawn, shade trees, footpaths and benches where families relax and children play, and old men play serious games of dominoes. Locals are called Martiniquaises.

Beaches

You can find a magnificent beach at **Grand Anse** in South Martinique. It is less visited by tourists than the beaches at Pointe du Bout, although it can get more crowded on weekends. Nearby is the petite pretty village of **Anse d'Arlets**. **Diamant Beach**, just south of Ande d'Arlets, is a paradisiacal stretch of 2.5 miles along the south coast dominated by the **Diamond Rock**, a famous volcanic rock that stands about a mile out to sea where the English stationed cannons in the 18th century (British ships still passing it salute her Majesty's "Ship Diamond Rock"). The beach is nearly deserted and fringed with coconut palms and almond trees. It is not advised for swimming since the currents are strong. From the town of Le Marin south, you'll find long white sand beaches fringed with palms trees and calm, clear seas. **Ste. Anne**, where the Club Med is, has its own fine beach, adjacent to the public one, where you can see a terrific view of the southwest coast. There are many places for shade on Ste. Anne under trees that sometimes overhang into the sea. There are lots of bars and restaurants here. There's a family beach on the road heading east from Marin called Cap Chevalier.

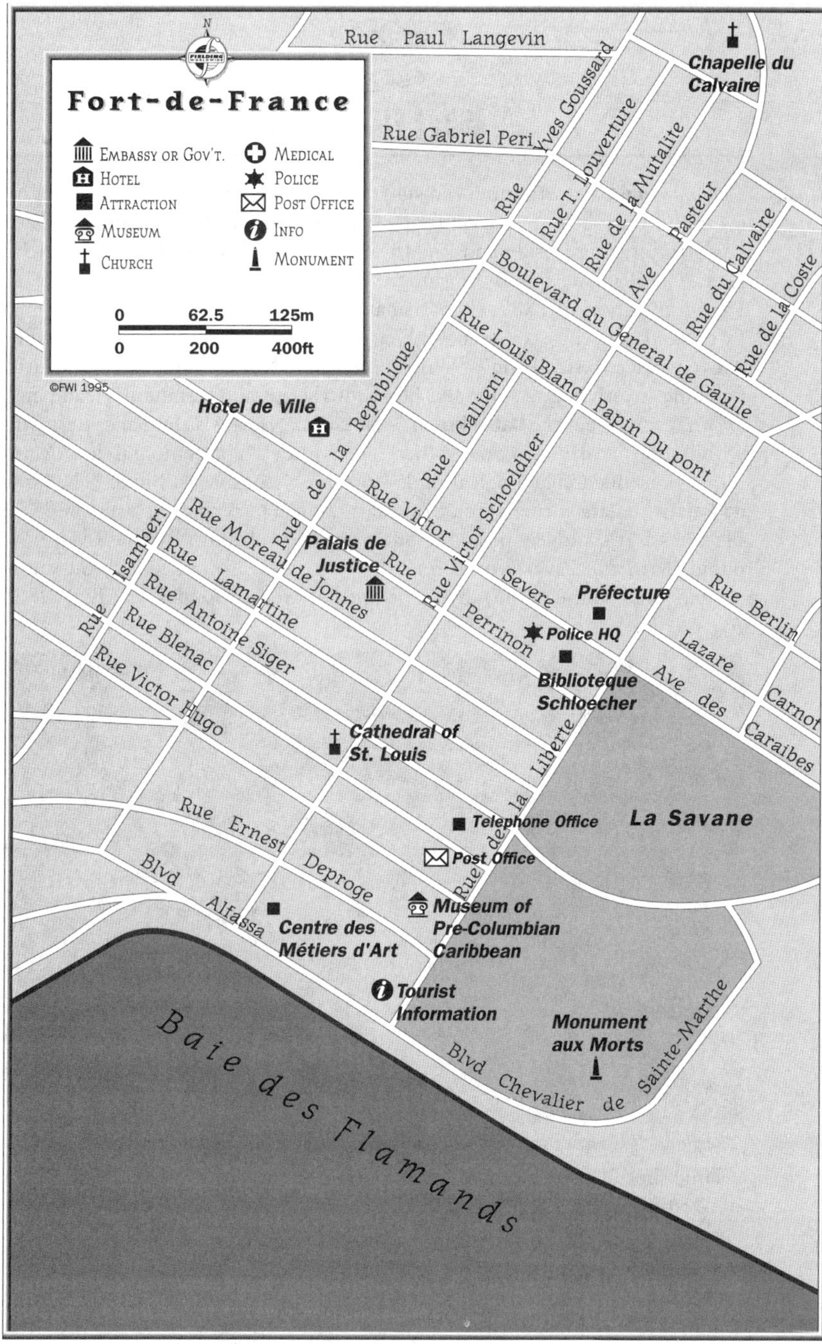

Fort-de-France
Embassy or Gov't.
Medical
Hotel
Police
Attraction
Post Office
Museum
Info
Church
Monument
0 62.5 125m
0 200 400ft
©FWI 1995
Rue Paul Langevin
Chapelle du Calvaire
Rue Gabriel Peri
Rue Yves Goussard
Rue T. Louverture
Rue de la Mutalite
Ave Pasteur
Rue du Calvaire
Rue de la Coste
Boulevard du General de Gaulle
Rue Louis Blanc
Papin Du pont
Hotel de Ville
Rue de la Republique
Rue Gallieni
Rue Victor Schoeldher
Rue Victor Severe
Rue Perrinon
Rue Moreau de Jonnes
Palais de Justice
Préfecture
Police HQ
Biblioteque Schloecher
Rue Berlin
Lazare Carnot
Ave des Caraibes
Rue Isambert
Rue Lamartine
Rue Antoine Siger
Rue Blenac
Rue Victor Hugo
Cathedral of St. Louis
Rue de la Liberte
Telephone Office
La Savane
Post Office
Rue Ernest Deproge
Blvd Alfassa
Centre des Métiers d'Art
Museum of Pre-Columbian Caribbean
Tourist Information
Monument aux Morts
Blvd Chevalier de Sainte-Marthe
Baie des Flamands

What Else to See

The capital of Martinique, **Fort-de-France**, is one of the most charming cities in the Caribbean to see on foot. Among the first sites to check out is the city's architectural pride and joy, the **Bibliotheque Schoelcher**, or Schoelcher Library, a Romanesque Byzantine treasure constructed a century ago for the Paris Exposition of 1889, then dismantled and shipped to Martinique piece by piece. It sits close to **Savane**, the city's central park, full of exotic flora; it's a lovely place to stroll and eavesdrop on locals. Narrow streets with beautiful balconies overhanging sidewalks filled with shops and restaurants lead you to another must-see: the **Cathedral of Saint-Louis**. Nearby is the Palais de Justice with its statue of Victor Schoelcher. The Musée Departemental de la Martinique presents archaeological finds from prehistoric Martinique. The **Jardin de Balata** (Balata gardens) is a tropical botanical park around a restored Creole house. It's a lovely place for browsing and relaxing. By the Riviere Madame (Madame River) you'll find the bustling fish markets. If you want a guided tour, you can find excellent ones offered by **Azimut** ☎ *(596) 60-16-59.*

The Fort-de-France market in Martinique has a plethora of fruits.

Time should also be carved out on your itinerary for travels outside the city of Martinique.

North along the coast, you'll discover **St. Pierre**, considered the "Paris of the West Indies" until 1902 when Mount Pelé Volcano erupted and flowed lava Pompeii-style all over it. You can see the full extent of the tragedy in the exhibits of the museum there. To get there with style, take the little train called **Cyparis Express**, which presents one-hour tours during the week and half-hour tours on the weekend. The drive from Fort-de-France is less than an hour, but make time to stop at such atmospheric fishing villages as **Case-Pilote** and **Bellefontaine**, as well as **Carbet**, where Columbus landed in 1502; Gauguin lived and painted there in 1887. A museum featuring his work is found in Carbet.

In the north, a dazzling route through the rain forest, called **La Trace**, is lush with banana and pineapple plantations, avocado groves, cane fields and lovely inns such as **Leyritz** and **Habitation Lagrange**. Le Précheur, the last village along the northern Caribbean coast, is known for hot springs of volcanic origin as well as the **Tomb of the Carib Indians**. Ajoupa Bouillon is an enchanting flower-lined town with a nature trail called **Les Ombrages**.

Rum is king on Martinique and most visitors enjoy sampling the island-brewed wares at distilleries. The St. James Distillery at Sainte-Marie in the north operates the **Musée du Rhum**. Nearby is a straw-weaving center called **Horne des Esses**. The **Fonds Saint Jacques**, a historically important 17th-century sugar estate in the north, attracts visitors with its museum, Musée du Pere Labat. A modern museum devoted to sugar and rum, called **Maison de la Canne**, is just outside Trois Ilets. Also near Trois Ilets is Joséphone Bonaparte's birthplace, **La Pagerie**, which has a museum chock full of her mementos.

Martinique is often known as the "Ilse of Flowers" and there are numerous floral gardens that are lovely to visit. Nearby La Pagerie is **Parc des Floralies**, a peaceful and pretty botanical park. One of the most beautiful is the **Jardin de Balata** on the Route de La Trace in the suburbs north of the capital. A short drive from here is the Sacré Coeur de Balata, a replica of the well-known basilica that dominates Montmarte in Paris. Other attractions south of Martinique include the H.M.S. *Diamond Rock*, a kind of Rock of Gibralter Caribbean-style rising 600 feet from the sea as used by the British in 1804 as a sloop of war. Anyone not venturing into the depths of the sea with a dive tank should really take a ride on the thrilling **Aquascope**, a semi-submersible craft that makes about an hour tour. One is located at the Marina Pointe du Bout and the other at Le Marin.

Museums and Exhibits

Maison de la Canne ★★★

Trois-Ilets, Fort-de-France.
Hours open: 9 a.m.–5:30 p.m.
You've probably always taken sugar for granted, but won't anymore after touring this museum dedicated to the history and production of sugarcane. Signage is in both French and English. Really quite interesting

Musee Departementale de Martin ★★★

9 Rue de la Liberte, Fort-de-France.
Decent exhibits on the history of slavery, clothing and furniture from the colonial period and artifacts from the pre-Columbian eras of the Arawak and the Carib indians.

Musee Paul Gauguin ★★★

Anse-Turin, Le Carbet.
Hours open: 10 a.m.–5 p.m.
Famed artist Paul Gauguin lived in Martinique in 1887. This museum pays homage to that period, with reproductions of works he created while here, letters and other memorabilia pertaining to his life. The museum also displays the works of other noted artists and changing displays by local artists.

Musee Vulcanologique ★★★★

St. Pierre, Fort-de-France.
Hours open: 9 a.m.–5 p.m.
American Frank Perrot established this museum in 1932, an homage to St. Pierre, the island's oldest city and a bustling one at that, until a devastating eruption of volcano Mt. Pelee on May 8, 1902. The entire town was buried in minutes and some 30,000 residents perished, all except for a prisoner whose underground cell saved him. (He later joined Barnum and Bailey's circus as a sideshow oddity.) Residents had been warned of the imminent danger but city fathers played it down because of an upcoming election. St. Pierre today is a modest village, but you can get a feel for its former glory days at the museum, which exhibits photographs and documents from the period.

Musee de Poupees Vegetables ★★★

Leyritz Plantation, Basse-Pointe.
Hours open: 7 a.m.–5:30 p.m.
Certainly the only one of its kind in Martinique (or possibly the world for that matter), this small museum displays sculptures made entirely of leaves and plants, designed to look like famous women in French history. It is located at the scenic Leyritz Plantation, which is detailed in the lodging section.

Musee du Rhum ★★★

Ste. Matie, Fort-de-France.
Hours open: 9 a.m.–6 p.m.
The St. James Distillery owns this monument to rum, located on a sugar plantation in an old creole house. After a guided tour showing the history and production of rum, you can taste-test the product yourself.

Musee le la Pagerie ★★★★

Trois-Ilets, Fort-de-France.
Hours open: 9 a.m.–5 p.m.
Located on the grounds of the birthplace of Josephine, Napoleon's wife and empress of France from 1804-1809, this museum is housed in a stone building that was formerly the kitchen (the rest of the estate was destroyed by hurricane). Memorabilia of her life, her childhood bed, and a passionate love letter by Napoleon are among the interesting exhibits.

Parks and Gardens

Jardin de Balata ★★★

Rte de Balata, Balata.
Hours open: 9 a.m.–5 p.m.
This tropical park, located on a hillside some 1475 feet above sea level, has stunning views and more than a thousand varieties of trees, flowers and plants. A lovely spot to while away the afternoon exploring winding walkways, lily pond, and breathtaking overlooks.

Tours

Martinique Aquarium ★★★

Blvd. de Marne, Fort-de-France.
Hours open: 9 a.m.–7 p.m.
Ths large aquarium has more than 2000 fish and sea creatures representing some 250 species. Of special interest are the shark tank and piranha pool.

Zoo de Carbet ★★★

Le Coin, Le Carbet.
Hours open: 9 a.m.–6 p.m.
Also called the Amazona Zoo, this park showcases 70 species from the Amazon Basin, including birds and big cats.

Sports

Sailing, scuba, snorkeling, golf, deep-sea fishing, windsurfing, horseback riding, squash, tennis, cycling and motorbiking, hiking—the list of sports on Martinique is endless and depends only on your skill, passion and time. Consider touring the island by bike. For more information contact the **Parc Naturel Régional**; ☎ *(596) 60-25-72*, which has designed highly unusual itineraries. You can even rent your own plane (have a license from back home in order to get the French equivalent at the Lamentin Airport). Then contact local plane owners through the **Aero Club de la Martinique** ☎ *(596) 55-01-84.* As for sailing, an enormous combination of excursions can be made to neighboring islands, among them Antigua, Dominica, Barbados, St. Lucia, St. Vincent and the Grenadines, and Mystique among others. Look for the comprehensive bilingual yachting manual "Guide Trois Rivieres: A Cruising Guide to Martinique" available in local bookstores, about $35 or from *Edition Trois Riviere, B.P. 566, 97242 Fort-de-France* ☎ *(596) 75-07-07.* Spectator sports on the island are weird but exciting if you have a taste for blood: mongoose and snake fights, and cockfights seem to be national pastimes and can be seen December to the beginning of August at Pitt Ducos, **Quartier Brac** ☎ *(596) 56-05-60* and **Pitt Marceny**. Horse racing can be found at the Carere racetrack in Lamentin ☎ *(596) 51-25-09.*

Golf

Trois-Ilets, near Pointe du Bont.

Martinique's only course, the Golf de Imperatrice Josephine, was designed by Robert Trent Jones. The 18-hole, par-71 course covers 150 acres and is quite scenic. The grounds include a pro shop (with an English-speaking pro), restaurant and three tennis courts. Greens fees are about $45.

Horseback Riding

Various locations, Martinique.

Several outfits offer trail rides: **La Cavale** *(76-22-94)*, **Ranch Jack** *(68-37-67)*, **Black Horse Ranch** *(68-37-80)*, and **Ranch Val d'Or** *(76-70-58)*.

Watersports

Various locations, Fort-de-France.

Scuba diving: **Bathy's Club** *(Pointe du Bont 66-00-00)*, **Sud Diamant Rock** *(Le Diamant, 76-42-42)* **Cressmal** *(Fort-de-France, 61-34-36)*, **Planete Bleue** *(Trois-Ilets, 66-08-79)*, Oxygene Bleu *(Lamentin, 50-25-78)*, and **Tropic Alizes** *(Le Bateliere, 61-49-49)*. Boating and sailing: **Soleil et Voile** *(Pointe du Bont 66-09-14)*, **Captains Shop** *(Pointe du Bont, 66-06-77)*, **Ship Shop** *(Fort-de-France, 71-43-40)*, **Carib Charter** *(Schoelcher, 73-08-80)*, **Caraibes Nautique** *(Trois-Ilets 66-06-06)*, and **Cercle Nautique** *(Schoelcher, 61-15- 21)*. Snorkeling: **Aquarium** *(Fort-de-France, 61 49 49)*.

Where to Eat

Fielding's Highest Rated Restaurants in Martinique		
★★★★	La Fontane	$30–$50
★★★★	Leyritz Plantation	$27–$50
★★★	Athanor	$11–$30
★★★	Aux Filets Bleus	$13–$30
★★★	Chez Mally Edjam	$11–$29
★★★	La Mouina	$15–$30
★★★	La Villa Creole	$14–$18
★★★	Le Colibri	$18–$27
★★★	Le Coq Hardi	$18–$36
★★★	Le Poisson d'Or	$25–$30

Fielding's Special Restaurants in Martinique		
★★★★	La Fontane	$30–$50
★★★	Chez Mally Edjam	$11–$29
★★★	La Mouina	$15–$30
★★★	Le Colibri	$18–$27
★★	Yva Chez Vava	$18–$27

Fielding's Budget Restaurants in Martinique		
★★★	Le Second Souffle	$8–$12
★★	La Dunette	$6–$20
★★★	La Villa Creole	$14–$18
★★	Le Cantonnais	$14–$20
★★	Diamant Les Bains	$16–$20

Perhaps it's the irrepressible French dedication to cuisine, but chefs in Martinique seem to take special care with their menus, overseeing both the preparation and the service. Throughout the island you will generally find one of two cuisines: traditional French or island Creole; many restaurants combine the two on their menus. Fresh seafood dishes are omnipresent, among the tastiest are *chatrou* (octopus), *langouste* (small clawless lobster), *lambi* (conch), and *cribiches* (large river shrimp). Red snapper is served in a variety of ways. *Coquille de lambi* (minced conch in creamy sauce served in a shell) is an island must; the *blaff de poisson* (steamed fish in local spices) is excellent at Le Mareyeur. Another island specialty, *pâté en pot*, is a thick creole soup made with mutton. A good afternoon drink to cool you off is *les planteurs*—a planter's punch in a sweet fruit juice base. Heart islanders tend to chug down *décollage*—aged herbal rum with a fruit juice chaser. Most restaurants have excellent selections of French wines. Prices per person for a three-course meal without wine range from $30–$45 and up. The French & English booklet *Ti Gourmet*, available from the Tourist Office, will give out more information about where and what to eat.

Fort-de-France

Diamant Les Bains **$$$** ★★

Le Diamant, 97223, Le Diamant,
Latin American cuisine. Specialties: Blaff, Coconut Flan.
Lunch: entrees $16–$20.
Dinner: entrees $16–$20.

Good local fare is served in a motel-like hostelry in Le Diamant, a cozy beach town whose claim to fame is the imposing Diamond Rock, majestically rising from the deep to an almost 600-foot height. The beach it fronts is nothing special, but it's a nice spot to dine on blaff fish (cooked with thyme, peppers, clove and other spices), boudin and coconut flan.

La Fontane **$$$** ★★★★

Km. 4 Rue de Balata, ☎ (596) 64-65-89.
French cuisine.
Lunch: entrees $30–$50.
Dinner: entrees $30–$50.

A highly-regarded French-creole restaurant, La Fontane is located in a restored gingerbread house surrounded by fruit trees. The service is formal, the interior is antique-filled and tasteful, with exotic carpets on the floors. Dishes have included crayfish salad with fruit, lamb and mango and red-snapper with a citrus sauce.

La Mouina **$$$** ★★★

route de Redoute, Redoute, ☎ (596) 79-34-57.
French cuisine. Specialties: Crab Farcis.
Lunch: Noon–4 p.m., entrees $15–$30.
Dinner: 7:30–9:30 p.m., entrees $15–$30.

This is suburbia Fort-de-France style—fine dining in a typical upper-class home in Redoute, high above the capital below. Guests are made welcome in a dining salon on a balcony with a garden view. The smart set likes to make La Mouina a regular stop for luncheons of stuffed crab backs, tournedos and crayfish. Dinners are served by candlelight.

La Villa Creole **$$$** ★★★

Anse Mitan 97229, Anse Mitan,
Latin American cuisine.
Lunch: Noon–2 p.m., entrees $14–$18.
Dinner: 7–10 p.m., entrees $14–$18.

A friendly and warm atmosphere permeates this gingerbread house with tables set on a seaside terrace in Anse Mitan, a beach resort famed for low-key, moderately priced hotels. There are several prixe-fixe meals to choose from, from plain to fancy, but all feature a bevy of side dishes, vegetables and dessert. The owner sometimes gives impromptu song and dance performances.

Le Cantonnais **$$$** ★★

La Marina,

Chinese cuisine.
Dinner: 6:30–11 p.m., prix fixe $14–$20.
Guests staying at the large resort hotels near the marina in Pointe du Bout can take a break from French-creole cuisine at this Chinese foodery serving a voluminous menu of unusual dishes including broiled shark's fin and bird's nest soup. Vegetarians also have a choice of several meatless entrees.

Le Colibri **$$$** ★★★
allee du Colibri, Morne des Esses,
Latin American cuisine. Specialties: Colombo, Tourte aux Lambis, Flan au Coco.
Lunch: Noon–3 p.m., entrees $18–$27.
Dinner: 7–11 p.m., entrees $18–$27.
A family-run operation, Le Colibri (The Hummingbird), located in the northwestern side of the island, could be named for the friendly bustling about hither and tither of Mme Paladino and her daughters, who are busy serving scrumptious creole meals to weekenders from Fort-de-France. These denizens often fill the veranda of the house for conch pie, crayfish stew and a dreamy coconut flan. Come early to nab these choice seats or you'll be seated inside facing the open kitchen (not so bad an idea).

Le Coq Hardi **$$$** ★★★
Rue Martin Luther King, ☎ (596) 63-66-83.
International cuisine. Specialties: Tournedos Rossini, Prime Rib.
Lunch: Noon–2 p.m., entrees $18–$36.
Dinner: 7–11 p.m., entrees $18–$36.
Red meat is god here, prepared *au bleu* (very rare) which is the French way. Master charcutier Alphonse Sintive regularly imports the choice cuts of T-Bone, filet mignon and entrecote from France. After you choose your own steak, it's cooked over an open wood fire. An old-fashioned tournedos rossini is prepared with foie gras and truffles, and is a favorite here. If you still have room after the huge portions served, there's still a wide selection of scrumptious desserts and sorbets.

Le Poisson d'Or **$$$** ★★★
Anse Mitan, Anse Mitan,
Latin American cuisine.
Lunch: Noon–2:30 p.m., prix fixe $25–$30.
Dinner: 7–10 p.m., prix fixe $25–$30.
This is a casual roadside seafood eatery set between the beach cities of Anse Mitan and Pointe du Bout. Tropical greenery and a bamboo ceiling make you feel like you're dining on an isle in the South Seas. A fixed-price meal for $25 is a good buy for an array of creole specialties including a Conch appetizer and an elegant dessert.

Le Second Souffle **$$** ★★★
27 Rue Blenac, ☎ (596) 63-44-11.
Latin American cuisine.
Lunch: Noon–3 p.m., entrees $8–$12.
Dinner: 7:30–10 p.m., entrees $8–$12.
A treat for the body and soul is a cleansing visit to this pleasant vegetarian restaurant after a tour of the Byzantine Saint Louis Cathedral nearby. Le Second Souffle (is there a first?) dishes up a salad of seasonal fruits with honey sauce, or a meatless plat du jour, which may include a christophene or callaloo souffle.

Leyritz Plantation **$$$** ★★★★
Basse Pointe 97218, Leyritz, ☎ (596) 78-53-92.
Latin American cuisine.
Lunch: 12:30–2 p.m., entrees $27–$40.
Dinner: 7:30–9 p.m., entrees $36–$50.

Dining at one of Martinique's prime tourist attractions sounds like a recipe for disaster, but surprisingly, the Creole cuisine remains first rate. Guests also get a lot of food for their francs, especially a set luncheon of stuffed crab, blood pudding, an entree (sometimes conch), rice and vegetables and dessert. The million-dollar setting amidst an 18th century sugar plantation is a fond postcard memory. Although lunch is the preferred time, come for dinner when the tour bus pandemonium becomes practically nonexistent.

Basse Pointe

Athanor **$$$** ★★★

Rue de Bord de Mer, Ste. Anne, ☎ (596) 76-72-93.
French cuisine. Specialties: Grilled Lobster.
Dinner: 7–10 p.m., entrees $11–$30.

This informal eatery located one block from the beach in Ste. Anne prepares tasty pizzas, salads and other casual meals from a large menu. Diners can choose a few fancier items including the specialty, grilled lobster, which is delicious. There's a choice of seating in a pretty garden behind the restaurant or in a greenery-draped dining room indoors.

Aux Filets Bleus **$$$** ★★★

Point Marin, Ste. Anne, ☎ (596) 76-73-42.
Latin American cuisine. Specialties: Delices de la Mer, Turtle Soup, Court Bouillon.
Lunch: 12:30–2:30 p.m., entrees $13–$30.
Dinner: 7:30–9:30 p.m., entrees $13–$30.

A restaurant of many contrasts—although Aux Filets Bleus charges haute cuisine prices, the place is so casual you can come here in a beach cover-up after a swim in the briny which is in full view of the tables. Also, dishes are mostly hearty West Indian dishes like *chatrous* (octopus) with red beans and rice, hardly justifying the stiff tab. Still, what you're served is usually very good, and the ambience is friendly and intimate.

Chez Mally Edjam **$$$** ★★★

Route de la Cote, ☎ (596) 78-51-18.
French cuisine. Specialties: Fruit Confitures, Colombo de Porc.
Dinner: entrees $11–$29.

It's a very pleasant drive to get to this home-style restaurant run by stellar cuisiniere Mally Edjam and her family. The surrounding landscape en route is dotted with pineapple plantations, and trees hung heavily with boughs of green bananas. That's just a prelude to the symphony of flavors on the fixed-price lunches served here, which may include *pork colombo* (local curry), conch and fabulous desserts. Don't miss the homemade preserves made from local fruits. Dinners may be arranged by appointment.

La Dunette **$$** ★★

Sainte Anne, 97227, Ste. Anne, ☎ (596) 76-73-90.
Seafood cuisine.
Lunch: entrees $6–$20.
Dinner: entrees $6–$20.

La Dunette is like a lot of pleasant seaside restaurants on the island that serves seafood specialties. Dine inside or out in a tropical garden facing the sea on poached sea urchins, curries or grilled fish. Connected to a pleasant, intimate hotel where you might consider staying if you're in the area, which is noted for gorgeous beaches and fine weather.

Yva Chez Vava **$$$** ★★

Boulevard de Gaulle, Grand Riviere, ☎ (596) 55-72-55.
French cuisine.
Dinner: entrees $18–$27.

This chez on the northern tip of the island is the domain of local legend Vava and her daughter Yva, who now continues the tradition of cooking family-style creole meals in their own residence near a river. As Grand Riviere is a fishing village, seafood appears prominently on the menu. Specialties include *accras* (cod fritters), *chicken colombo* and *z'habitants* (crayfish prepared Martinique style). After lunch, you might want to visit the fish market where your food originated, or stroll on the black sand beach.

Where to Shop

"Go French" is the password when trying to decode what to buy in Martinique, a place where you can find the best bargains among French imports—perfumes, cosmetics, clothes, china, and crystal—at prices 25-40 percent lower than in the U.S. If you pay in traveler's checks, you'll receive an additional 20 percent discount. You will never find these prices in France. Don't miss picking up a few bottles of Martinique-brewed rum. Craft buys range from folk-styled appliqué wall hangings to the Martiniquais doll dressed in the national costume, which can be seen in nearly every store and in every size imaginable. A conical bakoua straw hat does nicely as a sun-stopper. If you're interested in the bright gold Creole jewelry that seems to be around many women's necks, ears and wrists, you will be joining a long-standing cultural tradition.The special "convict's chain" called *chaîne forçat*, and the *tremblants*, gold brooches with special adornment, can be found in several stores, where you should be able to judge authenticity by the price. Among the most reputable are **Cadet Daniel**, **Bijouterie Onyx** and **Emile Mothie's** workshop in Trenelle. (The latter are for serious fans who want to observe his work.) For delicious French delicacies, wines, foie gras and chocolates, head for **Boutique Michel Montignac**. To pick up the latest in island music, try **Hit Parade** on Rue Lamartine. The latest Parisian fashions can be found at **l'Univers**.

Martinique Directory

BUSINESS HOURS

Stores open weekdays 8:30 a.m.–6 p.m. and Saturday 8:30 a.m.–1 p.m. Banks have varied hours but are generally open weekdays 7:30–noon and 2:30–4 p.m.

CLIMATE

Martinique's temperatures stay temperate all year long, hovering around 79 degrees F, with only a five degree difference between seasons. The air is cooled by constant wind currents (east and northeast); trade winds are called *les alizés*.

DOCUMENTS

For stays up to three weeks, U.S. and Canadian citizens traveling as tourists must show proof of citizenship in the form of a valid passport, or a passport that expired no more than five years ago, or other proof in the form of a birth certificate or voter's registration card with a government-authorized photo ID. For stays of more than three weeks, or for nontourist visas, a valid passport is necessary. Resident aliens of the U.S. and Canada and other foreign nationals other than those in the Common Market must have a valid passport and visa. All passengers must show an ongoing or return ticket.

ELECTRICITY

Current is 220 AC, 50 cycles. American and Canadian appliances require a French plug, converter and transformers.

GETTING AROUND

Taxi stands are located at the airport, in downtown Fort-de-France, and at major hotels. Rates rise 60 percent between 8 p.m. and 6 a.m. Eighty percent of the taxis are Mercedes Benz. There are also collective taxis (eight-passenger limousines bearing the sign TC).

Car rentals are available at Lamentin Airport, though hours are dependent on international flights. A valid driver's license is required, the minimum age is 21. Other agencies can be found in Fort-de-France. Among the best are **Avis**, *4 rue Ernest Deproge* ☎ *(596) 70-11-60*; **Budget**, *12 rue Félix Eboué, Fort-de-France* ☎ *(596) 63-69-00*; and **Hertz**, *24 rue Ernest Deproge, Fort-de-France* ☎ *(596) 60-64-54*.

Ferries, called vedettes, link Fort-de-France with Pointe du Bout daily from early morning until after midnight, and with Anse Mitan, Anse-a-l'Ane, Grand Anse d'Arlet from early morning till late afternoon. All ferries leave and arrive at Quai d'Esnambuc.

LANGUAGE

The languages of the isle are French and Creole. You'll find English spoken in most hotels, restaurants and tourist facilities, but you'll be happy if you remember to bring along a French phase book and pocket dictionary.

MEDICAL EMERGENCIES

There are 20 hospitals and clinics on the island, many well equipped; the best is **La Meynard** ☎ *(596) 55-20-00*. Ask the Tourist Office to assist you in securing an English-speaking physician.

MONEY

The official currency is the French franc, but U.S. and Canadian dollars are accepted almost everywhere. The rate of exchange, approximately five francs to the dollar, can change due to currency fluctuation.

TELEPHONE

The area code is *596*. To direct-dial from the U.S., dial ☎ *011-596*, plus the local Martinique number for station to station, or *01-596* plus local number for person to person. The best way to make international calls in Martinique is to purchase a "Telecarte" (a one-minute call to the U.S. is about $2.10. These credit cards can be purchased at all post offices and other outlets marked "Telécarte en vente Ici."; the booths you use them in are marked "Telécom." To use the assistance of an operator or to make a call from a hotel room will raise the price enormously.

TIME

Martinique is one hour later than New York (Eastern Standard Time). Time is related on the 24-hour hour schedule; i.e., 1 p.m. is 13:00 hours.

TIPPING AND TAXES

A 10–15 percent tip is the rule for waiters and waitresses.

TOURIST INFORMATION

The **Martinique Tourist Office** ☎ *(596) 63-79-60* is located in handsome quarters on the Boulevard Alfassa, which borders on the waterfront in Fort-de-France. Hours are Monday-Friday 7:30 a.m.–12:30 p.m. and 2:30–5:30 p.m., and Saturday 8 a.m.–noon. Pick up complimentary maps, magazines and information bulletins; the English-speaking staff is quite helpful. A tourist office information desk at Lamentin Airport is open daily until the last flight comes in. In the U.S. ☎ *(800) 391-4909.*

WHEN TO GO

Carnival begins on Jan. 7 for five days, a total-island experience with parties and parades. Ash Wednesday is a blowout affair on March 1, with jammed streets, flowing rum, wild dancing and a funeral cortege at La Savane, Fort-de-France. The Aqua Festival du Robert on April 15–22 is a sea extravaganza in this Atlantic coastal town with yawl races, regattas, and concerts. Jazz a la Plantation on June 2, for two weeks at Basse Pointe, is a New Orleans-meets-French Antilles affair, with concert jams, street bands, Creole nights, and jazz lectures and workshops. Images Caraibes, on June 2 for two weeks, is the 5th Caribbean Film Festival in Fort-de-France. Tour de la Martinique is July 7–16, a week-long bicycle race throughout the island. The tenth Tour des Yoles Rondes on July 30–Aug. 6, is a race of rawls used by Martinique fishermen. The Semi-Marathon, on Nov. 19, is a large race contest. Christmas Eve is celebrated with a midnight mass followed by a sumptuous supper, called Le Réveillon. New Year's Eve is another huge bash celebrated at hotels and restaurants.

MARTINIQUE RESTAURANTS	PHONE	ENTREE	CR. CARDS
Basse Pointe			
French			
★★★ **Athanor**	(596) 76-72-93	$11–$30••	MC, V
★★★ **Chez Mally Edjam**	(596) 78-51-18	$11–$29••	A, MC, V
★★ **Yva Chez Vava**	(596) 55-72-55	$18–$27••	None
Latin American			
★★★ **Aux Filets Bleus**	(596) 76-73-42	$13–$30	MC, V
Seafood			
★★ **La Dunette**	(596) 76-73-90	$6–$20	MC, V
Fort-de-France			
French			
★★★★ **La Fontane**	(596) 64-65-89	$30–$50	A

MARTINIQUE RESTAURANTS	PHONE	ENTREE	CR. CARDS
★★★ **La Mouina**	(596) 79-34-57	$15–$30	MC, V
International			
★★★ **Le Coq Hardi**	(596) 63-66-83	$18–$36	A, MC, V
Latin American			
★★★★ **Leyritz Plantation**	(596) 78-53-92	$27–$50	MC, V
★★★ **Le Second Souffle**	(596) 63-44-11	$8–$12	MC, V

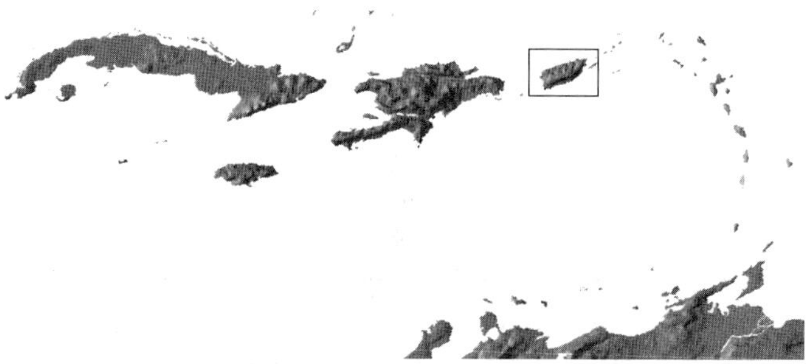

PUERTO RICO

Watersports of all kinds are available at Sun Bay.

Puerto Rico is probably the best kept secret in the Caribbean. Few people are aware that visitors from the U.S., Asia and South America reached a record four million for 1993–94, registering a 12.2 percent increase in hotel bookings. More than half of that four million were from the U.S.

The year 1994 was key for other reasons. A wet September enabled Puerto Rico officials to lift the drought restrictions in key tourist areas of the island following four months of such barriers. The surrounding areas of Old San Juan, Isla Verde and Condado—where many of the largest hotels are located—have returned to normal water service. Old San Juan, refurbished with a $41 million budget and another $41 million waterfront renewal project, is on a roll, though still a bit reeling from the 500th anniversary of Columbus' first sighting of Puerto Rico on Nov. 19, 1493. There are 16 historic blocks that compose this World Heritage site. Known as El Viejo, San Juan, embodies the spiritual heart of the island's nearly four million inhabitants. With centuries-old architecture, it symbolizes Puerto Rico's fight for identity in the face of 400 years of foreign assault and occupation.

Bird's Eye View

The farthest east of the four major islands that form the Greater Antilles, Puerto Rico is 110 miles by 35 miles in size. To the north lies the Atlantic Ocean, to the south the Caribbean. Three islands are situated off the coast of Puerto Rico: Vieques and Culebra to the east and Mona to the west. The island's terrain ranges from palm-lined beaches on four coastlines to rugged mountain ranges, gently rolling hills and dry desertlike areas. The island boasts 20 designated forest reserves and an additional six are in proposal. The most notable are the 28,000-acre El Yunque rain forest near San Juan, part of the Caribbean National Forest and the only tropical rain forest in the U.S. Forest Service; the Guajataca Forest, with 25 miles of trails through karst reserves; and the Guanica Forest Reserve, a dry forest with the largest number of bird species on the island. There are also two Phosphorescent Bays, one off the southwest coast and the other off the island of Vieques.

History

In 1493, Columbus arrived on the island of Puerto Rico in the company of one Ponce de León, who named the island for his patron saint, San Juan. The island, however, already had a name—Borinquen—a Taino Indian nomenclature and one that is still lovingly used today by native Puerto Ricans. Caparra, inland and across the bay, was the first choice for a capital in 1508 when Juan Ponce de León (the island's first governor) and his men with the permission of supreme cacique Agueybana, first scouted the island of San Juan Bautista. Eventually de León set off on his journey to discover eternal youth and never actually resided in the handsome home, Casa Blanca, that had been built for him. Thirteen years later, settlers decamped for the drier, windier islet fronting the Atlantic, where they permanently settled. During early years of colonization, the city repelled the British, French and Dutch corsairs. La Fortaleza, now the governor's mansion, and El Morro and San Cristóbal forts were built during those times with the specific aim of keeping marauders at bay.

By the early 1800s, the era of Caribbean piracy was finally brought to a halt. At the same time, Spain threw open her doors to immigration; subsequent increase in economic prosperity coupled with new aesthetic influences from abroad were soon reflected in the island's architectural styles. It was during this period that Old San Juan developed the colonial/neoclassic look that predominates today—all within the urban grid pattern envisioned by

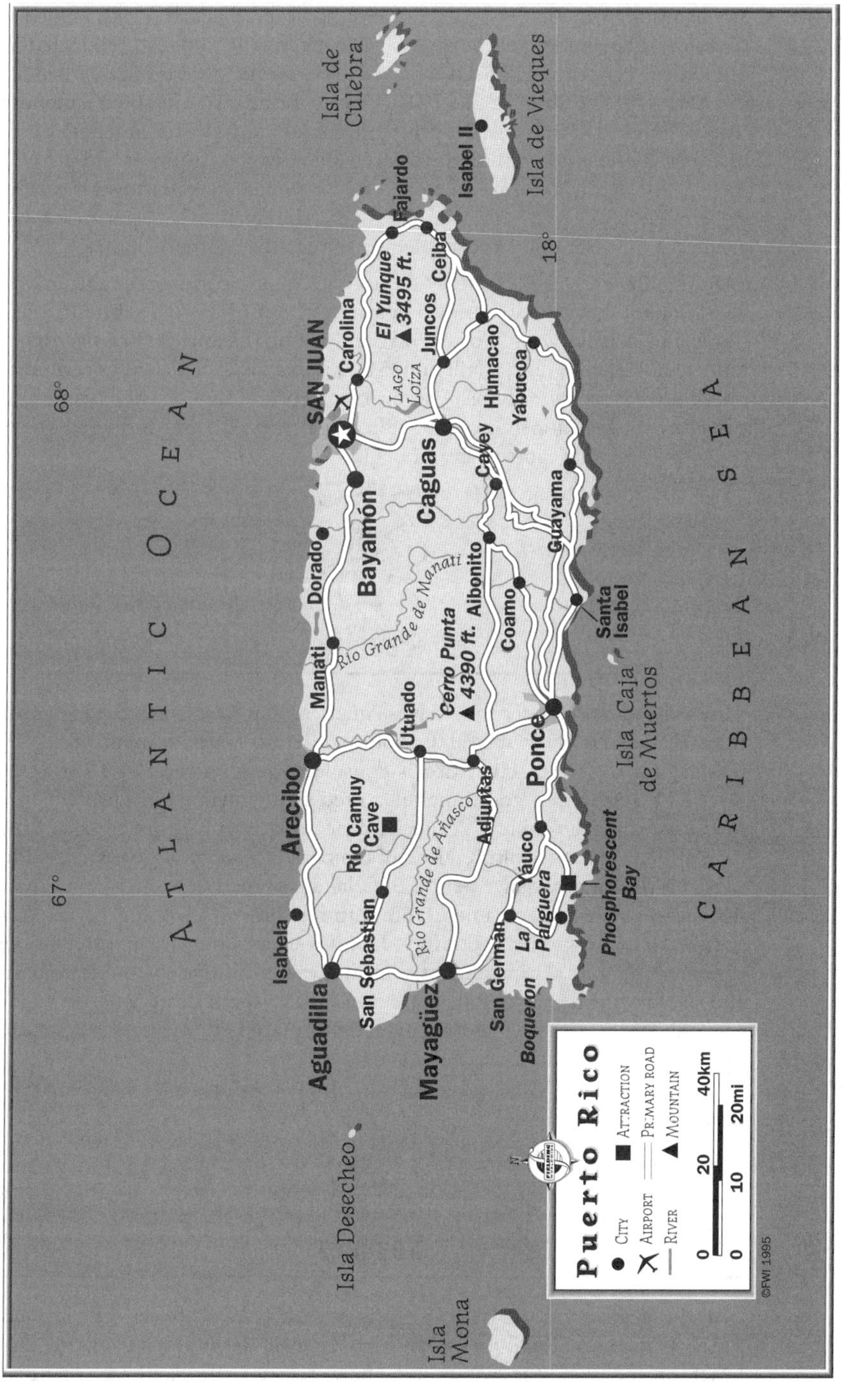
ATLANTIC OCEAN
CARIBBEAN SEA
67°
68°
18°
Isla de Culebra
Isla de Vieques
Isabel II
Fajardo
Ceiba
El Yunque
3495 ft.
Carolina
SAN JUAN
Juncos
Lago Loíza
Humacao
Yabucoa
Caguas
Cayey
Bayamón
Dorado
Guayama
Aibonito
Río Grande de Manatí
Manatí
Coamo
Santa Isabel
Cerro Punta
4390 ft.
Utuado
Isla Caja de Muertos
Ponce
Arecibo
Rio Camuy Cave
Adjuntas
Río Grande de Añasco
Yauco
Phosphorescent Bay
Parguera
La
Isabela
San Sebastian
San German
Aguadilla
Mayagüez
Boqueron
Isla Desecheo
Isla Mona
Puerto Rico
City
Airport
River
Attraction
Primary road
Mountain
0
20
40km
0
10
20mi
©FWI 1995

the original Spanish planners. In 1897 the island gained independence from Spanish rule in 1897. On July 25, 1898, however, Spanish troops landed in Guánica, in the middle of the Spanish-American War, and disturbed whatever modicum of peace had been achieved. The Treaty of Paris of 1899 handed the island over to the U.S. In 1917, Puerto Ricans were granted American citizenship; in 1952, the island achieved unique status by becoming the only member of the commonwealth to receive its own constitution and government. Although there have been several movements geared toward achieving complete independence, the 1993 vote to remain a U.S. possession has ensured a long-standing and stable future with the mother country.

During the early 20th century a burgeoning population brought growth beyond the Old City gates and soon after, the destruction of substantial sections of its massive walls. Today Old San Juan boasts only 5000 *residents*; no longer the financial hub, it still pulls 5000 *workers* to offices and government buildings, eateries and shops. A seven-block enclave that boasts a large number of art studios, florists, doctor's offices, galleries, etc., is considered one of the more desirable spots to live in island.

People

Puerto Ricans consider themselves American but have a fierce pride about their island and their special Caribbean identity. American products are ubiquitous; in fact, Puerto Rico is considered among the top 10 overseas markets for American goods manufactured on the mainland. Through such media as American cable TV, music, dance and fashion from the mainland have also invaded the culture, though tempered for tropical climes. Salsa, the music, is the biggest dance bet on the island, although it is often mixed with American rock'n' roll. Immense precautions, however, should be taken in regards to crime and petty thievery. Don't walk around with an ostentatious show of valuables, keep cameras tucked away in inexpensive-looking bags, and avoid wearing jewelry in the streets. Take special care when strolling through large cities such as San Juan, and in targeted tourist areas, such as Old San Juan.

Beaches

All the beaches on the island are public with one exception—the artificial beach at the Caribe Hilton in San Juan. **Luquillo Beach** is probably the best beach on the island for swimming. The waters are calm, and the coral reefs protect the pristine lagoon from the stronger waves of the Atlantic. Picnic ta-

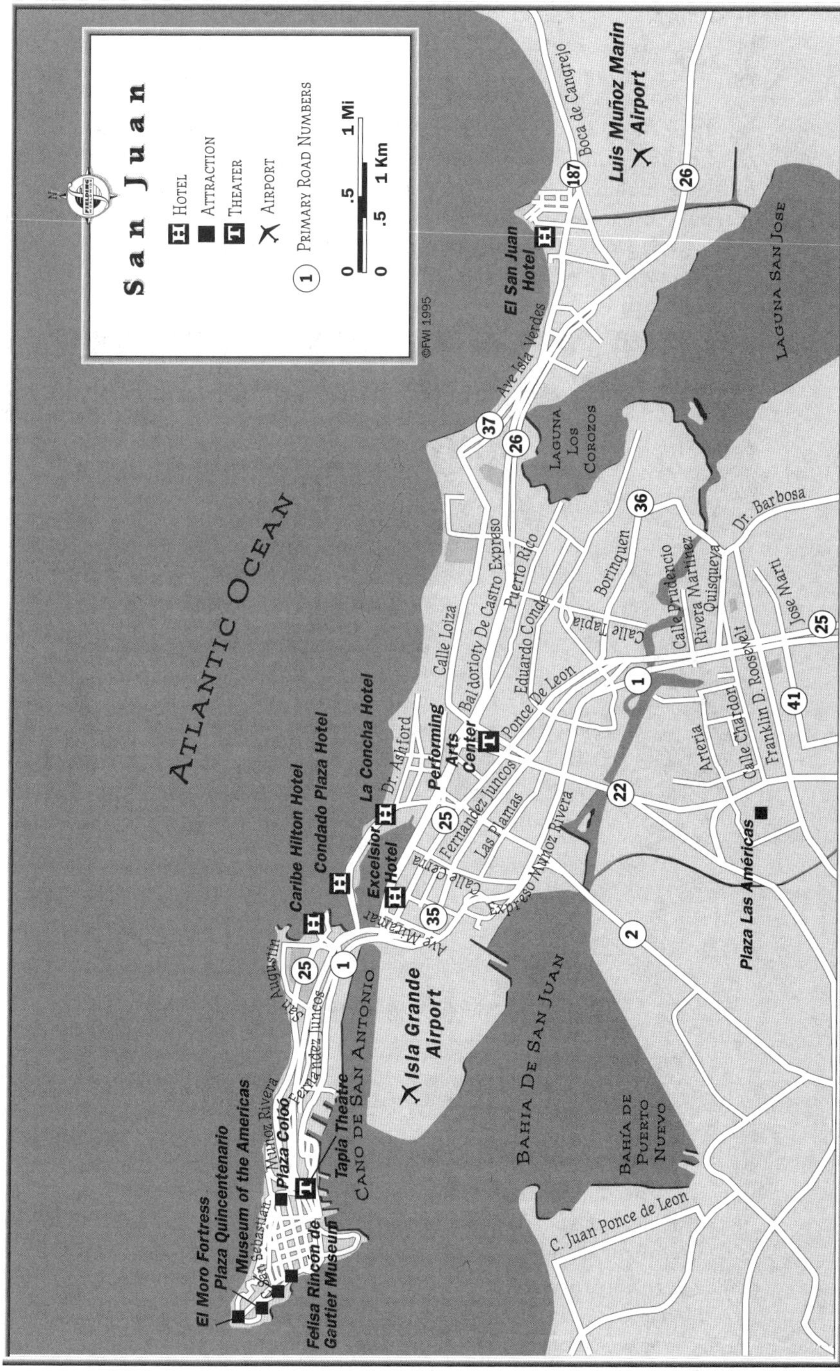
San Juan
Hotel
Attraction
Theater
Airport
1 Primary Road Numbers
0 .5 1 Mi
0 .5 1 Km
©FWI 1995
Atlantic Ocean
El Moro Fortress
Plaza Quincentenario
Museum of the Americas
Plaza Coloó
Felisa Rincon de Gautier Museum
Tapia Theatre
Caribe Hilton Hotel
Condado Plaza Hotel
La Concha Hotel
Excelsior Hotel
Performing Arts Center
El San Juan Hotel
Luis Muñoz Marin Airport
Isla Grande Airport
Plaza Las Américas
Cano de San Antonio
Bahia De San Juan
Bahía de Puerto Nuevo
Laguna Los Corozos
Laguna San Jose
San Sebastian
Muñoz Rivera
Fernandez Juncos
San Augustin
Ave Miramar
Calle Cerna
Las Plamas
Expreso Muñoz Rivera
Dr. Ashford
Calle Loiza
Baldorioty De Castro Expreso
Puerto Rico
Eduardo Conde
Ponce De Leon
Ave Isla Verdes
Boca de Cangrejo
Borinquen
Calle Tapia
Calle Prudencio
Rivera Martinez
Quisqueya
Dr. Barbosa
Jose Marti
Franklin D. Roosevelt
Calle Chardon
Arteria
C. Juan Ponce de Leon
187
26
37
36
25
1
41
22
35
2

bles are available as well as camp facilities. Also suitable for swimming is **Seven Seas**, a long strand with compacted sand. Trailers may be parked nearby as well as tents pitched. Water sports of all kinds can be arranged at **Sun Bay**, a sugar-white beach on Vieques. Vessels for sailing may be rented here. One of the most famous beaches is **Condado Beach**, along Ashford Avenue in San Juan. It's a beauty-watcher's delight, especially for those who want to see the latest trend in swimwear and the prettiest island girls. Within walking distance are the long beaches of **Rincón**, **Cabo Rojo** and **Paguera**. Surfers claim that the best waves are along the Atlantic coastline from Borinquén Point south to Rincón. The surf is best from October through April. In summer, La Concha and Aviones have the best curls. All these beaches have board rentals nearby.

The best beaches near San Juan, are at Isla Verde in front of the major hotels.

What Else to See Around the Island

The world's largest rum distillery is the famed **Bacardi Distillery**, a short hop across the San Juan Bay by ferry. Daily tours are offered through its 127 acres and plant, where 100,000 gallons can be distilled daily. Complimentary rum drinks are offered at the beginning of the tour, so by the time you've finished, you're bonkered enough to want to stock up at the gift shop. The prices of Bacardi rums are better here than in the U.S. and some rums not sold on the mainland are excellent presents for the "exclusive" sort.

The **Arecibo Observatory** (two hours west of San Juan) is the site of the world's largest radar/radio telescope, operated by Cornell University and the National Science Foundation. Here scientists monitor radio emissions from distant galaxies, pulsars, mysterious quasars and, perhaps, even more mysterious sources. This is also home base for **SETI**, the Search for Extraterrestrial Intelligence, and rumor has it that great strides has been made in that direction, although the results of research still remains difficult to obtain. A 600-ton suspended platform hovers over a 20-acre dish set in a sinkhole 565 feet below.

After 30 years of silence, the **Hacienda Buena Vista**, an early 19th-century coffee plantation, has been reopened to the public following a massive restoration. Located along the Canas River just north of Ponce, the hacienda is a step back in time, and visitors are invited to explore the plantation's mills and two-story estate house, observe original machinery in action, and enjoy a sensory feast—coffee drying in the trays, and pineapples and bananas growing on the hillsides. The ground floor of the manor estate, now a museum, contains old maps, photographs, bills of sale and other memorabilia of hacienda life. The rooms have been furnished with authentic period pieces from the 1850s, right down to the chamber pots, armoires, bathtubs and family portraits. Experts have considered the machinery—dating from the early days of the industrial revolution—of international importance because such machines rarely survived on the U.S. mainland. The entire estate resembles a hamlet of bygone days, including the manor house, the coffee and corn mills, a masonry storage shed that doubles as a hurricane shelter, and the former slave quarters that became a coffee storage and drying shed. Feel free to take a leisurely stroll on paths over which wagons once traveled carrying sacks of just harvested coffee beans or newly milled cornmeal. The hills surrounding Buena Vista (aptly named "beautiful view") are rich with gurgling streams, cascading waterfalls and a variety of plant and animal life. Ducks wander freely over the grounds. Also available for sighting are the Puerto Rican screech owl, the mangrove cuckoo and the hummingbird.

Historical Sites

Capilla de Cristo ★★★

Calle del Cristo, Old San Juan, ☎ (809) 721-2400.

The Christ Chapel was built in 1753 after a horse rider's life was supposedly spared after a tragic accident. (Supposedly, because historical records say the youth did, indeed, die.) In any event, the small silver altar is dedicated to the Christ of Miracles.

Casa de los Contrafuertes ★★★★

Calle San Sebastian 101, Old San Juan, ☎ (809) 724-5477.

Hours open: 9 a.m.–4:30 p.m.

Called the House of Buttresses (for obvious reasons once you see it), this is believed to be the oldest residence left in Old San Juan, dating back to the early 18th century. Inside are two museums, one devoted to graphic arts, the other displaying a 19th-century pharmacy.

Cathedral de San Juan ★★★

Calle del Cristo 151, Old San Juan, ☎ (809) 722-0861.

Hours open: 8:30 a.m.–4:30 p.m.

The San Juan Cathedral was built in 1540, destroyed by hurricane in 1529, looted in 1598, and damaged by another hurricane in 1615. Today it holds the remains of Ponce de Leon and the relic of San Pio, a Roman martyr. Sunday masses begin at 9:00 a.m.

Convento de los Dominicos ★★★

Plaza de San Jose, Old San Juan, ☎ (809) 724-5949.

This was Puerto Rico's first convent, started in 1523. It was home to Dominican friars until 1838, when it became barracks for the United States Army. Today, it is headquarters for the Institute of Puerto Rican Culture. Inside you'll find the old chapel, art exhibits and a fine gift shop.

Fort San Cristobel ★★★★

Calle Norzagaray, Old San Juan, ☎ *(809) 729-6960.*
Hours open: 9 a.m.–5 p.m.
This massive fort dates back to 1634. Its walls rise 150 feet above sea level, and it covers 27 acres. Now run under the auspices of the National Park Service, the site includes a replica of 18th-century Spanish troop barracks. Free tours are given daily from 10:00 a.m.–4:00 p.m.

Fort San Jeronimo ★★★

Next to the Caribe Hilton, Cordado Bay, ☎ *(809) 724-5949.*
This tiny fort was attacked by the British in 1797, 11 years after it was built. Now run by the Institute of Puerto Rican Culture, it houses a small military museum.

Fuerte San Felipe del Morro ★★★★

Calle Norzagaray, Old San Juan, ☎ *(809) 729-6960.*
Hours open: 9 a.m.–5 p.m.
This fort, commonly known as El Morro, guards the entrance to San Juan Bay. The Spaniards started construction in 1540, but it wasn't until 1787 that the fort was deemed complete. Now run under the auspices of the National Park Service, the six-level fort can be explored via guided tours (free, from 10 a.m. to 4 p.m.) or on your own. The dramatic fort contains dungeons, lookouts, barracks and vaults, as well as a small museum on its history.

Governor Mansion

Recito Oeste Street, Old San Juan, ☎ *(809) 721-2400.*
Hours open: 9 a.m.–4 p.m.
Puerto Rico boasts a lot of "oldest in the Western Hemisphere" —here's the oldest executive mansion in continuous use. It started as a fortress in 1553 and is the office and residence of Puerto Rico's governor. Now a U.S. National Historic Site, the mansion can be toured in the mornings, with tours of the gardens running all day.

Inglesia de San Jose ★★★

Plaza de San Jose, Old San Juan, ☎ *(809) 725-7501.*
Hours open: 8:30 a.m.–4 p.m.
The San Jose Church is the second-oldest in the Western Hemisphere, dating back to 1532. It was originally a Dominican chapel and was the family church of Ponce de Leon's descendants, many of whom are buried here. Among the highlights are a crucifix that belonged to the explorer, oil paintings by Jose Campeche and Francisco Oller, and ornate processional floats. Sunday mass is at 12:15 p.m.

Museums and Exhibits

Casa Blanca ★★★

Calle San Sebastian 1, San Juan, ☎ *(809) 724-4102.*
The land on which the "White House" sits was given to explorer Ponce de Leon by the Spanish Crown. He died before the house was built in 1521, but his descendants lived there for some 250 years. In 1779, it was taken over by the Spanish military, then used later by the United States as a residence for military commanders. Today the mansion is restored to its former glory and is a National Historic Monument. It houses two museums, one on the Taino Indians (believed to be Puerto Rico's first inhabitants) and one on the house's history, with emphasis on life in the 16th and 18th centuries. Casa Blanca is the oldest continuously occupied residence in the Western Hemisphere.

La Casa del Libro ★★★

Calle del Cristo, Old San Juan, ☎ *(809) 723-0354.*
Hours open: 11 a.m.–4:30 p.m.
Exhibits on printing and bookmaking are displayed at this 19th-century house. Noteworthy are pages from the Gutenberg Bible, a decree signed by Ferdinand and Isabella concerning Columbus' second voyage, and other pre-16th century examples of the art.

Museo de Arte y Historia ★★★

Calle Norzagaray, Old San Juan, ☎ *(809) 724-1875.*
This center for Puerto Rican arts and crafts displays works by local artists. It was a marketplace in the 1850s in a previous incarnation. Audiovisual shows in English on the city's history are shown daily at 11 a.m. and 1:15 p.m.

Museo de Pablo Casals ★★★

Calle San Sebastian 101, Old San Juan, ☎ *(809) 723-9185.*
Hours open: 9:30 a.m.–5:30 p.m.
The famed Spanish cellist spent his last years in Puerto Rico, leaving behind a collection of memorabilia from his long and distinguished career. The 18th-century house displays his cello, manuscripts and photos from his life, as well as videotaped performances, shown on request.

Parks and Gardens

Cabezas de San Juan Nature Res ★★★★

Route 987, Fajardo, ☎ *(809) 722-5882.*
Located on a peninsula, this nature reserve encompasses 316 acres and 124 acres of lagoons. It contains all of Puerto Rico's ecosystems except for the rainforest. A two-hour guided tour (reservations essential) will take you through a half-mile-long coral reef, mangrove swamps, beaches, a dry forest, and beds of turtle grass (thalassia). A highlight is El Faro, a lighthouse built in 1880 and still used by the U.S. Coast Guard. The small nature center in the lighthouse, which is a designated National Historic Place, has touch tanks, aquariums, and an observation deck. Bilingual tours are at 9:30 a.m., 10 a.m., 10:30 a.m.; the one at 2 p.m. is in English only. Well worth a visit.

Theatre

Centro de Ballas Artes ★★★★

De Diego and Ponce de Leon avs, San Juan, ☎ *(809) 724-4747.*
This fine arts center is the largest in the Caribbean. Call the box office or inquire at your hotel about events—from operas to plays—while you're in town

Teatro Tapia ★★★★

Ave. Ponce de Leon, San Juan, ☎ *(809) 722-0470.*
Dating back to 1832, this is one of the Western Hemisphere's oldest theaters. It is named after Puerto Rican playwright Alejandro Tapia y Rivera. Check with the box office for a schedule for upcoming plays and cultural events.

Tours

Bacardi Rum Plant ★★★

Poute 888, Catano, ☎ *(809) 788-1500.*
Located across the bay from San Juan (a short hop ferry), this plant offers 45-minute tours at 9 a.m., 10:30 a.m., noon, and 4 p.m. You'll see the distillery and bottling plant, and get to judge the results yourself.

Caribbean National Forest ★★★★★

Near Luquillo Beach, Puerto Rico, ☎ *(809) 887-2875.*
Known simply as El Yunque, this pristine spot encompasses 28,000 acres of virgin rainforest, with some 240 species of tropical trees, flowers and wildlife. It is home

to rare creatures like the Puerto Rican boa, which grows to seven feet, the colorful Puerto Rican parrot, and 26 other species found nowhere else. There are more than 20 kinds of orchids, 50 varieties of ferns, and millions of tiny tree frogs, who serenade visitors with their tiny croaks. Stop at the Sierra Palm Visitor Center on Route 191 to peruse the interesting exhibits and pick up a map. Numerous trails traverse the park, leading to waterfalls, natural pools and the peak of El Toro.

Rio Camuy Cave Park ★★★★

Route 129, near Arecibo, ☎ *(809) 898-3100.*
Hours open: 8 a.m.–4 p.m.
Located in Northwest Puerto Rico, 2.5 hours from San Juan, is one of the world's largest cave networks. Sixteen entrances have been found and seven miles of passages explored so far. A tram takes you to the cave, where you get out and walk through, passing sinkholes, one of the world's largest underground rivers, and giant stalagmites and stalactites. The Taino Indians, believed to be Puerto Rico's first inhabitants, also explored the cave. Reservations are essential, as this place is understandably popular.

Sports

Every water sport imaginable is played on Puerto Rico's 272 miles of beachfront. *Balnearios* (public beaches) offer lockers, showers and parking at nominal rates, though they are closed on Mondays, Election Day and Good Friday. For information about overnight stays call ☎ *(809)722-1551* or *721-2800.* The Puerto Rico Water Sport Federation sets standards and guidelines for members specializing in scuba diving, snorkeling, sailing, deep-sea fishing, windsurfing and other aquatic activities. Members, including the Caribbean School of Aquatics, Coral Head Divers, and many others, can make arrangements for surfing (the 1988 World Cup Surfing Championship was held in Aguadilla), scuba diving, sailing, etc. Arrangements can also be made at the island's many resort hotels.

Puerto Rico hosts many deep-sea fishing tournaments, in which 30 world records have been broken. The **Annual Billfish Tournament** is the world's largest consecutively held tournament of its kind. Deep-sea fishing boats can be chartered in San Juan, Fajardo, Humaco, Mayaguez and other towns. Lake fishing for largemouth bass, peacock bass, sunfish, catfish and tilapia is also popular. For more details, contact the **Department of Natural Resources** ☎ *(809) 722-5938.*

Horseback riding is tremendous on Puerto Rico—the island's palm-lined beaches are romantic settings. Riding and/or trail riding can be arranged through the Palmas del Mar Equestrian Center or the Hacienda Carabali.

Tennis is omnipresent here—there are over 100 tennis courts throughout the island, including 17 in San Juan's Central Park. A total of nine **golf championships** take place on Puerto Rico (public as well as at major resorts). The Hyatt Regency Cerromar and the Hyatt Dorado Beach resorts have two 18-hole Robert Trent Jones courses each. The newest 18-hole course is east of

San Juan at the Bahia Beach Plantation. The Berwind Country Club near Rio Grande has an 18-hole course open to the public on Tuesdays, Thursdays and Fridays (except holidays). Ramey Golf Club, an 18-hole course, is located on the former Ramey Air Force Base in Aguadilla, in the northwestern part of the island. Greens fees and prices of equipment rentals vary with the season.

Cockfighting is a popular native spectator sport in Puerto Rico, particularly in the Cordillera Central.

Boating and Cruising

Various locations, Puerto Rico.

Lots of firms will take you out on the high seas for a simple sail or snorkel trip. Most charge about $45 per person. Try: **Fondo de Cristal** *(☎ (809) 889-5891)*, **Island Safari** *(☎ (809) 728-6606)*, **Spread Eagle** *(☎ (809) 863-1905)*, **Erin Go Braugh** *(☎ (809) 860-4401)*, **East Wind Catamaran** *(☎ (809) 863-2821)*, **Captain Jack Becker** *(☎ (809) 860-0861)*, and **Land and Sea Excursions** *(☎ (809) 382-4877)*.

Golf

Various locations, Puerto Rico.

Unlike most of the Caribbean islands, which have just one or two golf courses (if any), Puerto Rico has a wealth of greens. All are 18-hole courses unless otherwise noted. Rio Grande: **Bahia Beach Plantation** *(☎ (809) 256-5600)*, **Berwind Country Club** *(☎ (809) 876-3056)*, **Club Riomar** *(☎ (809) 887-3964)*. Fajardo: **Conquistador Resort** (☎ *(809) 863-1000)*. Dorado: **Dorado del Mar Country Club** (nine holes, ☎ *(809) 796-2030)*, **Hyatts Dorado and Cerromar** (38 holes, ☎ *(809) 796-1234)*. Humacao: **Palmas del Mar Resort** *(☎ 852-6000)* Aguadilla: **Punta Borinquen** *(☎ (809) 890-2987)*. Call **Luiz Ortiz** *(☎ (809) 786-3859)* for access to courses in metropolitan San Juan.

Horseback Riding

Various locations, Puerto Rico.

Just hop on a horse and ride off into the sunset (or along the beach or through the rainforest) at **Hacienda Carabali** *(☎ (809) 889-5820)* or **Palmas del Mar's** Equestrian Center *(☎ (809) 852-6000)*.

Watersports

Various locations, Puerto Rico.

For general watersport equipment rentals, **Carib Aquatic Adventures in Miramar** *(☎ (809) 724-1882)* does everything from boat rentals to deep-sea fishing excursions. For scuba diving, call: **Adventure by the Sea** *(Cerro Gordo, ☎ (809) 251-4923)*, **Caribbean Divers** *(☎ (809) 722-7393)*, **Caribbean School of Aquatics** *(Condado, ☎ (809) 728-6606)*, **Coral Head Divers** *(Humacao, ☎ (809) 850-7208)*, **Dorado Marine Center** *(☎ (809) 796-4645)*, and **Mundo Submarino** *(Isla Verde, ☎ (809) 791-5764)*. For deep-sea fishing, try: **Benitez** *(San Juan, ☎ (809) 723-2292)*, **Makaira Hunter** *(Miramar, ☎ (809) 397-8028)*, **Southern Witch** *(Miramar, ☎ (809) 731-9252)*, **Western Tourist Services** *(☎ (809) 834-4008)*.

Where to Eat

Fielding's Highest Rated Restaurants in Puerto Rico		
★★★★★	Horned Dorset Primavera	$15–$45
★★★★★	La Compostela	$15–$29
★★★★★	Ramiro's	$24–$33
★★★★	Amadeus	$8–$16
★★★★	La Chaumiere	$22–$37
★★★	Ajilli-Mojili	$15–$25
★★★	Back Street Hong Kong	$15–$32
★★★	La Casona de Serafin	$10–$31
★★★	La Mallorquina	$14–$30
★★★	Parador Villa Parguera	$5–$20

Fielding's Special Restaurants in Puerto Rico		
★★★★★	Horned Dorset Primavera	$15–$45
★★★★★	La Compostela	$15–$29
★★★★★	Ramiro's	$24–$33
★★★★	La Chaumiere	$22–$37
★★★	AjilliMojili	$15–$25

Fielding's Budget Restaurants in Puerto Rico		
★★	Butterfly People	$5–$9
★★★	La Bombonera	$5–$8
★★★★	Amadeus	$8–$16
★★	Al Dente	$10–$15
★★★	Parador Villa Parguera	$5–$20

The first thing you must learn before sitting down to eat in Puerto Rico is the lively island equivalent to "bon appetit"—*¡buen provecho!* The phrase becomes easily prophetic here where traditional island fare as well as contemporary cuisine is lovingly and expertly prepared. Puerto Rican cuisine is a delicious blend of Spanish, African and Taíno Indian cooking. Each of these traditions have contributed in terms of seasonings, cooking methods and basic ingredients. *Cocina criolla* or creole cuisine, began with the Taínos, the indigenous tribe of the island. The Taínos cultivated many crops, notably *yuca* (yucca), corn, yam and *yautía* (taniers). Yuca was used to prepare *casabe*, a flatbread that was eaten daily and is still enjoyed today. Taínos also used yuca to make vinegar, which was an important seasoning since salt was not used in cooking. Foods introduced by the Spaniards include wheat, chickpeas, cilantro, eggplant, onions, coconut, garlic and rum. The African slave trade also brought important foods and techniques to the island, including pidgin peas, plantains and okra. The African population is also credited with developing many coconut dishes that remain popular today. Their favorite technique was frying, which quickly became the most common way of cooking on the island. The blending of flavors and ingredients evolved from generation to generation, combining to form the Puerto Rican cuisine today.

As for noshing, the island has no lack of things on which to while away your calories. Fritters are the favorite finger food, and are sold at fritter stands and even incorporated into the daily menus in most homes. The most famous fritters are *tostones* (fried green plantains), which are used as well as a side dish with rice and beans, onion steak or fried pork chops. Other favorites include *alcapurrias*, made from grated yautia, and green bananas, stuffed with *picadillo* (cooked ground meat), crabmeat or chicken, *empanadillas*, small deep-fried flour turnovers with cheddar or swiss cheese, ground meat or shredded chicken; *bacalaítos*, flour fritters made from salt codfish; *surrullos de maíz* or *surrullitos*, made of cornmeal, shaped like a cigar and served with a sauce made of mayonnaise and ketchup; and *rellenos de papa*, mashed potato balls stuffed with almost any filling and deep-fried to a crispy texture. Other traditional appetizers are chicken nuggets and marinated green bananas. The latter are now combined with the new ingredients such as flavored vinegars to create interesting variations found even in elegant restaurants.

Get used to the fact that side dishes are often as hearty as the main dish in Puerto Rico. In fact, if you are dieting and/or trying to save money, eating side dishes can be your vacation saver. Nearly standard for every meal in Puerto Rico is *arroz blanco* (white rice boiled in water and oil), and *habichuelas* (beans stewed in sofrito (piré of onions, peppers, cilantro, garlic, and salt pork), and a tomato and coriander sauce. *Mofongo* is also popular—fried green plantains mashed with garlic, salt and fried pork rinds and rolled into a ball. It's usually served with beef or chicken broth or *carne frita* (pork meat, diced and fried).

The national soup of Puerto Rico is *asopao*, a hearty chicken and rice gumbo-like soup which can serve as an entree. Sometimes it's made with lobster and shrimp. Roast suckling pig is a national dish, especially for holidays. Steak and onions is an everyday dish, as are pork ribs stewed or prepared with yellow rice and green pigeon peas. With such exquisite access to the sea, fish dishes are supremely fresh and display the island's Spanish heritage, as they are mostly prepared in a sofrito-based sauce or *escabeche* (marinated) style. Escabeche is a combination of olive oil, white vinegar and spices. *Bacalho* (salt cod) has been a menu staple for centuries; other seafood to look for are red snapper, shrimp, langostinos (saltwater crayfish), mussels, and the spiny lobster characteristic of the Caribbean. The national dessert is flan, a condensed milk and vanilla custard, variations of which can be made by adding any one of the following ingredients: cream cheese, coconut milk, mashed pumpkin, or breadfruit. Puerto Ricans also prepare bread pudding: *tembleqque*, a gelatin-like coconut milk and cornstarch custard often eaten sprinkled with cinnamon, *arroz con dulce*, rice pudding cooked with condensed coconut milk, ginger and raisins, and fruit sherbets made with tamarins and soursop. Other favorite desserts are green papaya or guava shells simmered in heavy syrup and served with white or cottage cheese.

Puerto Rican coffee is exquisitely aromatic, served either black or with frothy boiled milk. Since Puerto Rico is the leading producer of rum, you'll find the piña coladas on the island some of the tastiest you've ever had.

Ajilli-Mojili **$$$** ★★★

Calle Clemenceau.
Latin American cuisine. Specialties: Mofongo.
Lunch: entrees $15–$25.
Dinner: entrees $15–$25.

This is probably one of the most popular eateries for tipico Puerto Rican food. A specialty is Mofongo, fried plantain stuffed with seafood, beef or chicken (here it's usually shrimp), a dish you probably won't find outside of these isles. Although it's located in a Condado hotel, many local families make this a regular gathering spot, so the ambience is cheerful and festive.

Al Dente **$$** ★★

Calle Recinto Sur, Old San Juan, ☎ (809) 723-7303.
Italian cuisine. Specialties: Fresh Pasta.
Lunch: Noon–4 p.m., entrees $10–$15.
Dinner: 4–10 p.m., entrees $10–$15.

This restaurant is a touch of old Palermo in Old San Juan. Located in a historical building in the heart of the colonial city, the dining room features fresh pasta, chicken and fish in light sauces, utilizing fresh herbs and spices. The atmosphere is as unstuffy as the food.

Amadeus **$$** ★★★★

Calle San Sebastian, Old San Juan, ☎ (809) 722-8635.
Latin American cuisine.
Lunch: entrees $8–$16.
Dinner: entrees $8–$16.

A name like Amadeus connotes glittering candelabra, spinets and powdered wigs. Contrary to that idea, this restaurant and cafe is as modern as can be—the clever chef adds a dash of French flair to native dishes; for example, a combination of caviar and sour cream with green plantain. A version of cassoulet is made here with chorizo and black beans. Some people could make a whole meal from a plate of some very creative appetizers that a group of four or more can share; a sort of Puerto Rican dim sum. Call in advance to reserve space in the back room. It's open from noon to midnight.

Anchor's Inn **$$$** ★★

Route 987, Km. 2.7, Fajardo, ☎ (809) 863-7200.
Latin American cuisine.
Lunch: 11 a.m.–4 p.m., entrees $8–$15.
Dinner: 4–11 p.m., entrees $15–$20.

This unpretentious spot by the sea offers a scrumptious plate of paella and an equally appealing vista of the Fajardo harbor. It's an ideal stopping point for people driving around the island, with a location near one of Puerto Rico's prime boating and watersports areas. If you tire of the nine restaurants at the posh El Conquistador resort nearby, give this place a try; it stays open late.

Back Street Hong Kong **$$$** ★★★

Avenida de Isla Verde, Isla Verde, ☎ *(809) 791-1000.*
Chinese cuisine.
Dinner: 6 p.m.–midnight, entrees $15–$32.
This isn't your typical greasy spoon chop-suey, in fact, people like to dress up a bit to eat the savory Chinese food in a restaurant that recreates a Hong Kong back alley. The eclectic dining room was transported piecemeal from a Seattle World's Fair exhibition; it also contains a tropical aquarium that delights young children.

Butterfly People **$** ★★

152 Calle Fortaleza, Old San Juan, ☎ *(809) 723-2432.*
International cuisine.
Lunch: 10 a.m.–6 p.m., entrees $5–$9.
Notice to lepidopterists—you will be dazzled at this restaurant and gallery that sells butterflies under glass from one of the most extensive private collections in the world. While the prices for these winged beauties range from moderate to stratospheric, the mostly-Puerto Rican dishes here are fairly reasonable. You can also have a soup (gazpacho is good), or salad in a plant-filled patio.

El Patio de Sam **$$$** ★★★

102 Calle San Sebastian, Old San Juan, ☎ *(809) 723-1149.*
International cuisine.
Lunch: entrees $9–$25.
Dinner: entrees $9–$25.
This oft-visited eatery is remarkable for serving the juiciest burgers in town in the oldest building in town. Of course, there's a well-balanced menu of lobster tail, soups, desserts and tropical fruit libations. The late-night crowd likes to party here; it stays open till the wee hours on weekends.

La Bombonera **$** ★★★

Calle San Francisco, Old San Juan, ☎ *(809) 722-0658.*
Latin American cuisine.
Lunch: entrees $5–$8.
Dinner: entrees $5–$8.
Like its name says, this old-fashioned eatery proffers a plethora of bonbons both sweet and savory. You can have a plate of *calamares en su tinta* (squid in its own ink served with rice), while your youngster sips hot chocolate. This place serves as the corner malt shop and tryst spot for locals who have been flocking to it since 1902. It's great for breakfast, very crowded at lunch, and ideal for tea and snacks. Takeout available. It's open from 7:30 am to 8:30 p.m.

La Casona de Serafin **$$$** ★★★

Hwy 102, Km. 9, Cabo Rojo, ☎ *(809) 851-0066.*
Latin American cuisine. Specialties: Lobster.
Lunch: entrees $10–$20.
Dinner: entrees $21–$31.
Some people think the best seafood in Puerto Rico is served in this area of Joyuda Beach. Certainly the atmosphere at La Casona is great for eating peel-it-yourself shrimp or its specialty, lobster. Steaks and Puerto Rican dishes are also available, and there's a full bar and lounge. This restaurant is popular with local families who flock here on weekends, when the sleepy town wakes up to a noisy string of craft shops and oyster bars along the beach.

La Chaumiere **$$$** ★★★★

367 Tetuan Street, Old San Juan, ☎ *(809) 722-3330.*
French cuisine.
Dinner: 6 p.m.–midnight, entrees $22–$37.

This restaurant serves classic French cuisine to a faithful clientele in surroundings that transport guests to the Gallic countryside. It's the kind of place where you can order rarely-found specialties like floating island (merengues in a sauce of creme anglaise) or oysters Rockefeller. Perfect for a pre-show supper; it's located behind the famous Tapia Theater.

La Compostela **$$$** ★★★★★

Avenida Condado, Santurce, ☎ (809) 724-6088.
Spanish cuisine.
Lunch: Noon–3 p.m., entrees $15–$29.
Dinner: 6:30–10:30 p.m., entrees $15–$29.
Many repeat visitors recommend this Spanish restaurant with a French touch in a commercial suburb of San Juan. The owner has spent time laboring in the kitchens in both countries; he blends the styles effortlessly. The wine cellar is amazing: close to 10,000 bottles!

La Mallorquina **$$$** ★★★

Calle San Justo 207, Old San Juan, ☎ (809) 722-3261.
Latin American cuisine.
Lunch: 11:30 a.m.–3 p.m., entrees $14–$30.
Dinner: 4–10 p.m., entrees $14–$30.
This restaurant may be a bit of a tourist trap, but it's still worth visiting for the house special asopao, the Puerto Rican version of risotto, served with a choice of seafood or chicken. It's one of the oldest restaurants in town, founded in 1848. Service is gracious and attentive.

Parador Villa Parguera **$$** ★★★

Route 307, Lajas, ☎ (809) 899-7777.
Latin American cuisine. Specialties: Red Snapper Stuffed with Seafood.
Lunch: 7:30 a.m.–4 p.m., entrees $5–$20.
Dinner: 4–9:30 p.m., entrees $5–$20.
Simply prepared but very fresh seafood is a specialty at this seaside inn (one of the island's touted "paradores") surrounded by coconut palms on Phosphorescent Bay, on the West Coast. The Parador is an excellent base for viewing the local phenomenon—on moonlit nights, the bay is "lit" by thousands of tiny organisms called dinoflagellates. Come during the week, as hordes of families crowd the area on weekends.

Ramiro's **$$$** ★★★★★

Avenida Magdalena 1106, Condado, ☎ (809) 721-9049.
Spanish cuisine. Specialties: Lamb, Homemade Desserts.
Lunch: Noon–3 p.m., entrees $24–$33.
Dinner: 6:30–10:30 p.m., prix fixe $22–$33.
Patrons dress up to dine at this plush salon of cocina fantastica; owner Jesus Ramiro may be the island's most creative chef. Although he uses local produce and ingredients, his technique is distinctly French, especially in the elaborate constructions of his sinful desserts. Lamb is one of his favorite meats to work with, on the menu you will find it in ravioli or paired with buffalo or venison in a spicy sauce, or a perfectly roasted rack.

The Chart House **$$$** ★★

1214 Ashford Avenue, Condado, ☎ (809) 728-0110.
American cuisine. Specialties: Prime Rib, Mud Pie.
Dinner: 6–11 p.m., entrees $16–$25.
If the food here seems familiar to mainland guests, it is. The Chart House is a local link in the California-based steak and lobster chain, but what a link! The setting is in a historic turn-of-the-century homestead, which belonged to the Rauschenplat

family. The property is surrounded by well-tended gardens and a treehouse. The all-American food is very popular with locals as well.

Where to Shop

Puerto Rico has duty-free shopping at the Luis Munoz Marin International Airport and several factory outlets in Old San Juan. Both traditional and contemporary items can be bought in Old San Juan and out on the island, and you shouldn't go home without at least some representative of local craft. A day's excursion in a car could be spent touring the island to visit various craftsmen in their studios. (When you meet an artist and then buy his work, his personality and your memory of him or her always become indelibly entwined with the object itself—one of the true meanings of art.) The **Puerto Rico Tourism Company** ☎ *(809) 721-2400* offers a researched list of studios to visit along with a map to help you get there. Some studios are only open to the public at specific times, so make sure your itinerary fits the schedules. Possible workshops range from wood carvers to hammock-makers, to jewelry and furniture makers. It is always fascinating to visit the studio of an artisan who makes *santos* (saints); they are usually very spiritual people and the atmosphere of the saints themselves often pervades the workshop.

Even without the Biennial, Old San Juan has a remarkably lively arts scene. Walking along Cristo and San Jose Streets, you could lose count of the galleries. One of the best known is the **Galeria Botello** at *208 Cristo* with works by local artists as well as the Spanish artist Angel Botello and a fine collection of santos (small carved wooden figures of saints).

You'll find modern santos, carnival masks, pottery and the like at **Puerto Rican Arts and Crafts** at *204 Fortaleza*, old San Juan. And you can still get a Panama hat ($30–$50) at the **Casa Mendez Suarez**, which has been at *251 San Justo* since 1886, and elaborate flowered Spanish fans ($3.95 and up) at **La Nueva Opera**, *254 Fortaleza*. Another good place to check out is **La Piazoleta**, a Puerto Rican Craft Center, at *Pier 3, at the Customs House in Old San Juan.*

Old San Juan is also thick with antiques stores, including **El Alcazar** at *103 San Jose* and *109 Sol.* Both locations concentrate on 17th- and 18th-century Spanish art and 19th- and 20th-century French bibelots and brocante, and can ship home anything you buy.

The Book Store at *255 San Jose, Old San Juan*, has a good selection of English-language books as well as books on Puerto Rico, and CDs of Puerto Rican danza and salsa music.

Calle Fortaleza in Old San Juan is a treasurehouse of boutiques and stores. If you're in need of brightly colored resort wear made of special batiks and tie-dyes, stop by **La Casita**. On **Calle San Francisco**, the finest of the island's handmade lace can be found at **Aguadilla en San Juan**, including tablecloths and dresses.

East and Southeast Coast

Fajardo and Humacao

Full of small-town spirit, the seaport of Fajardo lies but five miles south of Las Cabezas on Route 3. The lifestyle is slower-paced than in San Juan, and you can take morning and afternoon ferries to Culebra and Vieques. Treks can be made to the **Caribbean National Forest**, of which El Yunque Mountain is a part (see "Treks" above) and Losquillo Beach. Special expeditions can be arranged through Las Cabezas Nature Reserve (see "Trek" above) which could last all day, especially if you are interested in bird-watching. Native sloops set sail for Iacos where you will find fine snorkeling and swimming conditions. Deep-sea fishing and other watersports can be arranged at the **Puerto del Rey Marina**. The region has a fine 18-hole golf course and myriads of opportunities for scuba (see "Dive Sites" above.) Also see "Sports" above for more information.

This part of the island can be reached by taxis (expensive from the international airport), by small planes that land at the airport of Palmas del Mar, near Humacao; or by ferry boat (the cheapest at $2.50).

Where to Eat

Best cuisine is found at the resorts; with so many facilities at **El Conquistador**, you may never have to leave the premises (that's their goal). Snacks can be found beachside (a cheap way to get through lunch on your way to a more expensive dinner). The best Italian food (if the most expensive) is at the **Azzuro** at the Palamas Mar Marriott hotel.

The South Coast

Ponce

Ponce is Puerto Rico's second-largest city, located about 70 miles south and west of San Juan. It dates back to 1692 when Ponce de Léon's great-grandson founded the small community. A high-speed road connects the two cities, which takes only about 90 minutes to traverse; you can also reach the area by plane from San Juan's International Airport. Many historical buildings, such as the stunning Cathedral of Our Lady of Guadeloupe, are masterpieces of construction, as are some one thousand colonial houses designated national historic sites in a 40-by-80-block area. Nineteenth-century gas lamps illuminate the marble-edged streets glimmering with a pink glow; at night the stroll is extremely romantic. A fine collection of Latin American artists and international masters can be found in the **Museu de Arte de Ponce**, a light, airy place to stroll and relax out of the sun. Particularly fine are the works by Rubens and Rodin as well as many pre-Raphaelite paintings and sculptures. Anyone interested in sugarcane production and plantations will find an interesting exhibit at the **Castillo Serralles**, a restored 19th-century mansion, which has been refurbished to its 1930s furnishings. On Route 10, you'll discover the **Hacienda Buena Vista**, a restored coffee plantation which is open to visitors.

BEST VIEW:

A terrific perspective of the surrounding countryside and town can be seen from the 100-foot-tall El Vigia, an observatory tower, next to Castillo Serrallés.

What Else to See

Historical Sites

Hacienda Buena Vista ★★★

Route 10, near Ponce, ☎ (809) 848-7020.

From 1833 to the 1950s, this thriving plantation produced corn, citrus fruits and coffee. Today, under the auspices of Puerto Rico's Conservation Trust, it is a reconstructed farm from the late 19th century. Reservations are required for 1.5-hour tours, which are conducted Friday through Sunday; call ☎ *722-5882*. The grounds include the estate house, former slave quarters, a 60-foot water slide, and working corn and coffee mills.

Tibes Indian Ceremonial Center ★★★

Route 503, near Ponce, ☎ (809) 840-2255.

Hours open: 9 a.m.–4:30 p.m.

This is the oldest cemetery in the Antilles, with some 200 skeletons unearthed from A.D. 300 and ballcourts and dance grounds from A.D. 700. The site also includes a recreated Taino village and a museum.

Museums and Exhibits

El Museo Castillo Serralles ★★★

El Virgia 17, Ponce, ☎ (809) 259-1774.

Hours open: 10 a.m.–5 p.m.

This Spanish-Revival mansion, Ponce's largest building, dates back to the 1930s. It is the former home of the Serralles family, producers of Don Q rum. Today it is a museum exhibiting elegant furnishings, the history of the local rum industry and a cafe. The lavishly landscaped grounds are a treat, and the views up here are breathtaking.

Museo de Arte de Ponce ★★★★

Ave. las Americas 25, Ponce, ☎ (809) 848-0505.

Designed by Edward Durell Stone, this fanciful museum exhibits traditional and modern art from the Americas and Europe, as well as contemporary works by Puerto Ricans.

Ponce History Museum ★★★

Calle Isabel, Ponce, ☎ (809) 844-7071.

Hours open: 10 a.m.–5 p.m.

The name says it all: the history of Ponce detailed in two wooden houses dating back to the turn of the century. Closed Tuesday.

Where to Eat

El Ancla **$$$** ★★★

9 Hostos Avenue, Ponce, ☎ (809) 840-2450.

Seafood cuisine.

Lunch: 11 a.m.–4 p.m., entrees $3–$28.

Dinner: 4 p.m.–midnight, entrees $3–$28.

This is an established family-owned restaurant perched over the water in Ponce Beach. Although it's long been popular with Poncenos and visitors, the welcome is always warm. That's probably what sets it apart from other restaurants serving seafood, which is the specialty of this eatery. Enjoy red snapper stuffed with lobster and shrimp served on a plate heaped with plenty of starchy side dishes.

Lupita's Mexican **$$$** ★★

Calle Isabel 60, Ponce, ☎ (809) 848-8808.

Mexican cuisine.

Lunch: 11 a.m.–4 p.m., entrees $7–$26.

Dinner: 4–11 p.m., entrees $7–$26.

The better-than-average Mexican fare served here is blended with local specialties—lobster is grilled and served with green plantain, but you can also have tacos and nachos. Entertainment is provided several times a week by mariachis. It's located in a historic building near Plaza las Delicias, Ponce's main square. Lupita's stays open until 2 a.m. on Saturdays and until midnight on Sundays.

The West Coast

Mayaguez

Mayaguez is the island's third-largest town, located about 10 miles from Rinceon on Route 2. Baroque and Victorian buildings make this pretty, bustling port even more charming. It's the launching pad for treks into the western and southwestern interior; routes into the mountains lead to some spectacular climbs and can be easily reached by car. Long a center of fine needlepoint, intrepid shoppers can still find some wonderful samples of fine island artistry in some of the older shops downtown. The island' s only zoo is located behind the University of Puerto Rico's campus. The city itself is centered around the impressive Spanish-style **Plaza Colón**, a tribute to Christopher Columbus, whose statue stands in the middle of the square. The **Cathédrale de la Virgen de la Candelaria** is also a fine structure, dating back four centuries.

About 50 miles west of Mayaguez, stands Mona Island, a rugged uninhabited island whose only residents are large colonies of seabirds and enormous iguanas. The stunning cliffs make excellent photo ops; years ago it was said they held the booty of pirates who combed these waters. Rustic adventurers can find perfect places for camping overlooking the sea. Permission to visit must be granted by the tourist office. Twenty miles south of Malagues is **Boqueón Beach**, a stunning mile-long beach that boasts balneario facilities and excellent low prices for lodging. The small cottages are owned by the government and must be applied for four months in advance through the **Recreation and Sports Department**, *Box 2923, San Juan, PR 00903;* ☎ *(809) 722-1551.* Avoid weekends when local families with noisy teenagers carrying boom boxes disrupt the peacefulness of the area. Excellent seafood restaurants can be found a bit farther north at **Joyuda Beach**. Along Route 301 can be found the **Cabo Rojo Wildlife Refuge** (see "Treks"). If you would like a guide, check at the visitor's desk, where you can also get maps and individual assistance. At the southwesternmost top of the island, the best place to watch sunsets is at the **Cabo Rojo Lighthouse** at El Faro. The lighthouse is not open to the public, but the promontory overlooking red cliffs and ocean make for a spectacular lookout.

What Else to See

Parks and Gardens

Puerto Rico Zoological Gardens ★★★

Route 108, Mayaguez, ☎ *(809) 834-8110.*
Hours open: 9 a.m.–5 p.m.
Check out the birds and beasts—500 in all—at this tropical zoo spread over 45 acres.

Where to Eat

Horned Dorset Primavera **$$$** ★★★★★

Route 429, Km. 3, Rincon, ☎ *(809) 823-4030.*
cuisine.
Lunch: Noon–2:30 p.m., entrees $15–$25.
Dinner: 7–9 p.m., prix fixe $45.

This plush, whitewashed hotel/restaurant stands quite alone in its glory in a frontier location catering to surfers and daytrippers. That isn't to say the area isn't sublimely beautiful; it is. Many visitors make a special trip to eat here; it's quiet, it's right on the beach and the $40 fixed-price, six-course dinner is served with great ceremony. Although it's named after a breed of English sheep, seafood is a specialty. Location is six miles northwest of Mayaguez. Lunch hours vary, call for information.

Puerto Rico Directory

BUSINESS HOURS

Shops open 9 a.m.–6 p.m. Banks open weekdays 8:30 a.m.–2:30 p.m. and Saturday 9:45 a.m.–noon.

CLIMATE

Coastal weather in Puerto Rico is warm and sunny year-round. During the summer, temperatures average in the mid 80s; during the winter, they hover in the low 70s to the low 80s. The rainiest months are May to December, generally heavier on the north than the south coast. Temperatures in the mountains tend to be 5–10 degrees cooler.

DOCUMENTS

Since Puerto Rico is a commonwealth of the United States, no passports are required for U.S. citizens. Visitors do need a valid driver's license to rent a car. If you are a citizen of any other country, a visa is required. Vaccinations are not necessary. U.S. citizens do not need to clear customs or immigration (other citizens do). On departure, luggage must be inspected by the U.S. Agriculture Department, as law prohibits the taking of certain fruits and plants in the U.S. Dogs and cats may be brought to Puerto Rico from the U.S. with two documents: a health certificate dated not more than 10 days prior to departure showing that the animal is certified disease-free by an official or registered veterinarian, and a certificate of rabies vaccination, dated not more than 30 days prior to departure, authenticated by the proper authorities.

ELECTRICITY

Current runs A.C. 60 cycles, 100 volts, single phase or 220 volts, three phase.

GETTING AROUND

Taxis, buses and rental cars are available at the airport and major hotels. All taxicabs are metered, but they may be rented unmetered for an hourly rate. *Publicos* (public cars) run on frequent schedules to all island towns (usually during daytime hours) and depart from main squares. They run on fixed rates. The *Ruta Panoramica* is a scenic road meandering across the island offering stunning vistas.

San Juan is the largest home-based cruise port in the world. Twenty-eight vessels use San Juan as their home port and each year new cruise ships either originate or call at the port.

Ferries shuttle passengers to and from Culebra and Vieques at reasonable rates. Car transport is also available. San Juan's harbor can also be crossed by the Catana ferry (50 cents) to the Bacardi Rum plant's free tours.

LANGUAGE

Spanish and English are both official languages of Puerto Rico. Many speak English—and many people don't, especially older people in outlying rural areas. In San Juan however, English is taught from kindergarten to high school as part of the school curriculum.

MEDICAL EMERGENCIES

Officially, the medical community of Puerto Rico meets the same standards as those required on the U.S. mainland (just explain why most rich Puerto Ricans come to the States for medical attention). Most physicians on the island are based in San Juan with almost all medical specializations represented. San Juan has 14 hospitals, most districts have at least one. Ask your hotel to recommend a physician on call.

MONEY

The official currency is the U.S. dollar and credit cards are widely accepted by hotels, restaurants and shops. Several foreign exchange offices are available in San Juan and at the airport.

TELEPHONE

The area code is *809*. Postage stamps are equivalent to those in the U.S. as are mail costs. You can dial direct to the mainland.

TIME

Atlantic Standard Time, year-round, which is one hour earlier than New York. During Daylight Saving Time, it is the same.

TIPPING AND TAXES

Gratuities on restaurant bills are not included, but a usual 15 percent tip is expected.

TOURIST INFORMATION

For more information about the island, contact the **Puerto Rico Tourism Company**, *La Princesa Building, Old San Juan, PR 00901;* ☎ *(809) 721-2400*. There are offices in New York, Los Angeles, Coral Gables, London, Madrid, Mexico City, Milan, Paris, Stockholm, Toronto and Weisbaden, Germany. In the U.S. ☎ *(213) 874-5991*.

WHEN TO GO

January-May the Puerto Rico Symphony Orchestra conducts its season with performances through May. January 6 is traditional gift-giving day in Puerto Rico, celebrated by island-wide festivals with music, dance, parades, puppet shows and caroling troubadours. Jan. 1–19 is the International Folklore Festival, featuring dance groups from around the world. February (usually 3rd weekend) is the Coffee Harvest Festival. Carnival usually happens the second week in February. The Sugar Harvest Festival takes place in May. The Festival Casals takes place in early June, honoring the late cellist. San Juan Bautista Day is June 23, celebrating the island's patron saint, as sanjuaneros walk backward into the sea three times at midnight for good luck. The Albonito Flower Festival takes place in July. The Barranquitas Artisans Fair is held July 16–18, the island's oldest crafts fair with 130 local artisans. The 42nd International Billfish Tournament takes place in September. The Inter-American Festival of the Arts takes place in September. The National Plantain Festival occurs in late October. The baseball season begins in October. The Festival of Typical Dishes lasts from November-December. Old San Juan's White Christmas Festival takes place December-January. Island-wide Christmas festivities with life-size nativity scenes are held December–January. The Bacardi Arts Festival featuring more than 200 craftsmen is in December. Lighting of the Town of Bethlehem occurs for three days in mid-December.

In general, spring is always a good time to visit San Juan. Old San Juan is less crowded with cruise ship day trippers than during the winter, hotels rates begin to drop, and many hotels offer inexpensive summer packages to lure visitors during the slowest months. Puerto Rico doesn't have extreme seasonal changes so you may see that quintessential Christmas flower, the poinsettia blooming and mangoes ripening in the same gardens. San Juan shuts down for much of Holy Week, but there are Easter celebrations. An annual sunrise Easter service is usually held at **El Morro**. For more information call Rev. Martha McCracken ☎ *(809) 722-5372.*

PUERTO RICO RESTAURANTS	PHONE	ENTREE	CR. CARDS
San Juan			
American			
★★ **The Chart House**	(809) 728-0110	$16–$25••	A, DC, MC, V
Chinese			
★★★ **Back Street Hong Kong**	(809) 791-1000	$15–$32••	A, MC, V
French			
★★★★ **La Chaumiere**	(809) 722-3330	$22–$37••	A, DC, MC, V
International			
★★★ **El Patio de Sam**	(809) 723-1149	$9–$25	A, DC, MC, V
★★ **Butterfly People**	(809) 723-2432	•$5–$9	A, DC, MC, V
Italian			
★★ **Al Dente**	(809) 723-7303	$10–$15	A, MC, V
Latin American			
★★★★ **Amadeus**	(809) 722-8635	$8–$16	A, MC, V
★★★ **Ajilli-Mojili**		$15–$25	A, MC, V
★★★ **La Bombonera**	(809) 722-0658	$5–$8	A, MC, V
★★★ **La Casona de Serafin**	(809) 851-0066	$10–$31	A, MC, V
★★★ **La Mallorquina**	(809) 722-3261	$14–$30	A, DC, MC, V
★★★ **Parador Villa Parguera**	(809) 899-7777	$5–$20	A, CB, D, DC, MC, V
★★ **Anchor's Inn**	(809) 863-7200	$8–$20	A, MC, V
Spanish			
★★★★★ **La Compostela**	(809) 724-6088	$15–$29	A, DC, MC, V
★★★★★ **Ramiro's**	(809) 721-9049	$24–$33	A, DC, MC, V
South Coast			
Mexican			
★★ **Lupita's Mexican**	(809) 848-8808	$7–$26	A, DC, MC, V

PUERTO RICO RESTAURANTS	PHONE	ENTREE	CR. CARDS
Seafood			
★★★ **El Ancla**	(809) 840-2450	$3–$28	A, DC, MC, V
West Coast			
Seafood			
★★★★★ **Horned Dorset Primavera**	(809) 823-4030	$15–$45	A, MC, V

Note: • Lunch Only

•• Dinner Only

ST. BARTHÉLÉMY

Waterskiing is only permitted in Colombier Bay.

One local island guide says it all: No bums allowed on St. Barts. And strangely enough, there isn't even one. Once known by its long nomenclature, St. Barthélémy, this thumbprint-sized isle is simply the antithesis of the ramshackle outpost. In fact, it could be easily considered one of *the* hoity-toitiest places alive on the planet. Try as you might, you won't find the seedy smells of West Indian life or the frenzied street markets that define Carib life. Instead, on St. Barts what you'll discover is a subculture of wealth superimposed on a native lore that is slowly but surely sinking into the sea. Even though there exists gorgeous scenery, pristine beaches and a seaworthy harbor, St. Barts remains a place to snooze, to "cruise," to pick new husbands and discard old ones—in high season the island makes L.A. look limp. If you're the kind of person who feels happy paying for social comeuppance, then St. Barts will be your biggest fantasy isle.

Bird's Eye View

St. Barts boasts white sandy beaches surrounded by lush, volcanic hillsides.

Shaped like a soprano sax or a backwards check mark, St. Barts covers only 9.5 square miles, making it half the size of Manhattan. A ten-minute flight from St. Martin, it is 125 miles from Guadeloupe, of which it is a dependency. There are six large lagoons scattered over the island, and no hill rising over the 920 ft. **Morne Vitet**. More than 20 tiny isles dot the surrounding water, the largest of which is Fourchue.

The harbor town of **Gustavia** puts the word quaint in the dictionary—a storybook setting for a fairytale. The eerily romantic streets are a mix of French, Colonial Creole, and Swedish style, so pristine that there's not even one piece of garbage sighted. Taking a road marked **Lurin** you can head out in a southeasterly direction and find achingly beautiful landscape. Latanier palms, imported for the straw hat industry, line the road, along with so many flowers—hibiscus, bougainvillea, dwarf poincianas, shell ginger flowers, baby orchids, flowering African tulips, frangipani—that you may feel overwhelmed. With trees bent permanently out of shape by the strong trade winds, the eastern side of the island, known as **Grand Fond**, resembles something out of *Wuthering Heights*, as tall grass waves hypnotically and stone walls that were constructed over a century ago by French immigrants continue to crumble. It's on this side of the island, nearly deserted, that you'll find one lone house perched on the rocks at ocean's edge—once owned by Rudolph Nureyev. At **Lorient**, on the east, local fishermen work as they have for centuries. As you travel northward, more buildings appear, though it is still largely residential housing around the northeastern tip at Petit Cul-de-Sac. The larger **Grand Cul-de-Sac** is a tourist enclave right out of *Lifestyles of the*

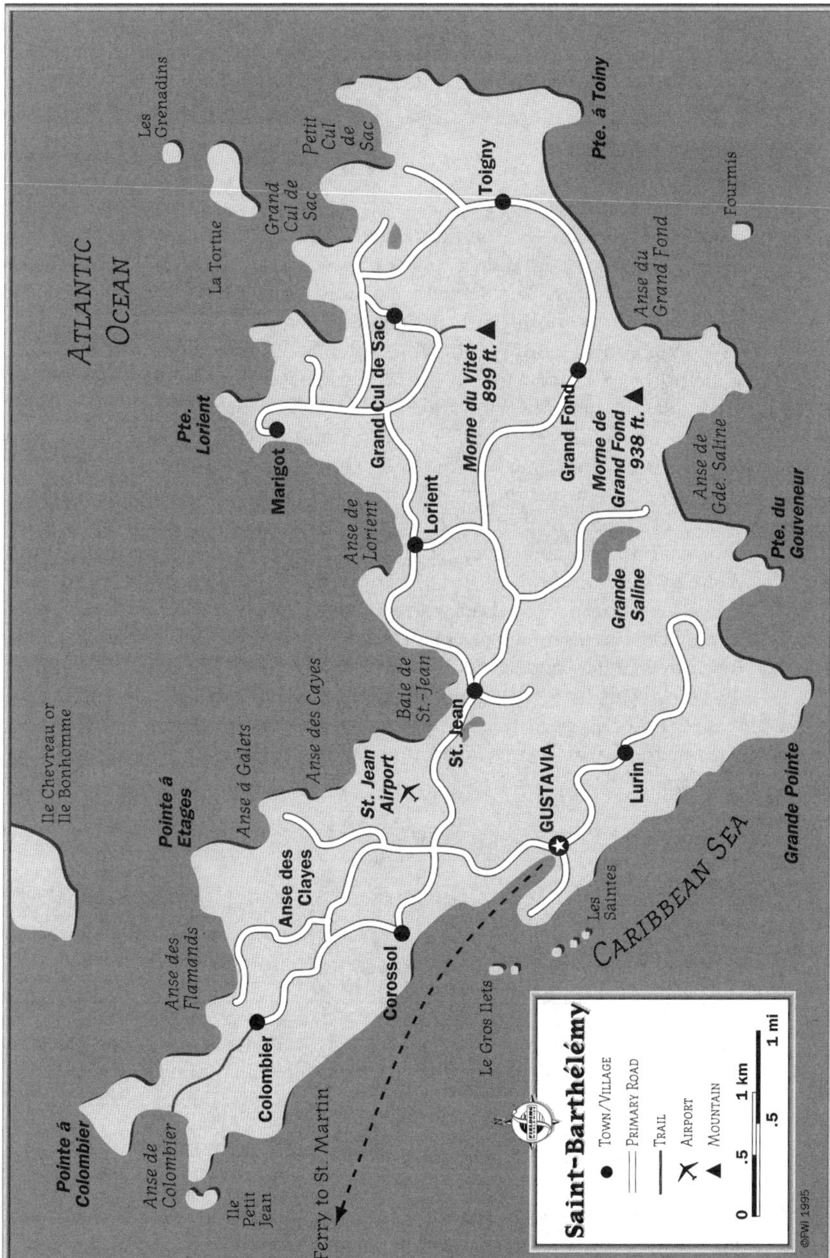
Saint-Barthélémy
Town/Village
Primary Road
Trail
Airport
Mountain
0 .5 1 km
.5 1 mi
©FWI 1995
Atlantic Ocean
Caribbean Sea
Les Grenadins
La Tortue
Petit Cul de Sac
Grand Cul de Sac
Pte. à Toiny
Toigny
Fourmis
Anse du Grand Fond
Morne du Vitet 899 ft.
Grand Cul de Sac
Pte. Lorient
Marigot
Grand Fond
Morne de Grand Fond 938 ft.
Anse de Gde. Saline
Pte. du Gouveneur
Anse de Lorient
Lorient
Grande Saline
Ile Chevreau or Ile Bonhomme
Pointe à Etages
Anse á Galets
Anse des Cayes
Baie de St.-Jean
St. Jean
St. Jean Airport
GUSTAVIA
Lurin
Grande Pointe
Anse des Clayes
Anse des Flamands
Corossol
Les Saintes
Le Gros Ilets
Colombier
Pointe à Colombier
Anse de Colombier
Ile Petit Jean
Ferry to St. Martin

Rich and Famous. An enclave of million-dollar villas dot the rocky tip of **Pointe Milou**, where it's rumored some of Prince Andrew's clan have nested.

History

Some people believe Columbus discovered St. Barts, naming it after his brother, but the island didn't appear on any map until 1523, when a speck of dirt was labeled San Bartoleme by a Spanish cartographer. After being summarily ignored by both Carib Indians and European pirates, St. Barts was finally explored in 1637, eight years after St. Kitts was colonized, though some of the first Norman and British settlers were scalped by Carib Indians. Over time the island became a secret hiding place for pirates, while the island itself became tenaciously French. When Louis XVI traded the flagging island to the Swedes for some warehouse in Goteborg, the island magically flourished with new management (Thomas Jefferson himself declared the port free of all duties). By 1847, the island had been ravaged by hurricanes, trade competition, fires and piracy, leaving Gustavia, the capital, dirt poor—a fact that convinced the Swedes in 1878 to dump the island back in the lap of the French. Not until 1946 did the French government declare St. Barts a commune in the department of Guadeloupe in 1946. In 1947, aviator/hotelier Rémy de Haenen landed the first airplane here on the short, grassy pasture of St. Jean. With the construction of the airport and the island's first runway (called a STOL, i.e., short takeoff and landing), the floodgates of tourism were opened, with most visitors flocking to St. Jean, on the central point of the island.

People

As the actress Ann Magnuson once wrote, everybody on St. Barts looks related—to Olive Oyl. In truth, there are fewer than a hundred blacks on St. Barts since the island was too small to support a large import of slaves. Moreover, the rocky terrain of St. Barts was so inhospitable to growing sugarcane that the slave ships simply passed the island by, leaving the northern French farmers who settled here to follow their own Breton way of life. Today, the most traditional sect of the population are the fiercely independent grandmothers (or *grandmeres*)—tough old ladies, thoroughly Caucasian, West Indian by birth and French by heritage, who singlehandedly raised their huge families in the absence of husbands who had to frequently leave the island to make ends meet. (Today you can see them wearing their straw *caleches* pulled low over their brows, a type of peasant bonnet that served to shield their faces not only from the sun but from the staring eyes of passing sailors.) Sadly, with the influx of more than a 1000 ex-pats (many of them French) and thousands of high-class international tourists, the old traditions are slowly dying out as the middle-aged generation is caught in transition while their children are looking solidly into a modernized future.

Anyone looking for political struggles or racial tension simply won't find them on St. Barts. An uncommon feeling of unity exists here among locals. Crime is unheard of (unless you call land developers thieves), simply because the cost of living is too high to support a petty thief. Instead, everyone seems to be gainfully employed, from fishermen, to builders, to shopkeepers to hoteliers and restaurateurs; even the dogs look well fed. As such, many visitors hitchhike around to see the island, which is said to be a completely safe way of passage, not to mention a great way to make friends. Between the native Bartians and the Euro babes and dudes who arrive during high season, rumor has it that there are ten men to every woman on St. Barts—and most of them are straight and very handsome. One word of warning: although the "genuine" locals are polite, if not unduly humble, the French ex-pats who run many of the hotels have an attitude that simply should be shipped home to Paris. Come armed with ammunition.

Beaches

St. Barts is famous for its pristine, white beaches—at present count, 14. Even during high season, they never become unbearably crowded, despite being public and free of charge. The **Grand Saline** is the only official nude beach, though stages of all levels of undress are seen throughout the island. (Grand Saline has been dubbed Indochine Beach, after the Manhattan restaurant frequented by the terminally fabulous. The unstated seating rule: hip and/or gay to the right side of the beach, conservative flanks to the left.) Both Grand Cul de Sac and St. Jean are the most developed beaches, with several hotels, restaurants, and water sports activities readily available; the two beaches are separated by the **Eden Rock** promontory. There is also a smattering of small hotels and restaurants at Flamanda to the west, a classic stretch of white sand fringed with lantana palms. For quiet seclusion, head for **Marigot** and **Lorient** on the north shore, where you'll see many island families on Sunday. Total privacy can be found at Gouverneur in the south. If you're walking, **Shell Beach** can be reached from Gustavia on foot; on the other side of town. The public beach is near the commercial pier but is good for a swim. The most difficult beach to reach is **Colombier**, a boat ride from Gustavia. If you're driving, go as far as the village of Colombier; from there, you'll have a half-hour hike down a scenic path.

What Else to See

St. Barts is blissfully free of tourist traps and boring museums. Anything worth finding will be your own special discovery, but a few hints will get you started. To find one of the last threads of traditional life, go to the once-isolated fishing village of Corossol on the southwestern coast, where you can still find old St. Bartian women weaving handicrafts from latanier palms. The wide-brimmed hats they're wearing, called *caleches,* may be hard to find, but you will find stalls of straw hats and baskets for sale. Second hint: Head for the northwest tip of the island, where the road dead-ends at Petite Anse. There's a goat path here that leads to **Anse de Colombier**. This rugged mountain trail is the sole land access to a beach that can otherwise only be enjoyed by island-hopping yachtsmen. A lizard-laden trail winds through the towering torch cacti and along the edge of a spectacular shoreline, ending up a paradise beach that is beyond description.

Museums and Exhibits

Municipal Museum ★★★

Le Pointe, Gustavia.

This winsome little museum tells the island's history through costumes, antiques, documents and artwork. It also has exhibits on St. Barth's vegetation and sea creatures.

Sports

If you are interested in deep-sea fishing, head for the harbor at **Gustavia**, where boat charters with fishing gear can be hired. As opposed to other Caribbean islands, spearfishing is permitted, as long as the spearfisher is fully equipped in scuba gear. Both diving and snorkeling equipment can be purchased in Gustavia. Among the most popular fish anglers seek in St. Barts are dorado, bonito, tuna, marlin, barracuda, amberjack, grouper and moray eel. Take time to talk to local fishermen and discover what are the best fish for the season and exactly which fish are edible—St. Barts has its own variety of edible fish. Local fishermen can also be the source of fascinating yarns that go on for hours, especially if they are inspired by a few beers.

Boating is more than a passion in St. Barts—it's a way of life, and sailors are often judged socially by the make of their boat. The ideal location of St. Barts—between Antigua and the Virgin Islands—gives sailors here a wide selection of destinations to choose from. In Gustavia, there are docking facilities and moorings for at least 40 vessels at one time. Other fine anchorages include **Colombier**, **Public** and **Corossol** bays. The calm winds of St.Jean and Grand Cul de Sac particularly take well to Sunfish; rentals are available there. It's very easy to pick up a full-day picnic excursion, leaving from Gustavia and headed to nearby beaches and islets (up to six passengers, usually). Full day sail to Ile Fourchue leaves the harbor at Gustavia at 9:30 a.m.

Surfing is terrific at **Lorient**. Always check the water conditions before you go; it will save you time and money, and sometimes your life, if the waves are too choppy. Most watersports facilities have boards for rent. Windsurfing equipment is also available at most facilities. Waterskiing is only authorized in Colombier Bay between 8:30 a.m. and 3 p.m.

Horseback Riding

Ranch des Flamands, Anse des Flamands.
Laure Nicolas is the person to see for trail rides and other excursions.

Watersports

Various locations, Gustavia.
La Marine Service *(☎ 27-70-34)* offers the island's most complete watersports center, with PADI-certified scuba diving, deep-sea fishing, snorkel excursions, and boat rides in the Aquascope from which you espy colorful coral, sea creatures, and a submerged yacht wreck. Also available are: **St. Barth Wind School** *(☎ 27-71-22)* and **Wind Wave Power** *(☎ 27-62-73)* for windsurfing instruction and rentals; **Club La Bulle** *(☎ 27-68-93)* and **Dive with Dan** *(☎ 27-64-78)* for scuba; and **La Maison de la Mer** *(☎ 27-81-00)* for deep-sea fishing.

Where to Eat

Fielding's Highest Rated Restaurants in St. Barthélémy		
★★★★★	**Le Toque Lyonnaise**	$43–$61
★★★★	**Ballahou**	$15–$45
★★★★	**Francois Plantation**	$16–$50
★★★★	**La Fregate**	$10–$19
★★★★	**Le Gaiac**	$30–$60
★★★★	**Le Sapotillier**	$45–$60
★★★	**Castelets**	$25–$35
★★★	**La Langouste**	$23–$42
★★★	**Marigot Bay Club & Art Gallery**	$40–$50
★★★	**Wall House**	$30–$45

Fielding's Special Restaurants in St. Barthélémy		
★★★★	**Ballahou**	$15–$45
★★★	**Eddy's Ghetto**	$15–$18
★★★	**Le Select**	$5–$10
★★★	**Wall House**	$30–$45

Fielding's Budget Restaurants in St. Barthélémy		
★★★	**Le Select**	$5–$10
★★★★	**La Fregate**	$10–$19
★★	**Santa Fe**	$10–$21
★★★	**Eddy's Ghetto**	$15–$18
★★★	**Pasta Paradise**	$10–$25

The food in St. Barts has to be good enough to suit the persnickety jetsetters who arrive, plus locals have to have the attitude to endure them. Cuisine usually runs to the French, often using the spoils of the sea, such as *langouste* (lobster) and redfish, but you can find a few West Indian kitchens, such as the casual Topolino, on the road to Salines.The harborside **Chez Maya** is the hippest celebrity hangout, where the atmosphere is relaxed and the exotic cuisine—from French to Creole to Vietnamese—is superb. Best dining can be found at **la Cuisine de Michel**, a tiny roadside takeout place on the Grand Fond road; many locals stop by to pick up their Sunday meals here from the

French chef Michel Brunet. **Eddy's Ghetto**, in Gustavia, is an open-air restaurant where everyone fits in, a funky lively joint where great meals come with good prices. When wallets get low, the village of Lorient proffers good hamburgers at **Chez Jo Jo**. Do your best to seek out the fresh-baked bread that a little old lady sells near the cemetery.

The club scene has slumped since the infamous club Au Tour de Rocher mysteriously burned down two years ago. Weekend nights at **Le Pélican** in St. Jean seem like a frat party. Every night except Wednesday is cabaret at **Club La Banane**, run by the French lady whose Parisian cabaret inspired "La Cage Aux Folles." Two of the favorite local bar hangouts—**Bar de l'Oubli** and **Le Sélect**—sit kitty-corner from each other on rue du Général de Gaulle in Gustavia, the busiest thoroughfare of the town, and are the places where you're most likely to meet new friends. If you are a young, drunken poet wannabe, drop in at **Chez Ginette S.O.S.**, and try the famous Punch Coco (a rum concoction whose ingredients are known only to owner Ginette). Wannabe sailors should try to get invited to dinner on one of the impressive yachts anchored in the match-box-size harbor—one even has the name *Octopussy*.

Adam $$$ ★★

Village St. Jean, St. Jean, ☎ (590) 27-84-56.
French cuisine.
Dinner: prix fixe $35.

On an island where fabulous eateries come and go, Adam prevails by proffering a seemingly infinite variety of three-course, prix-fixe dinners at a reasonable tariff. Entrees like filet mignon, lobster, or filet of pork with a coconut sauce are capped off with creme brulee or other heavenly desserts. The setting is also paradisiacal, high on a hillside with garden and lagoon views; there's art on the walls as well as on the plates.

Au Port $$$ ★★★

Rue Sadi-Carnot, ☎ (590) 27-62-36.
French cuisine.
Dinner: 6:30–10 p.m., entrees $19–$27.

Guests navigate a steep staircase to get to the second-floor dining room of this charming old house above the port of Gustavia. Cuisine is a fanciful blend of traditional French and creole—witness the popular colombo (Creole curry) of prawns or lamb served with seasoned rice. Ambience is understandably nautical.

Ballahou $$$ ★★★★

Anse des Cayes, Anse des Cayes, ☎ (590) 27-66-55.
French cuisine.
Lunch: 12:30–4 p.m., entrees $15–$30.
Dinner: 7:30–9:30 p.m., entrees $27–$45.

There's a lot of understandable ballyhoo (and hip-hooray) about this gorgeous restaurant in the sleek Hotel Manapany—architecturally, it seems to blend as one with the rim of the swimming pool. Specialties usually include seafood, but the menu changes often. Guests of the hotel and others dine here by candlelight only five months out of the year; it's closed in the warmer months. Manapany's Italian restaurant, Ouanalao, serves lunch and dinner all year round; try the gazpacho and risotto with prawns.

Castelets $$$ ★★★

Morne Lurin, ☎ (590) 27-6173.
French cuisine.

Dinner: 7–9 p.m., entrees $25–$35.

This long-established hotel went through a brief Italian phase as Sapore de Mare. Manager Genevieve Jouany returned and brought everything back to normal, including the chic dining salon presided over by two under-30s chefs (aren't they all?). These young wizards eschew heavy cream sauces in favor of fresh herbs and virgin olive oils. They also exhibit a propensity for wild morel and boletus mushrooms that show up frequently in pasta and seafood dishes.

Eddy's Ghetto **$$$** ★★★

Rue du General de Gaulle,
French cuisine.
Dinner: 7–10 p.m., entrees $15–$18.

When locals go slumming they go to Eddy's for simple grills, salads, ribs, beef ragouts and island music. The yacht crowd often fills the wicker and plant-filled restaurant the moment it opens at 7 p.m., if the locals haven't gotten there first. The place fills the need for light meals and casual ambience not found in some of the pricier establishments in town. The owner is Eddy Stakelborough (a member of the clan that founded Le Select across the street), who oversees the action from a perch behind the bar.

Francois Plantation **$$$** ★★★★

Colombier, Colombier, ☎ *(590) 27-7882.*
French cuisine.
Dinner: 6:30–10 p.m., entrees $16–$50.

No one doubts the serene beauty of this place—for exotic plantings, greenery and an interior boasting highly polished woods. But the food (lighter versions of traditional French favorites) and service have been slipping somewhat. It's hoped things will improve, as the innovativeness of the cuisine can't often be faulted.

Hostellerie Trois Forces **$$$** ★★★

Vitet, Vitet, ☎ *(590) 27-6125.*
French cuisine.
Lunch: Noon–3 p.m., entrees $10–$50.
Dinner: 7–9:45 p.m., entrees $10–$50.

Tarot readings and fine food commingle nicely at this surprisingly unpretentious holistic, new age resort-restaurant in the small town of Vitet, east of Lorient. Chef and chief astrologer Hubert Delemotte and family serve creole/French meals with a nod to organic and vegetarian diners, although there is red meat on the menu. There's a three-course, prix-fixe dinner offering nightly. Ambience is low-key and pleasant.

L'Entrepont **$$$** ★★

La Pointe, ☎ *(590) 27-9060.*
Italian cuisine.
Lunch: entrees $17–$25.
Dinner: entrees $25–$33.

Located in a newly fashionable area on the west side of Gustavia's harbor, this Italian restaurant owned by a Neapolitan family is renowned for unusual pizzas. Guests eat well in a garden setting that's open to the breezes. Other choices include beef carpaccio, pastas and veal.

L'Escale **$$$** ★★★

La Pointe, ☎ *(590) 27-8106.*
Italian cuisine.
Dinner: 7 p.m.–midnight, entrees $14–$29.

This mostly Italian trattoria on the west side of the harbor has many faithful followers who clamor for the wide variety of pizzas (some say it's the best in town), or lasagna and seafood. Lately it's been facing some competition from other eateries in the area serving similar cuisine, although it swings at night, especially in the hip bar.

La Fregate **$$** ★★★★

Flamandes Beach, Flamandes, ☎ (590) 27-6651.
French cuisine.
Lunch: Noon–3 p.m., entrees $10–$19.
Dinner: 7–9 p.m., entrees $10–$19.

Aim for an outside patio table at this excellent restaurant—if you still can. The word is out about the incredible edibles emerging from Jean-Pierre Crouzet's kitchen in a somewhat tacky beachfront motel in Baie des Flamandes. Island regulars know him from his past successes at Gustavia's La Sapotillier, where he was chef de cuisine. Here he continues to unleash a plethora of dishes utilizing the freshest local ingredients possible with a tried and true technique—although he is not yet 30, he has already worked his way through quite a few three-star establishments in France.

La Langouste **$$$** ★★★

rue Bord-de-la-Mer, ☎ (590) 27-69-47.
Latin American cuisine. Specialties: Langouste.
Lunch: Noon–2 p.m., entrees $23–$42.
Dinner: 7–10 p.m., entrees $23–$42.

The island's national crustacean (a clawless lobster) is the star at this pleasant creole/French eatery owned by Annie Ange, a member of a St. Barts landowning family (St. Barth Beach Hotel). The delectable seafood is dependably fresh, and other finny offerings include stuffed crabs and accra de morue (cod fritters). It's located is a traditional Swedish-style dwelling near several public offices.

Le Gaiac **$$$** ★★★★

Anse de Toiny, Anse de Toiny, ☎ (590) 27-8888.
French cuisine.
Lunch: entrees $30–$60.
Dinner: entrees $30–$60.

Nowadays, few great chefs stay in one place for long—Manapany's Jean Christophe Perrin has turned his talents to this small, very in spot at Le Toiny, a resort on a hilltop above a windward beach. It's very difficult to secure a seat in the 28-table outdoor restaurant (book way in advance) where such delights as conch cannelloni and rabbit with figs and pine nuts continue to dazzle guests.

Le Pelican **$$$** ★★

Plage de St. Jean, Plage de St. Jean, ☎ (590) 27-6464.
Latin American cuisine.
Lunch: 11:30 a.m.–3 p.m., entrees $20–$40.
Dinner: 6:30–1 p.m., entrees $20–$40.

This pleasant restaurant located a few steps from St. Barts' most popular beach satisfies on many counts. At lunch it's perfect for casual meals and ocean and people watching from a vast, covered terrace. Later, for dinner, the large dining rooms are awash in candlelight while sounds of piano music grace the background. Cuisine is a melange of creole and French favorites. Closed for dinner on Sundays.

Le Sapotillier **$$$** ★★★★

rue Sadi-Carnot, ☎ (590) 27-6028.
French cuisine. Specialties: Couscous with shrimp creole, fish mousse.
Dinner: prix fixe $45–$60.

Some fine chefs have emerged with an appreciative following from the kitchens of this memorable restaurant in a traditional old stone structure in Gustavia, including Le Fregate's Jean-Pierre Crouzette. La Sapotillier's reputation is still stellar, with classic French cuisine served with finesse in a small dining room or alfresco under the branches of a vast sapodilla tree.

Le Select **$** ★★★

rue de la France, ☎ (590) 27-86-87.
International cuisine. Specialties: Burgers.
Lunch: 10 a.m.–4 p.m., entrees $5–$10.
Dinner: 4–11 p.m., entrees $5–$10.

This old favorite (circa 1950) provides a safe haven for ordinary folk seeking refuge from the high prices and sometimes over-stuffed, precious atmosphere of some island dining establishments. Besides serving what is probably the best cheeseburger in town (it's called cheeseburger in paradise), the scruffy, poster-festooned old warehouse is great for loud reggae, zouk, or soca music. Newcomers can't possibly miss it—just walk around Gustavia during the day and you'll bump into it; at night you hear it before you see it.

Le Toque Lyonnaise **$$$** ★★★★★

Grand Cul-de-Sac, Grand Cul-de-Sac, ☎ (590) 27-6480.
French cuisine. Specialties: Grilled lobster with vanilla bean.
Dinner: 7–10 p.m., prix fixe $43–$61.

It's hard not to have a good meal here—chefs are from Lyon, which is the gourmet capital of France. This modern, oceanfront eatery, located a few miles out of Gustavia, boasts chefs who have trained with Paul Bocuse. Grilled seafood is the specialty, and the wine list is extensive and well-chosen. Closed June through October.

Marigot Bay Club & Art Gallery **$$$** ★★★

Marigot Bay, Marigot, ☎ (590) 27-7545.
French cuisine.
Lunch: entrees $40–$50.
Dinner: entrees $40–$50.

Two giant grilled langoustines appear on your plate here like creatures from Mars—yet they were freshly caught only this morning by a family of fisherfolk who own this popular restaurant at an intimate resort in the small bayside village of Marigot. You can have your crustacean plain or with a variety of sauces. Specialties rarely change, which is how most people who eat here like it. Closed for lunch on Monday and on Sundays from September through October.

Maya's **$$$** ★★

Public Beach, Public, ☎ (590) 27-7361.
Latin American cuisine.
Dinner: 6–11 p.m., entrees $27–$35.

Maya from Martinique serves savory creole cuisine with some spicy touches to an appreciative crowd; it's one of the more popular eateries on the island. The restaurant has a waterfront location in Public (west of Gustavia) with tables on a plant-filled patio. The menu changes frequently, but the salads are a standout.

Pasta Paradise **$$$** ★★★

Rue de Roi, ☎ (590) 27-8078.
French cuisine.
Lunch: entrees $10–$25.
Dinner: entrees $10–$25.

French-inspired Italian food is served at this very popular restaurant in a traditional, historic building in Gustavia. Formerly the site of La Citronelle, the jolly exterior features gingerbread trim, white shutters, tangerine and white railings and a tropical mural. Guests can dine on several different daily pasta offerings in air-conditioned insularity or in a breeze-cooled patio. The menu also features lobster in saffron oil and beef filets. Closed for lunch on Sunday.

Santa Fe **$$$** ★★

Morne Lurin,
American cuisine. Specialties: Burgers, steaks.

Lunch: Noon–2 p.m., entrees $10–$21.
Dinner: 5–10 p.m., entrees $10–$21.
Although the name evokes the American Southwest, the food served here is basically burgers (excellent), steak, and barbecue at American prices (reasonable). It's also a hangout for Anglais-speakers and sports fans of any stripe who come to watch their favorite teams play on wide-screen television, especially on Sundays. Located just a few miles east of Gustavia, it seems worlds away in atmosphere and in its isolation on a lofty hilltop. There's no ocean view; but that's not really necessary here. Closed for lunch on Sundays.

Wall House **$$$** ★★★

Gustavia Harbor, ☎ (590) 27-71-33.
French cuisine.
Lunch: entrees $30–$45.
Dinner: entrees $30–$45.
Almost every table in this whitewashed restaurant in the harbor has a lovely view; the wide picture windows in the dining room offer a panorama of swaying palms, small craft, azure waters, and a row of red tile-roofed, gingerbread-trimmed buildings. Diners can also sit outside to be closer to the action. The menu features lobster, rare lamb, duck breast, fabulous pates, and sinful desserts.

Where to Shop

To find one of the last threads of traditional life, go to the once-isolated fishing village of Corossol on the southwestern coast, where you can still find old St. Bartian women weaving handicrafts from latanier palms. The wide-brimmed hats called *caleches* may be hard to find atop their heads, but you will find stalls of straw hats and baskets.

Duty-free reigns in St. Barts, so if you're in the market for fine perfumes, china, crystal and liquor, you can find some of the best bargains in the Caribbean. Some French perfumes, like Chanel, are cheaper than they are in Paris. Due to the jetset crowd, a number of local crafts have found their way into international fashion magazines. Check around the small shops in Gustavia and in some of the outlying villages. **The Shell Shop** features unique jewelry, shells and coral found on the island. Yacht-owners and wannabes tend to congregate at **Loulou's Marine** in Gustavia, where everything you ever needed for a cruise is available— from clothes to rigs.

St. Barthélémy Directory

BUSINESS HOURS

Shops are open weekdays 8:30 a.m.–noon and 2–5 p.m. (some until 7 p.m.) and Saturday 8:30 a.m.–noon. Banks open weekdays 8 a.m.–noon and 2–3:30 p.m.

CLIMATE

St. Barts has an ideal dry climate and an average temperature of 72–86 degrees F.

DOCUMENTS

For stays of up to three weeks, U.S. and Canadian citizens traveling as tourists must have proof of citizenship in the form of a valid passport or that has expired not more than five years ago, or a birth certificate (original or copy) or voter's registration accompanied by a government authorized ID with photo.

For stays over three weeks, or for nontourist visits, a valid passport is necessary. Resident aliens of the U.S. and Canada, and visitors from countries other than those in the Common Market (E.E.C.) and Japan, must have a valid passport and visa. A return or onward ticket is also required of all visitors.

ELECTRICITY

Current runs at 220 AC, 60 cycles. American-made appliances require French plug converters and transformers.

GETTING AROUND

Car rentals are easy to secure on the island, but it is best to reserve one in advance, especially during the winter season. Roads are hilly, steep, narrow and winding, and drivers must know how to use a stick shift; your best options are VW Beetles, little open Gurgels, and Mini-Mokes. Daily rates go as high as $60 a day, which includes unlimited mileage, collision damage insurance (first $500 deductible) and free delivery. Gas costs about $3.25 a gallon. None of the two gas stations (near the airport and in Lorient) is open on Sunday. St. Barts' first all-night automatic gas station recently opened near the airport, requiring magnetically sensitized cards on sale at the station.

Some reliable agencies are: **Avis** at the airport ☎ *27-71-43*; **Budget** airport and town ☎ *27-67-43*; **Hertz** at the airport ☎ *27-71-14* or *27-60-21*. A few hotels have their own fleet of rentals, and may ask you to book through them because of limited parking.

Taxis stations (two) are located at the airport and one in Gustavia on rue de la République. To call a **taxi**, dial ☎ *27-66-31* on a local phone. For night taxis, call **Jean-Paul Janin** ☎ *27-61-86*, **Raymond Gréaux** ☎ *27-66-32*, or **Mathilde Laplace** ☎ *27-60-59*.

Motorbikes, mopeds, and scooters are easy to rent, but you must wear a helmet, required by law. You must also have a motorbike or driver's license. Rentals can be found at: **Denis Dufau's Rent Some Fun** ☎ *27-70-59*, which also carries 18-speed mountain bikes or **Fredéric Supligeau** ☎ *27-67-89*.

Sleek catamarans leave the marina on Dutch St. Maarten between 9:00 and 9:30 a.m. daily, arriving in Gustavia harbor less than 90 minutes later. One-way trips are possible, but the usual fare is one day round trips.

You can also arrive on St. Barts by ferryboats from St. Martin, such as the *St. Barth Express III*, which leaves at 7:30 a.m. and returns from Marina Porte La Royale in Mariot at 3:30 p.m. and Bobby's Marina in Philipsburg at 4:15 p.m., arriving in Gustavia 45 minutes later. To reserve, ☎ *(590) 27-77-24*, FAX *(590) 27-7723*. Two other ferryboats are the *Dauphin II* and the *Bateau Dakar*.

Private boat charters can be arranged through Sibarth in Gustavia ☎ *(590) 27-62-38* or its American affiliate WIMGO, Newport RI ☎ *(800) 932-3222* or *(410) 849-8012*.

LANGUAGE

French is the official language, spoken with a quaint Norman dialect. Most people speak English, but do plan to come loaded with an attitude to match that of the French employees at many hotels.

MEDICAL EMERGENCIES

Gustavia has a **hospital** ☎ *27-60-35*, eight resident doctors, three dentists, one gynecologist, and specialists in opthalmology, dermatology, etc. There are pharmacies at **La Savane Commercial Center** ☎ *27-66-61* and in Gustavia ☎ *27-61-82.*

MONEY

The official currency is the French franc; the official exchange rate (Aug. 1995) was approximately 5 francs to the American dollar. The rate is subject to change due to currency fluctuations. Dollars are accepted everywhere and prices are often quoted in dollars.

TELEPHONE

The area code for St. Barts is *590.* To call from the U.S. dial *011* (international access code), then *590* plus the local number in St. Barts. To call St. Barts from Dutch St. Maarten, dial 6 plus St. Barts's local six-digit number. To call St. Barts from other F.W.I (Martinique, Guadeloupe, and French St. Martin), you can dial direct.

Public phones require the use of "Telecartes" that look like credit cards and can be easily purchased at the Gustavia, St. Jean and Lorient post offices and at the gas station near the airport. Both local and international calls can be made from these phones using the card.

TIME

St. Barts is one hour ahead of Eastern Standard Time. When it is nine o'clock in St. Barts, it is eight o'clock in New York. During daylight saving time, there is no time difference.

TOURIST INFORMATION

The Tourist Board, called the Office de Tourisme, is located in attractive quarters on the Quai Général de Gaulle, across from the Capitainerie in Gustavia, open Monday–Friday 8:30 a.m.–6:00 p.m., and Saturday 8:30 a.m.–noon. From May to November, hours are a bit shorter. When writing to the **St. Barts Tourist Office**, use the address: *B.P. 113, Gustavia, 97098 Cedex, St. Barthélémy, F.W.I.* In the U.S. ☎ *(213) 658-7462.*

For what's happening weekly, pick up a current issue of *St. Barth Magazine*, distributed throughout the island. There's also an English program at noon on Mondays and Thursdays called "This Week in St. Barts."

WHEN TO GO

Three Kings Day on January 8 is celebrated with special ephinany cakes served at festivals. The 11th Anniversary of the St. Barts Music Festival is held Jan. 8–22, with jazz, chamber music and guests from the Metropolitan Opera. Carnival is celebrated Feb. 24, with a school parade, Mardi Gras pageant and parade, and the burning of Vaval, King of Carnival at Shell Beach.The award-winning cookbook author and instructor Steven Raichlen presents a one-week class on Caribbean cuisine at Hotel Yuana. The Festival of Gustavia is celebrated on August 20, with dragnet fishing contests, dances and parties.The Festival of St. Barthélémy is a feast day of the island's patron saint, celebrated with the pealing of church bells, a regatta, public ball, fireworks and the blessing of boats. The Fête du Vent on August 26–27 is honored with dragnet fishing contests, dances, fireworks and a lottery in the village of Lorient. The Swedish Marathon Race is held in December 6. The Réveillon de la Saint Sylvestre, on New Year's Eve, is a grand gala at the island's hotels and restaurants.

ST. BARTHÉLÉMY RESTAURANTS	PHONE	ENTREE	CR. CARDS
Gustavia			
American			
★★ Santa Fe		$10–$21	None
French			
★★★★★ Le Toque Lyonnaise	(590) 27-6480	$43–$61••	A, DC, MC, V
★★★★ Ballahou	(590) 27-66-55	$15–$45	A, DC, MC, V
★★★★ Francois Plantation	(590) 27-7882	$16–$50••	A, MC, V
★★★★ La Fregate	(590) 27-6651	$10–$19	A, MC, V
★★★★ Le Gaiac	(590) 27-8888	$30–$60	A, MC, V
★★★★ Le Sapotillier	(590) 27-6028	$45–$60••	MC, V
★★★ Au Port	(590) 27-62-36	$19–$27••	A
★★★ Castelets	(590) 27-6173	$25–$35••	A, MC, V
★★★ Eddy's Ghetto		$15–$18••	None
★★★ Hostellerie Trois Forces	(590) 27-6125	$10–$50	A, MC, V
★★★ Marigot Bay Club & Art Gallery	(590) 27-7545	$40–$50	A, V
★★★ Pasta Paradise	(590) 27-8078	$10–$25	MC, V
★★★ Wall House	(590) 27-71-33	$30–$45	MC, V
★★ Adam	(590) 27-84-56	$35–$35••	A
International			
★★★ Le Select	(590) 27-86-87	$5–$10	None
Italian			
★★★ L'Escale	(590) 27-8106	$14–$29••	MC, V
★★ L'Entrepont	(590) 27-9060	$17–$33	MC, V
Latin American			
★★★ La Langouste	(590) 27-69-47	$23–$42	MC, V
★★ Le Pelican	(590) 27-6464	$20–$40	A, V
★★ Maya's	(590) 27-7361	$27–$35••	A, MC, V

Note: • Lunch Only
•• Dinner Only

ST. CROIX

Straw hats of every style entice shoppers at the market in Christiansted.

If St. Thomas is the sophisticated cosmopolitan island of the United States Virgins Islands, and St. John is the nature island, then St. Croix is a cross between the two, a rustic environment with tinges of elegance. Columbus thought St. Croix looked like a lush garden when he first saw it. Today, the island is a combination of graceful Danish architecture, modern development and natural beauty. There are two main towns, Christiansted on the northeast coast and Frederiksted on the west. Christiansted, designed by the Dutch West Indies Company as a planned community, shows its Dutch influence plainly, but it is more than just historic buildings. There is modern shopping, excellent dining, wonderful little bars and numerous outstanding resort hotels. Guarded by Fort Frederik, Frederiksted is a very quiet community on the west seashore, differing substantially from Christiansted because many of the original buildings were destroyed by a hurricane and high waves in 1867 and the fire of 1878. The real pleasure in Frederiksted is its bustling, colorful port, attracting freighters, cruiseships and navy vessels, vying for sleeping quarters in the well-kept harbor. For years, divers and macrophotography buffs around the world have known the famous **Frederiksted Pier** as one of the Caribbean's premier dives for all kinds of marine life. The port of

Frederiksted has endured a major expansion, with vendor kiosks in Victorian gingerbread style lining the waterfront and two shaded bus stops installed in General Buddhoe Park. The old pump station has been converted into a hospitality lounge for tourists, a police substation, and a VITRAN bus token station. The best place to watch the glorious sunsets of St. Croix is now an old clock tower adjacent to the park that has been renovated to include a second-story observatory.

Bird's Eye View

Lying 75 miles east of Puerto Rico and 40 miles south of St. Thomas, St. Croix (rhymes with "boy"), is the largest of the U.S. Virgin Islands (which also include St. John and St. Thomas)—in fact more than two times larger than St. Thomas, but only 50,000 people live there. With a land mass 29 miles long by seven miles (82.2 square miles), St. Croix is separated from St. Thomas and St. John by 32 miles and a 12,000-foot oceanic trench. Rocky terrain fills the eastern sector, while the west end has higher elevation and more forests. Salt River on the north coast has now been approved as a National Park, including not only the sight where Columbus first landed, but also the underwater Salt River drop-off and canyon. Among the many natural attractions are wildlife refuges for birds and leatherback turtles, rain forest, botanic gardens, three nature preserves and three parks—one under the sea.

History

Columbus and his crew first came ashore at St. Croix's Salt River in 1493, but native Caribs did their best to fight them off. In haste he named the island Santa Cruz (Holy Cross) and sailed on to lay claim to St. John and St. Thomas. Eventually he renamed the entire group—including the British Virgin Islands at the time—for the legendary 11,000 virgin followers of St. Ursula. Today, we know that he wildly exaggerated the number of islands in the area. Soon after Columbus' departure, British, Dutch and French colonists began to establish farms on St. Croix, and in 1653, the island was awarded the crusaders' Order of St. John, better known as the Knights of Malta. France took control a few years later, and for the next 50 or so years, possession alternated between the French and the Spanish. As St. John and St. Thomas became acquired by the Danish West India Company and Guinea Company, St. Croix remained in the background. In 1773 the Danes also purchased St. Croix, attracted by its already burgeoning slave population

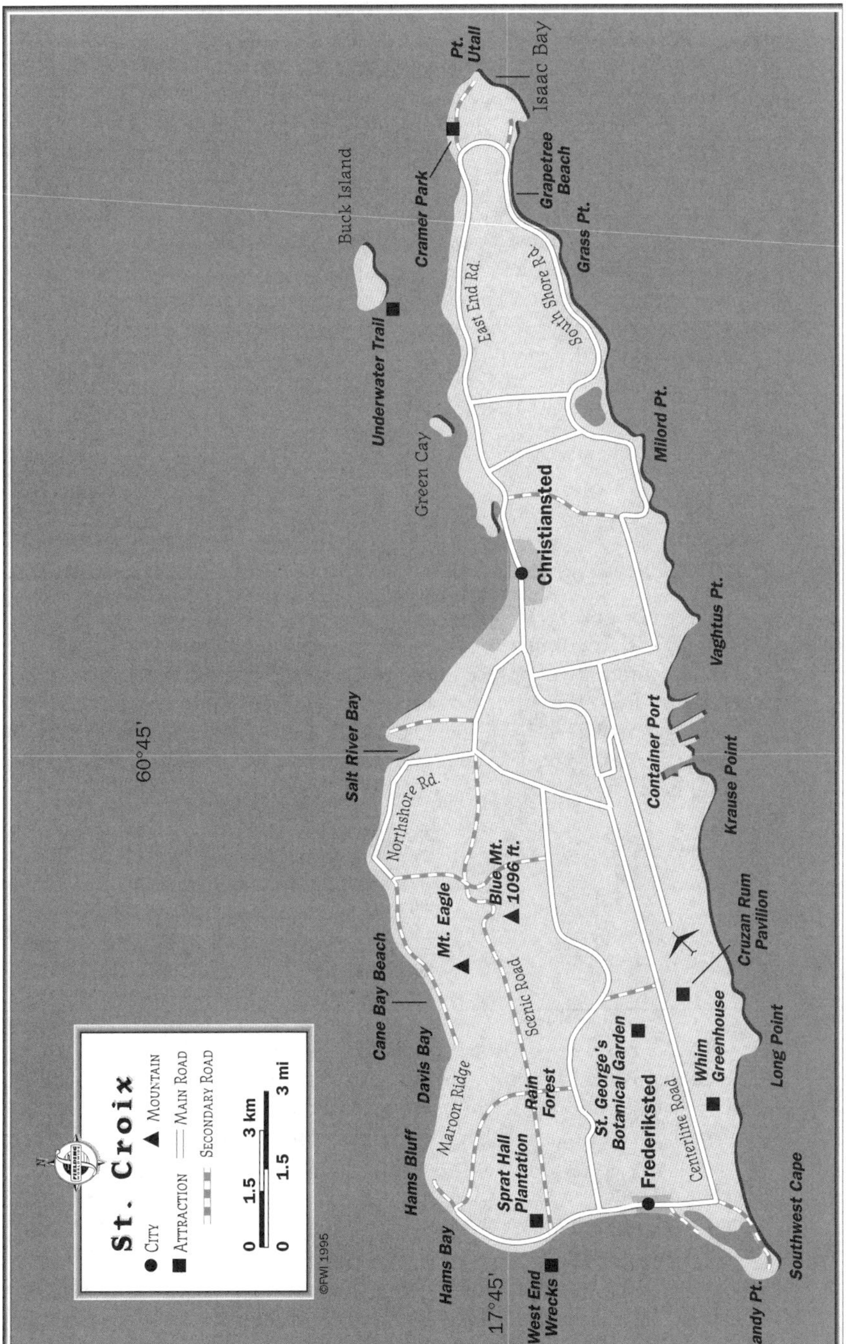
St. Croix
City
Attraction
Mountain
Main Road
Secondary Road
0 1.5 3 km
0 1.5 3 mi
©FWI 1995
17°45'
60°45'
Buck Island
Underwater Trail
Green Cay
Cramer Park
Pt. Utall
Isaac Bay
Grapetree Beach
Grass Pt.
East End Rd.
South Shore Rd.
Milord Pt.
Christiansted
Vaghtus Pt.
Container Port
Krause Point
Salt River Bay
Northshore Rd.
Blue Mt. 1096 ft.
Mt. Eagle
Scenic Road
Cane Bay Beach
Davis Bay
Maroon Ridge
Hams Bluff
Hams Bay
Rain Forest
Sprat Hall Plantation
St. George's Botanical Garden
Cruzan Rum Pavilion
Whim Greenhouse
Long Point
Frederiksted
Centerline Road
West End Wrecks
Sandy Pt.
Southwest Cape

and sugarcane fields. Planters and pirates mingled together during this golden age; some secluded coves are still said to harbor buried treasure. As the sugar beet was introduced to Europe, and the uprisings of slaves threatened the status quo, commercial interest in the island began to flag. Over the past 250 years, seven different conquerors took control of the island, though the Danish influence has remained the most lasting. During World War I, the Danes, sensing the sugarcane industry had all but dissolved, looked for buyers, finding the U.S. which was seeking a Caribbean base from which it could protect the Panama Canal. Eventually a great deal was struck between the two powers—$25 million dollars for three islands. The opening of the Carambola Beach Resort and Golf Club attracted a new wave of visitors to St. Croix starting in 1986. Though St. Croix was hard hit by Hurricane Hugo in 1989, islanders were not daunted and threw themselves body and soul into renovating the tourist facilities.

People

People born on St. Croix are called Crucians. The majority are of African descent, with a cultural mix from many other Caribbean islands. There is even a community of people from the island of Vieques (Puerto Rico). Lots of ex-pats from the U.S. also settle here. As well, there is a smattering of French, Germans and Italians who create their own small enclaves. A few Danes, stemming back to the original owners of the island, can even be found here.

Beaches

All beaches on St. Croix are public and free of charge, but if you go to a beach that is maintained by the resident hotel, you may have to pay a small fee for facilities. Lying 1.5 miles off northeast St. Croix, **Buck Island**, an 850-acre national monument, has some of the best beaches in the St. Croix area, reachable by boat from Christiansted; the six-mile trip takes 45 minutes to an hour. Some concessionaires that offer sail or motorboat tours also include a picnic lunch and an overland hike to the island's 400-foot summit with terrific views. Turtles also lay their eggs there. **Cane Bay** also has a stunning beach on the island's north side. Other fine beaches can be found at **Protestant Cay**, **Davis Bay**, **Cramer Park** on the east shore, and **Frederiksted Beach** to the north of town. The latter two have changing facilities and showers. Surfing is best on the north coast, and you'll find great shells on the northwest coast, from **Northside Beach** to **Ham's Bay**, as well as on **Sprat Hall Beach**.

Buck Island offers guided tours of underwater snorkeling trails.

What Else to See

There are two major towns to see in St. Croix, the largest which is **Christiansted**, and the place most ships dock, **Frederiksted**. Christiansted is a homey and culturally stimulating urban center, full of attractive 18th century buildings, many considered U.S. national historic sites. Covered walkways, mortar arches and colonnades lend an 18th century tropical ambiance. Take a look at the 17th-century French fortress, **Fort Chritiansvaern**, full of dungeons and cannons, from which there are excellent views of the harbor. A block away is the **Steeple Building**, today a historical museum with a small collection of Carib and Arawak relics and photos of the city from the 1800s. Also historically intriguing is the old **Scalehouse**, built in 1856 to house the huge scale used to weigh merchandise being shipped abroad, and the **Government House**, now home to the U.S. District Court, but still one of the most beautiful Danish colonial buildings in the islands. Saturday morning is the best time to visit the outdoor markets at **"Shan" Hendricks Square**, chock full of tropical fruits and vegetables for sale, including the island's favorite—green genips. The harbor itself is a joy to contemplate; nearby, on the waterfront and **Company Street**, you'll find lots of stores.

On the western end of the island is Frederiksted, usually asleep until a cruise liner docks at port. In contrast to the colonial Danish style of Christiansted, Frederiksted is more Victorian gingerbread. Pick up a free walking tour guide from the visitor's bureau at the end of the pier. **Fort Frederiks**, on the far side of Lagoon Street, was the site of the 1848 proclamation freeing the slaves. **The Market Place** is two blocks south and one block east of the fort. Feel free to browse up and down streets and alleys here—the best way to glimpse the stunning architecture. One especially pretty building on

Strand Street (along the waterfront) is the **Old Customs House** from the 18th century, now the headquarters of the Energy Commission, and the gingerbread-trimmed **Victorian House**. Not far from Christiansted is the **Cruzan Rum Factory**, which offers guided tour and drink samples.

North of Frederiksted, the shore road north will take you past **Sprat Hall**, an old plantation home turned guesthouse, all the way to the rain forest, and the **Scenic Drive**. Heading down Centerline Road you'll arrive at the fully restored **Estate Whim Plantation Museum**, dating back to the 17th century, and including a main house, and a half-dozen other structures including a windmill and cook house. Other places outside the urban areas include the rain forest at **St. Croix Leap**, where you will find a talented group of woodcarvers who create pieces carved in native mahogany. They practice a form of forest management, using wood from trees culled for specific purposes only. This is a lovely place to stroll and inspect the remains of a great house and a spectacular historical garden hosting some of the original crops of the native Indian tribes. Also worth a visit is the **St. Croix Aquarium**, notable for its ecological approach for staffing its tanks and fresh-food-feeding its "staff" daily, by recycling marine life after they have "performed" for a time in the aquariums. The aquarium houses about 40 species of marine animals and more than 100 species of invertebrates.

City Celebrations

Crucian Christmas Fiesta ★★★★

Various locations, Frederiksted.

This annual two-week festival celebrates the Christmas season with arts and crafts exhibits, food fairs, parades (one for children, the other for adults), the selection of Miss St. Croix, and the coronation of the festival's Prince and Princess. Most events take place in Christiansted and Frederiksted. Each town has a Festival Village complete with amusement rides and nightly entertainment.

Historical Sites

Fort Christiansvaern ★★★★

Downtown, Christiansted, ☎ (809) 773-1460.

Hours open: 8 a.m.–5 p.m.

This fort was built by the Danes in 1738 and rebuilt after hurricane damage in 1772. Its five rooms are decorated as they were in the 1840s. The admission charge (free for those under 16) includes entry to the Steeple Building. The fort's newest attraction is the St. Croix Police Museum, just opened in 1994. Created by Lt. Elton Lewis a 20-year veteran of the St. Croix Police Department, the idea behind the museum is to "promote high morale" and esprit de corps among police officers. Exhibits include weapons, photos, artifacts and an old police motorcycle from St. Croix's past.

Fort Frederik ★★★

Emancipation Park, Frederiksted, ☎ (809) 772-2021.

Hours open: 8:30 a.m.–4:30 p.m.

This fort dates back to 1760, and is now an art gallery and museum. It is best known as the site where on July 3, 1848, Governor General Peter Von Scholten freed the Danish West Indies slaves.

Steeple Building ★★★★

Downtown, Christiansted, ☎ (809) 773-1460.

Built by the Danish in 1754, this was their first Lutheran church, called the Church of Lord God of Sabaoth. Deconsecrated in 1831, it served as everything from a bakery to a school, and is now under the auspices of the U.S. National Park Service. Interesting exhibits tell the island's history, with emphasis on Native Americans and African Americans. The entry fee includes admission to Fort Christiansvaern.

Museums and Exhibits

Aquarium ★★★

On the waterfront, Frederiksted, ☎ *(809) 772-1345.*
Hours open: 11 a.m.–4 p.m.
Opened in 1990 by marine biologist Lonnie Kaczmarsky, this aquarium displays some 40 species of marine animals and more than 100 species of invertebrates. What makes it really unique is its "recycling" of sea life—after doing a stint in the tanks, creatures are released back to the open seas. Kaczmarsky is passionate on preserving the ocean environment; this is a good place to pick up hints before diving and snorkeling on how to minimize your impact.

Parks and Gardens

St. George Village Botanical Gardens ★★★★★

St. George Estate, Kingshill, ☎ *(809) 772-3874.*
Hours open: 9 a.m.–5 p.m.
Built among the ruins of a 19th-century sugarcane plantation workers' village, this little slice of paradise is not to be missed. The 17 acres were the site of an Arawak settlement dating to A.D. 100. Stop by the Great Hall to pick up a brochure for a self-guided walking tour, then feast your senses on the lovely gardens, which include 850 species of trees and plants. Each ecosystem of St. Croix is represented, from rainforest to desert. The grounds also include restored buildings from the plantation era, including workers' cottages, storehouses and a blacksmith shop. Warning: Don't buy the Aqua Venus bottled water in the giftshop. It's literally impossible to open! $1.00 for kids.

Tours

Buck Island Reef National Monument ★★★★★

Buck Island.
No trip to St. Croix is complete without a trip to this national monument island, located three miles northeast of the mainland. It's a volcanic rock comprising some 300 acres with hiking trails, an observation tower, picnic tables and lovely beaches. The real attraction, however, is its surrounding 550 acres of underwater coral gardens, home to more than 250 species of fish. This is a true snorkeler's paradise, with an underwater trail and visibility of more than 100 feet. Several operators will take you there and set you up with snorkel equipment: **Big Beard's Adventure Tours** *(☎ 773-4482)*, **Diva** *(☎ 778-3161)*, **Llewellyn's Charter** *(☎ 773-9027)*, **Teroro II** *(☎ 773-3161)*, and **Mile Mark Water Sports** *(☎ 773-2628)*. Not to be missed!

Cruzan Rum Factory ★★★

West Airport Road, Frederiksted, ☎ *(809) 772- 799.*
Tours of the rum distillery and bottling plant are offered Monday-Friday from 9:00-11:30 a.m. and 1:00–4:15 p.m. Check out the colorful mural in the tasting room, which depicts an old sugar plantation of the 1840s. You get to sample the product at the conclusion, but unless you're really interested and have never seen a rum factory before, skip this brief and relatively expensive tour (most such factories let you tour for free). One amusing sight: the mango tree, where workers write their names on the ripening fruit to keep the tourists from picking it.

Estate Mount Washington Planta ★★★

West coast, Frederiksted, ☎ *(809) 772-1026.*
Take a self-guided walking tour through the excavated ruins of a sugar plantation.

Estate Whim Plantation Museum ★★★★

Centerline Road, Frederiksted, ☎ (809) 772-0598.

Hours Open: 10 a.m.–4 p.m.

This partially restored sugar plantation gives a good look at what life was like in St. Croix in the 1800s. The handsome great house, built of lime, stone and coral and boasting walls three feet thick, is beautifully restored and filled with antiques. The grounds also include the cookhouse where you can feast on Johnny cakes ($1 each and well worth it, but the old woman who cooks them is a real crab and forbids pictures, and charges another dollar for the recipe), a woodworking shop, a windmill, and an apothecary. The giftshop is excellent; even if you're not interested in seeing the plantation, it's worth a trip just to peruse the interesting wares for sale. $1 for children.

Guided Tours ★★★

Various locations, Frederiksted.

If you choose to leave the driving to someone else, these companies are happy to oblige with guided tours of St. Croix's highlights. Be sure to check in advance if admission charges to attractions are included in the rates. **Eagle Tours** *(☎ 778-3313)*, **St. Croix Safari Tours** *(☎ 773-6700)*, and **Travellers Tours** *(☎ 778-1636)*. **Take-a-Hike** offers walking tours and hikes; call *☎ 778-6997*. For a birds-eye view of the island, call **St. Croix Aviation** *(☎ 778-0090)*, which offers sightseeing flights.

Salt River Bay National Historical Park ★★★★

Route 80 near Route 75, Frederiksted.

These 912 tropical acres were added to the national park system under the Bush Administration. The park remains in a pristine condition and is home to many threatened and endangered plant and animal species. It is the largest remaining mangrove forest in the Virgin Islands and a great spot for birdwatching. The site includes an old earthen fort, an Indian ceremonial ball court, and burial grounds. This is also the only documented site on U.S. soil on which Christopher Columbus landed. His ill-fated "discovery" in 1493 led to a skirmish with Carib Indians, with fatalities on both sides.

Sports

Sports on St. Croix run the tropical gamut of water games to golf, horseback riding, sailing and sportsfishing. Many visitors charter a sailboat to Buck Island or to other neighboring islands. Prices on charters and boats-for-hire are controlled by the National Parks Service, but they may change, so do your best to negotiate.

Golf

Various locations, Christiansted.

Duffers have three choices on St. Croix. **Carambol Golf Club** *(☎ 778-5638)* is a gorgeous, par-72 course designed by Robert Trent Jones. Located in St. Croix's northwest part, golfing on scenic 18 holes costs $50 per person per day (you can go around as many as you want), plus $18 mandatory cart rental for 18 holes. Near Christiansted, the Buccaneer course is a challenging 18 holes. Greens fees are about

$25. Call ☎ *773-2100.* **The Reef Club** at Tegue Bay *(☎ 773-8844)* is a nine-hole course. Greens fees are $8 for nine holes, $12 for 18.

Paul and Jill's Equestrian Center

Sprat Hall, near Frederiksted, ☎ (809) 772-2880.

Well-regarded for their high-quality horses, this stable takes folks out for two-hour trail rides through the rainforest and past Danish ruins. Jill's family has lived on St. Croix for some 200 years. Two-hour rides are about $50, and reservations are essential. Closed Sundays.

Watersports

Various locations, Frederiksted.

For scuba diving, try: **Dive Experience** *(☎ 773-3307)*, **Virgin Island Divers** *(☎ 773-6045)*, **Anchor Dive Center** *(☎ 778-1522)*, **Blue Dolphin Divers** *(☎ 773-8634)*, **Cruzan Divers** *(☎ 772-3701)*, **Cane Bay Dive Shop** *(☎ 773-9913)*, and **Dive St. Croix** *(☎ 773-3434)*. For deep-sea fishing: **St. Croix Marin** *(☎ 773-7165)*, **Captain Pete's Sportfishing** (☎ *773-1123*), and **Cruzan Divers** *(☎ 772-3701)*. For cruises and boating, try **Mile Mark Chaters** *(☎ 773-2628)*, **Sundance** *(☎ 778-9650)*, **Llwewellyn's Charter** *(☎ 773-9027)*, **Bilinda Charters** *(☎ 773-1641)*, and **Junie Bomba's** *(☎ 772-2482*). For windsurfing: **Lisa Neuburger Windsurfing Center** *(☎ 778-8312)* and **Minstral School** *(☎ 773-4810)*.

Where to Eat

Fielding's Highest Rated Restaurants in St. Croix

★★★★★	**Cafe Madeleine**	$18–$26
★★★★	**Kendrick's**	$14–$26
★★★	**Blue Moon**	$10–$20
★★★	**Harvey's**	$8–$20
★★★	**Le St. Tropez**	$10–$25
★★★	**Mahogany**	$26–$36
★★★	**Top Hat**	$14–$28

Fielding's Special Restaurants in St. Croix

★★★★★	**Cafe Madeleine**	$18–$26
★★★	**Blue Moon**	$10–$20
★★★	**Harvey's**	$8–$20
★★	**Comanche**	$9–$21
★★	**Picnic in Paradise**	$10–$20

Fielding's Budget Restaurants in St. Croix

★	**Mango Grove**	$5–$8
★★	**Tivoli Gardens**	$6–$20
★★★	**Harvey's**	$8–$20
★★★	**Blue Moon**	$10–$20
★★	**Comanche**	$9–$21

The best restaurants are in Christiansted, though you can find a handful of good ones in Frederiksted. New ones sprout up all the time. Prices are not cheap and could run you up to $100 for two (without wine) for the top-class options. Grilled fish are the specialty of the island, particularly **Comanche Restaurant**, which adds extremely exotic sauces. **Chart House** has a terrific view of the boat-filled harbor.

Christiansted

Antoine's **$$$** ★★

58A King Street, ☎ (809) 773-0263.
International cuisine. Specialties: Omelets, goulash, wienerschnitzel, lobster.
Lunch: 11 a.m.–2:30 p.m., entrees $14–$32.
Dinner: 6:30–9:30 p.m., entrees $14–$32.

Many visitors get their wakeup javas at this second-floor charmer in the Anchor Inn. The breakfast menu boasts at least a dozen omelets loaded with interesting combinations. But that's not all that's here—bartenders proffer tropical concoctions and a huge selection of beer to a lively crowd. At dinner, hearty and tasty German and Middle-European food appears on the generous plates—despite the restaurant's French name. From the terrace, there's a great view of seagoing vessels on the wharf below.

Banana Bay Club **$$$** ★★

44A Queen Cross St., ☎ (809) 778-9110.
Seafood cuisine.
Lunch: 7 a.m.–4 p.m., entrees $15–$25.
Dinner: 4–11 p.m., entrees $15–$25.

Sit surrounded by 18th-century buildings and 20th-century businessfolk who gather for gossip and low-key deal-making in this open-air eatery known for fresh seafood, burgers and steaks. The Banana Bay Club is located in the Caravelle Hotel, one of downtown's lodging bargains. You don't have to pay high prices for unsurprising, well-prepared food and a great view of the Christiansted harbor.

Cafe Madeleine **$$$** ★★★★★

Estate Teague Bay, Teague Bay, ☎ (809) 773-8141.
Italian cuisine.
Dinner: 6–10 p.m., entrees $18–$26.

The crowning glory of the Villa Madeleine, the romantic haven on the east coast of the island, this restaurant recalls a posh plantation house of bygone days. It's all dolled up in butter-yellow paint, and the patio bursts with bright blooms. The primarily Italian-continental cuisine is some of the finest on the island, with specialties like lamb served with rosemary and garlic in a Barolo wine glaze and open ravioli with fresh lobster in a sauterne sauce. On Sundays, brunch is served from 11:00 a.m.-2:00 p.m. for $16.

Chart House **$$$** ★★

59 King's Wharf, ☎ (809) 773-7718.
American cuisine. Specialties: Prime rib, mud pie.
Dinner: 6–10 p.m., entrees $14–$26.

Most stateside visitors are familiar with this chain restaurant based in California. Christiansted's version does not disappoint—the waitstaff is perky, the prime rib is cut the way you like it, the copious salad bar is one of the best on the island, and it's constantly mobbed. There's no outdoor dining, but the decor is nautical and it's so close to the water that it really doesn't matter, especially when you're lucky to get a seat with a harbor view.

Comanche **$$** ★★

1 Strand Street, ☎ (809) 773-2665.
International cuisine.
Lunch: 11:30 a.m.–2:30 p.m., entrees $9–$21.
Dinner: 6–9 p.m., entrees $9–$21.

A pianist tickles the ivories nightly at this intimate and consistently reliable terrace restaurant in the Comanche Inn. Decor is south-seas style, with wicker chairs and fans, and the cuisine runs the gamut from Chinese specialties to conch chowder. Serving three meals a day, the Comanche is also known for a filling West Indian lunch.

Dino's **$$$** ★★

4-C Hospital Street, ☎ (809) 778-8005.
Mediterranean cuisine. Specialties: Fresh pasta.
Dinner: entrees $14–$20.

After a tour of the nearby 17th-century Fort Christiansvaern, repair to this historical house serving thoroughly modern Italian fare. Chef Dwight deLude makes his pasta fresh every day, and he likes to experiment; sometimes there's ravioli made with sweet potatoes or other interesting vegetables. Sauces are always intensely flavored and made with fresh garden herbs.

Harvey's **$$** ★★★

11 Company Street, ☎ (809) 773-3433.
Latin American cuisine.
Lunch: entrees $8–$20.
Dinner: entrees $8–$20.

Motherly Sarah Harvey is the chef-owner of this small West Indian dinner house and local hangout. Timid diners won't remain so for long, because Harvey likes to visit at every table, and since there's no real menu, she'll discuss what's cookin' for the evening. Sometimes there's goat water or local seafood in butter sauce, and a mountain of island-grown veggies and starches. The decor could be described best as thrift-shop modern: plastic tableware and folding chairs.

Kendrick's **$$$** ★★★★

52 King Street, ☎ (809) 773-9199.
International cuisine.
Dinner: 6–10 p.m., entrees $14–$26.

Dine among the antiques in yet another restored old Danish home that's one of the island's toniest (and priciest) eating establishments. The nattily attired and well-trained wait staff keeps wineglasses full and dishes cleared deftly between courses. Chef David prepares island-inspired French cuisine and his specialties often include a luscious pork loin with a roasted pecan crust or rack of lamb marinated with crushed herbs and served with roasted garlic and thyme sauce. There are three dining rooms, and you'll be equally well-treated no matter which one you end up in.

Mahogany **$$$** ★★★

Kings Hill, ☎ (809) 778-3800.
Seafood cuisine.
Dinner: 6–10 p.m., entrees $26–$36.

This gourmet outlet at the Westin Carombola is open only on Tuesday, Thursday and Saturday. The formal dining room has a high, high beamed ceiling and pretty furniture for a gracious atmosphere. The menu features such delicacies as French snails sauteed in garlic, shallots and pernod and wrapped in chicken tenderloins; pan-seared mahi mahi encrusted with hazelnuts; and West Indian shrimp filled with backfin lump crabmeat and fine herbs. There are also beef and lamb dishes for carnivores. Men are requested to don collared shirts and slacks.

Mango Grove **$** ★

King and Queen Cross streets, ☎ (809) 773-0200.
American cuisine.
Lunch: from 11 a.m., entrees $5–$8.
Dinner: to late, entrees $5–$8.

I couldn't resist checking this place out after spotting their sign out front: "Hostess is getting a pedicure. Please seat yourself." That about sums up the casual atmosphere at this cool little spot in a nicely shaded courtyard. Munch on typical salads, burgers or sandwiches and quaff a cool beer at this friendly spot—and be sure to compliment the hostess on her perfect feet.

Picnic in Paradise **$$** ★★

Cane Bay, ☎ (809) 778-1212.
Italian cuisine.
Dinner: entrees $10–$20.

It's worth a drive up the north coast to dine at this lovely indoor-outdoor restaurant in a protected coral cove near Cane Bay. Whether on the deck or in a breeze-filled dining room, meals are generally well-prepared and often include conch fritters, filet mignon and other West Indian-Continental specialties. If not quite paradise, it comes pretty close, if only for an hour.

Saman **$$$** ★

Kings Hill, ☎ (809) 778-3800.
American cuisine.
Dinner: 6–10 p.m., entrees $15–$20.

The best reason to come to this restaurant at the Westin Carombola is to sit outside, enjoy the sea breeze, and groove to the excellent live jazz every Tuesday evening (other nights see steel, calypso and island bands). The menu offers up seafood, steaks, chicken and pasta dishes; the caesar salad with char-grilled shrimp, salmon or chicken is especially good. Wednesday nights are given over to a seafood buffet ($29), while Friday is a pirate theme night with limbo dancers and other entertainment (also $29).

Tivoli Gardens **$$$** ★★

39 Strand, ☎ (809) 773-6782.
International cuisine.
Lunch: 11:15 a.m.–2:30 p.m., entrees $6–$15.
Dinner: 6–9:30 p.m., entrees $11–$20.

There's a fairyland of lights and greenery on the spacious porch of this popular saloon facing Christiansted harbor. A surprising carnival of eclectic treats are prepared with aplomb—witness Hungarian goulash and a Thai curry on the same menu. The frequently served chocolate velvet cake is wicked on the waistline and heaven on the tastebuds.

Top Hat **$$$** ★★★

52 Company Street, ☎ (809) 773-2346.
Seafood cuisine. Specialties: Herring appetizers, frikadeller with red cabbage, gravlax.
Dinner: 6–10 p.m., entrees $14–$28.

Probably the only Danish restaurant on the island, Top Hat has consistently pleased visitors and residents for 20 years. The Danish owners—chef Bent Rasmussen and his wife Hanne—run a spic-and-span operation on the top floor of a charming gingerbread trimmed-house. Located above a shopping center, it's painted in muted, tasteful tones.

Frederiksted

Blue Moon **$$** ★★★

17 Strand St., ☎ (809) 772-2222.
International cuisine.
Dinner: entrees $10–$20.

Hot jazz and hot food draw folks to this restaurant and club in a quaint Victorian building in the heart of funky, laid-back Fredericksted. The place bustles Friday night for live jazz concerts and at Sunday brunch, and this bistro's creative chefs are always experimenting with different cooking styles. Some nights, specials could be Cajun, or at other times French-influenced Asian temptations. Usually there are one or more chocolate delights on the dessert menu. Closed July-September.

Le St. Tropez **$$$** ★★★

67 King Street, ☎ (809) 772-3000.
French cuisine.
Lunch: entrees $10–$25.
Dinner: entrees $10–$25.

This amiable bistro is a corner of Gallic charm in the center of the West Indian town of Fredericksted. Familiar favorites like quiche, roast duck and frog legs are served on a terrace or in a romantic dining room. The woodsy bar is a little dark, but that's how many people like it.

Where to Shop

Shopping only seems to get better on this island, though the brick or stone sidewalks and some hefty flights up may make it difficult for those with knee problems or the elderly. If you're healthy and able, pray that your ship docks at Christiansted's **Gallows Bay** (where there are more stores than at Frederiksted). Some new complexes near the water (**Pan Am Pavilion** and **Caravelle Arcade**) are more walker-friendly. If you are turned on by low prices, look for substantial savings on fine china and crystal (30–50 percent), perfume, liquor (60 percent cheaper), cigarettes (40 percent cheaper), watches, gold jewelry and imported cosmetics. If you're in need of resort wear and Indonesian style sarongs, head for **Java Wraps** in the Pan Am Pavilion. **Wayne James Boutique**, a famous native designer, offers excellent ladies' fashions. Also recommended are the gift shop at Estate Whim Plantation and the 1870 Town House Shoppes in Christiansted. U.S. citizens are allowed to bring home $1200 worth of goods tax-free and five-fifths of liquor (six, if one is locally produced, plus up to $100 in gifts.

St. Croix Directory

BUSINESS HOURS

Stores open weekdays 9 a.m.–5 p.m., some later in Christiansted. Banks generally open Monday–Thursday 9 a.m.–2:30 p.m. and Friday 9 a.m.–2 p.m. and 3:30–5 p.m.

CLIMATE

Temperatures during the summer, cooled by eastern trade winds, keep the temperature around 82 degrees F. Brief showers also keep things cool. Winter temperatures rise to 77 degrees F. Rainiest months are September–January, and about 40 inches of rain fall per year. A light sweater is needed in winter.

DOCUMENTS

U.S. citizens need not carry a passport, although some proof of identity will be required upon leaving the islands. A passport is a good idea since the nearby British Virgin Islands are so accessible from St. John and St. Thomas. If you wish to dive the Rhone or snorkel amid the fantastic granite boulders at the baths on Virgin Gorda, you'll need to first clear BVI Customs with a passport and an $8 entry fee.

ELECTRICITY

Current runs at 110 volts at 60 cycles.

GETTING AROUND

Transportation on the islands is handled either by taxi or rental cars. Remember, that driving is on the left side of the road. Many rental companies in Cuz Bay offer competitive rates. Expect to pay roughly $60 per day, plus gas and insurance for a Suzuki Sidekick (with four-wheel drive to accommodate the blind switchbacks and extreme mountain inclines).

LANGUAGE

The official language is English, but the special lilt to the accent is called cruzan. Some locals speak a musical patois called English Creole—a blend of English, African and Spanish. Many people also speak good Spanish.

MEDICAL EMERGENCIES

St. Croix has a 250-bed **hospital** ☎ *(809) 778-6311*, with 24-hour emergency service. Ask your hotel about doctors on call when you check-in.

MONEY

The official currency is the U.S. dollar.

TELEPHONE

The area code is *809*. Since USVI is an incorporated territory, toll-free numbers that operate in the U.S. work here. You can also dial direct to the mainland. Normal postage rates apply.

TIME

Atlantic Standard Time, one hour later than New York City; during Daylight Saving Time, it is the same as New York.

TIPPING AND TAXES

Leave a 15 percent tip for waiters and waitresses. Taxi drivers should receive a 15 percent tip if you are satisfied with the service.

TOURIST INFORMATION

The **St. Croix Tourist Office** ☎ *(809) 773-0495* is located at the Christiansted Wharf. It is open daily.

WHEN TO GO

The Fiesta Food Fair is held on Jan. 5 at the Agriculture Fair Grounds in Estate Lower Love, featuring native cooks and their cuisine, arts and crafts, and steel and quelbe bands. Organic Act Day is June 21. Oct. is one of the busiest months. The Champagne Mumm's Cup Regatta sets sail on Oct. 8–10. Columbus Day/Puerto Rican Friendship Day is celebrated on Oct. 6–10, a week-long celebration featuring parade, horse racing and native foods and music. The St. Croix Jazz & Caribbean Music & Arts Festival takes place in mid-October. The Golden Hook Challenge is slated for Oct. 21–23, a sportsfishing contest. Veterans Day is celebrated on Nov. 11,with island-style parades of steel bands, calypso and partying. The Crucian Christmas Fiesta, the traditional two-week event that features parades, pageants, food and music starts Dec. 11–Jan. 7. The Crucian Christmas Festival Food Fairs in Christiansted and Frederiksted is held in the third week of Dec. The Festival Village in Christiansted takes place on Dec. 29. Frederiksted's Village opens on Dec. 30, with nightly reggae, calypso and Latin music. A Carnival-like Christmas celebration takes place from several days before Christmas to about a week after New Year's.

ST. CROIX RESTAURANTS		PHONE	ENTREE	CR. CARDS
Christiansted				
	American			
★★	Chart House	(809) 773-7718	$14–$26••	A, DC, MC, V
	International			
★★★★	Kendrick's	(809) 773-9199	$14–$26••	A, MC, V
★★	Antoine's	(809) 773-0263	$14–$32	A, MC, V
★★	Comanche	(809) 773-2665	$9–$21	A, MC, V
★★	Tivoli Gardens	(809) 773-6782	$6–$20	A, MC, V
	Italian			
★★★★★	Cafe Madeleine	(809) 773-8141	$18–$26	A, DC, MC, V
★★	Picnic in Paradise	(809) 778-1212	$10–$20••	A, MC, V
	Latin American			
★★★	Harvey's	(809) 773-3433	$8–$20	None
	Mediterranean			
★★	Dino's	(809) 778-8005	$14–$20••	None
	Seafood			
★★★	Top Hat	(809) 773-2346	$14–$28••	A, MC, V
★★	Banana Bay Club	(809) 778-9110	$15–$25	A, MC, V
Frederiksted				
	French			
★★★	Le St. Tropez	(809) 772-3000	$10–$25	A, MC, V
	International			
★★★	Blue Moon	(809) 772-2222	$10–$20••	A

Note: • Lunch Only

•• Dinner Only

ST. JOHN

Constant trade winds off St. John thrill windsurfers.

For many die-hard ecotourists, St. John is one of the greatest natural wonders of the three U.S. Virgin Islands. In fact, the two major diversions here are climbing and "limin" (that is, "laying back," Caribbean style)—the latter preferably done before *and* after the former. Unlike so many other flat, arid Caribbean isles, the U.S. Virgin Islands (which also include St. Croix and St. Thomas), are beautifully sculpted and vividly green, and St. John has more than its fair share of emerald green bays, snow-white beaches, and lushly carpeted mountain peaks; in fact, almost two-thirds of the island's land area, plus another 5600 acres underwater, compose the U.S. Virgin Islands National Park, donated to the United States by Laurence Rockefeller. As such, there are terrific adventures both above and under water, so untrod that many visitors come for weeks and never get beyond the gorgeous **Trunk Bay Beach**. All it takes is a good pair of boots and a little guidance to mash one's way through densely packed rain forest or hike over well-marked nature trails that lead past 200-year-old plantation houses. Underwater the views are just as spectacular, with rock formations, grottoes and wrecks that rate as some of the best in the Caribbean. The absence of sales tax here has been known to drive some visitors to frenzy, but once the shopper's dust settles, they find that the most pleasant thing to do on St. John is just to lay back, drink in hand, shades in place, and soak up the rays.

Bird's Eye View

The U.S. Virgin Islands lie 1500 miles southeast of New York and about 1000 miles south of Miami. A mere 18 degrees above the equator, they are bounded to the north by the Atlantic Ocean and the south by the Caribbean Sea, except for St. Croix, which is surrounded by the Caribbean. St. John is two miles east of St. Thomas, and a mere 20-minute ferry ride away. A three-mile expanse called Pillsbury Sound separates St. John from St. Thomas, and between the two islands lie a few, smaller, mostly uninhabited ones, or so Christopher Columbus fantasized when he named the group St. Ursula and her 11,000 virgins. The highest peak is **Bordeaux Mountain** at 1277 feet. Most of St. John's 2500 residents live in the area surrounding **Cruz Bay**, a tiny, ramshackle town, where ferries and cruise-ship tenders dock, tourists shop, and islanders go about their very laid-back business. Scenic overlooks provide a glimpse of broad expanses of white sand lapped by a turquoise sea. Closer inspection reveals a sugary white sand and interesting snorkeling offshore. When the ferry landing was built in Cruz Bay, opening a gateway to St. Thomas and her airport, the closest to St. John, Coral Bay sank slowly into seclusion. It's a pass-through for those on their way to Salt Pond Beach or Don Carlos Mexican Seafood Cantina. The new eateries like Skinny Legs and Shipwreck Landing are beginning to lure crowds to Coral Bay.

History

Archaeologists have yet to decide whether the Arawaks or Caribs (the island's first pre-Columbian inhabitants), African slaves or a combination thereof were responsible for the primitive etchings along the Reef Bay trail. In 1493, Columbus discovered the islands of St. Croix, St. John and St. Thomas, and then shoved off to Puerto Rico. A hundred years later saw the arrival in St. John of Sir Francis Drake as he prepared to confront the Spanish troops in San Juan. While St. Croix changed hands between the French and Spanish, St. John (along with St. Thomas) was appropriated by the Danish West India Company, becoming a hub of business (St. Thomas), and a magnet for sugarcane, tobacco and cotton plantations (St. John). In 1717, the Danes established St. John's Coral Bay as a permanent port. In 1733, a great slave rebellion devastated the country, when a large mass of slaves, ostensibly carrying bundles of wood, were admitted to Fort Berg in Coral Bay. Once inside, they brandished cane knives and massacred hundreds of settlers and the entire Danish garrison. The rebels held the fort for nine months until the

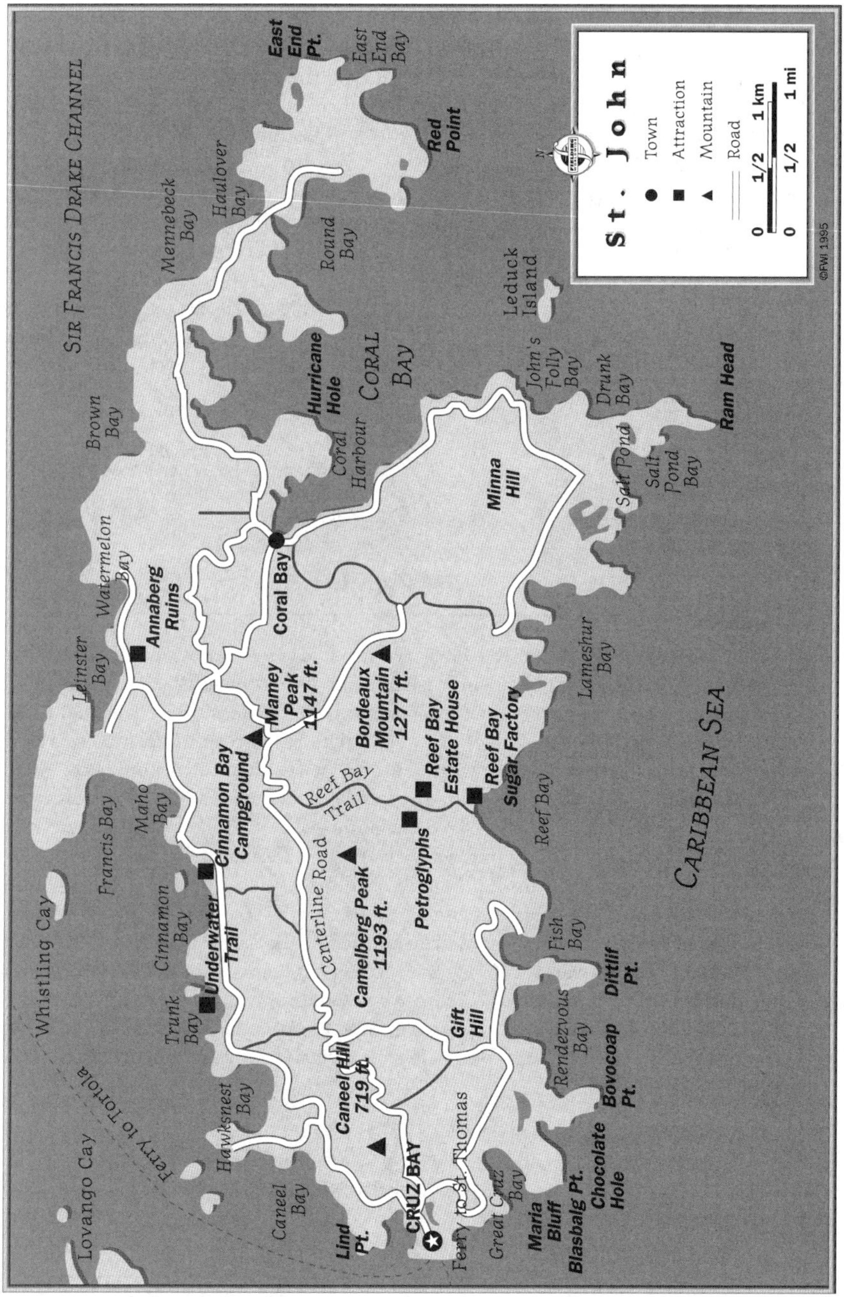
St. John
Town
Attraction
Mountain
Road
0 1/2 1 km
0 1/2 1 mi
©FWI 1995
Sir Francis Drake Channel
Caribbean Sea
Coral Bay
Lovango Cay
Whistling Cay
Ferry to Tortola
Ferry to St. Thomas
Cruz Bay
Lind Pt.
Caneel Bay
Hawksnest Bay
Trunk Bay
Cinnamon Bay
Maho Bay
Francis Bay
Leinster Bay
Watermelon Bay
Brown Bay
Mennebeck Bay
Haulover Bay
Round Bay
East End Pt.
East End Bay
Red Point
Leduck Island
Hurricane Hole
Coral Harbour
John's Folly Bay
Drunk Bay
Salt Pond
Salt Pond Bay
Ram Head
Minna Hill
Lameshur Bay
Reef Bay
Reef Bay Sugar Factory
Reef Bay Estate House
Reef Bay Trail
Bordeaux Mountain 1277 ft.
Mamey Peak 1147 ft.
Annaberg Ruins
Cinnamon Bay Campground
Underwater Trail
Centerline Road
Camelberg Peak 1193 ft.
Petroglyphs
Fish Bay
Dittlif Pt.
Gift Hill
Rendezvous Bay
Bovocoap Pt.
Caneel Hill 719 ft.
Chocolate Hole
Great Cruz Bay
Maria Bluff
Blasbalg Pt.

Danes, with the support of two French warships and an army from Martinique, recaptured the island and rebuilt the factories. In 1848, slavery was abolished, though planters tried to hold onto their crops until the advent of the European sugar-beet soured their profits. When the planters eventually left the island, the former slaves divided up their properties and relied on the land and the sea to provide their sustenance. In 1917, with a view to protect its interest in the Panama Canal, the U.S.bought the Virgin Islands package—St. John, St. Thomas and St. Croix—from the Danes for a mere $25 million. Starting in the 50s, tourism began to strategically raise the standard of living. In 1956, Laurence Rockefeller took a shine to the island and erected his Caneel Bay resort, which gave visitors full opportunity to enjoy the pleasures of the park. With the advent of the Maho Bay resort in 1976, more ecologically oriented travelers arrived on St. John's shores, ready to scale and sail the challenging resources. Luxury entered with the opening of the Virgin Grand, now the Hyatt Regency, with a slew of high-class condos following in its wake.

People

There are only about 3500 people who live on St. John, many of them not quite sure they want their small island overrun with tourists. That may be the reason why visitors are sometimes treated with a measure of distance. Locals take time to warm to conversation, and while they stop traffic talking among themselves, few may laugh with you. (To be fair, just one look at how American cruise passengers sometimes treat islanders—with an air of patronization left over from the master-slave dynamic—should fully explain their coolness.) Reggae is a major passion, as is the Rastafarianism influence, and belief in the supernatural runs high: natives still believe the jumbies (spirits) caused the closing of the Reef Bay Sugar Factory in 1916. You'll find a number of American ex-pats here, who, keen to the laid-back lifestyle, spend their days casually selling wares in Cruz Bay. If you can leave your cellular phone and datebook at home, it will take only a few days to understand the Virgin vibe called "limin"—a kind of wrinkle in time phenomenon that makes it impossible to do anything else but lounge, sip cool drinks and daydream.

Beaches

The island's best beach, **Trunk Bay**, is the most photographed spot in the Caribbean, but underwater it's beginning to show wear and tear. Non-divers can use a unique snorkeling scuba system (SNUBA) that involves an air-sup-

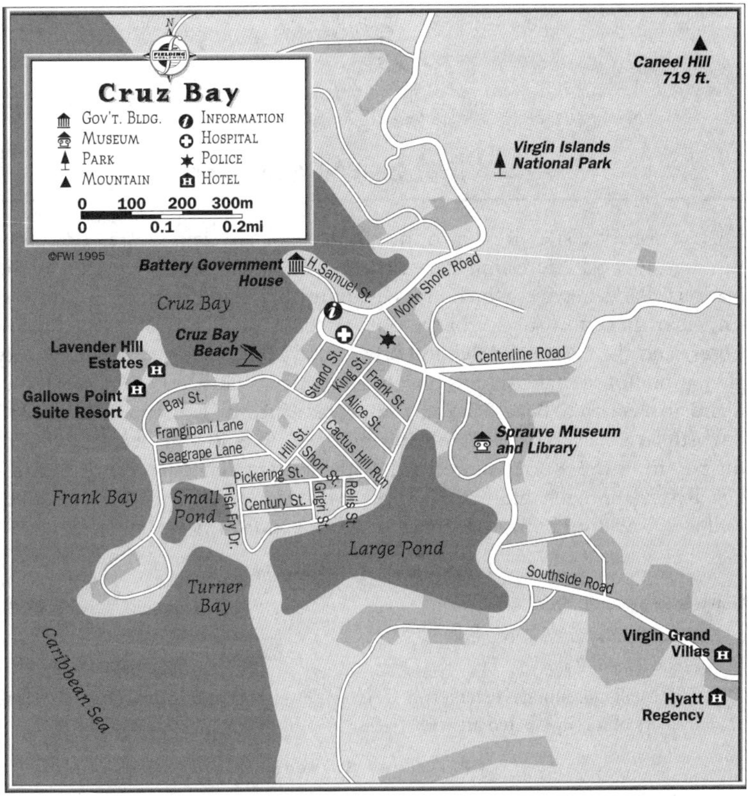

port raft attached to a 20-foot line allowing the snorkeler the thrill of diving. There are also snorkel rentals and lockers for hire, as well as snack bars. The beach, however, should be well avoided on days when cruise ships pull into port. **Hawks Nest Bay Beach**, a rollercoaster ride from Caneel, is a favorite beach. It's a 15-minute walk from the reception area of the **Caneel Bay** resort, and is usually very deserted. **Cinnamon Bay** is long and powdery, and the national park maintains a little historical museum. Difficult to reach over a torturous road, **Maho Bay** is beautiful and calm, full of turtles, and well worth the effort. Coves unreachable by car are **Solomon** and **Honeymoon** behind the Cruz Bay Center. The short hike will fill a morning (nudists prefer it, even if there is an official law against taking it all off). Palm trees fringe both coves and a rocky outcropping separates them, providing excellent snorkeling. **Reef Bay**, in the south, is reached by a 2.5-mile trail descending through a shady moist rain forest, after which comes a dry scrub forest. **Salt Pond** is also especially good for snorkeling and features a hearty climb to **Ram's Head**.

What Else to See

A few historical sites are worth the effort (some are even located on trails). Among the most interesting is the **Annaberg Sugar Mill Ruins**, operated by the National Parks Service, which gives living history demonstrations of how islanders managed to survive in the post-slavery years. The **Elaine Ione Spauve Library** and the **Museum of Cultural Arts** in Cruz Bay occupy an 18th-century plantation house that contains photos and artifacts illustrating the survival of island arts. A trip to **Caneel Bay**, the resort launched by Laurence Rockefeller, is worth a visit, even if you aren't staying there, to enjoy the dazzling view of the bay from the North Shore road. **Catherineberg Plantation** down Centerline Road, approachable from a rocky road, also has stupendous views, as well as a now crumbling windmill, full of stupendous views.

Museums and Exhibits

Elaine Ione Sprauve Museum ★★★

Cruz Bay, ☎ (809) 776-6359.

Hours Open: 9 a.m.–5 p.m.

This small museum has exhibits on St. John's Danish West Indian history, as well as displays of locally created artwork.

Parks and Gardens

Virgin Islands National Park ★★★★★

Cruz Bay, ☎ (809) 776-6201.

No visit to St. John—or any of the U.S. Virgins—would be complete without at least a day spent at the breathtaking national park. It encompasses 12,624 acres and has 20 miles of trails to explore. Stop by the Visitors Center (open daily from 8:00 a.m.to 4:30 p.m.) to peruse the exhibits, pick up a map, and get details of special ranger-led events. Highlights on the park include the Annaberg Ruins, a sugar plantation and mill from the 1780s; the Reef Bay Trail, which passes plantation ruins and petroglyphs); and Trunk Bay, a picture-postcard beach and the start of a marked underwater trail well-loved by snorkelers.

Tours

Guided Tours

Cruz Bay.

The St. John Taxi Association will show you around the island for about $30 for one or two people, $13 per person for three or more. The **St. John Island Tour** *(☎ 774-4550)* lasts two hours and costs $12 per person. Ranger-led tours are popular at **Virgin Islands National Park**; call *☎ 776-6201* for details. Finally, local personality **Miss Lucy** *(☎ 776-6804)* tailors private tours to individual interests, while **John Abraham** *(☎ 776-6177)* offers a friendly, insider's look at his island.

BEST VIEW:

Le Chateau de Bordeaux clings to the edge of a mountain top along Centerline Road, which gives spectacular views of Bordeaux Mountain, St. John's highest peak, and the serpentine Sir Francis Drake Channel, with the British Virgin Islands scattered below. And the cuisine is superb.

Sports

Watersports are an integral part of the St. John lifestyle. At Trunk Bay, a new sport called SNUBA has become very popular—a combination of snorkeling and scuba diving that doesn't require lengthy certification courses. Both campgrounds offer extensive sports packages, including scuba and trekking. The Virgin Islands are famous for spectacular deep-sea fishing for blue marlin, with many world records to prove it. Anglers from all over the world head here for the **Blue Marlin Fishing Tournament** in August. No deep-sea fishing is allowed in the National Park, but you can rod-and-reel fish from the beaches in St. John. Excellent sea conditions with balmy weather and numerous covers and sheltered anchors create unparalleled conditions for sailing. Every type of vessel, from sailfish to oceangoing yachts, can be hired. Boats may be chartered with a full crew or bareback, but know what you are doing if you choose to leave the crew behind. There are many half-day and full-day boat excursions; check first with your hotel, which probably has a full list and can recommend what will best suit your needs. Operators in St. John are based in Cruz Bay and Coral Bay. Because of the constant trade winds, windsurfing also finds a large group of fans. The winds, whipping down the **Sir Francis Drake Channel** north of St. John, are funneled by two hills through the Narrows to the Windward Passage. About five miles north of Trunk Bay, on the north side of **Johnson's Reef**, the conditions are simply perfect. Windsurfers can also sail cross **Pillsbury Sound** to St. Thomas.

Watersports

Various locations, Cruz Bay.

For general equipment rentals, try: **Coral Bay Watersports** *(☎ 776-6850)*, **Paradise Watersports** *(☎ 693-8690)*, **Low Key Watersports** *(☎ 693-8999)*, **Cinnam Bay Watersports Center** *(☎ 776-6330)*, and **Cruz Bay Watersports** *(☎ 776-6234)*. The latter four also offer diving instruction and excursions. For deep-sea fishing, try **Gone Ketchin** *(☎ 693-8657)*, **World Class Anglers** *(☎ 779-4281)*, and **Low Key Watersports** *(☎ 693-8999)*. For kayaking and windsurfing, in addition to other rentals, call **Paradise Aqua Tour** *(☎ 776-6226)*.

Where to Eat

Fielding's Highest Rated Restaurants in St. John		
★★★★★	**Equator**	$27–$32
★★★★	**Asolare**	$18–$24
★★★★	**Le Chateau de Bordeaux**	$20–$30
★★★★	**Paradiso**	$17–$25
★★★	**Chow Mein**	$11–$24
★★★	**Don Carlos**	$9–$17
★★★	**Ellington's**	$17–$25
★★★	**Mongoose**	$6–$50
★★★	**Morgan's Mango**	$7–$22
★★★	**Pussers**	$6–$25

Fielding's Special Restaurants in St. John		
★★★★★	**Equator**	$27–$32
★★★★	**Asolare**	$18–$24
★★★★	**Le Chateau de Bordeaux**	$20–$30
★★★	**Morgan's Mango**	$7–$22
★★★	**Vie's Snack Shack**	$2–$6

Fielding's Budget Restaurants in St. John		
★★★	**Vie's Snack Shack**	$2–$6
★★	**The Lime Inn**	$3–$20
★★★	**Don Carlos**	$9–$17
★★	**Cafe Roma**	$11–$16
★★★	**Morgan's Mango**	$7–$22

Restaurants in St. John favor American, British, West Indian and Italian cuisines. Atmosphere can range from an outdoor patio with neighborhood strays, a West Indian gingerbread house, the peak of a mountain, or the ruins of a sugar mill—almost all are open to the wind. The best selection is in Cruz Bay, where you can also find elegant dining. Outside Cruz Bay is **Le Chateau de Bordeau**, the island's most ambitious restaurant, a comfortable low-ceiling room set atop the 1277-foot **Bordeaux Mountain**, St. John's highest point.

The menu ranges from scrumptious pumpkin soup to West Indian curry to Peking duck. **Asolare** offers up spicy Asian-influenced fare in a lovely setting. **Etta**, at the Inn at Tamarind Court, is perfect for callaloo soup—a delicious, thick seafood porridge with okra and spinach—and other West Indian delights. Remember **Morgan's Mango** for creative neo-Caribbean cuisine in a gingerbread setting. One of the most romantic settings on the island is Caneel Bay's **Equator**, a pretty stone building open to the fresh air. Their pan-fried flying fish makes a memory. For a quick, agreeable pub lunch in Cruz Bay, try **Pusser's** waterfront balcony.

Asolare **$$$** ★★★★

Route 20, ☎ (809) 779-4747.
Asian cuisine.
Dinner: 5:30–8:45 p.m., entrees $18–$24.

When the owners of five-star Chateau de Bordeaux decided to open a second restaurant, they searched high and far for a name until stumbling upon the Greek work *asolare*, which means "the purposeless, agreeable and leisurely passing of time." Except for the purposeless part, the moniker perfectly sums up this new restaurant, just opened in November 1994. Dine on a large deck overlooking Cruz Bay and the twinkling lights of St. Thomas, or in a charming stone-walled room dominated by a rock fireplace. The eclectic menu has a decidedly Asian bent, with local fish seasoned with the herbs and spices of India, Thailand, Vietnam and China. Try five-spice barbecued tuna with chilled Szechwan noodles, dry-fried long beans and red onion crisps; glass noodle prawns with wok-crisp Chinese greens and a roasted tomato, garlic, red chili and cilantro sauce; or roasted swordfish with scallion vermicalli cake, braised greens and a black bean-clam sauce. The combinations may sound odd, but the results are spectacular. Afterwards, slip off to the nearby Bad Art Bar (Route 10, Cruz Bay, 693-8666), a lively joint that lives up to its name with the tackiest decor imaginable, including, of course, a velvet Elvis.

Cafe Roma **$$** ★★

Cruz Bay, ☎ (809) 776-6524.
Italian cuisine. Specialties: Pizza, shrimp with garlic sauce.
Dinner: 5–10 p.m., entrees $11–$16.

A touch of Italy in the tropics, this pretty trattoria overlooks the sights and sounds of Cruz Bay from a second-floor perch. No slouch on gustatory or olfactory senses either, the place is noted for dynamite pizza—there's a choice of a white or traditional tomato sauce as a base for several tasty toppings. Seafood is also a standout, especially shrimp with garlic sauce. An excellent choice for a varied selection of tropical drinks.

Chow Mein **$$$** ★★★

Great Cruz Bay, ☎ (809) 693-8000.
International cuisine.
Dinner: 6–9:30 p.m., entrees $11–$24.

This restaurant's name has changed a few times since its inception (it used to be called Ciao Mein), but the cuisine atop the sprawling, atrium-style Hyatt Regency St. John has remained a successful melange of Asian and Italian culinary concoctions. Guests can watch the lobby action below while dining on wok-stirred seafood, pot stickers, or pasta with vegetables.

Don Carlos **$$** ★★★

10-19 Estate Carolina, ☎ (809) 776-6866.
Mexican cuisine.
Lunch: 11 a.m.–4 p.m., entrees $9–$17.
Dinner: 4–9 p.m., entrees $9–$17.

This upscale cantina buzzes with zingy waiters delivering foaming margaritas and zippy fajitas (this stateside chain is famous for them) to happy customers. Don Carlos also features lots of lively entertainment three nights a week. You might see island favorites like conch fritters slipped in here and there on the menu along with south of the border staples.

Ellington's **$$$** ★★★

Gallows' Point, ☎ (809) 693-8490.
International cuisine.
Dinner: 6–10 p.m., entrees $17–$25.
Some of the best seafood on the island is prepared here at this view spot positioned near the ferry dock. On a clear day, you can see St. Thomas from a front-row seat on the terrace. After a tasty drink, dine on hearty seafood chowder followed by the daily special, which could be blackened something, or shrimp in an exotic fruit sauce. A light breakfast is also served from 8 to 10 a.m.

Equator **$$$** ★★★★★

Caneel Bay, ☎ (809) 776-6111.
International cuisine.
Dinner: 6:30–9 p.m., entrees $27–$32.
Dine in a restored horse-powered sugar mill located on the lovely Caneel Bay Resort grounds. It's a cavernous round room, formerly called the Sugar Mill, with a large terrace where many patrons begin their meals with a luscious peach daiquiri. The new menu features favorite foods and spices from countries close to the equator—specialties from such diverse locales as Morocco, Bombay, Indonesia and Brazil are among the eclectic choices. Especially appealing is the red chili-glazed calamari served on a curry noodle pancake and the red lentil-crusted snapper. Afterwards, take a stroll along one of the resort's seven spectacular beaches.

Le Chateau de Bordeaux **$$$** ★★★★

Junction 10, Centerline Road, Bordeaux Mountain, ☎ (809) 776-6611.
French cuisine. Specialties: Saffron pasta.
Dinner: 5:30–9.00 p.m., entrees $20–$30.
This petite dazzler clings to the cliffs of Bordeaux Mountain in the center of the island, and its terrace commands an unparalleled view of the setting sun and rising moon. (If you're on St. John during a full moon, dinner here is a must!) Despite its unprepossessing exterior, within is a cozy room with hand-crocheted tablecloths, flickering oil lanterns and eclectic chandeliers. It's no surprise many honeymooners end up here, as this place just oozes romance. The cuisine is as good as the atmosphere—don't miss the saffron pasta (shaped to resemble an angle fish) stuffed with smoked salmon and sauteed in a sauce of capers, leeks, tomatoes and white wine. Other choices include pan-seared Norwegian salmon in light fennel bouillabaisse with cultured mussels over bow-tie pasta, roasted rack of lamb, and grilled pork loin. This is one of the Caribbean's few nonsmoking restaurants, though there's a deck where smokers can slip off to get their fix.

Mongoose **$$$** ★★★

Mongoose Junction, Mongoose Junction, ☎ (809) 693-8677.
International cuisine.
Lunch: 11:30 a.m.–5 p.m., entrees $6–$10.
Dinner: 5–10 p.m., entrees $10–$50.
A pleasant refueling spot for tired shoppers souvenir hunting at the Tony Mongoose Junction arcade, this eatery and bar offers a bevy of cooling fruity alcoholic drinks and plates of fresh seafood. Patrons poise themselves on a tree-shaded wooden deck or at the bar, which serves light meals until midnight.

Morgan's Mango **$$** ★★★

Cruz Bay, ☎ (809) 693-8141.

Latin American cuisine.

Dinner: 6–10 p.m., entrees $7–$22.

There's often a crowd at this very popular dining spot in a gingerbread trimmed-house painted in pastels. One reason is an excellent bar and unusual Argentinian specialties interspersed with local seafood and chicken. Another is the woodsy patio where guests sit surrounded by trees and greenery. A plate-crowding hunk of prime beef comes accompanied by the piquant Pampas-style chimmichurri sauce—a spicy melding of oregano, peppers, lots of garlic and olive oil.

Paradiso **$$$** ★★★★

Mongoose Junction, Mongoose Junction, ☎ (809) 693-8899.

Italian cuisine. Specialties: Lobster fra diavolo.

Dinner: 6–10 p.m., entrees $17–$25.

The words "suave" and "chic" appropriately describe this Italian restaurant all dolled up in burnished woods and marble. Dine in air-conditioned comfort on lobster or a daily seafood special prepared with their signature fra diavolo sauce. Paradiso also has an impressive wine list and well-mixed drinks.

Pussers **$$$** ★★★

Wharfside Village, ☎ (809) 693-9080.

International cuisine. Specialties: Mud pie.

Lunch: 11 a.m.–6 p.m., entrees $6–$10.

Dinner: 6–10 p.m., entrees $15–$25.

The purveyors of the British Royal Navy's favorite rum have been successful in expanding their small chain of souvenir shops/pub establishments into U.S. Virgin territory with this open-air crowd pleaser. Offering special meal deals that should satisfy all but the very fussy, there are all-you-can-eat Alaskan king crab nights on Friday and Caribbean specials on Thursdays. Sandwiches, seafood plates, and gooey desserts are also available, including the famous mud pie. Don't miss the "Pusser Painkiller" drinks—good for whatever ails you.

The Lime Inn **$$** ★★

Cruz Bay, ☎ (809) 776-6425.

International cuisine. Specialties: All-you-can-eat shrimp.

Lunch: 11:30 a.m.–3 p.m., entrees $3–$10.

Dinner: 5:30–10 p.m., entrees $3–$20.

The local practice of limin' is strictly adhered to here (it means "hanging out") and the congenial group of limers include veteran travelers" as well as residents. Settle for a terrace seat to while away the hours with a bowl of goat water, seafood, or a sandwich. Hungry bargain hunters crowd the place Wednesday nights for the well-regarded, all-you-can-eat shrimp extravaganza, but no reservations are taken, so line up early.

Vie's Snack Shack **$** ★★★

East End, ☎ (809) 693-5033.

Latin American cuisine.

Lunch: 10 a.m.–5 p.m., entrees $2–$6.

This is probably the best local cooking in town—but it's only open four days a week, and only for lunch. But if you're in town when Vie's at the stove, don't miss it for fritters both sweet and savory, homemade fruit drinks and spicy chicken.

Where to Shop

Duty-free shopping is the major incentive to pull out your wallet here, and aside from attractive pricing on watches, china, gems, electronics and jewelry, there is no sales tax and a $1200 per person exemption from duty when returning to the U.S. Liquor is also a bargain and anyone over 21 years of age can return to the States with five bottles duty-free (or six, if one is produced in the USVI). Island clothing and T-shirts are also good buys. Stop by Bamboula in Mongoose Junction for ethnic folk art and artifacts.

St. John Directory

BUSINESS HOURS

Shops generally open weekdays 9 a.m.–5 p.m. Banks generally open Monday–Thursday 9 a.m.–2:30 p.m. and Friday 9 a.m.–2 p.m. and 3:30–5 p.m.

CLIMATE

Temperatures during the summer, cooled by eastern trade winds, keep the temperature around 82 degrees F. Brief showers also keep things cool. Winter temperatures rise to 77 degrees F. Rainiest months are September-January, and about 40 inches of rain fall per year. April-August are the calmest sea conditions with the best visibility, although days of stunning clarity in excess of 100 feet are not unusual in winter.

DOCUMENTS

U.S. citizens need not carry a passport, although some proof of identity will be required upon leaving the islands. A passport is a good idea since the nearby British Virgin Islands are so accessible from St. John and St. Thomas. If you wish to dive the Rhone or snorkel amid the fantastic granite boulders at the baths on Virgin Gorda, you'll need to first clear BVI Customs with a passport and an $8 entry fee.

ELECTRICITY

Current runs at 110 volts at 60 cycles.

GETTING AROUND

Many rental companies in Cruz Bay offer competitive rates. Expect to pay roughly $60 per day, plus gas and insurance, for a Suzuki Sidekick (with four-wheel drive to accommodate blind switchbacks and extreme mountain inclines). And be prepared to drive on the left.

LANGUAGE

The official language is English. Some locals speak a musical patois called English Creole—a blend of English, African and Spanish. Many people also speak good Spanish.

MEDICAL EMERGENCIES

Police ext. *915*, fire ext. *921*, ambulance ext. *922*.

MONEY

The official currency is the U.S. dollar.

TELEPHONE

The area code is 809. Since USVI is an incorporated territory, toll-free numbers that operate in the U.S. work here, normal postage rates apply. You can also direct dial to the mainland.

TIME

Atlantic Standard Time, one hour later than New York City; during Daylight Saving Time, it is the same as New York.

TIPPING AND TAXES

A 15 percent tip for waiters and waitresses should be sufficient. Taxi drivers should receive a 15 percent tip if you are satisfied with the service.

TOURIST INFORMATION

The **St. John Tourist Office** ☎ *(809) 776-6450* is located around the corner from the Cruz Bay ferry dock by the post office. It is open daily. In the U.S. call ☎ *(212) 332-2222*.

WHEN TO GO

St. John's Carnival events take place from June 18-July 4, including a food fair, boat races and the recreation of a carnival village. The St. John Carnival Parade takes place on July 4.

The area code is *809*. Since USVI is an unincorporated territory, toll-free numbers that operate in the U.S. work here, normal U.S. postage rates apply. You can also direct dial to the mainland.

ST. JOHN RESTAURANTS	PHONE	ENTREE	CR. CARDS
Coral Bay			
Asian			
★★★★★ Asolare	(809) 779-4747	$10–$24••	DC, MC, V
French			
★★★★ Le Chateau de Bordeaux	(809) 779-4078	$6–$28	DC, MC, V
International			
★★★ Chow Mein	(809) 693-8000	$11–$24••	A, DC, MC, V
★★★★★ Equator	(809) 776-6111	$27–$32••	A, DC, MC, V
★★★ Ellington's	(809) 693-8490	$17–$25••	A, MC, V
★★★ Mongoose	(809) 693-8677	$6–$50	A, DC, MC, V
★★★ Pussers	(809) 693-9080	$6–$25	A, MC, V
★★ The Lime Inn	(809) 776-6425	$3–$20	A, MC, V
Italian			
★★★★ Paradiso	(809) 693-8899	$17–$25••	A, MC, V
★★ Cafe Roma	(809) 776-6524	$11–$16••	MC, V
Latin American			
★★★ Morgan's Mango	(809) 693-8141	$7–$22••	A, MC, V
★★★ Vie's Snack Shack	(809) 693-5033	•$2–$6	None

ST. JOHN RESTAURANTS	PHONE	ENTREE	CR. CARDS
Mexican			
★★★ Don Carlos	(809) 776-6866	$9–$17	A, MC, V
Note: • Lunch Only			
•• Dinner Only			

ST. KITTS

Local and international regattas are held at St. Kitts.

Imagine empty beaches, the lushest of flora, dark, humid rain forests, spectacular dive sites, and even fat black ladies sashaying down country roads with pumpkin-sized washing atop their proud heads—St. Kitts has a little something for everybody. With its sister island Nevis, St. Kitts forms a Caribbean nation that just declared its first decade of independence, but the pace of life hasn't changed here in centuries. The epitome of the "limin' life," Kittian culture is still propelled by that "stop for a beer anytime" attitude—an almost ecological spirit, since, despite a lot of dream schemes, the coastline hasn't yet been marred by too much construction. Simply, unhampered tranquility reigns in St. Kitts, and the noisiest thing you'll ever hear will be the gentle skittering of the surf across the black and blonde sands. At one time, St. Kitts was distinguished only by its array of small inns fashioned from old plantations. Today, after the once-pristine Frigate Bay has been developed into an enclave of condos and package-tour hotels, Kittians are understandably nervous about change, even as the island struggles to recover from losses incurred from the demise of Pan Am and 1989's Hurricane Hugo, which did serious damage. Nevertheless, there's an unmistakable stir in the breezy Kitts air, and new luxury hotels are not the only signs of resurgence. A waterfront warehouse has been restyled into a lively duty-free mall, and concerned citizens are busily recycling fine old buildings in the capital city into boutiques, restaurants and offices. With just a few more trendy stores and cafes added to its vast array of water activities, St. Kitts could easily become the next Caribbean nexus.

Bird's Eye View

Untrammeled by tourism, St. Kitts is a stunning combination of volcanic mountains, rain forest and golden beaches.

Part of the northern chain of the Leeward Islands in the Eastern Caribbean, St. Kitts covers an area of 68 square miles, divided by three volcanic mountains split by deep ravines and a low-lying peninsula in the southeast. From the air, both St. Kitts and Nevis look like two green blips floating between St. Martin and Montserrat. St.Kitts' curious layout—three islands in one—recalls the shape over an oversized tennis racket. The "head" to the northwest is dominated by the 3793-foot **Mount Liamuiga** and a rain forest ringed by sugarcane plantations and a rugged shoreline; the neck is a low-lying isthmus known as **Frigate Bay;** and the "grip" is the hilly southwest peninsula, until 1992 reachable only by boat or four-wheel-drive buggy. For many years the Southeast Peninsula was considered the "Caribbean Shangri-La," blessed with palm-fringed coves that resemble lagoons, rugged, lush topography and a large salt pond. Today the peninsula is also a reserve for many of the green vervet monkeys and white-tailed deer that roam about.

The "last frontier of the Caribbean" was considered to be the beach of Sir Timothy Thornhill, once approachable only by a rugged stony trail that led to the southernmost tip of St. Kitts. The massive natural barrier, covered with steep slopes, thorn bushes and spiky acacia trees, daunted many a bather

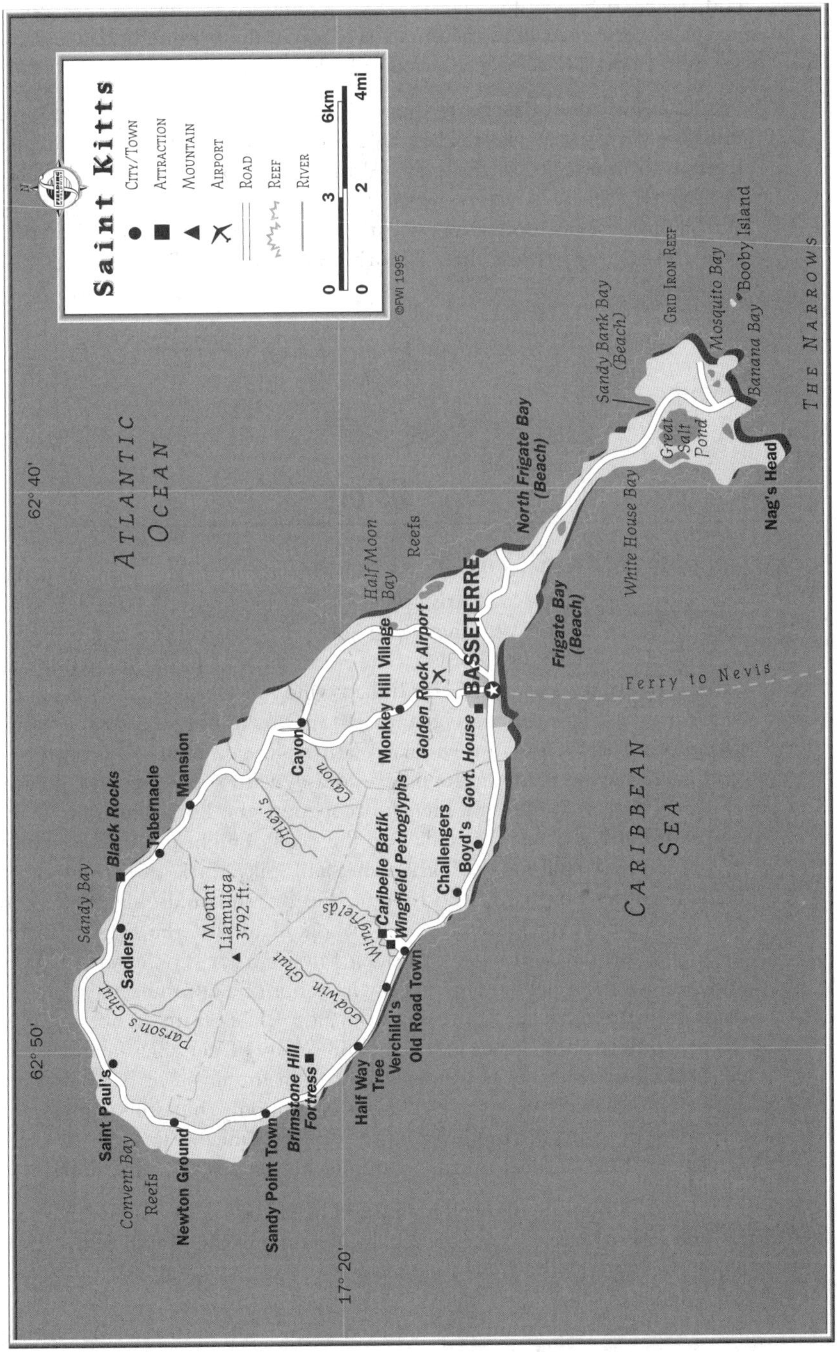
Saint Kitts
City/Town
Attraction
Mountain
Airport
Road
Reef
River
0 3 6km
0 2 4mi
©FWI 1995
62° 50'
62° 40'
17° 20'
Atlantic
Ocean
Caribbean
Sea
The Narrows
Ferry to Nevis
Saint Paul's
Newton Ground
Sandy Point Town
Brimstone Hill Fortress
Half Way Tree
Verchild's
Old Road Town
Sadlers
Black Rocks
Tabernacle
Mansion
Cayon
Monkey Hill Village
Golden Rock Airport
BASSETERRE
Govt. House
Boyd's
Challengers
Caribelle Batik
Wingfield Petroglyphs
Mount Liamuiga 3792 ft.
Parson's Ghut
Godwin Ghut
Wingfields
Ottley's
Cayon
Sandy Bay
Convent Bay
Reefs
Half Moon Bay
Reefs
North Frigate Bay (Beach)
Frigate Bay (Beach)
White House Bay
Great Salt Pond
Nag's Head
Sandy Bank Bay (Beach)
Grid Iron Reef
Mosquito Bay
Banana Bay
Booby Island

in search of the 23 beautiful peninsula beaches that had nearly become legend. Today the seven-mile Dr. Kennedy Simmonds Highway allows motorists to traverse the hill in minutes. To preserve the pristine beaches, only a few select hotels have been allowed to build on the site.

St.Kitts' capital of **Basseterre** (pop. 20,000) seems to boom with an irrepressible West Indian vigor. The traffic police are crisply dressed, and reggae blasts from music stores and cafes. Already being built is a $16.23 million deep-water cruiseship facility, which will include an expanded shopping area and sailing; the position allows debarking passengers to step off their ships and find themselves less than a block away from the Berkeley Memorial Clock.

History

Columbus first sighted the island of St. Kitts, dubbing it —with a touch of self-aggrandizement—St. Christopher. (The title was later shortened to St. Kitts by British tobacco planters, who ignored Spanish claims and moved in with their African slaves.) For years the island remained lost in obscurity, inhabited by cohiba-smoking Carib Indians who found nourishment from the island in the form of turtles, iguanas and mawby liquor. In 1623, a daring group of settlers led by Sir Thomas Warner plopped themselves on the island, soon having to share the beach uneasily with some French colonists. On June 20, 1690, during a French occupation, the Englishman Sir Timothy Thornhill led a party of soldiers in the dead of night through Friars Bay and over a rocky hill full of thorn bushes and spiky acacia trees to catch the French sentries off guard, who thought the British could only attack from the sea. After taking Basseterre, the island's main city, the English troops spiked the fortress cannons so that other English troops could land in safety. (The hill was later named Sir Timothy in honor of Thornhill, but remains a daunting natural barrier, stretching from steep cliffs on the Atlantic to even steeper cliffs on the Caribbean. (The 1783 Treaty of Versailles finally awarded sovereignty to the Brits.) Independent from Britain since 1983, St. Kitts is dealing peacefully with the challenges of economy, but still maintains affectionate ties with the mother country. In fact, Queen Elizabeth II visited St. Kitts in 1985 and her portrait continues to grace island bank notes.

Jewish communities on both islands can be traced back to the 17th century. The earliest date on the nineteen tombstones in the Jewish cemetery on Nevis goes back to the 1680s, and records in England suggest that the Nevis synagogue is older than the 1732 synagogue in Curaçao. Recently, a "mikvah," or ritual bath, was discovered by an island historian. When large populations of Jews fled to the islands to escape the Spanish Inquisition, the majority of those who came to Nevis were from Brazil.

People

Friendly and cricket-loving, Kittians are still living the remains of British gentility at the same time catering to the Caribbean rhythm of life. A little fishing, a little gardening, long pauses to chat—that's the pattern of a day's dally. Kittians were delighted with Queen Elizabeth's comments about the unspoiled beauty, an opinion shared by Christopher Columbus. The beauty, however, seems to have dazzled residents into a slumber that doesn't inspire too much art. A few are notable, such as the sculptor Valentine Brown, who lives in Dieppe Bay and is known for his finely crafted sculptures of faces and figures out of cedar. Style in St. Kitts is casual, but tourists are advised not to wear short shorts, bikinis or bare chests in public places. Today, the British are still aground, running many of the inns and hotels on the island.

Beaches

The southern beaches of St. Kitts, Frigate Bay and Salt Pond have long been considered the "Caribbean Shangri-La."

Most of the Kittian beaches are a dramatic black, born from rich volcanic sand, although the beaches at Frigate Bay and Salt Pond, on the southern peninsula, are brilliantly white. The best beaches are generally located in the south—**Major's Bay**, **Banana Bay**, **Cockleshell Bay** and **Mosquito Bay**—connected today by a new road that makes them fully accessible. Talcum white beaches can also be found in the southeast peninsula. Most of the watersports activities are centered around Frigate Bay, and swimming is especially good, as is snorkeling. Banana Bay and Cockleshell Bay are twin beaches, where conditions are also excellent for swimming, and there are cottage beach resorts with watersports facilities operated by Ocean Terrace Inn in Basseterre. **Conaree Beach**, two miles from Basseterre, and **Friar's Bay**, a peninsula where you can see the Atlantic and the Caribbean meet, are also considered user-friendly. Although all beaches are public, you may have to pay a small fee to use the facilities of a hotel located on the beach you choose. (For beaches in Nevis, see the chapter on Nevis.)

What Else to See

St.Kitts' capital of Basseterre (pop. 20,00) is in the midst of a booming revival. Decimated by fire in 1867 and rebuilt in the Franco-British colonial style, Basseterre today boasts such delightful Caribbean nuances as high-pitched, no-awning roofs (to lessen their vulnerability in storms); shutters (to reduce sun glare but retain the essential movement of air through the hot interior spaces); and occasional outbursts of carpenter Gothic trim. Many of the renovations are due to the efforts of the "Basseterre Beautiful" organization, which is working hard to restore sections of the old town, opening up new stores and courtyard cafes, and keeping the frilly, high-roofed architecture. A bit of the old St. Kitts can be seen in **St. George's Anglican Church**; its wood pews and dusty gravestones in the unruly cemetery point to another era. History buffs interested in the archaeological dig undertaken on the supposed site of a 17th century synagogue in Nevis should contact the historian **Dr. Vincent K. Hubbard in St. Kitts** ☎ *(809) 469-1817*, FAX *(809) 469-1794.*

Brimstone Hill Fortress, the most photographed tourist attraction on St. Kitts, is considered one of the most magnificent fortresses in the West Indies—the second largest of its kind in the hemisphere. Set on a mountainous ridge of volcanic origin, the fortress was adapted to the existing geological conditions of the hill, giving it a maximum potential for defense. Walking around the ruins, only partially restored and deep in weeds, you can easily imagine the violent struggles waged here between the British and the French, the latter who thought they captured the "Gilbraltar of the West Indies" in 1782, only to be ejected for the final time a year later. If you climb the hefty staircase, you'll discover a small museum that gives an overview of the island, and you'll be able to inspect the cannon; if you're lucky, you might even be visited by a local vervet monkey. The view from here gives a marvelous panorama of the ocean and the two cone-shaped islands of Saba and St. Eustatius.

Old Carib rock drawings can be found in **Old Road Town Village** and the ravine at **Bloody Point**, where more than 2000 Indians died in a massacre in 1626.

Twenty minutes north of Basseterre, along the west coast, stands the **Romney Manor**, home of **Caribelle Batik**, where island craftswomen use Indonesian techniques to create a dazzling array of fabrics and clothes unique to the Caribbean. Also, make a tour of the sugar refinery and taste the pride and joy of Baron Edmund de Rothschild, who distills his own subtle brand of CSR (Cane Spirits Rothschild).

Historical Sites

Brimstone ★★★★★

Main Street, Basseterre.

Hours open: 9:30 a.m.–5 p.m.

This national park houses one of the Caribbean's largest and best-preserved fortresses, called the "Gibraltar of the West Indies" due to its sheer size. It dates back to 1690, covers 38 acres, and saw several skirmishes between the French and the British, who alternated in their control of the fort. Today it is quite nicely restored, and you can see the officer's quarters, barracks, hospital and kitchen. A museum is devoted to military history. The park also includes numerous nature trails through its dense vegetation and stunning views of neighboring islands.

Romney Manor ★★★★

Old Road, Basseterre, ☎ (809) 465-6253.

Hours open: 8:30 a.m.–4 p.m.

Romney Manor is a beautifully restored 17th-century plantation great house, and is home to Caribelle Batik. You can watch local artists produce batik clothing and wall hangings in the same way it's been done for more than 2000 years. Prepare to drop a bundle in the duty-free shop. One of the best reasons to come is to stroll the ground's five acres of colorful gardens. The highlight is a saman tree said to be 350 years old.

Sports

Watersports activities on St. Kitts are focused on Frigate Bay, where you find options from sailing to scuba to windsurfing. Facilities for nearly any sport can be found at the **Jack Tar Village**; the 18-hole Robert Trent Jones-designed golf course is particularly popular. The best locations for windsurfing are **Banana Bay** and **Frigate Bay**, and equipment may be rented from watersports operators at hotels and resorts. The coast from **Cades Bay** and **Oualie Beach** to **Newcastle** is also excellent for windsurfing due to strong winds. Tennis courts can also be found there, as well as a few other resorts. Chartering a one-day cruise on a sailboat (picnic included) to Nevis is a wonderful way to spend the day. Horseback riding on St. Kitts can take the form of half-day outings available in Conaree from **The Stable at Trinity Inn**. Inquire whether the sport has been taken up again in the southeastern peninsula, temporarily stopped due to construction in the area.

Horseback Riding

Various locations, Basseterre.

Several outfits offer trail rides along the beach or through the rainforest: **Royal Stables** *(☎ 465-2222)* and **Trinity Stable** *(☎ 465-3226).*

Royal St. Kitts Golf Club

Adjacent to Jack Tar Village, Frigate Bay, ☎ (809) 465-8339.

Hours open: 7 a.m.–6 p.m.

St. Kitts' lone golf outlet is an 18-hole championship course designed by Robert Trent Jones. Greens fee are about $30.

Watersports

Various locations, Basseterre.

General watersports equipment and instruction can be found at **R.G. Watersports** *(☎ 465-8050)* and **Pro-Divers** *(☎ 465-3223).* **Tropical Tours** *(☎ 465-4167)* and **Pelican Cove Marina** *(☎ 465-2754)* offer deep-sea fishing excursions. For scuba diving, try **Kenneth's Dive Center** *(☎ 465-7043)* and **Pro-Divers** *(☎ 465-3223).* For boating and cruising, call **Kantours** *(☎ 465-2098)*, **Leeward Island Charters** *(☎ 465-7474)*, and **Tropical Tours** *(☎ 465-4039).*

Where to Eat

Fielding's Highest Rated Restaurants in St. Kitts

★★★★★	The Royal Palm	$8–$45
★★★★	Golden Lemon	$7–$50
★★★★	Rawlins Plantation	$23–$35
★★★	Ballahoo	$5–$55
★★★	Chef's Place	$5–$20
★★★	Fisherman's Wharf	$8–$22
★★★	PJ's Pizza	$5–$20
★★★	The Georgian House	$14–$21
★★★	The Patio	$26–$30
★★★	Turtle Beach Bar & Grill	$16–$24

Fielding's Special Restaurants in St. Kitts

★★★★★	The Royal Palm	$8–$45
★★★	Fisherman's Wharf	$8–$22
★★★	The Georgian House	$14–$21
★★★	The Patio	$26–$30

Fielding's Budget Restaurants in St. Kitts

★★★	Chef's Place	$5–$20
★★★	PJ's Pizza	$5–$20
★★★	Fisherman's Wharf	$8–$22
★★★	The Georgian House	$14–$21
★★★	Turtle Beach Bar & Grill	$16–$24

For such a small island, St. Kitts has a wide spectrum of dining experiences, from gourmet delights in historical settings to the homey kitchens of casual local hangouts. All four plantation inns have delightful outdoor patios for candlelit dinners. In Basseterre, dinner at the 400-year-old **Georgian House** is a leisurely elegant evening in a high-ceilinged salon, with aperitifs enjoyed in the walled garden beneath the big mango tree. At the **Ocean Terrace Inn**, the award-winning chef James Vanterpool makes a stunning Two-Flavor Soup (pumpkin and broccoli) and a carrot cake with local sugarcane sauce. Good West Indian food can be found at **The Ballahoo**, overlooking the town center.

Some typical delicacies of the island include goat dishes, fried plaintains, creole bean soup, boiled saltfish, goat water (actually, a rich lamb stew), conch chowder, and poached parrotfish with grilled yams. Don't miss an opportunity to try a swig of the island brew called **Royal Estra Stout**, or a glass of mauby, made from tree bark.

Ballahoo **$$$** ★★★

Fort Street, at the Circus, ☎ *(809) 465-4197.*
Latin American cuisine.
Lunch: 8 a.m.–6 p.m., entrees $5–$55.
Dinner: 6:30–10 p.m., entrees $25–$55.

This upper-level eatery overlooks the bustling downtown district that is Basseterre's version of Piccadilly Circus. The restaurant's customer base is a hodgepodge of cruise ship passengers, businesspeople and shoppers who are apt to find a wide variety of items to munch on, including fresh parrotfish fillets, rotis, burgers and yummy desserts. The place prides itself in presenting reasonably priced French wines. It's also a great location for West Indian or American-style breakfasts—be adventurous and have saltfish with your eggs instead of bacon.

Chef's Place **$$** ★★★

Church Street, ☎ *(809) 465-6176.*
Latin American cuisine. Specialties: Souse, lamb stew.
Lunch: 8 a.m.–6 p.m., entrees $5–$10.
Dinner: 6–11 p.m., entrees $5–$20.

Get friendly owner Oliver Peetes to describe the West Indian specialties on the daily blackboard—he'll probably oblige. Then settle down around picnic tables outdoors with a streetside view and await generous helpings of souse (pigs feet stew with a special sauce) or lamb stew. Main dishes will be rounded out with rice, a tasty salad and island vegetables. Beverages are also homemade and may include *mauby*, a bittersweet and spicy brew made from tree bark, or fresh ginger beer for the less adventurous.

Coconut Cafe **$$$** ★★

Frigate Bay Beach, Frigate Bay, ☎ *(809) 465-3020.*
American cuisine.
Lunch: 7:30 a.m.–4 p.m., entrees $6–$45.
Dinner: 4–11 p.m., entrees $25–$53.

Open to the sea breezes and steps away from the sand on the island's most popular swimming beach, this cafe dispenses three meals a day, but it's most popular for sunset cocktails and fresh seafood suppers to follow. There's steel band entertainment on Saturday evenings, and the bar stays open 'till the wee hours.

Fisherman's Wharf **$$** ★★★

Fortlands, ☎ *(809) 465-2754.*
Seafood cuisine.
Dinner: 7–12 p.m., entrees $8–$22.

Eating here is like a beach cookout, with diners choosing meat, fish, or chicken to be grilled to order, and serving themselves from a salad and condiments buffet. Orders are taken to long wooden tables facing the oceanfront. Everything is reliably good, but the fresh lobster and shrimp are standouts. A steel band entertains on Friday.

Golden Lemon **$$$** ★★★★

Dieppe Bay Town, Dieppe Bay, ☎ *(809) 465-7260.*
International cuisine.
Lunch: 11:30 a.m.–3 p.m., entrees $7–$12.
Dinner: 7–10 p.m., entrees $35–$50.

Some returning visitors would never dream of leaving the island without at least one visit to this exquisite boutique inn's fine restaurant. The three-course, prix-fixe dinners are rotated frequently; owner Arthur Leaman creates the internationally themed menus himself. Gleaming antiques and crystal chandeliers accentuate the dining room and a breezy patio is a gathering spot for Sunday brunch and cocktails. While touring by car, stop by for lunch, which features more informal offerings, including sandwiches, salads and fish dishes.

PJ's Pizza **$$** ★★★

North Frigate Bay, Frigate Bay, ☎ *(809) 465-8373.*
Italian cuisine. Specialties: Pizza, subs.
Lunch: 10 a.m.–6 p.m., entrees $5–$20.
Dinner: 6–10:30 p.m., entrees $10–$20.

A reputation for some of the most creative pizza toppings in the Caribbean chain is putting this small place on the culinary map. Refried beans embellish the Mexican pizza and a Rastafarian Ital pie is capped with island veggies in the Rasta colors of gold, red and green. The rest of the offerings are basically Italian, with hero sandwiches made on homebaked bread. Dinner plates usually include lasagne and chili.

Rawlins Plantation **$$$** ★★★★

Mt. Pleasant, Mt. Pleasant, ☎ *(809) 465-6221.*
International cuisine.
Lunch: 12:30–2 p.m., prix fixe $23.
Dinner: 8 p.m. Seating, prix fixe $35.

Cap off a tour of the island with lunch or dinner at this splendidly restored estate on the northwest coast. A varied buffet of creole specialties is served to diners on the terrace of the estate's great house, and offerings often include curries, fritters, salads, vegetables and several international specialties. Call before noon to make a reservation for a fixed-price dinner of four courses with soup, salad, entree and a tantalizing dessert—possibly chocolate terrine with passion fruit sauce. Closed mid-August-mid October.

The Georgian House **$$$** ★★★

Independence Square, ☎ *(809) 465-4049.*
International cuisine.
Dinner: 6–10 p.m., entrees $14–$21.

This beautifully restored home, decorated with Georgian-era reproductions, is a showcase for owner-chef Roger Doche, who prepares a continental menu of seafood, chicken, and steaks, prepared with West Indian flourishes. Peas and rice accompany some of the main courses. Dinner is served nightly on a patio behind the house.

The Patio **$$$** ★★★

Frigate Bay Beach, Frigate Bay, ☎ *(809) 465-8666.*
Latin American cuisine.
Dinner: 7–11 p.m., entrees $26–$30.

The father-daughter cooking team of Peter and Helen Mallalieu prepare island-inspired continental suppers served with a flourish on the patio of their Frigate Bay Beach home. Diners face one of the prettiest private gardens on the island while feasting on specialties like pepper pot stew, broiled fresh seafood, and tropical desserts. Wines and liqueurs are included with dinner.

The Royal Palm **$$$** ★★★★★

Ottley's Estate, ☎ *(809) 465-7234.*
International cuisine.
Lunch: Noon–3 p.m., entrees $8–$18.
Dinner: 8 p.m. Seating, prix fixe $45.

Possibly the most creative food on the island is served at this restaurant located in Ottley's Plantation Inn. Chef Pam Yahn's new "island cuisine" has been glossied on the pages of national magazines, including *Food and Wine*. Her ever-changing menu has included delights like lobster quesadillas and sweet treats like mango mousse with raspberry sauce. Lunches, dinners and Sunday brunch with champagne are served in a location that couldn't be lovelier—the dining room skirts a nearby rainforest. Fixed-price brunch is $20, and served from 12 to 2 p.m.

Turtle Beach Bar & Grill **$$$** ★★★

S.E. Peninsula Road, Turtle Beach, ☎ (809) 469-9086.
American cuisine.
Lunch: 8 a.m.–6 p.m., entrees $16–$24.

Combine an afternoon of snorkeling (the preferred activity), scuba diving, or just plain loafing on the beach with a notable barbecue of chicken, fish, meat, or lobster prepared at this solar-powered eatery on the southeast coast. Operated by the Ocean Terrace Inn in Fortlands, the Grill is also a cool place Sundays for a well-regarded West Indian buffet replete with live entertainment. Dinner is served only on Saturdays, from 7:30-10 p.m. Equipment for watersports can be rented here as well.

Where to Shop

Shopping is mostly concentrated at several shops and boutiques in and around the traffic circus less than a block from the waterfront. There are at least 57 stores on the island, including the famous **Caribelle Batik**, the island's world-famous designs manufactured at Romney Manor. Also good buys can be found at **Pelican Mall**, a 26-shop arena that features traditional Kittian architecture and pastel colors that resemble a Caribbean market. Duty-free items are available at **A Slice of the Lemon Duty-Free Gift Shop**, on Fort Street, where you can browse through pottery, teas, spices and condiments lower that those in St. Maarten or the USVI. **Splash** at the TDC Mall carries very attractive resort wear and colorful fabrics. Any groom in need of a tux can find one at **Valentino's Men's Wear** on Fort Street. **Windjammer & Caribbean Scents**, in the Pelican Mall, sells outstanding Caribbean resort wear and a fine selection of Caribbean perfumes, as well as **Jamaica's Blue Mountain coffee**. One gallery that shouldn't be missed is the **Plantation Picture House**, featuring the work of Kate Spencer, known for her portraits, landscapes and still lifes. Her designs are available on stone-washed silk and may be worn as scarves.

St. Kitts Directory

BUSINESS HOURS

Shops open Monday–Saturday 8 a.m.–noon and 1–4 p.m. Most close earlier on Thursday. Banks open Monday–Thursday 8 a.m.–3 p.m. and Friday 8 a.m.–5 p.m.

CLIMATE

The climate is pleasant and moderate, with an average temperature of 79 degrees Fahrenheit. Humidity is low and constant northeast trade winds keep the islands cool. Although there is no rainy season, annual rainfall averages 55 inches.

DOCUMENTS

U.S. citizens must present proof of citizenship (passport, voter's registration, or birth certificate), along with return or ongoing tickets. There is a departure tax of $8.

ELECTRICITY

The current runs 230 volts, 60 cycles AC. While the electricity supply at some hotels is 110 volts, AC transformers and adapters are generally needed.

GETTING AROUND

Local transportation is available via minibuses and taxis. Automobiles may be rented from a variety of agencies. A visitor's driver's license is required and can be obtained from the Police Traffic Department for a fee. Driving is on the left side of the street.

Among the agencies: **Avis**, located at South Independence Square ☎ *(809) 465-6507*, **Choice Car Rental** on Cayon Street in Basseterre ☎ *(809) 465-4422.*

The passenger ferry, *The Caribe Queen*, operates on a regular schedule between the two islands. The crossing takes about 45 minutes and costs $8 round trip.

LANGUAGE

The official language of both St. Kits and Nevis is English.

MEDICAL EMERGENCIES

There is a 24-hour emergency room at **Joseph N. France General Hospital** in Buckley ☎ *(809) 465-2551*. Also ask your hotel about physicians on call.

MONEY

The official currency is the Eastern Caribbean dollar. Make sure you understand which dollar is quoted on bills.

TELEPHONE

Area code is *809*. International calls, telexes and telegrams can be made from **Skantel**, *Cayon Street, Basseterre* ☎ *(809) 465-2219*, Monday-Friday from 8 a.m.–6 p.m., on Saturday 8 a.m.–2 p.m., and on Sundays and holidays from 6–8 p.m.

TIME

Atlantic Standard Time. That is to say, it's one hour ahead of New York time, except during Daylight Saving Time, when it is the same.

TIPPING

Expect a 10 percent service charge added to most restaurant bills. If it isn't, be prepared to tip 10–15 percent.

TOURIST INFORMATION

Good brochures and information can be found at the **St. Kitts Tourist Board**, *Pelican Mall, P.O Box 132, Basseterre*; ☎ *(809) 465-2620/ 4040*, FAX *(809) 465-8794*. In the U.S. ☎ *(212) 535-1234*.

WHEN TO GO

Carnival Celebrations take place in a week-long spectacle the last week of December, featuring calypso competitions, queen shows, street dancing and festivals. Tourism Week in Nevis is an annual fair in February. Museum Day is May 18, usually an open house at various museums. Culturama 20, in Nevis the last week of July, is a 20-year-old festival of native arts, crafts and music. Every other month the St. Kitts-Nevis Boating Club provides races and relays for residents and tourists alike. On the last Sunday of every month the Golden Rock Golf Club presents a day of fun golf played on a nine-hole fun course. The Nevis Jockey Club has scheduled nine race days throughout the year to coincide with national holidays.

ST. KITTS RESTAURANTS		PHONE	ENTREE	CR. CARDS
Basseterre				
	American			
★★★	**Turtle Beach Bar & Grill**	(809) 469-9086	$16–$24•	A, V
★★	**Coconut Cafe**	(809) 465-3020	$6–$53	A, DC, MC, V
	International			
★★★★★	**The Royal Palm**	(809) 465-7234	$8–$45	A, MC, V
★★★★	**Golden Lemon**	(809) 465-7260	$7–$50	A, DC, MC, V
★★★★	**Rawlins Plantation**	(809) 465-6221	$23–$35	A, MC, V
★★★	**The Georgian House**	(809) 465-4049	$14–$21••	A, MC, V
	Italian			
★★★	**PJ's Pizza**	(809) 465-8373	$5–$20	A, MC, V
	Latin American			
★★★	**Ballahoo**	(809) 465-4197	$5–$55	A, MC, V
★★★	**Chef's Place**	(809) 465-6176	$5–$20	None
★★★	**The Patio**	(809) 465-8666	$26–$30••	MC, V
	Seafood			
★★★	**Fisherman's Wharf**	(809) 465-2754	$8–$22••	A, MC, V
Note:	• Lunch Only			
	•• Dinner Only			

ST. LUCIA

Waterskiing and parasailing are popular activities around St. Lucia.

Watching a local cook an egg in steamy sulphur pools might be cliché now on lovely St. Lucia, but the rest of the island's attractions are far from worn out. Bit by bit St. Lucians are getting the ecotourism bug, finally figuring out that this Caribbean island's biggest draw is its lush natural resources—from exclusive beaches fringed with forests to waterfalls that change color from yellow to purple. In fact, it should be made mandatory for every visitor to drive the steep roads that wind the emerald hills at the island's southern end, where jungle flowers scent the air and giggling children soap themselves under roadside water faucets. To get the full Lucian experience, however, you must get out and trod toe to heel over the dramatic countryside, breathe in the rain forest, and even bathe in the volcano's hot mineral baths. But the spirit of St. Lucia lies not only in the land but in the people as well—friendly, musical and forever ready to party. Festivals carve the rhythm of life here, and ones such as the two flower festivals, La Rose and Marguerite, and Carnival—a calypso explosion two days before Ash Wednesday—shouldn't be missed.

Bird's Eye View

The second largest of the former West Indies Associated States, the avocado-shaped St. Lucia lies between Martinique and St. Vincent in the Windward Islands chain of the eastern Caribbean. It sprawls over a total area of 238 square miles, a majority of which is covered with dense tropical flora, such as hibiscus, frangipani, orchids, jasmine and poinciana. By contrast, the northern end of the island seems positively cosmopolitan. Castries, the capital, is still in need of beautification, but marinas and resorts are filling in the coastline. (The proliferation of all-inclusive resorts is starting to rankle local businesspeople—especially struggling restaurateurs.) Though tourism has been growing rapidly, the principal sector is agriculture (especially bananas and coconut) along with manufacturing, with more than 40 relatively diversified enterprises.

History

The first inhabitants of St. Lucia were surely Arawak Indians, and later Caribs, who did not appreciate the British invasion of their island in the early 17th century; for some time they managed to successfully fend off colonization. In 1650, the French overcame the resistance and settled a colony, completing a treaty with the Caribs in 1660. Over the next 164 years, the island exchanged hands 14 times between the French and British in an almost comical seesaw play of power. It was not until the issue of the 1814 Treaty of Paris that the British finally secured all rights. During this time, the Carib Indians were played as a pawn between the two powers until the British finally—and unceremoniously—exiled them to a still-existing reservation on Dominica. Although the island gained control of its own government on Feb. 22, 1979, its official head of state still remains the British throne, represented by a Governor General, who appoints the eleven members of St. Lucia's Senate. The House of Assembly is elected by popular vote.

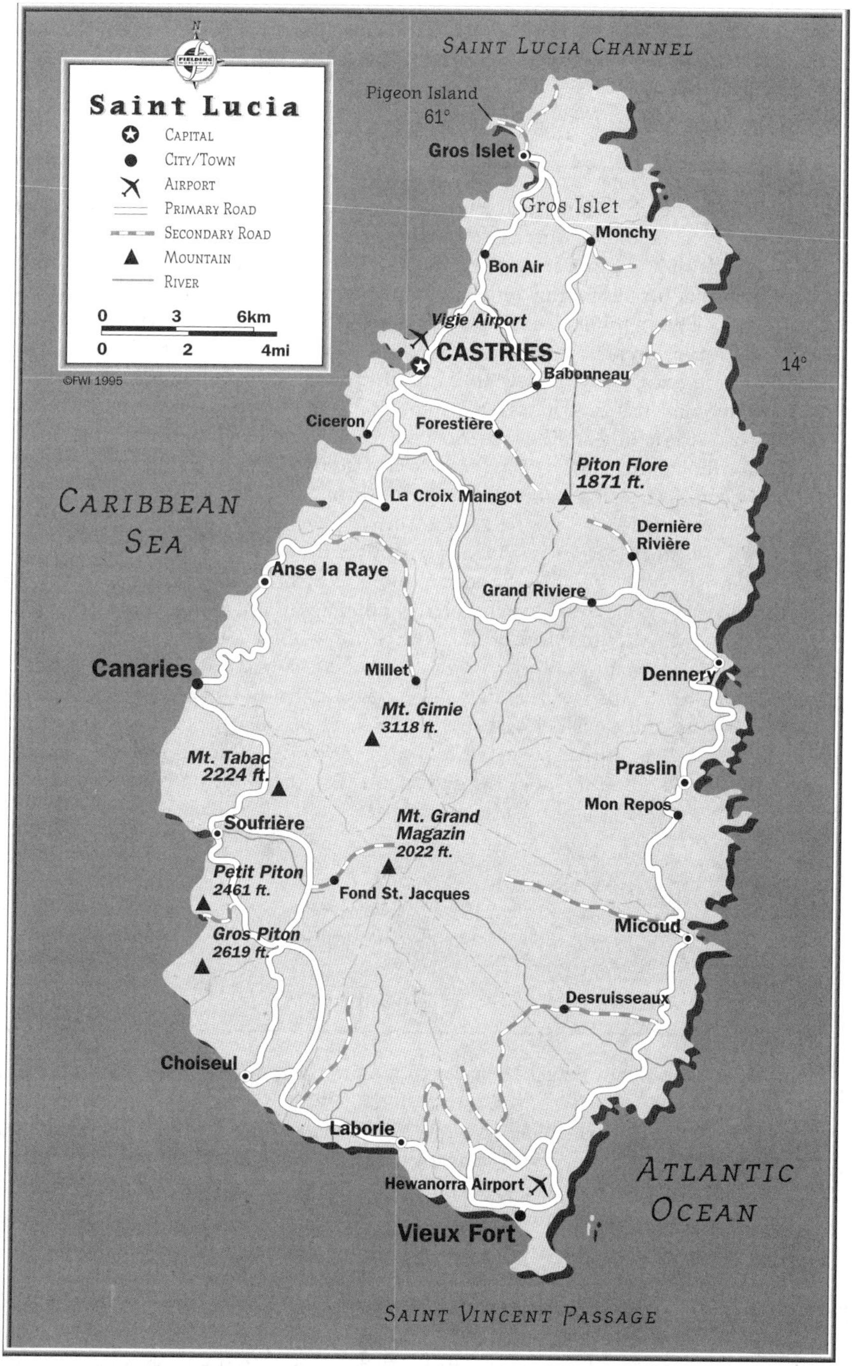
Saint Lucia
Capital
City/Town
Airport
Primary Road
Secondary Road
Mountain
River
0 3 6km
0 2 4mi
©FWI 1995
Saint Lucia Channel
Pigeon Island
61°
Gros Islet
Gros Islet
Monchy
Bon Air
Vigie Airport
CASTRIES
Babonneau
14°
Ciceron
Forestière
Piton Flore
1871 ft.
Caribbean
Sea
La Croix Maingot
Dernière
Rivière
Anse la Raye
Grand Riviere
Canaries
Millet
Dennery
Mt. Gimie
3118 ft.
Mt. Tabac
2224 ft.
Praslin
Mon Repos
Soufrière
Mt. Grand
Magazin
2022 ft.
Petit Piton
2461 ft.
Fond St. Jacques
Micoud
Gros Piton
2619 ft.
Desruisseaux
Choiseul
Laborie
Atlantic
Ocean
Hewanorra Airport
Vieux Fort
Saint Vincent Passage

People

As in neighboring states, about 75 percent of the inhabitants of St. Lucia are descendants of African slaves who were imported as plantation laborers in the 17th and 18th centuries. (Two percent are descended from indentured servants brought from India and another two percent are of European origin.) The rich mixture has produced a highly musical local patois, a combination of French, English and Spanish words utilizing a French and African grammatical structure. Although tourism is conducted in English, most private conversations, jokes, street jibe and some court cases are conducted in patois. Friendly and helpful, St. Lucians have retained a love of African and Caribbean rhythms; in fact, they so love to party that dancing has practically become a national sport. Every small town and village holds dances regularly, propelled by a little beer, rum, smoking weed, and ear-splitting speakers. Friday block parties in the village of **Gros Islet** are especially welcoming to tourists; other neighborhoods are more closed. Despite all the spontaneous partying, about 80 percent of the population still remains self-acclaimed Roman Catholics. Most of the older island women continue to wear the Madras head-tie and a modern version of the panniered skirt. A blend of French and British cultures, islanders share a passion for both savory French-Creole cooking and their beloved sport of cricket. St. Lucia has also given birth to two Nobel Laureates: Sir W. Arthur Lewis won the Nobel Prize in economics in 1979 and the poet Derek Walcott won the 1992 Nobel Prize in literature.

Beaches

St. Lucia's prime goal is to keep beaches open to the public but as pristine as possible; therefore, you'll only find a few with restrooms, changing facilities and snack bars. The best way to find *your* beach is to hire a sailboat and scope around the dozens of nearly deserted possibilities. Because shade is not always available, make sure you always travel to the beach with hat or umbrella, towel and liquid refreshment. Among the best beaches is **Anse Chastanet**, just north of Soufriere, which some claim offers the Windward Islands' only "perfect beach dive," with its steep dropoff, colorful fish, and variety of sponges (parts of *Superman II* were shot here). Anse Couchon beaches feature black, volcanic sand, calm waters for swimming, and a tropical, romantic setting accessible only by boat. Lying at the foot of the Pitons, the crescent-shaped bay of Anse des Piton rates as one of St. Lucia's most dramatic beaches. Facilities are few at Anse LaRaye, a small village beach just beyond Marigot Bay, but there are plenty of shady palm trees. **Cas en Bas**, just opposite Gros Islet on the island's north end, is a windsurfer's dream, comparable to the excellent conditions of Silver Sands on Barbados. Some of the island's major hotels are located on the nearly perfect **Reduit Beach**, chock full of shady palms, white sand and a full range of watersports facilities. Swimmers should avoid the strong currents at **La Toc Bay**, south of Castries Harbor, where the majestic **Cunard La Toc Hotel** lies, though the view is lovely for lunch and sunbathing. One of the most popularly frequented beaches is **Choc Bay**, a long, sweeping stretch of sand and coconut palms, not far from Castries and the major hotels along the northeastern coast. At the southernmost tip of the island you'll find **Vieux Fort**, where the beach makes up for the lack of facilities with gloriously white sand and miles of shady coconut palms.

What Else to See

St. Lucia's dramatic countryside includes emerald hills, waterfalls, rain forest, volcanic mineral baths and pristine beaches.

The best time to experience the hustle and bustle of West Indian port life in Castries, the island's capital, is on Saturday at the morning market, when small farmers and artisans lay out their tropical wares for serious barter. Not much else is of interest in the city, which has been rebuilt and decimated by fire several times over, except perhaps for **Columbus Square**, where a 400-year-old samaan tree shades the Cathedral of the Immaculate Conception built in 1897. Afternoons are the best time to visit the tiny fishing villages of **Anse-la-Raye** and **Canaries**, where you can watch the boats arrive with their daily catch. North of Castries, the **Pigeon Island National Park** offers the opportunity to relive the days when France and England waged over St. Lucia.

(George Rodney, the British admiral who defeated the French in the Dominica Passage, raised pigeons as a hobby—hence the name.) Friday nights, the fishing town of **Gros Islet** is a wild "jump-up" scene, noisy with soca and reggae, traditional beats of the Caribbean. The new marketplace at Soufriere in the south is also exceptional, decorated with colorful murals and gingerbread trim; the shabby town itself still retains a Third World aura. The dormant "Drive-in Volcano" of nearby **Mt. Soufriere** presents a face akin to a B-horror movie, complete with open pits of boiling sulfur. (You'll need a guide, available at the entrance of the park.) If you want to linger under cascading waterfalls and bathe in natural and more aromatic springs, go to the nearby **Diamond Falls**, where the Diamond Mineral Baths are located on the Soufriere Estate. Legend has it that King Louis XVI himself partook of the healing waters here during a French occupation.

Pigeon Island is a 40-acre islet connected by causeway to St. Lucia's west coast near the Rodney Bay resort area. The site of St. Lucia's annual jazz festival, the area also boasts two beaches, a restaurant and the remnants of the 18th-century British naval garrison. The new **Pigeon Island Museum and Interpretive Centre** is housed in the elegant former British officers' mess building and provides a hands-on display of the island's natural and political history.

BEST VIEW:

A startling panoramic view can be glimpsed from the Fort Charlotte fortress at the top of Morne Fortune, the same sight used by French and British troops alternately to defend the island. To the north is Pigeon Island, to the south the Pitons, and the entire scope of the capital's harbor and the Virgie Peninsula. While you're at the fort, notice the difference between the French architecture and the walls built by the British at different stages.

Historical Sites

Fort Charlotte ★★★

Morne Fortune, ☎ (809) 456-1165.

Set atop a hill 853 feet above sea level, this fortress was started by the French in 1764 and finished 20 years later by the British. Today it holds government and education offices, but it's worth a trip for the great views if nothing else. The grounds include a military cemetery that dates back to 1782 where French and British soldiers are buried as well as six former governors of the island.

Parks and Gardens

Maria Islands Nature Reserve ★★★

Half a mile offshore, ☎ (809) 454-5014.

Hours Open: 9:30 a.m.–5 p.m.

This reserve consists of two small islands in the Atlantic—one 25 acres, the other just four. It is home to a thriving population of birds and rare snakes and lizards. Great snorkeling off the larger island, Maria Major.

Pigeon Island National Park ★★★★

Pigeon Point, ☎ (809) 452-5005.

Hours Open: 9 a.m.–4 p.m.

This 40-acre island is connected to the mainland by a causeway. It has a long history and was used for all sorts of things before becoming a national park—pirates hid out here in the 1600s, the French and British militaries used it as a fort, and long before any of them, the Arawak Indians lived here. Ruins from some of these days still exist on the island, but this is primarily a place to picnic and hang out on its picturesque beaches.

Tours

Diamond Falls and Mineral Bath ★★★★

Soufriere Estate, Soufriere.
Hours open: 10 a.m.–5 p.m.
The water in these sulfuric mineral baths averages a toasty 106 degrees Fahrenheit. Louis XVI ordered them built in 1784 so French stationed in the area could soak in the supposedly curative waters. Bring your suit so you, too, can "take the waters."

La Soufriere ★★★

Soufriere.
Hours open: 9 a.m.–5 p.m.
Called the world's only drive-in volcano, this spot encompasses a seven-acre crater complete with pools of boiling mud and sulfurous waters.

The Pitons ★★★★

Soufriere.
These dramatic twin cones are St. Lucia's most identifying landmark. Formed by a prehistoric volcano eruption, Petit Piton rises to 2619 ft., Gros Piton (the fatter of the two) to 2461 ft. Most folks just admire them from the land or sea, but the truly hardy can climb through their lush foliage to the top. You'll need a permit from the **Forestry Division** *(☎ 452-3231)*, and it's best to hire a guide for the very strenuous hike.

Sports

Tennis courts and watersports facilities, including windsurfing, water skiing, and small sailboats are available for a fee at major hotels. Windsurfers all head for Anse de Sables, the bay on the southeastern tip of the island between Moule-a-Chique and the Maria Islands. Actually, conditions for windsurfing are ideal all along the entire south coast, on both the Atlantic and the Caribbean sides. Beginners normally like the calmer waters of the Caribbean while the more daring windsurfers take advantage of the rougher, choppy waters on the Atlantic coast. Golfers can enjoy two challenging golf courses. Half-day and full-day fishing charters are available and can be arranged through hotels and resorts, or at the marinas at Rodney Bay and Castries. The two main fishing seasons run between January to June (for tuna, kingfish and dolphin) and July to December (where the catch is closer to shore). As St. Lucians depend on fishing for their livelihood, the ways and means are many—you can join fishermen using lines and pots to catch snapper, lobsters and reef fish. Yachtsmen and day-trippers from Castries tend to congregate at Soufriere Bay. One of the region's major charters is **The Moorings**, which offers cruises for 4–6 passengers with lunch and drinks—bareboat or with crew. Other similar cruises can be found at Rodney Bay; **Stevens Yachts** is one of the foremost names in the region. Horseback riding through the forest is also available.

Golf

Two locations.

The choices for duffers are limited to two courses, both nine holes but set up so you can go around twice. **Cap Estate Golf Club** *(452-8523)* is open to the public while the course at **Sandals St. Lucia** *(452-3081)* is only available when not fully booked by guests at the island's two Sandals resorts.

Horseback Riding

Various locations.

Three stables await the horseman (and woman): **North Point** *(450-8853)*, **Trim's** *(452-8273)*, and **Jalousie Plantation** *(459-7666)*.

Watersports

Various locations.

Deep-sea fishing: **Mako Watersports** *(452-0412)* and **Captain Mike's** *(452-7044)*. Scuba diving: **Dive Jalousie** *(459-7666)*, **Moorings Scuba** *(451-4357)*, **Scuba St. Lucia** *(459-7355)*, **Buddies Scuba** *(452-5288)*, and **Windjammer Diving** *(452-0913)*. **Mistral Windsurfing** *(452-8351)* specializes in board rentals and instruction. For cruises and snorkel expeditions, call **Captain Mike's** *(452-0216)*, **Surf Queen** *(452-8351)*, **Brig Unicorn** *(452-6811)*, and **Cat Inc.** *(450-8651)*. Finally, **St. Lucian Watersports** *(452-8351)* offers waterskiing and parasailing in addition to general equipment rentals.

Where to Eat

Fielding's Highest Rated Restaurants in St. Lucia		
★★★★	**Dasheene Restaurant**	$35–$45
★★★★	**Jimmies**	$14–$28
★★★	**Bistro**	$14–$24
★★★	**Capones**	$11–$24
★★★	**Chart House**	$11–$30
★★★	**Chez Paul**	$20–$35
★★★	**Green Parrot**	$33–$40
★★★	**Hummingbird**	$9–$26
★★★	**Marina Steak House**	$13–$19
★★★	**San Antoine**	$15–$32

Fielding's Special Restaurants in St. Lucia		
★★★	**Capones**	$11–$24
★★	**Eagle's Inn**	$8–$10
★★	**Kimlan's**	$3–$5
★★	**Naked Virgin**	$15–$25

Fielding's Budget Restaurants in St. Lucia		
★★	**Kimlan's**	$3–$5
★★	**Eagle's Inn**	$8–$10
★★	**Ginger Lily**	$7–$11
★★★	**Paul's Place**	$7–$10
★★★	**Key Largo**	$6–$17

Excellent international cuisine can be found on St. Lucia. The fertile volcanic soil supports a cornucopia of exotic fruits and vegetables; the six types of bananas are particularly delicious. Island chefs make inventive use of papayas, soursops, mangos, passionfruit and coconuts. Most restaurants try to take advantage of the unparalleled natural beauty, so beautiful views have become almost commonplace. One of the most atmospheric eateries is **San Antoine**, perched in the hills overlooking Castries, which incorporates the walls of a 19th-century greathouse, with antique tableware to match. Try the delicious swordfish at **Jammer's** at Windjammer Landing, a villa complex, with pole beams, table linens and bridal-white cane furniture. **Naked Virgin** in Castries is a good bet for traditional West Indian and creole specialties such as callaloo, curries and pepperpot stew. Excellent jerk chicken, a Jamaican specialty, can be had at **Jimmie's**.

A-Pub $$$ ★★

The Waterfront, Rodney Bay, ☎ (809) 452-8725.
International cuisine.
Lunch: entrees $15–$30.
Dinner: entrees $15–$30.
A convivial yachtie hangout and local watering hole fronting Rodney Bay, the A-Pub serves up terrific steaks, fish and chips, West Indian specialties, and a few international dishes. Join the crowd for a friendly happy hour each evening.

Bistro $$$ ★★★

Waterfront, Rodney Bay, ☎ (809) 452-9494.
Seafood cuisine.
Dinner: 5–10:30 p.m., entrees $14–$24.
The British owners provide pub offerings like steak and kidney and shepherd's pie along with a varied, extensive seafood menu. Dining is on a wide elevated deck perched on the waterfront. Nautical types and others like the 20 percent discount on food items before 6:30 p.m., sort of a Caribbean early bird special.

Capones $$$ ★★★

Reduit Beach, Rodney Bay, ☎ (809) 452-0284.
Italian cuisine.
Lunch: 11:30 a.m.–4:30 p.m., entrees $11–$24.
Dinner: 4:30–10:30 p.m., entrees $11–$24.
Patrons are served by waitpersons dressed like 1930s mobsters who present the dinner check in a violin case. But it's all a lot of fun, and the Italian food is skillfully prepared. Dishes include fresh pasta, osso bucco, and juicy steaks. If the atmosphere is too heavy in the main dining room, there's a pizza parlor adjacent serving decent pies, burgers and sandwiches.

Chart House $$$ ★★★

Reduit Beach, Rodney Bay, ☎ (809) 452-8115.
American cuisine.
Dinner: 6–10:30 p.m., entrees $11–$30.
The most popular dining room on the island could be this all-American chain steakhouse overlooking the yacht harbor. Guests like the attentive service by a loyal staff (very little turnover here) and the food, which is steak, lobster (in season), tangy baby back ribs, and some Caribbean specialties, all familiar and well-prepared. The restaurant is a fern-filled wood-frame house that exudes warmth.

Chez Paul $$$ ★★★

Derek Walcott Square, Rodney Bay, ☎ (809) 452-3022.
International cuisine.
Lunch: 9 a.m.–4 p.m., entrees $20–$35.
Dinner: 4–11 p.m., entrees $20–$35.
Chez Paul is a more streamlined version of Rain, the South Pacific-themed restaurant that has held court on this spot since 1885. The drinks are still heady and rum-based, but the food, which was never the real attraction, is now a more sophisticated melding of European, Asian and Caribbean influences. It's open for sandwiches and lighter meals all day long. The tin-roofed house overlooks Derek Walcott Square, which is named after St. Lucia's distinguished Nobel Prize winner.

Dasheene Restaurant $$$ ★★★★

Ladera Resort, Soufriere, ☎ (809) 459-7850.
International cuisine.

Lunch: entrees $35–$45.
Dinner: entrees $35–$45.
The view from this hilltop aerie is unbeatable, nestled between the Pitons in Soufriere, an old French fishing community known for its sulphur springs. Located in a rustically chic villa resort, Dasheene is named after an exotic leaf used in cooking, and the menu, which changes often, incorporates locally grown produce, prime meats and seafood. The Austrian chef favors kingfish, which he likes to smoke and serve with mango or avocado and coconut sauces. Fish and shellfish are delivered to the restaurant daily.

Eagle's Inn **$** ★★

Reduit Beach Road, Rodney Bay, ☎ *(809) 452-0650.*
Latin American cuisine.
Lunch: entrees $8–$10.
Dinner: entrees $8–$10.
This small funky spot, which is one of a friendly string of similar joints in Reduit Beach, serves French-inspired West Indian food. The atmosphere is very low-key and romantic, with an eagle-eye view of Gros Ilet in the distance. A good place for curry and fish dishes.

Ginger Lily **$** ★★

Reduit Beach, Rodney Bay, ☎ *(809) 452-8303.*
Chinese cuisine.
Lunch: 11:30 a.m.–2:30 p.m., entrees $7–$11.
Dinner: 6–11 p.m., entrees $7–$11.
Cantonese specialties are on hand at this popular restaurant near the tourist hotels in Reduit Beach. There's always a long list of familiar favorites, which pleases residents who flock here often when the urge hits. Lunch specials are available, with several courses for under $8.

Green Parrot **$$$** ★★★

Red Tape Lane, Morne Fortune, ☎ *(809) 452-3399.*
International cuisine.
Lunch: Noon–3 p.m., entrees $33–$40.
Dinner: 7 p.m.–midnight, prix fixe $33–$40.
Chef Harry brought his years of culinary expertise learned at Claridge's in London home to St. Lucia, and now cooks and entertains nightly at this lively spot on a hilltop in Morne Fortune, overlooking Castries. His spiced pumpkin creation, "soup oh la la" will make you say just that when you taste it. Known for a scrumptious lunch buffet where you can heap your plate with West Indian goodies for under $8, Green Parrot is also a wild scene several nights a week when belly or limbo dancers (including Harry) reign. There's a well-chosen wine list.

Hummingbird **$$$** ★★★

Anse Chastenet Road, Soufriere, ☎ *(809) 459-7232.*
French cuisine.
Lunch: entrees $9–$26.
Dinner: entrees $9–$26.
Combine lunch with a plunge in the pool at this restaurant located in a rustic resort on the Soufriere waterfront. Visitors flock here when the house specialty, freshwater mountain crayfish, is in season. At other times, enjoy other seafood dishes, steaks, sandwiches and rich desserts.

Jimmies **$$$** ★★★★

Vigie Cove Marina, Rodney Bay, ☎ *(809) 452-5142.*
Latin American cuisine.
Lunch: 11 a.m.–4 p.m., entrees $14–$28.
Dinner: 4–11 p.m., entrees $14–$28.

Jimmies' bar has long been known as the place to meet and greet, but the cuisine, authentic West Indian specialties prepared by a local chef who trained in fine restaurants in England, is also worth noting. Jimmie cooks with a light touch, and his pancakes and crepes stuffed with vegetables and seafood are sublime.

Key Largo **$$** ★★★

The Marina, Rodney Bay, ☎ (809) 452-0282.
Italian cuisine.
Lunch: 11:30 a.m.–4 p.m., entrees $6–$17.
Dinner: 4–10 p.m., entrees $6–$17.

Sophisticated pizzas on a patio are served at this small restaurant with its own outdoor brick oven. All manner of Italian coffee drinks are dispensed here as well. Try the house specialty, a pizza made with artichokes and shrimp.

Kimlan's **$** ★★

Micoud Street, Rodney Bay, ☎ (809) 452-1136.
Latin American cuisine.
Lunch: 7 a.m.–4 p.m., entrees $3–$5.
Dinner: 4–11 p.m., entrees $3–$5.

A local family runs this upper-level West Indian restaurant with a terrace positioned directly across from Columbus Square. Steaming bowls of curry or fish stews are served with rice and salad. A good spot for people watching, and for lighter snacks and ice cream.

Marina Steak House **$$$** ★★★

The Marina, Rodney Bay, ☎ (809) 452-9800.
Seafood cuisine.
Dinner: 5 p.m.–midnight, entrees $13–$19.

You'll find steak and seafood in a series of dim rooms with a bar where jazz piano can be heard playing on Friday nights. The restaurant, a converted private home in Rodney Bay Marina, is a reliable spot for American-style meals with vegetables and a baked potato served alongside.

Naked Virgin **$$$** ★★

Marchand Road, Marchand, ☎ (809) 452-5594.
Latin American cuisine. Specialties: Flying fish.
Lunch: entrees $15–$25.
Dinner: entrees $15–$25.

This graceful West Indian building in the suburb of Marchand is the home of an excellent punch that gives the restaurant its provocative name. The brew is so potent, it might encourage you to take your clothes off. Be that as it may, the Virgin also has a loyal following of regulars who admire chef/owner John Paul's traditional creole cooking.

Paul's Place **$** ★★★

Bridge St., Rodney Bay, ☎ (809) 452-3398.
International cuisine.
Lunch: 9 a.m.–4 p.m., entrees $7–$10.
Dinner: 4–10 p.m., entrees $7–$10.

Paul's provides a tasty lunch buffet to office workers who crowd the place at noon. Those who don't want to brave the line can choose from a menu of rotis, sandwiches, and plate meals. Dinner is more subdued, with innovatively prepared fish, chicken and steak dishes. It's not always up to par, but when it is, it shines brightly.

San Antoine **$$$** ★★★

Old Morne Rd., Morne Fortune, ☎ (809) 452-4660.
International cuisine.
Lunch: 11:45 a.m.–2:15 p.m., entrees $15–$32.
Dinner: 6:15–9:30 p.m., entrees $15–$32.

The surroundings are old fashioned and gracious, with meals served in the main house of the old San Antoine Hotel. The dining room, lit by candles at night, is run by an English couple who keep things purring along smoothly. Those looking for a special night out often choose this salon, which overlooks the twinkling lights of the harbor. The menu includes French and continental specialties, including seafood in parchment, pepper steak, or filet mignon with crayfish stuffing.

Where to Shop

St. Lucia's shopping won't disappoint. A new harborfront shopping complex called **Pointe Seraphine** features a large variety of duty-free imports such as designer perfumes, crystal and china. You'll also find native crafts and resort wear there, but try to avoid the complex when a cruise ship has docked. Market day (Saturday) at the Castries' 100-year-old market will give you a chance to kibitz with farmer's wives displaying luscious tropical fruits and vegetables, spices and local crafts; don't be shy about asking to sample a bite of tamarind, but keep a watch on your handbag and wallet. Good buys are woven fruit baskets for the kitchen back home; a good place to shop is the **government handicraft store** at the waterfront. A number of shops also sell locally made baskets, wood carvings and pottery. Hand-screened clothing and colorful batik apparel are featured buys, especially at the famous **Caribelle Batik** store. St. Lucia's artists tend to specialize in designs and portraits of the island's flora and fauna. If you want to see craftspeople working in their studios, stop by the **Arts & Crafts Development Centre**, near Choiseul, on the southwest coast; baskets, dishes, tapestries and woodcarvings are good buys. Some shops are being developed on the west coast, south of Castries. In general, prices at hotel and resort boutiques run much higher than elsewhere.

St. Lucia Directory

BUSINESS HOURS

Shops open weekdays 8 a.m.–12:30 p.m. and 1:30–4 p.m. and Saturdays 8 a.m.–noon. Banks open Monday–Thursday 8 a.m.–3 p.m., Friday 8 a.m.–5 p.m. Some in Rodney Bay also open Saturday from 9 a.m.–noon.

CLIMATE

Temperatures year-round average between 70 and 90 degrees F. Constant trade winds keep the air cool and the humidity from becoming oppressive.

DOCUMENTS

U.S. and Canadian citizens need to show a full and valid passport. British citizens need no passport if their stay does not exceed six months. French citizens must show an ID card. An ongoing or return ticket must also be shown.

ELECTRICITY

Current runs 220 volts, 50 cycles, with a square three-pin plug. A few hotels use 110 volts, 50 cycles. Bring an adapter and converter plug.

GETTING AROUND

Travel between Castries and other towns including Soufriere and Vieux Fort can be done in minibuses, usually overcrowded and stocked with local produce; you may have to share your seat with a carton of tomatoes. Buses leaving for Soufriere and Vieux Fort can be picked up in front of the department store on Bridge Street. To get to Cap Estate, take the bus near the market on Jeremy Street in Castries.

Taxis are all over the island. They have excellent experience with the small, winding roads outside the capital. Many taxi drivers are guides and have been trained in showing tourists around the city and island. Cars are unmetered, but official rates have been set by the government. Before setting off for a destination, verify the price in advance, and in what currency. When someone says dollar, you must specify whether it is the American dollar or the Eastern Caribbean dollar that is being talked about.

Rental cars are available in St. Lucia, but roads are difficult in the countryside and driving is on the left—always a bit hazardous for drivers used to the right side of the road. A driver's license is required and may be obtained from the Immigration Office upon arrival. It remains valid for three months. Stick with the top American names in agencies. You have assurance that you can use your credit card, arrangements can be easily made in advance before you leave, and if anything goes wrong, you can easily contact the head office back home. **Budget** ☎ *(809) 452-8021*; **Avis** ☎ *(809) 353-2046*; and **Hertz** ☎ *(809) 452-0679*. Of the three Hertz is the most expensive. It's best to get collision insurance; membership in auto clubs may lower the price in certain circumstances. Budget is the least expensive. If it is the first time you are driving on the left-hand side of the road, it's a good idea to be traveling with a companion and allow him or her to spot the road for you.

LANGUAGE

The official language is English, though a local patois is spoken.

MEDICAL EMERGENCIES

A 24-hour emergency room is available at St. Jude's Hospital, Vieux Fort ☎ *(809) 454-6041* and Victoria Hospital, Hospital Road, Castries ☎ *(809) 452-2421*.

MONEY

The currency is the Eastern Caribbean dollar.

TELEPHONE

The area code is *809*. Local numbers have seven digits, all of which should be dialed. International phone calls, as well as cables, can be made at the offices of the **Cable & Wireless** in the George Gordon Building on Bridge Street in Castries ☎ *(809) 452-3301*.

TIME

Atlantic Standard Time, all year round, one hour earlier than New York time. During Daylight Saving Time, however, it is the same hour.

TIPPING AND TAXES

Sometimes restaurants add a 15 percent service charge, but check your bill carefully. In restaurants it is customary to tip waiters or waitresses 10–15 percent if it has not already been added to the bill.

TOURIST INFORMATION

The **St. Lucia Tourist Board** is located at Point Seraphine in Castries ☎ *(809) 452-5968*. It's always worth stopping by to see if they have any brochures or suggestions for hikes, excursions, etc. It is also a source to find out what is happening in the community. In the U.S. call ☎ *(800) 456-3984*.

WHEN TO GO

January 1 and 2, which is the New Year's celebration, culminates in a two-day street fair offering local foods, island music, and dancing and games for children. Carnival is celebrated February 14 and 15 with elaborate costumes, dancing before dawn and national calypso contests. The annual St. Lucia Jazz Festival usually takes place in the middle of May. June 29 is the feast of St. Peter, a Fisherman's Day, where priests bless the fishermen's brightly decorated boats. August 30 is the Feast of St. Rose of Lima, a spectacular flower festival dating back to the 18th century where members of the La Rose Flower Society sing and dance in the streets in costumes. September hosts an annual island-wide culinary competition. September 30–August 4 is an annual International Billfish tournament, with anglers from the region and North America participating. November 22 is St. Cecilia's Day, celebrated by musicians serenading the streets of Castries. Early December hosts the Atlantic Rally for Cruisers with the world's largest annual transocean yacht race. Christmas, on December 25, is usually celebrated by early morning serenaders visiting homes and sampling holiday gourmet fare.

ST. LUCIA RESTAURANTS	PHONE	ENTREE	CR. CARDS
Castries			
American			
★★★ Chart House	(809) 452-8115	$11–$30••	A, DC, MC, V
Chinese			
★★ Ginger Lily	(809) 452-8303	$7–$11	A, MC, V
International			
★★★ Chez Paul	(809) 452-3022	$20–$35	A, DC, MC, V
★★★ Green Parrot	(809) 452-3399	$33–$40	A, MC, V
★★★ Paul's Place	(809) 452-3398	$7–$10	A, MC, V
★★★ San Antoine	(809) 452-4660	$15–$32	A, MC, V
★★ A-Pub	(809) 452-8725	$15–$30	A, V
Italian			
★★★ Capones	(809) 452-0284	$11–$24	A, MC, V
★★★ Key Largo	(809) 452-0282	$6–$17	MC, V
Latin American			
★★★★ Jimmies	(809) 452-5142	$14–$28	A, MC, V

ST. LUCIA RESTAURANTS	PHONE	ENTREE	CR. CARDS
★★ **Eagle's Inn**	(809) 452-0650	$8–$10	A, MC, V
★★ **Kimlan's**	(809) 452-1136	$3–$5	None
★★ **Naked Virgin**	(809) 452-5594	$15–$25	A, MC, V
Seafood			
★★★ **Bistro**	(809) 452-9494	$14–$24••	A, MC, V
★★★ **Marina Steak House**	(809) 452-9800	$13–$19••	A, MC, V
Soufriere			
French			
★★★ **Hummingbird**	(809) 459-7232	$9–$26	MC, V
International			
★★★★ **Dasheene Restaurant**	(809) 459-7850	$35–$45	A, MC, V
Note: • Lunch Only			
•• Dinner Only			

SINT MAARTEN/ ST. MARTIN

Sailing excursions from St. Martin to other islands are easily arranged.

Half-Dutch, half-French, the island of Sint Maarten/St. Martin gives a bipolar vacation for the price of one. Sint Maarten, the Dutch side, is part of the trio of islands that make up the Dutch Windwards (including Sint Eustatius and Saba), while only a few steps away, St. Martin belongs to the French West Indies. A mere welcoming sign acts as the only border between the two sides—nary a customs officer in sight—but the contrasts are startling, if quite tantalizing. Not only are the native languages different (though most people speak English as a common dominator), the ambience of each sovereign state nation bears its own unique personality. Quiet and more refined, St. Martin's capital of Marigot is the place to go if you're looking for good (duty-free) shopping, fine Creole cooking, and French haute cuisine; if you're looking to sail, frenzied Philipsburg, Sint Maarten's capital, has the best port. The Dutch side also boasts a dozen casinos; the one at **Port de Plaisance** is the nicest. Beaches are good all around the island, and scuba divers and snorkelers will find very exciting conditions. Some of the Caribbean's most luxurious (and most expensive resorts) are situated on the island, but most tourists let themselves be lured to the sea at least for one day (if not a week) to sail to some of the other glorious islands nearby.

Bird's Eye View

Simpson's Bay lagoon is spectacular at sunset.

St. Martin/Sint Maarten lies at the top of the Guadeloupe archipelago, 144 miles east of Puerto Rico. The total land mass is 37 square miles. The main airport and seaport are located on the Dutch side, which occupies the southern part of the barely triangular island. The western coast is low-lying and mostly comprised of **Simpson Bay Lagoon**, where small craft find a safe harbor. The rest of the Dutch side is very hilly, almost conical scrubland, though a good strong rain can turn it into a lush garden. Two ranges cross the island, in-between lies **Great Bay** and its **Salt Pond**, the valley of **Belle Plaine**, and the smaller salt ponds at **Le Galion**. Dotting the coastline are numerous bays that make for excellent beaches.

History

Columbus discovered and named St. Martin in 1493, and by the 1630s both the Dutch and French had settled on the island. Pirates combed the craggy shores and secret coves of the island, burying treasure and booty they had won at sea. It was in St. Martin that Peter Stuyvesant (the last Dutch

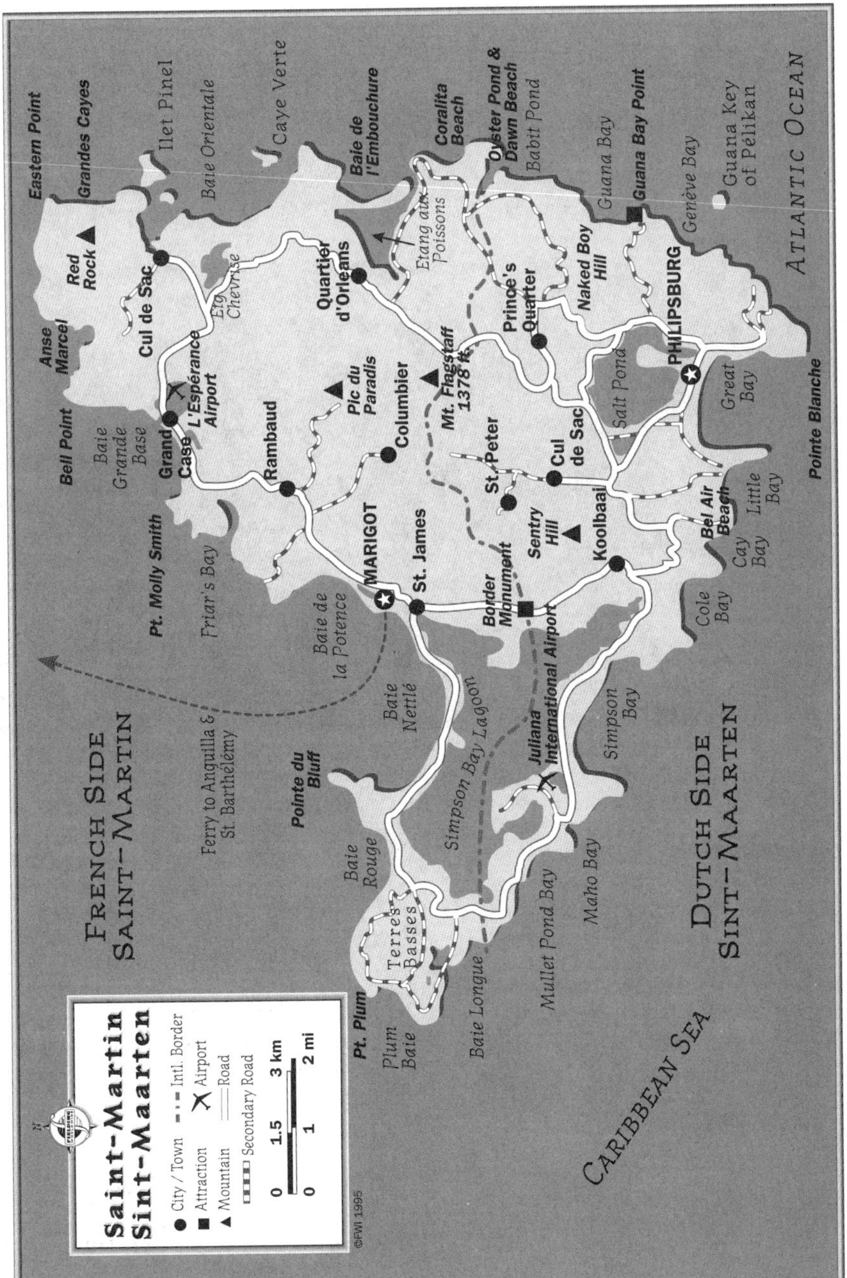
Saint-Martin
Sint-Maarten
City / Town
Attraction
Mountain
Intl. Border
Airport
Road
Secondary Road
0 1.5 3 km
0 1 2 mi
©FWI 1995
French Side
Saint-Martin
Dutch Side
Sint-Maarten
Caribbean Sea
Atlantic Ocean
Ferry to Anguilla & St. Barthélémy
Eastern Point
Grandes Cayes
Ilet Pinel
Baie Orientale
Caye Verte
Red Rock
Anse Marcel
Cul de Sac
Bell Point
Baie Grande Case
Grand Case
L'Espérance Airport
Etg. Chevrise
Rambaud
Pic du Paradis
Columbier
Quartier d'Orleans
Baie de l'Embouchure
Etang aux Poissons
Coralita Beach
Oyster Pond & Dawn Beach
Babit Pond
Mt. Flagstaff 1378 ft.
Prince's Quarter
Naked Boy Hill
Guana Bay
Guana Bay Point
Genève Bay
Guana Key of Pélikan
PHILIPSBURG
Salt Pond
Great Bay
Pointe Blanche
Cul de Sac
St. Peter
Little Bay
Bel Air Beach
Koolbaai
Sentry Hill
Cay Bay
Cole Bay
Pt. Molly Smith
Friar's Bay
MARIGOT
St. James
Border Monument
Baie de la Potence
Baie Nettlé
Juliana International Airport
Simpson Bay
Simpson Bay Lagoon
Pointe du Bluff
Baie Rouge
Terres Basses
Pt. Plum
Plum Baie
Baie Longue
Mullet Pond Bay
Maho Bay

governor of New York) lost his leg in a struggle with the Spanish in 1640. According to legend, the binational division of St. Martin was determined when a Dutchman and a Frenchman stood back to back, then circled the island until they encountered each other again, face to face. (Since the French side is somewhat bigger than the Dutch, leading devotees of this legend like to believe that the Dutchman was fatter and slower.) More legitimate historians tend to suppose that a small group of French and Dutch prisoners escaped their Spanish captors and drew up an agreement to divide the island between them. In 1946, Guadeloupe, of which St. Martin is a dependency, became an Overseas Department of France and in 1974, an Overseas Region of France.

A cannon on St. Maarten is a reminder of days when pirates roamed the shores.

People

As of 1994, there were about 28,000 residents on the French side and 32,000 on the Dutch side, but ask residents what they want to be called and nobody knows. The confusion lies in the multilinguistical nature that divides the island as well as the genuine amiability that unites it. On the Dutch side, children in primary school study in English, while students on the French side don't learn English until secondary school. Still, there's no real overt competition, and the signs separating the Dutch from the French side are truly ones of welcome, rather than declarations of partisanship. To make matters even more confusing, there are many different accents among English speakers (one distinctly Jamaican) and even a lively street dialect called *papiamento*, a hefty Caribbean mix of English, Spanish, Portuguese, Dutch and African languages. There's enough interest in Papiamento to warrant its own newspaper.

With all the French sophistication and the Dutch gentility, superstition and backwoods lore are still strong and thriving in St. Martin, including the belief in *jumbies* (evil spirits) and *soucouyants*, a kind of vampire woman. The fetish for calypso is also pure Caribbean, though the lyrics lack the political bite known on more dissident islands, and contests and parties are held regularly throughout the year. Lasana Sekou singularly upholds the literary tradition as the island's only published poet, rich in the local dialects and slang.

Beaches

St. Martin has 37 white sand beaches in excellent condition; many still wait to be discovered. Colors are dazzling, from deep blue to turquoise to emerald green. Take your pick from coastal crescent-shaped stretches noted for their seclusion to broad swatches of pristine virgin sand. Access to public beaches is easy, usually through little roads off the highway and even in high season, you won't find them uncomfortably crowded. In addition to the mile-long beach at **Great Bay** in Philipsburg, there is **Little Bay**, within a walking distance from town, with excellent watersports activities. At the west end of **Cupecoy**, you can bathe au naturel, but there are no facilities. Reachable more easily by boat are the more secluded beaches of **Plum Bay** and **Rouge Beach** (no facilities). You'll find a nudist beach (and clothes-optional hotel) at one end of **Orient Bay**. No roads go directly to the beach; rather, one must park on tracks off the main road at the north or south end of the beach and walk a few hundred feet to the water. Orient Bay also has lots of shops, restaurants and watersports facilities.

What Else to See

Unless you have a fort fetish, there's not much to see in St. Martin; better stay on the beach, cruise to a neighboring island, or go shopping in **Marigot**, a kind of St. Tropez of the Caribbean that sports its own jet-set scene, nude beach, sidewalk cafes and fishing boats. The **Port La Royale Marina** makes an interesting pitstop (you may be there anyway, chartering a schooner), and the museum Saint-Martin **On the Trail of the Arawaks** can be worth the trouble if you have any interest in Native American history. A good view of the French capital can be seen from the top of **Fort St. Louis** but be prepared for a hefty climb. To take your choice among the island's top restaurants, head for **Grand Case**, whose "Restaurant Row" has earned this tiny beachfront town the title "Gastronomic Center of St. Martin."

St. Maarten's shops at Simpson's Bay offer French fashions, batiks from St. Barts, jewelry, perfumes and quality gift items.

Don't miss the pastoral hamlet of **Orléans** (also known as the French Quarter), the oldest French settlement on the island. Here you'll find handsome small homes set among gardens alive with such tropical blossoms as bougainvillea, wisteria, flamboyant and hibiscus. **Roland Richardson**, a neighborhood artist, conservationist and historian, welcomes visitors to his studio on Thursdays.

Philipsburg, the capital of the Dutch side, boasts **Great Beach Bay**, perhaps one of the cleanest city beaches in the world. You can find more about the history of the city at the **Museum Arcade** on *111 Front Street*. Fauna and flora from the island can be glimpsed at the zoo, at **Madam Estate**, close to the New Amsterdam Shopping Center.

Historical Sites

Fort St. Louis ★★★

Just off Rue de la Republique, Marigot.

This old fort, dating back to 1786, is well preserved with some original cannons still intact. It's worth the very steep climb (bring water) for the splendid views of Marigot alone.

Museums and Exhibits

Courthouse of St. Maarten ★★★

Front Street, Philipsburg, Dutch Side.

Located north of the town square on bustling Front Street, this 1793 building was recently restored with glorious results. The second floor still functions as a courthouse, while the first floor is a post office. You'll definitely want to snap a picture of this colorful edifice.

Saint-Martin museum, On the Trail of the Arawaks ★★★★

Sandy Ground Road, Marigot.

This new museum is located next to the Royal Marina on the lagoon side. Exhibits focus on pre-Columbian artifacts, including remains of indigenous inhabitants dating back to 1800 B.C. and ceramics from 550 B.C. There's also a reproduction of a 1500-year-old Indian burial site (just discovered in 1994), early 20th-century photographs of the island, and displays on the plantation and slavery periods. Open Monday-Saturday from 9 a.m.–1 p.m. and from 3–7 p.m.

Simartn Museum ★★★

111 Front Street, Philipsburg, Dutch Side.

Hours open: 10 a.m.–6 p.m.

This small museum is housed in one of the few remaining 19th-century West Indian-style cottages on the island. Exhibits are on a changing basis, most focusing on the island's history and culture. There are some upscale specialty boutiques on the premises. Not worth a special trip, but a nice way to kill an hour or two if you're in the neighborhood.

Parks and Gardens

Butterfly Farm ★★★★★

Le Galion Beach Road, Orient Bay.

Hours Open: 9 a.m.–5 p.m.

If you're never given butterflies a second thought (or look) before, you certainly will after visiting this tranquil spot near Orient Bay. Hundreds of rare and exotic butterflies fly free in a large screened-in garden replete with fish ponds, fountains and tropical foliage. Interesting exhibits showcase their egg laying, caterpillar and pupa stages, and you'll get to see butterflies emerge from their cocoons and fly off into the great beyond (or at least around their 900-square-meter home). It's truly fascinating, and a tour, offered at no additional charge, is a must to really appreciate the exhibits. Butterflies are free...but this tour costs $10 for one or two people, $25 for three and $7.50 each for a group of four.

Tours

Pinel Island ★★★★

Cul de Sac Bay.

Just five bucks will get you a roundtrip boat ride to this tiny island off the coast of French St. Martin. There you can snorkel (they rent equipment), sunbathe or dine in the casual restaurant.

St. Maarten Zoo ★★★

Madame Estate, Philipsburg, Dutch Side.

Hours open: 9 a.m.–5 p.m.

This small zoo is especially suited to children (who get in for $2), with its playground and petting zoo. The grounds include botanical gardens, two walk-through aviaries, and caged animals from the Caribbean and South America.

Seaworld Explorer ★★★★

Grande Case Pier, Grande Case.

This semi-submarine has an open-air deck and underwater observatory hull that lets you view sealife in air-conditioned comfort—and without getting your hair wet. Trips depart from Grande Case Pier and explore the waters surrounding Creole Rock. A diver feeds the fishies to make sure tourists have lots to see. Tours cost $30 for adults, $20 for kids 2-12. Add $10 each ($7 for kids) for roundtrip transportation from your hotel.

BEST VIEW:

At 1278-feet, Paradise Peak, called Pic du Paradis, offers a breathtaking view of both the French and Dutch capitals.

Sports

Almost every beachfront hotel has facilities for windsurfing and sunfish sailing; windsurfing lessons average about $20. Waterskiing and parasailing are offered by a few hotels.

Sailing is one spectacular sport in St. Martin. From bases in Marigot, as well as Anse Marcel and Oyster Pond near the French/Dutch border, you can find any number of yacht charters. Recommended moorings on the French side of St. Martin include: **Bai Rouge** (good anchorage), **Nettlé Bay** near Marigot, **Marigot Bay** (for shopping), **Friar's Bay** (calm), **Happy Bay** (beach-grazing) and **Grand Case Bay**, a charming fishing village with a dock grocery, pharmacy and excellent restaurants. A top-class marina can be found at **Port Louvilliers** at Anse Marcel, with docking space for 60 boats (29–73 feet) and boutiques, grocery, cafe and **La Capitanerie**, a ship chandlery. At **Oyster Pond** you'll also find a large marina and **Captain Oliver's**, a popular restaurant and hotel, plus a small grocery and a ship chandlery. Sailing excursions from St. Martin to other islands (Anguilla is a favorite, but boats also go to St. Barts, Saba, St. Kitts, Nevis and St. Eustatius) can be arranged by most hotels. Rates for a day trip with snorkeling, open bar and picnics run between $65–$70 per person.

Caid & Isa, a horseback riding facility located at Meridien L'Habitation at Anse Marcel, is operated by longtime pro Brigitte Sacaze. Paso Finas can be hired for 2.5-hour excursions over the hills of Anse Marcel to the private beach of **Petite Cayes**. Other facilities include the **OK Corral** at the Coralita Beach (including one pony for children) and **Crazy Acres** at Cole Bay (on the Dutch side).

Sport-fishing finds big fans on St. Martin. Half-and full-day charters with tackle, bait and snacks are readily available at **Bobby's Marina**, **Great Bay**, **Simpson Bay** and **Port La Royale Marina**. December to April is the season for kingfish, dolphin and barracuda; tuna is available year-round.

Boating is available on two types of vessels: large catamarans holding 25 or more passengers that sail to St. Barts for the day, or small sailboats that hold six to ten passengers for excursions to secluded beaches. Boats depart from **Bobby's Marina** and **Great Bay Marina** in Philipsburg, **Simpson Bay Lagoon**, and **Port La Royale Marina** at Marigot Bay. A new marina is located at **Port Lonvilliers** at the north end of the French section.

There are numerous tennis courts on the island. **Le Privilege**, overlooking Meridien L'Habitation, has six lighted courses and **La Belle Créole** has four lighted Omni courts. **Laguna Beach** has three lighted hard-surface courts. Other hotels include **Nettlé Bay Beach Club**, **Mont Vernon**, **Simson Beach**, **Oyster Bay**, **Grand Case Beach Club**, **Coralita**, **Esmeralda Resort** and **Green Cay Village**.

Golf

Mullet Bay Resort, Philipsburg, Dutch Side.

The island's only links are an 18-hole course designed by Joseph Lee. It is quite scenic and very challenging, but often open only to guests at the Mullet Bay Resort—if your heart is really set on golfing, play it safe and stay at this well-run resort. Greens fee for nonguests (when they are allowed) are about $100, and considerably less for guests—another reason to stay here.

Horseback Riding

Various locations, Philipsburg, Dutch Side.
On the Dutch Side, horses can be rented at **Crazy Acres** *(☎ 5-42793)*. On the French Side, try **Caid and Isa** *(☎ 87-32-92)* and the **O.K. Corral** *(☎ 87-40-72)*. The going rate is about $40 for a two-hour trail ride.

Watersports

Various locations, Philipsburg, Dutch Side.
Dutch Side: for boating and cruises, try **White Octopus** *(☎ 5-23170)*, **Caribbean Watersports** *(☎ 5-42801)*, **Bobby's Marina** *(☎ 5-22366)*, and **Bluebeard** *(☎ 5-52898)*. For deep-sea fishing, try **Wampum** *(☎ 5-22366)*, **Sea Brat** *(☎ 5-24096)*, and **Bobby's Marina** *(☎ 5-22366)*. Scuba divers can call **Leeward Island Divers** *(☎ 5-242268)*, **Tradewinds** *(☎ 5-54387)*, **St. Maarten Divers** *(☎ 5-22446)*, and **Ocean Explorers** *(☎ 5-45252)*, which also runs a unique underwater walk on which non-swimmers can stroll with the help of special helmets that supply oxygen.

Where to Eat

Fielding's Highest Rated Restaurants in Sint Maarten/St. Martin		
★★★★	Bye Bar Brazil	$8–$19
★★★★	L'Auberge Gourmande	$15–$31
★★★★	Le Perroquet	$18–$26
★★★★	Saratoga	$16–$26
★★★	Antoine's	$15–$36
★★★	Captain Oliver Restaurant	$16–$24
★★★	Hevea	$22–$38
★★★	Hevea	$30–$50
★★★	La Nadaillac	$16–$32
★★★	Le Bec Fin	$16–$31

Fielding's Special Restaurants in Sint Maarten/St. Martin		
★★★★	Bye Bar Brazil	$8–$19
★★★★	Le Perroquet	$18–$26
★★★	Antoine's	$15–$36
★★★	La Nadaillac	$16–$32
★★★	The Wajang Doll	$21–$30

Fielding's Budget Restaurants in Sint Maarten/St. Martin		
★★★	Mark's Place	$3–$13
★★★	The Grill & Ribs Co.	$5–$11
★★★	Drew's Deli	$3–$15
★★★	Cheri's Cafe	$6–$17
★★★	David's	$6–$17

With its strong French influence, St. Martin almost has a legal obligation to serve world-class cuisine, and it doesn't disappoint. Out of 50 restaurants in Marigot, and another 20 in Grand Case and two dozen scattered throughout the island, many have top gourmet French kitchens; there are also fine Italian, Swiss, Vietnamese and Chinese eateries. Don't miss the **lolos**, family-run food stalls along Boulevard Grande Case. American junk food is always within reach. Seafood is omnipresent, and French wines are in abundance.

At some restaurants, you can dine to the tune of jazz, reggae and pop, and bars stay busy until midnight. In Philipsburg, the best French restaurant is surely **Le Bec Fin**, where the Dutch royal family dines. In Philipsburg, good burgers and conch chowder for prices that won't break can be found at **The Greenhouse**, and cheap Chinese restaurants can be found on Back Street. Reserve for most elegant dining, especially during high season. Prices for a three-course meal for two, without wine, can run from $60–$120 and upwards. Service charges are often added inconspicuously in the wrong place on credit card charges, so always peruse your slip carefully before signing or adding more tip. The legal age for drinking and gambling is 18.

Sint Maarten

Antoine's **$$$** ★★★

55 Front Street, Philipsburg, ☎ (599)5-22964.
French cuisine. Specialties: Fresh local crayfish.
Dinner: 4-10 p.m., entrees $15–$36.

A gorgeous setting on a breezy patio above Great Bay makes this restaurant a romantic choice for a celebration dinner. Cuisine is classic French with Italian touches. Some specialties offered bring back memories of an uncomplicated past; to wit, duck with cherries, lobster thermidor and chocolate mousse. When in season, fresh local crayfish makes a welcome appearance.

Cheri's Cafe **$$** ★★★

Cinnamon Grove Center, Maho Beach, ☎ (599) 55-3361.
American cuisine. Specialties: Steaks, seafood.
Lunch: 11 a.m.-4:30 p.m., entrees $6–$12.
Dinner: 4:30-1:30 p.m., entrees $12–$17.

Cheri Batson, owner of the legendary cafe and bar that bears her name, must share the honors for the success of her hugely popular eating establishment with her steak purveyor—customers are always raving about the quality and quantity of the grilled beef. A huge sirloin steak fills out a plate for a modest $10.95. A lot of customers think the place is just plain fun—nobody sits down for long when the house band, Ramon, starts to play. Great burgers are also on the menu, along with the inevitable grilled seafood.

Chesterfield's **$$** ★★★

Great Bay Marina, Pointe Blanche, ☎ (559) 5-23484.
American cuisine.
Lunch: 11:30 a.m.-2:30 p.m., entrees $7–$12.
Dinner: 5:30-10 p.m., entrees $7–$20.

Rub epaulets with the boating crowd at this pierside restaurant with a casual, congenial ambience. The food is well-prepared, with a host of seafood, duckling and beef dishes served with flair at lunch and dinner. A companionable group often gathers for happy hour on a daily basis.

Greenhouse **$$$** ★★

Bobby's Marina, Philipsburg, ☎ (599) 5-22941.
American cuisine.
Lunch: 11 a.m.-5 p.m., entrees $6–$10.
Dinner: 5-10 p.m., entrees $11–$25.

An all-purpose eatery that serves American favorites and exotic Indonesian specialties, the Greenhouse has a harbor location and a dining room lush with plant life. Guests can play pool, throw darts and dance as well as dine. It jumps daily at happy hour, which actually lasts a little longer; good for twofers and gratis hors d'oeuvres.

L'Escargot **$$$** ★★★

76 Front Street, Philipsburg, ☎ (599) 5-22483.

French cuisine.
Lunch: 11 a.m.-3 p.m., entrees $8–$23.
Dinner: 6:30-11 p.m., entrees $18–$29.
Snail fanciers will enjoy a meal at this venerable grande dame of a restaurant, which has been in the same spot for over 20 years. The delectable delicacy is a specialty, and it shows up stuffed in mushrooms and in various other ways. The rest of the menu is largely French, encompassing duck, seafood and meat dishes.

Le Bec Fin **$$$** ★★★
119 Front Street, Philipsburg, ☎ (599) 5-22976.
French cuisine.
Dinner: 6-10 p.m., entrees $16–$31.
Ascend a flight of stairs to this second-floor dining salon in the courtyard of the St. Maarten Museum. At night, the ambience is candlelit and intimate, during the day try to snag a table overlooking the sea; there are only a few of them available. The kitchen really shines with its seafood preparations, especially lobster, served grilled or flamed in brandy.

Le Perroquet **$$$** ★★★★
72 Airport Road, Simpson Bay, ☎ (599) 5-41339.
French cuisine.
Dinner: 6-10 p.m., entrees $18–$26.
This restaurant, situated in a typical West Indian house near the airport, serves very atypical meals. Once seated, servers wheel a cart to your table with a choice of nightly specials—which often include filets of ostrich or boar steaks. Surprisingly, ostrich tastes more like beef, rather than the expected chicken. For less adventurous palates, fresh red snapper or beef dishes are usually available. Simpson Bay Lagoon can be viewed from the plant-filled porch.

Saratoga **$$$** ★★★★
Simpson Bay Yacht Club, Simpson Bay, ☎ (599) 5-42421.
Seafood cuisine.
Dinner: 6:30-10 p.m., entrees $16–$26.
A perennial favorite, this yacht club restaurant in a mahogany-panelled dining room features a changing menu of very fresh seafood offerings. Although pricey, its faithful following returns for specialties like scallops seviche or salmon in puff pastry with spinach and mushrooms. Leafy salads feature at least two kinds of greens, served with two homemade dressings. Steaks and beef dishes are also available.

The Grill & Ribs Co. **$** ★★★
Old Street Shopping Cntr., Philipsburg,
American cuisine.
Lunch: 11 a.m.-4 p.m., entrees $5–$11.
Dinner: 4-10 p.m., entrees $5–$11.
This informal place is the island's best-known and best-loved ribarama. For a reasonable price of $12.95, diners can chow down on an unlimited amount of pork or beef ribs. The Grill & Ribs Co. has two locations to choose from: a second story alfresco terrace eatery at the Old St. Shopping Center, or the rib place behind Pizza Hut on Simpson Bay Beach. Other offerings include chicken fajitas, burgers, chicken and sandwiches heaped with a side of fries.

The Seafood Galley **$$** ★★★
Bobby's Marina, Philipsburg,
Seafood cuisine.
Lunch: 11 a.m.-3 p.m., entrees $7–$18.
Dinner: 6-10 p.m., entrees $7–$18.
Although this pier-side establishment has a clubby restaurant offering hot plates of fresh fish and seafood, some people bypass it and head straight for the adjoining raw

bar. There they can graze all night from a generous menu of oyster shooters, clams on the half shell, or crab claws. Lunchtime is popular for the view and the hearty sandwiches and egg dishes.

The Wajang Doll **$$$** ★★★

134 Front Street, Philipsburg,
Asian cuisine. Specialties: Rijstaffel.
Dinner: 6:45-10 p.m., entrees $21–$30.

It helps to come here with a big group and a healthy appetite for this restaurant's 20-item Javanese feasts. This cuisine, known as *rijstaffel* (rice table), originated in the former Dutch colony of Indonesia. Seemingly endless plates of savory and spicy seafood, meats and chicken are devoured over a mountain of fragrant rice. They can be embellished with "try them if you dare" hot pepper sambals. Couples and singles won't feel left out, as smaller and cheaper versions are available as well as a la carte dishes.

St. Martin

Bye Bar Brazil **$$** ★★★★

47 Boulevard Grande Case, Grand Case, ☎ *(590) 87-76-49.*
Latin American cuisine.
Dinner: 7–3 a.m., entrees $8–$19.

Locals love to hang out here and talk literature and politics with Michel, the opinionated (but gracious) owner of this laid-back spot in the heart of Grande Case. Michel is famous for his *caipirinha*—a wonderful concoction of rum, sugar and lime—as well as his selection of 38 whiskeys, including 16 single malts from Scotland. You can try three shots for $10. The Brazilian and French food is great, too, and the entire wine list is available by the bottle and by the glass, something we'd like to see more restaurants offer. Save room for the *manjar*, a coconut dessert, then try the *batita de coco*, a drink of coconut milk and rum that's an excellent digestive. This place is not to be missed!

Captain Oliver Restaurant **$$$** ★★★

Oyster Pond, Marigot, ☎ *(590) 87-30-00.*
Seafood cuisine.
Lunch: Noon–3 p.m., entrees $16–$24.
Dinner: 7–11 p.m., entrees $16–$24.

A popular outdoor restaurant/snackbar/store on a pier facing the sea, Captain Oliver's sits across from its namesake resort. A thoroughly democratic place, the good Captain has provided a choice of eateries to fit every budget. There's a snack shack dispensing le chili dog and other light meals, with a grocery store attached. The centerpiece, though, is the oceanfront restaurant, where creative international cuisine, with an emphasis on seafood, is served for lunch and dinner. Soups are delicious and different, and the fresh tuna, when available, is stellar.

Cha Cha Cha's **$$$** ★★★

Boulevard de Grand Case, Grand Case, ☎ *(590) 87-53-63.*
Latin American cuisine.
Dinner: 6–11 p.m., entrees $11–$20.

This colorful cafe draws the au courant set who like to behave a little outre. The menu is a melting pot of piquant Latin and Gallic specialties that usually taste as good as they read. Skillfully grilled or steamed fresh seafood is served with tropical salsas. Some people never make it to the dining room, preferring to graze on a daring tapas menu while sipping a blender drink in a whimsical garden. Come before 7 p.m. to save a little money on a generous prix-fixe, three-course supper for under $20.

Coco Beach Bar **$$$** ★★★

Orient Beach, Marigot,
International cuisine.
Lunch: entrees $15–$30.
Dinner: entrees $15–$30.

By day Coco Beach bar is just one of five plain open-air eateries competing for the tourist dollar on clothing-optional Orient Beach. But at night, it becomes a quaint little candlelit restaurant, with tastefully set tables and a diverse menu, which includes caesar salad, filet mignon, and lobster with pasta. Softly lapping ocean waves provide atmospheric background music. Despite an often-full house, service is among the best on the island.

David's **$$** ★★★

Rue de la Liberte, Marigot, ☎ (590) 87-51-58.
English cuisine.
Lunch: 11:30 a.m.–2:30 p.m., entrees $6–$17.
Dinner: 6–10 p.m., entrees $6–$17.

When it's crowded, David's can be a convivial place, with word games or darts providing the entertainment while waiting for light pub fare or full dinners. An interesting menu of hearty soups, meat and pasta dishes are all reasonably priced, and freshly caught seafood is a standout. The bar stays open until the witching hour and the scene can be boisterous or dull, depending upon who shows up.

Drew's Deli **$** ★★★

French Cul-de-Sac, Marigot,
American cuisine. Specialties: Cheeseburgers, cheesecake.
Lunch: 11 a.m.–3 p.m., entrees $3–$15.
Dinner: 7–9:30 p.m., entrees $3–$15.

North of Orient Bay lies the little community of French-Cul-de-Sac, where Drew from Wisconsin, a wonderful host, grills up some of the best bacon cheeseburgers around. Cole slaw and New York-style cheesecake with the burger provides a well-balanced vacation diet. The place is a little cramped, but the friendly reception might urge you to sit a spell. Full meals are also offered.

Hevea **$$$** ★★★

163 Boulevard de Grand Case, Grand Case, ☎ (590) 87-56-85.
French cuisine.
Dinner: 6:30–10 p.m., entrees $22–$38.

Set in a restored Creole mansion that is also an intimate inn, this 10-table French eatery is charming and romantic. The size of the dining room ensures the consistently fine quality of the French cuisine served here. The proprietors, who hail from Nice, use only the finest ingredients and believe that simplicity is key. Sauces made with fresh herbs, wine, or wild mushrooms are often used to subtly accentuate, never overpower, lamb, duck breast, or a signature red snapper en papillote. Closed Mondays from April 15-December 14.

L'Auberge Gourmande **$$$** ★★★★

89 Boulevard Grand Case, Grand Case, ☎ (590) 87-73-37.
French cuisine.
Dinner: 6:30–10 p.m., entrees $15–$31.

The setting is a quaint, converted residence sporting jalousied windows. Guests dine by candlelight in a comfortable room, although increased noise on the streets of Grand Case may affect a romantic tete-a-tete. Soups are a specialty and are interestingly prepared, including a brew of mussels with orange. Grilled fish is reliable, although the roast pork and roast lamb were only average on one occasion and the once-impeccable service has slipped of late.

L'ile Flottante **$** ★★

Boulevard Grande Case, Grand Case, ☎ (590) 87-89-46.
French cuisine.
This open-air French bakery is just about the only place to get breakfast in Grande Case. They offer up wonderful pastries and delicious cafe au lait, but don't expect service with a smile—unless you're a local. Open daily from 6:00-10:00 a.m.

La Maison sur Le Port **$$$** ★★★

rue de Republique, Marigot, ☎ (590) 87-56-38.
French cuisine.
Lunch: Noon–2:30 p.m., entrees $11–$14.
Dinner: 6–10 p.m., entrees $17–$34.
Chef Christian Verdeau presents impeccably prepared but rather small portions of duck, lobster and other prime meats and seafood on an outdoor patio with a harbor view. Prices remain stable, though, for the excellent quality of the ingredients, and a warm welcome is reserved for all comers.

La Nadaillac **$$$** ★★★

Rue de la Liberte, Marigot, ☎ (590) 87-53-77.
French cuisine.
Lunch: Noon–2:30 p.m., entrees $16–$32.
Dinner: 6:30–9:30 p.m., entrees $16–$32.
This intimate gem, albeit a very dear one (as in prices), is the province of Fernand Mallard, from the Perigord. Appropriately enough, most specialties involve products from that region of France, including preserved goose. The restaurant is on an attractive patio facing the harbor, nestled among the chic clothing stores in the Galerie Perigourdine.

Lolos **$** ★

Boulevard Grande Case, Grand Case,
Seafood cuisine.
The food stalls that line a section of Grande Case Boulevard are known as *lolos*. These mom-and-pop operations offer the freshest seafood and local treats each day for amazingly low prices. Most open from noon on, but it's a catch-as-catch-can type of business. Well worth checking out.

Mark's Place **$** ★★★

French-Cul-de-Sac, Marigot, ☎ (590) 87-34-50.
Latin American cuisine.
Lunch: 12:30–2:30 p.m., entrees $3–$13.
Dinner: 6:30–9:30 p.m., entrees $3–$13.
The West Indian food served here is hearty, plentiful and varied—on a given night you could have lobster bisque with a curry of conch or goat, or a crab back appetizer and swordfish, but sometimes the quality is unexceptional. It's hard to quibble with the reasonable prices, but you get what you pay for. And the crowds keep coming—Mark's Place is usually jammed.

Mini-Club **$$$** ★★

Rue de la Liberte, Marigot, ☎ (509) 87-50-69.
French cuisine.
Lunch: Noon–3 p.m., prix fixe $32.
Dinner: 7–10:30 p.m., entrees $18–$35.
Locals who like to stuff themselves silly with food as good as mother makes are grateful for the continuing success of the gargantuan French-creole buffet served here on Wednesdays and Saturday nights. The setting is lots of fun too: a jungly, tropical terrace suspended over the water. The feast includes all the wine you can drink, so bring a friend who can help you down the stairs. On other days sample an

unparalleled lobster souffle and other French specialties. The buffet is $40 per person.

Surf Club South **$** ★★

Boulevard Grande Case, Grand Case,
American cuisine.

New Jersey natives will do a double take as they come upon the Garden State Parkway, Turnpike and other highway signs prominently displayed on Boulevard Grande Case. Jersey expatriots run this funky spot, which boasts of a "New Jersey menu" (lots of burgers and cheese steaks). It's a happening spot, especially on Sunday, when they give out free drinks from 10 a.m.–2 p.m. and live music kicks in at 6 p.m. All the locals come and party, then head over to Jimbo's when the Surf Club closes at 10 p.m.

FIELDING'S CHOICE:

Little known to the outside world is the special purple and bittersweet guavaberry liqueur produced on the island ever since Dutch colonists settled in the 18th century. During the Christmas holidays, it's customary to go from home to home serenading for samples. Every family makes a different brew, which is usually fully consumed by the end of the Christmas season. The Sint Maarten Guavaberry Company now makes the liqueur locally, and offers shade, seating and a few samples at its midtown production area at the Guavaberry Shop on 10 Front St. Try a guavaberry colada (blended with cream of coconut and pineapple juice), or a guavaberry screwdriver (mixed with orange juice). A bottle of guavaberry sells for less than $15 and is considered duty-free because it is an island craft.

Where to Shop

St. Martin's duty-free port carries all the typical products one would expect to find at 25–50 percent discounts: china, jewelry, crystal, perfumes and fashions. Usually prices are quoted in American dollars and sales clerks speak English. Local art shown in galleries and artist's studios make great buys; besides **Roland Richardson** in Orleans, seek out the work of **Genevieve Curt** ☎ *(590) 87-88-52*, at the **Tropical Gallery**. Other fine names are the painter Alexandre Minguet and the Lynn family (husband, wife and two sons). Both the Dutch and French side have some of the most sophisticated fashion shops in the Caribbean, but be prepared to pay in francs on the French side if you want a good exchange. (Hours on the French side are iffy, but usually run Monday-Saturday 9 a.m.–12:30 p.m. and 3–7 p.m.) Some stores adjust their schedules to accommodate cruise ships on Sunday and holidays.

Philipsburg may seem more crowded and junk-oriented than Marigot, but you can find highly memorable leather (**Domina**), clothes (**Maurella Senesi**) and jewelry (**Caribbean Gems**). Shopping on Grand Case is limited to narrow main street. Best shops in Marigot are at the **Marina Royale**. Don't miss the lively **early morning market in Marigot** where locals sell their spices, handicrafts and tropical fruits and vegetables. **Port La Royale** is a beehive of activity after dawn; hang out here if you want to meet yachties and even local schooner captains cruising in from other islands with new goods. High-fashion designs can be found in the **Galerie Périgourdine** shopping complex, across from the post office.

Philipsburg, capital of Dutch St. Maarten, is full of shops and markets.

Sint Maarten/St. Martin Directory

BUSINESS HOURS

On the Dutch side, shops open Monday–Saturday 8 a.m.–noon and 2–6 p.m. Banks open Monday–Thursday 8 a.m.–1 and Friday from 8:30 a.m.–1 p.m. and 4–5 p.m. On the French side, shops open Monday–Saturday 9 a.m.–12:30 p.m. and 3–7 p.m. Some shops take a longer or shorter siesta, so call ahead. Banks open weekdays 8:30 a.m.–1:30 p.m.

CLIMATE

Sunshine prevails on the island and it is warm year-round. Temperatures during the winter average 80 degrees F, in the summer, it gets a little warmer. Constant trade winds keep the climate pleasant.

DOCUMENTS

U.S. citizens entering via the Dutch side for stays of up to three months need a valid passport, or one that has expired no longer than five years prior, or a notarized or original birth certificate with raised seal, or a voter's registration card. Canadian citizens must have a valid passport. U.S. residents and Canadians who are not citizens must have a green card or multiple re-entry stamp. Travelers must also show a return or onward ticket.

U.S. citizens and Canadians traveling as tourists and entering via the French side for stays up to three weeks must have proof of citizenship in the form of a valid passport, a passport that has expired no more than five years prior, or other proof of citizenship, in the form of a birth certificate (original or official copy), or a voter's registration card, plus a government-authorized identification with photo. For stays over three weeks, or for nontourist visits, a valid passport is necessary. Resident aliens of the U.S. and Canada, and visitors from countries other than those of the Common Market (E.E.C.) and Japan, must have a valid passport and visa. A return or onward ticket is also required for all visitors.

ELECTRICITY

Current runs 220 AC, 50 cycles. American and Canadian appliances require French plug converters and transformers.

GETTING AROUND

The taxi center in Marigot is near the tourist office ☎ *(590) 87-56-54*; in Grand Case ☎ *(590) 87-75-79*. Car rentals can be made at Juliana Airport or at hotels. Most have automatic transmission, many are air-conditioned. All foreign driver's licenses are honored. Major credit cards are accepted, and a tank of gas should last a week. Cars cost about $25–$55 per day, depending on make and unlimited mileage is offered. One rental company to try is **Sunset** ☎ *(590) 87-32-93;* book your car well in advance, especially in winter.

Scooters rent for about $18–$23 per day from **Rent 2 Wheels** in Baie Nettlé ☎ *(590) 87-20-59*, or **Moto Caraibes** ☎ *(590) 87-25-91*. Given the hilly terrain of St. Martin, mopeds, scooters and motorbikes should only be rented by experienced riders.

Buses run from 6 a.m.–midnight, leaving from Grand Case, and can be flagged down anywhere. Buses run to Marigot, Cole Bay, Simson Bay, Mullet Bay, etc., as well as Marigot/Philipsburg and French Quarter/Philipsburg. The fare is $1 within the French side and $1.50 if you cross to the Dutch side.

LANGUAGE

French is the official language of St. Martin and Dutch is the official language of Sint Maarten, but English is spoken everywhere.

MEDICAL EMERGENCIES

There is a hospital in Marigot ☎ *(590) 87-50-07* and another in Philipsburg ☎ *31111*. Hotels can contact English-speaking physicians for you. There are about 18 doctors practicing general medicine, six dentists, and specialists in many varied fields. In addition, French St. Martin has several pharmacies.

MONEY

The official currency on the French side is the French franc and the guilder on the Dutch side, but U.S. dollars are accepted everywhere. Prices are often quoted in U.S. dollars. The rate of exchange is subject to change due to currency fluctuation.

TELEPHONE

The international country code for St. Martin is *590*. To call the Dutch side, dial the code *599-5*. French side numbers have 6 digits, the Dutch side 5. The cheapest way to make calls is with a telephone card on public phones (8 on the square in Marigot and 2 in Grand Case in front of the pier). It's a toll call when phoning from one side of the island to the other.

TIME

St. Martin is one hour ahead of East Standard Time in New York. French St. Martin uses the 24-hour system of telling time; hence, 1 p.m. in the afternoon is 13 hours.

TIPPING AND TAXES

If no service charge is added, leave 10–15 percent on restaurant bills.

TOURIST INFORMATION

The St. Martin Tourist Office is located at the Waterfront in Marigot ☎ *(590) 87-57-21*, FAX *(590) 87-56-43*. A good source for history, architecture and art on the island can be found in the beautiful four-color magazines called *Discover St. Martin*, available free at hotels and tourist sites. A slew of other free publications are available, including *What to Do*, *St. Maarten Nights*, *St. Martin's Week* and *Focus*, among others. Some of the larger hotels distribute to guests free of charge a daily *Times* FAX in conjunction with the *New York Times*. In the U.S. ☎ *(212) 989-0000.*

WHEN TO GO

Mardi Gras is held on February 28, a frenzied carnival with dancing filling the streets of Marigot and Grand Case. Another carnival, with calypso, "jump ups," floats, steel bands and bright costumes takes place the last two weeks in April and early May, mostly on the Dutch side, but with some French participation. The Marlin Open de St. Martin on May 29–June 3 is an invitational organized by the Sailfish Caraibes Club. June 6 is the African Festival with arts, crafts, music and dance lectures. Bastille Day on July 14 is celebrated with fireworks, parades and sports contests. Schoelcher Day, on July 21, in honor of the French parliamentarian who led the campaign against slavery, is celebrated with boat and bike races. Halloween is a wild affair in Grande Case, when locals go crazy with exotic costumes. Concordia Day, on November 11, starts the season off with parades and ceremonies. New Year's Eve, called Réveillon de la Saint Sylvestre, is celebrated noisily with balloons, late-night dancing and dining at hotels and restaurants.

SINT MAARTEN/ST. MARTIN RESTAURANTS	PHONE	ENTREE	CR. CARDS
Marigot			
American			
★★★ Drew's Deli		$3–$15	A, MC, V
English			
★★★ David's	(590) 87-51-58	$6–$17	
French			
★★★★ L'Auberge Gourmande	(590) 87-73-37	$15–$31••	
★★★ Hevea	(590) 87-56-85	$22–$38••	A, MC, V
★★★ La Maison sur Le Port	(590) 87-56-38	$11–$34	MC, V
★★★ La Nadaillac	(590) 87-53-77	$16–$32	None
★★ Mini-Club	(590) 87-50-69	$32–$35	A, MC, V
International			
★★★ Coco Beach Bar		$15–$30	A, MC, V
Latin American			
★★★ Cha Cha Cha's	(590) 87-53-63	$11–$20••	MC, V

SINT MAARTEN/ST. MARTIN RESTAURANTS	PHONE	ENTREE	CR. CARDS
★★★ **Mark's Place**	(590) 87-34-50	$3–$13	A, MC, V
Seafood			
★★★ **Captain Oliver Restaurant**	(590) 87-30-00	$16–$24	A, MC, V
Philipsburg			
American			
★★★ **Cheri's Cafe**	(599) 5-53361	$6–$17	None
★★★ **Chesterfield's**	(599) 5-23484	$7–$20	None
★★★ **The Grill & Ribs Co.**		$5–$11	None
★★ **Greenhouse**	(599) 5-22941	$6–$25	A, MC, V
Asian			
★★★ **The Wajang Doll**		$21–$30••	A, MC, V
French			
★★★★ **Le Perroquet**	(599) 5-41339	$18–$26••	A, MC, V
★★★ **Antoine**	(599)5-22964	$16–$32	A, MC, V
★★★ **L'Escargot**	(599) 5-22483	$8–$29	A, MC, V
★★★ **Le Bec Fin**	(599) 5-22976	$16–$31••	A, MC, V
Seafood			
★★★★ **Saratoga**	(599) 5-42421	$16–$26••	A, MC, V
★★★ **The Seafood Galley**		$7–$18	A, MC, V

Note: • Lunch Only

•• Dinner Only

ST. THOMAS

St. Thomas has 34 dive sites and offers excellent snorkeling.

St. Thomas is the most cosmopolitan of the U.S. Virgin Islands, if not the most unabashedly commercial. Lots of Caribbean islands boast white sands, aquamarine seas and lush mountains, but few display luxury goods in such abundance. A commercial hub long before Blackbeard who prowled its waters, St. Thomas is now a prime destination for cruise ships, whose passengers rush ashore—not unlike the 19th-century buccaneers—in hot pursuit of duty-free booty.

Others still come to get away from it all, even if the wave of development that followed Hurricane Hugo in 1989 gave a jolt to urban American reality. Along with new resorts and fast-food restaurants there is now a K-mart and a Hard Rock Cafe, and luxurious homes have blossomed like frangipani on the northern and eastern hillsides. Gridlock in paradise today aptly describes the sidewalks and narrow alleyways of downtown Charlotte Amalie (pronounced ah-MAHL-ya), the territorial capital and St. Thomas's only real town. But beyond the city bustle, there lies another St. Thomas, with more than 40 beaches, rides aboard an Atlantic submarine, golf, tennis, parasailing, boardsailing, big game fishing—the activities of an endless summer. Simply, St.

Thomas is an ideal destination for the couple in which one shops and the other grumbles. Just one word of warning: whatever you do, avoid the cityscape when cruise ships dock in port (and if you're on a cruise ship yourself, duck!).

Bird's Eye View

The tram to Paradise Point gives a bird's eye view of the St. Thomas harbor.

St. Thomas lies about 40 miles north of St. Croix and 75 miles east of Puerto Rico. Only 14 miles by three miles long, it is literally built on a mountain—the reason it's called "Rock City"—with its one main town, Charlotte Amalie, situated on the central south shore. At its highest peak, **Crown Mountain**, it measures 1550 feet high. A scenic road around the island, **Skyline Drive** (Route 40), allows a simultaneous view of both sides of the island. Beach resorts dot most of the coastline; private homes with bright red, roofs of corrugated iron nestle into the hillside in the wooded interior. The island is easy to navigate by automobile, but there are the inevitable daily traffic jams that clog downtown Charlotte Amalie at rush hour. An excellent view of grassy hills, talcum-white beaches and blue waters can be glimpsed from the Crown Mountain Road, west off Harwood Highway. On the outskirts of town (follow Veterans Drive along the waterfront and turn left at the Villa Olga sign) you'll discover Frenchtown, a community of Swedish descendants from the time Sweden invaded St. Bart in the late 18th century. (Locals still speak a Norman French dialect.)

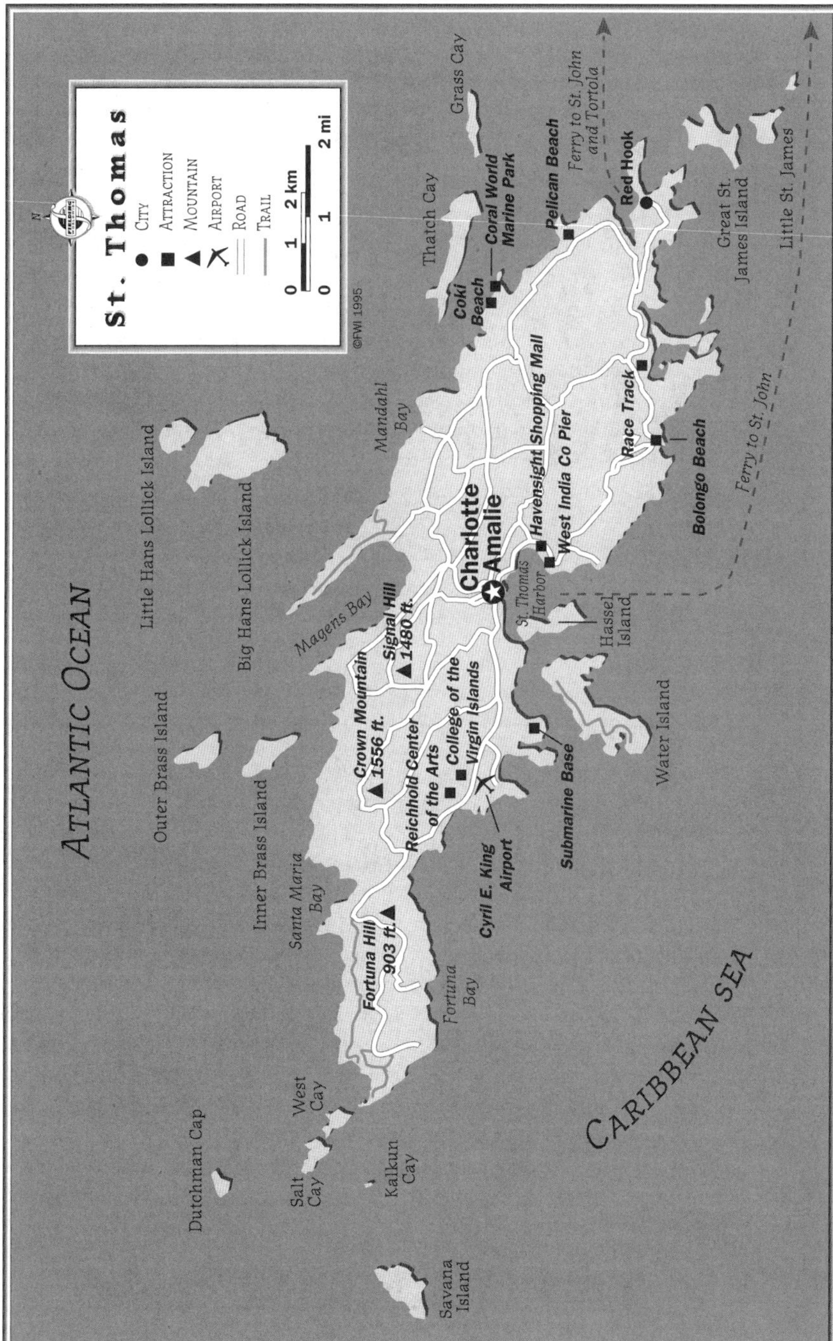
St. Thomas
City
Attraction
Mountain
Airport
Road
Trail
0 1 2 km
0 1 2 mi
©FWI 1995
Atlantic Ocean
Caribbean Sea
Charlotte Amalie
Crown Mountain 1556 ft.
Signal Hill 1480 ft.
Fortuna Hill 903 ft.
Reichhold Center of the Arts
College of the Virgin Islands
Cyril E. King Airport
Submarine Base
Havensight Shopping Mall
West India Co Pier
Race Track
Bolongo Beach
Red Hook
Pelican Beach
Coral World Marine Park
Coki Beach
Ferry to St. John and Tortola
Ferry to St. John
Magens Bay
Mandahl Bay
Santa Maria Bay
Fortuna Bay
St. Thomas Harbor
Hassel Island
Water Island
Little Hans Lollick Island
Big Hans Lollick Island
Outer Brass Island
Inner Brass Island
Thatch Cay
Grass Cay
Great St. James Island
Little St. James
West Cay
Salt Cay
Kalkun Cay
Dutchman Cap
Savana Island

History

As with St. Croix and St. John, Columbus discovered these islands on his third voyage in 1493. A plan for colonizing St. Thomas was signed by Frederick III of Denmark, but the first settlement failed. Charlotte Amalie, St. Thomas's first permanent European settlement, dates back to 1671. Set on a grand circular harbor, the town was laid out by planners in Denmark who had never seen the mountainous 32-square mile island. Danish control of the Virgin Islands ended when the U.S. bought St. Croix, St. Thomas and St. John for $25 million in order to protect its interests in the Panama Canal. Today, the self-governing unincorporated territory has a nonvoting delegate to the U.S. House of Representatives.

Beaches

Though St. Thomas endures a lot of visitors, beaches have remained appealing, with fine white sand sloping into beautiful bays. The heart-shaped **Magen's Bay**, the largest bay along St. Thomas' rugged northeast coast, is often considered one of the prettiest beaches in the world. It's also the only beach with an admission charge (50 cents, 25 cents for children under 11 and under, $1 for parking), but it also has all the conveniences of civilization, including parking, lifeguards, equipment rental, changing rooms, restaurants and bars. The calm waters are good for swimming, first-time sailors, and a small craft can be rented on the beach (for about $20 hourly). On the northeast shores, **Coki Point** is sterling (stop by the 80,000-gallon aquarium at **Coral World** and the underwater observatory), as is **Sapphire Beach** on the east coast, pointing toward St. John and the **British Virgin Islands**. In the south, two excellent beaches are **Lindbergh Bay**, in front of a hotel near the airport, and **Morning Star**, in front of a resort just east of Charlotte Amalie. There are few deserted beaches here, which is just as well, because isolated areas tend to attract more crime.

FIELDING'S CHOICE:

From January to April, pilot whales frequent the breeding grounds off the north end of the island. Inquire at your sports activity center about whale-watch tours.

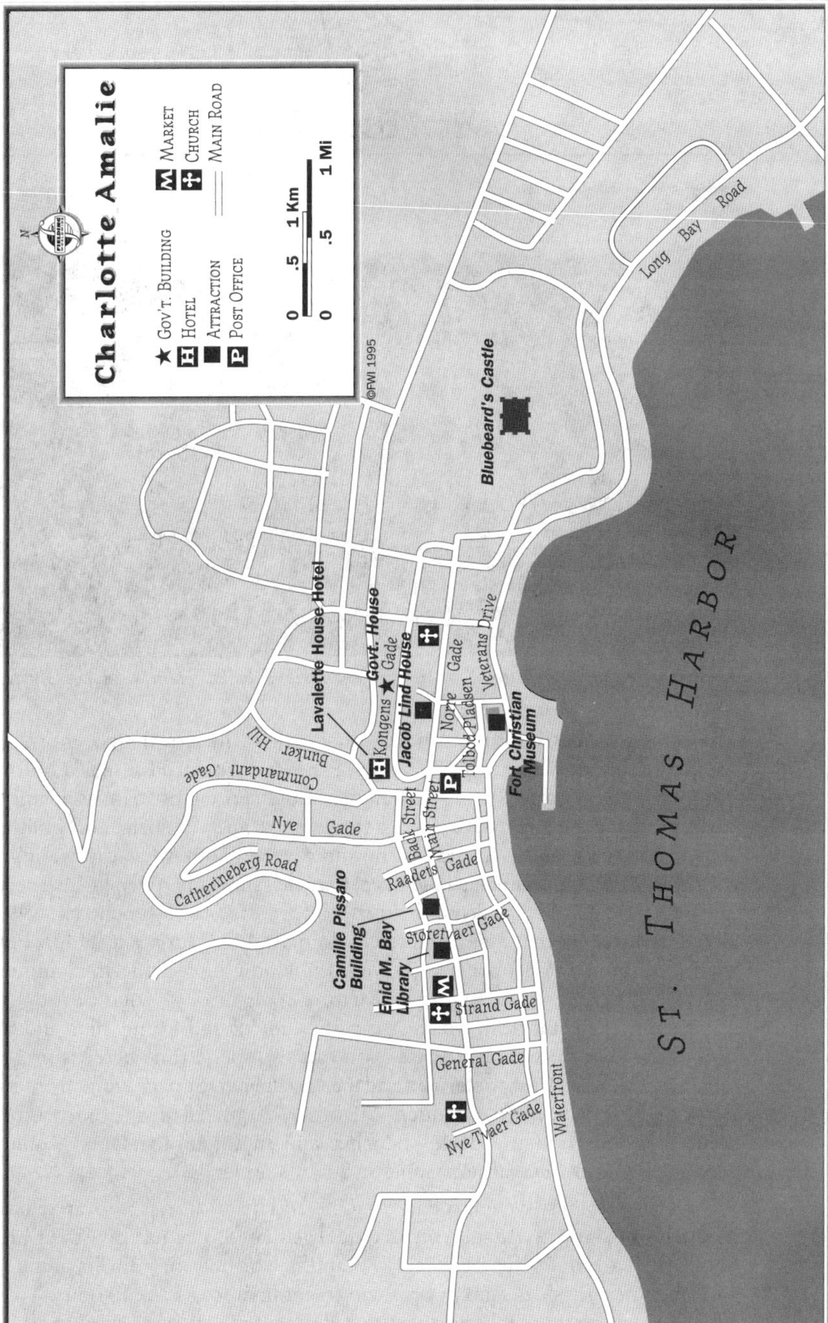
Charlotte Amalie
Gov't. Building
Hotel
Attraction
Post Office
Market
Church
Main Road
0 .5 1 Km
0 .5 1 Mi
©FWI 1995
Bluebeard's Castle
Long Bay Road
St. Thomas Harbor
Lavalette House Hotel
Govt. House
Kongens Gade
Jacob Lind House
Norre Gade
Tolbod Pladsen
Veterans Drive
Fort Christian Museum
Bunker Hill
Commandant Gade
Nye Gade
Back Street
Main Street
Catherineberg Road
Raadets Gade
Camille Pissaro Building
Enid M. Bay Library
Storetvaer Gade
Strand Gade
General Gade
Nye Tvaer Gade
Waterfront

What Else to See

Sailboats leave Charlotte Amalie for excursions to St. John and the British Virgin Islands.

A look around Charlotte Amalie can be done in less than a morning; choose a rainy day if you can find one. The Government House is a bit of a bore, as is the Virgin Islands Museum, though Fort Christian itself might harbor a few detectable ghosts since it was the center of social and political activity for the island over several hundred years. Somewhat captivating is the **Estate St. Peter Greathouse Botanical Gardens**, sprawling over 11 lush acres high atop the volcanic peaks of the north side of the island. Opened in 1992, after a renovation that was completely destroyed by Hurricane Hugo (and then renovated again by a hearty New England couple), the meticulously landscaped gardens offer self-guided nature trails through such exotic flora as the umbrella plant from Madagascar, the cane orchid from China and the bird of paradise from South Africa. You can also spend time here visiting an **orchid jungle**, **rain forest**, **waterfalls** and **monkey habitat**. Superb views from the outdoor observation deck renders 20 other Virgin Islands. Some visitors plant themselves on the deck's benches and sit for hours. Open 9 a.m.–5 p.m., admission is a rather steep $8 ($4 kids under 12).

The second-oldest synagogue in the U.S. and its territories is located at St. Thomas in Charlotte Amalie, picturesquely situated on a narrow street high above the harbor. It was built in 1833 and is worth visiting for its architecture and its fittings. Its sand floor is said to commemorate the Exodus. Tourists are welcome not only during the religious services but also during the week. An international Bicentennial celebration slated for 1995–96 is commemorating 200 years of Jewish life in St. Thomas. Visitors of all faiths will travel to St. Thomas in honor of the St. Thomas Synagogues' proud history. For more information contact the St. Thomas Tourist Board.

Coral World has an underwater observatory ☎ *(809) 775-1555* that provides a 360-degree look at coral life. At 2 p.m. divers hand-feed sharks in the Predator Tank. Admission is $16, $10 for children 3 and over. Open daily from 9 a.m.–6 p.m.

Reinhold Center for the Arts at the University of the Virgin Islands, located on a hillside overlooking Brewers Bay, holds many cultural events. Don't miss folk dances performed by the **Caribbean Dance Company**. Call ☎ *(809) 774-8475.*

Tillett Gardens in the Tutu area, the site of funky and fascinating arts and crafts studios, often hosts classical concerts ☎ *(809) 775-1929.* It's well worth a trip anytime for great shopping. Closed Sunday.

Carnival follows Easter in the Virgin Islands. The Carnival Food Fair offers a chance to sample dishes such as **kallaloo** (a stew of meat, seafood and greens) and drinks prepared with sea moss and soursop, a local fruit. A predawn dance through the streets, called the J'Ouvert Morning Tramp, is followed by the Children's Parade that day. On April 30, the Adults' Parade is led by Mocko Jumbies, stilt dancers in extravagant, brightly covered costumes.

Most tourists make at least one excursion to **St. John**, two-thirds of which is the Virgin Islands National Park, where each uncrowded beach seems to surpass the one before ($3 one way for a 20-minute ferry that leaves every hour from Red Hook on the East End, $7 for the 45-minute ride from Charlotte Amalie.)

BEST VIEW:

From atop the 1500-foot Mountain Top, on St. Peter's Mountain, you can see a panoramic view of both sides of the island as well as a multitude of islands stretching east to Virgin Gorda.

FIELDING'S CHOICE:

To experience the scuba thrill without getting wet, take a ride on the Atlantis Submarine, *a 46-passenger underwater craft that takes passengers for an hour's ride at depths of 50-90 feet. The sub's large windows give good views of corals reefs and a multitude of marine life. Hours are generally 10 a.m.-2 p.m., but call first for reservations. The boat ride leaves from the West Indies dock at Havensight Mall on the outskirts of Charlotte Amalie. For more information* ☎ (809) 775-1555.

Historical Sites

Fort Christian ★★★

At the harbor, ☎ *(809) 776-4566.*
Hours open: 8:30 a.m.–4:30 p.m.
This brick fortress is the oldest building in the Virgin Islands and a U.S. national landmark, dating back to 1672. It has housed everything from the entire St. Thomas colony to a jail to a church over the years, and is now home to an art gallery, police station, book store, and, in the former dungeons, the Virgin Islands

Museum, which traces the island's history. It's currently under renovation, so access may be limited.

Historic Churches ★★★★

Various locations.

Charming Charlotte Amalie is home to several historic churches well worth a look. The Frederick Lutheran Church (Norre Gade) is the Western Hemisphere's second-oldest Lutheran church. All Saints Anglican Church on Garden Street was built in 1848 to celebrate the end of slavery. The Dutch Reformed Church on Nye Gade was built in 1844, but actually dates back to 1744 (the original was destroyed by a fire in 1804). Finally, the Cathedral of St. Peter and St. Paul in Kronprindsens Alley was built in 1848 and is enhanced by murals done in 1899 by Belgian artists.

St. Thomas Synagogue ★★★★

Synagogue Hill, ☎ (809) 774-4312.

Hours open: 9 a.m.–4 p.m.

This is the oldest synagogue in continuous use under the American flag, and the second-oldest in the Western Hemisphere. The floor is sand, symbolic of the desert through which Moses and the Israelis wandered for 40 years. A bicentennial celebration, commemorating 200 years of Jewish life on St. Thomas, takes place in 1995-96, with art shows, celebrity guests, special events and Jewish cultural productions. Call for a schedule once on the island.

Museums and Exhibits

Seven Arches Museum ★★★

Government Hill, ☎ (809) 774-9259.

Hours open: 9 a.m.–3 p.m.

This Danish house was built in 1800 and is now a private home, but they'll let you in to see its historic furnishings and antiques. The grounds include a separate kitchen and a walled garden, the perfect spot to quaff the drink included in the admission fee.

Parks and Gardens

Estate St. Peter Greathouse Gardens ★★★★

Route 40 and Barrett Hill Road, Above Hull Bay, ☎ (809) 774-4999.

Hours open: 9 a.m.–5 p.m.

As you stroll the grounds of these new gardens, it's hard to believe this verdant spot was completely leveled by Hurricane Hugo in 1989. Owners Sylvie and Howard DeWolfe did an amazing job restoring everything to its former glory. These gardens, reopened in late 1992, are perched 1000 feet above Hull Bay and Magens Bay Beach on the island's north side. Self-guided trails lead through more than 200 varieties of Caribbean plants and trees, as well as imported treasures like the tropical day lily from Asia and South African bird of paradise. There are also ponds, waterfalls and a rainforest—not to mention sweeping views from the large deck, where you can spot more than 20 other Virgin Islands. The recreated great house is filled with contemporary Caribbean furnishings and locally done artwork. A treat!

Tours

Coral World ★★★★

Coki Point, ☎ (809) 775-1555.

Hours Open: 9 a.m.–6 p.m.

Nonswimmers can see what all the fuss is about at this five-acre marine park, home to 21 aquariums, a touch tank, an 80,000-gallon tank showcasing the world's largest living man-made reef, an exotic bird habitat, and semi-submarine rides. The highlight is the underwater observatory, an air-conditioned room 20 feet below sea level through which you can observe all sorts of sea life, an especially exciting sight at feeding time. The grounds also include duty-free shops, a bar and restaurant, and a pretty beach where they rent snorkel and scuba equipment (showers and changing rooms are available). Kids get in for $10.

Guided Tours

Various locations.

St. Thomas is easily explored on your own, but if you'd like to spare the expense of renting a car, take a guided tour. **Destination Virgin Islands** *(☎ 776-2424)* offers walking tours, beach and shopping trips, and excursions to St. John and St. Croix. Prices vary. The **St. Thomas Islands Tour** *(☎ 774-7668)* explores the island in two hours for $14 per person; another excursion takes in the many splendid views and costs $20. **Tropic Tours** *(☎ 774-1855)* offers various shopping and scenic tours; call for prices. Also try **Smitty Island Tour** *(☎ 775-2787)*, which goes to Coral World, Drakes Seat, Mountain Top and Magen's Bay ($35); and **Timmy Island Tour** (*☎ 775-9529*), whose 2.5-hour tour includes Red Hook, Sapphire Beach overlook, Coral World, Magen's Bay, Mountain Top, and Charlotte Amalie ($25).

Paradise Point Tramcom, Inc. ★★★

Havensight Area, ☎ (809) 774-9809.

Hours open: 8:30 a.m.–6:30 p.m.

When this $2.8-million tramway opened in August 1994, it brought back a popular attraction that ceased to exist in the 1970s. The 3.5-minute ride—not recommended for those afraid of heights—gives a bird's eye view of the harbor and stops at 697-foot-high Paradise Point, where you can wander among the shops, have a quiet drink or just soak up the scenery. When going up, try to snag the last car; when coming down, hop in the first car for the best unobstructed views. $5 for kids under 13; kids under six are free.

Robinson Crusoe Excursion ★★★★

☎ (809) 776-7880.

It's not cheap ($325 per couple), but if you're in love and solvent, here's a great day trip you'll always remember. A private helicopter takes you on a scenic ride to an uninhabited island, where you're left to your own devices for several hours. They'll give you a cooler of ice, but you'll have to pack your own lunch, drinks and towels. The four-hour trips leave at 9:30 a.m. 1:30 p.m.

Seaplane Adventure ★★★★★

Charlotte Amalie Harbor, Charlotte Amalie, ☎ (809) 777-4491.

Amazing views abound on this 45-minute flight aboard the twin-engine seaplane Vistaliner. Bring lots of film, because you'll be snapping away like mad as you fly over some 100 islands of the U.S. and British Virgin Islands. The entire tour takes 1.5 hours (it's exciting to take off and land from the ocean) and is greatly enhanced by extra-large windows, lively narration via headphones (which can also be plugged right into your video camera) and an interesting booklet that gives details on the islands spotted. Great fun!

Sports

All watersports activities are enjoyed on St. Thomas. Sportfishing on St. Thomas is devoted primarily to the blue marlin. In March, April, May and June they can be found in the south in the Caribbean, north in the Atlantic in July-September. On the Atlantic side of the Virgins is the **100-fathom drop-off**, bordering on the Puerto Rico Trench, the deepest hole in the Atlantic Ocean. Because the Virgin Islands lie in the Trade Winds Belt, fishing can always be done on the leeward side. **Redbook**, at the main center of St. Thomas, is the main center for boat operators. Many operators offer half- and full-day boat excursions on any number and variety of craft; full-day fishing expeditions can come with equipment, picnic, ice and beer. The waters northeast of St. Thomas are prime fishing grounds, helping the Virgin Islands live up to their reputation as a superb site to catch blue marlin. Surfing attracts lots of fans during the winter since the sea huskily rolls in with a blast at Hull Bay on the north coast of St.Thomas. Windsurfing here is best at the eastern end where winds peak during noontime; the roughest conditions are at Hull Bay, the gentlest at Morningstar in the south. Even novices are invited for a two-hour lesson of windsurfing at the Windsurfing St. Thomas/ School of Boardsailing at St. Pleasant. Kayaking is popular, as is sportfishing. Horse racing is a party event on St. Thomas, involving thoroughbred horses, panmutuel, and daily double betting. Events are approximately monthly, usually on a local holiday or Sunday. English-style riding lessons are available at **Rosenthal Riding Ring**, which also offers trial rides. St. Thomas has a spectacular 18-hole championship course, designed by George and Tom Fazio, at **Mahogany Run**. There are six public tennis courts on St. Thomas, as well as private ones at many hotels. Play in the early morning or late afternoon until you get used to the weather.

Mahogany Run Golf Course

Mahogany Run Road, North Shore, ☎ (809) 775-5000.
Hours open: 7 a.m.–4:50 p.m.

St. Thomas' only golf course is an especially scenic and challenging one, a par-70 known for its dramatic 13th and 14th holes, which hug cliffs overlooking the Atlantic Ocean. If you play holes 13, 14 and 15 (the "Devil's Triangle") without a penalty shot your first time on the course, they'll give you a prize. A new 270,000-gallon desalination plant keeps everything lush and green (in the past, the course was in a constant battle with Mother Nature). Designed by George and Tom Fazio, greens fees vary depending on the time of year, and range from a high of $70 for 18 holes to a low of $50. Nine holes can be played before 8 a.m. and after 3 p.m.; discount twilight rates kick in after 2 p.m. Tee times are taken 48 hours in advance and run daily from 7 a.m.–4:50 p.m. Several resorts, including Grand Palazzo, Renaissance Grand and Secret Harbour offer golf packages.

Watersports

Various locations.

For boating, try: **Island Yachts** *(☎ 775-6666 or (800) 524-2019)*, **Avery's Marine** *(☎ 776-0113)*, **Coconut Charters** *(☎ 775-5959)*, **Nightwind** *(☎ 775-4110)*, and **New Horizons** *(☎ 775-1171)*. For scuba and snorkel instruction and excursions, try: **Seahorse Dive** *(☎ 774-2001)*, **Adventure Center** *(☎ 774-2990)*, **Dean Johnston's Diving** *(☎ 775-7610)*, **Hi-Tec Water Sports** *(☎ 774-5650)*, **Aqua Action** *(☎ 775-6285)*, **Underwater Safaris** *(☎ 774-1350 or (800) 524-2090)*, and **Dive In** *(☎ 775-6100)*. Deep-sea fishers can call **Fish Hawk** *(☎ 775-9058)* and **St. Thomas Sportfishing Center** *(☎ 775-7990)*.

Where to Eat

Fielding's Highest Rated Restaurants in St. Thomas

Rating	Restaurant	Price
★★★★	**Cafe Normandie**	$25–$39
★★★★	**Craig and Sally's**	$11–$26
★★★★	**Cuzzin's**	$10–$20
★★★★	**Old Stone Farmhouse**	$23–$29
★★★★	**Palm Terrace**	$22–$32
★★★★	**Virgilio's**	$13–$39
★★★	**Hotel 1829**	$20–$32
★★★	**Palm Court**	$14–$32
★★★	**Raffles**	$15–$29
★★★	**The Frigate**	$15–$30

Fielding's Special Restaurants in St. Thomas

Rating	Restaurant	Price
★★★★	**Cafe Normandie**	$25–$39
★★★★	**Cuzzin's**	$10–$20
★★★★	**Old Stone Farmhouse**	$23–$29
★★★★	**Virgilio's**	$13–$39
★★★	**Victor's New Hide Out**	$9–$20

Fielding's Budget Restaurants in St. Thomas

Rating	Restaurant	Price
★★★	**Epernay Champagne Bar**	$6–$10
★	**Palm Passage**	$6–$12
★	**Glady's Cafe**	$6–$13
★	**Art Geckos**	$5–$16
★★★	**Cafe Sito**	$4–$19

Locals dine out as frequently as visitors on St. Thomas, which accounts for the extraordinary range of dining options, with cuisines hailing from nearly every corner of the world. Splurging on Sunday brunch is a national pastime. Restaurants are generally informal and open-air, but prices can rival those of Manhattan's most elegant dining rooms. Casual dress, even shorts, generally pass muster, but reservations are advisable. Each of the big hotels has several restaurants and a few have gained renown. One of the newest, most elegant spots is the **Grand Palazzo Hotel's Palm Terrace**, where excellent spa-style "light" cuisine dubbed "Floribbean" (Florida meets Caribbean) is serenaded by a pianist in a white diner jacket. A taste of France can be found at **Provence**, in funky Frenchtown, where you can sample such delights as hearty soups, casseroles and a fine antipasto bar. One delicacy not to pass up are the liqueur-flavored milkshakes such as the one with Jamoco-chocolate ice cream, coconut ice cream and Kahlua that you can find at **Udder Delite Dairy Bar** near Magens Bay. ☎ *(809) 775-2501.* Sorry to say, but St. Thomas is one of only two Caribbean islands with a **Hard Rock Cafe**. Go only if you feel homesick.

Agave Terrace **$$$** ★★★

6400 Estate Smith Bay, Water Bay, ☎ *(809) 775-4142.*
Seafood cuisine.
Lunch: 10 a.m.–6:30 p.m., entrees $18–$24.
Dinner: 6:30–10 p.m., entrees $18–$24.

It may be a little hard to find, with a resort-hotel location on the northeastern end of the island. But even nonguests should try to make it here for a leisurely breakfast or dinner on the patio while the light is still good for an unparalleled view of the Caribbean sea in the distance. The cuisine is mostly Mediterranean style seafood, and the chef is delighted to create any dish (within reason) that a customer requests.

Art Geckos **$$** ★

Tillet Gardens, Smith Bay Road, ☎ *(809) 775-4550.*
American cuisine.
Lunch: 11 a.m.–4:30 p.m., entrees $5–$8.
Dinner: 6–11:30 p.m., entrees $6–$16.

Enjoy burgers, sandwiches and salads at lunch, plus fresh seafood and grilled Jamaican jerk chicken at dinner at this casual open-air cafe in Tillett Gardens. If you're lucky, you'll get to watch the daily iguana feedings. The restaurant is a true oasis in a peaceful garden setting, though the real reason to come here is to check out the fascinating artisans' shops that surround it. Besides the famed maps and underwater seascapes by Jim Tillett, you'll find a goldsmith shop, African mahogany carvings, a tea shop and beautiful hand-painted gifts. A must!

Blackbeard's Castle **$$$** ★★★

P.O. Box 6041, Blackbeard Hill, ☎ *(809) 776-1234.*
American cuisine.
Lunch: 11:30 a.m.–2:30 p.m., entrees $8–$13.
Dinner: 6:30–9:30 p.m., entrees $18–$29.

Feel like Blackbeard the pirate surveying his domain from this stunning aerie with an eagle eye view of the harbor and the city. The international cuisine has won many awards from local publications several years in a row. It's hard to have a meal here without sampling from a varied array of homemade soups, salads or creative appetizers. Entrees include a choice of veal, excellent seafood, beef filets or a devilishly rich pasta. Lighter meals can be had in the lounge or by the pool, where non-guests can swim. There's a bountiful buffet Sundays from 11:00 to 3:00 pm.

Cafe Normandie **$$$** ★★★★

rue de St. Barthélémy, Frenchtown, ☎ *(809) 774-1622.*
French cuisine.
Dinner: 6–10 p.m., entrees $25–$39.

In an informal survey, island residents anointed this cozy, elegant French restaurant with a bright yellow painted exterior as their favorite overall dining out spot a few years ago. Food, service and location are all exceptional, but I suspect people return again and again for the sinful chocolate fudge pie. There's a well regarded five-course, prix-fixe supper available nightly that includes a palate-cleansing sorbet. Make sure to reserve in season, as it is small and popular. Closed Mondays in summer.

Cafe Sito **$$** ★★★

21 Queens Quarter, ☎ (809) 774-9574.
Mediterranean cuisine.
Lunch: entrees $4–$19.
Dinner: to 11 p.m., entrees $4–$19.

This new spot, just opened in 1995, is a real winner. The long dining room has wood-beamed ceilings, white-washed walls and pretty wooden cases displaying a good wine selection (featuring a $120 bottle of Dom Perignon). The cuisine is tapas, with such delicacies as sizzling shrimp in virgin olive oil with saffron and garlic, paellas, fish and chicken, and the most wonderful salad of vine-ripe tomatoes, hearts of palm and gorgonzola cheese. Highly recommended!

Chart House **$$$** ★★★

P.O. Box 3156, Villa Olga, ☎ (809) 774-4262.
American cuisine.
Dinner: 5–10 p.m., entrees $13–$37.

Salad bar lovers flock here for a huge spread of many items, including passable caviar. Dinner specialties include sizzling steaks, juicy prime rib, chicken and lobster; the salad bar is included. All this bounty is consumed on a terrace overlooking the sea, situated in a 19th century building which was once home to Russian diplomats. Don't overlook the famous "mud pie" if you still have room.

Craig and Sally's **$$$** ★★★★

22 Estate Honduras, Frenchtown, ☎ (809) 777-9949.
International cuisine.
Dinner: 6–10:30 p.m., entrees $11–$26.

A talented husband and wife team combine his knowledge of fine wines and her culinary expertise in the operation of this muraled restaurant in Frenchtown. Although there are several dining areas, it's often crowded; the word is out on the creative Mediterranean and Asian specialties prepared here. Sun-kissed tomatoes, broiled peppers or salsas made with market picked fruits are used liberally on plump scallops, chicken or swordfish. Sally's desserts recall a childhood learning to bake at mother's elbow; there's key lime pie and killer chocolate cakes.

Cuzzin's **$$** ★★★★

Back Street, Charlotte Amalie, ☎ (809) 777-4711.
cuisine.
Lunch: entrees $10–$20.
Dinner: 5–9:30 p.m., entrees $10–$20.

Authentic island cuisine awaits in this local's hangout, a cute yellow brick building with wooden shutters. Specialties include stewed conch, curried chicken and other local dishes and drinks like sea moss (milk, sugar, seaweed and nutmeg). Each entree comes with a choice of three side dishes such as potato stuffing, rice and beans, yams and macaroni and cheese. The daring will like the homemade hot sauce that accompanies some meals. Closed for dinner on Mondays.

Epernay Champagne Bar **$** ★★★

24 B Honduras Street, Frenchtown, ☎ (809) 774-5343.
International cuisine.
Dinner: 4:30 p.m.–1 a.m., entrees $6–$10.

Before or after a night on the prowl, nestle here for champagne by the glass; sample up to six different varieties. A grazing menu of sophisticated snacks covers the globe; there's sushi, caviar and goat cheese. Food is served from 5 p.m. to 12 a.m.; it's open later on weekends. Wine and desserts are also available.

Eunice's Terrace **$$$** ★★

66-67 Smith Bay, Route 38, Smith Bay, ☎ *(809) 775-3975.*
cuisine.
Lunch: 11 a.m.–4 p.m., entrees $6–$11.
Dinner: 6–10 p.m., entrees $10–$28.

Don't let the junk yard out back put you off. An island success story, Eunice's establishment grew like topsy from a simple food stand to a two-story building with a popular bar in Smith Bay. The West Indian cuisine that built her reputation is possibly the best on the island. There's a daily menu, but conch fritters and an incomparable tropical rum cake are usually available.

Glady's Cafe **$$** ★

17 Main Street, ☎ *(809) 774-6604.*
cuisine.
Lunch: entrees $6–$13.

This spot, set in an alleyway in Charlotte Amalie, is where locals congregate for breakfast (served from 6:30 a.m.) and Caribbean-style lunches. Besides the standard burgers and sandwiches, the menu offers up conch in lemon butter sauce and sauteed shrimp. The brick walls, covered in murals, feature pigs flying; check out the blackboard for Glady's thought of the day, such as the recent "The effect of hope is astounding."

Hard Rock Cafe **$$** ★★★

International Plaza, Charlotte Amalie,
American cuisine.
Lunch: 11 a.m.–4 p.m., entrees $7–$16.
Dinner: 4 p.m.–midnight, entrees $7–$16.

This memorabilia-laden retro-rock burger palace draws a more subdued crowd than those in mainland cities, but there's the requisite antique auto suspended over the entrance. Bob Marley mementoes are also included with the gold Beatle records behind glass frames. Among the wall exhibits is a red and gold neon sign proclaiming "No drugs or nuclear weapons allowed" inside. Good burgers barbecue ribs nachos and fajitas are served.

Hook, Line and Sinker **$$** ★★★

#2 The Waterfront, Frenchtown, ☎ *(809) 776-9708.*
International cuisine.
Lunch: entrees $5–$10.
Dinner: entrees $6–$20.

Yachties tie up to this seaside eatery that's nothing special, but it's a good meet and greet place. There's a nice outdoor deck, and offerings are reasonably priced. It's a convenient stop if you're in the area, especially for a burger or steak lunch.

Hotel 1829 **$$$** ★★★

30 Kongens Gade, Charlotte Amalie, ☎ *(809) 776-1829, (800) 524-2002.*
American cuisine.
Dinner: 5:30–10 p.m., entrees $20–$32.

Streamlined service and stellar food are served in a restored Government Hill hotel. Tables on the terrace are well-sought after for the terrific views, but wherever you sit, the cuisine is pleasing. Specialties include a wilted spinach salad and dessert souffles; and the raspberry chocolate is especially toothsome.

Il Cardinale **$$** ★★

Back Street, ☎ *(809) 775-1090.*
Italian cuisine.
Lunch: until 4 p.m., entrees $11–$19.
Dinner: 5:30–11 p.m., entrees $11–$19.

This air-conditioned spot offers a quiet and dignified respite from the teeming streets of Charlotte Amalie. Located upstairs in the Taste of Italy shopping mall, the decor is subdued, with large oil paintings dominating the walls and tables clothed in white linen. Among the choices are homemade crepes, salmon in champagne sauce, a highly regarded chicken salad and *pasta e fagiolo* soup. Nice. After your meal, stroll the adjacent gallery that spotlights local artwork.

L'Escargot **$$$** ★★★

#12 Submarine Base, Charlotte Amalie, ☎ *(809) 774-6565.*
Seafood cuisine.
Lunch: 11:45 a.m.–2:30 p.m., entrees $7–$15.
Dinner: 6–10 p.m., entrees $15–$27.
A long-established dining room, this classic French restaurant is one of a few eateries located at a submarine base west of Charlotte Amalie, near the airport. Meals are taken in a patio overlooking the ocean. Specialties are old favorites like rack of lamb or lobster thermidor; all simply and impeccably prepared.

Lemon Grass Cafe **$$$** ★★

Bakery Square, Back Street, ☎ *(809) 777-1877.*
cuisine.
Lunch: 11 a.m.-3:30 p.m., entrees $7–$16.
Dinner: 6–10 p.m., entrees $16–$20.
The menu changes often at this pretty spot located in a scenic courtyard. Dine outdoors next to the lily pond, or inside, where gleaming woods, stone walls and ceiling fans create a lovely atmosphere. Entrees range from salads and burgers to roast salmon, grilled swordfish and pork and lamb dishes. Sunday brunch (10:30 a.m.–2:30 p.m.) is followed by a "tea dance" with a mini menu from 5–9 p.m.

Old Stone Farmhouse **$$$** ★★★★

Mahogany Run, ☎ *(809) 775-1377.*
cuisine.
Dinner: 6:30–10 p.m., entrees $23–$29.
Considered one of St. Thomas' fining dining outlets, the Old Stone is built in the ruins of a 200-year-old dairy farm near Mahogany Run Golf Course (on the north side, 20 minutes from Charlotte Amalie). A pianist lends just the right amount of ambience to this lovely room of thick stone walls and varied antiques. Entrees include such imaginative offers as filet mignon with cheese and a red onion marmalade and snapper in a potato crust. Whatever you choose, you'll be well pleased.

Palm Court **$$$** ★★★

Red Hook, ☎ *(809) 775-1000.*
cuisine.
Dinner: 6:30–10 p.m., entrees $14–$32.
Located steps from the beach at the Elysian Resort, this fine dining spot offers tables inside or, better yet, out under the stars. Entrees run the gamut from fresh seafood to beef, lamb, poultry and pasta dishes. Such specialties as a grilled portabella mushroom served with carmelized onions and port wine sauce and swordfish in ginger lime butter with poached peaches in dark Cruzan rum keep patrons happy. Heavenly!

Palm Passage **$** ★

Off of Main Street, ☎ *(809) 779-2708.*
Italian cuisine.
Lunch: 11 a.m.–3:30 p.m., entrees $6–$12.
Located in a scenic courtyard and surrounded by art galleries, Palm Passage is a nice place for a tasty lunch of risotto, roasted garlic, pizza or grilled eggplant salad. The menu also features burgers and sandwiches.

Palm Terrace **$$$** ★★★★

Great Bay, ☎ *(809) 775-3333, (800) 545-0509.*
International cuisine.

Dinner: 6:30–10 p.m., entrees $22–$32.
A chef with a background in cooking for luxury health spas in California and Florida holds court at this, the Grand Palazzo resort's crown jewel. Weight watchers can delight in the fact that many of the delectable meals are prepared in natural juices and infusions, instead of heavy cream sauces. Alas, the calories await in the desserts, one of which is caramel ice cream encased in chocolate. Apparently, this ensures a return to the fat farm. The surroundings here are some of the most luxurious on the island; everything exudes a rosy glow and all is pretty in pink. A pianist helps further the romantic mood. Divine!

Piccola Marina Cafe **$$$** ★★★
6300 Smith Bay, Red Hook, ☎ (809) 775-6350.
American cuisine.
Lunch: 11 a.m.–5:30 p.m., entrees $5–$14.
Dinner: 5:30–10:30 p.m., entrees $13–$24.
This alfresco restaurant on a Red Hook Marina dock is a fun place, with a selection of pastas for your dining pleasure. Sauces range from tomato marinara to a creamy alfredo. Others can order sandwiches, chicken, fresh seafood or quaff a brew or two. Sunday brunch is served in the winter from 10 a.m. to 3 p.m.

Provence **$$$** ★★★
Honduras Street, Frenchtown, ☎ (809) 777-5600.
French cuisine. Specialties: Antipasto Table.
Dinner: 6–10:30 p.m., entrees $15–$19.
Chef and restaurateur Patricia La Corte, who created the well-regarded Fiddle Leaf on Government Hill is now roosting at this country-French bistro on the second floor of a wooden building in funky Frenchtown. The warmly-decorated room, with arched doorways and potted palms, offers a wharf-side view. Specialties include lamb shank with hearty chakerny and rosemary sauce on a bed of mashed potatoes and oven roasted garlic chicken. Nibblers go into grazing heaven with La Corte's reasonably priced antipasto table, served daily until 11:00 p.m.

Raffles **$$$** ★★★
The Marina, Compass Point, ☎ (809) 775-6004.
Seafood cuisine.
Dinner: 6:30–10:30 p.m., entrees $15–$29.
This south-seas themed restaurant is a favorite with residents, who enjoy the steaks flambeed at tableside. Ladies especially like the high-backed peacock chairs in a salon cooled by ceiling fans and ocean breezes. Other specialties include fresh fish, and stuffed leg of lamb.

Rain Forest Cafe **$** ★
Mountain Top Shopping Mall, Mountain Top, ☎ (809) 774-2400.
American cuisine.
The best reason to come to this new cafe is to check out its amazing views—probably the best on an island that abounds with sweeping vistas. The offerings are simple—deli sandwiches, salads, pastries—the better to leave room for at least one banana daiquiri. The frothy drink was reportedly invented here in 1949 by British restaurateur Conrad Graves. Cheers!

Terrace Restaurant **$$** ★
Next to the airport at the Carib Beach Resort, Lindbergh Bay, ☎ (809) 774-2525.
American cuisine.
Lunch: 11:30 a.m.–2:30 p.m., entrees $5–$7.
Dinner: 6–9:30 p.m., entrees $7–$19.
No need to make a special trip here (the food's merely adequate), but if you have a long wait at the airport, stroll on over to this pleasantly informal outdoor spot at the Carib Beach Resort. The menu features typical salads, burgers, steak, chicken and

the catch of the day. On Friday nights from 6:00-9:45, a steel band helps liven things up. A great place to catch the moon rise, and it sure beats sitting in the airport. Also open for breakfast from 7:00-10:30 a.m.

The Frigate **$$$** ★★★

P.O. Box 1506, Mafolie Hill, ☎ (809) 774-2790, (800) 225-7035.
Seafood cuisine.
Dinner: entrees $15–$30.
An awe-inspiring ocean view and tender steaks hot off the charcoal broiler continue to please the regulars that ascend to this small, charming hotel dining room on Mafolie Hill. Non-red meat eaters will be pleased with fresh seafood, chicken and a salad bar. There's a smaller branch in Red Hook (No 18-8) near the Marina, 775-1829.

Victor's New Hide Out **$$$** ★★★

103 Submarine Base, Charlotte Amalie, ☎ (809) 776-9379.
International cuisine.
Lunch: 11:30 a.m.–3:30 p.m., entrees $9–$11.
Dinner: 5:30–10 p.m., entrees $11–$20.
Chef Victor left quiet Montserrat for more action, and he cooks his West Indian specialties for an appreciative crowd of locals, tourists, and the occasional celebrity. The ubiquitous conch and curried chicken dishes are available, as well as his signature dish, Lobster Montserrat, cooked with fruit and cream sauce. Newcomers should probably arrive by taxi, as the hilltop hideaway is a little hard to find.

Virgilio's **$$$** ★★★★

18 Dronningens Gade, ☎ (809) 776-4920.
Italian cuisine.
Lunch: until 4 p.m., entrees $13–$22.
Dinner: 4–10:30, entrees $16–$39.
It looks like a dump from the outside, but a true haven awaits inside this wonderful restaurant. The walls are covered with eclectic artwork, the ceilings twinkle with tiny lights and display cases proudly spotlight the Caribbean's largest wine collection—400 bottles, plus an extensive collection of cordials. The food is as good as the atmosphere. The huge menu offers up 40 kinds of homemade pastas, fish, chicken and vegetarian specialties. Save room for a luscious dessert such as bananas foster or crepes suzette prepared tableside. You'll find few tourists among the upscale locals who dine here regularly.

Where to Shop

Since Charlotte Amalie was declared a free port in 1755, opening it for trade with the European powers and growing American colonies, the islands have moved to a mercantile beat. Jewelry, liquor and electronics stores, interspersed with shops offering china, linens and perfume crowd Main Street. Jitneys take cruise ship passengers downtown; most stores also have outlets at the Havensight Mall near the dock.

U.S. residents may bring home $1200 in goods free of duty, with the next $1000 each subject to 5 percent duty. Members of a household may make a joint declaration, entitling a family of four to a $4800 duty-free allowance. There is no sales or luxury tax. Best buys include unmounted gems (duty-free for Americans, no matter the price), gold jewelry and watches. Before stepping into a store, know what you are looking for and what the price is back home. Finesse in bargaining goes a long way.

Reputable establishments offer dealer warranties and certificates of authenticity and generally avoid the sidewalk barker come-ons that grow more shrill as one moves west on Main Street. Most visitors leave toting at least one bottle of rum. Local brands such as Cruzan cost less that $3 a fifth, and if you buy any spirits produced in the territory, you are allowed to take six bottles rather than the normal five bottles back to the States duty-free.

Must-see for shoppers are several specialty stores that showcase the impressive work of artisans from Jamaica, Haiti, Dominican Republic, Martinique and others. Start with **Down Island Traders** next to Post Office Alley on the Waterfront, where you can choose everything from edible delicacies such as marmalades and jellies to sweet Caribbean rum balls, fiery mustards, tasty fruit chutneys and exotic spices, as well as extensive Haitian and Jamaican wall hangings, handmade cloth and wooden dolls, including the legendary Caribbean worry doll. (According to an ancient island tale, these precious-looking figures will take away your troubles if you hand them over. The bigger the worry, the bigger the doll—one worry per doll.) Upstairs is **The Gallery**, a two-room studio featuring fine Caribbean folk art, including work from some of the island's top primitivists. The **Caribbean Marketplace** in Havensight Mall specializes in exotic condiments as well as "Sunsations," a new line of flower, fruit and herbal extracts for bath gels, body splashes and skin oils. Handmade steel-pan drums can also be found here. At **Mango Tango** in the Al Cohen Building (across the street from Havensight), you can stock up on wooden masks from Jamaica, wooden earrings from Trinidad and original and print work from the Virgin Islands. **Tillet Gardens Craft Complex**, located in Tutu across from Four Winds Plaza, features the work of Jim Tillett's screen-painted maps of the Caribbean, cruising maps of the Virgin Islands and abstract paintings by himself and other local artists. Also in the same complex is **Okidanokh**, where goldsmith Abel Fabri's original jewelry includes such precious stones as tourmaline, sapphire, topaz and agate. The **Color of Joy** is a boutique that features watercolors and prints by St. Thomas painter Corinne Van Rensselaer, as well as varied gifts from the islands; the **Caribbean Enamel Guild**—a small annex—features hand-painted jewelry, boxes and various accessories. The best time to visit Tillett Gardens is during the popular Arts Alive arts and crafts fairs, held on-site three times a year. For more information call ☎ *(809) 775-1929* about the next festival.

St. Thomas Directory

BUSINESS HOURS

Shops generally open weekdays 9 a.m.–5 p.m. Banks generally open Monday–Thursday 9 a.m.–2:30 p.m. and Friday 9 a.m.–2 and 3:30–5 p.m.

CLIMATE

Summer temperatures, cooled by eastern trade winds, hover around 82 degrees Fahrenheit. Winter temperatures range from 77 degrees, dipping to 69 degrees at night and rising as high as 84 degrees. The rainy season runs September-January, though the sun shines nearly every day. The average rainfall is about 40 inches per year, and showers are usually brief.

DOCUMENTS

U.S. citizens need no passport. But if you plan to visit the British Virgin Islands, you must show proof of citizenship (passport, or birth certificate with photo ID). Canadians must have a valid passport.

ELECTRICITY

Current runs at 110 volts, 60 cycles.

GETTING AROUND

Cabs are not metered but each driver must carry the most up-to-date list of fares. Rates quoted are for one passenger, extra passengers are charged more. If you decide to go to a destination not on the official list of rates, negotiate firmly ahead of time. And be warned they like to pile lots of people in the cabs, regardless of where they're going. You'll need to be patient!

There are public buses every 20 minutes from the terminal to the town (about $1).

Rental cars are widely available, including the large name agencies in the U.S. Rates are about $35 a day.

Ferry boats are an easy way to get around the islands. You can catch one from Red Hook to St. John (every hour from 8 a.m.- midnight); it takes 20 minutes one way, about $3. There's also a ferry at Charlotte Amalie to St. John (45 minutes, about $7), as well as one from downtown to Frenchman's Reef Hotel and Morningstar Beach ($3)—it's a cool way to get to the beach and only 15 minutes long.

Seaboard Seaplane *(☎ (809) 774-4491)* offers daily service to and from St. Croix for about $100 round-trip.

LANGUAGE

English is the official language. Locals also speak a native patois, a mixture of English, African and Spanish. Many people are bilingual in Spanish.

MEDICAL EMERGENCIES

Police ext. *915*, fire ext. *921*, ambulance ext. *922*.

MONEY

The official currency is the American dollar. There is no sales tax.

TELEPHONE

The area code is *809*. Since USVI is an unincorporated territory, toll-free numbers that operate in the U.S. work here, normal postage rates apply. You can also direct dial to the mainland.

TIME

Atlantic Standard Time, which means an hour later than New York City, except during Daylight Saving Time, when it is the same.

TIPPING AND TAXES

Leave a 15 percent tip for the waitress; bartenders and wine stewards should be tipped always. Taxi drivers should receive a 15 percent tip if you are satisfied with the service.

TOURIST INFORMATION

The **St. Thomas Dept. of Tourism** has information booths at the airport ☎ *(809) 774-8784*, at Emancipation Garden at Charlotte Amalie ☎ *(809) 774-8784*, ext. *147*; and in Havensight Mall near the cruise ship dock ☎ *(809) 774-8784*. You can also pick up brochures, rest your feet, and even check shopping bags at an island-sponsored hospitality lounge in the Old Customs House next to Little Switzerland.

WHEN TO GO

The Calypso Competition is held at the University of the Virgin Islands cafeteria on March 4. Arts Alive & Crafts Festival, where Caribbean vendors sell handmade crafts and arts, is held on March 17–19. The Caribbean Chorale, one of the most popular groups in the USVI, performs a blend of classical, West Indian and native compositions on April 2. The 10th annual Easter Bonnet Contest takes place on April 17. The Virgin Islands Carnival Events, with nightly competitions in music and costumes, takes place on April 18–22. The 22nd Annual International Rolex Cup Regatta is April 21–23 (tentative). Virgin Islands Carnival Village features local foods, drink, and rides on April 24–29. STARfest 1995, a star-studded tribute to Caribbean talent, is May 13. The 8th Annual American Yacht Harbor Billfish tournament is July 13–18. Arts Alive Arts & Crafts Festival is August 11–13. The Hebrew Congregation of St. Thomas Bicentennial Celebration Gala Opening Weekend, featuring a celebration of Jewish History, is September 15-17. Hebrew Congregation of St. Thomas Bicentennial Celebration Interfaith Succot Service is October 6–8. The Hebrew Congregation of St. Thomas Bicentennial Celebration Jewish Musical Performance starts October 24 for four weeks. St. Thomas/St. John Agriculture Food Fair is November 18–19. Arts Alive Arts & Crafts Festival is November 24–26. The Hebrew Congregations of St. Thomas Bicentennial Celebration, featuring an authentic Sephardic Service and Chanukah Celebration is December 22.

ST. THOMAS RESTAURANTS	PHONE	ENTREE	CR. CARDS
Charlotte Amalie			
American			
★★★ **Blackbeard's Castle**	(809) 776-1234	$8–$29	A, MC, V
★★★ **Chart House**	(809) 774-4262	$13–$37••	A, DC, MC, V
★★★ **Hard Rock Cafe**		$7–$16	A, MC, V
★★★ **Hotel 1829**	(809) 776-1829	$20–$32••	A, MC, V
Caribbean			
★★★★ **Cuzzin's**	(809) 777-4711	$10–$20	A, MC, V
French			
★★★★ **Cafe Normandie**	(809) 774-1622	$25–$39••	A, MC, V
★★★ **Provence**	(809) 777-5600	$15–$19••	A, MC, V
International			
★★★★ **Craig and Sally's**	(809) 777-9949	$11–$26••	A, MC, V

ST. THOMAS RESTAURANTS		PHONE	ENTREE	CR. CARDS
★★★	Epernay Champagne Bar	(809) 774-5343	$6–$10••	A, MC, V
★★★	Hook, Line and Sinker	(809) 776-9708	$5–$20	A, MC, V
★★★	Victor's New Hide Out	(809) 776-9379	$9–$20	A, MC, V
	Seafood			
★★★	L'Escargot	(809) 774-6565	$7–$27	A, MC, V
★★★	The Frigate	(809) 774-2790	$15–$30••	A, MC, V
Red Hook				
	American			
★★★	Piccola Marina Cafe	(809) 775-6350	$5–$24	A, MC, V
	International			
★★★★	Palm Terrace	(809) 775-3333	$22–$32••	A, MC, V
	Latin American			
★★	Eunice's Terrace	(809) 775-3975	$6–$28	A, MC, V
	Seafood			
★★★	Agave Terrace	(809) 775-4142	$18–$24	A, MC, V
★★★	Raffles	(809) 775-6004	$15–$29••	A, MC, V
Note:	• Lunch Only			
	•• Dinner Only			

ST. VINCENT AND THE GRENADINES

Picturesque St. Vincent's terrain ranges from rugged cliffs to lush valleys and beaches with golden and black sand.

The Grenadines is a small archipelago, a short boat hop south of St. Vincent that offers some of the best cruising possibilities in the Caribbean. Only a few of the islands have any touristic infrastructure, though many of them are so primitive and paradisiacal that most visitors arrive at least for the day to snorkel, trek and sunbathe in complete privacy. Collectively the islands total about 30 square miles of land mass, and while some are uninhabited, those that have residents are mostly populated by descendants of African slaves. The chain perhaps acquired its name from the French word for passionfruit, *grenadine*, of which there are many on the islands. Other historians believe that the chain was discovered at the same time Grenada was, hence "little grenada" or grenadine. The lifestyle in general is extremely laid-back and simple. Islands such as Mustique, Pal Island, Petit St. Vincent and Young are privately owned, and have the most luxurious resorts. Others such as Union, Bequia and St. Vincent are definitely for the vagabond on a budget.

St. Vincent

Boat excursions and hiking trails lead to cascading waterfalls and mineral springs on St. Vincent.

Green and volcanic, St. Vincent is the main island of the Grenadines, more rugged than Grenada and offering a vast array of nature-oriented activities. From Bequia, motor vessels make the nine-mile run to St. Vincent (locally called the mainland here). Although the area is just now awakening to tourism, yachtsmen and sailors have long used the island as a jumping port for fabulous cruises through the surrounding islets; recently many visitors are staying on the island to experience the superb nature trails, stunning waterfalls and the demanding hike to the crater of La Soufriere that last erupted in 1979. The western and eastern side of the island are wonderful areas to explore by bus; along the west, the coastline descends to beaches so golden they seem to glitter in the sun. At other times, the beaches turn coal black. In between are incredibly verdant landscapes flourishing with coconut, breadfruit, bananas, sweet potatoes and cocoa. Wild scenic excursions can be found along the rocky, rugged Atlantic coast, where, the farther you go, the more primitive the houses become. This is an island where you can see residents carrying their own water and pulling up arrowroot, a kind of skinny white radish which has become the island's major export (used for dressing wounds). The capital of Kingstown can claim the oldest botanical garden in the Western hemisphere, begun in 1765. Among its exotic specimens on the beautifully kept grounds is a breadfruit tree brought to the island in 1793 by Captain Bligh of the Bounty. Endangered St. Vincent parrots can also be found here.

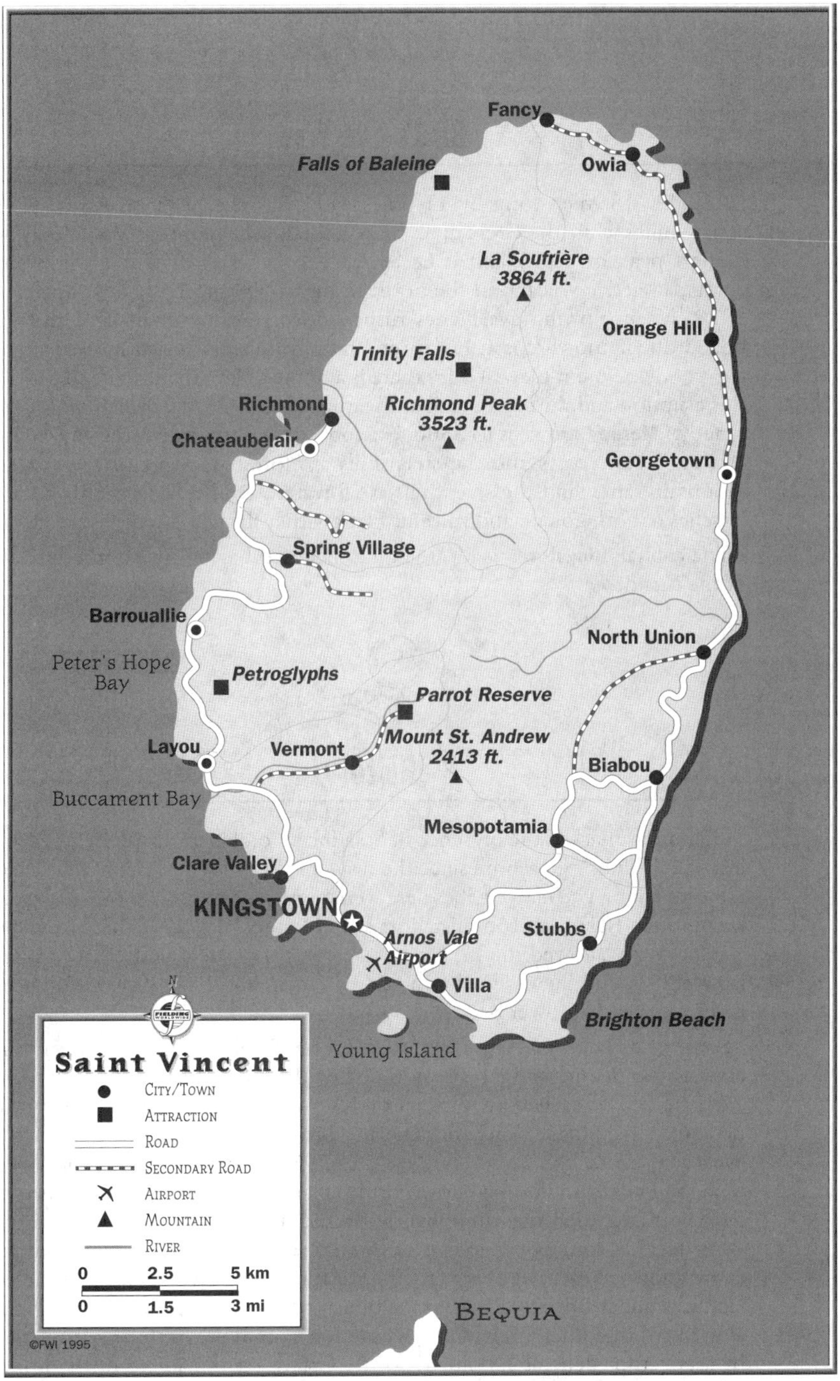
Fancy
Owia
Falls of Baleine
La Soufrière
3864 ft.
Orange Hill
Trinity Falls
Richmond
Richmond Peak
3523 ft.
Chateaubelair
Georgetown
Spring Village
Barrouallie
North Union
Peter's Hope Bay
Petroglyphs
Parrot Reserve
Mount St. Andrew
2413 ft.
Layou
Vermont
Biabou
Buccament Bay
Mesopotamia
Clare Valley
KINGSTOWN
Arnos Vale Airport
Stubbs
Villa
Brighton Beach
Young Island
Saint Vincent
City/Town
Attraction
Road
Secondary Road
Airport
Mountain
River
0 2.5 5 km
0 1.5 3 mi
Bequia
©FWI 1995

Bird's Eye View

Roughly 18 miles long by 11 miles wide, St. Vincent sprawls over 133 square miles while the Grenadines make a total of 17 more square miles. The highest peak on the island is **La Soufriere** on the leeward and windward coasts, an active volcano in the north rising to 4000 feet. It last erupted in 1979, when glowing avalanches rushed down the mountain and the sea boiled off the north coast, but careful monitoring succeeded in evacuating everybody before it blew. Today there is a dome of lava that extruded during this eruption and during an earlier disturbance in 1973. The steep mountain range of **Morne Garu** rises to 3500 feet and runs southward with spurs to the east and west coasts and the steep hills are forested. Most of the central mountain range and the steep hills are forested. Dominating the island are beaches of both golden and volcanic black with lush valleys and rugged cliffs.

The capital, **Kingstown**, is located on a sheltered bay, in the southern coast of the island.

History

Columbus marked the presence of St. Vincent on his third voyage in 1498, but luckily didn't go ashore since the resident Carib Indians might have cannibalized him. The native tribes here were more tenacious than other islands, keeping the European conquistadors at bay longer than any other island. In 1763 a treaty allowed the British to take control of the island. Sixteen years later, they found themselves battling the French, but the Treaty of Versailles in 1783 gave the power back to England.

Some years later, Captain Bligh took off for Tahiti from England with his crew of the *Bounty*, only to be mutinied by them and pushed out to sea. In 1793 he finally reached St. Vincent on his own, equipped with a canoeful of breadfruit seedlings, which became the progenitors of a crop that would eventually make the island famous. In 1795, the native population sided with the French and burned down British plantations during a ferocious battle; a year later the Brits triumphantly quelled the rebellion. At that time, the Brits decided to deport the rest of the native Indians to British Honduras (now known as Belize), where their ancestors live today. Until 1979 the island was under British rule, at which time it received independent statehood, along with the other Grenadines, within the Commonwealth. It is governed by a governor-general appointed by the Crown on the advice of the prime minister. The Parliament's House of Assembly is elected every five years.

People

Locals of St. Vincent and the Grenadines are unusually generous and courteous people, who have a gift for making others feel at home. A British formality, however, still runs through their behavior, a type of gentility that is also expected of visitors. Any trace of Gallic influence is tempered by a West Indies flavor, which is heard in the lilt of the language as well as the spices in the food. Service at most hotels, which are generally small, is characterized by enormous personal attention and care. Little serious crime ever happens on the islands, though valuables should never be left unguarded or ostentatiously displayed. The farther you travel into the interior, the more primitive the lifestyle.

Beaches

If you're looking for white-sand beaches, stay around Kingstown; the black ones are located around the rest of the island. Beautiful white sands can be found at **Villa Beach**, on the calm western coast. Also fine for swimming is the black **Questelle's Bay** and the black **Buccament Bay**. Dive shops are located at Villa beach and the CSY Yacht Club. The exposed Atlantic Coast is considered too rough for swimming, but the view of the crashing waves can be very exciting. None of the beaches here sport lifeguards, so take precautions; even experienced swimmers should have someone spotting them, particularly when the water is rough. No beach or changing facilities are located on the windward side.

What Else to See in Kingstown

As St. Vincent's capital and commercial hub, Kingstown bristles with the excitement of a busy port. A trip down to the waterfront is mandatory, to peruse all the island schooners and fishing boats delivering and exchanging goods with their colorful sails flapping in the wind. Take a pilgrimage to the 19th-century **St. Mary's Catholic Church**, which presides in the center of town, a strange concoction of architectural styles designed by a rather eccentric

Flemish monk, who loved to pit Romanesque against Baroque, Gothic and Moorish styles. On the north side of town stands the remains of **Fort Charlotte** (all cabs end up there, as does every cruise passenger, it seems). The winding road there passes through lush landscape, the view from the top, at 636 feet, is superb. "Charlotte" was the wife of King George III, whose countrymen built the fortress to defend themselves against French invaders. Driving east of the fort you'll discover one of the most placid places on the island—the **Botanical Gardens**, founded in 1765, and considered the oldest in the Western hemisphere. On the grounds is a breadfruit tree grown from the seedling originally brought to the island by Captain Bligh. Here you'll also find the **National Museum**, which contains ancient Indian artifacts.

Saturday mornings, take yourself down to the southern corner of town for the weekly market that draws farmers, vendors and fishermen from all over the island to sell their exotic-looking fruits, fresh fish and interesting crafts. If you are involved in self-catering accommodations, it's a good place to pick up your weekly rations.

Historical Sites

Fort Charlotte ★★★

Kingston, ☎ (809) 456-1830.
Hours open: 6 a.m.–6 p.m.
Construction on this fort was started around 1791, and it was completed in 1812. It's mostly in ruins today, but well worth a visit for the stunning views from its perch some 650 feet above sea level of Kingston and the Grenadines. Check out the murals that tell the history of black Caribbeans.

Parks and Gardens

Botanical Gardens ★★★★

Kingston, ☎ (809) 457-1003.
Hours open: 7 a.m.–4 p.m.
Located on a hillside north of town, this 20-acre garden is the oldest in the Western Hemisphere, dating back to 1765. Among the teak, mahogany and cannonball trees and exotic plants and flowers are breadfruit trees descended from seedlings brought over by Captain Bligh in 1793. The lush grounds also include a pagoda, lily pond, and the Archeological Museum, located in a West Indian house and displaying artifacts from pre-Columbian days. Admission to the gardens is free, but once there, it's well worth a couple of dollars to hire a guide for an hour-long tour. Garden lovers should also checkout **Kingston's Montreal Gardens** *(458-5452)*, which are not as well-tended.

Tours

Soufriere Volcano ★★★★★

The north side.
St. Vincent's dominant feature is the Soufriere Mountains, home to a volcano that has been active for centuries. The most devastating eruption occurred in 1812 and claimed some 2000 lives. Another in 1902 created the mile-wide crater; in 1972, still another eruption created the lava rock island in the crater lake. The latest eruption, in 1979, caused thousands to evacuate but happily took no lives. Two trails climb through rainforest to the crater rim; the easiest (that's a relative term) starts 26 miles out at Kingston at Rabacca. It takes at least three hours to get to the top, though it's only a three-mile trek. Hiring a local guide is strongly advised.

Sports

Sport fishing is only in its early stages of development in these parts, though there are abundant marine life, both in the waters around St. Vincent and in the Grenadines. Deep-sea fishing, however, can be arranged through watersports operators. Better yet, talk to a local fisherman and convince him to let you go along for the day's ride. As for sailing, the Grenadines hold a world reputation for some of the best conditions in the Caribbean. There is a windsurfing school on St. Vincent on the southern coast, and all islands in the Grenadines with resorts have windsurfing equipment. Horseback riding is available only in Mustique, at the Carlton House Hotel.

Watersports of all kinds can be arranged through hotels. Scuba certification is available on St. Bequia and St. Vincent, utilizing the terrific marine sources in the region. Sport fishing is not yet formally organized, but dive shops can arrange a fishing boat; you should bring your own gear. (Spearfishing is not allowed here except by special permission). Tennis is available on several courts on St. Vincent (Prospect Racket Club, Emerald Valley Hotel and Grand View Beach Hotel, among others. The Cotton House on Mustique also has one.) Windsurfing lessons are offered at the Young Island resort, as well as the Cotton House on Mustique. There is a squash court in Kingstown at the Cyril Cyrus Squash Complex on St. James Place.

Watersports

Various locations.

For boating and cruising, call **Barefoot Yacht Charters** *(☎ 456-9526)* or **Lagoon Marina** *(☎ 458-4308)*, both on St. Vincent. On Bequia, call **Frangipani Yacht Services** *(☎ 458-3255)*. For scuba, call **Dive St. Vincent** *(☎ 457-4714)* and **St. Vincent Dive Experience** *(☎ 456-9714)*, both on St. Vincent. On Bequia, call **Dive Bequia** *(☎ 458-3504)* or **Sunsports** *(☎ 458-3577)*. **Grenadines Dive** *(☎ 458-8138)* handles diving on Union Island, while **Dive Mustique** *(☎ 456-3486)* takes care of that island's needs.

Where to Eat

Fielding's Highest Rated Restaurants in St. Vincent and The Grenadines

★★★★★	Mac's Pizzeria	$7–$30
★★★★★	The French Restaurant	$6–$16
★★★★	Basil's Bar & Raft	$4–$28
★★★	Basil's Bar & Restaurant	$11–$15
★★★	Cobblestone Roof Top	$5–$6
★★★	Gingerbread Cafe	$4–$18
★★★	Heron Restaurant	$5–$10

Fielding's Special Restaurants in St. Vincent and The Grenadines

★★★★★	The French Restaurant	$6–$16
★★★★	Basil's Bar & Raft	$4–$28
★★★	Cobblestone Roof Top	$5–$6

Fielding's Budget Restaurants in St. Vincent and The Grenadines

★★★	Cobblestone Roof Top	$5–$6
★★★	Heron Restaurant	$5–$10
★★★	Gingerbread Cafe	$4–$18
★★★★★	The French Restaurant	$6–$16
★★★	Basil's Bar & Restaurant	$11–$15

No one visits these islands in search of the last great chef; he's not hiding out here. There is almost a unilateral menu for the island's casual cafés: a handful of West Indian dishes (callaloo soup, local fish or lobster prepared creole style), fried chicken baskets with french fries and hamburgers—what locals believe that tourists like. The most sophisticated food is found at the hotel restaurants. One island diversion is to visit as many bars as you can and make a serious study of the varieties of rum punch—each bartender takes great pride in his or her own unique recipe.

Basil's Bar & Restaurant **$** ★★★

Bay Street, Kingston, ☎ (809) 457-2713.
International cuisine.
Lunch: 10 a.m.–4 p.m., prix fixe $11.
Dinner: 4 p.m.–midnight, entrees $3–$15.

Those who can't get to Basil Charles' Fantasy Island overwater bar in Mustique make the scene at his second namesake hangout with food on the ground floor of the Cobblestone Inn. Lunchtime buzzes with hungry diners going back and forth from a tasty all-you-can-eat buffet. The spread includes salads and desserts, and a la carte burgers, sandwiches, egg dishes, and seafood are also available. Nighttime is more romantic, with candlelit tables and simple grills on the menu, plus French wines at decent prices. There's a Chinese buffet on Friday evenings.

Cobblestone Roof Top **$** ★★★

Bay Street, Kingston, ☎ (809) 456-1937.
Latin American cuisine.
Lunch: 7:30 a.m.–3 p.m., entrees $5–$6.
Whatever business is conducted on this leisurely island is usually done at breakfast or lunchtime from this eatery atop the Cobblestone Inn. Housed in a quaint, restored early 1800s-era warehouse, the restaurant serves substantial West Indian lunches along with good burgers and fish and chips.

Heron Restaurant **$** ★★★

Upper Bay Street, Kingston, ☎ (809) 457-1631.
International cuisine.
Lunch: Noon–1:30 p.m., entrees $5–$10.
Dinner: 7–10 p.m., prix fixe $5–$10.
A friendly local couple run this budget hotel and restaurant that's popular with residents for American bacon and eggs breakfasts. Lunch features soups, salads, and sandwiches, and a soup-to-nuts supper is served daily for a set price. Market fresh vegetables are a standout. There's always a lot of action here, and reservations are required for dinner.

The French Restaurant **$$** ★★★★★

Villa Beach, Villa Beach, ☎ (809) 458-4972.
French cuisine. Specialties: Lobster.
Lunch: 7 a.m.–9 p.m., entrees $6–$14.
Dinner: 7–9:30 p.m., entrees $8–$16.
Behind a homey white picket fence lies an excellent restaurant that dazzles with its simplicity. Guests sit on plain folding chairs, feet planted on rough wooden floors in a windowless structure open to salty breezes. Succulent lobster couldn't get much fresher, retrieved as they are live from an on-site pool. The Parisian chef serves the juicy crustaceans flambeed in brandy, sliced in crepes, or broiled. All dishes are prepared with island-grown herbs and spices. The dining room overlooks Villa Beach and Young Island.

Where to Shop

St. Vincent and the Grenadines is simply not a paradise for shoppers—there is no duty-free sport— but there are some interesting handicrafts to be discovered. Batiks and tie-died fabrics are the province of **Batik Caribe**, a famous name in the Caribbean. The **St. Vincent Craftsman** is a cooperative featuring the work of local artisans; the quality rates among the best crafts in the Caribbean. Many of the crafts represented here are a revival of very ancient techniques, rejuvenated through an unusual program sponsored by the United

Nations. If you're headed down the road leading from the banana-boat docks, stop at the shop on the **Old Cotton Ginnery**; while you're there, ask about how you can visit some of the artists in their own homes in the countryside. Other crafts can be found at **Noah's Arkade**, next to the Batik Caribe, where you can also pick up history books about the West Indies. Drop by the local markets to pick up a few bottles of sun-dried peanuts (great for the beach) and local spices. West Indian hot sauce is infamous for making eyes run. Philatelists will adore picking up a bunch of colorful stamps of the islands, available at the post office.

The Grenadines

Bequia

Bequia (BECK-we), a three-hour schooner-run from Union, is a chain of islets between St. Vincent and Grenada attracting escapists of all kinds— from advertising execs who live in homes carved from caves to writers and painters in search of a last-ditch inspiration. It has a great natural beauty, a warm, small world flavor, and an endearing innocence; everyone here seems to have a cousin who works on a ship or tanker. (Every time a Bequia grandmother has to visit her offspring on the mainland of St. Vincent, she has to brave the choppy seas on the two islands.) Port Elizabeth's main street bordering Admiralty Bay is but a few blocks of pavement, then turns into a footpath weaving past shops and small hotels and restaurants under the canopy of trees at the water's edge. Long a favorite of Caribbean insiders and yachties, the island was accessible only by boat until mid-1992 when an airport accommodating small planes was built. Some visitors, especially Americans, return to Bequia yearly. Local buses will get you around— actually, just pickup trucks with benches built into the truck bed with a canvas roof. Main beaches are **Friendship Bay**, **Lower Bay** and **Spring Bay**, the latter graced by restless coconut palms. Each has a restaurant or snack bar and sometimes even beach chairs.

In general, Bequia is a place for shuffling between beach and pool and, from bar to bar to dinner. The best way to sightsee is to stroll around, with your intuitive antennae out for a good round of spontaneous adventure. No major fortresses or historical plantations, but there are some interesting shops including the **Crab Hole Island** (artifacts), **Melinda's** (original handprints), **Maurice's Model Boat Shop** (model boat making is a renowned Bequia craft), the **Bequia Sailing Club** (distinctive T-shirts), the **Wearable Art Shop** and the **Bequia Bookstore**.

To get to Bequia, you can either arrive by small plane via LIAT, or by boat from Kingstown, St. Vincent. The mail boat is an option as is any one of a number of motor launches or chartered yachts.

Sports in Bequia

The **Frangipani** and **Plantation House** hotels have fully equipped dive facilities. You can also find windsurfing and sunfish sailing in **Admiralty Bay** and snorkeling around **Spring** and **Friendship Bays**. To find a new beach, hop on a water taxi to **Lower Bay**. Or rent a bicycle at the **Almond Tree** boutique and toot over to Spring or Friendship Bay. Evening entertainment revolves around whichever hotel is sponsoring a jump-up, a beach barbecue with bamboo bands and vigorous, sexy dancing.

Where to Eat

No great claims to chefdom here, but do get ready for home-style island cooking with lots of fresh seafood. Most of the eating places are along the waterfront within walking distance of each other.

Gingerbread Cafe **$$** ★★★

P.O. Box 1, Gingerbread Complex, Admiralty Bay, ☎ (809) 458-3800. International cuisine.

Lunch: entrees $4–$10.
Dinner: 7:30-6:30 p.m., entrees $4–$18.
This cute Hansel and Gretelish stone cottage is the place to go for Italian coffees, puckery-fresh limeade and fruit juices, and the appropriate cakes and breads to go with them. Sit here at leisure all day at an outdoor table with a book and gaze out at the activity in the harbor. Next door, the Gingerbread Restaurant serves full meals and sandwiches, and is a nice spot for happy hour rum drinks and music.

Mac's Pizzeria **$$$** ★★★★★
Box 23, Belmont Beach, Port Elizabeth, ☎ (809) 458-3474.
International cuisine. Specialties: Lobster Pizza.
Lunch: 11 a.m.-4 p.m., entrees $7–$30.
Dinner: 4-10 p.m., entrees $7–$30.
Bequia veterans daydream about the 15-inch lobster pizzas that this terraced restaurant is famous for. Besides the dream pies, Mac's homebakes all its scrumptious breads and bakery goods, and the banana bread, plump with raisins and flavored with rum, is especially toothsome. The menu also features East Indian samosas (fried pastries stuffed with curried vegetables or meats), crunchy conch nuggets, and chunky pita bread sandwiches. This place is a winner.

Where to Shop

Bequia isn't a shopper's fantasy, but you can discover a number of stores featuring various handicrafts and unusual clothing. Visit **Crab Hole**, next to the Plantation House, to watch cotton fabrics being silk-screened. **Garden Boutique** in Port Elizabeth features stunning batik dresses and hand-dyed blouses. Local artwork can be found at **Made in the Shade** in Port Elizabeth. At **Mauvin's Model Boat Shop** you can order a model made of your yacht.

Mustique

Where to Eat

Basil's Bar & Raft **$$$** ★★★★
Britannia Bay, Mustique, ☎ (809) 458-4621.
International cuisine.
Lunch: entrees $4–$26.
Dinner: entrees $4–$28.
Basil's is not just a bar, it's a way of life. Possibly the most beautiful watering hole in the world, this unique establishment is a thatch-roofed structure built over the turquoise waters of Britannia Bay in Mustique. Owner Basil Charles has a great thing going; this is the only nightlife spot on the island. Everyone ends up here sooner or later, including titled lords and ladies and *People* magazine cover girls and boys. There's good seafood served daily and a $28 barbecue on Wednesday nights. It's open from 10:00 am until the last guest goes home.

Union Island

Union Island is 3520 acres in size and attracts many American and Europeans, especially French, who are ready to fish, dive, beachcomb and sail. Many land at the airstrip and walk to the adjacent dock of the posh Anchorage Yacht Club, where they board their charter or private boats. Not much happens in tiny Clifton, so head outside town to deserted **Big Sand Beach** and to the crest of **Fort Hill** with its magnificent view. Trekkers are attracted to the jagged, slab-faced mountainous slopes, especially the 999-foot-high **Mt. Ta-**

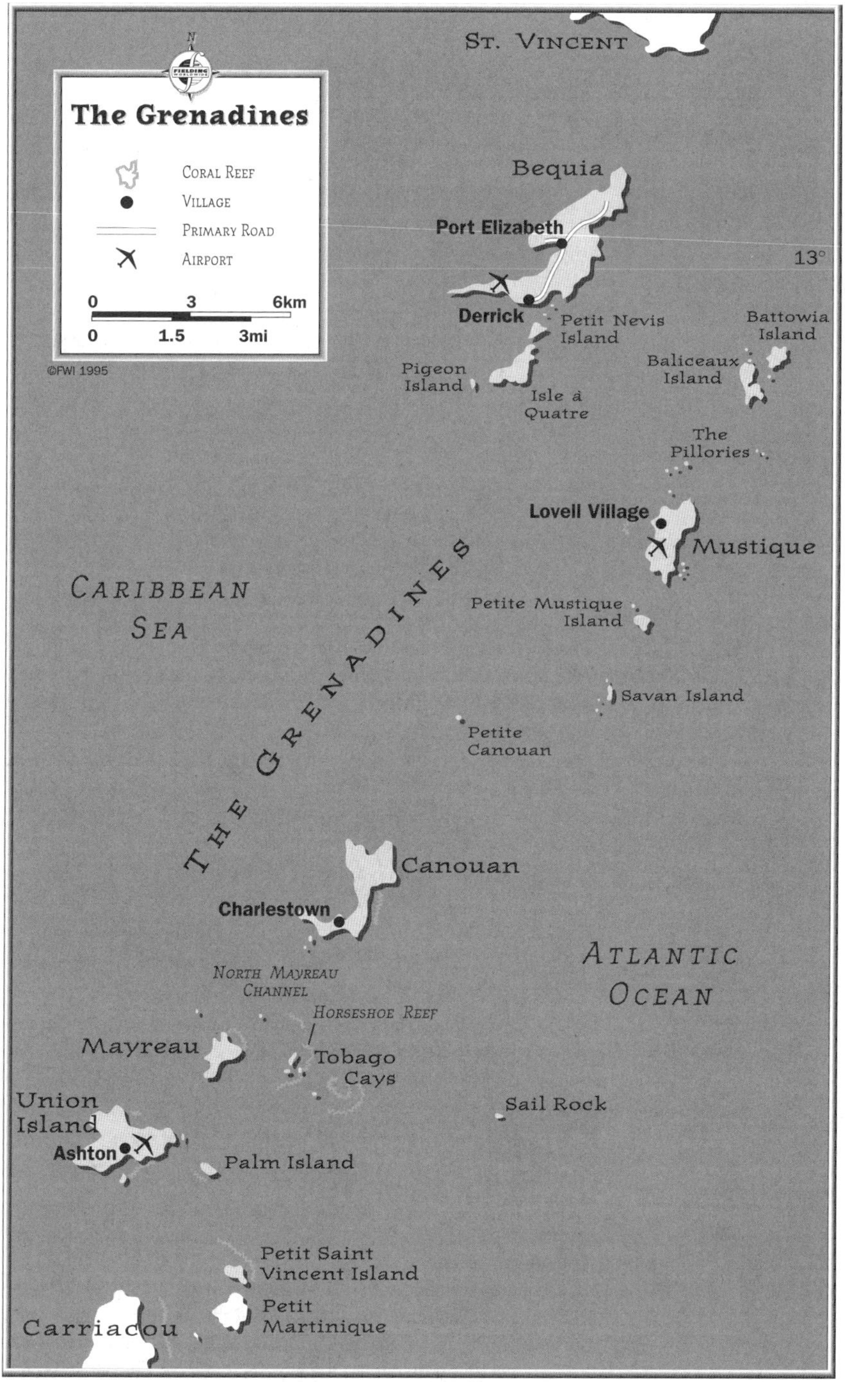

The Grenadines
Coral Reef
Village
Primary Road
Airport
0 3 6km
0 1.5 3mi
©FWI 1995
St. Vincent
Bequia
Port Elizabeth
Derrick
13°
Petit Nevis Island
Battowia Island
Baliceaux Island
Pigeon Island
Isle à Quatre
The Pillories
Lovell Village
Mustique
Caribbean Sea
The Grenadines
Petite Mustique Island
Savan Island
Petite Canouan
Canouan
Charlestown
Atlantic Ocean
North Mayreau Channel
Horseshoe Reef
Mayreau
Tobago Cays
Union Island
Ashton
Sail Rock
Palm Island
Petit Saint Vincent Island
Petit Martinique
Carriacou

bor, the Grenadines' highest peak. A foot trail leading inland from Ashton around Rock Fall ends up in Chatham Bay.

St. Vincent Directory

BUSINESS HOURS

Most shops open weekdays 8 a.m.–noon and 1–4 p.m., Saturday 8 a.m.–noon. Banks open Monday–Thursday 8 a.m.–1 or 3 p.m. and Friday 8 a.m.–5 p.m. Some banks take a two-hour break from 1–3 p.m. on Friday.

CLIMATE

Temperatures all year round are around 78–80 degrees F, cooled by gentle northeast trade window. Rain is heavier in the mountains of St. Vincent than in the Grenadines, which are generally flatter. Hurricanes can ravish the islands in the fall, while summers attract high humidity. Mosquito repellent is a must between July to November.

DOCUMENTS

U.S. and Canadian citizens must have a passport; all visitors must hold return or ongoing tickets. Visas are not required.

ELECTRICITY

Current runs 220/40 v. 50 cycles.

GETTING AROUND

Taxis fares run about $3–$4 around Kingstown, $8 from Kingstown to Villa Beach. A good way to see the island is to hire a taxi by the hour (about $15). Rates are fixed by the government, but most drivers try to get twice as much.

Public buses in the form of minivans are the cheapest way to get around; they tend to be boisterous, noisy and crowded, and full of local color. All you need to do is wave at the driver and he will stop for you. The terminal is at Market Square in Kingstown.

Rental cars run about $45–$50 a day. Driving is on the left. Since roads are not well maintained, do get as many directions as possible before you get behind the wheel. You might even take a minibus tour of the island first to get acquainted with the potholes. To rent a car, you will need a Vincentian license, unless you already have an international license.

LANGUAGE

English is spoken everywhere, often with a Vincentian patois or dialect.

MEDICAL EMERGENCIES

The government hospital, called **General Hospital** ☎ *(809) 61185*, is located at the west end of Kingstown. There is also **Bequia Casualty Hospital** at Port Elizabeth ☎ *(809) 83294*.

MONEY

The official currency is the Eastern Caribbean dollar, although U.S. and Canadian dollars are accepted at all but the smallest shops. Most establishments would prefer to take the Eastern Caribbean dollar. When quoted a price, make sure you know what dollar is being referred to. You can get a slightly higher exchange rate at banks; hotels are notoriously low and sometimes charge a fee.

TELEPHONE

The area code for St. Vincent and the Grenadines is *809*. At press time, only AT&T offered direct dial to the area, but check with the Sprint and the MCI offices in your area to verify the latest service. Before dialing other countries from St. Vincent, ask the operator; sometimes there are special codes. Also verify in advance the probable cost, surcharge and government tax; your hotel will probably also add another fee, which can send the bill sky-high. When dialing a local number from your hotel, you can drop the 45-prefix. Few hotels have phones in the rooms.

TIME

Atlantic Standard Time, one hour ahead of New York time, except during Daylight Saving Time, when it is the same.

TIPPING AND TAXES

Restaurants usually charge 10 percent for service. Tip taxi drivers 10 percent of the fare.

TOURIST INFORMATION

The **St. Vincent Department of Tourism** is located at Administrative Centre, Bay St., Kingstown, ☎ *(809) 457-1502*. Stop by and pick up brochures on lodging and sightseeing options. The St. Vincent and the Grenadines tourist guide called *Escape* contains useful tips and suggestions for excursions. The office is only open Monday–Friday.

Bequia has its own office on the waterfront in Port Elizabeth, ☎ *(809) 458-3286*, closed on Saturday afternoons. In the U.S. call ☎ *(212) 687-4981*.

WHEN TO GO

Carnival is a huge week-long celebration in early July, one of the most fantastic parties in the entire eastern Caribbean. Here you'll be able to witness and participate in calypso and steel-band competitions. Do be around when the queen and king of Carnival are crowned, a spectacular event.

ST. VINCENT AND THE GRENADINES RESTAURANTS	PHONE	ENTREE $	CR. CARDS
Bequia			
International			
★★★★★ **Mac's Pizzeria**	(809) 458-3474	$7–$30	MC, V
★★★ **Gingerbread Cafe**	(809) 458-3800	$4–$18	A, MC, V
St. Vincent			
Kingstown			
French			
★★★★★ **The French Restaurant**	(809) 458-4972	$6–$16	A, MC, V
International			
★★★ **Basil's Bar & Restaurant**	(809) 457-2713	$11–$15	A, MC, V
★★★ **Heron Restaurant**	(809) 457-1631	$5–$10	None

ST. VINCENT AND THE GRENADINES RESTAURANTS	PHONE	ENTREE $	CR. CARDS
Latin American			
★★★ **Cobblestone Roof Top**	(809) 456-1937	$5–$6•	A, MC, V
Mustique			
International			
★★★★ **Basil's Bar & Raft**	(809) 458-4621	$4–$28	A, MC, V
Note: • Lunch Only			
•• Dinner Only			

TOBAGO

The quiet turquoise waters of Tobago are great for swimming.

The sister island of nearby Trinidad, Tobago remains largely unknown, though its assets, cultural to ecological, are more than fantastic. Whereas Trinidad is emboldened by the rhythms and harmonies of steel pan bands, Tobago runs to the more subtle natural sounds of the jungle and countryside. The proximity to South America has given Tobago its Latin-based heritage that, combined with African, East Indian, Chinese and European influences, have created a rich cultural stew. And it's a heritage evident in every aspect of life, from the look of the people to the musical cadences of the language to the spicy flavors of the cuisine. A favored destination for South Americans and Europeans as well as Trinidadians, Tobago has remained somewhat a secret to North Americans, though that is beginning to change. What has saved Tobago from overdevelopment is 24,700 acres of rain forest set aside in 1765 by British growers, who intuitively realized more than 200 years ago that there was a connection between the amount of available water for crops and the number of standing trees. As such, the natural resources of Tobago have been ably preserved, today embodying a kind of frozen Fujichrome beauty—from rolling fields of tall, stately coconut palms swaying in the wind to steep, thickly overgrown, emerald-green hills, to the bright hues of fishing boats anchored on beaches that range in color from pale vanilla to rich butterscotch. If you stay in Trinidad, don't hesitate to take the ferry to Tobago, which, incidentally, has the best beaches in the region. The proliferations of plant, animal and reptile life residing within the island's several nature reserves make marvelous opportunities for ornithologists and biologists who can indulge in miles and miles of trekking. Divers should not miss the stupendous experience of swimming with Atlantic manta rays, usually dangerous marine creatures that have been subtly trained by locals to carry humans on their backs.

Bird's Eye View

Tobago, 27 miles by seven miles wide, lies in the extreme southeastern corner of the Caribbean, just 70 miles from Venezuela, on the northeastern shoulder of South America. It is separated from Trinidad by a narrow channel less than 20 miles wide; by plane the trip takes a mere 12 minutes. From the lowlands of the southwest end (home to Scarborough, Tobago's capital and center of population) the island slowly climbs in elevation until it reaches the northeast end. Here, the hills form steep, thickly jungled slopes populated by a wide variety of parrots and other birds. The end of this island is as popular with bird-watchers as it is with divers. Divers will be happy to know that the island is surrounded by fringing and patch reefs that take a broad variety of forms, including rolling fields of coral, sloping coral walls, huge blocks of invertebrate, and sponge-encrusted stone with offshore rock structures and pinnacles.

The island's development is concentrated in the southwestern corner, where visitors will find long, palm-lined stretches of beaches and a sea made for scuba, diving, waterskiing, wind surfing and snorkeling, especially at the spectacular **Buccoo Reef**, a shallow-water spot about a half-mile offshore. But the remaining two-thirds of the island is relatively untouched. Mountains rise to 1900 feet; hiking trails weave through stands of giant ferns, bamboo and calabash and saman trees. Farms and plantations of brilliant green dot the deeply indented coastlines. Fishing villages drowse in the sun, their brightly painted pirogues hauled up on beaches beneath coconut palms and sea grapes.

Several areas in Tobago have been designated as protected reserves or sanctuaries. The rain forest of the **Main Ridge** is the oldest forest reserve in the western hemisphere, dating back to 1764. Another important sanctuary is **Little Tobago Island**, which lies just offshore from the fishing village of Speyside. Here can be found important nesting grounds for an enormous number of species, including Audubon's shearwater, the red-footed booby, the sooty fern, the red-billed tropic-bird and at least 600 species of butterflies—a lepidopterists's dream.

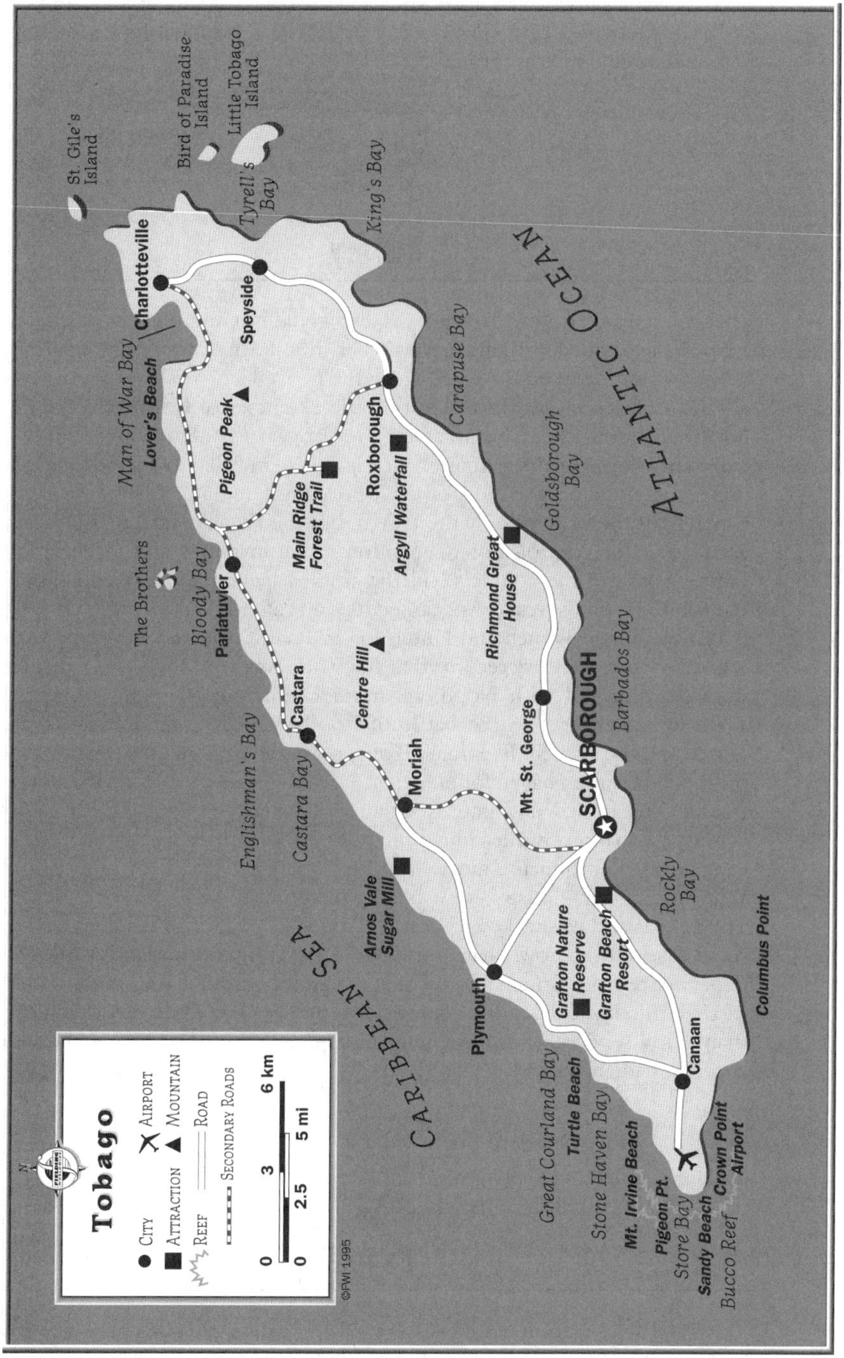
Tobago
City
Airport
Attraction
Mountain
Reef
Road
Secondary Roads
0 3 6 km
0 2.5 5 mi
©FWI 1995
St. Gile's Island
Bird of Paradise Island
Little Tobago Island
Tyrell's Bay
King's Bay
Charlotteville
Man of War Bay
Lover's Beach
Speyside
Pigeon Peak
Carapuse Bay
Roxborough
Main Ridge Forest Trail
Argyll Waterfall
Goldsborough Bay
ATLANTIC OCEAN
The Brothers
Bloody Bay
Parlatuvier
Richmond Great House
Centre Hill
Castara
Englishman's Bay
Castara Bay
Moriah
Mt. St. George
SCARBOROUGH
Barbados Bay
Amos Vale Sugar Mill
Rockly Bay
CARIBBEAN SEA
Plymouth
Grafton Nature Reserve
Grafton Beach Resort
Columbus Point
Great Courland Bay
Turtle Beach
Canaan
Stone Haven Bay
Mt. Irvine Beach
Pigeon Pt.
Store Bay
Sandy Beach
Crown Point Airport
Bucco Reef

Renovations and new constructions in recent years have spruced up Tobago's tourist facilities. A monster runway now makes it simple for visitors to arrive from Trinidad. In July 1992, a $20 million terminal for cruise ships was inaugurated in Scarborough.

History

Most historians believe Tobago was discovered by Columbus in 1498, who supposedly dubbed it "Bella Forma" (beautiful form). Its present name was derived from the word tobacco, which the native Caribs cultivated. In 1641 a Baltic duke received permission to settle a number of Courlanders on the north side of the island, but the Dutch took over in 1658, remaining in control until 1662. For the next few centuries the island changed hands at least a dozen times among world powers who considered the island a treasure worth fighting for. Not only the Dutch, but the French and English fought each other for control, not to mention pirate invasions and settlers from Latvia. Some of the conflicts had the stuff of legend about them. Bloody Bay, on the island's west coast, earned its name after a 17th-century clash between combined French and Dutch forces against a British fleet (the latter was the victor). History records that the battle was so "sanguinary" that the water became red with blood. In another ferocious struggle, more than 1700 lives were lost in the battle of Roodklyn Bay, fought between the Dutch and the French. Eventually Tobago was declared neutral territory and promptly became a haven for pirates and treasure hunters. (In fact, rumors of treasure still buried on Pirate's Bay abound today.) During the early 19th century, Tobago was a leading contender in the British and French sugarcane industry, producing more sugar per square acre than any other island. When the sugar industry went bust, Tobago also went bankrupt, and in 1888 the island was tacked to nearby Trinidad by a British colonial government that didn't know what to do with it. In 1962, both islands gained independence from Britain and became a republic within the Commonwealth in 1976. Today Tobago has its own 12-seat House of Assembly, which runs many local services. (For more information, also read the history section in the Trinidad chapter.)

People

Tobago's population numbers about 51,000; about 90 percent of Tobagonians are of African descent, and their food, folklore, music and religion are all African-based. Although the official language on both islands is English,

Tobagonians speak with a more lilting, softer accent than Trinidadians. In general, locals on Tobago are extremely friendly and helpful, and perhaps because the island's economy depends on tourism, visitors seem to receive special attention. There is also much less crime on Tobago than on Trinidad. Linguistically original, Tobagonians have invented their own rich local idioms, among them: *beat pan* (play the steel pan); *free up* (relax); *dougla* (a person of mixed Indian and African parentage); *maco* (a person who minds other people's businesses); and *lime* (spend time talking, laughing and watching the girls or boys go by).

About two-fifths of Trinidad and Tobago's people are descended from India, and major Hindu and Muslim festivals are recognized as public holidays. "Eid mubarak!" is the official greeting for Eidul-Fitr on March 14, marking the end of the Ramadan during which Muslims observe a daytime fast. Muslims celebrate this day by fasting and going to the mosque to say prayers, as well as giving alms to the poor. During this time, there is much hospitality extended, even to foreigners, homes are cleaned and decorated, and lavish meals mark the end of the abstinence. In November thousands of tiny deyas (clay pots with oil-fueled wicks) appear in parks and sidewalks to mark the Hindu Festival of Divali, in honor of Lakshmi, the goddess of light and beauty. If you drive through the towns and villages at sunset, you will find them transformed into a gentle wonderland. One of the most beautiful festivals to witness takes place on March 27, marking the Hindu New Year in India and the arrival of spring. Singing groups gather in villages and temples to perform the festive choral songs, and bonfires are lit to mark the triumph of light over darkness. Festivities the following day feature Phagwah bands, tassa drumming and singing, and colored water is sprinkled over everyone in sight. Hardly traditional, Easter is an enormously festive occasion, celebrated with goat and crab races.

To really tap into the traditions of Tobago, try to attend the Tobago Heritage Festival in July, when you can witness old-time weddings, hear traditional local music played with fiddles and tambourines, and hear about the complex courting rituals and codes and dances of days gone by. Each village presents one aspect of the island's heritage, showing off its own versatility in music, dance, drama, cooking and costuming.

Beaches

By all accounts, the best beach on the island is **Pigeon Point**, called by some the "archetype of paradise." Its quiet turquoise waters are good for swimming and the sunsets along the coast are fantastic. The land, however, is privately owned, and a small fee is charged for use, but you'll find seaside bars, boutiques, boats for hire and most watersports. Near the airport, **Store Bay** is Tobago's most happening beach, where young rastas sell locals arts and crafts; expect the vibe to be lively, if not noisy. The land, however, is privately owned, and a small fee is charged for use. Turtle Bay is also a well-kept beach. **Buccoo Reef** is excellent for snorkeling. **Salybia Bay** is delightfully secluded and good for swimming. Leatherback turtles can be seen nesting at certain times of the year on Matura Beach (see below). Surfers should head to **Mt. Irvine Bay**, home of the famous "Irvine wave"; the occasional whale has been sighted in this area.

For those who like clambering over slippery rocks, head for the so-called **Crusoe's Cave**, on the lowlands coast behind Crown Point Airport. The cave, which is gouged on to the coral, was originally the mouth of the tunnel that was thought to have twisted inland for miles. Today fallen rocks have blocked any explorations further than a few feet into the cave. Access to the cave is through private property. Expect to pay a small fee.

FIELDING'S CHOICE:

Leatherback Turtles, by the hundreds, come out of the water to nest during the months of March-June. This is one of the few places in the Caribbean where this occurs. Organized turtle watches allow visitors to witness the awesome spectacle while also protecting the nesting sites. Watchers help their guide measure each turtle and gather relevant statistics, which are sent to the U.S. turtle research stations. The primary location is along the southwestern shore from Great Courland Bay to Turtle Beach. On one June night last year, 80 giant leatherbacks as much as six feet long came up on Grand Riviere beach, while tiny hatchlings, emerging from eggs laid in the sand, were making their way to the sea. For more information, contact Thalia Moolochan of the Grande Riviere Environmental Trust ☎ (809) 670-8458, who is in charge of the program. Trinidad and Tobago Sightseeing Tours ☎ (809) 628-1051, FAX (809) 627-0856, has turtle-watching trips for $50, Caroni Swamp tours for $34, Buccoo Reef tours for $20, including hotel transport.

What Else to See

The star attractions on Tobago are mostly natural, but one of the main focuses of any excursion should be the delightful, though eccentric, little town of **Scarborough**, Tobago's capital. Market days on Friday and Saturday are an explosion of sights, sounds and aromas as the turbaned vendors lay out their enormous piles of fresh vegetables and fruits. Bargaining is the joy of the day; but don't try so hard to get a good deal that you miss biting down on a delicious papaya or a ripe golden tomato. From here, you can start the trek up to **Fort King George**, the city's most significant historical monument. Built in the 1770s, it stands a towering 450 feet above the town; today it houses a small but fascinating museum collection of colonial and Indian artifacts. Just below is the **Centre of Fine Art**, where you can peruse the products of local talent.

Even if you don't hike, take time to wander the island. Worthwhile is simply the joy of driving from Scarborough in the lowland to the fishing villages of **Charlotteville** and **Speyside** on the far side of the island. (While in Speyside, a visit to **Little Tobago**, the bird reserve, is highly recommended; see above.) As the road leaves the capital and enters the hills, it gradually narrows and becomes more and more convoluted until it becomes little more than a narrow, barely two-lane road, teetering along the edges of the seaside cliffs and plunging into palm-filled valleys, only to climb back again. The journey to the far side goes further back in time the farther you go. The town soon takes on that true Caribbean look of small fishing villages, covered with zinc roofs and animals wandering onto the road. Most watersports, golf, fine eateries and nightlife are all found in the southern region. If you want to stay in nature, stick to the "far side" of Tobago.

Not to be missed is **Charlotteville**, a picturesque fishing village embraced by high hills. Here, the bay is deep and sheltered; many head for a lively cove called **Pirate's Bay**, a 20-minute hike through the national forest. Legend has it that pirate treasure is buried here, but not a single piece of gold has ever turned up.

If you have time, the drive on the **Northside Road** will show you an uncommonly rugged but beautiful glimpse into rural Tobago. The starting point, where the ruins of the 17th-century **Fort James** are located, offers a wide-angle, windswept view of the west coast. This is the site of one of Tobago's earliest communities, settled by the Dutch in 1633. A requisite stop is the **Mystery Tombstone**, whose 18th-century epitaph for young Betty Stiven is as chilling as it is poetic: "A Mother without knowing it and a Wife without letting her husband know it except by her kind indulgence to him." Driving north from Plymouth, an excellent place to stop for a spot of tea is the charming **Arnos Vale Hotel**, an old estate house set in a beautifully lush tropical garden. A nature reserve is nearby (see above under "Treks."). As you continue north, you enter the heart of rural Tobago; the tiny mountain villages come alive with the rhythms of life. In **Golden Lane**, seek out the grave of Gang Gang Sara, an African woman rumored to be a witch who in olden days was said to have flown to Tobago, where she took up residence. When she tried to leave, it was said, she lost her power to fly because she had eaten salt while on the island.

BEST VIEW:

The view from the top of Fort King George is a panoramic sweep of the surrounding coastline, but for sunsets head for Flagstaff Hill on the island's northernmost tip, to watch the last golden rays penetrate the deep indigo sea. Deep-sea fishing is also available, as is horseback riding, with equipment provided by the Palm Tree Village Beach Resort. The leading beachfront hotels have their own watersports facilities.

Historical Sites

Fort King George ★★★

Scarborough.

Tobago's best-preserved historical building is this fort perched on a hill above Scarborough. English troops built it in 1779 and over the years it traded hands several times between the English and French. You can inspect its ruins and cannons, and on a clear day you can see forever, or at least to Trinidad. The Barrack Guard House is the site of the **Tobago Museum** *(☎ 639-3970)*, whose exhibits center on Amerindian pottery and relics, military artifacts, and documents from the slave era. It's open weekdays from 9:00 a.m. to 4:30 p.m.

Tours

Adventure Farm and Nature Rese ★★★

Anros Vale Road, Plymouth.

This 12-acre plantation grows mangoes, citrus, bananas and papaya, and rears sheep and goats in its pasture. You can come and pick your own fruit (they charge market prices) and for birdwatching. Open to the public every day but Saturday from 7:00 a.m.–9:00 a.m. and 5:00–6:00 p.m., when a caretaker acts as guide for an extra $1.

Sports

The leading beachfront hotels boast watersports activities. Deep-sea fishing is also available through the local **Gerard "Frothy" de Silva** ☎ *(809) 639-7108.* Other tour operators can be found in the vicinity of Pigeon Point/Crown Point; in the rural areas, arrangements can be made with local fishermen. The **Palm Tree Village Beach** resort also offers horseback riding (equipment provided) ☎ *(809) 639-4347*; it maintains its own stables. There are several professional sports associations, where like-minded athletes can find each other, such as the **Surfing Association** ☎ *(809) 637-4533*; **Windsurfing Association** ☎ *(809) 659-2457.* Anyone interested in yachting should contact the **Viking Dive and Sail/Yacht Chartering Limited**, inside Pigeon Point Resort at Crown Point; ☎ *(809) 639-9209*, FAX *(809) 639-0414.*

Mount Irvine Golf Course

Mount Irvine Hotel, Scarborough, ☎ *(809) 639-8871.*

Hours Open: 6:30 a.m.–3 p.m.

This 18-hole, par-72 course is among the Caribbean's most scenic, covering 125 acres of rolling hills and overlooking the sea. Great views from the clubhouse, too. Greens fees are about $46.

Watersports

Various locations.

Scuba diving: **Tobago Marine Sports** *(☎ 639-0291)*, **Dive Tobago** *(☎ 639-0202)*, Man Friday Diving *(☎ 660-4676)*, and **Viking Dive** *(☎ 639-9209)*. Boating: **Viking Sail/Yacht Chartering Limited** *(☎ 639-9209)*. Deep-sea fishing: **Gerald deSilva** *(☎ 639-7108)*. Windsurfing: **Windsurfing Association of Trinidad and Tobago** *(☎ 659-2457)*. General watersports: **Blue Waters Inn** *(☎ 660-4341)*, and **Mt. Irvine Watersports** *(☎ 639-9379)*.

Where to Eat

Fielding's Highest Rated Restaurants in Tobago		
★★★★★	Blue Crab	$4–$20
★★★★★	La Tartaruga	$9–$24
★★★	Dillon's Seafood	$12–$27
★★★	Jemma's Sea View Kitchen	$10–$27
★★★	Miss Jean's	$4–$6
★★★	Old Donkey Cart House	$3–$25
★★★	Papillon	$15–$25

Fielding's Special Restaurants in Tobago		
★★★	Jemma's Sea View Kitchen	$10–$27
★★★	Miss Jean's	$4–$6
★★★	Old Donkey Cart House	$3–$25

Fielding's Budget Restaurants in Tobago		
★★★	Miss Jean's	$4–$6
★★★★★	Blue Crab	$4–$20
★★★	Old Donkey Cart House	$3–$25
★★★★★	La Tartaruga	$9–$24
★★★	Jemma's Sea View Kitchen	$10–$27

While most of the big hotels and resorts offer "continental" cuisine—that means food that's recognizable back home—local cuisine is a flavorful combination of Indian curries blended with the more traditional Caribbean fare. Favorites include curried crab and dumplings, served in a curry sauce with hard dumplings (be sure to bring a bib, this is a messy one), and *rotis*, chicken or beef and potatoes in a curry sauce wrapped in a thin, unleavened bread. In the coastal areas, especially around festival times, indulge in a bit of *pacro*, a shellfish concoction that is reputed to have heady aphrodisiacal powers.

Down the street from the airport there are numerous stands advertising local food—**Miss Jean**, **Sylvia's**, **Alma's**, **Esme's**—offering some of T&T's most authentic cuisine. Here you'll be able to sample conch, crab and kingfish with roti, an especially Indian flat bread stuffed with ground chickpeas (a ubiquitous fast food in this country). At **Jemma's Seaview Kitchen** in Speyside, try the callaloo—a popular T&T "blue food" made from the leaves of the dasheen plant; her entrées of shrimp, kingfish, crab and chicken run a reasonable $10. Also unforgettable is the flying fish at the **Blue Crab** on Robinson and Main in the funky town of Scarborough ☎ *(809) 639-2737*, entrees from $10.

Blue Crab **$$$** ★★★★★

Robinson Street, Scarborough, ☎ *(809) 639-2737.*
Latin American cuisine.
Lunch: 11 a.m.–3 p.m., entrees $4–$6.
Dinner: 6–10 p.m., entrees $12–$20.

The hardworking family that runs this popular spot whips up tasty meals that combine the cuisines of East India, Portugal and Creole. Fresh vegetables and fruits from their own gardens are used in the preparation of such delights as pumpkin soup and homemade ice cream and fruit wines. Lunches are served on the wide terrace of the traditional West Indian building. Only fish caught that day is used in their seafood dishes. Treat an island friend to dinner here, which is available by advance reservation only from Wednesday through Friday.

Dillon's Seafood **$$$** ★★★

Airport Road, Crown Point, ☎ *(809) 639-8765.*
Seafood cuisine.
Dinner: 6–10 p.m., entrees $12–$27.

A charter captain and fisherman runs this modern restaurant cooled by air-conditioning, which assures that all fish and seafood are so fresh they snap back at you. There's lobster thermidor, or island kingfish in a tomato sauce, and fish soup. Some of the food though, could use a braver hand with the salt shaker or the spice rack.

Jemma's Sea View Kitchen **$$$** ★★★

Windward Road, Tyrell's Bay, ☎ *(809) 660-4066.*
Latin American cuisine.
Lunch: 9 a.m.–4 p.m., entrees $10–$20.
Dinner: 4.–9 p.m., entrees $10–$27.

The kids, big and small, will enjoy eating in a real treehouse overlooking Tyrell's Bay. They may have to fight for space though, as there are only 10 tables. The emphasis is on local dishes, served in generous portions by an amiable staff. Specialties include callaloo soup, grilled seafood, and crab and dumplings. It's a great place to stop on a circle-island tour or a day at the beach. Open Fridays from 8 a.m. to 5 p.m. only.

La Tartaruga **$$$** ★★★★★

Buccoo Bay Beach, Buccoo Bay, ☎ *(809) 639-0940.*
Italian cuisine.
Dinner: 7–11 p.m., entrees $9–$24.

Fresh is the key word at this intimate, friendly spot. The Italian owner and chef prepares delicious pasta that's homemade daily. Sauces are embellished with garden-grown herbs. Fish is delivered to his door from a reliable source. The service, by a well-trained staff, is as quick as it gets on the island. Recommended dishes include spaghetti with dorado in a sauce of olive oil and pepper, served with tomatoes. Stop by for a drink, an espresso, homemade ice cream or luscious deserts such as ricotta cakes, and amaretto cheesecake.

Miss Jean's **$** ★★★

Store Bay Beach, Store Bay, ☎ *(809) 639-0211.*
Latin American cuisine.
Lunch: 9 a.m.–4 p.m., entrees $4–$5.
Dinner: 4–10 p.m., entrees $5–$6.

Miss Jean's motto is if you love good food we love to feed you and she means it. All manner of seafood, soups and stews, including the island favorite, crab and dumplings, emanate miraculously from a small shed on the sand in Store Bay. If you like, sample a few things at Jean's and mosey on to Miss Esmie or Miss Trim's place next door. For a carbo load, try the macaroni pie, which is stewed chicken or beef with macaroni, if it's available.

Old Donkey Cart House **$$$** ★★★

Bacolet Street, Scarborough, ☎ (809) 639-3551.
International cuisine.
Lunch: 11 a.m.–3 p.m., entrees $3–$10.
Dinner: 6:30 p.m.–midnight, entrees $20–$25.

The Viennese owner of this charming restaurant is the island's only authority on German wines, which are a specialty of the place. These fine vintages accompany well-prepared local fish, steaks and pastas. Start your meal with some excellent cheese. At lunch, sandwiches are served on homebaked bread.

Papillon **$$$** ★★★

Buccoo Bay Road, Mt. Irvine, ☎ (809) 639-0275.
Seafood cuisine.
Lunch: entrees $15–$25.
Dinner: entrees $15–$25.

Chef Jakob Straessle's cuisine may not be on the cutting edge of chic, but the Swiss restaurateur always delivers reliably tasty old favorites like lobster thermidor, served with a choice of soup, rice and salad. Also featured are conch in season, cooked in coconut milk. Dine in air-conditioned comfort in a rustic, out-of-the-way lodge. Closed for lunch on Sundays.

Where to Shop

Compared to the cascades of goods available in Trinidad, Tobago's share represents a mere trickle. Three malls cater to the obvious and uninspiring: **Scarborough Mall** in the center of town, **IDC Mall** at Sangster Hill, and **Breeze Mall** on Milford Road. (Breeze Hall is perhaps a tad more fashionable.) You'll find more original items in the designer boutiques such as **The Cotton House** on Bacolet Street (with smaller outlets at Sandy Point Hotel and Pigeon Point, where you can pick up unusually beautiful batiks and tie-dyes). Tobago's own fashion mavens head for **Nairobi**, above the Starting Gate Pub off Shirvan Road. As for arts and crafts, you can find some of them at the malls (Scarborough and IDC), but it's more fun to buy them from vendors hawking their own wares in the market. Good buys are leather sandals, carved gourds and hand-wrought jewelry. Most hotels have small gift shops, but expect the prices to be exaggerated. A couple of nice craft stores can be found on the road leading to Pigeon Point, a fine beach. The jeweler **Jose Andres** is especially revered for his unique jewelry made from indigenous woods, bone, coral and seedpods. The duty-free allowance covers one quart of liquor, 200 cigarettes/50 cigars, and gifts up to TT$50.

Tobago Directory

BUSINESS HOURS

Shops open Monday–Thursday 8 a.m.–4 p.m., Friday 8 a.m.–6 p.m. and Saturday 8 a.m.–noon. Banks open Monday–Thursday 9 a.m.–2 p.m. and Friday 9 a.m.–noon and 3–5 p.m.

CLIMATE

Weather conditions are very comfortable, with temperatures averaging 83 degrees F. The wet season runs June to December, with rainfall in mostly short sharp bursts. Tobago is slightly cooler and less humid than Trinidad. A scant 11 degrees above the equator, the climate is decidedly tropical.

DOCUMENTS

A passport is required for entry, as is a return or ongoing ticket. A departure tax of about $12 in U.S. currency is collected at the airport. An international driver's license is required for car rentals.

ELECTRICITY

Current runs either 115 or 220 volts at 60 cycles. While many hotels have 115 volt current, it is advisable to travel with a small transformer just in case. These supplies are readily available at low cost.

GETTING AROUND

Although both Trinidad and Tobago are small, you'll need a car to get around. Try **Singh's** or **Amar**, and ask for maps. Driving is on the left side of the street. A ferry service links Trinidad and Tobago, about a 2.5 hour journey.

Taxis charge fixed fares to the major areas.

Car rentals are mostly local agencies. Among the best are **Auto Rentals Crown Point Beach hotel** ☎/FAX *(809) 639-0644* and **Singh's Auto Rentals, Grafton Beach Hotel** ☎ *(809) 639-0191.*

Bicycles, scooters and motorcycle rentals are available at **Blossom Enterprises**, *Milford Rd., Canaan,* ☎/FAX *(809) 639-8485.* **Toyota Rent a Car**, *177 Tragarete Rd.,* ☎ *(809) 628-5516*; and **Kalloo's Auto Rental** *32 Ariapita Ave., Woodbrook,* ☎ *(809) 622-9073.*

Among the best tour companies are **Pioneer Journeys**, *Man O'War Bay Cottages, Charlotteville,* ☎ *(809) 660-4327*; and **Bruce Ying Sightseeing Tours Around Trinidad and Tobago**, *Bacolet St., Scarborough,* ☎/FAX *(809) 639-4402.*

LANGUAGE

English is the official language and is spoken with a rich, melodious accent. The old French-based patois has almost died out; some Hindi is still used among the Indian community.

MEDICAL EMERGENCIES

There are hospitals in Port of Spain, Scarborough, Mount Hope (a large teaching hospital), and Fernando, and an extensive network of health centers and clinics, both public and private; both government and private doctors practice.

MONEY

The official currency is the Trinidad and Tobago dollar (written TT$), which floats against other currencies. Daily rates are listed in the newspapers. Credit cards are widely accepted in tourist areas, and by rental car companies, hotels, restaurants and major shops.

TELEPHONE

The country code is *809*. If dialing direct from the U.S. and Canada, and much of the Caribbean, dial the number "1" first; from other countries, including Haiti, Cuba and the Dutch and French Caribbean, dial "01." The phone system is digital, and international direct dialing and other standard services are available throughout the system.

TIME

Atlantic Standard Time, one hour ahead of New York City, except during Daylight Saving Time, when it is the same.

TIPPING

If the restaurant bill does not add a 10–15 percent service charge, feel free to do so.

TOURIST INFORMATION

Local information offices are at **Piarco Airport** ☎ *(809) 664-5196*; **Crown Point Airport**; ☎ *(809) 639-0509*; **Tobago: N.I.B. Mall**, Scarborough; ☎ *(809) 639-2125/3566*. In the United States call ☎ *(800) 232-0082*.

WATER

Tap water is safe to drink; bottled mineral waters are widely available and tasty.

WHEN TO GO

Carnival explodes in February with steel bands, parades and lots of local foods and drink. Tobago Arts Festival occurs March-April. The Round the Gulf Sailing Competition takes place in March. Goat and Crab races take place in April. The Indo-Caribbean Festival of Arts takes place in May. The Tobago Heritage Festival is in July. The Steelband Festival is in August and October. The Tobago Music Festival takes place in November and December. The Tobago Christmas Pageant, with local music and dance, is in December. For more information, contact the tourist board. Also check out "When To Go" at the end of the Trinidad chapter.

TOBAGO RESTAURANTS	PHONE	ENTREE	CR. CARDS
Plymouth			
International			
★★★ **Old Donkey Cart House**	(809) 639-3551	$3–$25	A, MC, V
Italian			
★★★★★ **La Tartaruga**	(809) 639-0940	$18–$24••	A, MC, V
Latin American			
★★★★★ **Blue Crab**	(809) 639-2737	$4–$20	A, MC, V
★★★ **Jemma's Sea View Kitchen**	(809) 660-4066	$10–$27	None
★★★ **Miss Jean's**	(809) 639-0211	$4–$6	None
Seafood			
★★★ **Dillon's Seafood**	(809) 639-8765	$12–$27••	A, MC, V
★★★ **Papillon**	(809) 639-0275	$15–$25	A, DC, MC, V

TOBAGO RESTAURANTS	PHONE	ENTREE	CR. CARDS
Note: • Lunch Only			
•• Dinner Only			

TRINIDAD

Trinidad's Carnival is the Caribbean's most celebrated annual spectacle with islanders working all year on floats and costumes.

Trinidad is the largest of the Lesser Antilles Islands, home to calypso, steel pan bands and some of the most spectacular aviary habitats in the Western World. Practically ringed with beaches, the island is a cultural smorgasbord of cuisines, festivals and religious rituals that draws tourists despite the almost studied indifference to their comfort. During the '70s, the two-island nation (which includes its sister island Tobago) became the wealthiest, if not the most cosmopolitan, nation in the Caribbean, allowing it to eschew tourism as an unneeded intrusion. As finances plummet in the early '90s, Trinidad is now courting tourism with an attractive come-on, and a special amiability toward foreigners is being seriously cultivated. Even without such natural resources as its fine rain forest, palm-fringed beaches and exotic nature reserves, simple daily life alone in Trinidad makes a fascinating diversion. The island's capital, Port-of-Spain is a vibrant, dizzying waterfront town of colorful gingerbread houses competing with ramshackle stalls and short high-rises as at least seven distinct nationalities stream down the narrow, winding alleyways intent on doing business somewhere between First

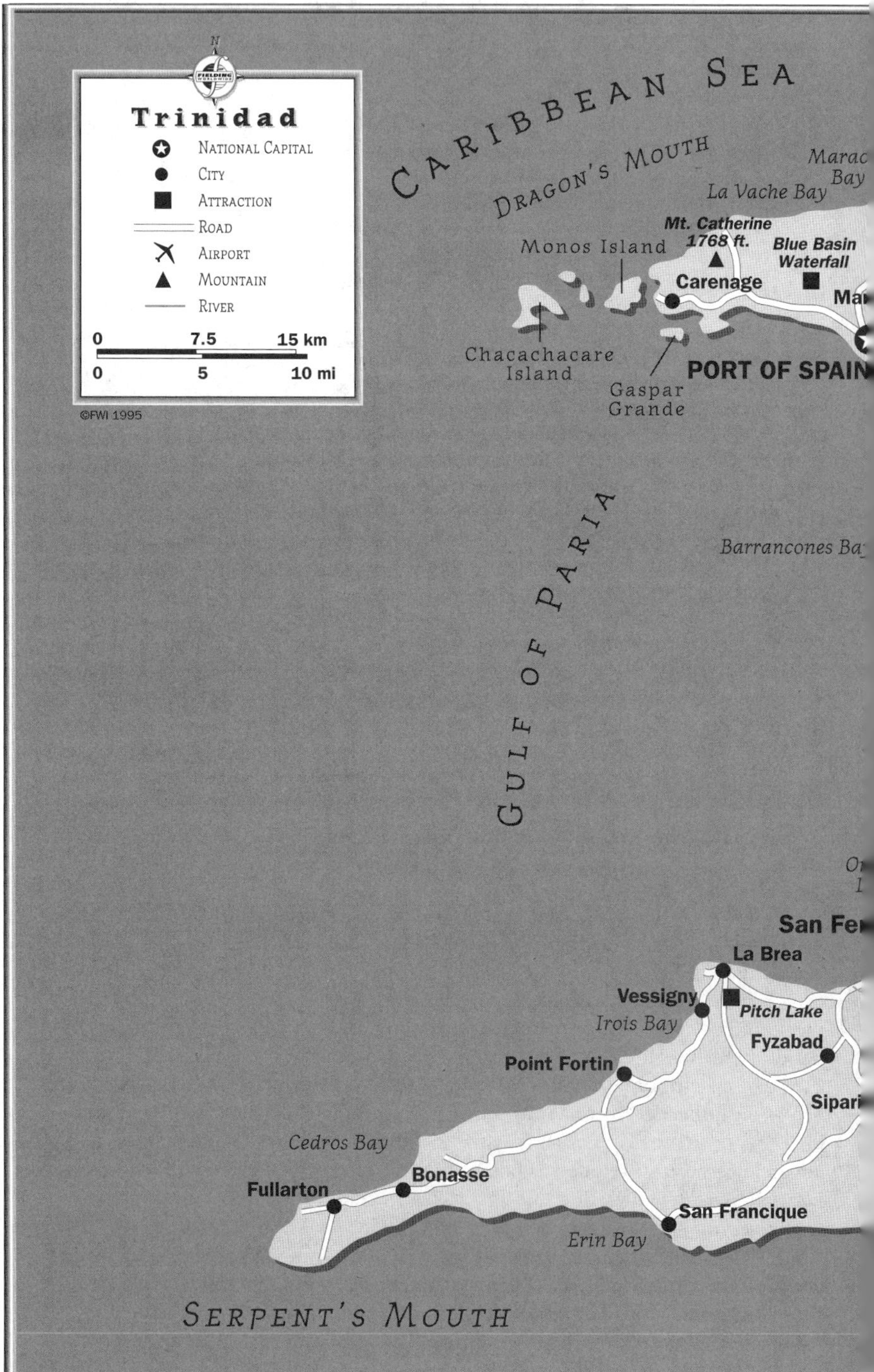
Trinidad
National Capital
City
Attraction
Road
Airport
Mountain
River
0 7.5 15 km
0 5 10 mi
©FWI 1995
Caribbean Sea
Dragon's Mouth
La Vache Bay
Mt. Catherine 1768 ft.
Blue Basin Waterfall
Monos Island
Carenage
Chacachacare Island
Gaspar Grande
PORT OF SPAIN
Gulf of Paria
Barrancones Bay
San Fe
La Brea
Vessigny
Pitch Lake
Irois Bay
Fyzabad
Point Fortin
Sipari
Cedros Bay
Bonasse
Fullarton
San Francique
Erin Bay
Serpent's Mouth

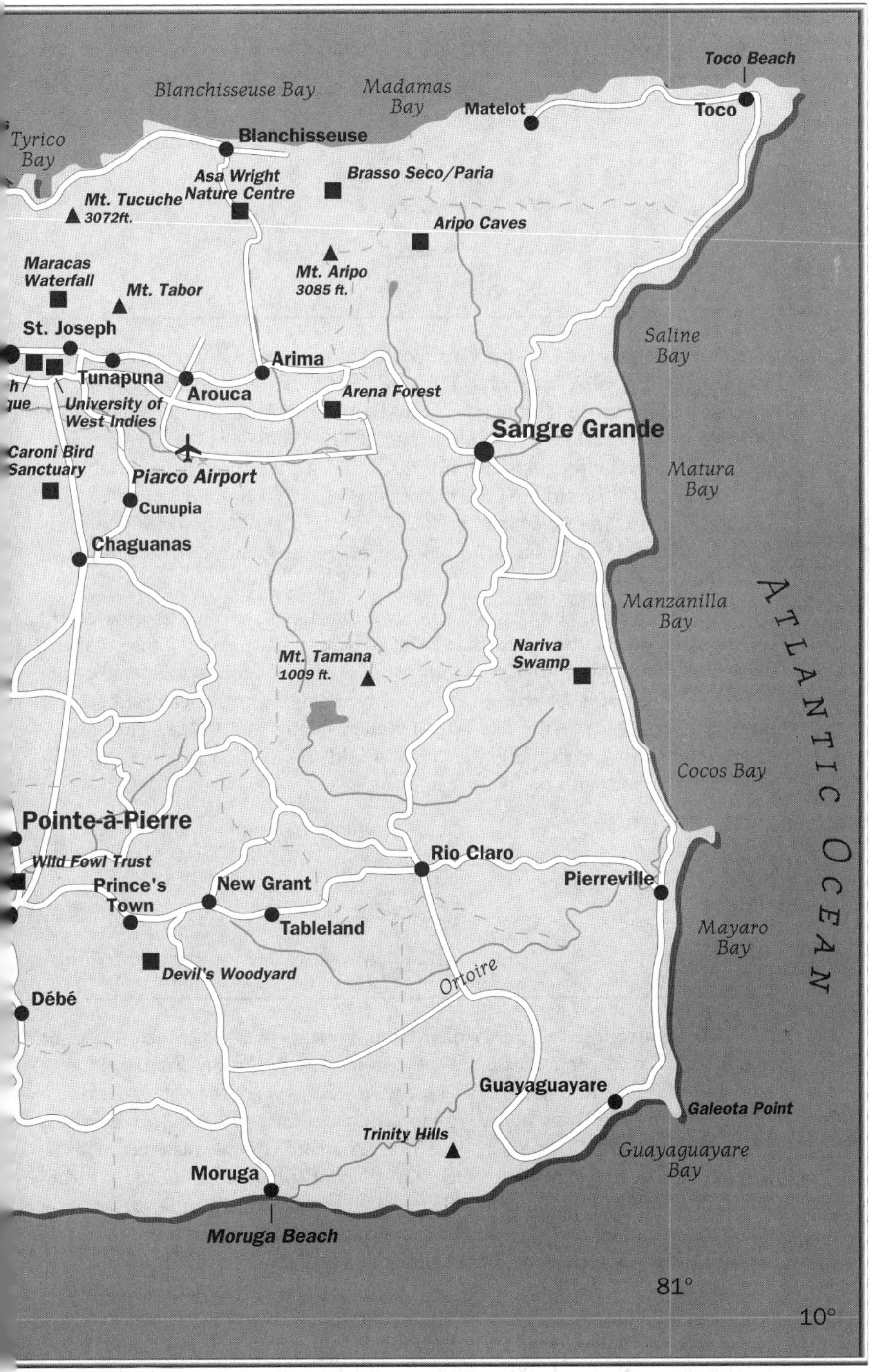
Toco Beach
Blanchisseuse Bay
Madamas Bay
Matelot
Toco
Tyrico Bay
Blanchisseuse
Asa Wright Nature Centre
Brasso Seco/Paria
Mt. Tucuche 3072ft.
Aripo Caves
Maracas Waterfall
Mt. Tabor
Mt. Aripo 3085 ft.
St. Joseph
Arima
Tunapuna
Arouca
University of West Indies
Arena Forest
Saline Bay
Sangre Grande
Caroni Bird Sanctuary
Piarco Airport
Matura Bay
Cunupia
Chaguanas
Manzanilla Bay
Atlantic Ocean
Nariva Swamp
Mt. Tamana 1009 ft.
Cocos Bay
Pointe-à-Pierre
Wild Fowl Trust
Rio Claro
Prince's Town
New Grant
Pierreville
Tableland
Mayaro Bay
Devil's Woodyard
Ortoire
Débé
Guayaguayare
Galeota Point
Trinity Hills
Guayaguayare Bay
Moruga
Moruga Beach
81°
10°

World and Third. Ecotreks are fabulous on the island, and especially on Tobago, which is a short ferry ride away. Carnival in Trinidad is one of the most spectacular events in the Caribbean, an annual blowout affair whose efforts can be seen year-round in the studious productions of floats, costumes and musical performances.

Bird's Eye View

Trinidad is situated in the Caribbean Sea about 12 kilometers off the northeast coast of Venezuela. Tobago is 30.7 kilometers farther to the northeast. The entire land mass of Trinidad covers 1861 square miles while Tobago has a mere 117 miles. Almost all of Trinidad's hotels and restaurants are confined to the foothills around Port of Spain, the capital city, which has more than 60,000 residents; the entire island has a population of more than 1 million. Below the **Savanah Park**, lined with gingerbread mansions, spreads the city, a jumble of wooden houses and tiny stores whose wares often spill onto the sidewalk.

Just an hour from the city is a primeval rain forest, arrived at by a coiled spring of a road that leads to **Arima Valley**, where wildlife is so profuse that the New York Zoological Society began its first tropical ecology center there in 1949. This was later turned into a neighboring coffee and cocoa estate and a hotel for bird-lovers—the **Asa Wright Nature Centre and Lodge**. The grotto here is the most accessible place in the world to see the rare cave-dwelling oilbird, equipped with batlike sonar.

History

Columbus stumbled upon Trinidad and Tobago in 1498. Since then, the two islands have been a battlefield of contention among the French, Dutch, British and Spanish. Trinidad was long viewed as a source for Amerindian slaves, so the island was fiercely guarded, in contrast to Tobago which was nearly deserted by the Spanish. In 1592, an inland capital was erected at St. Joseph, stimulating interest in the cultivation of tobacco and cocoa. During the middle of the 18th century, plagues swept through the area, decimating the settlement and forcing the Spanish governor to move to a more coastal location, less vulnerable to jungle diseases and Indian raids. Port of Spain took its time to develop, attracting a slow stream of settlers followed by Christian missionaries intent on civilizing the Indians. Both tobacco and cocoa production soon fell into disfavor, the former a victim of competition among the northern islands, the latter a victim of blight. In 1776, the Spanish government offered land grants and tax incentives to Roman Catholic settlers; in response, numerous French planters from French Caribbean countries poured in to establish farms. By the end of the century, prosperous Frenchmen had gained control of the government, spreading the lilt of their patois and their tasty cuisine islandwide. During the Napoleonic Wars in 1797, the British sent a fleet to Trinidad, who swiftly overcame the resident Spaniards who had been too distracted fighting off Indians. In 1815, Tobago itself came under British control and was made a ward of Trinidad in 1897.

In the 1970s, offshore petroleum discoveries propelled Trinidad to the enviable status of the wealthiest nation in the Caribbean. Literacy rose to 90 percent, roads were paved, electricity installed. Signs of abject poverty, common among West Indian nations, nearly disappeared. In 1962, Sr. Eric Williams, the father of Trinidad and Tobago's new independence from British rule, vowed to avoid what he called the mistakes of his Caribbean neighbors, which in his mind, was servile catering to tourists. As such, tourism lay fallow for several decades. However, during the mid-'80s, resources plummeted, and the challenge of the Trinidadian government in this decade will be to re-establish economic stability and ensure conservation of the island's natural resources.

People

Trinidad's population is well over one million people. Their facial features represent a mingling of characteristics from Africa, America, Europe, Asia and the Indian subcontinent. Calypso lyrics hold the soul of the people—often they are editorials that bemoan what the oil bust has done to the country. Yet by all standards, Trinidad and Tobago are prosperous nations; children are kept fed by plentiful fish and fruit, healthy by free medical care, and taught in schools responsible for a literacy rate higher than the United States. Today, the two-island nation is 40 percent black and 40 percent East Indian, plus Chinese, Arab, British and remnant Carib Amerindian stock—only with each passing generation are bloods mixing so much that you can't tell who's who. The cultural jetsam takes its biggest influence from the conquerors who stayed the longest—Spain, France and Holland. Important is the legacy left by the Africans who arrived as slaves, indentured servants from India brought to replace them after abolition, Chinese who proved unfit to harvest sugar but adept at everything else, Syrians bearing textiles, and former British estate owners whose descendants wouldn't leave for anything. Color is less an issue in this country, where intercultural cooperation has received lots of elbow grease. Race relations here are considered a miracle of worked-at harmony.

Music and Carnival are nearly year-round industries. A century ago, the British outlawed African drums in Trinidad, for allegedly inciting passions leading to violence. People switched to beating on bamboo, biscuit tins, hubcaps, and as local petroleum exploitation surged on, musicians used oil drums, which someone noticed tended to change pitch after much pounding, and particularly when dented. Pan music can now be heard everywhere from Sunday mass to jazz ensembles to 120-musician orchestras during Carnival's Panorama. Best of all is the ubiquitous pan yard, especially in the month preceding Carnival, where the neighborhoods gather to hear free rehearsals. Best jam is on Oxford Street. For more information, see the chapter called "Caribbean Culture" in the front of the book.

Beaches

On the subject of beaches, Tobago wins hands down over Trinidad. The latter, however, does have numerous ones—they are simply not as beautiful or as memorable as Tobago's. Most of Trinidad's beaches are on the Caribbean coast from Las Cuevas to Balata Bay, and on offshore islands such as Monos.

One of the most beautiful beaches is **Cyril Bay**, complete with a small waterfall and fantasy sites for picnics. The cove is made of pebbles and sand and can be reached only by foot. Surfers congregate at **Tyrico Bay**, but the beach is small for bathing. Swimmers who are not experienced should avoid the strong undertow. **Maracas Bay** is a favorite among locals who love the long stretch of sand and the ample parking spaces. You can also find food and changing facilities here. Along the north coast you'll find **Las Cuevas Bay**, a very pretty stretch of sand ringed by submerged and partially submerged caves. Some of the best fruit on the islands is sold across the street. Swimmers should avoid the waters because of a fierce current, but the beach is usually serene and uncrowded. **Blanchisseuse Bay** is located about eight miles east, with lovely palm trees for shade and no crowds. Lovers should enjoy the near absolute seclusion.

Northeast beaches take about an hour to reach by car. Bodysurfers particularly like the conditions at **Balandra Bay**. Good swimming can be found in the calm waters of **Salibea Bay**, just past Galera Point. A lovely drive can be had down **Cocal**, the road between Manzanilla Beach and Cocos Bay, lined as it is with towering palm trees who make an arch over the highway. The water at Manzanilla is sometimes polluted by the Atlantic overflow, so avoid swimming if the sea looks muddy.

What Else to See

Drive Saddle Road north from the Savannah for 30 minutes to beautiful Maracas Bay; continue east to Las Cuevas Bay. In the northeast the nicest beaches are **Ma Tura**, **Salybia**, **Pajes**, **Toco** (take the lighthouse road), **Grand Riviere**, **Shark River** and **Matelot**.

Nariva Swamp, the backdrop to Cocos Bay, is one of the world's great birding regions. **Canoni Swamp**, with its red ibis, four-eyed fish and other wonders, is 20 minutes south of Port of Spain on the Butler Highway toward San Fernando. Call Winston Nanan at **Nanan's Bird Sanctuary Tours** ☎ *(809) 645-1305.*

A stroll in **Queen's Park Savannah** in Port of Spain is obligatory. You'll ramble alongside training thoroughbreds, admire gingerbread mansions, watch sandlot cricket matches and buy fruit, corn or barbecued fish from park vendors, who also sell fresh coconut milk.

City Celebrations

Carnival ★★★★★

Port of Spain, ☎ *(809) 623-8867.*

Trinidad's famous carnival officially lasts just two days, from sunrise on Monday to midnight on Tuesday before Ash Wednesday. However, the unofficial season starts right after Christmas. Started by the French plantocracy 200 years ago, the festival was adopted by the island's blacks as a celebration of the end of slavery. Today, the joyous festival is eagerly anticipated by Trinidadians all year long. Most everyone dons elaborate costumes they've spent months making, then parades through the streets to the beat of steel bands. Tourists are welcome to join a troupe from a few hundred to literally thousands of costumed revelers.

Museums and Exhibits

National Museum ★★★★

117 Frederick Street, Port of Spain, ☎ *(809) 623-5941.*

Hours Open: 10 a.m.–6 p.m.

The museum's exhibits center on Trinidad's geography and history through the ages, with artifacts from pre-Columbian times. The highlight is a large art gallery with changing displays and a permanent exhibit on the works of famed 19th-century painter Michel Jean Cazabon.

Parks and Gardens

Royal Botanical Gardens ★★★★★

Queen's Park Savannah, Port of Spain, ☎ *(809) 622-3530.*

Hours Open: 9:30 a.m.–5:30 p.m.

Located in the two-mile Queen's Park Savannah, these lush gardens cover 70 colorful acres on land that was once a sugar plantation. The grounds include the President's House, an 1875 Victorian mansion home to the president of Trinidad and Tobago, and the **Emperor Valley Zoo** *(☎ 625-2264)*, named after the huge Emperor butterflies common in the area. The gardens, laid out in 1820, showcase specimens from around the world.

Tours

Asa Wright Nature Center ★★★★★

Spring Hill Estate, Port of Spain, ☎ (809) 667-4655.
Hours Open: 9 a.m.–5 p.m.

This 191-acre estate turned wildlife sanctuary is a must for bird watchers, with more than 100 species waiting to be glimpsed. The grounds include eight trails, one leading to the world's most accessible colony of nocturnal oilbirds. Guided tours are offered daily at 10:30 a.m. and 1:30 p.m.; reservations are suggested. They also take in guests here; see the entry under lodging for more details.

Caroni Bird Sanctuary ★★★★★

Butler Highway, Port of Spain.
Hours Open: 4 p.m.–6:30 p.m.

This sanctuary comprises 40 square miles of mangrove swampland bisected by waterways. Come at sunset to see the national bird, the scarlet ibis, come home to roost, an amazing, colorful sight. Boat tours are conducted by **David Ramsahai** *(☎ 663-4767)* and **Winston Nanon** *(☎ 645-1305)*.

Sports

Deep-sea fishing is available in the cliff-bound **Boca Islands** in the northwest where mackerel, kingfish, wahoo, yellowtail tuna, barracuda, red snapper and groupers are in abundance. Much sailing is done on a private basis in Trinidad, though it is in its infant stage commercially. Weekly races are held by the Yachting Association, and you may be able to inquire about renting or hiring boats among the owners. There is also a great interest in power-boat racing; the major annual competition is the Great Race (90 miles) between Trinidad and Tobago that takes place in August. Over the past several years surfing has become a passion on Trinidad. The Surfing Association of Trinidad and Tobago is very warm to visitors and will offer all the assistance it can. There is no particular season for surfing; conditions are favorable year-round. Four surfing breaks are available. The biggest swells happen around **Toco Point**, on the northeast coast of Trinidad. **Chaguaramas Bay** is the prime spot for windsurfing.

Golf

Two locations, Port of Spain.

Trinidad has two courses for duffers. The island's only 18-hole course is at **St. Andrew's Golf Club** in Maravel; ☎ *629-2314*. The **Chaguaramas Golf Course** has nine holes; ☎ *634-4349*.

Watersports

Various locations, Port of Spain.

A variety of companies are happy to assist with watersports. Deep-sea fishing: **Bayshore Charters** *(☎ 637-8711)* and **Trinidad and Tobago Game Fishing Association** *(☎ 624-5304)*. Boating and sailing: **Island Yacht Charters** *(☎ 637-7389)*. Windsurfing: **Windsurfing Association of Trinidad and Tobago** *(☎ 659-2457)*. General watersports equipment and instruction: **Ron's Watersports** *(☎ 622-0459)* and the **Surfing Association of Trinidad and Tobago** *(☎ 637-4355)*.

Where to Eat

Fielding's Highest Rated Restaurants in Trinidad

★★★★★	Veni Mange	$8–$10
★★★	Breakfast Shed	$5–$7
★★★	Cafe Savannah	$8–$17
★★★	Chaconia Inn	$12–$19
★★★	Hong Kong City	$8–$20
★★★	Michael's	$8–$25
★★★	Philip and Fraser's	$8–$20
★★★	Rafters	$6–$21
★★★	Tiki Village	$6–$13

Fielding's Special Restaurants in Trinidad

★★★	Cafe Savannah	$8–$17
★★★	Monsoon	$5–$5
★★★	Philip and Fraser's	$8–$20

Fielding's Budget Restaurants in Trinidad

★★★	Monsoon	$5–$5
★★★	Breakfast Shed	$5–$7
★★★	Singho	$5–$12
★★★★★	Veni Mange	$8–$10
★★★	Tiki Village	$6–$13

No fewer than seven distinct cultures have influenced the cuisine of Trinidad, from the Spanish settlers who cooked up pastelles to the French who introduced herbs such as broad-leaved thyme and basil. The British brought tamarind from the East Indies for sauces used still today in red snapper. A ten-alarm chile pepper called a *habañero* hails from Mexico. Spicy pastelles are a favorite snack—tamales concocted by placing meats, raisin, capers and fresh herbs atop grated corn or cornmeal and folded in bright green leaves instead of the usual corn husks. "Oil-down" is another local specialty, made from breadfruit, a round starchy yamlike fruit that makes a gooey thick stew when cooked. Before you go, check out the delicacies in *Callaloo, Calypso & Carnival*, a new cookbook from The Crossing Press in Freedom, California by Dae De Witt and Mary Jane Wilan. Most nights, calypso or pan music is heard at the exceedingly friendly **Mas Camp Pub** *(French St., at Ariapita Ave.,* ☎ *(809) 623-3745,* $2). There are also frequent concerts at **Spektakula Forum** *(Henry St.,* ☎ *(809) 623-2879,* about $5.)

Breakfast Shed $ ★★★

Waterfront, Wrightson Road, ☎ *(809) 627-2337.*
Latin American cuisine.
Lunch: 5 a.m.–3 p.m., entrees $5–$7.
Break bread with the wharf rats on huge platters of homestyle West Indian food near the cruise ship dock and the Holiday Inn. Fellow diners are working people and early risers who like the fish breakfasts served from 5 a.m. Lunch (the only other meal served) is accompanied by plantains, rice and peas and other plate stretchers. So down home, the hall-like room is called the "Holiday Out" by regulars.

Cafe Savannah $$ ★★★

16-18 Cotton Hill, St. Clair, ☎ *(809) 622-6441.*
Latin American cuisine.
Lunch: 11:45 a.m.–2:15 p.m., entrees $8–$9.
Dinner: 6–10:15 p.m., entrees $8–$17.
Possibly the best callaloo soup on the islands is served at this intimate restaurant on the lower level of the Kapok Hotel. Prepared with a rich stock of *dasheen* (taro leaf) and okra, it's filled with pumpkin, coconut and crabmeat. Other specialties include lobster Soucouyant and pork steak in zippy mustard sauce. There's a prix fixe lunch of several courses, but sandwiches and salads are available.

Chaconia Inn $$$ ★★★

106 Saddle Road, Maraval, ☎ *(809) 628-8603.*
Latin American cuisine.
Lunch: 11 a.m.–2 p.m., entrees $12–$19.
Dinner: 7–11 p.m., entrees $12–$19.
The dining rooms of this motel-like resort in a Port of Spain suburb serve a double purpose: at lunch in the Lounge, business folk gather for a no-frills lunch of fish, pasta, pork and some vegetarian offerings. Sandwiches are tasty and moderately priced. And once a week, a West Indian barbecue is the attraction at the modern, plant-filled alfresco Roof Garden atop the hotel. A bar serves drinks until 2 p.m.

Hong Kong City $$ ★★★

86 Tragarete Road, Newtown, ☎ *(809) 622-3949.*
Chinese cuisine.
Lunch: entrees $8–$20.
Dinner: entrees $8–$20.
Spicy, creative Tri-Chi food is served amidst gaudy red and gold trappings. Bright Oriental lanterns hang from an intricately decorated ceiling. Chinese-food loving Trinidadians favor pepper shrimp, pork with dasheen and other delights. Karaoke nights sometimes, for those who enjoy that sort of thing. For more Chinese food around town, try: **New Shay-Shay Ten**, *81 Cipriani Blvd., 627-8089*, and in San Fernando area **Soong's Great Wall**, 97 *Circular Road, 652-2583.*

Michael's $$$ ★★★

143 Long Circular Road, Maraval, ☎ *(809) 628-0445.*
International cuisine.
Dinner: 6–10:30 p.m., entrees $8–$25.
Michael's offers toothsome Italian food livened with local produce. His version of proscuitto is served with vividly-flavored fresh papaya instead of the more common melon. Pastas are a standout; they're all homemade. Filet mignon, fish and chicken are also served. Decor is modern, chairs are comfortable and hug the back, floors are

polished hardwood. Located in a townhouse in the suburb of Maraval, the service is notably efficient.

Monsoon **$** ★★★

72 Tragarete Road, Port of Spain, ☎ (809) 628-7684.
Indian cuisine.
Lunch: 11 a.m.–4 p.m., entrees $5.
Dinner: 4–10 p.m., entrees $5.

This brisk, but stylish East/West Indian restaurant is probably the most popular in town for curries and the flatbread (*paratha*). Lunch is a fast-paced affair, and very busy; many people take advantage of the take-out service. Complete meals built around shrimp, chicken, and fish include several veggies, lentils and rice. There are great rotis, or dough wrapped around spiced conch or chicken, and fresh squeezed, exotic drinks. The Wednesday night buffets are a good bet for a well-rounded feast in quieter surroundings.

Philip and Fraser's **$$** ★★★

16 Phillips St., Port of Spain, ☎ (809) 623-7632.
International cuisine.
Lunch: 11 a.m.–4 p.m., entrees $8–$12.
Dinner: 4–10 p.m., entrees $8–$20.

All meals are cooked to order at this bastion of new creole cuisine, which translates into smaller, but intensely-flavored dishes. Thankfully, vegetables are very lightly cooked, in the French style, rather than stewed out of all nutrients. Surroundings are tasteful and muted, with plenty of greenery and basketry. There's live jazz on Friday nights. Open Saturdays for dinner only, from 7 to 10 p.m.

Rafters **$$** ★★★

6A Warner Street, Newtown, ☎ (809) 628-9258.
Seafood cuisine.
Lunch: 11:30 a.m.–4 p.m., entrees $6–$21.
Dinner: 4–11 p.m., entrees $6–$21.

Meat and potatoes people and seafood lovers all get their culinary kicks here: On Wednesday, a buffet of fresh local sea creatures is featured, Thursdays, Fridays and Saturdays chefs carve hunks of roast beef and other meats nonstop until it's all gone. In an adjacent lounge snacks and sandwiches are available for folks with more prudent appetites and pocketbooks. The restaurant resides in a lovely old restored dry goods store.

Singho **$$** ★★★

Long Circular Mall, Port of Spain, ☎ (809) 628-2077.
Chinese cuisine.
Lunch: 11:30 a.m.–7 p.m., entrees $5–$7.
Dinner: 7:30–11 p.m., entrees $7–$12.

Solidly good Cantonese food is the star at this tony eatery in the gargantuan Long Circular Mall. Decor features an aquarium, and meals run on the lines of cashew chicken, spareribs in black bean sauce, and curries. Regulars and tourists like to stop in Wednesday nights for the Chinese buffet.

Tiki Village **$$** ★★★

16-18 Cotton Hill, St. Clair, ☎ (809) 622-6441.
Chinese cuisine.
Lunch: 11:30 a.m.–7 p.m., entrees $6–$13.
Dinner: 7:30–9 p.m., entrees $6–$13.

The island's version of Trader Vic's sits atop the plush Kapok Hotel, with a night vista of the glittering city lights; at lunch, Queens Park Savannah is spread out in all its glory. Food is good to average, with a dim sum lunch served from 11 a.m. to 3 p.m. on weekends and holidays. Management thoughtfully provides cards for diners to mark their choices on. The regular menu features Polynesian-style fish, steaks and chicken.

Veni Mange $ ★★★★★

13 Lucknow Street, St. James, ☎ (809) 622-7533.

Latin American cuisine.

Lunch: 11:30 a.m.–2:30 p.m., entrees $8–$10.

Come and eat, say local media star Allyson Hennesey and co-owner and sister Rosemary Hezekiah, in the local lingo. A cross between Julia Child and Oprah Winfrey, Allyson manages to run the best West Indian lunch spot in town and host her own TV talk show. Specialties include tasty crab backs, hollowed out crab shells filled with peppered meat and a spicy mix of peppers and tomatoes. Hearty soups, including pumpkin and callaloo, are also recommended. Open for dinner on Wednesdays 7:30 to 10 p.m., and for drinks on Fridays, from 7 to 10 p.m.

Where to Shop

Fabrics on the island of Trinidad are simply fantastic—a true art in themselves. East Indian silks and cottons come in high-class quality; the best bargains are found in downtown Port-of-Spain on Frederick Street around Independence Square. Even if you don't drink, stock up on local brews such as Angostura Bitters and Old Oak or Vat 19 rum, all which can be bought duty-free and make excellent gifts at Christmas time.

Local artisanry is quite skilled, ranging from fine straw work to cane-inspired creations to miniature steel pans (the large ones, of course are too bulky to ship home, but if you must, shopkeepers will have some interesting suggestions how to lug them home). Island-designed fashions are spectacular at **The Village**, near the Hotel Normandie, and you can find a top-class gallery, **Art Creators**, just around the corner on St. Ann's Road. The latest designs in batik work and island-inspired jewelry can be picked up at **The Cotton House** on Bacolet and Windward Roads. Calypso records are also a favorite buy here. The assistants at **Rhyner's Record Shop** on Prince Street will help you find the latest releases; ask to see some of the old classics. Soca music is also a great buy; many a traveler who just bought albums blindly has come away with great party music, only regretting he hadn't bought more at the time. **Metronome**, in Port-of-Spain, on Western Main Road, is also a good source for music.

Trinidad Directory

BUSINESS HOURS

Shops open Monday–Thursday 8 a.m.–4 p.m., Friday 8 a.m.–6 p.m. and Saturday 8 a.m.–noon. Banks open Monday–Thursday 9 a.m.–2 p.m. and Friday 9 a.m.–noon and 3–5 p.m.

CLIMATE

Trinidad has a tropical climate whose dry season runs from January to June, with a wet season the rest of the year. Temperatures are uniformly high year-round. In Port-of-Spain, average temperature in January is 78 degrees F, in July 79 degrees F. Annual rainfall is around 60 inches.

DOCUMENTS

U.S. and Canadian citizens, as well as those of the United Kingdom, may enter the country with a valid passport if they only plan to stay less than two months. An ongoing or return ticket is also required. An immigration card is handed to you upon arrival (or on the plane) which must be filled out and handed in as you depart. Do not lose it. A visa is required for longer stays. Long delays in clearing customs have often been reported. Visitors may bring in 200 cigarettes or 50 cigars, plus one quart of "spirits." To facilitate matters, pack as lightly and unostentatiously as possible.

ELECTRICITY

Current runs 110 or 220 volts, AC 60 cycles. Always inquire of your hotel when you are making reservations what kind of transformer or adapter you will need.

GETTING AROUND

Port-of-Spain is full of crazy drivers who taunt each other into dangerous maneuvers. Do your best to avoid driving yourself around the city, or at least downtown; better conditions are available in the countryside. You can explore the northern coast by taxi, but a car is more feasible.

Taxis run on fixed rates according to the destination. There is a set route that they follow and will drop off passengers anywhere along that route. There are minibuses as well as regular sedans. Before getting in the car, determine whether you are entering a route taxi or a private one, which will take you anywhere. Even though fares are fixed, drivers are not necessarily honest, and unless you're knowledgeable, expect to be stiffed a few dollars.

Private taxis do not pick up any other passengers and they take you straight to your destination. Take one for longer trips or destinations not on the regular route. Rates are usually not observed during Carnival, when anything goes since the demand is so high. Adjust and go with the flow or you will drive yourself crazy arguing.

Buses are an inexpensive way to get around the island, but they are often too crowded and dilapidated for comfort. Buses depart from the **South Quay Bus Terminal**. Cars can be rented from several agencies including **Auto Rentals** ☎ *(809) 675-2258* and cabs are available from **Bachhus Taxi Service** ☎ *(809) 622-5588*. Roads are fairly well-paved but turn narrow and tortuous in the backcountry. During the rainy season they may be dangerously washed out. Forget driving into downtown Port-of-Spain during rush hour—you'll never get out. Remember that all driving is on the left.

LANGUAGE

The official language is English, spiced with a rich slew of local idioms. There is also some facility in Chinese, Hindi, Spanish and French, due to the large amount of immigrants.

MEDICAL EMERGENCIES

There are several adequate hospitals in Port-of-Spain. Among them are the **Tobago Country Hospital** on Fort Street in Scarborough ☎ *(809) 639-2551;* and **Port-of-Spain General Hospital** on Charlotte Street ☎ *(809) 625-7869.* Ask your hotel to suggest the nearest pharmacy, but bring your own prescription medicine (an extra dose) in case you lose your luggage. Medicine made in the U.S. is far superior to any you could buy in the islands. Severe medical emergencies should be flown to San Juan or back home stateside.

MONEY

The Trinidadian dollar (written as TT$) has been devalued twice in the past few years. You can exchange money in the major hotels in Port-of-Spain, which offer rates comparable to banks. Most shops, hotels and restaurants will accept American dollars if you run short of local money, but they would prefer their own currency.

TELEPHONE

The area code for the two islands is *809*. Telegraphs, telefax, teletype, and telex, can be sent through the textel office at *1 Edward St., Port-of-Spain;* ☎ *(809) 625-4431*. Cables can be sent from the Tourism office and major hotels. To place an intra-island call, dial the local seven-digit number. To reach the U.S., dial 1, the area code, then the local number.

TIME

Atlantic Standard Time.

TIPPING AND TAXES

Restaurants add a 15 percent Value Added Tax (called VAT). Many restaurants add an additional 10–15 percent service charge; check your bill carefully. If they don't, do add your own tip, if you find the service satisfactory.

TOURIST INFORMATION

The **Trinidad & Tobago Tourism Development Authority** is located locally at *134-138 Frederick Street, Port-of-Spain;* ☎ *(809) 623-1932.* Stop by for brochures, maps, and advice and assistance in obtaining lodging, especially bed and breakfast situations. In the U.S. call ☎ *(800) 232-0082.*

WHEN TO GO

New Year's Day is January 1. Good Friday and Easter Monday are both holidays. Whit Monday is June 7. Corpus Christi is June 18. Labor Day is June 19. Emancipation Day is August 1. Independence Day is August 31. Republic Day is September 24. Christmas Day is December 25. Boxing Day is December 26.

Fielding's Choice:

Don't miss Divali, the Hindu Festival of Lights, usually celebrated in October. The beauty of pan music is epitomized by the world steel band festivals. The festival, called Pan Is Beautiful, is held in the last week of October. Check with the tourist board for exact dates.

TRINIDAD RESTAURANTS	PHONE	ENTREE	CR. CARDS
Port of Spain			
Chinese			
★★★ **Hong Kong City**	(809) 622-3949	$8–$20	A, DC, MC, V
★★★ **Singho**	(809) 628-2077	$5–$12	A, MC, V
★★★ **Tiki Village**	(809) 622-6441	$6–$13	A, DC, MC, V
Indian			
★★★ **Monsoon**	(809) 628-7684	$5–$5	A, DC, MC, V
International			
★★★ **Michael's**	(809) 628-0445	$8–$25••	A, MC, V
★★★ **Philip and Fraser's**	(809) 623-7632	$8–$20	A, MC, V
Latin American			
★★★★★ **Veni Mange**	(809) 622-7533	$8–$10•	None
★★★ **Breakfast Shed**	(809) 627-2337	$5–$7•	None
★★★ **Cafe Savannah**	(809) 622-6441	$8–$17	A, DC, MC, V
★★★ **Chaconia Inn**	(809) 628-8603	$12–$19	A, DC, MC, V
Seafood			
★★★ **Rafters**	(809) 628-9258	$6–$21	A, DC, MC, V
Note: • Lunch Only			
•• Dinner Only			

YUCATAN PENINSULA

Watersports of all types are readily available on the Yucatan Peninsula.

Until the 1960s, the Mexican Caribbean was a relatively undeveloped part of the world where people made their living by fishing or making hammocks, slippers, and rope from the henequen plant. Then the Mexican government (with the help of a computer) realized that the humble people of the Yucatan Peninsula were sitting right on top of what just might—with a little help from developers—turn out to be one of the world's most impressive playgrounds for the well-heeled tourists of the U.S. and Europe. So the pristine beaches were turned into hotel zones, cruise ships started making stops, divers started telling their friends that it didn't get much better than this, and—voila!—a few years later, the Mexican Caribbean was rivaling Acapulco as the country's tropical beachside hotspot. The rest, as they say, is history.

Bird's Eye View

The Yucatan Peninsula includes the states of Yucatan, Campeche and Quintana Roo, situated in southeast Mexico and bordered by the Caribbean Sea on the east, the Gulf of Mexico on the west, and Central America (Belize and Guatemala) on the south. Cancun, on the peninsula's northeast tip, and the island of Cozumel, south of Cancun and ten miles offshore, are the best-known resort areas, studded with high-class hotels and scads of tourists—the latter at a peak during the "on" season, which runs from late fall through March or April. Beaches are the main attraction, but the area is also rich in natural lagoons, sheltered bays, and coral reefs that make it a divers' paradise.

Playa del Carmen, approximately 40 miles south of Cancun and across from the island of Cozumel, is also in the process of developing into a major resort area, and is conveniently located partway between Cancun and Tulum. Ferry service connects Playa (as the locals refer to Playa del Carmen) to Cozumel, providing the final link between Playa and all major tourist sites, both coastal and inland.

The five-mile-long Isla Mujeres, located four miles off the coast, can be reached from both Cancun and Cozumel by boat or ferry, and offers lots of opportunities for exploring, as well as a plethora of premiere dive sites—including El Garron Reef—and incredibly gorgeous beaches. There are hotels on the island, but many prefer to visit Isla Mujeres as a day excursion.

Merida, capital of the state of Yucatan, is inland from the sea, but nearer to major archaeological sites such as Chichen Itza and Uxmal. It gets its own share of tourists, many of them on one- or two-day excursions from the resort cities, or as part of cruise ship shore excursions.

History

Before the Yucatan Peninsula was famous for its beaches, it was known as the land of the Maya, a people that lived in the region for approximately 1500 years, from the first century A.D. until the Spanish conquered Mexico in the early 16th century. By then, many of the Mayan cities had been abandoned, and others were in severe decline. What happened to the Mayan civilizations remains a mystery, but there are plenty of theories, and scientists continue to try and unlock the secrets of the magnificent temples and other buildings left standing—some still completely engulfed by the tropical jungle. The Spanish found that the Yucatan had little to offer in the way of riches, but small populations of people continued to live there, growing sugar

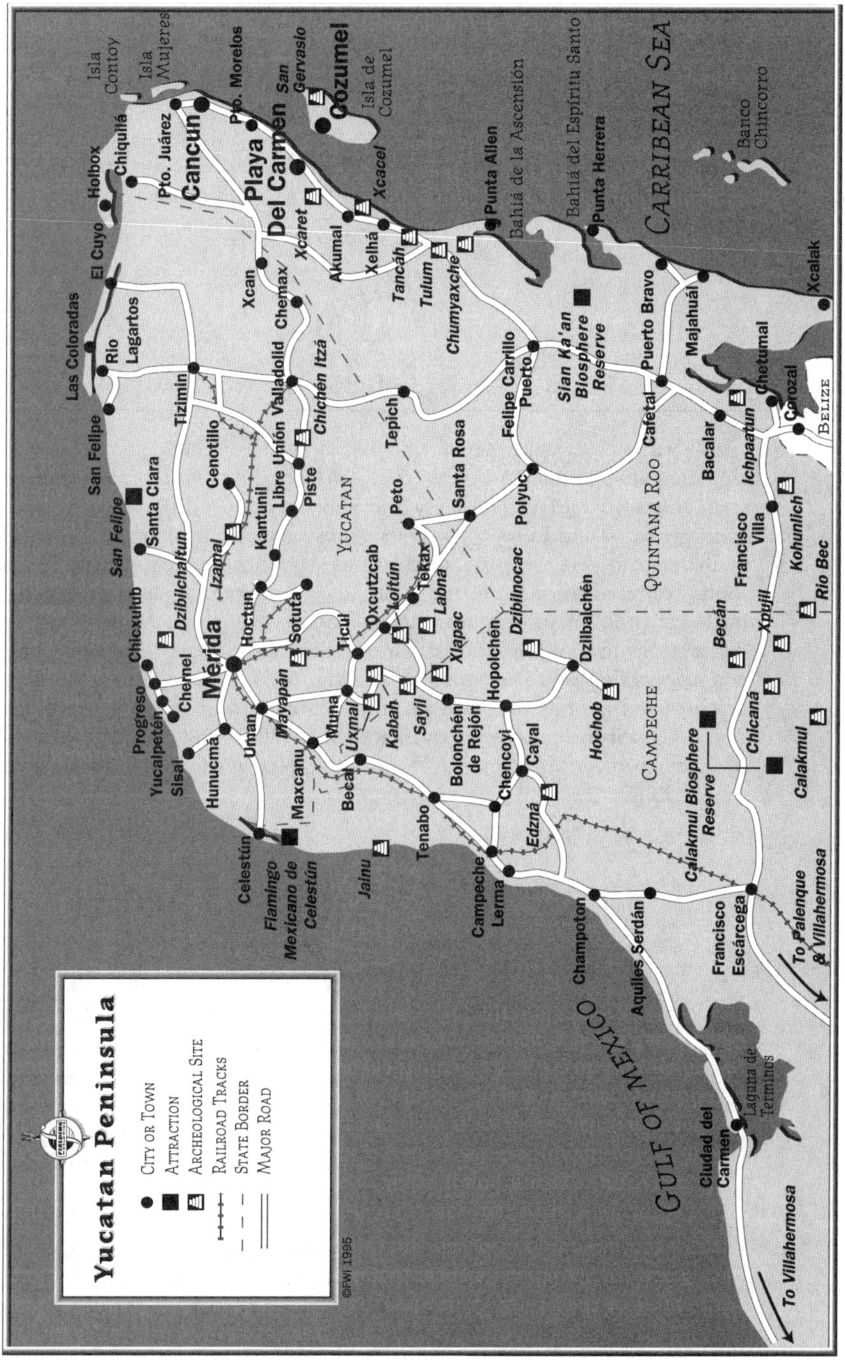
Yucatan Peninsula
City or Town
Attraction
Archeological Site
Railroad Tracks
State Border
Major Road
©FWI 1995
Gulf of Mexico
Carribean Sea
Yucatan
Quintana Roo
Campeche
Belize
Isla Contoy
Isla Mujeres
Isla de Cozumel
Cozumel
San Gervasio
Cancun
Pto. Juárez
Pto. Morelos
Playa Del Carmen
Chiquilá
Holbox
El Cuyo
Las Coloradas
Rio Lagartos
San Felipe
Xcaret
Xcacel
Akumal
Xelhá
Tancáh
Tulum
Chumyaxche
Punta Allen
Bahiá de la Ascensión
Bahiá del Espíritu Santo
Punta Herrera
Banco Chincorro
Xcan
Chemax
Valladolid
Chichén Itzá
Tizimín
Cenotillo
Santa Clara
Dzibilchaltun
Izamal
Kantunil
Libre Unión
Piste
Tepich
Peto
Santa Rosa
Felipe Carrillo Puerto
Sian Ka'an Biosphere Reserve
Puerto Bravo
Majahual
Xcalak
Chetumal
Corozal
Cafetal
Bacalar
Ichpaatun
Kohunlich
Francisco Villa
Rio Bec
Xpujil
Becán
Chicaná
Calakmul
Calakmul Biosphere Reserve
Polyuc
Dzibilnocac
Dzilbalchén
Hochob
Hopolchén
Xlapac
Labná
Tekax
Oxcutzcab
Loltún
Ticul
Sotuta
Hoctun
Mérida
Chicxulub
Progreso
Chelem
Chuburná
Yucalpetén
Sisal
Hunucmá
Uman
Mayapán
Muna
Uxmal
Kabah
Sayil
Bolonchén de Rejón
Chencoyi
Cayal
Edzná
Becal
Maxcanu
Tenabo
Celestún
Flamingo Mexicano de Celestún
Jaina
Campeche
Lerma
Champoton
Aquiles Serdán
Francisco Escárcega
To Palenque & Villahermosa
Laguna de Términos
Ciudad del Carmen
To Villahermosa

cane and raising cattle until Mexico freed itself from Spain's domination in the early 1800s.

By the middle of the 19th century, henequen, a relative of the agave plant, became an important cash crop, and was used to make rope, slippers, bags, hammocks and many other products. Later, roads (Mexico 186 and 180) were built to connect the peninsula to the rest of Mexico, and the newly "found" area began to grow, a process that ended with the marketing of Cancun and Cozumel as playgrounds for the rich and famous.

People

It's hard to classify the people who live and work on the Mexican Caribbean. The native population of the Yucatan Peninsula consists mostly of descendents of the Maya (Indians) and people who are the result of mixed ancestry (Maya and European). Today, most of the Indians are concentrated in the state of Yucatan, but populations of indigenous peoples are to be found scattered throughout the peninsula. A variety of dialects are spoken, but—except in the most remote areas—Indians can generally speak and understand Spanish. In the tourist zones, it is relatively easy to find someone who speaks English. The people of the Yucatan Peninsula are known to be gracious and friendly, but you are still cautioned to be on your toes if you don't speak Spanish; there are those few who will not pass up an opportunity to take advantage of a "gringo" who is completely clueless about financial transactions.

Beaches

All of the beaches on the Mexican Caribbean are gorgeous, some with fine white sand and crystal-clear, turquoise waters, others with a rocky shore and crashing surf. (In contrast, the beaches on the Gulf of Mexico side of the peninsula are quite unimpressive.) Overcrowding is one of the biggest problems, especially in the hotel zones, and some hotels advertise that their beaches are private in order to make them seem less crowded and more exclusive. In fact, all beaches are public, so a "private" beach is no guarantee that you won't be inundated with other beach-goers. Vendors add to the confusion at popular beaches, loudly hawking their wares and pestering tourists to buy. On many beaches, sand flies are as pesky as the vendors, so you may have to add a little insect repellent on top of that sunscreen.

Popular beaches in Cancun include **Playa Chac-Mool**, a lovely beach that's not associated with a hotel; and **Playa Delfines**, which is slightly off the beaten

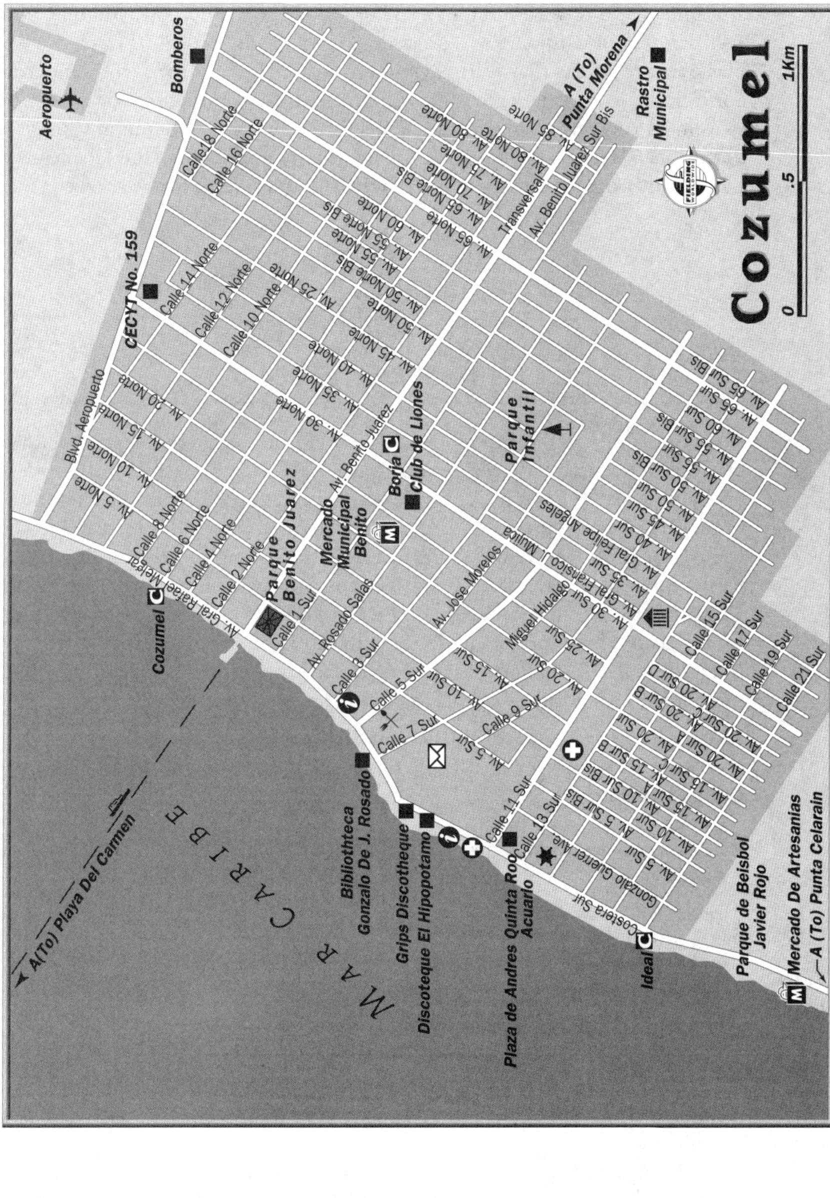
Cozumel
0
.5
1Km
Aeropuerto
Bomberos
CECYT No. 159
Blvd. Aeropuerto
A (To) Punta Morena
Rastro Municipal
Transversal
Av. Benito Juarez Sur Bis
Parque Benito Juarez
Mercado Municipal Benito
Borja
Club de Liones
Parque Infantil
Av. Benito Juarez
Av. Rosado Salas
Av. Jose Morelos
Miguel Hidalgo
Av. Gral Francisco J. Mujica
Av. Gral Felipe Angeles
Av. Gral Rafael Melgar
Cozumel
Bibliotheca Gonzalo De J. Rosado
Grips Discotheque
Discoteque El Hipopotamo
Plaza de Andres Quinta Roo
Acuario
Gonzalo Guerrer Ave
Costera Sur
Ideal
Parque de Beisbol Javier Rojo
Mercado De Artesanias
A (To) Punta Celarain
A(To) Playa Del Carmen
MAR CARIBE
Calle 18 Norte
Calle 16 Norte
Calle 14 Norte
Calle 12 Norte
Calle 10 Norte
Calle 8 Norte
Calle 6 Norte
Calle 4 Norte
Calle 2 Norte
Calle 1 Sur
Calle 3 Sur
Calle 5 Sur
Calle 7 Sur
Calle 9 Sur
Calle 11 Sur
Calle 13 Sur
Calle 15 Sur
Calle 17 Sur
Calle 19 Sur
Calle 21 Sur
Av. 5 Norte
Av. 10 Norte
Av. 15 Norte
Av. 20 Norte
Av. 25 Norte
Av. 30 Norte
Av. 35 Norte
Av. 40 Norte
Av. 45 Norte
Av. 50 Norte
Av. 50 Norte Bis
Av. 55 Norte
Av. 55 Norte Bis
Av. 60 Norte
Av. 60 Norte Bis
Av. 65 Norte
Av. 65 Norte Bis
Av. 70 Norte
Av. 75 Norte
Av. 80 Norte
Av. 85 Norte
Av. 5 Sur
Av. 10 Sur
Av. 15 Sur
Av. 20 Sur
Av. 25 Sur
Av. 30 Sur
Av. 35 Sur
Av. 40 Sur
Av. 45 Sur
Av. 50 Sur
Av. 50 Sur Bis
Av. 55 Sur
Av. 55 Sur Bis
Av. 60 Sur
Av. 65 Sur
Av. 65 Sur Bis
Av. 5 Sur Bis
Av. 10 Sur Bis
Av. 15 Sur A
Av. 15 Sur B
Av. 15 Sur C
Av. 20 Sur A
Av. 20 Sur B
Av. 20 Sur C
Av. 20 Sur D

path south of the Hotel Zone. In Cozumel, try **Playa San Francisco**, **Playa Chen Rio**, or the beach at **Palancar National Park**. On Isla Mujeres, **Playa Norte** has a generous stretch of beach and calm waters for swimming.

Not all of the Caribbean waters are as calm as they may look from shore, and unless you're swimming in a bay or along the inner coast, you may be at risk from strong undertows or large, hard-hitting waves. (Watch for the black and red flags that warn swimmers away.) Because of these dangerous conditions, calm, sheltered lagoons are often the destination of choice for swimmers and divers. In Cancun, **Nichupte Lagoon** beckons, and in Cozumel, **Chancanaab Bay** is a favorite spot for swimming and diving (the Chancanaab Lagoon is protected by the government and swimming is not allowed).

What Else to See

After you've seen all the ruins and done all the watersports, you could be overwhelmed with a "been there, done that" attitude—except that you'll probably want to do it all again. If you have your fill of the major stuff, try venturing inland into some of the smaller towns to see the real Mexico. Many places on the peninsula have their own charming celebrations, usually with a historical or religious bent (Tizimin, in Yucatan, holds the Fair of the Three Kings in early January; the first week of May, the Ceremony of the Holy Incense in Kohunlich, Quintana Roo, includes a reenactment of sacred Mayan rituals). There are also lots of lesser-known ruins scattered throughout the peninsula along the Maya Route, so get a map and go exploring.

City Celebrations

Cancun

Cancun Jazz Festival ★★★

Cancun.

This May celebration brings musicians of international renown to the resort town, and lots of festivities take place in conjunction with the great music.

Carnaval ★★★

Cancun.

It's Mardi Gras-cum-Cancun in this annual festival held on the three days before Ash Wednesday. Everything you'd expect from a Mardi Gras-style bash happens here, from parades to masked balls to dancing in the streets in authentic regional costumes. Hotels book up fast, so reserve early.

Cozumel

Carnaval ★★★

Cozumel.

There's a party going on in many parts of Mexico in conjunction with Carnaval, which happens on the three days before Ash Wednesday. Lots of colorful costumes, parades and dances mark the celebration in Cozumel.

Historical Sites

Cancun

Chichen Itza ★★★★★

125 miles east of Cancun, Merida.
Hours Open: 8 a.m.–5 p.m.

Not everyone is intrigued by ancient ruins, but Chichen Itza is the most famous Maya archaeological site on the Yucatan Peninsula—and maybe in the world. The nearly four-square-mile area encompasses hundreds of buildings, some still buried in the jungle or in a state of partial restoration. About 30 have been completely restored, and they are stunning. Stop at the visitors center before you explore the ruins; films and pamphlets will set the stage and explain the historical context of the buildings. And speaking of that stage, there's an impressive sound and light show presented nightly that bathes the ruins in eerie light and recounts the legends of the ancient inhabitants. Check the schedule to be sure you're there for the English-speaking version. There are charges for parking, admission, the sound and light show and for use of a video camera—though admission is free to all on Sundays. Guided tours are very big here, so you won't have any trouble arranging one. Call Mayaland Resorts *(☎ (800) 235-4079)* to arrange tours or lodging—which has been strategically placed in the center of Chichen Itza. If you're going on your own, try to get there early in the morning, wear sturdy shoes and bring water.

Teatro Peon Contreras ★★

Calle 60, Merida.

Built in the early 20th century, this ornate Italianate-style theater still hosts various performances. It's also the site of Merida's tourist information center, so you can check out what else there is to see in the area after you tour the theater.

Tulum ★★★

Merida.

Although it's a bit of a drive (more than 70 miles from Cancun), it's easy to snag a guided tour (from a cruise ship or otherwise) to Tulum, one of the area's best-known archaeological sites. It sits on the coast in what is probably the most stunning setting of any of the ancient Maya ruins. There are dozens of buildings that are quite well preserved, the largest of which is the Castle (El Castillo), perched above the limestone cliffs.

Uxmal ★★★★

50 miles south of Merida.
Hours Open: 8 a.m.–5 p.m.

The ruins at Uxmal are almost as famous as those of Chichen Itza, and are known for the beauty of the restored buildings. Highlights include the House of the Governor, the single largest structure in the Maya Empire, made up of a mosaic facade containing more than 25,000 hand-cut stones; and the Pyramid of the Magician, supposedly constructed by a mystical dwarf who hatched out of an egg. Like the ruins at Chichen Itza, Uxmal hosts a light and sound show every night that is designed to conjure up an ancient ambience of myth and magic. There is a charge for parking, admission, the sound and light show and for the use of a video camera—but come on Sunday, when it's free to all.

Cozumel

Balancanche Caves ★★★

three miles east of Chichen Itza.

Explore what is believed to be an ancient underground worship site of the Maya. The caves are lighted for convenience, but there's some rough going (and some crawling) required to get through them, so you may want to pass if that "closed-in" feeling gives you the creeps. Inside are various carved artifacts from the Maya era, probably used in religious ceremonies. Wear sturdy shoes and expect to get dirty.

Celarain Lighthouse ★★★

South end of Cozumel Island, Cozumel.

You'll have to drive several miles on a dirt road to the southern tip of the island (a four-wheel drive vehicle is recommended), but the views for the top of the lighthouse are grand—so bring your camera.

San Gervasio Ruins ★★★

11 miles east of San Miguel on trans-island hwy., Cozumel.

San Gervasio isn't on par with Chichen Itza, but it's one of the best-preserved archaeological sites on the island. Several small shrines and temples honoring the Maya goddess of fertility and childbirth, Ixchel, date from more than 1000 years ago. Guided tours are available. There's an admission charge plus a road access fee and an extra charge for using a video camera. Closed on holidays.

Museums and Exhibits

Cancun

CEDAM Museum ★★

Puerto Aventuras Resort, Playa del Carmen.

This small museum near Cancun salutes the members and finds of the Club de Exploraciones y Deportes Acuaticos de Mexico—in other words, local divers. Treasures retrieved from sunken ships, diving gear and other interesting exhibits are on display.

Museo Regional de Antropologia e Historia ★★

Paseo Montejo y Calle 43, Centro, Merida.

Maya art recovered from the ruins at Chichen Itza is on display at this regional museum, which focuses on gold and jade artifacts, stone carvings and pottery. The historic home that houses the museum is also of interest. Admission charged.

Cozumel

Museum of the Island of Cozumel ★★

Ave. Rafael Melgar, San Miguel.

Housed in a turn-of-the-century hotel building, this two-story museum chronicles the anthropological, cultural and natural history of the island of Cozumel. Exhibits show local flora and fauna, sea creatures and history from the Maya civilization to present day. Guided tours are available. Admission charged.

Parks and Gardens

Cancun

Centerario Zoo ★★

Along Ave. Itzaes from Calle 95, Merida.

This modest zoo provides a look at animals native to the Yucatan Peninsula as well as displays of more exotic animals and birds. The kids will particularly like the miniature train ride.

Cozumel

Chankanaab Lagoon & Botanical Gardens ★★★

six miles south of San Miguel, Cozumel.

You can't go swimming or diving in the saltwater lagoon, which is a protected habitat, but the diving is great offshore, where there's a sunken ship to explore. The Botanical Garden is wonderful, containing more than 300 kinds of tropical plants and trees from 22 countries around the world. Wander on the trail that leads into the botanical "jungle," then stop at the small museum or beachside restaurant for refreshments.

Palancar National Park ★★★★

south end of Cozumel Island, Cozumel.

The main attraction here is the Palancar Reef, a divers' paradise and the second-longest reef in the world. Marked by stunning coral formations, underwater caves and brightly colored fish, the reef is perfect for both snorkeling and scuba diving, which can be arranged as a shore excursion from a cruise ship or from your hotel. Non-divers can lounge on the excellent beach. From May to September, ask about guided nighttime excursions to watch sea turtles lay their eggs on the island's eastern shore.

Rio Lagartos National Park ★★★

End of Mexico 295 North.

Well off the beaten path, this national park, which includes more than 100,000 acres of protected habitat, sits in the middle of the Yucatan's northern coast. Home of one of Mexico's largest flamingo sanctuaries, the park is a birder's paradise, hosting many other species besides the big pink birds, which breed here from April into June.

Sian Ka'an Biosphere Reserve ★★★

South of Tulum, East of Mexico 307.

In 1986, the Mexican government set aside more than a million acres of native rainforest to form this preserve, which also includes offshore coral reefs and other precious habitat. There are more than 1000 varieties of plants here, many native animal species, birds and preserved archaeological sites. Much of the area is off-limits to tourists, but the outer buffer zone is accessible to those who want to explore the jungle habitat eihter on foot or by boat. Call for information and to arrange a guided tour—and bring insect repellent!

Theme/Amusement Parks

Cancun

Xcaret ★★★

35 miles south of Cancun.

Historical sites and natural wonders combine here to form the Yucatan's first-ever "eco-archaeological" theme park, although it's tame by Disney standards. There are real Maya ruins here, augmented by reproductions of other ruins, lagoons, dolphin ponds, dive sites, underground rivers, botanical gardens, a large aviary, horseback riding and other diversions. Facilities include picnic areas, restaurants, a visitor center, museum and changing rooms. Unlike Disneyland, most of this scenery is the real thing. Admission charged.

Sports

Watersports reign supreme in the Mexican Caribbean, but there are plenty of other recreational opportunities to keep you busy. Cancun boasts the 18-hole championship **Pok-Ta-Pok** golf course *(☎ (98) 830871)*, designed by Robert Trent Jones and situated in a stunning setting. Watch out for the Maya ruins, a definite hazard on this course! Tennis is always an option at the big resort hotels, which will also arrange horseback riding, or you can arrange your own ride by calling ☎ *(98) 840861.* In the way of spectator sports, jai ali is played every evening at the fronton at Km. 4.5 *(☎ (98) 839304)*, and bullfights (cruel but popular nonetheless) take place at the bull ring in Cancun City on Wednesday afternoons during the winter.

The island of Cozumel is almost exclusively a watersports resort, with tennis available at major hotels.

Watersports

Swimming, snorkeling, scuba diving, waterskiing, boating, parasailing, windsurfing and fishing await you at almost any port in the Mexican Caribbean. The most highly touted watersport is diving, and dive companies abound, all competing for the millions of tourist dollars that flow into Mexico each year. Hotels are usually set up to provide both diving instruction and diving excursions, but they may come at a premium. An independent dive shop may save you money, so ask around. In Cancun, call **Scuba Cancun** *(☎ (98) 831011);* in Cozumel, try **Chino's Scuba Shop** *(☎ 987-24487).*

Fishing can be arranged at the Cancun Yacht Club or the Pok-Ta-Pok Marina in Cancun, and in the harbor at San Miguel in Cozumel. Marlin, swordfish, sailfish, wahoo, barracuda, and tuna are all found in local waters, and in May, the billfish migration is celebrated with an International Billfish Tournament held in Cozumel. If you want to go shark fishing, it's best in **Laguna Yalahau**, at the northern tip of Quintana Roo. Get a boat in Chiquila, and head out for a day of trying to outsmart those sneaky denizens of the deep. Piers are obvious at all the large tourist areas, and offer boat trips to various local destinations. Get aboard on a scheduled fishing trip, or rent a boat and head out on your own.

Windsurfing and parasailing sites are generally clustered around the major tourist areas, and operators provide equipment and instruction. (There's a windsurfing school on **Playa Tortugas** in Cancun, ☎ *98-842023*). Waterskiing is excellent on the **Nichupte Lagoon** in Cancun, and there are various places to rent boats and other equipment everywhere along the Mexican Caribbean. Your hotel should be able to provide information on all nearby watersports, but the small hassle of arranging your watersports itinerary yourself can almost always save you money.

Where to Eat

Fielding's Highest Rated Restaurants on the Yucatan Peninsula

★★★★	Donatello	$5–$25
★★★★	La Joya	$1–$9
★★★★	Mirage	$1–$9
★★★	Acuario	$1–$9
★★★	Blue Bayou	$15–$35
★★★	Bogart's	$1–$9
★★★	Lorenzillo''s	$1–$9

Fielding's Special Restaurants on the Yucatan Peninsula

★★★★	Donatello	$5–$25
★★★★	La Joya	$1–$9
★★★	Bogart's	$1–$9

Almost every large, tourist-oriented hotel on the Yucatan Peninsula has at least one (usually expensive) restaurant, and many have several, so you can opt to eat at a hotel's dining room, or go restaurant hopping until you find a restaurant that appeals to you. No longer the secluded, exotic place it once was, the peninsula now caters to just about any taste, with its own pizza parlors, Mediterranean-style eateries, chain restaurants, and Americanized Mexican dishes. Middle Eastern cuisine is also to be found here, largely due to the influx of Lebanese and other Middle Easterners in recent years. There are still a few places to get authentic local cuisine, but you may have to get off the beaten path to find regional food that hasn't been dressed up to suit the American palate.

Cozumel

Acuario $ ★★★

Beach Road, ☎ (987) 21097.

Seafood cuisine.

This casual seafood restaurant has its own aquarium so that you can watch relatives of your meal swim by as you eat. Moderately priced seafood and a lively bar. The beach club is open from 10:00 to 6:00, offering swimming, sunning and dining. Open for lunch and dinner.

Carlos 'n Charlie's $ ★★

Ocean Promenade, Ave. Rafael, ☎ (987) 20191.

American cuisine.

The Mexico City chain strikes again. Dining (Mexican and American fare) is always a party here, with a happening bar and lots of decent seafood. No air conditioning—but have a few drinks and you may not notice. Open for lunch and dinner.

Donatello $ ★★★★

Ave. Melgar Sur 131, ☎ (987) 22586.
Italian cuisine.
This is one of the best restaurants on Cozumel, and it's all dressed up in Renaissance-style ambience—but you don't have to dress up. In fact, Donatello gives a nod to families with a children's menu and an attractive patio where you can corner the junior-sized spaghetti-flingers among you. This restaurant is extremely popular, which means you'd better make reservations during the high season.

Karen's Pizza and Grill $ ★★

Ave. 5 Norte.
Italian cuisine.
Pizza is the main thing here, and it's done well and delivered with a smile. Best of all, nearly everything on the menu is extremely affordable—so go for those extra toppings.

La Yucatequita $ ★★

9 C Sur y 10 Ave. Sur.
Local cuisine.
One of the best places in town to get real Maya food, La Yucatequita is a favorite for local cuisine at reasonable prices. Open only for dinner.

The Sports Page $ ★★

Calle 2 Norte 7 Ave. 5.
American cuisine.
When you get a hankering for a burger and fries—or just want to hang out and watch sports on satellite TV—come to this happening spot, which also caters to Americans with currency exchange. Open for breakfast, lunch and dinner.

Cancun

Bellini's New York Deli $ ★

Plaza Caracol Mall, 2nd level, ☎ (98) 830459.
Mexican cuisine.
It's New York-cum Mexico in this casual deli where Americans looking for a taste of home can order sandwiches and salads, or just hang out at the bar. There's no air conditioning, so dress lightly. Open for breakfast, lunch and dinner.

Blue Bayou $ ★★★

Blvd. Kukulcan Km 10.5, ☎ (98) 830044.
Cajun cuisine.
You're back on the bayou at this snappy Cajun restaurant located just off the lobby in the Hyatt Cancun Caribe. Expect all your spicy favorites, a lively bar scene and lots of mellow jazz. Very cool, but a bit pricey.

Bogart's $ ★★★

On the beach at Punta Cancun, ☎ (98) 831133.
Middle Eastern cuisine.
You'll think you've died and gone to Morocco at this upbeat spot. Most of the Middle Eastern cuisine is prepared at your table, and the music and ambience set an exotic mood. Open for dinner only.

Carlos'n Charlie's $ ★★

Km 5.5 at the lagoon, ☎ (98) 830846.
American cuisine.
Carlos and Charlie have an incongruous mix here, with American and Mexican specialties served in a party atmosphere. The restaurant, situated overlooking a marina, is part of a chain originating in Mexico City and features a decent variety of seafood at moderate prices. Open for lunch and dinner.

La Joya $ ★★★★

Blvd. Kukulcan Km 15, ☎ (98) 832900.

Mexican cuisine.

"Nouvelle" is the byword here, and Mexican cuisine goes upscale and sophisticated to suit the traveling gourmet. Evidence of the food-as-art fad lingers (at least until you eat it) on every plate, and you can expect to pay a pretty penny for dinner, but it will probably be worth it. Dress up, take advantage of the valet parking, and you'll soon be feeling like you're at some chi-chi L.A. hotspot.

Lorenzillo's $ ★★★

Hotel Zone, Km 10.5, ☎ (98) 831254.

Mexican cuisine.

Look out over the lagoon as you dine on regional specialties at Lorenzillo's, which does an especially good job with seafood. Open for lunch and dinner.

Los Huaraches $ ★★

Ave. Uxnal y Yaxchilian.

Mexican cuisine.

Located in Cancun City, this casual restaurant gives you an inexpensive taste of regional food and offers specials on empanadas and other local fare. Open for lunch and dinner.

Mikado $ ★★

Blvd. Kukulcan Km 16, ☎ (98) 852000.

Japanese cuisine.

This casual restaurant—a Japanese steakhouse that bears little or no resemblance to anything Mexican in either decor or cuisine—offers some good values, especially if you go for the early-bird specials. Open for dinner only.

Mirage $ ★★★★

Blvd. Kukulcan Km 15.5, ☎ (98) 851000.

Upscale cuisine.

One of the fanciest restaurants in Cancun—and one of four restaurants at the Fiesta Americana Condesa—the Mirage is open for dinner only, serving such upscale dishes as smoked salmon and other refined choices. The view is great, the surroundings sophisticated, the food excellent and the prices high.

Piemonte Pizzeria $ ★★

Ave. Yaxchilan 52.

Italian cuisine.

Pizza and other Italian specialties are served in this modest restaurant in Cancun City. Good value. Open for lunch and dinner.

Playa del Carmen

Playa Caribe $ ★★

Ave. 5.

Seafood cuisine.

If you're hanging out at the Plaza, stop in at this nearby casual spot for cheap eats and friendly service. Seafood is a specialty.

Where to Shop

Cancun

Cancun is a duty-free zone packed with tourists, so you probably have a good idea of what the shopping is all about: everything from the "My-mom-went-to-Cancun-and-all-I-got-was-this-lousy-T-shirt!" souvenirs to pricey jewelry and Mexican crafts. There are big shopping malls located in the Hotel Zone and large areas of shops in Cancun City *(Plaza Canzun, on Avenida Tulum)*, but if you're smart, you'll head for the open-air market *(Ave. Tulum 23)*, where you can have a ball dickering over the price on absolutely everything. There are especially good values to be had on jewelry, leather, locally-made clothing and other crafts, so don't chicken out—bargain!

If you take an excursion to Merida, visit the huge downtown market district or the government-run crafts market *(Mercado de Artesanias)*. Both of these areas can be crowded, and the vendors can be pushy and not always honest about what you're getting, so being able to speak (and understand) Spanish and knowing exactly what you're looking for is helpful. Be selective, look around, and comparison shop for the best deals. The most popular items for sale in Merida are hammocks, silver jewelry, sandals, leather goods and locally made clothing.

Cozumel

The main street in San Miguel—**Ave. Rafael Melgar**—is where most of the shops are situated on Cozumel. Although they are not as hoity-toity as the Hotel Zone shops in Cancun, shops along the Malecon are aimed at getting tourists to spend money on everything from junk souvenirs to jewelry and designer clothing. Get off the avenue even a block or two and you'll get better prices. No matter where you shop, remember that bargaining is a way of life in Mexico, so don't pay the asking price.

Yucatan Directory

BUSINESS HOURS

Stores open Monday–Saturday 10 a.m.–7 p.m.; many in the tourist areas are also open later in the evening and on Sunday. Banks are open weekdays 9 a.m.–1:30 p.m. and generally exchange foreign currency only from 10:30 a.m.–12:30 p.m.

CLIMATE

The Yucatan Peninsula is dry compared to the eastern Caribbean, but there's still lots of heat and humidity and the temperature consistently hovers at around 80 degrees F., peaking in the summer months at an average of 82 or 83, and dipping in the winter to the mid-70s. Rainfall is at its peak (an average of eight or so inches at Cancun) in the summer and early fall (the "off" season in the Caribbean), which means it's muggier than usual then. Hurricanes do occasionally spin in a direction that affects the Mexican Caribbean (Isla Mujeres took an especially nasty hit from Hurricane Gilbert), so pay at least moderate attention to the weather if you're traveling during the hurricane season (late summer—October).

DOCUMENTS

U.S. and Canadian citizens need proof of citizenship in the form of a valid passport or certified (not a photocopy) birth certificate. A Mexican tourist card should be obtained at the port of entry (or will be supplied by your cruise line) and carried with you while you are in Mexico. The card is valid for up to 90 days, and should be returned to Mexican officials when leaving the country. A valid drivers' license from either the U.S. or Canada is valid in Mexico.

ELECTRICITY

The current runs at 110 volts/AC 60.

GETTING AROUND

If you want to tour the area on your own, your cheapest transportation options are buses and taxis, which are all over the place. Bus travel is recommended if you are taking a tour to a specific destination, or if you can obtain "deluxe" service—buses on these jaunts tend to be comfortable and air-conditioned. Bus rides on a lower-class bus are exceedingly cheap, but are not always the most comfortable way to travel, as conditions are hot, crowded, smoky (smoking is allowed on buses)—and small farm animals may also be aboard.

Taxis get you where you're going without extra stops, but be sure to settle on the price beforehand, or you could be gouged for more money than you planned to spend. Dickering over fares is a way of life, so don't be hesitant about negotiating. The fee for several hours of local touring can run anywhere from $35 to $50.

Ferries are also a popular mode of transportation, especially between Cozumel and Playa del Carmen, Cozumel and Puerto Morelos, Cancun and Isla Mujeres, Kukulcan and Isla Mujeres, and Punta Sam and Isla Mujeres. Some of these trips can be long and uncomfortable; be sure to check schedules before departing, and realize that schedules are not always adhered to, especially during bad weather.

Several major car rental companies (including Avis, Budget and Hertz) offer cars for rent in major cities, but prices tend to be exorbitant ($50/day and up).

If you find that car rental rates are prohibitive, consider renting a moped for tooling around town. It's a popular mode of transportation, and is about half as expensive as renting a car.

LANGUAGE

Obviously, Spanish is the language of Mexico, and it helps if you can speak it. If not, remember that the economy of the Yucatan Peninsula is dependent on hosting lots of American tourists, so it's not difficult to find someone who speaks English in the resort areas. Once you get off the beaten track, you're on your own. No matter where you stay in the Mexican Caribbean, beware of being taken advantage of—especially if you don't speak English.

MEDICAL EMERGENCIES

There is no Mexican equivalent of the 911 call, but English-speaking emergency service is available by dialing 06. You can be directed to an English-speaking hospital by the Red Cross (called the "Cruz Roja" in Mexico), which also has clinics in several areas of the Yucatan *(☎ 987-21058 in Cozumel; 98-841616 in Cancun)*, and there is an American Hospital in Cancun *(☎ 98-846430)*.

MONEY

Mexico's monetary unit is the New Peso ("Nuevo Peso"), which replaced the "old" peso in 1993. The exchange rate varies from day to day, and you are likely to get the best exchange rate from banks (even though they charge a service fee) or downtown currency exchange booths; airports, hotels, and expensive shops in areas heavily traveled by tourists are generally not the most beneficent when exchanging currency.

You may take U.S. currency and traveler's checks into Mexico, but you should exchange small denominations of traveler's checks or U.S. dollars into Mexican currency as needed. Large Mexican banks generally have English-speaking personnel who can advise you on the exchange rate and help you with the conversion process. Most banks have limited hours during which they will exchange foreign currency, usually between 10:30 a.m. and 12:30 p.m. Regular banking hours are Monday-Friday, 9 a.m.–1:30 p.m., with banks in larger cities open in late afternoon and/or on Saturday mornings. Banks close on all national holidays, and smaller banks close for local celebrations.

TELEPHONE

The Mexican telephone system can be frustrating, and suffers from a lack of consistency, with phone numbers varying between five and seven digits, depending on where you are calling. The international code, to be used when calling Mexico from another country, is *011;* and the country code is *52*. (You can reach an English-speaking international operator by dialing *09*; a long-distance operator within Mexico with *02*.) Local area codes (*98* for Cancun; *987* for Cozumel, Playa del Carmen and Isla Mujeres; *99* for Merida and Uxmal) are used both when calling from another country or when calling within Mexico. If you plan on making a lot of calls, invest in a prepaid LADATEL phone card, which can be used at designated public phones throughout Mexico. Make as few phone calls as possible from your hotel, which will charge you plenty for the privilege.

TIME

The Yucatan Peninsula is in the Central Standard Time Zone.

TIPPING AND TAXES

Expect a 10 percent service charge to be added to your bill for basically all goods and services. Some restaurants also add a service charge, so check before you tip to be sure you aren't paying twice. The amount to be left for a tip is roughly consistent with what is expected in the U.S., and you should plan on tipping just about everyone who does a service for you. The exception is cab drivers, who don't really expect it unless they have gone beyond the call of duty enough to warrant a reward.

TOURIST INFORMATION

In Cancun, visit the State Tourism Office—open daily from 9 a.m. to 9 p.m.—in downtown Cancun City *(Ave. Tulum adjacent to the Municipal Palace; ☎ 98-848073)*, or stop in at one of the information booths at Plaza Caracol in the Hotel Zone, at the airport, and in Cancun City, where English is spoken. In Cozumel, the State Tourism Office—open Monday–Friday—is on the *Plaza Cozumel (☎ 987-20972)*. As in Cancun, there are information kiosks around the main square and in the resort areas.

WHEN TO GO

The best time to visit the Mexican Caribbean is from late fall to spring—unless you are a diver, in which case you should consider coming during the summer, when diving is best and hotel rates are lowest. Non-divers can also save lots of money by planning a trip in summer, but the heat and humidity associated with the rainy season can make a visit extremely uncomfortable. As far as what's happening, things are pretty much always a party in the tourist zones, so things are rockin' and rollin' at just about any time of year. Those interested in being around for Carnaval, celebrated in both Cancun and Cozumel, should plan to arrive the weekend before Ash Wednesday to get in on the celebration.

YUCATAN RESTAURANTS		PHONE	ENTREE	CR. CARDS
Cancun				
	American			
★★	**Carlos 'n Charlie's**	(98) 830846	$1–$15	A, MC, V
	Cajun			
★★★	**Blue Bayou**	(98) 830044	$15–$35	A, D, DC, MC, V
	Continental			
★★★★	**Mirage**	(98) 851000	$1–$9	A, D, DC, MC
★★★	**Bogart's**	(98) 831133	$1–$9	
	Italian			
★★	**Piemonte Pizzeria**		$1–$9	
	Japanese			
★★	**Mikado**	(98) 852000	$1–$9	A, CB, D, MC, V
	Mexican			
★★★★	**La Joya**	(98) 832900	$1–$9	A, D, DC, MC, V
★★★	**Lorenzillo's**	(98) 831254	$1–$9	A, D, MC, V
★★	**Los Huaraches**		$1–$9	
★	**Bellini's New York Deli**	(98) 830459	$1–$9	A, MC, V
Cozumel				
	American			
★★	**Carlos 'n Charlie's**	(987) 20191	$1–$15	A, MC, V
★★	**The Sports Page**		$1–$15	
	Continental			
★★	**La Yucatequita**		$1–$20	
	Italian			
★★★★	**Donatello**	(987) 22586	$5–$25	A, MC, V
★★	**Karen's Pizza and Grill**		$1–$9	
	Seafood			
★★★	**Acuario**	(987) 21097	$1–$9	D, MC, V

YUCATAN RESTAURANTS	PHONE	ENTREE	CR. CARDS
Playa del Carmen			
Seafood			
★★ **Playa Caribe**		$1–$9	

INDEX

A

B

C

D

E

F

S

T

U

V

W

Y

Z

Favorite People, Places & Experiences

ADDRESS:	NOTES:
Name Address Telephone	
Name Address Telephone	
Name Address Telephone	
Name Address Telephone	
Name Address Telephone	
Name Address Telephone	
Name Address Telephone	

Favorite People, Places & Experiences

ADDRESS:	NOTES:

Name

Address

Telephone

Name

Address

Telephone

Name

Address

Telephone

Name

Address

Telephone

Name

Address

Telephone

Name

Address

Telephone

Name

Address

Telephone

Favorite People, Places & Experiences

ADDRESS:	NOTES:

Name

Address

Telephone

Name

Address

Telephone

Name

Address

Telephone

Name

Address

Telephone

Name

Address

Telephone

Name

Address

Telephone

Name

Address

Telephone

Favorite People, Places & Experiences

ADDRESS:	NOTES:
Name **Address** **Telephone**	
Name **Address** **Telephone**	
Name **Address** **Telephone**	
Name **Address** **Telephone**	
Name **Address** **Telephone**	
Name **Address** **Telephone**	
Name **Address** **Telephone**	

Favorite People, Places & Experiences

ADDRESS:	NOTES:
Name	
Address	
Telephone	
Name	
Address	
Telephone	
Name	
Address	
Telephone	
Name	
Address	
Telephone	
Name	
Address	
Telephone	
Name	
Address	
Telephone	
Name	
Address	
Telephone	

Favorite People, Places & Experiences

ADDRESS:	NOTES:
Name Address Telephone	
Name Address Telephone	
Name Address Telephone	
Name Address Telephone	
Name Address Telephone	
Name Address Telephone	
Name Address Telephone	

Favorite People, Places & Experiences

ADDRESS:	NOTES:
Name Address Telephone	
Name Address Telephone	
Name Address Telephone	
Name Address Telephone	
Name Address Telephone	
Name Address Telephone	
Name Address Telephone	

Favorite People, Places & Experiences

ADDRESS:	NOTES:
Name Address Telephone	
Name Address Telephone	
Name Address Telephone	
Name Address Telephone	
Name Address Telephone	
Name Address Telephone	
Name Address Telephone	

Favorite People, Places & Experiences

ADDRESS:	NOTES:
Name	
Address	
Telephone	
Name	
Address	
Telephone	
Name	
Address	
Telephone	
Name	
Address	
Telephone	
Name	
Address	
Telephone	
Name	
Address	
Telephone	
Name	
Address	
Telephone	